A Modern History of Europe

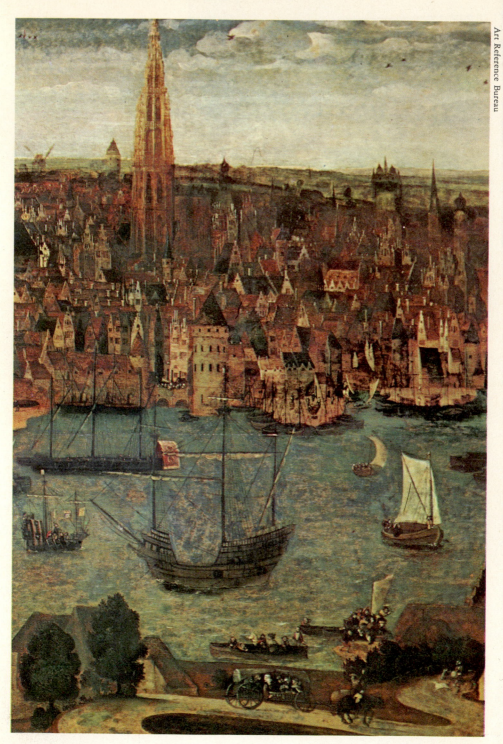

View of Antwerp, painted in the early sixteenth century by an anonymous artist. National Maritime Museum, Antwerp.

D 208 .W4

$12.50

Millions of persons

M 600 1700 1800 1900 1950
250

RUSSIA →
(TO 1970)

Millions of persons
80

GERMANY
(INCLUDES AUSTRIA
IN 1940)

200

70

150

WEST GERMANY

100

60

UNITED KINGDOM

ITALY

50

FRANCE
50

AUSTRIAN EMPIRE →

40

SPAIN

(INCLUDES IRELAND FROM 1800 TO 1910)

30

ANY
PRUSSIA)

YUGOSLAVIA
20

EAST GERMANY

CZECHOSLOVAKIA
NETHERLANDS

HUNGARY
10
BELGIUM
SWEDEN
AUSTRIA

(RELIABLE FIGURES BY DECADES NOT AVAILABLE FOR PERIOD BEFORE 1900)

1800   1850   1900 1910 1920 1930 1940 1950 1960 1970

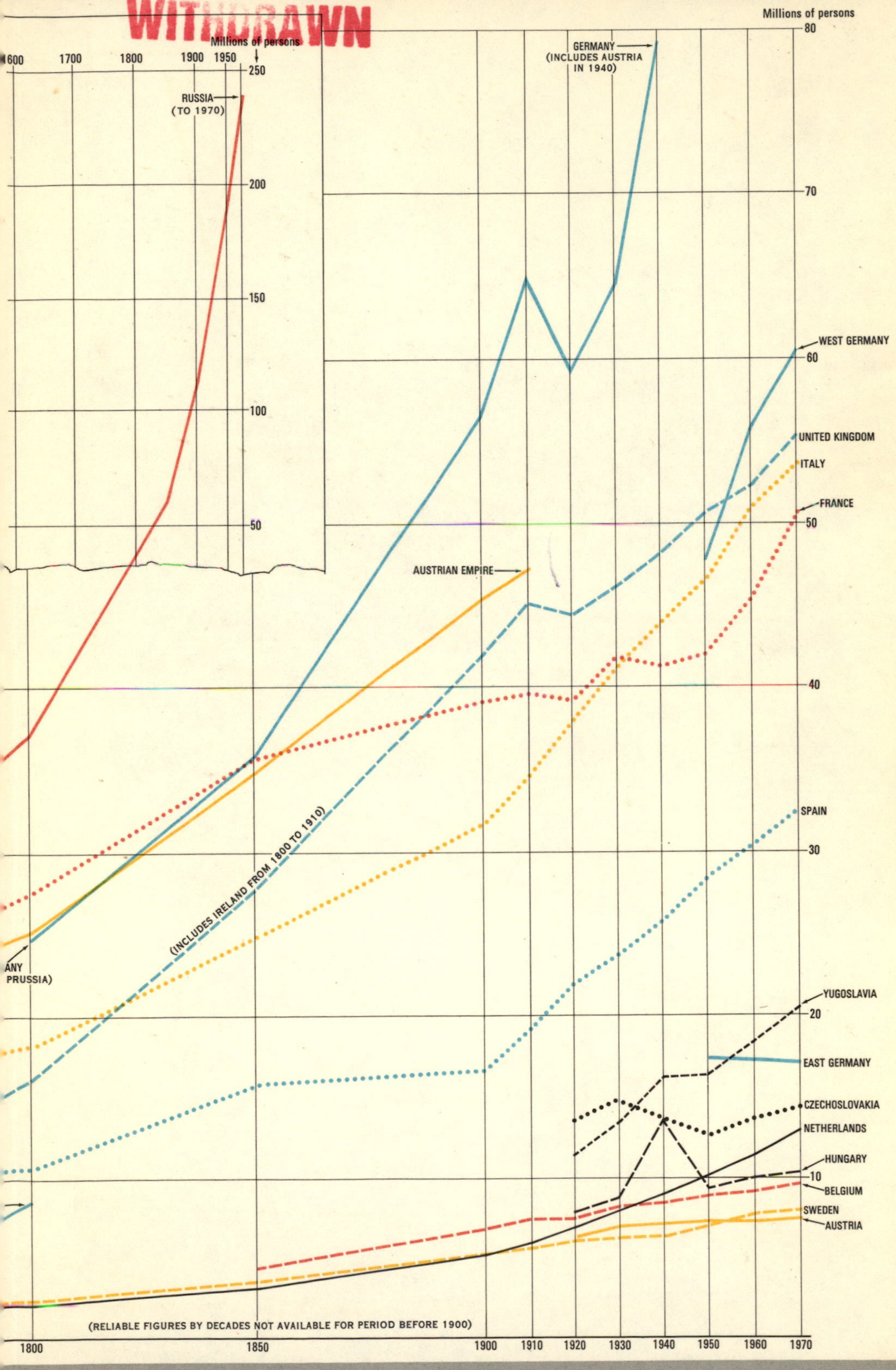

EUROPE • 1600 to 1970

A Modern History of Europe

Men, Cultures, and Societies
from the Renaissance to the Present

EUGEN WEBER

UNIVERSITY OF CALIFORNIA, LOS ANGELES

W · W · NORTON & COMPANY · INC · New York

For

Jacqueline

and

CONTENTS

PART II   Early Modern Europe: 1559-1715

PART III   An Age of Revolutions: 1715-1848

ILLUSTRATIONS

MAPS

PREFACE

This book attempts to tell the story of Europe in the past six hundred years and to reconcile the reality of the times themselves with what they mean to us. It is a compromise between historical narrative, synthesis, and analysis. It is divided into four major parts, each of which has a certain internal unity: the years to the middle of the sixteenth century when individuals learned to affirm themselves; the age running from about 1559 to 1715 when the structure of Europe's states and economy was organized; the revolutionary period 1715–1848 during which the ideological and industrial base of the contemporary world evolved; and the most recent period ending in our own day.

Each of these sections begins with some chapters that give an overview of international and political affairs in general: the continent and the world in which the events that it describes took place; the economic background, the atmosphere, the mentality of its times. Then follow sections devoted to internal affairs and to the development in particular states and regions—Britain, France, Northern or Eastern Europe—which had relevance to contemporary events.* Last, but not least, come the chapters about how people lived and the things that affected and reflected their way of life and thought. These chapters of social and cultural history take up at least half the book and will, I hope, prove its most useful contribution.

This organization is not strict. The pattern varies as it has seemed appropriate, and does so notably in the last part of the book, where 1945 marks a major limit. With the visible ending of Europe's hegemony (on the decline for a generation before), the continent reverts to its real dimensions and its history becomes a part of the history of the surround-

---

* Countries are mentioned in terms of the role they play. Thus, Russia does not appear until the second part and receives most attention in the fourth, while Sweden is not mentioned after the second part. Eli Hecksher remarks somewhere that a small country has no right to demand that its history be studied just because it happened. Space and prejudice both have persuaded me that he is right.

ing world with which it shares common problems, perplexities, and pressures. Hence the more general treatment of the years since 1945 when Europe ceases to hold the center of the stage.

An enterprise on this scale cannot be brought to a conclusion without the help of others. I am beholden to the resourcefulness of my research assistants: Mr. Ronald Behling, Dr. Vlad Georgescu, and Miss Vivienne Thomas, the last of whom especially afforded immense help. I have derived much profit from the comments of colleagues and friends who read and criticized portions of the manuscript: my friend and editor, Donald Lamm; Professors Lynn White of the University of California, Los Angeles, and Gene Brucker of the University of California, Berkeley, for Part I; Andrew Lossky of the University of California, Los Angeles, and Paul Lucas of Clark University for Part II; Isser Woloch of Columbia University and David D. Bien of the University of Michigan for Part III; Hans Rogger of the University of California, Los Angeles, and Charles Delzell of Vanderbilt University for Part IV. The fiercest arguments about the text, however, were with my wife, who stubbornly insists that what I write should be both readable and clear. The text will show that she got her way sometimes.

E. W.

Los Angeles, 1965–Bordeaux, 1970

INTRODUCTION

You should not expect to find here . . . the immense details of wars, of the storm of cities taken and retaken by arms, given and ceded by treaties. . . . All that was done, and does not deserve to be written. We shall only attend, in this history, to that which deserves the attention of all times, to that which can illustrate the genius and the customs of men. . . .

(Voltaire, *The Century of Louis XIV*)

A Modern History of Europe: the title is intended, first, to warn that here is *one* interpretation among several, not ultimate but tentative. It is *modern*—less as a part of the traditional triptych of ancient, medieval, and modern, whose arbitrariness becomes increasingly awkward, than in the relative sense of "recent": a contribution and response to ways of life and thought and action which are ours today. It is of *Europe,* not because the greater world is irrelevant, but because for the past five hundred years Europe was the most significant part of it. Not so naïve as to believe that the variety of mankind is exhausted by one of its physical incarnations, I am convinced that the mode and models evolved in Europe have provided the dynamo and the coloring of the modern world. Moreover, this period of European supremacy came to an end a quarter of a century ago and may be treated as a dramatic whole: the age when Europe found, organized, and affirmed itself, scattering its children, notions, and techniques over the world's surface. And it is history: *a* history.

What kind of history? A glance through the coming pages will show very soon. Above all it tries to touch on matters that fifteen years of teaching courses in so-called Western Civilization have made me feel students want to know. Not just the peaks but the valleys too. Not just the epic of collective deeds, but the tissue of the times. Not just what happened, but to whom and how. Not just wars and politics, the doings of a relatively restricted group, but the way people lived—humbler and middling people, and the rich as well—their food, their housing, the warp and woof of their existence. Not just great artists and philosophers and their works (and, it is to be hoped, not long, forgettable lists of dates and names), but the times and public to which they addressed themselves and to which they—somehow—responded. Above all, men and women.

Movements, ideologies, regimes, and trends are abstract. Great events are the poetry of fate. We remember them more for their lyrical impact than for the results that we attribute to them later. Only people are real, and what really matters is not Liberalism but Mill, not Cubism but Picasso, not electricity but its uses for factories and homemakers. History is the story of them, not as contributors to a present which soon becomes the past, but living their own lives. One can apply to history what General de Gaulle said about war: "No universal system, but only circumstances and personalities."

The difficult thing to understand is that past lives and events were not a preparation for what succeeded them, let alone for our own day, but autonomous: heavy with their own past but not with subsequent events, which only *we* now know would follow. Inevitably, knowing what happened, we look on Leonardo or Newton or Frederick the Great as predecessors, on events and situations as antecedents. In fact, they existed in their own right and deserve to be so considered: because otherwise they would not be free—not of history but of the future. Times make men, but men make ideas and make them in their image. After all, a time of distress could spark pessimistic reaction or optimistic escape; a time of change could suggest withdrawal or enthusiastic commitment. Man thinks alone and his thoughts, while affected by history and memory, by prejudice past and present, by circumstances social, economic, and physical, are still his own—not a social product, though they may become a social force.

History is not a sum but a synthesis, and one that goes on changing and accruing even while observed. The past, writes Marc Bloch, is by definition a fact that nothing can modify, but the knowledge of the past is a thing in process, which changes and progresses without end.

No account divided into chapters can really represent the continuing interaction between part and whole. An account on the present scale dwells too much on the general and only hints at ways in which the particular affects it. Those who lived through events cannot see them in perspective. Those who explain them cannot share their experience, reproduce the specific character of a given moment and its uncertainty. All we can do is *try* to distinguish the symptomatic and functional from the rest; attempt to approach situations concretely, by way of men and things; grapple with some of the living essence of history, of time, of the things men did and felt and wanted—the homely as well as the stately, not only those that were said in speeches, written in treaties and books, which have their place but not the exclusive significance so long attributed to them.

None of this is easy. When Rousseau proposed to write Prince Eugene's biography, Eugene warned him that history is a much more dangerous enterprise than poetry. Rousseau wisely forbore. Others are not so wise. In any case, it seemed to me worth doing, for the embarrassment of failure was outweighed by the possibility of some provisional truth. "Silence (Stravinsky *dixit*) will save me from being wrong but it will deprive me of the possibility of being right." Or, at least, suggestive.

Inevitably, things have been telescoped, compressed, omitted. The result is one man's view, one possible interpretation of events. No book can be all-inclusive. This one is far from it. Those who miss one thing or another may be moved to supply it for themselves. I hope they will concede that this was the particular story that I chose to tell. In telling it I have avoided singling out any particular theme: there are many themes, or trends, or views, but no dominant thesis. To impose one particular pattern on centuries so diverse would be to squeeze them into a corset built for one moment in time.

Despite such relativism, any account of such scale and nature is bound to be selective, and all selection is a form of prejudice. I have preferred to show my prejudices, without pretending to offer an ultimate or balanced chronicle. My presuppositions and my sympathies color choice and text. It will be for the reader to aim off for wind: take what he wants, leave or adjust the rest. He must not accept, but question: the facts perhaps (though those, I hope, are right); the interpretations certainly. He must invent his own questions too: is there a direction in history, or is the world spiraling in incoherence? Is there progress or eternal return? Is there coherence, can one make sense, and what is it?

The historian, said Lucien Febvre, is not the man who knows but the man who searches. His reader must search too.

PART I

The Renaissance and Reformation

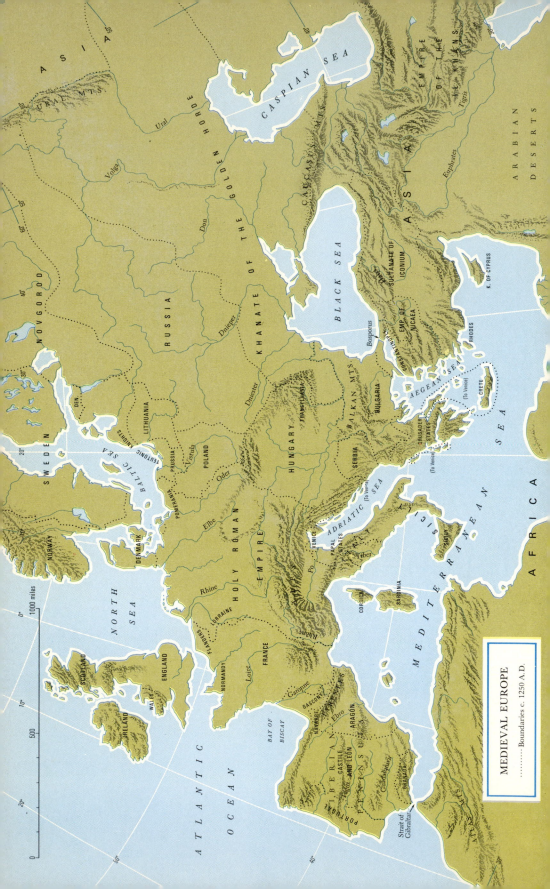

ASIA

URAL MTS.

Ural

Volga

NOVGOROD

RUSSIA

Don

GOLDEN HORDE OF THE

Dnieper

KHANATE

Dniester

CASPIAN SEA

CAUCASUS MTS.

ASIA

EMPIRE OF THE KHANS

Tigris

Euphrates

ARABIAN DESERTS

BLACK SEA

Bosporus

SULTANATE OF ICONIUM

CONSTANTINOPLE

EMP. OF NICAEA

RHODES

K. OF CYPRUS

SWEDEN

DEN.

BALTIC SEA

TEUTONIC KNIGHTS

LITHUANIA

PRUSSIA

POMERANIA

POLAND

Vistula

Oder

Elbe

TRANSYLVANIA

HUNGARY

SERBIA

BULGARIA

BALKAN MTS.

AEGEAN SEA

(To Venice)

CRETE

NORWAY

DENMARK

HOLY ROMAN EMPIRE

Rhine

LORRAINE

Po

VENICE

PAPAL STATES

Tiber

CRUSADER STATES

(To Venice)

ADRIATIC SEA

(To Venice)

ITALY

SICILY

NORTH SEA

ATLANTIC OCEAN

SCOTLAND

ENGLAND

WALES

IRELAND

FLANDERS

NORMANDY

FRANCE

Loire

Rhone

Garonne

GASCONY

Seine

NAVARRE

Ebro

ARAGÓN

CASTILE AND LEÓN

IBERIAN PENINSULA

PORTUGAL

Tagus

GRANADA

Guadalquivir

Strait of Gibraltar

BAY OF BISCAY

CORSICA

SARDINIA

MEDITERRANEAN SEA

AFRICA

ATLAS

1000 miles

500

0

MEDIEVAL EUROPE
Boundaries c. 1250 A.D.

Chapter 1

EUROPE IN THE

MIDDLE AGES

In the beginning was the land. A small peninsula at the western end of Asia. Mountains, great rivers and valleys, marshes and forests and coasts. Men put their hand to it, placed their mark on it, cleared and plowed and sowed, built and fought over it. By the thirteenth century conquerors had come and gone, great realms had risen and disintegrated, a wealth of dreams, ruins, and memories accumulated: a past. History. The soil in which the present plunged its roots, from which the future would rise. At the time when we begin to take a closer look at the background, the years before 1000 or 1100 A.D., man was absorbed by the Christian idea that his future life, for which the one on Earth was but a preparation, lay in another realm, a City of God, as St. Augustine put it. But we shall see that throughout the history of man there pulsed an enduring tendency to make man the measure, or at least the focus, of the universe in which he moved.

Of men there were few, terribly few by our standards, but their number was growing. Evidence is hard to come by, but what there is of it points to steadily rising numbers from the eleventh through the thirteenth century. In the Moselle Valley they had increased fourfold between 1000 and 1200 A.D. Along the eastern borderlands of Europe, settlers, merchants, adventurers, were exploiting a frontier that ran from the Baltic to the Balkans, landworkers from the overcrowded fields of Flanders, Luxembourg, and Lorraine for the grainlands, miners to work the ores of Transylvania for the King of Hungary, clerks less for holy rites than for administration and for law, knights to hold the castles and to fight the battles of Western Christendom and Western interests against the lesser breeds without the law.

In the South, too, Europe hard-pressed at the turn of the millennium by Viking raiders, Saracen invaders, and Magyar horsemen * was pushing forward now, sending its knights to capture or recapture positions held by the ancient Roman Empire remembered only vaguely in the bright lines and colors of myth. Beginning in the late eleventh century, the Crusades, which aimed to recover the Holy Land for Christianity from the Muslims, provided the leitmotif for four centuries of military and colonial enterprise—in the Iberian Peninsula, north and east around the Baltic, southward over and across the Mediterranean in all directions, shoring up, then biting off the proud but sickly remains of Eastern Rome. Along with the men at arms, ofttimes ahead of them, men of trade advanced on every side, *pieds-poudreux*, "dusty feet," as they were known from the essential feature of their calling, seeking out the dyes and silks and spices of the East, the honey, hemp, and amber of the Baltic, the heavier merchandise—grain, timber, wool, to feed, clothe, and equip the growing cities of the South and West, setting up a cat's cradle of economic relations to overtake and eventually to overthrow the equally complex but less productive structure of feudal society.

Feudalism: The Social and Political Matrix

The Middle Ages had elaborated an ideal social structure, often described as a great hierarchy linking together God, his creation, and the humblest creatures in it, through a long chain of authority and subordination, from Emperor to princes to lesser lords, orders and estates, each linked to the other, each with his proper function necessary to the functioning of the whole. But this was the ideal and, even though its very existence reflected and affected reality, reality was otherwise: more diverse, more confused as well, and nowhere as orderly or harmonious as the theory had it.

Feudalism—the system of political and social relationships within which Medieval man lived—was a complex, varied, and lengthy development. As Roman order disintegrated in the fifth and sixth centuries, its great structure of trade, administration, and communication fell to pieces, replaced by local improvisations. For centuries, Europeans lived in an agrarian society, lacking a market economy, where no political power could really protect its subjects or operate effectively over a large area. Under feudalism, a word related in origin to the word "fee," a hierarchy

* "From the wrath of the Northmen, O Lord, deliver us," prayed the ninth-century Frankish liturgy.

of lords and vassals evolved. It was based on military power and on the loyalty of lesser men to the ones immediately above them to whom they were bound by oath and whom they served mostly with horse and sword and lance. In return for this they received protection and payment—the latter, usually, in the form of a land grant (fee or fief).

Land was the basis of loyalty, life, and station, furnishing food and shelter, timber for building, kindling for fire, meager harvests often verging on famine yet providing the surpluses on which conspicuous consumption thrived. To begin with, the society it nourished divided quite simply into rich and poor, strong and weak, free and unfree, the tiny minority ruling or directing, the immense mass suffering and toiling. This primitive reality gradually evolved into more functional divisions, often described in familiar trinitarian terms. Christian society, said King Alfred the Great of England, was made up of "men of prayer, men of horse [*fyrdmen*], and men of labor": priests, warriors, peasants, we would say today.

The Men Who Prayed

In a wild, uncomfortable world the men who guarded the road to a consoling heaven came first among social orders: more organized, articulate, monopolists of culture and hence of propaganda, beneficiaries of an institutional network more broadly cast than any prince commanded. Rising above the ruins of secular authority, the Church had first replaced, then helped reconstitute it. Over centuries of darkness and chaos, its missionaries had spread the Christian message from Ireland to the Russian plains; its clerks had preserved small parcels of the ancient wisdom; its bishops, established in the old Roman cities, then in new burghs conquered from the pagans, had been among the first pillars of order, supporters of royal power, its counselors and representatives. Gifts, bequests, and sheer private enterprise made the Church a very great landowner, strong in its acres as in its treasury, in the loyalty of clergy that looked to Rome as much as to their territorial lords, in the devotion of masses it commanded, protected, served.

Parallel to the secular clergy there had risen regular monastic orders, descendants of hermits who had first fled from a corrupted world, organized and disciplined since the sixth century by the rules St. Benedict had given, renovated at intervals by devoted reformers, marshaled in monasteries and orders under the rule of abbots, self-contained, self-sufficient, respected, and prosperous. Inevitably, monks reflected the social divisions of the outside world, adopted its values, participated in its conflicts. Again and again contemplation had turned to idleness, retreat to exclusiveness, purity to corruption. Again and again men came to regenerate them and, by new foundations, instill new life in their enterprise.

In the twelfth century, one of the greatest reformers, St. Bernard of Clairvaux (in eastern France), launched a fresh offensive in favor of asceticism and manual labor. Under his guidance, the monastic order known as the Cistercians would build their houses far from the villages that furnished the serfs of other orders, clear their own lands, become great sheep and dairy farmers, turning out the wool and hides, cheese and meat, that a growing population needed. Austerity and hard work made them wealthy, grasping, resented for avarice where other orders were resented for idleness. It seemed that Satan had many ways to counter Christian commitments.

If Christian living posed recurrent problems, Christian thought did so no less. The God in Three Persons—Holy Trinity—of our hymns raised serious difficulties for thoughtful theologians, bothered less by His nature than by logical questions concerning equality or subordination between Father, Son, and Holy Ghost. This would be the source, among other things, of the break between the Greek and Latin churches, that is, between those Christians who looked to Latin Rome and those who followed the political and theological lead of Constantinople, whose Patriarch refused to recognize the supremacy of Peter's See.

Since 1054, the Greek Church was condemned by Rome as schismatic, the Byzantines holding that the Holy Ghost proceeded only from the Father, while Rome held that it proceeded both from Father *and* Son (the question of *filioque:* "and the son," as it is often referred to). The theological and institutional conflict between Western and Eastern churches reflected profounder differences: above all the resentment of poor, ignorant Western barbarians against rich, cultivated Greeks, whose language they could not understand, whose wealth they coveted, whose sophistication they despised. Ignorance and envy bred hatred, expressed most forcefully in 1204 when members of the Fourth Crusade launched an attack on Constantinople, massacre and pillage winning them, as their historian boasted, "booty greater than any seen since the Creation." Constantinople would be held by Latins until reconquered in 1261; but the Greek Empire never recovered from the blow dealt it by fellow-Christians.

Nearer home, differences of opinion could be more swiftly dealt with. The authority of tradition, repeatedly challenged, was as often reaffirmed—if need be by excommunicating the unregenerate. More dangerous were the heretics who insisted on leading a Christian life in an unChristian world, aspired to impossible perfection, rejected the material for a spiritual realm, sought salvation in poverty, chastity, and truth, affirmed a simple apostolic faith freed of institutional accretions needing no churches, altars, priests, or other dignitaries.

Such dangerous heresies—like that of the Cathars ("pure ones") or the Albigensians (from the city of Albi in France) which swept through southwest France in the second half of the twelfth century—were put

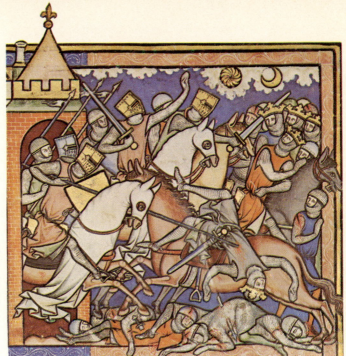

Kings in Battle. A French manuscript illumination, *c.* 1250, in which Joshua, in the center, battles the five kings of Canaan, raising his hand and commanding the sun and the moon to stand still. Morgan Library, New York.

down by military expeditions (Albigensian Crusade, 1208–1213) and by the Inquisition invented by St. Dominic on the same occasion. But the need for moral renewal that the heretics expressed and the yearning for a religion that stressed love over fear, charity over institutional alienation, were met by the foundation of new orders, less indifferent to the spiritual (and physical) needs of the masses, less self-centered, returning to the villages and, especially, to the urban poor. Beggars like the meanest of Christ's children, devoid of property or convents, wandering missionaries and preachers, Dominicans and Franciscans revived the evangelical ideals of poverty and charity, enlisting them this time in the interest of the Church, not against it. With the coming of the mendicant orders, it could be said that the great edifice was complete. The Church of Christ, the Church of Rome, was everywhere, richer than the greatest princes, more enduring than the greatest families, affirming the authority of bishop over parish priests, abbot over monks, superiors over friars, the Pope over all of them.

The Men Who Fought

Below this great and orderly elite came a less orderly crowd: the men-at-arms, another elite, for arms were a privilege of freedom and freedom as a rule the privilege of arms. Arms meant not only sword, lance, shield, ever more costly armor; they meant a horse as well, strong enough to carry its heavy rider, well-harnessed and well-fed. Rarities such as these required a long purse, plenty of land for revenue, the favors of a wealthy patron, or very simply a legacy. In a society where those who were truly free lived on the labor of others, knights fought or hunted but did no work. By the eleventh century their condition had become hereditary, an impressive ceremony ushering the knight into the privileged caste of warriors.

By the eleventh century, also, as too many sons crowded castle halls, the warriors began to burst the limited bonds of Europe and seek their fortunes far away: in Southern Italy and Sicily, in England conquered by the Duke of Normandy in 1066, in the reconquest of the Iberian peninsula from the Muslims and the creation of a new kingdom in Portugal, finally in the great armed pilgrimages called the Crusades which, beginning in 1095, fascinated the chivalry of the West. Delivering the Holy Land from infidels offered both spiritual and material profit, while taking pressure off the society left behind to enjoy more peace than it had known before. Meanwhile, the experience of colonial warfare, the proximity of civilizations more refined than theirs, transmuted knighthood into chivalry, superimposing on its original military virtues of loyalty and bravery, softer Christian ideals: righting wrongs, delivering prisoners, defending the weak and oppressed. The culmination of this attitude appears in the life of King Louis IX of France (1226–1270), the royal knight who "loved God with all his heart and followed His example . . . and placed his body in adventure many times for the love he bore his people." Louis, who went crusading twice, when crusades were rapidly going out of fashion, died as a martyr to his passion and quickly became St. Louis. There is little evidence that his public-

The departure of French knights during the Crusades. A French miniature of the Bourguignon school.

spirited faith or the fine ideals of chivalry had much effect on the conditions of the common people. But they left their mark on literature, on the manners of the upper classes and, through them, very gradually on those of society as a whole.

The Men Who Worked

If noble or, better, *gentle* birth predestined one, so did the destiny of being born unarmed. Peasants, or villeins, were so for evermore, as the Abbot of Vale Royal makes his serfs swear in 1336; "they and their sons after them, for all eternity." Villeins were vile: wild beasts, said the chronicles, fallen creatures destined for Hell, hideous, shaggy, their hair bristling, their cheeks black and tanned, "unwashed for six months and the only water ever wet them being the rain of heaven." "We are men made in the image of God," complained the peasant rebels Wat Tyler raised in England in 1381, "and yet we are treated like wild beasts." But for the masters, neither their physical nor their moral image recalled Christ. From villein comes villainy. There were no peasant heroes, no peasant saints, only clowns and rebels: rabid dogs a monk called them, malcontents sneered a Czech poet, desperately striking out, ferociously repressed: "Some had their teeth pulled out," recounts a Norman chronicle, "others [were] impaled, eyes torn out, hands cut off, ankles charred, others burnt alive or plunged in boiling lead. All were well-arranged. Hideous they were to see. Never were glimpsed again without being recognized."

A thirteenth-century German tale shows where an attempt to change one's lot can lead: Helmbrecht, the farmer's son, begins by imitating the young lords he envies, wearing his hair long and shiny (hence clean), under an embroidered bonnet. He refuses to carry heavy burdens or load manure on his father's cart, but longs for a lord's life, riding fast horses, hearing the stolen oxen moo as he drives them through the fields, enjoying the exhilaration of dragging villeins through thorn hedges by their hair. His father, a sage and prosperous man since he owns a cart, warns him that "he who rebels against his rank must fail, and your rank is the plough"; but Helmbrecht becomes a bandit instead—the nearest approximation of a lord—torturing and despoiling peasants. "I burst this one's eyes, hang another over the flames, bind this one on an anthill, tear out the other's beard with pincers, skin one, break another on the wheel or hang them by the sinews. All that the peasants own is also mine." Inevitably, the rash youth who imitated noblemen as closely as he could comes to a bad end; for "God never fails to punish him who does what he should not do." The lord's men catch Helmbrecht's gang, hang his fellow ruffians, blind and mutilate Helmbrecht himself, leaving the peasants to wreak on him the vengeance they could not inflict on their lords.

The Men Who Ruled

Above these orders or, better, in their midst, there stood the King: at first more predisposed to power than wielding it, gradually increasing his influence and that of the central authority that he represented. Anointed at his coronation, he carried a divine power, witness his magic touch that was supposed to heal the sick. Crowned master of a realm that could take weeks or months to cross, he was the only lord who owed homage to no other beside the Lord God, while all the greatest barons of his kingdom owed him allegiance. Master of great domains, like other barons, he was best placed to increase them when a line of succession failed or a vassal failed in his duties. Protector of churchmen and non-nobles who looked to him for support against closer hence more bothersome authorities, the King was also the first among his nobles, their natural liege and benefactor. Feudal society invented a theology in its own image: a royal God, ruling like a lord, enthroned in triumph or in judgment; a mutinous Satan, image of the disloyal vassal, rebel, and traitor. The lesson was clear: even if the present was sometimes doubtful, the future lay with the King.

There was also the Emperor, heir of the prestigious Roman title and of the puissant memory of Charlemagne, but in reality little more than the uncertain ruler of parts of Germany and Italy, often ignored by more powerful princes: first the kings of France, then those of Spain and England. Unlike other rulers, emperors held office not by hereditary right but by election and, since the thirteenth century, that decision rested with an Electoral College of seven German princes.* The *idea* of Empire maintained the ancient ideal of universal unity under one supreme head: the reality was disunity—at its most acute in the Emperor's own realm. His hold on Germany contested by civil war, his title controlled by the Electors, his power based on his own family domains, the Emperor was in effect the head of a confederation of German princes, a fact reflected by mid-fourteenth century in the new title of his realm: Holy Roman Empire of the German Nation.

But medieval Christendom—like one of the monsters that adorn the capitals of its pillars—had two heads: if the Emperor was one, the Pope was the other. And since two heads are seldom better than one, each attempted to establish his own supremacy. Kings or emperors claimed that the consecration of their coronation rites gave their office a religious, sacred character entitling them to rule priests as well as laymen, invest bishops, and draw the revenues presently running into Roman coffers. Popes asserted that the spiritual realm transcended and subsumed the worldly one. The papal tiara with its superimposed crowns joined pontifical and imperial sovereignty, the papal mantle was dyed

---

* The Archbishops of Mainz, Cologne, and Trier, the Count Palatine of the Rhine, the Duke of Saxony, the Margrave of Brandenburg, the King of Bohemia.

imperial purple, the papal chancery was the *curia*—reminiscent of Roman power and royal courts. Clerical propaganda likened the Pope to the sun, emperors or kings to the subordinate moon. As with these orbs, the light of royal power could only be a reflection of the papal sun.

Yet kings and emperors would not accept a secondary role or merely act as secular arm of a priestly caste which, in exchange, would consecrate their power. The theory of a single supreme ruler could be applied on their own behalf as well; and the long struggle this produced irremediably weakened the power of its chief contenders: both emperors and popes. Unable to maintain themselves against their northern vassals and Italian rebels, the German emperors dropped out of the race after a last attempt to assert themselves in the brilliant person of Frederick II (1215–1250). It would be a king of France, Philip the Fair (1285–1314), who finally checked papal pretensions and humbled Pope Boniface VIII in 1303.

After that date, Rome and all Italy were left prey to disorder and local resurgencies, while Boniface's successors sought refuge in exile at Avignon, where they remained from 1305 to 1378—some of them even longer, into the fifteenth century—reluctant protégés of the kings of France. We shall see that Rome's universalistic pretensions never recovered from this Babylonish captivity. Sacramental power remained with the priests, but secular supremacy stayed solidly in the hands of the princes. Yet, behind the great struggle, beyond all antagonisms, the two powers continued to collaborate. Men of prayer and men of war supported each other against the men of labor. Christ had advised that Caesar be given his due. The representatives of Christ were needed to repeat the point. "Good people," called a Bishop of Paris, "give to your earthly lord that which you owe him. Hear and believe that to your earthly lord you owe quit-rents, poll-taxes, forfeits, services, carts and porterage and horses. Render all, in the time and place required, integrally."

Lord and Manor

The economic unit was the manor. More than a mere homestead, the manor was a small self-sufficient entity, a tiny agrarian state ruled, judged, and administered by its lord. His subjects were his serfs, or vassals, their rights determined largely by his will and by tradition. It was the lord's land that the tenants worked and, in return for it and for his protection, they owed him certain services, many of them in kind: measures of grain or days of labor. The lord collected taxes, judged in peace, and led his men in war. He often had a say in what they did or whom they married; and he generally endowed the church and named its priest. But, in the end, feudal lords were always more than owners of land or managers of manors: above all, they were leaders of men. Greatness was expressed less in wealth than in swords and bows and lances; and many barons might echo the Highland chief who, on being asked what he got from his land, answered: "Five hundred men."

And if his men, bond or free, held their land from him, the lord in turn owed allegiance for it to some more powerful patron, head of his clan, count of a district, abbot or bishop, distributing their acres in exchange for allegiance, ultimately the liege lord of all: the king. One man could hold fees from several patrons, hence owe allegiance to more than one lord; and feudal estates, imbricated with one another, puzzle-like, were seldom well defined. Quarrels erupted over boundaries, contesting claims, rights of distributing justice, levying taxes or collective tolls, fights broke out between rival families or within them when disputes arose over inheritance or precedence, enduring vendettas stained generations and provinces with blood. All or nearly all raised dire questions of competing loyalties, of which lord a man was to follow when two were at loggerheads. Constant friction, warfare, raids, ambushes, and counterraids were part of normal life. The harmonious pyramid of vassals and lords was in practice closer to the organization of a lobster basket, disorderly and often desperate, in which the strongest gradually established their rights by the capacity to enforce them and upon the habit of familiar rule.

Custom and tradition dominated the Middle Ages. They provided assurance that survival is its own best justification, that what has long endured deserves to continue. From precedent to precedent, innovations, abuses, or gestures that sheer chance evokes can become traditions, rights, eventually even laws. Slowly, as the innovations of yesterday became the traditions of today, the luckier or more audacious asserted their grip over widening areas, unregulated warfare gave way before the rough justice of greater potentates, the relative calm they imposed gave scope to economic progress.

In a subsistence economy indifferent to productivity, economic growth could result only from demographic expansion: more people calling for more food, clothing, lodging, but also producing more, clearing more land, growing more crops, providing a greater quantity of energy as well, in a time when the basic power source in transport or labor was simply human muscles. Scarce animal traction also expanded. There was more fodder for horses, oxen, and donkeys. There were new harnesses and iron shoes permitting animals to pull greater weights, plow more deeply, move faster and farther, accelerating agricultural labor and facilitating the construction of the great religious and secular buildings of the High Middle Ages: castles, cathedrals, and palaces built of stone.

As numbers increased and as the fields pressed back forest and waste, exchanges between isolated communities became more frequent, manors and villages which had relied principally on their own products depended more on goods and services from outside, money economy replaced the natural economy of a closed subsistence. Where heretofore land had been the only source of power, a more organized world submitted to the power of money, which alone paid the price of expensive new arms and accoutrements, of mercenaries who did not slouch off when they had finished their forty days of feudal service, of fortifications which could hold back an enemy, of agents, and subjects, and of land itself. The little masters of little fiefs whose revenues could not keep up with all these new expenses gave way to the few great men—counts, dukes, princes—who controlled the fairs, the trade routes, or the cities whence the sinews of new power came. The advance of trade meant the promotion of greater realms in which the castle ward, once a concrete reality, would become only one more administrative division.

Gradually, services and payments began to be reckoned in terms of money rather than of land; military services, like goods, were bought and paid for in cash; the central power asserted itself increasingly, attempting to rule ever more directly and to dispense with the mediating authority of lesser lords. The restricted social structures of an earlier day began to crack before the appearance of a new estate, coolly received by representatives of the traditional orders. "God," says an English sermon of the fourteenth century, "made clerks, knights and laborers; but the devil has made bourgeois and usurers." A new diversity of professional functions and economic conditions was being shaped behind the stone walls of the cities. And, as the practice changed, the complex structures developed for earlier and vastly different circumstances became increasingly anachronistic.

The Rise of the City

By the thirteenth century, that Latin Christendom which survived the chaos of the Roman Empire's collapse eight centuries before had recovered the lost ground and more, had advanced the limits of the earlier Roman empire across great stretches of north and central Europe, which Rome had known only as threatening waste, and had incorporated the Germanic peoples and many other barbarians into its new society.

The dynamo of this very old but newly moving world was to be found in the cities, the centers of production and exchange that lay behind walls and towers scattered from Finland to Cyprus, from Scotland to Sicily. The cities of an earlier day, sacked, abandoned, ruined as the Roman Empire fell to pieces, had been left mere shells of past activity and use. It took a long time for them to resume their former function as markets and administrative centers. Urban activities had been mean-

ingless in a world ruled by the sword, fed by the plow; a world of warriors and peasants with no surplus for trade. When not laboring or
fighting, such men had mind for little else but prayer. Yet, sometimes
because they were left alone, sometimes because the feudal lord found
it convenient to strengthen them against more recalcitrant lieges, the
cities grew. The more ruthless lords established their rule, set up their
local peace, enabled their thralls to sow and reap free or freer of constant raids, their subjects and others to exchange their products and their
wares, to travel, to trade. In the ruins of Roman foundations, in the
shadow of lord's or bishop's peace, at a convenient ford or toll bridge,
markets were developed, ruined walls repaired, new ones built. Houses
went up, huddled together, often swept by fire, as often by pestilence or
famine, crowded for safety, for gain, eventually by the walls and towers
and also by the rules and regulations meant to ensure their safety. And
the citizens reached out from narrow shopfronts and tortuous streets
throughout the world for profits and recruits.

No more than 5 per cent of Europeans can have dwelt within the
towns of the eleventh century, when the Crusades began. Three centuries
later this proportion had quadrupled. The numbers were still small.
Around 1000 A.D., urban centers of 10,000 people or more were to be
found only in Byzantium and in Muslim Europe. By the twelfth century,
London counted about 20,000. Rome was the foul and perilous ruin of
its former self. Within the old Aurelian walls a million people had lived
under the Empire; by the fourteenth century, in the great expanse of
rubble, swamp, and briar, some 20,000 or 30,000 Romans still subsisted
in castles and in hovels built of and on the ancient ruins. The towers of
the nobles, the churches—not only those of Rome itself, were raised
out of marble and the stone salvaged from the rubble. The city which
Augustus had found of brick and left of marble was being stripped back
to its sources. These Romans lived chiefly by begging, crime, and fleeing pilgrims; they drank the foul yellow water of the Tiber and proudly
remembered the greatness of the past. But Milan, Europe's biggest city
in 1300, boasted a population of about 200,000; over 40,000 citizens able
to bear arms. "Its animals alone," says a preacher in 1228, "eat up as
much bread as the people of many big Italian towns." Venice, Florence,
Genoa, were smaller, between 50,000 and 100,000. Outside Italy, Paris
with its 80,000 dominated the north; in the Netherlands great cities like
Ghent reached 50,000 and so probably did Bruges. But figures before the
fifteenth century are speculative, and even after that uncertain. The
only certain thing, at this stage, is the impression of growth when cities
like Bruges, for instance, enlarged their boundaries in 1163, 1213, 1254,
1269, and 1299, to take in the suburbs that had grown up around
them.

"Soldiers busy themselves with their wars, people trade in peace and
the world belongs to him who takes it," writes a fourteenth-century

The Town Hall at Bruges.

Arab traveler in Palestine. The world belonged first and foremost to the Italians, who, by piracy, contraband, enterprise, and lower prices, had taken more than most. In 1315 the Bardi trading house of Florence showed an annual turnover of about 875,000 florins.* Compare this with the 80,000 florins Pope Clement VI paid in 1348 to buy Avignon from the Counts of Orange, or the 450,000 florins the French never managed to raise in 1360 to ransom their king, John II, taken prisoner at Poitiers. A great Italian merchant might count his fortune the equivalent of a king's ransom.

The cities fed on the great reservoir of rural labor and, of course, were fed by it. Most communes, the Italian ones first, abolished serfdom in their territory, chiefly so that free peasants should pay taxes, move freely into cities, provide cheap labor for the urban economy, produce the food and raw material cities swallowed. Here was another sign of the waning feudal order, and of the new mentality that went with it. For the abolition of feudal dues was sometimes justified by good intentions. In 1257 the Bolognese city charter declared that, just as in paradise man is born free, so the inhabitants of Bologna's territory have a right to be free. The commune "which has always fought for freedom" would pay serf owners damages of 10 lire per adult, 8 lire per minor under fourteen, and then place the free serfs on its tax rolls. The paradise was not exempt from taxes, but the condition of the peasants nevertheless improved.

Relative abundance made some thirteenth-century peasants better off than their kind would ever be again until the eighteenth century. The new or newly spreading, newly significant, money economy forced lords to convert their peasants' labor dues into fixed payments, though

*At today's valuation, the florin would be worth about $4.00, but its purchasing value was really greater by perhaps as much as twenty times.

A medieval village scene depicting plowing, grinding grain, and the slaughter of a boar. Two friars dispense bread and soup to the poor.

the growing inflation hollowed the value of these dues. Those who worked harder, made a good marriage, hid their gains more efficiently from the tax-collectors, or—best of all—became the lord's agents, paying no taxes themselves, exacting what they could from their fellows, grew rich. Some might even marry the dowryless daughter of a clerk or knight. Their sons could study to become clerks, their savings buy up noble land, the manor of some ruined squire. And, as the small rural gentry went downhill, rich peasants moved into the cities, began to trade and to assert themselves to the disgust of old established townsmen like Dante. Well would he have agreed with a fellow poet, a thirteenth-century Austrian, who complained that peasants lived like knights, married the daughters of noble families, grew too strong on their wealth. Within a generation, the battle of Morgarten (1315), in which Leopold of Austria's men-at-arms were thoroughly beaten by the infantry of Swiss forest cantons, would prove the poet's point.

The peasant who moved into town did not change his environment as radically as the eighteenth- or nineteenth-century worker pressed into the service of urban industry. Town and country life interpenetrated each other. There were fields within some cities and common fields outside most. Burghers stocked their larders with the produce of their farm, artisans stopped work to help with the harvest, the Hustings Court of London suspended its sittings during harvest time. And if to the medieval villager the city was a place of wonder, yet similar in a great many ways to what he knew at home, to us it seems in many ways still largely akin to a busy, backward village: the unpaved thoroughfares a-clang with blacksmiths' hammers, the trades carried on within the street or in sight of it as in today's bazaars, butchers doing their slaughtering in front of the shop. The horrid smell of Avignon—*odor terribilis*—was notorious; so was Bologna mud "that smells like corpses." But also there were luxuries. There was magnificence unknown in the country: rooms with great windows, hung with silk or leather, plenty of furniture and decorations—paintings and objects of art.

Amusements were simple and brutal: mock jousts in which students armed with poles fought others armed with eggs; boiled pigs thrown from a balcony to those bold enough to grapple for them under a shower of the boiling water in which they had been cooked; or the game in which a man bare to the waist, in a cage with a cat, had to kill the animal with his teeth alone. Bull fights turned into mass butcheries, young gentlemen starring as mounted matadors. One such held in 1332 in the Piazza Navona, the market square of Rome named after that popular vegetable, the turnip, saw the death of eleven bulls, but not before they had killed eighteen men and wounded nine. The cost of the festivities had been paid by a special tax on Jews.

One distinctive mark of the cities was their activity and the premium they placed on enterprise. Enterprise first spurred, then braked by a variety of associations. As cities grew, artisans and traders organized themselves into corporations designed to regulate working hours and conditions, define the quality of products, repress frauds, prevent underselling and cutthroat competition by imposing a "just" market price and limiting the number of enterprises within one town. Initiation ceremonies were hard, like those of journeymen in Norwegian Bergen who would be shoved down a chimney, thrown three times into the sea, then soundly whipped. But such stern exclusivism only made belonging more precious. Almost always a religious brotherhood under the protection of a saintly patron, the gild or corporation operated as a friendly society, assisting its members at times of sickness, contributing toward burial costs, or celebrating their successes.

Fraternities, charities, trades, arts, gilds, corporations, and societies, these associations—born spontaneously in the twelfth and thirteenth centuries for mutual aid and protection among men who could not think and would not dare to operate alone in parlous times—branched out in all directions. No professional could work outside their structure. Dante the poet had to join the doctors' and grocers' gild of Florence; sculptors belonged to the stonemasons' gild. Corporations provided the cadres for young men's societies devoted to games and military exercises. They organized feasts, mascarades, processions, and grand drinking bouts. They distributed food and alms to the needy on the feast of their patron saint, embellished their local churches with rich chapels or stained-glass windows, arranged jousts and matches between rival trades or quarters of the town—some of which survive for tourists to enjoy like the *Palio* horse race of Siena, or the *calcio* soccer game of Flor-

ence. Above the fears of isolated individuals, they raised the shield of
the patron saint, the embattled group, the team spirit that could form
or strengthen a faction or simply contribute a company to the city
militia.

By the fourteenth and fifteenth centuries gilds and corporations had
become a political force, operating too often to eliminate competition
or novelty, to put to death the inventor of a new loom in Danzig or
prohibit new wool-dyeing methods in Bruges, maintaining the monopoly of a minority of masters whose avarice, "abuses, conspiracies and
monopolies," numerous edicts mentioned. The years would bring ever
greater diversity and specialization, tighter organization too, permitting
closer control by the public powers. Thus, in 1613, even the lame, halt,
and blind of Rome were organized in a corporation whose members alone
had the privilege of begging, provided they paid regular monthly dues
to their "art." In the meantime, however, masters and journeymen had
evolved and refined a great many techniques from which their cities
benefited and which their apprentices learned and carried on: blast
furnaces worked with bellows and activated by hydraulic power, new
dyes and improved dyeing processes, engravings, etchings, copperplate,
enammeling, improvements in glass-making and glasswork, the special
ceramics of Faenza (*faïence*). The art of Murano glass blowers was one
of Venice's economic trumps, producing pearls, necklaces, strings of
glass beads, crystal goblets, above all Venetian mirrors with their novel
backing of lead-plating, spectacles whose lenses were first cut in rock
crystal, and only then in crystalline glass polished by the same technique that was used on mirrors, finally spyglasses and telescopes.

Enterprise existed in the countryside too, where conflict, need, and
inventiveness made for changes—albeit slow ones—and where the creativity of the common people expressed itself in concrete innovations
rather than chronicles. A glance at the agricultural history of the Middle
Ages, when one compares it to that of later centuries, suggests stability
almost akin to immobility. But below the appearance of enduring custom
and routine there surged uninterrupted movement and change: technical with the introduction of new plows, mills, crops, and methods of
crop rotation, clearing fields or forests, enclosing meadows for pasture,
draining marshes or improving land, parceling it out or tacking it together painfully over the generations; human and institutional with the
foundation of new villages or their disappearance, the shift from fallow
to cultivation and from that—sometimes—back to what the age called
desert, the rise of some nearby city and the market it offered, the raids
and destructions of war, the endemic risings, rebellions, or, simply, law-
suits, peasants nibbling away lordly rights, lords encroaching on those
of their subjects, the shift of wealth, power, and privilege.

Without the fundamental transformations taking place in the structure and organization of rural society, the rise of the cities would have

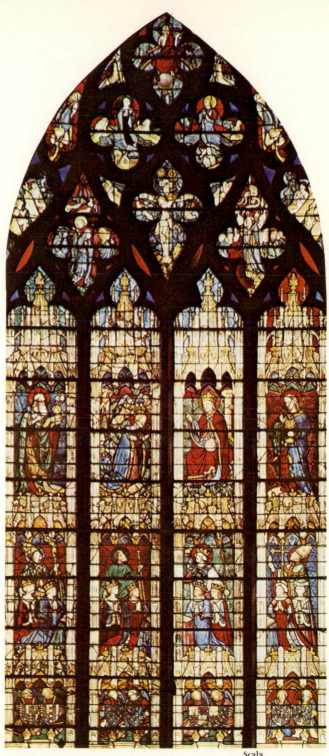

A stained-glass window
in Chartres Cathedral.

Scala

been impossible. This rise, in turn, led to further transformations in the country, calling for greater productivity and providing markets for the goods produced. The fourteenth century would see more and more burghers replacing barons as lords of lands and manors. They, their example copied by surviving nobles, their values carried into older families by burghers' daughters married for their dowries, worked to replace the old feudal mentality by a newly businesslike approach, counting profit and loss, undertaking investment for profit, on the land as in the counting house.

Yet the contrast between city and countryside endured. Change and novelty were part of the personality of the former; less evident, less easily accepted in the latter. The tempo of life was more intense in the towns; inertia—readily attributed to the rural hinterland—was scorned and banished from the bustling urban world. When Dante in his *Divine Comedy* was assigning regions, he placed the sluggish and the torpid in the most ignominious part of purgatory. Schooling mattered now not only to learn the recorded wisdom of the church but to keep accounts, take notes, engage in correspondence. In Florence around 1336, eight to ten thousand children were learning to read, over a thousand studied mathematics, some six hundred even such use-less subjects as literature and philosophy. For the first time in a thousand years enterprise, initiative, self-assertion, could find expression and success in realms other than those of God or war. Slowly, grubbingly and fumblingly, man as an individual was being rediscovered, in some ways reborn.

Medieval Man

The Medieval Environment

What, how, who were these men and women whose disembodied mass filled the churches and the streets, manned the walls, the plows, the galleys of these centuries, whom we meet mostly as statistics or as objects in stories whose heroes are always princes, prelates, noble warriors, saints, dominant or exceptional figures whose doings were considered worthy of record, whose gestures alone were significant and effective. There is no memorial for the masses, no chronicle of the commons. We have some tales of the poor who lived by poaching, some ballads that sang of villeins as well as nobles. We have from the 1370's *The Vision Concerning Piers the Plowman,* with its vivid portrayal of fourteenth-century life and social problems. But this is little to go by. The clerics preached, and the lords blustered, and the poets sang their songs, and the scholars taught and thought and wrote. But the humble merely lived—existed—

and how they did it they have not told us, because once they start telling us they are no longer the inarticulate masses, but something else.

First of all and obviously, the man of the Middle Ages was much closer to nature than we are today, and nature was not at all what we see today, softened, domesticated, and for the most part controlled. The countryside, where wild or fallow land took up the greatest part, bore little trace of human hands. Today, wild beasts haunt only our nursery stories and the safaris of our millionaires: in those days, bears, boars, and stags, and most especially wolves, wandered everywhere, including the village fields. For a long time, even the suburbs of great cities were not safe from wolves. In mid-fifteenth century they attacked the inhabitants of Montmartre. A little before that, in 1420, wolf packs had entered Paris itself through breaches in the walls. As late as 1640, wolves could roam the ducal residence of Besançon in Savoy, eating the children in the streets. More than a sport, hunting was a necessary defense and, of course, absolutely essential to provide nourishment.

Nourishment was a matter where all supplements were welcome. Farming practices made hay scarce and, hence, winter feed for cattle rare. Ill-fed, ill-fattened, cattle were costive beasts at best but under the circumstances many had to be slaughtered in autumn, their meat salted and used until the grass grew again in spring to fatten a new herd. Salt (or ill-salted) meat is not the most exciting dish, especially when it gets high—or slightly rotten. To hide its taste, or lend taste to duller fare, those who could afford it ate food highly spiced. In France, even peasants used imported pepper when they could, while garlic and onions were staples. A Byzantine author of the thirteenth century claimed that, when they stormed Constantinople in 1206, it was the breath of conquering French crusaders that undid the Greeks.

The staple food of the poor—that is, of most people—was pulse (something like lentils) and bread: rye bread was expensive, wheat bread a luxury. Vegetables, seldom eaten fresh, were used mainly in soups or stews. Dark, dangerous, full of wild beasts and sometimes of men no less wild, the forest was also an immense resource: not only for gleaning or hunting (when permitted, and sometimes when not), but for new additions to man's domestic store. Just as the pig is a domesticated boar, so the orchard is domesticated forest. First pears, then apples, appeared throughout western and northern Europe, contributing not only fruit but their juice products, perry and cider, to a limited diet. Another contribution of the forest: bees, or honey-flies, as they were called by those peasants whose sweetening on the eve of the French Revolution still came mostly from honey. Bees would be domesticated too. Meanwhile, however, people went out to gather wild fruit, wild herbs, and honey, much as they had done since the Stone Age. But the shortage of meat combined with that of vegetables made for a deficiency of fats and vitamin A, and a fairly widespread state of near scurvy.

And the nights were darker and the cold was colder than we can imagine, because there was practically no artificial light and there were few ways of heating. The fourteenth century knew few glass windows except in churches, and even those were scarcely transparent—more like bottle bottoms than windows. Even in Italy where glass was not so rare, it still passed as a luxury; a great flood in 1332 had a Franciscan preacher listing glass windows among the luxuries which had brought down God's wrath upon Tuscany. Panes were generally of parchment or oilcloth, guarded by shutters which could be opened on windless days, hence seldom in the darker season of the year. In the dark rooms those who could afford it hung draperies on the walls to keep the damp cold out,* tallow candles burned, smelling and in constant need of trimming. Wax candles were too expensive, except for church festivals or the dwellings of the great. Brass oil lamps gave but a feeble light. There might be more from the hearth, but that made troubles of its own, for it was often an open brazier or fireplace with no exit for the smoke. Chimneys were rare, as the Duke of Ferrara found when he visited Rome in 1368: "For fireplaces were not then in use, but people made a fire on the floor in the midst of the house, or some made fires in earthenware boxes." Two centuries later English authors still wrote of fireplaces as outlandish luxuries.

No light. No heat. No comfort. We need only think of the heavily clad figures in fifteenth- and sixteenth-century paintings, men and women who wore more clothes indoors than out, gowns, furs, hoods, piling layer upon layer to keep warm in counting house or study or hall, straining their eyes over script or ledger,** so constantly uncomfortable that they scarcely knew it.

Old wounds, ill-healed, that ached at every change of weather; a poor digestion, aggravated by unbalanced diet, by almost nonexistent hygienic facilities—there is no charting the role uneasy stomachs must have played in the uneven temper of medieval man. Frequent constipation. Endless scratching. The Middle Ages were rife with skin diseases, which coarse underclothing or the absence of underclothing must have made worse. It was only in the fourteenth and fifteenth century that body linen and linen shirts began to replace the rougher wool (and when worn

* In 1475 there died in Paris a dyer by the name of Gobelin, who had settled in the capital some thirty years before and had developed the secrets of a new art from which tapestry would grow. His name came to stand for tapestries of a magnificence that was never excelled.

** Spectacles seem to have been invented in the late thirteenth century, probably in northern Italy, and remained prohibitively expensive for a long time after that. Rare evidence of their use in the fourteenth century can be seen in a fresco painted by Tomasso de Modena (at Treviso) in 1352. In 1364 Petrarch began to use glasses. Early models, sometimes adorned with gold or jewels, were so expensive that they were generally mentioned in wills and property lists. By the sixteenth century, regarded as symbols of learning and wisdom, they came to ornament the portraits of ancient sages like Virgil or Pythagoras, saints like Peter, Paul, Jerome, Augustine, even occasionally the infant Jesus.

to rags, to provide raw material for paper). But if the absence of certain clothing might be unhealthy, its wearing with encrusted dirt might be worse. For washing, too, was rare and scarcely thorough. The ritual of knightly initiation which gave rise to the Order of the Bath was part of an ancient symbolism of purification. It was also connected with the exceptional nature of thorough washing and shaving.*

Beneath the current life we glimpse a grounding of primitiveness, a submission to forces not yet disciplined or tamed, a life of unattenuated physical contrasts. We glimpse the actors too: violent, nervous, emotive, sensitive to the lightest pressure on their passions, swift to anger and as swift to tears, a mass of contrasting moods that mirror the harsh contrasts of their lives, of day and night, of heat and cold, of famine and of plenty, in a world whose techniques had hardly intervened to ease transitions which we, today, so easily ignore; open to moods, but also to sounds, to scents, to omens, to every kind of experience which seldom meant to them what it would mean to us, in a puerile, "primitive" readiness to grasp the moment or be grasped by it, to live from moment to moment, in the moment, for the moment.

These people were rude and tough. Ill-mannered too. In mid-fourteenth century, when young Francesco Datini was in Avignon, even the Pope possessed only two forks, though he used golden skewers to spear his meat and crystal skewers for strawberries. A hundred years later, Aeneas Silvius, later Pope Pius II, relates in his *Commentaries* how his eloquence held an audience of high prelates so spellbound that for two hours no one even spat. This, too, was a world where every man carried a knife or dirk to be used in turn as tool, table utensil, or weapon. "The earth and the sea are full of robbers," wrote a fourteenth-century merchant to his partner, "and the greater part of mankind is evilly disposed."

Not content with the dangers of the outside world, many introduced hostile residents onto their premises by acquiring slaves. Countries within reach of the Mediterranean especially, counted few wealthy households without at least one slave. They came in the dowry of a bride, as part of a doctor's fee, in a bequest to monastery or church. The bill of lading of a Black Sea ship putting into Genoa in 1396 listed "17 bales of pilgrims' robes, 191 pieces of lead, and 80 slaves." ** Slavery would slowly

---

* Less exceptional, however, than it became with the sixteenth century, when even periodic bathing went out of fashion for two or three hundred years because of the appearance and spread of syphilis and also of a more puritanical attitude toward exposing the body. Around 1500, Nürnberg (population 20,000) boasted fourteen public baths with low admission prices, special hours set aside for city employees, and free admission once a week for prostitutes and children accompanied by their parents. Soon, however, the possibilities of infection, physical and moral, led to their progressive closing. The name of the public bath itself—*bagno*—became a synonym for brothel. By 1530, Lewis Mumford tells us, of the twenty-nine bathmen serving fourteenth-century Frankfurt, none were left.

** Iris Origo, *The Merchant of Prato* (1963).

waste away, but never disappear entirely until the end of the eighteenth century. Inclined though they might be to look upon the household slave more as an object than as a human being, few men and women could quite forget that in the amusing plaything or the scullery drab they had acquired a resident enemy.

No less volatile were the people at the top. Pope Alexander Borgia learns that his son has been murdered, breaks down, confesses his crimes before his cardinals. Cesare Borgia kills his father's favorite at his father's feet and the blood spurts up on the Pope himself. The Cardinal of Este, the Duke of Ferrara's brother, has the eyes of another brother torn out because a lady of the court found them too beautiful. Princesses and noble ladies knock one another about, spit on their dresses, quarrel like fishwives. The brutality of amusements has not diminished: fights between bulls and bears, men and pigs, men and men, provide public entertainment, as do executions, tortures, flagellations, and religious processions of every kind—all on a similar plane.

Less stable, less balanced, these people are also younger: not because hardship keeps men young, but because it kills them off. The people of these ages die sooner. Babies die in droves. We have no way of telling the rate of infant mortality, especially in the earlier period. But it has been estimated that among the highest classes of the sixteenth century, at least 40 per cent of children born alive did not live out their first year, and another 20 per cent died before twenty. Only three of Henry VIII's many children survived their father. Five of Queen Isabella's children died stillborn, by miscarriage, or in infancy; two more in their youth. Women died in childbirth, which is not surprising when one considers the early age of marriage, the frequency of pregnancies, the possibilities of infection. In the fourteenth century, Gian Galeazzo Visconti of Milan married Isabella of Valois at nine. By the time he was fourteen she had given him a son. The girl died at twenty-three. Three centuries later, the mother of the great Arnauld of Port Royal would die at thirty-nine, worn out after bearing her twentieth child. By then, eleven of her children had died at an early age.

Men also die: witness Chaucer's character, the Wife of Bath, who had five husbands at the church door and buried them all. In one of his dialogues, the poet Petrarch has St. Augustine tell him: "Most men do not reach your present age." His age at the time was thirty-eight. The best-fed princes, lords, patricians, died between forty-five and fifty-six. Men after forty, women after thirty, were considered old—and looked it. When Louis XII of France married Mary Tudor, sister of Henry VIII in 1514, people were surprised at such an enterprise on the part of a man considered *fort débile et antique* (very aged and decrepit) at fifty-two and, in effect, the King died of his overexertions within three months.

The Medieval Mentality

We cannot neglect the effects of an extraordinary sensitiveness to the supernatural, which may well have had something to do with the state of men's bodies and nerves, but which also affected this physical state in turn. Everybody seems to have been tensed all the time to notice every sort of sign or dream or hallucination. Particularly in monastic circles, fasts and repressions added their influence to a discipline and a reflection that were professionally and deliberately focused on the problems of an invisible world that only too often became visible. No psychoanalyst ever scrutinized his dreams with more ardor, with more loving care, than the medieval monk. But laymen had their share in this very emotional society, where there was as yet no code of manners that prohibited tears or fits or faints or swoons, and devils or saints were constantly intervening in everyday affairs. Prodigies, monsters, portents, angels, demons, the vast world of spirits impinged throughout on that of everyday, which must have seemed much like the visible portion of an iceberg, the ominous portent of the mass below. Miracles were omnipresent. Animals, natural phenomena, all prophesied. Statues would sweat or cry or nod. At Brescia in 1415 a statue of the Virgin opened and closed its eyes. At St. Maximin certain stones dyed with the blood of Christ brought there by Mary Magdalene herself would boil on Good Friday. At Naples the blood of St. Januarius still boils three times a year, though not apparently below 19 degrees centigrade.

The interpenetration of the visible and the invisible worlds, the constant interaction between spheres which we have since defined as different, categories we have distinguished and separated, was current on every plane of life. The law, the courts, seem to have recognized certain parallels between men and beasts, indeed between men and objects. The church bells which had tolled a village to arms against the king's officers were whipped by the public hangman; the pig who killed a man or ate a child was judged and hanged for his crime. How should we wonder then that witches were treated according to the same logic? A bolt of lightning, a comet in the sky, a strangely colored sunset, a score of other phenomena we connect with natural causes, were to these people *signs*, expressions of the constant deliberate logical intervention of the divine or diabolic powers. Logical, for the concept of cause and effect was not lacking; it was only applied in ways which to us would appear incoherent because they straddle planes of experience which we today consider alien to each other: trial by miracle for instance, the belief that the wounds of a murdered man will bleed in the presence of the murderer, a test applied in Breton courts until the

French Revolution; the magic aspects of medical practice where drugs and treatments only became effective when accompanied by ritual words or gestures; the frequent intervention of the dead in the world of the living, and the no less frequent intervention of the living in the other direction, all betray a different kind of logic, a different world view.

In a sense this may be attributed to too much logic: these people wanted to explain everything, connect everything. Trying to do so in a world where exact experiment was impossible, where the very notions of exactness or experiment were rough and rare, they created a vast network of logical but incoherent and to us improbable connections and explanations, the first hesitant steps toward a rational structuring of the world.

Meanwhile, when not expressed in religious rites, these fumblings toward scientific explanation diverged quite frequently into sorcery. Modern science is born of a marriage between mathematics and magic. This is obviously true of astrology, without whose motives we probably would not have astronomy; it is even truer of the alchemists, ancestors of our physicists and chemists, in their search for the philosopher's stone which would permit them to turn base metals into the perfect metal, gold, and above and beyond that to eliminate the impurities of matter at all levels, enabling man to rise from a worldly, unstable, and corrupt state to eternal perfection. Their search for purity would by the twelfth century lead alchemists to discover the distilling process and to turn out, first, sixty-proof alcohol, then, ninety-five proof brandy—effective both as a stimulant and as a disinfectant. Their search for gold, though less successful, would turn into the equally useful avenue of transmutation of metals and, on the way, produce other substances such as nitric and sulfuric acid.

Those who supported such experiments did it mostly for mundane ends. Henry IV of England, in need of money, granted royal permission to three alchemists searching for the secret of turning base metal into gold and for the elixir of immortality. Their failure only led to a long series of other researches under Henry VI and Edward IV. Elizabeth of England and Charles IX of France in the sixteenth century, Emperor Rudolph II, and Marie de Medici in the seventeenth century, were among the more eminent figures to sustain this interest.

But magic could be negative as well as (hopefully) positive. Pope John XXII (1316–1334), a considerable scholar, lived in terror of magicians and evil spirits. When one of his bishops started sticking pins in a wax image of him, he had to secure a serpent's horn at great expense to protect himself. It must have been effective, for he was ninety when he died.

In a society where the threshold of collective excitability was very low, where people flew off the handle very quickly and crowds easily became mobs in rage or panic, where knowledge of reality was approximate at best, preoccupation with magic could produce serious consequences. Books might be looked on as works of the devil, a particular talent as evidence of occult connections. Petrarch was accused of being a magician for reading Virgil, whom men considered a necromancer and, while Petrarch shrugged this off, Pope Innocent VI believed it.

The move toward accurate knowledge was fated to be painfully slow, not least in a world where the familiar notion of time was a strange and ill-conceived dimension. The measurement of time was impossible for most people and irrelevant to many. By the fourteenth century, sand-clocks, sundials, awkward and expensive waterclocks, were being replaced or, rather, supplemented by mechanical clocks, which eventually acquired hands and dials. Hours were divided into minutes and seconds. But these early mechanical contraptions were vast and clumsy, installed in bell towers or some other public edifice, and it was not until the fifteenth century that "many-wheeled watches out of small bits of iron" announced the appearance of the portable, small domestic clock.

Nor do they seem to have been gravely missed until about that time, by people who took approximation for granted and whose sense of chronology (let alone chronometry) was vague. In 1284 for want of any written record it took a major inquiry to establish—more or less—the age of one of the West's great heiresses, the young Countess of Champagne. The idea of exactness, the taste for exactness, with their essential basis in accurate figures, were foreign to the best of medieval and early modern minds. And perhaps this was just as well, in an approximate world in which the major hope or concept of survival, materially speaking, lay in living from day to day.

The Art of the Middle Ages

And yet, this world and these minds were responsibile for the wonderful artistic creations which remain today the most enduring glory of that period from the tenth to the fourteenth century. When one talks of medieval art one thinks of the cathedral. For once, the modern impression is perfectly correct, because the culture of the high middle ages did turn around the religious edifice, which was the expression of the most material aspirations, as well as of the most spiritual impulses. In a period of three centuries, from 1050 to 1350, France extracted several million tons of stone, in order to build eighty cathedrals, five hundred great churches and several tens of thousands of parish churches. The foundations of the great cathedrals go down as far as 40 or 50 feet (which is the average level of a subway station), and in certain cases these founda-

Chartres Cathedral with its thirteenth-century tower on the right, sixteenth-century tower on the left.

The interior of the Abbaye aux Dames, Caen, a tour de force of medieval vaulting.

tions form a mass of stone as great as that of the visible building above the ground. This means that the French quarried and carried more stones in these three centuries than ancient Egyptians in any period of their history, even though the Great Pyramid by itself has a volume of 2.5 million cubic meters.

During the high Middle Ages there was a church for about every 200 people, and the area covered by religious buildings took up a great part of every city. In Norwich, Lincoln, and York, which had between 5,000 and 10,000 inhabitants, there were respectively fifty, forty-nine, and forty-one churches. There might have been more and bigger churches yet, except that this would mean demolishing one or two neighboring shrines and building new lodgings for the people whose houses had been torn down; problems which tended to discourage the less enterprising.

The Cathedral of Amiens, which covered about 8,500 square yards, allowed the whole population of the city (about 10,000) to attend the same service. For a comparison on our own scale, one must imagine in a city of a million people a sports stadium, built in the very center, to accommodate the whole population. The same gigantic scale appears in the height of the walls, the towers, and the spires: you could build a fourteen-story building inside the choir of the Cathedral of Beauvais without reaching the roof, which is about 157 feet high. In the twelfth century, the men of Chartres built a spire 345 feet high; in Strasbourg, the Cathedral boasted a spire of 466 feet.

Here was a powerful form of self-expression, and one which literally dominated a good deal of life, towering over the squat crowded cities and visible for miles around, so that even today one sees the towers of the Cathedral when still half an hour's drive away from Chartres or from Rheims. Clearly, the spirit that planned and built these extraordinary enterprises was not altogether stulted and primitive and constipated. It was inspired by religious faith and religious awe, out to build temples to the Christian God more splendid than the heathens ever conceived. The twelfth century would see departures which facilitated greater size and capacity. The massive walls and sturdy lines of buildings based on Roman building methods, marked by round arches and cupolas, were replaced by higher, lighter structures best recognized by the use of pointed arches whose ribs crossed at the center of bays thus making the outer wall carry the weight of vaulting. Given support from flying buttresses outside the building, the heavy masonry of Roman architecture could be abandoned for more slender walls pierced by ever higher windows. The Gothic style, as it became known from the pejorative term applied to it by Renaissance artists, suggests a bold liberation of matter, an aspiration of man, pinnacles and arches springing upward, light flooding in, white or stained by colored glass, where shadows reigned before, a polyphonic harmony of God's creatures' skills. Style and scale may have been affected by what was going on in Syria and in Spain, in Arab architecture of which merchants and pilgrims brought back word. But it was also and above all inspired by fierce local patriotism and pride; and by a feeling very new in these surroundings: competitiveness.

Every abbey and community and city wanted a bigger, better, brighter church than everybody else, the most conspicuous possible mark of their piety, perhaps, but certainly of their success and wealth. All who could afford it brought in the architects and masons who could give them the greatest temple of Christendom. Funds were a problem. A rich abbey or chapter, drawing good and regular revenues from its sheep, crops, wines, or rents, could build fast—as at Cluny, where the great basilica begun in 1088 was almost finished in 1118. Most enterprises, however, lagged between fund-raising campaigns that had to be spurred by ever-fresh relics or miracles, leaving us monuments whose charm, as at Chartres, lies in the disparate architecture of parts that date from different generations and—sometimes—different centuries. Begun in 1134 on foundations going back to the ninth century, the cathedral of Chartres was burned in 1194, rebuilt by 1220; it integrates a romanesque portal of the twelfth century, gothic transept doors and porches of the thirteenth century, chapels and a muniment hall of the fourteenth century, a spire of the sixteenth century, and a choir screen finished in 1727. Intended to boast eight towers, it ended up with two: one romanesque and one gothic.*

---

* Here is a witness of the building of Chartres in 1145: "That year men began—first of all at Chartres—to draw on their shoulders chariots loaded with stone, with timber,

Again and again such towers and walls were thrust up to the sky, to the glory of God and confusion of the neighbors in the next town; again and again they collapsed, only to be put up again. City raced city and abbey raced abbey: in 1163 Notre Dame of Paris had the highest roof, 103 feet; in 1194 Chartres built up to 108 feet; in 1212 Rheims reached 113 feet, and nine years later Amiens topped them with 128. Finally in 1225 Beauvais beat the record with 157 feet, only to have the whole thing crash down half a century later. Fortunately, by then the architect was dead.

The amount of capital that went into these structures and other kinds of conspicuous consumption represented labor and resources denied the possibility of more profitable investment, and scholars have argued that cities like Beauvais, very prosperous in the thirteenth century, declined thereafter in part because of such Gargantuan endeavors.

In these wild sprees of enterprise and rivalry another side of medieval character appears, close to the kind of nineteenth-century America in which vulgarity and drive, robber barons and wide-open spaces, tore some things down as they built others up. The cathedrals bear lasting witness to this spirit. But besides this, appearing as they did at a somewhat clumsy and tongue-twisted moment in the history of man, these inarticulate creations were going to provide a language, a form of expression, for the highest forms of religious sensibility, of civic pride, of personal creativity—an interpenetration of sacred and profane that can be found in the naïve advertising of the local gilds in the stained glass windows; in the extraordinary elevation and sweep of arches and columns; in the grotesque caricatures that decorate stalls and capitals; in the impressive sculptures and murals that illustrate the familiar stories of the Bible—a mixture very characteristic of the times.

We might see medieval art as a compensation (at least sometimes) for certain values that could not find expression anywhere else but in these privileged places. The moderation and balance—so signally lacking in these times—we can sometimes find in their architecture. The exactness, the precision, the clarity that neither laws nor language could attain, we see presiding over the work of the great master-masons of the vast romanesque arches, domes, and vaults. Finally, the elevation, the grace, the purity, so often lacking in the ordinary life of this vulgar, brutal age, would be expressed in the soaring pinnacles and towers of the great gothic cathedrals.

---

with nourishment and other products for the work of the church whose towers were then being built. . . ." And another in nearby Normandy: "Kings, princes, men powerful in their time and weighed down with honors and riches, men and women of high birth, bent their proud and swollen necks to harness themselves to chariots and draw them with their load of wine, wheat, oil, lime, stone, timber and other products necessary for the sustenance of life or the building of the churches up to the shelter of Christ, in the manner of animals. . ." As late as the thirteenth century St. Louis would force his brothers to join him in doing as much at the abbey of Royaumont near Paris.

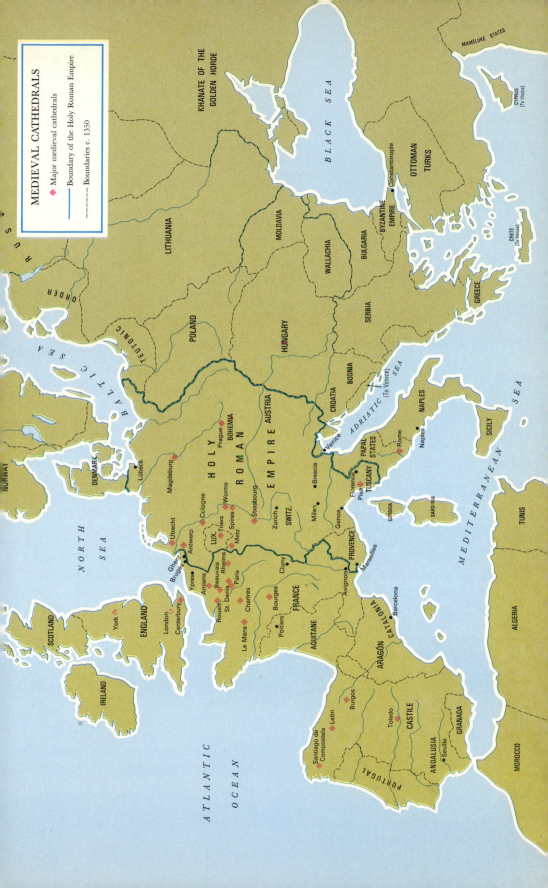

MEDIEVAL CATHEDRALS
♦ Major medieval cathedrals
── Boundary of the Holy Roman Empire
--- Boundaries c. 1350

ATLANTIC OCEAN

NORTH SEA

BALTIC SEA

BLACK SEA

MEDITERRANEAN SEA

ADRIATIC SEA

IRELAND

SCOTLAND

ENGLAND
London
Canterbury
York

NORWAY

DENMARK
Lübeck

RUS

ODER

TEUTONIC

LITHUANIA

KHANATE OF THE GOLDEN HORDE

POLAND

BOHEMIA
Prague

HOLY ROMAN EMPIRE
Magdeburg
Cologne
Worms
Triers
Spires
Strasbourg
Utrecht
Antwerp
LUX.
Metz
Zurich
SWITZ.
Milan
Brescia
Genoa
AUSTRIA

MOLDAVIA

WALLACHIA

HUNGARY

BULGARIA

SERBIA

BOSNIA

CROATIA

GREECE

BYZANTINE EMPIRE
Constantinople

OTTOMAN TURKS

CRETE
(To Venice)

CYPRUS
(To Venice)

MAMELUKE STATES

Venice

PAPAL STATES
Rome

TUSCANY
Florence
Pisa

NAPLES
Naples

SARDINIA

CORSICA

SICILY

TUNIS

ALGERIA

MOROCCO

Ghent
Bruges
Ypres
Amiens
Beauvais
Rheims
Paris
Rouen
St. Denis
Chartres
Le Mans
Bourges
Poitiers

FRANCE

Cluny

AQUITANE

PROVENCE
Avignon
Marseilles

CATALONIA
Barcelona

ARAGÓN

CASTILE
Burgos
León
Toledo
Santiago de Compostela

ANDALUSIA
Seville

GRANADA

PORTUGAL

The Waning of the Middle Ages

This flowering of the high Middle Ages, with their thriving peasantry and their booming cities would not last long.

Where the thirteenth century had been a time of relative prosperity, the fourteenth century begins badly and ends worse: rotten harvests, rotten weather, floods, deforestation in southern Europe, cold in the north bringing the icebergs down across established sea lanes, closing the Vikings' Greenland route and leaving Scandinavian settlements there to perish of hunger and cold; freezing the Baltic over in 1296, 1306, 1323; putting an end to grain farming over great parts of Norway and to vineyards in England; pushing glaciers across what had been Alpine pastures; helping to bring the lifespan down, for example, in England, from a thirteenth-century average of about thirty-five to below twenty-five in the fourteenth century.

In 1315–1317 a great famine, the first of many, devastated Europe. Rich cities like Ypres lost one-fifth of their population, 3,000 persons starving in six months. Malaria ravaged the countryside from Marseilles to Pisa. Worst of all, forgotten since the eighth century, plague returned (1348–1350, 1360–1363, 1371–1374, 1381–1384): lands lost to cultivation, capital lost to investment, hands lost to labor. The Black Death stopped the expansion of the previous two centuries: the new insecurity and mayhem, intensified by crop failures, scarcity and famine, affected trade and, hence, the prosperity of trading cities—especially after the kings of England and France defaulted on their debts, bringing about the bankruptcy of many great banking houses, like that of the Bardis, whose twenty-four branches had in mid-fourteenth century run from London and Seville to Jerusalem and Constantinople.

After 1320 the Ypres linen industry fell off badly. In Florence the textile industry declined so that the end of the century saw production at less than one-third of the figures of 1320. In places like Genoa and Marseilles, revenue from port duties at the end of the fourteenth century was less than half what it had been a century before. The expansion of trade, the distant adventures, even the advances of Christianity, all withered on the vine. Dante's Florence, about 100,000 strong, shrank to half that figure after 1350, never to rise above 75,000 in the fifteenth century, the great days of the Medici and Michelangelo. Rouen, in Normandy, which had built three new sets of walls to keep up with its expansion between 1150 and 1350, would build no more thereafter and, by Louis XIV's time, would not quite have refilled the space it occupied in 1350. Zurich, 12,400 strong in 1350, numbered only 4,700 in 1468. Altogether, after the fourteenth century, populations which had been growing rapidly now decreased, stagnated, or expanded only very slowly: England with over $3\frac{1}{2}$ million before the plague, counted some 2,200,000 in 1377, 3,200,000 in 1550. In France, the number of hearths in 1789 was only 10 per cent greater than in 1328. In Catalonia the population actually seemed to shrink: 95,258 hearths in 1369, 77,973 in 1379, less than 60,000 in 1497. 1375 marks the opening at Hamburg of the first madhouse—perhaps a symbol of the times.

In the cities, tension between townsmen and their feudal overlords, ecclesiastical or lay, friction between rich patricians and the lowest strata—between what Florentines called the *popolo grasso* and the *popolo minuto* (the fat and the little)—had several times exploded into insurrection even in the expanding and expansive decades before the plague. In the fourteenth century this became endemic. Bloody popular risings in countryside and city scarred fourteenth-century annals, in Flanders and Majorca, in Lübeck and in London, in Florence and in France, rebellion and reprisal heaping up the dead and the fuel for further resentments. All seemed connected with a catastrophic collapse of social progress which an Austrian observer summed up as a situation in which the coffers of the rich were full, the bellies of the poor were empty.

Against this background of material and social chaos, greater conflicts raged. There was war in Flanders. The Holy Roman Empire—re-creator of a Christian order—lay in anarchy from Naples to the Baltic. The great houses with royal pretensions struggled for the crown and even more for power, creating a situation in which the only trace of order left was to be found in the walled cities whose armed leagues dominated the north, the west, the south.

In the new lands of east and northeast Germany, the position of the peasants had been better than that of their fellows in the west (whence most colonists of these borderlands had come). Class distinctions were less sharp on the frontier, noblemen had often lived in towns, engaged in trade, become burghers and aldermen, while burghers in their turn had acquired fiefs and titles of nobility. Wars, plagues, famines, and feuds, now depopulated the countryside, making for an agrarian crisis which precipitated social and political changes.

Deprived of their regular source of revenue, encouraged by collapse of all higher authority, the nobles pressed harder on peasants and towns, the latter reacted in revolt and war, lost, and found themselves in the nobles' power. Heavier taxes drawn from cities stifled the incipient development of all but the strongest. Heavier labor services exacted from the peasants choked off the small-scale production and demand that were part of earlier patterns of local trade. Eager to raise grain production on their own estates and squeeze the peasants harder, the nobles, now short of labor, had to prevent the peasants from seeking better conditions elsewhere by tying them and their families to the soil and turning them into serfs. By the end of the fifteenth century the population had so declined and lands were so deserted that dire ordinances decreed that runaways could be hanged by their lord, runaway servants nailed by the ear to the pillory and given a knife to cut themselves off. Any servant idle for over thirteen days could be chained and forced to serve without wages for one year.

Farther east lay Bohemia, a land rich with fields and mines, described as the Nevada of Europe at the end of the Middle Ages. It, too, would be torn and ravaged by war between 1419 and 1436, this time a conflict sparked by religious issues, which exacerbated the friction between Germans and Czechs. These were the Hussite Wars. In fifteen or sixteen years of bitter fighting one-sixth of the country's population perished, many more sought refuge elsewhere. Refugees from Bohemia were often taken for gypsies, who also first appeared in west and central Europe about this time, and who also came from eastern parts as distant and as unknown—a confusion marked in the French word for gypsy, *bohémien.*

The wars in Bohemia had risen out of the collapse of authority in the one institution which dominated the Middle Ages: the papacy. Popes were once the richest sovereigns, bishops among the greatest lords of the medieval West. Humbled by the king of France (Philip the Fair) early in the fourteenth century, exiled in Avignon (1305–1378), where they had been regarded as echoes of the French king's will, torn by schisms (1378–1417) after their return to Rome so that at one time three popes contended for the suffrage and the revenue of the faithful while busily excommunicating one another, the papacy lost much of its prestige. In Germany, resentment against the foreign popes, the realization that over and over again the ambitions of German emperors had drained their resources southward across the Alps, led the Imperial Diet to proclaim in 1336 that imperial power comes directly from God and that a king elected by the people needed no papal confirmation. In 1356, the Golden Bull of Charles IV reconfirmed this and effectively limited both the electors and the power of the empire to Germany alone. From now on, not Germans, but Frenchmen and Spaniards would struggle for Italy; but only after an interval during which the Italians would be left to themselves, an interval that would prove of the greatest significance to Italy and all of Europe.

The greatest of medieval conflicts, however, raged in France, where over a hundred years of almost uninterrupted warfare (1338–1453, the Hundred Years' War) devastated the greatest of European powers. The struggle between the houses of Orléans and Burgundy, between the partisans of English pretenders and the last heirs of the Valois line holding out in dire straits, created a country which Petrarch described in 1360 as a heap of ruins; where another witness, about 1440, found nothing but desert between the Loire and the Somme. Wolves roamed what had been villages, orchards, fields and, worse than wolves, bands of mercenaries scoured the countryside for scarce provisions. Untilled lands returned to forest, scrub, or marsh. "The English," says a contemporary commentator, "brought the forest back to France."

In the midst of misery the conspicuous consumption of the great: rich processions, costly and vivid garments, men's shoes so elongated that French crusaders at the Battle of Nicopolis (1396) had to cut off their points the better to run away, women's headgear so tall that in 1418, when the French position in the Hundred Years' War was at its worst, the doors of the castle of Vincennes had to be heightened on the orders of the Queen to allow the ladies of the court to pass through. A country handed over to men-at-arms, cloaked in misery, sown with gibbets. And in the ruins a population half, sometimes one-third, of its former size, grubbed a thin and hazardous living from the broken earth.

The time of troubles would pass, the growth resume, production rise, trade would flow once more. Lands gone waste, cities drained under the touch of the Black Death, would fill again, though slowly. But somehow the early modern centuries—the fifteenth and the sixteenth—would lack the sanguine confidence of the thirteenth. One-third of the French kingdom was brought under cultivation between 1480 and 1510. Yet, even the population growth, providing labor and consumers once again, creating new markets and new demands, appears more obviously than before to create new problems too: chief among these the frequent

A 15th century city under siege. The cannon in the foreground, of the type used by Mohammed during the siege of Constantinople, had a vastly more powerful propellant than earlier weapons.

shortages periodically aggravated to the point of famine that ravaged whole regions throughout the sixteenth century—Castille and Portugal in 1521, Andalusia in 1525, Tuscany in 1528, all of Italy in 1583. After famine, plague again, cutting down one-third or half of a city's population: nine-tenths of Rome or Naples in 1525, so it was rumored, four-fifths of Marseilles in 1581, 50,000 dead in Venice between 1575 and 1577.

By the mid-fifteenth century the cities flourished once again: the small, like Basel or Frankfurt (8,000–9,000); the middling, like Nürnberg (25,000); the great like Cologne, Ghent, Bruges, each around 50,000; and in Italy the giants: Milan, Florence, Venice, each between 75 and 100 thousand. But from the roster of Christendom one city would soon be missing. At dusk on May 29, 1453, the people of Constantinople made for the walls, crying to the Virgin for aid. Besieged for fifty days by 160,000 Turks led by the twenty-one-year-old Mohammed II, they could not find the hands to man the long span of walls, mend the breaches wrought by the fire of 130 cannons (all built by European gunsmiths) and 250 ships. They crowded into Santa Sophia, to hear the patriarch celebrate the last mass and Emperor Constantine XI give a cool account of the situation before the final assault: "The Turks are superior in artillery, cavalry, infantry, and numbers, but we have on our side the help of our Lord and Redeemer, of our saints, and of all the strength that God can give." One hour after midnight the Turkish assault began. By noon Byzantium was no more.

Chapter 2

THE RENAISSANCE

The Renaissance: A Definition

"I was born," writes Petrarch of his birth in 1304, "just as the dawn began to brighten," and, while Petrarch meant his words to be taken literally, we may as justly choose to take them in a symbolic sense.

The word *rinascita* (rebirth), first used in Vasari's *Lives of the Most Excellent Italian Architects, Painters and Sculptors, from Cimabue to Our Own Day* (Florence, 1550), referred exclusively to the arts, Vasari asserting the progress "of the Renaissance of the arts, and the perfection to which they have attained in our own time." By the late eighteenth century the concept had reached its most extreme formulation as: " . . . this mighty deliverance, in which the moldering Gothic fabrics of false religion and false philosophy fell together . . . "

Since then, the idea of a renaissance has given place to endless discussions, each designed to show that the label is best attached to the thirteenth or the seventeenth century, that it applies here and not there, that it must be used only with serious qualifications or, better, not at all. Men of the fifteenth century seem to have had fewer doubts. "It is but in our day that men dare to boast that they see the dawn of better things," wrote Matteo Palmieri, a Florentine businessman and politician of the 1430's. "Now, indeed, may every thoughtful spirit thank God that it has been permitted to him to be born in this new age, so full of hope and promise, which already rejoices in a greater array of nobly gifted souls than the world has seen in the thousand years that have preceded it."

We shall consider the term an apt label of a time of change, discovery, and, yes, revival; a time when a significant part of Europe's heritage was indeed reborn, adapted, and reintegrated into the equipment, the tradition, of the West. Though it is impossible to limit or define precisely, one can suggest a pattern that begins in the fourteenth century when a few precursors like Petrarch began to re-think and review their world, its problems, and their attitude toward them; then follows a fifteenth-century flowering in the city states of Italy and, above all, in Florence; and a last phase, beginning in the sixteenth century, when the Italian Renaissance spread to foreign courts and countries—to France and Spain, Poland and Hungary, Germany and England—carried by artists and scholars, tutors and architects, soldiers and princes and merchants, precisely at the time when its fires were being banked at home. The Renaissance is not one event, like a battle or a coronation. It is a notion: an impression then, as it still remains.

The Renaissance: An Overview

Sometime between the thirteenth and the fifteenth centuries the coloring, the orientation, the *rhythm* of human activities changes; and at some point along this process of change first a few men, then more, then whole societies through their political and social elite, become aware of transformation, notice that things are altering around them, that (or so they think) after centuries of darkness and stagnation, the world is on the move and so are they. An exhilarating experience hard to recapture for us, when change is now the norm and frantic movement a part of every life and day. But then it must have been a little like the excitement and flurry of passengers at the rail of a steamer that begins to draw away from shore, the quiet, somewhat disturbing throbbing beneath their feet, the slow opening of space between them and the solid quay, the pang of venturing onto a new element, into a new realm not quite familiar, not altogether reassuring, toward change and who can know what wonders or what dangers.

A society of peasants, priests, and warriors was replaced by one of burghers, merchants, lawyers—soldiers too, of course, but increasingly professionals, armed differently and levied in larger numbers. A relatively simple social structure gave way to an increasingly differentiated, complicated one, in which precisely professionalism and specialization began to count. A society in which reality and ideal, fact and fancy, stood further apart than in any other, in which the most elevated aspirations contrasted with brutish facts, gradually altered into one where contrast and contradictions appear a whit less brusque, where theory and practice were more closely reconciled, if only by rationalization. A traditionalist mentality, where things are because they have always been and people do as they have always done, slowly, grudgingly, accepted a new curiosity in things for their own sake rather than for the part they play in a predestined order and even, at least in theory (for no society has really done so in practice), championed the pursuit of truth wherever it may lead.

"It is the quality of a noble and aspiring mind," wrote Petrarch, "to see many lands and the customs of many peoples and to observe and remember them." There had been curious travelers before but no medieval man had formulated views so appropriate to the questing generations of this new world, certainly no representative thinker of an earlier day could properly have done so when noble and aspiring minds were bent primarily on their own salvation or that of others—and *that* was not to be found on Earth.

Now, knowledge became something one acquired not by revelation or tradition, but by learning and experience. "Prayer, to be sure, is the stronger weapon," Erasmus was to write, answering those theologians who criticized his scholarship, "yet knowledge is no less necessary." "Knowledge," writes the future Pope Pius II, "which causes the learned to stand out above the unlearned makes the former like unto God . . . even those of the most humble origin it lifts to the level of the greatest."

Like knowledge, wealth and social promotion need not depend on birth and, hence, on fate alone. An able man like Giovanni di Bicci de Medici (1360–1429), founder of the Medici bank and Medici fortunes, could start life with practically no capital, rise from apprentice to manager and, finally, to heading his own bank. At the time of his death, his estate was appraised at the fabulous value of 180,000 florins, or nearly 1500 lbs. of gold. Whether the figure is correct or not, Giovanni's son Cosimo de Medici (1389–1464) would live to be the richest man in Florence, and the most powerful.

In the world of the Italian Renaissance and, gradually, in those societies affected by its values, success would become a matter of enterprise, capacity, and will, and just what these could do can be seen in the career of Aeneas Silvius—a clever country lad, of good family but penniless, pursuing legal studies in Siena where, too poor to buy books, he would sit up nights copying out passages from those his friends could lend him, so late and long that once he even set his nightcap on fire dozing off. The young Silvius became a cardinal's secretary and a high clerical diplomat. He came to believe and to state that ambition was the chief spur of every human activity, and chastity a virtue for philosophers, not poets like himself. He took orders only at the age of forty-two in 1447. Bishop of Trieste in 1448, of Siena in 1449, a cardinal in 1456, he was elected Pope in 1458—Pius II. His style and talent reflected everything the age admired: versatility, scholarship, eloquence, diplomacy, a curious, inquiring, and industrious mind. "Glorious deeds," he writes, "are not embraced by democracies, least of all by merchants who, being by their nature intent on profit, loathe those splendid things that cannot be achieved without expense." But this attack on merchants came mainly because merchant Venice refused to join in a crusade against the Turks on which he had set his heart. For his was, in a sense, an age of merchants.

Beginning in the society of Italian cities, we shall see that a new sense of property, a new sense of individuality, or an intensified one, combined in concord with the new atmosphere, with law, with economic structures, with political developments. The prince who was part of a traditional social and political structure, the clerk, the scholar integrated in tradition and traditional activities, the gildsman in his corporation, even the knight—these figures were joined and overshadowed by the man who forges his own fortune, the personal genius, the self-assertive, self-advertising individualist, man of letters or artist, soldier of fortune, or humanist official.

To each age its realism, to each its own ideals. The Middle Ages envisaged a universal Christian order, the new age ended with division and a diversity of reforms. Crusading dreams waned, along with those of Christian unity and universal empire, as Christian states warred with one another and popes turned ever more toward their small peninsular states. Universal empire was scarcely even the ideal it once had been for some. Colonial empires of a concrete kind replaced the golden imagery of vague, distant lands where riches lay ready to the intrepid traveler's shovel and unicorns roamed through perfumed flowery meadows. That was the dreamland of the rich, where ageless youths embraced in garden tapestries whose trees bore fruit and flowers all at once. The poor had more utilitarian dreams of blessed lands flowing with milk and honey. More concrete illusions too, of countries where, as Boccaccio tells us, mountains were made of Parmesan cheese and vines tied with sausages; where, as for Rabelais, men were paid five pence a day to sleep, and two more for snoring; where, as in Brueghel's Flanders, pigs wandered ready roasted carrying the knife for slicing, cooked eggs waddled past on tiny feet, pies fell off the roof on hedgerows festooned with sausages.

Henceforth, Utopias would be no more the land of Cockaigne,* an imaginary country of luxurious idleness, but sage political structures. As for the never-never lands, the Indies and Americas were now too well known to serve in such fairy tales, but there could still dwell in them the "noble savages" of newer myths. Likewise, medieval millenarianism and its attendant expectations of the Last Judgment never disappeared, but only changed its guise. Once it had spurred children and young shepherds to set off for the Holy Land; now it would spark the hopes and ravings of Anabaptists ready to build the City of God near the river Rhine or, in due course, the prophets of seventeenth-century

---

* Left as a nickname to the cockney's London.

England. Paradise had promised escape from medieval dark and danger; it offered as much in Renaissance times, equally insecure for many. But now the notion spread—as well—of earthly paradise: a city of Man akin to that of God, or preferable to it, a notion as strange to medieval thinkers as it would have been to St. Augustine himself, who in the fifth century had conceived the City of God. Perhaps here lies the crucial difference in mentality and temper: not that the new age was more *clearly* optimistic than the old, but that it was more *concretely* so; that it could conceive a better world or the means to improve and realize it here and now.

Not only improve, but master. Still at the mercy of the elements, of weather, drought, or fire, of his own weakness most of all, the Renaissance man admits ambitions he had not known (or publicly revealed) in the previous age.

The Middle Ages had known minds as agile and as subtle, scholars as profound as their successors. But their physical limitations had, as it were, built barriers to their imagining: what existed could only be transcended on an extraterrestrial plane. After the Renaissance, one could hope to do it here on earth. Man, said the scholarly Pico della Mirandola (1463–1494), was confined by no limit, defined by no one but himself. The world still overwhelmed him. But he no longer feared to admit his wish to dominate it, shape it to his will, become like to God. He thought of flying machines, of submarines, of chariots that moved by something other than animal power, of harnessing the winds and the tides. His ends were still far beyond his means, but he had broken through the shell of earlier days. In pursuit of his towering imagination, he would conquer far more than he could yet conceive.

"Heaven" says Poggio Bracciolini, Chancellor of Florence in 1453, "belongs by right to energetic men who have fought great fights and accomplished fine works on Earth." Marsilio Ficino (1433–1499) placed the human soul in the center of the universe. Pico affirmed man's freedom to choose his own destiny. The world remained as a divine creation, but the concept was slipping into second place. In the foreground now, there lay a man-made world, an object to be ordered and fashioned by the strong and able. It was still subject to obscure powers to be propitiated by astrologers and priests but liable, above all, to the will and initiative of man.

This was a new note, the slogan subversive of medieval Christendom, dredged up across a thousand years from an entirely different civilization, as when Vittorino da Feltre, the great schoolmaster of Mantua, quoted Cicero: "The whole glory of man lies in his activity." Family, profession, or trade, above all public affairs, were honorable now. The city of man was no longer an unworthy field for his endeavors; salvation did not necessarily lie in rejecting the world, virtue in withdrawal. "Undoubtedly," writes Matteo Palmieri, "some men are called to find their happiness in this way by devoting themselves to the contemplation of heavenly wisdom." But "no activity is so acceptable to God as that of sharing the task of guiding communities of men organized on the basis of social justice; to those who fulfill this duty He has given the promise of assured felicity hereafter."

To Palmieri's contemporary, Leon Battista Alberti, what man needs is "house, property and shop"—possessions, wealth, the source of wealth, are essentials of the good life, focused not on another world but on the here and now, on home, on friendship, on social and economic success. When the merchant Agnolo Pandolfini married, he knelt down with his wife and prayed, asking for himself "wealth, honor and friends," for her "blamelessness and honesty, that she might be a good housekeeper."

As for immortality, the most concrete certainty of that lay in the fame that ensured survival or, more immediately, in the family which would perpetuate name and possessions and in the monuments that could be left behind to do the same. Thus, Federigo da Montefeltro's inscription in the court of his great palace in Urbino, explaining that he had built it for his own glory and his posterity. Hence also so much of Renaissance art designed to publicize the wealth and glory of a man, of a family, of a state; the portraits painted to confer immortality on the features of princes and merchants; the narrative paintings of civic festivals and pageants, and of heroic moments of a family's or city's past that would impress all with their greatness. It has even been suggested that the sculpture of the time reflected a new individualism by detaching statues from the buildings of which they used to form a part, making them autonomous, leaving the free-standing work of art to be itself alone, like the men of the time, rather than fitted into a niche or into a greater architectural complex.

One need not go so far to be convinced of the relation between the new mentality and the new art. Even the polyphony of Renaissance music weaves a strand of voices or of sound into a new harmony reflecting the nature of the age: colorful, complex, seldom if ever simple. By the fifteenth century, liveliness, originality, vividness had replaced the austere simplicity of Gregorian chant. Counterpoint makes its appearance in song as in architecture: organic, logical but increasingly complicated, increasingly fantastic and subtle, straining after more exalted engineering feats.

The same is true of the connection between the new money and the new art or learning. The first great bankers of the fifteenth century—the Medici—were also the first great patrons of art. The first public library in Europe was set up because a book collector, Niccolo de Niccoli, who ruined himself with his passion, was given an unlimited overdraft at the Medici Bank and, after he died, Cosimo de Medici canceled the debt in exchange for the collection, most of which he gave to Florence. The man who was set to cataloguing the new library was Tomasso Parentu-

The Procession in the Piazza San Marco, by Gentile Bellini. Accademia, Venice.

celli. When Parentucelli became Pope Nicholas V he founded the Vatican Library, while the catalog he had drawn up in Florence became a guide to the founders of other great libraries, first in Italy, then in Germany, France, and England.

As men collected books or gold, they collected art as well—and also architects and artists. In the 1490's Ludovico il Moro of Milan, who already had Bramante and Leonardo da Vinci working for him, wrote to Florence asking for a talented painter and got from there a list to choose from: "Sandro Botticelli: very excellent artist, in easel as in mural paintings, his figures have a fine virile air in conception and proportions. Filippino Lippi: his heads have a suave and pleasing air, but we think he has less talent. Perugino: rare and peculiar artist, his figures have an air of the most angelic sweetness. Ghirlandaio: good master in panels and better in murals, industrious and productive master." Sad to say, Il Moro selected the sugary Perugino.

The worldliness was not in itself so new. One would imagine that ordinary men during the Middle Ages felt much the same. Only they did not say so. They did not show it. True, the virtues of unworldliness, of physical mortification, the superiority of the spiritual to the material, may have been respected more in the breach than the observance. At least, they were acknowledged. The change came when worldly values were proclaimed and accepted as respectable. And the change was now.

Paradoxically enough this change, this fresh mundanity, was not unconnected with the trials of the time, with the awareness that life is short, one's time is swift in passing. Death which used to be the soul's returning to its heavenly home becomes henceforth an exile from the earth. Physical annihilation, once a fulfillment, becomes a horrid threat. Out of this newly perceived challenge, human nature would draw a new sense of life as a struggle against death, against annihilation. The sense of death infused time lived with new meaning, gave man a new sense of temporality and hence, in a way, of life.

And this also can be seen in the art of the time. When we look at the fifteenth-century frescoes of Ghirlandaio, Pinturicchio, Botticelli, we may think that the painters sketched out their cityscapes from the new architecture going up around. In fact the position was just the opposite: architects followed the painters. The patrons of the Renaissance were in a hurry to realize their dreams and, while their great architectural ensembles were still in the planning stage or quite unfinished (for example, Urbino, or the Duke of Este's Palazzo Schiffanoja at Ferrara, or Pope Nicholas V's projects for reconstructing Rome), they had artists delineate the new cities and complexes which they had had neither the time nor the means to build. When Ghirlandaio and Botticelli painted, the great monumental compositions of the new style were still only projects: the Florence of their day was architecturally a medieval not a Renaissance city. The great Renaissance palaces were just beginning to rise, and those which stood, stood as isolated marvels. The new world was a-building, the artists anticipated it, their paintings one more way of overtaking time, forestalling death.

The new individualism, this haste to make one's mark, are found in the Italian admiration for a man's *virtù*—a term which refers less to virtue than to man's genius or demonic power, a quality reflected in striking gestures whose impressiveness rests not in good or evil but in their capacity to astound, to arrest attention. Evil fame is better than none: in 1537 Lorenzino de Medici, blamed for mutilating ancient Roman statues, sought some deed that would make men forget this and murdered the Duke of Florence, Alexander, his lord and kin.

That, of course, was not the official expression of the concept. The ideal was more the high-minded man of Aristotle's *Ethics*: "he who, being truly worthy of great things, holds himself thus worthy . . . For he who holds himself worthy of less than his merits is small-minded, the more so the greater his true excellence." A most unchristian view, but one which could be combined, in a new synthesis, with a perfectly Christian concern for personal salvation—and expression. For where tradition suggested that the self should seek to sink itself in God, a new vision suggested another, more exalting possibility. When Petrarch climbed to the top of Mont Ventoux, the first thought that came to him was that "nothing is admirable but the soul in comparison to which, if it is great, nothing is great." Not the soul to be saved—as in the past—but the soul aspiring to greatness and competitiveness. The soul and also now the man who bears it. The inspiration came from St. Augustine, and from Seneca, both scholars of another, older world which Petrarch and his contemporaries sought hard to recapture and which, as so often happens, would lead its captors captive, so that "Europe," in the words of the historian Huizinga, "after having lived in the shadow of antiquity, lived in its sunshine once more."

Economic Conditions: 14th and 15th Centuries

There is no understanding the intellectual and political revolution of this period without its economic side, without the development that set the tempo and the scale, furnished its means, its techniques, and sometimes its ideas.

The Rise of the Bourgeoisie

There has been much discussion about "the rise of the bourgeoisie"— that is, of free citizens dwelling in burgs or cities—the social and economic developments which, beginning perhaps in the twelfth or thirteenth century, brought to the fore new classes ignored in straiter times, new riches, new attitudes, new values, the very essence of what we call the Renaissance and then the modern world. That new men rise to wealth and power from humble circumstances is true of any age. That

The Strozzi Palace in Florence.

more of these did so outside the traditional channels of clergy or of arms is more characteristic. That these insinuated different social values it would be rash to state, for much of the social revolution we witness even in the urban world consisted of new men shouldering their way into the old positions or, when successful, seeking admission into the old ruling caste. At least until the turn of the eighteenth into the nineteenth century (in many places longer), success meant social promotion, and that only one thing: access to the nobility in which a successful family, arisen like the Medici or the Fuggers of Augsburg from the lower orders, finds a place—in which also it may simply melt and disappear. The rise of the bourgeoisie was not the triumph of bourgeois values for, consciously, the bourgeois accepted the values of the society in which he moved, conceived sanctions and rewards in terms of the traditional order, and capped the most successful of careers by rising into a class which, far from competing with, he aped.

Unconsciously, however, and in spite of this, as the cities grew, new values spread, spinning off the dynamo of civic activities. The number of men more or less consciously living by these values grew and their activities played a greater role in the world about them. The bourgeoisie did not challenge the Middle Ages: it grew in them, it was of them and always of its time, which it never tried to forge but rather to exploit. Yet this exploitation—the struggle for a living, then a profit, then for more—produced the forces and the energy which would explode the medieval world, produced also the wealth and the resources on which another kind of world would rise.

Surplus and Precapitalism

The first necessity for any but the very simplest economic activity is some kind of surplus, something which when set aside from the bare necessities of current consumption can be used to allow men to work at tasks that look beyond their mere survival or else exchanged for other surplus goods and invested in their production. Some kind of surplus there had often been in the Middle Ages, but ways of using it or, in another sense, a choice in how it might be used had long been lacking. Until the thirteenth century mere shortage of money—money in the obvious and convenient form of coins—a shortage due to the almost complete dearth of gold and the relative scarcity of silver, had meant that surplus income from land, rent, or taxes could only with difficulty be saved. Surpluses had to be eaten up or else invested in conspicuous consumption: servants, objects, or buildings. The discovery of new gold and silver mines in Germany, Bohemia, and Transylvania during the twelfth and thirteenth centuries began to make for change even as the Crusades and the enterprise of medieval trade began to funnel goods and profits westward. The appearance of the florin (1252) and the Venetian ducat (1284) provided both a symbol of new capital and a very practical means of saving or exchange.

Capital, yes. But capitalism, as some historians claim? We consider capitalism as the system in which the profit motive dominates, large accumulations of capital are both an end and factors, and the use of capital to earn profits (that is, more capital) is a standard practice. This was not always so.

> In moneys are matters much obscure
> They go high and low, one knows not what to do;
> When one thinks to gain, it's the reverse that's true

grumbles a disgruntled abbot as the fourteenth century opens. And the men—some men—who lived between the fourteenth and the sixteenth or the seventeenth centuries were only beginning to break through such puzzled and suspicious attitudes, which reflected their current possibilities and values.

The question in part is one of atmosphere. Great adventurers, entrepreneurs, very rich men of humble extraction already existed. We hear of a Dutch financier, William of Duvenwoorde (1290–1353) with an income of 70,000 livres (roughly a million dollars) per year. The fortune of Jacques Coeur (1395?–1456) is estimated at something like 9 million dollars (1940). Its purchasing power at ten or twenty times that sum. But not only were such men exceptions, as the very rich have been in all times, public opinion looked upon them as exceptions and, far from admiring or emulating them, disapproved of their doings and their values. This is one thing which changes between the fourteenth and the sixteenth century.

More men set out deliberately to fructify their monies. Moreover, they learned to reinvest their profits and to diversify their enterprises, as we can hear Antonio, Shakespeare's merchant of Venice explain:

> . . . I thank my fortune for it,
> My ventures are not in one bottom trusted,
> Nor to one place; nor is my whole estate
> Upon the fortune of this present year . . .

For traders, this kind of practice meant a margin of safety along with bigger profits, since funds were not allowed to lie dormant long. For society, it meant that, very, very slowly, the ownership of the means of production—goods, raw materials, equipment, labor, and, in some measure, land—passed into the hands of entrepreneurs who were neither craftsmen nor tradesmen in the medieval sense. Another change, not unrelated to the previous ones, was simply a difference in scale. Before we can speak of capitalism, a certain quantitative threshold must be passed, a level of production, a degree of exchange achieved which, so to speak, turns quantity into quality, makes for the difference between a shed and a house, a very big house and a palace; and obviously such a level of economic activity in turn depends in part on attitudes toward it.

"It was iron and wheat," Jean-Jacques Rousseau would write around 1750, "which civilized men and ruined humanity." Economists would probably add a few less ponderous things: silver and gold for one, but also and especially at this time textiles and spices. Even a subsistence economy in which men make do with goods which they themselves produce has room for certain specialties or luxuries—salt, weapons, or adornments. The more society evolves the greater the demand for these, the greater also the variety and the supply. A fourteenth-century Florentine trade manual lists 288 "spices," and includes not only Eastern products but also the most varied goods, like wax from Spain, Poland, and Riga, Italian paper, copper from central Europe, glue from Florence and Bologna. The greater this kind of commerce the greater also the attempts by people on the spot to bite into the profits by developing goods and specialties of their own, either to exchange for other things or to replace them. Thus in the thirteenth century the competition of Chinese silk, cheap and abundant at the time, had forced the weavers of Lucca to learn the use of waterpower to turn their silk-wringing machines, in order to increase production and lower costs.

Commerce

For a long time commercial activity had depended on wandering merchants (the *pieds-poudreux,* whence the Pie-Powder trade courts of medieval England) trailing across Europe with their caravans, meeting in fairs large or small to exchange their goods. In the thirteenth century the greatest of these fairs were held in Champagne, in northeast France, centrally located for the trading routes of the time. The wars of the fourteenth century brought about their decline and international trade turned toward other centers, such as Geneva and Lyons, where great fairs flourished in the fifteenth century. Meanwhile, however, everyday business was growing in the towns. The great trading cities had in effect become the home of never-ending fairs where buying and selling could go on all the year round.

This did not decrease the movement and exchange of goods. Rather the reverse. For in the towns were relatively vast concentrations of people, most of whom depended on others for supplies—not only the raw materials of their craft or the things that they would try to sell, but the barest staples of consumption: food, fuel, wine. Most of this clearly came from the nearby countryside; but such agglomerations of consumers might have to rely on sources from afar when the hinterland could not provide them in sufficient quantity, as in the case of the Dutch cities, say, or Genoa, or at times because the crops had failed. And there were always things that had to come from far away: fish or salt, timber for building and for ships, wool to be worked up into cloth.

Transport

Roads of course were few, dangerous, and bad. Land transport—by horse or mule or cart—was awkward and slow. The high cost of transport had its effect on prices, especially those of the heaviest and most essential commodities. At the beginning of the fourteenth century, carriage costs from Pisa to Florence increased the price of wine over 54 per cent. It was all a matter of weight and intrinsic value; four bales of silk sent from Lucca to Paris about the same time went up only 1.8 per cent. As late as the fifteenth century the transport of grain over the seventy-five-odd miles between Rouen and Amiens in Normandy would raise its price by a third.

While transport affected the price of bulkier goods (cereals, wine, or salt) by as much as 100 or 150 per cent, the lighter luxury goods never seem to have gone up more than 20 or 25 per cent. One result of this, and understandably, was the vast and early development of trade in luxury goods where profits were higher, efforts and difficulties relatively less. This was especially so in the case of Italy's trade with the Orient, whence most of these goods came. Another result was the tardier development of northern trade. But bulky goods had to be transported. They moved most conveniently on waterways, above all on the sea, open, free of rapids and of tolls. It takes thirty-five times less force to carry an equal weight on sea than on land. In spite of all its hazards the sea would hold the key to Europe's economic—and eventually political—development.

It may be that Europe was especially favored by its length of coastline, the depth of its watery indentations, the narrowness of a land mass which, unlike that of every other continent, places most of it within reasonable reach of a port. A glance at Europe, medieval as well as modern, shows three great maritime areas focusing and facilitating economic activity: the Mediterranean in the south, the Baltic in the north, the Atlantic in the west. Mediterranean and Baltic are in some ways replicas of each other, Lübeck a northern Venice, Baltic items the rougher, bulkier complement of Mediterranean cargoes. Through the Mediterranean, spices, silks, cottons, sugar, and small wares; through the Baltic, timber, potash, pitch, wax, furs, cereals, iron and copper, fish salted or dried. The wares are less glamorous in the north, the profits less impressive, the cities rise in brick where southern ones sport marble, still Lübeck and Hamburg lie at the center of a vast network that links Novgorod and Bruges, London and Cologne, Bergen and Riga. At the height of its greatness, in the fourteenth century, the confederacy which these cities led, the Hanseatic League, numbered some eighty cities. Its power, great enough to overawe some kings, did not decline until the sixteenth century, concomitant with the rise of central and western Europe and the decline of the Mediterranean in the south.

Before its rise to sixteenth-century predominance, the Atlantic-North Sea area was nowhere as important as the other two. It did provide wool for Italian looms and salt for Baltic fisheries, but it was less significant than a fourth economic complex developed in central Europe around the inland routes—the valleys of the Rhine, Rhone, and Danube and the Alpine passes—linking south and north, south and northwest, east and west. Since the fourteenth century, export of metals and textiles and transit trade would spur the growth of cities in the German south: Augsburg, Nürnberg, Basel. By 1500, the Great Company of Ravensbrück had branches in Bern, Geneva, Lyons, Avignon, Marseilles, Milan, Genoa, Barcelona, Valencia, Saragossa, Vienna, Budapest, Antwerp, Cologne, and Nürnberg. A new complex of trade was growing up, affected by the troubles of Mediterranean commerce when Egypt was conquered by the Ottomans in 1517, the opening up of sea routes to the Indies (west and east), the new colonial trade from Atlantic ports (especially the Portuguese factory set up at Antwerp in 1494), the wars and foreign invasions of Italy. The yearly galley fleet from Venice to Flanders sailed for the last time in 1532. Its abandonment was symbolic of northern Europe's emancipation from the Mediterranean.

Profits and Prohibitions

Before any flowering of commerce could evolve another emancipation had to be achieved: from the rule of a code which viewed commerce with suspicion, any but the most moderate profit with disapproval, and condemned most of the activities on which modern business enterprise is based. As we have noted, the world view of Medieval man was not, as ours, one of mobility, change, flux. Theoretically at least, the world was a stable place where men were expected and aspired to live out their lives in the position where God had placed them, son following his father, one generation in the footsteps of the next. Change, frequent enough, had to be justified in traditional terms; revolution not as an advance but always a return to ancient ways. Economic activity of any but the most limited kind threatened to upset stability. "He who has enough to satisfy his wants," a fourteenth-century writer tells us. "and nevertheless ceaselessly labors to acquire riches, either in order to obtain a higher social position or that subsequently he may have enough to live without labor, or that his sons may become men of wealth and importance—all such are incited by a damnable avarice, sensuality or pride."

Certain aspects of Christian doctrine concerning both law and life affected also the possibilities for investment, hence for production and profit. One was the doctrine of the just price, which held that a thing

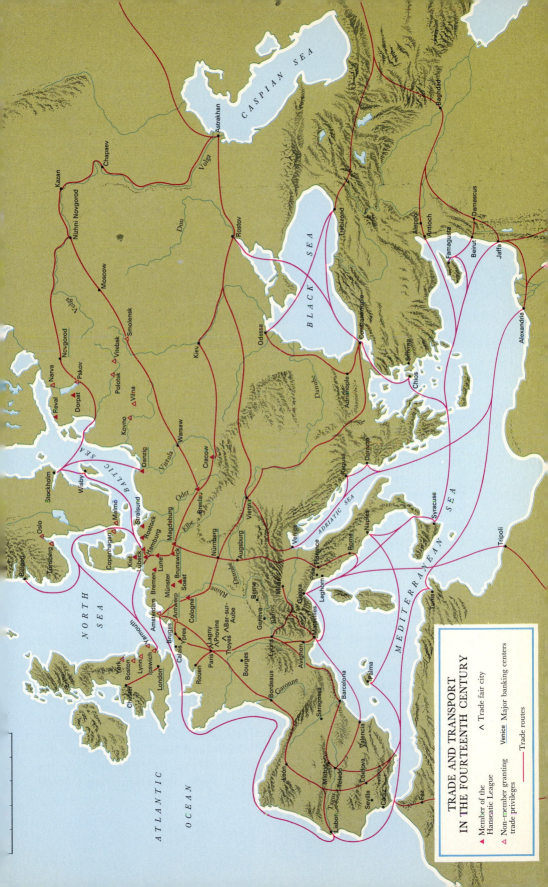

CASPIAN SEA

BLACK SEA

ADRIATIC SEA

MEDITERRANEAN SEA

NORTH SEA

BALTIC SEA

ATLANTIC OCEAN

Astrakhan

Chapaev

Kazan

Nizhni Novgorod

Volga

Rostov

Moscow

Don

Novgorod

Volga

Smolensk

Kiev

Narva

Pskov

Vitebsk

Polotsk

Reval

Dorpat

Vilna

Kovno

Warsaw

Vistula

Danzig

Cracow

Stockholm

Wisby

Oder

Breslau

Vienna

Malmö

Stralsund

Rostock

Copenhagen

Kiel

Lübeck

Hamburg

Lüne

Magdeburg

Elbe

Nürnberg

Augsburg

Danube

Bremen

Brunswick

Münster

Soest

Cologne

Rhine

Amsterdam

Antwerp

Bruges

Ypres

Calais

London

Ipswich

Lynn

Boston

Chester

York

Yarmouth

Rouen

Paris

Lagny

Provins

Bar-sur-Aube

Troyes

Bourges

Berne

Geneva

Lyons

Rhône

Garonne

Bordeaux

Avignon

Marseilles

Milan

Genoa

Pisa

Florence

Leghorn

Rome

Naples

Syracuse

Venice

Ragusa

Durazzo

Adrianople

Odessa

Constantinople

Trebizond

Smyrna

Chios

Tripoli

Alexandria

Aleppo

Antioch

Famagusta

Beirut

Damascus

Jaffa

Baghdad

Tunis

Palma

Barcelona

Saragossa

Valencia

León

Madrid

Toledo

Córdova

Seville

Cádiz

Fez

Lisbon

Tagus

Oslo

Tönsberg

Bergen

TRADE AND TRANSPORT
IN THE FOURTEENTH CENTURY

▲ Member of the
   Hanseatic League   △ Trade fair city

△ Non-member granting   Venice Major banking centers
   trade privileges

──── Trade routes

should not be sold for more than it was worth, but whose subjective basis allowed much leeway in interpretation. Another, more awkward, was the interdiction of usury, narrowly defined as the practice of lending money at almost any interest. St. Luke (6:35) had said, "Lend hoping for nothing again." Before him Aristotle, since promoted to the status of a father of the church, had pointed out that, unlike animals or land, money is sterile and cannot breed more money. Based on such authors, the doctrine of the church was clear enough: money is not consumed by use, it passes from hand to hand but can return as good as when it had been lent. Nor can it fructify (a view correct enough when opportunities for fruitful investment had been nil). This being so, the lender deserves no compensation, any more than the good neighbor does for loan of a shovel or a knife which are returned in good condition. If a fellow man needs money, it should be freely lent for the love of God. Whether they asked interest from the poor or from the prodigal, usurers sinned against God and nature; and the church could see no distinction between usury and commercial interest.

It soon became clear that views such as these had to be qualified. No large-scale enterprise was possible without loans, credit, various instruments of exchange, let alone profit. The gap between principle and practice was made good by tolerance, intolerance, indifference, rationalization, adjustment and, above all, final expiation. As a Ragusan merchant put it in his will which set apart 35 lire for ill-acquired goods: "Me-seems that having been a merchant, it is impossible that I should not have ill-acquired something." Trading companies kept a special account (*il conto di Messer Domeneddio*) for God and for his poor, or set aside a share of their capital whose fruits would go to charity. Rich men endowed churches and chapels, had themselves buried in Benedictine robes, like the great Arras usurer Baude Crespin, or planned crusades to salve their guilty souls, like the Genoese merchant-sailor Benedetto Zaccaria. They showed a strong interest in the poor and in the common good: they endowed hospices, asylums, hospitals (of which early fourteenth-century Arras—population 20,000— counted twenty-three with a total capacity of a thousand) and also bridges, fountains, aqueducts, even embankments and port installations.

Religious scruples were strong, but the determination to trade and profit was stronger. As early as 1208, Pope Innocent III, in a letter to the Bishop of Arras, admitted that it had become almost impossible to punish usurers as required because of the great numbers who would have to be chastized. Soon the painter Giotto, born poor, would grow rich, by his talent, of course, but also by hiring out looms to poor weavers with a profit of 120 per cent. In the University of Bologna, professors lent money to students at a high rate of interest and lined their pockets with profits from textbooks which they bought cheap and sold dear. By the fourteenth century, the rich merchant of Prato, Francesco Datini, could open his great ledgers with the words "in the name of God and profit." The merchants' world had become a vast counting house, due to end in the great day of accounting.

In cities where merchants ruled steps were taken to see that ecclesiastical anachronisms should not interfere with the interests of trade, as when debtors invoked religious prohibitions to avoid paying business debts. In 1369 Genoa promulgated a law "against those who pretend that contracts of exchange and insurance are illegal and usurious according to Scripture, and who have recourse to ecclesiastical tribunals to quash them . . . seeing that if such contracts were not honored, the citizens and merchants of Genoa would suffer great damages." The law condemned whoever invoked such arguments to pay a fine of half a lira for each lira he had refused to pay.

In insisting on a just price and condemning usury, the medieval church only reflected popular sentiment high and low. By the fourteenth and the fifteenth centuries, this sentiment was changing in important quarters and the church began to change with it. The humanists (to be discussed below, pp. 69–79) were among the first to find ammunition for their wealthy patrons, arguments for the new values against the old. Men, they pointed out, owed it to themselves, their family, the state, to be active, creative, generous—all virtues connected with material possessions which thus became a source of good. When in 1420 Leonardo Bruni translated a supposedly Aristotelian text for Cosimo de Medici, he commented that such possessions afforded "opportunity for the exercise of virtue." A little later at the papal court itself, another humanist conveniently explained that the poverty associated with Christ was only the reflection of socio-economic conditions in the Roman Empire, hardly appropriate for a Holy See whose duty in a more splendid age was to shine forth in material splendor.

This trend need not surprise us when we consider that the papacy, which had been the major economic power of the high Middle Ages, must have been the greatest capitalist of these centuries too. The origins of serious business accounting methods lie in the papal *curia* as much as in the Tuscan banks; and the economic orientation of ecclesiastical organization everywhere must have contributed to the growth of a secular spirit in the church itself. Alberti had taken it for granted that "all priests are in the highest degree greedy for money." This greed for money made the popes practically partners of the great merchant-bankers whose fortune as papal managers and agents rested partly on the collection of papal revenues and partly on the credit that they could extend to an institution much in need of it. By the sixteenth century the representatives of the great merchant houses worked hand-in-hand with the church, sometimes belonged to it: one Rome representative of a German business house was apostolic protonotary, the Fuggers' representative there accumulated numerous benefices and ecclesiastical dignities, the Thurzo family, the Fuggers' partners in eastern Europe, counted two bishops among their number. Pious merchants combined their business trips with edifying pilgrimages; and businessmen could at last relax in the belief that their labors served the highest ends: "The labor of merchants" asserts a book published in Venice in 1573 and soon translated into French, "is ordered in view of the salvation of humanity." In very Catholic Spain, the inscription over Valencia's new sixteenth-century exchange read: "A merchant acting thus overflows with riches and at last enjoys eternal life."

All this was firmly based in the work of fifteenth-century canonists, like St. Bernardino of Siena and St. Antoninus of Florence, who had a clear and novel notion of capital as the productive agent in investment and loans. "Capital," says St. Bernardino, "is more than money because of its 'creative power' and riches honorably acquired are agreeable in the sight of God and man." Talk of usury now intervened only where the lender took no risk at all, which must have been rare indeed, and interest was condemned only when it seemed excessive. As a matter of fact the first municipal pawnshop (*Monte de pietà*) designed to keep the poor out of the usurers' clutches by charging only 10 per cent interest, had been set up at Perugia (1462) under Franciscan inspiration and perfected at Mantua in 1482 by the blessed Bernardino da Feltre with papal approval.

In stressing the importance of possible risk involved as justifying interest, theologians seem to have been aware of the tendency of money to become increasingly abstract, with little or no relation to concrete values. They feared what we most prize today: the mechanization of relations between lender and borrower, the elimination of those human factors—charity, gratitude—which the church, at least in theory, counted above the mere efficiency of economic activity. How right they were we may see from a note Columbus has left scribbled in the margin of a book: "Gold is an excellent thing. When one has it, one does all one wants in the world, even to leading souls into Paradise."

Business Methods

So, people changed their minds. They also changed their methods. Slowly, beginning in the twelfth century, Arabic numerals had simplified mathematical operations. Starting in the fourteenth century, double-entry bookkeeping began to provide a really effective method of accounting. Guarded by Italians as a business secret for over a century, it affected business practices north of the Alps only very slowly. The first account of it, in Luca Facioli's book on mathematics, appeared in Venice in 1494; it was translated into French and Flemish over half a century later (1543), into English in 1547, into German in 1550. As late as 1581, Sebastian Gammersfelder, who had left his home at Passau on the Danube

CAPITAL · MANUFACTURING · TRADE IN THE LATE RENAISSANCE

Legend:

- ■ Fugger center
- ● Fugger branch
- ▲ Fugger mine
- ■ Medici center
- ● Medici branch

- **G** Gold
- **S** Silver
- **C** Copper
- **T** Tin
- **L** Lead
- **Z** Zinc
- **I** Iron
- **C** Coal

- Linen
- Wool
- Silk
- Furs and leather
- Grain
- Wine
- Herring
- Honey and wax
- Ⓢ Salt

Seas and oceans: BALTIC SEA · NORTH SEA · ADRIATIC SEA · MEDITERRANEAN SEA · ATLANTIC OCEAN

Rivers: Danube · Vistula · Oder · Elbe · Main · Rhine · Moselle · Seine · Loire · Garonne · Rhône · Po · Tagus

Cities: Warsaw · Danzig · Posen · Grünberg · Breslau · Cracow · Teschen · Neusohl · Kremnitz · Pressburg · Belgrade · Hochkirch · Dresden · Prague · Vienna · Salzburg · Schwaz · Botzen · Verona · Padua · Venice · Rome · Naples · Palermo · Hamburg · Magdeburg · Leipzig · Erfurt · Nuremberg · Augsburg · Hall · Innsbruck · Milan · Verona · Bologna · Florence · Lucca · Genoa · Frankfurt · Cologne · Deventer · Antwerp · Strasbourg · Basel · Geneva · Avignon · Marseilles · Amsterdam · Bruges · Ghent · Paris · Rouen · Lyons · Montpellier · Cahors · York · Beverly · Hull · Boston · Ipswich · Yarmouth · Lynn · Colchester · London · Canterbury · Southampton · Bristol · Salisbury · Exeter · Dartmouth · Plymouth · Poitiers · Bordeaux · Toulouse · Nantes · Saragossa · Valencia · Toledo · Almaden · Guadalcanal · Almagro · Seville · Lisbon

to teach school at Danzig, blamed critics of his bookkeeping manual for looking at modern accounting "like a cow at a gate." Even exaggerated by Gammersfelder's irritation, this serves to illustrate the gap between north and south, a certain delay in developing sophisticated business techniques or in paying serious attention to their possibilities.

But, north or south, all merchants scribbled and all merchants traveled. "A merchant," says Alberti, himself an architect and head of a great trading company, "should always have ink-stained hands." A trader's correspondence was immense and unending. Francesco Datini wrote interminably to his wife, his partners, his representatives, friends, and stewards, as well as to the many firms with which he did business. In his archives, rediscovered in 1870, 150,000 letters, thousands of bills of lading, bills of exchange, checks, hundreds of insurance policies and deeds, over 500 account books and ledgers had survived.

Correspondence in Datini's day went largely by private courier or chance messenger. Datini's messages from Florence to Venice seem to have taken about six days. The regular postal service that the Venetians organized between Venice and Bruges, however, took only seven days. By 1500 things had improved a bit. The average courier took two to three days from Rome to Venice, twelve from Rome to Paris. Louis XI had organized a royal postal service in France, whose couriers in their great boots rode in stages first of four and then of seven leagues (an advance that has gone down in legend) covering about thirty miles a day. One who, in 1342, took four and a half days to cover the 450-odd miles between Avignon and Paris set what was considered a record for a long time. In the sixteenth century the Empire had an official post organized by a Milanese family, the Taxis, whose services covered 135 kilometers a day and carried letters from Italy to Brussels in five and a half days.

But these were exceptional speeds, not available to the private trader. The merchant who wanted to keep an eye on operations, or to learn something of the markets and men that he was dealing with, had to go and see for himself. Thus merchants were inveterate travelers. Lucas Rem of Augsburg started out as a clerk and representative of the Welser Company at Antwerp and Lyons, Venice, Saragossa and, finally, at Lisbon—working and learning his trade the while. Here is the tally of his travels in three years: 1500: Lyons—Bourges—Paris—Rouen—Lyons; Lyons—Albi—Lyons; Lyons—Switzerland—Lyons. 1501: Lyons—Augsburg—Lyons; Lyons—Switzerland—Lyons. 1502: Lyons—Switzerland—Lyons; Lyons—Augsburg—Lyons; Lyons—Albi—Lyons; Lyons—Toulouse—Saragossa. 1503: Saragossa—Lisbon. From Lisbon he visited Morocco, Madeira, the Azores, and the Cape Verde Islands. It seems a lot of traveling, especially given the conditions of the time. But, as a Nürnberg merchant settled in Cracow would explain: "I am well content not to remain ever in the same town; he learns nothing, who remains thus ever settled in one town." Frederick Behaim of Nürnberg, had gone to Lyons at fifteen (1506) to learn his trade; he sent his son Paul to Cracow (1533) to learn a trade from the representatives of a Florentine firm—the De Nobilis. Paul would eventually represent a German firm at Antwerp.

This cannot have been much fun. Even the shortest trips were still fraught with hazards and difficulties: bandits or pirates, weather, the bad state of roads, at sea a total lack of control over the elements and lack of navigational instruments. Around 1500, swift trips from Venice to London by sea took twenty to thirty days, from Seville to Venice by sea fifteen, from Madrid to Rome by land and sea, thirty. A hulk would take a year for the round trip from Antwerp to Cadiz, the best time from Antwerp to Lisbon was fifteen days. Winds and weather made for tremendous, unpredictable variations: Venice to Constantinople could take between twenty-nine and seventy-three days, Tunis to Leghorn as little as six or as long as twenty days. Days and weeks could be lost waiting for a fair wind. Ships bound for Antwerp often ended on the Irish rocks; shipwreck and accident became matters of course. Even knowledgeable sailors, able by the sixteenth century to determine latitude, could do less well about longitude for lack of serviceable watches capable of showing time when on the move. This was the realm which the fifteenth century set itself to tame and which a hundred years later it began to conquer.

The Great Discoveries

In 1487, after seventy years of trial, error, and slow advance, a Portuguese sailor, Bartholomeu Diaz, rounded the Cape of Good Hope and opened a route to the Indies free of Venetian and Muslim middlemen. Ten years later Vasco da Gama sailed from Lisbon, to land in Calicut within a year, looking, as he explained himself, for Christians and for spices. Columbus, sailing westward, found neither: only islands (in 1492 he claimed San Salvador for Spain) and savages. Da Gama found both Christians and spices, but much more of the spices. His return to Lisbon

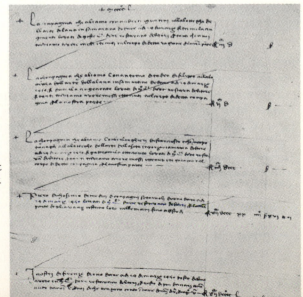

A page from the account book of the Medici bank in Florence.

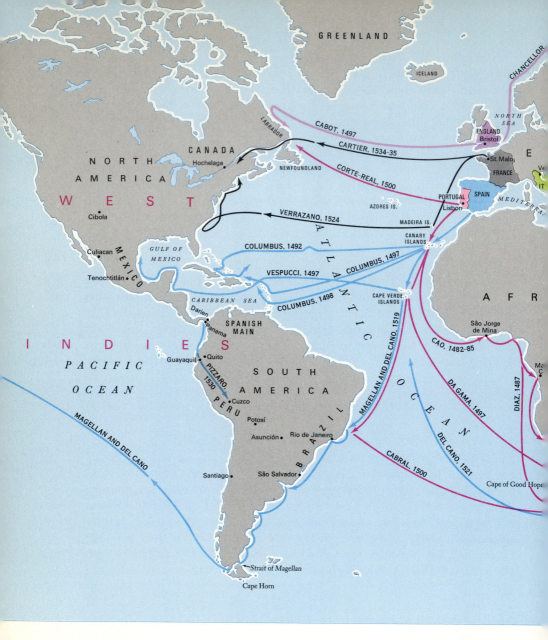

in 1499, laden with ginger, cinnamon, cloves, and other condiments, was the rich reward of a persistent quest.

For some generations intrepid Portuguese had sailed further and further into the South Atlantic, setting up forts and factories, trading for gold and slaves. The greatest figure in the history of these discoveries, their sponsor and their patron, was a son of the king of Portugal, Prince Henry the Navigator (1394–1460), who turned his palace at Sagres into a school of cartography and seamanship. From Sagres, Henry planned and sent out almost annual expeditions, each pressing farther than the last. Committed to spreading the word of God and to advancing Portugal's

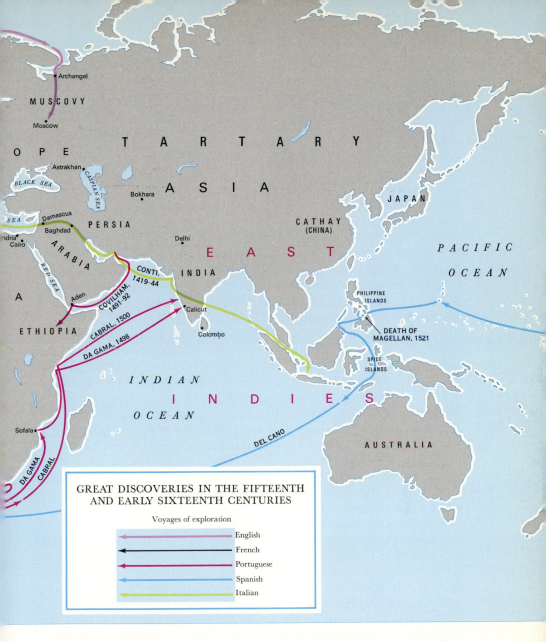

MUSCOVY

Archangel

Moscow

O P E

T A R T A R Y

Astrakhan

CASPIAN SEA

BLACK SEA

A S I A

Bokhara

JAPAN

SEA

Damascus

PERSIA

CATHAY
(CHINA)

ndria

Baghdad

Delhi

E A S T

PACIFIC

Cairo

A R A B I A

CONTI.
1419-44

INDIA

OCEAN

RED SEA

Aden

COVILHAM.
1491-92

Calicut

PHILIPPINE
ISLANDS

A

CABRAL, 1500

Colombo

DEATH OF
MAGELLAN, 1521

ETHIOPIA

DA GAMA, 1498

SPICE
ISLANDS

I N D I A N

I N D I E S

O C E A N

Sofala

DA GAMA

CABRAL

DEL CANO

AUSTRALIA

GREAT DISCOVERIES IN THE FIFTEENTH
AND EARLY SIXTEENTH CENTURIES

Voyages of exploration

English

French

Portuguese

Spanish

Italian

commercial interests, Henry turned his country's traditional crusading enthusiasm (and probably the funds that would have gone to serve it) to the profit of cosmography as well as that of Portugal itself. In 1454, Pope Nicholas V would write to Henry's nephew, King Alfonso, allowing him to enslave the natives of newly discovered lands for conversion's sake.

In general, the news of early Portuguese discoveries was stifled by an officially imposed conspiracy of silence designed to keep interlopers from poaching on their profitable and hard-won preserves. The possibilities of great ocean routes were not revealed until the very end of the fifteenth century. Then, with the voyages of Columbus, another Christian power having entered the exploration lists, a papal bull of 1493 divided such lands as exploration might reveal between Portugal and Spain, only to have its judgment revised by a treaty of the following year between the interested parties. The Treaty of Tordesillas (1494) gave Spain all discoveries west of a line running north and south, 370 miles west of the Cape Verde, and left the rest to Portugal, without bothering to say how the two halves would be adjusted at the other end. It came just in time to secure Brazil (discovered by Cabral in 1500) for Portugal, and left the two Iberian powers in almost undisputed mastery of the southern seas for over half a century.

Until the 1560's the northerners had been looking farther north. The Newfoundland fishing banks had been exploited since the 1470's by England, France, and sometimes also Portugal; and English expeditions sought an alternative passage to India by northwest and northeast, discovering Canada in the process (1534–1535) and also a new route to Russia through Archangel (1553–1554).

A concrete foundation was furnished by the tools with which the sailors worked. Ships were improving. New arrangements of masts and sails permitted ships of greater size by about 1400; the replacement of the steering oar by a rudder made for more wieldy ships; design itself produced narrower, more rakish lines, providing better speed, manoeuverability, and performance. Scale and capacity increased, from the caravelles that Diaz and Columbus used, to the galleons of the plate fleets and the vast carracks running to a thousand tons and more and capable of carrying as many people. Columbus's *Santa Maria* was probably 100 to 120 tons and measured 84 by 25 feet. The large ocean-going ship of Queen Elizabeth's time a century later would draw more like 500 tons and measure roughly 100 by 38 or 40 feet.

It is hard for men to travel, let alone for governments to rule, over any large area without maps. The Chinese had a map of China in 1125 B.C. The West had to wait longer, partly because cartography was either an unprestigious hit-or-miss affair or else a highly theoretical enterprise only loosely connected with experience. Strabo, the Greek geographer who was a contemporary of Christ, considered geography a province of philosophy. The results of this point of view were hardly satisfying. The understanding which men of the fourteenth and fifteenth centuries had about their world was very limited, or else strangely deformed by theories and myths perpetuated despite the information furnished by travelers like the Polos.

The Greeks—Pythagoras, Aristotle—had thought the earth was round. Most medieval men thought it was flat. The great second-century astronomer, Ptolemy, rediscovered after the thirteenth century, helped to turn the tide.* But there were other problems. Neither the Greeks

---

* He also, perhaps fortunately, made a gross error in calculating the circumference of the world, thus encouraging Columbus to undertake a voyage westward which he expected would turn out to be much shorter than it did.

nor medieval scholars could quite agree on how much of the unknown world was inhabited, how much of it indeed was habitable. In the great empty spaces of primitive maps men placed the land of Ophir, whence Solomon had drawn his treasures, and the Kingdom of Prester John, a legendary figure as rich as he was pious. Around Asia, they threaded a necklace of "Fortunate Isles"—5,000 of them—and, to the south, where so much of Europe's gold came from, they saw the Eldorado which they would seek first in Africa where the Rio de Oro flowed and, later, further west.

But such beckoning riches lay swathed in mystery and danger. The dreams of the Middle Ages fed on ancient fantasies of lands where fabulous creatures swarmed: men with dogs' heads who did not speak but barked, men who made up their lack of a head by carrying eyes upon their stomachs, others who used a single very large foot to shield them from the sun, griffins, and cranes that fought with pygmies, and giants like Gog and Magog whose cruel invasion would some day herald the end of mankind.

If land was hazardous, mariners were no safer. The ocean floor was thought to be strewn with lodestones whose magnetic pull drew all the nails out of passing hulks which foundered with all hands lost. Impertinent explorers might sail over the world's edge, be caught by clashing rocks, crushed in the coils of lurking sea serpents, or burst into flames where the sea was supposed to boil at the Equator. It took great courage, greed, or thoughtlessness to brave such perils.

Because more and more men braved them, in the late fifteenth and sixteenth centuries, maps, charts, and tables improved steadily. So did confidence. By the first decade of the sixteenth century seamen had fairly useful maps of Africa, South Asia, South America, and the Caribbean. Globes were being made of which that constructed by Behaim in Nürn-

Amerigo Vespucci with an astrolabe, used for measuring altitudes of celestial bodies, from which one could calculate latitudes or the time of day.

Warder Collection

A sixteenth-century map of the world, by Paolo dal Toscanelli, adviser to Columbus. Bibliothéque Nationale, Paris.

berg (1492) seems to have been the first. Cartography would take 200 years to improve on the stage reached by the end of the sixteenth century. Of course, coastlines were better known than inland regions where, as Jonathan Swift later put it,

> Geographers in Africa-Maps
> With Savage-Pictures fill their Gaps
> And o'er unhabitable Downs
> Place Elephants for want of Towns.

But, unlike the early Portuguese, Columbus and the navigator Amerigo Vespucci publicized their travels and the early sixteenth-century public was getting news of the voyages and discoveries broadening out its world. A famous Italian compilation, Montalboddo's significantly named *Recently Rediscovered Countries,* first printed in 1507, had six Italian, six French and two German editions almost at once, and was frequently reissued throughout the sixteenth century. Scores of other works brought historical, geographical, botanical, anthropological, and simply curious information to an avid public.

Even so, we should beware of envisaging the change that the discoveries wrought as swift and revolutionary. Economically, the New World was slow to affect the Old, and the first American gold was just enough for Pope Alexander VI to gild the ceiling of Santa Maria Maggiore. Socially, the Old World view persisted for a good half century after the specialists acquired a new one. As late as 1530, the fourteenth-century *Travels* of Sir John Mandeville with their tall tales of pre-Columbian worlds would be reissued three times. Between 1539 and 1558, there would be seven French reprintings of a geography book which had no hint of America and very little of African and Asian findings. Sebastian Brant's *Ship of Fools,* with its miraculous revelations, its comets, and its monsters, did much better than even *The Travels of Marco Polo.* Awareness of and interest in other worlds began to grow only after 1550 or 1560, and even then it was the nearer and more familiar East that intrigued, rather than the newer and more distant places.

The revelation, necessarily, came mostly from books, which spawned other books and hence new ideas. The influence of travel books can be seen in the works of men like Giordano Bruno (1548?–1600), eventually burned in Rome as heretic, like Rabelais and Montaigne in France, or Thomas More (*Utopia,* 1516) and Francis Bacon in England, suggesting not only new interpretations, but also the ambition, as Francis Bacon (1561–1626) put it in his *New Atlantis* (1627), to extend "the bounds of human empire to the effecting of all things possible."

Before very long a new type of traveler would appear, the tourist. Travelers who travel out of mere curiosity appear as early as Herodotus, the fifth century B.C. traveler, but their medieval prototypes had to be disguised as pilgrims. Now as facilities, temptations, and possibilities grew, they reappeared, from the compulsive restlessness of men like Francis I, always on the move, to the ambitious enterprise of a Thomas Coryate, who first walked across Europe to Venice, then from Constantinople to Aleppo and on to India (1614–1617), where he died from dysentery and overdrinking. Pietro Della Valle, driven from Venice by an unhappy love affair (1614), became a pilgrim to the Holy Land, went on from there to Baghdad, where, cured, he married a beautiful Circassian who accompanied him to Persia and who died (1622), only to be embalmed and carried on further travels by the faithful Pietro to India, Muscat, Basra, Aleppo, and back to Rome (in 1626).

Such sentiments, however, must have played a negligible part in the colonial exploration and settlement, conducted for the most part in the hope of profit, undertaken mostly by men who meant to improve their fortune, perhaps to find adventure, but certainly opportunities that Europe did not offer. The Pizarros who discovered Peru have been called "a bunch of illiterate thugs and conquerors of genius." The words could be applied to most conquistadores—to those men who, having nothing to lose or much to gain, pursuing their own fortune forged the fortunes of the world. Their enterprise brought about the greatest revolution between 1400 and 1600, removed a curtain of ignorance, indifference, and myth, and revealed a rich new world.

Concrete effects were even more obvious than intellectual ones: first the simple knowledge of the world, minute in 1500, radically expanded by 1515 to include West Africa, India, Newfoundland, the West Indies, and the Spanish Main. By 1530 Magellan's voyage proved once and for all that the earth was round, that America lay between Europe and Asia, that one could sail to the Spice Islands by doubling South America. All these places and the East Indies were not only a reality but a commercial battleground. By the end of the century, China, the Arctic, Equatorial Africa also had been integrated into a world view unimaginable three generations before.

The trade and trade routes affected by new discoveries, the relegation of Mediterranean ports to secondary place, the rise of northern ports and northern Europe to commercial and eventually political significance—first Antwerp, then, after 1576, Amsterdam and London, were paralleled by the development of capitalist enterprise in these places on a new scale, with new or perfected instruments: commission selling, joint stock companies, marine insurance, modern specialized banking. The prizes lay not only in Spanish bullion and Portuguese spices, but in Newfoundland codfish, Virginia tobacco, Canadian furs, Caribbean sugar (and from sugar, rum), and African slaves. The reflection of all this appeared in peoples' lives: not only in vastly expanded horizons, not only in more lavish, more ornate furnishings, architecture, interior decoration, and utensils down to cutlery, but at the humblest most everyday level—cheaper textiles from the Indies, muslin from Mosul, gingham from Malaya, calico from Calicut, permitting among other things the more general use of cotton underclothes and handkerchiefs; porcelain and wallpaper from China, chocolate from Mexico, potatoes, tomatoes, pumpkins, maize, gradually entering the diet, along with sugar and rice, already familiar like other tropical products—dates, melons, bananas, pineapple—but now more readily available.

Italy: *The Beginning of the Modern Age*

The modern age begins in Italy. That peninsula during the waning Middle Ages, provides a case of the backwater which profits from a relative isolation to become a focus of wealth and culture, the cynosure of all surrounding eyes, in due course the prey of the greed which its success arouses, and which the foreign grip returns to its former insignificance like fairy gold that turns to dross in unworthy hands.

Conquered, overrun, divided, early medieval Italy had long hung in the margin of a world whose cultural and political center lay in France, whose great decisions were made north of the Alps. Italy was a dependency of the Holy Roman Empire, whose rulers regularly wasted their resources but also those of the lands they visited on the assertion of their imperial rights. In the twelfth century the reforming papacy enlisted the rising cities against the Empire. For over a hundred years, Italy was polarized into Guelphs and Ghibellines, supporters of Pope or Emperor; and the labels divided not only states but clans, and parties within cities identified themselves by them even as the terms themselves began to lose their original meaning.

By the beginning of the fourteenth century, the Guelphs had driven the Germans out of Naples, the French had driven or enticed the popes to Avignon. For seventy years Italy was left to herself, to develop as she wished or could, without outside interference. When at last in 1377 the popes came back to Rome to stay, it was in the guise of secular princes, taking their chances with the other secular states that had grown up and learned to assert themselves in their absence. From Naples to Venice, Italian states were not the fruit of tradition, heirs of that feudal system which had ruled Europe for five centuries and still held sway north of the Alps, but the creation of free men—free, that is to say, of certain medieval institutions and restrictions, to engage in a more explicit kind of power politics than the north could or would yet acknowledge, a kind of politics in which what counted was neither spiritual values nor ancient institutions, but ingenuity, energy, and force. Such states were *communes:* joint enterprises based on a common oath of mutual aid among their citizens. Commitment among equals replaced the old feudal oath in which an inferior swore fealty to a superior. Of course, in these urban communes or republics (from the Latin *res publica* meaning almost literally *commonwealth*), as in ancient Athens, or in George Orwell's *Animal Farm,* some were always more equal than others. Nonetheless, here was a new model of society which escaped the feudal structure and challenged it.

The great substitute for feudal conventions came from a source that was native to the land. The memory, sometimes the practice, of Roman law, had survived the intervening centuries. What men of law, of state, and of affairs appreciated about it were its centralizing and authoritarian tendencies, but also the strong consciousness of private property and the individualistic concept that society does best when its individual members take care of their own interests. Italy was not the only place where Roman law lived on. But in the south of France the hazard of a heresy, the opportunity of a profitable crusade, the brutal intervention of northern feudalism, crushed its brief flowering. At the very time this happened, in the first half of the thirteenth century, the interests of men like Emperor Frederick of Hohenstaufen, eager to humble his overly powerful subjects, sponsored the civil cause in Naples and Sicily, expressing the strange but valid paradox that authority appreciates equality before its law. The theoretical assertion that subjects were equal under the princes' law introduced a revolutionary concept of equal justice for all, departing from the hierarchic approach for the sake of political efficacy, administrative efficiency, and economic organization.

When Frederick and his sons were gone, the principle proved useful to batter down old privileges and powers in cities further north, and lay down the legal basis for the new society and the new economy developing in them. But the temporary abolition of traditional privileges was only the prelude to establishing new ones, those of a new urban patriciate, replacing or absorbing the lords of an earlier age and using their new power just as voraciously as they.

Medieval politics wanted to dominate men on behalf of reputedly impersonal forces. The new age wanted man to dominate. But what? Other men and society; above all, processes and nature. This meant that even men were dehumanized to make process more perfect, declared free the better to harness their labor. It is as if the great faceless masses of the medieval fields were briefly incarnated, allowed a personality and a will for theory's sake, only to be enrolled in a new equation—subordination to which did not even imply the old man-to-man feudal relations of master and servant, vassal and lord.

Novelty is always upsetting, especially of habit which makes even acute discomfort easier to bear. The new society was to many people no more agreeable, to some far less agreeable, than the old. Italy was a divided land—a thousand varieties of dialect, Dante had estimated in his day; a host of little states, all riven by internal cleavages between, in the most general terms, nobles, the merchant class, the *popolo minuto*—little people of all sorts. All this in flux, every political division coveted or coveting, the city governments with their perquisites, above all with the power of excluding foes from earning, from affairs, from the community itself—the utter instability of life and fortune, great opportunities for some, great insecurity for many.

The trade and industry that made the cities' wealth also made for internal instability: creating a large and diversified labor force which did not fit traditional hierarchies and structures, weakening established gilds and institutions, causing social tensions, exposing society to the effects of competition from other trading centers in Italy itself, Germany, and the Netherlands. Economic pressures of all kinds were soon translated into political terms, especially in times of crisis when power meant the ability to redistribute suffering: my friends losing less and gaining more than others.

The inner contradictions, therefore, meant growing struggle for political control. Only firm government, only strong and able rulers, only force, could impose some kind of order, bring a semblance of stability and peace. Where the Middle Ages wanted princes to be good, the Renaissance wanted them effective. Maybe both ages shared the same ultimate concern to combine the two: the difference lay in what they

Donatello's statue of Gatta-melata, one of the greatest of the Condottieri, stands outside St. Anthony's Basilica in Padua. The work took its inspiration from a second-century statue of the Emperor Marcus Aurelius.

Metropolitan Museum of Art, New York

chose to stress, what they acknowledged as the dominant motive. Above all was the knowledge that the strength, initiative, cleverness, which had *made* what was, were its only support. Religious faith and superstition in no way precluded this extraordinary sense of self-reliance, not new but newly conscious, expressed, admitted, increasingly emphasized at the expense of purely religious references and increasingly overshadowing them. Self-reliance—hence when successful, self-assertion and glorification; self-reliance—hence to be successful, calculation and also feverish activity, for God helped those who helped themselves. Activity, impatience—hence, as we have seen, a new realization that time is money, power, a precious capital to be saved, invested, profitably *used*—so that overfrequent church attendance even was seen by one commentator as "useful" enough, but "most detrimental to a thorough exploitation of the day's time."

So, from the thirteenth-century age of chaos we find ourselves by the late fourteenth century in an age of despots cutting out the benchmarks of new patterns in politics, economics, and religion: the consolidation of government, and government increasingly centralized, increasingly based on dynastic principles around whose ambitions and interests internal politics and foreign struggles turned; the authority and the unity of the church dissolving under pressure of the secular state and of private intellectual attitudes; the reclassification of the nobles—all processes in which Italy seems to have led the world.

Beginning in the fourteenth century, important changes in the mode of warfare emphasized first infantry—the arm of the lower classes, then

artillery—the arm of princes and central governments. Companies of professional fighting men appeared, offering to do better what the city
militias did only clumsily, what in the absence of regular armies princes
could not do. They sold their arms and skills to the highest bidder and
sometimes sold them again in the midst of a campaign, but generally
did the job for which they had been hired as long as they were paid for
it and, by exacting pay for what had been the noblest of pastimes—
fighting—devaluated it for the noble knights. Despised at first, the greatest of these *condottieri* became popular heroes, had statues raised to
them by grateful employers or, like Sir John Hawkwood, Giovanni
Acuto, their life-size portrait on a horse painted over the door of the
Cathedral in Florence. Some ended poisoned or otherwise eliminated
by suspicious masters. Others, more fortunate or more able, won a domain, sometimes even a throne, in Rimini, or Fermo, eventually in
Milan. While, taught by their example, some of the lesser princes,
rulers of poor domains—the Gonzagas of Mantua, the Montefeltros of
Urbino, took up the trade of *condottieri* too.

The nobles lost their monopoly of military practice at the same time
as they were losing their feudal hold on the land. They remained an
important factor but no longer the principal. In Italy and in the Netherlands, where urban activities and urban wealth first prevailed, feudal
and bourgeois, political and economic attitudes interpenetrated and,
consciously and deliberately, the business mentality began to affect politics. As the social historian Alfred von Martin put it: "Business methods
served political ends, political means served economic ends. Political
and economic credit were already inseparable. The fame and the glory
of a state (also increased by successful wars) were reflected in profits."
And the profits of a family like the Medici, or of vast import-export
enterprises like those of Venice and Portugal, were reflected in fame and
glory while they lasted. A last permutation on this theme: the military
capitalism of families like the Montefeltros, the profits of whose mercenary activities kept their poor state prosperous and enabled them to
combine efficient rule with lighter taxes.

Money (as fourteenth-century Italians were the first to put it) is the
sinews of war, and war the source of power. War now became a kind of
business and politics a kind of war, until the calculating intellect was
seen as the master of all. J. C. Burckhardt has wisely pointed out how
much the new states of *quattrocento* Italy resembled works of art. Their
sanction came not from tradition but from opportunity and power, their
very existence and nature depending on a creator—the prince: a wholly
artificial situation, man-made and man-centered, developing new structures, new sanctions, new methods and attitudes, and suggesting or
imposing them on others.

By mid-fifteenth century, out of the confusion of wars, alliances, and treacheries, some salient facts emerged: the rise of Venice, after the exhaustion of rival Genoa, and her establishment as a mainland power, the richest and most stable of the peninsula; at the other end of the scale, as of the Italian boot, the realm of Naples, wrested from the Germans by the Angevins, then from them by the Aragonese, a bridgehead for future Spanish intervention but meanwhile the most backward of feudal realms; Milan, the greatest city amid its fertile plains, disputing Lombardy to Venice which tried to expand westward while Milan moved east and briefly laying claim to most of north Italy; Florence, grasping yet irresolute, threatening all neighbors—Pisa, Siena—with her greed and in turn threatened, especially by Milan; and in their midst the popes basing their territorial ambitions on the great machinery and prestige of their office, seeking to affirm their suzerainty on a host of restless cities—Perugia, Bologna, Ferrara.

Among these greater powers, lesser ones—Mantua, Genoa, Lucca, Urbino—trying even harder to preserve themselves against the encroachments of the great, to keep in existence from one year to another, obeying now this tyrant now the next. And, in all but Venice, the rulers changing according to the fortune of arms, of leagues, of insurrections or of plots, very much the parallel of a free market ruled by enterprise and luck, very much a contrast with the still feudal north, where even rebellious vassals tended to preserve their fundamental rights.

All this was possible only because the greater powers were employed elsewhere. Italian politics moved in a microcosm isolated by the chance of war among its neighbors. Encouraged by their success in conditions which habit seemed to make the norm rather than the exception, Italian rulers lost all sense of proportion, tried to embroil the foreigner in their conflicts, forgot that they were calling in giants to redress the balance of minor factions. Some called in the French, some the Spaniards, some the Swiss. Then they called on the French against the Spaniards and on the Swiss against the French, twisting about in a tumult of treachery that could only end—when one barbarian had turned on the other and had been turned out by a third—in the triumph of the strongest, cunningest, luckiest: in this case the Spaniards. The French passed like gaudy, destructive comets through the Italian sky. The Spaniards, grimmer, more steadfast, more ably led, more steadily paid, remained at least for two centuries holding first Naples and then Milan.

The Humanists

While economic and political developments influenced life and thought, they would in turn be first spurred, then hampered by the philosophers

ITALY IN THE RENAISSANCE

Papal states

States claimed by the pope

whom they subsidized. Each new society seeks and evokes appropriate spokesmen. The men who first formulated Renaissance values, then taught and inflected them, were known as humanists.

The revival of antiquity is one of the most striking aspects of the Renaissance. It was a fashion and a long campaign which, in a century or two, restored the West to the possession of those ideas and achievements of the ancients that had been left forgotten or ignored since Rome collapsed into barbarism. From this position it could go forward to greater achievements of its own. The process had begun quite slowly and unselfconsciously, and its earliest protagonists had been the lawyers who, in a Christendom ruled by canon law, and especially in Italy where Justinian's Code * had never disappeared, began as early as the eleventh century to study and refurbish the Roman civil law. As we have seen, they came to serve the needs of rising cities, of princes that disputed with the papacy and sought a rival and more ancient authority against it, and of bright young men in search of a career outside the church.

There were in Italy none of the cathedral schools which, further north, served to foster, to focus, and to perpetuate the scholarly activities of the Christian Middle Ages. Until the eleventh century, medieval Italy was culturally backward compared with France which excelled in scholarship, in literature, and art. The University of Bologna, founded in the eleventh century, set the pattern for what was really a new kind of trade school, specializing in civil law—not, as in the north, theology— and classical studies on their own account continued to be comparatively neglected until the second half of the thirteenth century. Perhaps, even then, the classics were introduced in Italy from France. When this happened, they were welcomed by those then trying to discern the basic traits of human society and of the laws that rule it.

The leading role which men of law played in the early development of Italian humanism is not surprising. They constituted of course one of the most literate sections of the laity. But also their studies and profession kept them in contact with Roman tradition and made them look on Roman civilization as a living thing whose values they constantly applied to contemporary problems. As the use of law became more widespread and its study too, so did the new attitude toward ancient literature, an outgrowth of the attitude toward ancient law. Parallel with this, the growing use of rhetoric in politics led to further study of the subject in ancient literary sources, especially Cicero. The new approach seems to have been sparked by very practical considerations, especially the search by professional rhetoricians—the representatives, diplomats, lawyers, teachers, and publicity agents of certain cities or courts—for new sources of eloquence and polish in classical models. Classical studies benefited from this even before Petrarch and Boccaccio came along to accelerate their development.

Classical studies had been part of the seven liberal arts (grammar, rhetoric, dialectic, arithmetic, geometry, astronomy, and music) taught

* Emperor Justinian (527–565) presided over the collection and publication of all existing laws and constitutions (*Codex*), of juridical opinions concerning them (*Digest*), and of a basic law textbook (the *Institutes*). This great work of codification, too impressive to tamper with, hampered the further development of Roman law for centuries thereafter, but ensured its survival and enduring prestige.

A French manuscript of the late fifteenth century, translating the works of Virgil. Houghton Library, Harvard University.

in medieval monastic and cathedral schools. The new fascination with the classics led to more emphasis of the first three of these arts. In the fourteenth century they became known (from a Ciceronian expression) as humane studies (*studia humanitatis*)—the field of studies specially befitting a human being. The humanities included, in general, grammar, rhetoric, history, poetry, and moral philosophy, and they were studied as they had been treated by the ancient writers, in Latin; and, eventually, though always to a lesser extent, in Greek.

Late in the fifteenth century the men who taught these humanities came to be called "humanists," first as a term of student slang, then as a professional label like that of other specialists: artists, legists, or canonists. Humanists in the exact sense would always remain professional teachers and representatives of this particular branch of learning, not to be confused with the tenets of "humanism," a term coined only in the nineteenth century to denote a special philosophy of man.

Though some humanists developed philosophies of their own, Renaissance humanists were not necessarily philosophers. All were men of letters, some as writers (Petrarch, Boccaccio, Erasmus), some as teachers in schools and universities (Vittorino da Feltre), many in the professions, serving as secretaries of cities or princes (Coluccio Salutati or Niccolò Machiavelli), some again as clerics, or as dilettantes like Pico della Mirandola. But it would be wrong to attribute to them a common point of view; the more so since we speak of men who lived, some in the fourteenth century, some in the fifteenth or sixteenth, in different cities and different societies. All did, however, share a common attitude and played a major part in formulating the concept of that Renaissance of which they remained a major feature. As described by the historian

Kristeller, "they believed that classical antiquity was in most respects a perfect age; that it was followed by a long period of decline, the Dark or Middle Ages; and that it was the task and destiny of their own age to accomplish a rebirth or renaissance of classical antiquity or of its learning, arts and sciences."

Their rediscoveries of Latin texts, lost or neglected for centuries, vastly extended the available mass of Latin literature which had been used during the Middle Ages but with great blind spots. More important perhaps than their resurrection of manuscripts and authors was their activity in spreading them abroad. There are probably more fifteenth-century manuscripts of Latin classics than those of all previous centuries combined, a fact suggesting how widely the Renaissance read and spread the classical authors.

Humanists were copyists and editors. They were helped by the contemporary introduction of paper, which furnished a writing material cheaper than parchment or papyrus, and by the organization of a regular trade in manuscript books; then in the late fifteenth century, by the printing process. They were also textual and historical critics and commentators, both as men of letters and as teachers. Above all, perhaps, they were translators, turning their chase for Greek texts into new gains for Western libraries and into more accessible Latin editions. The Middle Ages had studied and even translated some Greek authors: Plato, Hippocrates, Galen, Ptolemy, not least Aristotle. Now some of these were retranslated, and to them were added most of the Greek poets, historians, and non-Aristotelian philosophers whom medieval scholars had neglected: Homer, Sophocles, Herodotus, Thucydides, Xenophon, Plutarch, Epicurus, Plotinus, and such.

While Latin letters had been quite thoroughly studied in earlier ages, the recovery of Greek literature and philosophy was one of the humanists' greatest contributions—not unaided by the presence of refugees from Constantinople, providing both teachers and a new wealth of original texts. One result of renewed interest in Greek thought was a philosophical current—restricted but influential—that centered above all in fifteenth-century Florence.

Platonists (or Neo-Platonists) like Marsilio Ficino and his brilliant pupil Pico, were humanists in their education, their classicism, their respect for the ancients and for the arts, ideas, and institutions of the ancient world. But for them this return to sources did not stop with the age of Caesar and Augustus. Perhaps because they had been trained in scholastic philosophy at universities like Padua or Paris, such men were more aware of and more affected by the medieval inheritance of serious philosophical speculation. They refused to be satisfied with the superficial rhetoric of a Cicero, preferring to revivify and press further the possibilities of textual studies and interpretation long explored by medieval schoolmen. Through them, Aristotle and Augustine, as well as Plato and his heirs, were reintroduced, current religious interests were blended with scholarship and philosophy. The soul's striving toward God was turned into a reaffirmation of the freedom of man, whose almost existential ability to determine his way of life was asserted in Ficino's *Platonic Theology* or Pico's great *Oration* on the dignity of man (1487).

Once again, the dignity of man was connected with his ability to think his way through a problematic world. Christian concern to reestablish the harmony of faith (Christian) and reason (ancient); civic concern in the training of good citizens able to accept responsibilities; intellectual concerns of thinkers straining to provide a secular philosophy of life more valid than the scholastic theology of yesteryear; didactic concerns of teachers wanting to provide guidelines for their students, models to improve their taste, their eloquence, their reasoning, their character; all testify to a felt need to redefine the rules of life and action in a world no longer content with custom.

Not surprisingly, therefore, the fifteenth century witnessed something close to an educational revolution. Schools multiplied everywhere; literacy spread (relatively of course: in Thomas More's London, three out of every five persons could read); the number of university students increased three- and fourfold. By the end of the fourteenth century there were forty-five universities (*studia generalia*) in Christendom. Thirty-three more were founded in the fifteenth century and as many again in the next fifty years, mostly in areas heretofore neglected like Scotland, Spain, and Portugal. The Empire, which had had five universities in 1400, boasted eighteen by 1520. Obviously, an important motive behind this flowering was material. Scholarship was the surest key to social mobility. For men who lacked birth and money or who, with money, lacked status, education was the resource that would carry them upward into the administration, into the courts, into the church. Throughout the Middle Ages the church had been the greatest avenue for personal ability. Only in the ecclesiastical hierarchy were the highest positions open to talented and ambitious men of humble birth. This situation did not change very quickly, but the secular orientation spreading from Italy revealed the vista of many new careers.

Secular did not necessarily mean material: Guillaume Postel (1510–1581) the orphan son of a peasant, worked his way from farm boy to scullion in a Paris college, to priesthood and education. Postel traveled all over Europe and the Orient, learned Greek and Turkish, Arabic, Coptic, Armenian, collected manuscripts from Middle Eastern monasteries, was appointed by Francis I lecturer at the Collège de France (1538), published the first Arabic grammar and the first attempt at a comparative grammar, and dreamed of an ecumenical concord of all religions and all men. As a contemporary poet put it, "he meditated in him the concord of the world." The Venetians took him for mad, the

THE RISE OF THE UNIVERSITY

● Founded before the 14th century
● Founded in the 14th century
● Founded in the 15th century
------ Boundaries c. 1500

BLACK SEA

OTTOMAN EMPIRE

POLAND

Cracow 1364

HUNGARY

Pressburg 1467

Buda 1389

Fünfkirchen 1367

SWEDEN

1477

BALTIC SEA

Copenhagen 1478

DENMARK

Greifswald 1428

Rostock 1419

Vienna 1365

Prague 1348

HOLY ROMAN EMPIRE

Leipzig 1409

Erfurt 1379

Würzburg 1402

Heidelberg 1385

Ingolstadt 1472

Freiburg 1455

Cologne 1388

Trèves 1454

Mayence 1476

Tübingen 1477

Basel 1459

Louvain 1425

VENETIAN REPUBLIC

ADRIATIC SEA

Treviso 1318

Padua before 1000

Vicenza 1204

Reggio 1188

Pavia 1361

Piacenza 1248

Bologna 1088

Ferrara 1391

Modena before 1300

Arezzo 1215

Perugia 1308

Siena 1246

France 1349

Pisa 1343

Rome before 1000

NAPLES

Salerno 1059

Naples 1224

CORSICA

SARDINIA

Palermo 1394

SICILY

Catania 1444

Vercelli 1228

Turin 1405

Besançon 1485

Dôle 1422

Grenoble 1339

Avignon 1303

Aix 1409

NORTH SEA

Aberdeen 1494

St. Andrews 1411

SCOTLAND

Glasgow 1450

ENGLAND

Cambridge 1233

Oxford 1167

IRELAND

Paris c. 1150

Orléans 1235

Caen 1432

Bourges 1464

FRANCE

Lyons 1330

Valence 1452

Orange 1365

Perpignan 1349

MEDITERRANEAN SEA

Bordeaux 1441

Cahors 1332

Toulouse 1229

Montpellier 1140

Nantes 1460

Angers 1229

Barcelona 1430

Palma 1483

BALEARIC IS.

Huesca 1354

Lérida 1300

Saragossa 1474

Valencia 1245

Palencia 1208

Valladolid 1250

Sigüenza 1489

Alcalá 1459

Salamanca before 1230

SPAIN

Toledo 1474

Ávila 1482

Seville 1254

Coimbra 1307

PORTUGAL

Lisbon 1290

ATLANTIC OCEAN

Roman Inquisition imprisoned him, the magistrates of Lyons pursued him, the Parliament of Paris finally interned him in an abbey. A visitor there has described him for us, aged but still grand, passionate still, long white beard and fiery eyes, saying mass with a kind of smoke surrounding his head—"so much was his soul tensed towards this mystery."

Postel's case may be extreme but he was not alone in his vehement dedication or in the obsessive pursuit of his scholarly goals. The annals of humanism are full of tales of men who worked hard and suffered long to acquire what they sought: learning. There is the Belgian Jean Standonck (1443–1504), again the son of a poor working man, brought up hard by the Brethren of the Common Life where he learned "the fear of God, the horror of hell fire, the love of the heavenly fatherland," and that also of books. He came to Paris in 1471, worked in a convent kitchen and as bellringer in order to see himself through school. At night, too poor to afford light, he studied in the belltower by moonlight. Fourteen years later he was rector of the Sorbonne and principal of one of the great colleges of Paris. There is Thomas Platter (1499–1582), son of poor Swiss peasants, who left home to roam as the acolyte of a wandering student—of whom there were many in those days—begging for his master and earning a poor pittance while he slowly learned something himself. With incredible persistence, Platter taught himself Latin, Greek, Hebrew, became a private tutor, then a rope-maker by which he earned a living while translating the Bible and teaching the Hebrew he had taught himself to humanists who came to seek him out. Such men were no exceptions. Just one more category to take into consideration when considering an age where many seemed drunk with knowledge, with discovery, with the effort and exhilaration of it all.

There had been other lives spent in scholarship. There had been classical scholars in the Middle Ages. But their studies were seldom if ever of literature for its own sake, but rather designed to press it into the service of philosophy and theology. Latin and even Greek were there, but they were there to be used and not to be enjoyed. When chairs in classics and oriental languages were founded (but never filled) in fifteenth-century Paris, it was with the specific object of facilitating the conversion of the infidel. It needed a society prosperous enough and leisured enough, like that which first appeared in Italy, for men to think that use and pleasure could somehow be combined.

Everywhere, however, and especially in the north the idea that education could improve capacity caught on more easily than the suggestion that it could improve leisure too. In any case, men had to live. Observers have compared the humanists with their contemporaries, the *condottieri*, those soldiers of fortune on a different stage but set like them to assert their genius, uniqueness, singularity, trying to influence others, to forge not only their fortune but their fame, like Petrarch—in, we might add, the free market their forebears had ignored. The economic parallel has its uses too, for early humanists reflected and strengthened the values of the new economy—stressing the productive uses of learning, critical insights, and independence, criticizing the Christian depreciation of riches with the *distinguo* that riches well employed on books, on beautiful things, on the gentle life, both reflected and affected fortune and also that indefinable new quality, *virtù,* combining intelligence, enterprise, self-control, the will to create one's own destiny, which alone (wrote a friend of Lorenzo the Magnificent) "makes men noble."

But humanistic education was useless for business and for the aristocracy, most of whom cared little enough for learning. On the other hand most students lacked the income for a life of leisure. Public service was the chief direction left, and toward that most humanists oriented themselves by taste as much as need, preaching and sometimes practicing the new civic virtues: integrity, patriotism, self-respect, dedication to the well-being of the community. Fifteenth-century Florentine writers on education sketch the ideal portrait not of the medieval saint or knight but of a cultivated man of affairs. They tried to develop body as well as mind, but looked upon the dangerous and ostentatious entertainments of feudal nobles, such as tourneys and bullfights, as useless and they despised mere physical excellence without a moral and intellectual counterpart. Theirs was a non- if not an anti-aristocratic view, and they disprized the values of the older world—the idle brutality of hunting, the vain pride of men tracing their descents, as Poggio put it, from a "long line of bold miscreants." Not birth, not consecration, not broad acres, but wealth and erudition were the things they honored. All, or almost all, things a man can get for himself. It was their task to point out the new directions and furnish the equipment with which they could be reached.

A Concept of the Past

One great change that humanism introduced was the idea that literary and scholarly interests could be pursued without explicit reference to religion. An alternative but no less revolutionary change came from those men whose very real religious convictions combined with their humanistic training in an insistence on original sources—in this case the Bible and the church fathers. Going back to sources meant going back beyond the scholastic theology of the Middle Ages, beyond the dusty out-of-context compilations, to the Christian classics and above all the Bible itself. It also meant the duty of criticizing and restoring Scripture in much the same way as one would do with Cicero, and for similar reasons; because these works were authoritative and fundamental, and therefore must be purged of errors and accretions. Texts accepted for centuries began to be questioned and revised when Lorenzo Valla (1406–1457) criticized Jerome's *Vulgate* on the basis of the original Greek text, when Erasmus edited the Greek New Testament, when Luther translated the Bible from Hebrew and Greek into German, when Catholic scholars revised the *Vulgate* late in the sixteenth century and English scholars produced the King James Version early in the seventeenth.

Reference to authentic contemporary documents, textual criticism, value judgments of available evidence would also be applied to history, ecclesiastical as well as secular. What this could do when applied to church history may be seen from Valla's attack on the Donation of Constantine, a spurious gift whose authenticity was based on medieval parchments which he showed to be forged.* By the sixteenth century, Protestants and Catholics were rewriting church history from their particular points of view. Their sharp criticism of the opponent's evidence, while it may have convinced the converted, also provided a new store of critical techniques, and of evidence for more skeptical approaches.

Meanwhile, the tenor of history had changed in other ways as well. Not only church history was being written or rewritten. The political problems of Renaissance Italy challenged political thinkers and historians to adjust traditional assumptions to contemporary realities, to devise a framework of thought, a way of looking at society and politics, suited to the situations facing them. A sense of the permanent interests behind the actions of friends and enemies—indeed, of those that influenced or that should influence their own decisions—could only be provided by an analysis and understanding of the past. The age of pictorial perspective was also the age when historical perspective came to be recognized as meaningful.

The earliest humanists—Petrarch, Poggio, Ficino—had indicated how the ethics of the ancients could be reconciled with Christian tradition, how classical philosophy could be applied to modern politics. Their heirs carried this further. From rhetoric to politics, the transition was obvious. Appointments to public office, the social position of businessmen, the hiring and firing of mercenaries, were all discussed in the context of classical notions. Speculation about utopian societies and perfect institutions had its uses, but there were historical forces which you had to understand and estimate: money, trade, arms, the use of force in politics and the effectiveness of different kinds of governmental machinery, personalities in their unpredictable (and sometimes demonic) individuality.

Writing in the dangerous climate of sixteenth-century Florence, sur-

---

* The "Donation of Constantine" had been "discovered" by the papal chancery some time in the eighth century. By it, the Emperor Constantine I resigned his authority to the Pope only to receive it back to wield as servant of God and of God's church. "The sacred See of Peter shall be gloriously exalted above our empire and earthly throne." As for Rome and Rome's western dominions, they would be ruled by the Pope and his successors while Constantine ruled Constantinople in the East.

The charter, which embodied and buttressed the theory of papal supremacy, was shown to be not, as it claimed, a fourth-century Roman document, but a forgery of later date. Valla proved that the Latin used did not belong to the age of Constantine, when it was supposed to have been written.

rounded by revolution and war, men like Francesco Guicciardini (1483–1540) and Niccolò Machiavelli (1469–1527) were no longer content with abstractions, for their concerns were too pressing to admit such luxuries. There had to be a working art of politics, applicable to public affairs as law was used in court or medicine in dealing with human bodies. The humanists had clarified and codified the ancient principles of art, and law, and healing. Why not do the same for politics? This was what Machiavelli tried to do, only to find (what we now know) that historians, whatever they intend, cannot but write contemporary history. Like his *Prince* (1532), his *Discourses on Livy* (1531) was less a textbook of past politics than reflections on (and of) the present. Amoral, relativistic, his insights and conclusions ran away from his original intentions.

Machiavelli's approach reflects not only the changed circumstances of a less sanguine age than Petrarch's, but also an intellectual evolution that made for greater subtlety. If history was to be—as early humanists had thought—a school of heroism and virtue, teaching men less what they are than what they ought to be, its negative findings were bound to spoil the desired effect. Meanness, passion, vice, or simple human weakness are hardly edifying. Thus, while research and facts and a certain critical attitude regarding the credibility and value of documents had their importance, moral implications and elevated lessons were to be heavily stressed. Historians did not scruple to insert into their account set speeches which were not attempts at realistic reconstruction but moral tracts and rhetorical decorations.

Only slowly was the truth, the variety and richness of events admitted as relevant. In the new view, men could be intelligent and good, yet be defeated; or find success despite their faults—perhaps because of them—or simply because of chance. No one model, no one given rule, could apply to all circumstances. History now was less the poetry of universals than a record of particular events, unique yet interdependent. Thus, factual accuracy became important because sixteenth-century men looked less for elevation than for information. History was recognized as a major instrument not of moral but of political instruction.

What did it seem to show? Guicciardini, writing in 1532, noted "the instability of all human affairs, like a sea whipped by winds." Not constancy but change ruled the world of men. Thus, at least for some, history which had begun as a tool for action became a lesson in resignation, teaching the relativity and unpredictability of fortune. Its role was to mitigate the impotence of man by the stoic sense that a dignified and philosophical attitude can save something from the uncontrollable forces whose prey he otherwise appears. Men *can* be studied in history, which reflects not only their failures but also their achievements, their potential, their (limited) hopes. Here was a lesson in dignity, in relativism, in political flexibility: a readjustment, yes, but also a reaffirmation of the Promethean hopes of an earlier age.

Renaissance Science

There are those aspects of a time that matter most to men living at the very time, the commonplaces of everyday life which seldom stand out in retrospect or which fail to survive at all. There are those aspects which often pass unperceived by most contemporaries but prove enduring, and end by providing the main material with which to color in the outlines of an age. This is the case with the history of thought, a subject to which most men have always shown a steadfast and perhaps proper indifference, unaware that sooner or later they or their sons would be affected by it and, at the very least, the picture later generations have of them.

The Basic Tools

A movement of men of letters in which books and studies played a major part accorded much attention to philosophical problems. We should do well to remember the peculiar difficulties which these men had to cope with, not only in the relative rarity of their raw materials (paper, books), the insecurity of their times, the discomfort of their lives (ink often freezing in the inkwell) but, more important, in the indigence of their essential tool: language.

There has been much debate concerning the beneficial or stifling quality of Latin as the humanists purified it, the flexibility of medieval Latin as against the frozen structures of a dead language revived, the alternative virtues of Latin and vernaculars. But whether Latin or vernacular, a reading of most texts up to and including the sixteenth century, perhaps later, leaves the impression of grammar just finding its feet, confused syntax, tenses all mixed up, subordinate clauses unreconciled, and order wanting. Slow to come to the point, thought wanders off into irrelevant detail, clumsy, obscure, meandering into endless explanations. These are not—or only with few exceptions—professional writers. They are talkers prating with more time than skill, led on by the very excitement of using words, of handling this new and still unwieldy instrument—language, still like experience full of mystery, full of meaning, and quite devoid of precision. There is no better reflection of mind and time than language, and the language of the fifteenth and the sixteenth centuries reflects rawness, excitement, striving, the development of a thought still searching for its form.

Nevertheless, or perhaps for this very reason, some of the philosophical trends appear attractive. The Renaissance inherited a Greco-Roman tradition in which reality is outside oneself, truth a being not becoming, and thought simply the pursuit of perfect ready-made universal ideas. The great task of Renaissance philosophy was to turn man from a distant and rather unsuccessful beholder of truth into the agent who lives, forges, and assimilates the truth. It had, in other words, to put man and thought, thought and truth, on one single and accessible (hence perhaps relative) plane.

The Application

As we have seen, doctrines were now defended less on religious (that is, revealed), or traditional grounds than in the name of nature and of reason. There was less reference to otherworldly authority: the central position of man in the universe strengthened the suggestion drawn from Plato and the Stoics that virtue is its own reward. New interest in man's happiness and comfort placed practical intellectual pursuits above theoretical and speculative ones. Renaissance science, too, turned from magic to mechanics: from an attempt to operate by breaking through nature, or casting a spell over nature, to an attempt to understand its processes and laws, so as to use them. An excellent example of this can be seen in the work of Leonardo da Vinci (1452–1519). Leonardo outlined all sorts of original discoveries: like the fact that you can see a red light through mist where you cannot see blue, a perception he used to give his landscapes more depth. He explored numerous different mechanical devices: bridges, excavators, life-jackets, automatic file-cutters, machines for grinding needles, or mirrors for measuring the speed of wind.

The attempt to understand nature and its laws could take many directions. One of the most popular may still be seen today on the ceiling of a room decorated by Raphael in Agostino Chigi's Villa Farnesina in Rome. There the artist painted for his patron a vast chart of the northern sky on Chigi's birthday, December 1, 1466, illustrating his horoscope in mythological terms. The old gods had been driven out of the temples. They had survived as planets and constellations affecting the lives of men as powerfully as ever. Astral influences were not invincible: a professor of astrology at Bologna was burned alive in 1327 for maintaining the contrary. Yet it was well to know their influence on one, a knowledge which was arduous to acquire but available also to men of modest means from rapidly calculated horoscopes. The astrologer of those days appears as a collaborator of the doctor, often a doctor himself, like Arnaldo da Villanova, personal physician of a king of Aragon, philosopher and alchemist. believer like many of his colleagues in psychosomatic medicine, recommending that soul and body should be treated at the same time and as a whole. Astrologers of course have continued

to be consulted and in the highest quarters down to our own day.*

Jules Michelet, the nineteenth-century historian, credits the Renaissance with two discoveries: that of the world and that of man. We might add in the sixteenth century the discoveries of the heavens, and of man, not only as an individual but as a physical being, if we remember the tremendous influence of Andreas Vesalius (1514–1564), the Belgian physician whose great anatomical treatise of 1543, *De Humani Corporis Fabrica,* with its splendid woodcuts, survived to be quoted with only slight modifications in the pages of Diderot's *Encyclopedia* of the eighteenth century. We might note, too, the line from him and Ambroise Paré, court doctor of four French kings (1517–1590), to William Harvey (1578–1657). It was Paré, writing in 1545, who formulated the new scientific approach when he maintained that we have to use the ancients as stilts or towers perched on which we can see further, but that whenever experiment contradicted them, we had to follow what we saw. Tradition is no use, argued the French physician, if it leads you astray, if it encourages you to go on making other men's mistakes because you are too lazy or too timid to strike out for yourself. "I should prefer to do everything by myself than to fall into error with the sages and even with all mankind," he said. "Knowledge is a great thing, but only if it is based on experience."

The name most frequently mentioned in this connection is that of Nicolaus Copernicus. Although born in the fifteenth century (1473), his great work only appeared in the year of his death (1543), and his

* If we scorn Adolf Hitler's dependence upon soothsayers as mad, it is harder to discount the fact that the most radical government Ceylon has known since independence set the date of the 1965 elections in that island according to astrological advice. It was not re-elected.

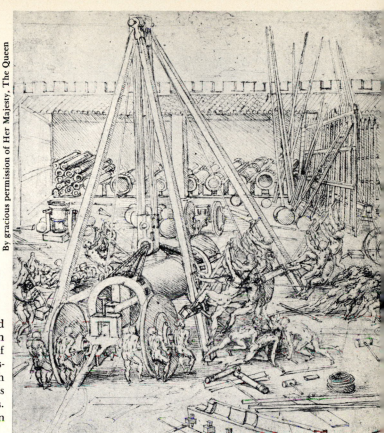

By gracious permission of Her Majesty, The Queen

Machines of war as sketched by Leonardo da Vinci. On the left, the wheels of the vehicle rotate the suspended maces at a high speed as the machine is pulled by a team of horses. On the right, a cannon foundry.

influence was not really felt until the end of the century. Essentially, Copernicus tore earth from its foundations, removed it in our thinking from the center of a universe which turned no longer around man but around the sun. This was strong meat. But his geometry was luminous, his calculations elegant; his astronomical tables, though later found to be incorrect, more attractive and more accurate than the current Ptolemaic model of planetary spheres. His book, dedicated to Paul III, was prefaced by a Lutheran divine. Apparently nobody minded. Hardly anybody saw the implications of his theory and the threat it bore to geo- and anthropocentric views. Soon it would be too late to do anything about it: first Tycho Brahe (1546–1601), then Johannes Kepler (1571–1630) perfected the astronomical tables; then Galileo Gallei (1564–1642) expressed the mechanical implications of further observations. A Pole, a Dane, a German, and an Italian upset the uniform model of a closed and stable universe, insisted that movement, change, infinite possibilities ruled an open and inexhaustible world. The stable patterns of Genesis and Aristotle had been overthrown. Galileo's contemporaries likened him to Columbus who had also revealed new worlds.

It wasn't Copernicus's system that was revolutionary, but its implications; and the arguments needed to defend or impose it against the accepted geocentric theory—to explain why, if the earth moved, objects and buildings upon it remained stable—shook the very foundations of physics, mechanics, and common sense, not to mention theology. It made more sense to assume that the earth was fixed, while sun and stars revolved around it, than to argue that it moved while the sun stood still. If Copernicus was right, Aristotle was wrong and so were our senses. The calculations of Copernicus were more elegant than those of Ptolemy; but sound scientific thinking could not be sacrificed to mathematical style nor the old natural philosophy be jettisoned before a new one took its place. And there would not be a new philosophy of nature before Galileo suggested the possibility of one in the early seventeenth century.

Clearly, the men of the Renaissance did not find the arena of thought unencumbered, the sand swept, the enclosure bare. They were the inheritors not only of the ancients but of many generations of Christian sages whose work and speculations had forged the intellectual universe into which they were born. Dante, in the *Divine Comedy,* summed up the fourteenth-century view of a natural order in which

> . . . all things incline, by diverse lots, more near and less unto their principle; Wherefore they move to diverse ports o'er the great sea of being, and each one with instinct given it to bear it on.
> This beareth the fire toward the moon; this is the mover in the hearts of things that die; this doth draw the earth together and unite it.

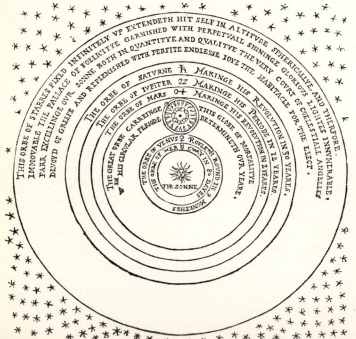

A diagram from the *Revolutions of the Celestial Spheres* by Copernicus, showing stars in a fixed position and Saturn, Jupiter, Mars, Venus, and Mercury in their orbital patterns around the sun. Folger Shakespeare Library, Washington, D.C.

Here was a world where substance and nature were clearly visible to those who gave them thought, where things had a principle of being (rain to bring up crops, stars to light the heaven, man "to know God and enjoy him forever"), an essence which explained their tendency (downward for water which was heavy, upward for steam which was light, or fire), and a purpose, which was—ultimately—to serve and enlighten man on earth. Even the planets in their course, said Dante, are set "to satisfy the world that calleth on them": man's world, God's man.

Aristotle's first principle regarding the Unmoved Mover had posited that "all things whatsoever observe a mutual order; and this the form that maketh the universe like unto God." Now, the prime mover of the ancients had become one with the Christian God, also the All-Mover in Dante's poem, whose "glory penetrates through the universe," who "made whatsoever circleth through mind or space with so great order that whoso looketh on it may not be without some taste of him."

Thus, understanding nature was to come close to God, understanding God's purpose was to understand nature and its phenomena. Inevitably, it seemed more important to know God and God's will for man and for the world, for, knowing these, all else would be illumined. Hence natural science was subject to theology and largely speculative, proceeding by deduction from the ultimate certainty that all phenomena had a purpose and meaning. Chiefly deductive, science was non-experimental. Ideas were stronger than facts.

However, it was also possible to argue that one could proceed from the lesser to the great as, in the twelfth and thirteenth centuries, when study of Aristotle and of St. Augustine spurred this point of view. Its great protagonists were Oxford men like Robert Grosseteste (1168–1263), who eventually became bishop of Lincoln. Fascinated by the analogy between the divine and the physical nature of light, Grosseteste came to feel that mathematics, optics, and astronomy (tools for analyzing and for measuring light) contributed to philosophical understanding, that physics and metaphysics were one, and that positive knowledge was worth acquiring even for its own sake.

Pupils of Grosseteste, like the Franciscan friar Roger Bacon (1219?–?1292), learned from him the uses of observation and experiment that could be analyzed and verified and, further, the usefulness of mathematics as an instrument of exact description. Unconventional, experimental, positivistic, this school's repute survived into the seventeenth century.

In its own time, its influence merged with that of Aristotle's nominalist critics (best known among them the English schoolman, William Ockham, (1280?–?1349), who maintained that the only reality was individual and specific. There were no universal categories, as Platonists asserted, only words. Horses existed, horseness was a man-made notion. Armed with this rather skeptical approach, the nominalist insisted that assumptions were only justified by unanswerable arguments, by demonstrable fact. They went on to spark a new interest in natural science. Nominalist practitioners, especially scholars of the University of Paris, successfully attacked the cosmology of Aristotle, disemboweled his purpose-filled universe, came close during the fourteenth century to some of the discoveries that marked the sixteenth and seventeenth.

Then came the fifteenth century and the humanists, whose intellectual attention we have seen turned from science to literature. Interest shifted from the possibilities of the experimental approach back to ingenious hypotheses and dialectics. The humanists were critical enough, but little inclined to experimental methods. They used their eyes and they used their heads. But applied science did not appeal to them. In any case physical contact with material things was an activity less elevated than speculation. The thought was purer than the act, the idea closer to perfection than any concrete image of it. We have seen that medieval philosophy and science had subordinated physics to metaphysics. The properties of matter were subject to immaterial laws and powers, the meaner to the higher, exactly as in everyday society the humble were supposed to carry out the purposes of those of nobler station. The humanists now took this over. The student of physics therefore, and of the natural sciences in general, became a student of philosophy—not matter. His approach was not, as in our day, quantitative; but qualitative—deciding, for example, by the use of logic, which bodies and which elements must be subject to others in terms of relative nobility or meanness within a kind of sociophysical hierarchy.

One aspect of nobility that all could see was detachment from manual labor. Likewise, the nobler a science the purer it would be of experiment and of material contacts. Medicine, for example, was best practiced as a reflection of philosophy too, and remedies prescribed in terms of a tradition to be learned from books or of esoteric and symbolical interpretations. The practical tasks of healing or relief were carried out by unschooled and unexalted medicasters working on empirical lines, surgeons often doubling as barbers, who pulled teeth, cauterized, applied leeches, practiced surgery and perhaps a little cut-rate magic.

Abstract and applied sciences lived apart. To the extent that anatomy and surgery were the less noble aspects of medicine, and thus relatively removed from medical-philosophical theory, they did progress. The same held true for mathematics and astronomy, which also advanced in the sixteenth century in pursuit of very concrete ends but without affecting traditional natural philosophy. The abstract and the experimental would not really meet until the coming of Galileo who, himself a mathematician and astronomer, claimed to be a natural philosopher too. Galileo trespassed onto the noble sciences' domain and argued that new physics, true physics, had to be based not on logic but on calculation and experiment, substituting quantity (that is, mathematics) for quality (that is, philosophy). What we today call science describes, analyzes, and explains natural phenomena. In the fifteenth and sixteenth century, however, the process of explanation was still overlaid by Aristotelian logic and reference to ancient authority. The "modern" emphasis of observation, experiment, and demonstration would not really appear until the seventeenth century.

Nevertheless, unimpressive though it might look when compared with the discoveries of later days, Renaissance speculation was subversive enough. When the humanists said that one authority was superior to another, that a Roman author was a better source of wisdom than a doctor of the medieval church, they implied the right to decide between different authorities and therefore the possibility of judging for oneself. And where some humanists simply replaced blind faith in one set of books because they were holy, with blind faith in another set of books because they were old, others decided to place experience and experiment above any book, above any second-hand authority. This, too, was something new.

Truths and Consequences

We should not wonder that Pope Paul II (1464–1471) accused the humanists, especially officials of his own papal chancellery, of paganism, denial of immortality, and other sins. The Pope was an ignorant curmudgeon, but his judgment was sounder than it might appear. In time —however long it took—the acids of the newer views would corrode and disintegrate the old. When Petrarch had laid down as a fundamental rule that "Nothing happens contrary to nature, even though things may seem contrary . . . nothing is a portent among men," he fired a trail that would explode in the libertinism of a Cyrano de Bergerac (see Part II, p. 392), who declared in 1641 "one should believe of a man only that which is human."

The Renaissance was a time of strong religious beliefs but also of growing nonreligious intellectual interests which did not set out to contradict religious doctrine but, sooner or later, came into competition with it. Even the religious Middle Ages had known nonreligious interests in literature, scholarship, and the arts. The change was one of degree as these interests, growing as the bounds of the world and its possibilities grew, began to show greater vitality and more appeal than simply religious ones.

The scope of Christianity was broadened. Marsilio Ficino, the Florentine humanist who translated Plato, held Christianity to be the most perfect religion, but found some kind of truth in every faith. Pico, his disciple, thought every religion and philosophy was part of one vast universal truth; and both men held that religious variety enriches the world. Religion, they thought, is part of human nature, distinguishing men from animals, which have no religion and need none. Such views, though not unchristian, appeared to some too tolerant of alternatives. Ficino's idea of a common humanity, a common human community, led him to argue that men are most fully men when they love other men as their fellows and equals—when they are humane. Cruelty, inhumanity, remove man from the human community as they reflect his loss of human dignity. The cruel are less men than others, they are inhuman—the young, the stupid, the imperfect, sick, fail to see the relation and the likeness of one man with all others, and his duty to treat all men as brothers.

A century after Ficino, a Silesian shoemaker, Jakob Böhme (1575–1624), would liken the variety of religions to that of flowers, of which all kinds grow side by side without dispute over their color, taste, or scent. "And each grows according to its essence and to the qualities proper to it. Thus is it with the children of God." Intolerance is as absurd as it is inauspicious, contrary to the most obvious natural laws: "Who would dream of finding the birds in the woods, who praise the Lord of all things in their songs? Will the spirit of God punish them because their voices are not in perfect harmony? Let them rather sing with all their might and play in His presence."

Next to Nature, Art

In one direction only did the new spirit succeed in expressing itself unequivocally. The men of the Renaissance loved beauty and appreciated its elevating value. Theoretically, beauty was prized because it could guide its lover toward those higher realms where its own source lay. Beauty is the mirror that man holds up to nature and himself. But it is a mirror through which we must pass on our quest for the absolute, the highest kind of beauty being the most subtle, as the ethereal girls of Botticelli, permitting the lover to glimpse the ideal through the material envelope. The appreciation of appropriateness, of a certain rhythm or agreement between character and form, between the seen and the unseen—where, as the English poet Edmund Spenser put it, "soule is form and doth the bodie make"—gave to some men a very rich and broad vision. A biographer who knew him speaks of "the singular and most intense pleasure" which affected the talented architect Alberti in the presence of beauty: "an old man of venerable aspect, vigorous and active under his years, had marvelous attraction for him. The genius

The Tempietto di San Pietro in Montorio, Rome, by Donato Bramante, regarded by later architects as the perfect classical building.

or skilled craftsmanship of the artist, the curve and distances of landscape, the light and color of gem or flower—in their beauty he saw something of the divine nature itself. To look upon the smiling face of the land would not seldom cure him of a malady."

But man did not need to remain a passive spectator, he could create beauty of his own. The art of the Renaissance tried to apply human reason to discover and express the natural laws of proportion and harmony. The aim was to integrate the works of man in the grander creations of nature but, above all, to mobilize that which nature puts at our disposal for the joy and self-assertion of man.

Proportion, Perspective, and Light

Art was discipline and order. Aristotle had recognized its gift to express and "purge" the passions, but insisted that it should not only move the feelings but discipline them as well. This ideal would play an important part in an age which was challenging and shaking the traditional orders into which it came. In its pursuit, nature could suggest the rules; while the classics—rediscovered, re-examined—served as interpreters or go-betweens. Although they borrowed their principles from nature, the works of man retained a logic of their own, speaking the language of human order and calculation.

The results partook little of Rome and less of nature's apparent mystery and disorder. In their rules of proportion, Renaissance architects like ancient ones, expressed their organic view of nature by comparing the relations of the parts of a building with those of the members of the human body, which are related with one another and with the whole. Man being created in the image of God, they reasoned, his proportions must reflect the ideal proportions of a harmonious universe, and their study could provide a model for creations which would best fit into this universe. The geometrical relations between the different parts of the body could be applied to the relations between parts of the structure of a building.

Vitruvius's architectural treatise of the first century B.C. provided the basic principle that all parts should be so interrelated that any addition or subtraction would spoil their harmony. The best means of solving the problem of integrating parts into a whole was by mathematics. Perfection thus became a geometrical affair of balance, unity, and proportion through which the cosmic harmony could somehow be reproduced on earth. The first place in which to do this would be churches. In Brunelleschi's church of San Lorenzo in Florence (finished 1470) and Bramante's circular chapel or *Tempietto* in Rome (finished 1502), the resources of ancient art and classic forms were adapted to new, personal conceptions of volumes. clearly articulated and rigorously distributed according to the noble principles of geometry. Here were sites where man and God could meet—centralized by combining that square and circle which (Vitruvius had shown) encompassed man; rounded in perfect circles which, having no end, provided fitting symbols of divine eternity; crowned by vast domes, triumphs of balance, of man's homage to and his achievement before God.

But if the master plan must subordinate parts to the whole, in architecture, in literature, as in the perspective of the painter, this meant not only calculation but selection. The supremacy of one dominant idea suggested the elimination of irrelevancies from the background of Italian Renaissance paintings, from the capitals of columns stripped of their medieval fancies, or indeed from the increasingly planned, rationalized state, also a work of art. The new classical synthesis aimed to subordinate parts to whole in monarchy as well as art, in urban planning as in literature, trying to establish the organic connection of the different parts, their subordination to a center.

It would be wrong to see all of this only (or even mostly) as a matter of philosophy. It was much more a style and a mood; and the conditions which made the mood also offered the opportunities to express it. The curiosity for strange and exotic things, for odd costumes and animals from overseas, expressed the current quest for the unknown and the mentality of discoverers pressing on to ever further horizons—and ever greater gains. The technical exhilaration of the artists, their relish of mathematical and scientific problems, their joy in experiment and discovery, from Paolo Ucello's pursuit of perspective to the problems Leonardo sought and solved, are all very much of their time.

Arts and artists mirror their times. Like goods, like men, forms and

The Virgin of the Rocks,
by Leonardo da Vinci.
Louvre, Paris.

styles moved farther and faster, their new insistence and self-affirmation
reflected the new assertiveness of personalities, cities, states. Life is exciting, but it passes fast; the world is an adventure, and art, like life, aims
to grasp all it can of both in heroic terms and, often, as with Michelangelo, on a heroic scale.

The great discovery of the Italian *quattrocento,* or fifteenth century,
was that space can be rationalized and dominated by the artist in every
kind of creation from cameos to cathedrals. Intelligence and reason
triumphed in the pure linear tensions opposed to the agitated ornament
of the late gothic. They triumphed, above all, in the conquest of space
by skill and illusion, which would be the great contribution this age
made to modern art.

Medieval space was limited: by walls and roof arches, by stone and
glass, more fundamentally by a limiting conception in the men who han-

dled it and the society they served. Space was not a juncture but a partition between compartments as separate as the parts of a world which had a way of ending abruptly at the edge of a forest, of a map, of a sea—of the unknown. Now, as these margins were pressed back and human experience began to acquire greater proportions, the artist's view of space broadened as well. Its first conquest would be perspective.

Not unknown to the Middle Ages, perspective, the ideal network of lines converging toward an imaginary point, becomes relevant because it indicates the proper place and scale of men and things, something increasingly important as the world expands. Proportion is divine, as the title of a book on the subject suggests, because it indicates the proper place of parts in the whole. Both proportion and perspective were part of the new science derived from study of the ancients, from a conjunction of archeological findings and explorations in geometry. The dome that Brunelleschi constructed over the nave of the Florence cathedral was not just the solution of mathematical and technological problems that earlier generations could not solve. It was the expression of a world no longer closed but open, no longer hemmed in but related to all within the mind or scope of man.

It would not be long before space itself became constraint. The forms of Michelangelo strain at their bonds, cry out against the limits that stones or frames impose, attempt the breakthrough that light and optics actually achieved in the sixteenth century with works like those of Leonardo, in which light was enlisted to solve the problem of space. While architects—by dint of their profession—generally stressed the solid,

The Expulsion of Adam and Eve from Paradise, by Masaccio. Santa Maria del Carmine, Florence.

opaque nature of their structures, painters—enlisting perspective in the service of fantasy—worked to increase the illusion of space and to prolong the limited world of hall or chamber in all directions. The general trend can best be followed through some of the painters whose works are most accessible and speak most clearly to our time.

Giotto (1267?–?1337) closed an era preoccupied especially with God, and opened one that looked above all to man. Yet his proportions, as in medieval painting, reflected the importance not of real figures and objects in nature but of an ideal scale in the painter's mind. With Masaccio we get human figures, their feet firmly planted on the ground, their humility before supernatural powers gone, their proportions greater, their bodies acknowledging a weight and a concreteness that were not there before. Even when—as in his painting of Adam and Eve expelled from Paradise—they flee the wrath of God, they are energetic, vital, and appealing in their human suffering. Masaccio, born in 1401, died in 1428, nearly a century after Giotto, having imparted a new reality to painting and a sense of divinity to man—a heroic quality like that which was stressed by contemporary humanists.

A generation later, by the time of Piero della Francesca (1420?–1492), the dignity of man had become more complex and more solemn. Its expression now turned toward a new aristocratism, obeying the ideals of geometry and perspective discovered at the beginning of the century. The transcendental rules commanding the construction of a work of art made a fit setting for transcendental mysteries: Christ's resurrection becomes a luminous, almost an abstract, scene devoid of the gentle humility of Giotto, as of Masaccio's forthright earthiness. Above all, we see that the eye has conquered its surroundings. It has learned not only to trace forms more precisely, but how to place them in perspective. This intellectual victory so fascinated its first discoverers that painters like Paolo Ucello (a contemporary of Piero's, who died in 1475) preferred his perspective studies to his wife. As late as 1505, the young Albrecht Dürer could still journey from Nürnberg to Bologna especially to study what he called "the secret art of perspective."

Earlier artists had used space to place their figures in, but it was the actors that mattered, their surroundings only scenery. Painters, sculptors, and architects could now demonstrate the new awareness that things, space, and man are an integrated whole. In a painting like Leonardo's *Virgin of the Rocks,* characters and landscape are one, the latter used to reflect and enhance the mood of the former. Light itself has been promoted to an active role. It had been no more than a transparent receptacle for the shapes in it. It now became *lighting,* dynamic with a personality of its own which modifies what is simply perceived in terms of the will, imagination, intention of the artist.

Masaccio, Piero, or Leonardo's fellow-apprentice Sandro Botticelli, all outlined their figures with well-defined strokes of the brush. Now the

The Birth of Venus, by Sandro Botticelli. Uffizi, Florence.

very line becomes vaguer so that things, beings, and tones merge into one another, a certain indefiniteness permitting light and shade to dominate the canvas. The force of the painting lies less in the figures than in the atmosphere. The creator, who had enlisted one technique to reproduce the vision of his eyes, now taps another to evoke the visions of his mind and senses: thought, feeling, atmosphere. With Leonardo (and after him with painters like Caravaggio, Rembrandt, Georges de la Tour) the subtlest senses find their place on canvas, soaring highest in the contrast of light and shade which turns matter into spirit.

Idealization could move in several directions. With Raphael (1483–1520) it often went toward academism: beautifully composed yet somehow less elevated than edulcorated, so that even the cherubs of his Sistine Madonna seem to smirk at the sugariness of the scene. With Raphael, reality scarcely intrudes, and harmony rules over a delicate world divorced from the harsh disorders beyond its artificial bounds. There is beauty still, but less evocative and less spiritual than its predecessors, aspiring toward the fleshly, aristocratic dignity in the subjects of Titian (1477–1576), almost all of them plumper and looking very expensive. Pre-Renaissance painting, often realistic enough, nevertheless had lacked life in its figures. They were stiff and emblematic: general rather than individual or exact. Now, naturalistic realism took over, individuality was increasingly stressed along with faithfulness of reproduction. Art learned to copy nature down to the dew drop on the blade of grass and to the fur of every little hare. Oil painting, known in principle but little used before the fifteenth century, furnished the opportunity to show detail, texture, with a precision impossible in fresco or wash techniques, to indicate depth, weight, opaque or reflecting surfaces, roughness, smoothness of skin or materials to the delight of admirers who liked to finger and weigh what they beheld.

The Artist

The conquests of art were the conquests of man over nature, but also the symbols of a wider glory: if artists were proud of their achievements, so were cities, stressing their greatness over other competitors but also over the past. Social appreciation of artists, and the reflected glory their work shed on the community, can be seen from the public honors that were showered upon these heroes. For the funeral of Fra Filippo Lippi, the shops in Florence closed just as they did for funerals of princes. Genius, like death, was a great equalizer.

One should observe that the majority of artists, even among the greatest, were not concerned with expressing creative genius or providing social comments. They were, as Kristeller has told us, in the first place craftsmen; many of them of humble extraction, like Mantegna, who herded sheep in the fields near Padua until discovered by Squarcione; many poor, like Piero di Cosimo, who lived on eggs which he hard-boiled fifty at a time along with his varnishes to save time and money; some rough and violent like Andrea del Castagno, who killed another painter out of envy. Some took up "science" because they needed anatomy, or perspective, or mechanics in their work. But their science was practical, not theoretical. Many were sculptors who belonged to the bricklayers' gild, or painters belonging to the apothecaries' gild. The workshops in which many worked turned out curtains, flags, tombstones, decorations for horses, furniture, or festival floats.

Painters, like stonemasons or goldsmiths, were part of society and worked for it. The painter, says Alberti, tries "to please the multitude" and should heed them "when it is possible to satisfy their opinions." The multitude, in turn, admired creativeness, the capacity to produce full and forceful works of art, masterpieces in the sense of that term, appreciating the quality of detail, of imagination, and craftsmanship as well as the distinction of the work.

As the sixteenth century drew on, the craftsman became an artist proud of his talent, indulging his temperament and his increasingly extravagant tastes, while the employer became a patron aware of a special kind of greatness not accounted for by birth or station, acknowledging "the humors of such men of genius" as Julius II and his successors did those of Michelangelo (who was even forgiven his part in the anti-Medici rebellion of Florence provided he continued work on the Medici family tomb), or stooping like Charles V to pick up Titian's brush. But that was in Italy where, as a Portuguese painter noted with wonder: "In Italy one does not care for the renown of great princes; it is a painter only that they call divine."

Europe at the 16th Century: *A New Capitalism?*

We must now return to the economic developments of the early modern age, the fundamental background for all other developments of a busy time.

The economic enterprise of one age, with its dynamism and challenge of existing practices and attitudes tends, if successful, to create new vested interests, defensive of their acquired positions and possessions, prizing stability over enterprise, consumption over production. For the most successful of the bourgeoisie, trade which had made the fortune of their families soon took second place to stabler investments: city real estate or land beyond the walls. Land itself was no longer a means of subsistence only, something to be lived off, but property like any other—a source of income or, perhaps, prestige. But it was also and would remain for a long time, along with urban real estate, the most stable and sometimes even the most fruitful source of income.

Soundly established bourgeois no longer sought gains in risky enterprises. They wanted to stabilize what they had, be it the craft, the trade, the profits: not expand them. Already, as the fifteenth century ended, the policy of the great urban centers had become restrictive, limiting the economic activity of merchants, traders, producers in a tight corset of municipal regulations designed to protect the vested interests of gilds and trades. In the older trading centers, like Ghent and Bruges in Flanders or Nürnberg in Bavaria, the trade regulations that had made their reputation began to wear it down, gild protection came to mean protectionism, hurting the workers outside the closed shop of the gild and hampering enterprise, novelty, development.

Soon, however, the modification of trade routes following on new discoveries, inflation, the rise of monarchies restraining the authority of great old cities reluctant to obey, encouraging the activities of newer centers, cutting and slashing at local protectionism and particularism on behalf of wider interests, ushered in an economic revolution best reflected in the rise of new ports like Antwerp, surpassing Bruges and Ghent, a new spirit of economic freedom and enterprise, speculation and adventure. Here were the beginnings of a new capitalism.

While the privileged crafts of medieval cities languished their way to ruin, the new centers spurred the rise of newer manufacturers resting on free labor and capital investment. In England, the Netherlands, and parts of France, the enclosure of common village lands by noblemen dislodged some of the peasants who had drawn their living from them and furnished the manpower for new enterprises whose profits in turn would provide the capital of commercial expansion. Already in the early fif-

teenth century the arsenal of Venice—an early example of state capitalism—boasted 3,000 ship's carpenters and as many caulkers. Now industrial concentration made its appearance in trades like printing, textiles,
metallurgy, shipbuilding, and especially in mines where the new machines needed to dig, pump, or shore up deeper shafts called for more
capital than small-scale entrepreneurs could find.

At Liège, today in Belgium but then an independent bishopric, the
proximity of iron and coal deposits fostered the growth of an important
arms industry: Liège became the city of miners and muskets, which it
long remained. In 1515, a mining disaster nearby killed eighty-eight
men and inaugurated a grim series of great mining accidents.

High furnaces fed by coal, whose use spread from Germany and
reached England by the end of the fifteenth century, proved able to turn
out 100 to 150 tons of cast iron a year. English salt pans became vast
capitalist enterprises, like one with a capital investment of 4,000 pounds
sterling which employed 100 workers. The sixteenth-century English
ballad of Jack of Newbury tells us of a cloth factory owner employing 200
weavers and 400 other workers.

Production rose generally at the expense of workers called on to labor
increasingly longer hours now that medieval gild protection wore away.
The printer-journeymen of the sixteenth century, a relatively well-off
group, worked twelve to sixteen hours a day, turning out from 2,500 to
3,500 sheets—an average of one printed sheet every twenty seconds, a
rate not improved upon until the late eighteenth century, and not
greatly until November 29, 1814, when the London *Times* brought out
the first newspaper printed on a mechanical press which turned out 1,100
sheets an hour.

Printers and Books

The printing industry is a good example of mass production and mass
consumption in a field which was itself the vehicle of revolutionary
changes. Books of sorts had existed since the most ancient days, but the
lack of a means of mechanical reproduction severely limited their numbers and kept up their price. One of the leading factors was the cost of
parchment made from skins—the best kind, vellum, from skins of unborn
calves. Paper, made in China before the beginning of the Christian era,
and used by the Arabs around the ninth century, was manufactured in
Moorish Spain three centuries later and introduced into Italy by
merchants who traded with the Arabs. It only began to replace parchment in the fourteenth century.

Paper was made of rags or bits of hempen cordage. The extension of
flax and hemp cultivation in the late Middle Ages, the substitution of
linen for wool in underclothing, and eventually the wider use of linens
which Portugal imported from the East helped to make the necessary raw

A sixteenth-century printing shop. Gutenberg Museum, Mainz. Right: a page from the Gutenberg Bible.

materials more readily available. Paper manufacturers would be established first in Italy and France (thirteenth century), then in Germany (fourteenth century), facilitating the multiplication of books. To carry the story forward, paper, of course, facilitated the introduction of printing, but this in turn was going to create such a shortage of raw material that by the seventeenth century desperate attempts to find some substitute led to experiments with nettles, mulberries, palm fronds, and seaweed. The solution would only be found in mid-nineteenth century, when rags were at last replaced by pulps of wood and straw.

Late in the fourteenth century, seventy years before printing from movable type appeared, engravings and broadsheets printed by wooden blocks provided the mass of pious images, cheap and very popular, bringing the saints from church into the home. Woodcuts allowed the poorest to contemplate the miracles of Christ, the stories of the Bible, or simply to decorate their walls with the image of a patron—St. Christopher, protector of travelers, who guarded against sudden death; St. Rocco, against the plague; St. Sebastian, against wounds; St. Apolline, against toothache.

By the fifteenth century, manuscript copyists had set up mass-production workshops which could turn out impressive quantities: an order of 1437 recently found at Leyden refers to 200 copies of the *Psalms of Penitence,* 200 of Cato's *Distics* in Flemish, 400 of a small prayer book— all presumably for a university bookshop. Most of the books the copyists turned out were used by scholars and clerics, but many went into bourgeois households. Such were the *Travels* of Sir John Mandeville, first brought out in 1356, of which 250 manuscript copies still exist—73 in German and Dutch, 50 in Latin, 40 in English, 37 in French, the rest in Spanish, Italian, Danish, Czech, and Irish.

To go beyond this stage and make a printed book, the basic problem was how to compose a page by using independent movable type that could be put together, used to do a job, then separated and used again and again. The solution came not, as one might expect, from the wood-cutters, several generations of whom had been using a primitive form of printing, but from the metal workers, probably goldsmiths like Johann Gutenberg himself (1400?–?1468), and many of the first generation of master printers, who applied the experience gained in engraving seals and small-scale figures.

The exact origin of the invention, or even the precise person of the inventor, remains a mystery. We do know that by 1400 the three essential elements of printing were already in use: wire presses and presses for expelling moisture from paper; ink on a varnish base, on the same principle as fourteenth-century oil paints; "movable type" as used in letter stamps or punches. The first printers were Germans, all from one or more workshops in the cathedral city of Mainz where the first presses appeared around 1445. In the next decade, printing and the book trade spread abroad, first in Germany—rich, full of cities, metal workers, and merchants in a position to finance the new ventures; then, throughout the world. 1465 marks the date of the first book printed in Italy by German printers; 1470, the first book printed in Paris; 1473, the first book in Louvain; 1474, the first book printed in Cracow. In 1476 William Caxton, an English merchant who had learned printing at Cologne and run a press at Bruges, settled at Westminster. About the same time books began to appear in Spain. By 1480 printing shops had been set up in over 110 European towns. By the end of the fifteenth century, fifty years after the first printed book appeared, at least 35,000 editions had been published, some 15 to 20 million books printed. At a time when the total population of Europe numbered less than 100 million and only a minority of it could read, this was an honorable record.

It is true that the German printers who carried the new art to Italy and France met with a hostile reception from established editors and copyists at first. There was snobbery and there was sheer inertia, but also the sort of prejudice that all new machines elicit from old-fashioned crafts-men and wealthy amateurs. Manuscript makers and collectors looked askance at developments which threatened to reduce the value and, since some of the first books were rather rough, the aesthetic appeal of existing libraries. As late as 1482, we find the librarian of the Duke of Urbino, a great humanist, Vespasiano da Bisticci, declaring that his master would be ashamed to have a printed book in his library. But this hostility did not endure. Printers soon showed that they could rival the most handsome manuscripts. Humanists realized the advantage of cheaper, more numerous books. Above all, to start with, the church gave enthusiastic support to a technique of great didactic value which, properly employed, could help bring many more people close to God. To a mid-fifteenth-century ecclesiastic, printing was "the art of arts, the science of sciences. Thanks to its rapid diffusion, the world has been endowed with a magnificent, hitherto hidden, treasury of wisdom and of science. An infinite number of works that very few students could consult until now, in Paris, in Athens, and in the libraries of other great university towns, are now translated into all languages and spread among all nations of the world."

Who read these early books and what were they about? The immense majority were either religious or literary: roughly 45 per cent of existing books printed before 1500 are on religious subjects, 30 per cent are works of literature, either current medieval works or ancient classics. Most of these (77 per cent of the total) are in Latin, and thus directed to the relatively cultivated public acquainted with that language. Few of the ephemeral publications intended for the ordinary man survive. But fly sheets, posters, pamphlets bringing news of comets, public events, discoveries like those of Columbus, victories in war, princes' exploits, or the impending visit of an indulgence-seller, were being sold at fairs or in the streets, and preparing the paper warfare of Reformation and Counter-Reformation.

Certainly a revolution was taking place. If by 1500, about 20 million books had been printed, the sixteenth century saw at least ten times more. This is no greater than the annual production of a great European country like France today, but enough to make the printed book available and accessible to any sixteenth-century person who knew how to read. And whereas at the end of the fifteenth century this had been mostly clerics or clerks, by the sixteenth century it meant more and more magistrates, bourgeois, merchants, and tradesmen. The size of book collections also went up, comfortable lawyers or merchants boasting 500 or 700 books, and barbers, apothecaries, tanners, grocers, also possessing very respectable collections. A whole industry catered to the needs of simple people whom it provided with almanacs, saints' lives, books pious and entertaining in such numbers that the inventory of one bookseller in 1522 shows 50,000 such works, of another in 1528, 102,285, of yet another in 1545, 271,939.

There were bestsellers in those days. The writings of Rabelais may have passed the 100,000-mark; Erasmus's *Colloquies* and *Adages* alone went into several hundred thousands in the half century after their publication. More's *Utopia* sold tens of thousands. Most popular of all, were the religious works. Luther's German Bible (1522–23) must have reached the million mark in the first half of the century and done better than that in the second half (one printer alone sold 100,000 copies between 1534 and 1574). The total of Luther's works—sermons, polemics, catechisms—marks the beginning of mass literature, addressed to all and accessible to all, not just to small cultivated circles. The Psalms in their French translation met with similar success, though on a lesser scale. They were sung by the rebel Huguenots in their conventicles, or at the stake, or on the battlefield. Though they were repeatedly forbidden by royal edict, nevertheless Francis I liked and read them, Henry II, his successor, sang them and had them sung. In 1561 Henry II's widow, Catherine de Medici, permitted their reprinting and within a few months, 50 or 60,000 copies had been placed—one in the hands of every Protestant.

We might also consider the extent to which the future conquistadores' dreams of adventure, glory, fame, and gold fed on the knightly romances turned out in massive numbers by Spanish printers. Vulgarized in hundreds and thousands of printed books, shipped to America by the case in almost every ship that sailed there, the new literature did its part in inspiring the further exploration of the New World. Soon the presses started turning in Mexico, where 116 works were printed in the sixteenth century, 1,228 in the seventeenth century, and in Lima, Peru, which, with five colleges and one university boasting eighty professors, wanted more books than Spanish ships could bring.

Neither the church nor governments ignored the use of print in propaganda. The first book printed in Russia dates from 1663; in Constantinople, 1727; in Greece, 1821. But much earlier books had appeared in Abyssinia in 1515, printing shops were set up at Goa in 1557, in Macao in 1588, and in Nagasaki in 1590. In 1494 two German printers had already been sent from Lisbon to the Congo, to which the Portuguese had exported books since 1490—books which were part of the cargo of all early Portuguese explorers.

The Portuguese sovereigns never forgot that grammar and catechism provided excellent support for canons and, like the canon-founders, the men who printed books ranked among the busier capitalists of the age. Great printer-publishers like Christopher Plantin in Antwerp or Koberger in Nürnberg, who specialized in liturgical books for churches and books for university use, were large entrepreneurs, with over a hundred men in their workshops, twenty-four presses, and warehouses or representatives from Danzig to Lisbon. No greater publishers would arise before the nineteenth century. And, naturally, the great printing houses were in the busiest cities—in Venice, Paris, Basel, Nürnberg, and Antwerp—where they could benefit from the greater availability of capital.

The Merchants

From land to city; from noncompetitive, price-fixing, restrictive and exclusive gild organization to competition and an increasingly free market;

from regulation based on traditional values to increasingly rational treatment of economic problems—management, production, exchange, investment; from emphasis on consumption in a scarcity economy to that of production and exchange; from regard at least theoretical for justice, to interest in profit and profit from interest. These, by the sixteenth century, were the economic trends which played such an important part in the making of the modern world.

It was the merchants who really introduced a sense of exactness, so lacking in the sixteenth century. Constant use of measures and of calculations developed a greater capacity to think in quantitative terms. The importance of time when it came to contracts, options, and other operations focused attention on its more precise measurement and recording. We ignore the precise birth date of Erasmus, Rabelais, and Luther, but sixteenth-century merchants noted the birthdays of all their children, all major events of their lives, their trips, and illnesses. Time now is valuable—time is money.

It is a long slow way from magic to mathematics, but merchants were among the pathfinders. To shelter their commercial activities, all cities built exchanges. Antwerp, which opened one in 1460, replaced it with a more splendid building in 1531. Sir Thomas Gresham, Queen Elizabeth's agent in Antwerp, would build the London Exchange, which the Queen herself opened in 1571. Medieval exchanges, such as the one at Bruges, had been glorified fairs; new ones operated more on a paper economy—credit, loans, insurance, or goods not at hand—thus both concentrating and abstracting the nature of business transactions.

Business was venture and adventure. In a world quite irrational and unpredictable, there was much superstition. Gambling was widespread, and card games and dice were everywhere. The connection between gambling and business was close, both reflecting a view of an unpredictable world. Speculation was rife: trade in futures, attempts to corner the market, to manipulate foreign exchange and interest rates.

Business was a gamble, and betting part of business. In 1502, two businessmen of Lubeck bet whether the Duke of Guelders would or would not capture a castle he was besieging; in 1534, a contract specified that it would only be valid if, by a certain date, the seller had married a nun or the daughter of a nun. (He did, but the clause was voided in court.) Other bets referred to stock-market prices or the sex of children about to be born.

Many took a dim view of the whole thing. "Lottery—trumpery," writes an Antwerper who buys a lottery ticket nevertheless. "Finance is a fine word for theft," notes Matthäus Schwarz, Jakob Fugger's chief accountant. This was particularly true of the insurance business—also much organized and expanded in these years. Marine insurance dates back at least to fourteenth-century Italy. The sixteenth century saw the standardization of contracts and premiums, the appearance of regular insurance brokers, 600 of whom were working in Antwerp by 1504, the development of fire insurance, which first appeared in Hamburg, and also of life insurance, with endless opportunities for fraud. Sailors were insured without their knowledge and then murdered, old men kidnapped, sequestered, and starved to death. The records of the time abound in litigation and legislation which the new possibilities for enterprise called up.

As the sixteenth century opened, old-style companies still dominated the field in the north of Europe, combining trade and banking, great family enterprises with branches run by a member of the family or by a trusted factor, like the Welsers of Augsburg, whose eleven branches stretched from Lisbon to Nürnberg and who, in the 1520's would even try to colonize Venezuela. Soon, however, new trade associations appeared enabling lesser men to embark on costly but promising enterprises. In 1525 at Antwerp, we find two German merchants joining up, the better to carry on their business: Kilian Rietwieser of Würtzburg had his office in Leipzig and traded chiefly between central Germany and Antwerp; Joachim Pruner of Berlin dealt mostly between Lisbon and Antwerp. Between the two of them, the new company could hope for a wider field.

We might also look at the association established in 1535 in Antwerp by five merchants of Aix, Tournai, and Bois-le-Duc, all in the Lowlands, to join together for a trading voyage to Spain, in which profits and expenses would be shared in proportion to the capital contributed by each. To check expenses, all agreed to limit their dress "to what normal usage, their estate and condition requires," to produce an expense account every fifteen days, to keep food bills as low as possible, to be personally responsible not only for any "banquets or extraordinary expenses," but also for money lost gambling or in "dissolute places," or fines thereby incurred. If in Spain the partners found that a voyage to Peru would be profitable, they would embark upon it; if not, they would sell their goods in Spain. If any one of them, in Peru or elsewhere, should peradventure find "gold, silver, precious stones or jewelry," this should be shared equally among all. And if there should be in Peru some war against the infidel, and if one of the partners joined in it, any loot he garnered should also be shared—one-third for the man who got it, the rest to his associates, even if they should have cautiously kept out of it. Note here the combination of business-like forethought and the vast dreams of riches far away.

The dreams, however, were not entirely baseless. The profits of successful ventures could be vast. Lukas Rem, who started out as a Welser clerk in the 1490's, then set up his own house, notes in his diary: "On 15 June, 1525, at Augsburg we established the general balance . . . by the grace of God I found a gain of 30%."

The grace of God worked most effectively on behalf of those who traded in money rather than in goods. In fifteen years, between 1511 and 1526, the Fuggers who traded jewels, spices, clothes, minerals, but above all money—taking the revenue from mines as security for the cash they lent, earned over 54 per cent per year. Rivals dealing more in goods than loans had to be content with a regular 9 or 10 per cent. At its height,. the Augsburg firm of Fugger disposed of a capital of 4,700,000 gold florins equivalent to 13,000 kilograms of pure gold. We may compare this with the riches of the Florentine Peruzzi, great fourteenth-century bankers, who could lay their hands on only 135,000 florins, equivalent to 147 kilograms of gold. With sums of the former kind, a threshold had been passed beyond which comparison with medieval capital becomes impossible.

There was a new spirit about the sixteenth-century commerce of the north, a new kind of rapacity as well as risk long known to southern businessmen. There was, above all, a new kind of scale which affected prices and also business opportunities. The quantity of spices imported from overseas allowed them to be sold five times as cheaply at Lisbon as they had been at Venice. In 1548 the Fuggers prepared to furnish the Portuguese for their African trade nearly four tons of brass bracelets, over 40,000 cauldrons, and various other tools. This presupposes gigantic stocks. A French group which at this time tried to take over the whole of France's salt trade by gaining control of Spanish imports, was involved in chartering 30,000 tons' worth of shipping.

And yet it would be wrong to stress all this too much. Compared to their predecessors these men were modern; compared to their successors they were not. Their methods, spirit, enterprise, are the forest murmurs of capitalism; but no more than that. Even the scale of their operations bears witness to the limitations under which they worked. All the freight crossing the Saint Gotthard Pass in one year could be carried on one of our freight trains; and the thousand tons of Portuguese spices sold in Antwerp in 1504 would scarcely be noticed in one of our cargo lists.

Modern capitalism consists in the search for greater profits by the extension of the volume of business, of greater gains by greater sales even if profit per unit should be smaller. From this point of view the very high rates of profit in spice trade or banking suggest not so much early modern capitalism, but a comparatively primitive economic structure, where under-developed markets, disorganization of public finance, and shortage of capital and credit made for vast risks, vast losses, and vast gains. The economic and social structures of the time often appear more "medieval" than "modern," more "feudal" and less capitalistic. The "new capitalism" was still predominantly commercial, involving no significant changes in business techniques. Mass production was still generally impossible for lack of technological means. Subsistence agriculture continued to provide much of the economic activity. The scattered offer could not always meet an equally scattered demand: consumption could not rely on or conjure up production. Economic concentration was less connected with production than with distribution and exchange. Still, it seems clear that things were changing. Those who have argued the modernity of the sixteenth century have a case. So have their opponents who point out the backward state of business, the paucity of means, the scarce opportunities. Two kinds of men have always written history and read it: those who emphasize similarities and those who insist on differences. The reader must decide according to his inclination whether the changes we have seen count more than the enduring bonds which linked this time with the preceding age.

How did economic activities affect men and their attitudes? The answer in this case seems to be, relatively little. The society in which merchants moved had been materially affected by their enterprises, but not toward a restructuring of fundamental values. Even the most enterprising merchants contended against contradictory forces—inertia, conservatism, hostility to innovation, sheer conformity—at work not only around them but *within* them. The new men were part of a society of castes, orders, and corporations that they never thought to question but only to exploit (or circumvent). They had set wealth in circulation and increased it, sparked fresh activity, introduced new business methods, more accurate records, swifter communications, greater precision even in everyday life. But they did not dispute the existing order, only sought to be part of it; they did not challenge the existing hierarchy, only aspired to rise in it.

The characteristic representatives of economic success sought nobler employment, taught their children Latin, which marked a move from trade to higher things—in law, administration, the councils of princes, leaving the field to new groups of parvenus. In later generations, scions of merchant houses might become humanists like Hans Jakob Fugger in the 1560's, who knew Latin, Greek, Hebrew, Italian, French, Hungarian, Czech, and Polish; patrons of art like his brother Ulrich, who spent so much on his collections and his protégés that his family got an injunction against the spending. The Fugger House at Rome was decorated by a pupil of Raphael. In 1508, Giorgione and Titian were engaged to paint the frescoes of the *Fondaco dei Tedeschi* (the German Merchants' House) in Venice. (Titian actually got a place as broker there in 1516.) The Medici, of course, became noble—dukes, popes, princes—ruined themselves and rebuilt their fortunes not out of trade but out of the revenue they acquired in their capacity as rulers.

The greatest financial success of fifteenth-century France was Jacques Coeur, who might serve as the prototype of what has come to be called the "Renaissance man." His enterprises were everywhere. He minted money, manufactured textiles, was first to exploit French mines on a large scale, owned ships for which he obtained a papal concession to transport pilgrims to the Holy Land even while making immense profits from selling contraband arms to Egypt. His talents made him indispensable to the King, Charles VII, and put him in a position to make or break cities and firms all of which eagerly sought the favorite's favor. Part of his income came from bribes, part of it went on bribes to the King's mistress, his chief officers, perhaps to the King himself, whom he made a partner in his ventures and thus interested in their success (as Queen Elizabeth was in Sir Francis Drake's). But the palm of his prosperity came when he was ennobled, married his daughter to a noble, had his son named Archbishop of Bourges, his brother Bishop of Luçon, three of his best friends to other Episcopal sees. Disgraced in 1441, arrested, condemned to ruinous fines and to imprisonment, Coeur's end was worthy of his record. Escaping from prison, he took refuge with the Pope, who gave him command of a fleet to fight the Turks in Chios, where he would die in 1456, a strange and wonderful creature.

The Prince

Jacques Coeur's motto had been a pun: *A vaillans cuers riens impossible*—nothing impossible to valiant hearts (*coeurs*). It stands as one of the representative statements of a time when strong personalities had better opportunities of affirming themselves than a less mobile, less urban, more hierarchized society had offered. Not long after Coeur's death another merchant banker, Jakob Fugger the Rich, decided the results of the imperial election of 1519. Still another, Cosimo de Medici, ruled over the destinies of Florence. Small noblemen like Francisco Pizarro and Hernando Cortes cut out for themselves empires overseas. *Condottieri* like Francesco Sforza wrested the duchy of Milan from its Visconti masters. Landless bastards became princes: Sforza himself, Alfonso of Aragon in Naples, Sigismondo Malatesta at Rimini on the Adriatic.

Though such destinies may be found in other lands, Italy was the choice stage of their unfolding. In the years between 1494 when the French of Charles VIII first rode down into Italy and 1559 when Henry II at last renounced his costly pretensions there—the peninsula remained a cockpit of experiment and private initiative, unlike any other part of Europe. It is instructive to compare a prince of the *quattrocento* whose power was revolutionary with rulers north of the Alps whose position was quite traditional. The Duke of Burgundy struggling against his feudal lord, the King of France, wanted to be like him only more so, to take over a traditional authority. A Cosimo de Medici, a Sforza of Milan, founded himself on a new conception of principate based only on personal power and wealth.

The absence of the papacy, the weakening of imperial authority, had opened the way to personal adventure. Traditional wealth stemming from land, from craftsmanship, from local gilds, had given way to wealth from new enterprise—the handling of money, speculation, the exploration also and exploitation of new space. The novelties suited and matched the novelty of the Renaissance princes. Inevitably a kind of *entente* would be established between political and economic, political and intellectual, political and artistic adventurers. Politics and imagination are not so far apart. The intellectual and artistic flowering proved it. Soon, however, a certain stabilization appeared. Usurpers became dynasts and surviving tyrants, princes. Exploration of possibilities came to an end as the stability grew. The era of adventure dissolved into conformism, a new courtly culture, an adaptation of aristocratic values to the needs of new princes, new courts, new authorities not so very different from those which they displaced, not too different either from the aristocratic monarchies developing in the north.

In this evolution, late-fifteenth- and sixteenth-century princes found useful allies in the very men who had formulated and expressed the values of the preceding age: the humanists. Fourteenth- and early-fifteenth century humanists had praised the civic virtues of an active, public-spirited bourgeoisie. When they looked to Rome they had gloried in the valor of the Republic, stern, brave, hard-working, highly moral, and with a strong sense of social responsibility. As the fifteenth century drew on, the humanists seemed to advance, or perhaps retreated, much as their fellow citizens did, from the demanding freedom of the Republic to the constraint, authority, and order of the Roman Empire. A growing interest in the less public aspects of life, the special skills of scholarship, the search for seclusion and quiet away from the vulgar crowds, all drew the humanist from city to court, from their earlier public activities to private dependence on a patron, from republicanism to the admiration and service of those who bestowed both patronage and distinction—princes and great prelates.

Once they had disapproved of idleness, now they praised leisure; once they had sung activity, now they asked only for a tranquil life. Simplicity was good, but better allied with comfort; gain, at least when the result of work, once more became vulgar. Realism, too, was changing. Dante's dreamlike Beatrice of the thirteenth century had been followed in the fourteenth by Petrarch's more concrete, fleshly Laura and even by Boccaccio's tales for a bawdy public. Now this naturalism gave way to idealization once more, to images higher, purer, less harsh, suited to a new aristocratic public, as we can see if we compare the works of the courtly Pisanello (1395?–?1455) or Antonello da Messina (1430?–1479), with their naturalistic depiction of garb and gear and horses, with that of Raphael or da Vinci, who exclude such details as irrelevant.

The humanistic orator, philosopher, or chronicler participated in reviving old chivalrous ideals now being adapted to the needs of the new elite. He emphasized the role of women, no longer mere housekeepers

Niccolo Machiavelli, by Santo di Tito.

and child-producers but, in an aristocratic culture, fit students of the
higher things, dispensers of pleasure, ornaments of manners, objects
of conspicuous consumption. He polished up the image of the modern
knight, the urbane, gallant, and cultivated man of the world or, rather,
of the court, as Castiglione has described him in his *Courtier.* New
courtly ethics looked down on gain as Castiglione did, despised middle-
class values, calculation, and frugality. Waste and heedlessness were
rated much more highly than any dignity that work or business could
provide. This kind of code, so similar to that of northern aristocracies,
though more refined, lent itself to being borrowed in more backward
lands and Castiglione's book, first printed in 1528, laid down what would
become the moral code of the sixteenth-century gentry.

At the center of the court was the prince. Early in the fifteenth century
already, humanists had been found to argue that "security, prosperity,
efficient government" were to be found only in the rule of a single man,
that letters really flourished "only in the ordered progress afforded by a
prince." Their heirs had gone much further on this road. The concept
of philosopher kings stood in the forefront of their preoccupations, in an
age when learning and absolutism were both setting out on fresh careers.
Machiavelli was not the only humanist to concern himself with princes.
There were more acceptable attempts by men like Juan Luis Vives,
writing for Catherine of Aragon, who was just then bringing up the
princess Mary, heiress to the English throne, and even by Erasmus in his

Education of a Christian Prince.

Some princes were both Christian and educated: Federigo da Monte-feltro of Urbino (1444–1482), a devout prince, had two chapels—one Christian and alongside it, with the same proportions, another dedicated to the muses. In the portraits of famous men that lined his study, saints and biblical characters alternated with ancient sages—Homer and Aquinas, Seneca and Solomon. Yet many princes lived lives of mayhem and bloodshed. "Horror waits on princes," the English dramatist John Webster was soon to write. In 1402 the chief members of the ruling family of Lodi were burned alive by their enemies in the public square. In 1445, when the Bentivoglios of Bologna were murdered by members of a rival faction, the people hunted down their enemies and nailed their steaming hearts to the gates of the Bentivoglio palace.

In 1478, a conspiracy inspired by the Pope himself tried to take over Florence, murdered Giuliano de Medici in the cathedral while he was hearing mass, succeeded only in wounding his brother Lorenzo (1449–1492), and failed in its larger aim. Two hundred and seventy conspirators headed by the Archbishop were hung from the battlements of the Signoria, or thrown into the square and cut into small pieces by the populace. Furious at his failure and at his Archbishop's death, Pope Sixtus IV excommunicated Lorenzo, placed Florence under interdict, and, allied with the King of Naples, went to war against it. Hard-pressed after eighteen months of fighting, Lorenzo slipped off to Naples, won over his enemy there, and lived to be called Lorenzo the Magnificent. He died thirteen years later, afflicted by gout and an abdominal disorder that had been aggravated by a physician's prescription of powdered pearls.

Lorenzo, who spent more than half the annual income of the state on books and art, seems to represent the better kind of prince. As Guicciardini put it, "although the city was not free under him, it would have been impossible to find a better or more pleasing tyrant."

One cannot say as much of Cesare Borgia (1475–1507), favorite son of a corrupt, rapacious Spanish pope (Alexander VI) and of his Roman mistress, murderer of his brother-in-law and probably of his elder brother. Archbishop of Valencia at seventeen, Cardinal at eighteen, Cesare renounced the cloth to marry the sister of the King of Navarre and take command of his father's armies at twenty-three. Between 1499 and 1503 his campaigns carved out a large Borgia domain in central Italy, but its disintegration was as swift as its rise had been vivid. With Pope Alexander's sudden death in 1503, Cesare found himself deprived of support, isolated, himself too sick to attempt a rally. His followers melted away. His principality built on murder, bribery, and treason, collapsed along with his fortunes. His ruthlessness had established a brief reign of order-by-terror within the Pope's disorderly domains. It had also earned him untold enemies. Prison and an inglorious death in ambush were the final lot of the man whom Machiavelli holds up as a model for those who "by fortune or the arms of others arrive at sovereignty."

"Wit, superstition, atheism, massacres, poisons, murders, a few great men, an infinite number of cunning yet unfortunate rogues," Stendhal has written of Renaissance Italy. "Everywhere passions ardent in their savage pride: that is the fifteenth century." How could the humanists accept such patrons?

One easy explanation is that they were idealists, their eyes on a glorious past, their exuberant rhetoric concealing from them the facts of present conditions. Certainly their scholarship, their theorizing, their love of symbol, allegory, obscurity for its own sake, removed them from the realm of everyday, encouraged them to subordinate reality to ideal or, rather, to regard ideals as higher realities. By the late fifteenth century, the humanist's philosophy of man dealt not with men and women, but with abstractions, ethereal like the figures of Botticelli, heroic like the superhuman creations of Michelangelo. Where were the solid bourgeois of yesteryear, the human scale of even transcendental scenes we find in the paintings of Fra Angelico (1378–1455)? They had been lost from sight in the great gilded halls, the cool tiled loggias where graceful courtiers held discourse with wise philosophers.

But the humanists fished other lessons out of the ancient pond. Like the ancients, they saw the state not as given once and for all, but as the work of men, the natural expression of social forces, of individual creativity; and its success, as the result of human virtù and of human will. Machiavelli studied the relations between individual and state, state and state, not with regard to morality or law, but rather ends and means, the application of means to ends, the calculation of how human beliefs and passions can be enlisted to aim toward one final goal: the foundation, the stabilization, the aggrandizement of the state. The state, for its part, is for Machiavelli no longer a feudal realm or a medieval commune, not even or not quite the city or the empire of ancient days, not yet the monarchy to be found in Western lands. The state is theoretically a republic or commonwealth, ideally a burgeoning nation state, practically a work of art, a political model and machinery created in all its parts by the effort of tenacious wills in the fluid chaos of the Renaissance world.

Machiavelli's analysis is brutally realistic in its acceptance of violence and fraud; power politics are simply the art of harnessing and using whatever lies at hand. His work contrasts with More's *Utopia* or Erasmus's *Adages,* also written in the second decade of the sixteenth century, also concerned with issues of political and social morality, but not as means but ends, both persuaded that Christian morality should govern relations between rulers, as between ruler and ruled. Machiavelli for his part believes in *men,* their action, their response to destiny, their courage, their collaboration with luck. Not that he thinks men good. He sees that "they are thankless, fickle, false, studious to avoid danger, greedy of

Lorenzo de Medici, by Bronzino. Gabinetto Disequo, Florence.

gain . . . and ready . . . in the hour of need [to] turn against you."

One could not be more pessimistic. Withal, man has one great virtue, or some men have, and that is energy. Machiavelli despised the nobles, idle on their lands, far away from the city, its civilization and activities, proud of their class and of the barbarous and gothic distinction of men who do not work and do not earn. "No culture, no profession, no contribution to civil society, and that is what they call a gentleman!" * His own hero has nothing of the saint or knight. He is the active statesman. Chivalry is for books, for poets, for those who can afford it. Skill, cunning, and astuteness are the new virtues. As for religion, indifferent to its dogmas, Machiavelli does not underrate its uses. Religion is a useful tool in a statesman's hands to be enforced even if considered nothing but imposture, to be used the better to harness subjects to his yoke. Before Marx, Machiavelli had already formulated the concept of religion as the opium of the people.

Yet, cynical or realistic as he tried to be, Machiavelli revealed the extraordinary unworldliness of his caste. Though he had helped run the affairs of one of the major cities of the world, a pioneer in capitalist

* He was right, of course, but the fact that he could say it or even think it, and saying it express a widespread view, meant that the nobles had lost their function in society: that of professional soldiers.

industrial and banking enterprise, he knew little and cared less about industry, trade, finance. He neglected the whole social side of politics. Material realities, "the obscure struggle of material interests," for him played no more part than intellectual activities in a view of politics in which men and laws—that is, institutions—alone seem to matter. Machiavelli's *History of Florence* says nothing of arts or letters! Politics, diplomacy, war, and laws are the factors which the humanist historian notes. This tendency would mark historical interpretation right to the eighteenth century.

There is a letter from Machiavelli, cast out of his native Florence, in which he tells a friend how in a country inn he passed his time of exile as best he could in endless games of backgammon with the innkeeper, the miller, and two bakers: quarrels over a penny, railings, shouts, and curses. But then the sun went down, and the sometime Secretary of State of the Florentine Republic made for his room, took off his dirty clothes, and dressed as for a princely court. Settling down with his books, he was going to consort with princes: with the greatest minds of the past, who received him with amenity and, dwelling with him for hours, restored his self-respect.

Humanistic culture and humanistic values began by serving and justifying the bourgeois society which sparked them. Yet, after successfully formulating and applying bourgeois virtues, humanists and merchants abandoned them for more courtly ways, because their vision of fulfillment was still an aristocratic one. We have seen how the successful businessman acquired land, or title, or an office, ceased so far as he could to be a bourgeois and became a *rentier,* a noble small or great. Even if he could not always pass, these were and these had been the values he accepted. The bourgeois who praised work, consistently despised manual labor. "Those things which by their nature call for studies and more knowledge," writes Giorgio Vasari (1511–1574), "are infinitely more noble than those which involve physical force." And his sixteenth-century contemporary, the French lawyer Loyseau adds: "artisans are those who exercise the mechanical arts and we call mechanic that which is vile and abject. Artisans being properly mechanics are vile and abject." Journeymen printers denied being mechanics and they wore swords to prove it.

It is almost as if the sixteenth century came to mark the break between the cultivated man and "the rest," as culture, like other callings, became increasingly specialized and theoretical The rise of a new class, the bourgeoisie, made less for emancipation of its members than for differentiation. Society became more complex, its categories more diverse. Scholarship, talent, skill, and wealth began to join birth or clerical rank as agents of distinction. And, slow at first, then with increasing speed and brilliance, over the new society there rose the monarch's star.

Chapter 3

PRINCIPALITIES
AND POWERS

If much historical writing treats of kings and queens, it is because history turned around them to such a degree and for such a long time. Their whims and their personalities (and those of the great men who served or withstood them) influenced policy, made treaties and wars, and generally affected the lives of other men.

This was not true, of course, in the Italian communes of the early *quattrocento,* though even there it would become so once the fluid situation of the fourteenth century had hardened into the one-man states of the later fifteenth. And we have seen that the respite Italy was granted occurred to a great extent because the emperors had problems with their great German vassals, while across the Rhine the internal quarrels of the house of France and the attempts of English princes to seize the French crown also diverted attention for a while. From this time of trials, the kings of France would emerge stronger than ever by the end of the fifteenth century. So would the English monarchy, once it had settled its internal affairs, once the battle of Bosworth (1485) put an end to the bloody wars that the houses of York and Lancaster waged for the English throne, and left the victorious Tudors, heirs to both families, to set their house in order.

It is as the fifteenth century turns into the sixteenth that modern monarchs and modern monarchies appear. They are or aim to be all-powerful; and that is how men look upon them. "All depends on the monarch," writes Claude Seyssel, a counselor of Louis XII; and Thomas More: "from the prince as from a perpetual wellspring comes among the people a flood of all that is good or evil." A great fifteenth-century scholar thought that royalty were allotted guardian angels of higher rank than those of other men. And worldly exaltation effectively reflected immensely vaster powers. "Eveyone knows," a late fourteenth-century book on war had stated, "that in the matter of deciding on war, of declaring it, or of undertaking it, poor men are not concerned at all." In the fifteenth century as in the fourteenth, in the sixteenth as in the fifteenth, ordinary men and women had nothing to say of war, peace, foreign policy, and, where the king was strong enough, even taxes. Politics were the preserve of a special class: princes, nobles, their servants and advisors. Hence, when we survey the political scene, it is to their activities that we have to look, sparing only an occasional glance for those who, objects rather than subjects of these affairs, intrude from time to time, turning their preoccupations, their needs, their rebellions, into matters of state.

Spreading from Italy in the thirteenth century, Roman Law had been taken up by the lawyers whose task it was to bolster the arguments of the king against the vassals and the clergy with whom he competed for dominion. It brought with it the idea of an absolute ruler—the *princeps* whose person had all power, whose will was law. This combined with another classical ideal—that of the hero who is practically a god, always a dominant and benevolent figure. Together these evolved with the contemporary growth of a literary, semihistorical "nationalism"—a sentiment of patriotic pride in origins and past glories which seemed to justify present dominion and future greatness.

As the fifteenth century turned into the sixteenth, Italians, Spaniards, Frenchmen learned to sing the glories of their separate countries, to vaunt a national character or a national tongue. German humanists praised the German past as nowise inferior to that of ancient Rome. Around 1500, the need to assert this led to the editing of Tacitus's first-century *Germania* and of other texts that would reflect Germany's past glories and suggest her present claim to greatness. Spenser's *Faërie Queene,* a chivalric romance alluding to Arthurian legend, was one of many national epics. A number of sixteenth-century plays, like those of Shakespeare, praised the country, denigrated neighbors, exalted patriotic sentiment. In Germany Joachim Sandrart invented a tenth muse —Teutillis—exclusively engaged in superintending German art.

The reference to the past which colors and inspires the present, could focus on the ideal figure of the prince, personifying the nation. The prince answered the contemporary need for some strong central authority, imposing unity and order on a disparate medley of provinces, cities, estates, and individuals, suppressing their divisions, co-ordinating their activities, enlisting all for the common good.

In practice the beginnings of the modern age would see a marked consolidation of the central power not only in England, France, and Spain, where this is evident, but also in Germany, where a few princely houses achieved it at the expense of medieval survivals—the Holy Roman Empire, the cities or the knights. It is hard to tell whether the ideal answered new circumstances or whether these sought and found their justification in refurbished notions dredged out of the past. As the feudal system disintegrated through its own success in settling the old anarchy into some kind of order, as population increased, and growth of cities quickened, greater numbers called for greater power. The reaction against civil war and internal chaos turned to the advantage of the monarchy. The same was true in Russia and in the Turkish Empire, which were, or strained to be, autocracies more absolute than any in the West. In Poland, Hungary, Bohemia, Italy (except for Venice), where this was not the case, divided lands faced serious threats to their survival or their independence.

The Lengthened Shadow of One Man

The job of centralization was not an easy one. Medieval states were more a verbal expression than a fact. Their territory was a jigsaw puzzle of holdings, in which the king of England might be the vassal of the king of France, and German princes the suzerains of territories in Provence, Bohemia, or the Netherlands. When Clement V settled in Avignon (1309) the city was a possession of the king of Naples, adjoining the papal territory of the Comtat Venaissin, just across the Rhone. When in 1316 Petrarch went to Montpellier to begin legal studies, a section of that city was ruled by the king of Majorca and another by the king of France.

No central government could maintain a far-flung authority without the fiscal income denied it until about the twelfth century, which meant that effective power and jurisdiction were left in the hands of local lords or other corporate groups. This local autonomy which was the essence of the feudal period became increasingly meaningless as commerce and city life revived in the twelfth and thirteenth centuries, as subsistence economy turned to money economy, and as wealth from overseas trade, a larger richer bourgeoisie, and land seized from rebels, began to concentrate in royal treasuries. Kings and princes were in a better position to reassert their rights, whittle away independent feudal, ecclesiastical, or urban jurisdictions, and turn what had been loose claims for allegiance into increasingly enforced control. This they would do aided by economic crises which sapped the position of great landed nobles, and by the urban classes, some of whom saw their immediate enemy in some feudal lord, whether clerical or lay, while others hoped the territorial state would afford them a larger sphere for capitalist enterprise.

The central power did try by every means to unify the realm. Kings of France like Francis I (1515–1547) and his son Henry II (1547–1559) tried to establish uniform standards of weights and measures. Their efforts failed at first but set a precedent for later rulers. A common language was advanced when in 1539 Francis I prescribed the use of French in all his courts of justice.

To master the opposition, princes needed standing armies which could enable royal officials to assert their will and especially to collect the taxes that went in good proportion to maintain and enlarge the very forces that collected them. Very simply put, royal government needed power to establish and enforce its writ. The relation between money and royal supremacy is clear. Kings and princes seeking to impose central authority had to face ever greater governmental and military expenses. These they tried to finance by taking loans from merchant bankers, and sometimes by improving the financial machinery of the state with the advice of men of the same class as those who lent the money. These last in turn found in the circumstances opportunities for large profits and new sources of enterprise in supplying the needs of royal court and royal army.

Extending the frequency and the amount of feudal revenues also played its part in the development of national ideas. Under the feudal system, taxes had been raised to cope with immediate, well-defined needs (defense, ransom, the marriage expenses of a suzerain). As taxes evolved from feudal aids into increasingly frequent contributions raised not from vassals alone but from all subjects, they became more personal and also territorially more inclusive. The modern relation between the central power and the individual paying taxes as a subject and resident of a state began to take shape, as did the representative institutions— councils, parliaments, estates—which mark the modern West.

When states and rulers turned for aid no longer to vassals who owed it them by contract, but to all their subjects, they had to win consent. Assemblies could not function when numbers became too great. This happened first in some Italian communes and, in due course, in greater realms. Hence as a substitute for personal attendance there developed a new concept of representation, with the idea that certain men could somehow, by election or appointment, speak for other men or cities or estates. The monarchs of the thirteenth century developed the principle which Justinian's sixth-century Code expressed, that "that which concerns everybody should be approved by everybody"—the words Edward I of England quoted when summoning barons, knights, and burgesses to his Parliament of 1295.

Some of these representative assemblies became instruments of opposition to royal authority, as a result of which they ceased to function in several kingdoms. But for the most part, their very existence, the measures they approved concerning great regional wholes, gave disparate territories a sense of unity which they had not had before. The "perverse habit" of a permanent impost (as a fifteenth-century Frenchman called it) affected not only the purses of those who henceforth paid it, but their minds as well.

The princes needed administrative officials: in France, whose kings were best served in these matters, there were some 12,000 of them in 1505, about 1 to every 1,250 people or 1 per 40 square kilometers (about 25 square miles). Four hundred years later there was one civil servant for every seventy French men and women, or 56 per 40 square kilometers. The princes needed soldiers, not only to back their officials but also, perhaps especially, for war, which was the greatest industry of their time as it is of ours. Sixteenth-century Europe, incessantly tormented by conflicts, counted only twenty-five years without important wars; the seventeenth century would count twenty-one. And what wars! One thinks of Philip II of Spain on horseback, looking on at the sack of San Quentin, which he was powerless to prevent, and vomiting, vomiting . . .

They also needed representatives for negotiations—for diplomacy, which is the continuance of war by other means and which the Renaissance was just beginning to evolve, along with an international law, a code governing relations between sovereigns and sovereign states now that feudal conventions and the medieval concept of a united Christendom were disappearing. Once there had been the superior authority of the Holy See and the Holy Roman Empire. Now the Pope was another princeling, the Emperor only a German king. Disputes between parties no longer recognizing a superior could not be referred to some impartial authority. Only war ·or direct negotiation could settle the debate; and both war and the new diplomacy, with its envoys, its newly permanent residents in foreign lands, its embassies, were consequently elaborated beyond the relatively limited possibilities of more primitive days.

Thus the demands of centralization made for new expertise, the rise of specialists, professional diplomats (from the fifteenth century), professional soldiers (after the sixteenth century except in Italy), professional civil servants. These specialists were laymen. Their growing availability emancipated princes from their dependence on the clergy and encouraged another aspect of centralization, the final affirmation of the secular arm.

Anachronisms and Adaptations

Unsupported by the people, a majority of whom showed themselves increasingly indifferent to its sanctions and resentful of its riches and immunities, abandoned by the Pope who made his own deals with other princes, the clergy fell into the hands of territorial rulers—emperors, kings, or dukes—who controlled appointments and benefices with an eye to their political interests. This is what medieval princes always longed for, attempting to restrict or refuse privileges the church demanded, seeking to control the church in their territories and nominate its prelates. How far they succeeded depended on circumstances, but by the fifteenth century, in England, in France, and in Spain, the crown had come to dominate the church and to use it insofar as possible for its own purposes of unification, administration, and control. In Germany the story was much the same, except that provincialism took over from the central power and ecclesiastical princes, just as at Rome, acted as secular rulers before, in some cases, becoming such as well.

In the mid-fifteenth century Fouquet (1415?–1485) painted a diptych of the Madonna, one panel showing St. Stephen and the donor, Charles VII's treasurer, Etienne Chevalier, and the other the Virgin attired in the fashion of contemporary ladies and with the features of Agnes Sorel, mistress of the king, with whom Chevalier was passionately in love. Men who did not shrink from blasphemy would surely not hesitate from trespassing on more concrete rights which other generations had respected. Clerical privileges were a major obstacle to the assertion of the central power: a criminal in the most minor orders, like those of many university students, could claim benefit of clergy, be allowed a first crime free, seek the more lenient justice of episcopal courts thereafter. Escaping criminals could find sanctuary in churches and other quarters under the jurisdiction of the church. Royal justice could not tolerate such alien enclaves. Legislation was passed to limit their effects, abolish the right of sanctuary, incorporate the ecclesiastic structure into that of the rising state.

The medieval communes also fell under royal subjection, their privileges increasingly subject to the ruler's will. The gilds with their restrictive practices declined before new trades or unrestricted cities. New capitalists sided with the king because the monarchy opposed older exclusivism and favored (at least temporarily) economic liberty. The rural population opposed the older cities because they prohibited or restricted rural industries. In the cities themselves, different factions sought the king's support and municipalities tried to secure it in their disputes with rival boroughs. Urban militias became ever less effective when faced with professional troops which their improvised bands, training on the week end, could not withstand. Under the touch of monarchy municipal autonomy began to wither. The great age of municipal republics was drawing to a close. In 1530 Florence, in 1540 Ghent, in 1548 Constance, in the following decade a score of free German cities lost their liberties.

This did not go without reactions. For a long time each favorable moment—the minority of a prince, the weakness or division of his servants—would see attempts by only imperfectly subjugated groups to rise, rebel, re-establish their former liberties. In 1477, for example, as soon as news of Charles the Bold's death spread, the first concern of his Burgundian cities and provinces was to restore the local "liberties" usurped by the growth of the Burgundian state. Their success, like that of similar attempts elsewhere, was only temporary. Local entities struggled against the state and went on struggling at least a century longer, sometimes two. They could not in the long run withstand the greater power which profited from growing resources and from the exigencies of international conflict to strengthen its hold on the separate parts and orders of the realm. But the opposition to royal centralization remained a fundamental issue of sixteenth-century politics and a fundamental factor of political instability.

The nobility throughout this time was rising, though no longer in the old feudal guise. The nobility was still the reservoir of men whose earliest and sometimes only training befitted them for the career of arms. It was, however, much less independent. The state set out to harness and to discipline the nobles, and much internal policy until 1800 would turn around the effort to integrate them, like the other subjects only more important, into a more orderly structure, to offer new outlets for their energies and ambitions at court and in the service of the prince. War was obviously one pursuit in which they could be used. But there was not always war and not everybody could fight in it all the time. The nobles had to be kept occupied, offered other satisfactions than the military ones in which they excelled.

The less useful nobility became, the more ornamental it waxed; the more its teeth were drawn, the greater the display to which it would be treated, with which it was encouraged to express itself. The functional reality of yore now turned into a game. Display and make-believe became the great business of the noble life and of the courts where it could best be led.

As we have noted, the late fourteenth century and the fifteenth saw a revival of chivalric notions. New knightly orders were set up, by which the rising monarchies hoped to bind the nobility of their disparate provinces with conventions and symbols that would appeal to them, and with activities that would do least harm. The most brilliant center of this new knightly culture was found at first at the Burgundian court, whence it would spread to culminate perhaps in the famous meeting when Francis I courted Henry VIII's support on the Field of the Cloth of Gold (1520), a pompous joust of conspicuous consumption the nullity of whose political effects reflected the emptiness of the long, costly trend.

Immense amounts of money, imagination, and energy were absorbed by the games which princes and nobles played. Behind them lay the legends, the literary inspiration: the tales of knightly valor in ancient days, absorbed in education, expressed in manners and in politics. When in the 1470's Caxton set up his press at Westminster, the mass of his publications consisted of this literature—King Arthur, Charlemagne, the scores of English versions of ancient "histories"—the favorite reading matter of contemporary courts. The Trojan War, the fabled splendors of Alexander's court, the deeds of ancient heroes—mostly imaginary, served as a model for the modern knight. "It is hard to think that they were men and not great children," writes Henri Pirenne, in his *History of Belgium,* describing the exuberant show of the Burgundian court, the wedding in 1468 of Margaret of York and Charles the Bold; the tourneys, display and costumes, the sixty-foot long "whale" with forty men inside it romping round the banquet hall, the elephants, the thirty gilded trees each eight feet high, the pelican disgorging wine for all to drink, "in short a mass of marvelous toys, graceful or strange but always sumptuous and whose accumulation leaves one dizzy." There are feasts with twenty-eight-piece bands baked in a pie, birds flying out of the mouth of a mechanical dragon, the representation of a tower 41 feet high with mechanical boars blowing trumpets from its battlements and goats singing motets while toy wolves played the flute. There are Gargantuan decorations prepared by artists who, at other times, painted the great altarpieces of their day—just as in 1488 the painter Gérard David would be brought to Bruges to decorate the bars and the shutters of the prison in which the Archduke Maximilian was jailed. There was—precursor of the Cloth of Gold—Charles the Bold's great camp at Neuss, a town of wood and canvas, equipped with baths and churches. Glittering and glistening as it did in a dazzle of banners, it must have brought to mind as Pirenne said, a vast box of toy soldiers. Soldiers all very brightly painted, as everything seems to have been in this gaudy age.

Behind these splendid games there lay a serious crisis: the crisis of the nobility. Their military monopoly was giving way to foot soldiers and guns. Their incomes from land could not keep up with expenditures. The Burgundy of Charles the Bold fell before the peasant levies of the Swiss, before the mercenaries of the king of France. And so, here too, the old order was giving way to new. Many of Europe's old noble families did not survive these changes. They were replaced by rich burghers who bought patents of nobility, estates, and offices. Nobles who persisted in the anachronistic games were doomed. The new nobles were a more ruthless and more efficient group of officeholders, military captains, and estate managers.

The Northern Renaissance

As a general rule that "dawn of better things" referred to by the Florentine Palmieri in the 1430's appears across the Alps almost a century later. "In my youth the times were still gloomy and dark, redolent of the infelicity and the calamity of the Goths who had put all good literature to the sack," Gargantua writes to Pantagruel, his son: "but, by divine grace, dignity and light have been restored to letters in my time . . . now all disciplines are restored, the languages established, Greek without which it is shameful for a man to call himself wise, Hebrew, Chaldean, Latin; and all the correct and elegant expressions in use which were invented in my time by divine inspiration . . . " All this in 1532. A generation later, Pierre de la Ramée (the humanist Ramus) could declare: "in one century we have seen greater progress among men of science than our ancestors have seen in all the preceding centuries." It is the language, the excitement of the *quattrocento,* reflecting the delayed reaction and experience of the North.

The North was far from sterile and, even in its time of troubles, had a busy culture of its own; but one which showed little interest at first in what was going on in the Italian cities. The first Italian renaissance was urban, bourgeois, speaking for and through lawyers, merchants, teachers. Before the aristocratic society in the North could feel that there was something for it to borrow, the Italians had to develop an aristocratic culture of their own, intelligible and attractive to the Northerners. This only happened, as we saw, late in the fifteenth century. It is significant that this was when the North began to look for light in Italy, just as it is that some of the more remarkable figures of the Northern renaissance were princes and princesses, who were among the first to learn the fashions of Italian courts.

In 1499, the French archers of Louis XII entering Milan had used the great clay model of Leonardo's statue of Francesco Sforza for target practice. Seventeen years later Leonardo was journeying to the royal castle of Amboise, where he lived until his death in 1519 as the honored guest of the French king. In France, Francis I, his mother, his sister, his mistresses, sang, danced, versified, protected the letters and the arts. Margaret of Navarre, the sister of the King, would write a bawdy Boccaccian collection of stories, the *Heptameron,* several very spiritual hymns, and a short mystical treatise, the *Mirror of the Sinful Soul.* Margaret was patroness of both Erasmus and Rabelais, protected both Protestants and Catholics provided they represented the intellectual and artistic values of the humanism for which she stood. The mother of the King, Louise of Savoy, was something of a poet in her own right, wrote many of her letters in verse, and taught her children to do the same. Characteristically though, this may well have been because she felt that the letters of princes should be somehow couched in another style than that of mere mortals.

In England, Henry VIII, who composed music, fancied himself as something of a Latinist and theologian. His wife, Catherine, princess of Aragon, knew Latin; his children Edward and Mary knew Latin and

French, Elizabeth also Greek and Italian. When Francis I set up royal Readers in his new Paris College (today the *Collège de France*), Henry, not to be left behind, founded chairs for Greek and Hebrew at Cambridge University.

One could also see a renaissance in another rising monarchy: Spain, where Salamanca, founded in the thirteenth century, was one of the greatest European universities by 1500. Not unreceptive to new ideas, allowing anatomists to dissect human bodies and Copernicans to teach their system, Salamanca was almost unique in opening its courses and its degrees to women. Between 1472 and 1526, nine other universities were set up in Spain. The most famous of them, Alcalá de Henares (1498), birthplace of Cervantes, provided the first instance of a planned university city. Cardinal Jiménez, who founded Alcalá, also sponsored the great project of the *Polyglot* or *Complutensian Bible* (after the Latin name of Alcalá—Complutum), in Hebrew, Aramaic, and Greek, as well as in the Latin vulgate text.

Though Ferdinand of Aragon was a strong contender for the title (and Machiavelli certainly thought of him in this light), Francis I appears as the model Renaissance ruler—not the best but the most striking—from beyond the Alps; and his most notable characteristic is his fascination with things Italian. To France he brought not only artists and architects, painters and sculptors, but magistrates, jurists, prelates, soldiers, sailors, financiers, traders, humanists, professors, and artisans of various skills. He brought his children up in the "progressive" Italian manner, married his eldest son to an Italian princess, infused not just art but government and jurisprudence with Italian ideas—and used art and artists as part of the propaganda for his struggle with his contemporary, the Emperor Charles V.

The striking point is that the new fashions appeared in North and Western Europe a hundred years or more after they had developed in the Italian cities, and all were introduced largely from the top. The fact suggests the crux of the whole matter: the North, even the Netherlands, was never free or quite so free of aristocratic masters as the Italian communes where the Renaissance began. The social code throughout remained the noble—which for a long time meant medieval—one. A French Augustinian friar of 1412 is known to have called for a social reform in which all non-nobles who did not devote themselves to a craft or labor on the land would be banished from France. Clearly, nobles did not need to work. Just as clearly, trade or law or study were not considered socially useful, or indeed very significant at all. In 1444, when literature in Italy was an acknowledged art, respected and some-times practiced by the noblest princes, the future Pope Pius II writes home from Germany that magnates there "pay more attention to horses and dogs than to poets—and thus neglecting the arts they die unremembered like their own beasts."

At this very time, however, the beginnings of a Renaissance could be discerned in the German cities. Well-situated athwart the north-south trade routes of the continent, exporting the iron, the copper, above all the silver of central European mines, dealing as easily with London and Antwerp as with Venice or Milan, places like Nürnberg, Augsburg, and Innsbruck entered a period of spectacular prosperity. As they did so, German music, not very significant before mid-fifteenth century, rose to a rank comparable to that of Italy and the Netherlands. From clumsy beginnings, German folk songs grew to furnish a vivid picture of the busy, flourishing society that produced and enjoyed them, its mechanical skills reflected in the ever-improved organs of its churches (one blind organist, Konrad Paumann (1415–1473), being actually knighted by the Emperor), its burghers' self-confidence matched by the vigor of Hans Sachs's Nürnberg with its society of mastersingers, its sculptors, painters, and goldsmiths, thriving on commercial enterprise. In due course, France and England recovering from their wars would follow in this wake. And the exhilaration affected learning as well as the arts.

The scholarship which played such a great part in the Italian Renaissance, was less a part of everyday life in lands where the light, the landscape, the ruins incorporated in the living world were not, as in Tuscany or Rome, still those of classical antiquity. The classical revival here was mostly the preserve of clergymen, of professional scholars and teachers whose interests affected the masses and the classes very little. Antiquity was the realm of legend. Huizinga has given us an inkling of how the North envisaged antiquity, in telling us that when Charles the Bold was being buried at Nancy, the young Duke of Lorraine came to honor him "dressed in antique style, that is to say wearing a long golden beard which reached to his girdle," and in this costume representing one of the nine worthies, prayed for a quarter of an hour.

By the sixteenth century, when no Italian gentleman who could, remained without at least a veneer of culture, the more advanced men further north began to realize that learning could serve for more than just a clerical career, that letters could prepare for office, preferment, even for the everyday business and litigation of a landowner. But bluffer men remained who would sooner die than read a book and said so; and, as for artists, honored further south, their social status continued to be rather low. The painter Albrecht Dürer, in Venice in 1506, was loath to leave an Italy that was quite another world. "How I shall long for the sun in the cold," he wrote, but also especially: "here I am a gentleman, at home I am a parasite."

Yet Dürer's life reflects the change by which, in the sixteenth century, the artist-artisan became the erudite or artist-humanist, owner of a stately home, keeping company with scientists and scholars, bishops and noblemen. Dürer's best friend, the humanist Willibald Pirkheimer, was a scion of the Patriciate of Nürnberg. Dürer studied languages and mathematics, tried his hand at verse, showed the omnivorous curiosity of a humanist in his attraction for strange beasts and costumes, even in his last excursion into the mosquito-infested marshes of Zeeland to see a whale which had been washed ashore and where, instead, he caught malaria of which he died.

But in his art Dürer also showed the scrupulous attention to minute detail which the Italians were abandoning for more general and sweeping lines; and his attitude to the trade, too, was more straightforward. One of the reasons for his trip to the Netherlands in 1520 was, as he put it, "to sell art," and at Antwerp he drew quite a number of portraits costing one florin apiece. In his diary he noted, "I have sold two Adam and Eve, one sea monster, one Jerome, one knight [the portrait of the son of a German merchant], one Nemesis, one Eustace, one whole sheet and seventeen engravings, eight quarter sheets, nineteen other woodcuts, and seven poor woodcuts, two books and ten small passions on wood, the lot for eight *florins*."

If Dürer saw himself as an art-seller, in ways that the great Italians would not have conceived, this was because of the social and business orientation of his northern world. Likewise, his religious preoccupations marked him as a member of another culture, referring as they did to matters little heeded in cultured Italy. Religious concerns, so characteristic of the Middle Ages, played an immense part in the northern Renaissance: in art, literature, and scholarship alike. The humanists of Germany, Switzerland, and the Netherlands were quite explicitly Christian, and so for a long time was the art of these countries, quite unaffected by Italian developments. Throughout the fifteenth century, at the beginning of the sixteenth, religion continued to provide the dominant inspiration. We can see it in the great altarpiece carved by a Nürnberger, Veit Stoss, for the Cathedral of Cracow (1493), with a dramatic realism quite uninhibited by the new idealism taking over in Rome. We recognize it in the disquieting canvases of Hollanders like Bosch and Brueghel. We meet it above all in the mystical intensity of Matthias Grünewald (1460?–1528), whose vision of Christ's sufferings came not from the restrained, increasingly formalistic south, but from the Christian mysticism of Thomas à Kempis. The young Dürer sought for Grünewald and, while he did not find him, he probably saw the greatest of his works, a picture of Christ's passion painted for the Abbey of Isenheim in Alsace (1512), which expresses an anguish whose terrible intensity contemporary Italians would have excoriated as bad form. Grünewald was very much involved in the religious concerns of his time and, for religious and moral reasons, with its social problems. He may even have been involved with the peasants' revolt of the 1520's. In this tradition Dürer, who was committed to Luther, used all the possibilities of medieval symbolism, and of new humanistic symbolism too, to enrich the Protestants' pictorial propaganda.

Melancholia, by Albrecht Dürer, 1514. Metropolitan Museum of Art, New York.

All this was hardly very modern, though we can trace in it some clearly modern trends and though it too found its resources in economic activity and commercial wealth. Stretching from the Alps to the North Sea and the English Channel, the realms of Burgundy were populous and wealthy, boasting a highly developed urban life. The urban population in the fifteenth century almost matched that of the countryside. The cities—Arras whence came the curtain through which Hamlet stabbed Polonius, Cambrai which gave its name to cambric, Lille and Valenciennes for lisle, thread, and lace, but most of all Bruges and Ghent and Ypres, and the rising port of Antwerp—were second only to those of Italy and destined to overtake them in the sixteenth century.

Before the death of Charles the Bold in 1477 and the collapse of his realm, the court of Burgundy had briefly dominated the art and fashion of the West. Its dukes were richer than kings and, after 1420, when Charles's father Philip the Good (1419–1467) moved his household from Dijon to the Netherlands, art and music flourished in the Low Countries as they had never done outside Italy.

It is no longer believed today that the Italians learned the techniques of oil painting from the Netherlands. But Jan van Eyck (1385?–1441)

The Isenheim Altarpiece: *Crucifixion,* by Matthias Grünewald. Unterlinden Museum, Colmar.

and Rogier van der Weyden (1400?–1464) were admired in Italy, and painters like Botticelli and Mantegna were influenced by Flemish innovations. What is certain is that the fifteenth century looked to the Netherlands for its best music. Josquin Després (1440?–1521) the greatest musician of his time, was courted in Italy and France. Charles the Bold himself composed *motets* and *chansons.* And eventually the slender Italian madrigal, light and airy, would blend with the linear severity of Burgundian art to achieve the new precision and grace that we connect with the vivid tones of Roland de Lassus's *motets* or Palestrina's music in the mid-sixteenth century.

Painters, however, are better known than musicians, and their works more accessible. A glance at these suggests that the *ars nova* of the north which southerners admired was *sui generis*—very much of its own kind —and the language they spoke drew on different references. Botticelli's *Birth of Venus,* painted about 1480, substitutes woman for Virgin, uses diaphanous but classic beauty to affirm the triumph not of heaven but of life. Its allusions, its allegorical idiom, were comprehensible to Botticelli's Medici patrons and to a society that had assimilated the values of the ancients along with their myths. The northerners—whether Botticelli's contemporaries or his predecessors—were modern in their own fashion: less classical, more Christian.

Jan van Eyck's characters, compared with those of Masaccio, lived in another world: one that seems clearer, simpler, older somehow than that through which the younger man's massive figures move. A painting like Van Eyck's canvas of the merchant Arnolfini and his bride is a pioneering work in its psychology as in its concern with the life of ordinary people. But even this, with its meticulous realism, radiates a mystery which suggests the ever-possible irruption of metaphysical agents. Although the architecture of his scenes is often that of the Renaissance, Van Eyck remains a Gothic painter, the radiance of his angels' wings as magnificent as the polyphonic inventions of fifteenth-century Dutch music. The masters of later generations (Hans Memling, Dirk Bouts, contemporaries of Piero della Francesca and even Botticelli) emphasize this difference between Italy and Flanders in an austere geometry whose Gothic arches often stress the distance between the North Sea and the Mediterranean. The faith and the popular fantasies of the North appear even more clearly in the canvases of a man who painted less for the ducal court than for local religious brotherhoods: Hieronymus Bosch (1450–1516). Bewitched and eerie landscapes, haunted forests, skeletons on the march, flying fish and strange composite plants, their colors as disturbing as their shapes, grotesque representatives of evil tortuously tempting or tormenting fallen man—Bosch's work is a popular picture book rooted in everyday life, one of the last expressions of the medieval world view.

Meanwhile, and late in the day when compared with Italian developments, the Netherlands were slowly abandoning the original and mystical local tradition illustrated by Van Eyck and Van der Weyden. The advance of humanism, the growing Italian influence first glimpsed in the work of Quentin Metsys (1466?–?1530), with his portraits of bankers, money lenders, tax collectors, but also of scholars (such as Erasmus, 1517), became apparent with Jan Gossaert (known as Mabuse, 1478?–?1532) and Bernard van Orley (1492–1542), both of whom had studied in Italy. There was one interesting national deviation, however. For, while Italian painting tended increasingly to reproduce less a scene than an abstraction, less what the painter saw than what he thought, Metsys and Mabuse insisted on a more precise realism, emphasizing matter in its most concrete forms. Linen, silk, satin, granite, or sandstone, the scales of a fish or the crust of a pie rendered in faithful detail became as relevant as any ideal value.

The new artists conceived of themselves no longer as artisans like the previous generation but, like Leonardo or Hans Holbein the Younger (1497?–1543), as artists and philosophers, the friends and peers of literary men. With the exception of the paintings of Pieter Brueghel (1525?–1569), some of whose finest works are bitter or ironic comments on the men and society he knew, the sixteenth-century Netherlands, and especially Antwerp, became a great factory and marketplace of Italianate paintings, with dynasties of painters passing the trade from father to

The Garden of Earthly Delights, by Hieronymus Bosch. Prado, Madrid.

son and, finally, exporting painters to Spain, England, Germany, and France—even to Italy, until in the century's second half Belgian painters seem like the counterpart of Swiss mercenaries.

Like other mercenaries, this meant that they served the men with money; and in this age, though there was plenty of money in the cities, there was still more of it, more ready to be spent, in noble hands. When not expressing a local mysticism and fantasy, when not serving the rather insulated ends of scholarship, the northern Renaissance served the nobility and its themes reflected its values.

The Major Powers

France

Now let us turn toward the internal politics of the major powers and seek a general overview, a survey of the affairs of Europe.

The center of European politics was France—partly because of its size and population—about fourteen million around 1500, twice as many people as in Spain, four times as many as in England, ten times as many as in Venice. The rulers of the Holy Roman Empire, larger and more populous, could not tap the resources of an atomized realm but only those of their hereditary lands. After 1459, the King of France could not only raise a royal army but also, and without consulting his Estates, the taxes needed to support the military and the policies he chose.

Between about 1450 and 1560, France was at peace internally, waged most campaigns abroad, and thus could build up the prosperity which a century of war had seriously impaired. Grain production improved; revenue from the royal *taille,* a tax on income and on real estate, quadrupled between 1462 and 1481. The death of Charles the Bold removed the Burgundian threat, allowed the kings of France to round off their domains in north and east, a process they perfected by marrying the heiress of the last great feudal province, Brittany, and by the end of the fifteenth century annexing it to France. Charles VII (1422–1461) had planned a regular army to make himself independent of mercenary companies. In the sixteenth century Francis I realized his dream: first a cavalry corps (gendarmes), then a fine artillery, lastly an infantry corps of regional "legions." For this he needed money, and his reign, like those of all contemporary crowned heads, was a continual hunt for resources. When in 1518 Francis I reorganized the finances of the realm, the three departments of the financial administration concerned themselves with royal domains, extraordinary revenues (aids, duties, etc.), and finally *inventions*—fiscal expedients the most lasting of which would be the creation and sale of offices, a dangerous institution but one which, even so, to start with, helped swell the number of those who had a stake in the stability of crown and state.

Meanwhile, an old concept and new policies helped bring the church to heel. Gallicanism, which evolved in the fourteenth century, harked back to the conciliar view of the Pope as only *primus inter pares* (the first among equals), without jurisdiction or rights of revenue over different national units of the church and especially over the kingdom of France. Less a doctrine than an attitude and the rationalization of practices convenient to the king, to the king's lawyers, and to some sections of the clergy, Gallicanism would color relations between France and the papacy down to our own day. The first measure to reflect the Gallican spirit was the Pragmatic Sanction of Bourges (1438), in which Charles VII settled a new statute for the French church without reference to the Pope, abolishing papal taxes, appeals from French ecclesiastical tribunals to the Roman court, and Roman approval for election to episcopal sees and other benefices henceforth largely in royal hands. The Gallican Church was thus almost self-governing, its hierarchy far more powerful than the voice of Rome.

The new regime did not last very long. The Concordat of 1516 returned formal control to the Pope, but it did hand it in practice to the King, who would henceforth have an interest in maintaining control of the clergy, as an instrument of power and a source of benefices for his servants and his favorites. As we shall see in Spain, the French church became a court and noble institution, but also to all effects and purposes a national one.

Revenues, soldiers, servants. There is a well-known saying of the Emperor Maximilian that he was a king of kings, for nobody obeyed him; the king of Spain was a king of men, for men reproached him and yet did his bidding; but the king of France was a king of beasts, for no man ever dared refuse his orders. The wry tone cannot conceal the rueful envy of the speaker who, like other European princes. would have been glad to rule over beasts of his own as numerous and as rich.

England

The long-time foe off France's northwest shores, whose kings' pretentions to the country's crown had helped to keep it in a century of disastrous wars, had been beaten off in the 1450's. Thereafter England had plunged into a costly internal war, the houses of York and Lancaster struggling for its crown. The battles between the white rose, emblem of the house of York, and the red rose of Lancaster had given this conflict the name of the War of the Roses. Of roses the dreary tale of murder, slaughter, battles, and betrayals had nothing but the thorns. In 1485, at last, victory at Bosworth over the last Yorkist king, Richard III, brought to the throne a man who meant to keep it: the last surviving claimant of the Lancasterian line, Henry Tudor. He solidly grasped the crown which a soldier had picked up on Bosworth field, where it had fallen on a thorn bush and, the better to secure it, promptly married Elizabeth, heiress of the house of York.

Henry VII (1485–1509) became king in a country where thirty years of warfare had decimated the aristocracy to such an extent that one-fifth of the land was left without a master, to be reclaimed as royal domain and added to such holdings as had been confiscated for rebellion. This left the King once more the greatest landowner and the greatest power in his realm. That realm had once grown moderately rich on médieval exports first of wool, then cloth; and, protected by the sea, it had lived and worked in the relative peace its forceful kings compelled. Now it had wasted its substance in long years of war. At the end of the fifteenth century, England stood in the margin of European economy and culture. Charles V expressed it: "I speak Latin to God, Italian to musicians, Spanish to ladies, French at court, German to servants and English to my horses."

What Henry VII wanted was to keep the country at peace, revive its prosperity, restore its finances, and solidly establish the new ruling house. He kept out of continental quarrels and not only saved money by doing so, but received payment for abstaining. The policy was unexciting but it paid. His successor Henry VIII (1509–1547), was more active, more flamboyant, and much more troublesome. Six wives: two beheaded, two divorced, one dead in childbirth and one surviving him; a brutal break with the Catholic church which would not grant him the divorce he sought; the persecution of those who did not accept his supremacy over the church in England and the execution of Catholic martyrs like Sir Thomas More (briefly Chancellor, 1529–1532); the Gargantuan meals and Rabelaisian manners; these are the images of him that survive. Three centuries after his death, Henry VIII was still "a spot of blood and grease on English history." His contemporaries saw him in another guise. Well-educated, willful, handsome, he was determined to put England on the map. To do this and especially to compete with France, the traditional rival, and the obvious one since it was ruled by an equally flashy and ambitious prince, Henry engaged the country in a long series of useless and costly enterprises, wasting on them and on his court's display the treasure which his father had accumulated.

As king, however, he pursued the task of all contemporary monarchs: the enforcement and broadening of absolute royal power and the development of its institutions. Aided by chance, by his stubborn will, by able and devoted chancellors like Cardinal Thomas Wolsey (1473?–1530) and Thomas Cromwell (1485?–1540), and by the English peoples' resentment of the Pope, he was the first prince to take over the church and subject it openly and in theory totally to the state. Along with this, partly in his reign, partly in those of his successors, came an administrative revolution that gave the centralized state the instruments to govern and enlisted the nobility and the gentry into the service of the king in a structure that still remains peculiarly English.

Within the institutional structure then a-forging, the country's economic life gathered new speed. Political and ideological changes affected commercial interests but little, as can be seen with the fishing industry, very important for this island nation, which was less a source of food perhaps than a training ground for sailors and a naval reserve. Henry VIII, who created a royal navy (as other contemporary princes set up regular armies on the continent), was never indifferent to the sailors' interests. The coming of the Reformation meant the disappearance of the religious requirements to eat fish on Friday. This could hit hard at the fishermen. Laws passed in 1549 under Edward VI and in 1559 under Elizabeth I enforced the fasting to protect the fisheries and, in 1563, a new law required eating fish on Wednesdays as well as on the usual Friday. Some Londoners were pilloried that year for eating meat during Lent.

The major economic change came as part of the attempt to cope with the pressing problem of inflation. During the late fifteenth and the sixteenth centuries, throughout most of Europe the prices were rising, affecting the buying power of the poor but also of the nobles who lived on the rent income of their lands. In parts of France eight out of ten noble families were ruined. Documents from late fifteenth century Provence refer to nobles begging. Production of food and staples espe-

Henry VIII, by Hans Holbein (the Younger). National Gallery of Art, Rome.

cially could not keep up with the demand swelled by the increasing amount of unproductive investments: soldiers, more costly armaments, more conspicuous consumption, and also (relatively speaking) more comforts for the better off.

The major problem was how, within a rather stiff, old established structure, producers and property owners could adjust to the new situation. In England and in other places, landlords sought to answer the money problem by turning their tenants' customary payments, long rendered in services or goods, into cash rents or lump-sum payments, or by changing long-term tenures into shorter leases whose rates could be adjusted as the money values dropped. Antother method was by enclosures: surrounding land with a hedge or fence for more intensive exploitation, producing not for use or for subsistence as had been the practice but for the market where crops or wool could bring the needed cash. Landlords enclosed their own demesne or wasteland (draining fens, plowing the moors), or former tenanted lands that could be more profitably exploited, or even common lands—encroaching on the peasant's right to use them. Procedures such as these were not unknown in earlier days, but generalized and practiced on a vaster scale they created a serious problem of able-bodied men forced off the land, into beggary, and rebelliousness.

The government tried to stem both beggary and enclosures without much success. The law, made and dispensed by men of property, inevitably reflected their interests. "The rich men not only by private fraud but also by common laws do everyday pluck and snatch away from the poor some part of their daily living . . ." we read in More's *Utopia*.

"Now they have to this their wrong and unjust dealing . . . given the name of justice, yea, and that by force of a law."

A long series of risings reflected the resentment of rural populations against the landlord's greed: the Pilgimage of Grace in 1536, Ket's rebellion in 1549, Wyatt's rebellion in 1554 were part of the much wider unrest throughout Europe. Savonarola's brief rule in Florence (1497–1498); Fiesco's plot at Genoa (1547); the *Germania,* or brotherhood rising, in Valencia (1519–1522)—all these mark not necessarily depression but the misery of some while others forged ahead; or again as in the German peasants' risings of the 1520's, the resistance of a sturdy peasantry to the kind of pressures and encroachments we have seen succeed in England.

In England these reactions were complicated by others which followed in the wake of Henry VIII's appropriation of church property to pay for his fantastic undertakings. The confiscation and secularization of church and monastic lands often meant that peasants and properties which had vegetated for generations began to be squeezed hard to cover the debts and needs of new secular owners. A development economically much more productive, turned out much more unpleasant on the human plane. Suffering was the price paid for economic opportunity and the creation of vested interests of those who profited in the economy and the state. It is true that sheep were eating men, as More protested. Their meat and wool were feeding others. A busy bourgeoisie, a fairly prosperous gentry, were rising on the ruins of an older world.

Spain

Economic and political problems just as acute were solved quite differently in the lands of the Spanish crown. The heiress to the throne of Castile, Isabella (1474–1504) had the choice between marrying the heir to Portugal or the king of Aragon, Ferdinand (1479–1516). She chose the latter and, in 1469, their marriage linked together two crowns and a diversity of institutions. The political guile and genius of King Ferdinand could rule but hardly integrate the string of varied states that stretched from the Atlantic and the Pyrenees to the Mediterranean and across it to the Italian colonies of Aragon. The difficult task was left to Ferdinand's grandson, Charles, who through other alliances and successions came to be the ruler of the Spanish, Habsburg, Burgundian, and Austrian domains, including their overseas possessions. It would be Charles (1516–1556), then his son Philip II (1556–1598), who gave to Spain efficient government, and strengthened the bonds and structure of the realm the Catholic kings had linked.

The groundwork had been laid by Isabella—called "the too Catholic"—and by Ferdinand who conquered Granada, last bastion of Islam (1492), sponsored the fateful expeditions overseas, forced their Muslim and their Jewish subjects into Christian conformity or exile, enlisted in their service the support of the clergy and the intense popular religious feelings bred by centuries of religious warfare, and subordinated the church hierarchy to the crown. One of the major instruments in their organization of disparate estates was the Inquisition, set up in 1478 by Pope Sixtus IV at their own request to hunt down cryptoheretics among, especially, Moriscos and Marranos, the baptised Moors and Jews whom they had forced into the church and who quite often and understandably preserved their faith in secret. Religious intolerance had its practical side in lands and at a time where religious orthodoxy and political loyalty were identical. This was the more so when the religious instrument began to be applied to secular ends, cutting across traditional laws, customs, privileges, bringing all men, whatever rank or riches, into subjection to the crown and to its law.

Nothing good can be said about the Inquisition, be it an instrument of religious or of political conformity. But it was only the outstanding example of current practices. By the standards of the fifteenth century when the Inquisition was set up and even of later times, its judicial procedure was careful, its tortures moderate, its executions no more horrible or numerous than in England, for example, where burning was the penalty for many crimes and a woman was burned for coining as late as March 18, 1789. The Spanish Inquisition may be seen as a counterpart of the witch hunts which scarred the rest of Europe.

The activities of the Inquisition helped unify the realm and also sterilized it. Vast numbers of the most productive and most enterprising were killed, exiled, or suppressed. And this was part of a broader trend, the power of the Inquisition and that of the church going hand in hand, encouraging an almost medieval orientation toward economically unproductive occupations. Trade or industry could mean covetousness, money-making was un-Christian, a bad Christian was certainly no gentleman, possibly disloyal, likely to attract the scorn of neighbors and the dangerous attentions of the Holy Office. The ambitious young of

Warder Collection

The Spanish Inquisition, a contemporary print.

Silver mining at Potosí. Hispanic Society of America, New York.

fifteenth-century Spain looked for advancement in *Iglesia, o mar, o casa real*—the church, or the sea, or the royal household—and we see that the phrase quoted puts the church first. By 1570 about a quarter of the country's adult population was in holy orders, almost a million men (not counting the women) out of a total population between nine and ten million strong. Such enormous figures indicate a problem that would bode ill for a society's health.

Even in what has been called its golden century, roughly the sixteenth and the beginning years of the seventeenth century, this orientation toward consumption not production, toward fruitless but prestigious occupations, sapped the well-being of the peninsula. Castilians in particular, Spaniards in general, prided themselves on their gentility and their Catholicism. A gentleman would be demeaned by work; and every man who had been forced to work but fortunate enough to profit bought state annuities, entailed them to his heir, and thus enabled his descendants to live poorly but nobly on an unearned income. Henceforth they were *Hidalgos*—the "sons of someone," not of common men. The noblemen, too, entailed their estates and thus froze them generally into unproductivity. Less land was bought or sold, and those who owned it showed little interest in newer agricultural methods. Production declined, wheat imports went up to feed the population, but the country was short of goods with which to pay for them since the mentality described above scarcely encouraged enterprise.

The country's greatest industry itself bore down on agricultural interests. Sheep-farming was the one enterprise invested in by nobles, and

Charles V, by Titian. Alte Pinakothek, Munich.

in its interest many fields of grain were sacrificed and grain producers too. Not only in England but in Spain the sheep were eating men, and impoverished peasants made poor buyers of those manufactures cities could turn out. But in Spain, in addition, taxes falling wholly on the non-nobles least able to pay them kept the towns small, their industries underdeveloped, their trade uncompetitive until, in 1546, the future Philip II would write his father that Spaniards were keeping away from any kind of commerce, leaving the opportunities of expanding trade to foreign enterprise.

Spaniards did go into the army, swelling the ranks of the king's forces —loyal, brave, proud of their ancestry but not too proud to trail a pike or hoist an arquebus in the *tercios,* the new infantry units, that were the terror and admiration of Europe.

Men and resources were being drained from Spain. In the meantime, she sucked what she could from her dependencies. Bullion came in from overseas, first the loot of Aztecs and Incas, then a trickle of silver from Mexican silver mines which became a flow with the discovery in 1545 of the deposits at Potosí. All this bullion, briskly coined, increased the currency and raised prices, of all of Europe and first of all of Spain, making its paradoxical contribution to the country's economic problems as her higher prices discouraged buyers and encouraged sellers from abroad.

We should not exaggerate the contribution of American revenue to Spanish royal income, much of which came throughout the century from what was still under Charles and Philip a European continental empire.

If American bullion was important, no less important were the loans based on the vast resources of German bankers with whose aid the king of Spain in 1519 won the imperial crown—or the credit of international financiers in Antwerp and Genoa and Augsburg which financed his endless campaigns; or the central and east European mines, which provided the firmest base of Habsburg power and laid down some essentials of their policies.

But it cannot be denied that overseas treasure provided essential support for undertakings so grandiose and so costly that they must have collapsed without it. "Seven Perus wouldn't suffice for the emperor's needs in Lombardy," wrote the Spanish representative in Genoa in 1537. And Henry II of France would say that American gold arrived in Spain, passed on to France to buy goods, then on to Italy to keep up soldiers, and thence to the Orient for the luxury goods which were then bought by the same emperor in whose realm America lay. The Spaniards in this equation are forgotten, or else included with the soldiery.

Where new goods or processes appear, the entrepreneurs who organize the sales and draw their profits will make such gains that they may, if the novelty be great enough, change the social balance by becoming richer and stronger faster than either the existing rich or the existing workers and producers. This is what seems to have happened to the traders and merchants of sixteenth-century Europe. But in Spain and Portugal the wealth of the Indies flowed not to an entrepreneurial class but to the established aristocracy, state and court. It was harnessed to their interests and to their conspicuous consumption—a fact which raised wages rather than prices and failed to create any new class. It is enlightening to compare the bustle and the wealth of sixteenth-century Antwerp with the Spanish and Portuguese ports of the time. A Belgian traveler to Lisbon described the natives parading the streets escorted by negro slaves, and then returning to their shabby homes to dine off some miserable vegetables, but ashamed to engage in any useful profession. This they left to the northerners. At Antwerp, meanwhile, the citizens worked and played, earned and enjoyed, their appreciation of luxury and comfort spurring them on to ever greater effort. Of course, the king of Spain—who would be king of Portugal too after 1580—was also Duke in Antwerp, drew revenues from there, just as he did from Italy and from his German lands.

In the person of Charles, the king of Spain was also German emperor.* This was a disadvantage that his son Philip was spared but one which bore heavily on his policies and which, when Charles was gone, and his

* He was a good many other things too. In 1519 a list of his titles read as follows: "King of the Romans; Emperor Elect; Semper Augustus; King of Spain, Sicily, Jerusalem, the Balearic Islands, the Canary Islands, the Indies and the mainland on the far side of the Atlantic; Archduke of Austria; Duke of Burgundy, Brabant, Stiria, Carinthia, Carniola, Luxembourg, Limburg, Athens and Patras; Count of Habsburg, Flanders and Tyrol; Count Palatine of Burgundy, Hainault, Pfirt, Roussillon; Landgrave of Alsace; Count of Swabia; Lord of Asia and Africa." It is as Holy Roman Emperor that he has gone down in history as Charles V.

great realm had been divided between a Spanish and Austrian branch, nevertheless influenced the strategy of Habsburgs and the affairs of Europe for another one hundred and fifty years.

The Germanies

In Germany the tendencies that we have seen at work in England, France, and Spain suffered defeat or appeared at another level, in another guise. The empire was a medieval institution. Any number of attempts to modernize it could not adapt it to the modern world. Too many separate, too many sovereign powers had too much interest in preventing the development of effective central rule. Two hundred and forty states, hundreds of quasi-independent knights, besides the private territories of the Habsburgs, clashed in discordant clamor whenever such an attempt was made. There would be no unified empire under Charles, nor under his successors, not for some centuries. There would be states instead, quasi-independent, owing only a formal allegiance to the Emperor, maneuvering between the greater powers to serve their interests —Saxony, Bavaria, Prussia; and then the great dominions of the Habsburgs, kernel of what became in the seventeenth century and was named in the nineteenth, the Austrian Empire.

Germany, like Italy, was hardly a political term: a geographical expression only, and one which allowed for great variety. The north, from Netherlands to Stettin, the long Rhineland alley between Alps and North Sea, the Upper Danube Valley, were thickly sown with cities, part of the economic and cultural mainstream of the West. The numerous towns provided nearby peasants with an accessible market for their products and, in due course, with the means of emancipation. Beyond the Elbe, where Germany melted into east and northeast Europe, towns were few, their economic activity (with notable exceptions) weak, their political and cultural influence slight. Getting the grain to the market was a more difficult and costly job than the peasant with his cart could undertake alone. There, the development of commercial agriculture spurred by the increased demands of western urban centers, fostered the wealth and power of wholesale merchants and noble landowners who fastened serfdom on the farmers whose products went to feed not shabby nearby towns, but distant hungry cities. The proceeds of the land strengthened overlords not peasants, exploiters not producers.

The fact goes far to explain the different situation in eastern Europe: waning or extinguished further west, feudalism persisted and thrived in the eastern states of Germany and beyond. In contrast to what happened in France, England, or Spain, where the nobility weakened and gave way before the encroachments and the self-assertion of the crown, what occurred in the eastern borderlands of Europe is quite the opposite. There we see the greater prosperity—hence power of resistance

—of Polish nobles to the weak attempts of their kings to install a central power, the successful resistance of Hungarian magnates against the similar policies of their kings. In the latter country these struggles, with royal power dissolving before the self-assertion of the nobles, would bring dire results. From 1458 to 1490 one of the most brilliant courts in Europe, comparable to that of the Estes at Ferrara, had been that which Mathias Corvinus had set up at Buda. There was a splendid library, a brilliant circle of humanists and artists, even a standing army. The power of the magnates broken, the revenues of Transylvanian silver mines worked by German miners made Hungary for a while the dominant state in eastern Europe.

With Mathias's death, all this melted away in factional struggles whose winnings were ultimately taken off the peasants' backs. In early sixteenth-century Hungary, a young king reigned but did not govern, the magnates struggled for the spoils of power, the peasants enslaved, resentful, rose up only to be brutally crushed. In 1515 a decree of the Diet (made up of nobles only) placed all lands firmly in noble hands, the peasants in "perpetual servitude." No wonder that so many of the latter welcomed the Turks, just as some southern Slavs had done in the previous century. In 1521, Belgrade, key to the Danube valley, fell into Turkish hands, there to remain for two centuries. In 1525 the Battle of Mohacs with its vast slaughter of the disorganized Magyar army, the death of the last ineffective king of an independent Hungary killed in the battle along with ten thousand of his peasants and vassals, divided the country between Turks and Habsburgs, left Buda a Turkish fortress, and turned the eastern territories of the Habsburgs into the bastions of Christian Europe under siege.

The Turks

The siege had developed slowly. Ottoman tribesmen called in to help in the internal struggles of the Byzantines had first appeared in Europe in mid-fourteenth century and, by its end, established their dominion over Bulgars and Serbs. A series of crusading enterprises was wrecked on the foolhardy gusto of western knights unwilling, at Nicopolis (1396) as at Agincourt (1415), to sacrifice bravery to tactics and good sense. Constantinople fell, as we have seen, in 1453, and the Ottomans began to press forward toward the decaying Muslim states of the eastern Mediterranean and by sea to the Aegean and Adriatic holdings of Venice —even to Italy, where in 1480 a Turkish force briefly occupied Otranto and, twenty years later, Turkish cavalry raided to the walls of Vicenza in the valley of the Po.

They would not get Italy but they did get Syria (1516), Egypt (1517), and Rhodes (1522). The Turks now ruled the eastern Mediterranean and commanded what they did not rule, controlling the traditional trade routes which fed the commerce of Italy; while Belgrade, captured in 1521, opened to them the gate of central Europe. 1529 would see a Turkish army laying siege to Vienna and the beginnings of constant campaigning on the Danube. 1534 found them moving into the western Mediterranean. No history of Europe can be complete if it leaves out the Turks, the pressure they exerted on the Habsburgs—hence on the Germans, the dread their coming roused, their serious effects on the safety and the wealth of Italy, their role as allies of the French against the great Habsburg power, as challengers of Spanish power in the west and, finally, as prototypes of the absolute power which western monarchies were straining to achieve.

The Turkish Empire was a vast military organization, set up specially for conquest, feeding on subjugated lands, recruiting its best troops and administrators from its subject peoples, converting and integrating them into the ruling group. The Sultan was omnipotent, his slaves were ministers and ministers his slaves. The absolute rule and the relative order imposed by the Sultan, coming after the anarchy and the oppression which the Balkans and the Near East had known before the Ottoman conquest, made·their burden more acceptable. The Turks were no harsher than their predecessors, their exactions were no greater, their troops more disciplined.* Their rule was less intolerant, their peace was more secure. Greek Orthodox subjects paid heavy taxes but did not have to contend with the persecution and the pressures they felt under the Catholic Venetians or the Knights of Saint John.

The great sixteenth-century problem—the struggle between a hereditary, landed nobility and the developing bureaucratic absolutism of the monarchies—was one which the Turks at first ignored. Their empire was based on and served by officials with no hereditary claim to power or position. A Flemish gentleman, Augier Ghislain de Busbecq,* * who served as Austrian ambassador to the Ottoman court, has left us a famous dispatch of 1555 which deals with this essential point:

> It is by merit that men rise in the service, a system which ensures that posts should only be assigned to the competent. Each man in Turkey carries in his own hand his ancestry and his position in life, which he may make or mar as he wills. Those who receive the highest offices from the Sultan are for the most part the sons of shepherds or herdsmen, and so far from being ashamed of their parentage, they actually glory in it and consider it a matter of boasting that they owe nothing to the accident of birth; for they . . . believe that high qualities are . . . partly the gift of God and partly the result of good training, great industry and unwearied zeal . . . Among the Turks therefore, honors, high posts, and judgeships are the rewards of great ability and good service. If a man be dishonest or lazy or careless he remains at the bottom of the ladder, an object of contempt;

---

* Ottoman soldiers on the march were strictly forbidden to tread on roses.
* * Responsible, among other things, for introducing into Europe the lilac and tulip he found in the Levant.

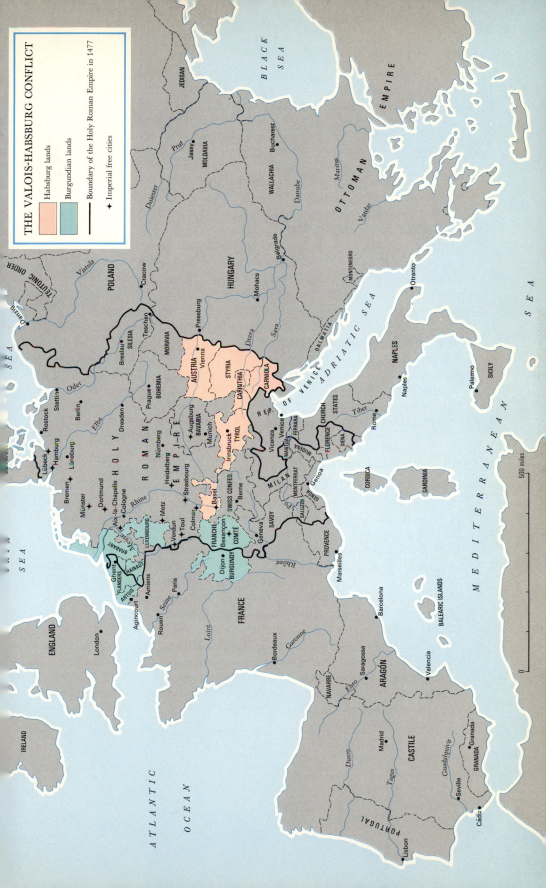

THE VALOIS-HABSBURG CONFLICT

☐ Habsburg lands
☐ Burgundian lands
— Boundary of the Holy Roman Empire in 1477
✦ Imperial free cities

TEUTONIC ORDER

POLAND

JEDISAN

BLACK SEA

Vistula

Danzig

Cracow

Teschen

SILESIA

Breslau

Stettin

Berlin

Oder

MORAVIA

Prut

Dniester

Jassy

MOLDAVIA

Bucharest

WALLACHIA

Danube

Pressburg

HUNGARY

Mohacs

Drava

Sava

Belgrade

Maritza

OTTOMAN EMPIRE

Vardar

Rostock

Lübeck

Hamburg

Lüneburg

Bremen

Münster

Dortmund

Cologne

Aix-la-Chapelle

HOLY

Elbe

Dresden

BOHEMIA

Prague

ROMAN

Nürnberg

Heidelberg

Strasbourg

EMPIRE

Augsburg

BAVARIA

Munich

AUSTRIA

Vienna

STYRIA

CARINTHIA

CARNIOLA

TYROL

Innsbruck

SWISS CONFED.

Basel

Berne

Geneva

MILAN

Vicenza

Venice

REP. OF VENICE

MANTUA

FERRARA

MODENA

Genoa

GENOA

MONTFERRAT

SALUZZO

Po

SAVOY

PROVENCE

Marseilles

Tiber

Rome

CHURCH STATES

FLORENCE

SIENA

DALMATIA

ADRIATIC SEA

MONTENEGRO

Otranto

NAPLES

Naples

Palermo

SICILY

CORSICA

SARDINIA

MEDITERRANEAN SEA

500 miles

Rhine

Metz

Toul

Verdun

Colmar

LUXEMBOURG

Besançon

FRANCHE-COMTÉ

Dijon

BURGUNDY

Rhône

BRABANT

LIÈGE

HAINAUT

Ghent

FLANDERS

ARTOIS

Amiens

Agincourt

Paris

Seine

Rouen

Loire

FRANCE

Bordeaux

Garonne

ENGLAND

London

IRELAND

ATLANTIC OCEAN

NAVARRE

Saragossa

Ebro

ARAGÓN

Valencia

Barcelona

BALEARIC ISLANDS

Madrid

Duero

CASTILE

Tagus

Guadalquivir

GRANADA

Granada

Seville

Cádiz

PORTUGAL

Lisbon

SEA

for such qualities there are no honors in Turkey! This is the reason that they are successful in their undertakings, that they lord it over others, and are daily extending the bounds of their empire. These are not our ideas; with us there is no opening left for merit; birth is the standard for everything; the prestige of birth is the sole key to advancement in the public service.

No wonder Busbecq dwells at such length on the questions of birth and merit which long continued to bedevil the efficiency of the West.

Until at least the death of their great Sultan Suleiman (1520-1566), the Ottomans—more rational, flexible, and authoritarian—had the advantage of their western foes. After Suleiman died, the mediocrity of succeeding rulers in a regime whose crucial part they were, the relative stabilization of the Turkish borders, and the growth of hereditary castes would usher in decline. Authority becoming rigid, practical institutions stiffening into burdens, checked Turkish effectiveness while Europeans forged steadily ahead. This becomes clear with hindsight. It was not soon or easily evident at the time. And, though declining slowly, the Turks remained a factor of tremendous importance—a danger which the states of Europe jockeying for power were forced to take into account.

Against this background—warfare, revolts, and treaties—the two great dramas of the sixteenth century: the dynastic contest between the Valois and Habsburg, and the religious struggle, would unfold.

Valois and Habsburg

It was in 1494 that Charles VIII (1483–1498) rode into Italy to claim the heritage of the ousted Angevins of Naples from the Aragonese ruler of that land.* His cavalcade ushered in over sixty years of fighting for dominion over what was, at least to start with, the most advanced, most civilized, the richest part of Europe. The rivalries of the Italian states had often led them to appeal for foreign aid against their enemies. When finally the intervention came, it introduced more trouble than it solved, a power that could outmatch the brittle forces of Italian princelings and turn campaigns into a promenade (as Machiavelli said of Charles VIII).

Italians who had hoped to use the foreigners found that they were used by them instead. One intervention could only breed another. The French could be dislodged by bringing in the Spaniards, whose hold proved even more tenacious. Between 1494 and 1559 the land became a prize in a tug-of-war between these two powers. City militia and mer-

---

* From 1268 to 1435, Naples had been ruled by kings of the French House of Anjou, related to the House of Valois. This Angevin dynasty had been evinced by Alfonso V of Aragon, who secured the Napolitan crown in 1435. It was against his heir that Charles VIII, of Valois, attempted to reassert the dynastic claims he had inherited.

cenary armies melted or broke before the *tercios* or the French *gendarmes;* the Pope cowered in the Castel Sant'Angelo while Rome was sacked by German mercenaries; the only effective counter to the foreigner would be the plague.

One expedition followed another from France, invited now by Milan against Naples (1494), now by Venice against Milan (1499), now by the Emperor Maximilian against Venice (1508), now by the Pope against his Spanish foes (1526 and 1556). In every case the prize slipped through French fingers, their allies fell away. Leagues formed against each victorious power, dissolved as much in success as in defeat, reformed again to bring together the combatants of yesterday against a new objective until, finally, the settlement of 1559 left the country a satellite of Spain, which held its two extremities in Naples and Milan.

Historians have written of these wars as rational ambitions, arguing that France needed Sicilian wheat to feed her cities, coveted a market, grasped at the Alpine passes or simply at the riches of Milan. Such considerations, if they existed, played a very secondary role. More convincing is the explanation advanced by the contemporary historian, Philippe de Commynes (1447?–?1511) who concluded that Charles VIII went into Italy because he was young, silly, and ill-advised. He was certainly all three. But there is more to it. Charles had claims to Naples (as Louis XII had to Milan and Francis I, who was their heir, to both) which were perfectly well-founded. He had been invited, not for the first time, by the ruler of Milan. Above all he wanted to divert the wild energies of his nobles away from France and into foreign channels where he and they might hope to put them to some profitable use. It is most doubtful if he even thought about his subjects' economic interests, Mediterranean commerce, or the grain trade. The profits of the merchants did not enter into the calculations of kings. They fought and Charles

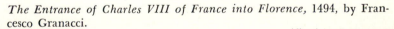

The Entrance of Charles VIII of France into Florence, 1494, by Francesco Granacci.

Alinari-Art Reference Bureau

fought for dynastic interests, for glory, for ill-assayed dreams of conquest and loot, for the satisfaction of vanity and pride. These were the components of the golden and gory mirage four French kings * pursued south of the Alps from 1494 to 1559, only to see it fall finally to Spain.

After the 1520's however, Italy was a counter in a much greater game in which the kings of Europe struggled for higher stakes. The world was moving. The Ottomans pressed forward in the east. In 1509 Henry VII died, in 1515 Louis XII, in 1516 Ferdinand of Aragon. A new generation was coming to the fore and, to begin with, the princes talked of peace. In 1518 the treaty of London between the kings of England and of France, soon ratified by all great European powers, meant to ensure the perpetual peace of Christendom and common defense against the Turkish menace. It embodied age-old dreams of united and crusading Christendom and also humanist ideas of peace and general enlightenment. The treaty lasted thirty months and preceded the great wars which rent both Europe and Christendom more deeply than before.

The Spanish realm had passed in 1516 to Ferdinand and Isabella's grandson. Elected Emperor in 1519 (though not crowned until 1530) as Charles V, he tried to fulfill the implications of his string of titles which meant on one hand a universal empire and on the other dismemberment of France to recover the Burgundian provinces grabbed by Louis XI, and which he claimed as part of his inheritance. But the lost lands of Burgundy meant less to Charles V than northwest Italy. Milan, for Charles, was the indispensable link of an empire which stretched from Spain and Naples to the Baltic and North Sea and whose communications ran through Lombardy. Key of the empire for the emperor, Milan for Francis I was the lever with which he might break it up. Francis had also hoped for the imperial crown and, losing it, had not abandoned hope of winning (or winning over) Germany. France was surrounded by Habsburg territories and threatened on all sides—but threatening in turn, strong in her manpower and in the resources with which to hire more from the apparently inexhaustible warlike cantons of the Swiss.

Around these rivals revolved the German princes, the Italian powers, the ambitious English king. England, traditionally hostile to France, just as traditionally close to her Lowland markets, seemed the predestined ally of Spain until Henry VIII's marital imbroglio, his desperate attempts to divorce his wife who was a daughter of Isabella and aunt of Charles V, made him the Emperor's enemy. The Pope turned either way. In search of dependable allies, Francis recalled Louis XI's motto that the end justifies the means. Defeated by the Emperor, he turned to Suleiman, the Emperor's eastern foe, opened his ports to Muslim corsairs, finally concluded a formal alliance with the Turks (1536). Caught in continuous war, pressed from every side, Charles could never build on his successes. In the Mediterranean he fought the Turkish fleet,

---

* After Charles VIII, his successors Louis XII, Francis I, Henry II.

the pirates of North Africa, mounted great expeditions against Tunis, Algiers, and others of their ports. In Germany he was harried by the princes, by religious problems, by the Turkish threat, only fitfully able to intervene. The French gave him no peace: Francis I died in 1547, but his son, Henry II, continued to fight the Habsburgs in Germany and in Italy.

The dream of empire became a weary holding operation; and Charles was growing old. He had been born in 1500. The spiced dishes which he favored gave him gout and asthma. He grew steadily more pious, his only indulgence being overeating, so that in the eyes of his courtiers life seemed to oscillate between mass and board (*de la missa a la mesa*). At last in 1556 he abdicated, leaving his German lands and the imperial burden to his brother Ferdinand; Spain, Italy, and the Netherlands to his son Philip. The means of the sixteenth century were not sufficient to cope with the scale of the possessions which Charles had tried to rule at once. Centralization worked best within a large but not too disparate area. Size could be a source of power, but sprawling separate territories were still too hard to rule. The modern state grew up as a compact territorial unit (France ,England, Spain) and even Philip would find it hard to keep the distant duchies of the Netherlands.

Charles retired to end his life in a Spanish abbey, where he would die in 1558, one year before Philip and Henry II concluded peace at last at Cateau-Cambrésis (1559). Yet the Emperor's long and weary efforts had not been ineffective. The treaty marked the end of French attempts to conquer Italy and the beginning of Spain's hegemony in Europe. The death in the same year of Henry II, killed in a jousting match—in what a contemporary French historian calls an *accident sportif*,*—delayed the French from pressing forward their more fruitful conquests in Lorraine, and ushered into France a difficult period of religious wars, just when the Germans had managed temporarily to settle their religious troubles (Augsburg, 1555), just when the Protestant offensive had run down elsewhere. In 1558 also, the English lost Calais, their last continental possession, and gained a new queen—Elizabeth, daughter of Henry VIII and of his second wife Anne Boleyn, who had ended her short reign on the scaffold at the age of twenty-nine. With France temporarily weakened, they would again play a more important role.

Mercantilism

The needs of constant warfare, especially its costs, had encouraged every power to develop and marshal its resources, attempting to become self-sufficient, especially in the sinews of war. Arms and ammuni-

* Edward III had banned such sports from England in 1340.

tion were essential: saltpeter, sulfur, metals; so was the bullion that paid for them, for warriors, for fortifications, and for the enterprises of diplomacy. Each state's ideal now was to be economically independent. Friends could not be trusted. Neighbors even less. States to survive had to build up production in industry, agriculture, commerce; secure a favorable trading balance; encourage enterprise by privileges, monopolies, controls, tariff protection; accumulate the bullion that was all important, prevent it from leaving the country and funnel in more by every means.

This economic nationalism, generally described as *mercantilism,* is less a theory than a weapon—the use of economic means to serve political ends. The practice was not new. The medieval kings of England had used their control of wool exports to put pressure on the lords and cities of Flanders and Brabant. In 1381 an English navigation act had tried to keep all trade with English ports for English ships. Now, what had been an occasional practice became a policy of state, trying to use control to increase prosperity and power.

One way of tapping wealth, was by securing it overseas—poaching on Spanish and Portuguese preserves. The king of Portugal's oriental empire was joined to Spain's when Philip donned the Portuguese crown in 1580. By then it had turned, as the historian Garrett Mattingly expressed it, into a bankrupt wholesale grocery business. In it and in the ports of Spain, overorganization, overregulation, increasing restrictions, invited interlopers. As England, France, later on the Dutch, began to sail into areas which Spain and Portugal looked on as exclusive reservations, they had to forge arguments with which to counter the claims of the possessing powers, arguments which in effect asserted the free right of trade and navigation, thus going counter to current mercantilist ideas and to the practices of those who uttered them themselves.

Mercantilist at home, Francis I, Henry VIII, Elizabeth especially, spoke a new language when they looked abroad, asserting that the sea was free and that men could not by mere prescription be excluded from the use and enjoyment of half the earth. In 1540 we hear Francis I of France declaring that the sun shone for him as it did for others, that only occupation could create a right to territory overseas. It took some time before the English and the French acted on these principles, but Francis's refusal to recognize the established system laid the foundation of free colonial enterprise and the struggle for colonial power which marks the rest of the modern period.

Meanwhile, however, mercantilist ideas and the notion of balanced trade which they implied, spurred the competitors of the Habsburgs into colonial enterprises of their own where they might find the wares they presently bought from others, perhaps a basis for self-sufficiency. By 1614 the English Levant Company was exporting East Indian pepper and spices from London to Turkey. The old days when oriental goods had reached Europe via Suez and Venice were well and truly buried.

Chapter 4

THE CRISIS OF CHRISTIANITY AND CHRISTENDOM

On October 31, 1517, a provincial clergyman nailed ninety-five theses against papal misuse of indulgences and absolution on the door of the castle Church of Wittenberg in Saxony. The gesture was contentious but hardly revolutionary. Proposing a debate on theological theses was accepted practice and the language of Dr. Martin Luther was perfectly academic. Yet the swelling echoes of his gesture would travel far and wide. By 1518 the great German cities were joining in the issue: Nürnberg, Strasbourg, Basel; in Zurich a priest with humanistic leanings, Ulrich Zwingli, was launching a movement of his own. By 1520 Germany was buzzing with contention and the rest of Europe woke up to a new issue which it could not avoid. Religious war and religious rebellions cut into the political conflicts, providing old enemies with new battle cries and contributing new and profound causes of friction. Religious conflict ravaged Germany until the 1550's, France and the Netherlands during the second half of the century, and threw England into political confusion. Within one generation the seamless robe of Christendom was rent. Henceforth, men stood divided by Christian faith as much as by political allegiance or economic interest. That was the Reformation.

Religion in the 15th and 16th Centuries

The vast reverberations of a religious issue can be understood only in the context of a society and a world in which religious matters were of prime concern. Where today Christianity is a religion among others, a matter of taste or choice, in the sixteenth century it was the very definition of Europe, the air one breathed, inseparable part of the tissue of life, a matter of choice for no one, inescapable, omnipresent. Degrees, wills, treaties, even sometimes contracts were religious acts. Baptism gave man his birth certificate, marriage at the church door set up the family, burial in the parish churchyard marked the end of a life in which church bells spelled out the time for work or meals or rest; in which the calendar was a succession not of dates but of saints' days. Whether in day or night these men were Christians, continually reminded of its implications: "Rise, rise, Christians from your sleep," cried the night-watchman of mid-sixteenth century Besançon, "and pray for the dead that God may forgive them."

Because it was so encompassing, religion was a matter for grave concern. Men, some men at least, were becoming more demanding, more critical of the prevailing theology which held the mystery of God and of his salvation to be ultimately incomprehensible and the Christian's duty to believe without much thought and carry out the rites in the way the church prescribed. To an earlier age which pressed less hard into the why and how of things, the Christian doctrine seemed to offer a reasonable explanation of reality. Now it became a kind of magic ritual, or turned into a formalism, an impersonal pattern of observance and gestures. No wonder men appeared who, far from wanting to abolish religious rites, tried to revitalize them, to return them from symbolic gestures to the real communion they signified.

Rites were not all. Christianity is a way of life and reformers have always sought to revitalize it by living it and encouraging others to do so in ways as close as possible to the simplicity, the charity, the love of Christ. Throughout the Middle Ages reformers tried to cut through the worldliness of institutionalized Christianity to primitive simplicity and dedication. The failure of St. Francis in the thirteenth century and the emphatic assertion of fourteenth-century popes that the doctrine of Christian poverty was heretical (decrees of John XXII, 1322–1323) turned many toward apocalyptic compensations and forced others into "heresy."

In the fourteenth century, a Dutchman, Gerard Groote of Deventer (1340–1384) founded a brotherhood of devout men who, without monastic vows, without the habit of an order, lived chaste and pious lives, trying to renovate religion as the humanists just then were renovating learning. The characteristic expression of what became known as the New Piety (*devotio moderna*) is to be found in Thomas à Kempis's (1380–1471) *Imitation of Christ;* the diary of a soul that sought in Christ "the love which alone makes what is heavy light." Mystical yet vigorous and clear, intellectual humility replaced dry scholastic reasoning, arguing that the way to Christ has to be lived and felt.

Practical, ethical, stoical, not very speculative, the Brethren of the Common Life, as they came to be called, emphasized the importance of self-knowledge and the practice of Christianity in everyday life. Not very interested in liturgical forms, they encouraged meditation on the life of Christ and of the Virgin, suggested methodical exercises that used psychological association to focus the believer's attention and help the mystic toward the Divinity with which he sought to merge: "the immense desert, one, impassable, where the truly pious heart . . . wanders without losing itself, loses itself without straying, is overwhelmed in delight and continues unyielding . . ." As they spread from the Netherlands along the Rhine and into Northern Germany, the Brethren set up printing presses, founded schools and hostels for poor students. Their interest in education was responsible for men like the future Cardinal Nicholas of Cusa (1401–1464), Rudolph Agricola, "Father of German Humanism" (1443–1485), Erasmus, Luther, and a host of German humanists, all trained or affected by them.

The mystical side encouraged by the Brethren could, however, express itself in other directions, in the contemporary enthusiasm for the Virgin and St. Anne, the devotion to the passion of Jesus, the cult of his Bleeding Heart and of the Rosary, all rising at this time, all answering a popular need for warmer, more personal religion—but also letting loose a wealth of pious fancies that could easily run awry. Thus the great Breton visionary, the Dominican Alain de la Roche (1428–1475), one of the first promoters of the Rosary Cult, was not only a friend of the Brethren of the Common Life (in one of whose houses he would die) but teacher of Jacob Sprenger, who, while propagating Alain's Brotherhood of the Rosary in Germany, actually made his name as one of Germany's chief witch-hunters, co-author of the nefarious *Malleus Maleficarum* (1489), the witch-hunters' bible.

Reform attempts could take a more forceful and, to the church, a more disquieting form when mingled with political campaigns and interests. In fourteenth-century England, resentment of papal demands for subsidy and suspicion of the popes of Avignon during the war with France lent popular (and more important, royal) support to the theories of John Wycliffe (1320–1384). Wycliffe's argument ascribed all authority to Grace, and connected this with personal character and this in turn with predestination. Salvation could not depend on the services of the church, pope or priest could not excommunicate the righteous or absolve the unworthy—let alone provide them with indulgences. The church is simply the community of all believers and the authority of secular government had to be conceded in everything temporal, which necessarily included such things as church property, patronage, and politics. As for religious authority, that came from the Bible—especially from the Gospels, the only certain guide. It followed that these should be made available to everybody in the language which they understood —their own.*

The logic of Wycliffe's arguments eventually led him to propose disendowment, since divesting the church of her property would be a first step to church reform; and then to challenge even the doctrine of transubstantiation by arguing that Christ's presence in the bread and wine was spiritual or symbolic, rather than actual and substantial. His chief influence would be felt in Bohemia, where national and radical reformist sentiments similar to those in Wycliffe's England culminated in the heresy and martyrdom of John Huss (1370?–1415).

John Huss believed that the church is the community of those whom God has predestined for salvation, and called for the reform of a corrupt, undisciplined, simoniacal, clergy. His death at Constance at the hands of the emperor who had promised him safe conduct to the council there only precipitated the clash between his Czech followers and the Catholic party, identified with the German Emperor. The ensuing struggle, with Hussites at first victorious, saw a developing claim of the laity's right to receive communion in both kinds—not only bread but also wine which the church reserved for the priest alone. The doctrine, whose adherents took the name *Utraquists,* was one more assertion that all believers are equal and the clergy no more so than anybody else. More radical Hussite groups in the fifteenth century rejected all beliefs and practices not explicitly based in the New Testament, denied the existence of Purgatory, the validity of either indulgences or masses for the dead, condemned worship of saints, relics, and images, and finally rejected a special status for priests, whom they proceeded to elect themselves.

The Humanist Reformers

More moderate criticism, but in some ways thereby more effective, came from the humanists. Some historians have cited their pagan or

---

* There would be nineteen editions of the Bible in high German and twenty-four of the Old Testament in French printed by the opening years of the sixteenth century.

paganizing influence. And certainly study is a subversive thing when it develops critical vision and detachment, creates awareness of the contrast between what men say and do, or results in the cynicism with which Lorenzo Valla in 1440 told the Inquisitors: "I believe as Mother Church believes. It is true she knows nothing. But what she believes I believe."

There was little sign of irreligion. In a period of devotion and active religious sentiment, the Reformation was hardly pagan but rather an explosion of the liveliest faith. It was not as cynics or agnostics that the humanists harmed the interests of the church, but as Christians whose activities were often continuations of medieval interests. True, textual criticism contributed to the revision and rethinking of traditional texts and doctrines and, hence, to the Reformation current. Humanist rationalism helped expose the contradictions and the frequent failures of established religious institutions. Yet, wrote the French humanist Mathurin Cordier (1479–1564), "a devout and Christian life . . . comes before purity of speech. Without piety there can be no true progress in learning." *This* was the spirit of Christian humanism and this perhaps its most subversive aspect.

The humanists tended toward reform perhaps, but hardly Reformation. The humanistic spirit was far from the theological position of the great reformers. Humanistic optimism and anthropocentrism rejected the emphasis on original sin, the utter helplessness of man to save himself, the Lutheran denial of free will. The great reformers were not the apostles of a new tolerance, which the best humanists were, but of a new and newly intolerant interpretation against the old. Humanists sought a morality. Reformers affirmed a faith. The humanist search revalued the Scriptures, devalued the traditional rites and formal-

Bulloz

Rabelais, an engraving by an unknown artist.

ities, stressed the personal and internal decision and choice, all of which prepared the way for reform. But their insistence on free will and free choice clashed with reformed dogmatism as much or more than it did with that of the Catholic Church. The greatest of Luther's humanist supporters, Philipp Melanchthon (1497–1560), would put it very well: "What do we ask of theology? Two things. Consolations for death and for the last judgment. Luther provides them. Erasmus wants a lesson of morality and civility."

More and John Fisher would be beheaded by Henry VIII for their loyaly to Rome, Servetus burned by Calvin for subversive antitrinitarianism, Erasmus would refuse the Cardinal's hat and die unshriven, attacked by both sides. On the other hand, an important humanist like Sadoletus became a cardinal, and Melanchthon, another quite as learned, the educational leader of Lutheran Germany. As for Calvin, a humanist by training, and a good one, we know he founded Calvinism. So humanists went in every direction, and there is no point in connecting them with one party or another.

Desiderius Erasmus (1466?–1536) was the acknowledged prince of sixteenth-century humanists. In all his works (especially the *Praise of Folly*, 1509), one finds the effort to bring ancient wisdom to the men of his day, experience of the past within the reach of the present. His Christianity itself was connected with this, and the model Erasmus set up is that of the Christian knight—the decent, wise, and virtuous man who follows Christ's teachings, free to develop his personality, to become a useful member of society, through his own interpretation of the Scriptures. Erasmus wanted no married priests, no monks, no superstitions, no asceticism. He tried to reconcile the critical spirit born of the Renaissance and the traditional acceptance of dogma and authority without which the church would not have withstood the buffeting of ages. In attempting this, however, he moved, at least in theory, away from dogma because he minimized the importance of dogmatic differences * and emphasized the essential implications, applications of the Christian faith, the living morality of the spirit, its expression in love and faith, in charity and joy. His Christianity was not literal but practical, different both from the sterile disputes of the schools and from the stern injunctions of the protestant rebels.

It would be this living interpretation of the New Testament which inspired his friend Thomas More's utopian religion—simple, tolerant, and free. Broadcast in a mass of publication, by a vast correspondence, copied and circulated throughout Christendom, the message of Erasmus inspired many with respect for classical studies, with dislike for hollow ritual and useless monks, above all with respect for Scripture. One must have recourse to Jesus, without reference to human or supernatural in-

* —whether the Holy Ghost proceeded from the Father, from the Son, or from Father and Son together, for example—

Desiderius Erasmus, by Hans Holbein (the Younger). Galleria Nazionale, Parma.

termediaries in quest of salvation in a world where every hope exists for men who are willing to express their fundamentally good (not wicked) nature and use their fundamentally positive capacities. When Rabelais's wise giant Gargantua devised the one clause of his Thelemite Foundation: "do what you will," he explained himself: "because people who are free, well-born, well-bred, and easy in honest company have a natural spur and instinct which drives them to virtuous deeds and deflects them from vice; and this they called honor."

Note here the contradiction with the pessimistic doctrine of original sin. Man is corrupt and can do nothing good by himself, Luther was saying. Man is evil and full of sin, Calvin was saying. Man is born to love wisdom and to do good deeds, says Erasmus. For Erasmus, man is Promethean—free spirit, free will, free agent, able to penetrate to truth and apply it in a good world—good by nature and hence able to reach whatever (human) levels, fulfill whatever (spiritual) tasks he sets for himself, if only his individual personal potential is allowed, encouraged, trained to develop freely.

Such was the thinking of Erasmus and after him of Rabelais and More; eventually of many others. But that would not happen for some time. As Luther remarked in 1517, "the human avails more with Erasmus than the divine." Perhaps this is what leaves him attractive to our day. In his time the harsher virtues were appropriate. More was executed. Erasmus pushed aside. Rabelais survived only as a clown. We shall see that the men who triumphed were the armed prophets Machiavelli once referred to.

The Clergy

More dangerous to religion, more likely to spur attacks against the church, was the ecclesiastical personnel itself: the papacy, the bishops, and the clergy. As we have seen, the popes had degenerated into secular princes, their states a crazy quilt of feudal holdings whose rulers were either tyrannical or ineffective, before they became bigoted as well. The long Avignonese exile had been followed by the demeaning period of the papal schism and by the unsavory struggle for power between popes and ecclesiastical councils. When the papacy at last revived, around 1500, its new authority was not based on Christian virtues but on eminently worldly ones: money, arms, and diplomacy. Alexander VI, a Borgia, was the first to show what a pope could do with money and with men. He also showed how little he cared about papal interests compared with the worldly activities of his family. But the conclusion of his and his son Cesare's efforts was nevertheless the restoration of papal power on the secular plane.

This had its useful and its awkward aspects. Secular power lends prestige, provides the concrete means of furthering spiritual ends. The function of the papacy, Erasmus could still write in 1514, was "to compose the quarrels of Christian princes." In fact, of course, it had long been merely a party to these quarrels. The old prohibition against making Christian slaves was dead; the old idea of crusade against the infidel lingered on more as an excuse for taxation or expeditions that led into Italy rather than Palestine. However much some rulers struggled to revive crusades, the crux of the matter was expressed by Henry VIII when he told a Venetian ambassador that "no general expedition against the Turks will ever be effected so long as such treachery prevails among the Christian powers, that their sole thought is to destroy one another."

The Holy See was deeply engaged in costly policies to advance its temporal power and the interests of the family of the ruling pope. Like other princes, to meet the costs of their monarchic policies, popes had to trade in what merchandise they had: ecclesiastical appointments, dispensations, indulgences. These latter, which would provide the immediate cause of Luther's theses, were an old device, based on a thirteenth-century doctrine officially formulated by Clement VI in his bull *Unigenitus* (1343). According to this doctrine the church disposed of a great treasury of good deeds, those of Christ and of the saints, which Christ had entrusted to St. Peter, and this vast capital of goodness increased daily by the further accumulation of other merits. Upon this treasury the pope could draw in order to reward some other meriting Christians, and this he did in the form of the indulgence which was in fact a check drawn on this bottomless account, made out to relieve the bearer of the consequences of his sins.

The device proved very popular. As early as 1300, when Boniface VIII promised special indulgences for pilgrims coming to Rome to celebrate the jubilee of that year, the crowd of pilgrims was so great that traffic on Sant' Angelo Bridge had to be channeled by making people walk on the right: the first known example of traffic regulations. The popes had struck oil: in this case, holy oil. They did not scruple to exploit it, either to attract pilgrims to some favorite shrine,—* or to raise money for their current schemes—from works of charity or public utility to the building of Saint Peter's Basilica in Rome. Inevitably, this led to criticism, of which a famous example can be found in Erasmus's *Praise of Folly*:

> What should I say of them that hug themselves with their counterfeit pardons; that have measured Purgatory by an hourglass, and can without the least mistake demonstrate it—ages, years, months, days, hours, minutes and seconds, as it were in a mathematical table? And now suppose some merchant, soldier or judge parts with some small piece of ill-gotten money. He at once conceives all that sink of his whole life quite cleansed; so many perjuries, so many lusts, so many debaucheries, so many contentions, so many murders, so many deceits, so many breaches of trust, so many treacheries bought off, as it were, by compact; and so bought off that they may begin upon a new score . . .

Remission of sins, of course, could also come from relics of some particularly holy object or of a saint. The faithful who tore to pieces the corpse of St. Elizabeth of Hungary in 1231 knew this, as did the monks of Fossannova who made sure of keeping a bit of St. Thomas Aquinas by cutting off his head, boiling the body, preserving the bones and the fat; or King Charles VI of France, distributing the rib bones of his sainted ancestor Louis IX in 1392.

Petrarch has written about St. Romualdus, who had to feign madness to escape from France because his admirers meant to kill him to make quite sure that they would get his remains. Luther's own patron, Frederick the Wise of Saxony, had gathered 17,443 relics in his castle church at Wittenberg—a great museum of edifying objects housed in twelve galleries that ran along the nave, whence pious and penitent sightseers could gain 128,000 years' worth of indulgences.

Among those most in need of indulgence were the clergy who lent their authority to such dispensations. The unworthiness of its representatives could not but diminish the prestige of the church. In 1479, the testament of Bishop John VI of Cambrai enumerated a long string of bastards; and the Abbot of the Monastery of St. Aubert mentions as a matter of course in the Monastery's memorial how he acted as godfather to a child the Bishop had fathered by the daughter of the Provost of the

* St. Julian's Church in Rome, where confession brought 8,000 years' remission of Purgatory, offered an excellent bargain.

Cathedral. In 1547 a local vicar appeared before the aldermen of Ghent to leave his house to his five bastards. The Bishop of Basel, one of the rare reforming prelates, enjoined his clergy "not to curl their hair with curling tongs, not to carry on trade in churches or to raise a disturbance there, not to keep drinking booths or to engage in horse dealing and not to buy stolen property." His neighbor, the Bishop of Chur, "chose his mistresses from the nunneries of his diocese," while his colleague of Constance made great profits by raising the fine for priests' children from 4 to 5 gulden. In Scotland the greatest piety went hand in hand with great abuses. Schools, churches, and hospitals were being founded by the dozen between 1450 and 1550. On the other hand, Cardinal James Beaton had nine children; Hepburn, Bishop of Moray, had ten —all by different mothers.

Even when their morality went unquestioned, too many clerics neglected the duties of their office, like Rupert von Simmern, Bishop of Strasbourg from 1440 to 1478, who in all his long career said not one single mass. Men such as these had bought their office or else secured appointment as a reward for services or simply for their family connections. And by the sixteenth century the concordats signed between popes and monarchs further developed this alliance by exchanging fiscal advantages for the Vatican for royal control of clergy. This meant that more than ever royalty would use high clerical benefices for its ends. In Scotland the illegitimate progeny of the Stuarts occupied archbishoprics, bishoprics, and abbeys—like James IV's eleven-year-old illegitimate son Alexander, appointed to the Archbishopric of St. Andrews in 1504. In France, Jean de Guise, created Cardinal in 1518 at the age of twenty, received as benefices by grace of Francis I five great abbeys, nine bishoprics, and three archbishoprics, all among the richest and most important in France. His style of life was notoriously sumptuous, so much so that a blind Roman beggar feeling his alms one day cried out "you are either Christ or the Cardinal of Lorraine." A less Christlike aspect appears in the remark of a contemporary chronicler that there was hardly a lady or maid at court who had not been debauched or snared by the Cardinal's enterprise.

The high clergy now became a privileged and aristocratic body of courtiers who saw only the profits of their charges and tended to ignore their diocese for the royal court where the source of favor and advancement lay. Between them and the lesser clergy relations were distant and hostile. The latter, left to pick up what crumbs they could from their superiors' table, lived miserable, discontented lives and either added to the discredit of their cloth or swelled the criticism. In 1512 the Lateran Council summoned by Pope Julius II (1503–1513) bent its attention to possible reforms—to restrain rather than abolish obvious abuses such as the accumulation of benefices, simony, and monastic license. Yet Francis I's Chancellor, Duprat, could still acquire two abbeys, five bishoprics, one archbishopric, and finally, in 1527, the cardinalate with, three years later, the title of Papal Legate.

The rise of late medieval mysticism showed well enough that official channels were insufficient for those whom faith thrust on to slake their thirst for God in a communion without ritual and without middlemen. As for the clergy, they stood dishonored—although the great among them were still prestigious in a secular sense and the good respected while belittled by their failure to measure up to the exigencies of their office.

If the church was criticized for its greed and corruption, it was even more resented for being foreign. The Pope was an Italian bishop, the church was seen as an Italian church. There were 301 episcopal sees in Italy alone against a total of 267 in Germany, France, Spain, Portugal, and the British Isles. And many foreign sees were in Italian hands. Not only benefices but even sainthood seemed to be an Italian prerogative. In three and a half centuries since 1300, the church recognized over 200 Italian saints, only 60 Frenchmen and 26 from Spain. And then there was the money—annates, Peter's pence, the price of legal business and indulgence. Charles V, a far from hostile witness, complained that the Pope made more money out of Germany than he, the Emperor.

The Church's Role Curtailed

Last but not least important, while failing in its spiritual functions, the church was being replaced in its more worldly ones. For long the principal provider of education, it was being challenged by laymen in that field where most serious scholarship went on outside its ken.

By the beginning of the sixteenth century, the most sought-after schoolmasters were laymen—humanists, Brethren of the Common Life, teachers in municipal colleges widely sponsored by local authorities: the Collège de Guyenne in Bordeaux, St. Paul's School in London, or Sturm's Academy in Strasbourg. Their pupils also were destined less for clerical positions than for the many functions lay society was beginning to offer in administration, teaching, business, and law. But the new schools did more than compete with the old: they cracked the shell of the old culture through. Medieval Latin schools had served the needs of the Church which founded or protected them, training chiefly clerks versed in a Latin that was still the living language of Christian society. Renaissance teachers substituted a much purer Ciceronian Latin, whose use set "men of letters" apart from current usage and the common herd. A gap thus opened between the language of "culture" and that of daily life; and, what is more, between educated laymen and the poor priests and friars, many of whom could hardly write, let alone read.

The church had also been the major channel for charity and social aid, activities very relevant at a time when beggary and vagrants presented serious social problems. The decay of trades, industrial crises, discharged or invalided soldiers, all increased the number of displaced persons in need of charity just when the chaos and maladministration of foundations, the decay of the monastic houses, made these least able to cope. Municipal and royal authorities had to intervene. They reorganized, simplified, amalgamated, took over the administration of schools, hospitals, workhouses, founded the first public assistance systems, put children to work, edicted dire penalties against valid beggars, abandoning Christian charity for rough empiricism. In cities like Nürnberg, where the Bishop was far away and his prerogatives slight or nonexistent, where the Council supervised the local church and its members managed the affairs of churches, convents, monasteries, and charitable institutions, the foundations of a state church practically existed already.

As secular institutions meddled increasingly in church affairs in order to reform, to force bishops to devote more of their revenues to the diocese, to take over some of the charitable and educational tasks which the church used to fulfill, more and more Christians tended to find spiritual guides in secular leaders. As the Council of 1431 met at Basel, the Hussites posted a manifesto on the cathedral door: "Why should God pay more attention to the prayers of priests than to those of other

The title page of Brant's *Ship of Fools.*

Warder Collection

men?" it asked, among other things. "Would it be because of their thick lips and red cheeks, or perhaps because of their brilliant apparel, their avarice and their luxuriousness?" Half a century later, the Orator of the Clergy at the Estate of Tours found "laymen better than clergymen." If so, perhaps a saintly layman was more truly a priest than a corrupt cleric. Above all, did the dialogue between man and God need the mediation of this rather disconsidered body? "The papal dignity stems from the emperor," Huss had contended; "papal primacy and institutions come from imperial power." The Council of Constance had found this proposition heretical. Now it seemed to make sense to many. Luther began by appealing from pope to council, but ended (at Leipzig in 1519) by rejecting the Council of Constance's condemnation of Huss. A Christian might be right albeit against pope or council if God was on his side. He would be right more safely if by him stood the prince.

Popular Religion

Corruption, irreligion, decay, secularism, and sometimes secularization, the scholarship and criticism of humanists, discontent with and among the clergy, all played their part in the mood where Reformation became a burning issue. But most effective must have been the popular concern fed on popular religious works with a wide circulation. A great preacher stated that you could no more put the Bible in the hands of the common man than a carving knife in those of a child. The printers did. With clergy and church devalued, God remained the only sure authority and of His will one document existed: Scripture. In the half century before 1520, over 150 Latin editions of the Bible appeared, paralleled by almost as many in vulgar tongues: the first German edition came out in 1466, the first Italian translation in 1471, Dutch in 1477, Castilian in 1485, the first full French Bible was published by the King's command in 1487. Sebastian Brant's *Ship of Fools* (1494) saw Germany overflowing with "Bibles, doctrines of salvation, editions of the Holy Fathers and such like books." And if books were referred to in the first place because of dissatisfaction with clerical services, they rendered these services less necessary, they allowed every man to hear God's word directly and interpret it as he would and could. Every man his own priest.

People cared too much, there were too many of them who cared, there were too many of them eager to ask questions, there were too many ready to respond. Perhaps this is where the crux of the whole question lies, where we might seek the origins of the Reformation.

In effect, recent historians of the Reformation present it above all as the religious expression of a great anguish, the widespread insecurity and distress of a time of troubles and catastrophes—the thirty-nine years of schisms, the Wars of the Roses in England, of the Hussites in Bohemia, the meteoric rise and fall of Charles the Bold and of his realm, the growing Turkish menace, and everywhere plagues, famines, an apparent accumulation of ills that dismayed the masses. Such visitations must be the punishment of grievous sins. Of sins every man and woman had enough to feed the furnace of his guilt, the fantasies of even worse retribution ahead. As the fifteenth century ended, many came to think that, since the time of the great schism, not a soul had entered paradise.

What awaited them elsewhere could be seen in the complicated horrors of Hieronymus Bosch's paintings and a good many other works in the same vein. Judgment and hell had always been part of the fresco cartoons that edified the medieval churchgoer. After the Black Death in mid-fourteenth century the detail, the horror of infernal pains grew in intensity, the menacing stature of Satan grew until he became the gigantic monster feeding on the souls of the damned who appear on one of the illustrations of the *Très Riches Heures du Duc de Berry,* ornate mirror of early fifteenth-century ways.

Before damnation, death; and death was everywhere, looming with its scythe, its hourglass, its bat's wings, its skeleton grin—sinister, *macabre* (the word appears in the fourteenth century), inevitable, dragging off in its grim equalitarian jig kings and bishops, plowmen and burghers. Frescoes, and flysheets, woodcuts, and songs and masques made death the constant companion of every man in a world where the reality of it was anyhow close enough. And why not the final catastrophe which so many preliminary ones seemed to predict, why not the apocalypse which Savonarola announced, which Dürer engraved (1498), which Lucca Signorelli painted in his terrible frescoes at Orvieto (1504)—that end of the world foreshadowed by the ruin of Rome (which all could see), the rise of Antichrist (which many thought they saw), and the doom of all those wandering preachers with their ominous prophecies?

In these straits, men reached out more than ever for what security they might find against death and damnation: the help of Christ, first and foremost—no longer the calm Lord of the great cathedrals, henceforth tormented, twisted, sweating tears of blood, expiating the sins of men, the man of sorrows and tormented with grief whom we find in Grünewald, and then in Dürer, in Michelangelo's *Pietà,* in the statistics preachers furnished who knew the very number of lashes Christ endured (5,475), until the Passion almost edged out the Resurrection in impact. Like that of contemporary Aztecs, the religion of an anxious Christendom sought expiation in blood, in suffering and tears. Unlike the Aztecs, though, they sought protection, too, in softer figures—the Virgin above all, whose great cloak ofttimes spread out to cover a mankind in distress, whose cult saw an extraordinary development in the fifteenth century

The Inferno, the right-hand panel of the *Garden of Earthly Delights,* by Hieronymus Bosch. Prado, Madrid.

along with the belief in the immaculate conception, the recitation of *Aves,* the pilgrimages to her special shrine at Loretto, the increasing attention paid to her mother, St. Anne.

After the Virgin, the saints, whose cult was particularly widespread in the fifteenth and early sixteenth century, verging almost on a new kind of polytheism. After the saints, indulgences, amulets, pious images and relics. And even this arsenal which men accumulated according to their means (the aging Louis XI going to his reward amassed a vast collection) did not reassure them against the wrath of God whose terrifying ways they felt and saw around them everywhere.

The late fourteenth century had expressed this in what still remains the great and fearsome death hymn of our day, the *Dies Irae*:

> Day of anger, day of mourning
> When to ashes all is burning,
> Seer and Sybil gave the warning.
> Oh what fear man's bosom rendeth,
> When from heaven the Judge descendeth
> On whose sentence all dependeth!*

No intercessors appeared to ease the lot of man alone before his Maker. Alone, as Luther felt, alone as he must be when the crutches and rationalizations he had accumulated were discarded and only his life remained, his self, small and mean and devoid of virtue before God's terrible majesty. What good were the forms and baubles of this world in a situation where only the grace of God availed, the free gift of salvation and man's own faith in the Giver and the Gift? Therein lay Luther's answer—and that of the other reformers—to the anxieties and obsessions of their time.

To sum the matter up, in the sixteenth century the bonds and conventions that govern relations between men and men, men and society, men and rulers, were snapping everywhere; and in Germany more than elsewhere, as we shall shortly see. Corruption, anarchy, and misery were in the saddle but evidently going nowhere. Princes and prelates were in disrepute. Among the learned, the best called for change while the rest floundered in meaningless ruts. Among those who were beginning to think, to question, to expect, the sense of restlessness and absurdity around them swelled, making for cynicism or rebellion. But rebellion for what? If one was not cynical or supine a new faith could be garnered from the old, a new commitment suggested by the betrayals of the old, reaction against present failures could affirm—reaffirm—the ancient prom-

---

* Compare this with a fifteenth-century ballad quoted by Johan Huizinga in *The Waning of the Middle Ages* (New York: 1954), p. 33: "Time of pain and of temptation/ Age of envy, tears and torment/Time of langor and damnation/. . . Age of sadness shortening life."

ise which clerks, politicians, lawyers had hidden with their travesties: that of God's love and of salvation through him.

A world whose most thoughtful denizens had lost all faith in it offered no alternative and no escape. This could only exist in God and in the private, inner communion with him that could be re-established by re-establishing contact with his word and will, brushing aside if need be the institutional barriers that seemed to obstruct the way. Here was the source of what Norman Cantor has called the existential doctrine of Luther and his friends. Set man right with God and he will once again be right with himself and—hopefully—with his fellows.

Luther

Dr. Martin Luther (1483–1546), professor of theology at Wittenberg, was thirty-four years old when he nailed his theses to the castle church door. He was, in his way, a good example of the social and intellectual promotion open to a bright boy of his day. His father, a simple Saxon miner, had shown sufficient enterprise to set up in a business of his own and send his son to the University at Erfurt to study canon law. But law and profit were not what young Martin wanted. Torn by a variety of impulses, subject to severe emotional crises, in conflict with his father and the worldly values the tough old man represented, he left his legal studies and (he thought) the world. Joining the Augustinian friars in 1505, Luther went on to become a theologian, philosopher, and scholar,

Martin Luther, an engraving by Melchior Lorch.

in due course a university teacher. Vulgar, violent, impatient, argumentative, impulsive, the man made an effective lecturer and an impressive preacher, as his superiors were not slow to recognize.

One thing tormented him: the question of salvation—the inability to see how the sinful, corrupt, fallible, human creature could ever overcome its *damnosa hereditas,* transcend its human bondage, save its immortal soul. Fears of damnation led Luther to despair until he found an answer in St. Paul's assurance to the Romans that the just shall live by faith. The phrase was far from new and the idea hardly seems subversive. The French humanist Lefèvre of Etaples had put forward the doctrine of justification by faith in his new edition of St. Paul's Epistles as early as 1512. Both Louis XII and Francis I, as well as the latter's sister, Margaret of Navarre, thought highly of Lefèvre and supported his later work, which culminated in the French translation of the New and Old Testament (1523 and 1525). To Luther the view came as release and revelation, so that he felt himself "to be born anew and to enter through open gates into Paradise itself."

In 1515, three years after Lefèvre had expressed his views in France, Luther began to teach along similar lines. If faith were pre-eminent, then any dogmatic and formal superstructure was a deviation, an obstacle, a maze in which man lost himself, stumbling away from God's simple call, forgetting to listen to God's word, which could be found not in the libraries, the courts, the learned disquisitions, but in God's own statements recorded in the Scriptures and echoed in man's own heart. Out of this grew the idea of "the priesthood of all believers," which contributed to the uprisings that followed in Luther's wake. It further followed that the church conceals rather than reveals divine salvation and truth, its mundane activities so many compromises with evil, its rites and promises misleading. Only faith could save. Only God grants faith. Man is God's creature, he is in His hands, his will God's will, his salvation God's will also. If salvation comes from Christ and Christ cares only for faith, indulgences are blasphemies, their sale misrepresentation—a shabby confidence trick.

Luther's arguments echoed so far and fast throughout Germany and then beyond that they must have appealed to strong and varied yearnings or resentments: the intellectuals who criticized ecclesiastical laxness and corruption; the ordinary people weary of paying for the upkeep of an unsatisfactory, often foreign church; eventually, the princes who could profit from the elimination of papal authority, the confiscation of church property, the domination of the new church structure in their states; above all many believers hard-put to save their souls.

Why this peculiar susceptibility of the Germans to his message?

In 1517, Germany, as Lucien Febvre has described it in the best of the books we have on the young Luther, was an anarchy. It had riches, pride, hard work, good profits, great cities, but no unity, no stability, nor the capacity to do anything about it. One also feels a vague, diffuse sense of humiliation, of unease that amid the national states taking shape around it the Empire remained a medieval nation not a modern one, a medley of dialects, privileges, parochial rivalries, ruled over by an emperor poorer than his bishops, weaker than neighboring kings, and by territorial princes grasping for a power whose reality they were beginning to organize in their own lands.

There were more men, but they lived harder lives and their lives counted for little, perhaps for less than ever since the Black Death. This was especially true of the lives of common men. Fernand Braudel quotes the words of Charles V at the siege of Metz in 1552—or at least words that were attributed to him: "The Emperor asked who were the people who were dying, and if they were gentlemen and men of note. He was answered that they were all poor soldiers. Thereupon he said that there was no danger if they died, comparing them to caterpillars, locusts and June bugs which eat the sprouts and other goods of the earth . . ."

In the countryside, feudal lords were turning the loose manorial system into something more centralized and more methodically administered, changing hereditary leaseholders into serfs, reasserting old feudal rights and inventing new ones. The unrest and dissatisfaction caused by these changes frequently broke out into riots, sometimes even into millenarian movements that promised a resolution of grievances and the true application of divine justice. Luther's revolt against one authority suggested the fresh possibility of revolt against another. Religious aspirations became interwoven with secular cravings, contributing fresh impetus for a rebelliousness already endemic in the land.

Rural revolts were no novelty in the sixteenth century. They were as much a part of the old regime, Marc Bloch has suggested, as strikes are a normal aspect of capitalist enterprise. The annals of the Middle Ages, of all the centuries into the eighteenth, are full of peasants rising, setting castles or manors on fire, electing "kings" or "popes" to lead them, always advancing much the same demands concerning their tithes or gleaning rights, the hunting rights, and all the privileges of their lords and priests, often moved by millenarian hopes, by evangelic memories of a basic human equality, by religious sentiments that did not wait for the Reformation. And such sentiments, such grievances, such hopes, were often articulated by priest-leaders, poor country priests no better off than their followers but slightly more educated, more capable of seeing particular miseries in general terms, of providing the intellectual ferment, the yeast without which revolt could not turn into rebellion.

But spread of the word from Wittenberg was greatest in the independent cities where Lutheran preaching was most concentrated and the councils more responsive to popular clamor for reform than territorial princes who knew and cared less about it. In the cities, journeymen were finding it harder to become masters, craftsmen were being turned into mere wage-laborers, social and economic groups were hardening. There, too, social grievances would find it natural to express themselves in religious terms.

The men and factions that could not agree on the political reform could agree on religious, for in this realm all could hope for some gain and none need fear a loss. The Emperor, traditional rival of the papacy, could look for an increase in authority; the cities and the common people hoped for a stop of the flow of gold into Roman coffers; the princes for the loot of church property. Then came an event which focused all these motives: the death of Emperor Maximilian in 1519. The question of his succession had been debated for a long time. Would the next Emperor be Maximilian's grandson, Charles of Spain and Burgundy; would it be King Francis I of France, or the Elector Frederick of Saxony whom the Pope favored, or that playboy of the Western world, Henry VIII of England? Of all these, only Habsburg and Valois had the means to contend seriously for a crown that had to be bought and bought again from every elector.*

Echoes of the campaign which kept all Germany on its toes stoked the fires of nationalism or, at least, of xenophobia. Away with all these foreigners who, not content with constant interference, would seek to rule as well. As we have seen, Charles of Habsburg would finally be elected as the most German of the candidates, on a real tide of national sentiment. Here, too, Luther echoed and amplified the anger and humiliation of the popular masses. "There is no nation more despised than the German," he cried out, denouncing the Italians—too clever by half—who sucked the marrow from the country's bones. If Germany was overrun and drained by foreigners, too many of them were there because of Rome.

In 1520, Luther published his three most famous pamphlets: the *Address to the Christian Nobility of the German Nation* called on the Germans to resist the exactions of Rome and to reform the church through a general council. *The Babylonish Captivity of the Church,* the only one in Latin, dealt with the question of the sacraments and, finding only baptism, the Eucharist, and penance ** to be necessary, attacked the papacy for long misleading Christians. The third, *Of the Freedom of a Christian Man,* discussed justification by faith.

Ideas of this sort, presented with increasing eloquence and force, were bound to bring first conflict and then a break with Rome. For Luther's friends, like Ulrich von Hutten, knight, humanist, friend of the robber barons and foe of the papacy, Luther's struggle was one for German liberties, a German struggle for freedom and self-affirmation. Less partisan observers like Erasmus declared that it was not for his

---

* One elector sold his vote six times: thrice to Francis, thrice to Charles, who got it in the end.
** The last was eventually dropped.

heresies that Rome pursued the friar, but because he had raised his hand against "Papal crown and monkish bellies." And it does seem that, eager to defend its German interests, its position in the Empire, its authority, its revenues, Rome treated Luther not as a Christian soul but as an insubmissive nuisance not to be convinced but crushed. Thus, it drove him into the rebellion it had feared, and his countrymen with him.

Luther rejected papal infallibility, then even the infallibility of councils. Excommunicated in December, 1520, he invited the students and the burghers of Wittenberg to witness his public burning of the papal bull. He was summoned by the Emperor to retract but affirmed that he could not and would not deny the truth as he saw it (Diet at Worms, 1521). Outlawed, his protector, the elector of Saxony, hid him in the Wartburg, a castle, where he translated the Bible into German, forging during his year of banishment the greatest weapon for the popularization of a doctrine now spreading rapidly among all social classes. First under Hutten's pen, then under Luther's, the polemic had shifted from Latin to German, from an appeal to the powerful and the learned to rallying the popular will—the German will—against the common foe.

From Worms the papal legate, Aleander, had to inform his master who expected an early settlement of the "monkish quarrel" that nine-tenths of the Germans were for Luther and the remaining tenth against the Pope. Perhaps the proportions ought to be reversed; the gospel of reform, at any rate, forged rapidly ahead until it suddenly appeared that its refreshing breezes had ushered in a hurricane of revolution.

It is impossible to attack existing structures, to bring about a radical alteration of belief and institutions, and not stir up some calls for further changes still. It is impossible to use your judgment boldly, to assert free will against authority, without clearing the way for others who want to do the same and who, authority removed, reach different conclusions from your own. Nor is it possible, once having called on Christian

New York Public Library

An illustration from a German translation of the Bible by Martin Luther, depicting the trials of Jonah.

principles which are fundamentally quite subversive of ordinary social order and injustice, to prevent the poor and the oppressed from taking them up in their own cause and using them as flags for revolution that can easily be transferred from the spiritual to the social plane.

Luther had faced the problem of salvation, the crucial concern of Christian souls that others took for granted. Painfully, he had broken through the accretions of centuries to return to the original promise of the church—that faith saves and that salvation is free—a view both disturbing and unconcerned with institutional needs. This led to mutual excommunication. The church cast out Luther's followers as schismatics and they in turn denounced the church for having lost the spirit and forgotten the word of God. Two rights—one spiritual, the other historical—quite easily made two wrongs. And now the profoundly subversive tenor of Luther's thought poured out not only against Rome, the "whore of Babylon," but in its implicit reaffirmation of life and of the world which, though full of sin, must yet be good since they were of God's making. The tasks that men accomplish, however humble, are the will of God. Every Christian—peasant, artisan, maid, or knight—is just as worthy as the priest and preacher. Indeed, they are all priests, all witnesses to the glory and the might of God, far more than monks or nuns who in their retreat deny life.

Here were revolutionary ideas appealing to burghers and villeins and gentry, but reactionary ideas too: profoundly conservative in their insistence upon the place and task in life allotted everyone by God at birth. According to their bent, different minds interpreted them differently. Communities like Nürnberg or Strasbourg, little affected by the social agitation of the time, responded eagerly to the spiritual appeal. Humanists and cobblers heeded Peter's advice (I Peter: 5, 7) to cast all their care upon the Lord, felt better for it, lighter, stronger, more confident. Social resentments, economic strains, drove others to insist on the call for man to become an instrument of God, sweeping away corruption, restoring the good life that had been meant for man, establishing God's kingdom here on earth. By 1520–1521 Germany was in turmoil. The pamphlet war raged everywhere. There was trouble in the streets and in the churches. Priests were attacked and monks insulted. The word—which had been sufficient for Luther—was now made flesh, in acts, in agitation and, lastly, in rebellion.

Inevitably, many preachers carried Luther's evangelical ideas much further than he would want to see. Men like Karlstadt (1480?–1541) and Thomas Münzer (1489?–1525), envisaging a Christianity of the Elect, living in saintly communism, awaiting an early end of the world, soon came to preach what amounted to social revolution. It was the powerful and the rich, they said, who kept the masses from salvation by keeping them too poor, too ignorant, too harassed, to pray and read the Bible. Religious reformation could only come through social reformation,

hence social revolution. Such arguments encouraged first the great peasant rising of 1524–1525, then the rise of Anabaptism which culminated
in the terrible siege of Münster (1534–1535).

Anabaptists and Evangelical Reformers

The story of the Anabaptists provides an instance of the lengths to which
the radical Christianity of some reformers could extend. Born in southern Germany, where it was equally persecuted by Lutherans and Catholics, Anabaptism very quickly made converts among peasants, workers,
and the poor. Carried into northern Germany and the Netherlands, by
the 1530's it had been recognized as a dangerously corrosive force.
Short on doctrine and long on mysticism, its prophets announced the
end of the world when God would come to judge the quick and the dead.
Their news appealed to the yearnings of the popular masses. Apocalyptic, the spokesmen rejected the established order, dismissed together
church and priests, property and government with its structure of magistrates, soldiers, and contracts. All these were worldly and, being
worldly, evil. The just, the pure, the saved would set up their own
city of God, where men would be equal and free, where all distinctions
would dissolve in a community of charity and love.

One sees the profoundly revolutionary nature of such concepts and
why their holders were soon persecuted by a society and a state only too
well aware of their menace. Consciously or unconsciously many welcomed religious arguments for ceasing to pay taxes, denying the jurisdiction of the secular courts, rejecting the authority of social superiors
and opposing them. All this took concrete shape with the appearance in
1533 of one Jan Matthis of Haarlem, who, setting aside the earlier mood
of Christian resignation, began to preach the kingdom of God established
by the sword, the new Jerusalem founded on terror. In 1534 a rising by

The Siege of Münster. Landsmuseum, Münster.

his followers in Amsterdam proved a failure. In 1535 a disciple of Matthis, John of Leyden, would find his Jerusalem, his death, and that of many others at Münster, a city in Westphalia. When Münster had fallen and John with his lieutenants hung in iron cages from the cathedral towers, all Christendom knew that Anabaptists had to be hunted down like mad dogs, even though most of those surviving reverted to a softer apocalysm. Until mid-sixteenth century, Anabaptists would furnish the majority of the victims of the Inquisition, with even advocates of tolerance considering them too dangerous to have around.

The bulk of evangelical reformers had long before that dissociated themselves from such activities. So had Luther. Rebellion, democracy, social transformations, were not what Luther wanted, nor what he preached. Outside the heart, the work of reform was to be performed not by Mr. Everyman—*Herr Omnes*—whose task was to obey, but by the proper authorities: if not the Pope, then the Emperor; if not the Emperor, the territorial princes. This is one reason why Luther reacted violently to the rebellion of men who not only went far beyond his purpose but who denied those authorities which alone could and should apply the values he refurbished.

It would be fair to say that Luther was no Lutheran: not the man of a new church, let alone of a radical revolution. The peasants had looked to him as champion of the oppressed and foe of tyrannies. Profound misunderstanding: he could not countenance their brandishing the gospels against their lords and princes. God alone, who made them, could humble secular authorities. Man's only true freedom is spiritual. All else must lead to anarchy and must be the devil's work. The bloody chaos of the first peasants' rising had persuaded Luther of the political incompetence of common people. In such extraordinary times, Luther declared, "a prince could earn the kingdom of heaven more easily by shedding blood than others by their prayers." Had he come by 1525 to contradict his earlier positions? It is more likely that he was reaffirming his belief that the city of God lay elsewhere and that men in this world could only try to merit it, not install it. Citizens of the heavenly city—at least by aspiration—men must live the lives they can while they are here below. Accepting, not rebelling; carrying out the function God has assigned to them. Here was the groundwork of Lutheran Germany.

Men could not simply resign from the secular order, set up their own communities and rule themselves according—as they saw it—to the law of God. They must be ruled by those whom God had set above them, the magistrates and princes entrusted with the task. Man's relations with divinity could be direct. He needed no intermediary but, often, a teacher. This was the didactic function the church had to fulfill. The church was not a representative or governing institution but part of the social structure, subordinate to the secular magistrate or to the prince, a state church loyal to the state it served.

Such views were reassuring to the men of power and of property alarmed by the apparent connection of reformed ideas and social upsets. Even a friend of Luther and Erasmus, the Nürnberg patrician and humanist, Willibald Pirkheimer (Dürer's best friend), had bitterly criticized the evangelicals in the 1520's for being "altogether disunified and divided into sects, which must run their course, like the fanatical peasants, until they at last go mad. God preserve all pious men, lands and people from such a doctrine that where it enters there is no peace, quiet or unity."

The stand taken by Luther in 1525 discouraged the popular radicals who did not count for much as a political force, but quieted the fears of the men who did. Saxony, Prussia, Hesse, Brandenburg, Schleswig, Brunswick, Mansfeld, besides a score of cities, supported Luther. By 1529 their protests against the Catholic majority at the imperial Diet of Speyer provided the party with a name (Protestants) and with a statement of principle*: "in matters which concern God's honor and salvation and the eternal life of our souls, everyone must stand and give account before God for himself."

The movement continued, in war as well as peace: Cleves, the Palatinate, Würtenberg joined the Protestants. So did the Scandinavians, by mid-century firmly in the Lutheran camp. In Antwerp and in Paris, the first reformation martyrs were burned in 1523; in Scotland five years later. In England, Thomas Cromwell, who helped Henry VIII break with Rome, did not conceal his Lutheran sympathies. In every case, however, church reform worked in the direction of strong monarchy. It is significant that where, as in Spain and in France, the crown had secured control over the national church (or where, as in Italy, the church was most obviously national) Protestantism could not really win. If Luther, after 1517, liked to sign his name as *Eleutherius*—the Liberator—the liberation that he brought was strictly qualified, from the political and also from the spiritual point of view.

The enthusiasm of German humanists who hailed Luther as the German Cicero or Hercules should not make us forget that the emancipation which he brought from mass, religious vows, ecclesiastical celibacy, fasts, and other traditional forms was only most distantly related with the humanist emphasis of man's individuality and dignity. True, Luther's man reflects the God of truth and beauty who created him in His image, who gave him reason and learning as He gave flowers and sunshine to the world. But the mirror is cracked, man's relation to God flawed beyond repair, or at least, beyond human repair, by the original sin and the inevitable corruption resulting therefrom. From this there could be no escape without the further intervention, without the grace of God. It is not enough (as Erasmus would have it) for man to will, for man to work his way to Christianity and to salvation. It is not enough for

* The theologians had been unable to agree on a declaration of faith.

John Calvin.

man to perform his given duties, rituals, conscientiously (as the church would have it). God must intervene uncalled, arbitrary, and free before man can be saved. The initiative does not rest in man but in the call of God. And this would be carried to its logical extreme in John Calvin's theory of predestination.

Calvin

Misogynist, insomniac, monomaniac like all geniuses, a powerful will in a sickly body, articulate, stubborn, well-educated and drawing on an excellent memory, John Calvin (1509–1564) represents, so to speak, the following generation—the men who drew the conclusions of the revolution which gripped them while they were still young. A Frenchman who had pursued humanistic and legal studies, Calvin broke with Catholicism in 1534, sought refuge in the Protestant cities to the east of France, finally in 1541 settled at Geneva, a city then hardly 10,000 strong. There he would work and fight until his dying day, turning his new home into the fortress of a new protestantism.

Luther had rejected one tradition by appealing to an older one, broken with one institution only to turn to another, rebelled—it seemed to many—only to end in a new conformity. Calvin abandoned institutions and traditions to rely on Scripture, on Christ alone, on grace and faith, above everything else on all-powerful God. Though he agreed with Luther that man was justified by faith and works availed him nothing, logic carried him to formulate the harsher implications of predestination—of man's dependence on the eternal plan of God.

There can be no salvation without predestination. Men picture God in their own image and Calvin outlined one who reflects himself: self-sufficient in his unlimited power, implacably strong-willed, coldly intelligent, a god who never changes and never changes his mind.* There is no knowing God for "his majesty is hidden far from all our senses." The only glimpse we get of the divine mystery is through the Scriptures, His revelation to us, a mirror of God for those who have faith. But faith is a free gift: "the mysteries of God are only understood by those to whom it is given." God elects men to eternal life or condemns them to be eternally deprived of him, hence damned, according to His pleasure, to His grace, which nothing but His own will affect, which man can do nothing to deserve or, for that matter, reject; and which manifests itself in the life, the character, in every action of the elect. Right thinking, right living, good works, are not the means but the expression of salvation; constant self-interrogation, self-examination, the only way to ascertain whether God has chosen one or not. But once the conviction has been gained, the joy, the gratitude, can only act as a powerful spur to the service of the Master, of His word, to sacrifice and sanctification of self and of the world which owes God obedience and praise as its creator, its ruler, and its lord.

Here was a view of God cut out for very strong men, tough, vigorous, confident, who accept the image because they might have invented it themselves. It—too—reflected the warlike, knightly, monarchic ideas of its time. It turned the convert into a Christian soldier, offering him a doctrine of energy and action, reviving the holy wars of the Old Testament to defend the New, transposing current theories of knightly honor onto a Christian plane. No wonder Calvinism appealed to the nobility—in France, in Scotland, Poland, Transylvania, and the Netherlands. It also prospered among artisans and peasants in France, Scotland, and the Netherlands; but did less well among the prosperous bourgeoisie, reluctant to strike out where it did exist. By 1570, 50 per cent of the French nobility, 30 per cent of the bourgeoisie were Protestant. Yet a good number of the refugees pouring into Calvin's Geneva were neither poor nor noble. Merchants, printers, manufacturers, physicians, lawyers, scholars, reflected both the greater commitment of educated men and their greater readiness to uproot themselves when compared to peasants or to gentry, tied to their land by necessity as well as choice.

Perhaps the Calvinist appeal is best understood less in a purely social than in a political context. To know oneself saved is good. To know one's foes damned is better. Contrary to Lutheranism which allied with rulers where it could, helping them to assert or to increase their power, Calvinism appeared in the guise of a fighting faith, often allied with the po-

* Nor did Calvin. In his dying speech to the pastors of Geneva, he asked them to make no changes or innovations, "because all changes are dangerous."

litical opposition. Calvin himself respected secular authority as much as Luther, reserved the punishment of wicked magistrates to God, prohibited resistance to their orders. But God's authority was above the princes and where He could not prevail, the Calvinist found the ultimate authority no longer outside but within himself, and this only too often drove him to revolt.

Predestinarian and congregationalist, the Calvinists made up their own political order where Lutherans respected established institutions. Where Lutherans were opportunistic, Calvinists were totalitarian in their creed. Their certainty, their independence, the kind of self-determination they affirmed within the world, imposed a change of character wherever it was established for some time, turning self-indulgent Geneva into a sober, earnest town; turning the Scots from a bunch of improvident, dissolute toughs, into a nation of dour, enterprising citizens; instilling all with a sense of progress—since, progress being measured by the degree of change, the change which they imposed convinced beholders that they were engaged in moving forward.

If this was the case, the first stages of the move were effected in great confusion. In England Parliament and Convocation (the church assembly) took the Church of England out of Rome at Henry VIII's behest in 1534, toward Geneva under Edward VI (1547–1553), back to Rome under Mary (1553–1558), and finally settled into a middle ground between Catholic and Calvinist under Elizabeth (1558–1603). The final break with Rome came only with Elizabeth's excommunication, to be confirmed in 1588 by the failure of the Spanish Armada to reconquer the kingdom for Catholicism. In Scotland reformed ideas spread under James V (1528–1542), were repressed under Mary Stuart, revived after mid-century in triumph with John Knox and the establishment of the Presbyterian Church only in 1560.

The situation was just as unsettled in other countries, and sometimes expressed itself in paradoxical acts. When Henry VIII died in 1547, Francis I ordered a funeral oration delivered in the Catholic cathedral of Notre Dame. The French explorer Villegagnon, who traveled to Brazil in 1555–1558, though favorable to reformed ideas, never thought this implied a breach with Rome. In sixteenth-century Germany, Catholic traditions and Protestant sentiments often went together. Many villages ignored the label under which they worshiped, priests officiated according to Lutheran or to Catholic rite as pleased the local lords. In Zurich, the local reform leader and sometime priest Ulrich Zwingli kept all the festivals dedicated to the Virgin Mary and the Angelus Bell tolled to commemorate the incarnation. Princes like William the Silent of the Netherlands passed from Catholicism to Lutheranism to Calvinism. Henry IV, born a French Protestant, became a Catholic after the massacre of St. Bartholomew, returned to Calvinism as soon as he could, recanted to the Roman church in 1593 to be crowned as most Christian King of France in 1594.

The Catholic Reformation

Meanwhile, the Catholic counteroffensive was getting under way. The Protestant challenge which first made talk of reformation suspect, had to be met with serious attempts at reorganization and reform.

The Reformation had grown out of a religious revival which, after and beyond its destructive outbreak, continued to run its course among the Catholics as with the Protestants. The fifteenth-century mystics had sixteenth-century heirs who culminated with St. Theresa of Avila (1515–1582) and St. John of the Cross (1542–1591). They seized on that portion of God to be found in every human soul as a kind of Jacob's Ladder on which to raise themselves into communion with God, annihilate themselves in God, in love, in ecstasy of oneness with Him—experiences which, once they have been enjoyed, leave the heart and soul uniquely dedicated to God's service. A similar experience, within a much more highly disciplined structure, would be enlisted by Ignatius Loyola into the service of his Society of Jesus, founded in 1532, approved by the Pope eight years later, destined to become the most dynamic and effective support of Roman Catholicism.

Open to the individualism of the mystics, more accessible to the public in the cultural and charitable work of the Oratorians (founded 1516) or the didactic and political labors of the Jesuits, the Catholic reaction became repressive with the foundation in 1542 of the Holy Office of the Roman Inquisition. It was Cardinal Caraffa (later Pope Paul IV, 1555–1559) who reformed the old Roman Inquisition, shaping it on the more successful Spanish model. In 1543 the Holy Office moved against subversive books and printers. In 1559 appeared the first index of forbidden books. Strict censorship and the activities of the Inquisition forced the unorthodox into conformity or exile, helped stifle Italy's busy intellectual life and turn it into the cultural desert which it remained (outside the plastic arts) until the nineteenth century.

All culminated in the work of the Council of Trent (1545–1564), where the authority of tradition, of the church, and of the hierarchy were reaffirmed. Scripture, indeed, is holy but it is not everything. Christ himself said that there would be further revelations through the agency of the Holy Ghost. Christian doctrine is not something given once for all times, but a progressive revelation interpreted, publicized, and applied by the church away from which no salvation is possible, only heresy. A catechism of belief published in 1556, an approved edition of the Bible—the *Vulgate* (1592), embodied this reaffirmation; the Inquisition affirmed it; the Catholic princes applied it in Poland, in the Empire, and throughout the Latin world.

The Break Established

It is well to remember that the Reformation of the early sixteenth century—the first reformation that ends with the death of Luther in 1546 and that of Calvin in 1564—did *not* mean to break with the church, to set up a new church or churches, to divide Christendom, but to reform quite literally church and religion, to purify, revive, reintegrate them into lives, souls, and societies. There was certainly no intent to secularize (this came from laymen) and, if the reformers suppressed monks and priests, it was because they wanted all to be monks and priests living lives dedicated to God, praying and laboring in his praise in great convent-cities such as Geneva (briefly) aspired to be.

However, the unintentional and the unexpected happened. That this created a new situation was not immediately evident; but it is clear now that by the second half of the sixteenth century Europe was settling into the new situation. Not without trouble, not without dismay, not without painful struggles which scarred the remainder of the century. But ideological differences could not suppress a unity more basic, for it was founded on a common culture and on common economic needs, a vast community of civilized intercourse (even in war) which could be dissolved only by dissolving civilization itself.

English Newfoundlanders continued to furnish Catholics with their Lenten fish. The papal mines at Tolfa still furnished English dyers with the alum they needed for their trade. In the great church at Gouda, in the Netherlands, Protestant stained-glass windows follow the Catholic ones: Philip II and William the Silent face each other despite the fury of their conflict. Protestant artists decorated Catholic churches or, like Rembrandt (in some of his etchings, such as those of the Virgin's Death) bid for the Catholic trade. Rubens and Van Dyck, friends of the Jesuits, worked for the English court. The Jesuits in their schools used the books of Erasmus and even of Melanchthon, the Lutheran divine.

Thus, when we speak of what the Reformation left behind, we speak not of two cultures but of one. There was for instance an anti-intellectual trend in both the camps. The Catholic counter-reformation suspected the subversive activities of scholars, only mildly devoted to the church at best. Among the Protestants, too, many preachers inveighed against study, teaching that children should be trained rather to manual labor. Study was good when limited to Scripture, a dangerous diversion otherwise and one not favored by the princes, who, following the territorialization of education as of the church, were now increasingly in control. Besides, many of the simpler people had in the past been

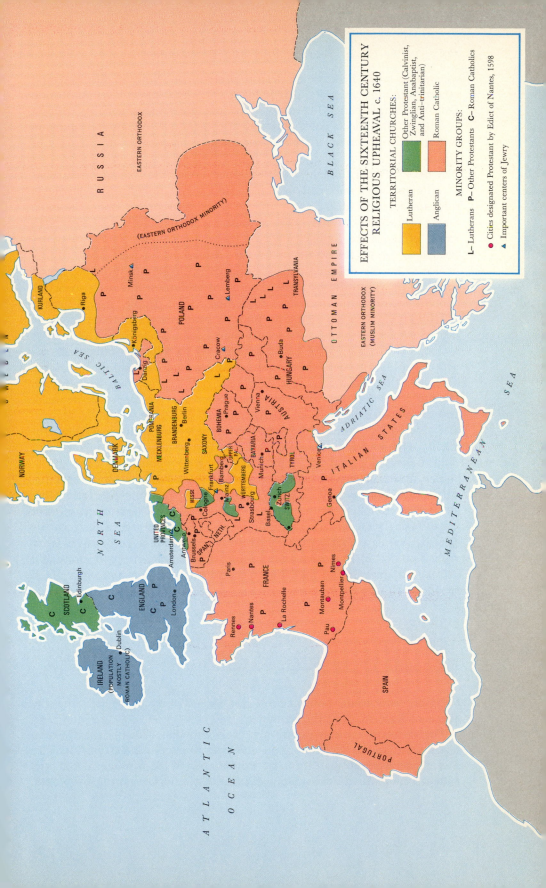

EFFECTS OF THE SIXTEENTH CENTURY
RELIGIOUS UPHEAVAL c. 1640

TERRITORIAL CHURCHES:

Lutheran

Other Protestant (Calvinist,
Zwinglian, Anabaptist,
and Anti-trinitarian)

Anglican

Roman Catholic

MINORITY GROUPS:

L– Lutherans   P– Other Protestant   C– Roman Catholics

● Cities designated Protestant by Edict of Nantes, 1598

▲ Important centers of Jewry

RUSSIA

EASTERN ORTHODOX

(EASTERN ORTHODOX MINORITY)

BLACK SEA

OTTOMAN EMPIRE

EASTERN ORTHODOX
(MUSLIM MINORITY)

KURLAND

Riga

Minsk ▲

Lemberg ▲

POLAND

Königsberg ●

Danzig

Cracow ▲

POMERANIA

BRANDENBURG

Berlin ●

MECKLENBURG

SAXONY

Wittenberg ●

BOHEMIA

Prague ●

SILESIA

HUNGARY

Buda ●

TRANSYLVANIA

AUSTRIA

Vienna ●

BAVARIA

Munich ●

TYROL

Venice ▲

HESSE

Frankfurt

Bamberg ●

Mainz ●

Cologne ●

WÜRTTEMBERG

Strasbourg ●

Basel ●

Zürich ●

SWITZ.

Genoa ●

ITALIAN STATES

ADRIATIC SEA

NORWAY

SWEDEN

DENMARK

BALTIC SEA

NORTH SEA

UNITED
PROVINCES

Amsterdam ▲

Antwerp ▲

Brussels ●

SPAN.
NETH.

Paris ●

FRANCE

Rennes ●

Nantes ●

La Rochelle ●

Montauban ●

Pau ●

Montpellier ●

Nîmes ●

SPAIN

PORTUGAL

SCOTLAND

Edinburgh ●

ENGLAND

London ●

IRELAND
(POPULATION
MOSTLY
ROMAN CATHOLIC)

Dublin ●

ATLANTIC OCEAN

MEDITERRANEAN SEA

spurred to study in hope of clerical preferment. Now, in England and other Protestant countries, this inducement would be lacking. As Bishop Latimer complained, "There are none but great mens' sons in colleges and their fathers look not to have them preachers." In Catholic countries ecclesiastical preferment, too, depended more on birth than on study or ability.

A new political thought also developed under the strains and stresses of religious war: not really new in essence, but delving into medieval tradition to stress ideas appropriate to the changed conditions. Catholics facing Elizabeth or Henry IV, Protestants facing Philip II, needed a frame of reference to justify revolt. Both Jesuits and Protestants concerned to prove the right to depose irreligious princes declared the prince to be the delegate and minister of the community, which could remove him rightfully by force if he tried to impose his religion or his heresy upon it. Authority comes from God to the people, argued French Calvinists and also the Spaniard Juan de Mariana (1536–1624). It is the people who entrust authority to the prince, who keeps it just as long as he keeps God's law. When he no longer does so, when he fails them, the people acting through their elders and through magistrates (through the estates of the realm, says Mariana) can deprive him of his rule. Having become a public enemy, the prince may be opposed, deposed, and even killed. Rebellion or tyrannicide could be a public service; and this would prompt the murders of heretical princes (William the Silent, Henry III, Henry IV) and justify political rebellion on every side: in Scotland, England, France, and the Netherlands.

The traditional right to rule was being replaced by a new reasoning, which called on natural rights derived not from custom but from God, and vested no longer in the prince but the people. This concept did not help to clarify the situation, it only introduced more arguments into the existing welter of ratiocination. However, it made certain that, faced with a choice of doctrines, men would draw their interpretations and deductions according to their interests and to the circumstances in which they found themselves.

Economic Effects of the Reformation

Religion, education, politics, one last strand remains to describe the effects of Reformation: the economy.

The sixteenth-century public was gross and materialistic: the German lands were famous for eating and drinking to excess; a sixteenth-century Florentine warned that his city would end by drowning in Chianti; Rabelais symbolized the contemporary heroes in his *Gargantua* and *Panta-*

gruel. No wonder the great reformers were also great apostles of temperance; and, like them, the Catholic counter-reformation waged war against alcoholism as it did also against beggars.

However, some of the economic virtues seem to have been more marked among the Protestants. The relative sobriety instilled by their ideas, the avoidance of ostentation and of the brilliant gewgaws of baroque art, encouraged saving and the accumulation of capital. It has been suggested that the property losses suffered by the church which once directed a considerable part of its revenues to artistic investment forced artisans and artists in Reformation countries to turn from quality to quantity production—thus explaining "a first industrial revolution" in the 1540–1640 period in Protestant countries like England, Sweden, and the United Provinces of the northern Netherlands.

But this is a very relative consideration. Some of the greatest sixteenth-century capitalists were Catholics; and even Luther's first German opponent, John Eck (1486–1543) of Ingolstadt in Bavaria defended commercial capitalism and interest on loans. Luther, the economic conservative, denounced greed, usury, and avarice with all the fire of a medieval preacher, but left economic decisions to the individual conscience. This opened the door to every transgression of old-fashioned Christianity. Calvin, more modern, was no more "progressive" than the fifteenth-century Franciscans who had launched the municipal pawnshops to protect the poor. He would have liked to banish usury from the world but "since this is impossible" resigned himself to come to terms with what he called common utility. In 1547 Genevan regulations allowed loans at no more than 5 per cent. In 1568 the state of Geneva organized a loan service with an interest rate of 10 per cent. The Calvinist virtues themselves so often quoted remind one of the fourteenth-century Florentine Alberti who praised economy, blamed idleness and prodigality, advised that expenses should never exceed revenues, and insisted on doing everything with a "holy spirit of order."

The world was changing fast, the Protestants were expressions of this change before they changed even further with it. All over Europe a new mentality was taking shape: individualism, rationalism, interest in efficiency, in gain, in new techniques permitting both, but also in administration, in law, in history and accuracy and exact knowledge as opposed to tradition, approximation, and hearsay. None of these did Protestantism create, all of them it accelerated.

It was once thought that Protestantism fostered the rise of the capitalist mentality by removing doctrinal obstacles to every kind of gain and giving the profit motive free rein. But there is no necessary connection between Protestant fervor and capitalist enterprise. Scotland, Norway, Sweden, remained backwaters although reformed; France and Milan continued to thrive despite their allegiance to Rome; Spain and the Italian cities entered economic decline only in the seventeenth century, for largely political causes. It might be best to forget direct correlations of an economic kind and look at the excitements—and eventual cooling— of religious passions. What did occur in the long run was a secularization of values. Most recent students of the sixteenth century agree that Protestantism was born out of desperate efforts to return to sources, to apostolic teachings, and to apply the message rediscovered to private and public life in order to bring about both spiritual and institutional reform.

When the reformers brought salvation out of the cloister into everyday life, when they replaced private mortification by social duty, contemplation by striving, the virtues of poverty by those of work, they went counter to accepted Christian concepts which looked on the beggar as an image of Christ and on the world as evil or, to say the least, regrettable. Yet the tendencies they formulated were already there. The reformers rationalized and justified practices increasingly common throughout the West, Catholic or not. Having provided them with justification, they released men from the necessity of shame and of dissembling, advanced the development of a new mentality, encouraged the formulation of quite new concepts, unsuspected by the reformers, far more secular, far less religious than Calvin or Luther would have contemplated.

PART II

Early Modern Europe

1559-1715

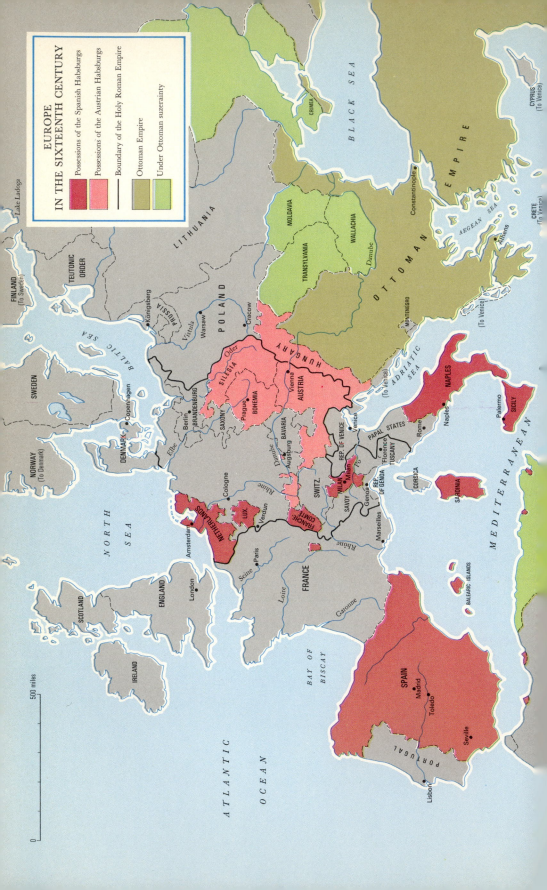

Possessions of the Spanish Habsburgs
Possessions of the Austrian Habsburgs
Boundary of the Holy Roman Empire
Ottoman Empire
Under Ottoman suzerainty

Lake Ladoga

FINLAND
(To Sweden)

TEUTONIC
ORDER

NORWAY
(To Denmark)

SWEDEN

DENMARK
Copenhagen

LITHUANIA

PRUSSIA
Königsberg

POLAND
Vistula
Warsaw
Cracow

BALTIC SEA

Elbe
Berlin
BRANDENBURG
SAXONY
Prague
BOHEMIA

SILESIA

HUNGARY
Vienna
AUSTRIA

BAVARIA
Augsburg
Danube

LITHUANIA

MOLDAVIA

TRANSYLVANIA

WALLACHIA

Danube

BLACK SEA

CRIMEA

OTTOMAN EMPIRE

Constantinople

MONTENEGRO

(To Venice)

AEGEAN SEA

CRETE
(To Venice)

Athens

CYPRUS
(To Venice)

NORTH
SEA

SCOTLAND

IRELAND

ENGLAND
London

NETHERLANDS
Amsterdam

Cologne

Rhine

Verdun
LUX.

Seine
Paris

FRANCHE
COMTÉ

SWITZ.

MILAN
Milan

SAVOY

REP.
OF GENOA
Genoa

Marseilles

Rhône

REP. OF VENICE
Venice

PAPAL STATES
Florence
TUSCANY
Rome

Po

CORSICA

SARDINIA

NAPLES
Naples

Palermo
SICILY

MEDITERRANEAN

ADRIATIC
SEA

(To Venice)

FRANCE

Loire

Garonne

BAY
OF
BISCAY

BALEARIC ISLANDS

SPAIN
Madrid
Toledo

Seville

ATLANTIC
OCEAN

PORTUGAL
Lisbon

500 miles

0

Continuity and Change

ON APRIL 3, 1559, the representatives of Henry II of France and Philip II of Spain affixed their signatures to the Treaty of Cateau-Cambrésis. A century and a half later, on April 11, 1713, France, Spain, England, and the United Provinces of the Netherlands agreed to the Treaty of Utrecht. During that time, we situate the beginnings of modern Europe: the crystallization of much that had gone before, and many new developments that no one in the Renaissance would have predicted.

One thing remained stable, and it explains the arbitrary limits chosen to mark the era. Almost everywhere, whether at Cateau or Utrecht, states were still personified by, identified with, their rulers. Collective memory bears this out when it divides history into reigns, and textbook chapters, like ancient chronicles, begin and end with the sound of coronation trumpets and the tolling of funeral bells. A number of such occasions converge around Cateau and Utrecht. In 1559, Elizabeth of England had reigned less than one year; Philip II had been king of Spain since 1556, after the abdication of his father, the Emperor Charles V, who died in 1558, just before the negotiations at Cateau began. Henry II of France died in June, 1559, less than three months after the treaty. In 1713, on the other hand, Louis XIV, who had been responsible for the great war that Utrecht ended, had two years left to live, Queen Anne of England, one. The two lists of names can easily symbolize two different eras: the former redolent of Renaissance (and Reformation), the latter already modern. They also reflect great changes in the status of the realms these princes ruled.

In 1559, the king of France was still an uncertain contender for European supremacy, overshadowed by his rivals: the Spanish Habsburgs. But the power of the French crown, weakened in the wake of Henry II's death, was to be reasserted after a new dynasty—that of the Bourbons—acceded to the French throne in the person of Henry IV (1589–1610). In 1713, King Henry's grandson ruled over France; and Louis XIV's own grandson reigned in Spain, where the descendants of Charles and of Philip II had petered out by 1700. Thus, two of the signatories of the Treaty of Utrecht were Bourbon princes, symbolically erasing the Pyrenean barrier between erstwhile rivals and marking the achievement of one dynastic dream.

The Habsburg dynasty survived in Vienna, where Charles V's imperial crown had gone in 1556. Slowly, painfully, the Vienna Habsburgs affirmed their power, less in divided Germany than by enlarging their own domains. In 1714, Charles VI (1711–1740) ruled in Vienna. He had claimed the throne of Spain, fought long and hard for it. Charles sent no emissaries to Utrecht, but continued the war with France alone, despite the settlement which denied his Spanish ambitions. The next few months saw the reward of his persistence. Cateau-Cambrésis had marked France's abandonment of her Italian dreams in Spain's favor. With the Treaty of Rastatt, signed in 1714, and included in the general peace of Utrecht, Austrian garrisons replaced Spanish ones in Italy, and the Spanish Netherlands that lay like a slender barrier between the United Provinces and France were taken over by Austria. Spain in Europe had been reduced to her territorial limits. In the long rivalry between Bourbon and Habsburg, the old role of Madrid henceforth fell to Vienna.

A third signatory of 1713 had not existed in 1559, when the Netherlands (and Utrecht itself) had been part of the dominions of the King of Spain. Revolt in the 1560's split the Netherlands in twain, long drawn-out war forged a new republic in their northern parts: the United Provinces, or Holland, as it was also known from the greatest of these provinces.

Queen Elizabeth of England, on the other hand, had been represented at Cateau-Cambrésis. At that time, her kingdom weighed only lightly in the balance compared to those of the other signatories, and Henry VIII's younger daughter had to tread warily. Since then, England had risen in the world. The Treaty of Utrecht confirmed her status as a world power, France's challenger for European supremacy, able to weight the balance of international conflicts in favor of the side which she chose to take.

England, too, had undergone dynastic changes. The Tudor strain, exhausted with Elizabeth's death in 1603, had been replaced by that of Scottish Stuarts. Their marriage alliance with a great Dutch family—the house of Orange—permitted the ouster of the reigning Stuarts in 1688, ensuring a Protestant succession without a formal change of dynasty. From 1688 to 1702 England was ruled by a Prince of Orange (William III) married to a Stuart princess, Mary. At the time of Utrecht the crown had passed to Mary's sister, Anne, but the essential had been preserved: Anne was Protestant, and so were her eventual successors.

Here was another novelty. In 1559, Protestantism had still been a menacing heresy. By 1713 it had become part of the general order of things. Philip II and Henry II composed their differences in part because each wished to be free to turn against the reformed heresy inside his territory, and Philip never ceased to hope that he might extirpate it in England, too. Since then, France and Spain had indeed been preserved for the Roman Church, but by 1713 the existence of Protestantism was no longer an issue of international politics. Profoundly anchored in popular sentiment, religion on the public plane had now become an affair of state, an item on the agenda of government rather than an integral part of life. The royal function was still placed under divine protection, the welfare of the realm was still ensured by the prayers of the local church, but even these conceptions were turning into pious rites, part of the armory of would-be absolute princes and of increasingly encompassing states.

All this came about through toil and bloodshed. Like men, kingdoms and institutions are born in pain and grow in labor. Our survey of early modern times will dwell on the pains and labor, but also on the positive results that they produced. The crystallization of the monarchy, the formulation of royal absolutism and the difficulties this encountered, the new roles of men and classes in society, the ideas and institutions such evolutions sparked, no less than the great episodes of international politics will be the major themes of the next three chapters.

Chapter 5

THE SEARCH FOR

NEW STRUCTURES

In Search of Order

We have seen that the opening chapters of the modern West appear as a rediscovery, a reassertion of individual man: the exceptional, heroic figure of the noble knight, the enterprising self-creating merchant, banker, and venturer, the artist asserting his will and imagination on plastic matter or political structure, the refined consciousness of the humanists and, finally, the individual conscience whose rights the Reformation affirmed, bear witness to an all-engrossing theme. The following period, by contrast, is more impersonal. It sees a search for structure, or, rather, many different quests to renew or replace the structures of a world that had become much broader, more complex, more confused; a world in which the reassuring routines of worship, habit, and social groups had broken down; in which new forces, problems, and values had been added to the old but never integrated. Social groups had changed their function, states had grown, economies had altered, units had broken down and other units formed. Change had wrought confusion—of place and duties, of authority, of who did what and how and by what right. The late sixteenth and the seventeenth centuries seem, in overview, to be devoted to a reordering task, the forging of attitudes and institutions—political and religious, social and mental—which would bring some means of control in this new-wrought world.

We shall see that the process was, like every historical process, painful, complicated, and haphazard, affected by the vision or ambition of a few, the inertia or malleability of many, by chance and accident and

185

sheer catastrophe. It took place piecemeal, so that only hindsight can suggest coherence. Yet it can be traced for some two hundred years, setting its mark on kingdoms and literature and church, on trade and science, and on the minds of men.

Diversities were gradually diminished: local particularisms swallowed by central authorities; medieval liberties and privileges—oppressive to outsiders, anarchic at home—suppressed. Bureaucracy developed—more laws, taxes, tax and census rolls, more, and eventually more secular, public servants who would take care of them. Religion, which reformation had brought into confusion, was disciplined. So, with a new stress on form, were the plastic arts and urban planning; and the pursuit of knowledge in academies. War, more terrible and on a vaster scale than ever, also suggested the need for regulation—by international law which grew out of its horrors and gradually by the self-discipline of the participants.

The sixteenth century was a time of revolution, the seventeenth was a time of war—organized, massive, its intense demands suggesting and enforcing the more effective structuring of the units taking part in it: states, subjects, armies. By 1700, the days of untrained rabble, temporary service, disparate small contingents, or enthusiastic knights lay in the past. Victory went to the large battalions, armed, trained, drilled, equipped, and uniformed as well as uniform.

Societies, like armies, became more specialized, the classes more exclusive. The social hierarchy of the Middle Ages had been part of a connecting chain between God and people. The social hierarchy of modern times became a kind of obstacle course—a series of enclosures for separate elites. Mobility increased as wars and the economy stirred up and shuffled men, but social barriers rose with social definitions. There was mobility and promotion from class to class as from place to place, but consciousness of status also changed and, with it, the will to defend this status and affirm it by keeping others out of it. Education, like society, became more exclusive, making the same divisions as social hierarchy, considering the station for which it should train men. It also became more systematic, reflecting the general concern for method and discipline.

The new ideal was order—new order thrusting out the old, drawing new maps, new plans for the heavens, new anatomies, envisioning nature and society and state as mechanisms, so that we can find the philosopher Leibniz recommending a new system of state administration to Peter the Great of Russia by likening its mechanism to that of watches—a simile which others used of men. But this order was evolved and imposed only imperfectly and by incredible efforts upon the men who bore it restively. The greatest struggles of the seventeenth century were waged between the partisans of custom and those of change, between the upholders of tradition and those of power. Yet it was need that made princes trespass upon local privileges in the name of *salus populi* (the

good of the people), which had to be *suprema lex* (the supreme law).
Only what that good was—and whose—was not agreed upon by all.
Method and system, symmetry and restraint were less the reward of good
administration than of exhaustion, coercion, and constraint. Discipline
appeared as the obverse of wildness, the self-curbing extremity of a
brutal world.

The Way of the World

The shape of states without and their institutions within, their international rivalries and the solutions they find for internal strains, im-
pinge on private life and, even more heavily, on men's consciousness.
Men retain the names of warriors and statesmen more readily than those
of thinkers or inventors. Battles prove more memorable than reforms,
and coronations than agricultural improvements. And, yet, we know
that the evolution of attitudes, techniques, social groups, institutions—
less striking as a rule than wars, less definable than a given reign—reveal
the benchmarks of another and perhaps profounder history.

Like ideas, politics receive their meanings from people. The bare account of politics comes to life because men act, interpreting and applying ideas in laws, works, gestures, and controversies. This is where we
must search for the substructure of the traditional tale, beginning not
with wars and monarchies but with more pedestrian themes: the world
and the everyday life of early modern man.

Not that, in this as in any period, politics were separate from everyday affairs. Far from it. But they affected them from outside, external
agents very much like the weather; and it is well to describe the stage,
the living, aching base, on which soldiers and priests, princes and
scholars, played out their costly and complicated game. Most men, of
course, spend most of their time just making a living. Their values
would be the values which helped them do this; and the higher aspirations which we note and study, while influential in certain spheres, had
somehow to come to terms with the harsh necessities of operating in a
difficult material world in which the chief business of man was to stay
alive.

Population

During the sixteenth century this task had been pursued with impressive
results and population had risen notably. In Castile it doubled between
1530 and 1594, from 3 to 6 million; in Sicily it increased by two-thirds or
better: 600,000 in 1501, over 1 million in 1570. By 1600, the population
of Spain reached around 8 million, that of Portugal 1 million, that of
France 16 million, that of Italy 12 or 13 million, that of Turkey 16 million (half in Europe and half in Asia), that of England and Wales 4

million. Across the Mediterranean, Egypt held 2 or 3 million, North Africa as many.

The most densely populated countries were still inhabited quite sparsely: in Italy an average of seventy-one people lived in one square mile, in France fifty-five, in Portugal and Spain only twenty-seven. This is a very light population density; between relatively heavily settled zones like Lombardy or the Loire Valley there stretched regions practically deserted—much of Aragon, parts of Andalusia and Provence, mountainous districts everywhere, in Corsica, the Balkans, or the French Cévennes—occupied by wild animals and a few humans no less wild. Fifty years later, in mid-seventeenth century, the population of Europe numbered some 100 million. Much of the sparsely inhabited countryside ran under forest or squelched in undrained marshlands, treacherous to strangers. The gentry lived in fortified manors or castles, the peasants in huts of mud or wattle more often than of stone. The roads, difficult at all times, impassable in bad weather, were threatened by wolves and lined with the dangling bodies of robbers, reminders of the danger from their living mates.

The advance by the mid-seventeenth century that we can witness in some countries favored by peace, weather, and economic enterprise—France, England, the United Provinces of the northern Netherlands—was more than matched by the decline of others: Spain, Italy, Poland, Hungary, southern Germany, and the southern or Spanish Netherlands, where war and economic decline caused population to decrease. The balance of population, like that of wealth and power, shifted from the south to the west and northwest of Europe. How this happened, the following chapters will show.

Warder Collection

A model plan of the city of Münster drawn in 1641.

The Corn Harvest by Pieter Brueghel (the Elder). The countryside and those who work in it become a subject fit to hang on the walls of princes. Metropolitan Museum of Art.

Agricultural Conditions

The limits of a population are set by the capacity to feed it. With the exception of England and the Netherlands, the agricultural economy of the sixteenth and seventeenth centuries did not differ much from that of the fourteenth or fifteenth. The Middle Ages had introduced horse-shoes, stirrups, more effective harnessing and yoking methods, wind-mills to supplement water mills. Short sickles had been replaced with more efficient scythes for harvesting (though the former survived in parts of France until the eighteenth century and in the east far longer); churns were improved to turn milk into butter more efficiently. The greatest changes after the fourteenth and the fifteenth centuries were less technological than structural, and stemmed from the inflation which ruined feudal landowners living off fixed rents: not inventions or inno-vations, but piecing together land for more efficient exploitation. Where this happened, especially in Italy and the western lands, the former landlords were usually replaced by buyers belonging to the merchant *bourgeoisie* which profited from the price rise. Under their management, subsistence agriculture gave way to production for profit, less for consumption than for sale. Bourgeois landowners kept only a small part of their harvests and sold the rest. In Florence one can still see the wickets beside palace gates through which the porters sold the wine or oil produced on family domains.

The new structure suggests that these domains grew larger at the expense of the small farmer. Bourgeois or noble, as the sixteenth century turned into the seventeenth, large landowners squeezed out small. Land was the most profitable and safest of investments. Men bought it as they would buy state bonds in the nineteenth century or blue-chip stocks in the twentieth. They pieced it together slowly, painfully, sometimes taking over a century to accumulate a respectable estate out of scores of tiny parcels. Poor landholders found it harder to survive bad years, ran into debt, had to sell out to their better-off neighbors. Even when given lands, they had to sell them to their creditors so that, as Christopher Hill has put it, the rich inherited the earth.

> The law locks up the man or woman
> That steals the goose from off the common;
> But leaves the greater villain loose
> Who steals the common from the goose,

so ran the traditional jingle.

In mountainous or rugged country unfit for large estates, many small poor landowners survived. Swiss mountain cantons, the Tyrol, the Black Forest, Pyrenean valleys, Cévennes in south-central France, were abodes of free peasants and even free peasant communities. Plains and bottomlands lent themselves better to the constitution of large estates and there, while free peasants also increased in numbers as a rule, more and more of them might be landless, squeezed or bought out by wealthier farmers, moneylenders, or lords both secular and ecclesiastic.

Venerable legal practices contributed to the accumulation of land: *entail,* declaring estates inalienable in a particular line of succession, *mortmain,* placing lands in the "dead hand" of some corporation—usually an abbey or a chapter. Such trends, however ruinous to small men, dealt not with bodies (as in earlier centuries) but with property.

Meanwhile, cities, armies, the growing population everywhere in Western Europe, depended on food, far more than local lands provided and which had to come from the wheatlands of Poland and the Balkans, Romania and the Ukraine. Large estates producing for export needed many hands and these were tied to the soil by the interest of lords and of the princes who surveyed them, so that from the Baltic to the Black Sea and the Adriatic a new serfdom came to be established or asserted where freedom, anarchy, or local liberties once reigned. Thus, roughly east of the Elbe River personal servitudes on their way out elsewhere were being established or reinforced. There, large estates based on forced labor adapted an earlier manorial economy to new economic needs. Feudal forms and legalisms could be used to serve modern political objectives.

The knights of northeastern Germany—the Junkers—provide a prototype of conditions in the "colonial" areas east of the Elbe. There, the gentry whose chief business had been fighting turned to farming and used their political power to harness once-free peasants, their labor, animals, and tools to the noblemen's agrarian enterprises. Thus, peasants became serfs and were subjected to manorial justice at the very time when elsewhere tenure was shifting from men to real estate. We can contrast the growing economic dependency and legal subservience of serfs or sharecroppers on these *Gutsherrschaften* where lords practically owned their subjects and their subjects' property with the relative emancipation heralded by developments in the west; it is clear that they both reflected and affected differing political structures in these two parts of Europe.

In general, however, it is safe to say that more and more possessions were concentrated in the hands of a few powerful landowners, above all in northeast and eastern Europe but also in Italy, Spain, and the European west. The cities had expanded not only at the expense of the neighboring gentry but of the peasants too. Wherever possible, the bourgeois who replaced older feudal lords became lords and exploiters in their turn, more distant, more impersonal, and more persevering than the nobles they displaced, so that in some Swiss cantons and Netherland provinces peasants were not emancipated until the eighteenth century at the time of the French Revolution.

The new owners were interested in revenue, not innovation. Here and there new methods were tried, such as planting root crops like turnips and clover to provide cattle fodder through the winter. This afforded a supply of fresh meat in winter, scarce when most cattle had to be slaughtered and salted down before the hollow months. It also increased the supply of fertilizer that could be strewn on land which need no longer lie fallow and useless one year out of every two or three. The possibility of crop rotation was a great boon to production. So was the use of manure, as we can see from an agricultural reformer's hymn to compost: "It is manure," wrote Olivier de Serres in his *Theater of Agriculture* (1600), "which rejoices, warms, fattens, softens, sweetens, tames and makes easy lands which are angry and tired from being overworked, and those which are by nature cold, thin, hard, bitter, rebellious and difficult to work."

But for the most part compost remained scarce and lands difficult, as did their laborers and masters, reluctant then as now to change the time-tried practices inherited from their fathers. By the seventeenth century, the greatest advances had been accomplished in the Netherlands, where climate and urban development encouraged production for market and, especially, cattle-breeding. Holland exported so many milk products that at the court of Louis XIV the Dutch were known as "cheese-merchants"— an insult in French eyes, but to us evidence of their renown. But, until the end of the seventeenth century, until the eighteenth in fact, such enterprises remained exceptional. Food production by traditional methods stayed limited and utterly at the mercy of nature and of ill-disposed men: wasteful fallow lands cut up into small parcels, oversown with dirty seeds, scratched with wooden implements, were harvested with sickles for lack of scythes. A minority owned plows, let alone a team of cattle to provide traction power and manure. For those who did, 800-lb. oxen were considered fat. (Our cattle today average twice as much.) Such conditions meant that periodically population outran resources and famines were endemic, balancing off a birth rate which otherwise would have doubled the population every quarter century.

Food and Hunger

The crux of seventeenth-century economics lay in the capacity to produce more food. But the basic producer, the peasant, was drained and exhausted by the demands of his masters: lords trying hard to keep up with rising prices and standards of luxury, cities increasingly

Peasant women, a drawing by Hieronymus Bosch. Staatlichmuseen Preussischer Kulturbesitz, Berlin.

hidebound in management and views, states calling for more taxes to maintain their machinery, their wars and courts. None of these looked far beyond known methods of exploitation and peasants could think of no way out: all they knew was the pressure of landlords and tax-collectors and the relentless round of harvests, of which the better only bred too many mouths to feed and the worst resolved this crisis by killing them off.

Attempts were made to produce a surplus. The first handbook on crop rotation came out in mid-sixteenth-century Italy, where maize also began to be grown in the Po delta, Lombardy, and Piedmont, and rice cultivation expanded tremendously so that by 1710 it covered as much ground as it does today. By 1700, maize and also cotton had spread throughout the Balkans, potatoes were being eaten in Ireland and England. Eventually the economical potato, with its high yield of nourishment per acre and per man-hours needed to plant and harvest it, moved into northern Europe, too. It would spread slowly through the eighteenth century, become a staple in the nineteenth, an important factor in the expansion of Europe's population. But for the moment and for a long time to come, agriculture—especially the serf economies of eastern Europe—continued terribly inefficient and would remain so until the agricultural revolution that began in mid-eighteenth century.

For example, unrelieved cereal culture exhausted soils which manure seldom enriched. Land lay fallow every other year in the south, every two years in the north, so that at least two-fifths of working lands remained unproductive. Productivity was universally low, farmers underemployed, ill-fed, poor in health, short-lived. Half the infants died before they were one year old, one in four might live to be twenty, and survivors aged fast: a man would be considered old after the age of forty, a woman in poorer regions or classes after thirty. Recent population studies give the average life span of western Europeans in 1656–76 as twenty-one years, in 1700 as thirty. Their numbers were limited by the simple fact that every increase diminished the quantity of available food per head and raised mortality in consequence. The periodical shortages and famines disorganized agriculture, killed the working men or sent them wandering off to increase the pool of tramps and thieves and beggars. Their absence from the fields caused a further fall in production, further food shortages, further price increases, while the hunger, poverty, and underemployment which they carried outward from their sorry fields disorganized the urban economy after ravaging the countryside.

Death and hunger punctuated the life of most Europeans until about two hundred years ago, rising again and again to peaks of homicidal famine.*

---

* A recent work on the world's food has left us a partial list of the most important European famines in this period: 1556: France; 1558: England and France; 1560: France; 1563: Ireland and Great Britain; 1565: France; 1572–74: France; 1586: Ireland,

Oule gresle Maigret, fait boullir la marmite, Le Le gtos frere Lubin, s'en depesche a la fuite. **Maigre Cuisine.** | **Mager keucken.** Daer mager-man Cock is, boutmen sober bancketten. Waer om dat Broer Lubbert, neemt fijn vlucht byden vetten. bruegel inu. H. exendit.

An engraving that was roughly entitled *Slim Pickings,* by Pieter Brueghel (the Elder). A verse beneath the picture reads: "Where the gaunt, scrawny man stirs the boiling kettle, Fat brother Lubin makes off in fine fettle." Bibliothèque Nationale, Paris.

Most of these disasters were only local or regional, sharpened by transport difficulties and internal customs barriers, but some raged over whole countries, like the catastrophe which swallowed a third of Finland's sparse population in 1696–97. France, one of the richer lands, counted thirteen general famines in the sixteenth century, eleven in the seventeenth, sixteen in the eighteenth. Between 1375 and 1791 Florence experienced 111: one every four years as against only sixteen really good harvests over the same period. In 1662, a third of the people of Burgundy were eating grass and herbs.

Hunger in itself was nothing extraordinary. A Roman newsletter of February, 1558, records: "In Rome, nothing new, except that they die of hunger," and goes on to mention a banquet given by the Pope. Periods of scarcity were common. When bread was made of fern or bran, the strong survived and only the old or sick died off more quickly. Famines were times when entire villages, whole provinces, were ravaged; when bakers fought for flour at the city gates; when a seventeenth-century doctor found "a boy who had already eaten one of his own hands"

England, Hungary; 1587: France; 1588–89: Ireland; 1590–93: Paris (a hundred thousand died in three months); 1594: Hungary; 1594–95: England; 1595–98: France, Germany; 1601–03: Ireland; 1610: Saxony; 1621: France; 1629: Paris; 1630: England; 1649: Scotland and North England; 1693: Scotland; 1698: England, France; 1700: England; 1709: Scotland, England, France.

to keep alive; when populous villages were left deserted, the weak dying, the stronger wandering off to seek for nourishment or death elsewhere.

Nor was hunger all, for after hunger came sickness and plague. In the Catalan valley of Urgell, bad harvests in 1627, 1628, and 1629 were followed by an epidemic in 1630. In the countryside, notes the chronicle of the little town of Cervera, people "were eating nothing but grass and they arrived here all black or pallid and defunct, so that it caused pity to see them . . ."

Even when there was no famine, *especially* when there was no famine, population pressure alone increased demand for grain, so that Spain and Sicily, for instance, which once exported grain, imported it by the end of the sixteenth century in Dutch and English and Hansa ships, but also by cart and mule. This meant more trade; it also meant more transport and that in turn more horses and mules for traction. But this meant more fodder was consumed, thus taking up for fodder the land once used for grain, and thereby contributing to the grain shortage, the higher prices, the general distress.

Cities, too, which had begun by playing a liberating role, became exploiters, leeches, weighing heavy on the countryside both near and far. Each city, it has been said, was a vast stomach. The greatest of them, Constantinople—about 700,000 strong—devoured the wheat of the Black Sea, the fish of the Bosporus, the herds of the Balkans, the fruits of Anatolia, never-endingly and never satiated. In March, 1581, eight shiploads of Egyptian wheat sufficed to provide Constantinople with exactly one day's food. But ships were scarce, provisioning marginal. Even Madrid, far smaller, was said around 1600 to consume 50,000 sheep, 12,000 oxen, 60,000 kids, 10,000 calves, 13,000 pigs a year. No wonder cities were always on the verge of famine.

All over Europe, the period between 1650 and 1750 was one of especially acute agricultural and general economic depression, punctuated by violent ups and downs that marked the psychologically depressed mood of the time. Climatic conditions contributed to frequent crop failures under violent rainstorms or severe drought. Yet, the grain imported from eastern Europe to allay the threat of famine depressed the cereal prices in the west, ruining many farmers. Over great stretches of Italy, Germany, and France farms lay abandoned, villages deserted, fields untilled, bare to wind and rain, prey to erosion, producing nothing but thistles, dust, and despair.

This had broad repercussions. Business suffered. Economic instability stifled development. In a world confined by physical limits, the causes of the instability were almost built-in, while one remedy—the previous influx of precious metals from European and overseas mines—grew scarce. Stocks of gold and silver which had increased tenfold in the sixteenth century hardly doubled in the seventeenth, while the need for them rose with the growth of commercial exchanges. Prices reflected this: they rose until about 1650, then they began to fall. Profits followed suit, capital accumulation became difficult, investment sources and possibilities shrank, economic expansion dragged, some enterprises foundered while others merely lagged, production diminished, unemployment rose with consequent social disorders and economic difficulties. Entrepreneurs pulled in their horns, looking for technical changes that might lower their production costs but avoiding also any enterprises which implied some risk. To bring some remedies to economic problems, to cope with social ones, central authorities increasingly intervened, either to arbitrate in social conflicts exacerbated by hard times or to initiate enterprises no longer spontaneously undertaken. But to do this, the king's officers must interpose more often, the king's taxgatherers must collect more taxes. On them most resentments focused and riots or rebellions became almost endemic in their turn—directed in almost every case against the royal agents and often led or sparked by local notables, whose functions the newcomers tended to usurp on behalf of the central power.

This was the grim background of the political unrest that marked the time, the scores of minor risings, the greater revolts in Naples, Catalonia, and Portugal within the Spanish Empire of the 1640's, the Ukrainian revolt of 1648–54, the Swiss Peasant War in 1653, the rebellions of the Cossack Stenka Razin in Russia (1672), of Irish or Bohemian peasants in the 1640's and 1680's. It is striking how rebellion, endemic in the countryside for centuries, would become much rarer in the west after conditions improved in the later eighteenth century. The main thing to note, however, is that all this time was often seared and gashed by terrible hunger crises, whose death rate may be compared to the worst figures of Auschwitz (30 per cent per year, one-third of the population) and that this dominated the life and mind of men. There would be fewer massive famines in England after the 1690's, in France after 1710, to cut the population as soon as it began to grow, to force men into eating children to keep alive, to set impassable limits to expansion. But, until then, food would remain the major issue of life.

Food means bread. Today, a working-class budget shows 1 to 3 per cent of expenses going toward bread and other cereals, and only a relatively small portion of total income devoted to all the food consumed. Before 1830 more than half the money spent on food went for bread; in working-class families it accounted for one-third to one-half of the total family budget. The prayer for daily bread reflected an overwhelming fact of life. With food consisting largely of soup and bread, most people spent their lives in what we would call a scorbutic condition. True, the situation differed in different regions and climates, yet it would seem to have varied largely between bad and worse.

The Swedish peasant's staple diet consisted of coarse bread, turnips,

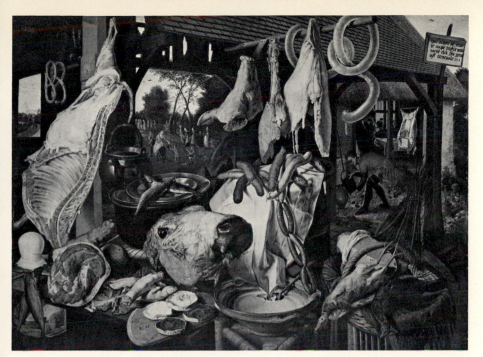

The Meat Stall, a painting by Pieter Aertsen, 1551. University College, Uppsala, Sweden.

and porridge. Civil servants working at Uppsala castle lived on bread, salt fish, salt meat, and beer. Half of the year no fresh meat was available. Milk was turned to butter and butter was salted and generally rancid. Bread made of bark was normal in bad times as late as the nineteenth century, and this seems to have been the least desperate of expedients to which hungry mouths were driven. In Iceland they used bones, heather, and horse droppings, as well as moss and flax seed. Some peasants made a regular practice of eating the bark bread, knowing that otherwise their stomachs could not digest it when, the harvest having failed, they had no choice.

If men did not live by bread alone, it can almost be said that they lived by grain alone. Beer and ale, both derived from grain, were consumed in vast quantities: soldiers on campaign got two gallons a day (Dutch soldiers in 1582 were issued two and a half gallons, Queen Elizabeth's men only one). Drunkenness was a normal feature of life almost everywhere and the introduction of distilled alcohols only facilitated it. There was little variety in food, as well, and only slight improvement. The introduction of potatoes in seventeenth-century Ireland allowed the Irish population to escape tithes based on grain production and live more cheaply, thus undercutting the English and Scottish immigrants brought into the north by Cromwell and his successors, who would eat only bread made of wheat or oats. Similarly, the introduction of maize in the southern Balkans about that time and in the Romanian principalities a hundred years later allowed the peasants to raise food for themselves which Ottoman consumers did not want and which the government did not tax. It gave them a new and plentiful food supply on which they increased in numbers and decreased the discontentment based on hunger, thus calming social unrest for awhile.

All this, of course, concerns the poor—that is, the great majority of the people. The comfortable minority could do much better, though even they ate rather much than well. Vegetables were generally despised, except for truffles and for artichokes—prized as aphrodisiacs—cabbages which were supposed to prevent baldness and give nurses milk, and, for some unfathomable reason, turnips. Dishes on the richer tables tended to spiciness, sometimes because the meat was not fresh, most often simply because palates enjoyed a spicy taste and doctors believed hot food to be good for the digestion. Mustard, ginger, honey, pepper —sometimes separate and sometimes mixed—titillated the palate, purified the blood, and cleared the bile of those who could afford them. In 1600, sugar was still a great luxury, so that if it appeared on a table it would be sprinkled even on the meat. The poor ignored it, using honey for sweetening when they could get it. Sugar only became a staple for the richer classes in the course of the seventeenth century, which is also when other exotic items were incorporated: coffee, useful against the creeping drowsiness of sermon-time; tea, good for nerves and vapors; tobacco, first used as a medicinal herb, snuffled as far back as 1558, widely smoked by 1600, provoking James I's *Counterblast to Tobacco* (1604) and a papal ban on its use in church.

Tea, too, first shipped to Europe by the Dutch in 1609, began as a luxury appreciated for its medicinal qualities: "Home and there find my wife making of tea," notes Samuel Pepys, on June 28, 1667, "a drink which Mr. Pelling, the potticary, tells her is good for her cold and defluxions." A popular beverage by mid-eighteenth century, tea competed with coffee, which had reached Paris by 1643 by way of Italy, Europe's staging point to Turkey and the Middle East. By the end of the seventeenth century Paris had two hundred and fifty coffeehouses, England, Germany, and Holland following suit. They took longer to spring up elsewhere and story has it that it was the vast quantities of Turkish coffee seized in the Ottoman camp when Vienna was delivered in 1683 which gave the Viennese public a taste for the new brew and launched their famous coffeehouse tradition.

Chocolate remained a luxury for a long time, although in 1657 a Frenchman opened the first chocolate-house in London and Pepys tells us he drank it in a coffeehouse in 1664. All these beverages needed sweetening and increased imports would reduce the price of sugar and make it increasingly accessible—though only in the eighteenth century. Wines, too, improved, though nowhere near their present-day level, and the 1670's are marked by the first production of port wine and also of what we now call champagne, when Dom Perignon, cellarer of a Benedictine abbey, not only invented the bubbly wine but replaced the hemp stoppers of his bottles with corks which made the fizziness possible. The success of champagne would be ensured by the favor of women, who loved its tingle and foam, and of Englishmen, who praised its sparkle. Yet, whatever the available luxuries, these were only for the few. Tainted meat, stinking fish, rancid butter, bread, wine or beer adulterated and eventually faked with poisonous chemicals, filthy water, these were the staples of the urban poor and, often, of the rich as well.

The peasants, we have seen, were often even worse off. St. Vincent de Paul, who knew the peasants well, called them "savage peoples." In England, where they were better off, they were called "beasts." In 1613 a French jurist who despised them reflected incidentally that they were "so oppressed by taxes . . . that one wonders how they can subsist and that husbandmen can still be found to feed us." The unconscious sting, as always, is in the tail. These oppressed husbandmen fed the rest, the little world that alone counted and which rested on their labor.

A Perilous Environment

To people such as these the hostility of nature seemed to present a threat that was continual and direct. Today our chief anxieties are rooted in human causes. Natural threats have not been eliminated but they have been explained, so that thunder or comets, while they may frighten us for a moment, are not the cause of significant and prolonged worry. This was not so before. In the countryside especially, all was a cause for fear. A sudden panic, generally focused on an innocent figure, could set off the murder of a lonely traveler suspected of God knows what, the lynching of a tax-gatherer, even a riot, which church bells could turn into a rising. There was no need of a specific source when there were so many latent insecurities always ready to burst out like the plague, which also slept but lightly beneath the harrowed surface. Superstition never slept in a world where everything continued to remain conceivable, where our differentiation between what is natural and what is not had hardly been formulated, where spells killed cattle and charms secured love, where processions wound through parched fields in order to bring down rain or secure fair weather for the countryside.

Taxes, famines, struggles between lords and cities, lords and kings, lords and other lords, war and the destruction in its wake, poor harvests, all brought recruits to bandit gangs which dominated much of the countryside, using the multitude of jurisdictions to pass from one into another. Don Quixote and Sancho Panza were to meet one of them just outside Barcelona and to be much impressed by the discipline

Hanging Thieves, an engraving by Jacques Callot, 1633.

which its leader, Roque Guimaro, imposed on his numerous followers. Italy especially was full of bandits, so that, particularly after a bad harvest, Rome and the other cities stood like isolated islands lapped by waves of outlawry. From the mountains into the plains, when hunger drove or opportunity allowed, brigands enlisted the hungry peasantry to whom pillage offered a last hope. They followed some rebel baron, sought to enlist in some army or other, entered into negotiations with popes or grand dukes eager to facilitate their movement out of their lands.

The soldiers who sometimes pursued the brigands were no better than they. Soldiers, peasants, bandits: here was a savage, brutalized world at the very base of society but at the margin of existence. Violence and precariousness marked its days and miles, its time and space and values. Torture was the standard method of inquiry, punishments were of the most gruesome kind: cutting off nose, ears, or the right hand, burning the tongue, putting out the eyes, opening the cheek, branding. Death could be by hanging (garrote in Spain) or beheading, drowning (sometimes in a barrel), burning, or burying alive. An Englishman traveling from Dresden to Prague found "above seven score gallowses and wheels" by the roadside, "where thieves were hanged, some fresh and some half-rotten, and the carcasses of murderers broken limb after limb on the wheel." When Huygens, the scientist, left Holland for Italy in 1620, he counted no less than fifty gibbets in about a hundred and twenty miles along the Rhine. Public executions stoked the slender store of entertainment. The strange shapes that punctuate the landscapes of the painter Hieronymus Bosch are wheels on stakes for highwaymen who were strung up on the spot where they had been caught. Burning cats in a sack suspended over a pyre provided another popular amusement.

The Way They Lived (and Died)

Most people, then, were less concerned with politics or diplomacy, with kings and wars, than they were with keeping alive. And most people, most of the time, when they were not toiling, were giving birth or dying. Married women normally produced a child a year, except when suckling delayed conception to a two-year pattern. The French historian Pierre Chaunu points out the difference between the birth rate of rich and poor—"dominants and dominated"—that of the former much higher because of better food and earlier marriage. The practice of putting upper-class babies out to nurse freed their mothers for fresh pregnancies—and also created a new avenue of social promotion: milk brotherhood. What this meant can be seen in the case of Cardinal Mazarin, the effective ruler of France through most of the 1640's and '50's, whose mother nursed a scion of the princely Colonna family, establishing a relationship that led her son, a mere commoner, to royal preference and, finally, to secret marriage with the daughter of a king of Spain and widow of a king of France.

On the other hand, the richer women who gave their children out to nurse conceived more but also often sicklier children, and themselves ran the risks and discomforts of pregnancy more often. "An honest woman must always be pregnant or just delivered of a child," writes the Marquise de Villeneuve-Arrifat of her eighteenth-century youth. There was no question of choice and even less of free decision. The Princess Palatine, sister-in-law of Louis XIV, found "the task of manufacturing children . . . a nasty, dangerous, stupid business from no stage of which did I ever derive the slightest pleasure." But those who thought to question the iron laws of nature were pitifully few and very ill-supported. In the seventeenth century some of the English began to apply birth control methods and the upper classes on the Continent took it up late in the century despite clerical condemnation. Among the poor, as one might expect, birth control was practically non-existent; but other factors entered in. Thus, drunk or slumbering parents overlaid and stifled babies to death so frequently that it has been suggested that this was one seventeenth-century method of limiting families.

When contraceptive techniques are lacking, only late marriage or abstinence can serve to limit births and both were widely practiced. Spinsters and bachelors, nuns and priests, were very numerous. Colbert, minister of Louis XIV, anxious to mobilize all hands for the industry he was trying to develop in France, estimated that 12 per cent of the relevant population wasted away in ecclesiastical celibacy. Others simply did not marry, in order to facilitate the education of a few of the boys and the betrothal of a few of the girls in the family. Despite Shakespeare's evidence which makes Juliet's mother marry at twelve and Miranda in *The Tempest* at fourteen, the Cambridge historian Peter Laslett has found the average age of Elizabethan and Jacobean brides to be about twenty-four and of their bridegrooms nearly twenty-eight. He adds that "the higher the social status, the younger the age at marriage."

The average man would see only half of his five or six brothers and sisters grow up and would have lost one of his parents in his teens (the average age at loss of the first parent was fourteen). He would marry for the first time around twenty-seven and have five or six children of which only two or three would outlive him. If, unlike most people, he reached his fifties, he would remember the death of most of his immediate family: brothers, sisters, parents, children, very possibly a spouse. His grandparents had probably died before he was born, although one of the four might have survived to later add to the death roll of the child's experiences.

The rich, of course, who ate better and lived better, probably grew both fitter and faster. But riches had hygienic drawbacks of their own. In this age of excess those who could, gorged themselves; those who couldn't, aimed to. Frequent apoplexies rewarded the gluttony of nobles and the rich. Louis XIV's brother, the Duke of Orléans, was struck down by a heart attack at the dinner table. The great King's own post-mortem revealed a stomach and digestive tract double the normal size. Many others succumbed to fatty degeneration of the heart.

Whatever the diet, then, the most effective way of family limitation was through death—if not from hunger, very probably from disease. Diseases were many and cruel, especially deficiency diseases like scurvy and pellagra, and contagious ones that ran like brush fires through organisms weakened by want, excess, or the ministrations of contemporary doctors. Smallpox and measles were current and often mortal. Diphtheria was known in Spain as *garrotillo* after the garrote with which condemned criminals were slowly throttled. Syphilis was widespread and murderous: one early account by Alexander VI's court physician describes seventeen cases treated in the Pope's court and family in September and October, 1497.

Worst of all, perhaps, was typhus: epidemic since the sixteenth century, known by names like "Hungarian fever," or "Jail fever" because it frequently spread by jail lice passing from prisoners to audience at assize courts. At Oxford assizes in 1577 it killed over 500 people and the danger persisted in the next two centuries, climaxed by the death of John Howard, a prison reformer, who caught typhus during inquiries he made for his treatise, *The State of Prisons in England and Wales* (1770). The disease spread the more readily since most sixteenth- and seventeenth-century people carried lice, but the role of lice or indeed of germs in epidemics was still ignored. Sir Francis Bacon attributed the infection to "stinks" insinuating themselves into men's bodies, other theories blamed "vitiated air," and popular opinion credited papistical winds devised at Louvain and loosed in Oxford. Bubonic plague was also widespread. These and other fevers were spurred and spread by misery, famine, and warfare. They culminated in the Thirty Years' War (1618–1648), which a historian of diseases and their carriers de-

The Plague, a six-teenth-century painting by an unknown German artist. The arrows are symbolic of the disease striking various parts of the body.

scribes as "the most gigantic natural experiment in epidemiology to which mankind has ever been subjected." The first half of hostilities was dominated by typhus, the second half by plague; but neither eliminated the other and both were reinforced by dysentery, typhoid fever, diphtheria, smallpox, scarlet fever, syphilis, and several more. The results were utterly devastating.

When sickness came and went in such formidable and mysterious ways, it is not surprising that panic and prejudice joined ignorance in devising the most extraordinary explanations. The great epidemics that Milan underwent in 1576 and 1630 set the scene for accusations that plague was spread by servants of the devil (actually seen by many in a coach drawn by six black horses) who anointed doors and walls with a deadly unguent, or dropped their poison in the holy water of the churches. When the devil was not blamed for this, some chosen alien was. The French and the English seem to have been the favorite scape-goats at Milan, as heretics had been in Lyons in 1564, the English in France during the Hundred Years' War (1384), the French over most of Italy at most times, and Jews everywhere.

In Austria the imperial court chaplain, Abraham a Sancta Clara (1646–1709), attributed responsibility for the great plague that ravaged Vienna in 1679 to Jews, witches, sextons, and gravediggers (the latter because they benefited from having many corpses to bury). In one of his works, Sancta Clara explains that these people used a mirror to poison the moon, whose rays then could be reflected by the same mirror at wax images of persons selected for infection. He does not explain why such a cumbersome method should be needed by such ingenious sorcerers. Sancta Clara also believed in werewolves, corpses that blushed, bells that rang by themselves, signs in the sky, and the like.*

Nowadays, when we refer to plague, we are more inclined to blame it on poor nutrition and bad hygiene. We must remember that, even today, most human beings are a breeding ground for vermin; and that until very recently men and women spent a good deal of their time simply scratching. Westerners have forgotten this by now, but not even the most exalted ignored it in 1700 when a young French princess was taught that it is not done to scratch by habit rather than necessity, and quite improper "to take lice, fleas and other vermin by the neck to kill them in front of other people unless in private." Young George Washington would be similarly advised. It has been suggested that wigs were introduced into seventeenth century attire as an attempt to cope with vermin: cropped hair would house less of it. If so, this proved singularly unsuccessful. Wigs, of course, were often full of nits: "Thence to Westminster to my barbers," notes Pepys, "to have my Periwigg he lately made me cleansed of its nits, which vexed me cruelly." Some people even developed a certain affection for familiar parasites. The ladies of the French and Spanish courts affected to train and feed pet fleas. The future Louis XIV as a little boy had a tiny set of gold cannon drawn by a team of fleas. The richest clothes housed a vermin no less rich.

In cities especially, improper drainage was a great source of infection. Sewers and cesspits seeped into wells or cisterns, ran off into nearby rivers, poisoning the water sources. Hence, the increased consumption of wine, of beer, and of tea made from boiling water marked the retreat of deaths from typhoid and other infections. But the basic danger remained. Madrid had the wind of the *sierras,* Naples and Rome the Mediterranean sun, Amsterdam benefited from the tides, but other cities wallowed in their refuse, the excrement of daily life lapping round the feet of their citizens. Pollution is no new problem.

Most of the time, of course, water was scarce, hard to get, and used chiefly for cooking. There was little washing and baths were for the very sick or the very rich. Public baths, popular in past centuries, had been banned as dens of vice. The seventeenth was a remarkably dirty century and proud of it. People cleaned the dirt off themselves by rubbing or by scratching. Even hands were seldom washed. The first wife of

---

* Such beliefs could sometimes prove useful. In his *Conquest of the Plague* (Oxford: 1953), p. 27, L. Fabian Hirst tells of a comet which appeared over Russia in 1664. When the Tsar inquired what it portended, he was told there would be a plague in autumn, but one less dangerous to Russia than to other lands. He therefore set up a sanitary cordon at his borders and banned foreign, especially English, ships from Russian ports. The story may be apocryphal, but Russia appears to have escaped infection at that time.

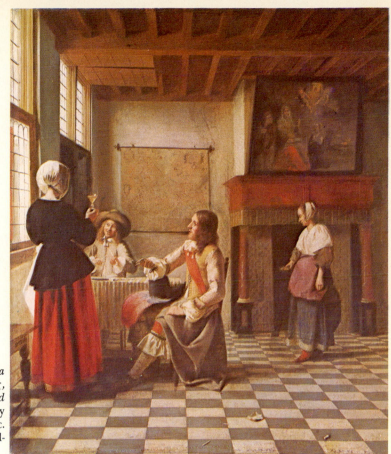

An Interior with a Woman Drinking, with Two Men and a Maidservant, by Pieter de Hooch, c. 1658. National Gallery, London.

Henry IV, Princess Margaret of Valois, joked about her hands "unwashed for a week"; two generations later a lady visiting Queen Christina of Sweden found it impossible to tell how her hands looked because "they were too foul." Cleanliness was so exceptional that the biographer of the painter Guido Reni (1575–1642) made special mention of the fact that his hero was so clean that he never smelled. The smell of Henry IV was so ferocious that his wife had to brew special perfumes to stand him, and Louis XIII prided himself on taking after his father. Those who could, sucked aniseed lozenges to improve a breath affected by torrid digestions and the absence of any dental hygiene. The tremendous smells, not only human but horsy, drove all who could to drench themselves in strong scents, which must have mingled in strange dissonance with the persistent odors of candle grease, sewerless houses, and sewerlike streets.

Within this splendid breeding ground the medical profession practiced its deadly trade. "More people perish at the hands of doctors," notes Casanova in his eighteenth-century memoirs, "than are cured by them." A glance at the doctor's arsenal of bleedings and purges, emetics and cauteries, unguents and balms, should convince us he was right. Despite the invention of forceps, which saved thousands of lives where adopted in England and Holland, seventeenth-century surgeons must have shed more blood than soldiers ever did, since bloodletting was the favorite of their remedies. Even a very good surgeon like Ambroise Paré boasted of having bled a youth twenty-seven times in four days. Cupping and purging must have sent more men to their doom than war, and shortened the lives of many, among them probably Louis XIII, his chief Minister Cardinal Richelieu, and Richelieu's successor, Mazarin.* That contemporaries realized the murderous possibilities of medicine may be seen from one of the more popular plays of the Spanish dramatist Pedro Calderón (1600–1681), *The Doctor of his Honor (El Médico de su Honra)*, in which the hero who suspects his wife, unjustly, as it happens, of having besmirched his honor, forces a surgeon to bleed her until she dies.

Less bloody in their relative ineffectiveness, even their more benign remedies give us pause. Copernicus has copied out one medical prescription with the following ingredients: Armenian sponge, cinnamon, cedarwood, blood-root, dittany, red sandalwood, ivory shavings, crocus, camomile in vinegar, lemon rind, pearls, emerald, sapphires, a deer's heartbone or a pulped heart, a beetle, the horn of a unicorn, red coral, gold, silver, and sugar. A learned London physician claimed to have cured himself of plague in the great outbreak of 1665 by applying to his stomach a large dried toad which drew out poison; and dried-toad lozenges were very popular, one doctor treating one thousand cases with them, although another considered them better for prevention than for cure.

The Family

Given the number of births and also of deaths, it seems that attachment to, affection for, children were less and their very significance as individuals was smaller than today, when they are a rarer commodity but also a more lasting one, likely to develop a personality to which we may attach ourselves. There must have been in child-parent relations a sort of emotional gap which eventually affected the whole of society. They knew each other less; they loved each other less. A society almost half of which was made up of children would be much concerned with the quest for order and authority.

The Roman law, administered by bourgeois lawyers, insisted on paternal authority and masculine rights. Children were subject, women

---

* The personal physician of Louis XIII, Héroard, a veterinary surgeon by training, kept a detailed record of his tasks for twenty-seven years. One year at random we may note the King was bled forty-seven times, purged two hundred and twelve times, and given two hundred and fifteen enemas.

perpetual minors, men alone recognized by law.

Law, of course, was not everything. Great ladies had been praised by medieval troubadours and glorified in the courts of the Renaissance. They would be educated by the Christian humanists of the sixteenth century, as were the learned daughters of Sir Thomas More, or Margaret of Navarre, sister of King Francis I. But such exceptions are no more representative of the woman's lot than the great queens of this and earlier periods: Isabella the Catholic, Catherine de Medici, Elizabeth of England.

More to the point, the average woman who had performed important economic functions managing the medieval household began to retreat into idleness, hence into a kind of irrelevancy, as the bourgeoisie sought to ape noble standards which excluded work. There had been printers' wives in the early sixteenth century who knew enough Latin to help their husbands in correcting proofs. A successful printer of the seventeenth century would not wish his wife involved in menial occupations. And even the first girls' schools, which Ursuline nuns had founded in Spain and France as early as the sixteenth century, taught piety and social graces rather than classical learning or useful arts.

In a sense, this reflected a social and ideological promotion. The Middle Ages had little good to say about women, responsible for the Fall and vessels of further temptation; or about marriage, which theologians considered inferior to chastity. It had been humanists like Erasmus who rehabilitated the idea of married love, and all the great reformers (Luther, Zwingli, even Calvin) married, thus setting an impressive example for their followers. A writer could now praise his beloved even if she was not some noble, unattainable, or lascivious lady, but simply his spouse. Edmund Spenser's *Epithalamion* (1594) was a paean to his own wedding day. A contemporary Polish poet sang of the wife he married for love, for she had little money, whose tresses were fair as the bark of a young birch tree. One could love one's wife and not be ridiculous. One could be a respectable woman, though not nobly born.

Yet it would seem that, despite occasional political or literary appearances, seventeenth-century women played a less important role than they did in the Middle Ages. Especially in the growing middle classes, they served to gratify the pleasures of the men or to perpetuate their line; they provided objects for trade and contract, part of an alliance in which dowry and girl were added up like the courses on a restaurant bill, with no indication of a difference of kind between them. Thus, in September, 1698, Jean Racine writes to his son concerning a match proposed for him: "They were giving you a girl with 80,000 livres . . ." It might as well be two acres and a cow. Not enough for Racine.

Since most children lost their fathers before growing up, a youngster had to take over responsibilities and duties before he had been much trained, and there was no opportunity to cast around for a career:

following in father's footsteps, taking up his profession or trade, was the obvious way to cope with a situation that allowed little leisure or choice. One had to benefit from whatever experience the family could furnish, to serve, as it were, one's apprenticeship within the family itself. And just as personal inclinations were hardly in question with reference to a career, so they were little considered in choice of a spouse, selected not with personal taste but with the interest of the family in view.

Not God, not self, or profit was the chief base for action, but *family,* as a lasting entity to improve and maintain whose wealth and status all efforts were bent and all members would make sacrifices, not least the children brought into the world to help and support it, if possible by marriage alliances. When young Elizabeth Paston refused to marry an elderly misshapen widower, her mother beat her "once in a week or twice, sometimes twice in one day, and her head broken in two or three places," over a period of three months. Compatibility was irrelevant in the utilitarian view; the spouses would maintain a formal relationship at best which would be reinforced by the frequent difference in their ages. Thus, La Fontaine at twenty-six married a girl of fourteen; the forty-year-old Molière, a girl of sixteen; the Count of Evreux, who needed money to pay his gambling debts, married the twelve-year-old daughter of a financier and spent her vast dowry while she was in convent school learning to write and sing.

The Old, the Young, and the Poor

With survival so rare, old people in their fifties or sixties would enjoy great prestige simply for having lasted that long. Their experience would be the more useful since society changed so slowly that the views of oldsters seemed less anachronistic, more in tune with social and economic realities, than they seem today. And the slow rate of change itself was probably connected with the relatively small numbers which reached full intellectual maturity, let alone had any time or training to think or to apply their knowledge. Not only were intellectuals scarce, but, relatively speaking, so were grown men and women whose experience, imagination, enterprise could contribute to the pool of social techniques even in the simplest way. Men's intellectual activities before the age of ten or twelve are limited and the immense mass of young people itself must have weighed heavily on the minority that had to keep the wheels of society turning, while keeping an eye on the dependent section within it. In other words, the pool of energy and skills was limited not only by immaturity but by the need to rear the children themselves.

On the other hand, since the young formed the greatest portion of society, more of them had to work sooner. In any case, when people die so young, life brooks no delay. Young men entered upon apprenticeship at an early age—not only in shop or store but also in the army: Cinq-Mars, the favorite of Louis XIII, began to serve at thirteen, Turenne, one of the century's great soldiers, at fourteen; the future marshal of Saxe at twelve, while at thirteen he was present at the Battle of Malplaquet and marched on foot from Saxony to Flanders. Another young man, whose father had taken him on campaign at nine, received a saber cut when twelve while fighting like a man. Another, midshipman at thirteen, received his first wound at fourteen. So, in the royal services and in the courts of law, scores of officers, magistrates, and officials must have been in their twenties and even in their teens.

The progeny of the poor were even more thoroughly exploited. The children of the poor, wrote John Locke in 1697, must work at least part-time from the age of three; and mostly, it would seem, living on bread and water. In seventeenth-century Leyden, a great textile center second only to Lyons, children, sometimes six years old, toiled in the mills. Orphans from the municipal asylum were brought in to lend a hand and, during the textile boom of 1638–48, four thousand children were imported from the bishopric of Liège. A city ordinance of 1646 limited child labor to fourteen hours a day and an inspector appointed by the municipality was supposed to supervise the children.

We get some idea of general working hours from Queen Elizabeth's *Statute of Artificers* (1563), which, reflecting contemporary practice, expected workers to work from sunrise to sunset. Almost a hundred years later (1648), a judge at the York assizes expected them to "continue from five of the clock in the morning till seven at night in the summer and from seven till five in the winter." In the eighteenth century, men in the ironware factory of the philanthropist Ambrose Cowley worked thirteen and a half hours a day, six days a week—over eighty hours. It has been said that no one can explain how wage-earners lived on wages alone. It is even harder to understand how any of the poor survived.

Repeated strikes and mutinies achieved nothing but the leader's punishment. The poor had no rights. They were proletarians: the class of people who contribute nothing to society except offspring—*proles*. But if there was a use for them, they would be sought after. In 1618, a hundred boys and girls were picked off the London streets to be shipped to Virginia. Fifteen years later a monopolist was allowed to conscript labor in this random fashion for his Welsh mines. Paris workhouses and jails were scoured to furnish settlers for Louisiana, but in 1719 when this source ran short, able-bodied vagrants of both sexes were conscripted straight off the street. Authority ruled over the poor as it did over children. Isolation, illiteracy, and widespread poverty preoccupied with sheer survival made for resignation; and this was bolstered by official propaganda. The Church of England *Catechism* of 1549, which every parish priest taught and every parishioner had to learn by heart, culminated in the wish "to do my duty in that state of life unto which it shall please God to call me."

What counted were authority and rank—degree. In a world where the rich were very rich and the poor very poor, the latter were held to be of no account and their existence attracted little attention except when it erupted into trouble. Then, history records its reverberations: disorders, insurrections, sporadic risings, brigandage, reflecting the rising tide of misery, the price revolution which left wages behind living costs, the nightmare procession of beggars, maimed, vagabonds, migrants to the Indies,* pilgrims, thieves, drunks, the long convoys of galley slaves and bloody chronicles of banditry up to the very gates of cities and within.

The "idleness" and vagrancy which the powers that be denounced were typical of backward economies in which men had neither regular employment nor adequate reward for their labor. In such circumstances, it is not surprising that manual labor was held in low esteem. What with land concentration, shrinking trade, church and bureaucracy must have been very appealing and in countries like Spain almost inevitable. As the English historian J. H. Elliot has put it of Castile: "The nature of the economic system was such that one became a student or a monk, a beggar or a bureaucrat. There was nothing else to be." It is a strange thought that, as leprosy, the scourge of the Middle Ages, disappeared, the leper houses were assigned to the poor: workhouses, reformatories, madhouses, and foundling hospitals, the former prisons of the lepers inherited by the new lepers of the modern world, hid or confined the products of unemployment or underemployment, tried to relieve the pressures on primitive economies, to get potential criminals and agitators off the streets, sequester lunatics, cripples, and the poor as members of similarly asocial groups which one could only institutionalize. Such were the poor, and it would seem that, before the French Revolution, about half the population was considered poor by the other half, judging by standards immeasurably lower than our own.

Society in the 16th and 17th Centuries

Estates

Survivals and changes, heredities and mobilities, appearance of classes defined by revenue, the persistence of orders defined by traditional function: well into the eighteenth century the structures of European societies remained closer to those of the Middle Ages than to those of the Industrial Revolution. Men who were not nobly born could be-

---

* "Refuge and protection of all the *desperados* of Spain," writes Cervantes, "church of the rebels, safe conduct of the murderers." Is that why the seventeenth century was colonialist?

come rich and influential by investment and trade. Yet this growing class whose material success seems to mark it out for power, seems more concerned with security or status: the security of annuities or land rents, the status that could be bought with a patent of nobility, a royal office, ultimately the life of men living "nobly," that is, idly. In terms of such values, not economic power but the dignity of one's estate determined one's degree. Within each estate, its own hierarchy: from Cardinals through bishops, down to parish clergy and humble friars; from princes of royal blood to the latest buyer of some patent of nobility.

Jurists still divided men into the three formal functions of a society not as bygone as we sometimes think. There were still those who prayed, those who fought, and those who labored: the last useful, of course, indeed indispensable, but not noble and much too diversified to treat as a single whole. In actual practice, the three categories were a swarm of subdivisions. The peaks of the social hierarchy were sparsely covered: a few princes of the Church, a few great nobles, with the remainder of clergy and gentry at quite another level. Around 1600, thirty-two Spanish grandees could call the King "my cousin"; fifty-eight peers of the realm sat in the English House of Lords. Below them came what we can loosely call the gentry: knights, squires, gentlemen, *Junkers* or *hidalgos,* men of noble descent rather than mere purchasers of titles.

Below them, again, came the highest reaches of the Third Estate: officers of the crown, men of law and letters, merchants whom a seventeenth-century jurist described as "the last of the people to be considered honorable, being qualified as honorable men or honest persons or bourgeois: qualities attributed neither to workers nor to bailiffs, nor to artisans, and even less to laborers, who are all reputed vile persons." It would be from this class that the parallel nobility of office or "of the robe" would be recruited.

In the simplest sense, the Third Estate might be divided into those who worked with their hands and those who didn't. Formally, greatest prestige attached to "men of letters": university graduates destined for official functions or professional practice as doctors, lawyers, notaries, and such. In practice, these vied with the rich merchants, shippers, merchant-bankers and financiers, with apothecaries, jewelers and goldsmiths, and were probably related to them. All such were *bourgeoisie,* with the charges and privileges this entailed: access to municipal office, right to exercize and regulate their professions, control of local militia bodies, and whatever exemptions or immunities might obtain in their locality. Below them came artisans, shopkeepers, every kind of menial trade, laborers, and peasants.

Such divisions were not watertight. Several generations, more often a century or two, might see a family rise from one order to the next. But in the meantime, men lived in the compartments defined by birth, subject to the different limits this entailed.

Privilege

There were many social gradations in the hierarchy of the seventeenth century, but only one essential difference: that between privileged * and unprivileged. The former might be noble, they were not necessarily so. Members of the clergy and even some commoners enjoyed special prerogatives, exemptions from all or certain taxes, peculiar treatment under the law or escape from it into particular courts, advantages of every sort, from being able to keep a private pigeon loft to permission to keep their hats on in the royal presence. These were the people who counted in some way. Seventeenth-century *freedom* really meant privilege, the right to have something others did not have and keep them out of it. The freehold of an estate, the freedom of a town, was the grant or charter of a privilege which carried with it rights and immunities: the parliament members' immunity from arrest, the freeman's immunity from conscription and flogging. So when the seventeenth century speaks of freedom it speaks of the exceptional rights of the propertied minority, or the particular rights of some particular group.

Beyond and far below them, in another realm, stirred the unprivileged, the mass of proletarians whom Sir Thomas Smith described in 1560 as "the sort of men who do not rule": day-laborers, shoemakers, bricklayers, and such, owning no property and having, by rights, no rights in anything. No say and, indeed, no personality. When King Henry IV of France was murdered in 1610, the judges who questioned his assassin under torture would not believe that a simple man would have the idea and the courage of such a deed if he had not been put up to it by someone of high estate. In 1614, a London tailor who said he was as good a man as the gentleman-customer who would not pay his bill was fined double the amount which the gentleman owed him.

As if to symbolize the difference, the greater part of common folk had no family name: only their Christian names followed by a descriptive surname, identifying Peter as Carter or Smith, or else as Steven's son. Englishmen began to carry regular surnames in the sixteenth century, other Europeans following in due course, though slowly. Many Dutch only acquired surnames in the nineteenth century, as did the Jews. In Denmark, surnames of common folk only began to be handed on in 1828. Essentially the only people who mattered were the privileged minority.

There were, of course, the bourgeois: summit of the Third Estate. They played a significant part in the affairs of England and the Netherlands, even those of France. But the bourgeoisie as such declined in importance just as independent cities declined before the growing power of central authority. The end of the fifteenth century saw the end of

* Those who, as the Latin had it, benefited from *privatae leges:* private laws.

cities as independent political units (1453, Constantinople; 1472, Barcelona; 1492, Granada) and the replacement of urban by territorial states, alone capable of facing the costs of modern war and furnishing the space and men to cope with it. We have already seen the problems cities faced in feeding themselves. Food problems meant political ones. The overpopulated cities of the sixteenth century had to go ever further for their food, to scour the countryside, to seek the support of territorial lords who could provide or facilitate fulfillment of their needs. They either increased their agricultural hinterland and their possessions, swallowing up others, as Florence, Milan, or Venice did, or shriveled, or became the subjects of some greater land power. Outside the Netherlands, the medieval city with its suburban fields, master of its fate and of the nearby roads and shores, passed out of reality into history (at last in seventeenth-century Germany as well).

The influence of urban patriciates waned, the more successful among them fusing into the nobility which reinforced its position in the seventeenth century when land recovered its value as the safest investment and source of spare but regular revenues, when new abysses yawned between rich and poor, when great indifference or ruthlessness marked relations among all the classes. Many who lived in smaller cities were simply wealthier peasants owning a town house. Conversely, as had long been the case, townsmen often owned land outside the walls—perhaps a house and orchard in the town where they plied their trade and a vineyard outside it—and prosperous merchants, doctors, drapers, all put some of their capital in that safest of investments: a plot of land. In countries where land brought nobility, the bourgeois bought it to secure a title. But while social promotion was attractive, freedom from tax was equally so. In countries like Sweden, where the bourgeois could only acquire land subject to taxes and where titles came by crown patent, like a decoration, not from land, the bourgeoisie proved much slower to acquire estates. On the other hand, all bourgeois were eager to "live nobly" and nothing came closer to this than a manor or country house.

Mobility

The most ambitious made their way toward nobility and the franchises, prerogatives, and exemptions that went with it. A great lord has described the age of Louis XIV, that is, the second half of the seventeenth century, as "a long reign of vile bourgeoisie." But the bourgeois he resented were men promoted to a kind of nobility, as public servants or magistrates, and this metamorphosis for themselves or for their offspring (if need be by way of a dearly bought marriage) was their constant aim: a title, exemption from taxes, the promise of a surviving family name available to noble dynasties. Throughout the sixteenth and seventeenth centuries the sale of titles paralleled the sale of offices, the sale of privileges, the sale of tickets of admission to greater security or higher status. The English public was scandalized in 1616 by the discovery that the common hangman of London had purchased a coat of arms for 22 shillings.

Opportunities for social promotion there were aplenty but, ultimately, not through business enterprise; though this too continued important at a certain stage in the ascent. Some of the great merchants who founded the East India Company in Amsterdam had started out as penniless laborers or refugees. One of these, Jan Poppen, who died in 1616, left the enormous amount of a million guilders, at a time when Dutch workmen earned half a guilder a day, master carpenters just under one guilder a day, and sailors on East India ships ten guilders a month. But it is worthy of note that Poppen had long before abandoned the risky ventures that made his fortune for solid investments in drained farmland, city real estate, and safe East India Company debentures, and that within eight years of his death his daughter married a nobleman.

Poppen's career, in republican Holland, is typical of the new mentality for which business was only a step to security and wealth a key to status rather than to more enterprise. At least it was based on trade to begin with. More characteristic of the new age would be the rise of other families. The Perrenots: great-grandfather a village blacksmith, grandfather a small-town notary, his eldest son, Nicholas (1468–1550), enters the service of Emperor Charles V, does well, and buys the domain of Granvelle. The eldest of Nicholas's fifteen children, Antony (1517–1586), is placed in the household of Philip II, becomes Bishop of Arras, Chancellor of Burgundy, Archbishop and Cardinal of Malines. Or the Fouquets: the grandfather a merchant at Nantes, the father a councilor of the Paris Parliament; his son Nicholas (1615–1680) enters the service of Cardinal Richelieu, then of Mazarin, becomes Superintendent of Finances, a marquess, the patron of men like the dramatist Corneille and the writer La Fontaine, while his castle of Vaux inspires the young Louis XIV to build Versailles. At a less exalted level, there is André Bossuet, the son of a small provincial official in Burgundy, who makes a fortune buying and selling offices and estates, then uses his wealth to protect and advance a young relative from Dijon, Jacques Bénigne Bossuet (1627–1704), the future bishop and preceptor of the Dauphin.*

The Households of the Great

Always the court, always the prince's service. In the sixteenth century the courts of princes take over the role which cities played at an

---

* In 1349 King Charles V of France had bought the southeastern province of Dauphiné from its lords and granted it to his eldest son, the future Charles VI. Thereafter, *Dauphin* became the title of the heir apparent to the French crown.

earlier stage, become the new centers of power, wealth, and culture. Cities themselves now prosper insofar as they become a royal residence or learn to serve the court. No longer citizens in any significant way, men pride themselves on being servants of princes, and great servants can indeed serve greatly their own interests and their master's too. But if a prince wished to assert his power, he had to count with that of his greatest subjects: the high aristocracy, the men whom one modern historian has likened to "little kings." We shall see in another chapter how this struggle went which was the foremost internal issue of the three centuries before 1789.

One may compare the great lords of 1600 to great wild beasts—lions, tigers, or buffaloes, noble and fierce. There is a strange pleistocene quality about them. They are often uncultured, the greatest of them sometimes unable to read or write. They are dissolute in morals and violent in manners. But they are unbridled in courage, in arrogance, in splendor. Truculent, brutal, greedy, prodigal, sensitive to the least imagined slight, generous to their own, ruthless to all others, utterly devoted to their House, name, repute, unpredictable in mood, trumpeting their glory, riches, amorous conquests, dressing like Christmas trees bedecked with so many precious stones that one could hardly glimpse the material beneath. The Duke of Nevers, sent by Henry IV as ambassador to the Holy See, makes Rome marvel at his black velvet suit embroidered all over with diamonds. Henry IV's mistress, Gabrielle d'Estrées, attending a baptism, wears a frock of black satin so charged with pearls and precious stones "that she could not hold herself up under it." When the future Louis XIII was baptized at Fontainebleau in 1606, the sword of the Duke of Epernon was encrusted with eighteen hundred diamonds, while one of Henry's Marshals wore a dress of violet gold cloth sewn with fifty pounds of pearls. Louis XIV, sumptuous in youth, dressed fairly simply in his middle age. But even then, he sometimes affected grandiose costumes, as when to dazzle the Persian ambassador he received him in a suit bedecked with twelve million livres' worth of diamonds. "He bent under their weight," Saint-Simon recorded.

Ostentatious display was a badge of greatness.* When the Duke of Buckingham visited Paris in 1625 he brought twenty-seven gala suits. The most notable one was of white velvet sewn with diamonds and with strings of pearls. The pearls were allowed to slip off one after the other for lackeys and courtiers to pick up. The same was true of ceremonial horseshoes, sometimes made of silver and only lightly fixed so that the bystanders could pick up what the horse cast off.

Susceptible and mettlesome, men such as these and many lesser

---

* In 1636 King Charles I of England prohibited imitation jewelry because it made social copycatting too easy and confused those differences of degree essential "in a well-governed state."

Elizabeth I, a painting by an unknown artist, showing the queen in a sumptuous robe embroidered with jewels. National Portrait Gallery, London.

ones engaged in endless squabbles over titles and questions of etiquette, precedent, or imagined slights. One Italian general in 1625 was surprised by the enemy and defeated because he refused to read a message which had omitted some of his titles. In 1632 the deputies of the city of Barcelona brought the Catalan *cortes* to a halt because of a dispute on the right of municipal councilors to keep their hats on in the presence of the king. An apparently petty issue such as this laid the ground for the Catalan revolt of 1640. Under Louis XIV such issues would become matters of state, leading practically to war.

No one seemed to doubt that a great lord was different from others, moving on a level where normal laws and rules have no hold, surrounded by quasi-religious prestige and a great horde of dependents. Of course, footmen and maids made up for technical backwardness; but, even more, they symbolized the wealth and power of their master, the splendor of their apparel reflecting the splendor of his fame. The Duke of Osuna, who had made a fortune as Viceroy of Naples, appeared at a tourney in Madrid toward the end of Philip III's reign escorted by a hundred lackeys dressed in blue and gold and by fifty officers clad in suits of costly stuff embroidered with precious stones. And there were others like him.

The greater the lord the greater the number of his servants. The Duke of Sully had so many in one of his country houses alone that eighty could be ill without their absence being noticed. Before the English Civil War (1642–1646), the Herbert household counted over one hundred servants and retainers, the less grand Howards kept forty or fifty in one country house. A seventeenth-century ambassador had to have one or two secretaries, a chaplain, cooks, lackeys, footmen, pages, coachmen, stablemen, and a few other domestics and gentlemen who danced attendance on him. A small ambassadorial household at a simple court, such as The Hague, might number thirty; a great embassy in Rome, Paris, or Madrid would number over a hundred. In 1690 a medium-sized Holstein Junker employed forty-five lackeys and servants, apart from any serfs about the house. By mid-eighteenth century this kind of staff would shrink but still represented an important proportion of the public. In absence of worker-buyers, the market in many places depended on domestics and on how shrewdly these managed to steal from their masters.*

This merely stresses the economic position of great nobles, parasites whose parasites made up a significant proportion of the solvent community and of the buying public, so that the arrival or departure of a great household could enrich or impoverish a whole town. It could also shake it, for the noble beasts and their attendants had sharp teeth and claws. War had long been the chief occupation of the nobility and the justification of their otherwise unproductive existence. As war became increasingly professional and grubby, as central authorities stamped out private feuds, the nobles' bellicosity had to be expressed in other ways: blood sports in which whole menageries were goaded to death, hunting, which from a useful enterprise became an expensive obsession, above all dueling—the noblest and most murderous of games.

In the nineteen years from 1585 to 1603, 7,000 gentlemen who had killed their opponents received letters of grace from Henry IV. In 1606 alone, 2,000 swordsmen were killed in France. In 1607, 300 men met in a mass encounter between two clans of the Poitou from which only fifteen escaped without serious wounds. From mid-sixteenth to mid-seventeenth century, men fought at the drop of a hat, in twos or fours or more, with sword and dagger, using every dirty trick they could to kill their opponent. Two noblemen at the court of Valois get into an argument over whether the embroidery on a lady's muff is in the shape of an X or a Y. They fight and one dies. Schoolboys fight to the death. The future Henry IV writes: "We live ready nearly always to cut each other's throats. We carry daggers, wear mail jackets and often light armor under our capes."

The Growing Refinement of Life

Such wild and murderous manners, though they persisted for a long time, sparked a reaction. The early seventeenth-century turning against these turbulent, rowdy ways began to stress courtesy and good manners.

---

* Stealing was an intrinsic part of the system, since many of these servants were only seldom paid (as *The Marriage of Figaro* reveals). When the Duchess of Berri, daughter of the Duke of Orléans, Regent of France, died in 1719 the wages of her 800 servants were £17,000 in arrears.

A straw in the wind was Honoré d' Urfé's romance *Astrée* (1609), which stresses the precedence of "soul" over "body," of refined feeling over brutal strength. Another was the increasing discipline inculcated by the new classical education. Obviously, counsels of balance and moderation in all things were put forward the more pressingly the less these virtues were in evidence. It was because it was so remote from existing realities that moderation was held in high regard. As the seventeenth century drew on, everything mirrored the new trend: even noble skins grew whiter when compared to those of suntanned courtiers always on the move, on horseback, carriage, or barge, from one castle to another. With Louis XIV a courtier's life shifted increasingly indoors, the corridors of power took on a literal sense, and soft, sensitive skins became proof of gentility, so much so that young noble ladies likely to be touched by the sun in their excursions into the outer world wore a mask against it.

Growing comfort and refinement would gradually affect more and more peole, more and more walks of life. Already in 1600 small dolls carefully dressed in exact imitations of court costumes carried the latest fashions into the provinces. And its effects were sometimes revealed in unexpected ways. Thus, we have seen that houses were cold, and continued frigid, especially in winter, so that most people piled several layers of clothes on top of each other to keep warm. In mid-eighteenth century, Oliver Goldsmith (1728–1774), visiting prosperous Holland, found Dutchmen wearing seven waistcoats and nine trousers, their womenfolk so many petticoats that their hips seemed to start at the armpits. Window glass continued rare until the seventeenth century; in Scotland as late as 1661 even royal palaces had glass only in the upper part of windows, while lower ones were closed with shutters. Those who could afford it lit fires in winter; but generally they took refuge in the kitchen. Even great houses seldom heated more than one room where the whole family sat on stone benches beneath the fireplace. The Germans had stoves, but their porcelain tiles were scarce outside central Europe until the seventeenth century and nonexistent further south.

Throughout the seventeenth century, however, houses became more comfortable, more richly decorated, more opulent. The Dutch, for instance, found new luxuries soaking up so much capital that rumor accused Louis XIV of a plot to weaken them by spreading Paris fashions in their once-sober land. Even peasant homes added more rooms, equipped them with grates, began to burn coal, replaced benches or stools with chairs. At every level except the very poorest, relative comfort increased and so did privacy. Privacy suggested and permitted introspection, the keeping of diaries and journals, the development of self-consciousness and self-examination so characteristic of the age of René Descartes (1596–1650) and of Thomas Browne (1605–1682), the London physician whose *Religio Medici* was "a private exercise dedicated to myself." More mirrors may have contributed to this. Glass mirrors had been made in Venice since the fourteenth century but they remained very expensive until more widely manufactured in England and France by mid-seventeenth century. Mirrors permitted men (and especially women) to see themselves more closely as they were. But privacy also permitted more differentiation between those who dwelt together. As middle-class houses added living and dining rooms, as more rooms in all houses began to be heated, the kitchen—once the common meeting-place—was left to servants; and servants were increasingly confined to separate quarters.

This trend was only starting in the seventeenth century and we shall meet it again later, at a more advanced stage. It was, however, part and portent of new divisions which would henceforth affect society and color its attitudes. The lower classes were increasingly banned from the quarters, the districts, the contact of the rich. At Dijon in 1674 the fruit market was moved to a less fashionable part of town so that its hubbub should not disturb the magistrates who lived near the old site. In Rome, the gorgeous shows rich Romans offered in the fifteenth and sixteenth centuries were progressively closed to the public. Where in the 1560's papal tourneys were still public and many plays, banquets, and other festivities were held in the open for the vicarious enjoyment of the common people, the end of the century saw the crowd excluded, the streets closed to the vulgar. Mystery plays were no longer presented to mixed audiences; troops of strolling players performed for commoners in the Piazza Navona, but for the mighty in their *salons*. In 1600, guests at a banquet offered by Cardinal Aldobrandini to the visiting Viceroy of Naples had to show their invitation cards at the door. The break between rich and poor was now extended to excluding the latter from even a vicarious share in the pleasures of the rich.

The possibility of contamination affected even seventeenth-century gardens, from which useful plants were banished. Good taste rejected anything practical—fruit trees and even more so vegetables. Medieval gardens had been orchards and kitchen-gardens as well as pleasure places. Modern gardens aspired to be parks, adorned with statues, pavilions, formal lines and perspectives, as fashionable taste demanded. Like useful plants, practical instruments could not be tolerated in good company. Even the spindle, once to be found in every middle-class living room, was by the end of the seventeenth century relegated to the kitchen.

Decorum prohibited useful work—especially manual labor. As we have seen, this was one basic criterion of social identification. Artisans, mechanics, peasants above all, were "vile persons," their occupation "dishonest and sordid." Loyseau's influential *Treatise of Order and Simple Dignities* (1613) makes clear that no one could claim an honorable position in life who worked with his hands. Work itself was sufficiently demeaning, but there were degrees of baseness. Retail business was considered as menial as any handicraft. Wholesalers, on the other hand, could pass as "merchants"—a more honorable calling. Obviously, men who bought and sold at wholesale were better able to amass the fortunes that could be invested in the land or office which would bring status, rank, and social promotion. Once again, the yearning to be a gentleman or pass as one, proved the obsessive guide of ambitious commoners.

Yet a gentleman's lot, apparently, was not an easy one. Greater refinement and luxury, new products, gewgaws or necessities, a costlier, more complicated way of living, all these added up to more expense. Wrote Sir John Oglander in 1632:

> It is impossible for a mere country gentleman ever to grow rich or raise his house. He must have some other vocation with his inheritance as to be a courtier, lawyer, merchant or some other vocation. If he hath no other vocation, let him get a ship and judiciously manage her, or buy some auditor's place, or be vice admiral in his county. By only following the plow he may keep his word and be upright, but will never increase his fortune.

All over the west, there were "poor gentlemen," as Cardinal Richelieu called them, all of whose wealth consisted in land, which was little to go on with when rents were going down and real wealth came from other sources.

Aware that inability to engage in trade put them at a disadvantage, nobles sometimes strove to remove the stigma that attached to it. French nobles pleaded the distinction between retail and wholesale trade, obtaining permission to engage in the former without derogation. In the Duchy of Brittany, nobility could be set aside and left to lie dormant until its possessor had made enough money to gild his escutcheon again. Then he reassumed it. Certain ventures could be attempted without losing caste: the grain trade, where German, Polish, and Danish landowners appear as great capitalists; mining and metallurgy, which enriched Swedish and German noblemen, and where noble ironmasters were sometimes found in association with Dutch or Hanseatic or Nürnberg merchants; naval enterprises of every kind along the Atlantic coast, from shipbuilding to piracy, in which again noblemen would frequently associate with commoners.

But all this was more exception than rule. Ideals, inclinations, and social prejudices combined to restrict the number of such enterprises and their scope. In 1626, Catalan noblemen sought royal permission "to have a share in shops and in every other kind of trade or business without losing anything of their status," but failed. And even commercial undertakings and trading ventures proved more an occasion for commoners to rise in the world by participating in a noble venture than for noblemen to become richer. The nobler the enterprise, the smaller the profits. No wonder most nobles put their trust in royal appointments and pensions.

Sovereignty and Kingship

At the summit of the social pyramid, kingpin of it all, stood the king.

European kingship has been traced back to the Roman Empire, and also to the early customs of Germanic tribes. The former furnished a tradition of absolute power, the latter that of an authority derived from investiture by people or peers. To these, Christianity added the notion dear to Charlemagne that kings held their office by the grace of God. Medieval clerics who wrote on such matters insisted on the holy aspect of the office, which was emphasized by the holy oil used to anoint royalty. The kings of France were Most Christian Kings because the oil used in crowning them had been a heavenly gift to their Merovingian forerunner, Clovis. But all royal office was looked upon as semi-divine: a kind of priesthood, including the power to cure certain ills.

Kings ruled by what came to be called divine right, therefore, long before the sixteenth century. And this, especially when reinforced by the revival of Roman law with its maxim that "what pleases the prince has force of law," provided theoretical justification for absolutism. Institutional and practical considerations could—and did—limit the conclusions of this. But the theory was there to support, justify, and prompt those who had the power to apply it.

There was the rub. For kings ruled not only by divine right but by worldly rights arising out of contracts between them and their subjects: covenants whereby private rights (of feudal nobles, for example) were subordinated to public ones in a mutual bond between governor and governed. The terms of such contracts varied, according to the capacity of parties to enforce them, defend them, or encroach upon them. In the dominions of the kings of Spain, the *cortes* of Castile alone recognized the power of the crown to make and interpret laws "whereinsoever they shall think it convenient to do so"; those of Aragon swore that "the people has as much right and more power than the king." In France, as in Spain, the king was not equally king everywhere in his kingdom. According to the terms that had been recognized, provinces or cities, corporations and social groups, abbeys or cathedral chapters fared differently. Taxes were higher in certain provinces, lower in others, laws differed from place to place and so—often—did the courts that administered them.

Limitations

In any case, if ruling meant making, interpreting, and applying laws, the concrete possibilities for doing these things were severely limited.

The great chain of the feudal system survived in its legal forms—bonds between men and men, suzerains and vassals, fiefs and benefices—but also in loyalties, in troops of clients, in great households, in followers beholden to a lord or patron, expecting his aid and protection albeit against the officers of the king.

The king's powers were further circumscribed by ruling notions about the functions of civil authority, which has been described as "merely the police department of the Church"; and by the prevailing view of law as a kind of revelation, expressing the command of God validated by scripture. In the wake of Plato and Aristotle, the Middle Ages had regarded man-made laws as reflections of the eternal laws of God, the order that laws imposed as a reflection of God's universal order. "Natural Law is that which nature, that is to say God Himself, teaches to all animals . . . ," declared the English thirteenth-century legist, Henry Bracton, "a certain regulated impulse arising out of the nature of a living thing." Each particular creature follows the law of its own being. The law of man and of human society "regards the state of the body politic," and imposes its pattern on society.

Strictly speaking, men—even kings—could not *make* laws: only apply the insights and deductions drawn from the laws of nature—that is, the observable results of God's commands. And, as if this were not enough, even the divine prerogatives of kingship dimmed somewhat before the claims of a more manifestly priestly figure: that of the Pope, against whose pretensions to supremacy medieval monarchs struggled long and hard.

All this meant that kings could be challenged in theory as well as practice, either on behalf of papal claims to greater authority than theirs, or on behalf of mundane laws, contracts, and customs, like the mutual duties of vassal and lord in feudal society.

The Reformation had removed the first argument in states like England and Sweden, where kings became supreme heads of local churches. The civil troubles following the Reformation subordinated traditional limitations to the need for order. Absolutism, writes the Belgian scholar, Emil Lousse, "is a monarchy which once was, but does not remain, limited." Subject to theoretical qualifications, medieval kings had been absolute too. However, their power and their means of asserting it were not absolute, depending as they did on nobles and estates. During the fifteenth and sixteenth centuries, the crown freed itself from dependence on the feudal nobility's monopoly of military power. The proud *cortes* of Aragon were humbled by Philip II in the 1590's. Around that same time, in France, in Naples, in the Spanish Netherlands, estates and assemblies ceased to meet and hence to limit the power of the rising princes.

The assemblies of estates representing the orders of the nation, born after the thirteenth century to provide monarchs with exceptional subsidies, could bolster a king's power or brake it. As a rule, kings appealed to estates in hope of material or political support, sought to leave them dormant when they could (or wished to) do without them. This is very clear in France, where strong kings like Francis I and Henry II ignored the Estates-General (as these national assemblies were called there). The Estates revived when royal power weakened during the period of religious wars, but did not meet again for 175 years after 1614 when the Court determined to afford potential opposition no opportunity to express itself.

In England, on the other hand, the Tudor Revolution of the sixteenth century needed the legal endorsement of a great representative body. In 1485, at the end of the Wars of the Roses, it was Parliament that validated Henry VII's succession to the crown. In 1534, Henry VIII appealed to it to confirm his break with Rome, appoint him head of the Church of England, and establish the line of succession. Thus, statutes legalized by Parliamentary approval formed the basis of the modern English state, and sovereignty in England came to rest not solely in the crown but in Parliament too: the ultimate constitutional authority being "the King-in-Parliament." But this was an exceptional departure and, even in England, its implications did not reveal themselves until the seventeenth century (see pp. 302–311). That "dread and fear of kings" Shakespeare alludes to, endured:

Bibliothèque Nationale

The convening of the Estates-General in 1614.

Not all the water in the rough rude sea
Can wash the balm from an anointed king;
The breath of worldly men cannot dispose
The deputy elected by the Lord.

The Dynastic Hold

The prestige of hereditary succession, the feeling that kingly estate was vested in a particular family, strengthened the claims of dynastic legitimacy. God's choice was manifest in royal birth; and analogy to a father's "natural" authority suggested that kings should be respected and revered like fathers by their children. Whatever the strength of such arguments, hereditary succession tended to create strong attachments to the ruling family. In the dynastic states of the sixteenth century and after, loyalty to the king, respect for the sacred character of his office, fulfilled the function that patriotism does today. Dynastic states were more or less ancient patrimonies, to be defended as legacies from the past or out of the "love and loyalty" their subjects bore to their rulers and to Christ whose regents princes are on earth.

Such states would be managed like very large family estates, patrimonial rights displacing and replacing—as far as could be done—the particular rights of vassals, feudal tenants, and provinces. As this happened, dynastic conflicts—at least on the legalistic level—turned more and more on questions of inheritance, of dowries, of rights acquired by marriage or birth, so that the claims of princes, asserted or defended as they had always been by force of arms, were justified by reference to marriage contracts rather than feudal ones, and the territory of future national states, as we shall see, was pieced together like a family holding. The best example of this will be found in the house of Habsburg, whose greatness stemmed less from the imperial title to which it clung than from its patient accumulation of territories around its original Austrian possessions. It is not surprising that, within a realm held as the hereditary assets of a family, kings stressed rather a father's overweening rights than those of feudal lords.

Kingship preserved some of its magic and mystical aspects—especially to the popular mind—but after the sixteenth century theory stressed less God's will in the king's making or the king's responsibility to govern according to God's wishes and to his coronation bond than the subject's duty to obey his king. "We may not resist, nor in any wise hurt, an anointed king, which is God's lieutenant, viceregent and highest minister in the country where he is king," admonished one of the homilies of the Church of England, meant to inspire preaching in all the churches of the land. Even in distant Muscovy, the ever-present monks affirmed that the Tsar, "though he be in body like all others, yet in power of office he is like God."

The Contract

Yet there were certain limits even to this. The first lay in the surviving notion of a royal power based on agreement. But even where such contractual views gave way to the absolute prerogatives of divine right, respect for natural law or established custom limited the sovereignty of the king—that is, his freedom to meddle in certain spheres, like private life or public worship. There was just so much that the king could do, and even theoretical demands for absolute obedience to him were qualified by particular rights.

The other limit was to be found in the political writings of certain Christian theorists like the Jesuit Juan de Mariana and—much more circumspectly—John Calvin. Blending memories of the old feudal right to resist a liege that does not carry out his bargain with the traditional image of the Christian monarch's duty to defend true religion and repress heresy, such men argued that, while magistrates must be obeyed and not least the king, highest of all magistrates, in certain circumstances inferior magistrates might maintain God's order and true Word against superior ones, even against the king, should he become a tyrant.

This argument would be enlisted in England against the Stuart kings who insisted on their divine right to rule absolutely, at the expense of their contractual duties to their people. By the end of the seventeenth century, English kings had become the first magistrates of their realm within the King-in-Parliament structure, which combined hereditary and elective authorities, partners (if unequal ones) in the rule of the realm.

Elsewhere, the result was different. Men came to feel that no social contract could last long without a strong power to enforce it, a power freed of all restraints except those of expediency—like that of Machiavelli's *Prince*. In a world where the existing order seemed constantly threatened by some change or challenge, survival was seen as society's chief concern. It was crucial that sovereignty—the absolute, final power of decision—should be defined at last. A single will must·be supreme, free to make and enforce law as he pleases for the welfare of society, not as a delegate of a sovereign people but as the ordained agent of God.

Sovereignty has to do with ultimate authority and the power to enforce it. In the Middle Ages, sovereignty rested in the law of God and political disputes turned on the interpretation and application of laws, not on their creation. The king enforced laws. He was never above the law. Now, religious wars, internal disorders, external threats, grief and despair like that which moved the Englishman Thomas Hobbes in later but similar circumstances "for the present calamities of my country," argued in favor of a monarchy so strong that no resistance could disturb the order it imposed. "If he is to govern the state well," wrote

The title page of *Leviathan*, by Thomas Hobbes. British Museum.

Jean Bodin in 1576, as French religious struggles raged around him, "a sovereign prince must be above the law."

Yet even Bodin still felt that, above the law or not, the prince was bound by God's and nature's laws. Not really accountable but still —as with Aristotle—theoretically bound. A hundred years later Thomas Hobbes (1588–1679), as shocked as Bodin had been by civil warfare, "giddy people," and ambitious men, would free the prince of bonds and of Aristotle. Hobbes will reappear in another context later (see pp. 402–404). Here he represents the lengths to which the search for order and authority would go, his reasoning founded on disabused observation subjecting the traditional notions to devastating criticism.

The old notion of contract is no use, argued Hobbes in his *Leviathan* (1651). Treaties, promises, or oaths are meaningless, incapable of securing peace among men because men will always break them. The only thing that can repress the savage instincts of mankind is force, and the fear that force alone inspires. The absolute king must have the power of arms, and that last word in settlement of disputes which we entitle justice. However arbitrary or tyrannical, a master such as this is better than no master and his despotic rule the only logical alternative to the savage freedom of catch-as-catch-can from which it saves us. We must not try to hobble the ruler's authority by limiting institutions or by opportunities for effective criticism, because anything that affects his power is just a step back to anarchy. The king is not responsible to anyone. He is everything. And, though we sacrifice our freedom to him, we must realize that liberty and life cannot be reconciled, and it is therefore better to choose life because, without it, liberty is entirely impossible.

To presuppose a natural law is to admit some outer standard of criticism. But states are no longer part of some theoretical Christendom. The *Respublica Christiana* in whose context such arguments could hold water had disintegrated. States could be seen to be—and were—independent societies, subsisting in terms of power alone, knowing no right or wrong but those defined in laws made by the sovereign. The only law of nature Hobbes recognized was survival. This could only be achieved by escaping the natural state of war into a society ruled by a sovereign power that protects its subjects' lives at the expense of their freedom—including the freedom to judge. Sovereignty and tyranny had become identical, and even the traditional hatred of tyranny was banned as bad for society.

Hobbes' views were shared by few and generally rejected as excessive. Yet they proved prophetic. By his day, in any case, the kind of natural law regarded as transcendental was being discarded, natural law was being gently divorced from theology and discussed in terms of a government which alone can create an ordered civilization and which finds justification in its satisfactory operation. Social convenience vindicates governments more forcibly than divine will, and governments, that work presumably conform to natural law.

Thus, as the power of natural law was gradually loosened and the hold of religion weakened, law was no longer seen as the expression of a higher morality but as the servant of particular objectives, rationally appraised. Legislation, like policy, was justified less by the will of God than by the will of the sovereign, moved by "reason of state." What James H. Billington in his *The Icon and the Axe* (1966) has said of Peter the Great's revolution in eighteenth-century Russia applies to the seventeenth-century changes of the West: "Political expediency based on impersonal calculation replaced a world where ideal ends and personal attachments had been all-important." And the absolute monarchy, represented by Louis XIV and (at least theoretically) by his heirs, turned into a more secular absolutism, increasingly divested even of its religious mantle in the hands of the so-called Enlightened Despots to come.

Government

Sir Thomas More, writing in the days of Henry VIII, had defined government as "nothing but a certain conspiracy of rich men procuring their own commodities under the name and title of a Commonwealth." In the sixteenth and seventeenth centuries government proceeded from the court. In effect the court served as a means of distributing among the wealthy the revenue from the country's taxes. Yet income dwindled and expenditure swelled as old feudal sources of revenue decayed, as an

increasingly sedentary court could no longer pass on its expenses to aristocratic hosts who entertained the king on his travels, as armaments became
more costly and wars "a financial disaster." Still, the king had to be
liberal, "to multiply," as James I's councilors put it, "and confer affection
and duty." Bounty, explained Secretary Cecil, was "an essential virtue of
the king." A generation later, a royal servant reasoned that it was "as
necessary for princes to have places of preferment [for] servants of merit
as money in their exchequer." Actually, it was because they had no
money in their exchequer that they needed places, or what we would
call "offices," filled by political appointment.

To tame the great nobles or to intimidate them, to employ or pension
off his hungry gentlemen, the king needed armies, places, and resources.
To raise resources he needed armies which, once in being, were certain to devour the resources. It was a vicious circle and one that no
prince, no statesman in this period, ever resolved. Princes had no ready
money. This could come only from taxes. Since adequate or trained personnel was lacking, most taxes were farmed out to financiers who paid
a lump sum down and perhaps promised a rent from future collections
for the right to gather what they could. In effect, governments mortgaged
their tax income for ready cash, and they did this on very onerous
terms which left them little better off than when they started.

Yet there were favorites to reward, servants and officers to be paid,
loans to be redeemed, armed forces to maintain, supplies to be collected. To pay for these they granted monopolies or privileges, gave
lands away or leased them for a nominal sum, borrowed money or raised
it at a discount, sold offices to men who proceeded to recoup their investment at the country's expense, and altogether garnered what resources they could in whatever way they could. While these ways varied
widely, they were always cumbrous and inefficient.

We might look upon the development of governments in the early
modern period as an attempt to introduce order and efficiency into a
chaotic structure. But any interpretation that presented changes as de-
riving from a consistent purpose or intent would only superimpose
anachronistic motives on the confusion of reality. Men—including
princes—struggled with their difficulties in piecemeal fashion and tried to
solve them in often contradictory ways. No single rule—except perhaps
the absence of a rule—presided over their policies beyond tradition,
which, like the Bible, can lend itself to any interpretation at all. And if
the absolute power of a royal prince eventually triumphed in most societies (though not in all) it did so as the result of hit-or-miss advances
and, by our standards, only imperfectly.

And this was probably just as well! What really triumphed, as we
shall see, over most of continental Europe, was less the absolute king than
a notion of absolute power and, to some extent, a structure to support
and extend this power. Meanwhile, from the very first, the development
of the modern state obeyed not theories but immediate needs; above

all, like everything and everybody else, the need for money which—all agreed—was the greatest power in the world next to Divine Providence.

Revenues

Inflation, high and rising prices, growing expenses, faced state governments no less than individuals. Revenues grew: Charles V's tripled, Philip II and Philip III's doubled in the course of their reigns. But debts grew fourfold and over. Constant treasury deficits had to be made good by loans, unpaid loans led to bankruptcies, the finances of the state seemed ever verging on disaster, and fiscal struggles dominated all others. From this point of view, Spain's policy in the Netherlands of the 1560's (see below pp. 287–290), the arbitrary taxes, the exactions that ignored traditional rights of cities and estates, appear as an increasingly desperate attempt to tap the riches of a great marketplace, and the revolt of the Netherlands far less a rising in defense of religious freedom than an insurrection against heavier taxation.

This brings up once again one of the most striking facts about this age: the limits of its possibilities and means, the contrast between all-powerful potentates and their effective reach, between the scale of empires and their power—sapped by primitive technology, inadequate communications and administrative structure. The explanation of why so many wars and policies collapsed halfway lies in the limited means of those who undertook them. Limits in food, in treasure, in productivity, in transport, and in speed. Victorious campaigns petered out because armies could march only just so far; great states went bankrupt for loss of one bullion fleet; cities and provinces lay at the mercy of the elements; emperors were helpless to police their realm, and ruling was the most haphazard kind of process. Again and again great enterprises ran out of breath, imperial aspirations were scotched, plans otherwise logical enough were stifled by the narrow possibilities reality allowed. Nothing ever quite went on beyond a certain scale in time and space.

A certain scale in money too, which could affect the rest. Gold and silver coinage was "the blood of the economy," the substance of the state: cut off its circulation and the state would weaken, its powers fail. Yet the available quantity of coinage was still remarkably small: the greatest banks held only little gold by our standards and precious metals circulating in all of Europe in 1660 probably amounted to less than two tons of gold. Contemporary notions of value prevented the widespread utilization of mere tokens, and attempts to introduce coinage of baser metals, such as copper in Spain after 1600, created peculiar situations in which great wagon trains were needed to haul a moderate sum and the price of wax candles took up as much room and weighed far more than the candles themselves. In 1653, to pay for 100 lbs. of candles or cheese, one had to use copper coins weighing 400 lbs.

Shortage or awkwardness of coins meant that many exchanges and payments were still made by barter. In 1573 only 6 per cent of Swedish royal revenue was paid in cash, the rest in goods of every kind from grain and ale and butter to skins and ore. By the beginning of the seventeenth century, most taxes, wages, and exchanges were still in kind, not cash; and as the century ended, after great efforts to put royal revenues on a cash basis, almost a third of them were still received in kind. True, Sweden was peculiarly backward and out of the way, and the countries of north and northwest Europe were more advanced. But her case was not so utterly exceptional in a world in most of whose parts a natural economy persisted well into the eighteenth century.* It is striking to see the difficulties states faced, even more than individuals, in collecting and distributing revenues, keeping accounts, making payments, becoming and remaining solvent.

In some ways, shortage of specie spurred the search for ways to get around it. European trade grew not on coin but credit. Forebear of the check, the bill of exchange, invented in the Middle Ages, was increasingly put to use. There was a great expansion in the use of promissory notes —especially notes payable to order, rather than on a fixed date. The expansion of negotiable credit instruments was the key to the commercial expansion of Europe. And seventeenth-century men understood quite well that advances in instruments of credit—the increasing sophistication of notes, bills, and discount—were the foundation for the extension of commerce, industry, and agriculture and, hence, for the strengthening of the state.

The Sale of Offices

One way of raising ready money was the sale of offices: in France especially, but gradually in many other countries too, the traditional gift made upon appointment to some public function—exciseman, alderman, or magistrate—became a fee, a price; the office a commodity that could be bought, sold, inherited (also for a fee), an object of investment and speculation, a source of revenue for the monarchy which could always invent more posts, as governments today can print more money and with similar results.

The practice seemed to kill two birds with one stone: it supplied needed administrators and personnel for an ill- or unstructured state and made them pay for the privilege. In the long run it proved costly, for, like all mortgages, it had to be paid off eventually, not only in the salaries of officers which were meager and irregularly doled out, but in restricted freedom to reform the haphazard machinery created according to no administrative logic, and in the poor quality of administration itself. "The ministry of the judges," explained a speaker in the French

---

* Hungarian peasants could hardly gather the specie to pay their taxes. As late as 1783, several Hungarian counties asked to be allowed to pay their taxes in kind. It has recently been argued that much popular—especially rural—unrest, even in the West, arose from unwonted demands for taxes to be paid in cash by men whose economic activity gave them very few spare coins.

Estates of 1568, "their jurisdiction and distribution of justice are nothing but a shop where the offices they have purchased wholesale are sold
at retail." Yet, as the hard-pressed princes grasped at any straw, more
and more offices were created and the class of officers—owners of their
office—grew.

"Every time your majesty creates an office," one of his ministers
told Louis XIV, "God creates a fool to buy it." It is worth remembering that, as a matter of fact, the buyers were not such fools as all that.
Purchasers gained not only in social prestige but in concrete advantages: relief from the obligation to billet troops and feed them, from
militia and guard duties, from communal taxes, sometimes even from
the poll tax and salt tax. Since there were other ways of acquiring privileges by buying immunities and exemptions or holding municipal office,
this left ever fewer households subject to taxation and, while taxes themselves went steadily up, they had to be borne by those very households least able to support them. More and more functions kept being
invented, some sold to two or three persons at once, so that the same
post might be filled (and its revenues cashed) by different men every
second or third semester or year. At last, in 1706, the French government proposed to sell life exemptions and privileges *without* office, so
many of them per parish.

The multiplication of offices went to mad lengths. Few could live out
their lives without appeal to myriad legal officials, from scriveners to
the most exalted judges—barristers and solicitors, notaries, ushers, sher-
iffs and bailiffs, registrars, recorders, clerks of municipalities or courts,
each with his fees and also with what the French called "spices," those
little gifts without which nothing would advance. None could ignore the
tax farmers and their minions, or the toll gatherers along rivers and
roads, at the gates of towns or marketplaces. These last swarmed everywhere. Along the Seine alone, the owner of a shipload of goods would
have to pay dues to thirty-five different persons levying tolls, weighing,
stamping, checking, inspecting, accounting, listing at one locality after
another. The effect this had on prices was tragic: many doubled
during the twenty years before 1715, while farmers, vintners, and other
producers got less for their products. Thus firewood cost half as much
again in 1715 as in 1695, while forest land fell in price by a third to a
half. The difference went to bureaucracy and taxes.

The Bureaucrats

The sale of offices was a fiscal expedient peculiar to some countries.
The rise of the bureaucracy was a development common to all. Over
the centuries, the retainers of the medieval prince had become administrators, his household had spawned a bureaucracy increasingly specialized as the scope and complexity of governmental affairs increased.
Temporary public service by clerics or by knights turned into long-
term employment for more-or-less regular pay, by university-trained

secretaries, officials, councilors. The increasing scale and intricacy of problems facing the modern ruler demanded an ever more numerous and specialized administrative staff to help him govern. As we have seen, one reaction to this had been to employ private persons to carry out many public functions. The sixteenth century, however, brought an increasing concern to get a better grasp of the administration and especially of affairs in the provinces. With it, there came increasing use of men charged with a temporary commission—commissioners—to perform one particular task: carry out an investigation, submit a report, oversee royal troops in an area, organize police or constabulary forces, inspect or improve highways, above all exploit sources of revenue, surveying fairs, tax rolls, royal properties, and such.

Where officeholders exploited their offices primarily for themselves and their families, the new bureaucrats—though not above bribes—were direct servants of the prince and state from whom pay and advancement would come and toward whom they directed their loyalties. These officers could be recruited among commoners, as in France or Denmark, among the petty nobility as in Germany or Sweden, among both as in Russia, Italy, or Spain. Ultimately they became a new class, cut off from older feudal standards which hampered and hamstrung royal initiatives: a new service nobility, formally recognized as in Russia, integrated in the old as in France, but enlisted in the service of the state. And, as the old nobility lost its function though never its place in society, a new class grew, grew and proliferated, its upper reaches merged with the nobility but functionally different from it: the bureaucracy of the modern state.

Thus, parallel to the great web of semi-independent officers and placemen, there grew another network of commissioners, commissaries, inspectors, comptrollers, and even governors, who were more truly the king's stewards—*intendants* as the greatest of them came to be called—in constant struggle against the traditional authorities, officials, placemen, provincial courts and estates, which sought to protect their prerogatives from the encroachments of the new bureaucrats.

Like any great, growing enterprise, the state was striving and fumbling for a more efficient grasp of its affairs, more effective control of its subjects. The difficulties were huge. In 1613, we hear Philip III's secretary declare that no human being, not even the King himself, knew the amount of royal revenues. The King would very much like to know, he had given orders that a report be prepared, but his orders had not been carried out. The only consolation was that the task was probably impossible, so that whether an inquiry was undertaken or not made little difference in the end. Over and over again the kings and statesmen of this age appear in this strange light, bound as it were by invisible threads of ignorance, inefficiency, inability to act beyond very narrow limits—the limits of their time and means.

An Imperfect Centralism

To mobilize resources, the seventeenth-century state had created a staff of public servants who sought efficiency and, in its service more and better information, the kind of intelligence that Philip III could not get: statistics, population census, registration of births, deaths and marriages, tables that showed the movement of prices. Ideally, they were supposed to direct and control everything. In practice, there was no general plan, no efficiency, a great deal of interference, and much local control.

The government did not seek so much to increase production as to ensure the provisioning of cities and armies and the collection of taxes. The chief means for doing this was by requisition. Farmers were bound to carry their products to the market. If that did not provide sufficient resources, the farms were searched and goods confiscated. It followed that farmers hid a good deal of their produce and the supply machinery worked badly, the more so since difficulties of transport did not allow the cities to draw supplies from very far away. Shortages could soon turn into famine, as we have seen, and successful tax raids into the countryside, depriving farmers of the grain needed for seed, could produce scant harvests in the year to come, peasants taking to vagrancy in search of the food which cities denied them.

Incompetence and technological backwardness saved Europe from the totalitarian implications of bureaucratic absolutism. However, as machinery grew, as administrative techniques were refined by experience, as government came to encompass more and more, one ominous development occurred: a real bureaucracy implied fixed regulations which would gnaw away the crown's power of decision. Decisions, by their very number and frequency, passed out of the hands of the central authority (kings, secretaries of state, *intendants*) into myriad offices, to the lesser officials who operated in terms of precedents and rules. Royal power had created bureaucracy in order to affirm itself. In due course it would find itself limited by the growth and efficiency of its own administration, which came to operate increasingly as an independent organism with its own life and ends and power.

The same held true of the judiciary structure, and especially of the great magistrates. Already in the 1580's Montaigne deplored the rise of a "fourth estate" of judicial officers. By the time of Richelieu, as we shall see, one generation later, the force of the judiciary, with its own *esprit de corps* and sense of power, could not be ignored. It had acquired both a dynamic and an inertia of its own.

The crown had cast off the influence of its overmighty subjects—proud clerics and rebellious nobles—but the royal administration, so much of it made up and carried on by private office-owners, escaped its control.

It existed by virtue of the royal sanction and constituted no threat to the king's political position, as great nobles once had done. But its interest was vested in a situation to which it opposed all change, obstructing all reforms as menaces to its own existence. Having defeated all royal innovations designed to bring the system up-to-date by administrative or financial reform, the magistracy had its share in the eventual ruin of the Old Regime that went to its death after 1789. The king could do anything except touch the privileges on which he had founded his absolutism and the servants on whom he had founded his state. In the long run this was bound to weaken both the state and his own hold on it. But all this was not yet; and what there was, was slight, as we shall see, and slow to develop.

Meanwhile, when all criticisms against the new system are taken to account, the fact remains that royal officers were preferable to "little lords and barons who usually tyrannize [the villages and the little people] and gnaw them right down to the bone with unjust taxes," as a French memoir put it in 1643. In places where the royal writ did not run, because crown forces were weak or local and noble privileges strong, "the state of nature" prevailed—that is, chaos. A Castilian noble, the Marquess of Almazan, would comment in 1613 on the state of Catalonia: "They say that the *caballeros* here are free. But in my opinion they are more oppressed than those of Castile, because they cannot go out of town without a large number of men, whereas I could travel from Madrid to Almazan alone, or with a single servant, without being afraid of anybody. That is what I call freedom, and not what passes for freedom in Catalonia." When it cut across particular rights, the royal power was challenging what amounted as a rule to licence for members of the ruling classes to do as they pleased at the expense of the rest. When the king's servants and the king's writ cut across this, they did so usually for the sake of revenue, but also for the sake of what we would regard as justice and orderly government.

In any case, it is important not to exaggerate the range and scale of these innovations. The very term "state" only begins to be used in its present sense around mid-sixteenth century. Seventeenth-century government was still highly informal, still the concern of king and favorites, advisors, servants, and their creatures. Everything was a matter of improvisation and expedients, reactions to external pressures and predicaments. Ministers like Richelieu, favorites like the Duke of Buckingham, "ruled" by virtue of their credit with the king, through men personally devoted to them, who, in turn, preferred to use loyal subordinates: possibly relatives from whom, by tradition and interest, the truest loyalty could be expected. And while so many things escaped attention, a host of petty issues cluttered the highest levels of government. Louis XIII and Richelieu concerned themselves with fixing the price of bread or with the numbers and pay of small provincial garrisons. Things which today would be settled by subordinate clerks were considered

Cardinal Richelieu, a painting by Philippe de Champaigne. Louvre, Paris.

and discussed by the king and his secretaries. Philip II of Spain, determined to control the web of his vast holdings, labored day and night, "sitting forever over [his] papers" as his subjects complained, submerged by their mass, submitting his subordinates to interminable delays. Over half a century later, the best-administered country in Europe—the France of Louis XIV and Colbert—was run by only a thousand men or so. If we consider this meager executive overwhelmed by the number of decisions to be made, by the number of tasks to be carried out, the paucity of agents and resources—a slenderness of structure reflecting and affecting the slenderness of its means—we may well wonder not at how much they let slip by them but how much they managed to achieve.

The king's secretaries themselves, very important persons, had no place of their own in the royal palace or any official buildings. They came in to confer with the king and went home carrying their papers to work there with their retainer-clerks. Only as the century advanced did this begin to change, chanceries being allotted special quarters for offices and archives, rulers setting aside office space in their palace or some other public building. Philip himself set up the royal archives at Simancas, but it took a century before his Habsburg cousins followed suit. By the end of his reign Louis XIV employed 900 "royal secretaries," and still "himself remained his own first minister" and not the least hard-working. Yet, as his Grand Almoner had advised Philip II, "God did not send your majesty and all the other kings, his viceroys on earth, to waste their time reading or writing . . ." The function of the king was vaster,

Louis XIV, a painting attributed to Hyacinthe Rigaud. John B. Wolf Collection.

more important, could not be trammeled by administrative concerns and yet could not be carried out effectively until a solution for them had been found.

The Royal Cult Amplified

What Charles I's minister, the Earl of Strafford, said of England applied everywhere: "The authority of a king is the keystone which closes up the arch of order and government, which, once shaken, all the frame falls together in a confused heap of foundation and battlement." But the authority of a king depended on his resources. Rid of his debt, Strafford told Charles I, "You may govern as you please." Shakespeare had said as much in an earlier generation and his repeated references to order and degree reflected the contemporary concern that they might not endure. Thus, Ulysses in *Troilus and Cressida* explains:

> The heavens themselves, the planets, and this center
> Observe degree, priority and place,
> Insisture, course, proportion, season, form,
> Office and custom, in all line of order . . .
> . . . but when the planets,
> In evil mixture, to disorder wander,
> What plagues and what portents, what mutiny!

Too many mutinies, too much disorder plagued the times for such words to be taken lightly. Again, the authoritarian orientation of the age was in direct proportion to its need for some direction, the threat of chaos constant over it, the faith placed in a supreme figure to reassure protect, provide—symbol of the unity and order so evidently lacking, so sorely missed. Habsburgs in Spain, Stuarts in England, Bourbons in France, lesser monarchs elsewhere, sought to elaborate an ideal and practice based on such needs, the institution of absolute monarchy which culminated in the person of Louis XIV.

The power of the king could be filtered through the person of a minister; but such a man, like Richelieu for Louis XIII or Olivares for Philip IV, could become a mayor of the palace, a rival power threatening to supplant the increasingly formal power of the crown. Louis XIV, like Philip II, resolved to be his own first minister, alone to know all secrets and hold all strings of power. The effort needed to achieve this was enormous and could scarce have been borne by a lesser constitution. Even so, the monarch's life became increasingly disciplined, routinized, his time and gestures rationed, so to speak, with a view to effective production, so that one could always tell where and when to find him doing what. Like the Spanish Escorial but more so, the palace at Versailles was more than just a royal fancy: it was the retreat and workplace of the monarchy, the center of its bureaucracy, where two whole wings were filled with offices, where the King received his secretaries of state one after the other.

Since he wanted no overweening minister, no indispensable servant of the state beside himself, Louis divided and mingled functions—and functionaries too—feeling his safety depended on their rivalries, pitting one minister against another all the time. Rid of a first minister by the death of Mazarin in 1661, Louis found it harder to control the royal officers whom purchase had rendered independent, masters of their charges. Against them he created a staff of his own, appointed by him and liable to dismissal, a whole new civil and sometimes military hierarchy in the provincial administration, fiscality, police, and justice—first and foremost the *intendants.* And to enforce his will directly, without time-wasting recourse to the courts, he used his personal warrant, the *lettre de cachet,* by which the King could order any individual, any body, to carry out his sovereign and arbitrary will. A *lettre de cachet* could be an order for an arrest or exile; it could scotch a plot real or assumed, remove an obstacle from the royal path, or simply grant the request of a family shocked by the misbehavior of some fractious member. These orders were carried out, and the general order was enforced, by an increasingly elaborate network of police and by an increasingly efficient army, created, maintained, improved according to Louis' will by the men who served him, no longer drawn from the rebellion-prone older nobility but promoted from the bourgeoisie, their fortune focused wholly on the King's commands.

The older nobility did not like this. Gentlemen who could trace their ancestry further back than the Crusades, further than Charlemagne, felt offices and public functions to be theirs by birth, and resented seeing them filled by men whose birth was far from noble. They also resented the competition of more recently ennobled families: nobility of office or, as the French called them from the magistrate's garb, "of the robe." The fact is that, when the King could get educated and loyal men of noble birth to do his bidding, he preferred them to commoners.

Pope Alexander VII had remarked that, just as earthly kings liked to have wellborn men about them, so the King of Heaven would prefer them too. A king without nobles, decreed the Duke of Savoy, was like a diamond set in lead. Royalty had brought them to obedience by making them useless or dependent while maintaining their privileges; but it could not touch these privileges which were the price of their support, and hence of its own power, yet hampered its actions and weighed on its income. A king without nobles might be a diamond set in lead; a king with nobles was like a diamond behind bars.

Some absolute rulers even founded their rule on nobles themselves: the Elector of Brandenburg; or Charles XI of Sweden, whose bureaucratic absolutism was introduced in 1680 with the support of the petty gentry who backed the crown's campaign to recover estates alienated to great magnates so that the royal domain could provide reliable revenues for the salary of their offices. But many French nobles, especially those of the highest aristocracy as contemporary writers observed, lacked the instruction needed for administrative posts—or the self-discipline. Their letters testify to this: ill-written, childish, full of misspellings. They also lacked the means to buy those places which princes wished to sell for revenue. In any case they had never liked the sort of policy that cut into their status or their privileges as any must that sought the public good. So, Louis set out to domesticate and harness his nobles, assembling them at a court whose costly routine made them increasingly dependent on his good will, on the pensions, posts, or bene-

An illustration from a contemporary souvenir book for Louis XIV's carrousel of 1662, giving a general view of the square at Versailles and of all the participants. The Art Institute of Chicago.

fices he might grant them. He gave them the impression that the functions of the state were divided between nobility and crown but actually kept the essentials for the new bureaucrats who depended on him, while dazzling the court aristocracy with splendid games which persuaded them that Versailles was a kind of Mt. Olympus and they the heroes and the demigods attendant on the Sun King, greatest of them all.

The need to enlist the nobles into this splendid and deceptive masquerade explains some aspects of the royal cult. The King had to be very great so that his reflected greatness should make the courtiers feel more than decorative parasites, endow them with a particle of his own high significance. The analogy of the sun came readily to mind. Nor was it an analogy only applied to Louis. A courtier had already likened Henry IV to the sun: "You who are that great sun who gives life, light and strength . . ."; and Henry's heir, Louis XIII, though cruelly beaten like all children of his time to the point where he fainted under the blows, was nevertheless brought up like a kind of demigod: foreign ambassadors came to greet him, poor people came on pilgrimage and begged permission to touch him to be cured of scrofula, at times he was presented from a balcony to crowds which knelt at his sight, drums rolled and flags waved at his passing.

The grandson of Henry IV was even more the center of the world. At Louis XIV's estate of Marly, near Versailles, built between 1679 and 1686, the whole design reminded the beholder of the role the monarch was supposed to play. The plan of Marly is theatrical but unambiguous: Louis XIV dwelt in the center, in a pavilion decorated with solar symbols and dedicated to Jupiter, king of the gods. Around this, twelve other pavilions pressed other gods or virtues to his retinue: Renown, Abundance, Apollo, and so on. On one side the chapel, at the other side the guardhouse, as though, comments Roland Mousnier, "the Lord God too were one of the officers of the Lord King." And it is true, the king becomes alike to God, as he had been in the later Roman Empire and especially in Byzantium. Inversely God becomes increasingly like a king, an imposing patriarch reminiscent of Jupiter, divine majesty providing a reflection of the earthly kind.

This centralism appeared at every level. The city planning of the seventeenth century mirrored the royal desire to establish within the city the same order as within the state—symmetrical plans, regular lines for streets, squares, buildings. Just as in the government the nation focused on the sovereign, just as in thought subsidiary ideas must be subordinated to the major premise, so urban patterns tended to order buildings round a central point, applying hierarchy in city as in state.

The world of learning was enlisted too. In the 1630's, Cardinal Richelieu found out that a group of literary-minded friends had been meeting since 1629 at the home of one of the King's secretaries, Valentin Conrart. In 1635 he made these people into a public and privileged body, the French Academy, whose protector he appointed himself. Academicians received pensions. Their duty was to sing the praises of the King, provide polemicists against Spanish or Dutch critics of France, purify and regulate the language for which they began a dictionary and a grammar. In 1671 Colbert made this privileged group into an official public body, the King its protector, allotting it a yearly budget, quarters in the Palace of the Louvre, and all this bent ever more to the publicity of the King. As the dramatist Racine wrote, on their behalf: "All the words of the language, all its syllables seem precious to us, because we look upon them as so many instruments which shall serve the glory of our August Protector."

Absolutism and its Rivals

This new exaltation of royal power and the efforts to develop a machinery to serve it, reflect the overwhelming issue of security which dominates the time, the feeling voiced by Hobbes that covenants are fine, but covenants without the sword are but words. Hobbes and Louis XIV were contemporaries, each in his way expressing an absolute dread of anarchy and disturbance, which only unlimited sovereignty could counter. Since natural men are violent and brutish, hope could lie only in an artificial structure run by a supreme master—a superhuman trainer in a lion cage—whose arbitrary power would need to know no bounds. Different men arrived at this conclusion by different roads. In Louis' thinking the power of the state was justified by its existence, in that of Hobbes by the needs of individuals who, advised by self-interest and pressed by fear, accepted its all-engrossing protection. Such utilitarian justifications for absolutism differed both from the theological rationalizations of the time and from the populist references of modern totalitarianism. Yet if the justification differs, the results are similar: in each case, the state's authority becomes paramount, its validity is ultimate, its services are held indispensable. The subject abdicates all responsibility, including moral or religious, in exchange for a security of the most material kind.

Divine right had never been absolute. Its limited power, rendered legitimate by tradition, would now be challenged by a despotic rule justified by logic and by force. As to its necessity, most agreed. An English republican, speaking in 1653, observed that the question was not "whether we should be governed by arbitrary power, but in whose hands it should be." The ultimate aim was order, and only arbitrary power could ensure it, whether it was wielded by Louis XIV or by the man who had Louis' uncle-in-law executed: Oliver Cromwell. Of course, the Leviathan of Hobbes never materialized. The totalitarian dictatorship Hobbes envisaged was neither good nor, in its time, feasible. The mood of anxiety and gloom which it reflected, and (like so many other works written in the first half of the seventeenth century) with reason, waned in the relaxed second part of the century. The great heritage of Hobbes, in the end, would be his pessimistic view of human psychology and his suggestion that political thought be based on its analysis and application rather than on the unproved and irrelevant assertion of ancient and biblical law. However, this would only become clear later. For now, the shock was administered by Hobbes's utter totalitarianism, articulating what working politicians never voiced but rather tried to apply.

By the seventeenth century, the changes introduced to cope with the challenge of change evoked deep resentment and bitter opposition. People felt the need for absolutism, yet rebelled against its consequences; they sought the stability it promised yet resented its novelties. Some lines from James Harrington's *Oceana* (1656) reflect a struggle for power and survival between crown and estates:

> What is become of the princes of Germany? Blown up. Where are the Estates or the power of the people in France? Blown up. Where is that of the people of Aragon and the rest of the Spanish kingdoms? Blown up. Where is that of the Austrian princes in Switz? Blown up. . . . Nor shall any man show a reason that will be holding in prudence why the people of Oceana have blown up their king, but that their kings did not first blow up them.

Innumerable revolts and conflicts sprinkled the seventeenth century. Not risings of the poor against the rich alone, but rather of those dissatisfied with change and especially with royal taxation. Nobles rebelled against the King's attempts to trim their influence and their claws; provinces protested against the crown's attempt to abridge local liberties and integrate them into a centralized whole; peasants rose against the exactions of royal tax-collectors and the ravages of royal armies; workers rioted when bread was dear and work was lacking, killed the hated royal officers, sacked their offices and their homes; parliaments, estates, bodies of magistrates, expostulated against the growing number of royal officials whom the King could make and unmake at will and whose activities cut increasingly across theirs. All sides pleaded the public good, one in the name of the state and its head, the King, whose interest was one with the general interest of all; the others in the name of a structure where particular interests balanced one another to the general good.

Finally, religious conflicts capped all, fed upon and fanned all other frictions, setting Protestant against Catholic, Puritan against moderate, Catholic against Dissenters, persuading the kings of France that they will never be masters in their land until special Protestant privileges have been stamped out, English and Scottish Dissenters that their religious and economic interests were one, Spanish kings that their imperial ambitions went hand in hand with the service of Christ. For the religious contest we examined in Part I was not over and the hundred years before 1650 would see the full bloom of Counter-Reformation, the several-sided conflict of Catholicism and the Protestant sects complicating the political conflicts of princes avid for power and territory.

The Reformed Religions

The Social Function

In one sense, there is something very strange about the religious disputes that rend the age, a windmill-fighting quality in which oddly shaped arguments are turned against what seem oddly irrelevant issues. The modern reader feels disoriented before so much heat, such passionate attention bestowed on issues which he finds hard to recognize as such. Men waxed violent and bitter over quibbles, too often losing sight of larger matters, scoring points by philology or force which we today can scarcely credit. Yet behind the arguments which ·time has dessicated, behind the long rows of collected pamphlets and sermons and disputes, rise the important questions of power, social order, the place and duties of man and state and rulers, and of the reason for believing all these things, drawn from a total vision of God's plan for man and of its implications.

Since ultimate authority was suprahuman, it was essential to interpret its will and purpose. The great debate turned on these interpretations, on the deductions that were drawn from them, and, since the protagonists were human, on the attempts to reconcile existing interests and intentions with this superior law.

In all countries during this period, the Church played a crucial role, provided a pivot on which much of life still turned. The church building itself was central to the community—meeting hall, trysting place, sometimes storehouse, or passageway. The *Duomo* of Milan was typical of a thousand churches, and not in Catholic countries only, its great interior full of women sewing or spinning, of food and fruit sellers, of masons hewing stones for the unfinished parts, of people taking shortcuts—St. Carlo Borromeo who consecrated it in 1577 soon had to close the side doors to keep wheelbarrows and men on horseback from using it as a throughway.

The services themselves provided a resort and meeting place in an age when distractions were few and news at a premium. When illiteracy and primitive administration prevailed and there was scarcely a printed press, the pulpit was an essential platform for publicity of every sort. Uncultivated as they often were, priests and parsons were still likely to be the best educated men in the parish, speaking with authority on every aspect of life and politics from the length of hair to taxes. It was from the pulpit that most men learned about new laws, imposts, or great

A sixteenth-century Protestant conception of the cluttered interior of a cathedral showing the wide range of activities performed by the Catholic Church. Bibliothèque National, Paris.

events; and parish priests everywhere acted as representatives of civil authority, devoting sermons to the issues they had been directed to treat, passing on governmental proclamations and explaining them as best they could, exhorting the parishioners to comply. The cleric was a small but crucial cog in the secular machine, and priests often had to act as government agents in keeping public records, drawing up tax assessments, or administering the parish and its institutions.

No wonder everybody agreed that religion had a social function, a view crudely expressed by the London alderman who in 1650 proposed as the first remedy to contemporary problems, including that of decay of trade, "able and Godly ministers . . . that will teach the people to fear God, to obey their superiors and to live peaceably with each other . . ." Since "tuning the pulpit" was so important to politics, control of the levers through which this was done was a basic political issue.

The Political Struggle

The Reformation itself was part of this political struggle to control the pulpit, to control the men who controlled and effected the ideological orientation of society. It is striking that the first stirrings and the most lasting successes of the Reformation came around the fringes of Latin Christendom, almost as a kind of provincial (or protonational) revolution against the dominion of the Catholic *Roman* Church in Germany and Transylvania, around the Baltic and the North Sea. Today we are struck by the success of the Reformation in economically more advanced areas. But this was not so at first. It was the more backward or, at least, the more peripheral lands which felt its effect.

Everywhere political issues played a great part in determining the outcome of religious ones. German princes had found in Lutheranism a convenient way of asserting their independence against the Catholic Emperor and their power over their subjects. In France and Spain, on the other hand, the crown, solidly in control of the church, felt little need to break from Rome: while in England, the struggle to establish such control led to a break the crown had not envisaged. The Austrian Habsburgs wavered for a while: as emperors they were Romans; as men they were sometimes attracted by Protestant views; as central European princes they reflected the varying prejudices of their subjects, frequently Lutheran in the Austrian provinces or Utraquist in Bohemia, as well as Catholic. Only with Ferdinand II (1619–1637) was the final orientation of the dynasty settled and, while Ferdinand's Jesuit education and private prejudices cannot be underrated, the decision was evidently based on a judgment of what would be the most profitable alliance, what would furnish a firmer support to the Habsburg cause.

It is interesting to note that Lutheranism always remained a provincial and specifically German creed, which spread in the trail of the German diaspora, in central, eastern, and northern Europe, around the Baltic, along the Rhine, wherever colonies of German merchants or settlers lived or traded. This largely set its limits. And the provincialism was further emphasized by an almost principial subjection to the state. The theory that the state should direct church affairs and determine church policies was not new. It had been formulated in the great medieval struggles between Philip the Fair and Boniface VIII and strongly expressed when a similar controversy set the Emperor against the French-controlled popes of Avignon. In his *Defensor Pacis* (1324), Marsiglio of Padua argued that society exists in terms of the state which draws its authority from the people, whose actions and interests rule the outward existence, jurisdiction, and hierarchy of the church, whose province is in the souls of men, not in their worldly affairs. John Wycliffe's work had been in the same tradition and so had Luther's.

Erastianism

These ideas were going to be reformulated in the sixteenth century by the Swiss theologian Thomas Erastus (1524–1583), for whom the Church seemed but a department of the secular government, religion a private area policed by clergymen who were simply state employees. Erastianism, named after him, affected all Protestant churches and furnished matter for heated debates for some three centuries. But the debates took place mostly among Calvinists, since Lutherans on the whole accepted the spirit, if not always the applications, of the doctrine. Lutheran churches soon became and remained an arm of the secular power —conservative, intellectually unenterprising, socially irrelevant (except in a negative sense), and theologically overlaid with arid formalism. Their most striking effects were in supporting provincial isolationism, linguistic and cultural; and, by frequent reference to Mosaic law, to introduce bloodthirsty penalties for venal offenses, such as swearing and blasphemy, which were an ingrained part of life, and thus create new social and penal problems without solving old ones.

The Spread of Calvinism

Where Lutheranism was culturally and geographically circumscribed, socially and politically conservative, Calvinism was universalist, dynamic, highly subversive, less by deliberate purpose than because of the beliefs it inculcated and of their effects. As represented in John Bunyan's *Pilgrim's Progress* (1678), Christian life consists of continual effort, a trail of ambushes, endless struggle with evil, with the devil, with temptation, with corruption. Politics are no different. The struggle with Satan and his worldly minions is simply an extension of internal spiritual conflicts.

Puritans * lived in an age of chaos and crime (though perhaps no more so than any other). They knew that men are wicked, ever in need of control and restraint. They wished to train their conscience and will to withstand the sinfulness around them and triumph over it. The only way to this was by self-repression, self-discipline, stifling inward iniquities and weakness; and that by discipline, voluntarily accepted, which was furnished by the holy commonwealth—and immediately expressed by one's fellows in the congregation. Self-control suggested control of others. Self-repression suggested the repression of others: political discipline, watchful, critical, of the kind Puritans instituted whenever they could in the communities they set up in Geneva, in North America, and elsewhere.

Here was a new type of man, his own master after God, rejecting the traditional loyalties that still obtained for one loyalty only—to his faith, abandoning the passive attitude typical of common men for vigorous activity and strong assertiveness justified by faith. Puritans had an extraordinary training in criticizing themselves and others, debating, voting; and in a pious, rigorous, self-imposed routine. It gave them self-assurance based on more than mere fanaticism, and kept their morale high under the most difficult circumstances. Christian life was war and war was part of their calling. Some of the greatest military innovators of the time were moved by this sentiment—not least Oliver Cromwell. But, more important, it inspired their men, made them obey more readily, fight more effectively. Collective discipline prepared them for military discipline.

Yet, if faith was a form of war, so that John Bunyan's brave Christian Mr. Valiant-for-Truth would wish to carry his marks and scars with him

* This term was first used in the 1560's as a contemptuous description of those who wanted to purify the Church of England of all taints of popery: Presbyterians, Congregationalists, Baptists, eventually Quakers. Here it is employed in a broader sense to describe the "pure" and separatist tendencies of Calvinism.

into death "to be a Witness for me, that I have fought his Battles who now will be my Rewarder," faith came only by persuasion. To be committed, men must be convinced. Salvation was propagated by argument.

First and foremost an intellectual current, Calvinism was carried by books even more than by men; and books conveyed its message into circles and areas particularly open to its proud, demanding appeal— book-reading circles of intellectuals, merchants, artisans, gentry families unsuccessful in the competition for patronage and places, ready to turn their grudges, their earnestness, their opposition to an unheeding court, into a kind of self-assertive nonconformism. Looking back, with all the distortion such anachronistic parallels entail, Calvinists appear as the Bolsheviks of the Protestant camp, small in numbers, strong in faith, theory, and organization, highly dogmatic: a dangerous, potentially explosive, generally revolutionary force wherever they appeared.

The Calvinist network spread outward from Geneva to Scotland and Poland, Hungary, Holland, and Brazil. In France, as we shall see, the Huguenots (as they were called there, probably by a popular corruption of the German word *Eidgenossen*: confederates) attracted numerous converts, found support and leadership in royal princes like the Bourbons and in the Colignys, who were related to the greatest families in the country, and even threatened the security of the crown. Everywhere, their provincial structure of colloquies, churches, and synods enabled them to muster troops rapidly, with local congregations acting as recruiting units. In 1561, Admiral Coligny claimed there were 2,150 congregations in France and the forces they could muster for the religious wars that ran from 1562 to 1598 reflected their importance. But Calvinists remained a minority group and their church never held exclusive power for long outside Geneva, Scotland, and the Netherlands. As an opposition movement Calvinism concentrated too many disparate interests whose representatives might be discouraged by failure, softened by success, bought off, or diverted. In France, England, Scotland and Holland, where the Calvinist drive was strongest, religious and political concerns became inextricably mixed, so that political factions became religious ones and religious factions fought for political ends.

In the end, Huguenots, Presbyterians, and Puritans were defeated by the defenders of established political order. Those who were not defeated became the representatives of established order as in Geneva itself, or reconciled themselves to some kind of conservative compromise as in Transylvania. Not that Calvinism in its pure form was necessarily revolutionary. It could be that too, as when the poorer classes—sailors, laborers, the urban proletariat of the Dutch cities—seized upon the uncompromising doctrines of Pastor Gomarus (see p. 291) as a stick to beat the wealthy patricians. Proletarian groups sprang up here and there, following some local prophet who appealed to the principle of toleration and the equalitarian revelations of the inner light, denounced

The interior of a Protestant church which depicts a simplicity of worship and décor not found in the same artist's illustration of the Cathedral (p. 243).

worldly wisdom, laws and taxes, demanded a new freedom which might soon become anarchy or, if briefly successful as it had been at Münster, arbitrary oppression and mayhem.

None of these got very far. They were soon dispersed or eliminated by the forces of order, but they reflected a strong divisive tendency bound to affect a creed that stressed the individual conscience. Seventeenth-century Calvinism would break up into groups and sects, some of which rejected selective predestination for the notion that, God being a God of love, his grace must be available to all so that even the most humble could hope to be saved. In England, an official report of 1634 listed "Brownists, Anabaptists, Aryans, Traskites, Familists and some other sorts" as people on whom it would be well to keep an eye for their low-class membership, democratic ideas, and subversive refusal to conform. But the Puritan Parliamentary leaders were conservative and so was Cromwell; and the noble leaders of the Huguenots were quite reactionary. The Huguenot gentry of sixteenth-century France opposed royal encroachments on their feudal rights and dreamed of whittling down the growing power and efficiency of central government. The Parliamentary gentry in seventeenth-century England opposed royal "innovations" in appointments, taxation, and the administration and interpretation of law.

The most interesting result of religious divergencies was the founding in North America of colonies designed as havens for believers who could find no peace at home. Mid-sixteenth century had witnessed an unsuccessful attempt to settle French Huguenots in Brazil. The reigns of James I and his son Charles in England, with their increasingly determined persecution of nonconformists, drove a small band of Puritans, mostly humble people from East Anglia, first into Dutch exile and then to face the long, dangerous journey to America. (This at a time when the gentry of the Isle of Wight would make their wills before undertaking a journey to London, less than a hundred miles away.) On November 11, 1620, the *Mayflower* brought them to harbor at Cape Cod and shortly they were tilling their first fields around Plymouth Bay.

As their leader, Governor Bradford, put it: "as one small candle may light a thousand; so the light here kindled hath shone unto many . . ." There would be a new England overseas, a refuge sanctioned by royal charters for those who, having entered into a covenant with the Lord, meant to live out their lives in His way. By 1640, some 20,000 settlers straggled along the New England coast from Massachussetts (1629), through Connecticut (1639) and Rhode Island (1636–1638), with their own forms of self-government, their own printing presses, and even a college founded in 1636 and named after John Harvard two years later. In Rhode Island especially, separation of church and state meant toleration and the freedom of all—irrespective of their religious beliefs—to participate in government. Here were practices unheard-of elsewhere, and least of all in England, for centuries to come.

Yet, for a long time little would be known in Europe about these distant places; and their unusually democratic institutions remained peculiar to themselves. As for Calvinism, which some scholars consider a highly democratic movement because of its self-governing organization, it was actually aristocratic or oligarchic, emphasizing the role of lay elders who played a large part in managing churches and electing their pastors. Since Calvinist congregations, like everybody else at that time, were accustomed to defer to their betters, the most prominent members of the community were usually elected to head it. The possibilities of the structure attracted the gentry in France, Hungary, and Poland, who could provide protection and leadership and who thus took over positions of leadership in most congregations. This was the tendency that triumphed in eastern Europe. In the west, the tension between democracy and oligarchy was eventually resolved when political failure or persecution in the seventeenth century made Calvinism unfashionable and rather disreputable, and gradually drove away its most prominent adherents in England and France, while in Scotland and Holland the Calvinism of the state itself became moderate, acceptable, but so narrow as to be unattractive to the more sophisticated. Having begun by being considered dangerously radical, the image of Puritans and Puritanism became that of dreary hypocrites who, in Samuel Butler's lines

> Compound for Sins they are inclin'd to
> By damning those they have no mind to;
> Still so perverse and opposite
> As if they worshipped God for spight.

They were hypocrites who cramped fashionable style, bores who talked one into the ground. It was their unfortunate practice of long sermons which probably accounted for the tendency so often denounced of sleep-ing in church; and, as a matter of fact, in Sweden, a special official armed with a long cane performed the duty of awakening worshipers who dozed off. One positive aspect of the new importance of sermons is the fact that shorthand was probably first devised to take down the ser-mons of Puritan preachers.* Still, the most pungent and convincing por-trait of a sectarian Puritan can be found in a poem by George Crabbe (1754–1832):

> Grave Jonas Kindred, Sybil Kindred's sire,
> Was six feet high and looked six inches higher;
> Erect, morose, determined, solemn, slow,
> Who knew the man, could never cease to know;
> Himself he viewed with undisguised respect,
> And never pardoned freedom or neglect.
> Peace in the sober house of Jonas dwelt,
> Where each his duty and his station felt:
> Yet not that peace some favored mortals find
> In equal views and harmony of mind;
> Not the soft peace that blesses those who love,
> Where all with one consent in union move;
> But it was that which one superior will
> Commands, by making all inferiors still;
> Who bids all murmurs, all objections cease,
> And with imperious voice, announces—Peace!

In 1722 we find the testament of a Geneva burgher offering thanks to God for the infinite graces he had bestowed upon him by an ex-traordinary benediction on his *business*. The works of man were insuf-ficient to provide salvation, but the works of God were sufficient to prove it. What might be the Calvinists' greatest contribution was their relation with economic development. The kind of direct relation be-tween work and virtue, thrift and capitalist enterprise, that has often been propounded is highly debatable. What seems more obvious is the role of political-religious factors in the migrations of men and groups that played a major part in the development of industry and finance. Mi-gration has always been an important factor in the spread of skills and the movement of capital. Through the sixteenth and seventeenth cen-tury, the frontier areas of European economy were developed by the en-terprise of emigrants from the great merchant centers of Italy, Spain, South Germany, and Flanders: Catholic bankers and merchants, Jew-ish refugees, Calvinist exiles. From the capitalist centers of an earlier age, from Seville and Lisbon, Augsburg and Lucca, Antwerp and Liège, masters and workmen spread over Europe to seed the development of un-exploited, undeveloped regions whose growth paralleled the decline of older areas, where enterprises had hardened into bureaucracy and free-dom into despotism, in economics as in religion or society.

* John Cleveland, the royalist poet, refers to "the accursed stenography of fate."

People such as these were not necessarily Calvinist, but peculiarly open to the language of Calvinism: self-conscious, self-reliant, independent, dynamic. The Jews, whose structures were equally strong, whose drives were equally dynamic, labored under peculiar social and political disabilities. While individual Jews might attain wealth and power, the Jewish communities ever on the razor's edge of toleration could never hope for more than grudging acceptance, a stifling situation which only gradually improved. The Catholics, on the other hand, when successful, would merge into the surrounding society as immigrant Italian bankers did in France or in the Spanish Netherlands and would adopt this society's aristrocratic hence uneconomic views. Protestants also integrated into the societies which accepted them; but they carried with them a religion that favored industry, condemned unproductive activities, insisted on man's duty to labor for the glory of God. They replaced the cult of charity by the cult of labor. Pious Catholics would aid the poor to keep them alive; pious Calvinists would give them work.

Calvinism gave capitalists the means of glorifying God by the exercise of their economic function. No wonder then, that Calvinists played a major role in developing the industry, commerce, and finances first of Holland and of North German cities, then of Denmark, Sweden, and the Baltic, of England and France, of Bohemia, where the Catholic Emperor's armies were financed by a Calvinist banker who had moved from Antwerp to Prague; and, finally, Prussia. But most of them were migrants, and it was this, rather than a religious identity that marked the Belgian refugees who spread all over Europe to develop French

Amsterdam in the seventeenth century, an engraving showing merchants' homes.

New York Public Library

and German industry, but especially into the northern Netherlands and thence Sweden and Denmark; or the Huguenots who fled the persecutions of Louis XIV to play the same role a century later, in Switzerland and the Germanies, always carrying the skills and enterprises of more advanced societies into less developed lands, or, as in England, contributing new skills and dynamism in more developed ones.

The rulers of Catholic countries drove their more critical and less conformist townsmen into emigration. There, in the process of rebuilding their own fortunes, they also built those of the societies that sheltered them. And yet these same Catholic rulers who drove their nonconforming subjects into exile had to rely on them in money matters. The Habsburgs muddled through the seventeenth century with the aid of Calvinist financiers they had expelled from their Flemish lands; Louis XIV's great banker, Samuel Bernard, was a Protestant renegade; and in the eighteenth century Louis' heirs struggled to make ends meet with the help of Huguenot money men who, expelled from France, had set up shop in Switzerland. Colbert himself, opposed as he was to the heretics, set out to introduce policies which were effectively similar to those of Calvinists, to banish "idleness," alms-giving, pilgrimages, religious holidays which cut into production, religious foundations whose denizens were lost to the labor force; to substitute work for alms and individual recognition for traditional privilege. He did not realize the parallels, any more than contemporary Jansenists (see pp. 260–262) acknowledged the similarity between their doctrines and those of Geneva. But the resemblance is clear and it suggests the appropriateness of Calvinist attitudes to social needs, the uses of economy and austerity in a society ailing for want of either and bloated with glorification of consumption and display. In effect, though, the capitalist "ethic" often attributed to Calvinism was less peculiar to one religious group than to a time adjusting to the needs and possibilities it glimpsed.

One may conclude that, by being considered subversive, by being persecuted, some Calvinists were forced into the kind of effort which we associate with alien or persecuted minorities, which must be more cohesive, more energetic, more enterprising, more productive, if they wish to survive and to assert themselves. Make no mistake: persecution is *not* a creative challenge. It stifles and destroys more often than it spurs. The Jews, pursued, hemmed in, oppressed, barely survived and only flowered in the relative freedom of the nineteenth century. Those Calvinists who reacted positively to persecution—and they were a minority among the many who broke or bent or withered or gave up—did so because they found haven, because the net of the persecutors had gaps, their thoroughness was imperfect; and because in the patchwork quilt that Christendom became in the seventeenth century men could escape from the domain of one prejudice to that of another to which they could more easily adjust.

Pope Innocent X, by Velázquez, 1650.
Doria-Pamphili Collection, Rome.

Counter-Reformation and Catholic Reform

The Catholic camp, too, reflected and sometimes combined trends toward both conformism and dynamic movement. On the one hand it
sought to restore order in a structure shaken and rent by questioning and
schism; on the other it tried to recapture the initiative, adjust to the
times, respond to the challenge of Protestant Reformation with a
Reformation of its own. We have already seen (p. 175) that internal
reform went hand in hand with measures to counter the challenge of
Protestantism. Catholic Reformation and Counter-Reformation were com-
plementary. Throughout the second half of the sixteenth century especially, a series of energetic pontiffs devoted themselves to fighting
Protestantism, to the spiritual restoration of Catholicism, and the progressive reform of Church administration.

Vigorous and forceful men like Pius V (1566–1572) and Sixtus V
(1585–1590) strengthened the central control which the Council of
Trent had reaffirmed, enforced a rule requiring diocesan bishops to report to the pope in person at regular intervals, turned the once-tur-
bulent Cardinals into a kind of council of ministers directing a systematic
structure of departments known as congregations, developed an expanded ecclesiastical bureaucracy into a buttress of papal supremacy.
By the end of the sixteenth century a regular system of diplomatic representation by papal *nuncios* had been set up, and a new official, the Papal
Secretary of State, had taken in hand the major activities of the *Curia.*
In 1622, a special Congregation for the Propagation of the Faith

was founded to manage the many new missionary enterprises undertaken in the last decades. In Italy itself, the papal states, enlarged and consolidated by 1600, furnished the economic support for budgets once dependent on foreign contributions and, notably, for the great building projects which turned Rome from a medieval into a baroque city.

In reasserting their supremacy, the popes faced not only Protestants but also Catholics: the great Catholic monarchs, in particular, who insisted on controlling ecclesiastical appointments in their territories, hungered for a slice of the Church's wealth, and supported theological and legal doctrines advocating restriction of papal power. Such a tradition, generally described as Gallicanism and insisting on a kind of autonomy for the French church, had existed since the thirteenth-century struggle between Pope Boniface and King Philip the Fair of France. The University of Paris, with its European prestige, continued to support theses that subordinated papal power spiritually to that of the Church as a whole (or represented by a Council), and made the king (or the law courts, or both) supreme in matters secular, such as the appointment of bishops. And tendencies of this kind appeared elsewhere: in Spain, or in the Habsburg dominions, when they suited their rulers' interests. Rome had to keep up a continual struggle against its allies, who increasingly placed their secular interests ahead of its religious ones.

All this may be considered part of the Counter-Reformation, whose political aspects we shall see elsewhere. Parallel but integral part of it were more strictly religious initiatives. Serious attempts were made to further learning and to improve the education of the clergy, research into early Christian history was stimulated,* the Vatican library was improved and enriched. In 1582, Pope Gregory XIII promulgated a new and improved calendar.** National seminaries were set up in Rome for the training of priests. By the seventeenth century, the Church could rely on a secular priesthood much better trained, versed in theology, able to read, write, preach, and to impart a better religious culture to their congregations. By way of this militia of the lower clergy, ill-paid but devoted, the religious experience of the popular masses themselves would become less elementary and more pervasive.

Two tendencies appear in the great figures of the Catholic Reformation, sometimes separate, sometimes commingled. One is the reaction against Renaissance worldliness and the humanistic enjoyment of na-

---

* The Catacombs of Rome were discovered in 1578.

** The Gregorian Calendar Reform added a chronological variant to other contemporary schisms. The improved calendar was rather reluctantly adopted by Spain, Portugal, Italy, and France in 1582, while Catholic Germany waited until 1583. Denmark, the Dutch Republic, the Protestant states of Germany, and the Protestant cantons of Switzerland did not accept it until 1700, England until 1752 (the English mob, explained Voltaire, preferred their calendar to disagree with the sun than to agree with the Pope). Sweden adopted the Gregorian Calendar only in 1753 and Orthodox Russia after the Revolution, on January 31, 1918. The difference between the old Julian Calendar (established in 45 B.C. by order of Julius Caesar) and the new was ten days.

ture and the senses, whose irresponsible meddling and criticism had prepared the way to rebellion. This made for an insistence on discipline, restraint, repentance, and for suspicion of spontaneous expression, even in the arts, as we shall see, where discipline and technique turned into mannerism and sometimes into stodginess. In this view, schism was attributed to sentiment and enthusiasm; the best defense against heresy was the cold dominion of reason and the mind over the body with its unruly passions. The other trend was militant, enthusiastic, ardent, passionate, prone to heroics and emotion, the very contrary, it would seem, of the official view, yet its necessary concomitant if Catholic Christianity was to survive as a fighting creed.

It was the second of these trends that outwardly dominated Counter-Reformation politics, and whose fervor colors the impressions we retain of it. Nor are these impressions wrong. The heroes of the Counter-Reformation were passionate men. Unable to convince a fellow traveler that Mary was really a virgin, Ignatius Loyola was tempted to stab him. He fought the temptation and won, and then hung his dagger on the wall of the Church of Monserrat, consecrating it to the Virgin. Only passionate men could wage the necessary campaigns in the great conflict, mount to the assault of enemy-held territory, face the hardships, the dangers, and the horrors, the narrow priest-holes designed as hiding places in the houses of the Catholic gentry holding out against the pressures of Protestant England; the possibility of being caught, tortured, executed, mobbed by angry crowds or skewered by indifferent natives, the strange escapes like that of Fr. Greenway across the English Channel hidden in a cargo of dead pigs, the disguises, the nervous business of enlisting hotheaded or grumbling gentlemen to perish miserably in some plot, the dank and weary voyages to distant lands.

Only enthusiasts could face martyrdom and rejoice; and martyrdom itself was a necessary component of the Counter-Reformation arsenal. The public had to be impressed, novices preparing to go out into the heretic or pagan jungle must be hardened and inspired by graphic images of the long tale of Christian sufferings for the faith. The English College in Rome had a quasi-chronicle of England in the tortures and maimings painted on its walls. The frescoes of the German College Church, Santo Stefano Rotondo, provide a history of persecutions: Christians in animal skins torn up by dogs, others torn to pieces by red-hot pincers, by wild horses, by bent trees, by iron claws, thrown into furnaces or vats of boiling lead, pierced with arrows, crushed beneath rocks, cut to pieces, their eyes poked out, their breasts cut off, or, mercifully, despatched in more traditional ways. "We must not fear to paint the Christians' torments in all their horror," wrote Cardinal Paleotti in 1594, "the wheels, the gridirons, the wooden horses, the crosses. The Church wants thereby to glorify the courage of the martyrs but she wants also to inflame the soul of her sons."

A whole descriptive literature, the erudite inspiring the vulgar, was spawned by this intent and seems to have satisfied contemporary yearnings, strange fantasies of sacrifice, suffering, and extraordinary violence.

It worked, though Catholics had no monopoly of it. "How many men and women have we not seen," writes Montaigne, "who have patiently endured to be burnt and roasted for misunderstood and vain opinions which they have borrowed of others."

Saints and Mystics

But this is the visible side of the Counter-Reformation. Far from unimportant, far from basic too. The Catholic Reformation was above all a spiritual movement. It was dominated by the great mystics of Spain, France, and Italy, some harsh and anguished, like St. John of the Cross (1542–1591), some joyous and practical, like St. Philip Neri (1515–1595) or St. François de Sales (1567–1622). The Florentine Philip Neri, founder of the Oratory of Divine Love, seems to carry on the Franciscan tradition of a faith that is happy as well as thoughtful, committed to salvation but also to intellect and art. François de Sales, from Savoy, appears as the suaver apostle of devotion softened for French consumption, a devoutness "for the artisan in his shop, the prince in his court, the couple in its household." His realistic appraisal of possibilities and needs would inspire the career of Jeanne Frémyot (1572–1641), offspring of a magistrate family from Dijon, widow of a certain Baron Chantal, who founded the order of *Visitandines* (devoted to the visit and care of old and sick and needy) and became Sainte Chantal.

Among these kindly saints, works seemed the best reflection of enthusiasm. But in the arid, wind-battered plains of Castile a ruder tradition gave birth to the great mystics whose visions would rekindle the "flame of lively love" (St. John of the Cross) in the "castle within," as St. Theresa (1515–1582) described it in her *Book of the Castle Within or the Internal Dwellings of the Soul*. Their supersensitive dreams, pious hysteria, supplied the poetry and inwardness, slaked the thirst for intimacy with God, which Protestants had offered when the Church had failed.*

Whatever their orientation, all, however, stressed the nothingness of man in terms inspired by St. Augustine and curiously close to Luther and to Calvin. It is on this human insignificance that Pierre de Bérulle (1575–1629), founder of the French Oratory, based his idea of abnegation: self-renunciation, self-annihilation in the service of Jesus, for the sake of a perfect union with him. The Oratorian Order, which he founded in 1611, taught respect for God, self-examination and self-understanding, and presented a theocentric image of life and of the world whose insistence on complete submission to an omnipotent God could be transferred to the sovereign, God's Vice-Gerent on earth. Cardinal de Bérulle was a member of the Council of Louis XIII. On the other

* Not that St. Theresa was not human (and apparently eloquent and charming as well). In her travels she noted that "God gives us so much to suffer for Him, if only from fleas, ghosts, and bad roads." She wrote long letters of advice to King Philip II, and did not even hesitate to address God himself in familiar terms. "No wonder," she says to Him on one occasion, "you have so few friends when you treat the ones you have so badly."

hand, since works were important (as the Council of Trent insisted in 1564), a thread of practical common sense runs through most, blending austerity with action even in the lives of mystics like St. Theresa of Avila, but especially in a figure like St. Vincent de Paul (1581?–1660), with his insistence on charitable action and his life devoted to convicts, the poor, and the most helpless.

Order and learning with the Jesuits, devotion and liveliness with the Oratory, devotion and works with Salesians and Paulists, ecstasy with the mystics, the Church reformed could compete again and offer all whatever they might seek.

Of course, the new orders (and the old regular ones revived), while they fulfilled a social function, also created new social burdens. They had to be kept up with men and resources which might have been used in other more productive ways. Colbert thought so, though when considering the constant underemployment of the time one would doubt it. Perhaps religious orders fulfilled a function that universities do today: of keeping a portion of the working population off the employment market, so that the remainder can find work. They certainly kept .a portion of the nubile population from marriage, and this group method of birth control was useful, too. Besides, the new orders, though they increased the economic burden of the societies in which they operated (which meant that Protestant countries had more spare capital for other purposes), also reconciled the society to these burdens, to the existing order, and to the crown they (nearly) always supported. So they paid off

The Ecstasy of St. Theresa, an altar piece by Bernini. Cornaro Chapel, Church of Santa Maria della Vittoria, Rome. *"It pleased the Lord that I should see this angel* in the following way. He was not tall, but short, and very beautiful, his face so aflame that he appeared to be one of the highest types of angel who seem to be all afire. . . . *In his hands* I saw *a long golden spear* and at the end of the iron tip I seemed to see a point of fire. *With this he seemed to pierce my heart several times so that it penetrated to my entrails."*

in order and stability what they may have cost in resources and socio-economic inertia.

The Jesuits

Most widespread of all was the influence of Jesuit education, which shaped the heart and mind of so many Catholics: Bérulle himself, Descartes, Corneille, Bossuet, Colbert, were taught by Jesuits whose whole system was bent to train intelligence and will so that its products could find and apply Christian solutions to all worldly situations. Since man can by his will avoid sin and attain salvation, Jesuit education aimed to reinforce will by habit, impose order and discipline, teach punctuality and polite manners, so that students would get used to doing what they should, not what they wanted. Pride, ambition, even vanity, could be turned to the service of religion, of the sovereign, of the state. So could the classics and the lessons of the past when properly expurgated, commented upon, and brought up-to-date.

Natural instincts were the gift of God: they should not be stifled but harnessed, hierarchized, harmonized, above all trained. Men could be taught to lead a Christian life and to this end no means should be ignored. Drama was a major instructional instrument in Jesuit hands. In the twenty-one Jesuit colleges of the Lower Rhine province, 502 plays were performed between 1597 and 1761; 213 including ballets between 1635 and 1761 in the Paris College of Clermont. Even in distant India in 1624 a dramatized *Life of Saint Francis Xavier* was put on in the square before the church at Goa, while at Pondicherry, *The Triumph of David over Goliath* or the tale of *Josaphat* were enacted in Tamil for the benefit of native audiences. "Let all plays be suited to the end intended by the Society, to wit, to move men's souls to detest lewd manners and perverted habits, to flee from the occasion of sin, to apply themselves to virtue, to imitate the saints," said an instruction of the Upper Rhine province in 1619. Jesuit drama would culminate in the *Polyeucte* of Corneille, himself the star pupil of the Jesuits of Rouen, in which the *will* to do the right thing triumphs over both desire and fear.

By 1580, the Jesuits boasted 5,000 members, 21 provinces, 144 colleges: the most internationally active and certainly the most effective of the new orders. When one day in 1592 Cardinal Odoardo Farnese visited the Jesuit College of Rome, he noted that in the refectory twenty-seven different idioms were being spoken. So Jesuits were widespread and they were effective, but they also found their critics. The lessons they taught were said to rationalize piety, to "normalize the supernatural," to make everything too easy and straightforward to be true. Their pious gymnastics in casuistry failed to satisfy the more anguished and concerned. The relativism of their arguments, the laxity of the discipline they imposed on charges too important to be distressed by sternness, all lent themselves to criticism not only by schismatics but by rival orders.

Here was an order tightly organized on military lines and one whose motto, "For the greater glory of God," challenged the contemporary rise of national consciousness and the self-centered orientation of modern states. But it also had another drawback. The Jesuits were clever. Their scholars had the dangerous habit of carrying arguments to their logical conclusions, and logical conclusions are too often extreme. This meant that the most subversive theories could be ascribed to Jesuits; and they were, including that of justified regicide. Cardinal Manning, the nineteenth-century English prelate, once noted how little difference there was between Presbyterians and Jesuits in the great disputes that tore the seventeenth century, when the two classics of regicide were the work of a Spanish Jesuit, Mariana, and of a Presbyterian Scot, Buchanan, both of whom insisted that the contract that made a king implied that, if he broke it, he could be cast out or slain. This was not calculated to make Jesuits popular with crowned heads, the more so since Jesuits were found to be involved in plots, some successful, to murder Henry III and Henry IV of France, James I of England, William of Orange, and several less important figures.

To him who hath it shall be given: Jesuits were credited with more conspiracies than they knew about. The ill-repute of Machiavelli was shifted onto their shoulders, not without cause. Against Machiavelli and his remark that means may be justified by results, the Jesuits had advanced a theory that not results but intention alone can justify means; that worthy ideals can justify even unworthy means intended to serve them, no matter what results; that what counts ultimately in politics, as Giovanni Botero phrased it, is "reason of state." The pragmatic remark of the practical politician was replaced by the ideological justification for almost anything. And this helps to explain why Catholic governments generally ignored the subversive possibilities of the Jesuits and sought their aid. They knew them as the best-organized, most effective, and probably the most intelligent of regular orders, and wanted them on their side. Even the converted Huguenot Henry IV relied on their support.

Pomp and Circumstance

So the Catholic Church gathered itself together, recovered lost positions, and strengthened shaken ones. It did this by tightening discipline, improving structure, and mobilizing the enthusiasm of the regulars. Public piety was revived by missionary propaganda and by stronger emotional appeals. Martyrs, saints, relics were refurbished and re-emphasized, their ranks increased by new arrivals. Men risked their lives to preserve a spine of the Crown of Thorns, a chip of St. Thomas à Becket's skull, a piece of St. Vitus's armbone. Traditionally, European Christendom (especially in the south) inclined toward a kind of polytheism, reflected in the place saints played in Christianity. Protestants attacked the saints, and such iconoclasm only rendered Catholic devotion to them and to the Virgin more fervid under fire.

Saints must have played a useful role in worship as intermediaries between a distant God and an insignificant sinner,* much as confessors dispense many Catholics today from recourse to other means. It is also possible that the cult of saints, rising at times to fanatical heights, channeled off *some* of the passions which in the saintless north had to be stilled in bloodstained witch hunts. The supernatural does not let itself be eliminated easily. In any case polytheism is no Catholic preserve. In out-of-the-way parts of Lutheran Scandinavia, Nordic gods were still worshiped as late as the eighteenth century, while old and new gods met in spells and rites. Such survivals, in any case, became not rarer but less obvious in time, increasingly integrated in liturgical and theological structures which custom reinforced. On the whole, the application of the decrees promulgated at Trent eliminated medieval fantasies that lent themselves to Protestant criticism, free manners of service, the possibility to interject observations or questions during the sermon. The faithful were silenced, ceremony was purified, everything became more solemn, more refined, more distant, more impressive, but also more strange.

In addition, religious grandeur and ostentation were increased to impress the worshipers. Images of saints were provided with sumptuous vestments and with no less sumptuous homes. If great nobles lived in magnificent palaces, wore rich robes and precious jewels, how much more elegantly bedecked and housed should be the symbols of the holy family and their court! The materialism of such conceptions soon penetrated a hierarchy which naturally shared current views concerning the proper state and privileges of office. As Cardinal Mazarin murmured before the statue of Pope John XXII at Avignon: "He was a great pope, he left eight millions!" By his end, Mazarin could boast over twice as much. But such a view called forth its obverse: a generation later, when Louis XIV seized the Pope's territory of Avignon, the Cardinal d'Estrées reflected: "How can the Pope resist a King who has 200,000 soldiers?" The remark would not have occurred—not in this form—a hundred years before.

Formalism

Along with ostentation there went formalism. The deep and anguished piety of Philip II, the serene devotion of Louis XIII, became a series of gestures whose performance had little significance but, supposedly, some automatic efficacy. King Philip IV of Spain, for instance, repeatedly

* A recent anthropological study of Brazil refers to the most popular of Brazilian saints, St. Anthony, envisaged as the colony's protector against the foreign invader to the extent of being appointed Lt. Colonel of Brazilian armies, with the pay of his rank. One of his many tasks during the nineteenth century was to help locate fugitive slaves; and sometimes his statue would be thrown into a dark hole or turned on its head and left there until the slave was found, in order to encourage it to help.

requested the nuns of Agreda to perform penance for his sensual sins, while the Abbess vainly tried to explain that penitence calls for some effort on the part of the sinner too. Criminals said their prayers and their rosary, not to free themselves from thieving but to gain safety from punishment and lawmen.

A striking aspect of the new formalism is to be found in the frequent references to confession. The newssheets of Madrid bear witness to its importance. "This night Fernand Pimentel was killed by a rapier stroke without having had time to draw his sword. He called loudly for Confession . . ." (August 8, 1622). "At eight in the evening, some gentlemen awaited Diego de Avila as he left a house to kill him; they threw themselves upon him and cut him down; he was loudly crying for Confession . . ." (December 1, 1622). "Christoforo Bustamante has been killed in Paredes Street, without having had time to confess himself." (October 3, 1627). And a historian of seventeenth-century Italy tells the same story: "A priest of the Bardi family shot another member of the clan against whom he had a grudge. His dying victim implored him not to take his soul as well as his life, but to confess and absolve him, and the murderer did as requested."

A century after the Reformation the Church had revived so well that it was back where it started. The new display, formalism, above all distance between religion and behavior, could seem as revolting as in Luther's day. Another reaction was inevitable and it arose, as it always has, from its own midst.

Jansenism

The Council of Trent had sought to help sinners by making Communion more frequent, absolution more accessible, penitence more easy. This tendency to indulgence and "laxness" revolted more austere believers, among them an ardent Basque, Duvergier de Hauranne, Abbot of St.-Cyran, who directed the reform of the Cistercian convent of Port-Royal near Paris. In the 1630's Port-Royal became the center of a new ascetic revival, in which salvation by grace alone was considered able to redeem man. Men, it was thought, are utterly damned by Original Sin but for the intervention of Grace, which alone can bring conversion and salvation. But Grace is predestined, inaccessible by our unaided efforts. Here was a predicament which not even the intervention of the Church could help.

In 1640, centenary of the foundation of the Jesuits, the presses of Louvain turned out the three vast volumes of the *Augustinus,* a posthumous work of St.-Cyran's friend Jansenius, Bishop of Ypres, soon condemned by Rome. In 1643 a Port-Royal supporter published a discussion, *Frequent Communion,* which attacked that practice while carrying the battle from Latin into French. Antoine Arnauld's book recommended that penitents abstain from Communion until contrition was proved.

This left religious responsibility to individual penitents or priests, and seemed to deny the claims of the effectiveness of ritual and even of superior clerical judgment. The religious quarrel now became involved with political rivalries and Port-Royal identified with the defeated nobles of the Fronde, which only a few years before had sought to curb the royal will by armed resistance. Mazarin, securing condemnation of Jansenist doctrines (1655), had their schools closed and the "solitaries" who had gathered round the abbey dispersed. Then, between 1656 and 1657, Jansenism found a powerful new champion: Blaise Pascal's *Provincial Letters* (burned by the public hangman in 1660) argued the case of Christian morality against Jesuit casuistry in a style which brought the Jansenists wide attention and swung public sympathies toward the persecuted sect.

So the dispute continued. It fed in part on the Gallican tradition and on the feeling that, while Jansenists were a native breed, the Jesuits, who were their chief doctrinal opponents, represented the interests of Rome. Yet the debate had another dimension. In retrospect it appears as a clash between rigorists who had thought over St. Augustine and concluded with him that man is nothing, that he counts for nothing before God's grace, human merits being quite vain when compared to those of Christ crucified; a clash between rigorists and those, Jesuits foremost, who found in this doctrine a mere rehash of Calvinism. The critics of Jansenism cut close to the bone, but the persecution of the Jansenists came rather because they insisted on a moral rigor as awkward for the more indulgent Jesuits as it was for the state. The Jansenist belief in predestination allowed man freedom to choose good, not for reward but for his own satisfaction: a kind of gratuitous commitment with high moral possibilities, unlikely to appeal to many and, above all, subversive of authority—pontifical or secular—since in this view truth lay in the heart. Here was a doctrine ill-equipped to compete against the supple rationalizations of the Jesuits, but attractive to the sterner consciences: educated bourgeois, magistrates, nobility of the robe, even some members of the highest aristocracy who sought truth and right for themselves. Even when quashed, its center at Port-Royal closed, its followers imprisoned or exiled, and all the French clergy required to sign a loyalty oath, Jansenism survived, publicized by persecutions, turned from a theological dispute into a major affair of state, providing Catholics with a non-Protestant alternative to laxness, a Catholic variant of the high moral and intellectual critical tone that could be found among the Calvinists.

Like high-minded Protestantism, however, Jansenism could develop in less attractive directions, exerting an influence its founders never expected. In an age when the religion of some began to be affected by common sense, when the faith of cultivated men started to turn into moral philosophy and virtue to become a sort of prudent wisdom, the Jansenists reacted by denying man's freedom or his capacity to work out his own salvation. Man is too torn by passions, subject to the senses, enthralled by a nature which is evil, to reach good or an awful God whose Grace was only vouchsafed to a few elect souls. This pessimistic view identified even natural beauty with sin to the extent of recommending its adherents to "close their eyes when praying in a church that is too beautiful." Angélique Arnauld declared "I like all that is ugly; art is but vanity and lies; who gives to the senses takes away from God." There were no flowers in the abbeys of Port-Royal—only medicinal plants; no ornaments in the houses of the elect, no columns, and no statues. This break between the world and God, this separation between physical and metaphysical, contributed to a separation between those things which concern both: conscience and the world, spirit and business carried on in a world one knew to be irremediably lost, so that one need concern oneself only with private salvation; until the conclusion was reached which Richard Steele voiced in *The Tradesman's Calling* (1684): "Prudence and piety were always very good friends . . . you may gain enough of both worlds if you would mind each in its place."

Quietism

A less broadly influential development, but potentially an insidious one, was the appearance of quietist doctrines first expressed in the works of a Spanish theologian, Miguel de Molinos (1628–1696). Quietism denies the use of any exterior activity, insists on the total passivity of the believer, a passiveness which God can use to turn his soul toward pure love. This glorification of inertia was typical of situations in which no activity was the best activity, and it appropriately reflected conditions prevailing in the homeland of its most influential advocate. It spread after 1670 among societies where somewhat similar conditions prevailed: in Germany, where the Elector of Brandenburg was its most notable convert, and in France where its most enthusiastic leader, Madame Guyon (1648–1717) made converts at the court of Louis XIV, including the powerful Madame de Maintenon and (though only briefly) the future Archbishop of Cambrai, François Fénelon (1651–1715), tutor of the Duke of Burgundy, grandson of the King and heir to the throne.

The French quietists stressed love and childlike simplicity in a rather attractive way. But a creed which equated passiveness with sanctity and whose antirationalism argued against theological controversy—indeed, against theology of any sort—went against the very structure of the Church. Nor, despite its emphasis upon submissiveness, could quietist notions of withdrawal from mundane tasks be accepted by the state. The ideas of Molinos were condemned by Rome in 1687; those of Fénelon in 1699 after a great dispute with Bishop Bossuet. In a worldly sense, this was right. Society could not permit men to opt out of it, the Church could not survive by worldly abdication. The question remained whether Christians needed to care about such things. But it was always answered on non-religious grounds. Meanwhile, the temper quietism reflected, the yearning for peace and for the simple homely virtues, the reaction against the cold and calculating grandeur or the institutionalization of religion, survived to re-emerge in the eighteenth century in sentimentalism and romanticism.

God and Caesar

The Church proved itself able to deal with internal challenges, but at a price. When it drove out heresy, it drove out variety, too. In earlier centuries the Church had been relatively adaptable and tolerant. In the new age, having withstood Protestant rebellion by stiffening its ranks and allying with the state, it would tolerate rebellion no more.* Renovation was to be followed by bigotry. Humanism hardened into dogmatism. Unlike the Beghards or the Brethren of the Common Life, Jansenists or Quietists were better eliminated, not assimilated. Socially and politically this marked an ominous change.

Among Protestants, Catholics, and Orthodox Christians, the fundamental problem remained the division between God and Caesar, the authority of a Christian conscience facing that of organized church and state, the authority of the church defying that of the state, the demands of a God to whose will everything must be subordinated confronting the right to voice, interpret, and apply this Divine Will. Some preferred to live out their salvation privately and utterly; others sought to reconcile the demands of heaven and those of the world. Established churches generally chose the latter: the flesh was weak, and strong the world's demands; pious austerity did not suit the immense majority of men and women however well-intentioned, nor did it fit the plans or needs or tastes of most of those who ruled them. But the uncompromising ideal of Christian devotion inspired enough men and women to challenge the more accommodating: Puritans and Independents in England, Protestant pietists in Germany, Jansenists in France, "Friends of God" and fundamentalist Old Believers in Russia—penitent, rigoristic, eternally at grips with God, the Devil, and a Divine Providence working within themselves, often (as the Archbishop of Paris said of the nuns of Port-Royal) "Pure as angels and proud as the Devil."

There was the rub: for state and church could not countenance a faith which left too many in the cold and rejected their own authority. Men could not always tremble before a terrible God. Bishop and king wanted to be obeyed without constant reference to private conscience. But, while repressing these unbending and occasionally subversive purists, they also tried to purge the Church of laxities and weaknesses which

* Or even dissent. Professors at Prague University had to take an annual oath of faith in the Immaculate Conception of the Virgin, even before this had been proclaimed a dogma.

laid it open to criticism: form and faith were reformed, the Church was reordered and regulated, no longer a warehouse or a trysting place, increasingly specialized in purpose and purified in fact. As this took place, gradually but surely, the earlier confusion of sacred and profane was unraveled, the naïve intimacies of the Middle Ages waned, and purified religion, separated from secular concerns, was relegated from a social to a political function. Once the money-changers were excluded from the temple, the temple began to slide out of daily life— slowly, gradually, sometimes in the most paradoxical fashion which left the Church a part of life but separated from it, so that ordinary men could *prey* for six days and on the seventh *pray* without qualms, while the few elect in their withdrawal left the world to its perdition. The established churches clung to structures increasingly devoid of content, bodies from which the soul seemed about to flit at any moment.

Secularism and Erastianism advanced apace. If Paris was worth a mass to Henry IV, London was worth dispensing with it where Charles II was concerned. So Henry abandoned Protestantism for the crown, and Charles refrained from Catholicism to retain his. Religious issues now became clearly political: matters of state in every respect. This was so for a thinker like Spinoza (1632–1677), whose *Theologico-Political Treatise* (1670) insisted that "religious worship in our day rests solely on the competence of the high authorities and that no one, unless with their authority and their approval is entitled or has the capacity to regulate religion, to select its servants, to determine the basic principles and doctrines of the Church, to pronounce on morals and acts of piety, to excommunicate a person or to admit him to the church, or finally to care for the poor . . . whoever wishes to deprive the authorities of this power is trying to push his way to supreme power."

It had been so for the Englishman, John Selden (1584–1654), to whom church and clergy were what the people made them. But if the office of priest was a mere profession, so was the office of king. "A king," asserted Selden, "is a thing men have made for their own sakes." No Divine Right for kings balanced no Divine Right for priests. And the growing pressure against religion by secular authority, while temporarily strengthening the latter, menaced it in the long run.

In the two centuries following the Reformation, religious concerns waxed very bright indeed, then waned. The crusading ideal, so strong in the late sixteenth century, decayed. After Don Juan of Austria (1547–1578) and King Sebastian of Portugal (1557–1578), Christian passions were reoriented to internal struggles: the Wars of Religion, which we shall study next. The last of these were fought in the first half of the seventeenth century: in Bohemia and Germany, in attacks by Catholic Poland and Lutheran Sweden on Orthodox Russia, in France, and then in England. The Peace of Westphalia in 1648 would be concluded without the Pope. Henceforth Europe defined itself by other characteristics than those of Christendom.

Chapter 6

THE STRUGGLES

FOR EMPIRE

These centuries which witnessed so many changes can be divided into two major political periods: the first, which runs roughly from mid-sixteenth to mid-seventeenth century, sees the hegemony of Spain, the second (which is shorter) that of France. During the first, the dominant Spanish Habsburgs, too weakly balanced by a divided France, were challenged only by the maritime activities of Protestant England and, above all, of their own rebellious subjects in the Netherlands. Sufficient to singe the king of Spain's beard, such forces could not really humble him. The political predominance of Spain throughout this period was reflected in the preponderance of its culture. French and Italian filled with Spanish terms; translations from Spanish abounded; so many learned Castilian that in 1617 Cervantes' latest work was immediately reprinted in Paris even before it was translated into French. At the court of Louis XIII, the manners, perfumes, women's make-up, gloves, and fashions were for the best part Spanish. When in 1624 Philip IV of Spain introduced certain sartorial reforms for economy's sake and banished the expensive ruff from his household, the ruff's exclusion from the Spanish court was quite enough to drive it out of Europe. This kind of influence lasted through the 1630's and did not end until the next decade when France, having at last put her own house in order, wrested military and political supremacy from Madrid.

It was then France's turn to dominate Europe, helped by the Habsburg weakness in Vienna and Madrid, by England's internal troubles, by the resources of what was potentially and for a while in fact the richest and best organized state in the world. But French hegemony in turn stumbled against the same obstinate David that had worn down

Spain: the rich mercantile power of the Dutch. And French ambitions which threatened all these neighbors had the effect of forcing them to league against France and fight her to a standstill. Britain, ruled by a Dutch prince, would take the lead in this great struggle and keep it long after the 1715 Peace of Utrecht, which provided that no one power should impose her will on everybody else.

But Britain did not seek hegemony. Her interests were best served by a balance between the various nations. The imperial ambitions of Spain and France, of Habsburg and Bourbon, defeated for the moment, would give way to the principle of a balance of power, which had orig- inated in Italy long before. Just as the squabbling states of Renaissance Italy which had sought to swallow one another failed, and had to accept an uneasy balance where none could grow too strong and where the su- periority of one state or camp brought forth a league against them, so the competing states of late seventeenth- and eighteenth-century Europe learned to calculate the equations and combinations of international affairs. And just as Venice, a shrewd trading power, with her maritime vested interests and her mercantile oligarchy, had launched the new idea in Italy, so Britain, similarly maritime, mercantile, and businesslike, would represent it in Europe.

The Treaty of Utrecht proclaimed its purpose "to confirm the peace and tranquillity of the Christian world through a just equilibrium of power . . .," and this Anglo-Dutch idea, for which war had been waged (at least by these two countries which had been its core), became for a hundred years the moving idea of international affairs.

The Dominance of Spain

The imperial ambitions of the Habsburg dynasty had begun with Charles V's attempts to realize the possibilities of his Burgundian heritage, reconstitute the ancient kingdom of Lothar, the Carolingian, join the divided territories of the dukes of Burgundy in a realm running between Rhine and Rhone from Mediterranean and Alps to the North Sea. To do this he had to recover the territories lost to France after the death of Charles the Bold, and that, despite his victories over Francis I, he could not achieve. The Treaty of Cambrai (1529) had registered his failure and the abandonment of the Burgundian dream.

After Cambrai Charles turned toward Italy, where Spanish needs in- spired a new policy: Sicily could furnish the grain the Spanish peninsula lacked, the lands of the Neapolitan crown could stand as security for German bankers' loans, the Duchy of Milan provide a firm base for crossing and control of Alpine passes, and Genoa supply the credit of

Philip II of Spain, a painting by Lucas
de Heere. Prado, Madrid.

its banks and the facilities of its fleet and harbor. Italy became the
turntable of Habsburg policy.

After Italy, Germany. Spanish troops secured the German Empire for
the Habsburg princes, but a realm cannot rest on pikes alone and the elite
infantry of the *tercios* could not persuade the Germans, even Catholics,
even the Austrian Habsburgs, that Charles' heir, a Spanish prince,
should succeed his father there. Spanish troops had to be withdrawn in
1551 and when, in 1556, Charles abdicated the imperial crown, it went
to his Austrian brother, Ferdinand, not his Castilian son. In many
ways this was advantageous in a world where the greater the realm the
harder it was to rule. After the universal pretensions and disparate territories of Charles V, the power of Philip II could be somewhat more
concentrated. The father's policy had been based on Italy and the
Netherlands; the son took his stand on Spain and on its crown. Charles
had had to put up with the running sore of Germany; Philip abandoned imperial pretensions there, but had the Netherlands to plague
him. His empire was more solid, more coherent, less diverted by territorial preoccupations from the seas across which his chief concern
and source of power lay; but it was an empire only in fact, not name.
The imperial title had gone to his Vienna uncle (and his heirs). Philip
had reason to rue this when quarrels for precedence opposed his embassies to those of other kings, especially the French; reason enough apparently to consider assuming an imperial title of his own: Emperor of
the Indies. Rumors to this effect circulated several times and, while the
project was never realized, it indicates the persistent importance of an
Imperial title in an age much concerned with appearances and with
prestige.

But, failing the title, Philip had the possessions and they—dominion
of sea and land, riches in quantities never seen before—held him in

their grip, governed his policies, affecting henceforth his whole style of life. Unlike the wandering Charles, Philip established himself in Spain, and directed more and more of his energies to Atlantic affairs. The bureaucracy, the masses of paper and secretaries that grew around him may have been a result in part of new stability, itself a reflection of the king's close watch over the main resource and basis of his power.

Philip's European policy, when it was not a reflection of his primary Spanish and Atlantic interests, was largely an effect of the Counter-Reformation, which took a generation to ripen but which, when ready, attacked the Protestant North and West with sufficient dynamism to carry even Philip along, involving him in conflicts he may have preferred to avoid. But Philip was an uncompromising son of the Church. Unyielding in allegiance to it, his policy raised a hornet's nest in the Netherlands, lost him English friendship, involved him in war with France but failed to keep the heretical Henry of Navarre from its throne. Eventually, the Franco-Spanish Treaty of Vervins (1598) and the Spanish truce with the rebellious Dutch (1609) would place Spanish ambitions in suspended animation, until the weary wars of the seventeenth century scotched them finally.

Meanwhile, Spain's Mediterranean possessions made her the chief defender of Europe against the infidel threat. Crusader for the faith against the Protestants, Philip was also cast in the role of its defender against the Turks. Though more modern minds envisaged even religious strife in a pragmatic manner, the crusading ideal of earlier times persisted, not least in the Iberian peninsula with its recent memories of religious war. The defeat of the Turkish fleet at Lepanto (1571) was seen as a crusade both by the Pope and by the Spanish admiral, Don Juan of Austria (Philip's half brother); though neither Philip nor the Venetians saw it in this light and judged their running fight with Muslim fleets and corsairs largely in terms of military and commercial necessities. But crusades had their uses and the last Iberian crusade was yet to come: in 1578 young King Sebastian of Portugal, haunted by chivalrous ideas, followed their will o' the wisp to Morocco, there to die together with the knighthood of his country on the parched plain of Alcazar Kebir. Two years later, Philip was king of Portugal and of its empire.

By this time Spain had become involved in a revolt which would drain much of her resources. We shall examine this in detail further on. The thing to note at this point is that the Netherlands revolted because they objected to their privileges being trampled upon by an alien prince who wanted his dominions more sensibly and more effectively managed and exploited; and this was complicated by the rise of Calvinism which Philip was determined to crush. Political troubles reinforced by religious ones could only be dealt with by force. The troops which the Duke of Alva (1508–1582) brought with him to the Netherlands in 1567 cost money and this meant new taxes. It was the taxes that set off a rebellion which, as the 1570's ended, had divided the seventeen provinces into an "obedient" southern group of ten and a united northern group of seven. The south was disciplined, Catholicized, and ruined. The north, dredging its riches from the sea as it did its land, learned to become a country; urban, mercantile, and open, diametrically and aggressively opposed in every way to everything Spain was or stood for.

The way in which the rebels managed to survive and prosper, withstanding the might of the greatest European prince, bears witness to the problems Philip, his ministers, and their successors faced, especially the nagging problems of communication in a world much broader than it seems today. Passage for troops, for supplies, for treasures, for news, and orders was lumbering and hazardous. Philip's governor in Brussels might be left without dispatches for weeks and even months at a stretch. At the end of the sixteenth century, the carriage of 100,000 gold *écus* from Florence to Paris took seventeen heavy carts escorted by two hundred footmen and five companies of cavalry. In view of this we may imagine the problems involved when Spaniards tried to move money to pay their troops in the Netherlands and found the sea routes closed.

The Spanish strategy has to be seen in this perspective, its sea lanes at the mercy of pirates in French and Lowland ports, later of the English; its land communications stretching along a tenuous path through Italy, the Alpine passes, and the Rhineland, risking attack from France and sometimes dependent on the latter for speedier passage. French neutrality on land, English neutrality at sea, were necessary to keep the lines of communication open. The hostility of either power could deal a serious blow to Spanish strategy, cutting a lifeline as the English (with the Dutch) did in the 1590's, as the French tried but never succeeded in doing for half a century more.

Spanish policy sought to keep England friendly, France divided and weak. In both cases it succeeded for a time, only to fail in the end. England had been brought back into the Spanish orbit by Philip's own marriage with Mary Tudor, who ruled from 1553 to 1558; it remained friendly in the beginning of the reign of her successor, Elizabeth (1558–1603) but in the 1580's this changed radically. Religious and dynastic considerations, the pressure of Protestants in France and the Netherlands, of piratic ventures on the high seas, of Philip's commitment to Elizabeth's Catholic competitor for the throne, Mary Stuart, all cast Elizabeth as the Protestant champion against Philip, whom the Counter-Reformation bound. Between 1587 and 1604, England and Spain were reluctantly at war.

Philip and his advisers now recognized in England what seemed to them the key to all their problems: a priceless base which, friendly to or occupied by Spain could drive the Lowland rebels from the Narrow Seas, deny them the support which kept them going, a nest of pri-

A contemporary print illustrating the defeat of the Spanish Armada by the English.

vateers who harassed the Spanish treasure fleets and whose disappearance would leave Spanish ships in freedom of the sea. It was decided that an attack on England would easily overcome the ill-armed, ill-defended island and solve a great many issues at one blow. A monstrous fleet was gathered in Iberian ports: 130 ships, over 30,000 men, who were expected to repeat the triumph of Lepanto against the Turkish fleet. But 1588 was not 1571, nor was Atlantic fighting like that in the Mediterranean, as many galleys particularly found, which had been built to sail in calmer seas. When the Armada sailed at last after interminable delays, its destiny was failure and defeat.

Harassed through the Channel by trimmer, more seaworthy English vessels which carried better guns and could sail much closer to the wind, the lumbering Spanish fleet disintegrated. It sailed on into the North Atlantic, almost to Norway, round by the Shetlands and the Hebrides, then south past Ireland, a prey to winds and storms in unfamiliar seas, until its remnants limped into home ports at last, more than half the ships lost en route or unfit for further service, a third of the men dead —mostly of shipwreck and disease. The loss was shattering but it was not final. Spanish naval power, badly maimed, was far from broken. Philip too, more gloomy but more firm than ever, would carry on, although with his Armada's failure had also sunk whatever hopes of victory he had. The Protestant base in England had proved impregnable and, soon, the English challenge would be paralleled on land by the reviving forces of Spain's continental foes.

France, it is true, had been kept weak for a good long time. The death of Henry II in 1559 left the crown in the hands of his widow, Catherine de Medici (1519–1589) and of three lads who succeeded only in frittering away the royal power. The land was torn by religious and political strife, with Spain supporting the Catholic party headed by the family of Guise, and England supporting the Protestants, whose leader, Henry of Navarre, eventually succeeded to the throne in 1589 as Henry IV. Attacked by Spanish troops from the Netherlands, Henry eventually declared war on Spain (1595) and the underhand conflict became an official one. But Henry's contested authority affirmed itself and France regained her strength. The only ones to benefit from the war were the Protestants: London, Bristol, Amsterdam gained—the English at the expense of Spanish trade, the Dutch from the ruin of Antwerp and of the Spanish Netherlands. Dutch and English sailors entered the Mediterranean, reached India to the east, conquered the Atlantic to the west and, while the northern seamen parceled out the world, Spain and France contested over small portions of devastated ground in Europe. In 1598 Henry IV and Philip II both out of money and out of breath resigned themselves to peace and signed the Treaty of Vervins by which the situation of Cateau-Cambrésis (1559) was re-established, France abandoning positions in the Alps, which threatened Italy and the Spanish routes, while keeping Calais and the three bishoprics in Lorraine.

In 1604 peace between Spain and England followed, and in 1609 a twelve-year truce signed between Spain and the seven United Provinces of the northern Netherlands admitted the fact if not the principle of their being. The truce might very well have been a peace, but for the efforts of French diplomacy. The French, feeling their strength, were planning new advances, and did not want the Spanish to be free from their entanglements in the north. They succeeded, but whatever Henry had planned shall not be known, for he was murdered in 1610 and the general war for which he was preparing was postponed for a decade. When it broke out, it came in an area which had been spared from major conflicts for some time: the Empire. The years of war from 1620 to 1648, proved that it had lost nothing by waiting.

The Thirty Years' War

The shift of war from France to Italy in the fifteenth century, from Italy to Germany, then to the Netherlands and France in the sixteenth century, and from the Mediterranean to the Atlantic, thence back to central Europe in the seventeenth century suggests that war, which in those days had to feed upon the place where it was waged, tended toward

territory which would sustain it. A minor Italian historian reflecting
on the destruction such a war had brought to his native city after a century of peace and prosperity had this to say about it: "I have always
heard it said that peace brings riches; riches bring pride; pride brings
anger; anger brings war; war brings poverty; poverty brings humanity;
humanity brings peace; peace, as I have said, brings riches, and so the
world's affairs go round."

In mid-sixteenth century, Germany had put an end to the religious
conflicts sparked by the Reformation. In 1555, the Treaty of Augsburg
had re-established peace by giving princes and free cities the right to vary
in their worship, each territory taking the profession of its ruler as expressed in the formula *cujus regno, ejus religio.*

Since 1555, Germany had had time to fatten. As the focus of trade
and conflict shifted westward, the Empire had become something of a
backwater, but not unprosperous and little the worse for that. The Emperor's authority had declined and reached a low point in Charles V's
grandson, Rudolph II (1576–1612), a strange prince whose eccentricity
bordered on madness and whose court at Prague provided a haven for
artists, alchemists, astrologers, but little leadership. Nor did his successor,
Matthias (1612–1619) improve matters. While the rulers of Spain and
France and England advanced their rule and centralized power in their
lands, the Emperor faced and hardly ruled a fragmented realm united
only in opposition to change and in its determination to prevent
any assertion of imperial power. But Matthias's successor, Ferdinand II
was a pupil of the Jesuits, devout and profoundly imbued with a
sense of his rights and duties: the latter drove him to assert his authority,
the former to re-establish Catholicism in dominions where the tide of
Reformation had been rising for a century. His firm stand on his rights
and his unwillingness to make concessions drove his Bohemian subjects to rebel. They deposed Ferdinand from the Bohemian throne
to which he had been elected and offered it to a Protestant (1619):
Frederick V, Elector Palatine, a son-in-law of James I of England. The
rebellion and Frederick's acceptance of a crown which he had no means
of defending gave Ferdinand his chance. While imperial troops crushed
the Czechs (1620) and bent Bohemia to the Habsburg yoke, their
Bavarian allies expelled Frederick from the Palatinate. James could not
intervene. Frederick's electoral dignity and most of his lands passed to
the Catholic Duke of Bavaria. The issue seemed settled, but it was only
the first act.

Ferdinand would not be content with such an economical victory. With
the electoral college now heavily weighted on the Catholic side, the Emperor set out to crush Protestantism in his empire, and, at the same
time, establish his dominion in it. He would apply the Treaty of Augsburg, but in a Catholic sense, would refuse to recognize any secularization that had occurred since mid-sixteenth century, take over such

lands and goods from Protestants and enforce his will by means of a great army raised for him by a Bohemian *condottiere*, Albrecht von Wallenstein (1583–1634), and paid from the proceeds of his policy. Ferdinand's Spanish cousins financed and supported this course of action. Their truce with the United Provinces ended in 1621 and they had to secure a route for their troops from Italy through the Alpine passes along the Rhine to Luxembourg and Belgium. Spanish and Austrian troops made sure of this, while Spanish ships found new bases of operation against the Dutch in North German ports occupied by Wallenstein's men.

This threatened not only the German Protestants, too weak and disunited for effective opposition, but the interests of neighboring states. The king of Denmark's revenues depended on duties that he levied on the Baltic trade passing through the narrow channel before Elsinore. As duke of Holstein the king of Denmark was also a magnate of the Empire and his policy aimed to secure control of German river mouths and possibly of northeast German trade. The king of Sweden, Gustavus Adolphus (1594–1632), who had long fought for control of the eastern Baltic, entertained similar aims, spurred by the hope of leading a league of Protestant German princes. He was involved in war in Poland and the conflict of Protestant against Catholic raging there could not be separated from the similar conflict in Bohemia and Germany.

The German war inevitably involved northern and eastern Europe just as it involved its southern and western parts. The Dutch, directly threatened by the Spanish armies, believed their survival to depend on continued closing of the port of Antwerp, whose blockade they could not maintain if harassed by hostile bases to the north. Swiss independence hung on a balance of neighboring powers, failing which they might fall under the sway of one. Spanish occupation of the Valtelline —vital link between Italy and Germany—filled the Swiss with suspicions amplified by the knowledge that juridically their cantons still belonged to the Empire, thus falling under the theoretical rule of the Emperor when he was strong enough to assert his rights. France, above all, had reason to fear Spanish ambitions. The troops of Philip IV stood all around her borders and there was no saying when they might strike for Dijon or even Paris. While imperial generals scored successes in Germany and the Spanish in Italy, French diplomacy took the initiative in organizing opposition to them, throwing into battle against them first the Danes and then the Swedes.

The Danes were soon defeated. In 1630, Wallenstein's threat to the Baltic and Richelieu's intrigues finally saw Gustavus Adolphus of Sweden appear in Germany for two meteoric years. His death in 1632 forced the French closer toward intervention. In 1633 they occupied the Duchy of Lorraine; then, as the combined Austro-Spanish armies defeated the Swedes at Nördlingen (1634), they finally decided to declare war (1635). They subsidized every single enemy who might oppose the Habsburgs: they paid the Dutch, the Catalan insurgents asserting provincial liberties against the Spanish crown and its Castilian agents (1640), sent arms to the Portuguese in their successful war of national independence (1641), supported a Neapolitan rising against Spain (1647), encouraged the prince of Transylvania to invade Austrian lands, finally allied with Cromwell to defeat the Spaniards at the Battle of the Dunes (1658). Once they had openly entered the war, French armies gained control of Alsace, the Alpine passes, Catalonia. In 1638 they captured Breisach by the Rhine, thus cutting the vital Milan-Flanders route. Germany was devastated but France preserved.

By this time war had become big business; quite possibly the biggest industry in Europe. Wallenstein, now Duke of Friedland, was the greatest of contractors, the numbers of his army (camp followers included) no less than those of a modern town, his officers entrepreneurs purveying the ill-paid rank-and-file into a business in whose success they invested all their efforts; the revenue, plunder, and reward of war recouping the fortunes of many a gentleman. Yet employees have to be paid. These armies were paid seldom and irregularly. The difficulty in finding funds to pay them, or often to pay them off, could prolong a war; and armies sometimes forced their masters to continue fighting because, unable to pay them wages and dismiss them, they feared the ravages which might ensue. Ravages in any case were standard. The English physician William Harvey, traveling across Europe in 1630 in the suite of the Duke of Lennox wrote of the miseries of the countries which he passed, where "by

The defeat of the Swedes at Nördlingen, 1634.

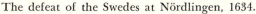

Bibliothèque Nationale

The Treaty of Münster, a painting by Ter Borch.

the way we could scarce see a dog, crow, kite, raven or any bird, or any thing to anatomize, only some few miserable people, the relics of the war and the plague, where famine had made anatomies before I came."

"For what can Warr," asked Milton, "but endless warr still breed?" Only exhaustion of the combatants could put an end to it. Nördlingen in 1634 had been the last Spanish victory, won against the Swedes. At Rocroi in 1643 French arms dealt the final blow to the long myth of Spanish invincibility. France's growing power convinced Spain and the Dutch to come to terms in 1648. A few months later, the negotiations which had been dragging on for four years in the small Westphalian towns of Münster and Osnabruck resulted in the treaties of West-phalia, which settled the fate of Germany for two hundred years. The Empire would remain divided, its "liberties"—that is, the near-independence of German princes—guaranteed by the kings of France and Spain, the Emperor's powerlessness in the Empire safeguarded by an Imperial Diet which, bound by its rules to be unanimous on all important questions, could never settle any. The son of Frederick V recovered his father's electoral title and a portion of his lands, while the Bavarian Duke kept another part of his gains and *his* electoral title.

Within the Empire, which the United Provinces and the Swiss now left for good, a balance of power was established between Catholics and Protestants. The *cujus regio* provisions of the previous century were re-established, secularization up to 1624 accepted, Swedish power in the Baltic secured by the accession of Pomerania and the bishoprics of Bremen and Verden, which gave it control of the major north German rivers: Oder, Weser, and Elbe, and the king of France saw his eastern borders safeguarded by territorial gains in Alsace and recognition of his sovereignty over Metz, Toul, and Verdun, which Henry II had grabbed. The Court of Vienna remained the head of an empire but an increasingly non-German one. The firm base of the house of Habsburg now rested in Austria, Bohemia, and in Hungary, and looked toward south and southeast. Its imperial ambitions in Germany disappointed, it now turned more resolutely in the opposite direction, principally at the expense of the Turks.

Only Spain held out. Its conflict with the United Provinces now settled, war with France dragged on for ten more years, to be concluded by the Treaty of the Pyrenees (1659). The Franco-Spanish War had lasted twenty-four years. Advantageous territorially for France, the settlement with which it ended also avoided the possibility of a new Austro-Spanish alliance: the Infanta of Spain, Maria Theresa, who was to have wed the Emperor, married Louis XIV; and though she abandoned her succession rights to the Spanish throne this was only subject to the payment of 500,000 gold crowns, a sum which the ruined Spanish exchequer never found. The Infanta retained her rights, which passed to her husband, Louis XIV, and which Louis would not fail to claim, along with his own rights as grandson of Philip III of Spain, when the right moment came. As always, the seeds of future conflict lay in the covenant. For the time being, though, Europe had received a settlement based on the balance of contending powers and the exhaustion of religious conflict. The Spanish bid for empire had been defeated and France emerged (much challenged) as the great power of the coming age.

The French Hegemony

From the 1660's to the 1680's France dominated Europe more completely than any single power since Rome. But her strength reflected more the weakness of her rivals and her neighbors, divided internally and unable to mobilize their resources as they might.

France, which had gone through twenty years of troubles after the murder of Henry IV and through ten more (1643–1653) after the death of his son Louis XIII, had come into her own under the rule of powerful ministers. Cardinal Richelieu triumphed over the rebellious Protestants (1628), Cardinal Mazarin brought the overweening nobles and ambitious magistrates to heel (1653), the crown ruled supreme in the kingdom of which Emperor Maximilian used to say that God would have given it to His younger son, if He had one. It was a splendid young king who wore that crown, a king determined to be not only his own master but also to enforce his mastery on all that he surveyed.

Most specifically, Louis XIV seems to have cast his eye on the inheritance of Lothar and of Burgundy: the Spanish Netherlands and Luxembourg in the north, Lorraine and Alsace, the Free County of Burgundy (the Franche Comté) on the Swiss border, the strong places commanding passage into Italy. This apparent grab-bag makes some sense if we think of it first as an inheritance Louis claimed because he was the grandson of one Spanish king, the son-in-law of another. But if dynastic legalism furnished excuses, more concrete calculations suggest that we interpret his acts, first in terms of the route which Spanish forces had to follow going north and which the French for a century had tried to close, then as a defensive wish to shift the border from the exposed capital of Paris and, above all, to hold the great entry ports through which enemy troops had often invaded France: the Flanders plains, the plateau of Lorraine, the cities of Alsace with the great Rhine bridge of Strasbourg, the Alpine passes. And while Louis did not obtain all he coveted—not all of the Netherlands but only Flanders with its dense population and rich economy, not all Lorraine (which would only be gained in 1738), not all the passes (the essentials had been secured in his father's time)—he did by 1678 round out French territory quite remarkably.

But gates that can be closed can open too; the garrison can emerge to ravage and raid outside. While the internal safety is preserved, the troops can fall upon a defenseless neighbor. Louis' ambitions went far beyond security or else his view of security was vaster than contemporaries could safely tolerate. His vision of dominion grew to overcast the Dutch, the Empire, Italy, even at some times Spain. At least, that is how it looked to some enthusiasts in France and to prudent observers outside her. And, while official policy disclaimed such views, French troops campaigned or nibbled their way forward in a disturbing way. The Dutch feared with some reason the prospect of dynamic France on their southern border replacing the reconciled and cowed administration of the Spanish Netherlands; the Emperor and other German princes drew their conclusions from French advances on the Rhine; the Duke of Savoy feared for his independence, the king of Spain for his Italian lands. Even beyond her shores France claimed, as Louis' minister Colbert put it in 1677, "that all other nations must bow to her at sea as at the court of kings." Genoa was twice bombarded (1678, 1684) to enforce the claim, and full-scale sea battles waged in time of peace between the French and Dutch (1687, 1688), made the point. It was a point the English could not miss and, while the friendly and dependent Stuarts tried to ignore it, their fall in 1688 left England free to pit her interests and even more her pride against the arrogant French.

Long before that, the European powers had begun to combine against their threatening might. In 1668 an alliance of England, Holland, and Sweden forced Louis to halt his advance in Flanders and conclude peace at Aix-la-Chapelle (1668). A few years later, his attack on the Dutch brought into being a Grand Alliance (Holland, the Emperor, Spain, the Duke of Lorraine, later joined by the German diet and by Denmark) which saved the Low Countries from being devoured by France and moderated French gains (Peace of Nymegen, 1678).

Nymegen persuaded Europe that Louis XIV was bent on unlimited conquest. His annexation of Strasbourg with its important bridge over the Rhine confirmed this (1681). French pride in Louis' achievements and their own could only stress the point. French imperial power would be universal, as the sway of the French language already was: the Danish envoys at Nymegen wrote their dispatches in French, even the Spanish ambassador expressed himself in it. But the imperial ambitions of the Bourbons faced the imperial reality of the Habsburg clan, led now by the Emperor in Vienna. The Treaty of Westphalia had turned Habsburg ambitions east and south where the Turks provided more tempting possibilities and also more immediate dangers than the German princes. This meant that Habsburg forces were diverted from full-scale intervention on the Rhine, but paid off handsome dividends for the future. In 1683 with Polish help the armies of Leopold I stemmed the last great Turk assault on Vienna and turned to the offensive. By 1699 they had recovered Hungary and Transylvania, so that the Austrian border stood on the Carpathians and the Danube.

But, while the Emperor's power grew, his very commitments made him less than fully effective as an opponent to French ambitions in the west. He needed allies and found them in the maritime powers, threatened by the mercantile imperialism of France. England and Holland had waged a long struggle for supremacy overseas, which ended in the 1660's with the English winning on points, the Dutch evacuating almost all their American territories (including New Amsterdam which became New York) and concentrating henceforth on their eastern holdings. The Stuart kings of England had been sympathetic to France, whose absolute monarchy and Catholic faith they hoped to introduce into their kingdom. But when they failed in this attempt, their place was taken by a prince of Orange and the forces of Britain and the United Provinces joined in an alliance profoundly hostile to the French, who in the meantime pecked and gobbled on, in Alsace, along the Rhine, and in the Alps. In 1686, the Emperor, Spain, and Sweden had associated with some German princes to form the League of Augsburg and ensure the maintenance of the treaties of Westphalia and Nymegen. In 1688, after England and Holland joined them, began the War of the League of Augsburg, which succeeded in fighting the French to a standstill and even depriving them of some of their past gains (Treaty of Ryswick, 1697).

The greatest of the wars was still to come. It came about, for once, against the will of Louis, weary of war and doubting he could win. But the inheritance of the Spanish Empire was at stake. The last of the Spanish Habsburgs, Charles II, was dying without a direct heir. The chief contenders were in Vienna, in the junior branch of the Habsburg family, and in France, where the royal princes were direct descendants in the female line. A compromise candidate, the Elector of Bavaria, was briefly mooted but died; Vienna would not accept any scheme which cheated the Habsburg candidate (Archduke Charles, later Emperor Charles VI, 1711-1740) of his full rights; finally Louis, the English, and the Dutch agreed among themselves on an arrangement which left the Archduke Charles the principal heir, the French claimants receiving consolation prizes in Italy and Spain. The details of the scheme were very complex but not unfeasible. The chief gain of France and the maritime powers would be the maintenance of peace, while Habsburg interests came off better than by anything they could have done themselves. But Vienna was still reluctant to agree and, above all, the Spaniards would not stand by and let their empire be carved up by outsiders.

In 1700, Charles II of Spain died. They had brought the mummy of St. Isidore, an urn containing the remains of San Diego of Alcala, and basketfuls of relics; had put warm fresh-killed pigeons on his head and the steaming entrails of animals on his stomach, but nothing availed and the cretinous king passed away leaving behind a testament which designated as his sole heir Louis' grandson, the Dauphin's younger son, Philip of Anjou, or, failing him, his younger brother, or then the Archduke Charles. Spanish territories were to remain united.

Louis faced a deadly alternative: to break his word and go to war for Philip of Anjou or have the Spanish empire pass to Charles and see the threatening might of Charles V recreated. His almost forced decision for the former course did not precipitate war, but the French-dominated policies of the new French-born King Philip V of Spain (1700–1746) did. The War of the Spanish Succession broke out in 1702 and lasted for twelve years, with France fighting almost all of Europe not for herself but Spain. It ended with France ruined but entire, Philip V in possession of Spain and her empire, and the Archduke Charles, who in 1711 had succeeded to the empire, receiving Spain's Italian holdings

The War of the Spanish Succession, a contemporary engraving showing the encounter between the French and Austrian forces at Turin, September 1706. The French defeat at Turin practically ended the fighting on the Italian front.

and the Spanish Netherlands as well. The Emperor had obviously increased his power, but not without concession to his German peers—especially among the Protestants. In 1700, in return for his help, the Elector Frederick of Brandenburg had been recognized king in Prussia. In the treaties of Utrecht, Louis XIV had given up his support of Stuart pretenders to the English throne and recognized the Protestant succession in England. This meant that in 1714 the Elector of Hanover, George Louis, became King George I of England (1714–1727). The European powers, above all France, had accepted the legitimacy of the Revolution of 1688, the Anglo-Dutch view of contract, and of Prince William of Orange's bargain with the British people by virtue of which he, then Queen Anne (1702–1714), then their Hanoverian successors, ruled not merely by right of descent and blood but by a constitutional contract. The real winner of the war was England, less in terms of concrete gain (she got Gibraltar and Minorca from Spain, Newfoundland, Acadia, and Hudson Bay from France) than in terms of policy and prestige. Spain conceded the British right to South American trade (if only temporarily), and British ships had in any case garnered during the war a goodly portion of the overseas market. Her constitutional views now met with general acceptance, not only for home consumption, but abroad. Thus, English negotiators had imposed on Philip V the renunciation of his French succession rights, and on his cousins, the Dukes of Berry and Orléans, a similar renunciation to the succession of Spain which would avoid the possibility of the two crowns being united. Such gestures were impossible in absolute right but perfectly possible in the more flexible eyes of contract law which henceforth would hold sway. The change was fundamental and symbolic of the defeat of the divine-right theories of sovereignty which Louis XIV had incarnated.

France remained a great power, but no one power could henceforth claim to dominate Europe without raising a coalition of opponents. Princes remained the masters of their realms but never again *sole* masters. The monarchy continued sacred, but human conventions—treaties and compacts—weighed more heavily than divine right. The poisons of modernity were seeping into the veins of the old system. The balance, and also the imbalances and tensions, of *powers* would be one of the characteristics of the modern age.

Internal and Constitutional Changes

Italy

Italy in the sixteenth century was but a shadow of her former past, a backyard of Spain. After 1559, the peninsula was dominated by Spanish establishments in Milan, Naples, Sicily, and Sardinia. The Genoese were their bankers, the Medici in Florence (grand dukes of Tuscany since 1569), their protégés. Parma and Mantua were overawed by the *tercios* of the Milanese; the Pope was grudgingly acquiescent. Brigandage and malaria ruled over Roman territories. The sophistication of the early 1600's when prelates were still enlightened men waned as the century advanced. Clerical narrowness replaced the open curiosity which inspired Galileo's friends and patrons. Intellectual and scientific activity were stifled. Tight censorship was clamped upon the Roman press. Universities which had been great and active wasted and shrank. The year of Galileo's death, 1642, was also that of Newton's birth; the two events serve to symbolize the waning of intellectual and scientific enterprise where it had once flared so bright and its new intensity in the once barbarian northwest.

Politically too, as national and international affairs became increasingly secular, papal influence declined. Pious popes were rigid, lax ones were corrupt, all were feeble images of past prestige. The treaties of Westphalia were concluded with no reference to their wishes. It was an ominous portent. After 1648, the popes would be disregarded in all the main peace treaties of the modern age.

Of the Italian states (for "powers" would be a misleading term) only Venice and Savoy retained some semblance of independent policy. Genoa, a Spanish vassal, would see her fortunes affected by Spain's decline and, humbled by France, would shrink to a lagging city of great palaces and of lesser houses that stank, as Charles Dickens eventually reported, "like very bad cheese kept in very hot blankets." In Florence, the erstwhile luster of the Medici was sadly dimmed. John Evelyn, the English traveler, found the Grand Duke at the Pitti Palace "selling what he can spare of his wines, at the cellar under his very house: wicker bottles dangling over even the chief entrance into the Palace, serving for a vintner's bush."

Venice was caught between the great new trading powers whose competition sapped her merchants' wealth and the Turkish pressure to which her eastern interests exposed her. Her long wars with Turkey meant the loss of almost all her trade in the Levant to French, English, and Dutch competitors. The great patrician families transferred their capital from trade to land. No longer businessmen but landowners, the ruling oligarchs became increasingly conservative, allies of the papacy and of their Habsburg neighbors to the north, their city more a tourist than a trade resort. In the far northwest, the Duchy of Savoy was still a barren backwater, yet so strategically placed that its masters "could not," as Prince Eugene of Savoy explained, "afford to be honorable." They maneuvered shrewdly between Spain and France, selling the Alpine passes they commanded to the highest bidder, taking advantage of every opportunity to improve their precarious position and to avoid fall-

ing irretrievably under the sway of any one great neighbor. The end
of the War of the Spanish Succession brought the Duke of Savoy the
crown he coveted: he became king of Sicily, soon exchanged for Sardinia,
poorer but also carrying the royal dignity.

Thus Italy was a kind of colony whose fate was settled by outsiders.
In 1574 already an Italian patriot bewailed the fate of the land "which
had been queen of all kingdoms and is now enslaved by foreign and
barbarous nations." Some generations later we find a telling comment
scribbled on a report from the Spanish governor of Milan: ". . . these
Italians, although they are not Indians, have to be treated as such, so
that they will understand we are in charge of them . . ." The influence
of Spain was paramount. An early seventeenth-century sonnet took the
funereal black garb Italians were adopting from their masters to be
symbolic of the country's state.

The cities which had been the glory of the Renaissance became
principally the residences of landowning nobles or the administrative
centers of petty princes and prelates. Enterprise, industry, economy,
which had laid the fortune of the bourgeoisie, gave way to waste, idleness, and display. Money went not into savings or investments, but to
conspicuous consumption. Cultural activity of an indifferent order flourished on the time and energy such men could spare.* New academies
were founded where many spent their time in poetic and rhetorical
pursuits, improvising verses and orations of no social or artistic significance—"amazing futilities," as one observer called them who failed to
see their function: taking up time which could not usefully or safely be
spent on other things. The backwater soon turned into a museum and a
deer park for upper-class foreigners on the Grand Tour.

By about 1660, Italy was a depressed area. The industrial structure
had collapsed so far that the economy had become almost wholly agrarian and agriculture was fossilized by trusts, entails, and the indifference
of the greatest landowner: the Church. The major invisible exports
(banking and the carrying trade) had been abandoned to Dutch and
English competitors. The Spanish market decayed, the German market was laid waste by war, the French was forfeited with the rise of native industry there. Ravaged by plague in 1630 and 1657, the great
Italian cities lost about one-third of their population. By the end of
the century the losses were being replaced, but now there was no use
for them, no call for labor or demand for what could be turned out.
Overpopulated, underemployed, backward, and unindustrialized: the
new Italy would remain so until the twentieth century.

---

* Economic decay may be as great a spur to cultural life as economic activity.
Sometimes greater. In Rome, the bankers' quarter was also the artists' quarter and
Valencia would become, at the turn of the sixteenth century, one of the great in-
tellectual centers of Spain.

Spain

The year 1559 was not only the year when the peace of Cateau-Cambrésis was concluded, but the year when Philip II left Flanders for Spain, never to return. Not for Spain only, but for Castile in the midst of which he set his court, from which he henceforth "governed the world from a chair," as a seventeenth-century Aragonese document had it, imposing upon it not quite the will of Spain but rather of Castile with its more backward, more sober, more arrogant aristocratic and autocratic ways. The kingdom remained a congeries of provinces, each with its characteristic personality. Aragon, with its nobility and *cortes* jealously asserting wide feudal "liberties" and claims at least until the end of the sixteenth century; Catalonia (part of the lands of the crown of Aragon), more mercantile, more "modern," proud of its great port of Barcelona, its Catalan speech, and the particular rights of *its* estates; the south with its vast domains and semicolonial atmosphere; Castile, largest and most populous but also most effectively subject to the crown. Aragonese lands looked north and east to France, to the Mediterranean, to the King's possessions in Italy and the intervening islands. Castile looked more to Africa and across the Atlantic to the Americas, but conceived itself above all else as the conquering kernel and base of the monarchy.

His court established at Madrid, Philip began construction fifty miles away of a great monastery, the Escorial, which he had vowed to San Lorenzo to build in thanks for the victory of St. Quentin and whose plan would imitate the grill on which the martyred saint had been roasted. There within the gray granite walls of what an American historian saw as being a palace, monastery, and a tomb in one, among Hyeronimite monks, above the great family mausoleum, in view of the gardens that he loved, the prudent king worked, prayed, and hesitated, while piles of paper rose high about him awaiting a decision.

"Time and I are a match for any two," said Philip; but the asso-

El Escorial.

ciation stood on a firm base of treasure and of arms. The Spanish *tercios* were as famous as they were feared. When, in 1566, the young French writer Pierre de Brantôme (1540–1614) heard that the armies of the Duke of Alva would cross Lorraine on their way from Italy to the Netherlånds, he took a post chaise to go and see "this gentle troop of brave and valiant soldiers . . . all aged and inured to war, so fine in dress and arms that one took them rather for captains than for soldiers . . . and you would think that they were princes, so proud they were and marched arrogantly and with fine grace." But, as we have seen, such fine men cost money. The Spanish crown spent more in every year of the Netherlands' rebellion than it had got in yearly revenue from the Netherlands when trade was flourishing. And there were other conflicts that made for other costs: particularly the war at sea. Just the one great Armada, although its total tonnage (57,868) was rather less than that of the *Queen Mary*, piled up astronomical expenses.* Yet its loss was only the prelude to the building of a new Armada, no more successful than the first.

Such enterprises were financed by ever heavier taxes and, of course, by the flow of riches from across the sea. While this should not be exaggerated, it must have been impressive and contemporaries certainly found it so. We can see what happened from one example, culled from a chronicle late in Philip's reign. On March 22, 1595, ships of the Indies plate fleet drew up to the Seville quays and began to unload 332 cartfuls of silver, gold, and pearls. On April 8, the main galleon of the fleet disgorged 103 cartloads by itself. The Admiral's flagship had been blown into Lisbon by a storm and its contents were moved overland to Seville. For six days beginning May 23 the carts loaded with gold and jewels continued to roll through the city gate, until the Casa de Contratacion where all the wealth piled up was so full that bars of precious metal and cases crammed with it had to be stacked in all its courtyards.

Yet neither the flow of treasure from the New World, nor the taxes from the old, sufficed for Philip's vast commitments. The crown got into the habit of repeated bankruptcies and Philip II alone had to repudiate his debts seven times in the course of his reign. At his death in 1598 he left the country ruined and exhausted, a state which would get worse throughout the seventeenth century.

Philip at least had imposed some order in his realm, had firmly settled the crown on a bureaucratic structure, inefficient by our lights but effective enough in its time. His death reopened the issue of political supremacy, allowed the aristocracy to rise again and reassert itself in the machinery of the state. Under Philip's degenerate successors his realm became the prey and plaything of avid favorites. The Duke of Lerma

---

* In 1612, Thomé Cano's *Arte de Navegar* explained that a 500-ton ship which cost 4,000 ducats in the days of Charles V now ran four times as much.

(1552–1625) under the bigoted Philip III (1598–1621), the Duke of Olivares (1587–1645) under the more frivolous and artistic-minded Philip IV (1621–1665), were not without some talent. The favorites of Charles II (1665–1700) and his queens were utterly disastrous and dedicated only to pillaging the country. Throughout the seventeenth century the royal court, brilliant and useless, ruinous and immoral, was probably (as a Spanish historian has described it) the greatest of the national calamities. But there were others. The most productive sections of the population, Jews and Moors, had been expelled or forced into conversion soon after 1492. But the remaining converts—*Marranos* and *Moriscos*—were generally suspected of having shed their old faiths only on the surface and they were pursued by bitter popular racism as well as by the long arm of the Inquisition. Most of the converted Jews (Marranos) had left during the sixteenth century. In 1609–1614 several hundred thousand Moriscos, who were especially productive farmers, were expelled, amid great popular enthusiasm, with disastrous consequences for an economy already in dire straits.

In 1600, the government, hard-driven by its needs, debased the coinage, introduced copper coins, drove gold and silver out of circulation. We have seen that copper money was so bulky that it created serious cartage and storage problems. Worse, foreigners would not accept it, and with silver at a premium, foreign trade withered along with the remains of economic activity. Even the Pope insisted on silver and the *Cortes* of 1624 complained that bulls, indulgences, and other papal documents could not be obtained with the result that many people "failed to gain papal indulgence and the dead do not enjoy suffrage because there is no silver money to pay for bulls."

Between 1620 and 1650 prices rose by 200 per cent. Taxes by more. And taxes were being paid by ever fewer people and ever fewer people were in a position to pay them. In 1591, the tax rolls of Burgos show 3,319 heads of households; among them, 1,722 *hidalgos,* of gentle birth, 1,023 members of the clergy, only 574 taxpayers who were economically active and productive: 17 per cent of the whole. No wonder population declined: between 1594 and 1646 Toledo's population shrank by half, its hundreds of textile workshops dwindled to scarcely better than a dozen; Burgos which had been the chief market of uncarded wool for export fell from 2,600 "hearths" or households (counting approximately five souls to each) to 600; Medina del Campo, once the site of great fairs, was ruined: 3,000 hearths in 1570, 650 in 1646. City after once-prosperous city became a semirural township whose inhabitants lived on the income from land rather than industrial production or trade. Fields lay abandoned, villages decayed, houses crumbled. The livestock in some places fell by as much as 60 percent, the human population by about a quarter. Don Quixote and Sancho could ride for days without seeing a soul. "In Aragon, near the Pyrenees," remarks a

French traveler in 1617, "one walks and walks without finding an inhabitant."

The number of priests and monks was growing, the wealth and power of the Church (owning about one-fifth of all the land) seemed to increase in inverse proportion to the country's welfare. A royal circular of 1689 shows King Charles II complaining to the Episcopate that in many places it was hard to find a young man *not* in holy orders: "Almost all do this to enjoy exemption from the law, to live in great freedom, to avoid taxes, and from other worldly interests."

Probably an exaggeration, but the argument is a telling one: enterprise consisted of avoiding productive labor, of managing to live without contributing to the increase of social wealth. Idleness was noble; a contemporary social theorist wrote proudly of Spain's sloth: "All nations produce craftsmen for Madrid . . . she is the queen of cities, since all serve her and she serves nobody." With indolence went slackness: *Don Quixote* has been called "a discourse on lack of method," contrasting with the rational methods increasingly in vogue elsewhere. Not reason but passion, not efficacy but nobility were the Spanish style and we may wonder whether the stress upon them was not a compensation for lack of thought and of action and for the country's growing ineffectiveness.

Economic decline checked economic, hence social, mobility; it accentuated the contrast between social groups and led to increasing ostentation and formalism. Increasingly rigid, Spanish society grew increasingly concerned with impression and outward show. An exaggerated sense of honor confused uprightness with reputation, integrity with vanity. "Honor," said the Code of Castile, "is the reputation that a man has acquired by the rank he fills, by his high deeds, or by the valor he shows . . . and there are two things which are equal: killing a man or besmirching his reputation, for the man who has lost his reputation, even through no fault of his own, is dead as to the values and the honors of this world; and for him better death than life." This kind of honor depends on others: on their actions and on their opinions. A man's mind is ever on his fellows, concerned to impress them and impose himself upon them. Says Lope de Vega:

> No man is honorable in himself
> He holds his honor from others.
> It is not honorable to be a virtuous man
> And full of merit. Hence follows
> That honor rests in others, not in self.

Thus honor is less a private than a social value, exaggerated and highly verbalized, a mechanical reflex devoid of individual virtue, an outward show like those Spanish houses, so often sordid or bare behind the gigantic coats of arms on the facade.

Yet, Spain lived on, proud, as Felipe de Meneses writes in 1554, of her isolation and spiritual security behind "a fiery wall, which is the holy office of the Inquisition." The importance of American treasure kept shrinking. In 1647 Spain withdrew her Caribbean fleet and buccaneers entered their golden age. But if the warships were withdrawn, the reason lay in the insignificant quantities they had to protect by then, the falling productivity of South American mines and higher costs of production there, the frauds which withheld even what treasure was found, the commercial circuits which sent it west to the Philippines and China instead of east to Cadiz and Seville. And the drought of precious metals would be reflected in a new anemia of Spanish power.

With overseas income shrinking and governmental costs rising, the economy passed by default into the hands of heretical Dutchmen, Portuguese Jews, and the "white Moors" of Genoa. This seems to have caused a kind of nationalist reaction, inspired partly by the growing sense of inferiority and partly by inability to find a way out of besetting difficulties. A new aggressive Castilian nationalism inspired the reforming politics of Olivares, chief minister of Philip IV from 1621 to 1643, and subsequent attempts to reaffirm past greatness in new wars which proved even costlier and even less successful than the old.

Bankruptcy became a way of life. Not that it prevented ostentatious spending. In 1637, to celebrate the election to the Empire of the King's Viennese cousin, Ferdinand III, the Madrid court spent 300,000 ducats on great festivities: "They say that a manifestation of such importance had another aim than sheer amusement and that such ostentation was meant to let Cardinal Richelieu, our good friend, know that there is still money to spare to chasten his king." Behind the proud facade, realities were harsher. "There are many days," writes a chronicler in 1654, "when the households of the King and of the Queen lack everything, even bread"; and a note of November, 1657, from Diego de Velasquez (the painter had been appointed intendant of the royal palace in 1652) complained that his pay is one and a half years in arrears, sweepers and servants unpaid have stopped work, and there is no money to buy wood for their majesty's fire. The days of Spanish greatness were over.

The Netherlands

The brightest gems in the crown of Charles V had been the provinces of the Burgundian circle on the lower Rhine, where trade and industry were further advanced than anywhere outside Italy. The center of economic activity was Antwerp. By mid-sixteenth century, as the Belgian historian Henri Pirenne has said, the Netherlands were practically its suburbs. So were the other centers of the trading world: English wool, Portuguese spices, expensive goods from Italy, bulky ones from the Baltic, the manufactures of Germany and Flanders, drained into it down the Rhine or across the sea. At the height of its prosperity, in the 1560's, every day some five hundred ships went up or down Antwerp's river, hundreds of coaches brought in travelers, thousands of wagons rolled in with goods and with provisions. A good proportion of its population were foreigners, many Protestants, protected by the city's policy of toleration and even more by the awareness that the Netherlands' prosperity rested on the freedom, the coming and going, the cosmopolitan activity of their bourgeoisie.

The seventeen provinces that focused on Antwerp were ruled from Brussels as an autonomous unit by a royal governor. Each was represented by deputies in a general assembly—the Estates-General—which dated back to 1463 and which alone could vote the taxes and the subsidies requested by the governor or king. The Estates were very insistent on their privileges and rights. So were the different provinces represented in them. Charles V had treated them with tact and caution, avoiding friction and sparing their interests. Philip II, more stubborn, made no concessions. He was a Spaniard, he was modern; without his father's sympathy for the medieval survivals which the Netherlands called their liberties, the ancient customs which preserved a confusing medley of privilege and interest. Philip, for one thing, wanted a simpler, more efficient tax structure which could bring him more revenue. He also sought to eliminate heresy, introduce the Jesuits and the Inquisition, and set about rationalizing the ecclesiastical machinery through which this could be done. His measures cut across established interests, threatened the wealth of the burghers, the pride of the nobles, the freedom of the market, the rights of the Estates. Calvinism was spreading, appealing both to the merchant classes and to the urban poor. The royal efforts to prohibit it stirred further disquiet over the crown's authoritarian plans. One excess was bound to bring another: Calvinist iconoclasm evoked royal repression, royal repression riot and unrest. Philip resolved to bring his rebellious subjects to obedience. In 1567, the Duke of Alva arrived in Brussels bringing 10,000 costly troops from Italy— sufficient numbers, it would seem, to chastise insurgents and introduce a Spanish discipline among the restless Netherlanders. A reign of terror followed, with thousands executed; rebellion and heresy were being extirpated.

Alva might have succeeded had he not, in dire straits for money, imposed the intolerable series of taxes—the *alcabalas,* including a 10 per cent duty on every sale—copied on Spanish practices but bound in a commercial country to ruin industry and trade. Alva's tax was meant to be rational and uniform, paid by all alike, no matter what their class or their ancestral privilege might be. It was an equalitarian measure which ignored social and provincial distinction for better as for worse. It was not all bad. But it was Spanish and it was thoughtless. In 1572 the Netherlanders rose against the prospect of commercial ruin, against

THE NETHERLANDS

The United Provinces before 1648

Spanish Netherlands in 1579

Boundary of the Union of Arras in 1579

Lands ceded by Spain to the United Provinces in 1648 (known as the Generality)

NORTH SEA

ZUIDER ZEE

HOLLAND

Leeuwarden

FRIESLAND

GRONINGEN

DRENTHE

Emden

Haarlem

Amsterdam

OVERYSSEL

Devender

The Hague

UTRECHT

Utrecht

GELDERLAND

Arnhem

Rotterdam

Münster

ZEELAND

Cleve

GENERALITY

THE

Antwerp

Herenthals

Mechlin

Rhine

Meuse

HOLY ROMAN EMPIRE

Dunkirk

Bruges

Ghent

Schelde

FLANDERS

Ypres

BRUSSELS

BRABANT

Cologne

Aachen

Calais

Lys

Lille

BISHOPRIC OF LIÉGE

Liège

Boulogne

ARTOIS

Arras

HAINAUT

NAMUR

Cambrai

CAMBRESIS

Guise

St. Quentin

Amiens

LUXEMBOURG

Moselle

Trier

Sedan

Luxembourg

FRANCE

Verdun

Meuse

Metz

ENGLAND

GLISH

NNEL

50   100 miles

the principle of a permanent tax imposed from above without consultation or consent of their Estates. The "Placard of Dismissal" by which the Estates-General deposed Philip from dominion over his Netherland provinces appealed to the old feudal contracts between prince and subjects which, the Estates claimed, Philip had broken by ignoring their rights. Religious considerations here were incidental to medieval traditions, though the Calvinist assertion of individual rights fitted the spirit of the principles and provided the energy to carry them through.

This was only a beginning. Sporadic but bitter fighting raged over the land for nearly forty years. The long struggle between the Spanish forces and their supporters and the rebels would not be settled until the following century. Chance and geography eventually determined the outcome. The south was easier to conquer, the northern parts more inaccessible behind their watery barriers. Protestant refugees from the south moved north, away from Spanish arms; Catholics from the north fled the rebels and the Protestant inconoclasts. Antwerp, sacked in 1576 by the Spaniards, in 1583 by the French, finally captured by Spanish royal troops in 1585, sent thousands of enterprising refugees into the north, and many of those who had not been Calvinist to begin with converted in due course, especially as the Calvinists became indentified with the party of resistance to Catholic Spain. By 1579, the Low Countries had become divided roughly on present lines, the ten provinces of the south making their peace with Philip and with Rome, the seven northern ones (Holland, Zeeland, Guelders, Utrecht, Overyssel, Friesland, and Groningen), easier to defend and less accessible, shortly to form the United Provinces.

One man above all others played a crucial part in the successful stand the rebels made and in their organization into a working body: William, Prince of Orange (1533–1584), heir of a great family, who placed his persistence, his humane personality, his talents in the service of the Protestant cause, held its divergent parts together through the most difficult times, and guided it to statehood. After his murder by a Catholic, probably in the pay of Spain, his office of Stadtholder (governor and military commander) continued to be filled by other members of the Orange clan: his son, Maurice of Nassau (1567–1625), Maurice's half-brother Frederick Henry (1584–1647), Frederick's son, William II (1626–1650), finally William III (1650–1702).

Able though sometimes unsuccessful soldiers, the Orange-Nassau princes reorganized the armies of the Estates putting them on a modern footing, and tended to become leaders of the war party, averse to the conciliatory and pacifistic policies which the mercantile patricians generally favored. Around these two poles two parties grew: the Republicans, led by the Grand Pensionary (Chief Civil Magistrate) of Holland and by the urban bourgeoisie, stood for municipal rights, for commerce, and for peace; the Orangists, based on the officers and gentry and on the lower classes attached to the Orange name and hostile to rich merchants, tended to bellicosity and centralism.

Almost unique in an age of absolutism, the Dutch in effect set up a federation of oligarchies, where local liberties counted for more than national power. Efficient enough while no grave danger threatened, this loose state structure proved cumbersome and slow at times of serious danger. Then, the rule of a small group of wealthy men would be exchanged for Orange leadership and parochial preoccupations would be subordinated—for a while—to centralism imposed by military needs. Such reversals were spurred, and sometimes facilitated, by the identification of the Republican faction with Holland; so that the Orangists became a kind of "country party," standing not only for opposition to merchant rule but expressing the more widespread resentment of other Dutch provinces against the predominance of Amsterdam and Hollanders.

Political interests were complicated by social struggles between rich and poor, between commercial interests and the army-country party, and by religious conflicts. The sizable Catholic minority had little say, but Protestants themselves split into many sects. Among the dominant Calvinists two tendencies developed: one more rigorous headed by Pastor Francis Gomar (1563–1641), and a more moderate wing, led by Arminius (1560–1609), for whom religion had social aspects subject to the civil authorities. The Gomarists seem to have got the better of the Arminians at first, yet were not able to introduce the strict religious measures which they envisaged. The memory of William's stand for tolerance lived on, the mixed cosmopolitan cities did not lend themselves to sustained religious repression, and the Republic soon became a haven of religious tolerance. In a world dedicated to uniformity and exclusiveness, the seven Provinces were first to allow variety of religious observance and belief and to profit from it. Among the religious exiles who found refuge there were numerous Jews and Marranos who had fled Spain for Lisbon, thence to Antwerp, and, finally, escaped to Amsterdam where their talents and new skills (as in the diamond business) made them a useful leaven in commerce, industry, and banking.

The possibility of freedom, the liberty of thought and even, though more limited, of dissent, turned the Dutch Republic into an intellectual center, a safe resort for scholars and scientists, philosophers and theologians, a crossroads of European intellect. The freedom of expression, the absence of censorship, spurred the publication of newsletters and journals. Many of these were in French, to reach a wider public; and their function proved especially important when, in the 1680's, Louis XIV's anti-Protestant persecutions increased their public and turned them into weapons of argument and criticism.

The greatest, strongest, wealthiest of the United Provinces, contributing 58 per cent of the national budget, was Holland (a name which came to be synonymous with the United Provinces). The greatest city of Holland was Amsterdam. With Antwerp despoiled by the Spaniards and further ruined by the exodus of its most enterprising citizens, Amsterdam inherited its place. It became the great exchange and money mart, the printing and bookselling center, the greatest fur market and sugar-refining center in Europe, and its most thriving port. In 1609 the foundation of the Bank of Amsterdam affirmed it as the center of European capitalism and further accelerated its growth. The Bank provided an invaluable credit institution which would accept deposits and make loans, handle foreign exchange, provide convenient means of pay-

The Harbor of Amsterdam, by Willem van de Velde (the Younger), 168(?). Rijksmuseum, Amsterdam.

ment (bank notes, checks) by which sums could be transferred from one account to another without money needing to change hands, and an apparently unlimited source of capital for business and the state.

But the United Provinces were full of ports and full of enterprise; short of land they placed their capital in industrial and money-making ventures, particularly on the sea. A contemporary of Charles V had commented that "Hollanders fish more gold and silver out of the sea than other countries dig out of the ground"; a hundred years later the Estates-General declared fishing "One of the chiefest mines of the Netherlands." Not fishing alone, however. Dutch entrepreneurs, often southern refugees, built up all kinds of industries, dug mines, farmed out taxes, founded banks, throughout the western world. From Antwerp to Amsterdam, then to Copenhagen, Gabriel Marcelis became the chief purveyor of the Danish king; his kinsman, Louis de Geer, developed the Swedish iron industry, the iron mines, dealt in armaments, finally in 1644 equipped an entire fleet for Sweden. It was the Dutch who taught the North how to build cities that were comfortable, efficient, clean, and laced with canals: the Copenhagen of Christian IV (1588–1648), so reminiscent of Amsterdam in parts; Oslo, which Christian rebuilt after a fire in 1620 and called Christiania; Göteborg, newly created that same year by his rival Gustavus Adolphus; sections of Berlin; and even St. Petersburg, where the Tsar's first plan had been a canal town to resemble Amsterdam.

The Dutch were traders, shippers, entrepreneurs. They carried grain from the Baltic to the Mediterranean, stores from the north to the south, and spices from the south to the north. They carried exotic goods from the Indies and slaves from Africa and sugar from Brazil. For a while they turned the Baltic into a Dutch preserve, and almost did the same with the southeast Asian seas. They traded with their enemies as they did with friends, never ceasing their connection with Spain and Portugal through the eighty years of official war, smuggling when they could not do things straightforwardly, fighting when they had to, to enforce their will.

Politics and war became instruments of trade, religious tolerance a function of economic need, as was the doctrine of the open seas. The East India Company, the greatest force in the country, with a monopoly of trade with the Indies, sought to enforce its rule over seas from which it tried to keep or sweep ships of other nations, maintaining a fleet of forty to sixty ships, an army over ten thousand strong. The profits from the sale of the merchandise imported sent dividends up to 25 and 30 per cent, shares quintupling and sextupling in price by 1670. No wonder there was speculation, sometimes carried to extraordinary lengths, as in the case of the tulip craze of the 1630's.

Tulips had been first imported from Turkey to Germany around the 1550's. They were brought to the Netherlands as an exotic curiosity in 1593, and became the reigning queens of gardens after 1615 on news that they were fashionable in Paris. Speculation in bulbs and varieties—of which hundreds were developed—rose to mad heights by 1636, when a house could be bought for three tulip bulbs, a carriage and pair of horses for one. In 1637 came the crash which ruined a great many people. Many suffered in the wake of this and similar debacles, like the painter Jan Van Goyen, ruined when the tulip bubble burst, and one wonders how far the somber paintings of Rembrandt's later years are due to the fact that he lost most of his money in East India Company shares. Yet many also enriched themselves, and the Netherlands prospered enough to bear the burdens of long warfare without collapsing. In 1665 Colbert estimated that the Dutch owned three-quarters of the world's ships—some 15,000. Actually, their fleet numbered far less, but still remained eight or ten times more numerous than the French.

What really counted is that between 1568 and 1648 a nation had been forged in the seven provinces between the North Sea and the Rhine, a new type of federal state without geographical unity, without an original religious or ethnic sense, but one whose members had in effect done great things together and were prepared for more. They had successfully withstood the might of Spain, held off the Catholic offensive, created political and economic institutions, provided opportunities for intellectual, scientific, and artistic enterprise of the most significant kind. Religious tolerance and military success had given them a consciousness of unity and telescoped historical experiences which elsewhere took much longer. It is true that the Dutch Republic could only act as a great power when its greater rivals were temporarily weakened (as in 1659–60); and then it did so with caution. But it could cause great powers to act. Through most of the seventeenth century the Dutch throve, as it were, in a relative vacuum of power. When first France, then England asserted itself, this situation changed. Public institutions and private wealth were both affected by the strain of warfare carried on too long. Prosperity endured, but limited resources could no longer match the scale of world affairs. After the Peace of Utrecht the United Provinces, as Frederick II would put it, "were no more than a dinghy in the wake of British ships."

France

No country could offer a more striking contrast to the United Provinces than France: an extensive kingdom, committed by long historical evolution to a strong crown, proud and contentious nobles, an enterprising, legalistic middle class; a power which expanded on lines its predecessors had laid down, whose wealth came largely from the land, whose force rested on her armies, not her fleets. Where the Dutch estates had the problem of building a new nation, the French kings were concerned with structuring an old—harnessing a variety of social and provincial groups within their power and their authority. The greatest obstacle they met was the nobility—proud, rebellious, disparate, but fiercely jealous of its privileges and rights. Traditionally, nobiliar rights were the reward of function, primarily armed service in the field, but also any other service to the crown in the administration or in law. The rise of mercenary armies and of an administrative and legal corps recruited among commoners who owed their posts to the crown, not to their birth, made many of the old nobles useless and restlessly conscious of new insecurities, especially as growing inflation cut into their incomes and their way of life.

Affected by the price revolution of the sixteenth century, the nobles were even more affected by the termination of the wars, when these left them without employment. In Germany at least, their social functions increased; in Spain, the king's service or emigration offered valid alternatives; in England and the Netherlands economic enterprise, in trade or agriculture, was possible for many; but in France trade was out of the question, social functions were increasingly usurped by the lowborn servants of the crown, wealth was diminished by absence of entail with consequent breaking up of family estates and, finally, after 1559, peace closed the possibilities of warlike enterprises. No wonder that, with the disappearance of Henry II, killed in a tourney, nobles turned to banditry, rebellion, and civil war, as a means of amusement but even more of restoring their sagging fortunes.

Protestantism, particularly in its French Calvinist form, spread rapidly through France, especially in the west and south, attracting converts from every walk of life but generally led and protected by the local gentry. By the mid-sixteenth century Protestantism was a force

Catherine de Medici, by an unknown artist.

that not only threatened the Catholic establishment but also the authority of the crown. Henry II disliked the Calvinists but found himself hampered by the war with Spain which he concluded in 1559 especially to free his hands at home. That same year a first Protestant synod met in Paris, enforcing the King's suspicion of the heretics and spurring him to take measures against them. But Henry's death put an end to his restrictive measures. Under the regency of his widow, Catherine, a daughter of the Medici dukes of Tuscany, the power-hungry nobles gathered strength, the hopes and credit of the Protestants increased. The Protestant (Huguenot) party was headed by the junior branch of the royal family, the princes of the house of Bourbon. Against them stood another interest group, identified with the Catholic cause and led by Lorrainer princes of the house of Guise. The Queen tried to maneuver between them by using a third party grouped around the magnate family of Montmorency, whose vast domains stood in the center of the country and who, while Catholic, preferred a policy of compromise and tolerance to a clash which might bring civil war. These men, eventually known as *politiques,* deplored both Huguenot Puritanism and Catholic fanaticism, "preferred," writes a contemporary historian, "the repose of the kingdom and their own homes to the salvation of their souls; who would rather that the kingdom remain at peace without God than at war for him."

Yet such a delicate balance could not last. One religious fanaticism faced the other and the constant friction exacerbated both. The nephews of Montmorency, the Colignys, turned Protestant, bringing fresh force and leadership to the Calvinist camp whose gains were frightening the Catholics. It was probably only the common people's attachment to the old religion that saved the Church in France; but not before its defenders had precipitated civil war. Massacres and countermassacres, raids, murders, sieges, and pitched battles scoured the country. Thousands of victims were "stabbed, stoned, thrown down from heights, strangled, beaten, burnt or starved to death, buried alive, drowned, suffocated . . ." These are the words of a Calvinist, but they apply as well to Catholics, although the latter were responsible for the worst massacre of all, starting in Paris on St. Bartholomew's Day (August 24, 1572) and spreading throughout France. Murders only called for further murders. The Protestants killed the Duke of Guise, the Guises killed Coligny, Henry III had two other Guises murdered, was murdered in his turn by a monk *—the French stage ran with blood. A kind of Protestant state grew out of the Protestant party: a counterstate which faced the Catholic league in civil strife, the two opponents vying for royal support, which went now to the one and now to the other.

The authority of the crown itself was waning. One after another the three sons of Henry II succeeded to the throne (Francis II in 1559, Charles IX in 1560, Henry III in 1574), but not to effective power. With the murder of the last in 1589, the house of Valois was dead and Henry III's successor was a heretic, Henry of Bourbon, king of the little kingdom of Navarre, leader of the Protestant forces. At this point Spanish troops intervened in the civil conflict, supporting the Catholic league

* His killer, Jacques Clément, would be commemorated in the popular ditty, *Frère Jacques.*

The St. Bartholomew's Day Massacre of Huguenots, when over 3,000 died.

Henry of Navarre, the future Henry IV of France, by an unknown artist. Carnavalet Museum, Paris.

against Henry, and thirty years of civil troubles were followed by a decade of general war. Gradually, Henry IV pacified the country, drove out the Spaniards, settled the conflict. The *politiques* who wanted peace and order rallied round him. He himself realized that the crown would be his only at the price of conversion. The principle that subjects must follow the king's religion was reversed and Henry IV adopted the religion of the majority of his subjects before being crowned and re-entering Paris as a Catholic (1594). Four years later, common exhaustion made for peace with Spain (Vervins, 1598).

Peace at home was even more important. Promulgated a few weeks before Vervins, the Edict of Nantes recognized full liberty of conscience for Protestants, freedom of worship in designated places and a number of strongholds as a guarantee. Here was one more of those religious treaties which the time knew well (similar to the Peace of Augsburg) and generally disliked because religious passions were too strong to sanction coexistence. Designed to reconcile the Protestants to a Catholic king and kingdom, the Catholics to the existence of a Protestant minority which, untolerated, could cause chaos, the Edict of Nantes satisfied neither side (as previous similar royal measures had also failed to do) but lasted because both sides were exhausted.

Meanwhile, forty years of ruin had to be restored, the growing poverty mitigated. Henry set to do this aided by two Huguenot nobles: Maximilien de Béthune, later Duke of Sully (1560–1641), and Barthélémy de Laffémas (1545–1611), who became the head of a new Bureau of Commerce, founded significantly as soon as peace returned, to spark new enterprises, shake gilds and corporations out of sluggish routine. Agriculture was reanimated, roads and canals built, industry revived, new industries encouraged; France became an economic power once again. But her prosperity was fragile. It hung, as such things always did

Marie de Medici, a painting by Scipione Pulzone. Pitti Palace, Florence.

in those days, on the vagaries of nature and also upon peace and order, which were absolutely needed if the land should thrive. Warfare could bring fresh devastation, heavier taxes; a change of government could allow unrest to breed, weaken the rule of law, disrupt the economy, slide the country back into ruin. In the seventeenth century, the contemporaries of Richelieu and Mazarin would look back on the good times of King Henry as a golden age: it was less than that, but it was prosperous.

But in 1610 Henry was murdered by a mad fanatic, and the government, in the hands of a regent, his widow Marie de Medici (1573–1642), was once more at the mercy of factions and royal favorites. King Henry's heir, Louis XIII (1601–1643), was only nine years old, a sickly, troubled child who grew into a troubled, sickly man but one deeply devoted to his task. In the mid-1620's he found to help him a shrewd and forceful servant of the Queen Marie, Armand du Plessis (1585–1642), known to history as Cardinal Richelieu. Richelieu set out, as his *Political Testament* would put it, "To reduce all [the King's] subjects to their duty and to revive his name among foreign nations to the level at which it deserves to be." The first in order of his tasks was to bring the Huguenots to heel. The King's minority and the new time of troubles had increased their credit and their tendency to treat with the King's foreign enemies as if they were an independent power. "So long as the Huguenots in France are a state within the state," writes Richelieu in a private memo of 1625 to his king, "the King cannot be master within his realm, or achieve great things outside it."

In a few years but after a difficult struggle, the Huguenots were humbled and deprived of their strongholds, their military power broken, reduced to political impotence. The nobility also was being tamed, enlisted in the service of the King, its deadly claws filed down or put to use

Cardinal Mazarin, an etching by Huret from the Champaigne portrait. John B. Wolf Collection.

in the campaigns which reasserted French interests and power abroad. Richelieu's successor, Giulio Mazzarini (Cardinal Mazarin 1602–1661), pursued his work, though hampered by a recrudescence of the rebelliousness which always marked royal minorities. Louis XIII had been nine when his father died; his son was four years old when he succeeded him as Louis XIV. From 1643 to his death in 1661 Mazarin was Louis' first minister, the manager of the country. A good part of this time rebellion boiled up against the crown, a last attempt as it turned out to violently assert the privileges of princes and great nobles, of magistrates, municipal assemblies, and *parlements,* against the royal authority. Greatest of these explosions—the *Frondes* (1648–1653), as they were called after the slings which city urchins often used to pelt carriages and riders with stones and mud, left an indelible impression on the young king's mind. He grew up determined that this would never recur, that the royal power must be placed on firm foundations, and that no class in the state should challenge it again.

Louis le Grand   Louis XIV moved his court out of unquiet Paris to the safe isolated hamlet of Versailles, beyond the reach of popular rebellion; he domesticated the proud nobility, turning their pretensions from politics toward his glittering court, persuading them that there alone amid the artificial pomp of its stage effects lay beauty, profit, and real life. The courtesans were shut in a gilded cage of ceremonies and pensions, of gifts and dowries, benefits and places; the public was awed by power, dazzled by the scale of buildings and displays, charmed by royal style, affected by official propaganda. In the end, Louis persuaded every estate—clergy, nobility, and that famous Third Estate which really represented lawyers, magistrates, and officeholders rather than the masses —that they owed their existence to the King, functioned in terms of the

299

crown and on its terms. The persuasion was not final, opposition boiled up in fits and starts, old rights and new interests were asserted or, at least, recalled, especially when the great king had died. But it would be rebelliousness, not rebellion.

Louis cared deeply for his realm and felt his responsibilities keenly. It is doubtful if he ever pronounced the phrase attributed to him, *l'état c'est moi*, (I am the state), although it has been suggested he might well have said "the state is mine," since kings of this time regarded their realm as one great estate. This is reflected in his remark that "When one cares for the state, one works for oneself. The good of the one makes the glory of the other." The King fulfilled himself in a state which realized its full potential through his efforts. That is the theory of absolute monarchy. Its weakness, not then apparent, was that the monarch being human his abilities were limited, the state lived longer, its machinery went on turning even when that of the king might fail.

Short of stature (hence the high heels and wigs he favored), Louis schooled himself to become the very embodiment of royal power: handsome, courteous, majestic and—by all accounts—immensely impressive to all who approached him. Yet even this energetic and industrious man, whose devotion to his royal duties recalls his descent from Philip II of Spain, would weaken and die. In the long run the state outdeveloped and outlived the king, first subjected and then sacrificed to its theoretically unlimited interests and power.

Louis' excellent intentions could not make up for his human shortcomings, above all his pride. His fame is based largely on enterprises sparked by delusions of grandeur, of which he repented before his death: buildings and wars, both endless, both ruinously costly yet playing a logical role—the latter offering an opening for idle energies and reassurance of greatness (as long as they were successful), the former providing a scenic framework for royal pomp and order, both furnishing opportunities for display and for the great royal ballet of precedence and power.

All this cost money. An efficient minister of finance, Jean Baptiste Colbert (1619–1683), increased the royal revenues throughout the 1660's, but the long wars on which Louis embarked drained all excess away. The last budget surplus vanished in 1672; a few years later Bishop Bossuet, tutor of the Dauphin, was writing to the King to point out the misery of his people. The government had recourse to ever more desperate expedients. The great men who had served Louis in his youth died off, to be replaced by men of lesser stature. The King himself was growing old and pious. Foolish economics were aggravated by persecution of the Huguenots (about 10 per cent of the total population), whose presence spoiled the uniformity of France and seemed to mock the authority of the King. The Edict of Nantes was revoked in 1685 by the Edict of St. Germain. The mass of Huguenots was forcibly and only super-

Jean Baptiste Colbert, an engraving by Jacques Lubin. The Art Institute of Chicago.

ficially converted; many fled. As we have seen, the country lost thousands of its most skilled, loyal, enterprising subjects, whose energies and resources were henceforth devoted to improving the resources of France's neighbors and competitors instead.

By 1694 the famine in the country was so bad that in some provinces people were eating corpses. The War of the Spanish Succession turned misery into disaster. Shortly before the Battle of Malplaquet (1709), the French armies were left breadless for thirty hours, a reflection of the famine that raged throughout the land. By 1713 expenses were almost twice what revenues brought in, the royal debt thirty-four times the size of annual income, and taxes had been mortgaged for the next eight years.

The French hegemony had lasted only little and been jeopardized for empty dreams. France had indeed grown larger, more imposing, and Louis had given it religious uniformity which, if uneconomic, tallied with most contemporary views. Royal authority would not be seriously questioned until the 1780's and the coming years of peace allowed the economy to recover. French might would constantly be challenged but French dominance on the cultural plane could not be gainsaid. Louis died deplored by all, but the memory of men who build great monuments or who kill many people endures when the details wear away. "Every crime is permitted when it makes us great," declaimed the hero of a seventeenth-century tragedy. Louis XIV is still remembered as Louis the Great.

England

If France provides the prototype of dynastic absolutism, England provided the stage of its refutation and, even more important, eventually suggested a working alternative to it. The Reformation had made national sovereignty "absolute" by making it absolutely independent of any authority outside the realm. Spiritual supremacy was henceforth vested in the monarch, civil supremacy shared between crown and Parliament. The lawyers of Henry VIII and his successors established the omnicompetence of Crown and Parliament, without pressing too far the question how prerogatives would be divided between them. The main thing at first was that both church and state were merely different aspects of one Commonwealth and that the High Court of Parliament (as a text of 1583 would have it) "legitimateth bastards, establisheth forms of religion, altereth weights and measures."

Such formal unity, absent in continental countries, facilitated government and internal peace. It also provided matter for acrimonious debate when, in due course, king and Parliament came to loggerheads over their respective spheres and powers; and a base for their reconciliation in a refurbished Commonwealth.

Already in the sixteenth century, the long reign of Queen Elizabeth (1558–1603) had suggested the possibility of a monarchy reconciled with its estates, living within its means, and treating religion chiefly as a political factor: allowing Catholics to worship privately, provided they paid a fine and acted otherwise as loyal subjects of the crown. When her great minister, Sir William Cecil (1520–1598), had pressed the Queen to "scotch the papists' humors," she had refused to make, as she put it, "windows into men's souls."

Men who pay fines to worship as they please and not to worship as their neighbors want them may nevertheless be tempted into disloyal ways. Elizabeth had to beware of Catholic conspiracies, of plots in which Spanish money and Jesuit enthusiasm played a part, and of the dissatisfied gentry which could be found in England and elsewhere and which might gather behind some rebel magnate—Duke of Norfolk or Earl of Essex. From 1569 to 1587 Elizabeth held as her guest and prisoner the fugitive Queen of Scotland, Mary Stuart, who also claimed her crown and who provided a livid focus for conspiracy. Mary's execution in 1587, followed by the defeat of the Spanish Armada in 1588, removed the major threats to her security. The Catholics muttered but remained quiescent, the gentry found employment and gain in ventures over the sea, the country prospered free of heavy taxes.

Like Holland's, English prosperity was connected with the sea which, encompassing the island, facilitated not only defense but transport and exchanges. It cost as much to ship goods from Norwich to London by land, just over a hundred miles, as it cost to ship them from Lisbon to London by sea, about ten times as far. English sailors began to range all over the Atlantic, into the Mediterranean and the far eastern seas. In 1577 Sir Francis Drake set off to duplicate Magellan's voyage, ravaged the Pacific coast of South America, established a British factory among the Spice Islands, returned to Deptford in 1580 in his ship, the *Golden Hind*. He was knighted on his ship's deck having "encompassed the world" and enriched the Queen, shareholder in his venture, whom the exploit paid off forty-seven-fold. Companies were being formed to trade or venture, joint-stock companies enlisting the capital of several—sometimes of many—investors who could spread the risk of possible losses, or profit from a share in successful ventures they had staked.

The last Venetian galleys cast anchor off Southampton in 1587; already English ships were invading the Mediterranean, competing for its trade with French and Dutch, with Spaniards and Italians. The Levant Company had fifteen ships in 1595, thirty-one in 1600; and there were other companies sailing to the Baltic, to Archangel, to North America, to the East Indies. The Steelyard, London factory of the Hansa merchants, closed in 1597. It was the Londoners who sailed the Baltic now. A company for trade in the East Indies was chartered in 1600. And in all these ventures nobles and commoners worked together. Great nobles owned soapworks, breweries, glassworks. The Sidney family were ironmasters. Even the Earl of Leicester, Queen Elizabeth's favorite, drew part of his fortune from his ironworks. In 1598, Gresham College had been founded in London, to serve the needs of trade and manufacture, technicians, and navigators. The college, out of which the Royal Society for the Advancement of Science would eventually grow, had been endowed in the will of Sir Thomas Gresham (1519?–1579), Queen Elizabeth's chief financial expert. It had a governing board controlled by London merchants, a far cry with its utilitarian structure from the clerical-dominated Sorbonne or the Italian schools soon to be stifled by papal censorship.*

It was such men as these, merchants, seafarers, gentlemen hungry for treasure and gain, who sailed the slight, trim ships which harassed the Armada into failure. Elizabeth had a fleet and expert sailors who disposed of faster, more maneuverable ships, superior in armament and rigging, thanks to sea hawks like John Hawkins and Drake and to her treasurer, William Cecil, but thanks too—at least in part—to this pursuit of "useful arts" and profit.

The Stuarts   Elizabeth died in 1603, the last of the Tudors; to be succeeded by the Stuart James VI of Scotland, son of the murdered Mary, who became king in England as James I. James lacked the authority combined with tact and conciliation which Elizabeth enjoyed. He also lacked her economic sense. His political philosophy, expressed in several works (such as the *Basilicon Doron*—the Book of Kings), called for absolute royal rule based on a strong ecclesiastical hierarchy,

---

* The college probably suggested one feature in Sir Francis Bacon's *New Atlantis* (1627) , an account of an utopian state which includes a college, the House of Solomon, dedicated to the study of sciences and useful arts.

which alone could secure order and prosperity for any country.

James raised the hackles of his Parliaments, displeased the commercial classes, disorganized trade. His favorites and their retinues had to be paid in offices, monopolies, trading privileges, and in gifts of land from the royal domain which reduced royal income and made the king demand more from outside. Elizabeth and her counselors had managed Parliament, retaining its loyalty and that of the country for which it stood. James drove many of the best men of his time into opposition, widening the gulf between king and Commons, and creating a potential threat to the monarchy itself.

The royal administration was riddled with even more corruption than was usual: this was an opening for Parliament, which, hostile to the King, indicted his Lord Chancellor, Sir Francis Bacon (1561–1626), on charges of bribery, had him imprisoned and heavily fined (1621). No wonder that, whenever they could, the King and his favorite, the Duke of Buckingham (1592–1628), dispensed with Parliament, raising their money in any way they could. The economic policies of James and of his son and successor, Charles I (1625–1649)—or rather their lack of policy, their reliance on expedients designed to bring in revenue at any cost— plunged the country into economic confusion. Both James and Charles were continually pressed for money (hence probably the former's inability to aid his Palatine son-in-law against the Emperor, see p. 272) and their policies continued too rigid and erratic to permit solution.

Anywhere outside England (and Holland), disastrous economic policies affected chiefly the less influential section of the community: the poor, of course, the merchants, the middle classes. In England they also affected the gentry and sometimes the great nobles as well. England in the first half of the seventeenth century was remarkably industrialized for her time, a relatively large proportion of the population being affected. Mines especially employed numerous workers. In the century before 1640, English coal production increased seven- or eightfold to equal that of all the rest of Europe. Mines whose annual production had averaged several hundred tons in 1550, turned out between 10,000 and 25,000 tons in 1640. Metal industries grew apace, iron production rising fivefold over the century. By the 1630's the Keswick smelting works employed 400 men, the cannon foundry of the small town of Brendeley 200, the Dartford paper mills 600. Sugar and salt refineries, breweries, and dyeries, brick-making, soap-boiling, glass-blowing, called for coal, for equipment, for pumps, and for much capital.

In 1540 a brewery could run on a capital of £25; sixty years later the capital of a London brewer stood at £10,000. In the textile industry, especially in Lancashire, great merchants dealt with hundreds, sometimes thousands of spinners and weavers in their cottages. Enclosures also continued to replace grainland with pastures, to expel tenants, to raise the number of vagrants, and to provide recruits from the displaced for urban

Charles I of England, by Sir Anthony van Dyck, c. 1635. Louvre, Paris.

industry, but also for the ranks of the dissatisfied. While wages doubled between 1603 and 1650 the number of wage-earners among the growing population diminished. Hence, social conflict: between workers and employers, between old-fashioned landlords and the new entrepreneurs of cities and enclosures, between the business classes and the poor or poorer groups. The new men insisted on their right to exploit and create property as best they could, the right of free enterprise to serve itself regardless of consequences to others. The old criticized them in terms of the traditional view of society as an organic body whose members must cooperate and aid one another, not seek to grow at one another's expense.

In this struggle between the old communitarian and the new individualistic conceptions of society, this last might have found itself at a loss for arguments (at least of an ideological sort) had it not been able to appeal to Puritan ideas of work, of man's duty to labor for God. Man's first relationship, in this view, was not with his society but with God. If he was called to business, his duty was to tackle it as best he could, carry it on as a discipline and a dedication. Success came as the proof that he had done his duty. Hence, profit was the sign of duty done, success an indication of God's grace, as poverty was a proof of God's rejection. Laws which protect the poor, mitigate misery, cut across God's will, which was not to favor idleness—itself a source of sin—but to reform it. In any case, the rich were stewards of the wealth that God bestowed on them, distributing it to the deserving poor or using it to build chapels, endow schools and charitable foundations. Charity and social service too were part of God's plan for mankind.

Such views provided advancing capitalists, bourgeois and noble, with a good conscience should they need one. They clashed, however, with Stuart policy which tried to maintain the old type of society in which, as God decreed, each class fulfilled its function and was assured of means appropriate to its estate. Crown, state, courts, as temporal agents of God, must see his will be done, not undone, remedy injustice, repress usury, control production and prices, condemn speculators responsible for scarcity or landowners responsible for enclosures or extortionate rents. Absolute royal power to apply these views, to legislate in this sense, raise taxes without reference to Parliament, keep up the army to enforce their will—and God's—would bring the Stuart kings into conflict with Puritan businessmen and squires whom the economy had brought much closer together than in other countries, with squires' sons turning apprentice in London, the sons and daughters of merchants or yeomen marrying into the gentry, midshipmen on the craft of the great trading companies coming both from the gentry and from rich city families. Puritanism and economic interest could unite as well as divide and, against the King who sought to preserve social balance at the expense of the more enterprising, first in Parliament, then in the field, the wealthier classes rebelled (1640–1660).

Yet, while economic difficulties laid the groundwork for rebellion, they were not its spring. Sir Robert Filmer, the royalist pamphleteer, spoke of the monarchy being crucified between two thieves: popery and the people. This gives an indication of the more obvious issues, of which religion certainly was one. Yet, in the end, the Stuart monarchy was caught rather between its own absolutist views and the fierce reactionary opposition they aroused. The Stuarts' absolutist policies were more than a form of self-indulgence: they were, at least with Charles I, an attempt to balance various social needs and pressures, temper the wind of change to the shorn sheep, protect his poorer subjects against the richer and more enterprising ones, realize a kind of medieval good society. Archbishop William Laud (1573–1645) argued that the state is "the temporal expression of spiritual obligations." If society was an organism, the end of government was to make sure that its parts worked together smoothly.

The Stuarts therefore opposed political parties, factions which "have always private ends." They did not like individualism, whether economic or religious—the former tending to ignore the public weal, the latter introducing private vagaries in a sphere vital to the state's execution of its mandate. Hence their sympathy for Catholicism, whose social views were similar to theirs and which could place its hierarchy at the King's disposal. Hence also their insistence on clerical alliance. James had said "No bishop, no king"; and the ideology this represented was borne out by his son's fate.

Oliver Cromwell, by an anonymous artist.

Civil War   Having quarreled with the English Parliament, Charles I precipitated trouble by trying to impose an episcopal structure on the Presbyterian Scots. When the Scots rebelled, he had to call on Parliament for subsidies to oppose them; and Parliament, in due course, turned against the men who had carried out his absolutist policies, then against him and his prerogatives, against his bishops, his taxes, his special courts, his control of the military. There was a break and civil war flared up in 1642 which only ended with the King's execution seven years later.

The friction had been fiscal and constitutional: who should control the state, what were its functions, who would pay for it, who should have the final authority in deciding all these things? The issues were religious and they continued so even when the King had been captured: should all Englishmen or Scotsmen be members of one single church, should this be the Church of England or the Presbyterian Church of Calvin and Knox, could diversity in religious matters be tolerated? All these combined in the revolution and in the republican years that followed under the Protectorate of Oliver Cromwell (1599–1658).

Cromwell has been called "the most typical Englishman of all time," which suggests that we may at least find out what contemporary Englishmen were like whom he resembled though on a larger scale: country gentleman, keen on poetry and flowers like so many of his generals who wrote the former and cultivated the latter, knowledgeable about husbandry and horses, capable of sudden passions and great geniality, unusually tolerant toward and curious about odd nonconformist types, though himself capable of conforming and dissembling as well as the next man, deeply patriotic and above all religious. It is worth remembering that, when bishops were among the King's most reliable servants in Parliament and throughout the country, the religious issue was an integral part

of secular politics—the question of who should have power in the land
and for what, of who should raise taxes in the land and how and how
much, of a man's rights over his property and how far they went and how
far he could, or should, go to assert such rights.

Just how far religious belief could go in challenging the civil order was
demonstrated by the sects which sprang up and very briefly flourished in
the troubled atmosphere of the civil war. There were the Diggers,
agrarian communists who wanted lands distributed to the poor; the
equalitarian Levellers, who sought to "level men's estates"; the Fifth
Monarchy Men, extreme Puritans awaiting the impending reign of
Christ and of his saints. Such small groups of radical reformers combined
religious doctrine with advanced democratic and equalitarian ideas, the
former justifying the latter. Social differences were a result of the Fall.
Before it,

> When Adam delved and Eve span,
> Who was then the Gentleman?

After it, hierarchies became "natural" to an imperfect world striving for
a balance. Yet Messianic hopes of re-establishing the harmonious unity
of mankind, the primordial equality of a lost Eden, were swelling all
the time into millenarian revolts like that of the Anabaptists in Germany.
Such tendencies found strong meat to feed on in seventeenth-century
England as they had done in sixteenth-century Germany. Faith and will
could build Jerusalem here and now, in England's green and pleasant
land. "Every man by nature being a king, priest, prophet in his own
natural circuit and compass, whereof no second may partake but by
deputation, commission and free consent from him whose right and freedom it is," declared a Leveller leader, government should be equalitarian and representative. Since "the earth was made by Almighty God
to be a common treasury of livelihood for whole mankind in all his
branches," equality of condition and a fair division of land should match
equality of political rights, contended the Diggers.

What was due to men as Christians and claimed for them on religious
grounds could, in time, become the right of men as men, claimed for
them on ethical grounds. Democracy in politics, socialism in economic
organization, were prefigured by the religious extremists of the English
Revolution. For the moment, their claims were rejected, their activities
stifled. Such aspirations went far beyond anything that even Puritan
rebels, fearful of anarchy, were ready to envisage or to tolerate.

At any rate, Cromwell's religious fervor stopped far short of radical
innovations. His faith in God was paralleled by a sharp eye for the ways
of men. ("If you don't want to be betrayed by your enemies," he once
said, "stop trusting your friends") and great organizing talent. He forged
the instrument of rebel victory in a military force which combined the

discipline and tactics of the military revolution with the fervor and self-discipline of Puritan commitment. Having defeated the royalists, his New Model Army went on to sweep aside the Presbyterian Scots as well (1650, 1651) and to "pacify" Ireland (1649–52) by merciless methods of warfare which left long bitter memories behind. It built a fleet which could defeat the Dutch (1652–1654), and sent an expeditionary force to fight Spain together with the French and win Dunkirk (1659). It was in effect the army which governed England during the Interregnum, cowed or eliminated Parliament, named Cromwell Lord Protector (1653–1658), then briefly his calm ineffective son Richard (1626–1712), and finally called back Parliament (1659), and Parliament the dead king's son: Charles II (1660).

The Restoration   The restoration of a Stuart king did not, however, mean the restoration of Stuart policies. The score of years just past had seen important changes, above all the destruction of royal absolutism. With absolutism defeated, the victors had naturally fallen to quarreling. Men of property wanted freedom for themselves, but not for the rabble. Men of birth resented the power of lowborn officers risen up through military service. The advocates of efficiency raised the hackles of local gentry; the advocates of democracy and communism the fears of all. Eventually, men who had followed their consciences learned to obey their interests or were eliminated. Religion was sacrificed to social order, republic to apprehensions, compromise defended property, restored the gentry, brought back the king, paid off the army, rendered the rabble and sectarians harmless. It was no good crying over spilled ideals; the revolution was over.

Yet, in some ways, revolution was only just beginning. As Laurence

A news vendor in the late seventeenth century.

Stone points out in his *Crisis of the Aristocracy* (1965), "the seventeenth century revolution, with its outburst of pamphleteering and of radical political theory, took place in what was perhaps the most literate society in the world." There is no underrating the dangers this carried for stability. Milton had called for "liberty to know, to argue and to utter freely according to conscience." Levellers had insisted that we are all originally equal and have the same rights to a say in society. Although the Restoration quashed them, their memory survived in a kingdom where the absolute pretensions of the crown had been defeated along with the democratic pretensions of the mob. Meanwhile, utility, expediency, had shown themselves stronger than either theology or tradition, and that was revolution enough to go on with.

Pessimistic and clever, shrewd and sensuous, Charles II was a more dexterous politican than his father. His twenty-five years of reign were a period of peace for England and of political stability in the midst of struggle, stability maintained by ceaseless maneuvers at home and abroad. The major issue of the reign, once its safety had been ensured, became once more religion. Charles was no enthusiast, but need for money drove him to sign a pact with France (Treaty of Dover, 1670) which promised toleration for English Catholics and his own conversion at the earliest possible moment. The majority of his subjects feared and detested Catholicism, as a subversive and un-English creed, and Catholics as disloyal cat's-paws of hostile foreign powers. They would tolerate neither Catholics nor Dissenters and wished to forbid succession to Charles' brother James, Duke of York (1633–1701), converted to Rome and married to a Catholic princess.

The Glorious Revolution   In 1685, nevertheless, when Charles II died (after his own conversion), James II succeeded without trouble. England now had a Catholic king who strove by every means to impose his religion and his absolute views of royal rule on it. But the old king had no son and his eldest daughter, married to William, Prince of Orange, held out the hope of sound Protestant government when he died. In 1688, however, just as James' conflict with Parliament and bishops rose to new heights, his queen presented him with a male heir. The prospect of a Catholic succession, now made concrete, drove some of the great lords to invite William of Orange to save their country for Protestantism. In the summer of 1688 William set sail for England. With the army hostile, James fled to France and Parliament called to the throne his Protestant daughter Mary (1662–1694) to rule conjointly with her husband, William III (1650–1702). The Scots refused to support James, the Irish who stood by him were defeated (Battle of the Boyne, 1690). A second revolution, known to history as the Glorious Revolution, had secured the hopes and the achievements of the first.

The new joint monarchs swore to observe the Parliament's Bill of

A contemporary engraving of William and Mary.

Rights (1689), affirming the supremacy of law over the sovereign, the power of Parliament, the rights of individual citizens. The Habeas Corpus Act of 1679, forcing authorities to bring all prisoners speedily to trial, was reaffirmed. The Mutiny Act subjected the army to Parliament and to the regular courts. Lastly, the Toleration Act liberated religious belief and vouchsafed nonconformists the public practice of their religion. The tolerance granted was still quite limited. It excluded Catholics and Unitarians. It only opened *public* office to those ready to make a show of occasional conformity or able to secure a special act of indemnity for themselves. Nonconformists would protest and agitate against these survivals. But the Toleration Act was a great departure nevertheless. Observers did not fail to contrast it with Louis XIV's Edict of St. Germain and the religious uniformity that act imposed on France. In fact, the measure broke with the old view that the state was necessarily identified with a single church to which all citizens must belong. The English clergy were no longer a very special order, but merely the members of an ill-paid profession. And public office, like public worship, would gradually be opened to all Englishmen who were considered loyal whatever their religious persuasion.

Here was the culmination of what the historian Macaulay described as "the great English revolution of the seventeenth century, that is to say the transfer of supreme control of the executive administration from the crown to the House of Commons." Its basis rested on the steady expansion of the economy. Parliamentary control of taxation, of military expenditure, of customs and excise, meant that policies would not often be allowed to hinder profit. Taxes paid by all (though still inefficiently tapped and unfairly distributed) meant greater and more elastic yields. The long series of Navigation Acts, beginning under Cromwell, sought to foster shipping by forcing goods to be imported and exported only in English vessels. From 1660 to 1688 the tonnage of the English merchant fleet had doubled and it continued to grow, with profits flowing in not only from the freight but from the freight rates and the insurance business that developed to serve them.

Agriculture also prospered and became more diversified. Enclosures ruined some, enriched others, evoked the first reasoned statements of utilitarian individualism; "Everyone, by the light of nature and reason will do what profits him more," wrote one of their defenders in 1656. "The advantage of every one in particular will be the advantage of all." The farmers driven off their land to molder in the cities did not agree, but wool and dairy merchants did. The textile industry also was growing, finding its markets overseas. A statute of 1666 had ruled that English corpses should not be buried in imported fabrics but in English cloth. Soon such protectionist measures proved unnecessary as increased production and lower prices made English textiles triumph wherever the marketplace was free. Dairy production rose: milk, butter, eggs got cheaper. The economy shifted away from self-sufficiency and barter to specialization and exchange. In 1680, John Bunyan's Mister Badman, invited to get married, replies "Who would keep a cow of their own that can have a quart of milk for a penny?" Bad morals but good economics, and suggestive reflection of economic change. Produce and goods were being sold at retail in established shops based on a money economy. The retail stores which Daniel Defoe (1660–1731) found in many villages of early eighteenth-century England were harbingers of progress. The scornful accusations that the late eighteenth century would raise against England—that it was a nation of shopkeepers—suggests a nation of customers as well, of people with money enough to keep shops going, with a mentality and socioeconomic structure which had broken from the barter and simplicity that lingered on elsewhere.

London in 1700 had 800,000 inhabitants, almost twice as many as Paris. It outstripped Amsterdam in wealth and energy. It stood as the symbol of the coming world: a world where wealth not birth commanded, where privilege existed but as the reward of enterprise, where utility was coming to dominate ideology. Addison and Steele wrote in *The Spectator:* "We merchants are a sort of nobility which has risen in the world this century past . . . an accomplished merchant is the best kind of gentleman in a nation."

The Baltic

Northeast of England, across the northern sea, lay the backward Baltic, frozen or unnavigable half the year but a passageway for goods essential to the economy of the west and south and to their existence. Here were great granaries and, above all, essential naval stores. Without the Baltic (which North America supplemented only in the eighteenth century), Europe would not have been able to caulk, line, or mast its ships.

The sea had long been dominated by German trading cities whose league, the Hansa, had made its influence felt from Finland to the Danish Sound, from Bergen to Poland. The Baltic lands were primitive and backward. The first books printed in Stockholm date from 1483, those in Copenhagen ten years later. The economic structure of the bordering countries was of the most homespun kind. The sixteenth century saw Hanseatic predominance wane. Dutch and English ships appeared in Baltic waters and for a time, as we have seen, the Hollanders even turned the sea into a closed preserve. The local powers—Danes, Swedes, Poles— found it convenient to ally with the interlopers to shake off the German hold on their economy. Even though the king of Denmark controlled the narrow straits between the Baltic and the North Sea, and enriched himself by levying tolls on every passing ship, he had to come to terms with the naval power of the Dutch.

Poland-Lithuania   The kings of Poland, rulers of vast territories butting on the Turkish Empire, were also interested in the Baltic trade. By way of Danzig and of lesser ports the plains drained by the Vistula supplied the urban west: cereals, timber, tars, pitch, cordage, ashes; importing in return salt, wine, textiles, luxury articles for the nobles who sold the produce of their great estates and extended them further, putting wastelands to plow or taking over peasant properties.

Sixteenth-century Poland-Lithuania was probably the largest state in Europe after Russia, endowed with universities and a brilliant court, full of Italian artists and scholars who fostered the development of native literature, art, and humanism. The Reformation had strongly affected the country, but had been pressed back by the Jesuits. A growing identity arose between Catholicism and a Polish nation self-consciously embattled against the pressures of Islam and of its schismatic orthodox Russian neighbors. But the needs of great estate agriculture stifled the rising cities, tied the free peasants to the lands, increased the power of the landed magnates, deprived the Polish kings of any solid base on which to expand or modernize their power. In mid-sixteenth century, the end of the Jagiello dynasty left the crown in the hands of the assembly of the nobility, dominated by a few great families. The elected kings, while sometimes quite able, could never reform a structure which denied continuity and stability to Polish politics. The crown of Poland and its policies became the stake of other powers, whose diplomats sought to win the support of noble factions for their own designs. War, foreign and civil, rent the nation and, while the wealthy prospered, the population declined. So did the significance of this invertebrate kingdom which became a battleground for foreigners before it became their prey.

The Swedish Empire   Sweden was the most backward of all the Baltic countries, isolated by geography and climate from the outer world, its economy in the sixteenth century not far from that of Carolingian France six hundred years before. The Union of Calmar (1397) had joined the kingdom with Norway under the rule of Danish kings. But in the 1520's a Swedish noble, Gustavus Eriksson Vasa (1490–1560), managed, with the support of Lübeck, to expel the Danes, and had himself crowned king of an independent Sweden (1523), to which he joined the territories of Finland. The wars all this entailed, his debts to Lübeck, the sheer necessities of political survival, drove Gustavus to introduce the Lutheran Reformation in his lands and confiscate the holdings of the Church (the king of Denmark would shortly imitate him). His death in 1560 ushered in conflict between his sons, one of whom, John III (1568–1592), had married a daughter of the king of Poland and sought to gain the Polish succession by reintroducing Catholicism. In this he was unsuccessful, but his son Sigismund (a Catholic) was in effect elected king of Poland in 1587. A few years later, after his father's death, Sigismund became king of Sweden also. But not for long. The Swedish Protestants would brook no Catholic king. Sigismund was replaced by his uncle, who became Charles IX (1599–1611) and whose advent ushered in a long-drawn-out struggle between the Swedish and Polish branches of the Vasa house, a political conflict with strong religious overtones, and which would not be settled until the Peace of Oliva (1660).

Warlike, brutal, and energetic, the Swedish Vasas had not neglected the economic side. While the immense majority of Sweden's small population (around one million) were fishermen and farmers, the mining industry was the base of royal wealth. Their iron ore, which in the seventeenth century provided one-third of total European production, furnished raw material for export and soon for mills and foundries developed by Dutch capitalists in Sweden itself. Swedish copper supplied important revenues, especially after Spain had turned to copper coinage in 1599. The revenues from copper, the products of the iron industry, enabled Vasa kings to equip small but effective armies, which they organized in the most modern ways, tempered and tried in long campaigns against the Russians, Poles, and Danes.

It was the son of Charles IX, Gustavus Adolphus (1611–1632), who really affirmed the significance of Sweden in the modern world. He recognized the importance of education, founded new schools, refounded the University of Uppsala, created the post of Antiquary Royal, whose chief task would be to glorify the memory of the Goths. He reorganized the courts of justice, encouraged the ventures of English, Scotch, and Dutch immigrants, assured himself the confidence and loyalty of the four estates (nobles, clergy. burghers, peasants). All this, however, was secondary to his main concern. A great and able leader, brave, proud, sober,

King Gustavus Adolphus of Sweden,
a bronze bust by George Petel, 1632.
Royal Collection, Stockholm

pious but unbigoted and tolerantly unwilling to constrain the conscience of men, Gustavus Adolphus was a formidable warrior. Trained in a hard school of unceasing warfare, the Lion of the North had come to think that his task, having secured his dynasty and kingdom, was to ensure the safety of Protestantism in Germany. His death at the Battle of Lützen left Sweden imperial but overstrained, her territories ringing all the Baltic, her forces ranging from Narva to the Danube.

The daughter of Gustavus Adolphus, Queen Christina (1632–1654), inherited her father's intellectual curiosity, his love of music, his gift for languages and rhetoric, but not his talent for ruling. She abdicated in 1654 and left the country, soon to announce her conversion to the faith of Rome, where she lived on respected and eccentric until 1680. Christina was succeeded by her cousin Charles X (1654–1660), whose reign was a long succession of campaigns. The country was getting short of men and of resources, Swedish possessions, fleets, and armies could only be maintained with French support, and Sweden at this time tended to become a belligerent follower of France. This situation culminated under Charles XI (1660–1697), whose need of funds enlisted him in Louis XIV's wars. Defeated by the Prussians at Fehrbellin (1675), by the Danish fleet at sea, the Swedes survived without very many losses thanks only to the protection of the French. Thereafter, Charles attempted to give Sweden the peace she badly needed. Playing the lower orders and the smaller gentry against the great nobles, he enlarged the royal domains, established royal absolutism and bureaucracy, tamed the uppity nobility, developed trade and shipping, administered the country and its economy with a despotic hand.

The threatened Swedish Empire now ran from Finland, taken from the Danes; through Ingria and Karelia at the head of the Gulf of Finland, conquered from the Russians; Livonia and Estonia, wrested from the

Poles; western Pomerania which Brandenburg coveted, controlling the mouth of the Oder; Bremen and Verden further west, between the Elbe and Weser and dominating north German trade into the North Sea. It was enough to evoke the greed or enmity of many. In the late 1690's risings in Livonia, precipitated by local nobles displeased at Charles' authoritarian policies, began the greatest of Sweden's wars. The Livonian rebels managed to spark a coalition of all of Sweden's enemies: Denmark, Russia, Poland, and Saxony all turned against the Swedish Vasas, when once again a warrior-prince arose to save them from their straits. Charles XII (1697–1718) was young, tall, slender, ruthless, incomparably brave. The great Northern War (1700–1721) in which he distinguished himself saw him defeat in quick succession the Danes, the Russians, and the Poles (1700–1702), impose a new king on Poland (1705), defeat Saxony (1706). But the war was not over and Peter the Great of Muscovy inveigled Charles ever further forward into the Russian plains and finally defeated him at Poltava (1709). For several years Charles strove to turn the Turks against the Russians; finally unsuccessful he returned home (1714) to find the Swedish Empire had disintegrated: Finland and Livonia lost to Russia, most of the German possessions fallen to Hanover or Brandenburg, the annual revenue half the costs of war, one-third of the male population lost. Yet, fighting still continued until the King was killed in the siege of an obscure Norwegian town. Then Sweden was free to conclude peace, giving up her overseas territories except for a small part of Pomerania. The strange adventures of a tiny nation * straining to hold vast areas of land were over. The memory and the fatigue of greatness alone remained.

Russia

In May, 1717, Peter Alexeyevich Romanov, Tsar of Russia since 1682, spent six weeks in Paris. He visited the Gobelins, the Sorbonne, the Academy of Sciences, and Versailles, but above all he sought to negotiate. Sweden, France's northern ally, was finished; Russia was rising. Let France abandon her old ally and take a new. The French did not heed Peter, but the boldness of his approach was typical of the man, the fact that he even made it reflected the appearance of a new figure on the checkerboard of international affairs.

The Byzantine Inheritance   Muscovy was not a recent realm, but one which had long seemed so far away and alien that her existence and her affairs appeared irrelevant to the rest of Europe. It had been formed by a slow and relentless process of colonization, the Eastern Slavs spreading

---

* The population of Sweden at the end of the Great Northern War is estimated at a million and a quarter, one-eighth of that of Poland, one-fifth of that of England, one-half that of the United Provinces.

ATLANTIC

OCEAN

300 miles

LAPLAND

Tornia

Uleåborg

GULF OF BOTHNIA

JEMTLAND

Trondheim

HERJEDALEN

Umeå

Vasa

FINLAND

KARELIA

SWEDEN

Lake
Ladoga

NORWAY

DALECARLIA

Christiana

Uppsala

ÅLAND
ISLANDS

Helsingfors

GULF OF FINLAND

INGRIA

Stockholm

DAGÖ

ESTONIA

Lake
Peipus

BOHUS

ÖSEL

Göteborg

GOTLAND

LIVONIA

HALLAND

Calmar

ÖLAND

Riga

SCANIA

BLEKINGE

BALTIC

Copenhagen

SEA

Dvina

Malmö

DENMARK

Nieman

RÜGEN

Königsberg

Bergen

Kiel

WEST-POMERANIA

Oliva

Lübeck

WISMAR

POMERANIA

Danzig

BREMEN

Hamburg

Stettin

Bremen

Fehrbellin

BRANDENBURG

POLAND

Berlin

Breitenfeld

Elbe

Bautzen

Lützen

Oder

HOLY ROMAN EMPIRE

THE RISE OF SWEDEN

Under Gustavus Vasa (1523–1560)

Acquisitions under Gustavus Vasa's sons (to 1611)

Acquisitions under Gustavus Adolphus (1611–1632),
and Christina (1632–1654)

Acquisitions under Charles X (1654–1660)

× Battle sites

outward into the wild forest regions to the north and east, and also toward the Volga river. J. H. Billington has entitled his history of Russian culture *The Icon and the Axe*:—while the latter cleared the land, the former provided a sense of basic unity which would otherwise have been absent.

In the ninth century, two Greek missionaries from Constantinople, the brothers Cyril and Methodius, brought Greek Christianity to the East Slavs along with an alphabet that expressed vernacular speech in a written language—Slavonic—using letters many of which had been borrowed from the Greek. The Orthodox Church introduced the East Slavs to the culture of Byzantium. Its dogma, its liturgy, and its Cyrillic script separated the Russians from Western Christendom, but intensified their self-consciousness as members of one people that identified itself *against* Catholics to the west and Muslims to the south and east.

From the Byzantines, the Russians inherited not only Orthodox Christianity and the Cesaropapism of an empire whose ruler was also supreme head of the church in the image of Roman emperors, but the dual nature of a polity that straddled East and West: a western tradition in oriental garb, the latter with its splendor, display, and exuberance often on the ascendant. As in Byzantium, so in Russia, the tension between Eastern and Western influences provided the dynamic and the framework of an enduring and peculiar society whose position is well-expressed in the fact that, in the 1660's, the great throne of the Tsar, flanked by mechanical lions that rolled their eyes and emitted roaring sounds like those by the throne of the Byzantine emperor, was designed in Poland and built in Persia.

The quandary of a "national" personality continually forced to assert itself against alien threats and continually forced to borrow from abroad in order to survive would be further intensified by the long interlude of subjection to Mongol rule. This, which ran roughly from 1200 to 1400 (or even 1480), never "Tartarized" the people, but had profound and lasting effects. The Tartars' contempt for human dignity, their obscurantism, their cruelty, and their political methods of violence and cunning colored the moral standards of their Christian subjects and, above all, of the ruling class.

The beginnings of Russian modern history have generally been identified with the reign of Ivan III, or Ivan the Great, (1462–1505). A contemporary of Louis XI of France, Ivan showed the same taste for intrigue, the same piety, the same cunning, the same drive to piece together the dispersed territories of his realm. It was he who subjugated the great northern trading city of Novgorod in 1478 and who put an end in 1480 to Mongol domination over Russia. He too who, having married in 1472 Sophie Paleologus, the niece of the last emperor of Constantinople, brought to Moscow a host of Greek and Italian scholars, craftsmen, architects, and artists who, among other things, rebuilt the primitive Kremlin.

Ivan the Great, as depicted in an early woodcut.

He was thus directly responsible for Moscow's taking over the Roman inheritance and imperial mission of fallen Byzantium. He introduced the two-headed eagle of the Paleologos into his own coat of arms; took up the title of Caesar (Tsar), heir of the Roman Empire and of Orthodoxy; oriented Russia toward Constantinople, and Moscow to her destiny as a new, third Rome.

But the vast realm was isolated and distant, threatened by Turks and Tartars south and southeast, by the strong expansive Catholic kingdom of Poland from the west. The Poles particularly seemed to menace it, ruling great masses of orthodox Ukranians and trying to bring them into the Catholic camp if not by straight conversion then through the Uniate Church—a section of the Orthodox Church which accepted the Latin creed and papal supremacy in 1596, retaining Greek liturgy and rites, but passing otherwise into the realm of Rome.

Russia and the Western World   Ivan III's grandson, Ivan IV, "the Terrible" (1533–1584), contemporary of Queen Elizabeth, began the work of actually bringing Russia into contact with the West. It was during his reign that English merchant venturers opened Archangel on the White Sea (1553), providing a link with the outer world free from Polish supervision, and opening new trade routes to Moscow and the Caspian and to the Persian silks beyond. Ivan welcomed the English and the Dutch merchants who soon followed. The foreigners could spur the lagging economy of a land most of whose folk lived from hunting, fishing, and the most primitive kind of agriculture; they could teach new techniques, disturb the sluggishness of landowning *boyars,* and provide the Tsar with added revenues.

Like other contemporary princes, Ivan's first task was to control the nobility and to endow his territories which reached uneasily from the

Baltic to the Urals and beyond, with a working structure of authority. He tamed the great princely families, though only precariously, turning unruly *boyars* into a nobility of service to the state—that is, to the Tsar, whose autocratic rule would be enforced by terror. Everyone of any consequence had to be or became an agent of the state. With the rich old trading towns of the northwest conquered and stifled, he set up new towns that would not challenge his authority, towns founded not by burghers but by the state and ignorant of municipal liberties or pride. The burghers like the *boyars* were servants of the state; the greatest merchants traded or administered for the Tsar. Only such men or the state itself disposed of significant capital. Withal, Ivan encouraged traders, brought soldiers and skilled artisans from abroad, spurred colonization to the east and south, made sure that Baltic affairs would henceforth have to count with a new contender.

Despite his title it would seem that Ivan was not much more terrible than his predecessors. The peasants did not mind the way in which "he skinned alive all the lords and princes," and "boiled the *boyars* in a large kettle." The *boyars* did. Attempts to modernize clashed with tradition and with their interests rooted in the old ways. "A realm without dread," wrote one of Ivan's apologists, "is like a horse beneath a Tsar without a bridle." The Russian realm would seldom lack this dark bridle. Politically as well as culturally, obscurantism became the national alternative to Western rationalism, which never ceased being denounced as alien to the national spirit and to the Orthodox faith.

The death of Ivan in 1584 ushered in "the time of troubles," dominated by the massive figure of Boris Godunov, who stood for reform and centralization. The *boyars* who opposed Godunov were led by a nephew of Ivan's first wife—Fiodor Nikitich Romanov—soon to become Patriarch of the Russian Church. Elected Tsar in 1598, Godunov was soon faced by revolt, which the Poles and the papacy supported—and which was led or at least focused upon a pretender called Dimitri who claimed to be a son of Ivan IV.* Polish invasion, civil and foreign war, the death of Boris Godunov and of his son, the brief rule of Dimitri based on Polish arms, attempts to Catholicize the Russians, an anti-Catholic revolt which culminated in utter chaos, all these concluded in 1613 with the coronation of a new Tsar, Michael Romanov, son of Fiodor Nikitich.

The Romanov Dynasty   Starting from small beginnings the Romanov dynasty would last over three hundred years. The Poles were thrust back again. Michael's son, Alexis (1645–1676), won back Smolensk and Kiev, negotiated the reunion of the Ukraine, whose Cossack masters had previously looked to Poland, encouraged colonization on the steppes, attempted once again to improve and centralize administration. One of the most arduous problems mingled religious and social griefs in an

* The son actually died or was murdered at the age of eight in 1591.

explosive mixture. From the end of the sixteenth century and for a hundred years Russia was torn by social conflict pitting the peasants against the feudal nobility and, sometimes, nobles against the Tsar. The great agrarian and social revolts of the time of troubles were aimed first against the *boyars* and only marginally against the monarchy. They were quashed soon after the accession of the Romanovs, but the resentments they reflected broke out in a catastrophic religious conflict in mid-seventeenth century. Attempts to improve and revise the liturgy and holy books of the Church aroused the opposition of many clergy and people wedded to traditional religion and established forms of worship. Reform and "westernization" (however relative) were anathema to millions of "Old Believers": xenophobic fundamentalists, puritanical and hardworking, but utterly opposed to all foreign influences and to the modern world in general. The persecution of the Old Believers would mark the next two centuries and a half; their obstinate resistance would embody on the religious plane resentments and tensions repressed on the political plane. And on the ruins of a church weakened by internal dissension and schism there rose a secular state to which all clergy would henceforth be subordinated.

Yet, though the realm was strengthened and revivified, it remained a barbarous state in Western eyes. Autocracy functioned through bureaucracy, centralized but ill-structured, ill-controlled, riddled with inefficiency, brutality, and corruption. Russian legislation was still promulgated with the formula "The Tsar has decreed, the magnates have assented," yet the power of magnates was decaying, being replaced by the personalities surrounding the Tsar, his personal favorites and servants, selected by him, not by their birth. Society consisted of a few masters and of many serfs, unfree, oppressed, and backward; the margin of society, the frontier, relieved the social pressures, providing temporary refuge for the outcast, the rebellious, or the independent man, but also an advance guard of the empire. Where Cossacks rode and camped, south and east, Muscovy followed in due course.

Peter the Great   Under Alexis, Russia had reached out (as well as spread) and tried to learn some of the Western skills she sorely lacked, especially on the military and technical plane. But the advance was hesitant and the great kingdom remained an oriental monarchy, profoundly different in costume, custom, and every kind of structure from the West which it would have to ape in order to advance. Alexis' son Peter (1689–1725) precipitated a change. By 1700 Muscovy thrust forward and change had been thrust upon her: government and finances were reorganized; education, dress, and customs were in a turmoil; industry and armament on the upswing; a modern standing army and a fleet had been created—all made for war and for the power of the state.

The gentry were forced into state service and ordered in a new com-

Peter the Great, a mosaic showing Byzantine influence by Mikhail Lomonosov, 1754. Hermitage
Museum, Leningrad.

prehensive table of ranks in which all officers and officials found their
place within a bureaucratic hierarchy encompassing all the upper classes,
preceding even birth or wealth within the social scale. Beneath them
moved the great mass of commoners—townsmen tied to their trades or
crafts, peasants tied to land and serfdom, subject not only to taxes but to
the weary and demanding burdens of conscription and forced labor. For
Peter's revolution turned out costly, as it was bound to be: new fleets,
new armaments, new armies, roads, canals, above all the new city on the
Gulf of Finland—Saint Petersburg—built from nothing by a conscript
force laboring in the northeastern marshes, now frozen, now squelching
and mephitic. All had to be pressed and beaten out of reluctant subjects.

The ideal was duty, responsibility, public spirit, law: a "police state,"
a "regulated state," which really meant a "policed" state, well-ruled,
law-abiding, fulfilling every kind of social and economic function. The
practice was haphazard, the system run either by mediocre foreigners or
by worse Russians; fear, brutality, arbitrariness, routine, and rigor were
now mitigated, now exacerbated, by incompetence. Suffering, waste,
and terrible conditions of labor were standard at the time; yet they seem
to have been even worse in Russia, and the strain and pain must have
been immense. The balance of the account is hard to draw: Peter succeeded in his herculean task. He defeated Sweden, humbled Poland,
opened new windows to the Baltic trade. His Muscovy became a European power, its foreign trade quadrupled, its industry expanded, its
position firmly established on the Baltic, its claims on the southeast
less successfully asserted but nevertheless reinforced. A feudal Russia

ЗИМНЕЙ ДВОРЕЦ

The Winter Palace of Peter the Great in St. Petersburg, an engraving by Alexei Zubov, 1717.

persisted long after Peter's reforms, but one of Catherine the Great's nobles would calculate that, without Peter, Russia would have taken until 1892 to reach the stage of civilization and power which was hers by the latter part of the eighteenth century. It is not clear what weight misery and lives played in his calculation.

The Ottoman Empire

It is possible to compare and contrast Russia and Turkey at this time, both facing the challenge of alien efficiencies and new techniques, both in need of reform to keep up with or assert themselves in the seventeenth-century world, both hampered by established interests opposing innovation by reference to historical precedent in tradition and religion. This is where the Russians, who had no memory of a great imperial past, could be more flexible, abandon ways less hallowed by success, copy the foreigner. It is possible that if the Turks had been less successful in their earlier enterprises they would have been readier to change. The notion seems borne out by the long tale of military successes that spans Ottoman history into the sixteenth century, followed by increasing rigidity and failure to adjust in subsequent times.

Islam on the Ascendant   The conquests of Islam were paralleled by the attraction which it exercised on the West. In France between 1480 and 1609 there were twice as many books about Turks as on America. The Turks were soldiers; they needed technologists, administrators, artisans, and still more soldiers. They welcomed renegades, offered privi-

323

leges and high rewards to converts from their Christian provinces, captives of their armies or of Barbary pirates, deserters from opposing forces. Between 1453 and 1623, of forty-eight Grand Viziers, only fourteen were of straight Turkish descent, one a Ghirghiz, ten of unknown origin, and thirty-three Christian renegades—among them six Greeks, eleven Albanians or South Slavs, one Italian, one Armenian, and one Georgian. Under Selim II (1566–1574), eight Grand Viziers out of ten were renegades and so was the Viceroy of Algiers, the famed Barbary Corsair, Euldj Ali. Not only were three out of four viziers of foreign extraction, but the Sultan himself was, too—"son of the slave," as the people of Constantinople called him, that is, of some harem favorite: the mother of Selim II was Russian, that of Mohammed III (1595–1603) Venetian, while Osman II (1618–1622), Murad IV (1623–1640), Ibrahim I (1640–1648), and Mustafa I (1695–1703) were the sons of Greek women.

The Sultan was the richest sovereign in Europe, his revenues double those of Charles V or Philip II, his manpower resources vaster than those of any rival. Even when they did not breed men, the great open spaces of the Empire provided grazing grounds not only for the inmates of imperial menageries but for the thousands of horses and camels that formed the base of their armed mobility. Yet, with all its wealth of men, livestock, and other riches, the Muslim Empire lacked technicians. All useful knowledge was thought to lie in the Koran and the most worthwhile occupation could only be its study or else its application in holy war. The best minds among Muslims were bent in these directions. Fatalism, suspicion of novelty and of knowledge not based on the Koran, religious divisions just as bitter as those of Christendom, finally a family structure which caused serious succession problems in society and state all weakened Islam and prevented it from dominating the world.

New wealth was not created; old wealth was annexed, consumed, its creators attracted from abroad and parasitically exploited. The Turkish culture was a drab one, lacking the qualities we call imagination and initiative. Its mosques were merely Byzantine churches with architectural goiters and minarets added; its administrative structure was one vast family of slaves. Life and color lay only in the bazaars, thronged with foreigners—Christians and Jews. Islam rejected European civilization, yet could withstand it only by adopting its products and techniques. Mundane skills had to be imported. This could be done successfully as long as the Empire continued to expand, its rulers to act as effective leaders of a military camp perpetually on the move. Such was the case during the sixteenth century when Austria and Venice were only saved by the logistic impossibilities of large-scale campaigning,* and by the Turks' interminable wars with other Muslim powers, especially Persia. By the seventeenth century, however, Ottoman power was running down,

---

* In 1566 Suleiman took eighty days to reach the Danube, dragging behind him convoys of 24,000 camels. Supplies set the limits of material expansion.

GROWTH OF THE OTTOMAN EMPIRE
1480–1699

Ottoman Empire in 1481
Added 1481–1699
Tributaries added 1481–1699
Territories lost in 1699

500 miles

PERSIAN GULF

CASPIAN SEA

DAGHESTAN
KARABAGH
AZERBAIJAN
ARDILAN
LURISTAN
GEORGIA
Kura
Aras
Baghdad
Tigris
Mosul
ARMENIA
KURDISTAN
MESOPOTAMIA
Euphrates
ARABIA

CAUCASUS MTS.

Don

KHANATE OF CRIMEA
KUBAN
CIRCASSIA
CRIMEA
Balaklava
BLACK SEA
Sinope
Trebizond
TAURUS MTS.
ANATOLIA
Kizil Irmak
Angora
Konia
Adalia
Smyrna
SYRIA
Beirut
Damascus
Jaffa
Jerusalem
Nicosia
CYPRUS
Cairo
Nile
Alexandria
EGYPT

Dnieper
Bug
JEDISAN
Dniester
Akkerman
PODOLIA
BESSARABIA
MOLDAVIA
Jassy
TRANSYLVANIA
Bucharest
WALLACHIA
Danube
Varna
Constantinople
Gallipoli
BULGARIA
Sofia
SERBIA
RUMELIA
MACEDONIA
Salonika
Athens
MOREA
Leganto
CEPHALONIA
ZANTE
Candia
CRETE
RHODES

CARPATHIAN MTS.

BANAT
Belgrade
HUNGARY
Pest
Buda
Karlowitz
Save
SLAVONIA
CROATIA
BOSNIA
Ragusa
MONTENEGRO
ALBANIA
DALMATIA
ADRIATIC SEA
Vienna
AUSTRIAN HUNGARY
Drave

MEDITERRANEAN SEA

ITALY
Rome
SICILY
Benghasi
TRIPOLI
Tripoli

though only very slowy. The Portuguese were soaking up the gold of India, English traders were equipping Persian troops with cannon; above all, the economic indifference and ineptitude of the Ottomans were exacerbated by poor leadership and tumultuous power struggles stemming from the uncertainty of succession to the throne.

Factors of Decline   In the polygamous family of the Padishah there was no obvious right or sequence of succession. Each sultana intrigued to get it for her son and to eliminate his rivals; each ruler sought to corrupt, soften, and eliminate his possible challengers; the struggles of the harem ended in civil wars, risings, and massacres. Mohammed III had nineteen brothers strangled, Murad III only five. Many sultans were infants, others were deranged, debauched: Selim II was a drunkard, Murad II epileptic, Ibrahim I completely mad. Murad III (1574–1595) was focused chiefly on the harem, whence he turned out a hundred and three children, forty-seven of whom survived him, twenty of them males. With so much competition no wonder there was slaughter. Many sultans were massacred by military revolts. All were erotomaniacs, distorted by their upbringing, swayed by the harem politics of eunuchs, women, slaves, who ran the Empire through them and put it to the sack.

Since the Empire had practically no institutional structure but depended wholly on its head and army, consequences were fatal. The decay, however, was only gradual. Turkey's enemies faced problems of their own, ultimately similar to hers—problems of means and scale—and Turkey itself had moments of revival. In the 1630's, for instance, one such revivification took back Baghdad (1638) from the Persians, Azov from the Cossacks, and even began the twenty-year campaign which eventually wrested Crete from the Venetians. But as the Ottoman's power of attraction diminished, as the temptations and the rewards they offered shrank or disappeared, as their expansion halted, probably when the conquest of Crete was with difficulty achieved in 1669, their sources of skilled labor and initiative tarried, their own incapacity of assimilating and applying European techniques weakened them.

A last great offensive was defeated before Vienna in 1683 and the event was commemorated in a German song meaningfully titled "The Turk Is Sick." Thereafter their ebbing power became visible to all in the series of defeats that culminated in the Treaty of Karlowitz (1699) * and loss of Hungary, Transylvania, Croatia, and Slavonia to the Habsburgs, Dalmatia and parts of the Peloponnese to Venice, Podolia to Poland. The Christian peoples of the Balkans, Transylvania, and the Romanian principalities had never ceased to struggle against the Ottomans. Over the centuries they had thrown up legendary heroes, like the Albanian Skanderbeg in mid-fifteenth century and the Romanian prince, Michael

* Signed on January 26, 1699, the hour of signature was fixed to suit the astrological convenience of the Turks. Apart from that, it suited only their enemies.

the Brave (1593–1601), who for a while resisted Turkish might and even threw it back. But in the past such setbacks had been temporary. Now, the far-flung Empire began to wither at the edges. The Barbary states of North Africa asserted their quasi-independence, the Mameluk rulers of Egypt did so too; in Oman and in Yemen local dynasties expelled the Turkish garrisons, while in Constantinople itself the official hierarchy, no longer recruited only from renegades, slowly filled with Orthodox Greeks who did not even take the trouble to convert. The Orthodox subjects of Islam began to look to Russia, while to the northwest rose the new and threatening power of the Austrian Habsburgs.

The Holy Roman Empire

Divided and weakened by religious wars, the German lands had recovered a measure of prosperity as the sixteenth century ended. An agricultural economy is at the mercy of many factors, but also capable of quick recovery when circumstances are not hostile. This was the case in Germany, where the inflation which struck hard at the small landowning gentry did not seem to have harmed the trade of the many little urban markets which dotted the land. But trade routes were shifting, and money getting scarce. In 1614 the bankruptcy of the Welsers reflected the straits of the great money and merchant houses whose scions when not bankrupt preferred to place their capital in land or the acquisition of a noble title.

The Effects of War   The Thirty Years' War dealt a withering blow to this declining structure. When it was over the population had fallen from some sixteen to some six million inhabitants, the cities lay in ruin with wolves roaming their streets, half—sometimes three-quarters—of their population gone. Between 1648 and 1680 one-third of German soil was not cultivated for lack of manpower, the peasants living on linseed and oilcakes, or bread of bran and moss.

Politically, the Treaties of Westphalia enshrined the division of the land, the symbolic nature of the imperial title, and the regalian rights of German princes, who could not only collect taxes but coin money, raise armies, and conclude treaties like independent states. Habsburg hopes of hegemony having been warded off, the Empire turned into a sort of international federation, its Diet a permanent conference of ambassadors who talked a lot but lacked effective power, its "internal" affairs open to foreign intervention, heavily affected by Sweden and even more by France. The many princely families crumbled further, dividing their estates among all heirs until most families could boast seven, eight, or more ruling branches, each with its own court and capital, armies, and policies. This mélange provided fertile ground for outside ambitions, for the diplomacy and intrigues of all the powers, and frequently a battleground as well. It also turned out a rich recruiting ground, not only for mercenaries but for thrones: Denmark and Sweden, Holland, England, Poland, eventually Russia too, took princes or princesses from the German courts, until in the eighteenth century the provincial rivalries of central Europe had been transferred onto a wider stage.

The Holdings of the Princes   The Brunswicks who ruled Hanover obtained the electoral title (1692) and then the English throne (1714); Augustus of Saxony converted to Catholicism to gain the Polish crown (1696); the Hohenzollern Elector of Brandenburg obtained first the title of sovereign duke in Prussia (1657), then that of king (1700). The firm base of Hohenzollern power was laid by Frederick William I (1640–1688), the Great Elector who had been educated in Holland, at Leyden, and in the armies of the Republic. Determined to regenerate and people his poor north German lands, he opened them to all the persecuted—Jews, Catholics, Socinians, Protestants from Savoy. He attracted Dutchmen who taught his peasants better agricultural methods and Huguenots who developed industry. Efficient, better-paid civil service, reformed taxation, increased his resources fourfold and enabled him to train the best army in Germany—which proved its worth in 1675 by defeating the Swedes at Fehrbellin.

The scattered holdings of the Hohenzollerns stretched across the north of Germany from Poland to the Dutch border. Most of them were poor

A contemporary engraving depicting crowds gathered to honor Frederick William of Brandenburg, the Great Elector.

Ullstein Bilderdienst

and all were exposed to attack. But their very insecurity seems to have inspired their rulers to make the most of everything they had: developing the bureaucratic structure, improving all means of marshaling manpower and production, encouraging science and the schools and universities. A minor state was being forged into a progressive independent monarchy, a protector of German Protestants, and ready to step into the place of the weakening Swedes.

The Habsburg Empire   The mightiest house in Germany remained the Habsburgs, who came out of the Thirty Years' War weakened in their German aspirations but much strengthened in their own Austrian and Bohemian lands. There the aristocracy had been temporarily tamed, the clergy reinvigorated, the official servants of the crown increased in strength and numbers, trained in schools and universities founded or reorganized especially by the Jesuits, who provided clergy and administrators with a firm and common basis of values, ideas, and skills. Leopold I (1658–1705), who modeled himself on his bureaucratic uncle Philip II and signed more than 300,000 letters in his life, established a regular army and police, set up the legal and administrative structure of a modern state, beat back the Turks with Polish help, reconquering most of Hungary. Pious and hard-working, though his ambitious schemes were often paralyzed by the penury which plagued all heads of state in this ill-ordered age, Emperor Leopold seems to have been surrounded by a stagnant moat of rapacious courtiers, utterly ineffective for any but negative tasks. He knew that his far-flung lands with their backward economies and poor communications had all the greater need of good administration and tried to assert his authority within his varied states. Treasury revenues were increased after long struggles by taxing privileged clergy and aristocracy, a new civil service recruited among the better educated lower gentry and middle class who sought to advance themselves by personal merit.

But the conservative nobility, jealous of its rights, concerned with building great palaces, hunting, and social pursuits, remained an inert millstone for the monarchy. Its power and privileges were maintained in inverse proportion to its usefulness. The service function was left to foreigners, the greatest of whom in the seventeenth century was an exiled Frenchman, Prince Eugene of Savoy (1663–1736), a cool, resourceful soldier driven by his resentment against Louis XIV, who had refused him a chance in the armies of France. Commander-in-Chief of the imperial forces in 1697 at thirty-four, President of the Imperial War Council at thirty-nine, Eugene remained thereafter not only the Empire's greatest general but almost a Prime Minister, responsible for the most important victories won against French and Turks, but also for the diplomatic strategy of the Habsburgs.* It was in part thanks to Eugene that Leopold dur-

---

* Montesquieu's Usbek in the *Persian Letters* refers to him as the grand Vizier of Germany.

Prince Eugene of Savoy. Heeres-
geschichtliches Museum, Vienna.

ing his rule saw his dominions grow by half again their size, from 6,800 square miles to 9,100 square miles. The struggle against Louis XIV, his enemy and chief opponent throughout his reign, divided his attention and his strength as it did that of his successors, Joseph I (1705–1711) and Charles VI (1711–1740). But Austrian arms advanced in east and south, gaining provinces which Ottomans had held for a century and a half.

The War of the Spanish Succession ended with Spain and her empire lost for good (Treaty of Rastatt, 1714). But Italy had been won, and Austrian garrisons in Milan confirmed a new imperialistic vocation, while only a few years later the exhausting fight against the Turks concluded with new accessions of land (Treaty of Passarowitz, 1718). The Austrians had drawn victory from defeat. On the continent of Europe their power henceforth counted more than that of the Emperor.

But the wars and struggles of the century left more contenders for power. Turkey and Poland declined when Russia entered the lists, the Swedes passed like a brilliant comet and expired, the states of Holland which had shone so bright dulled, and Spain retired to a backwater. Never unchallenged, England ruled on the sea and interfered on land; France, fought to a standstill, remained strong; Austria defied her across the central European lands, while in the north the Prussian armies drilled and fought.

Costs and Consequences of War

A century of almost continuous war in many countries, of warlike preparations when no war was in progress, of serious strain affecting even regions which escaped the fighting, was bound to mark all Europe far and wide. By the 1620's, Gustavus Adolphus, king of Sweden, felt that "all European wars are being interwoven into one knot, one universal war." The Thirty Years' War cut broad swathes of destruction through central Europe, the southern Netherlands once so prosperous were drained and stifled by the Dutch and French, the Turkish wars left the southeast exhausted, the French burned and devastated the Palatinate, Spain was racked and ruined by interminable struggles, the weary murderous drag that ended in 1713 and 1714 raked Italy and Germany and France. Raimundo Montecucoli, Emperor Leopold's general, noted in 1668 that within living memory there had not been real peace in his part of the world. Many could echo that in many other places, other years.

Disruption and Mobility

Campaigns were far from all. More people died of the conditions war creates than ever died in battles. More cavalrymen fell from broken legs or knees suffered when they collided with comrades charging alongside them, than from shot and shell. More soldiers died of plague, pox, and a score of other ills than perished on the field of battle. And many perished, but more than merely soldiers. Warfare disrupted agriculture and transport, caused famines and migrations. We read in Richelieu's *Political Testament* that "states need wars at certain times to purge themselves of evil humors," and some observers have referred to the rising population and strained resources of the seventeenth century to explain its wars, viewing them as a method of deferred infanticide as its growing armies absorbed an increasing proportion of the population. A historian of the seventeenth century has compared the France of the 1680's, more populous than ever before, to that of 1715, which slaughter and famine had cut down by some 5 per cent, removing the pressures and instabilities of earlier days while creating others. This cannot have been what Corneille meant when he made Oedipus declare that "The people is only too happy to die for its kings."

The seventeenth century must have been a terribly and terrifyingly mobile age, when the self-contained units of regional society broke down under a score of strains, when marching armies, disbanded soldiers, itinerant preachers, migrant artists and tradesmen, roaming bands of va-

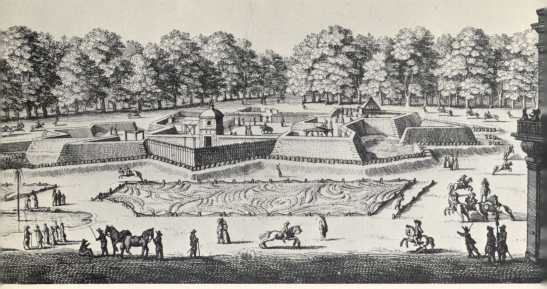

Model of French fortifications displayed at the Palais Royal, Paris.

grants and refugees—Calvinists, Catholics, royalists, Irishmen, Moors or Jews expelled from Spain, Huguenots escaped from France—crisscrossed Europe from Ireland to Russia, carried by deadly political, religious, and military tides. And war could be exported, either by hiring out organized units, as the German princes and the king of Denmark were wont to do, or by the movement of individual soldiers into the units of the fighting states. Feudal military service had almost disappeared and, if one had to hire troops, it might be more convenient to pay professionals than natives who were needed in the fields and workshops. In any case, professionalization was called forth by the new needs and methods of warfare.

The New Army

Roughly between 1590 and 1630, the massive weight of Swiss infantry or Spanish *tercios* found its match in the innovations of generals like Maurice of Nassau in the Netherlands and Gustavus Adolphus in Germany. What has been called the military revolution was an attempt to introduce flexibility and movement into combat, to combine firepower and mobility in smaller, less unwieldy bodies of troops, to use each fighting man to the maximum. Soldiers were drilled to maneuver and to march in step, disciplined by long training and practice to use their weapons and their firepower most effectively, equipped with lighter artillery, sheltered behind more ambitious fieldworks. This meant more officers, more what we would call noncommissioned officers, more technicians, and, even at the humblest level, more intelligent subordination than had been required of a pikeman in the massive square formations like those of the Swiss infantry: practically solid bodies of armed men. It meant that temporary levies would be finally replaced by standing forces, made up of and framed by skilled professionals. It meant, at least in theory, the transformation of generals from leaders slashing away in the vanguard of combat to strategists and engineers planning and conducting complicated operations from the rear.

The new armies were no longer the anarchic collections of individual fighters that feudal armies fielded, nor compact masses of men like those the Swiss had marshalled, but flexible and articulated bodies, more regularly supplied, more regularly financed, like the new state itself. Arms plants, foundries, arsenals, drill books, military manuals, engineers for artillery and fortifications, constituted a growing investment in a self-perpetuating enterprise headed by rulers increasingly identified not only as commanders-in-chief, but as the engineers charged with the operation of this cumbrous machine.

As this gathered momentum, the consumption and turnover of troops was so vast that recruiters grasped after every man. As the Thirty Years' War rolled on, the Swedish army came to include more and more Germans, the Spanish army more Walloons, Irish, English, and Scots. At the Battle of the Dunes in 1658 the French army had English and Scottish regiments and so had the Spaniards. After the Battle of the Boyne (1690), Irish refugees formed a brigade that continued in French service until 1789, as did the German regiment formed in 1654. William III won the Battle of the Boyne with an army that included Danes, Swedes, Huguenots, Prussians, and Dutchmen, as well as English, Scots, and Ulstermen. And in the Russian navy all officers had to speak Russian, English, and Dutch.

Grotius and International Law

Here is an illustration of Milton's vision of war ever breeding endless wars again. The times took war for granted, so much so that efforts were made to regulate it like any part of life. Henry IV had been the first modern prince to try to limit the license of his troops, placing peasants and cattle under his royal protection and cutting down the sack of conquered places from three days to one. The horrors of the Thirty Years' War inspired Hugo Grotius, (1583–1645) a Dutch refugee in the Paris of Louis XIII, who undertook his *Laws of Peace and War* (*De jure Belli ac Pacis*) in 1625 to mitigate the collapse of old restraints and harness the unrestricted warfare of his time.

To limit warfare, medieval authors had elaborated a theory of "just war," insisting on legitimate causes (defense, reparation, punishment), proper motives (above all the establishment of justice), and permissible means. War was one expression of the Fall. There could be nothing good about it: only mitigating circumstances. A "just" war involved "mournful" combat, avoiding hatred for the foe, eschewing indiscriminate slaughter, pillage, or rape, and shunning conquest. At least injunctions had existed. By the 1620's they had been lost from sight. The significance of Grotius's book, soon taken up by scholars and diplomats, was that, by indicating the principles of international law, it made such a law possible, laid the groundwork for civil relations between states, suggested that the horrors of war could be alleviated and routines of diplomacy regularized, all this by reference to the need of preserving society from collapse. Respected largely in the breach, such injunctions nevertheless exercised some ideal influence in controlling or limiting war. The limits Grotius set out, in what is regarded as the first modern treatise of international law, are wider than earlier centuries would have envisaged. They permitted the devastation of enemy lands and massacre of civilian population, sanctioned by what Grotius saw as logistic needs, and also by the 137th Psalm ("Happy shall he be that taketh and dasheth thy children against the stone").

Devastation had grown proportionate to armies. The armies of Philip II numbered some forty thousand; those of Philip IV, a generation later, twice as many. Louis XIV needed ten times that number to dominate Europe for a much shorter time. The soldiers must be paid. Even under Charles V, it has been reckoned that four-fifths of Spanish revenues in 1543 went into war expenses. By 1629, "The soldiers die of hunger", reads a report from Flanders to Madrid: "They go half naked and beg from door to door. . . . We have come to the limits of misery, destitution and want, especially the Spanish, of whom an infinity have died and not a single one of wounds." The new scale of warfare meant new problems for rulers, new burdens for subjects, new strains on economies already creaking under old. The demands of warfare forced governments into fiscal policies which they had neither the legal powers nor the administrative machinery to enforce. The great powers could somehow cope with the new needs; lesser ones had to sink or swim, and it was by copying the French that Brandenburg raised its defense forces from 900 men in 1627 to 80,000 a century later.

The Fallout of War

It was this need, itself justified by the horrors of war, that persuaded Estates in lands which warfare threatened, to abandon their liberties to absolute rulers capable of defending them. Only in countries like England where geography provided natural fortifications could mixed governments, with liberty and inefficiency inextricably connected, survive without catastrophic results. In other lands, threatened or devastated by recurrent wars, traditional representative institutions had to give way to military bureaucracy and to a state based on crown officials. In the second half of the seventeenth century, Bavaria, Brandenburg, the Palatinate, eventually also Denmark and Sweden, followed the French example of a centralized supreme authority as the best way toward efficiency and security.

Greater armies also needed greater resources. During the siege of Magdeburg (1631) the imperial general Tilly's cannon fired 12,000 to 18,000 balls every day; and this was only a beginning. Iron production had to be increased. So also the coal industry, which in industrial centers like Liège or London grew about twentyfold between mid-sixteenth and mid-seventeenth century. The soot from kilns and breweries, furnaces, refineries, and workshops in the growing cities struck contemporaries as incredible. The mass of London smoke shocked and dismayed foreign visitors, who failed to understand how men could live in it. John Evelyn (1620–1706) compared this darkling sky with Troy's after it had been sacked by the ancient Greeks. But there were only few places yet like Liège or London or Saint-Etienne, far fewer than the hungry maw of war would need, far less productive than ambitious administrators would have liked to see.

War by Other Means

Workers, too, were soldiers in an industrial army which labored for the power and the greatness of the state. Like older-style armies, however, they lacked discipline. Efficiency was rare, output (even by contemporary standards) too low, attendance sporadic, conditions of work too relaxed. This was particularly true for those who worked at home, receiving the raw material of their labor from a "putter-out" and being paid on piece rates for what they returned. In a society with few facilities for large-scale organization there were advantages to the putting-out system, with its informality. Its development in the countryside, particularly, tapped the manpower and relieved the underemployment of the peasantry without depriving agriculture of the hands it needed. But village industries, cottage industries, threatened urban ones, so that in England, Flanders, the Spanish Netherlands, and elsewhere, the practice was apt to cause unemployment and to set off protests and food riots.

Such problems had to be tackled, even though they were seldom if ever remedied. Production had to be regulated, in the shops at least if not in the cottages. The labor force must be harnessed, disciplined, if necessary chastised and forced to work. The employer, supported by the state, was free to impose fines, use corporal punishments of every sort (whip, pillory, stocks, strappado) to repress lateness, idleness, disobedience, drunkenness, blasphemy, adultery or loose behavior, and anything that could affect production or lead the worker to demand higher pay. Wages were low and often paid in kind, the workday lasted 12 to 16 hours, strikes and unions were prohibited, workers who complained about wages were put in prison, and any mobility was stifled by the need to obtain written permission before they could leave their jobs. Even religion was enlisted to serve production: the workday opened with prayers, meals were accompanied by pious readings, psalms replaced the chatter forbidden in the workshops.

Such desperate attempts to mobilize labor and increase production butted against tough survivals: gilds which aimed first and foremost to establish monopoly by eliminating competition; restrictive ideas of limited output, controlled quality and steady prices; the structure of an agrarian society which changed little and of a feudal society which, as we have seen, fought all change. The gilds, though increasingly regulated by the state, changed their attitude only reluctantly, when and where they were forced to give way. The labor force did not shift from agriculture to industry. The dominant values ignored investment and production; industry was developed more to serve aristocratic demands than the mass market, which alone can spark an industrial revolution. Businessmen sought their profit, as they had always done, in the production, distribution, and sale of a few expensive things; and this seemed both easier and more natural. But it called for no particular social or technical changes. Through the eighteenth century, the most profitable business was still in luxuries, a parasitic trade based on the existing social order and serving its masters. Meanwhile, the great masses continued to live in poverty and scarcely to use money, while even the middling people, especially yeoman peasants, accounted for little demand for goods, replacing their clothes and utensils only seldom.

As long as aristocratic fashions and refinement remained the watchword, as long as consumption was limited by the poverty of the masses and the particular taste of the few, the industrial structure was condemned to languish. Yet states could not ignore it—could not ignore it and survive. That much they knew, but they did not know what to do about it without cutting one anothers' throats. They were used to struggling with one another over a limited amount of land: that which one held, another could only covet. Economic expansion followed the same pattern, no one realizing that commerce could be expanded, that competitors did not have to destroy in order to thrive, that trade could reproduce the miracle of the loaves and fishes and divide greater production and consumption without war. Seventeenth-century economic thinkers envisaged a static world in which the quantity of gold or goods, the number of consumers, the level of demand, were always constant and one man's gain was bound to be another man's loss. It followed from this that to enrich a country it was necessary to impoverish her competitors, a point of view which led to three wars between England and Holland (1652–1654, 1665–1667, 1672–1674) and to the Franco-Dutch war of 1672–1678.

Trade was a major source and great consumer of precious metals needed to pay for essential armies and supplies. And their continuous shortage was the nightmare of every government. It led to a running money war between states, all seeking a favorable trade balance to attract bullion and keep it home. Mercantilism was the pursuit of war by other means (see Part I, pp. 145–146). And it meant development of industry, low or no tariffs on raw materials for it, cheap agricultural products to keep food prices down, hence industrial wages on which a man could eat, hence production costs. It meant low interest rates to provide easy access to capital, low wages for the worker, high profits for entrepreneurs. It meant colonies to provide cheap raw materials and a protected market for manufactured goods. When wisely applied, as in Holland which became the exchange of the Western world, trade could provide an abundance of capital that turned a small country into a great power. In England, the same ends inspired a long series of navigation acts (for example Cromwell's in 1651 and Charles II's in 1660 and 1663) designed to reserve overseas trade for British ships, raise freight rates, encourage investment in shipbuilding, and increase the available number of potential warships. They led also to the formation and encouragement of trading companies, commercial treaties, and commercial wars. Finally, Britain, too, became one great market, undivided by internal trade barriers especially after the act of union with Scotland (1707) and serving as a warehouse for products bought cheap in the colonies, sold dear abroad.

It was in France that state intervention went furthest, in a policy often connected with Colbert, who said, "Commercial companies are the armies of the king, manufactures his reserves." A vast machine grew up to spur or supplement the merchants' lack of enterprise, the state regulating consumption, production, exports and imports. It created new enterprises either by subsidizing entrepreneurs or by setting up its own enterprises. It ensured labor by encouraging the birthrate, prohibiting emigration, mobilizing vagabonds and idle hands. It provided technical training in schools and royal works, sponsoring technical manuals and experiments and keeping all of this alive with state orders, loans, and privileges.

The Rise of National Loyalties

Interest in industry and armies produced a new concern for manpower, which in turn spurred a new awareness of demography and the use of such administrative statistics as would facilitate the raising of money and men on an unprecedented scale. And while such political logistics began to develop, military tactics concerned itself with occupation of the territory needed to sustain the soldiers, or its devastation to deny it to the enemy. Supplies came to be seen as a logistical necessity and so did fear techniques. The menace of devastation by wandering armies, the need to deny them access to territory and preserve one's own territory from their raids, caused a new consciousness of borders, strengthened to meet strategic needs. Through a chain of fortified places built by the great military engineer Vauban (1633–1707), Louis XIV attempted to close the entry gates to France and to set up border strong points for campaigns beyond. Frontiers in the modern sense appeared: lines, more or less definite, drawn on maps and preferably based on rivers or other identifiable physical barriers, reinforced by chains of fortresses, replaced the old borderlands, broad stretches of uncertainty and struggle where dominion went to whoever could enforce it. As lines replaced zones, rulers and administrators began to think in terms of a uniform language and society within no-longer-fluid borders; and we can recognize the rudiments of conscious nationalism.

Local patriotism has always existed: men's love for their city, valley, and region, and the pride they take in it, is nothing new, nor the concomitant dislike and suspicion of outsiders. But identification with larger wholes, the pride of the Roman in his citizenship however far from Rome, is a rarer thing, more difficult to arouse or instill. The subject of the medieval state directed his loyalty to, drew his pride from, his city or his lord—eventually perhaps emperor, king, or prince, ultimately, of course, God. By the seventeenth century, God was becoming local or personal. The prince was still the focus of "national" loyalties, but a prince progressively identified with the more abstract notion of the fatherland, a concept from the classics translated from Latin in the sixteenth century. The French philosopher Renan has defined national sentiment as "having done great things together and wishing to do more." The more great things a state could pride itself on, the sooner national sentiment awaked. It is not surprising to find it wakening in Spain, and even Michael Servetus (1511–1553), fugitive from the Inquisition, born in Navarre and educated in Aragon, called himself *Hispanus*—a Spaniard, not a Navarrese. The dramatist Lope de Vega makes one of the famous Spanish captains of the Italian wars declaim:

> I am Garcia de Paredes, and besides . . .
> But it is enough to say: I am Spanish.

The English of Elizabeth and James I knew the same feeling and raised it to a principle. "There is a necessity," wrote the poet and playwright Ben Jonson (1573–1637), that "all men should love their country." By the seventeenth century such sentiments were widespread. In the geography manual of Philip Clavier (1629), a Protestant from Danzig teaching at Leyden, we glimpse the beginnings of pan-Germanism. His greater Germany included Alsace, Lorraine, Belgium, Holland, Prussia, Bohemia, Scandinavia, and, of course Danzig itself. The work went through twenty-six editions. French geographies published in the 1630's and the 1640's envisioned the country's borders on the Rhine, that river which Spanish ambitions reserved as highway to Spain's lowland dominions, if France itself could not be incorporated into the realms of the Castilian crown. Gustavus Adolphus, who had dreamed of turning the Baltic into a Swedish lake, trasnferred his sights to Germany, where he hoped to head a vast Protestant confederation from Alsace to Bohemia, perhaps to take the Emperor's place.

The naval powers had their own brand of imperialism: the Dutch pretending to impose a freedom of trade which suited their developed economy, the English proclaiming their exclusive sovereignty over British seas and arguing that this domain was limited only by the shores of other nations. Even the Catholic Church was affected by national particularism. When a converted Brahmin, Matteo de Castro, was admitted to priesthood in Rome in 1634 and sent to Goa in Portuguese India, the local archbishop did not allow him to work there because he lacked the approval of the Lisbon chancellery. De Castro returned to Rome, was consecrated bishop in 1637 and went off as apostolic vicar to Christianize the Indian kingdom of Idalcan, where there were no Portuguese priests. Even there, however, the hostility of the Goan archbishop and of the king of Portugal pursued him and forced him to leave India for Rome, where he died in 1677.

While, clearly, none of this was yet codified and developed into doctrine, it was a beginning. The sentiments were there. National pride sparked national consciousness. Political definition emphasized national definition. Societies more sharply separate from others became conscious of their particular identity and particularism spread from the narrow level of the province to the broader level of the land. The men who had heaved a rock at the passing stranger learned to heave more lethal things at foreigners from further lands. It was an advance and a dangerous regression. And they would reap the whirlwind in centuries to come.

Chapter 7

EARLY MODERN CULTURE

Languages and Letters

The most obvious vehicle of culture is language. Throughout most of the seventeenth century as through the sixteenth, the language question was still unresolved, the situation confused, the problem of communication cumbersome and awkward. Latin continued to provide the language of scholarship and sometimes of diplomacy, Italian and French the tongues of cultivated people and polite intercourse. The painter Rubens preferred Italian and signed himself Pietro Paolo, even at the end of letters in his native Dutch. But French was gaining. Even Montaigne, brought up on Latin by a German tutor who knew no French at all, preferred to read his Plutarch in Amyot's French translation and to write his *Essays* in that tongue. Most national languages and cultures, though, were still despised in educated circles, unless they coincided with a political interest. Castilian, for example, was respected and its use encouraged on the highest grounds. Nothing could serve so well to forge or to assert a nation. Hence, works like Du Bellay's *Défense et Illustration de la Langue Française* (1548) or the Antwerper Jan Van De Werve's *Tresoor der Duitsche Tale* (1553). It was well-known that, as the Bishop of Avila remarked to Queen Isabella when presenting her with a new Spanish Grammar in 1492, "Language is the perfect instrument of empire," of the assertion of a culture over others and also of a cultural unity which could serve and enforce political unity as well. That was the motive of the Royal Ordinance of 1536, imposing the use of French in all judicial acts,* and of the efforts of Mazarin's ambassadors at Münster in 1648 to get French recognized as a diplomatic language on a par with Latin.

But all these tongues were fated to remain for some time longer the idioms of minorities. This was particularly true of Latin, which ordinary people never knew and which ever smaller numbers showed any readiness to use. Besides, as George Sarton once remarked, "No language can be truly alive that is not used by women"; and Latin was used only by men. But even national tongues like French or English or Castilian were isolated in a sea of local dialects; and the plaintive report of a French bishop in 1709 laments that the sermons of itinerant preachers and even of parish priests pass over the heads of peasants and artisans who understand only their own *patois*.

The problems of oral communication can be seen in more acute form with writing. We are only just beginning to realize that history has focused on the writings of societies which lived a largely oral life, where very little was recorded because very few could either record or refer, where most transactions were by word of mouth and most activities were hardly available to literate record. There were exceptions. Protestants were "people of the Book" and of books, Protestant societies were more literate: Presbyterian Scotland of the seventeenth century began to build up a network of parish schools and high schools; mid-seventeenth century England, covered with a flood of pamphlets and newspapers, had a male literacy rate of about 30 per cent. But these were exceptions, and it is safe to say that before 1700, some three-quarters of the men and nine-tenths of the women in Europe could not even sign their names. Nine out of ten men of property never owned a book. Writing from his Neapolitan prison, the heretical philosopher Thomas Campanella (1568–1639) rejoiced that "more books have been published in the last century than in the five thousand years before it." He was right; but even so their total impact was very limited.

With reading and writing highly restricted skills, oral memory remained the prevailing method of handing on accumulated knowledge. Records about techniques, about events (wars, floods, changes of master), about the weather and its vagaries, were scarce or nonexistent. But information about such things matters and, where records were lacking (almost everywhere outside the cities), it had to be passed on by word of mouth from old people to younger ones—a random, awkward system, apt to break down in times when old people were almost as rare as educated ones.

Since the common speech was rude and unattractive, the cultivated classes insisted on its very opposite, seeking to assert the distance between them and the common herd by the convolutions of their style. Late

---

* In England, a century later, petitions clamored for a similar reform.

sixteenth-century literature swells and bloats with overmannered graces —Marinism in Italy, Gongorism in Spain, Euphuism in England. The first draws its name from the exaggerated style of Giambattista Marino (1569–1625), soon imitated by a canon of Cordova, Luis de Góngora y Argôte (1561–1627), whose ornate allusive works addressed themselves only to the *cultos*—to cultivated people as opposed to the popular public other writers wooed. Lyly's *Euphues or the Anatomy of Wit* (1578) spread the fashion to England with the mannered tale of an Oxford undergraduate lost in Italianized London. French preciousness would be delayed by the Wars of Religion but when it came, at the beginning of the seventeenth century, sentiment would be refined almost to the point of metaphysics, floridity and fustian joined in the *precious* style. Honoré d'Urfé's famous pastoral novel, *Astrée* (1610), brought forth a new world of shepherds sighing for delicate shepherdesses in the romantic setting of a past that never was, first of a long line of works which today seem unreasonable or insipid but which charmed contemporaries, such as the Elector Palatine, Frederick, the Winter King of Bohemia, who addressed his wife in terms taken from *Astrée*.

Of course, there were other writings, more down to earth, more straightforward. There were the ancient classics in new translations, like the *Plutarch* which Jacques Amyot translated into French in 1559 and whose tremendous success inspired not only a conventional view of Greek and Roman virtues, but a stoic conception of life. There were the *Essays* of Montaigne (1580), shrewd and skeptical, reminding their readers that "even on the highest throne we sit but on our behind," great favorites of Henry IV. There were the Spanish *picaresque* novels, beginning with *Lazarillo da Tormes,* placed on the Index in 1559 but so popular that an expurgated edition had to be brought out in 1573. At the turn of the century, *Guzman de Alfarache,* became the ideal *picaro* type: now student, now soldier, beggar or pander, now robber, now robbed, rowing in the galleys, trailing a pike, serving as the pageboy of a Cardinal, full of guile and courage, pious but devoid of any conscience. Told with immense verve, Guzman's story leaves one with the grim impression of a society all of a piece with the rogues it spawned and spurned.

The picaresque novel attacked and deflated the pompous notions and the humbug of a time and a society when self-delusion held sway. A more moderate effort in this same direction achieved international fame in the work of a man whose life bears out some of the apparently extraordinary tales of the *picaros*. Miguel de Cervantes Saavedra (1547–1616), fourth son of a poor surgeon from Alcala de Henares, studied at Madrid and Rome and Naples, joined the Crusade of 1571, lost a hand at Lepanto, was captured by Barbary pirates (1575), languished in Algiers until ransomed five years later. Petty clerk in Seville, he eked out a living by writing plays, was imprisoned for debt (1601, 1602) and there

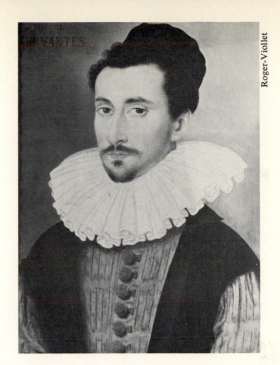

Miguel Cervantes.

conceived *Don Quixote,* which first appeared in 1605. This tale of a would-be knight out to perform anachronistic deeds of valor in a world where there is no room for them ridiculed the chivalric values and novels current at the time, but with a certain tenderness for the Don's ideals, better surely than the mediocrity and the self-satisfaction all around him. *Don Quixote* was an immense success, perhaps because its readers enjoyed the very romance Cervantes satirized.

Even more successful were the comedies of the Golden Age dramatists: Calderon, Tirso de Molina and above all, Felipe Lope de Vega (1562–1635), a veteran of the Armada and of less glorious situations, said to have written 1,800 plays of which 470 survive. The fame of Lope de Vega, like that of William Shakespeare (1564–1616), reminds us again that, in an age of few books and much illiteracy, the word of mouth remained the great means of communication. Lope's plays were made to be performed and improvised rather than published and read. So, in effect, were those of Shakespeare who, between 1590 and 1613, must have produced far more than the thirty-seven or thirty-eight scripts that still survive in print. The popular theater consumed plays at an extraordinary rate and actor-playwrights or actor-directors turned them out *en masse.* In Paris, Alexandre Hardy who died in 1631 wrote some 800, of which few survive.

Best adjusted to the predicament which vast demand created was the *commedia dell'arte* born in Italy, probably in Mantua, sometime in the 1560's, whose players improvised the action as they went along, on the basis of the traditional personages they incarnated. The characters and roles became fixed by custom, rather as in a Punch and Judy show: the

William Shakespeare, an engraving which first appeared on the title page of the First Folio, 1623.

Spanish captain, the Venetian pantaloon, the Neapolitan punchinello, the Columbine, and many others. The commedia competed with an older tradition of religious mysteries, passion plays and knockabout farce, from which the modern drama has developed.

As we saw in considering the society of early modern times, as social distances grew, the erstwhile patrons of this older theater lost interest in shows where they performed before the vulgar mob or rubbed elbows with it. Masques and mysteries, written and acted by clerks and bourgeois, presented in public places, declined and almost disappeared. They were replaced by paying theaters in the hands of traveling showmen who addressed themselves to those who could afford an entrance fee. One side effect of this would be that, since entertainment was no longer provided by respectable citizen-amateurs, professional actors, wandering purveyors of entertainment, always hovering on the margins of stable society, came to be looked upon as akin to gypsies (Bohemians). They were identified with license and immorality, denied the sacraments of the Church. including the right to be buried in sacred ground. This, however, did not prevent them from thriving.

The first permanent theaters in London opened in 1576, in Madrid in 1579, in Paris somewhat later. They called forth at once works of quality and power which give us some idea of what the public could take. Many of Lope de Vega's plays seem to have been harsh criticisms of the injustice and inequalities that prevailed in Spain. Those of English writers appear to favor characters strong sometimes to the verge of madness, like Christopher Marlowe's *Tamburlaine;* as passionate, amoral, and power-hungry as his *Doctor Faustus,* or Shakespeare's *Macbeth.* But if they are mad with *Lear* or almost so with Prospero (*The Tempest*), they can also be hard-headed and hard-hearted; and so we see them in the second part of *Henry IV* or in Ben Jonson's comedy *Volpone*.

Perhaps the most striking thing about the plays of this period, as indeed about all plays written for a popular public avid for entertainment, for action, and for excitement not necessarily very sophisticated, is the intensity of immediate effects, the violence and complication of the action, the highly colored and improbable nature of the scenes. In a French comedy of 1635, the heroine disguised as a young knight sets off in pursuit of her lover, finds him on the shores of Barbary thanks to a storm and shipwreck, uses her trusty sword to rescue him from an Arab ambush, after which the lovers are captured by pirates whose leader turns out to be her father. End of Act I. Even the plots of Shakespeare's comedies turn often on improbable events which only served to feed the public's appetite for sensation.

In Richelieu's France, however, fashionable *précieuses,* noble bluestockings (so-called from the blue stockings Paris students wore with their breeches), began to attend the theater and to impose their standards on the stage. The kind of women who attended the theater had, until then, been neither respectable nor cultivated. Their appearance in the public of the 1630's and 1640's pressed the demand for new proprieties and a new decorum. By the middle of the seventeenth century, the Parlement of Paris had banned those mysteries and farces that survived because they were the work of "ignorant, unlettered people . . . a carpenter, an upholsterer, a fish-seller, who have played the Acts of the Apostles." Such "mechanic artisans, who know neither A nor B, who were never instructed and have neither eloquent speech nor proper, nor pronounce in decent accents . . ." could be left to entertain in fairs or villages. Real theater, real art, were elsewhere; and there not naturalism but refinement prevailed, and facts gave way to superior ideals. From a lively, vulgar art full of improbable adventures and intrigues, the patronage of the cultivated rich turned the theater onto different lines, not always more seemly, but everywhere more highly structured and in many ways more conventional, concerned less with incident than with sentiment and passion. The last popular theater company in France (revealingly called The Brotherhood of the Passion) was suppressed in 1676, and the Comédie Française was set up in 1680 to perform the plays the new society approved. In 1696 a royal decree prohibited whistles and catcalls in the theater. The popular stage was buried. Decorum was king.

But preciousness withered too. By mid-seventeenth century the overornate tradition, holding reality at arm's length, was wearing thin. Educated people now expressed themselves more clearly in writing and in speech, as can be seen even of poetry written before and after the 1640's: the former circumvoluted almost to flatulence, the latter simpler and to the point. The French public therefore appreciated Molière's attacks on prissy aesthetes in his *Précieuses Ridicules* (1659) and his sturdy new naturalism, just as the English public of the Restoration welcomed a generation of bawdy dramatists.

More important, language itself was changing along with literary style. The *Académie Française* (founded in 1635), the Royal Society of England (founded in 1662), set up committees to modify, clarify, and purify the language. As more men learned to read, literary style adjusted itself to a public keen on information rather than on learned allusions. Just as the literacy explosion of the nineteenth century begot a simpler style (as in journalism), so that of the seventeenth century did too, a style increasingly functional, designed to convey precise facts briefly and plainly. One result of this would be the dissociation of poetry and prose, the former made up of "pleasant pictures and agreeable visions in the fancy" (John Locke) but likely to mislead, the latter the chosen vehicle of straight thinking and serious enterprise, unadorned, "bringing all things as near the mathematical plainness as they can," wrote Bishop Thomas Sprat (1635–1713) in his *History of the Royal Society* (1667), and "preferring the language of artizans, countrymen and merchants, before that of wits and scholars."

The Arts

Mannerism

Where words, even spoken, and knowledge, even publicized, can speak only to some, the language of the arts can be addressed to many. Of course, it is not always so. The High Renaissance inclined to look on art as something only a few refined spirits—intellectuals, aristocrats, princes, prelates, and patricians—could properly appreciate and enjoy. The last expression of this esoteric view of taste as the preserve of an elite, alone open to pleasures of the mind and senses, had been the late-sixteenth-century flowering of rare and precious works which can be loosely labeled *mannerism* in painting, as in music or in literature: a search for strangeness, for the abnormal, a kind of sensual and intellectual alchemy. Where Renaissance taste tried to clarify reality, the mannerists departed from reality, distorted it, shifted into the realm of fantasy, where artifice contributed new excitements and sensations. Gongorists and Euphuists favored the obscure allusion, the ornate, convoluted mode. Architects, such as the Italian Palladio (1508–1580), complicated the clear lines and volumes of an earlier style, making a building something of an intellectual game. Musicians preferred polyphony, the colored blend of several notes and voices, increasingly subtle and fastidious as in the work of Palestrina (1526?–1594), or in the vivid, clever tones of the motets of the Belgian Roland de Lassus (Orlando di Lasso, 1532?–1594). Painters abandoned the geometric logic of lines and perspective, broke up form and surface by contrast, light, and shade (Tintoretto, 1518–1594), painted portraits in distorting mirrors (Parmigiano, 1503?–1540), indulged expressionistic tendencies (El Greco, 1548?–1614), sought out the grotesque (Archimboldo, 1527?–1592), or the refined romantic (Nicholas Hilliard, 1537–1619).

This view of art as dedicated to the delight of the chosen few was not to last. We have already seen in the case of literature that it had been criticized and paralleled by more popular and straightforward works. The world was wider than the marbled halls and flowered bowers of a refined elite. The things that could be said to it and about it could be expressed with less deliberate obscurity, and presented in a form accessible to many, not only to a select few. Truth was more important than abstraction; life, even everyday life, better than fantasy: hence realism. Caravaggio (1565?–1609) appears as the great representative of this reaction against the nervous delicacy and distortions of mannerism: sober, intense, and as highly conscious of the living world as the mannerists had been concerned to exclude it from their ken. Where Renaissance painters had painted saints as ancient statues, where the mannerists had presented them as noble lords and ladies, Caravaggio saw them as living persons drawn from the street, the countryside, the world of everyday.

But Caravaggio was never very popular, though he was influential—especially in the north, where his social conscience found a readier echo than in the aristocratic south. The antielitist, antiaristocratic views he painted into his pictures were more pungently reflected in the Northern Reformation, bitterly opposed to the worldly pride of the Renaissance, contesting its glorification of man, insisting on man's fall, denying the right of some to privileges and pleasures which were refused to others. The social arguments of the Protestants affected art the more, since so much art had been devoted to the service of religion. The house-clearing of the Catholic pantheon swept out the aristocracy of heaven, and left the churches bare. Protestant iconoclasm was not mere philistinism, though it was sometimes that—sometimes rowdy and destructive, sometimes blind fanaticism. Its attack on images also reflected a disgust that these dead objects should be bedecked with riches, while poor live beings went hungry, thirsty, and cold. Statues and images were broken but, wrote a man of Ghent, the Church had broken men. So the iconoclasm had a social and humanitarian meaning which would appeal to intellectuals, to radicals, and sometimes even to the poor they sought to help.

But Protestants tended to severity. They stripped worship and churches of ornament, laid bare the walls and the believer's soul, moved toward abstraction on the material as well as on the spiritual plane. The

The Calling of St. Matthew, by Caravaggio. Painted for the altarpiece of a Roman chapel, Caravaggio's "vulgar" treatment of a saint was considered close to sacrilege. Church of San Luigi dei Francesi, Rome.

Counter-Reformation almost naturally took the opposite view. A decree of the Council of Trent demanded that "by means of the stories of the mysteries of our Redemption portrayed by paintings or other representations, the people be instructed and confirmed in the habit of remembering, and continually revolving in mind the articles of faith." The dogmas heretics denied would be insisted on. The significance of holy rites—mass, sacraments, prayers for the dead, intercession of the saints— had to be affirmed, stressed, proclaimed over and over again. The images and idols Protestants condemned were necessary not only in polemic but in doctrine, an essential part of the Church's armory.

Art could touch the senses, hence the soul. It could place wholesome examples before the eyes of the faithful so that, said the Council, they "may be incited to worship and love God and cultivate piety." Art would acquire the techniques of persuasion, appeal to the masses not to the elite, address the heart and nerves, adopt a theatrical quality, emphasize scenery, consider the effect that atmosphere has on the senses, which it seeks to charm, to elevate, to terrorize. This was the basis of the style we call Baroque or, at least, of its alliance with Catholicism.

The Baroque

Baroque is an offspring of the Counter-Reformation; it is not all of Counter-Reformation art. The first reaction to the Protestant challenge had been in the direction of austerity and functionalism, seeking to answer reformed criticisms with internal reform, concentration, almost severity. The ardor of such reactions could lead to the intensity of an El Greco, as to that of St. John of the Cross. Its more obvious culmination is to be seen in the morose rigor of Phillip II's Escorial. Counter-Reformation art has been described as a long, exalted meditation on suffering and death. Corpses, skulls, whole skeletons, brought back the Dance of Death into a death-obsessed seventeenth century, no longer concerned with social criticism but ominous, shocking, the continual reminder of what awaits us. The humanist serenity of the Renaissance was now replaced by absorbed contemplation of an awful fate. Repose and harmony gave way to painful striving; reasoning to revelation; scholarship to mysticism; sensuousness (sometimes camouflaged as ecstasy) to chaste dignity. In the past, martyrs seemed calm and triumphed over their pains. Now we get the most graphic descriptions of horrid torments endured by Christians past and present, including one of monks buried to their necks, their heads providing targets for a game of bowls. Their very agonies—frescoed, sculpted, or engraved—were paradoxically meant to solace, console, exalt, and, finally, instruct.

The Council had not only decreed, it had also prohibited. Images which evoked impurity or erroneous dogmas were to be suppressed; saints and martyrs should not be painted as ordinary men lacking supernatural dignity. Great subjects must be treated greatly; triviality and vulgarity must be banned. Thus it was that in 1573 the Holy Office reprimanded Paolo Veronese for introducing into a painting of the Lord's Supper figures unworthy of the dignity of the occasion—a servant with a bleeding nose, armed men dressed in the German fashion—and gave him three months to revise his picture. Caravaggio got into trouble for his vulgar realism; his painting of St. Matthew was criticized for coarsely showing the saint's feet, his Virgin of Loretto, condemned for the Virgin's simplicity and nearness to her common worshipers. This would be the prelude to a stylization of religious art, too often sweetened, softened, and soppy.

The ideal instrument for the new kind of art burgeoned in Bologna— a city only recently annexed to the papal states and one with a strong intellectual tradition based on its ancient university, yet one which had eschewed the worldliness of merchant Venice or the sensual frivolities of Florence. Bologna furnished the Holy See with two of its most didactic-minded popes: Gregory XIII (1572–1585), the sponsor of the Gregorian calendar and of a score of colleges and schools, and Gregory XV (1621–1623), founder of the Congregation for the Propagation of the

Faith, an educational enterprise on a universal scale. It also bred the most typical and influential painting school of the Counter-Reformation, that of the Carraci: two brothers, Agostino (1557–1602) and Annibale (1560–1606), and a cousin, Lodovico (1555–1619). It was this talented family, especially Agostino, who first insisted that forms should be not complements but servants of ideas. Ideas were to be in command, guiding the artist's hand, subordinating his images to what they have to say. No more irrelevant preoccupations, then, like Raphael's, with the elegance of a pose or the charm of a figure; no more the driving concern of Michelangelo with the possibilities of the human body in all conceivable attitudes; no more the distracting dwarfs or dogs or courtesans of Veronese, but the clear reproduction of edifying scenes, rendered as dramatic and as moving as one could.

Giotto and Fra Angelico had been Christian painters too, but not sufficiently accessible to please the public or the patrons of a latter day. Their Renaissance successors were masterly, but often irreligious. The Carraci produced works that all could grasp and all appreciate, paintings that still survive in religious imagery because they are infused with strong religious feeling. Characteristically, Lodovico had studied in the University of Bologna, a rare accomplishment in the world of artists, and the Academy he founded in the 1580's along with the many paintings of the trio spurred on the work of like-minded followers: Il Guido, Guercino, Domenichino and many others, the favorite decorators of Counter-Reformation churches, who made their walls once more the Bible of the people.

All painters traveled widely. Artists had always been wanderers, gathering round a project which offered employment, dispersing just as quickly, going from place to place—church, villa, palace—often picking up where others had left off on a fresco, a dome, an altarpiece; now interior decorators, now public works designers, but always, even the humblest (masons or stonecutters), carriers of taste and fashion which would be imitated for generations in the provinces or towns touched by their brush, their chisel, or, simply, by their tavern talk. Flemish artists could be found in Italy and Spain (where they decorated the Cathedral of Seville), Portuguese in Brussels, and we all know the peregrinations of a Cretan lad, Domenico Theotokopulos, who—having learned his trade in Venice under Titian and Tintoretto—moved to Toledo where he became famous as El Greco. El Greco's mixture of fantasy and realism conveyed to Spain not only the mannerism of Tintoretto, retouched by his own genius, but also the sulfurous, metallic magic of Venetian colors.

Many Spaniards drew their inspiration from Italy more directly: Ribera (1588–1652), who left Valencia for Rome, finally settling in Naples to paint in the violently realistic style of Caravaggio; Velasquez (1599–

1660), admirer of Correggio and Ribera; Murillo (1617–1682), who learned so much from the Carraci. Not only Spaniards, though: the inspiration of seventeenth-century Europe was Italian, just as it would be French in the eighteenth. Nicolas Poussin and a host of Frenchmen; Rubens, Van Dyck, and many other Flemings; all drew their color from Venice, their sentiment from Bologna, their Christianity from Rome. And when in mid-seventeenth century the Church militant gave way to the Church triumphant, it was these men who helped replace its gravity with joy, its sternness with exuberance—though ever more refined, with majesty and riches.

Rubens, Ribera, Murillo. Zurbarán, and many lesser figures were told just what to paint, their subjects outlined by theologians who knew exactly what they wanted to show. This was not a revolutionary departure, except for the detail and precision of instructions. Nor did many artists object, for most of them shared the piety of their fellow citizens: Lodovico Carraci made amends for an unedifying life by spending his last days with the Capuchins of Bologna, praying and painting a picture of St. Peter lamenting his sins; Domenichino (1581–1641) always began a painting of a saint by praying to him; Jacques Callot (1592–1635) began every working day by attending mass; Philippe de Champaigne (1602–1674), painter to the Queen of France, had a daughter cloistered as a nun at Port-Royal, where he himself retired to end his days; Murillo, who spent most of his life in convents and churches, belonged to a Seville confrery devoted to burying bodies of men drowned or murdered and to consoling those condemned to death. Where piety was standard, instructions were no burden. In any case, as the sculptor and architect Bernini said: "Submission is necessary only in matters of faith; otherwise man has complete freedom in all spheres of life."

If paintings should be purged, so should the churches. They were cleared of the darkness, the screens and pillars which prevented people from joining as one in worship or in sermon. The new design sought visibility, light, good acoustics, for a congregation which should be able to follow every movement of the liturgy, every word of the preacher, every line of their missals. The first to devise such new forms, emphasizing simplicity, economy, and convenience, were the Jesuits. Just as some twentieth-century architects thought of the house as a machine for living, they thought of the Church as a machine for worship and for preaching, functional and eloquent, only later to be overlaid by the ornaments of baroque which gilded and embellished the barer simplicities of the first Tridentine buildings.

Between 1568 and 1575, while St. Peter's was being finished, the Church of Jesus—the Gesù—was built in Rome, first and prototype of all the Jesuit churches whose spare geometry and grand design would soon be imitated all over the Catholic world. Initial sobriety, however, would

The façade of the Gesù in Rome. Right: the ceiling fresco of the Gesù, *The Triumph of the Name of Jesus,* by Gaulli.

soon give way to sumptuousness. The Protestants stood for soberness, hated image and ornament. The Church would contradict them. Where God was present, no magnificence was too great. "The Church," a Catholic chronicler would write, "is an image of heaven on earth. God fills it all. How could we not ornate it with all that is most precious?"

The Gesù filled with riches. Aristotle's *Rhetoric* was the crown of Jesuit college studies. It also guided the art which Jesuits directed: from poetic it became highly rhetorical. The most striking images possible insinuated or hammered in the truth of disputed dogmas; popular devotion was spurred by and demanded exuberant decorations, vast dimensions, chapels and altars rich with color and movement, attended by a horde of statues; dramatic in the fashion of the Mediterranean where the counteroffensive was based; voluptuous in the blood-and-death idiom of the peninsula where Loyola was born; theatrical in a theatrical age when all, including the stage, brought grist for the Jesuits' mill. The more popular, the more so: as can be witnessed in the flamboyant work of the Spaniard José Benito Churriguera (1665–1725), in the whipped-cream and gingerbread pilgrimage cloisters of Austria and Bavaria, in the gaily cluttered art of Latin-American churches. Baroque works and buildings seem to be in perpetual motion: they teem, shimmer, surge, strain, swell, and overflow with movement. Even what seems solid, stable, is an illusion: part of a constant spectacle of constant change.

Music sacred and profane also changed, and also in two contrasting directions, though sharing the same aims: above all else, the desperate desire to communicate. Composers—declared Vincenzo Galilei, father of the astronomer, in a work of 1581—should "express the conceptions of the mind and . . . impress them with the greatest possible effectiveness on the minds of the listeners." At the religious level this meant that profane themes were abandoned for motives from Gregorian chants, and Palestrina for example insisted that words (lyrics) should be audible. It also led to the birth of modern musical drama. Songs and tunes had been associated with drama at least since medieval miracle and morality plays. Around 1600 the first opera, with dialogue set to music, was performed in Florence, and the genre was at once enlisted to serve the needs of clerical propaganda. The same year an allegorical opera would be performed at Philip Neri's Oratory in Rome; *oratorio* was the name applied to these lyrical and allegorical religious dramas, widely performed on the steps of churches for the edification of the public. Public concerts, mostly of sacred works, would appear first in England (1672) and Germany (1673), then in France. Public opera performances outside Italy appeared in the second half of the seventeenth century.

In England, meanwhile, another medieval entertainment, the masque —an expensive and exclusive court spectacle combining music, poetry, and miming dance—developed into an art form that mobilized poets like Ben Jonson and Milton, composers like Henry Purcell (1659–1695), and set designers like Inigo Jones (1573–1652), whose stage settings brought him fame long before he became known as an architect. Poetry evidently sounded better to music (indeed, much of it was written to be sung), and plays—whether didactic or merely entertaining—would affect more people when accompanied by mime and dance.

Splendor, scale, and desire to affect people strongly stand out in all the manifestations of the time. Perhaps the contrapuntal harmony that we associate with Johann Sebastian Bach (1685–1750)—great organist and composer as prodigious in output as in quality—is emblematic of it: an accumulation of musical images, a grand architectural organization, elaborate structures achieved through the working out and the embellishment of a few basic themes.

The didactic and edifying would contrast with the more exuberant, more elitist mannerist tradition. Color and sweep triumphed, contrast and impressiveness deliberately meant to dazzle. This affected the painting of Tintoretto and Veronese as much as the music of the Venetian Giovanni Gabrielli. Radiant on canvas, radiant in sound, picturesqueness transferred from painting to *chorales* with the same qualities of light and shade, polychoral effects in one answering polychromatic effects in the other. The monumental and ornate pomp of Veronese was comparable to that of the new festival masses, like those Orazio Benevoli composed for the inauguration of the new

Johann Sebastian Bach. From a painting by Elias Gottlieb Haussmann.

Salzburg cathedral in 1628, the sudden contrasts of *fortissimo* and *pianissimo* in the first chorus of Bach's St. Matthew Passion, the elaborate structures in his Brandenburg Concertos, the fancies of his Chromatic Fantasy, reminiscent of the interest in color effects that we can find in a Monteverdi opera like *Orfeo* (1607).

The *Paradise Lost* of Bach's English predecessor, John Milton, leaves a similar impression of power and magnificence. Deeply involved in politics and pamphleteering, rising in 1649 to serve the Commonwealth as writer and translator of diplomatic documents, encompassed by blindness, disgraced by the Restoration, Milton set out to tell

> Of man's first disobedience, and the fruit
> Of that forbidden tree whose mortal taste
> Brought death into the world, and all our woe.

This poem of the Fall, written by a deeply religious man fascinated by the majesty of the fallen Satan, "confounded though immortal," is the most typical of baroque epics: its organlike harmonies similar to Bach's; its richness of simile and metaphor, the grandeur and vividness of its images, recalling Rubens; his claim to sing "things unattempted yet in prose or rhyme," worthy of the heroic dimensions of his age.

There was a contemporary echo on a humbler level. John Bunyan (1628–1688) used the fashionable mode of allegory to describe Christian's journey through the temptations of life in *Pilgrim's Progress* (1678). Tinker, rebel, veteran of the English civil war and of a dozen years in Bedford jail, nonconformist preacher, Bunyan's style echoes that of King James's Bible, earnest yet striking, addressing the simple audiences with which he was familiar in simple, concrete, and majestic terms to give us one of the classics of reformed Christianity and of the English language.

Thus the baroque was many things. Populist, realistic, and concrete with Caravaggio, Bunyan, or St. Philip Neri; rhetorical and theatrical with the Jesuits and the Carraci; spiritual and dramatic with Milton in England, Zurbarán in Spain, or Georges de La Tour in France; Jansenist and sober with Philippe de Champaigne; vigorous and delicate with Velasquez; luminous and rich with Peter-Paul Rubens. The paradox of what has been called the democratic art of an aristocratic society can be seen in the latter's *Last Judgment,* painted in the second decade of the seventeenth century. In this sumptuous painting, the violence of movement, the richness of form, the heat of the colors, the contrast of light and shade, create an Apocalypse whose victims are plumper and more desirable than most of its probable beholders. Today, Rubens appears as the great representative of the baroque style, combining in his exuberant output vivacity and pomp, eloquence and subtlety, north and south, a brush which would in due course enchant Watteau and Delacroix, Renoir and Picasso.

Such a diversity of styles reflected a diversity of patrons. The Church was no more alone in patronage in the seventeenth century than it had been in the fifteenth. On the contrary, this was the great age of aestheticism and collecting. Rubens made an excellent diplomat because so many people admired him as a painter. In 1630, he was able to bring about peace between his patrons, the king of England and the king of Spain. Marie de Medici and Richelieu were rivals in collecting as in politics, Cardinal Mazarin when dying sighed not for his soul but for his art collection. Elector Maximilian in Munich, lover of Dürers; the eccentric Emperor Rudolph II in Prague patron of Archimboldo and Bartolomeus Spränger; Queen Christina writing to her generals to ship home the books and paintings of ravaged central Europe, are only the more avid collectors of the time. Topping them, King Charles of England was, says the historian Trevor-Roper, "perhaps the greatest royal patron that art has ever found," his court "the last Renaissance court in Europe." Charles I's collections, his patronage of Rubens, Van Dyck, Inigo Jones (royal surveyor of buildings), his buying of Rembrandts and Titians (he visited Spain to win the Infanta's hand but got a set of Titians instead), his placing and pensioning of poets and musicians, goaded the English nobles into imitation, importing European sculptures, amassing vast galleries of paintings, building Palladian houses with gardens laid out in the Italian style, perfect settings for the performance of Milton's *Comus* or Henry Lawes' music to it. It was not thought or intellect that moved these men but aestheticism and theatrical effect, but that was enough to spur a brief flowering soon doomed by the outbreak of Civil War.

The Last Judgment, by Peter-Paul Rubens. Colorful, fleshly, sensual, Rubens' worldliness could not be banished even from religious subjects. There would be none of this in the highly disciplined compositions of his contemporary, Poussin. Alte Pinakothek, Munich.

The Classicist Reaction

Meanwhile, the pendulum of public taste was swinging back toward a different point of view. Some thought there was too much variety about baroque art and too much fervor; many felt a sense of artistic anarchy. Shocked by such disorder, as they were by the disorder in the political sphere, men turned increasingly to reason for discipline and structure in the arts as in society. Too much subjectivity makes for chaos. Thought was the antidote which Descartes glorified, which the coming age respected. Thought, not feeling. "Intelligence alone can perceive truth," wrote Spinoza: can seek to grasp reality "in an eternal form" according to the laws "of fixed and eternal things . . . by which all particular things happen and order themselves." Philosophy now offered the unity which religion no longer provided. Descartes, Spinoza, Newton, all proposed an "effective philosophy"—the order and rule which the world had lost.

The plastic result of the search for a universally valid order would appear in the harmonious paintings of Poussin, the restrictive codes of

Landscape with the Burial of Phocion, by Nicolas Poussin. "My nature forces me towards the orderly," explained the artist-philosopher who spent much of his life painting and pondering in the Roman hills. His quest for perfection made his work the model of French classicism. Louvre, Paris.

Le Brun's Academy of Art, the noble buildings of Le Vau, the elegant gardens of Le Nôtre, the monumental order personified by Louis XIV. The classical ideal called for uniformity of style, abhorred the fantasy of Gothic, from Molière who rejected "the insipid taste of Gothic ornaments" to Rousseau who found "the portals of our Gothic churches subsist only for the shame of those who had the patience to make them." In the seventeenth century the canons of the royal Abbey of St. Denis had the façade hammered off; in the eighteenth century, dislike of vulgar medieval colors led some stained glass windows of Rheims Cathedral to be replaced by white panes. Nothing could serve this purpose better than reference to ancient models. Already for Louis XIV's coronation, the interior of Rheims had been hung with draperies which tried to turn the Gothic nave into a Greek temple. On the eve of the Revolution, a major project was still being seriously considered which would remodel the façade of Notre Dame Cathedral so as to make it resemble the Pantheon in Rome. Here was the reaction to baroque ecstasy. The baroque, as the art historian Heinrich Wölfflin has defined it, is a *musical style,* meant to excite emotions and perceptions, emphasizing color and suggestion, light, mobility, and atmosphere; the classic style is *architectural*: it seeks stable definitions, stresses form and line, symmetry, and unity. The wheel had come full circle from the classic revival of the Renaissance to yet another classical revival.

The palace of Versailles bears witness to the rightness of Wöllflin's views. In painting as in politics, the new ideal which it incorporates is static not dynamic. Reason, as the new architects and artists saw it, is neither a highway nor a roller coaster, but a magnificent structure. From the greatest works of the age, movement is almost excluded; symmetry, symbolism, chaste abstractions take over, as they do in the aseptic lucidity, the cool forms and colors of that most intellectual of painters, Nicolas Poussin (1594–1665). Poussin, who spent most of his life in Rome, drew his clients from the highest bourgeoisie in France. One of his followers has described his method: "When a painter has made a drawing from the living model, he should make another study of the same figure on a separate sheet and should try to give it the character of an ancient statue." Painters, in other words, should not imitate life but paint nature, "not as it ordinarily appears, but as it ought to be in its greatest perfection." Nature, not as it is, but as it should be: eliminate the accidental, the incidental, the irregular, the distracting. Concentrate, select, simplify, purify. Like a corset which restricts, the recipe also affirms. In paintings, as in the theater, the dramatic intensity grows as the action is concentrated. As vocabulary becomes more rigid, as the rhyme inexorably marshals the verses of the poet and the line constricts the painter's forms, a certain richness seems to be not lost but gained. The richness is largely internal—symbolic, psychological, sentimental—the wealth of a new elite. Both painting and the theater are interested not in events but in character; and this can best be seen by glancing at the stage.

The kind of events which fill picaresque novels now become fortuitous accidents within a more significant fate. The ones that really matter take place essentially within a person, where they can be controlled, where (at any rate) the significant action lies. Since time and place tend to be distracting, they are best concentrated in a reasonable unit—twenty-four hours—which will force the playwright and the spectator to focus upon what really matters—not irrelevant adventures but psychological problems in which the will is really the hero of the story.

The first great exponent of this different style had been a Norman lawyer, Pierre Corneille (1606–1684), whose *Cid* (1637) is the tale of a girl's love for the murderer of her father, rendered important by the heroes' struggle to submit their passions to the will and their vulgar reason to the higher dialectic of duty. But Corneille's situations were still too complicated and the high perfection of the tragic style would be achieved by Jean Racine (1639–1699), the action of whose plays is clear, simple, and largely devoid of incident, concentrating entirely on the psychological analysis of the motives and passions of the characters. The psychology of Racine is no more profound than that of

Shakespeare: but its setting is barer, more abstract, the light thrown on spiritual and mental processes more intense because more isolated. That is why his plays stand as the high point of classical drama.

It almost seems as if the classical style suited the new centralization of the state, the assertion of monarchic primacy, the stately dignity of the new order. It served them in minor ways as we can see from an ode written as early as 1645, which rejoices that

> Now changing scenery on stage replaced
> The turmoils which the state disgraced.

It entertained and instructed, reflecting the ethos of the new order. Thus in France, after 1660, Lully's operas, once frothy and light, took on the solemn glitter and monumental structures of Versailles, majestic, impersonal, rather cold but severely impressive. Nor could there be a more impressive monument to the royal power than Versailles itself. The gigantic undertaking had entailed tremendous cost: on a state budget of about 120 million livres the building of the castle began by costing some 5 million yearly, went up to sums between 15 and 25 million a year after 1678; 22,000 workers labored upon it in 1682, 36,000 in 1683. In 230 acres of its gardens, 1,400 fountains, 25,000 trees had been transplanted in one year alone, so that the King could enjoy them full-grown. Wonder of the age, the waters of the Seine were raised to supply its

Alceste, an opera with ballet by Lully, performed for Louis XIV in the marble court of the palace at Versailles. The stage is illuminated, top to bottom, with myriad lights.

waterworks by the great machine of Marly: 14 hydraulic wheels and 223 pumps. At last, in 1682, Louis XIV moved to Versailles for good. From 1693 to 1700 he never set foot in Paris again. His last visit there would be in 1706. Versailles became the monument of his splendor but also his retreat, his Escorial. "With him there is only grandeur, magnificence and symmetry," complained Madame de Maintenon, "and it is better to bear the bitter draft of the doors, as long as they face each other . . . You have to die symmetrically!"

Beyond Versailles, as well, the splendid stage designs which never failed to exalt Jove or the Sun were reproduced in urban architecture. In Rome, in Paris, in Turin, great places rose (like the Place Vendôme, completed in 1686); designed to serve a scenic rather than an organic purpose, their plan centered on the statue of the monarch who presided over the site as he did over the state. The spirit of Descartes presided over them. The *Discourse* had criticized cities which had grown at random and whose separate buildings, even if handsome, were ill arranged so that "chance rather than the will of a few men using their reason has thus disposed them."

Both baroque and classicism, however, ran a risk which neither would eschew: festive and grand, they could confuse magnificence with opulence, pomp with pompousness, dignity with pretentiousness, and fall into the very vulgarity which they wanted to avoid. The academies set up to codify arts and letters dessicated them;* the rigor of new rules, once invigorating, dulled and parched, discipline became pedantry, bold illusionism turned to artifice, and only scale and gilt were left to cover reality and crush initiative. That would be the negative side of classicism, against which a new reaction would rise in the eighteenth century.

Realism?

Meanwhile, the core of the reaction still to come was to be found among the realists—heirs of Caravaggio in Italy or Spain—painting scenes from popular life (often for the amusement of nobles wondering at their clownish vulgarity), and most effectively in the bourgeois Netherlands. The realistic presentation of humble things and people had always survived in the north. The social concerns of the Reformation revived this interest. In Holland particularly a new secular art developed, often individualistic, generally insisting on free observation and choice, catering to a free market whose patrons were not ecclesiastic or royal but middle-class laymen, shifting to man the attention elsewhere accorded to God.

---

* We can see how the breach between artisan and artist grew while academies codified the work of the latter. In France in 1671, glaziers were expelled from the corporation of stained-glass painters, sculptors left the carpenters' guild. Painters and sculptors were no longer manual workers but something higher, nobler, sometimes literally so. Le Brun was ennobled in 1662, Le Nôtre in 1675, Mansard in 1683: Mignard, the King's painter, left over half a million livres when he died.

The Night Watch, by Rembrandt van Rijn, designated by Rembrandt's contemporaries as "the great corporation piece." Originally entitled *Sortie of the Shooting Company of Captain Frans Banning Cocq,* many coats of dirt and varnish turned Rembrandt's bright canvas into a night scene. Finally cleaned in 1947, *The Night Watch* shows once again Rembrandt's interweaving of chiaroscuro and brilliant color. Rijksmuseum, Amsterdam.

Painting is a trade, and paintings are merchandise which can be used for publicity or for investment, above all to fill an empty wall. Shopkeepers, innkeepers, peasants buy paintings, sometimes at a fair. One wealthy Amsterdam bookseller in the 1670's owned forty-one canvases, although engravings which cost far less hung probably more often on a wall than oils. Painters worked to order: all of Vermeer's forty known canvases were turned out on somebody's command. If artists were wise, they turned out what the public liked: still-lifes, sights from daily life, the familiar landscape, above all self-glorifying portraits of which one workshop alone painted 5,000. All over the seventeenth-century west, but in the Netherlands more than elsewhere, portrait painting answered the need for ancestors and status characteristic of the age. Family portraits hung where family photographs might serve later generations. It also, at higher levels, served the political and diplomatic needs of statesmen and financiers who wanted to connect names and faces. In Paris, Catherine de Medici collected a vast mass of drawings for just this purpose.

Genre painting flourished depicting characteristic episodes or furnishing a conversation piece, favoring themes that were popular or even "low," like tavern brawls, lower-class festivities, or the vulgar doings of the marketplace. The Reformation had banned religious scenes, and the church market was quasi-nonexistent. Subtle, allegorical symbolism was out. Objective, concrete, local, the typical Dutch painter was anti-heroic. His paintings, full of meticulous detail rendered with few or no embellishments, were a constant homage to materialism.

This realism had sharp social implications. The group portraits which testified to the civic and corporate activity of the new society;* the polemical quality of genre paintings by Van Ostade or Jan Steen, which contrast the free untidy lower classes with the sombre sober bourgeois and whose revolutionary tones Louis XIV sensed; the lively and evocative novelty of real landscapes; the cozy cleanliness of a comfortable bourgeois home—all these were far distant from the dominant values of the outer world. This cheerful materialism would be transcended in the work of Rembrandt (1606–1669), more spiritual and incandescent than any of his contemporaries. But Rembrandt's greatness was little appreciated in his time. Problems of light, shade, and dramatic composition so obsessed him that most of the people he portrayed could not find themselves on the canvas, while the strange, enigmatic quality of his painting bothered observers. He was admired for his technical skill, but criticized for the way his spiritual torments and his plastic researches affected his style. A Dutch literary leader referring to Rembrandt twelve years after the painter's death regretted the poor man's failure to use his great gifts properly, his obstinate choice of vulgar models like washerwomen and peasants, rather than "a Greek Venus." And Samuel van Hoogstraten (1627–1678), once one of Rembrandt's pupils, insisted on the significance of the rules and values which Rembrandt had ignored, concluding: "The art of painting is in my opinion such a noble one that one comes near to disgracing it if one makes it serve to picture an object that is not in itself worth contemplating. Nothing but what is charming and elegant should be placed before our eyes by it."

The generation of Hals and Rembrandt, Terborch, Van Goyen, and Solomon van Ruysdael was followed by a distinguished band of men born between 1620 and 1640—landscapists like Jacob van Ruysdael (1628?–1682) and Meindert Hobbema (1638–1709), and painters of intimate scenes like Pieter de Hooch (1626–1679) and Jan Vermeer (1632–1675). But the influence of France and Italy could not be withstood. Artists who clung to the old tradition fared ill. The taste of the prosperous years following the Peace of Westphalia favored them little. Rembrandt went bankrupt in 1658 and was forced to sell his collections. A few years later Haarlem granted Hals a small annuity to eke out his old age in memory of his earlier fame. Steen had to work as an innkeeper, Vermeer was forced to pawn his paintings for bread, the landscape painters could not sell their canvases, Ruysdael and Hobbema fell on charity. The fashionable style was at first the Italianate one subsisting in the

---

* Most of the output and reputation of Frans Hals (1580?–1666) were based on single and group portraits, many of civic guard companies or governing boards of various institutions.

south, with its tenants summoned from Antwerp to The Hague to decorate the new palaces of the Orange family; and then the French-inspired academism, copied from Poussin and Le Brun. Clear light, sharp outlines, noble subjects, elegance, marked the decoration of Amsterdam Town Hall as much as the palaces of the nobility. It was the architects who built in the classic manner who got the orders for the great houses and the civic buildings of the new age. It was the painters who painted in the French or Italian manner who got the orders and who sold their wares: Biblical and mythological subjects, landscapes whose denizens—nymphs and satyrs, shepherds, and shepherdesses —contrasted strongly with the realistic vision that we associate with Dutch seventeenth-century art.

Precariously poised between comfort and crisis, the Dutch lived here and now in their thriving cities, their elegant but narrow houses so different from the emphatic palaces of other realms, their own oft-flooded land, not on Olympus or in some lurid heroic past. They lived in the present. Hence the realism. Hence also its devaluation, as the new oligarchy developed aristocratic pretensions of their own and soberness gave way (here too) to ostentation. Holland, which withstood its enemies, triumphed only to become like them; and, when it did, its contribution to European culture had been made. The classical style had triumphed. For a while.

Science

The development of a critical spirit in the literary arts, the growth of rational attitudes, the progress from exciting and adventurous but random strivings to order and system, are even more evident in the realm of science.

The Traditional View

The medieval view of the material world had been based on that of the ancient Greeks and especially on that of Aristotle. Guardian angel of the medieval schools, Aristotle taught that the world was a closed, stable entity, fixed once and for all inside a sphere studded with fixed stars. Within this outer sphere, two parts: the heavens and the "sublunary" world—one made up of incorruptible ether through which heavenly bodies carried by invisible spheres turn in eternal, uniform, circular motion; the other, ours, situated in an inferior position below the moon, unstable, corruptible, and made up of four basic elements: earth, water, fire, and air. Deep down within it, in the earth's entrails, Christian scholars situated Hell, through whose vents Satan's minions issued forth to trouble mankind.

In a world where all celestial forces and bodies behaved as men behave, loving, hating, mating, having their particular friends and rivals, good-natured and helpful when their course brought them close to their constellation-home, angry and inauspicious when clashing with some rival star, material and spiritual forces interpenetrated so that the astrologers' heaven reflected on a vaster scale the passions and possibilities of the world below.

Everywhere, obscure sympathies and corrrespondences ruled between stars, minerals, plants, and organs. Like the heavens, nature around us was anthropomorphic—alike to man—its parts like those of our own bodies corresponding to one another in a mysterious network of attractions and repulsions similar to that seen in the stars. In the great chain of being, the world of men, and that of nature, were related, interpenetrating and interdependent, disorder in society reflected in natural disorders like plagues or droughts, disorders in the heavens foretelling its counterpart on earth. "The heavens themselves blaze forth the death of princes," Shakespeare tells us; and no one could forget that Christ's own birth was heralded by a star.

The connection between heavenly and human bodies, heavenly motions and human activities, could be divined by logic and analogy. "These late eclipses in the sun and moon portend no good to us," mumbles a character in *King Lear*. The Sun dominated the heart, the Moon the brain, Mars imparted courage, Venus sensuality. The conjunction of particular planets during their courses created special circumstances: Saturn and Mars could bring syphilis, Saturn and Jupiter the plague, the phases of the moon were relevant for bleedings, purgings, haircuts, and, of course, for the farmer's calendar. Material causality, if perceived, was equated to and overlaid by the activity of such invisible magic forces, so that Catherine de Medici consulted Nostradamus the soothsayer, and Popes fixed the day and time of their coronation according to the auspices of stars.

The scientific thought of the Renaissance (see Part I, pp. 80–87) had made its greatest contribution in two directions. It had accepted the notion of change itself, been ready to discard old ideas for new, shaken the hold of ancient stereotypes. At the same time, the contemporary demand for more accurate description and control of time and space had set off a search for structures and regularities in every sphere, and stressed the importance of mathematics. The Renaissance had also seen a revival of interest in Platonic thought; and Plato's works, now made available in good Latin translations, reflected that philosopher's high regard for mathematics—a key to God and to his universe. The original meaning of mathematics had been simply "learning." They would once more come to be identified with learning in its most embracing sense. The God of Renaissance Neoplatonists was a geometrist, and scientists eager to discern the regularities of nature looked to geometry and to arithmetic to open the way.

Galileo, a painting by Sustermans.
Uffizi Gallery, Florence.

The Scientific Revolution

By the end of the sixteenth century such interests had improved the mathematical framework of science: decimal fractions had been introduced, letters were being used to represent quantities. But the instrument was not enough: a new attitude toward its use was needed. Aristotle, too, had admired mathematics for its precision and the elegant economy of its explanations. But he had held that different aspects of life or nature had different "sciences," different forms of learning, each with its appropriate language and methodology. Medieval "scientists" had agreed with him, attempting to accommodate their reasoning and approach to the special nature they attributed to the objects they investigated, according to the quality of the elements supposed to be part of their make-up. Clearly, stars were made up of different matter than stones, or men. The rules of their behavior must also be different.

Before a modern science could develop, a new attitude, a new way of thinking, had to develop too: above all, the admission that the same approach based on observation and reasoning could be applied to all branches of science, that this universal method could be used in dealing with every kind of datum and problem, and that it could yield not a collection of "curious observations," but a single, interconnected body of results. Diversity subsisted, but a diversity that was part of one integral whole subject to similar laws. Not "quality" but quantifiable data would matter in the new view, its collection and use facilitated by the common language of mathematics, and by the operations of reason, also common to all men.

This radical change in the structure and the avenues of thought, which is generally referred to as "the scientific revolution," would come about in the seventeenth century, and its greatest figures would be Galileo Galilei (1564–1642), Johannes Kepler (1571–1630), and René Descartes (1596–1650). By mid-seventeenth century, their work and that of others they inspired had done away with the moral connotation of physical events and with the anthropomorphic interpenetration of natural phenomena, had established the rule that physical experiments should be expressed in mathematical terms, had prepared science for specialization and formal organization in terms that we can recognize today.

Novelties and Survivals

The seventeenth century has been called the heroic age of rationalism in the West. And one can see newly discovered and speedily fashionable theories of mathematics and mechanics reflected in theater and state, philosophy and economics. Yet, we must beware the temptation to envisage the scientific activity of that pioneering time as akin to ours. A scientist of the twentieth century could not discuss his subject with a man of 1500, however learned. By 1600, he could find a very few men, by 1700 a good few more, with whom he could conduct a useful conversation. Men were still scrambling in the dark, grappling with mysteries whose very extent they could not conceive, grasping at what they could, advancing sometimes by accident incidental to ends which we today should count most strange. Napier of Merchistoun, the great Scottish mathematician, invented logarithms to speed his calculations of the number of the Beast of the Apocalypse. Before him, Michael Servetus had described the pulmonary circulation of the blood, although he did not grasp the role of the heart in it, but the purpose of his studies had been to prove that the "soul" lies in the blood. Infused by God through our mouths and nostrils, the soul, Servetus thought, passes from the left ventricle and lodges in the liver. This was the heresy (compounded by heterodox views of the Trinity) that led to his burning in 1553. As E. A. Burtt expressed it while explaining the connection of physics and metaphysics: "One of the most curious and exasperating features of this whole magnificent movement is that none of its great representatives appears to have known with satisfying clarity just what he was doing or how he was doing it."

Another basic difference between the science of our day and that of the sixteenth and seventeenth centuries was the divorce between theory and practice, between science and technology. Philosophers examined and explained natural phenomena, craftsmen tried to put them to practical use. The former produced ingenious theories, the latter objects and techniques often no less ingenious, but theory interested the latter as little as application concerned the former.

By the seventeenth century a few men began to see that knowledge is power in the most pragmatic sense, that to harness nature you must undestand its workings and its laws on more than a haphazard level. A growing number of philosophers and scientists tried to understand what craftsmen did, to serve both science and "technology" by uniting them. René Descartes was an artillery man; his analytic geometry could serve not only physics but ballistics. Rules of perspective that craftsmen and artists used affected the study of optics, and optical innovations were put to concrete use by painters and designers. If Napier's logarithms were meant to identify the Beast of the Apocalypse, calculus which they facilitated served surveyors, engineers, architects, and astronomers. Thus it was that awareness spread—slowly and gradually—that science could learn from experience and craft from theory, that skill could benefit from analysis and precision, and that pure science and systematic research could profit from and contribute to economic activities.

But while such views were held, sometimes unformulated, by men like Galileo or like Francis Bacon, in whose *New Atlantis* (1627) labor was eased by wonderful machines and production enriched by "diverse mechanical arts," they gained ground only slowly until the nineteenth century. The traditional way of acquiring control over nature was by magic or religious means and this view only wore away very slowly. Throughout the seventeenth century, the advances of natural science suggested a working alternative to magic, itself magic to many. If stars did not foretell the fate of men, they could aid the navigation of ships; if events were unpredictable, weather was no longer entirely so; if witches' cauldrons were unreliable, steam could at least be harnessed and put to work, and chemical substances also. If men with manmade lenses could work out the course of planets or see the minute organisms swimming in the blood, perhaps they could control their destinies. Certainly they could try. And science which gave them the courage also gave them the means.

But the process took a long, long time. From the first, its results evoked extraordinary excitement among the few who knew them, and parallel apprehensions. No one expressed the cosmological exhilaration of the late sixteenth century more ardently than Giordano Bruno, whose treatise *Of the Infinite Universe* appeared in 1584:

> Thus is the excellence of God magnified and the greatness of his kingdom made manifest; He is glorified not in one, but in countless suns; not in a single earth, but in a thousand, I say, in an infinity of worlds. Thus not in vain the power of the intellect which ever seeketh, yea, and achieveth the addition of space to space, mass to mass, unity to unity, number to number, by the science that dischargeth us from the fetters of a most narrow kingdom and promoteth us to the freedom of a truly august realm, which freeth us from an imagined poverty and straineth to the possession of the myriad riches of so vast a space, of so worthy a field, of so many culti-vated worlds. This science does not permit that the arch of the horizon that

our deluded vision imagineth over the Earth and that by our fantasy is feigned in the spacious ether, shall imprison our spirit under the custody of Pluto or at the mercy of a Jove. We are spared the thought of so wealthy an owner and subsequently of so miserly, sordid and avaricious a donor.*

But Bruno was burned as a heretic in 1600 and the German Faust story of 1587 shows Doctor Faustus as a godless rebel, seeking things he should not delve into, aspiring to powers and to knowledge not meant for him, pactioning with the devil and condemned to Hell. He would pay for free thought and rebellion just like the searchers and the scientists of the time who came to be suspected and reproved by Catholics and Lutherans alike.

More people felt like John Donne than like Giordano Bruno, when the future Dean of St. Paul's in his "Anatomy of the World" (1611) averred that

> . . . new Philosophy calls all in doubt,
> The element of fire is quite put out;
> The sun is lost, and th'earth, and no man's wit
> Can well direct him where to look for it.
> And freely men confesse that this world's spent,
> When in the Planets, and the Firmament
> They seek so many new; then see that this
> Is crumbled out againe to his Atomies.
> 'Tis all in peeces, all coherence gone;
> All just supply, and all Relation.

The New Cosmology

The first of these great mutations came in man's view of the heavens and of our place in them. For one thing, the structure of the universe had long been held as given once and for all, unchanging except in the world itself—the sublunary sphere where alone change, generation, and decay belonged—while the starry heavens remained immutable in their perfection. But in 1572 a new star appeared in the sky, suggesting the possibilities of change in a realm where, because of its perfection, no change had been imaginable.* A few years later, the Danish astronomer, Tycho Brahe, showed another newly discovered luminary to be no comet but a real star, far further than the moon, hence also contrary to the theory which had hitherto rationalized the phenomenon of comets by placing them in the corruptible sublunary sphere. Wrote Donne:

* *Giordano Bruno, His Life and Work,* translated by D. W. Singer (New York, 1950), p. 246.
* The star was noticed at the beginning of November, only three months after St. Bartholomew's Massacre (see p. 296), and many took it as an omen of worse things to come; perhaps, as a German painter explained, a condensation of the vapors of human sins, the mark of a poisonous fallout bringing evils of every sort, including "bad weather, pestilence and Frenchmen."

> Man has weav'd out a net, and this net throwne
> Upon the Heavens, and now they are his owne . . .

It was not nets that conquered the heavens, but calculations and lenses. Rudimentary telescopes, probably invented in 1608 by a Dutch oculist, Hans Lippersheg, would be used by Johannes Kepler in Tycho Brahe's wake to furnish a firm base for corrected Copernican theories, to draw up planetary tables, and establish the heliocentric pattern of a planetary system centering no longer about the earth but about the sun. In 1609, the Italian Galileo Galilei's superior knowledge of optics enabled him to build a much stronger telescope with which in 1610 he discovered the satellites of Jupiter, the spots of the sun (confirmed within a year by the observations of an Austrian Jesuit, Fr. Scheiner), and observed the moon, which he found similar to earth with its mountains and valleys. Observation of Jupiter and its satellites convinced Galileo that (by analogy and inference) the heliocentric theory must be correct and led him to try to re-establish the harmony of a world picture which new discoveries had sorely troubled. Kepler had observed that objects in themselves are inert and that they react in a predictably uniform manner to forces exerted upon them. Galileo put this to the test in a series of experiments which established the principles of inertia and the laws of movement that ruled not only inanimate objects but all the elements and—it soon appeared—even the circulation of the blood, which William Harvey's *De Motu Cordis* publicized in 1628.

Medicine

The practice of medicine had long been set in a restrictive traditionalism, the great authority of Galen and to some extent of Aristotle reigning unquestioned over the profession. Serious advances could not be made while the chemical function of drugs remained confused with magic and while the human body itself was considered unfit for scholarly research. Surgery was looked down on, partly because surgeons were not trained in universities and often knew no Latin. In 1215, the Fourth Lateran Council had forbidden clerks in holy orders (who until that time combined medicine and surgery) to practice surgery in order that they should not spill blood. Surgery was left to men who were neither scholars nor gentlemen and a distinction grew up between physicians, members of a learned profession, and surgeons who practiced a menial trade, often doubling as barbers or as dentists. Anatomy was studied in the most perfunctory manner, and rare dissections were carried out by assistants—not physicians or professors of medicine.

The sixteenth century saw the growth of a new inquiring spirit, especially with the great Flemish anatomist Andreas Vesalius (1514–1564), whose *Fabric of the Human Body* appeared in 1543, the same year as

Copernicus's *De Revolutionibus Orbium Celestium*. Vesalius had almost perished in Madrid for daring to dissect a man. By 1580, we find a Basque physician in Bilbao asserting that "in medicine, experience has greater force than reason, and reason more than authority." People were beginning to look before they reasoned, and to reason about what they actually saw rather than read.

In 1615, William Harvey (1578–1657), professor at the London College of Physicians, announced his theory of the circulation of the blood, which became more widely known when published thirteen years later. Harvey disagreed with the Galenic tradition in which veins and arteries were thought to form separate systems in the body. He assumed that capillaries allowed blood to pass from arteries to veins, and his theory, based on vivisection, embryology, and serious comparative research practiced what his contemporary, Bacon, preached: "The observation of concrete nature." It remained a working hypothesis questioned by many until in 1661 the development of microscopes enabled Marcello Malpighi (1628–1694) to actually *see* the capillary vessels and prove Harvey's theory.

Microscopes did for the infinitely small what telescopes did for the infinitely vast. Although high-powered microscopes were not developed until the 1830's, those that existed, magnifying things sixty to eighty times, opened up new worlds to biology and suggested great needs and possibilities in description, enumeration, and sheer discovery. Malpighi himself is considered to be the founder of animal and plant histology (the anatomical study of tissues). More important perhaps was Antonius van Leeuwenhoek (1632–1723), a citizen of Delft who, with no university training, pursued his hobby of microscopic anatomy to become the father of protozoology. In the mid-1670's Leeuwenhoek was to discover first microbes, then spermatozoa, and to shake very seriously the current assumptions of the origins of life and of living beings.

The Significance of the New Discoveries

Such discoveries were still in the future, but in Galileo's own lifetime movement had taken over from inertia, change from stability. Blood was no longer thought to be motionless in man's veins, a stagnant element in which animal spirits moved their bearer. Subject to the muscular contractions of the heart, it entered by veins and left by arteries whose obstruction could prevent its circulation. The world was no longer a limited entity, the earth standing still in the midst of a harmoniously revolving circle of celestial bodies—perfect, incorruptible, and at a uniform distance from it—but one of the diverse yet similar satellites of a sun whose spots showed it to be corruptible too, imperfect like the earth itself. New telescopes revealed new stars at incredible distances incapable of fitting into the old Aristotelian model. The calculations of Kepler had shown their movements to be not circular but elliptical, once again re-moved from what contemporaries imagined as perfection. The world itself moved around the sun like other planets, and objects on it moved according not to their intrinsic nature but to mathematical laws of gravity and weight. Not spirits but gravity and inertia affected their behavior. And Galileo dared suggest that, far from a criterion of per-fection, changelessness—if it were possible—would be an ill. It was more noble, certainly more exciting, to move, to grow, to change; and change was everywhere, not the hierarchic ordered stability of the Aristotelians, but change and movement proceeding all around according to the same natural laws, affecting the heavens as they did the earth.

A very revealing letter written by Kepler in 1605 shows that this had been a deliberate hope of the great inventors:

> My aim is to show that the heavenly machine is not a kind of divine, live being, but a kind of clockwork (and he who believes that the clock has a soul, attributes the maker's glory to the work), in so far as nearly all the manifold motions are caused by a most simple, magnetic and material force, just as all motions of the clock are caused by a simple weight. And I also show how these physical causes are to be given numerical and geometrical expression.*

Here was a new world, a limitless universe opening on infinity, united by laws applicable everywhere but no longer set. Neither settled nor, to those who understood the implications of these novelties, stable. John Donne's curious mind, always hungry for new fare, was fascinated by the news of Kepler's and Galileo's discoveries as much as by American ones; and his letters list Virginia and fresh-found stars in the same breath. In his poem on the first anniversary of the death of his patron's daughter (1611), the tone is sad less on account of the girl now one year dead than for the sake of an order and a world-image irretrievably lost, a new proportion with troubling implications of other worlds, where there arise

> New starres, and old doe vanish from our eyes.
> As though heav'n suffered earthquakes, peace or war,
> When new Towers rise, and old demolish't are.

The finite Aristotelian world, finite in its possibilities as it was in space but reassuring in its completeness and coherence, would give way to the infinite possibilities the new discoveries and even more the new suggestions opened. But not without a struggle. The challenge it implied to Genesis and to the Aristotelian predilections of the Church created the first and perhaps most powerful obstacles. Scheiner's superior in the Jesuit order, reassured by references to Aristotle, attributed his discovery of sunspots to a fault in the lenses or in the seer's eyes. The

* A. Koestler, *The Sleepwalkers* (London, 1956).

The dedication page of Galileo's *Dialogue*. Left to right are Aristotle, Ptolemy, and Copernicus.

Holy Office found the view that the sun stands still at the center of the universe "mad, philosophically false and wholly heretical, being contrary to Holy Writ" (1616). Galileo was arrested by the Inquisition (1633), the *Dialogue* (1632) in which he attacked Aristotelian doctrine placed on the Index, he himself forced to retract or face torture.

Since a great deal has been written about Galileo's recantation it is essential to understand that his trial for expounding Copernican views was chiefly triggered by his quarrelsome insistence on being right against all comers, that his judges were careful to spare him unnecessary trouble or humiliation, and that his brief imprisonment was first in a five-room apartment overlooking the Vatican gardens and then in even more comfortable quarters furnished by the Grand Duke of Tuscany, the Archbishop of Siena, and his own house in Florence. His punishment consisted largely of penitential psalms, which he was condemned to recite once a week for a period of three years; and these were actually recited, by consent of the authorities, by his daughter who was a Carmelite nun. If the verdict of the Inquisition formally quashed Copernican argument, its actions little injured the famous septuagenerian and did not even prevent the Jesuits from going on teaching the Copernican theory which he had defended. Galileo lived on in comfort, able to settle the new science of dynamics in his *Dialogues Concerning Two New Sciences* (1636) published in Leyden before he went blind in 1637, "so that this heaven, this earth, this universe, which I, by marvelous discoveries and clear demonstrations, have enlarged a thousand times beyond the belief of the wise men of bygone ages, henceforward for me is shrunk into such a small space as is filled by my own bodily sensations." But he continued working, dictating, receiving visitors (including Milton in 1638), and died in 1642 surrounded by friends and pupils.

What was much worse than the intimidation of Galileo is that proponents of the new views which he represented found no integrated system to replace the Aristotelian phenomenology. They knew they were advancing but they did not know quite to what. Their sense of conquest was reflected on the title page of Bacon's *Novum Organum* (1620) showing a ship in full sail trying to pass the columns of Hercules which had set the limit of the ancient world. And Francis Bacon's works, like *Of the Increase of Science* (1623), attacking Aristotle and Plato who had too long set up a screen between Nature and man, advised his readers to query nature directly by experience whereby they would learn to order it by obeying it, that is, through having learned to know its laws.

Bacon's empiricism provided a vigorous impulse to scientific investigation but failed to provide the structure and the system needed by his age. Similarly, Galileo too appears as something of an empiricist. He insisted that mathematics could interrogate nature, that nature's laws and language are mathematical, that geometry can dominate and illumine physics. But his experiments and calculations left too much out: the resistance of air, the force of gravity. The principle of inertia had not been worked out in a way that could be generally applied, but merely stated. The connection between mathematics and reality remained to be established. In the meantime, the "natures" of Aristotelian physics would be replaced by "forces" of a would-be more scientific kind, especially magnetic ones explaining repulsion or attraction and providing the basis of movement which had, as we have seen, itself become the foundation of new physics. But forces of this kind were only a re-edition of the older anthropomorphic views and lent themselves to fresh efforts to endow the stars with life. So, while old structures crumbled and new discoveries generated endless speculation and debate, their contradictions only increased the chaos and disorder of the time and, by seeming to show the insufficiencies of reason, spurred the arguments and the speculations of the skeptics and of the "libertines," whom we shall examine shortly.

Science and Philosophy

Descartes

The new achievements of scientific research suggested further research. They also suggested what the scientific approach should be: "The wit and mind of man," wrote Bacon in his *Advancement of Learning*, "if it work upon matter, which is the contemplation of the creatures of God, worketh according to the stuff, and is limited thereby; but if it work upon itself, as the spider worketh his web, then it is endless and brings forth indeed cobwebs of learning, admirable for the fineness of thread and work, but of no substance or profit."

The deduction seemed reasonable enough: things not words, observation not rationalization, should be the subject matter of scientific investigation; and a young Frenchman from Touraine applied these views in his own development, seeking experience and reflecting upon it, going to the sources of knowledge in the men who had it rather than in books, thinking that he "should find much more truth in the reasonings of each individual with reference to the affairs in which he is personally interested . . . than in those conducted by a man of letters in his study, regarding speculative matters of no practical moment . . ." But René Descartes (1596–1650) was fated to give the problem of experience and experiment a fateful twist, shifting it brusquely from a search for positive experience to a query as to what positive experience consists of.

The triumph of heliocentrism, based on the expanded scale of observation, paradoxically suggested that the experience of the senses was to be distrusted. Our senses gave us the impression that the earth was flat, that constellations turned around it, that space was limited, and the moon a disc in the sky. All this had been proved wrong, and, while some found in this exhilarating proof of man's faculties, Descartes was struck rather by their failings, and especially by the shortcomings of our oft-misleading senses. Since we cannot trust experience and impression, we must rely on reason. But reason itself can be misleading unless handled critically. Descartes began by doubting everything that lent itself to doubt: the learning of the past, the statements of others, the evidence of his senses, and came down to rock bottom in his own existence, which he could not doubt, for who would do the doubting if he did not exist. He doubted, that is, he thought, and, if he thought, then he existed. *Cogito ergo sum.* I think, therefore I am.

Think by all means: but how think right? For Descartes, the answer was evident. On the night of November 10, 1619, the Angel of Truth had appeared to him and verified his own belief that "mathematics was the sole key needed to unlock the secrets of nature." Within a few months, the young man had invented analytical geometry, an important tool for relating numbers and space. If space, like time, could be expressed in exact quantitative terms, it should be possible to think straight. The world of approximations and fumbling, the superficial semblances of sense perception, guesswork, inference, could be abandoned in favor of a "universe of precision, of exact measure, of strict determination." Mathematical studies convinced him that all sciences are one, all amenable to mathematical treatment once they are purged of (qualitative) irrelevancies, so that order and measurement can reveal essentials.

From this base Descartes proceeded to reconstruct the world he had just torn down, but on new and, to him, more valid principles. He thought. He could conceive greater perfection as well as his own imperfection. This suggested a perfect being, God, from whom the idea of perfection derived. The perfect God would not deceive and, since He had formed his mind (else where would the concept of perfection within it come from?), neither would his mind deceive him, although his senses might if they were not watched and checked by the mind. "All the things which we clearly and distinctly *conceive* are true." Notions and ideas which are clear and distinct proceed from God and hence are real and true. And the closest we can get to clarity and distinction is by mathematics, which enables us to check and measure things that otherwise might deceive us. Mathematics is the philosopher's key to reality. Sense experience is less trustworthy than abstraction: taste, smell, vision are less "real" than weight or measure, which are subject to exactness and lend themselves to the kind of mathematical expression that reason can grapple with independent of the senses.

Thus it appeared that the empirical investigation of matter had led to a new disdain of it; and that the reaction against the abstract reasonings of traditional scholars had bred a new worship of abstraction. The full title of Descartes' most famous work (which he drew up in Latin and then translated into French in order to reach a wider public) is *A Discourse Concerning the Method for Proper Use of Reason and Search for Truth in the Sciences* (1637). The Truth he used his method to discern was, of course, the nature of God, man, and the universe. Briefly, God was good, the universe infinite, man a kind of machine, different from animals in that he had free will—a soul. Man like other animals is a mechanical contraption within a world that is one too, with all particles of matter measurable and predictable according to laws of motion and mechanics. But man's soul, acting on the mind, affects the

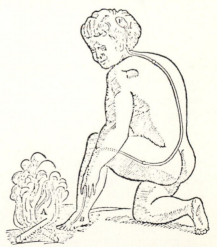

An illustration of the human reflex from *De Homine,* by Descartes.

Warder Collection

body too through the mysterious pineal gland, and thus unites the otherwise separate and distinct realms of mind and matter.

It would be soon argued that there was no way for an immaterial soul to affect the material body, and that Cartesian dualism begged more questions than it solved. One suggestion, known as the theory of occasionalism, was that "the purer spirit" was not actually "united to this clod" of corporeity but that they only seem to interact, like two clocks set to tick parallel to each other but working separately although the chimes of one seem to respond to the time shown on the other's face. Another was the *idealistic* argument, generally identified with the eighteenth-century philosopher George Berkeley, Bishop of Cloyne in Ireland, who denied the very existence of matter. Berkeley held that material objects exist only as the reflection of mental events, and that what we think we perceive outside ourselves is only the result of something going on within our minds. Continuity in nature, as well as our own existence, reflects God's existence as an eternal being continuously perceiving everything. Hence the well-known limerick exchange in which Mgr. Ronald Knox presented Berkeley's theory:

> There was a young man who said, "God
> Must think it exceedingly odd
> If he finds that this tree
> Continues to be
> When there's no one about in the Quad."

This evokes a reply:

> Dear Sir: Your astonishment's odd:
> *I* am always about in the Quad.
> And that's why the tree
> Will continue to be
> Since observed by
> Yours Faithfully, God.

Thomas Hobbes, on the other hand, had already evolved the diametrically opposed idea in which mental events do not exist independently at all, but are themselves called forth by matter in motion. Here was philosophy calling all in doubt with a vengeance.

The pious conclusions could not make up for the skepticism of the method, the excellent intentions for the subversive results. Placed on the Roman Index of Prohibited Books in 1665, condemned by the Sorbonne in 1671, the works of Descartes had already caused a rumpus in the schools. In 1656, professors at Leyden University in the freest of all seventeenth-century states were required to take a kind of loyalty oath "to leave off propagating the philosophemata drawn from Doctor Cartesius's philosophy, which today give offense to a number of people."

New Abstractions

But the new vogue of mathematics could not be held back. Nature was seen no longer as an organism but as a machine, natural processes as based on motion, capable of expression and subject to analysis in quantitative terms which triumphed over the qualitative distinctions of Aristotelian tradition. The laws of reality became equivalent to the laws of motion and the idiom of the new laws would be mathematics. Where in 1644 Descartes had entitled his major work *The Principles of Philosophy*, in 1687 Isaac Newton (1642–1727) would write the *Mathematical Principles of Natural Philosophy*. Slowly space and time, even then, became calculable: seven years after John Napier had published his invention of logarithms, the slide rule appeared, based on logarithmic principles. Mathematics was applied to actuarial science, used in public finance and the private insurance business. Life tables began to appear, the first really good ones calculated by the astronomer Edmund Halley in 1693; but already in 1671 Holland could reform its state scheme of life annuity bonds on the basis of actuarial calculations. Statistics were recognized as a useful tool. In 1662 John Graunt published his *Natural and Political Observations upon the Bills of Mortality, with Reference to the Government, Religion, Trade, Growth, Ayre, Diseases, and the several Changes of the said City of London,* based on records of deaths that had occurred in London, and which would provide the root of modern statistical studies. An English statistical office was set up in 1696. Sir William Petty (1623–1687), the first man to use vital and trade statistics, published his *Political Arithmetic* (1683), which assumed that human actions are measurable in mathematical terms and can be projected and interpreted in order to predict, understand, and control.

Newton

The crucial role in validating such assumptions was played by Isaac Newton. The puny orphan prematurely born on Christmas Day who, said his mother, might have fitted into a quart mug, grew up to be the greatest scientific genius of his century. He did not seem likely to make a good farmer, so he was sent to Cambridge University when he was eighteen. By twenty-two, just after the great plague and fire of London, he had developed the methods of infinitesimal and differential calculus, essential for the study of motions. He had also invented the law of gravitation, having watched an apple drop and concluded that it fell as it did because the earth pulled it, and that the moon would likewise drop were it not kept from doing so by the centrifugal force of its motion in a circle. Departing from this hypothesis, he then calculated the magnitude of the forces involved, in order to deduce the inverse law of gravitation.

The point about Newton's explanation of why planets move the way they do was not—or not only—that it came nearer truth than previous explanations, providing a simpler and more precise solution to the conundrums tackled by Copernicus, Kepler, and Galileo, but that his very concept of an explanation was new. His predecessors tended to say that a planet moved because of a moving principle. As a medical student in a contemporary play by Molière explains, opium sends men to sleep "because there is in it a dormitive virtue whose property is to soothe the senses." This kind of nature, intelligible to men in terms of familiar qualities, was simply not good enough. "To tell us that every Species of Things is endow'd with an occult specifick Quality by which it acts and produces manifest Effects," he wrote in 1669 in a text that would be printed only in 1704 (his *Opticks*), "is to tell us nothing." He devised laws which could be verified by mathematical calculation. There would be no more conjectures: only proof "by Reason and Experiments." Experiment, observation, produce simple laws that anyone can test. If the tests check out, you have scientific truth. Here was a method that did no concern itself with *causes* (who moved the planets) or philosophically ultimate reasons (to what purpose did they move), but only with ascertainable facts, accessible to any trained mind, and able to be worked out quantitatively.

Newton's *Mathematical Principles* followed this course. The work claims to "demonstrate the frame of the System of the World" by deduction from simple mathematical laws. No higher wisdom was needed to explain how the universe behaved than that of the mathematician.

John Maynard Keynes, the twentieth-century economist, who owned many of Newton's manuscript notes, found that many of them dealt with the transmutation of elements, the philosophers' stone, and the elixir of life, and decided that the philosopher's deepest instincts had been "occult, esoteric, romantic." But if magic and mysticism show Newton as a man of his time, his scientific discoveries show how men of his time could (and did) transcend its limits, asserting other values and opening doors into another age.

In the old view, natural phenomena had carried moral lessons, analogies between celestial and worldly harmonies had argued from the ones to justify the others. Now Edmund Halley (1656–1742) calculated the course of comets, showing that those of 1305, 1456, 1531, 1607, and 1682 were one and the same star, traveling on the same track, and predicting that it would appear again in 1758, as it did. Obviously, a calculable star lent itself but ill to ominous interpretations. The supernatural machinery by which, as in Shakespeare's world, man bent beneath "the yoke of inauspicious stars," was left to run down.

There were even greater consequences arising out of the revolution Copernicus began and Newton perfected. Since laws governing the motion of bodies on earth and in the heavens were the same, pendulums and projectiles could be used to learn about the movements of the planets. Mechanical experiments could help explain celestial motions, mathematical equations could reveal the structure of a world machine where observations of the heavens could be applied on earth and mundane experiments illuminate the sky. The work of Newton made this very clear. The Aristotelian universe had taken over a century to crumble into pieces. Newtonian physics replaced it with a comprehensive mechanism where heaven and hell had lost their place, miracles which went counter to mechanical laws were unnecessary, and God who made those laws was slowly separated from the grand clockwork he had set in motion.

Even at the most vulgar level, the passion for figures created a new interest in dates. Henceforth individuals of a certain standing, beginning with richer peasants, liked to record events even on furniture and objects which would be carved or painted with the date of the birth or marriage or other festivity that called them forth. Dates suggest chronology and chronology itself suggests a new sense of time, of sequence, of order and division, concepts characteristic of modern man.

The Seats of Learning

These principles preside over the culture of the seventeenth century. But with a difference. Whether in Jesuit, Protestant, or Oratorian schools, the educational structure imparted a classical culture based on Greek and Latin, turning out men infused with the thought and works of Plutarch, Xenophon, Pliny, and Cicero.

Universities also taught the classics, but were less progressive. They continued to function but hardly to foster intellectual advances, or disseminate them. The traditional establishment feared the effect of novelties on theology, on faith, and on their courses. At the University of Utrecht the ideas of Galileo, or Harvey, and of Descartes were long refused admittance. The professor of medicine had to promise on appointment that he would keep to currently accepted doctrines. The first man to publicly touch on the circulation of the blood raised a storm in the university. Throughout the seventeenth and eighteenth centuries, the many schemes to foster scientific research, set up observatories, found museums or laboratories, had nothing to do with universities, but with private or state enterprise, with new-founded academies or institutes, with bodies like the Royal Society in England or the Academy of Sciences in France. Most important, perhaps, were the activities of more or less private discussion groups meeting in some drawing room or collector's cabinet. It was through them, or through the many small associations—assemblies, *conférences, conversaziones*—that the first laboratories and observatories were set up, that the greatest number of instruments were perfected and standardized, that scientific tracts, essays, and discourses were printed or circulated in manuscript from hand to hand, that groups of science-minded men could meet and collaborate among furnaces and telescopes and microscopes. Universities and colleges still offered professional training in law, theology, and other branches of traditional scholarship, but innovations of every kind would be opposed by the regular faculty.

Popular education, widespread in the Middle Ages when every parish tried at least to have a school, when cathedral or abbey schools had been open to all worthy comers so that Suger, son of a serf, had been taught at St. Denis together with the future Louis VII—all this had been ruined by religious wars. Few rural parishes still maintained schools and many cities had none or only a fraction of what the past had known. The new system which grew up on the ruins of the old was based on colleges for boys whose parents could afford to pay their fees. Free education limped along as best it could, nor was it supposed to go too far: no classical Latin, no classics at all, no bourgeois pupils. The poor, as Richelieu's *Testament* remarks, should not be too knowledgeable, for then vanity and presumption would banish obedience and labor.

In the colleges, education was devoted to developing faculties of mind, of thought, of abstraction. Personal experience was seen as most valuable when intellectual, most demeaning when involved with manual labor. Experiments were banished, just as the physicians banished the vulgar activities of surgeons. "All our dignity," as Pascal explains, "lies in the mind." But in the thinking mind: intuition, like concrete experience, is secondary to logical deduction, to the theories and principles to which it must be fitted. Just as jurists had substituted the logic of Roman law for the fumbling disorder of custom, so Descartes substituted the logical progression of reasoning and mathematics for the accepted traditions of the past. Facts might contradict principles, as the discoveries of Harvey or Newton contradicted those of Descartes, but facts had to adjust to principles or be ignored. It was a philosophy for times when, as Pascal had it, "there is nothing which is entirely in our power except our thoughts."

Since such times are frequent, Cartesianism spread and with it, or with its variants, the kind of intellectual convictions that, ignoring history, tradition, and concrete experience, claim a superior objectivity and a universal validity to which particular nonconformities are irrelevant in logic and undesirable in fact. The principles suggested the rules to which human activity should conform, among these the rules of aesthetics, the ideal of artistic beauty inspired by the ancients and confirmed by reason: harmony, unity, order, mastery of all elements in a given equation, including those unruly feelings and passions which always threaten and sometimes overthrow the perfect balance, spoiling the unity of the whole.

To the code which could be deduced from such basic principles, the arts also owed allegiance, excluding external irrelevancies and adventures to come as close as possible to an ideal and noble whole, as appreciated by those elevated souls, that cultivated taste, alone worthy and able of perfection. Nicolas Rapin (1540–1608) had defined these: "Truth is nearly always defective by the mixture of singular conditions which compose it. Nothing is born in the world which does not depart from the perfection of its idea in being born. We must seek the origins and models in the likelihood and the universal principles of things where nothing material or singular can corrupt them."

Here we might note that even in the very sensible fables of La Fontaine there is no trace of the personal experience of animals and land which La Fontaine certainly acquired in his post as royal inspector of waters and forests, but rather the memory of Aesop's Fables. As always, vicarious experience was held more valuable than one's own. Yet, along with rationality and rules, another thread appears as important as the others, and as firmly based on the ancients: that of common sense, of moderation, of "that constant observation of measure" which Charles de St.-Evremond (1610?–1703) recommended, which Montaigne praised, which Descartes practiced when he chose those "opinions most moderate and furthest from excess . . ."

Empiricism

Quite apart from traditionalist opposition, Cartesianism was not the only major doctrine of its time. Its rationalism, insisting on clarity and logic but resting on *a priori* argument, challenged and was challenged in turn by another attitude, which we have met already and which we now meet again: empiricism. Where rationalists doubted the value of sense experience, the empirical approach, on the contrary, sought sensory evidence from which it could generalize and denied the validity of intuitive revelation and of the deductions derived from it. There was a humanistic tradition, going back beyond Montaigne, which tried to replace the metaphysical view of man current in its day with a positive, empirical study of *men* in the infinite variety of their types and customs and beliefs: not automata subject to mechanics but individuals calling for a kind of sociology. The chief instrument of their inquiries had been erudition—history and literature, travelers' tales and chronicles —which tended to clash with the sterner rationalism, the stricter rules of evidence that the Cartesians set forth. For the Cartesians knowledge began with self-knowledge; for the humanists self-knowledge was best attained through learning. The paradox was that Cartesian rationalism was too highly systematic to permit the untrammeled development of scientific thought, while the methods of relativistic humanism were too naïve and credulous in treatment of evidence to base a science on.

In effect, to begin with, scientists seemed fascinated by the varied possibilities of experiment, but in an incoherent, rather childish way, seeking often to amuse rather than understand, to spark or satisfy curiosity rather than build an organized theory. This reflects the mentality of men who are interested in scientific activity or knowledge, but have not yet defined it, do not quite know what it is. A French traveler of 1660 records his fascination with hydraulic machines, telescopes, thermometers, and barometers but also with old wives' remedies; he is intrigued by Mr. Hobbes, whom he visits in London, and by Descartes, but also by hearsay and legend. There were so many ideas abroad that it was hard to tell yet which were facts, which science, hard to apply exact standards, hard to know how measuring and testing could be used on different things. It is possible that more machines were devised to move scenery, amaze, delight, surprise the public, and provide entertainment than for scientific research or technical production.

We must remember that the science of this period still retained close connections with alchemy and astrology. Tycho Brahe's island estate of Uraniburg, which attracted a stream of distinguished visitors, including James VI of Scotland, seems to have been a magic Disneyland, full of gadgets and automatic wonders, statues that turned on invisible mechanisms, bells which brought men running from far away as if by magic and, behind this, the careful, precise, hard-drinking astronomer, rather like the Wizard of Oz, with his notorious silver nose, the man who revolutionized astronomical method by insisting on accuracy and continuity in what was still a very hit-or-miss affair.

Alchemy continued to mingle superstition, prejudice, and research. Johann Rudolph Glauber (1604–1668), who discovered sodium sulfate (Glauber salt), the best purgative of a purge-conscious time, also devised really effective laboratory kilns which he called "philosophical furnaces." The Frenchman Jean Rey found that calcination increased the weight of metals; the Fleming Van Helmont discovered carbonic gas and founded the study of gases as part of his alchemistical research. But it was a Swiss charlatan and genius, Paracelsus (1493?–1541), who first insisted that the purpose of alchemy was to make not gold but medicines, and introduced the preparation and use of mineral as well as herbal drugs. The confusion between chemistry and magic was hard to kill. Richelieu and Louis XIII themselves patronized an alchemist who promised to turn base metal into gold, and Louis attended a demonstration in the Louvre where two musket balls were turned into a bar of gold. Given the budget difficulties of the time, anything was worth trying. As late as 1708 a charlatan persuaded the finance minister of Louis XIV that he was on the track of the philosopher's stone; he had a laboratory set up at Versailles and became the cynosure of all eyes until arrested two months later.

Perhaps court boredom had as much to do with this as persistent

An engraving after a drawing by
Tycho Brahe of an equatorial model
from his Magic Garden at Uraniburg.

credulousness and persistent need. Yet, for a long time, even to scholars
and scientists, the Copernican universe remained "an ingenious absurdity." For the future Cardinal de Retz passing his doctorate in the Sorbonne
(1631) there continued to be three skies, of which the lowest was a liquid
one. Was this divorce between men and science an application of the
dictum that nothing should be accepted without evidence, or a negation of
belief in common sense? Only in 1654 do we find Cyrano de Bergerac
(philosopher-swordsman) insisting: "We must not believe all things of
a man, because a man can say all things. We must believe of a man only
that which is human," that is, only that which seems possible. It was the
first inkling that the impossible would soon be banished from serious
thought. A few years later Robert Boyle's significantly titled *Sceptical
Chemist* (1661) divorced chemistry from alchemy. Insisting that chemistry's only function was to investigate natural phenomena, Boyle explained the nature of chemical combination between different substances and elements, and laid the foundations of organic chemistry.*

The inclination to reason and argue your way through problems is
characteristic of an age when the mind is subtle but techniques are rough
and not sufficiently elaborate to permit refined observation and experiments. But the method of arguing one's way through problems created
a kind of mentality which, highly skilled in this particular technique of
analysis and construction, tended to reject all others and resisted attempts to use more empirical ways as both misleading and demeaning. In
the second half of the seventeenth century, however, the challenge of
the empiricists pressed back not only the limits of knowledge but such

* Yet even the great experimenter went as far as Ireland to be "touched" by a famous
healer of the time, Valentine Greatrix.

attitudes toward it. The Royal Society, founded in 1660, was hailed by the poet John Dryden as ". . . truly Royall who behold the Law and rule of beings in your Maker's mind." That applied even more strongly to the Royal Academy of Sciences, founded in Paris a few years later. But such Cartesian views of scientific enterprises were balanced by an ode of 1666 rejoicing that the Royal Society concerned itself not with *words* but *things.* We can find the Society parodied in *Gulliver's Travels* (1726) as the Grand Academy of Lagado, whose members' projects included the extraction of sunbeams from cucumbers, the calcination of ice into gunpowder, and the placing of sundials on weathercocks balanced so that the motions of the earth would counteract the impulsions of the wind.*

One important function of such academies and scientific societies was the rapid expansion, not of activity and research alone, but of publicity for new discoveries and ideas. International scientific journals were founded—in England and France in 1665, a few years later in Italy and Germany—which spread the news of important work, allowing researchers from Italy to Holland to compare their findings. Like the scholarly world of the Middle Ages, the scientific world knew no frontiers, spoke a common language, followed a common goal, however diverse the paths. The empirical experimental methods they accepted implied willingness to weigh probability and to accept tentative answers based on limited observations and calculations. They also implied toleration of other views, subject to experiment and confirmation.

Science and Religion

A cosmopolitan community transcending political boundaries, a pursuit which sets man's judgment over against traditional authority: no wonder the new science was connected and sometimes compared with Protestant mentality; the more so since the Protestant stress on personal religious *experience* was not very far removed from the experimental spirit. Such sympathies had been noticeable from the first. Paracelsus, the

* The Florentine *Academia del Cimento* (the Academy of Experiment) had been set up as early as 1657 by two Medici brothers—the Grand Duke Ferdinand II and his brother, Leopold—who had been pupils of Galileo and of Torricelli, discoverer of the principle of the barometer, and who were themselves amateur scientists and experimenters. When Ferdinand became a Cardinal in 1667, however, the Academy was discontinued, possibly because its pursuits did not jibe with those of a Prince of the Church. In Germany, a number of lesser societies founded in the course of the seventeenth century divided their attention between scientific experiment and the study and cultivation of the German tongue. The most enduring was the Berlin Academy, instituted in 1700 through the efforts of Leibniz, one of the last academies to be founded.

alchemist and doctor, admired Luther and imitated his burning of the papal bull by a bonfire which he made out of the works of medical authorities. Luther in turn appreciated the allegorical lessons of the alchemist's art, whose chemical processes he likened to the resurrection of the dead when God's fire would separate the righteous from the ungodly. The careers of Galileo and Gassendi show that Protestants had no monopoly of scientific enterprise. In time, however, the conservative pressures of the Counter-Reformation Church, the livelier, freer, more inquiring atmosphere of Protestant countries—not so much because they were Protestant but because they were in the van of economic enterprise—stressed the coincidence. Of ninety-two foreigners elected to the Paris Academy of Sciences between 1666 and 1866, only sixteen were Catholics, five were Jews or of indeterminate faith, seventy-one were Protestant.

The Calvinist Mentality

The Calvinist mentality in particular seems to have lent itself to the new approach. The Calvinists saw God as a great legislator, the universe as a vast structure of divine laws which men have to discover. As Francis Bacon put it, himself the son of a devoutly Puritan mother, "we cannot command nature except by obeying her." This attitude could easily be transferred from theology to science, from moral to natural laws, which were seen as interconnected. The historian of the Royal Society of London, for instance, held that the Royal Society and the Church of England "may lay equal claim of the word reformation; the one having compassed it in religion, the other purposing it in philosophy." Both, he observed, rejected "corrupt copies" for original sources, ancient traditions for novelties; both "suppose alike that their ancestors might err" and "follow the great precept of the apostle of trying all things." A Puritan divine preaching before Charles I attacked the notion of papal infallibility by arguing that "we may learn to take nothing merely upon trust, nor to think things are so, only because the Church hath said." Like the new Philosophy, Puritanism, too, called all in doubt (at least all things tradition had enshrined), seeking to replace tradition with a coherence truer to God's will and nature, looking deliberately "to overcome the necessities and miseries of humanity," and asking with Bacon that knowledge be devoted to "the relief of man's estate."

More important, Protestant reformers challenged the reigning concept of hierarchy which, in nature as in politics, envisaged a graded chain of beings and relations, each intermediate to the next, each more perfect than the next. The coincidence here with the new scientific thought was not one which religious men would necessarily favor, but it could not help affecting the minds of men. The old hierarchical universe had become a neutral one, whose laws applied as well on earth as they did in heaven. All parts of nature and of man were equal, none were more *base* or *noble,* not spirit more than matter, not mind more than body, not even manual labor inferior to nonmanual. Such theories and their implications took long to be exploited, but they were available henceforth for equalitarian use.

Meanwhile, Calvinist theology eliminated the gradations of authority and replaced them by the absolute power of a Deity whose decrees were predeterminate, orderly, unchanging, allowing for no miracles. "God alters no law of Nature," wrote the Puritan Master of Emmanuel College at Cambridge, in the beginning of the seventeenth-century. His decrees were what Descartes called the "laws established in nature by God": from predestination to mechanical determinism. And the elimination of hierarchical intermediaries from theology, which pushed angels and other miracle workers out of theological and scientific speculation, went side by side with new theories of sovereignty in which the absolute monarch dispensed with intermediaries and exercised his power directly, just as the divine lawgiver was supposed to do.

The Thinkers and Their Impact

The new absolutist theories found analogies in the central role of the sun in the universe, the central role of the heart in the body. William Harvey in 1628 had already compared Charles I to "the sun of the world around him, the heart of the republic," and he had made this view explicit in a striking passage:

> The heart is the beginning of life; the sun of the microcosm, even as the sun in his turn might well be designated the heart of the world; for it is the heart by whose virtue and pulse the blood is moved, perfected . . .; it is the household divinity which, discharging its function, nourishes, cherishes, quickens the whole body, and is indeed the foundation of life, the source of all action. . . . The heart, like the prince in a kingdom, in whose hands lies the chief and highest authority, rules over all; it is the original and foundation from which all power is derived, on which all power depends in the animal body.

A century later, Joseph Priestley, a chemist and a Unitarian, felt that the Pope had "reason to tremble even at an air pump or an electrical machine," for the effect they might have on the Church he headed.

But such possibilities, in the long run, affected more than the Roman Church. In the first place, those who voiced or demonstrated them were never popular within the schools or with the Churches that dominated them. Scientific trail-blazers were always forced out of their academic posts and generally found shelter under the patronage of some benevolent prince who appreciated their astrological or medical skills: Kepler became imperial mathematician, Harvey the court physician of James I,

Galileo, as we have seen, was protected by the Duke of Tuscany. This too only changed slowly, as the seventeenth century drew on. John Aubrey, the English memorialist, places the watershed in mid-century and writes: "Till about the year 1649, 'twas held a strange presumption for a young man to attempt an innovation in learning."

Yet the defenders of the old order had perfectly good reason to feel disturbed. The new ideas had intensely subversive implications. Those who, like Donne, were troubled by them were right in ruing the passing of old relevancies. Within a century of Copernicus's death the finite universe was gone, replaced by an infinity of space and stars and suns with their own planet systems, in which man's own unique earth was just another "speck of cosmic dust."

As the new cosmology perfected its mechanistic view of the way the world works, God became less and less essential to the operations which it postulated. Predestination in religion matched cosmic mechanics in natural science; and this meant that God had irrevocably decided all that is to be once and for all. It could turn an omnipotent God into an impotent observer bound by the laws he himself decreed, unable or unwilling to intervene in the fixed course of his own creation. The absolute ruler could become the constitutional head of a cosmic system with which, as Newton reassuringly pointed out, there was no need to tinker and, in due course, a *Roi fainéant* (an idle king), formally deferred to and increasingly ignored. At last, when Napoleon asked the great mathematician and astronomer Pierre Laplace (1749–1827) what role God played in his world system, Laplace replied, "Sire, I had no need of this hypothesis." Demoted to the rank of a hypothesis, God would be banished from observatories and laboratories where, apparently, he was no longer needed.

Skeptics and Libertines

The first to entertain such notions were to be found among those intellectuals described by their contemporaries as *libertines*: free thinkers who exercised their critical spirit on the accepted authorities, ways, and values of the world around them, sometimes with disintegrating results. They were of different kinds and came to different conclusions: some merely skeptical, suspending judgment on unproven claims; others Deist, believing in a gentle, tolerant God—first cause and creator of first principles—indifferent to sects and cults; others atheistic, denying God altogether; some more, some less discreet about the gist of their beliefs. But—doctors, lawyers, men of letters, or dissolute noblemen, often very young—they always remained a tiny minority of the thinking public and they are mentioned here more in the light of their future significance than of their contemporary strength. For, in their works, drawn up while Louis XIII and Louis XIV reigned, we may find the roots of most of the philosophical positions of the eighteenth century.

The philosophical developments we have already seen and those that we are still about to notice did not take place in isolation, any more than the scientific developments just discussed. Both were close reflections of the world around them and both, in particular, were strongly affected by contemporary religious attitudes which they in turn affected. The universe of Western Christendom had burst asunder. A mental structure in which religious diversity had no place was shattered and hustled into accepting variety as a real possibility. Once the division within Christendom itself was accepted, once the possibility of coexistence began to be admitted, other diversities followed or were discovered and were eventually integrated in a new model of reality. The Wars of Religion contributed to the change.

Reason and Relativity

The various essays Michel de Montaigne wrote between 1572 and his death dealt with a world in which the traditionally Christian hierarchy has been replaced by luck, by chance, and by a kind of reasonable opportunism. Religion's place shifted from the center toward the margin of everyday life. Rules of morality and behavior, no longer essentially religious or even established by laws of nature which must remain obscure, were seen as the creation of men and of their reason, and this last recognized as the unsatisfactory yet solitary guide and rule in an uncertain world.

Montaigne's attitude was one of humanistic skepticism, observing all with a tolerant but critical eye, taking for granted the vagaries of human prejudice and passion, while trying to forge his own philosophy of common sense and kindliness and learning. Montaigne did not think that men could force others to be good. It was hard enough to live the good life for oneself, and quite impossible to tell for certain what the good life is. All one could do was to be oneself wisely, distrusting invitations to be or to force others to be something else according to an alien pattern of principle or faith.

The new doubts about the possibilities of reason had also been sparked by current religious controversies. Many Protestants contended that human reason could interpret the Scriptures correctly and find authority for its interpretations in Divine Revelation. Faced with such arguments, some of their opponents had fallen back on skeptical criticism of the possibilities of human reason. Truth, they said, could not be attained or defined by human means. Many Jesuits used this particular

Michel de Montaigne.

argument to refute their Protestant opponents and went on from demolition of rational truth to the assertion of a revealed truth which the
church preserved. This meant that libertine skeptics were in good company. Besides, the thorough skeptic denied the human mind's capacity
of knowing what is true, which meant that he could never insist on the
positive truth of his views and, holding nothing right, could never
be really wrong. He accepted the laws and customs that prevailed and
would therefore be a good Catholic, like Montaigne, whose inner skepticism took cover behind outward conformity. The libertine refused to
sacrifice anything (or anyone) for any cause, preferring living safely to
living well.

> Each wise man first best loves himself
> Lives close, thinks and obeys . . .

wrote Alexander Brome in the Cromwellian England of 1656.

> That side is always right that's strong,
> And that that's beaten must be wrong;
> And he that thinks it is not so,
> Unless he's sure to beat them too,
> Is but a fool to oppose them.

There were, however, men less cautious than Montaigne or Brome, who
felt disgusted by the poor morals of the clergy, the dirty linen of religious
disputes aired in public, the senseless violence of religious wars, who
began to wonder whether religion might not actually be an evil and
whether the pretended verities of the churches might possibly be untrue.

The Christians claimed their faith was founded on reason; they held that the existence and nature of God could be proved by logical argument, and that rational historical criticism would not disprove the divinity of Christ. But the effectiveness of reason was set in doubt both by the clash of opposing reasons on the religious and the scientific plane and by the followers of Montaigne, the greatest of them a cleric and professor of mathematics, Pierre Gassendi (1592–1655), who, in his significantly titled *Apology for Epicurus,* described a universe composed of continuously moving atoms capable of joining to create an infinity of worlds which could be compared to our own. Objects, bodies, even what we call soul or spirit, are all composed of tiny atoms, which means that when our body and its component atoms dissolve, so does the soul and the individual comes to an end. Sensations felt by the body would also be felt by the soul. These sensations are interpreted by the imagination to produce ideas which may quite easily be mistaken, and belief in the supernatural is simply an error of judgment, like many others that we are capable of making. Essentially, we can never know what is true, since our senses offer us only a relative truth which is sufficient for nothing more than practical activities. This is not an adequate basis for ambitious speculations on Being, on God, on Ultimate Truth, which, when they do not reflect the highest lessons and aspirations of purely human experience, are simply invitations to error.

Historical experience, too, had to be treated with care. Ancient leaders and politicians often claimed divine authority to justify their actions or to affirm their power. If careful criticism showed these to be political subterfuges, what should we make of the evidence contained in the Bible, which new discoveries revealed no longer as the record of God's intercourse with humanity but simply as a history of an ancient people? Why, then, the Bible rather than Cicero or Seneca, who taught the bounds of possibility, the wisdom of limiting one's desires to these possibilities, in order to secure the happiness of achieving one's desires? Why not epicureanism, placing absence of pain and worry above all things, counseling moderation, frugality, honesty, and justice as the best means of attaining and retaining the *voluptuous* state which gratifies the senses, when there is nothing else to gratify?

The possibilities of these views appealed to cultivated bourgeois, magistrates, royal officers, ecclesiastics to such an extent that alarmists saw these people taking over. In the 1620's fearful observers counted 50,000 atheists in Paris, a million lost souls in France. It was a vast exaggeration. The fears were premature. But the phenomena were significant.

A New View of Man

The formulation of such views could lead from sheer skepticism to more positive positions. Young poets and nobles like Théophile de Viau (arrested in 1623 for his subversive views) saw man as just another animal, subject to the same natural-physical laws as other animals, dominated by humors, passions, never constant nor consistent, lacking any real free will. Men should learn to live "like God," that is, like free souls—free from the human bondage of their bodies and above all free of reigning prejudices; they could then discover "the natural reason of things." Men such as Viau or La Mothe Le Vayer, secretary of Richelieu and one of Louis XIV's tutors, did not accept the explanations and moral theories on which society rested, despised its hierarchies, its social values, above all its worship of wealth. Against such illusions they insisted on a virtue available only to a few: generosity—a word they used to mean great-heartedness—a quality of the spirit "which resists all the assaults of fortune and which lets nothing low affect its actions." If God has given us natural thoughts, inclinations, passions, there is no more harm in following them than there is in eating, drinking, sleeping, an unbelieving physician insisted on his deathbed in 1661. So, have fun, or, as St.-Evremond would put it, make pleasure the end of life. This is what he wrote to Ninon de Lenclos, the celebrated courtesan, in the 1680's: "Love of pleasure and flight from pain are the first and most natural movements one notes in men" and pleasure "the true end to which our actions tend."

Newly discovered worlds added their disturbing influence to what the libertines could draw from the ancient classics and from a critical look at their own times. The sixteenth century had discovered America. The seventeenth discovered China. In each case, the revelation sent intellectual as well as economic tremors right through the body politic. From America, Europeans drew the image of noble savages, purer and finer in their state of nature before it was corrupted by European men, an idea which would provide the basis of a view of human nature that culminated in the eighteenth century with Rousseau. Then, more immediately eventful, after the memoirs of Jesuits and other travelers began to circulate in the seventeenth century, China provided the image of an advanced society whose wisdom and whose institutions were superior or at the very least comparable to those of Europe, and yet had been developed outside the ken of Christianity. Here was a country excelling in "Antiquity, largeness, Ritcheness, healthynesse, Plentyffulnesse," as a visiting English sailor informed the reading public of the 1630's: "For Arts and manner off governmentt I thinck noe Kingdome in the world Comparable to it. Considered altogether." It was left to a Frenchman to introduce the sacrilegious note: *"Sancte Confuci, ora pro nobis!"*—Holy Confucius, pray for us—wrote La Mothe Le Vayer, convinced of the superiority of the Chinese sage.

If Confucianism offered a morality comparable to ours, what should we think about original sin—indeed, about salvation? Did virtuous Chinese go to Heaven, or were they condemned to Hell? If, as La Mothe Le Vayer argued, the sages of such nations as the Apostles had not reached were saved by their inborn virtues, then original sin could be escaped by mere good works and neither Grace nor Church were necessary to ensure salvation. Besides, it seemed that Chinese history made hay of the history recorded in the Bible, demoting it from a divinely inspired record of mankind to the provincial chronicle of a little people. What then became of Genesis and Biblical revelation? The authority of the Bible was severely shaken.

Deism

On the other hand, some scholars and philosophers found it impossible to conciliate their high idea of what God might be with Christian dogmas in which the Infinite Being becomes flesh and the Supreme Goodness condemns mankind to eternal damnation; in which, again, Immutable Perfection could alter its designs in response to a diversity of prayers. Here we have the beginnings of a deism which would expel God from the world because its view of God was too exalted to allow for a God involved in the everyday affairs of men, and which meanwhile criticized existing "superstitions" that diminished the Divinity it claimed to adore. Humanist tradition on the one hand, experience of the Religious Wars on the other, persuaded thoughtful men that confessions of faith divided mankind where the worship of a superior being should unite them. But thoughtful men were few and they must be cautious. They looked upon different creeds chiefly as masks of political interests; they insisted on thinking through dogmas and traditions which the masses accepted without any discussion; they met in a few small groups and referred to themselves as "illuminated"—that is, enlightened—cured of popular errors by the light of their reason, a reason that revealed the impostures and illusions which blinded most of their fellows. But they doubted that their fellows could or would do as much, doubted even their own capacity to do more than criticize existing misconceptions, and limited themselves to discreet analyses leaving others to draw conclusions. Nor did they really wish to disturb the public order. On the contrary, they wanted a firmer, more effective order, a public power handled by enlightened but authoritarian rulers, such as they themselves frequently served.

Cyrano de Bergerac, who died in 1655, was inspired by similar ideas but, having read Gassendi, he concluded that the apparent order of the universe was due to chance, the possible number of combinations and permutations of the available atoms being infinite but the number of valid combinations limited, so that eventually a valid combination could occur and so establish a lasting phenomenon. In such a world there was no need for God. Religions, once again, were seen as social or political inventions which served to establish an authority over a people; good insofar as they were socially useful, but not otherwise superior to one another.

A generation later, in the second half of the seventeenth century, St.-Evremond carried these views further. For this Norman gentleman who had distinguished himself in the Thirty Years' War and who now lies buried in Westminster Abbey, the basic drives and motives of mankind are rooted not in reason but in passions and, above all, in their anxieties, men's quest for pleasure being no more than a vain attempt to escape the misery and real awareness of our hopeless state: an amusement, a *divertissement*. Thought and sensibility were best avoided, thoughtlessness and lack of feeling were to be envied, involvement or commitment had best be jettisoned, not because life is not beautiful but because it is fragile and vain. Man is not the only mortal creature—all creatures are mortal, of course—but man has received the poisoned gift of self-consciousness in his cradle. Flowers die too, but they do not know it. We do; and all our life is one long struggle and plaint against this fate.

Such a philosophy found its logical conclusion in the abdication of desire, of awareness, of thought: in quietism (see pp. 262–263) and its attempt to merge in the flow of an order that one could not resist, a point of view which Archbishop Fénelon partially reflected. But the God of the quietists was almost a pantheistic universal spirit, part of all nature, present in all its aspects and hardly different from the Supreme Being of the deists. This kind of sweet acceptance, this refusal of specific definitions and commitments, with which quietists would solve the problem of the world, was unacceptable to those who felt that man *had* to go on in the world, operate in it, hence shape and define it according to his desires, needs, and will.

In spite of the strains involved, religion was too much a part of social order to be abandoned to philosophical speculations. Philosophy affected religion, religion affected society, and society, or the men who ran it, could not afford to abdicate. Nor were they going to. The debate between Fénelon and Bossuet was a debate between proponents of withdrawal and acceptance: the former praising the wisdom of surrender to God and renunciation of self, the latter suspicious of the passiveness this implied and significantly ignoring the long mystical tradition of the Church. In the end, the doers, the rulers, the active and committed had their way. The quietists were defeated. But the analytical side of their philosophy survived and it expressed itself in two directions: in one, the acceptance of religion as a matter of social utility while taking it to pieces as a creed: the argument that religion was a useful part of the state machinery led to the argument that a state religion was indispensable to the social order. But if religion was justified by the state, then the state could define, indeed invent its own religion, and this the state proceeded to do when it replaced the Christian cult by a national cult: patriotism.

Historical Criticism

If philosophical analysis threatened the integrity of religious beliefs and political interests menaced the primacy and independence of religion, the progress of historical methods held out possibilities even more ominous.

The study of history had continued (see pp. 77–79) as a mirror men hold up to themselves. The past did not only weigh upon the present; it helped interpret it, just as the present furnished lessons to understand the past. The same psychology that Shakespeare, Corneille, and Racine applied to the heroes of their plays illuminated the actions of ancient (and less ancient) heroes, inspired the gestures, conflicts, postures of contemporaries. Why not? Human conditions differ, human nature does not—so it was thought—in time or space. The passions, interests, and calculations of mankind are the same, always and everywhere, whether in Plutarch's *Lives* or at the Tudor court. Hence, history is useful (for knowledge was not pursued for itself alone), as Renaissance men had found it, not only because it permits a better understanding of human character, but as a servant of speculation and of political action. "The first utility of history," declared the French philosopher Jean Bodin in the midst of his country's religious wars, "is to serve policy. Philosophy would die of inanition amidst its principles, were they not vivified by history." An age in which tradition was respected could not but use traditional references. Both those who challenged and those who defended what existed, bolstered their arguments with demonstrations based on what (they claimed) had happened in history.

No wonder that, amidst violent religious and constitutional conflicts, political and theological legitimacy was sought beyond abstract arguments in documents, that lawyers and clerics studied whatever sources could be dredged out of the past, that the critical ideas of the fifteenth century were applied ever more rigorously and methodically to confute the assertions of opponents and to ensure against their criticism. In seventeenth-century France, especially, the Benedictine scholars of the Congregation of St. Maur, drawing on the vast resources of their order's houses; the Oratorians inspired by the Catholic reformation and the needs of controversy; the Bollandist Fathers—created the foundations of new scholarship. The Bollandists were Jesuit scholars who took their name from the Belgian, Jean Bollandus (1596–1665), who initiated their great study of saints' lives, purged of spurious materials and intended to show their true importance for the Christian church. The Bollandists and their fellows would lay the groundwork of systematic textual editing, founding a great tradition of research on national and provincial antiquities as well as church and medieval history.

But enterprises of this nature, while meant to defend and purify existing beliefs, could also explain them away if pressed too far. In the 1670's an Oratorian priest, Richard Simon, decided to apply the philological and historical methods which had long been used on classic texts to the Bible. The outcome was a *Critical History of the Old Testament* (1678), which caused a great scandal and founded Biblical exegesis in France. The book was banned, its author punished, but Biblical criticism went on from there. The example of Simon as well as that of the libertines worked on a young Protestant theologian, Pierre Bayle (1647–1706), himself the son of a pastor and a refugee in Holland since 1685, where he would publish his famous *Historical and Critical Dictionary* (1697). The Simon-libertarian-Baylist influence was carried on by Fontenelle and the Encyclopedists in the eighteenth century. In hands such as these, religion became a subject not for theologians but for historians, ethnographers, anthropologists, and sociologists, who studied and compared the different myths of very different peoples and ages, seeking to understand the ones by the others. Libertinism, with its denial of revelation, turned into the comparative study of religions.

Pascal's Faith

One further alternative would be recognized by one of the seventeenth century's finest minds, that of Blaise Pascal (1623–1662). Scion of a great parliamentary family from central France, the young Pascal early distinguished himself as a mathematician and physicist. He turned his inventiveness in a number of directions, elaborating the theory of probability, joining in a venture to create a new form of public transport on the lines of an omnibus, inventing the roulette wheel and organizing a lottery that exploited its possibilities. At twenty-one, however, a mystical experience revealed the limits of reason and turned him to religious faith. Convinced that both science and the world were vain, Pascal became a radical Jansenist, abandoned all hope in worldly institutions—including the Church to which he nevertheless submitted, and affirmed the meaninglessness of all but God, whom he sought in terror and despair.

More than the *Provincial Letters,* in which he defended Jansenism against contemporary attacks, his posthumously published *Pensées* (*Thoughts,* 1670) indicates that in this tormented man the moral and religious problems of the time found both their culmination and their contradiction. The new dimensions of space and time, the new possibilities of the natural and physical sciences, convinced the precocious logician and mathematical genius only that they could tell him nothing about ultimate things, that however much you search and reason the surface of life will remain opaque, and that man must gamble in the end: either on the here and now, or on infinities of beatitude or pain, belief in which can only rest on irrational decision—faith. Having decided that the odds stood in its favor, Pascal counseled betting on eternal life.

PENSÉES

DE

M. PASCAL

SUR LA RELIGION,

ET SUR QUELQUES

AUTRES SUJETS,

*Qui ont esté trouvées aprés sa mort
parmy ses papiers.*

A PARIS,

Chez GUILLAUME DESPREZ,
ruë Saint Jacques à Saint Prosper.

M. DC. LXIX.

Avec Privilege & Approbation.

Title page of *Pensées*, by Pascal.
Bibliothèque Nationale, Paris.

Avid reader of Montaigne, alumnus of libertinism and its subversive speculations, Blaise Pascal suggests the possibility that skepticism may lead beyond reason, beyond doubt, to a firm conclusion. "The last step of reason is to recognize the infinity of things beyond its grasp. Reason is but weakness if it does not lead to that knowledge." Not for Pascal the rationalization of Descartes, or the suspended judgment of the libertine that leaves man bereft in a void of unknowing. Admitting the mystery of life, the converted skeptic chooses affirmation and thereby finds a faith that permits him to escape from absurdity. No wonder that he is regarded as one of the ancestors of twentieth-century Existentialism.

We must bear this in mind: All such views, eventually influential, were long the preserve of very small minorities everywhere, whose members generally maintained a prudent discretion about them and preferred outward conformity to the likely discomforts publicity might bring. Libertinism—freethinking—was the distinction of the few, discussed in narrow circles, seldom and slowly trickling into the world outside. One side effect of this situation was that nonconforming thinkers heartily despised the society in which they moved, its priests, professors and, above all, the cloddish, ignorant, superstition-ridden commoners, apt at any moment to fall upon nonconformists.

The Supernatural

We should not forget that this great age of scientific and philosophical speculation was equally a great age of superstition, witchcraft, and of burning stakes. Eschatological speculation was widespread. The end of days was widely expected, especially among Protestants. Melanchthon expected Gog and Magog to appear in 1600 or 1607. The predestined age of the earth—6,000 years—had pretty well run out. In 1572 the apparition of a brilliant new star had persuaded many that this ushered in the end of the world. In 1606, Pope Paul V dreamt that Paris was collapsing in flames and news of the papal dream set off a minor panic in the capital, whole families fleeing the city to escape the divine fire. Relics and amulets were everywhere, encouraged by Counter-Reformation propaganda in Catholic lands but no less popular in Protestant countries. Those who could not afford the real thing carried about them bits of parchment, chunks of dead animals, or pieces of blessed bread guaranteed to "put the devil to flight, heal the body's maladies, preserve from rabies and destroy rats."

Equally ubiquitous were witches, consorts of the devil, an infernal fifth column sapping the fragile world of men. Against the witches no effort was too great, no weapon too blunt, no suspicion too sharp. *Exodus* (22:18) decreed "Thou shalt not suffer a witch to live"; and the sixteenth and seventeenth centuries seemed determined to carry out this injunction, sacrificing great hecatombs of victims on the smoking altars of faith. Between 1575 and 1590, the inquisitor of Lorraine, Nicho-

The hanging of three notorious witches at Chelmsford, 1589. Lambeth Palace Library, London.

las Rémy, had some 900 sorcerers and witches burned to death. In old age his conscience bothered him because he had spared several children. Rémy's record was bettered by a contemporary bishop of Trier, Peter Binsfeld, who ordered the death of some 6,500 people. Small cities could be hit by witch mania as by an attack of plague: Leonberg in Würtemberg, about two hundred families strong, burned six witches in the winter of 1615; neighboring Weil, Kepler's birthplace, and no larger than Leonberg, burned thirty-eight witches between 1615 and 1629. Kepler's own mother, one of whose aunts had perished at the stake, was pursued for witchcraft and probably only her son's intervention saved her after six years of trials.

A few thoughtful men in every age had doubted the reality of witchcraft. Montaigne, moved by curiosity, had gone to see a coven of imprisoned witches but found only some women who seemed simply mad. In 1563, a Dutchman, Jan Wier (1516–88), published a refutation of contemporary beliefs in demons and incantations, explaining witches as mental cases and their aberrations in medical terms. Jean Bodin, just finishing his study of *The Demonomania of Sorcerers* (1580), saw a copy of Jan Wier's book and was much incensed, refuting it "to defend God's honour against sorcerers" in whom this otherwise wise and well-informed man firmly believed on the basis of Holy Writ, the Christian fathers, and the judgment of Paris theologians. Between 1580 and 1601 there were at least one dozen editions of Bodin's *Demonomania*—two in Latin, two in Italian, and the rest in French* The specialists of the Inquisition also had their doubts, holding reports of witches to be "dreams and illusions and not true reality," as the Bishop of Vic wrote King Philip III of Spain in 1622. But the common people believed in witches, and not even the Inquisition could sometimes prevent great witch hunts to slake the popular thirst for scapegoats in a miserable world.

Increasingly, the prejudices of learned and unlearned drew them apart, strengthening their mutual distrust. In 1649 we find the libertine Gabriel Naudé denouncing the foolishness of believing that poor mad women "had done a thousand childish, ridiculous, impossible extravagances for which they would better deserve to be healed or shut up in a madhouse than to exterminate them as one does by fire and rope." All this only demonstrated to Naudé the power of impostures that could affect the popular mind, than which nothing was less reliable and more foolish. And he quoted Seneca: "The worst argument is the approval of the crowd." But while a few doctors and intellectuals thought so, the crowd thought otherwise; and it had to be satisfied over and over with burnt offerings.

* Bossuet agreed with Bodin: "I hold that sorcerers could raise an army equal to that of Xerxes which was eighteen hundred thousand strong. For if, under Charles IX, they numbered 300,000 in France alone, what should we estimate the number that could be found in other countries?"

The vulgar mob was stupid and dangerous, dangerous because stupid. Everywhere the cultivated few feared the religious excesses of the unreasoning masses and, by a natural reversal, came to make light of the religious lapses of cultivated nonconformists. "Atheism did never perturb states," reads Bacon's essay on superstition. "But superstition has been the confusion of many states, and bringeth in a new *primum mobile* that ravisheth all the spheres of government. The master of superstition is the people; and in all superstition wise men follow fools . . ." Thus skepticism grew as a posh reaction against vulgar "enthusiasms." "There is nothing that can prevail more to persuade a man to be an atheist," said Samuel Butler, "as to see such unreasonable beasts pretend to religion." In Restoration England, Dryden's political satire in verse, "Absalom and Achitophel," laughed at the variety of gods "of every shape and size that God-smiths could produce, or Priests devise," and especially at "the herd of such, who think too little and talk too much. These, out of mere instinct, they knew not why, ador'd their father's God, and Property; and, by the same blind benefit of Fate, the Devil and the Jebusite did hate." Nor did he spare the Puritans who "wisely from expensive Sins refrain and never broke the sabbath, but for Gain . . ."

Of course, there were two currents: the restrictive and the rebellious; and one worked upon the other. Under the assault of Counter-Reformation, orthodoxy became increasingly stifling, moral and religious conformism ever more intolerant of independent thought. In this atmosphere, even sincere Christians learned to dissemble and, dissembling, shifted onto common ground with the critics of religion whose discretion and outward conformity concealed their scorn of vulgar crowds and ignorant clerics. With freedom of inquiry, a new relativism was growing up under the effect of skeptical ideas, travelers' tales, and comparative thinking, which would culminate in what A. S. Eddington has called Dean Swift's "elementary treatise on relativity"—*Gulliver's Travels* (1726)—but which Pascal, in his *Pensées,* expressed more poignantly.

> We are floating in a medium of vast extent, always drifting uncertainly, blown to and fro; whenever we think we have a fixed point to which we can cling and make fast, it shifts and leaves us behind; if we follow it, it eludes our grasp, slips away, and flees eternally before us. Nothing stands still for us. This is our natural state and yet the state most contrary to our inclinations. We burn with desire to find a firm footing, an ultimate lasting base on which to build a tower rising up to infinity, but our whole foundation cracks and the earth opens up into the depths of the abyss.

Pascal had found a firm footing by placing rational thought as a barrier against chaos. On a less eminent level, others did so too. Among the cultivated, superstition waned. The Duke of Buckingham, like Wallenstein, had had his own private astrologer and necromancer. A generation later this was no longer so. An astrologer who offered his services to Charles II was carried off by the King to Newmarket Races and light-heartedly invited to pick the winners. By 1693 a clergyman proclaiming the second coming was treated not as a heretic but as an unbalanced man. The last witch trial in England took place in 1712. That was also the year when Good Queen Anne "touched" young Samuel Johnson to cure him of scrofula. Queen Anne was the last English ruler to perform such "cures." Charles II had "touched" nearly 100,000 who hoped his royal magic would cure their scrofula. It is doubtful that he himself believed it. The great change seems to have come around the middle of the seventeenth century. The English memorialist, John Aubrey, placed it there: "When I was a child and so before the Civil Wars, the fashion was for old women and maids to tell fabulous stories, night-times, of spirits and of walking of ghosts, etc. . . . When the wars came, and with them liberty of conscience and liberty of inquisition [i.e., of inquiry], the phantoms vanished. Now children fear no such things."

The more scientific knowledge grew, the wider grew the gap between learned and uncultivated, the greater the mutual distrust and dislike. Nothing good could come from majorities. "The reason . . . for which all government was at first appointed was . . . to prevent mobs and rabbles in the world," wrote Daniel Defoe. The "new dictators of the streets" should be put in their place "and if persuasion won't the gallows will." Even the gentle John Locke, in writing *The Reasonableness of Christianity,* drew the division between educated men for whom "reason must be our judge and guide in everything" and "the day-laborers and tradesmen, the spinsters and dairymaids" who "cannot know and therefore they must believe." Reason only meant what men of a given class and education thought reasonable; but more of them thought toleration so.

If religion was reasonable, politics was rational: the universe was a machine constructed by God, the state a structure constructed by man. God was bound by his own laws; so was the state. But the laws were the work of man. In the new heliocentric universe everything turned on man; and it is symptomatic that in 1691 already the chemist Robert Boyle endowed a set of lectures designed to defend the truths of Christianity. They needed defending.

Toward the 18th Century

In little more than a hundred years running from the last quarter of the sixteenth century to the end of the seventeenth, political theories

mirrored the clash of old and new attitudes and the omnipresent search
for order and reason. Loosely speaking, order was the dominant concern
during the first part of this period, reason during the second part; and,
before long, it would become quite clear that the medieval ideals of
order founded on reason and justified by it had to be abandoned because reason, which could marshal arguments supporting any order,
could prove just as easily to be a disruptive force.

The religious struggles of the sixteenth century had spawned sharp
theories that rulers could be challenged by their subjects in the name
of God, that political power lay with the people rather than the prince.
The rebellions and disorder roused or justified by arguments such as
these bred their counterparts in fresh references to the divine authority
investing civil power. Political stability, it was argued, took precedence
even over religious faith. Only the state could safeguard property
and order, wrote Jean Bodin (1530–1596), appalled by the wild chaos of
the Huguenot wars. Absolute sovereignty alone could assert its will over
all others, force rival interests to keep the peace, bend religious fanaticism
or noble factions to its rule, provide peace and security for the realm.
Here was the theory of the sovereign state on which Bourbons and
Stuarts both relied, and which the *politiques* in France believed in.
And this was capped by the right of kings to rule, wielding a sovereignty vested in them by God, a divine right which turned rebellion into
sacrilege. The office of king, said James I of England, much given to
philosophizing on that score, was a "mystery," out of bounds to philosophers or lawyers who sought to discern its reasons or its limits. The
right of kings to rule was not a matter of argument but of obedience
and unquestioning faith.

But, obviously, whatever else it was, the seventeenth century was not
an age of unquestioning faith. Even the divine right of kings had to find
arguments to justify itself, and the most scholarly of these would be
provided by Bishop Bossuet, tutor of the son of Louis XIV, in his
Politics Drawn From the Very Words of Holy Writ, a treatise which
he began to write in 1679, although it was not published until 1709.
Bossuet's main conclusion from the Scriptures was that the person of the
king is sacred, and no one has the right to hurt him or attack his power.
"The royal throne is not the throne of a man, but of God himself."
The king, of course, is subject to the law of God and will be called
to account on Judgment Day. But, while reponsible to God, he is not
responsible before his subjects. Subjects have been created to obey as
princes are created to command, and nothing could relieve a people
from the divine duty of submission to their lord. The actions of the
king reflect the secret designs of God and, if the subjects cannot agree
with them or understand them, they must remember that this is due to
the limits of their worm's-eye vision. What looks to men obscure or
bad makes better sense when viewed from the transcendent seat of
the Divinity that willed it.

Yet arguments such as these were challenged. Indeed, it was to answer current challenges that Bossuet composed his *Politics*. The point is that the theories of absolute sovereignty had been evolved and welcomed for very concrete ends: the search for peace and order. The arguments of Bodin and of the *politiques* had removed political power from the province of theology (since theological dispute had been at the root of the disorders they wanted to avoid) and placed it in the realm of secular argument which rested, in the end, on utility and reason. Now, reason could formulate new definitions of utility, and challenge old arguments with new.

Hobbes

The most brutal challenge came in the *Leviathan* of Thomas Hobbes. That was ten years after Descartes' *Discourse on Method*, and Hobbes relentlessly applied Cartesian method to the analysis of politics. The book which the old philosopher presented in 1651 to the exiled Charles II, was, like the *Discourse*, the result of private logical thought, discounting experience and the vicarious experience of reading (Hobbes said that if he had read as much as other men he would only know as much as they), glorifying mathematics and its application to society. His findings were grandiose, frightening, and ultimately destructive of the old philosophy, dismantled by the corrosive skepticism of his approach.

Leviathan was a disturbing book because it is the product of a rational, calculating mind at work upon a subject which Hobbes took up anew, discarding all the norms accumulated about it through the ages. The basis of Hobbes' argument is man's psychology, the standard of his judgment is utility. He brings the two together in cold assessment of what the state can do for man and do *to* him, and forces his readers to reconsider it.

For Hobbes, men are by nature evil: men are wolves to men. This was the view of a philosopher who moved in high political circles and mixed with powerful men—first secretary of Francis Bacon, then tutor to the exiled Charles II—a wandering refugee fascinated by power as much as by the problem of his own security.

Men are not, says Hobbes, as so many philosophers describe them, gregarious beings made for social life. Ambitious and selfish, men are in society only for what they can get out of it—gain or glory—and, since a lot of men want the same things at once, society is marked above all by "a mutual will of hurting." Man is depraved. A society based on any other view must crack to bits; a society which accepts this view must rest on naked power. The world knows no such thing as spiritual principles or higher aims. There is no good save pleasure, no evil except pain, no aims but selfish aims, and freedom is simply the license of following your passions. The basic principle of life is self-regard. As everybody struggles to attain his ends, the natural state of man is a state of war: that is, a constant struggle of man against man. And the life of man in this unregenerate state of nature, says Hobbes in a famous phrase, is solitary, poor, nasty, brutish, and short.

If this be so, the only thing that keeps the human race from killing itself off is philoprogenitiveness. But that is not enough and, given the state of nature, the last two men seem fated to die with their teeth firmly fixed in each other's throats. Something must be done. And Hobbes suggests the artificial remedy which helps mankind get over the evils of its natural state: the natural equality of all murderous men, equality tempered only by fortuitous physical differences, is replaced by a regime of inequality, the only thing that can save them from themselves, from the discomfort and destruction free men naturally inflict upon one another. In other words, a political society is set up, under the authority of a monarch who, by evident necessity, must be absolute.

Of course, the society this postulates is highly artificial. But it is not beyond the powers of men, which a glance around shows to be very great. Men can make robot toys that are remarkably like living beings; they have in the same way made an artificial society, a strange and vast machine that takes the place of natural society.

> Nature (the Art whereby God hath made and governs the World) is by the Art of man, as in many other things so in this imitated, that it can make an Artificial Animal. For see life is but a motion of limbs, the beginning whereof is in some principal part within; why may we not say that all Automata (Engines that move themselves by springs and wheels as doth a watch) have an artificial life? For what is the Heart, but a spring; and the Nerves, but so many Strings; and the Joints, but so many Wheels, giving motion to the whole Body, such as was intended by the Artificer? Art goes yet further, imitating that rational and most excellent work of Nature, Man. For by Art is created that great Leviathan called a Commonwealth, or State (in Latin *Civitas*), which is but an artificial man, though of greater stature and strength than the natural, for whose protection and defense it was intended.

Self-preservation justified the state and the unbridled power of the prince who ruled. Such savage arguments appealed to very few, though practical politicians who had more sense than to formulate them accepted them in practice readily enough: human beings might easily be treated like interchangeable parts of an impersonal machine. This was in part what Archbishop Fénelon opposed when he opposed royal autocracy: the impersonal repressive state which had abandoned Christian love for discipline, which strove for order, not for the good life. But love has never been dispensed by governments. A somewhat ordered life was easier to enforce than the good life to conceive.

Right now, the first concern was to tame the wildness of the sovereign state, to moderate these monsters which, absolute at home, vied with one another in that natural state that still prevailed in international relations. War was regarded as the natural pastime and relationship of states. "No body can be healthful without exercise," wrote Chancellor Bacon, ". . . and certainly to a kingdom or estate a just and honorable war is the true exercise. A civil war is like the heat of a fever; but a foreign war is like the heat of exercise and serves to keep the body in health . . ." Some of those who witnessed the Thirty Years War dissented from such views. Thus we have seen (p. 333) how the horror Grotius felt at the debauch of war that ravaged the so-called Christian world had sparked his *Law of Peace and War*. There the treachery and barbarism which reason of state excused had been transcended by the law of nature that made all men gregarious, socially conscious, and responsible. Here was a law that went beyond the bounds of states, that provided a base for relations between men and also between states. Yet Grotius's arguments suggested one more thing: that human law could supplement the obscure will of God, that worldly chaos could be cleared up by man-made means, that international conventions devised by lawyers and politicians could soften or abolish the ills impenetrable Providence decreed.

Spinoza

This was more clearly stated in the disturbing works of a Portuguese Jew living in Holland, and of a German Protestant teaching at the University of Lund in Sweden: Baruch Spinoza (1632–1677) and Samuel Pufendorf (1632–1694), each of whom formulated a theory of political obligation, based not on God but on social utility.

Spinoza is one of the most attractive seventeenth-century figures, one of those tough-fragile beings who flee all conflict, yet attract it by their unwillingness to yield their principles. Strongly influenced by Cartesian thought as well as by his rabbinical training, Spinoza found himself excommunicated from the Jewish community for heterodoxy and suspected by his Christian fellows for the dangerous implications his ideas carried. But his study of science and optics proved useful: he was able to earn his living grinding lenses, while pursuing his philosophical speculations. This frugal, slender, kindly man, with courteous ways and many friends, was a fearless champion of the freedom of all thought. His most important work, the *Theologico-Political Treatise*, was published anonymously in 1670; two other essays appeared only after his death. Like Grotius, Spinoza stressed men's sociable instincts. Like Hobbes, he believed that the search for security and self-preservation resulted in a sovereign state. But here Spinoza parts company with Hobbes, whose analysis of human personality justified a lion-tamer state.

For Spinoza, men need not be led through fear or pride alone. They can be brought or allowed to fulfill themselves in intellectual and spiritual self-awareness: "to persevere in the nature of their being." He did not see men as separate entities in relation with outer authorities (worldly or divine), but as parts of a pantheistic universe every portion of which can be seen, and can operate, only in connection with the whole. The political conclusion of this view was that, far from existing to glorify God or serve a king or state, men are themselves the reason of their being, that their fulfillment is their highest aim, and that they should defend themselves against anyone or anything who thwarts the fullest possible development of what they have. "It follows," he says in the *Treatise,* "that the ultimate aim of government is not to rule or restrain by fear, not to exact obedience, but on the contrary free every man from fear, that he may live in all possible security." There could be no more deliberate contradiction of Hobbes' views: "No, the object of government is not to change men from rational beings into beasts or puppets, but to enable them to develop their minds and bodies in security and to employ their reason unshackled; . . . in fact, the true aim of government is Liberty." The state is a convenience, made for man; man should obey it insofar as it·promotes that self-fulfillment which is his proper end. "Every man should think what he likes and say what he thinks." Here was a novel and sophisticated twist of utility, and one which we need not wonder caused horror among right-thinking people in its time.

Spinoza glorified man and man's values, which might even prove to be the instrument of God's self-realization. God, for Spinoza, like the state, becomes almost a means to man's accomplishment. Pufendorf did not go so far: he merely relegated divine power to another plane which does not concern us. God's realm was in the heavens, Pufendorf's down here; and here on earth natural reason rules, which does not need to bother with theology. Pufendorf's *Laws of Nature and of Men* (1672) advances the old idea of a social compact, a covenant between the members of a society, upon which the society is based. Society, says Pufendorf, rests on such conventions. Men agree among themselves to unite in society and, once united, to regulate their lives and actions by common consent. Those who are entrusted with sovereign power must ensure public safety and utility, in return for which their subjects promise to obey them. Such a concept had been current in the Middle Ages and it was still familiar to the Catholic Church; but now it was presented in a secular grab. As seen by the Lund University professor, the idea of a contract between people and God turned into a double contract: first among the governed and secondly between the governed and the governor, a modern version of the feudal contract. Natural law provided a secular approach to social disciplines and political practice.

The Revocation of the Edict of Nantes

But such ideas lacked the sanction of reality until, in 1685, the revocation of the Edict of Nantes raised a case in point in which a sovereign found himself at odds with a vociferous section of his subjects. The Protestant exiles took refuge in Holland and, thence, proclaimed the right of rebellion against Louis XIV, who had used his power to force his will on consciences that were entitled to be free. Louis had transgressed the natural law, proclaimed the exiles, and thus become an outlaw; rebellion against him became legitimate. Here was more than a quarrel between Protestants and Catholics; for, casting around for arguments, the Huguenots relied less on religious revelation than on the theories of Grotius and Pufendorf. And, in the pamphlet war which followed, Bishop Bossuet countered with an alternative between Divine Right and the totalitarianism of Hobbes. If society arose out of a natural state, how could the barbarous men, who lived in it at first, have ever got together or conceived the original contract to live as one in peace? Either men learned to live together because God willed it so, the self-same God who set a king to rule over them and to enforce his will; or else the only way they found their way out of the natural state was as Hobbes described it, and Hobbes' arguments justified Louis XIV as much as Bossuet's.

A New View of Natural Law

Logically speaking this was quite impressive and, while political polemics are not very logical, no ideology can endure on shaky theoretical foundations. Those who appealed to Natural Rights against Absolutism had to find an answer to the argument of Bossuet; and the answer came, in

Bulloz

The second page of the document revoking the Edict of Nantes signed by Louis XIV.

theory and practice, in the English Revolution of 1688. James II, King by the Grace of God, was cast out and replaced by a new king, who ruled by an explicit contract passed between him and his subjects. And the new arrangement, as well as the right of subjects to rebel against their sovereign, found a philosophical sanction in the *Treatise on Civil Government* (1690), published by John Locke (1632–1704), who had sailed back to England in the very fleet of William III.

Locke took up the same ideas which we have already met and started off from a state of nature. But in his view this last is not the reign of brutishness and violence, as Hobbes would have it. Yet it is far from perfect and, in effect, to remedy its imperfections men get together and agree on a social contract into which they enter for their own advantage and which implies playing the game of social living according to established rules. If anybody breaks these rules, he will be outlawed. And if the appointed ruler breaks the rules, then any member of society and, of course, society as a whole has the right to appeal to the rules agreed on and, if necessary, to do this by force. The conclusion is simple: if the executive power does not act according to the ends for which it has been set up, if it infringes on the liberties of the people, then this power must be removed from those to whom it has been entrusted. Furthermore, if the subjects have reason to suspect that a would-be tyrant is preparing to enslave them, they have the right to take preventive action and, by open rebellion, keep him from carrying out his plans.

By this line of argument Locke succeeded in justifying the Glorious Revolution. He also answered Bossuet and the political pessimists, by postulating a natural man who was on the whole decent enough to come to terms with his own kind. Those who found Locke convincing did so as an act of faith in the moderate perfectibility of man—and probably of a man whom they conceived to be as reasonable and decent as they thought themselves. The changed conditions of the late-seventeenth century, a far less lawless time than the early 1600's, must have played their part. So, too, no doubt, the successful outcome of 1688. The result was twofold: on the one hand, by the association of Lockian arguments and political success, the brilliance of the Glorious Revolution reflected upon the doctrine of Natural Law, enhancing its prestige. On the other hand, the idea of Natural Law and also Locke's conception of man as naturally decent came to provide the essence of England's new constitutional and legal thought. By way of Locke and 1688, Natural Law entered into the politics of its time and most especially into the politics of England, whose influence in the centuries to come would be preponderant.

Other results followed. 1688 had been a Protestant triumph. Locke's theories, not only on government but also as seen in his *On Toleration* (1689) marked an alliance between Natural Law and the reformed religion. They influenced the reformed religion far more than they were influenced by it, so that gradually and increasingly the conception of man's fall would be abandoned in favor of a new idea of perfectibility: man's perfectibility *of* man, and society's perfectibility *by* man. And, finally, from now on, men could know that Divine Right, as soon as it pretended to establish the absolute rule of a man or a regime, was no longer supernatural but antinatural, and should be scorned and attacked as such. 1688 and 1690 were only a beginning. But they marked a decisive stage because the theory of natural law, the theory of the rights of man (which, for the moment, meant simply the rights of Englishmen), and the reality of hard facts had been fused in the ideas and institutions arising out of the Glorious Revolution. The following century would write their concrete epilogue.

Looking Forward

Arbitrary terminus for the study of an age, as we began by saying, the Treaty of Utrecht and the death of Louis XIV symbolize perfectly the transition from an era when princes and treaties could be taken as the major factors of history to those later periods when more diverse factors assume a major role. Through the seventeenth century, social and economic tensions, crises, catastrophes, are attributed to the king. The problems of the nobles, the misery of the poor, the shortage of specie, the famines when harvests ran short, the low prices when grain or wine overflowed storage space, the breakdowns in trade, were all laid at his door. Rightly, to a great extent, since the king's hand was everywhere, his wars, his taxes, his regulations, his policies, ruined or favored regions and social groups. What changed in the eighteenth century was not so much the tendency of state machinery to interfere and control, but the capacity of its subjects to affect in their turn the realm in which they operated. In different terms, their capacity to exploit the world around them and especially the earth, improved. Friction between classes—between nobles and king, nobles and new nobles, rich and poor—did not cease. But it took place in a more diverse world where it was clear that there were other factors of prosperity than the policies of the crown. Typically, the economists of the eighteenth century would turn toward the land and toward the problem of rural structures and productivity; the thinkers would begin to note (if only to refute) the claims of common men, even those who were not noble, rich, or lettered; the politicians would address themselves to laws and institutions rather than to men alone; and the dominant power, England, would show the world that to wage war for mercantile rather than dynastic interests was no less proper for being profitable.

Neither laws nor men, neither society nor its rulers, would become "better"—whatever that means. But the accumulation of experience, the increase of resources, intellectual and material, would reveal new possibilities and make men (some men) freer: to envisage alternatives to the present, to choose, sometimes even to act.

PART III

An Age of
Revolutions
1715-1848

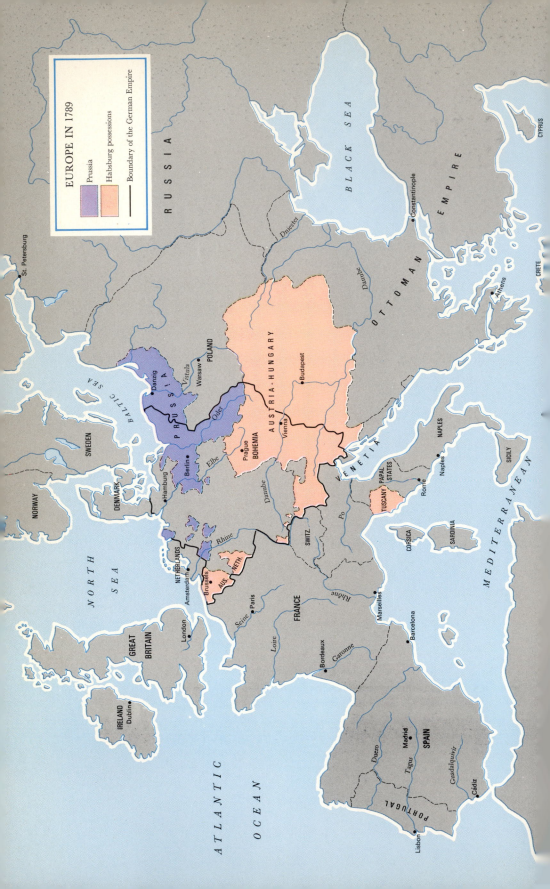

EUROPE IN 1789

Prussia
Habsburg possessions
Boundary of the German Empire

RUSSIA

St. Petersburg

BALTIC SEA

SWEDEN

NORWAY

DENMARK

NORTH SEA

GREAT BRITAIN

London

IRELAND
Dublin

ATLANTIC OCEAN

Hamburg
Berlin
Elbe
P R U S S I A
Danzig
Vistula
Oder
Warsaw
POLAND

Amsterdam
NETHERLANDS
Brussels
AUS. NETH.
Seine
Paris
FRANCE
Loire
Bordeaux
Garonne
Rhine
SWITZ.
Danube

Prague
BOHEMIA
Vienna
AUSTRIA-HUNGARY
Budapest
Danube

Dniester

BLACK SEA

O T T O M A N   E M P I R E

Constantinople

Athens

CYPRUS

CRETE

Po
VENETIA
PAPAL STATES
TUSCANY
Rome
Naples
NAPLES
Naples

CORSICA
SARDINIA
SICILY

Rhône
Marseilles
Barcelona

Duero
Tagus
Madrid
SPAIN
Guadalquivir
Cádiz

PORTUGAL
Lisbon

MEDITERRANEAN

The Great Lines of Change

The turn of the eighteenth into the nineteenth century is generally regarded as the focus of a revolution which has its roots in the preceding hundred years and whose effects are still felt today. For Robert R. Palmer the period 1760 to 1800 is *The Age of the Democratic Revolution;* for E. J. Hobsbawm, *The Age of Revolutions* runs from 1789 to 1848. Without quibbling too much over dates, one cannot deny the number or importance of the changes and convulsions of this time. They led from absolute monarchies to constitutions and republics, from feudal institutions to representative ones, from political passivity alleviated by sporadic risings to participation and reform, from the speed and productivity of men and beasts to that of machines, from cottage industries to great manufacturing hives in factories and cities, from parochialism to world vision. Change has today become a part of life. It was not so in the eighteenth century, when stability was the norm, even in a life and world beset by the murderous spasms of war and insurrection, famine and plague. At the beginning of the period we are about to examine, environment, way of life, institutions, altered so little, so slowly, that to most men they could have seemed unchanging. By the time the period ended, for most Europeans this would never be so again.

Perhaps this shift from stability to mobility was the greatest revolution of the age and we still live within its shadow. Its groundwork was laid within the eighteenth century, its decisions were made by the middle of the nineteenth. One generation laid the foundations for the advances of the next, one generation worked on foundations laid down by the last. Not without trouble, convulsions, and pain. Here is a time of ideas in turmoil, techniques in transition, society in evolution, economies in flux, the whole world view modified. Religion collapses into privacy or secularism. Institutions, hierarchies, long taken for granted, are questioned, criticized, exposed, overturned, replaced by others. Against the background of international conflicts, social conflicts acquire new importance, forging new worlds in the embers of their fires. Wars themselves change, in mood and scale, from professional and dynastic enterprises to ideological crusades or national undertakings; and politics, no longer the preserve of a restricted circle, take the same coloring as war. The wars of princes become the wars of nations; the politics of courts come down into the street and marketplace, assemblies, and exchanges. Their mood, scale, tempo, also change; and so do the terms in which they are conducted as more and more people are involved.

The seeds of novelties to come had been sown in Holland and in England and in France, where new attitudes to state and trade, to administration and finance and public opinion (a term first forged at this time), had been formulated and, sometimes, even felt. In England especially, the political institutions, the social structures, bent to new winds; and England it would be which, after Utrecht, dominates not only the seas but the affairs of the century It was to England that the French philosophers looked, who formulated the criticisms and yearnings of the time, who lent their pens to the campaign for change which, in due course, would bring much change about. It was in England that the rebels inspired by French examples to gain their liberty often took refuge and, from these wards and offspring of the English realm, others would draw the hope that they could do as much. England, her colonies, then France, provided example, inspiration, and then proof that radical change could be brought about, new institutions set in place of old. Many would want, many would have, to follow.

Meanwhile, another revolution was taking place. What we now call the Industrial Revolution brought radical change in business and in industry—again a change in scale but also in conditions, frames of mind, and life—no less important than what happened in politics. Based on new wealth acquired and new stability achieved during the prosperous decades of the eighteenth century (roughly 1730–1770), this development took off in England, surged to the continent, holding out prodigious expectations for a new well-being belie at first by its ferocity. Carried on the new tide of wealth and opportunity, some grew affluent, the middle classes settled more firmly in power. But the poor workers who provided the human capital of the new industries felt little gain. Their clamor, their incipient struggles, introduced a new note in the cacophony of politics. Their very presence was a new factor which after 1848 would not be discounted again.

Their growing number was another. The population explosion is one of the great events of the late eighteenth and nineteenth centuries. Demographic pressures worked on political structures, burst out in revolutions and political unrest, spread outward from Europe in a vast exodus whose scale would make it the greatest migration that history has known.

In 1848 all these conflicts came to a head: the sheer weight of increasing numbers of people and their growing demands, notions of popular sovereignty and national consciousness, the political ambitions of the middle classes, the social claims of the workers, the feudal leftovers in many parts of Europe, traditional authorities and new interests, clashed, crashed, and were in great part settled. Not always resolved but, for a while, decided. The trends which the eighteenth century announced were fulfilled at last, the feudal age was buried, the middle classes or their values eclipsed the older hierarchies for good, the new contenders for a hearing and a say on class and national grounds had put in their claim, and their defeat set the pattern of struggles yet to come. The hopeful affirmations of the eighteenth century had been fulfilled with all the disillusions only fulfillment brings. Europe believed in progress because it had been proved. The questions progress begged were still unsettled in 1848; their innings would come later.

Chapter 8

THE WORLD
AND ITS HORIZONS

Industrial Revolution

"In every country a traveller can pass through," writes an English voyager of the 1780's, "he will find some mechanical contrivances, some modes of expediting work, which are of late invention, or at least new to him . . ." The Industrial Revolution has given rise to almost as many arguments as the Renaissance: was there an industrial revolution or was there an industrial evolution? Should events strung out over a century and sometimes more be described as a sudden, radical change? The debate, suggestive though it is, need not detain us here. G. M. Trevelyan seems to have solved the problem by calling the vast changes in the means and results of production which had their start in the second half of the eighteenth century a *process*, not an *event*. If we think of the Industrial Revolution in that way, we shall have no need to waste time on quibbles.

What actually happened seems to be fairly clear. It all started in Britain where, beginning in mid-eighteenth century, better medical schools, better midwifery, more orphanages and lying-in hospitals, kept more children alive, provided more migrants to the growing towns, a bigger reservoir of labor and consumers, above all a lower-middle class with the education and the technical background gathered in schools, and ready to take advantage of the opportunities held out by expanding markets.

Early in the eighteenth century Abraham Darby had discovered how to replace charcoal by coke in smelting iron, thus opening the way to expansion now that timber no longer commanded fuel needs. In 1759

413

The Duke of Bridgewater Canal. Opposite: the Staffordshire collieries. The "whimsey" or engine at the right is used to draw coal from the mines at the left.

the Duke of Bridgewater began the famous canal leading from his colliery to Manchester, and its success persuaded others to invest in the fundamental base without which a spurt in production would have been impossible. Then, in 1784, the puddling process to convert pig iron into malleable iron doubled and redoubled production, providing lasting iron rails to replace frailer wood.

Puddling and rolling made cast iron cheap. England rose to first rank among European iron producers—a handy accomplishment when sixty years of war lay ahead. John Wilkinson, the greatest of ironmasters, built the first iron bridge (1779), the first iron boat (1787), a Methodist chapel in iron, and was buried in an iron coffin (1805). At his works at Coalbrookdale, where coke first replaced charcoal in a blast furnace, even tombstones were made of iron. Wilkinson seems to have been an epic figure: he had a ballad written about him in his lifetime, and after his death the legend spread that he would rise again in seven years. But iron itself caught the imagination of the age; and a utopian novel of 1849 presents an ideal city erected entirely of iron. Perhaps more important, by 1825, cast iron cost two and a half times less in England than it did in France, and lower costs meant extraordinary possibilities for its use.

Iron called for coal, coal called for power and hence for steam, and steam spurred the mills. By 1757, the new industrial areas of the English Midlands set the imagination of the poet soaring:

> Thus all is here in motion, all is life:
> . . . th'echoing hills repeat
> The stroke of axe and hammer; scaffolds rise
> And growing edifices . . . and new streets . . .
> So appear
> Th'increasing walls of busy Manchester,
> Sheffield, and Birmingham, whose redd'ning fields
> Rise and enlarge their suburbs.

As shallow ore veins became exhausted, mines had to go deeper, engines were needed to pump out the water or provide ventilation. Power engines were devised to work the pumps—driven by human beings, horses, goats, and dogs. Something more sturdy was needed. The first successful piston steam engine appeared around 1712, the brainchild of two English engineers, Thomas Savery (1650?–1715) and Thomas Newcomen (1663–1729). But a really commercially successful design would be the work of James Watt (1736–1819), and did not come until 1776.

A poor man's son who had obtained a post of laboratory assistant and instrument maker at Glasgow University, Watt had to repair a Newcomen steam engine and was shocked by the heat it wasted as it worked. To remedy this, Watt devised a separate condenser (patented in 1769), which would subsequently be patented into the rotative steam engines that became standardized in the 1780's. By 1800, some 500 of these had been built by Watt and by his partner, Matthew Boulton (1728–1809) at their great Birmingham plant, in Soho.

Boulton and Watt sold, as the former put it "what all the world wants —Power." But the source of this power came from coal, and coal consumption jumped as the demand increased by leaps and bounds. So, coal, the need for which had spurred development of steam engines, would be needed even more as steam engines spread. And rising coal consumption, for quantities no longer small enough to be shipped by cart or packmule, in turn sparked the construction first of canals, then railroads, to link main rivers and industrial towns with ports, and also with the mining areas. Coal became the first raw material to be measured and carried by millions of tons; and, after coal, bricks and iron followed, and all the other heavy goods that stood as the foundation of heavy industry.

There was one industry where demand was even greater. Overseas trade and a growing home market called first of all for textiles to clothe the swelling masses of the globe. Increasing demand, in this field as

James Watt's first "sun and planet" steam engine, named for the manner in which the driving gear rotates around the flywheel gear. Right: the spinning jenny, invented by James Hargreaves in 1767.

in others, incited men to search for more efficient methods: division of labor, which replaced the craftsman's slow and careful work by a series of simple processes enabling unskilled labor to turn things out much faster; simplification of the product, by eliminating decoration and refinement; last but not least, technological improvements—the development and introduction of machines.

The first weaving machines may be dated back to the 1730's, when John Kay devised his flying shuttle, although they took some two decades to come into wider use. When they did, the faster rate of weaving increased the demand for yarn, which part-time spinners still spun on spinning wheels, and which tended to run especially short at harvest time when home producers left their cottages for the fields. In the 1760's, when British victories in India opened the Indian market to Lancashire cotton goods, this shortage became particularly acute. Result: the jenny of James Hargreaves (1767) enabling one man to work first eight then eighty spindles; then Robert Arkwright's water frame driven by water power (1769); then Samuel Crompton's mule (1774–1779) combining previous ideas to produce a much finer yarn. Greater yarn production pushed weavers to catch up, lest excess yarn be exported to continental competitors. Cartwright's power loom followed in the 1780's, using the possibilities provided by Newcomen and Watt.

The English textile industry progressed and expanded because the markets it supplied grew rapidly. Economic historians have expressed doubts whether before the nineteenth century the world market could have accommodated more than one industrialized economy able to provide (or needing) mass-produced goods on a modern scale. Holland, France, and Britain struggled for a market that the seventeenth and eighteenth centuries still regarded as fixed and unvarying. They assumed that one man's gains cut down the possibilities of other competitors; and perhaps this view, proved wrong in the nineteenth century, fitted the conditions of earlier times. The Dutch lacked the territorial base and the industrial tradition. French possibilities were limited by the weakness of the money market which hamstrung industrial expansion, but also by the fact that in the crucial eighteenth century France lost potential colonial outlets to Britain. By the late eighteenth century the British had captured or controlled most of the world's colonial areas; and this victory gave their industrialization a flying start, both from windfall profits and from demand.

Again, English settlements were more likely to provide such demand than the purely trading and mining posts of earlier days. Even more, the slave trade. Importation of slaves into the Americas grew five- or tenfold from about 10,000 a year in the 1640's to 50,000 and 100,000 a century later. The increase created a great demand for European goods in Africa, and plantation products increased demand for these and other goods on the plantations themselves and throughout the hinterland. In 1700, about 20 per cent of English exports were going to colonial areas; by 1759 over one-third of all British exports went to British colonies alone; by 1784 about half, if we include the new United States. And if we take the staple of the new Industrial Revolution—cotton goods—then the colonies, including Ireland, took almost 90 per cent of Britain's products until 1770.

Capitalism

But if all this brought in money, it also cost money. Machines need capital much greater than the tools of individual artisans. Raw capital was flowing in from overseas. Nationalist historians and some others have asserted that the capital of England's Industrial Revolution was supplied by Indian plunder, funneled back by returning nabobs. In actual practice, another source was far more important. Through Portugal, which in the eighteenth century became almost a British economic preserve,* Brazilian gold flowed into London banks to the tune, sometimes, of 50,000 pounds a week. The consequent accumulation of gold reserves enabled London to wrest the financial supremacy of Europe from Amsterdam, and provided the treasure which permitted England to carry on her wars without facing ruin. Meanwhile, English manufacturers were clothing and equipping Brazil as well as Africa.

But, while the bullion imports afforded much needed liquidity, the basic capital came out of the societies which it served, much as the spider's web is spun from the very substance of the beast. Serious indus-

---

* The British had supported Portugal's long seventeenth-century struggle to assert its independence from Spain, and in 1662 Charles II of England married a Portuguese princess whose dowry included Bombay. The two countries' alliance was enshrined in the Methuen treaty of 1703, promoting the exchange of port wine for English woolens and giving English merchants a commanding position in Portuguese trade.

trialization on a large scale required more money than even Brazil could provide. If the capital to set up one large enterprise might not seem overwhelming, the economic substructure of roads and docks and buildings and various means of transport was still largely lacking. It continued to be so everywhere until the eighteenth century, and in most places much later than that. Government after government tried to industrialize, but few really succeeded until—as in eighteenth-century Britain—the initial equipment had been accumulated for the Industrial Revolution to get off the ground. So England had a basic foundation which other countries had to build up while she thrived on hers.

There was, however, one obvious way to accumulate capital which others too could use. Throughout this time, and even more on the continent than in England, prices seem to have risen way ahead of wages, thus providing profits—that is, capital—with which the country's industrial and manufacturing strength could be built up. This stern lesson is clearly drawn in Earl Hamilton's *War and Prices in Spain 1651–1800**: "By involuntarily sacrificing real incomes through the price-wage squeeze, the laboring class bore the burden that implemented material progress, just as laborers and peasants in Soviet Russia, sacrificing through governmental directives, have largely financed the mechanization of industry . . . Along with other social groups, later generations of workers have reaped the rewards."

Capital now appeared, massive, mobile, created by labor rather than by land, available for reinvestment, circulating rapidly, contrasting with the rather stiff and stolid land economy in a society where money and men are on the move. And so appeared modern capitalists, whom one of Rousseau's correspondents mentioned in 1759 ("I am neither great lord nor capitalist"), whom Turgot defined in 1777 as "possessors of money," whom a speaker in the Convention of 1792 denounced: "Of whom is our republic composed? Of a small number of capitalists and a large number of poor. Who carries on the grain trade? That small number of capitalists. Why? To get rich. How can they get rich? By raising the price of grain. . . ."

There was one other source of capital and, in the late eighteenth century perhaps the most important, and this was trade. In the sixteenth and seventeenth centuries, shares in business ventures had come to be sold on the open market and impersonal capital, in shares of enterprises, began to take over the functions previously exercised by individual investors. Companies organized for periods longer than single voyages or ventures, warranted and acquired a separate impersonal "personality" of their own. Directors, investors, "managers," became replaceable, interchangeable, no longer absolutely crucial as the Fuggers or the Medicis had been.

In 1602, the foundation of the Dutch East India Company had brought into being the first giant stock-holding corporation. Others fol-

* (Cambridge, Mass.: 1947), p. 225.

The Royal Exchange in London.

lowed. The London Stock Exchange was incorporated under William III, the English Board of Trade set up in 1696, the French Council of Commerce in 1700, "The wealth of the nation, that used to be reckoned by the value of land, is now computed by the rise and fall of stocks," wrote Jonathan Swift in his *Examiner*. Large corporations and private trading ventures provided the original accumulation of modern capital, especially in France and England where overseas trade flourished. This was particularly true of England, where profits of trade tripling between 1715 and 1790 helped subsidize much of industry: Welsh iron works were backed by the money of London and Bristol colonial shippers, the Clydeside industry grew out of Glasgow's tobacco trade.

Where merchants would not lend a hand and private capital was lacking, there were banks. The seventeenth century saw state and private banks set up throughout the west, whose paper—guaranteed by their deposits—provided credit at more or less moderate interest. Holland had led the way, but Holland concentrated more on trading and finance operations than industrial production. In France, the crash of speculative banking schemes in 1720 discouraged the development of banking activities, and thus restricted investment credit there until Napoleon founded the Bank of France in 1800. So England had an advantage here as well. To carry the story forward, since industrial development fed on capital, banks became its mainstay and the indispensable turntables of modern economy. The nineteenth century would be the age of bankers—or else of usurers like Balzac's Grandet or Gobseck, Dickens' Murdstone or Sir Ralph Nickleby, men who made a fortune out of a credit-hungry world. "The bank heads the state," noted the French novelist Stendhal in the 1830's. "The bourgeoisie has taken over from the nobles and the bankers are the nobles of the bourgeois class."

The Rothschilds must have been the greatest of these bourgeois nobles and the origin of their fortune throws a useful light on the services that bankers could provide. In the 1790's, the landgrave George William of Hesse-Cassel—a colossal brute who had shut his wife in a fort in order to be free to enjoy his mistress in his Cassel palace—worried that the invading French revolutionaries would take his fortune accumulated largely by Hesse's trade in soldiers, entrusted it to Meyer Amstel Rothschild of Frankfurt, who paid regular interest on the wealth and returned it to the landgrave when the danger had passed, much increased. The landgrave then turned over the management of all his financial affairs to Rothschild, and publicized his trustworthiness all over Europe.

In the meantime, Meyer's sons, established in Frankfurt, Vienna, London, Paris, and Naples, had rendered signal services to the princes allied against France by conveying British subsidies to Britain's allies, and had increased their capital as well. Their reward came after the war was over, as Metternich helped secure baronies for all of them, and also moved to improve the condition of the Frankfurt Jews. Karl Rothschild, head of the Naples branch, was decorated by the Pope himself. Baron James, in Paris, supported composers like Meyerbeer and Berlioz, novelists like Balzac, poets like Heine, while his balls and dinners were no less famous than his artistic interests. Lionel in England, elected to the House of Commons in 1847 by the City of London, could not take his seat because of his religion; he was re-elected in 1858, and the form of the Parliamentary oath was changed partly to accommodate him.

These men provided the capital for French railroads and United States bonds, for steamship companies on the Danube and railroad enterprises in Bohemia, for paying Austrian troops in Lombardy and equipping the rebel student corps in Vienna in 1848. They seemed indispensable, omnipotent, and omnipresent. In 1844, G. Toussenel, a follower of Fourier, the socialist reformer, published a significant attack, *The Jews, Kings of Our Time,* in which he argued that it was not the people but the Jews who reigned and governed, above all the Rothschild Bank. Toussenel's allegations would echo down the ages. Of course, it was not the Jews who reigned; but, to some extent, the bankers—of whom some of the more visible were Jews. They were, true enough, the harbingers and symbols of great changes which, without capital, without a banking structure that could collect and distribute it, could not have taken place. And they were hated as representatives of change —of that change which, for better or for worse, was affecting all people in its turmoil.

The Price of Change

With the nineteenth century, the price of change, the pressure of progress, seemed to increase. In France the textile worker's wages in the second quarter of the nineteenth century were half what they had been in 1800; the wage index for miners, 100 in 1792, was 49 in 1850. In England, the domestic weaver who made thirty shillings a week around 1820, was making seven or nine shillings twenty years later. Industry, once dependent largely on home production, was organized in factories: "This temple, where is offered up/To gain, the master-idol of the realm,/Perpetual sacrifice"; and factories reminded observers, and not least their inmates, of barracks, or convents, or prisons.

In 1817, Mary Shelley invented *Frankenstein* as a symbolic tale of science creating slaves out of men and also creating monsters that could master and destroy them. It seemed as if Leviathan had been reborn. The ideal factory was, in the words of one of their leading advocates, "a vast automaton," its various organs—mechanical or human—"subordinate to a self-regulated moving force." Machines fitted well enough in this, but workers were less reliable; and the main difficulty lay in "training human beings to renounce their desultory habits of work and to identify themselves with the unvarying regularity of the complex automaton."

The author of these remarks, Dr. Andrew Ure, even advised mill owners "to organize their moral machinery on equally sound principles with their mechanical," meaning presumably that moral discipline and religious enthusiasm could help chain or channel passions and emotions which could otherwise endanger the regularity and discipline of work, productivity, or social order.

This could go a long way. Wordsworth, in his *Excursion* (1814), described the boy deprived of "the short holiday of childhood":

> Creeping his gait and cowering, his lip pale,
> His respiration quick and audible;
> And scarcely could you fancy that a gleam
> Could break out from those languid eyes . . .
> —Can hope look forward to a manhood raised
> On such foundations?
>   Hope is none for him!
> And tens of thousands suffer wrong as deep.

Yet

> Economists will tell you that the state
> Thrives by the forfeiture—unfeeling thought
> And false as monstrous!

When the great French wallpaper manufacturer, Oberkampf, was ennobled in 1787, the decree congratulated him for employing in his factory many children "from the age of five and six." In fact, even babies of three and four could be put to work plaiting straw or making lace. By 1804, the poet William Blake was singing bitterly about "those dark

Children at work in a textile factory.

Satanic mills" to which little boys and girls trudged at three in the morning, from which they tottered home after ten at night, after a day in which the hour off for meals was partly spent cleaning the machines.

Apprentice children from workhouses or bankrupt enterprises were sold in batches like slaves to factories where the day shift often collapsed into the night shift's bunks without giving them time to cool. Small boys worked from dawn till dusk in squalid, filthy shops. Many toppled from weariness into the machinery to be maimed or killed. Many were flogged or tortured, had weights hung down their backs, heavy hand-vices screwed to their ears, or were tied, three or four at a time, "on a cross-beam above the machinery, hanging by our hands, without shirts or stockings," as a witness told a British Commission of Inquiry in 1833.

Not only boys squatted solitary daylong in the dark beside the shaft trap of a mine, beaten to keep awake, facing walks of a mile or more to and from work. Girls and women, man's earliest beasts of burden, did so too. More and more of them worked in factories and mines where some, bare to the waist and crawling on all fours through the long, dark shafts. pushed or pulled the wagonets of coal, then carried huge loads of it on their backs up long ladders from pit to surface. They cried as they climbed, one witness tells us, all the way. Draught animals. Or drudges like the little sweeps sent up to clear chimney flues in which they often stuck and died, even as late as 1863 when Charles Kingsley wrote his *Water Babies,* based on a Royal Commission report of that year. This should remind us that the worst conditions were not necessarily in industry, but among small masters and independent journeymen struggling to survive in the new industrial world.

However much mechanization increased, at this stage it was still only a portent. The greatest raw material of the Industrial Revolution was human, and human brawn and sinew long continued to be its chief source of power: the backs of men to carry coal, the arms of men to push wheelbarrows full of sand for nine miles sometimes and nine miles back empty for one shilling a day, the ditches dug, rails laid, coal chipped, wool and cotton woven and pottery turned by the fists and the picks and the skills of human beings, hundreds of thousands of them, more and more of them, competing with one another for jobs when the economy faltered, for demeaning, exhausting, abasing, occasional and seasonal and casual labor, immolated on the altars of supply and demand. As the men who sowed and plowed and harvested went hungry, so the men who wove the cloth went in rags, the men who baked the bricks lived in cellars, the men who mined the coal went without fire, the hundreds of thousands of domestics who catered to the increasing comfort of their masters were banished to basements and garrets.

"It is as if the English nation entered a crucible in the 1790's and emerged after the wars in a different form," writes E. P. Thompson. Contemporary observers, too, reflect this sense of catastrophic change, in class relations, in economic activities, in political and social attitudes, in scale and speed of movement, of change and of transition. The catastrophic view of industrial revolution has been much challenged of late by an almost semantic re-evaluation of phenomena: enclosures are not harsh dislocating measures, but contributions to agricultural efficiency; starvation wages and squalid slums are seen as part of a necessary process of capital accumulation and relocation of labor, shaking a whole new world into place; popular unrest becomes social tension, and the grim horrors of unemployment and hunger disappear behind tables of statistics, cycles, food prices and wage scales which document a steady improvement.

It has been argued by W. W. Rostow that all this was the price that society had to pay before it could "take off into self-sustained economic growth," that present consumption and existing welfare had to be sacrificed to accumulate the capital base, the long-term investments and substructure, buildings and equipment and roads and railways, without which expansion and future prosperity would have been impossible.

But maybe we should forget the determinism that we read into events after they have happened, think less about standards and more about ways of life: loss of independence, loss of status, monotony, discipline, conditions of work, the conscious sense of becoming a machine like others, or a bookkeeping item rather than a person. In the end, people suffered. Lives were dislocated, social relations disrupted. The industrial development multiplied and practically created before it ground them down, domestic workers, miners, factory workers, transport workers, and plantation slaves, all of whom increased in numbers to answer the demand for cotton and calico, iron and coal, stuffs and steam. It crowded them together in horrid lives no less awful for being necessary and, if their conditions of life in earlier days may not have been more sanitary, they were almost certainly less unpleasant, less ugly, and less open to disease and crime.

The Agricultural Revolution

In the age of the Industrial Revolution, the greatest industry remained agriculture; and agriculture also was revolutionized, so that fewer men on the land were eventually able to supply and feed far greater populations. The seventeenth century had counted seven important agricultural inventions; the eighteenth brought forth thirty-eight, the greatest part during its second half; and sixteen more would see the light between 1815 and 1848. A new, much heavier plow, allowing deeper plowing, was being widely used by 1800, so were manure to improve the soil, and forage corps to see more cattle through the hungry winters. Cattle breeding and animal husbandry made great strides, so that in Germany and the Netherlands where cows had given 150 gallons of milk a year in 1750, by 1800 cows gave up to 400 gallons a year. Butter churns, cheese presses, also were improved and wool production rose to meet demands—permitting, for example, British imports to rise from an average of 2.5 million pounds a year before 1799 to over 35,000,000 pounds in the 1830's.

The crux of agricultural changes lay in the fact that, sometime in the eighteenth century, an industry geared to provide subsistence turned to production for markets and for profit. The seventeenth-century Dutch had already set this trend; and soon the English followed. In 1733, Jethro Tull's book on horse-hoeing outlined the new principles: rows cleaned of weeds, economy of seed, a sowing machine sowing in regular rows. A great reforming landowner fascinated by the possibilities of root crops, especially turnips, Viscount Charles Townshend (1674–1738) inspired by Tull and by Dutch methods, showed that practical improvements could bring a profit. Then, in the 1760's Robert Bakewell (1725–1795) turned attention to stock-breeding.

The new root crops provided better fodder. Sheep, once bred for wool, would now be bred for meat, to answer the needs of a growing population. The average weight of oxen sold at the London slaughterhouse between 1710 and 1795 more than doubled, that of calves trebled, that of sheep went up two and a half times. Breeding and fodder made the roast beef of old England. Last, came the most impressive of the land reformers: William Coke, Earl of Leicester (1752–1842) who made 48,000 acres of poor Norfolk land at Holkham fertile by turning the subsoil to the top, surrounded his estate with a high wall and turned it into an experimental farm for trying out all sorts of crops, which do not seem to have done too badly, since we learn that his revenue increased from £2,200 a year to £20,000. What was, perhaps, equally remarkable, this gentleman married at sixty-nine a girl of eighteen and produced five sons and a daughter.

While English reformers showed an empirical bent, the French seem to have been more theoretical. Tull's ideas spread to France in mid-eighteenth century, but few took them up. More popular were the new physiocratic doctrines put forward by François Quesnay (1694–1774), personal physician to the royal mistress, Madame de Pompadour. Quesnay, who had set out to find a way to improve the tax yield, concluded (rightly for his time) that the best source of revenue was land. *Physiocracy* (from two Greek words meaning the force of nature) was a reaction against the mercantilist insistence on industry which the French associated with Colbert. Not industry but land, argued Quesnay's followers, is the real basic source of riches. The existing fiscal system discouraged intelligent enterprise by undertaxing land and overtaxing trade and industry. Landowners were stupid, selfish, and protected. Their lack of enterprise slowed down the growth of industry and commerce, and left these to bear the charges of the state. The only remedy was for all existing taxes to be abolished and replaced by a single tax on land property, estimated not on the revenue the land might bring but on the value of the land itself—that is, on its capacity of production. Landowners would then be forced to draw out of their ill-exploited lands profits proportionate to their real potential, or else to sell them to those who could and would.

Going beyond this, and carried by the logic of their arguments, the physiocrats became the advocates of free trade and *laisser faire*, calling first of all for abolition of restrictions on the internal movement of goods, especially of grain, and on its export too. They reasoned that a free grain trade would raise prices, encourage grain production—especially large-scale cultivation, which would be most economical and productive—and hence bring larger crops and also better revenue from taxes. The physiocrats stood against all anachronistic trammels: mercantilistic regulation, feudal privileges and exemptions; and on this they agreed with their Scotch contemporary, Adam Smith, who also objected to the artificial distribution of social resources under the existing system but, being British, thought more about encouraging trade and industry.

Under the impact of argument in France and proof in England, under the more direct pressure of population growth and economic need, the surface of land under cultivation increased throughout western Europe. Drainage and irrigation brought into use fens in Yorkshire and Lincolnshire, polders in Holland, marshes in Italy, Germany, and France. The English, Dutch, and Belgians led the field. But men like Frederick II in Prussia, Turgot in France, Grand Duke Leopold in Tuscany, did their best to stimulate agricultural progress. Veterinary schools were founded, some before 1789; between 1770 and 1850 new tools and techniques appeared, especially on large estates, where—sometimes in a lifetime—factory-made cast iron plows replaced the local product, seed no longer broadcast would be sown by drills, harvesting and threshing came to be done by machines which drove out flails and sickles. McCormick's reaper, patented in 1834, began to be mass-produced in 1846.

Clover, turnips, and other fodder crops increased supplies of animal feed for winter. More and fitter livestock provided larger quantities of manure to fertilize the soil, but increasingly artificial manure came into use as fertilizer: waste, shreds, peat, turf, crushed bones especially (to such extent that old battlefields were scoured for more), had to serve until the 1820's saw the first shiploads of Peruvian guano and Chilean nitrates. England was using 220,000 tons in 1847. That same decade, the artificial fertilizer industry was taking shape, with the manufacture of calcium superphosphate in England by Sir John Bennett Lawes (1814–1900) and in Germany by Justus Liebig (1803–1873). Agriculture was becoming scientific. *The Journal of the Royal Agricultural Society* was founded in 1838. Justus Liebig published his *Organic Chemistry in its Relations to Agricultural and Plant Physiology* in 1840.

The Napoleonic wars and the British blockade of continental Europe led to a search for substitutes for articles that the blockade cut off. Sugar was so rare that in those rich homes which could still secure it, a piece was sometimes hung from the ceiling so that everyone could plunge it for a few seconds into his cup. The first factory to make sugar from beet roots was built in 1801; by 1836, Europe produced three-quarters of a million tons. By then the agricultural market had broadened and altered quite a lot: freight trains and steamships were carrying prod-

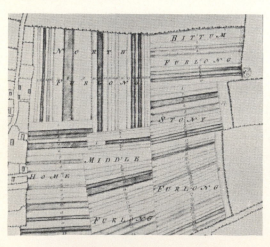

An excerpt from a survey book of Strettington, Sussex, showing individual landholdings in 1781.

uce and cattle, Odessa was shipping almost as much wheat as Danzig.

All this took money. That was partly why initiative for innovations came from the authorities (as we have seen already), from agricultural societies, rare landowners with progressive views, and, only very rarely, from peasants themselves, little inclined to any innovation. Gentlemen or vicars fired by reading the works of agronomists, some country iron-master, frequently postmasters eager for sources of fodder to feed their horses, might venture on applying the newfangled methods. In any case, modern agriculture called for capital which the smaller farmer could not hope to find. Rural credit appeared first for the rich, and smaller men were driven to the wall or left to linger in their backwardness.

This was true in all countries, but especially true as one moved eastward or southward across Europe, and the different levels of development can be discerned from the way in which population shifted from the country to the cities. By 1830, only 25 per cent of English population lived in rural parts, France and Italy had 40 percent of their population in cities, Belgium and Holland more than that. But over 70 per cent of Prussian population, over 90 per cent in Spain, over 95 per cent in Russia and eastern Europe still lived on the land—and off it. And there, as on the small, chopped-up, impoverished holdings of central and southern France, sowing and harvesting were still done by hand, with gestures that an ancient Egyptian would have recognized; livestock remained costive; goats, the poor man's cows, nibbled away at everything they could; average productivity remained low. The revolution in agriculture progressed like that in industry and, if it went at a slower pace, it left behind as many casualties.

This had significant results and for a while Europe, which had always been an agricultural economy, lived on two levels: with part of its economy industrial and part still agricultural. Agricultural and industrial economies have a different incidence on general well-being. The former is less flexible. Politically, every bad harvest could become a civil danger. Any grain shipments, carts on the roads, barges on rivers and canals, government convoys, or merchants heading for the highest market, gave an impression of abundance in the midst of scarcity which persuaded the common people that the high prices were not due to shortage but to speculation, conspiracy, and ill will.

Popular notions are always anthropomorphic, their economic conjectures always come down to personalities: the government, the brokers, or the owners are to blame. What bad harvests really mean is high prices, when the farmer has little to sell after deducting his own needs for food, seed (one-fifth or a quarter of the average old-fashioned harvest), and dues; and the high price of bread affects both the landless laborers and industrial workers at the very time when lower revenues would shrink demand and cause unemployment. Only very large farmers with reserves, or landlords cashing in on fixed rents, could prosper while all others suffer. Industrial prices on the other hand rise with greater demand which reflects greater possibilities—that is, greater prosperity. In agricultural societies high prices mean low production. In industrial societies (except when raw materials run short, as cotton would do in the 1860's high prices mean prosperity and invite greater production.

Higher agricultural prices cannot be answered with greater production by small farmers, whose flexibility is limited by capital, means, land, and shortage of seed. Only large landowners can put more land to the plow and they are reluctant to do so, thinking that they are doing well enough as it is. From this there follows unemployment, which only aggravates the economic crisis. This was the situation in 1789 and it appeared again in 1847 and 1848. But by then it was an exception; and railroads, steamships, international trade, would soon be turning it into an anachronism. Agriculture like industry was becoming modern and, in the age of industry, it would become a secondary factor, no longer dominant, no longer threatening the livelihood of men or the stability of industrialized society.

Society and Societies

More Food, More People

A historian of Britain in the 1750's begins his description with a revealing phrase: "To understand how human life looked and felt," he writes, "we have to begin by removing six out of seven persons in its present population." The world of 1700 or of 1750 was a much less crowded world, for objects and for people. But it would become more crowded, it was growing so, and this is when demography changes gears. In 1750 the process was only starting; by 1850 it was rolling fast.

Estimates of population figures in the eighteenth century are still somewhat approximative, especially beyond western Europe; but it would seem that the world population, about 600 million in 1700, stood around 900 million in 1800. Within this population, that of Europe increased faster than Asia's, much faster than Africa's, spilling over into the Western Hemisphere, where American rates of population growth were a magnified reflection of those in the European homeland. European population, which probably hovered around 100 million in 1650, about 140 million a hundred years later, has been estimated at 187 million in 1800 and 274 million in 1850. Within Europe itself demographic relations were changing: the British Isles went up from 9 million in 1700 to 16 million in 1800 and over 27 million in 1850; Italy rose from 18 million to 25 million between 1800 and 1850; Germany without Austria almost matched France's 35 million in 1850, second only to the 57 million of Russia. But some nations had higher birth rates than others: the French birth rate fell; the British stabilized around 32 per 1,000 in 1850, while the Germans boasted 40 per 1,000 and the United States 43.3.

Life expectation figures can also be revealing, though only in a very general way: life expectancy seems to have risen from 33 to 40 years in Sweden between 1755 and 1840, from 35 to 41 years in the United States between 1789 and 1850. In France the average life span increased from 21 in the years around 1660 to 32 in the years around 1780, and averaged 38 in 1832. Such figures can easily be misleading, for they ignore the vast variations between the rich and poor, the fact that at a time when the average age was 38, that of an Alsatian cotton spinner would be 22; and that in 1830 in an industrial center like Lille in northern France, half of the children died before they reached the age of five. They tell us one thing, however: people lived longer, though nowhere near as long as they do today. When at 46 Diderot visited the town where he had been born, he found that most of his childhood friends were dead. Life was still brief in 1759.

What caused the population explosion, we do not know. Did the death rate decline because of better medical practice, better drugs, and better midwives, improved housing, water, food supplies and general hygiene? Did the birth rate rise because social taboos were breaking down and the illegitimacy rate was soaring, or because of a conscious attempt to produce more potential wage earners for a family?

There was more food: not greater food consumption *per capita,* but there were more regular supplies and fewer periodical shortages. Some people may have eaten worse, but most ate more regularly. Endemic illnesses disappeared, especially smallpox, which had killed almost a third of children before the age of four. Yet scholars tell us that mortality remained terribly high. Undernourished, unresistant, recurrent epidemics knocked down the poor like ninepins. Smallpox drew back as vaccination advanced, but typhus, cholera, syphilis, and consumption raged, while malaria ruled over Mediterranean countries. The terrible thing about death, Proust has said, is that it nearly always simplifies life for the survivors. This was a young society (in France in 1815 44 per cent of the population were below twenty, only 7 per cent over sixty), and one where the weak went to the wall.

As for the survivors, they went to the city. In England where the population was growing 30 per cent in every generation, the cities grew still faster. Manchester had some 12,000 inhabitants in 1760, 50,000 in 1780, double that by 1801, 400,000 in 1850, doubled again in time for the First World War. Liverpool had 26,000 in 1670, 77,000 in 1800, 375,000 in 1850. Glasgow, 30,000 in 1750, was ten times as populous a hundred years later. Such figures may not seem overwhelming in twentieth-century America; they were so then. The crux of the demographic revolution lies in the migration of country people to the towns and in the growth of big cities at the expense of small ones. In 1850 England, of the 3,336,000 inhabitants of London and the sixty biggest cities, only 1,337,000 had been born in the cities where they lived. In London, as in Paris, far less than half the people had been born there. *This* was a revolution.

As we have seen, the basis of the eighteenth-century economy was still agricultural. By increasing the mass of workers in an economy which had little flexibility because of its agricultural basis, the demographic revolution of the eighteenth century may be said to have worsened the workers' lot. In industrial societies high prices mean high demand and encourage the employer to grant higher wages; in agricultural societies dependent on the harvest, high prices generally mean low production and low demand, so that the employer is readier to fire workers than to give them more pay just when they need the money to buy the dearer bread, while periods of prosperity mean cheaper bread, hence less pressure to improve a pay which seems relatively more adequate.

In Padua in the eighteenth century, masons earned 384 lire a year, foremen 512—the same as the cost of a theater box for three months. In the countryside, the day-laborers, the *braccianti,* when fully employed, earned 161 lire, of which a minimum of 128 were needed for food and 20-30 to pay for lodgings. That left little or nothing for taxes, heat, or emergencies. In France, on the eve of the revolution, an agricultural laborer made 10-12 sous a day, an artisan 15–18 sous, skilled workers 26–30. With bread at 3 sous a pound, beef 7 sous a pound, coffee (a luxury) 27 sous a pound, wine 4 sous a bottle and milk 2 sous a pint, the cost of a day's food came to a minimum of 18–19 sous at least. Some workers worked for eighteen hours a day—when they found work. The printers and bookbinders who worked only fourteen hours were regarded as the aristocracy of labor. In 1808, the English House of Commons was told that a skilled workman made eight shillings a week for ninety hours' labor (fifteen hours a day for six days a week). No wonder that within a few years textile workers like the Luddites were rioting through the Midlands, breaking up the machinery which put them out of work or chained them to it.

Unlike today, the price of food was even more important than a worker's wages. Wage rates stayed fairly steady: prices varied. When a poor harvest made food prices rise, popular effervescence would begin. That was what happened in 1787–1789, in 1838–1840, and in the hungry 40's. In 1847 and 1848 the price of bread doubled, and sometimes worse than that: a catastrophe for those whose diet consisted largely of bread. As a greater proportion of working-class income had to turn back to food (assuming it had ever been spent on something else), the industrial sector was affected, sales receded, unemployment rose, and a revolutionary situation was created.

DURING THE
INDUSTRIAL REVOLUTION
1820-1840

▲ City populations over 200,000 in 1820
▲ City populations over 200,000 by 1840

POPULATION INCREASES
BY PERCENTAGE, 1820-1840

10–25
25–50
50–75

Industrial areas

▼ Coal mining

BLACK SEA

OTTOMAN EMPIRE

GREECE

RUSSIA

Moscow

SWEDEN

NORWAY

DENMARK

Copenhagen

Hamburg

Berlin

Warsaw

Breslau

Prague

GERMANY

Munich

AUSTRIA–HUNGARY

Budapest

Vienna

BALTIC SEA

NORTH SEA

ADRIATIC SEA

Venice

Milan

Turin

Genoa

Florence

ITALY

CORSICA

SARDINIA

SWITZ.

NETHERLANDS

Amsterdam

Brussels

Lux.

Paris

FRANCE

Bordeaux

Marseilles

MEDITERRANEAN SEA

GREAT BRITAIN

Glasgow

Edinburgh

Leeds

Manchester

Liverpool

Sheffield

Nottingham

Birmingham

Bristol

London

Dublin

SPAIN

Madrid

PORTUGAL

Lisbon

ATLANTIC OCEAN

"No one ignores," wrote a Lyons manufacturer in 1786, "that price of food sets the price of labor," and that low cost of labor makes the low price of goods and hence better sales. But "it is necessary that the worker should never grow rich, that he should have precisely what he needs to clothe and feed himself." For "in certain classes too much ease dulls industry, breeds laziness and all the vices that depend on it." Most of this time there was little chance for ease to dull industry. The buying power of the working classes depended on the harvest—we might say on the weather. Meat in the eighteenth century was still considered a luxury by most. It would be only in 1789 that the French National Assembly mentioned it as "an aliment of secondary necessity." A family would eat 2–3 pounds of bread a day in good years, less than one pound in bad, and little else. To make clear what this means, one must know that two and a half pounds of bread are the equivalent of 3,000 calories, which would be the absolute minimum required by a family of five. They could expect to get this one year out of four. Potatoes in northern and western Europe, corn in the southeast, enabled more people to survive on smaller wages and possibly put off revolt until production increased or society organized enough to give some satisfaction or crush dissatisfaction. Yet the poor must have lived all the time on the verge of hunger. The specter of famine returned every bad harvest year. Fear of the panics and riots which might arise from this accounted for the cumbersome and complicated system of regulations and surveillance, which were intended to keep markets and bakers supplied with flour, but which hindered and clogged agricultural development, movement and initiative, and burdened the state with heavy charges and with the worst suspicions too.

The Dark Side of the City

By the nineteenth century, living space in the cities had become horribly restricted. A German visitor to England compared working-class quarters to the worst ghettos of the continent. In Bristol, half the families visited by official investigators lived all in one room. In London, the proportion was much greater. In Paris, a mason who came to town in 1830 lived in a room where twelve lodgers shared six beds. Martin Nadaud who remembered this, worked hard, got rich, and became a deputy. Others did not, like the old woman quoted by Blanqui: "I am not rich, but I have my heap of straw. God thanks." By the 1820's, research conducted in Paris had established a direct relation between the height of men and their position on the tax rolls—that is, between wealth and physical development. Death rates in the poorer quarters were two and three times those of the wealthier ones. An official French report of 1840 found that where four out of ten conscripts from agricultural regions would be rejected as unfit for service, the proportion among recruits from industrial departments was nine in ten.

Wentworth Street, by Gustave Doré, a print depicting "the dangerous classes" in the slums of nineteenth-century London.

Thousands lived underground, in cellars and in basements with no light or heat, only the eternal bone-searing dampness. In Manchester, in 1832, the Board of Health found 20,000 such lodgings; in Liverpool, Engels counted 45,000 troglodites and, thirty years later, Taine found that things had not changed. In France, at Lille, thousands were crowded in basements with earthen floors full of filthy puddles, lying on beds of straw that crawled with vermin or on potato parings or, even, sand and ashes. Privies were scarce: one for 120 people in Manchester's Little Ireland, so that most used the courtyard, the stairs, or hallways. Piles of excrement stood in yard or close, rising sometimes as high as fifteen or twenty feet, awaiting the contractors who carted if off once a week, or even once a month, to sell to farmers.

Fed on adulterated provisions, their sugar mixed with soap boiler's refuse, their flour mixed with gypsum and with chalk, their pepper with pounded nutshells, their cocoa with brown earth; clad in rags they seldom took off and even more seldom washed, freezing in the cold, stifling in the heat, dying like flies in recurrent epidemics or just of anything that can attack worn and weakened constitutions, to be buried in loosely covered ditches from which the putrefaction spread to the neighborhood; misshapen, brutalized, unwashed (of course, since few houses had water and some streets had no pumps), untaught, and hopeless—these were the cholera-incubators of the early 1830's and the late 1840's, the men and women with reference to whom the moralists justified the moral depravity of the lower classes.

"The workers" wrote a French observer, "are as free of duties towards their masters as their masters are towards them; they consider them as

The Stonemason's Yard, by Canaletto. National Gallery, London.

men of a different class, opposed to them, even hostile. Cut off from the nation, cast out of the social and political community, alone with their needs and their misery, they agitate to escape this frightening solitude and, like the barbarians to whom they have been compared, perhaps they meditate an invasion." Savages and outcasts, these people were both a threat to society and a necessity, a little like the black laborers of South Africa today: potential criminals whom circumstances continually turned into actual ones. One observer estimated some 115,000 criminals living in London around 1800, when the population was somewhat less than a million: Not only thieves and harlots, coiners and receivers, but wonderful types whom he enumerates, like scroungers, mudlarks, scuffle-hunters, bludgeon men, morocco men, flash coachmen, grubbers, bear baiters and strolling minstrels.* There was little security, and less sense of it, since the general assumption held people without a steady job or source of income to be actual or potential criminals; and the general assumption was not far wrong. This is the age that gave birth to the revealing description "poor *but* honest."

"The laws are spiders' webs through which the great flies pass and in which the small are caught." This phrase, written by Montesquieu in the eighteenth century, would be Balzac's conclusion to his epic of nineteenth-century finance: *La Maison Nucingen* (1837–1838). Police were extremely scarce; smugglers, bandits, highwaymen pullulated. As

* Patrick Colquhoun, *Treatise on the Police of the Metropolis* (1797), quoted in Edward P. Thompson, *Making of the English Working Class* (New York: 1964), p. 55.

late as the 1830's, great pitched battles were fought on the English coast between smugglers and newly organized coast guards. Cutpurses and criminals existed in every street. The arm of the law was short but its penalties were terrible, making up in savagery what they lacked in efficiency. In Paris in the 1830's, criminals were still exposed at the stake before the town hall, to be publicly branded with a red-hot iron. It was in the 1830's, also, that public executions were shifted from that central spot toward the city gates, and began to take place at dawn, which only partly discouraged attendance in this early rising age. In the 1820's Hans Christian Andersen and his schoolfellows near Copenhagen were taken to witness a triple execution as an edifying sight. Similarly, in *The Fairchild Family,* a juvenile best-seller of those days, the father takes his children to see a man hung in chains, in order to warn them by example.

When police were almost nonexistent, spies and informers provided an essential cog in the machinery of government. Since they were paid by results, such men tended to become *agents provocateurs,* stirring up the very crimes they were hired to detect—whether by planting forged bank notes to collect blood money or by sparking conspiracies to do better still. Paradoxically, the more police, the more humanity. The London metropolitan police was founded in 1829, and policemen called bobbies after Sir Robert Peel who organized them. A rural police appeared only after 1839. Capital offenses became restricted in the 1820's and 30's, the pillory went out in 1837, about the same time as cockfighting, bull- or bearbaiting; but public executions continued until 1865.

If sewers play such an important part in the writings and the terminology of the time (as in the novels of Victor Hugo), it is because never have sewers resumed and subsumed so utterly the hidden realities of city life. Crime was no longer a sort of marginal waste—the offal, so to speak, of urban life; no longer an exceptional but a normal part and consequence of it. The memoirs of Vidocq, criminal and policeman, published in 1828, inspired Balzac, Hugo, and Sue; became a legend that struck sparks off the everyday reality of crime to inflame the popular imagination. "If we write terrible things," a correspondent wrote to Sue in 1843, "it is because everything around us is terrible. If we are anxious, ill at ease in our society, it is because the future is here, more terrible and perhaps more bloody than the past."

The suicide rate rose. Illegitimacy and infanticide went up by leaps and bounds, until one enthusiastic English Malthusian suggested that all working-class children after the third should be asphyxiated, which caused some debate. On the other hand, of babies in the Paris foundling hospital —which received twenty a day in 1835—a quarter died in their first year. Slower than infanticide, perhaps, but more legal.

Death, banished from the imagery of the lighter-hearted eighteenth century, reappears in the nineteenth as symbol and as fact, hovering over the minds, the works, the lives of the Romantics, but more concretely over the masses, whose mortality rate rose to fearful peaks, running wild in the great cholera epidemics of 1832 and 1848, cutting its widest swath where misery, overwork, and underfeeding had prepared the ground. There was no equality there, and no fraternity either: the cold and death which Victor Hugo evokes in *Les Misérables* as leading to the barricades, turned disease into revolt and social malady into political malady. When people speak of revolution as a fever, the fact shines through the image to reveal the biological basis of social unrest.

Social unrest there was aplenty, often what Eric Hobsbawm calls "collective bargaining by riot." Where the machines appeared, low wages, unemployment—first of all in England, but also in France and Belgium, Switzerland, the Rhineland, and Saxony—the workers struck or rioted. In French textile towns the revolution of 1830 flared up to cries of "Break the machines!" The workers claimed to fight for bread and work. But the bourgeoisie was not about to grant them bread without work, and it would give them work only when it needed them. No interference was tolerated with the free operation of the market (except occasionally in order to impose tariffs), labor must be free, unorganized, unconstrained, divided before employers. Calls for regulation, maximum hours, minimum wages, or anything that interfered with the laboring man's freedom were similarly opposed. Interference to defend the poor was denounced as tyranny; and if the poor preserved from tyranny rebelled, they must be crushed. "No quarter," ordered the French prime minister, Thiers, in 1834; "All must be killed," decreed General Bugeaud who carried out his orders. "No quarter, be pitiless . . . we have got to slaughter 3,000 rebels." The figure would be upped in 1848, and a year later we find Bugeaud muttering to Thiers: "What brute ferocious beasts! . . . there are the true enemies, not the Russians or the Austrians!"

So, poverty was a crime. But it was also an economic phenomenon, an outgrowth of market oscillations, of demand and supply, or growth of population. This point of view was new and its effects insidious. Having become a factor of production, the poor man would soon move ahead to a larger role. In the medieval or Catholic view, the poor man is the image of Christ, the one who is sure of a place in heaven. Beggars are hallowed by the begging friars, by St. Francis, and by the opportunity which they afford all men to exercise charity. In the modern view, poverty is not virtue but a vice or the result of vices; charity only an encouragement to idleness, not just a social ill but the Devil's playground. The best kind of charity is work, or giving work. Where there were many mansions in Christ's father's house, now there was just a workshop.

This kind of attitude could be, and generally was, very harsh indeed, providing a good conscience to those in comfortable circumstances who could look down on misery and disapprove it without feeling involved by it. But those who did feel involved, affected, now found that charity was not enough. Resignation to individual and mass misery, which beggar and philanthropist both accepted, was not possible to minds for which poverty was evil and must be cured not by benefactions but by labor, discipline, social organization, and education. If poverty is a failure of character, reform would be the training of character: schooling and, if need be, forced labor. But if labor is a duty, it is also a right which society cannot refuse to those who ask for it. Asking for charity had been dishonorable, asking for work was honorable and manly. Here lay the justification of new social claims.

The Brighter Side

The obverse of this suffering was profit, progress, and prosperity. Between 1800 and 1851 the English population grew 111 per cent, coal output increased 470 per cent, the production of pig iron 946 per cent, cotton imports 1400 per cent. Power looms had become really serviceable only in 1803; by 1820 there were 14,000 of them in England, by 1829, 55,000, by 1833, 100,000. Domestic industry gradually disappeared; small workshops gave way to larger ones. Workers no longer owned their instruments, much too costly to be bought by one man, too demanding to be used only by one. The new dominant class would be that of machine owners. And not only machines started being shipped all over the world, as far as India, as far as Peru; so was the know-how. The French and Germans sent their young men (like Friedrich Engels) to learn industrial techniques in England, the English sent operatives and entrepreneurs to teach skills or found new firms, like those of Thomas Cockerill whose Belgian works would be the largest on the continent by 1830.

Standardization progressed and so did mass production. From Josiah Wedgwood's potteries, at Etruria in Staffordshire, popular chinawares flowed out, serviceable, cheap, to replace the trencher, the pewter plate, the tin cup. Many backward villages remained outside the distribution network, depending on a subsistence economy and on traveling hawkers. But Balzac in 1833 describes the portent of things to come, the commercial traveler Gaudissart, as "one of the most curious figures created by the ways of the present," announcing "the rule of uniform but levelling power, equalizing products, throwing them out in masses . . ." And Cobden, the English radical, had ridden twenty-five to thirty miles a day in his youth, trying to sell muslin. Bazaars, chain stores, department stores appeared, with shopwindows, clearly marked prices, periodic sales; retailing cheap, ready-made clothing more or less mass-produced, and even, at the end of this period, foods (Felix Potin's stores in Paris, 1850); or cutting prices by eliminating middlemen and selling direct from manufacturer to consumer. Advertising appeared—publicity posters, eye-catching in color and design, forerunners of a whole new art form—and advertising agencies (the first set up in Paris in 1845, by followers of the philosopher Saint-Simon), as well as newspaper publicity, which set the press free from political backers before enserfing it to business ones.

A way of life was dying. By mid-nineteenty-century it had died. And with it died a certain speed of life, of life and of experience and perception. Perhaps the Industrial Revolution lay not in *change,* but in the *rhythm* of change it introduced. Change had existed before, and change would be more vertiginous later. But here in this harsh period, the *rate* of change altered in spectacular fashion. So did the energy available to man. The Industrial Revolution set on foot the use and the production of new energy sources beyond the plants, the elements, and animals which men had harnessed some time during the Stone age. Coal and steam were only a beginning. The more energy produced, the more was sought, the more consumed. Nor have we seen the end of the revolution.

The Urban Environment

"In this great town," Descartes had written from seventeenth-century Amsterdam, "where apart from myself there dwells no one who is not engaged in trade, everyone is so much out for his own advantage that I should be able to live my whole life here without ever meeting a mortal being." Evidently, the sense of alienation amidst the impersonal vastness of great cities did not first appear in the twentieth century. Yet it would be in the eighteenth that such cities really grew in size and problems to proportions which we today would recognize as urban.

Urban agglomerations had grown higgledy-piggledy until the central power began to rationalize them in the late seventeenth and eighteenth centuries, to light, straighten, and pave streets which until then had catered rather to their dwellers than to traffic, and to eliminate or regulate refuse disposal, gutters, signs, stalls, outbuildings, and projections. Special oil lanterns for public places had begun to appear in the last third of the seventeenth century, but were primitive and rare.* Oil lamps steadily improved throughout the eighteenth century, were fitted with better wicks, glass mantles, and reflectors, and were eventually overtaken by gas lamps, burning first wood- then coal-gas. By the first decade of the nineteenth century, English industrialists were lighting their works and houses with new gas lamps. We have to make an effort to imagine the utter revolution which artificial light produced in public and private life, the hours which it added to the day, the possibilities it opened. In Louis XIV's time, the friends of Madame de Sévigné used

---

* Naples, whose king had tried to introduce street lights, only succeeded when holy shrines were set up at every convenient street corner, and the inhabitants persuaded to keep lamps burning below them—the only regular illumination which the city had from the 1750's to 1806, when street lamps actually appeared.

two candles a day, which suggests that, at least in winter, such noble households must have dined before five and gone to bed about six. The safety of the streets, the comforts of the home, the possibilities of study, play, or movement were all immeasurably increased.

Even in daytime, light could be a problem if it found no way of shining in. The eighteenth century would see the spread of window-glass in the urban west. Indeed, the economic advance of a city or region can be related to delays in its appearance. By the time of the Revolution the lodgings of the poorest Paris workers could boast windowpanes, but in the provinces oiled paper still held sway. In Serbia, glass windows became the norm only in the nineteenth century. The bright hues in which furniture, walls, and ceilings were often painted, or peasant rugs woven, reflected the hunger for light, for some liveliness and color in dark places—the homes, or hovels, palaces, churches, or stores where men had to live and work.

Much more than lighting, straightening of streets was one of the passions of an eighteenth century which wanted to replace "Gothic" disorder with rational uniformity. Demolished city ramparts were replaced by malls, boulevards, gardens, promenades. Urban improvement flourished—at least in theory—and English urban architects in particular built towns or sections of them in squares and terraces, planned as coherent wholes whose charm and harmony still survive today. The regulation of shop signs (many of which impeded traffic on narrow thoroughfares) and straightening out of streets also removed the peculiar personality of houses, which had to be given a new identity in numbers. In Paris this began under Louis XVI, but only spottily and inconspicuously. In 1780, the painter Greuze lived in the "Rue Pavée, first door on the left after the Rue St. André des Arts" and Fragonard in the "Rue de la Bucherie, the gate after the corner of the Street of Rats." The official and compulsory numbering of houses would come only in Napoleon's time. In Rome, the first street signs with names on them appeared only in 1803, and houses would not be numbered until midnineteenth century. Until then, addresses seem to have been indicated as "the house with green painted shutters in the street which goes from X to Y."

Streets were not only nameless, they were also dirty. Stendhal, in Napoleon's Paris, once had to spend the night at a friend's house, having his trousers dried for having tried to cross the street gutter and got them completely muddy. Yet, slowly, mud was being paved over (first in London), new sewers built which drained the filth from streets into some river, cemeteries in the churchyards of residential quarters transferred into the suburbs, to the indignation of priests and relatives and to the benefit of sanitation. In mid-eighteenth century steam pumps and iron pipes improved water supplies. Wells and fountains in insufficient number (Lyons under Louis XIII had only six public fountains) were supplemented by new aqueducts, fountains, and water towers. Public washhouses for the laundry, public baths for people, were built at municipal expense. Water also served to put out fires and, while the water flowed only at certain hours, a messenger could be sent to the offices of the water company to have the mains opened in an emergency. At least the eighteenth century would see the equipment of trained fire companies with real pumps, as well as the spread of fire insurance companies.

Since most people still got around on foot, cities could not grow too much without solving the transportation problem. Sedan chairs served only the wealthy few. Tradition attributes the invention of omnibuses to Pascal, and public transportation vehicles appeared in the 1660's. By the end of the eighteenth century they had been replaced by cabs and hansoms, catering to those who had the means for transport but not for keeping a carriage of their own. Poor people had to walk until cheap public transportation developed in the following century.

The cleaner, more orderly cities that the eighteenth century sought to build were soon overrun by the pressure of growing population. The cities of the Industrial Revolution were a jumble of houses put up without order or reason, obeying only profits. Space shrank again and dirt advanced, ugliness triumphed, house piled on house, street on street, with no plan, no open space except the waste allowed by hazard, factories in the midst of residential quarters, workshops taking over great houses with no reference to history, art, let alone aesthetics. Fine old buildings were demeaned or completely destroyed. In 1817, William I of Holland handed the Castle of Seraing over to John Cockerill the ironmaster; even Louis XIV's elegant pavilions at Marly were turned over to a cotton weaver and, in the new urban maze, no one knew his neighbor or his name. Speculators built fast and speed pared quality just as it would do in the early days of Soviet Russia, when passage from underdeveloped economy to intense industrialization would cause somewhat similar conditions.

Cleanliness, too, had its ups and downs. Country squires, like Richardson's Sir Charles Grandison or Fielding's Squire Western, were coarse, brutal, stinking and hard-drinking, gluttonous and dirty, seldom changing their linen or their shirt. Yet there was more soap about. And, now that cottons and calicoes replaced wool and silk, cotton cloth could be boiled without damage, thus killing lice and vermin. As snuff became the passion of all who could afford it, handkerchiefs became a necessity, soiled shirts began to be changed more often. Not by the poor, of course, and many even of the better off still wore them fifteen days at a time. But beaux and dandies changed as often as three times a day, and impeccable linen became the mark of the fastidious man, good personal hygiene a sign of social status. The eighteenth century rediscovered the possibilities of cleanliness. Thomas Sheraton designed washstands. Lavabos and bidets appeared—one Paris dealer of the 1740's advertising the latter as "a porcelain violin case on four legs" and

Boucher painting a portrait of a lady using one. As soap became cheaper, patents were taken out for mechanical washing machines. Lavatory stools, sometimes quite sumptuous, which played such a conspicuous part in the appointments of well-furnished rooms that we find important personages granting audience while seated on them (it was on his *chaise percée* that Louis XIV announced his forthcoming marriage to Madame de Maintenon), began to be replaced by water closets. An English cabinet maker had made 6,000 such by 1797, and W.C. became one English term to enter universal speech.

Baths caught on more slowly. Fifteenth-century Nürnberg had had thirteen vapor baths, and it was one of these that Dürer sketched in 1496. The Reformation and the Counter-Reformation, with their prejudice against nakedness and sin, stifled medieval respect for the body's welfare and equated sin and "stews." Concern for physical well-being returned only slowly, as eighteenth-century doctors and nature-lovers worked on the public mind. Rousseauist and therapeutic views spread the vogue of cold baths, even of sea-bathing. On the educational front, reformers like J. B. Basedow (1724?–1790) and J. H. Pestalozzi (1746–1827) were coupling swimming with gymnastics. Ludwig Jahn's gymnastic societies sought to harden German youth after 1807. "Military exercises," declared Jahn in 1816, "even without guns, build a manly character, awaken and stimulate the sense of order, and inculcate obedience to leadership." These too went with cold baths, and the English public schools—that.is, those private schools in which the upper classes were brought up to muscular Christianity—soon applied a variant of Jahn's point of view.

Water had other uses too. It could be drunk at spas and, in 1765, a private lunatic asylum in Norwich used baths both hot and cold to calm unruly inmates. The sane followed more slowly, but it seems that Napoleon liked very hot baths indeed and, since Wellington liked them cold, it has been suggested that Waterloo may have been won in the bathroom. Yet, in most places, baths had to be limited to pails and sponges, while tubs and showers long remained rare luxuries for the rich. A French writer, we are told, "died of a cold caught by washing," and Joseph II would pay his brother-in-law, the king of Naples, a dubious compliment: "He is clean, except for his hands; and at least he does not stink." When Voltaire built a bathroom at Ferney, with hot and cold water, he placed it in the park, rather like a privy, which made it awkward to use and suggests that use was not his first consideration in its building. In 1837, Victoria found no bathroom in Buckingham Palace and Parliament had to vote an allocation to meet the cost of conveying water to the portable bath in the young queen's bedroom. Public baths appeared in mid-nineteenth century, in conjunction with public laundries, but did not really catch on until the century's end. Running water only began to be common in the second half of the nineteenth century, and then it took its time reaching the upper stories.

Running hot water only really came with the turn of the nineteenth into the twentieth century—wash basins equipped with taps as well—and permanent bathrooms with tubs and running hot and cold water are really twentieth-century installations beyond a very few rich houses.

Meanwhile, drainage and sewers posed pressing problems. Sewage from cesspools and privies seeped into wells, or ran into rivers, thence to be drunk by those living on their banks, while noxious gases from the cesspits gave residents in the houses above them vapors, sore throats, and worse ills. At Buckingham Palace in 1845, " a room in the basement painted freshly with white lead paint was blackened by the next morning owing to putrefactive gases. The kitchens were fitted with charcoal fires with no flues, the fumes going straight up to the royal nurseries." In mid-nineteenth century, the smell from the Thames "was sometimes so bad," noted Lord Malmesbury, "as to make it questionable whether Parliament could continue to sit." And Prince Albert alone had the drive to replace the overflowing cesspits under Windsor Castle with more modern conveniences.

We shall soon see that these descriptions apply largely to the better off. Yet, before leaving this class, it should be noted that many of the changes taking place were indeed for the better. More jobs, more salaries, more quarters, encouraged young couples to move out of the parents' house into independent lodgings where husband, wife, and children formed a separate unit, one in which the children in their turn stood out more clearly, as also did the cost of their upkeep and education, an argument in favor of family limitation and planning. Apartments and houses grew smaller, and their design reflected the new interest in privacy. Rooms no longer opened one into the other, so that everyone was always passing through, but onto a corridor or hall. Beds, once present throughout the house, were concentrated in specialized rooms and such specialization was marked by the English prefix indicating the function a room might serve—bedroom, dining room, etc.

Servants were given their own quarters, increasingly distant from their masters' lives, and hand-bells which could only be heard from nearby were replaced by bells that could be rung to summon help from a distance. Privacy was increasingly preserved. Not only against servants but against all intruders who formerly could come and go much as they pleased. Now "family quarters" appeared, and also "days" or hours when people were "at home" to visitors. Light, comfort, privacy, are very modern concepts—and modern conquests too—for which we might give thanks. Yet for most of this period, their enjoyment was limited only to narrow sections of society. Now we must turn to the rest.

The Populace

The immense majority of Europeans lived on the land. East of the Rhine, more often of the Elbe, these people were serfs and remained so until mid-nineteenth century or, in Russia and Romania, later. In 1842 the *Farmer's Magazine,* defending British Corn Laws, referred to the low wages "paid to German boors, Polish serfs and Russian slaves." Further west things were different. By the late seventeenth century countries like England and France knew hardly any serfs, only villeins. Was it much better? It is hard to say. Peasants were the invisible men of their time. "One sees certain wild beasts," La Bruyère had written in the golden years of Louis XIV, "males and females, scattered about the countryside, dark, leaden, and all tanned by the sun, bound to the soil which they dig and stir with invincible stubbornness; they have something like an articulate voice, and when they rear up on their legs they show a human face, and in truth they are men. At night they take refuge in lairs where they live on black bread, water and roots; they spare other men the trouble of sowing, toiling and reaping to live, and thus deserve not to lack the bread which they themselves have sown."

Wheelless plows made labor harder; rye bread full of bran was black and heavy as lead, so that little girls of four had stomachs round as pregnant women. There is little difference to be found in the living conditions appearing in the seventeenth- and eighteenth-century paintings of peasants like those by Le Nain and Fragonard, and those illustrated in fourteenth-century works like the *Riches Heures du Duc de Berry*: the furnishings sparse, the clothes worn, ill-fitting and rough, the bread gray. In Auvergne peasants baked 20- to 30-pound cartwheels of bread that could be kept for a month. In Dauphiné, the bread was baked twice a year and kept as long as eighteen months. Little country lads sent to city schools took bread for six months, broke it with a hammer, and soaked it in order to eat.

That was under Louis XV. Under his heir, the English traveler Young was struck by the poverty of peasant houses, the lack of windows and of chimneys—the smoke getting out by a hole in the roof; at Souillac, the women were "walking dunghills"; near Amiens, in Normandy, men, women, children had neither footwear nor stockings. A year later in Brittany, Young found "a hideous heap of wretchedness" round the home of a future romantic hero: "To Combourg the country has a savage aspect; husbandry not much further advanced, at least in skill, than among the Hurons, which appears incredible amidst enclosures; the people almost as wild as their country, and their town of Combourg one of the most brutal filthy places that can be seen; mud houses, no windows, and a pavement so broken, as to impede all passengers, but ease none. Yet here is a chateau, and inhabited; who is this Mons. de Chateaubriand, the owner, that has nerves attuned for a residence amidst such filth and poverty?"

On his way to Metz, on July 12, 1789, while walking up a long hill to ease his mare, Young would fall in with a poor woman who complained of the hard times: "God send us better, for the *taille* and the services crush us."

"This woman, at no great distance, might have been taken for sixty or seventy, her figure was so bent, and her face so furrowed and hardened by labor,—but she said she was only twenty-eight. An Englishman who has not travelled cannot imagine the figure made by infinitely the greater part of the country women in France; it speaks, at the first sight, hard and severe labor. I am inclined to think, that they work harder than the men and this, united with the more miserable labor of bringing a new race of slaves into the world, destroys absolutely all symmetry of person and every feminine appearance. To what are we to attribute this difference in the manners of the lower people in the two kingdoms? To *government*."

Such people have no recognizable personality and their contemporaries seem to have allowed them none, not even surnames which, in the common people, began to be handed on only in the early nineteenth century. The same was to some extent true of servants—an immense proportion of the working force,* who seem to have been regarded more as objects than as beings, so that Voltaire's mistress, the enlightened Marquise du Châtelet, bathed before her *valet* just as the Madisons, in this country, did not bother to conceal their marital affairs from the slave sleeping on a pallet at the foot of their bed.

The urban poor (and this included most workmen) lived, as we have seen, close to the margin of starvation, often over it. And things in the countryside were not much better. Thomas Smart testified before the Select Committee of 1824 on the Rate of Agricultural Wages that he had "by good luck and hard work" always enjoyed steady employment and received relief only to bury six of his thirteen children. "He lived almost entirely on bread and cheese, had often touched no meat for a month, got now and then a little bacon and sometimes a half-penny worth of milk, but the farmers did not like selling it." Those who were not as lucky or hard-working "mostly lived on bread" or bruised bean porridge.** It was in the 1790's that the agronomist Antoine Parmentier (1737–1813) published his famous *Treatise on the Uses of the Potato*, which would provide a base for economical soups and keep people alive when wheat was scarce. And in the early 1800's, when popular pretensions had begun to rise, horse meat would be the answer: a popular source of cheap meat for the people, its use encouraged by philanthropists and by the armies for whose old horses the horse butcher provided a perfect end. Yet fresh horse meat was sometimes inaccessible and, in the hungry 40's, we hear stories of weavers unburying the carcasses of dead animals and fighting over dogs and cats. Scrofulous, rachitic, consumptive, syphilitic, these people—working people unable to find work and sometimes to find relief—looked on prosti-

---

* In 1795, Vienna, with a population of 260,000, counted 40,000 domestic servants— 15 per cent of the population—a proportion often repeated in many central and east European towns.
** Quoted by John Burnett, *Plenty and Want* (Edinburgh: 1965).

tution as a welcome addition to the family income and on drink as one of the few escapes from grim reality.

Gin was the opium of the eighteenth-century masses, a passion that swept over England, ruined their health, their morals, their sanity, and what little respect they might have had for the law. From the classic sign "Drunk for a penny, dead drunk for twopence," to Hogarth's illustration of *Gin Lane,* gin was the poison and the sop of the poor, "the principal sustenance (wrote Fielding) of a hundred thousand people in this metropolis."

From 1714 to 1733, English consumption rose from two to five million gallons of gin a year, and only receded in the 1750's when stringent laws began to restrict sales. The rich, of course, drank too: "All the decent people in Lichfield," recalled Dr. Johnson, "got drunk every night and were not the worse thought of." But where the poor drank gin, the rich drank port and brandy in incredible quantities. Five or six bottles a man were par for an evening; and Dr. Johnson once drank thirty-six glasses of port without moving from his seat—a feat in more ways than one. Addison and Steele, Goldsmith and Boswell, Sheridan and Fox and Pitt—and Walpole before them—were bottomless wells of liquor, frequently drunk, often dead drunk, and little the worse for it, except in health and that only eventually. It was, evidently, an age of titans.

Where the wealthy drank for pleasure, the poor drank for solace; and not only in England. Around 1700, Vauban estimated 40,000 taverns and cabarets in the 36,000 parishes of the French kingdom. In 1789 one country parish of 400 souls counted eight taverns, beside lesser cabarets. In 1875 France would have more than one dram shop for every hundred inhabitants.

Gin Lane, by William Hogarth. Courtesy of the Metropolitan Museum of Art, New York.

No wonder life, like men, was coarse and callous. Beneath the exquisite veneer of eighteenth-century manners, behind the screen of polite punctiliousness, the mass of men appear as savages, much closer to their savagery (and to its results) than we. Barbarians, savages, nomads, are terms which recur endlessly in the press and the social novels of the early nineteenth century when they describe those who dwell, in Eugène Sue's words, in "the sinister regions of misery and ignorance," those sinister depths which Victor Hugo plumbed in his *Les Misérables,* which he began to write in 1842. Such wretchedness could not but stir some response. The poor who begged and stole and robbed among their betters, as Fielding, magistrate and novelist observed, also starved and rotted and froze among themselves; and if a man were to hang for stealing, why should he hold back from murder, which would not kill him twice? Like Smollett's Humphry Clinker, they stood convicted of sickness, hunger, wretchedness, and want.

Going by Somerset Maugham's notion that "the degree of a nation's civilization is marked by its disregard for the necessities of existence," all nations of this time appear excruciatingly civilized. Yet, of the three great elements of modern civilization—gunpowder, printing, and an effective system of police and law—the last was still missing.

"To civilize" is an old legal term describing the transfer to civil law of a case which had been classed as criminal. Given the barbarous penalties of eighteenth-century criminal law, we may well say that law, and then society, would be civilized by legal reforms undertaken at the behest of the enlightenment but also under the pressure of utilitarian arguments. "We live in an age of commerce and computation;" wrote the *Annual Register* of 1759: "Let us, therefore, coolly inquire what is the sum of evil which the imprisonment of debtors brings upon our country . . . What shall we say of the humanity or the wisdom of a nation that voluntarily sacrifices one in every three hundred to lingering destruction?"

"We live in an age when humanity is in fashion," a London magistrate observed in 1787. Humanity maybe; utilitarian concerns certainly. The shocking thing was the waste of imprisoned men who might have been productively employed. Whatever the motivation, reform advanced: in prisons, in penalties, even in madhouses. Then it was stifled by fear and counter-revolutionary hostility. Then it began again, again on utilitarian lines, less to save lives—of which there were too many—but effort and resources, save souls, induce sobriety and order, make better citizens. The poor were still expected (as Edmund Burke had put it in 1795, which was a famine year) to rely on "patience, labor, sobriety, frugality and religion . . ." But, increasingly, their claim to better things was voiced and heard. However bad their conditions, never had there been so much talk *about* them: "One of the most marked characteristics of the present time," wrote the *Edinburgh Review* in 1846, "is the large amount of public attention which is given to the working classes." Here, too, change had broken the web of habit; and poverty, which had been taken for granted until then, became a subject for comment and concern. The poor were after all the people, as Carlyle and Michelet argued with a new pride and love. And the very fact of this new attention seemed to foretell a firmer future hope.

Transport and Communications

It would be in the eighteenth century and most especially in the nineteenth that the scale of time cut down the scale of space, broadening the horizons of the latter by lowering the time it took to get from one place to another, making journeys not only shorter but safer and more comfortable, improving means of conveyance and the ways by which these moved, contributing yet one more factor of mobility to a rapidly fluctuating world.

Transport in the seventeenth century had still been risky, primitive, and costly. In 1612 Barbary pirates inflicted 40,000 pounds' worth of damage on Newfoundland fishermen. Coastal shipping in the Atlantic was continually threatened by them, the coal flow from Newcastle to London was interrupted for a year or two together, and at one time measures against the Mediterranean pirates planned by the admiralty in London were suspended because the Lord Admiral had been bribed by English pirates. The Barbary pirates were no fiction. Robinson Crusoe, in Defoe's novel published in 1719, was a slave at Salee, near Rabat. Robinson was fictional but Salee-men were not: in 1625, off the Newfoundland banks, they seized forty ships from Le Havre and many others besides. In 1631, Algerian pirates captured the whole able-bodied population of Baltimore in County Cork; in 1634 they got 800 slaves in Iceland; and mid-seventeenth century Cornwall lived in fear of them. In 1679 still, Algerian pirates based on the Scilly Isles took thirteen Virginia ships; and Barbados sugar shipments to London had to sail around Scotland instead of taking the southern route.

Slave raids on the coasts of Spain, France, and Italy—not to mention the Mediterranean islands—remained a commonplace of seafaring life until the French conquest of Algeria in 1830. But, by the eighteenth century, trade in coastal Atlantic waters had become fairly safe and long-range voyages increasingly so. Besides, canals were being built which did a lot to cut the freight rates, as in the case of the late eighteenth-century ship canal built between Manchester and Liverpool which cut the cost of shipping goods to and from Manchester 700 per cent. The late eighteenth and early nineteenth century was the great age of canals, when all of western Europe was crisscrossed with them; but perhaps the most successful of them all was dug not in Europe but in America, where in 1825 Lake Erie was linked to the Hudson River, opening the west to trade, and cutting the cost of shipping a bushel of wheat from Buffalo to Albany from $108 to $7. The Erie Canal brought cheap western flour to the northeast, thus integrating the midwest with the east and driving immigrants into the Great Lakes basin, before it created a whole new grain shipping situation in the western world.

The eighteenth century was still an age, as one chronicler has described it, that was short on lamp posts and long on highwaymen. The latter only disappeared with railroads, but the safety and structure of the roads improved. Slowly: parts of Sweden would only see their first wheeled vehicles in 1790; and Odensee, where Hans Christian Andersen was born, less than a hundred miles from Copenhagen as the crow flies, was, at his birth in 1805, two and a half days by coach and ship from the capital. But on the major routes the speed and comfort got much better. In France, in the 1780's, coaches took five days from Paris to Bordeaux, about 400 miles, two and a half to Lille, about 150. Half a century later they took thirty-six and fifteen hours respectively. In 1750 England, the journey from London to Edinburgh (comparable to that from Paris to Bordeaux) lasted ten or twelve days; by 1786 reforms improving postal and passenger services had reduced this to seventy-two hours. Eighteenth-century roads introduced one of the great revolutions of the time: the taming of space, the liberation of land transport, the opening of possibilities which dominated eighteenth-century warfare before defeating Napoleon's armies, lost in the roadless spaces beyond the Elbe and the Vistula when their triumphs had been based on facilities unknown outside the West.

Still, travelers took accidents, spills, or getting stuck for granted. Traveling was an adventurous enterprise. Then, in the early nineteenth century, McAdam's method of surfacing roads with a layer of granite lumps and chips improved surfaces, hence safety and speed. The French had led the way in establishing the first body of public works experts in the Road and Bridge Corps of civil engineers, who were given their own training school in 1747. Stone highways took the place of ruts and trails in France, Germany, Austria; traffic increased. In 1830 coaches logged 500,000,000 passenger-kilometers (1 kilometer = .62 mile); and by then protests were being heard against the speed at which they traveled. Trains pulled by steam engines were beginning to run. In 1840 the railroads carried 113,000,000 passenger-kilometers, 800,000,000 in 1851, 4,270,000,000, in 1870.

At the same time, roads with really strong foundations were spreading over Europe, built by men like Telford and McAdam. In the cities the presence of more wheeled vehicles demanded better pavements: bricks,

George Stephenson's "Rocket." The winning entry in a competition among railroad engines in 1829.

cobblestones, wood coated with tar and pitch, were pressed to use, although concrete, tar, or asphalt roadbeds caught on more slowly and hardly counted until the advent of the motorcar. Roads were a symbol of liberalism and progress: Sicily had no real ones before mid-nineteenth century; in Russia the first modern highway, between Moscow and Petersburg, was finished only in 1834; the Spanish corps of highway engineers, set up on the French model by the reforming Charles III, was abolished by Ferdinand VII on his restoration in 1814, re-established by liberal revolutionaries in 1820, dissolved again by the reactionary king in 1823, and only came to stay when re-established again by liberals in 1834. Italian disunity was reflected in the disjointedness of the Peninsula's transportation network. In 1849, Giuseppe Verdi, leaving Naples where he had overseen the first production of his opera *Louisa Miller,* would take five days to reach his home near Parma, by steamboat, then by coach. Today, by train or car, the journey takes less than one day.

Yet Verdi took a steamship from Naples to Genoa, and that probably helped shorten his journey. Steam had appeared first on rivers and canals, ruining haulers and barges, but developing river traffic on the Rhine, the Elbe, the Vistula, the Danube, and the Mississippi—which latter river boasted 200 steamboats in 1830, over 1,000 in 1860. One could not cross oceans as yet by steam alone, with no port of call for refueling, but it was possible to combine steam and sail. The first such lines began in 1816, and Samuel Cunard's steamers took only seventeen days from Liverpool to Boston. But in 1848 sailing ships still dominated navigation: 10,-000,000 tons of sail towered over 750,000 tons of steam-driven ships.

Steam transportation on land and sea appears as a significant fact only after 1850. Before that time one could regard it as hopeful or as ominous as one might choose. Still, it was a fact. In 1814, George Stephenson's engine *Blucher* had pulled eight carriages weighing 30 tons at five miles an hour; in 1825 the Stockton-Darlington Railway had opened in England, with trains that could do up to 26 m.p.h. going downhill; in 1830 Manchester and Liverpool were linked by rail. By 1850 trains could do 35-40 miles an hour, and passenger fares were about half those of the former coaches. The United States took the invention up: in 1830 there were 316 kilometers of rail in Europe (279 in England) and 65 in the United States; by 1840 Europe had 3,534 kilometers and the United States 4,509. In the political crisis of 1834, Sir Robert Peel, returning "at the utmost speed" from Rome to London, took twelve days to do it. Thirty years later the same journey would take two and a half days. That was the sense of the revolution in transportation. The leisurely pace of coaches and of barges was left behind for good. Perhaps for ill, as some critic said who saw in the new speed the ruin of carters, a danger for cattle, and madness for men. But more thought differently: "The iron rail has proved a magician's road," wrote Samuel Smiles, the popular moralist. "The locomotive gave a new celerity to time. It virtually reduced England to a sixth of its size. It brought the country nearer to the town, and the town to the country . . . it energized punctuality, discipline, and attention; and proved a moral teacher by the influence of example."

Better means of transportation encouraged specialization in agriculture, modified techniques, replacing the habits and trade of past centuries with new ones they evoked. In the next decade, American wheat, Argentine meat and leather, Australian wool, Egyptian and American cotton, Japanese silk, Asian rice, the oils and oleaginous grains of Africa, would begin to compete with European products and eventually push them out. Equally important, as road and then railroad networks spread, their tracery had profound effects on the economic and social geography of the lands they covered. Old cities withered from want of transportation, villages grew into towns, great cities were allowed to expand unreasonably because food could be shipped in from very far away, the provinces—once so distant—were much more closely tied to metropolitan centers, and the metropolis itself, its shops, its cultural life, even its politics were affected in turn by the far greater facility with which provincials could now visit them—even for the day. Men traveled more: for every Englishman who had gone abroad under the first two Georges, ten faced the glories and the weariness of foreign travel under the third George, a hundred under Queen Victoria. Men traveled more, and more men traveled, and far more kinds of men.

Power and Profit Overseas

Now we must turn to the colonial struggles which played a growing part in the history of this time. Some of the major conflicts of the eighteenth century, many of the major enterprises of the next, took place on the seas or across them. The old colonial powers—Dutch, Spanish, Portuguese—gradually lost their grip on colonies and trade, while France and Britain struggled for colonial power and the latter won.

European countries had had colonies in Europe before they ever struck out across the oceans: in the Baltic, in the Mediterranean, even in the Aegean. The crushing of the population, the withering of the cities in these areas during the sixteenth and seventeenth centuries, narrowed the outlets for western manufactures and redirected the attention of some merchants toward more distant colonies in the Americas and Indies. The chief purpose of colonies, a Bristol merchant declared in 1717, was "to take off our product and manufactures, supply us with commodities which may either be wrought up here or exported again, or prevent fetching things of the same nature from other places for our own home consumption, employ our poor and encourage our navigation." *

At first the need for naval stores, raw materials, and "colonial" goods, could be fulfilled by a few planters controlling a large subject labor force. But colonies, it was thought, could also provide a safety valve for population problems caused by a laggard agriculture, a point of view voiced by many writers of the early seventeenth century. When that century ended, the idea of drawing off the surplus population or funneling the discontented overseas had worked only too well. Greater economic stability brought new appreciation of human material and the fear that too much of this was being lost by emigration. Already an English pamphlet of 1674 had complained about "the ruinous numbers of our men daily flocking to the American plantations, whence so few returned . . ."

In due course, those who did not return would win independence. By that time, at the end of the eighteenth century, the North American colonies which became the United States had built a sizable trading activity of their own (see pp. 486–492). Less economically enterprising, but no less relevant, Spanish colonies in Latin America would be moved by Yankee example and by the opportunities offered by the French revolutionary wars to assert their own independence in the first quarter of the nineteenth century see pp. (572–575).

Sugar and Slavery

For a long time, however, influential men in the city of London, in Paris, Nantes, or Cadiz thought less of the American plantations or, indeed, of territorial possessions *as such* than of the profitable trade to be conducted in the southern seas. There, two things dominated: bullion and

* Quoted by J. F. Reese, *The Cambridge History of the British Empire* (Cambridge: 1929), Vol. I, p. 566.

sugar. Brazil had both: sugar in the north, gold mines inland and also diamonds, which sent a seemingly inexhaustible flow to Portugal and thence to her ally, England. Spain had silver in Mexico and Peru, whose flow revived remarkably in the eighteenth century under the impact of new technologies, and sugar in her Caribbean islands.

This last commodity stood at the center of a complex trade. Sugar had come to America from the cane-producing islands in the East Atlantic—Madeira, the Azores—first to Brazil in the sixteenth century, then to the Caribbean isles where the introduction of cane in the early seventeenth century promised prosperity to planters and to their backers in the metropolis. Sugar was scarce and very highly prized. British Barbados began to export it in 1646, the French from Martinique and Guadeloupe, the Spaniards from Cuba and San Domingo in the next decade, Jamaica in the 1660's. But cane plantations needed a large labor force, able to stand the heat and hardships of back-breaking work in equatorial sun. So did the refining process. European settlers lent themselves ill to these needs; the native Indians were either soon exterminated, as in the Caribbean, or ill-adapted to the labor, as in Brazil. Sixteenth-century Spaniards and Brazilians sought a solution in the importation of black slaves, stolen in Africa, as the historian David Williams put it, to work the lands stolen from the Indians in America. Between 1570 and 1670 an average of 4,000 slaves entered Brazil yearly, who seem to have enjoyed an average life span of about seven years. There and in other colonial territories, slave labor permitted the development of a large-scale mining industry, sugar refining, and agricultural plantations. Exploited by the whites, the blacks in turn affected local culture—the language, literature, art, and culinary taste of Brazil and the Caribbean—which turned into an Euro-African society, mixed in blood and mentality.

Slaves being ordered into the hold of a ship. A pathetic but edulcorated view fit to move the magazine-reading public.

Warder Collection

A print from revolutionary France which asks the question, "Am I not your brother?"

By the seventeenth century, the slave trade had passed largely into the hands of French, Dutch, and English shippers, and these nations, too, were using slaves for their own account. By 1701, the slave population of the French Caribbean islands was double that of whites, by the end of the eighteenth century the proportion would be ten to one: half a million to 50,000.

The slave trade was a link in a great trade triangle which shipped shoddy goods and textiles from European ports to Africa, thence slaves to America, and sugar, precious metals, or other colonial goods from there to Europe. The African captives not only facilitated production by their labor, but exchange by their very being. Bought from African chiefs who captured or who pressed them, men, women, children were crowded below the decks of slave ships for the two- or three-month-long voyage to the isles. Mortality of a slave cargo would vary between 5 and 34 per cent, and probably averaged 12 or 15 per cent.* Trade grew with demand. In 1725, Bristol ships alone carried 17,000 slaves, London ships more. By 1750, ships from Liverpool—close to the Lancashire textiles which provided the main source of payment and exchange—carried 35,000. In the thirty years before 1793 some 80,000 slaves a year were shipped out of west Africa, a quarter of them in French ships and over half in British.

Soon, slaving became the preserve of a few large shippers in ports like Liverpool or Nantes. Profits were very high, sometimes as much as 300 per cent, but turnover was slow, losses were large, and enterprises risky. Opposition was appearing, invoking Christian principles or the Rights of Man, but also arguing that labor which did not appeal to personal profit would be less productive. Here was an ominous note. The enlightenment had not criticized slavery. Montesquieu's *Spirit of the Laws,* which rejoiced that slavery had been banished from Europe, considered it natural in certain countries and pointed out that sugar pro-

* A figure somewhat higher than that in other long-range voyages on the high seas at that time.

duction, for example, would become too expensive if not done by slaves. The *Encyclopedia*—most influential compendium of the age—treated slavery as a colonial necessity. In 1774, one French slave ship owner even named the three slavers of his fleet: the *Artless*, the *Huron* (after the noble savage), and the *Social Contract*. The French National Assembly refused to abolish slavery at the expense of the property rights of owners. It even refused to enfranchise mulattoes and free negroes. However, neither enlightened relativism nor property could hold out very long against the Rights of Man, and especially against evangelical reformism. For a brief moment, the Convention of 1794 abolished slavery

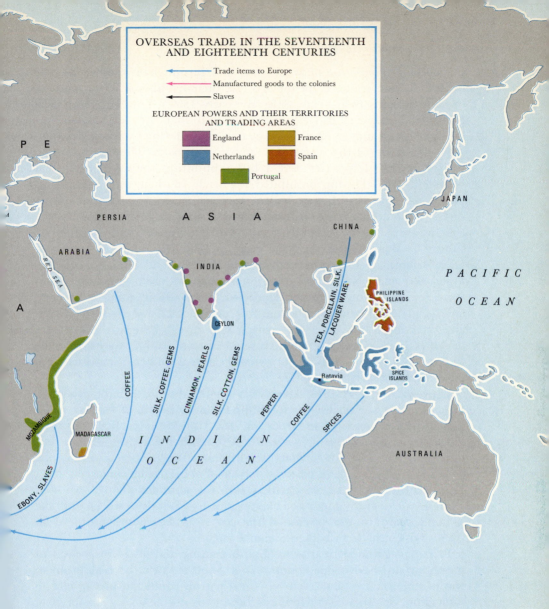

OVERSEAS TRADE IN THE SEVENTEENTH
AND EIGHTEENTH CENTURIES

Trade items to Europe
Manufactured goods to the colonies
Slaves

EUROPEAN POWERS AND THEIR TERRITORIES
AND TRADING AREAS

England
Netherlands
Portugal
France
Spain

and declared all men, whatever their color, French citizens with all a citizen's rights. This did not last and slavery was restored, at least partly, by Napoleon, while in Haiti the first black independent modern state arose in 1804, out of revolt and torment.

In England meanwhile, the antislavery campaign inspired by evangelical enthusiasm and under the determined management of William Wilberforce (1759–1833) progressed. Since 1787, annual motions to abolish the slave trade drew ever stronger support in the House of Commons, until their passage was only prevented by the merchants' opposition and the sugar interest in the House of Lords. Almost half

455

the working population of Manchester and Birmingham produced goods for the African trade. Were they to lose their livelihood, it was argued, or ship captains their cargoes? By the early 1800's, however, most merchants and shippers had become convinced that they could make as much or better money in other ways, now that they had won almost complete dominion of the seas and of overseas markets. The opposition to reform became less bitter and a bill prohibiting the slave trade was passed in 1807. Having prohibited the trade in their own vessels and possessions, the British now had every interest to prevent others from carrying it on. Hence, we shall see that they applied great pressure at the conclusion of the peace treaties of 1815, though only with delayed results. The Danes had banned the trade in 1804, the Americans one year after Britain, in 1808, the Netherlands in 1814, and other powers followed. But many still found the opportunity for profit irresistible; and more or less open smuggling flourished, especially in French, Spanish, and North American ships, to feed new demands arising in Brazil, Cuba, and the American south where cotton now revealed a great new source of riches in need of slave labor. Instead of diminishing, the slave trade increased, so that by 1840 about 135,000 slaves were being imported into the Americas yearly.

Between 1831 and 1838 slavery was finally abolished in British territories and the Second French Republic followed suit in 1848. But, while the institution persisted in Brazil and the United States, little improvement was to be expected; nor were the English themselves without second thoughts. "We know that for all mercantile purposes we are one with the States," said an editorial leader of the London *Times* in 1857, "and that, in effect, we are partners with the southern planter; we hold a bill of sale over his goods and chattels, his live and dead stock, and take a lion's share in the profits of slavery . . ." The same people who cried over Uncle Tom backed Simon Legree.

Britain negotiated treaties to abolish trading and allow inspection of merchant ships with one country after another. But the real problem was to stifle slavery at the source. Naval patrols could not put an end to smuggling. So, antislavery interests began to seek some legitimate rival to compete with the deadly trade, to develop a new climate among Africans themselves and suggest new sources of wealth both to the Africans and to those who preyed upon them. One way or another, this led to the exploration of an African interior that Europeans had hardly plumbed before, and to progressive involvement in the new continent which, in its turn, created new situations and new problems. From this point of view, African colonialism was born of good intentions.* We shall return to this situation at a later stage.

* And so, quite specifically, in the 1820's were the settlements of freed slaves at Freetown (Sierra Leone) and Monrovia (Liberia), the former a British, the latter an American abolitionist enterprise.

A street in Canton at the time of the Opium War, from a painting by Thomas Allom.

The Farther East

While empires in America were collapsing, others were being won in Asia. There, the quest for spices had sent the Dutch after the Portuguese, and the English and French after the Hollanders. During the seventeenth century, the Dutch succeeded in defeating all their rivals and set up a great spice-carrying and producing empire that stretched from Batavia (1619) to Colombo (1636) and the Cape (1652), with trading posts radiating outward as far as Nagasaki and Isfahan. But, as the century ended, the Hollanders were getting out of breath. Their great joint-stock East India Company, set up in 1602, still made impressive profits, but greater resources and a broader base enabled the English East India Company to forge ahead. Dominion of the east would be disputed not between the Dutch and English, but between English and French; and it would turn not on possession of the Spice Islands but of India, control of which could provide control of the eastern seas.

Part of the issue was that the trading companies needed both goods and bullion to secure the silks and porcelain, the tea and spices and the lacquer wares that they would sell at home. Far Eastern trade, though most impressive, was not yet carried out on a scale which could supply sufficient capital for significant expansion, and until the middle of the eighteenth century Europe's bullion shortage starved eastern traders of the major means of exchange Asiatics would accept. To put the matter blunt, things would be better if they could find a source of loot with which to finance their operations, and this India provided.

There, the great Mogul Empire which Shah Akbar had founded in the seventeenth century was slowly disintegrating. Akbar had done his best to reconcile the Hindu peoples of the peninsula to Muslim rule. Those who followed Akbar were increasingly intolerant and rapacious, until the disastrously bellicose Aurangzeb (1659–1707) ruined the peasants and the administration, while his religious fanaticism raised the Hindus and the Sikhs against him. The army, on which Mogul power rested, deteriorated as its Hindu and Sikh contingents broke away. Revolts broke out throughout the Mogul empire, while Aurangzeb's successors struggled for throne and treasury. Chaos reigned. In the south-center, the marauding Maratha federation grew; in the north, the Persian Nadir Shah took Delhi and almost put an end to Mogul rule (1739). Afghan raids seared the northern plains. The empire fell to pieces into a series of principalities.

Amid this chaos, the English and French companies, trading mostly in the south of the continent at first, were caught both in the rivalries of local rulers and in the wars precipitated by governments at home. Competing for the support of native princes, they found themselves in turn supporting them, then putting up their own candidates against others, then ruling through their puppets, or alone, in territories secured in exchange for aid. Both the French and the British used these methods, drawn ahead most of the time insensibly, without deliberate purpose, to turn a trading interest into a political one. Eventually, superior leadership, as well as the fortunes of naval warfare, enabled the English East India Company to establish its power firmly in Bengal (Plassey, 1757) and then in the Carnatic in the south (Wandewash, 1760). Political commitment became military occupation. By 1800 the British had a serious problem on their hands, a problem not only political but moral: they had come to India to trade. Should they stay to govern?

By what reason were they entitled to inflict themselves on the Indians? And what would they get from it? The latter question was most readily answered: gain. And this in turn would suggest a justification for the first. It was God who willed that the enlightened British should rule benighted Indians for their good, and such imperial destiny could not be lightly evaded. The evasion might have had to take place, had Divine Providence not provided opium, which, prohibited in India, could be exported to China in large quantities, so that the profits of the China trade might pay for governing India, a subcontinent full of heathens unable to rule themselves—a self-enforcing argument if ever there was one.*

---

* In 1839–1840, the first Opium War opened five Chinese treaty ports to British trade and consuls, gave Britain a firm base on Hong Kong Island, and assured the East India Company of a sound means of exchange for its Chinese trade. Through the breach that the English blasted in Chinese isolation, other nations soon followed, led by France and the United States.

The seventeenth century had admired Chinese and Hindu cultures, learned from them that virtue and society could be founded even without Christianity, adopted practical ideas like that of the Chinese national census. Now all this changed. Once the Asians had been conquered they did not seem so admirable anymore. The philosophical count of Saint-Simon discouraged research in the history of Hindus or Chinese, peoples —he said—which had remained in a childish state. Another philosopher, Auguste Comte, seeking the "laws of social development" would pay attention only to "the major part of the white race," since other societies "have not followed the march of progress." Everyone apparently felt confronted by childish races, to be paternally governed, missionized, and taught. The old colonial system that collapsed in America would be replaced by a new one, more moral, or at least more moralistic, more committed, and, on the whole, more profitable. This is the time when English colonists turn from being nabobs into sahibs, from buccaneers to moralists with a sense of mission, from tolerated merchants to a ruling caste. The crude old greed and swagger is overlaid by a sense of duty; the appetites, though no less great, are now indulged in for the sake of authority rather than of wealth; the eighteenth-century expediency and openness to local institutions, natives, and native cultures is overcome by sentiments of class, caste, and racial superiority.

By mid-nineteenth century, Sir Fitzjames Stephen would see the British task as "introduction of the essential part of European civilization into a country densely peopled, grossly ignorant, steeped in idolatrous superstition, unenergetic, fatalistic, indifferent to most of what we regard as the evils of life, and preferring the repose of submitting to them to the trouble of encountering and trying to remove them." All this must mean a vast social revolution imposed upon the Indians and unpopular with them, bound to go against the feelings, opinions, prejudices of most of the population. Yet such a revolution must be tried. "The English in India," wrote Stephen in 1883, "have been by circumstances committed to an enterprise which is in reality difficult and dangerous to the last degree, although its difficulties and dangers have thus far been concealed by the conspicuous success which has attended their efforts. That enterprise is nothing less than the management and guidance of the most extensive and far reaching revolution recorded in history. It involves the radical change of the ideas and institutions of a vast population which has already got ideas and institutions to which it is deeply attached . . ." Thus it was that imperialism, which had begun as a series of expedients, became by the nineteenth century an emotional commitment, its secular objectives translated to a religious plane and pursued with evangelical zeal.

Chapter 9

STRUCTURES IN TRANSITION

The State in Flux

Mid-eighteenth century saw European economies refloated on a tide of gold from Brazil and silver from the Spanish Indies, where new extractive methods improved lagging yields. The stock of precious metal doubled, then tripled, quadrupled even, sending new energy coursing through the arteries of exchange and trade. Even more important, the eighteenth century saw the stabilization of currency first in England (1719), then in France (1726), where the gold value of the pound and of the *livre* (which would become the *franc* in 1801) remained unchanged for two centuries, until the aftermath of the First World War. This monetary stability, already achieved by Holland, would eventually be attained by most countries of western Europe and would provide a base of stable values and certainties on which liberal economy and liberal society could be founded. The state no longer manipulated currency, no longer expropriated cash by nibbling at its value, no longer imposed its will on economic exchanges based on currency. The autonomy of the economy vis-à-vis the state would parallel and render possible the autonomy of the individual, and the growth of capital.

There was stability and confidence in another way as well: the social massacres of the past few centuries spaced out, became rarer, milder, then disappeared. 1848 saw the last great famine, more horrible because people had grown unaccustomed to it. Meanwhile, an economy based wholly on agricultural revenues, flourished as agricultural production increased and, with it, population. Even the poorest, who in the past had been decimated by recurrent famines, now survived in greater numbers, their fate commuted from death to hard labor. The massive birth rate began to overtake the death rate, creating more hands and more mouths, but also more revenues, however low, at every level. As long as the land paid off, these changes vitalized all sectors of the economy. The rural population began to buy the clothes and tools which it had always needed but never could afford. Industrial production grew even more for, while few could eat twice as much bread, many wanted to dress better or improve their lodgings. Colonial trade brought in luxuries—sugar, coffee, spices—which all coveted and more could now afford. Manufacture and trade prospered most of all, and the bourgeoisie increased in numbers and in power, spreading its hold further over the land in which it also invested. Gold and silver, decreed Dr. Johnson in 1778, destroy feudal subordination. The men of substance who felt they had a stake in their country's fate wanted a voice in its government but were excluded from it. The owners of government bonds and of annuities, the various creditors of the crown, were deeply concerned in public finance, wanted a say in it, had such a voice in England and Holland, claimed it elsewhere, and finally grappled to get it.

Prosperity made people feel that the economy would take care of itself, that it did not need state interference which only hamstrung enterprise. Machinery created for periods of scarcity and need began to look anachronistic in times of affluence: corporations, monopolies, subventions, regulations, appeared a nuisance when expansion ruled. Free the artisans, free the trades, free industry, allow enclosures and agricultural enterprise, and let profit reign. Nature will take care of its own if you open the doors to market economy, sweep out the bureaucrats and the fetters that hinder free movement and free enterprise. Reflection of an expanding economy, this was the mentality of liberalism from the eighteenth to the nineteenth century, from Turgot, in the 1770's, through Camille Desmoulins at the turn of the century, to François Guizot in the 1840's.

Such views clashed with existing institutions and traditions elaborated by secular experience, with the anarchic structure of rules and regulations accumulated over the centuries, with the absolutist tendencies and the interventionism of almost every European state and of the monarchies which the state machinery served.

With few exceptions—like the United Provinces, Genoa, Venice, or the Swiss cantons, all on their decline—monarchy and state were still pretty much identical. The monarchy was, was expected, or tried to be all-powerful. Though waning, the old idea of kings as agents of God and fathers of their people had left behind the image which Lord Bolingbroke described in 1738 as "that of a patriarchal family." And this was supplemented by the utilitarian view that a strong monarchy alone could develop an effective bureaucracy and a powerful army, guarantee civil peace and security, overcome provincial particularism, introduce necessary reforms. Strong or not, all governments sought to do these things in part as continuations of earlier policies. For monarchs had long tried to secure control over their territories, unify their administrative and legal institutions, subject all classes, corporations, and provinces to their writ, ensure a larger and a steadier flow of revenue for their treasuries and recruits for their armies from a more prosperous, more productive, and more pliable body of subjects.

Most of the rulers tried very hard to introduce reforms, but found that the very conditions of their power restricted their ability to move with the times. Monarchy had become absolute by depriving the intermediary authorities of the feudal world of their independent power, but guaranteeing their nonpolitical privileges. Public power, once divided among a host of lords (religious and secular) and of corporations, had become concentrated in the state, that is—England excepted—in the *entourage* of the ruler. What survived was *property,* a hierarchy of revenues and benefits, in which the right of property was guaranteed and whose existence became the chief obstacle in the way of the exercise of royal power. Privilege itself became a property of which the possessors could not be deprived without risk for the whole system; and this paralyzed royal power by forbidding change in the existing society and economic order.

Having suppressed the organized representatives of orders and groups which could have facilitated reform, monarchy found nothing but opponents to innovation. Having failed to suppress these orders and groups, it found them ranged against any reform. Only in a country like England, where politically significant and effective bodies existed and where economic and social differences were not underscored by law, could social relations be recognized to operate on a basis of ability and wealth, and reforms keep up (however sluggishly) with contemporary needs. In England, the nobility was actually a politically effective class, as in some countries of eastern Europe, but one whose members were prepared to work for their position and even to tax themselves. This was the fundamental distinction that saved them when others crumbled before the revolution in France and this is why many of the following generalizations do not apply to England, or do so only with a difference.

Enlightened Despotism

Absolute monarchy of the traditional kind—the sort which culminated in Louis XIV—had to respect rights, privileges, and property. "The first rule of justice," argued the parlement of Paris against the King's reforming minister, Turgot, "is to conserve to everyone that which belongs to him"; and that included the prerogatives of rank and birth. Despotism, on the other hand, need recognize no difference between its subjects and could assert the interest of the state, superior to any prior right an individual subject might refer to. Some despots may indeed have been benevolent or enlightened, as described in the term which still survives today; the fact is that all were autocratic and that their main characteristic was less the adjective than the noun. The Belgian historian Henri Pirenne has defined enlightened despotism as the rationalization of the state; and that is why it was called benevolent or enlightened. Frederick II in Prussia, Charles III in Spain (and before that in Naples), Joseph II in Austria and then his brother Leopold, Gustavus III in Sweden, all sought to achieve prosperity, efficiency, and reform.*

A good example of enlightened despotism may be found in Gustavus III of Sweden (1771–1792), who began his reign with a *coup d'état* that put an end to the long struggle between the aristocratic and popular factions which had enfeebled Sweden for two generations. The King imposed a new constitution, abolished torture, granted foreign immigrants freedom of worship, freed the grain trade, developed elementary education, founded the Swedish Academy, reformed army and navy, finally increased the taxes to the point where he lost popular support and allowed the nobles to rise again. Force allowed him to defeat his enemies, but in the end force killed him: a dagger at a masked ball. Here in a capsule we have most of the measures such men were concerned with, most of their methods too.

Almost all these rulers felt that the best source of wealth lay in a numerous population, and the best way to ensure this was to make the population prosperous. The mass of the people being on the land, the crux of things lay in improving the lot of peasants; and royal administrators everywhere sought to advance and protect the peasants against those who exploited them and the land without working and, above all, without paying the same taxes. "Populationist" doctrine stressed this new concern for the welfare of the masses: a concern which tended toward an alliance of people and prince against the nobles who both exploited the people and opposed those measures that reason of state suggested to the prince. It drew support from natural law ideas which saw the prince's absolute power as an economic necessity: the crown being the natural supporter of the people against an arbitrary and spendthrift feudalism. It also leaned on the progressive ideas of the period and, most particularly, upon the arguments of contemporary Physiocrats who advocated a single tax on land, sweeping away old exemptions for those best able to pay (nobles and clergy), old exactions from those most likely to produce (peasants), old restrictions upon the free movement of grains and goods and persons.

* Catherine II in Russia talked better than she did in practice; while King Stanislas of Poland meant well but could achieve very little indeed.

Of all existing institutions none was more hated by all "enlightened men" than serfdom. Wherever they could, therefore, progressive rulers sought to change labor service into cash payments. This did not always work: sometimes because of the fierce opposition of landowners dependent on the labor services of peasants, sometimes because the peasants lacked the cash which would release them from their obligations. One of Maria Theresa's advisers went so far as to suggest the use of black slaves to ease the lot of serfs in Habsburg territories; but even he could not devise a way to solve their credit problem. Generally, results were highly uneven. It might be said that where (as in Austria, Bohemia, and Hungary) rulers really insisted on their emancipation programs, they failed; and that where they did not fail (Prussia or Russia) it was because they did not insist.

Nevertheless, almost everywhere, reforms went some way in improving the peasants' lot. Not much east of the Elbe, where, despite all the efforts of Frederick the Great, a Frenchman commented that while in France the peasant held the land, in Prussia the land held the peasant. And the situation was the same in Russia and Poland. But in the Habsburg lands, in Denmark, in many German and Italian states, some dues were limited, some services commuted, the peasant gained freedom of movement and from manorial justice, and certain rights of tenure in the land he worked. On behalf of the crown—and against the landlord if need be—local government would protect the peasant: at least in theory, for in practice local government itself was often administered by local noblemen. In theory, too, the government got more eager cultivators, more prosperous taxpayers, fitter recruits. That was in principle and, sometimes, in practice.

Trade was a second source of wealth for the ruler and very much in evidence at the time when world commerce and shipping were undergoing a tremendous change of scale, with British exports doubling between 1720 and 1763 and French exports quadrupling in the seventy years before 1789. The fortune and prestige of maritime companies were so great that even inland states would seek to set them up. After the kings of Denmark and of Prussia, the rulers of Russia and Austria, Saxony and Bavaria, founded their own companies, none very successful, but an indication of the hopes that trade held out.* But trade not only promised; it demanded. More and more, merchants and producers criticized the old controls of prices, quality, movement, and production. They wanted to turn out all they could as cheaply as they could, sell all they could on the best terms they could, when and where they could. Political economists agreed. Jurists and legislators should do in politics "what the philosophers of our times do in the physical and natural sciences": free themselves from prejudice and tradition, revise existing laws according to "the natural rules of right and reason," give way

---

* They did lead, however, to the creation of new ports at Trieste and Ostend.

tion of opportunities, was natural and sacred. Liberty was not necessarily so. Political freedom was not for the great mass of the people. For them, thought Voltaire, "a yoke, a goad and plenty of hay" should suffice. Joseph II of Austria drew the conclusions of enlightened philosophy: "all for the people, nothing by the people."

Rulers and Churches

There were other conclusions that rational men would draw from the enlightened pursuit of their self-interest. Private morality did not apply in politics, reason of state ruled supreme and, in its service, the virtues and the worst passions of mankind might properly be enlisted. To strengthen and to modernize the state, religious tolerance and religious persecution were both valid methods, to be used if necessary for secular ends. "Any religion is as good as any other," declared Frederick II, "provided that it teaches obedience to men." Napoleon, in due course, agreed. Inevitably, in this process, some of the despots clashed with the established church. They were determined on social and economic development, and insisted that the church should make its financial and physical contribution. The typical example is afforded by Joseph II (in so many ways a prototype of his kind), who abolished the contemplative orders in his dominions, because, he claimed, the realm could not afford their cost. What Austria and Bohemia needed were "virtuous, educated priests who teach love of one's neighbor; not beggars, barefoot and ragged." Orders which nursed the sick, maintained schools or some scientific activity were welcome. Others were turned away. While founding new parishes and churches, Joseph was determined to force the church to use its vast wealth for the social purpose for which—many argued—it had originally been intended.*

The negative side of this appears in the fate of the Jesuits, resented by a great many governments as an obstacle to their policy and a rival focus of influence and opposition in the state. In the Iberian peninsula especially, they had also incurred the popular ire by being among the very few to stand out against the brutish anti-Semitism that other religious orders encouraged and the Inquisition exploited, pleasing the masses and stripping Spain and Portugal of some of their most enterprising elements. For this and other sins the Jesuits would pay in the eighteenth century. In 1758, a Jesuit missionary had the bad inspiration to describe the terrible earthquake which in 1755 laid low most of Lisbon and killed thousands of people as a divine punishment of the Portuguese govern-

* After 1945, communist regimes have referred to the Josephist tradition in their policy of restraining the material power and spiritual influence of the Catholic Church.

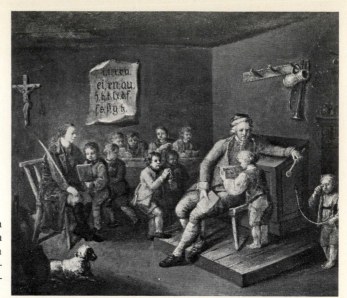

Instruction in an Austrian classroom in the time of Maria Theresa. State Historical Museum, Vienna.

to a market economy. Trade was, indeed, freed from old restrictions, in Tuscany and France and even in the dominions of the king of Spain; though only partly and in piecemeal fashion, which did not satisfy either those who resented change or those who called for more.

It was a complicated situation. Economic freedom is seldom the true ideology of private interests, which are generally inclined to deny to others the freedom demanded for themselves. Complaints against the rigidity of protectionism do not mean that the plaintiff is liberal, only that he wants his particular interest freed from some anachronistic burden, while protected from somebody else. Business interests tend to be liberal in general, protectionist in particular, each with its own interest to defend. Liberalizing moves at this time seem to have come more often from the royal administration than from any interest groups. The royal administration was ahead of business, ahead of landed interests, ahead even sometimes of intellectuals; and it came up against the jungle thickets of rights and customs where everyone had something to defend—even the poorest peasants, concerned to preserve the common lands, their wood-gathering, gleaning, and grazing rights. This is why enlightened opinion could think only of a despotism equally enlightened (that is, of the same mind) to cut through the mass of particular privileges and carry through a revolution for the public good, not against the monarchy, but by and for it.

Monarchs and governments agreed, and were determined that nothing should stand in their way. It was a question, as a French philosopher put it, of "joining absolute authority to the force of reason." Men, equal before God, should be equal before the law as well: same taxes, same courts, same opportunities to show their talent. But, equal before God, men are not equal before nature. Their unequal capacities must be reflected in their unequal fortunes. Property, born of the free exploita-

ment. The Portuguese government at that time was headed by the Marquis of Pombal (1699–1782), who had played a great part in destroying the flourishing Jesuit colonies in Paraguay. Pombal, a ruthless authoritarian, was a typical "enlightened" minister in a backward, poor, priest-ridden state.* Pombal established the absolute power of the crown by humbling the great noble houses, strengthening state control of the church, harnessing the Inquisition in his service. Robert Southey, the English writer, who found no conscience or humanity in the great minister, thought him devoted to restoring Portugal if not to greatness at least to plenty. But Pombal did not get far with this, failing to develop the home manufactures that he hoped for, and his most concrete achievement was the rebuilding of Lisbon after the earthquake. At any rate this was the man the Jesuit was attacking.

Pombal retaliated in a pamphlet denouncing the Jesuits as exploiters of the natives of Paraguay, and arguing that the state which the Jesuits had set up in South America, at the natives' cost, was but a pattern of the way in which they planned to enslave the world. The pamphlet achieved great effect in enlightened circles. In 1759, the Jesuits were expelled from Portugal, followed in 1760 by the Papal Nuncio, while the Portuguese Inquisition was used to scourge supporters of the Jesuits and of the Pope who vainly tried to stand by the Order. Reconciliation between the Pope and Portugal could only be achieved at the cost of accepting their expulsion. Once the Pope agreed, other governments followed. Expelled from France in 1764, suppressed in Spain in 1767, in other Italian states in 1768, the order was finally dissolved by the Pope in 1773, under the steady pressure of its royal enemies.** The latter much preferred the "Jansenists" (see p. 260 ff.) or Febronians (after the name of an Erastian German Bishop), who combined a simpler, sterner, more scriptural moralism with opposition to papal supremacy, support of local bishops and of the secular power. In the long struggle between church and state it seemed at last as if the state was winning clear decisions.

Enlightened despots regarded the state as the ultimate touchstone of all policy, declared themselves the servants of the state, seeking to be its masters only in order to serve it better. Frederick the Great defined the sovereign as the first magistrate, the first general, the first financier, the first minister of the community: "He is only the first servant of the state, obliged to act with integrity, wisdom and complete disinterestedness as if, at any moment, he were bound to render an account of his

* In early eighteenth-century Portugal, the church owned two-thirds of the land and boasted nine hundred religious houses in a population of three million. Prelates were as thick on the ground as Kentucky colonels, the King having invested much of the gold of Brazil to turning his court chaplaincy into a cardinal patriarchate and securing special privileges for the canons of his new foundation in Lisbon.

** The Jesuits survived in Russia until expelled from there in 1820, because Tsar Alexander found them converting too many of his Orthodox subjects. The order was revived in 1814.

administration to his fellow citizens." This was confirmed from an even better source, a letter that Leopold II of Habsburg wrote to his sister in 1790, on the eve of his accession to the Imperial crown:

> . . . I am firmly convinced that each country needs a constitution, that is a contract between the people and its sovereign . . . I am convinced that the sovereign who does not respect that contract, renounces thereby his throne . . . I am convinced that the executive power belongs to the sovereign, while the legislative power belongs to the people and its representatives . . . I am convinced that the sovereign is accountable before his people . . . I am convinced that the supreme reason for the existence of societies and governments is the happiness of individuals . . .

There is little evidence that Leopold really believed all this, but every reason to think he was convinced it was the right thing to believe at this time. Constitutional monarchy in the English fashion was obviously in the air, and the French Revolution would go to war against an emperor who seemed to hold much the same views as many of its leaders.

Yet revolution came. It came because reforms were too slow and sporadic, because the enlightened despots, however much they tried, could only scratch the surface of their problems, because in many places—and especially in France—no reforming despot could appear. It came to some extent because, especially in countries like France, changes had been taking place, things had been getting better, and revolutions, at least according to Tocqueville, "spring not from despair but from rising expectations." It came, above all, perhaps, because too many rulers, heedless of real priorities, indulged in ruinous wars which aggravated the debts and financial difficulties of their treasuries, the social and economic tensions between classes resulting from their incapacity to reform, or else frustrated those reforms they had managed to introduce. The beginning of the end was precipitated by costly conflicts which showed no real awareness of how precarious was their position and that of the existing order in most countries.

International Conflicts: Wars and Revolutions

Most international conflicts of the early eighteenth century turned on inessentials. The ideological wars of an earlier day, to be revived as the century ended, the great power struggles like those in which Bourbon and Habsburg had locked horns, do not appear until midcentury or later. Only one power, England, followed a line of conduct which, despite twists and turns, consistently reflected its national interests. In peace and war, with the one sometimes not very distinct from the other, England struggled to assert her naval and colonial supremacy, not as a matter of royal policy but as reflection of trading and manufacturing interests which showed a familiar mixture of selfishness and rectitude, and of popular policies in which self-interest was salved by good conscience. The moralization of self-interest was a practice in which the eighteenth and nineteenth centuries excelled. Here, as in other areas, England was supreme.

On the continent, the powers kept their eyes fixed on dynastic rather than economic objectives. There is a reality about dynastic conflicts which our day may be tempted to underrate, yet there is no underrating the great dynastic clashes of the fourteenth or the sixteenth century when lives, thrones and the control of kingdoms were at stake. The dynastic interests of the eighteenth century appear less consistent and less basic, their contests less tuned to the realities of an age of markets and finance; and the succession problems of Poland, Austria, or Parma were of little direct concern to the subjects of the princes who pursued them. If that itself was no novelty, the rise of a public opinion which formulated and expressed such an impression was. As a result, subjects felt little involvement in, and less commitment to, their masters' wars: in 1733, Goldoni, the Venetian playwright, joined the citizens of Parma watching the battle fought beneath the city's walls—a battle which ended with 25,000 dead, including the Austrian commander; in 1744, the Romans on their walls watched Austrians and Neapolitans slaughtering one another below; a year later, at the battle of Fontenoy, the trees were full of curious onlookers. In more favorable circumstances, ladies actually got seats on fortification bastions to watch hostilities from a comfortable place.

War was for the soldiers; a rabble of rankers, the sweepings of city streets and country taverns, officered by professionals who recognized one another across the fortuitous barriers of war as members of the same fraternity and caste. "No man in his right senses," William Pitt told the House of Commons in 1759, "would ever enlist in the army." * So, armies were made up largely of jailbirds released on condition they joined up, of paupers, of "any sturdy beggar, any fortune teller, any idle, unknown, suspected fellow in a parish that cannot give an account of himself"; and, in central Europe, of recruits called up, kidnapped, or captured among the prince's subjects or his foes.

In the nation, such troops were a foreign body. In the seventeenth century, the greatest punishment one could inflict on a city had been to quarter troops in it. There are cases of the inhabitants fleeing their cities at the soldiers' coming, deserting their houses and shops to save

---

* In Dr. Johnson's opinion no man would be a sailor who could get into jail, for the ship was equivalent to a jail plus the risk of drowning. And not only drowning: in the Seven Years' War, 1,512 seamen were killed in battle, 133,708 were missing or dead of disease.

what they could. Then came barracks, first for the garrisons in border towns, then, in the eighteenth century, inland too. Barracks were a relief for the citizens; but they only emphasized the isolation of the soldier, with his dissolute and brutal manners and his point of view oriented to, and by, what was in those days a lifetime occupation from which only age or desertion offered an escape.

To guard against desertion, discipline was tightened, marching and battle order organized to keep the soldier in the ranks, affording the least possible chance for a man to slip off unnoticed. There would be no marauding or foraging expeditions, during which troops could desert in droves. Magazines, stores, ovens, heavy supply trains, regular arrangements with contractors en route, limited mobility, excluded winter campaigning, precluded swift movement or pursuit, made sieges rather than battles the preferred form of war, imposed parade ground order even on the battle ground, and thus enhanced the importance of drill.

The ragamuffin soldiers learned to move with the precision of automatons. Their officers, versed in drill, convinced of the superiority of position over movement, unaccustomed to initiatives which their cumbersome machine discouraged, became used to fighting by the book, deciding some encounters by rule and precedent rather than waste their shot and men. An enemy in a strong position meant that you should march away. A city meant a siege to the attackers, or else a breadbasket to protect with stout fortifications. Supply lines became all-important, and soldiering an enterprise from which the civil population should ideally be left out. Gone were the days when the soldiers of Louis XIV, sent to put down a French peasant rising, roasted the children on spits. War was still full of atrocities; but mostly in the somber east where the Russians, for instance, hung the inhabitants of conquered Memel after cutting off their noses and ears, "tore off legs, opened innards and heart." Further west, hostages, requisitions, reprisals, were part of the logistical arsenal, brought in to secure order or supplies; no longer the commonplace of every land where troops appeared.

So, there were wars and the horrors of war, but there was no fighting for sheer survival or for a dominant ideal. War was part of the business of the state—perhaps the greatest part. Like every business, it often turned around land and trade but—like a business too—its directors generally knew when they should cut their losses. One did what one could, and gave up when one had to without too much fuss. And, since the actual fighting and the duration of the wars were relatively limited, the suffering they caused was less than that to which the seventeenth century had grown accustomed.

Men have called this relatively mild period the time of lace-cuff wars—*la guerre en dentelles*—even though thousands of corpses still strewed the battlegrounds whose hideousness only gave way to the rich meadows grown out of their bones, so that old battlefields offered a lush contrast with the sparse-cropped fields nearby. Perhaps this only stresses how alien the servants of war and their pursuits were to the society of that time. Rather than war in lace cuffs, European alliances and entanglements in the eighteenth century evoke a minuet, that superficial dance in which partners pair and separate, evolving gracefully and somewhat gratuitously amid the scenery of a stately world.

As in the days of Louis XIV, the great perennial contest for dominion in this time was waged between England and France, the richest and most powerful nations of the West. No great wars broke out while they were at peace; but no tenuous *entente* could conceal for long the power struggle between them. From 1715 to 1740 and from 1815 to 1848 peace between the two powers, if it put no end to European wars, at least kept them from spreading. The rest of the time, France and England were the core of more widespread power struggles, which rose to a great climax in the Napoleonic wars. When these ended, the issue had been settled. France lay defeated, decimated by two decades of murderous campaigns, humbled by foreign occupation. And Britain ruled the seas. In a sense the long years of unrest and war that began in the 1790's provide a natural transition from the "old regime" which had evolved out of the feudal order, to the new conditions of the "modern" nineteenth century. The transition would only be accomplished in 1848, when the agitation and convulsions of fourscore years culminated in revolution continent-wide.

The next few pages carry the chronicle of major international events to the eve of the French Revolution. Subsequent chapters will sketch their background in more detail, and bring the story to the watershed of 1848.

From Utrecht to the Peace of Versailles

The Peace of Utrecht, the accession of a Hanoverian prince to the English throne, the death of Louis XIV, all drew England and France, so long at daggers drawn, closer together. Louis XV (1715–1774) was a child, and the Regent sat uneasily in his place. George I (1714–1727), was the occupant of a contested throne. French recovery depended on British co-operation. The peace of both countries hung on maintaining the terms agreed at Utrecht, keeping the Stuarts from the English crown and the Spanish Bourbons from the French. Spain and Austria, on the other hand, were both dissatisfied with the Utrecht settlement. Charles VI had been frustrated in his Spanish aspirations; Philip V, encouraged by his Italian wives, sought further gains in Italy. When in 1717 Spain opened the attack in Italy at last, England and France intervened on Austria's side, forcing Philip V to moderate his ambitions and to accept a settlement which promised the succession of the duchies of Parma and Piacenza to one of his younger sons (1720).

Italy was not yet over her troubles. The young king of France had been affianced to an even younger Spanish Infanta. His kingdom could not wait for her to grow up before the succession problem was resolved. In 1725, the Spanish engagement was broken off, the incensed Infanta returned to her parents in Madrid, and Louis XV was married to Marie Leczinska, the plump and pious daughter of the pretender to the Polish crown. When, in 1733, Augustus II, the reigning king of Poland died, the French naturally supported the claims of their king's father-in-law, the Austrians a rival candidate—Augustus's son. War broke out with France and Spain on the one side, Russia and Austria on the other. Stanislas Leczinsky was soon driven out of Poland, the French armies occupying Lorraine—Empire territory—while the brunt of fighting took place in Italy, where Spaniards vied with Austrians for territorial gains. In 1738, the Peace of Vienna gave Stanislas the Duchy of Lorraine for life, after which it would revert to France to complete her eastern border. Francis, Duke of Lorraine and husband of the Emperor's daughter, Maria Theresa, was compensated with Tuscany and Parma, while Prince Charles of Spain gave up Parma for the Kingdom of the Two Sicilies.

Like the wonderful game that Alice witnessed in Wonderland, everybody had won, everyone must get prizes—though no one consulted the inhabitants of places which rulers were treating as musical thrones. Everybody had won—except England. England had kept out of war and saved her resources for business. Now she began to feel that her interests were threatened. France was increasing her power once again, not only in Europe but in the Mediterranean too, where French merchants were elbowing Englishmen out of the Levant trade. Spain, too, was regaining strength, and her refurbished fleet interfered with the multitude of English smugglers who had long poached so profitably on her South American preserves. In 1739, the government of England was forced to give in to popular outcry and mercantile pressure and to declare war on Spain, whose fleets in the South Seas would shortly receive support from French warships.

Then, in 1740, Emperor Charles VI died, to be succeeded by his daughter, Maria Theresa (1717–1780). Charles had spent much energy and money to secure recognition of the Pragmatic Sanction by which the Salic Law, banning succession in the female line, was laid aside and his daughter's right to the family heritage assured. But the agreements Charles secured were written on the wind. The young king of Prussia, Frederick II, considered the opportunity too good to miss and marched into Austrian territory, occupying Silesia. In Frederick's wake, the Elector of Bavaria asserted his rights to the Austrian succession, Spain attacked Austrian lands in Italy, finally France—not to be outdone—attacked the

Austrian Netherlands (i.e., Belgium). This brought England into the general war.

The English, already at war with Spain, might have kept out of the wider conflict but for the French threat to their interests overseas and—through Belgium—to their own coasts as well. Having been drawn into war, they fought it mostly overseas, where French and Spanish forces divided by the continental war did not show up in a good light. Fighting in Europe as well as overseas, the French and Spanish had to scatter their forces over several fronts, apportion their resources between the fleet and the army. The British, of course, did too, but nowhere near as much. This disproportion, and her freedom to concentrate on colonial questions, stood Britain in good stead in this as in future conflicts. And we shall see that the only war she lost was lost when France was free to concentrate on fighting her enemy of long standing, free of commitments on the continent.

Despite British support, the weight of the enemies leagued against her told against Maria Theresa; and the Peace of Aix-la-Chapelle was concluded in 1748 at Austria's expense. Spain received Parma and Frederick received Silesia. France gave up Belgium, which her forces had occupied, and left the war no better off than when she started, partly because her merchants were clamoring for peace and the reopening of sea lanes which the English had cut. Britain made no gains either, although she had asserted her power in the Western hemisphere.

But the peace was only a truce. None of its signatories felt quite satisfied or quite secure. Maria Theresa wanted Silesia back. Frederick was waiting for the first opportunity to defend himself by attacking her. England, her attention focused overseas, wanted an effective guardian for her king's Hanoverian possessions and thought she could find one in Frederick, who hoped that, already assured of the French alliance, he could detach England from Austria and thus achieve the isolation of his chief enemy. But the rapprochement of England and Prussia threw France into the arms of Austria, herself in search of an ally who could help check the dangerous might of Prussia. The secular hostility of Bourbons and Habsburgs was abandoned and a diplomatic revolution brought Paris and Vienna together, turning the tables on Frederick, who found himself isolated, with no great expectation of effective armed support from his new British allies.

Yet both France and Britain were less interested in Europe than in their struggle overseas, where population pressure and the search for markets spurred their imperial ambitions, leading to frequent clashes. In 1754, the long-standing friction between French troops and trappers moving south and west from Canada and British settlers and traders moving north and west from the seashore colonies exploded into fighting. The interest of France was to concentrate her forces against Britain, in America and in India, where trouble also brewed. Yet, once again, she would be caught between her continental commitments and her colonial interests. In 1756 the colonial war became a general one, as England and Prussia faced Austria, Russia, and France in what became known as the Seven Years' War. While Frederick fought a series of brilliant but desperate holding actions against Russian and Austrian armies, the French were losing their empire to the British. Quebec fell in 1759; Canada was forfeited soon after; most of the Caribbean sugar islands too; in India, Pondicherry surrendered to the British in 1761. When Frederick had been saved on the brink of defeat by the death of the Tsarina Elizabeth (1762), whose successor preferred to leave the war, France's hope of redeeming her losses overseas by European victory had to be given up. So had Maria Theresa's hope of recovering Silesia. Frederick was left in possession of his loot and the Treaty of Paris (1763) gave England Canada and effective, if temporary, dominion of the North Atlantic. France recovered the sugar islands, which her merchants and economists regarded as far more important than "a few acres of snow," as Voltaire called Canada.

Two things came out of the Seven Years' War quite clearly. The first was its impact on the finances of all participants, an impact which had a great deal to do with subsequent events. The budgetary troubles resulting from the conflict inspired the legal and administrative reforms of the Habsburg empire; the British policies which eventually set off rebellion in their American colonies; the fiscal reforms of Louis XV and his clashes with the privileged orders and institutions; not least and most successful, the various reforms of Frederick II in Prussia. The second effect of the Seven Years' War was on the international scene: it left Prussia ruined but one of the great powers. Her population had been quite literally decimated, her land devastated, both friends and funds seemed to have melted away, the state of her provinces—wrote Frederick—resembled that of Brandenburg at the end of the Thirty Years' War. But she was a power now, and none could count without her. Her isolation imposed one course: alliance with Russia, whose change of front in 1762 had saved Frederick and with whom Prussia shared a common greed for Poland. This alliance would dominate Prussian diplomacy for a hundred and fifty years.

The Anglo-French struggle had remained unresolved; and the French prepared for the next round in it by buying Corsica from the Genoese (1768), hoping to use the island as an advanced Mediterranean base, and by feverishly rebuilding their navy. Meanwhile, with British and French attention focused on a future naval conflict, Prussia, Russia, and Austria were free to prey on their weaker neighbors. Poland and Turkey would have to pay the price of the preoccupation of the western powers, their fate strangely interconnected as Catherine of Russia and Frederick of Prussia, reluctantly joined by Maria Theresa, stepped in—they claimed—to rescue Christians from benighted Ottoman opression, or from Catholic intolerance and governmental anarchy on

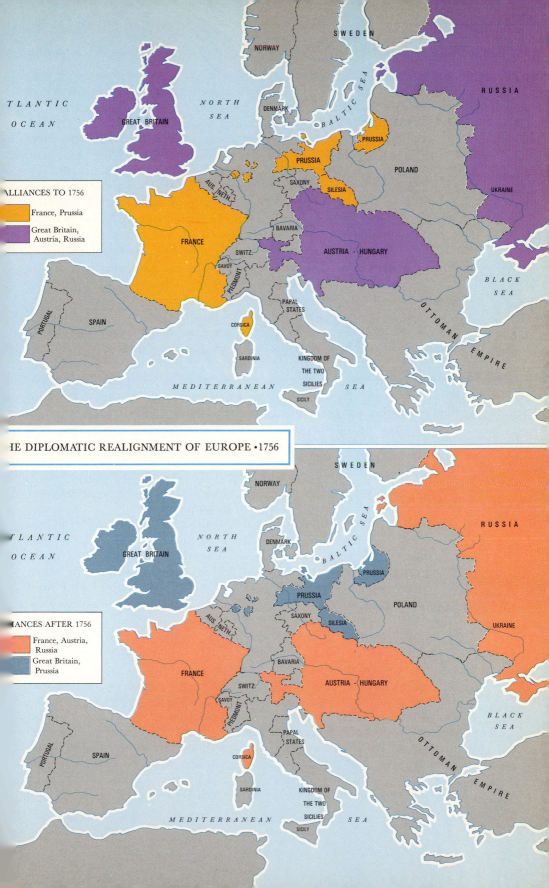

ALLIANCES TO 1756
France, Prussia
Great Britain, Austria, Russia

NORWAY
SWEDEN
GREAT BRITAIN
ATLANTIC OCEAN
NORTH SEA
DENMARK
BALTIC SEA
RUSSIA
PRUSSIA
PRUSSIA
POLAND
UKRAINE
AUS. NETH.
SAXONY
SILESIA
FRANCE
BAVARIA
AUSTRIA - HUNGARY
SWITZ.
SAVOY
PIEDMONT
PORTUGAL
SPAIN
CORSICA
PAPAL STATES
SARDINIA
KINGDOM OF THE TWO SICILIES
SICILY
MEDITERRANEAN SEA
OTTOMAN EMPIRE
BLACK SEA

THE DIPLOMATIC REALIGNMENT OF EUROPE · 1756

ALLIANCES AFTER 1756
France, Austria, Russia
Great Britain, Prussia

NORWAY
SWEDEN
GREAT BRITAIN
ATLANTIC OCEAN
NORTH SEA
DENMARK
BALTIC SEA
RUSSIA
PRUSSIA
PRUSSIA
POLAND
UKRAINE
AUS. NETH.
SAXONY
SILESIA
FRANCE
BAVARIA
AUSTRIA - HUNGARY
SWITZ.
SAVOY
PIEDMONT
PORTUGAL
SPAIN
CORSICA
PAPAL STATES
SARDINIA
KINGDOM OF THE TWO SICILIES
SICILY
MEDITERRANEAN SEA
OTTOMAN EMPIRE
BLACK SEA

the banks of the Vistula.

The War of the Polish Succession had not closed the tale of that kingdom's woes. Further succession struggles in the 1760's had turned Poland into something close to a Russian protectorate. A Polish rising at the end of that decade brought Turkey into war with Russia, when Russian troops pursuing Polish foes violated Ottoman territory. The war went badly for Turkey, and in 1774 the Treaty of Kuchuk-Kainardji deprived her of vast territories between the river Bug and the Sea of Azov. Before that, however, as Russian troops advanced in the southern Ukraine, Prussia and Austria came to feel that the balance of power could only be maintained if they secured compensation for the Russians' gains. Where could this be found better than in Poland? The first partition of Poland, therefore, was carried out in 1772 and gave all three of Poland's neighbors important chunks of new territory.

A new Russo-Turkish war (1787–1792), which ended with more annexations of Turkish territory by Russia, suggested further compensations at Poland's expense in 1792, when France, deep in the throes of revolution, was once again incapable of intervening. It has been suggested that, in turn, preoccupation with the affairs of Poland saved the young French Revolution from being crushed to death by an effective Austro-Prussian intervention. At any rate, in 1794, the Poles who understandably enough refused to accept the role of victim with equanimity, were finally dispatched and their kingdom, which once had stretched from the Black Sea to the Baltic and even reached out to Moscow, fell victim to Romanov, Hohenzollern, and Habsburg greed.

While all this happened in the eastern borderlands of Europe, France and England had gone to war again when England's American colonies had rebelled against her. Between 1778 and 1783, French military and economic aid on land, the skillful use of the rebuilt French fleet at sea, ensured the defeat of the British. In 1783, the Peace of Versailles lost England an empire: thirteen colonies, the island of Minorca to Spain, several islands and African lands to France. Leopold of Tuscany noted sadly that the great power which had balanced the might of France had fallen completely and forever. But if the American war brought England defeat, it brought economic and political collapse to France. Unable to face the financial problems which the cost of war had exasperated, France broke into revolution, thus apparently removing yet another counter from the international checkerboard.

Several revolutions had preceded the French: in Geneva, in 1766 and 1781 French intervention had curbed serious risings; between 1774 and 1783 Britain's North American colonies had gained their freedom; between 1783 and 1787 there had been civil war in Holland, and in 1789 a revolt in Austria's Belgian provinces. But the troubles which began in France in 1787 would set fire to Europe, then to the Caribbean, and, finally, to Latin America, adding their own fuel to existing conflicts and fundamentally affecting the international situation itself.

Chapter 10

CONSTITUTIONAL EVOLUTION IN BRITAIN

Like Italy in the fifteenth century and France in the seventeenth, England seems to have been the pilot country of the eighteenth century, its economic and industrial advances, its political institutions, the ideas it generated, inspiring envy or emulation elsewhere.

To trace the internal policies of European countries during the century and a half in which an older order fumbled for new forms, it seems best to begin with a look at Great Britain (so called since the official union with Scotland in 1707, when the crosses of St. Andrew and St. George were joined in the Union Jack), and at her American offspring whose self-assertion played an important role in subsequent events in Europe.

Both England and France underwent "revolutions" which were to leave their mark on their neighbors and on the whole world. But England's "revolution" was both similar to and different from that of France: less immediately evident, yet in some ways more far-reaching. Above all, it began sooner.

The eighteenth and nineteenth centuries saw England preserving extraordinary stability in the midst of changes no less extraordinary. Popular agitation, political and industrial riots, rebellions and invasions, as well as bitter and wide-flung wars, did not manage to shake either the Protestant settlement or the parliamentary system, each of which underwent profound reforms that strengthened rather than endangered the established order. Government by cabinet, party politics,

477

a wider franchise, radical social and economic changes, a demographic explosion which increased the population from six million in 1750 to eighteen million a hundred years later, and the total national income in far greater proportion, succeeded only in affirming the dynasty and increasing attachment to a system which, with all its faults, had proved able to adjust to fast-changing conditions and to accept the new world rather than battle it.

When Queen Anne, last of the Stuarts, died in 1714, she was succeeded by her nearest Protestant relative, the Elector of Hanover, first of a string of Georges destined to rule for 116 years.* One consequence of their accession was a revival of Jacobite** hopes for a restoration of the Stuart dynasty. In 1715 James II's son—James III—landed in Scotland, only to flee after defeat a few months later. Further attempts to raise the Highland clans in the 1720's met with no success. But in 1745, while France and Britain were at war, Louis XV supported a fresh attempt to upset the Hanoverians: James's heir, Charles Edward (1720–1788)—Bonnie Prince Charlie—landed in Scotland, rallied the clans still faithful to the Stuart cause and even invaded England. By spring of 1746, however, he too had been defeated and hopes of Stuart restoration dashed for good, while the Scots, crushed and persecuted, were forced out of their secular isolation to win a paradoxical revenge in their increasing share of the trade and administration of their English victors and of England's empire.

Another result of the Hanoverian settlement, and one which affected the kingdom's European policy, was that fifty-two years after giving up her last continental possessions England had once more to bear in mind the interests and security of her king's electorate. The interlude was brief. The fate of Hanover only mattered to the first two Georges, still close to their German roots. George III showed little interest in what he called "that horrid electorate;" and this progressive detachment culminated in 1837 in the accession of another branch of the family to what had by then become a kingdom, to whose throne Victoria, as a woman, was not entitled to succeed. But for a while, the Hanover connection affected the policies of England.

Much has been made of the idea that George I could speak no English, which left his ministers very much to themselves and allowed cabinet government to develop unpresided by the King and increasingly independent of his direct authority. Despite tales of George I communicating with his ministers in dog-Latin, it would appear that he did know a bit of English, and quite a lot of French, which he generally used like many other monarchs of his time. State documents destined for the King's examination were translated into French, and George's

* George I, 1714–1727; George II, 1727–1760; George III, 1760–1820; George IV, 1820–1830; followed by William IV, 1830–1837, and Victoria, 1837–1901.
** From Jacobus, Latin for James: partisans of James II, exiled in 1688, and of his direct heirs.

George I of England.

conversations with English ministers were in that language.

The situation changed under his son, less boorish than his father. It was said that the sight of a book made George I angry; his grumpy "I hate all boets and bainters!" has often been quoted. George II liked books and patronized their authors—and musicians too. What is more important, the new king was familiar with English ways. Thereafter, and to the end of the century—even though George II long left his affairs in the hands of his father's great minister, Robert Walpole—the crown once more dominated British policy. Yet, with a difference: for it never ruled with the arbitrary power wielded by the kings of France, let alone of Prussia; or long ignored the wishes of the lords, the money interests of the city of London, and even of public opinion taken in the broadest sense. So that, henceforth and quite significantly, the tale of English politics would be told in terms of ministries, not reigns.

King and Parliament

England was ruled by the King-in-Parliament, and for most of the eighteenth century this meant that to rule England the king—or rather his ministers—had to manage Parliament, and the great families or interests which controlled elections to it, so as to secure a majority in the House of Commons. This turned politics into a vast spoils system, in which support was bought with offices and the perquisites of office supported the cost of politics. In 1726, one quarter of the English peerage held either court or government office, and most of the offices left over went to peers' friends, their clients, or their relatives, in a great round of venality, nepotism, and corruption. Archaic survivals, like the post of Taster of the King's Wine in Dublin, became sinecures in the gift of ministers eager to ensure the loyalty of some man or clan. Failing office, bribery would do. The visiting Voltaire recorded the remark of an English member of Parliament, threatening that if he did not receive a bribe he would be forced to vote according to his conscience. On the other hand, Walpole once explained he was obliged to bribe members, not to vote against their conscience, but for it. One way or another, it may be argued that the system seems to have worked; and that, bad as it was, corruption was better than force.

Walpole and Pitt

The man who made it work was Robert Walpole (1676–1745), a country gentleman of great managing ability, who held office from 1715 to 1717 and again from 1721 to 1742. In Louis Kronenberger's words "he ascertained that men are vain, self-interested and stupid, and proceeded to act on the information." Most people are content to bewail the fact. Not that many did so in those days, when most generally admitted that they went into public affairs for what they could get out of it. As one of Walpole's chief opponents put it, speaking of his own Tory party, "our principal views were the preservation of this power, great employment to ourselves, and great opportunity of rewarding those who had helped to raise us, and of hurting those who stood in opposition to us." Hence, the matter-of-factness with which Walpole could remark about the House of Commons "All these men have their price." Much the same could be said of any other ruling group of the time, but it is significant that it was said in England.

Controlling the Commons and strong in the King's support, Walpole kept England at peace as long as he could, avoiding commercial wars and higher taxes. After he resigned in 1742, influence, patronage, and low taxes were followed by influence, patronage, and high taxes raised to pay for aggressive enterprises which were designed to exploit every possibility of commercial expansion. The change in policies can be seen in the comparison between the two great prime ministers of the time: solid, all-too-human Walpole, the politicking country squire, himself the scion of an old established country family; and the man who succeeded him, dynamic William Pitt (1708–1778), grandson of an East India merchant who promoted himself from interloping buccaneer to governor of Madras. Cold, aggressive, egoistic, and unstable, Pitt believed in his destiny and in that of England—which meant that of her sailors and her merchants. William Pitt had learned from his fierce grandfather that trade and wealth came by risk and war. In 1735, at twenty-seven, he entered the Commons from the family borough of Old Sarum, where proprietorship of a mound of earth on which a village had once stood gave the right to a seat in Parliament. In 1739 he spoke for war with Spain: "When trade is at stake, you must defend it or perish." It was a language which the merchants of London and Bristol, and the city people whose livelihood depended on them, liked. For the next fourteen years, England would be almost constantly at war, in India, in America, and over all the seas, conquering the empire that would serve her trade; and Pitt—later the Earl of Chatham—would be the symbol of her imperial gains.

Yet Pitt would be removed from power in 1761 and reduced to protest bitterly against the mealy policies of lesser men,* and against the Peace of 1763, in which, he complained "We retain nothing although we have conquered everything" and which, above all, failed to curb France's power at sea. His warnings went unheeded and Britain paid the penalty in the American war, during which the old statesman died, the empire he had helped build foundering, his son William reading to him from the *Iliad* the death of Hector. Burke wrote the inscription of his tomb in Westminster Abbey, praising the first statesman by whom commerce was united with and made to flourish by war.

G. M. Trevelyan, the English historian, has called the days of Pitt "an age of aristocracy and liberty," when law and money ruled but reform was kept at bay. Such stability could rest only on prosperity and expansion, and figures bear this out. Between 1720 and 1802 the value of British imports increased fivefold, that of British exports sixfold. "Our ships," Addison boasted in his *Spectator* in 1711, "are laden with the harvest of every climate: our tables are stored with spices, and oils, and wines: our rooms are filled with pyramids of china, and adorned with the workmanship of Japan: our morning's draught comes to us from the remotest corners of the earth: we repair our bodies by the drugs from America and repose ourselves under Indian canopies . . . nature indeed furnishes us with the bare necessities of life; but traffic gives us a great variety of what is useful, and at the same time supplies us with everything that is convenient and ornamental." That year, the penny post introduced in London and nearby facilitated letter writing and business communications, providing frequent and regular deliveries of mail. That year too had seen the foundation of the South Sea Company, set up less to trade in the southern seas than to finance the taking over of the national debt and strengthen public credit.

The wave of speculation that the maneuvers of the South Sea Company set off, and the eventual crash in which they finally resulted when this and other bubbles burst in 1720, threatened for a while to have just the opposite effect. Yet Walpole's astute policies righted the situation and, as the 1720's ended, trade was booming once more and public credit had been restored. The very venality of the administration approached that of the business interests and, while ministers made no bones about their greed, rapacity did not prevent scrupulous discharge

---

* Like George III's tutor, the Earl of Bute; or, briefly, the Duke of Newcastle, of whose bumbling ways Louis Kronenberger quotes some characteristic examples: "Oh— yes—yes—to be sure—Annapolis must be defended—troops must be sent to Annapolis —pray where *is* Annapolis?" "Cape Breton is an island! Wonderful! —show it to me in the map. So it is, sure enough. My dear Sir, you always bring us good news. I must go and tell the King that Cape Breton is an island."

of governmental debts. This policy paid off. Public confidence in the government enabled it to draw on private resources to an amazing extent. The national debt, one million in 1688, was nearly eighty million in mid-eighteenth century, and yet government securities which paid 5 per cent in 1717 paid only 3 per cent in 1749. Government was constitutional; propertied men knew that their peers controlled expenditures and made accounting public. Public obligations would no more be canceled. That was why the government could borrow cheaply and use what it got for policies which only advanced the interests of its merchant creditors.

Perhaps England was ruled less exactly by an aristocracy than by an oligarchy—or a plutocracy. Rank meant wealth and wealth brought rank. The English, as Burke put it, were "entitled to equal rights, but to equal rights to unequal things." Magnates grew rich on the rents of their lands; lesser gentry yearned for a better past and turned against them, but prosperity tempered social animosity. Among the rural lower classes many went hungry but some prospered. Workhouses fed, housed, and hired out the poor to manufacturers or landlords, who got cheap labor for the cost of their keep. Some workhouse children wore manacles, or rings round their necks, to keep them from running away. Riots were commonplace in leaner years, but the countryside was well in hand.

The pivot was the volunteer Justice of the Peace, who acted as neighborhood administrator and supervisor, licensing inns, fixing wages, supervising the jail and the workhouse, meting out rough justice, setting the rates, and keeping highways in indifferent repair. The J.P. could become a petty local tyrant; he was certainly a very influential man.

"You are the slaves of laws," Voltaire remarked wistfully to Boswell. "The French are the slaves of men." Any reader of *Tom Jones* will know that some English magistrates were also arbitrary and unjust. But they were the stern defenders of the order they incarnated. As late as 1763 a seventy-three-year-old schoolmaster would be put in stocks and thrown in jail for translating Voltaire and publishing freethinking tracts. But that itself reflected a new public, for which the literature of this kind was meant. As early as 1727, a Swiss traveler had been impressed by the way English workmen started their day by going to a coffeehouse to read the newspapers, discussing politics and even the King. By that year the English provinces boasted twenty-five newspapers. By 1753, seven and a half million newspapers were being sold in England: forty years later this number had more than doubled. Literacy grew, thanks largely to charity schools for children of artisans, small shopkeepers, the lower middle class. Clubs sprang up devoted to discussion and debate. Political awareness increased in London and the provinces. And all this would be reflected in the Wilkes affair.

John Wilkes (1727–1797) was the son of a parvenu distiller: a great talker, winebibber, and womanizer, a brash and exhibitionistic man.

Robert Walpole Before the British Cabinet, a painting by Joseph Coopy. British Museum, London.

But he was also the owner of a newspaper and member of Parliament, in which he supported the politics of Pitt. In 1763, angered by the peace which made too many concessions to France and none to the city merchants, Wilkes denounced the treaty, the ministry, and even George III, in his *North Briton,* in ferocious terms that brought charges of seditious libel and a general warrant to arrest both him and his printer. George III had used general warrants much as the king of France used *lettres de cachet,* but with explosive results. The English public were not about to see a printer, let alone a Member of Parliament, arrested and pursued against what seemed to them the law of the land. From the Tower, Wilkes claimed wrongful arrest and instituted a countersuit. Popular imagination sizzled, "Wilkes and liberty" became the slogan of the day and, when a friendly judge declared general warrants illegal, Wilkes triumphed and won his damages. But the King had other strings to his bow, and Wilkes was expelled from the Commons on obscenity charges and had to flee the country. In 1768, he returned to stand as candidate for Middlesex. Elected, rejected by the Commons unwilling to displease the King, he became a hero once more, was repeatedly re-elected by Middlesex votes and repeatedly rejected by the Commons which finally declared his defeated opponent elected in his stead.

Wilkes lived on to become Lord Mayor of London, proof that blundering governments could not blunder too far and that popular temper could not be denied too long; but also that—in the end—England was not fated to revolution but to adjustment. Meanwhile, the long battles waged around him established the right to report Parliamentary debates; political agitation, complete with public meetings and propaganda

John Wilkes, as depicted by William Hogarth. British Museum, London.

organization, indicated that politics could not remain the preserve of a narrow coterie; and Parliament itself was discredited for the prejudice, corruption, and unrepresentativeness which had been taken for granted until then. A new mentality was appearing, fertile ground for the reform agitation to come, and one soon to be raked over by the great controversy that would arise over the rights of Britain's American colonies,

From Colonies to Nation in America

By a curious paradox, the land which today symbolizes the western hemisphere and arrogates to itself the name of America was one of the last parts of the New World to be discovered, settled, and organized. English colonists reached Virginia almost a century after Columbus had sighted Cuba; French travelers preceded English ones in the Canadian wastes. While English settlers were scrabbling between the Bay of Fundy and the Savannah River, empires had been built to the south and an empire was growing in the north. Yet, unexpectedly, it would be the latecomers who triumphed, to build new Jerusalems throughout the continent.

More than any other country, the history of North America is that of men tackling nature, wrestling with the physical environment and with the elements, taming and shaping them to their will and being shaped in turn by the experiences they encountered and the challenges they overcame. Men, not states; men, not heroes; men who turned a continent of forest and waste into the immense demonstration of what men can do.

Two great cohesive forces seem to have dominated the formation of these new societies: the one was the pressure of the environment, the hostility of Indians and Frenchmen; the other idealism, diversely manifested, but chiefly—to begin with—in religious terms. Many colonists, especially in New England and the middle colonies, had left their homelands or been forced from them to be free to follow their conscience, to worship in their own way. Seeking freedom of conscience and worship for themselves, they denied it to others, as it had been denied to them. Their new societies would be founded on a common faith, which, once responsible for their own exclusion, now suggested the exclusion of others. Religion provided unity and counseled intolerance, as well as the moral right of society to intervene in its members' private lives, private morality becoming a matter of public concern. And though this applies largely to the New England colonies, religious beliefs would inspire other settlements, including that of the Quakers in Pennsylvania, who would be tolerant on principle as others were intolerant, and who would also leave their mark on American minds in centuries to come.

Since so many immigrants were nonconformists, they left their mark in yet another way: in their interest in popular education, in reading, in libraries and printing presses, above all in representative institutions from the town meeting to the colonial assembly, whose members consented to the taxes levied by the royal government. Conditions varied immensely among settlements stretching for nearly 1,500 miles across fifteen degrees of latitude; but one thing is evident: the colonies were growing fast. The twelve colonies of 1713 numbered about 360,000 people; in the thirteen colonies of 1763 the population had increased fivefold and the area of settlement had tripled. Much of the increase can be attributed to favorable conditions in a country where land was plentiful, and large families useful and easy to feed. Most of it, however, came from immigration: Huguenots, Highlanders, Swiss, about a quarter of a million Ulstermen, Germans driven by war or poverty or religious persecution, black slaves who numbered some 300,000 by the close of the Seven Years' War. The population seems to have doubled every generation. By 1775 it was approaching two and a half million; the first census in 1790 counted nearly four million, including 750,000 Negroes.

"You may depend upon it," said an American patriot, "that this is one of the best Poor Man's Country's in the World." Driven by land hunger, by dissatisfaction with the rule of churchmen in New England or great planters in the south, the poor men moved inland, pushed forward an irregular but ever-advancing frontier which served both as a safety valve and as a source for further development. Where the tidewater was prosperous and sophisticated, the hinterland was rebellious and self-reliant. Indifferent or hostile to the English culture of the seaboard, to the mercantile preoccupations of wealthy merchants and planters, to religious or political conformism, frontiersmen were nomadic, homespun, tough; they looked west across the continent, not east across the sea. Only the threat of Indians and the competition of Frenchmen held them back.

There were only 60,000 Frenchmen, but enterprise and military organization allowed them to hold their own. Sixty thousand against seventeen times as many. But not all British colonists were confronting the French, and most of their militiamen preferred to remain close to home rather than fight in the Canadian wastes. The so-called French and Indian wars of the 1750's which led into the Seven Years' War, would not have gone against the French but for the troops shipped over to do the fighting, and for the British fleet commanding the sea lanes over the Atlantic.

No wonder the British general, James Wolfe, did not mince his words: "The Americans are in general the dirtiest, the most contemptible cowardly dogs you can conceive. There is no depending on 'em in action. They fall down dead in their own dirt and desert by battalions, officers and all." As long as the French Empire lasted, the fate of the colonies, especially their chances of expansion, remained in doubt. Once the French threat had been removed in 1763, they would have little use for government from the outside, still less for taxes that might keep it up.

Issues of Conflict

Hardly more than a decade passed between the Peace of Paris and serious trouble in the colonies. The most evident sources of trouble were two: trade and taxes. The first was connected with the basic principle of the old colonial system, according to which colonies were supposed to supply the home country with raw materials and provide a market for its exports, never competing with them. American colonists could buy only English goods or foreign goods imported by way of England, could sell their goods only to the English, who might not want them if they competed with their own, or who would make a profit reselling them to others. So, the Americans fell back on smuggling, which became so successful that it enriched the colonists and angered the English.

Incapable of stopping contraband, the English sought at least to cash in on the prosperity it fostered, by taxing the colonists. Walpole tried it and caused such a stir that he retreated. Then, after 1763, the cost of war and of its aftermath counseled other attempts, especially a stamp tax whose revenue should pay for the upkeep of British troops in America. But the victorious war had just removed the chief need for such troops, and the colonists felt that for defense against Indians they could do as well more cheaply, the more so since the presence of the British troops also hampered their own attempts to encroach on Indian territories. Moreover, they would not be taxed without their consent and there were many men in England who agreed.

Here we come to the second issue, that of taxes. After 1763, the British government felt that economies were in order and that these could best be achieved by stopping westward expansion which would avoid Indian wars, and by devising means whereby Americans assumed the burden of their own defense. The government's effort to raise revenue by customs and taxation caused opposition and protest which remained only local until the Stamp Act of 1765, requiring revenue stamps to be fixed on legal documents, bills, and newspapers, roused the most vocal classes among the colonists and produced a violent reaction. Repealed in 1766, chiefly because revenue did not live up to expectations, the Stamp Act was followed by new import duties, which raised a fresh uproar and a boycott that frightened conservative interests in the colonies as much as it did the government in London. For the moment most of the duties were repealed and protests simmered down again until, in response to the East India Company's financial needs, the Tea Act of 1773 permitted the company to ship its tea direct to American ports and retail it there more cheaply, thus injuring both established colonial merchants and the smugglers who had supplied them.

These two influential groups now joined with the constitutional radicals who opposed the measure on principle. The Boston Tea Party of December, 1773, which destroyed the cargo of tea ships in Boston harbor, shook the British government out of appeasement into coercion, attempts at which in turn united the remaining colonies in support of Massachusetts, groaning under the British Coercive Acts of 1774.

Growing resentment and distrust of London in the colonies was matched by growing exasperation in London over the obstreperousness of the colonists. By 1774, as Burke reported to the New York Assembly, not only government but opinion felt the need to assert themselves by *"some* act of power." Such acts, when they came, unleashed first a storm of popular fury against the supporters of imperial authority in the colonies and, then, armed conflict.

Meanwhile, as the American debate grew ever more heated on both sides of the Atlantic, Parliament, discredited by recent events, bore the brunt of criticism. Old William Pitt, now Earl of Chatham, supported the colonists, arguing that there could be no taxation without representation.* A high judge, Lord Camden, formulated their greatest argument: "Taxation and representation are inseparable; this position is founded on the laws of nature"; and quoted Locke: "The supreme power cannot take from any man any part of his property without his own consent." In British eyes government was a trust, a *delegation,* not an absolute, unchallengeable force as on the continent. Yet, in defiance of nature and of Locke, this was something to which no government of the

---

* The friends of liberty took their watchword from a pamphlet by James Otis, *Rights of the Colonies* (1764): "No parts of His Majesty's dominions can be taxed without their consent."

day could resign itself.

The issue had ceased to turn on taxes. It was now one of Parliamentary and governmental supremacy facing the traditional and theoretical rights of free men. If the Americans "would submit and leave to us the constitutional right of supremacy," Lord North told Parliament in 1775, the quarrel would be at an end. The colonists, on their part, would not give way to what George Washington—in a letter of 1774—called "a systematic assertion of an arbitrary power, deeply planned to overturn the laws and constitution of their country, and to violate the most essential and valuable rights of mankind . . ." To do so would mean that they were no longer free. "None of them will ever submit to the loss of those valuable rights and privileges which are essential to the life of every free State, and without which life, liberty and property are rendered totally insecure."

In May of 1774 the first Continental Congress, meeting at Philadelphia, petitioned the King for redress and organized to withstand the mother country, while provincial congresses collected stores, organized militia, and prepared for trouble. In April, 1775, at Lexington, British troops sent to seize the arms and stores which colonists had gathered at nearby Concord, were fired upon. These were the shots heard round the world. By the end of the day, the British were besieged in Boston. By the end of May, a second Continental Congress had authorized a Continental Army "of the United Colonies," which George Washington was soon appointed to command. In July, 1776, after a year's fighting, Congress approved the Declaration of Independence.

If the language of this great document is familiar today, it is worth noting that it was familiar in its own day as well, and that much of its success came from the fact that it voiced in magnificent terms the basic tenets which Locke and his successors had inculcated in educated westerners since the beginning of the century:

> We hold these truths to be self-evident, that all men are created equal, that they are endowed by their Creator with certain unalienable Rights, that among these are life, liberty and the pursuit of Happiness.—That to secure these rights, Governments are instituted among Men, deriving their just powers from the consent of the governed.—That whenever any Form of Government becomes destructive of these ends, it is the Right of the People to abolish it, and to institute new Government . . .

These things were worth repeating. If they were not original, that only meant that they could be the more effective on minds prepared to receive them and on which their effect was electrifying.

For the moment the issues were to be decided not by words, but arms. Chiefly, it might be added, French arms; for the news of the first real rebel victory in forcing General Burgoyne's surrender at Saratoga (1777) persuaded the French government that the time had come to take revenge against the British. Four years later, another surrender—that of Cornwallis cornered in Yorktown by the French fleet and the Franco-American army—would persuade the British to open negotiations for peace, which was finally signed in 1783.

"New Government"

Independence had been won. Patriots had actually shown that the ideas of Locke and Montesquieu could be put into practice and that governments could be founded by social compact. They had developed the arsenal of revolution, from correspondence societies and clubs to constitutional conventions. The Declaration of Rights (1776) stated the basic rights of men or, at least, of American citizens, for slaves were still excluded; the Articles of Confederation (1781) organized the new republic as a federal state; finally, the Constitution (1787) laid down the working structure of the state to be: the separation of powers (executive, legislative, judiciary), the separation of church and state and the disestablishment of the church; the faith (as every dollar bill reminds us) that they were ushering in a new order of ages.

The new order did not apply to slaves or to indentured servants; and, oddly enough, it was a reactionary swing back to an older order, a reaction against modernist reforms which had inspired those who fought for it. Yet the state whose first President was inaugurated just four months before the fall of the Bastille, was a new thing: it was republican, it was federal, it was a symbol of hope. This new hope, this promise, this American myth, would be as strong in Europe as in the new federal republic. Here was the proof that philosophical ideas could really be put into practice: in Budapest a Masonic lodge called itself *American,* the new American Constitution was translated, commented upon, and set a pattern for the future. "We talked of nothing but America," Talleyrand would remember later; and Benjamin Franklin in Paris provided a dubious but impressive example of republican virtues for everyone to see.

What was less obvious at the time, the long debate during which the Constitution was hammered out gave a prophetic foretaste of future conflicts which the Republic—and other democracies too—would have to face. To oversimplify, it was conducted between "Republicans"—defenders of state rights against the central power, of small free men, preferably landowners, against the ambitions of some selfish faction of the powerful and greedy—and the Federalists, who stood for stronger federal power, for an executive which could maintain order and run a modern state. The former, with Rousseau and Jefferson, believed in the individual; the latter in order, hierarchy, and sound laws. Elitist, the Federalists wanted the minority's rights protected from the possible oppression of majority rule. Democratic, the Republicans wanted the majority freed from the oppression of the powerful and rich. The Federalists looked to England and to a National Bank to maintain sound money; the Republicans looked to France, to schools, and newspapers, and easier credit. The former would rule with Washington and John Adams; the latter with Jefferson, Madison and Monroe between 1801 and 1825. But while Republicans stood for a small man's democracy, and sympathized with the French Revolution, neither party really envisaged social revolution on these shores.

"A little rebellion now and then," thought Thomas Jefferson, "is a good thing." The author of the Declaration of Independence was the new republic's minister in Paris in 1789, and General Lafayette, who had won his spurs on Washington's staff, gave him a key of the Bastille to convey to his old commander. But conservative Federalists like Washington did not like the way in which the French Revolution evolved, or the Jacobin propaganda of Citizen Genêt, the French Republic's representative in the United States. Washington stood for neutrality, American opinion shifted from sympathy for France to co-operation with England, and the Alien and Sedition Acts were voted to defend this neutrality.

America, "kindly separated by nature and a wide ocean from the exterminating havoc [in Europe]," as Jefferson would put it, meant to keep further revolution from its shores. That was not easily done. Napoleon's Berlin Decree of 1806 was to be answered by the British Orders in Council of 1807: blockade by counterblockade. These led to Jefferson's Embargo Act (1807) forbidding U.S. ships to sail outside their territorial waters. And, while this hurt the French and English, many of whose imports came in U.S. vessels, it hurt American shipping more. After Madison took office in 1809, the Embargo Act was repealed and replaced with the Non-Intercourse Act, permitting trade with all but Britain and France, which was itself revoked in 1810. The Americans needed to trade, as the Europeans needed their goods.

Then, Napoleon managed to trick the Americans into thinking that their continued difficulties were to be attributed solely to the British refusal to withdraw the Orders in Council, pretending that he was willing to withdraw his own blockade decrees. This suited the anti-British partisans of western expansion, the war hawks, who seized on these differences as a pretext for war with Britain, hoping to annex Canada and, anyway, to put a stop to aid which the Indians received from there. Despite British anxiety to avoid conflict, war was declared in 1812, just two days after the Orders in Council had been withdrawn. This, in a way, illustrates the most remarkable aspect of a war begun after its ostensible reason had evaporated and ended two weeks before its most important battle, since the news that peace had been signed did not reach New Orleans in time to prevent the bloody fighting there.

Distances were so great and news so sluggish, that things like these were bound to happen. The one great result of the war was that the young United States became conscious of themselves as one nation that stretched from Erie to New Orleans, complete with a war hero (Andrew Jackson) who would become one of her great Presidents.

"These United States"

When the thirteen ex-colonies had given themselves a new federal Constitution in 1789, their total population was below four million, less than that of Switzerland today, less than that of contemporary Spain (ten million) or Mexico (six million), and including several hundred thousand Negro slaves. This tiny nation held immense territories, which were increased by the acquisition of Louisiana from Napoleon for $15,000,000 in 1802, and of Florida from Spain in 1819. With Texas acquired in 1845 and the Pacific Northwest wrenched from England in 1846, the Southwest from Mexico in 1848 and 1853, finally with Alaska, bought from Russia in 1867, the continental empire would be complete. The continent soon filled with people, for not only immigrants came but more people were born and fewer died in the spacious new republic than elsewhere. It was the economist Adam Smith who had noted in 1776 that the population of the North American colonies tended to double every twenty or twenty-five years, whereas in Britain the same process took twenty times as long. This continued to be true in the nineteenth century; and the disproportion, although less striking, remains marked: the American rate of population increase in recent years being still twice that of France, nearly three times the German, three and a half times the British.

The American colonies had early produced most of their necessities. The development of the sugar islands in the Caribbean provided Northerners with a hungry market for wheat, rum, fish, and lumber, and stimulated their shipping. The war of independence, interrupting imports of manufactures from England, further stimulated home production. Then came the Revolutionary and Napoleonic Wars, which left the new United States the only neutral with a large merchant fleet, a fleet that grew sevenfold between 1789 and 1810. Its earnings alone could pay for more imported goods than the colonies had used before the Revolution. Eli Whitney's invention of the cotton gin in 1793 turned the South into a cotton kingdom and established a new symbiosis beween the Southern states and Lancashire, which was soon taking about three-quarters of all the raw cotton they exported. Expansion of textile industries in continental Europe also created a vast and growing market for American cotton. The British mills alone increased their consumption from 2,000 to 250,000 tons a year, between 1780 and 1850. In the United States the number of spindles rose from

8,000 in 1808 to 500,000 in 1815. The parallel rise in American production went with large-scale productivity, which, cutting the price of raw materials, allowed the price of British manufactures to be cut by two-thirds in the same years. Cotton exports and those of similarly bulky goods like timber and wheat meant that ships sailing westward, back to the United States, had lots of space which they could sell at low rates to passengers from Europe. Lower passage fares encouraged immigrants who might otherwise find the journey's cost impossible to bear, while the expanding market for American goods meant that the immigrants could sell their labor and its products when they arrived on these shores. The demand fed not only an increasing supply of goods but of people too.

The decade following 1815 is known in U.S. history as the era of good feelings. It was perhaps more, as the historian George Dangerfield suggests, an era of mixed feelings, when geographical divisions would take the place of political ones, when slavery began to threaten the delicate balance of the union, when the Missouri Compromise of 1820 prohibiting slavery north of 36°30′ provided a temporary solution to the conundrum whether a nation can exist half slave half free, and an introduction to the sectional controversies which colored the rest of the century. In 1823, with the Monroe Doctrine, the new nation had established the basis of a diplomacy which unilaterally—though taking the Royal Navy for granted—kept both Russians and reactionary Europeans from enterprises in its hemisphere.

The greatest land power in the West—modest though its real power still was at that time—was the first to have farmers who thought in terms of movement not stability, of cash when they talked of crops, of markets and enterprise. The first, too, effectively to offer equal chances to all (although not to slaves) in the great economic race that now opened up. The Jacksonian confrontation of the 1820's would revive the two-party system which had faded away during the era of good feelings. The Democrats now stood for Jacksonian equalitarianism, freedom of enterprise and trade, states' rights. The Whigs, heirs of the Federalists of yore, had no real program but shared a common distrust of the masses. With Andrew Jackson (1829), the transition from East to West, from mansion to log cabin was established, and democratic politics rose on a firm foundation of spoils and wider suffrage.

American democracy was rude, its structure was clumsy, its politics were wasteful, but it worked. Or so it seemed to foreign observers like Alexis de Tocqueville who saw in it, with little enough satisfaction for some of them, the shape of things to come. Not only did American democracy work; it moved: Louisiana in 1803, Florida in 1819, Texas in 1845, Oregon in 1846, California and New Mexico in 1848. After 1853, only Alaska and Hawaii would be missing from the present constellation.

The year 1850 would actually see the United States reach its continental limits. From 9 million in 1820, the population by 1850 had grown to 23 million. The sprawling union was still a colony of its eastern seaboard. The railroad only reached Chicago and St. Louis in 1853. In this expanding land, where every tenth man was an immigrant, a new nationalism was taking shape. "We have listened too long to the refined muses of Europe," wrote Ralph Waldo Emerson. "We shall walk on our own feet, we shall work with our own hands, we shall speak according to our own convictions."

Britain Resurgent

"A great empire and little minds go ill together," Burke had said. Events had borne him out. As the American conflict unfolded the spectacle of division at home and incompetence abroad, the King's bid toward a "despotism" only dimly lightened ran on the rocks. So did his supporters. In 1780, the Commons narrowly passed the famous motion "that the influence of the crown has increased, is increasing, and ought to be diminished." By 1783, this was done.

Domestic reforms introduced salaries for public servants whose services had formerly been paid by fees, bit into political patronage and sinecure-appointments, diminished the influence of the Court—partly by the Civil List Act which fixed a yearly sum for the king's expenditures, simplified the tax structure and the funding of government debts. Parliament resisted its own reform, but the country's administration was gradually rationalized. The executive became less corrupt, more stable, more sensible too. Economies were effected, revenue was increased, a financial reconstruction was achieved which would stand the country in good stead in the years ahead.

The Americans had saved Britain from monarchic despotism, if such a threat existed. They had also shaken her badly. But that did not last long. The 1780's would be a time of economic and industrial boom, and the loss of empire soon proved to be no loss to trade and, hence, to prosperity. But the war had portentous effects in many ways. One concrete issue raised by the loss of the American colonies was that convicts could no longer be transported westward and had to be shipped southeast instead, to Botany Bay from which Australia grew. Another was that British responsibilities in India would be taken more seriously than those in America had been. Soul-searching following defeat attributed the insurrection to a failure to realize and face imperial responsibilities, which were to bring up the colonists in paternal fashion from childhood to maturity. This implied a mission highly suitable to an increasingly Christian and moralistic society that preferred its economic and strategic interests presented in moralistic terms.

Reform: For and Against

Not unconnected with this mood was the growing agitation for reform—reform of a discredited Parliament, but also of an institutional structure increasingly criticized by vocal friends of liberty and of efficiency, foremost among them the members of the country's dissenting sects.

The Glorious Revolution of 1688 had brought toleration to dissenters (and to Catholics too) but not full citizenship. The Catholics, held to be potential enemies and almost resident aliens, lived very much at the margin of society, their low status emphasized by the poverty of Irish immigrants, most of them Catholic. Decent people loathed and feared members of a church connected with the Inquisition and other dark mysteries.* Dissenters had a much easier time. They were generally accepted but the Test and Corporation Acts hamstrung and hampered them, preventing them from taking municipal office (except in some unincorporated provincial towns) and keeping them second-class citizens. Anyone wanting to get on in public life had to be an Anglican: many became so, more or less sincerely, translating religious into social divisions. Others—among them some of the best and best-educated—lived apart from political activity, depriving the country of their services and concentrating on economic activities in which they were not hampered at all.

Naturally, able men excluded from political life and most aspects of government would be the more critical of them, and the keener to secure the rights of individuals, the civil and religious liberties they needed for themselves. Excluded from the universities, they founded dissenting academies, livelier and more progressive than the old foundations. Excluded from city corporations, they were active in the new unincorporated cities like Manchester and Birmingham. They were moral and rationalistic, and developed a social conscience in localities which had sprung up so quickly, mobilizing the rising middle classes, with no regard for creed, to work for efficient administration and orderly local government. Such men had sympathized with the colonists because they were "virtuous" and with Wilkes because he represented the cause of Parliamentary reform. They were for democracy because they thought it meant their own emancipation: the rights of sober, rational, enterprising men like themselves. English radicalism began as the venture of an assertive middle-class minority group.

The first measure calling for comprehensive Parliamentary reform was introduced in the Commons while war raged in America. It was in 1776, the same year in which Adam Smith's *Inquiry into the Wealth of Nations,* Jeremy Bentham's *Theory of Legislation,* and the first volume

---

* As late as the 1830's a lady alone in a railway compartment with the architect Pugin, who saw him cross himself, cried, "You are a Catholic, Sir! Guard, let me out— I must get into another carriage."

Canvassing for Votes, by William Hogarth. Astor, Lennox, and Tilden Foundation.

of Edward Gibbon's *Decline and Fall of the Roman Empire* also appeared. Members of the Commons were elected in boroughs which had been and were no more, or not elected in boroughs which were but had not been when seats in Parliament were first allotted. Rotten boroughs, pocket boroughs, made nonsense of representativeness. Deserted or near-deserted villages retained two seats in the gift of whoever owned their land; while Manchester and Leeds returned no one at all. Twenty or fifty electors in one borough were as well represented as thousands in some shire. Seats could be bought, and so could their incumbents—paid in sinecures, in pensions, or favors of some kind. No wonder enlightened men thought there was room for improvement.

Yet the agitation for reform, like that for repeal of the Test Acts, which began well, soon ran into the backlash of the French Revolution. The example of France inspired the rise of Jacobin clubs, such as the one in Sheffield where 2,500 "of the lowest mechanics" were enrolled in a constitutional society where "they read the most violent publications and comment on them," keeping up correspondence with other societies in neighboring towns and villages and all over England. Laboring men of every kind were reading Thomas Paine and talking of equality. This was not calculated to reassure men of property.

Burke's *Reflections on the Revolution in France* (1790) denounced the dangers of radicalism which left organic growth behind for destructive and unnatural changes. It was answered by Tom Paine's *Rights of Man* (1791), which found the institutions Burke respected (aristocracy and monarchy) anachronistic, and called for popular sovereignty and universal suffrage. Both books were popular: the one with propertied men and most respectable people shocked by revolutionary excesses; the other with the reform societies and lower-class radicals. The government moved against the latter, suspended the Habeas Corpus Act late in 1790, arrested radical leaders on charges of treason, passed Treason and Sedition Acts in 1795 and again in 1799, suppressed the reform groups, and, by the Combination Act of 1799, closed those clubs which workers had founded to improve working conditions and their wages. Henceforth manufacturers could keep down wages and claim conspiracy if workers organized to protest against them. Any tendency toward unionism was savagely suppressed.

War against France, which came in 1793, meant war against English liberals at home. To face Jacobin subversion, freedom of meeting and expression were suppressed. England was no more threatened by native Jacobins in the 1790's than the United States by home-grown Communists in the 1950's, but the label was convenient and there are always awkward dogs about, to whom it might be well to affix a bad name. There was no revolution in England and there would be none, in the first place because the ruling class was confident and seldom so disunited as to lose its grip on power.

Lenin has pointed out that worse conditions for the masses and wider, more intense political activities can only result in revolution if the rulers are going to pieces and are challenged by men who can make and lead a revolution. In England nothing went to pieces except the party of reform, which split in its reaction to events in France. The failure of the more moderate revolutionaries in France, drove their English counterparts, the manufacturers and commercial classes, into an alliance with landowners and with the Establishment against the prospect of any reform at all. "I wish," wrote Coleridge to Wordsworth in 1799, "you would write a poem in blank verse addressed to those who, in consequence of the complete failure of the French Revolution, have thrown up all hopes for the amelioration of mankind, and are sinking into an almost Epicurean selfishness, disguising the same under the soft titles of domestic attachment and contempt for visionary *philosphes*."

The Pursuit of Grace

Another reason why the revolutionary ideas that spread from France to England never caught fire there was the influence of Methodism, implanted since the late 1730's by pious and passionate creatures, above all John Wesley (1703–1791), whose 40,000 sermons—to deliver which he rode 224,000 miles in fifty-five years—preached salvation by faith and spread evangelical fervor among the masses which, hungry for hope, were ready to renounce a bitter world for a sweeter Providence. The incandescent eloquence of the Methodists* provided the enthusiasm, emotion, and release, which the established church withheld. The wealthy and educated found little need for such febrile escapes from a world quite comfortable enough. The poor found it irresistible. Seventy

---

* Who soon adopted the contemptuous nickname inspired by the regularity of their lives and their strict observance.

thousand English men and women had joined Wesley by the time he died, and far more in the New World, where the new religion spread like wildfire with the nineteenth century.

The Wesleyan revival improved manners and released emotions; as such it was a harbinger or part of the romantic turn against decorum and against the cold emptiness of reason. Yet its core and focus was God, and in this too it forecast a century when God became anthropomorphic once again, and religious concerns were more closely personal than in the rather detached or indifferent eighteenth century. Frenzied revival meetings, the anguish and burden of sin, the exaltation that a sense of salvation brought, would furnish the days and the feelings of millions in the century to come.

Wesley set up classes—today we might call them cells—bands, societies, a highly co-ordinated pyramid of soul-searching fervent Christians, autocratically ruled by him. By 1784, when he broke with the Church of England which would not ordain his ministers, and began to ordain his own, his followers had built nearly four hundred chapels. Thrifty, industrious, anti-intellectual and narrow-minded, obscurantist in education, abstinent, the Methodists were a dynamic novelty in society but a reactionary force in politics. As Wesley himself noted a few years before his death, diligence and frugality increased their goods but diminished their spirit. That is often the case, but here it was more to be expected, since the movement was the image of its leader.

Wesley would make his followers more respectable but also more grim, suspicious of worldly pleasure, mistrusting worldly rank, hostile to beauty or diversion in any form which could turn the eyes from the supreme concern of personal salvation. This implied the dreary shape of austerities to come, but also an equalitarian and responsible spirit; and the very idea which so revolted the Duchess of Buckingham, that she might have a heart as sinful as that of a wretched commoner, could turn attention to the commoners' wretchedness. If most Methodists, persuaded that equality before God rendered equality before the law irrelevant, were as stoutly conservative as their masters, their interests operated in progressive ways: a more fervent religion, a cleaner, more pious, more decent way of life, built a cleaner, more prosperous, more decent following, although a narrow and a strait-laced one.

In the Church of England itself meanwhile, an evangelical awakening was taking place, which would do for middle-class conversion what the Methodists did among the lower classes: suggest a religion of the heart rather than the mind, but also eventually a formidable social conscience. Conviction of sin and expectation of Grace combined to forge a dynamo of reform: moral, social, and political. The evangelicals criticized the public and private laxness of eighteenth-century morals, the savagery of the criminal law, the selfish mess of anachronistic local government and opportunist industrial conditions, the inhumanity and injustice of slavery which the world had taken for granted time out of mind. They sought to enforce new moral standards, pass new laws, make England a cleaner, safer, more just, more decent country; but also one more prurient, more hypocritical, more dreary.

In pursuit of Grace, the so-called Clapham Sect gathered in the 1790's at Clapham in South London, around the parish rector John Venn: William Wilberforce, Henry Thornton, James Stephen, Zachary Macaulay, Hannah More (a Bishop in petticoats as Cobbett described her).* The party of the saints, as the evangelicals were called after their puritan predecessors of the 1640's, was small but influential. In 1809, the prime minister of the day gave up calling Parliament on Mondays so that members should not have to travel on the Sabbath. The Church Missionary Society (1799) and the British and Foreign Bible Society (1804) cast their net wide throughout the country, where 2.5 million Bibles were distributed between 1804 and 1819, and far beyond its shores, where a free Negro colony was set up at Sierra Leone in 1784.** The African Association (1806) promoted the antislavery cause, while missions and bishops were also sent to India. Beyond the new spirit which they helped to promote, one interesting legacy which the evangelicals left was the organization and propaganda pattern they evolved—tracts and pamphlets, public meetings and voluntary societies, which provided the armory of the organized political activity of the nineteenth century.

Immediately, however, religious revivalism—Episcopal or Nonconformist—provided an alternative to radical politics: sometimes a training for them, sometimes a refuge from them, sometimes a consolation for their failure—a socially sanctioned issue for despair which might otherwise have rocked society gravely.

The Restive Populace

Despair was running strongest in England's nearest and worst-governed colony, across the Irish Channel. There had been troubles in Ireland in the early eighties, echoes of the American Revolution. Reforms sought to restore calm by improving the condition of the Irish. The Test Act was abolished in the island, Catholics allowed to purchase land, the Irish Parliament declared autonomous, the two kingdoms equal. Further reforms came up against the King's conviction that his coronation oath precluded Catholic emancipation and, after 1787, when George III had got down from his carriage in Windsor park and addressed an oak tree as the king of Prussia, his minister, Pitt, Chatham's son, hesitated to press him on any issue that might bring on new attacks of madness. Hence George III ruled on, and Ireland boiled. The Catholics wanted the vote, which Pitt wanted to give them but could not. The nationalist

* Her two cats were called "Non-resistance" and "Passive obedience." There is no mention of whether they came when called.
** And a draft from British prisons made good the shortage of women among early settlers.

United Irishmen, led by Wolfe Tone, sought the help of the French, but the projected French invasion went awry and Tone's rising of 1798 was put down with the utmost brutality, while Tone himself committed suicide. The Irish Parliament was abolished, and Ireland "indissolubly" bound to Britain by the Act of Union of 1800, to bedevil British politics for another century and more.

Meanwhile, social unrest was reviving in Britain, born of vast economic changes enhanced by the difficulties of war. The country weathered the storm, the wars with France were won, but never had the situation seemed so uneasy. Shelley portrayed:

> An old, mad, blind, despised and dying king,
> Princes, the dregs of their dull race, who flow
> Through public scorn—mud from a muddy spring—
> Rulers who neither see, nor feel, nor know,
> But leech-like to their fainting country cling. . .

Popular agitation, food riots, machine-breaking, rick-burning, calls for reform, continued in the postwar years, culminating in the Massacre of Peterloo (1819), when armed horsemen cut down a great reform meeting in Manchester's Saint Peter's Fields.

Yet, whatever the misery and sporadic recessions, economic activity poured oil on troubled waters. In spite of Napoleon's Continental System, the value of British exports quadrupled between 1805 and 1811. The volume of international trade had doubled between 1780 and 1800; it would double again by 1840. Between 1700 and 1750 real income per head had grown at an average rate of 0.30 per cent a year. This average rate would increase to 0.45 per cent between 1750 and 1800, 1.1 per cent between 1801 and 1831, 1.5 per cent between 1831 and 1851. In 1830, real wages stood 50 per cent higher than in 1780. Agricultural improvements allowed a smaller number of rural laborers to feed a population which had doubled in number, increased trade revenue took care of the rest. During the first half of the nineteenth century about a quarter of the whole world's trade was in British hands. The exports of

The Massacre of Peterloo, 1819, a contemporary drawing.

Mansell Collection

the next largest trading power, France, were less than half the value of the British. Britain was the dynamo of the Industrial Revolution, the center of the world's banking structure, the school and inspiration of things to come.

The face of the country was altering at a rate that had not been seen before, population was growing, factories springing up, farming methods changing, masses of people shifting from country to town, crowding around the new manufactory-barracks of production, creating slums, brewing discontent, calling ever more harshly for a remedy to their misery. The young Benjamin Disraeli compared the problems caused by teeming population with those which toppled down the Roman Empire and found the troubles of his day incomparably greater: "What are your invasions of the barbarous nations . . . to our Population Returns!" Already in 1798 a pessimistic country clergyman, Thomas Malthus, had warned that population was increasing faster than the means of subsistence. Laborers who dined on bread and apples, or tried "to make potato flour by grating the half-rotten potatoes into a large tub full of water," plowmen who made tea with burnt crusts of bread and shared a herring among five for Sunday dinner, families subsisting on nauseous messes "that made your inside feel as if it was on fire and sort of choked'ee," bore him out.

Yet reform, sparked by evangelical propaganda and by the arguments of utilitarian thinkers, spurred by popular pressure, was on the march again. In the very year of Peterloo, revision of the criminal law ended the death penalty for over a hundred offenses, such as fraud.* Beginning in 1825, Factory Acts, rudimentary at first but growing increasingly effective, regulated the employment of women and children, the hours and conditions of labor, and provided inspectors to enforce the new regulations. In 1828, the Test and Corporation Acts were at last repealed and Dissenters fully integrated in society.** In 1829, Roman Catholics followed. But the greatest issue remained unsolved: that of Parliamentary reform.

Whigs and Tories

The authority of the Crown had been declining, along with its popularity. George IV and his brothers were, said Wellington, the "damn'-dest millstone about the neck of any government that can be imagined." Crown influence shrank as administrative and fiscal efficiency increased. But, while patronage declined, parties were only just taking shape and, without a disciplined party machine, Parliament was bound

---

* The law continued harsh, though not as harsh as some traditionalists would have liked. In the 1840's, a twelve-year-old girl could be sentenced to fourteen days' hard labor for stealing a small prayer book from school, with the magistrate expressing his regret that he could not order her to be whipped as well.

** Although it was not until the 1850's that they could take university degrees.

to flounder amidst a welter of groups and factions.

"Foreigners think parliamentarism a form of government," Oswald Spengler has written: "It is nothing of the kind. It is an English game, like cricket, which only English people can play." The game was played by Whigs and Tories. The latter, on the whole, were the party of landed interests, of the smaller gentry, of opposition to change, to Dissent, to Catholics, to industrial and agricultural developments for which they lacked both sympathy and means. As we might expect, they also opposed parliamentary reform. Their inarticulate loyalties would soon be enlisted in a new Conservative Party, first by Robert Peel (1788–1850) and then by Benjamin Disraeli (1804–1881). The Whigs were not a party that you joined but a connection into which you were born—preferably in a great country house. It was their liberal and radical allies —the City money interests, the manufacturers, the Dissenters—who mobilized them to support· the cause of "civil and religious liberty." Although highly exclusive and aristocratic, the Whigs' roots in the Glorious Revolution of 1688 identified them with the cause of constitutional government. They had no particular sympathy for democratic government, let alone for the masses, but would accept innovations in order to avert more catastrophic change. Whig leaders therefore listened to liberal industrialists who wanted representation for their interests and for their growing cities, and to the radicals who expected a reformed Parliament to prove more responsive to the demands of the urban masses; but they were undecided as to what to do.

Reform of Parliament threatened entrenched interests in both parties. It had been fended off for a long time with the argument that even an unreformed House of Commons responded to public opinion and demands; but such a plea sounded less convincing every year. News of the French revolution of 1830, in which the reactionary Bourbons had been swept out with ease, furnished fresh arguments to enemies of aristocratic privilege that seemed embodied in the existing composition of the House of Commons. Shortly thereafter, King George IV died; and the general election following his death turned on the issue of parliamentary reform.

Although the new Whig cabinet, headed by Lord Grey, turned out to be the most aristocratic of the century, its members were persuaded that they must make some concession to popular demands by bringing in a measure which would put an end to further innovations. The bills introduced to this end ran into heavy opposition. While Parliament debated, public tempers rose. There were mass meetings, riots, strikes, and mobs clashed bloodily with army units. Through most of 1831 cholera raged in England, further fraying nerves that brought the country to the verge of rebellion. Business was upset. Some people refused to pay taxes. The radicals talked of setting up a national guard. The Tories saw the struggle as—no longer one for office on traditional lines—a battle between "the conservative and subversive principles."* At last, in 1832, the Reform Bill became law.

Today, the measure which had given rise to so much contention and which was greeted with widespread rejoicing seems a very moderate one. It suppressed the most unrepresentative among the closed or rotten boroughs and gave representation to new ones. It lowered the property qualification for the franchise, thus broadening the Commons' electoral base, and increased the electorate by about 50 per cent—from 435,000 to 652,000: a figure which the country's rising wealth and population would by the 1860's carry beyond the million mark. There was some shift of electoral power from countryside to towns, but this was only slight. The urban electorate was only really strengthened by the second Reform Act, of 1867, which more than doubled the number of electors. For the moment, the composition of the House of Commons changed but little: the landed interest almost held its own, and so did members of the aristocracy, into the 1860's.

New measures needed time to change old mentalities. In 1835, Florence Nightingale's father—a reforming Whig—lost the parliamentary seat he was standing for because he refused to bribe the voters of Andover. They, for their part, felt that, since a vote had always been bought for cash, extension of the franchise simply meant cash for more people who now had the vote: a kind of social subsidy. "How I hate Tories, all Beer and Money," wrote William Nightingale. But, in effect, beer and money flowed on both sides, when the means allowed. Just because candidates talked so much alike and because electors had to choose more between personalities than between policies, money talked and would go on talking until, in 1883, election expenses were limited by the Corrupt Practices Act.

New Politics

Yet 1832 *was* a turning point. The larger franchise drew into politics a mass of new participants, and persuaded others that their turn must come. The new official lists of voters spurred the development of party organizations which would keep registration up and increase the party's voting strength, build local associations, keep in touch with the small voter, and nurse constituencies along from one election to another. Politics were no longer the preserve of a small, charmed circle and of their clientele. Politicians had to adapt to new conditions or face defeat. As

* The prevailing mood may be guessed from the fact that many property-owners expected a bloody revolution followed by confiscation. At Durham, where the Cathedral was fabulously wealthy, the agitation persuaded the chapter to sacrifice some of their revenues in endowing a University, hoping that this at least might survive the coming cataclysm and the confiscation they expected. The cataclysm never came, but the University of Durham was chartered in 1837.

closed boroughs disappeared, patronage crumbled. It would collapse altogether after the introduction of the secret ballot in 1872. The majority of Englishmen were still voteless, and radical reformers still dissatisfied. But the rising middle class had been acknowledged, the growing power of industry and commerce recognized. Many utilitarian liberals, like Walter Bagehot the economist, or the novelist Anthony Trollope, who wanted the vote for the educated few but not for the uneducated many, could rest content.

The uneducated many were going to be taken care of by the Poor Law of 1834, which forced relief recipients into workhouses: the paupers' bastilles.

In order to discourage malingering and ease the burden on the taxrolls, the condition of paupers sheltered in workhouses was intended to be worse than the worst they could expect outside. "Our intention is to make the workhouses as like prisons as possible," declared an assistant commissioner charged with enforcing the law. "Our object . . . is to establish therein a discipline so severe and repulsive as to make them a terror to the poor and prevent them from entering," explained another. Meals had to be eaten in silence, a strict timetable strictly observed, sexes and families were kept apart, mothers and children separated, work was endless. This is how the poet George Crabbe described "the pauper palace":

> That giant building, that high-bounding wall,
> Those bare-worn walks, that lofty thund'ring hall!
> That large loud clock, which tolls each dreaded hour,
> Those gates and locks, and all those kinds of power:
> It is a prison with a milder name,
> Which few inhabit without dread or shame.

By 1843 workhouses had nearly 200,000 inmates. "The most eloquent testimony to the depths of poverty," comments E. P. Thompson, "is in the fact that they were tenanted at all."

It is easy to see why sensitive men should find the regime disgusting—hypocritical, corrupt, costly, and squalid. It is just as easy to see why men who did well by it wished to retain it, and men who were not actually maimed by it accepted it as they always had and always would, by force of inertia and habit. The trouble is that many whom it oppressed and injured were so stupefied that they could conceive no resistance. Only a few idealists—radicals, born of Jacobinism, or, like William Cobbett, of Toryism *—set out to redress the wrongs of the great, obscure, and

---

* Like Wilkes, William Cobbett (1763–1835) provides another illustration of the English talent for assimilating critics. He began as a Tory and ended as a radical opponent of the Establishment and of the bad new times, as well as of "bloody old *Times*." But, before his death, the Establishment had got him: he had become a Member of Parliament and a Public Figure; his son, a Chartist at first, became a supporter of Disraeli; and their descendants, good solid Manchester conservatives, would be the very image of the values the old man had fought.

much-wronged masses.

Meanwhile, the Whig administration, feeling that reform had gone far enough, knew only how

> To promise, pause, prepare, postpone,
> And end by letting things alone:
> In short to earn the people's pay
> By doing nothing every day.

Exports might be growing, but so was misery; and so was immigration by which some sought to escape it. By the 1840's the trickle had become a flood, directed toward New Zealand and Australia, Canada and the Cape, or the United States. The 60,000 yearly immigrants of the early forties, had grown to 250,000 a year in 1847, and in 1848 some thousand people were leaving the country every day. These figures reflected the depression which began in the late 1830's and rose to a climax in the famine year of 1848.*

Against this sorry background, two parallel agitations developed: the first was directed against the Corn Laws which protected the high price of English grain and kept out foreign foodstuffs by high tariffs. Corn Laws, originally designed to maintain fair prices by regulating the grain trade, had been known in England since the Middle Ages. They had begun by restricting exports to keep bread cheap; then, in the seventeenth century, a sliding scale of import duties had been imposed in order to protect the English farmer. By the end of the Napoleonic wars this had come to operate against the consumer, encouraging speculation and keeping prices high by excluding almost all foreign grain. This was hard on the poor at any time; but in the late thirties a series of poor harvests intensified their hardships and sharpened the agitation for repeal and cheap bread.

The Anti-Corn Law Association, founded in Manchester in 1838, was supported by the manufacturing interests led by Richard Cobden and John Bright, and by the more productive landlords. Its propaganda insisted on free trade and free competition, not only in industry but in the products of the soil; arguing that cheap bread would improve the worker's lot and, also, the competitive position of his employers. What the *Times* called the "incendiary claptrap" of Cobden and Bright stirred up riots and strikes in working-class areas, and consciences at Westminster, including that of Robert Peel. Tea parties and bazaars flanked great free trade meetings; and propaganda, which put out as much as a hundred tons of printed paper a year and made full use of the penny post of 1840 to mobilize middle-class opinion, triumphed with repeal in 1846.

---

* Ireland, dependent on potatoes, suffered more than England. Its population in 1845 was eight and a quarter million; in 1851 six and a half million. About a million had died and another million had emigrated.

Defeat of the Chartists at Newport, 1839.

Repeal of the Corn Laws was seen as the triumph of free trade, and of industry over agricultural interests. It was also a triumph of social consciences stirred by bad times. Robert Peel—"an iceberg with a slight thaw on the surface," said a contemporary, but a deeply conscientious man— had reorganized the old Tories into a Conservative Party which Disraeli would eventually steer toward unwilling reforms. His first Conservative administration in 1841 included a promising young man, William Ewart Gladstone (1809–1898), who would become the heir of his policy though under a different label. It was a great reforming ministry. The Coal Mines Act of 1842 forbade the underground employment of women and of boys under ten; the Factory Act of 1844 set a maximum working day for children under thirteen (six and a half hours) and women (twelve hours); finally, the Ten Hours Bill of 1847 gave workers an endurable working day. Repeal was part of this long list, not unconnected with the second great agitation of those years, that of the Chartists.

Workmen, especially craftsmen, had long tried to organize themselves in associations and unions designed to advance their interests, secure shorter hours, higher wages, effective education, above all universal suffrage which alone would make these things possible. "You have heard, I doubt not, of the trades' unions," wrote Dr. Thomas Arnold of Rugby to a friend in 1834: "A fearful engine of mischief, ready to riot or to assassinate." Some of these people argued that the English middle class, having made its revolution in 1832, was now making a counterrevolution against its erstwhile allies of the working class. It was up to the workers to save themselves and the revolution, by carrying the latter to a logical conclusion in the destruction of the new oppressor class.

In 1838, the London Workingmen's Association drew up the People's

Charter, whose six points demanded universal male suffrage, equal electoral districts, no property qualification for Members of Parliament, payment of wages for Members of Parliament, a secret ballot, and annual general elections, that is, direct democracy. Similar reforms had been advocated in 1780 by a reform committee of the House of Commons, and talked about before the great disillusion of 1832, when radical craftsmen found that the Whigs would not give them the vote. So there was a tradition of reform to which the Charter appealed, and current difficulties and disillusions brought it solid support.

The First Petition its supporters presented to Parliament in 1838 bore nearly 1,300,000 signatures. The second in 1842 bore over 3,300,000 signatures. The third, in 1848, with economic depression at home and revolution across the Channel, claimed 6 million and probably got half or two-thirds that many. Parliament rejected them all. Political leaders denounced the Chartist movement as a threat to property. The long series of strikes, riots, demonstrations, and insurrections that marked the hungry forties sharpened class fears so that, as Charles Kingsley—Queen Victoria's future chaplain—tells us "young men believed (and not so wrongly) that the masses were their natural enemies, and that they might have to fight any year or any day, for the safety of their property and the honor of their sisters." Above all, perhaps, repeal of the Corn Laws had satisfied the middle classes and turned them into supporters of order once again. As a result, 170,000 special constables and a considerable military force under the Duke of Wellington faced the Third Petition on "a glorious day, the Waterloo of peace and order" and the great Chartist petition fizzled out in rain and apathy, while Lady Palmerston congratulated herself on "the good spirit of our middle classes."

No wonder the English were complacent. To a nineteenth-century Englishman's mind the best thing between England and Europe was the sea. A widely used elementary text of mid-century reflected English delight that they were not as other people were, certainly not like the French who sometimes "have a king, and sometimes they send him away and will have none." English children could happily

> . . . thank the goodness and the grace
> Which on my birth have smiled.
> And made me in these Christian days
> A happy English child.

Enterprise had made England great. Compromise kept her at peace. But it was the kind of compromise that Tom Brown favored, as Thomas Hughes described him in *Tom Brown's School Days* (1857): "He never wants anything but what's right and fair; only when you come to settle what's right and fair, it's everything that he wants and nothing that you want. And that's his idea of a compromise. Give me the Brown compromise when I'm on his side."

Chapter 11

REVOLUTIONARY CHANGE IN FRANCE

French history did not run so smoothly, or—rather—the French seem to have lacked the English talent for channeling the streams of change to constructive rather than destructive purposes. This would appear as clearly in the vicissitudes of the "Old Regime" as in the ventures of the new.

The last fourscore years of the French monarchy could be divided roughly into three parts. The first of these was the Regency, when from 1715 to his death in 1723, the Duke of Orléans ruled on behalf of his small and sickly nephew, Louis XV. Three important developments originated in these years, each of which was to affect the country's fortunes. First in time was the increased importance of the Paris Parlement whose support Orléans invoked in order to secure full authority as Regent, despite the contrary instructions of Louis XIV's will. In effect, Orléans gained his power by a minor coup, legalized by Parlementary sanction. Louis XIV had confined the Parlement to an insignificant role. Henceforth, it would constantly intervene in politics, providing the opposition with leadership and a focus. When it did not represent the King, this high court of law represented nothing more than itself. Yet these magistrates who owned their offices would become the defenders of all the privileged classes and, against their determination, few reforms which threatened their interests would get by. Nevertheless, the majority of Frenchmen took them at their word when they claimed to stand against monarchic despotism, and rallied to their cause again and again. Only too often, Voltaire would jeer, the people are like flies who take the side of spiders.

The second development was the nobiliary reaction. Released from the stern rule of the old king, the nobility sprang up like a jack-in-the-box and with about as much consequence, to reassert their rights and claim back the influence and revenues of which they had been deprived. Orléans' own prejudices were on their side and, at first, he tried to govern

507

A contemporary print depicting unrest following the crash of the South Sea Bubble

through councils of nobles rather than through baseborn ministers. This did not last. The necessities of government, the frivolity and inexperience of the nobles, threw Orléans back on the old administrative structure. But the nobles were never jammed back into the box where Louis XIV had squeezed them, or disciplined by his listless successors. Their pretensions and their rebelliousness, allied with the pretensions of the Parlementary nobility, would in due course bring everything crashing down.

The third development stemmed from Orléans' disillusion with his fellow nobles and his search for a more effective policy. The Regent's major problem arose from the heavy debts Louis XIV had left behind. Across the sea, in England, the South Sea Company was booming, apparently taking over the national debt. A Scotsman, John Law (1671–1729), persuaded the Regent that he could do as much, absorbing the national debt and spurring general prosperity. Exchanges, Law argued, depend on currency. Let him create a bank which would accept deposits and issue paper currency redeemable against its deposits. Since depositors seldom claim their deposits back *in toto,* or all of them at once, this meant that the bank could issue more paper than the deposits held, thus creating an inflation that would stimulate economic activity. The principle was sound and Law's bank, founded in 1716, prospered. So did the companies he bought or founded to trade in the East and West, especially the Mississippi Company for the exploitation of Louisiana, where fabulous fortunes were held out to settlers and investors. At last, in 1719, Law proposed a scheme to take over the national debt, converting its obligations to those of his company. The shares soared, speculation ran riot, consumption and prices rose as predicted, Law became head of the state's finances, hailed as the savior of France. Then, in 1720, speculative complications and political intrigue brought a crash, and Law fled to die in poverty at Venice.

The state's debt had, indeed, been very much lightened and, after a brief recession, economic activity returned. Fortunes had changed hands:

many had been ruined, but others (including Law's own coachman) had become wealthy in their stead. But the speculative fever had dealt a hard blow at the idea of economic improvement by hard work and savings; * while its collapse had dealt a harder one at the concepts of paper money or a state bank, thus depriving France of essential instruments of economic activity for a long time to come. Public interest in America also collapsed. The lands which Law had described as choking with gold, emeralds, and diamonds no longer tempted anyone. Only transported convicts made up cargoes for these Godforsaken colonies; and it was soon said that the best thing Louisiana ever produced was the story of the little prostitute, Manon Lescaut, who was deported there. No wonder the empire was lightly abandoned, and Louisiana itself eventually sold to the highest bidder.

This crucial period, during which most subsequent problems were sketched out, ended with the Regent's death in 1723. It was followed by the long, peace-minded ministry of Cardinal Fleury, during which conflict with England was avoided, while French influence and trade slowly increased. The half-century following Fleury's death in 1743 would, on the contrary, be marked by ministerial instability, constant friction between the privileged orders and governments seeking reform, the ever more evident inability of the Crown to put its house in order.

The two latter periods—the final years of the French monarchy—were deeply affected by the personalities of the two kings whose reigns bridged the time between the death of Louis XIV and that of the Old Regime: Louis XV (1715–1774) and Louis XVI (1774–1793). The fact that both had been orphaned at an early age may help account for many of their quirks and inadequacies. It remains that their failings helped demonstrate the awkwardness of entrusting a nation's fate to the arbitrary decisions of birth.

The two men were quite different. Handsome, spoiled, and self-indulgent, Louis XV was five when his great-grandfather died, fifteen when he was married to Marie Leczinska (1703–1768), an unassuming woman seven years older than himself, who gave him ten children in ten years, and whom he soon replaced with a long string of mistresses. The best-known and longest lasting of these was Madame de Pompadour (1721–1764), the most charming of the King's indulgences, intelligent, ambitious, friend and protector of artists and philosophers, but no more effective than her royal lover.

Louis XV lives on in the notorious remark *"Après moi, le déluge."* The words, whether he ever uttered them or not, correctly reflect his

* One of the Persians in Montesquieu's *Persian Letters* of 1721 tells of a visit to a coffeehouse where he meets a landed gentleman who could never collect his rents, a townsman whose house is full of devalued money and who wishes he owned a little country estate which alone produces security, a bitter man complaining that his best friend has had the unkindness to pay him back the money he had lent him, and a genealogist who alone delights in the new society where he expects to grow rich by providing parvenus with fictitiously honorable family trees.

Madame de Pompadour, by Francois Boucher. Wallace Collection, London.

rather hopeless detachment and the image of cynical indifference which he left his subjects. Yet there was more to him than that. Louis was intelligent, cultivated, and even his boundless sensuality seems to have been directed toward charming objects. But, as the effective head of a great kingdom, he functioned only reluctantly and spasmodically. This meant that after the death of his tutor and first minister, Cardinal Fleury (1653–1743), the affairs of his kingdom moved in fits and starts, pulled every which way by the passing influence of short-lived advisers. Policy rested in the hands of a small clique at Versailles, whose world turned on the King and on his favorites.

There would be no royal mistresses in the following reign, but a more fatal queen and a king even less fitted for his task. Deprived of parental care, isolated in a hostile and corrupt court, despised by brothers who were his intellectual and physical superiors, Louis XVI was a weaker vessel altogether, decent, dull, awkward, and slow on the uptake. His favorite pastimes (bar one) struck his contemporaries as menial or childish: that he enjoyed forging keys, hammering nails, sweeping out his workshop, or reading police reports was not unusual in his time, or even in our own. But he also liked shooting cats from the terrace of Versailles, or throwing pellets of dirt from between his toes at the courtiers attending his *lever.** Perhaps the fairest comment on the

* The ceremony of the king's rising, washing, and dressing. The *lever* was a fashionable and well-attended spectacle, and so was his going to bed.

man came from his brother-in-law: "His intellectual faculties are weak," reported Joseph II in 1777, "yet he is not altogether an imbecile."

This weak, well-meaning man, admirer of Fénelon and of Rousseau, seriously concerned about his people, lacked the decisiveness or energy to make up his own mind, let alone impose his authority. His marriage in 1770 to Marie Antoinette of Austria accentuated his deficiencies and the crown's incapacity to respond to the country's needs. Marie Antoinette (1755–1793) struck her contemporaries as lightheaded, frivolous, unreliable, interested in politics only as the cat's-paw of Austrian interest, or to find money and places for her friends. She was probably less bad than she has been painted. Gay, warm, loyal, the fifteen-year-old bride found herself isolated in the midst of a court where many opposed the sterile Austrian alliance she represented, married to a man she could neither respect nor love. These two mediocre beings might have performed quite adequately in less demanding times. They would, in due course, pay with their lives for the crime of having been cast in roles that were too great for them.

Only one thing both kings had in common, and that was their devotion to hunting. Both men seem to have invested in this passion time and energies which, some contemporaries felt, might have been more profitably employed elsewhere. "The King is really doing a dog's work for his dogs," complained one of Louis XV's ministers. "From the beginning of the year he arranges all that these animals will do until the end. They say that his majesty would run the finances and the war with far less trouble than all this. But the meetings of the Council weary him, because he has got to remain inactive and because affairs of state bore him." What had been an engrossing hobby for Louis XV was in his grandson a devouring passion. Louis XVI noted in his diary every hunt and every head he got: 1,274 stags and 189,251 lesser trophies between 1774 and 1787. As for his wife, herself a great equestrienne, hunting seems to have offered one more opportunity for diversion and display. In November, 1781, alone, tailors delivered thirty-one riding costumes for the Queen's use.

The Economic Impasse

Since the crux of France's troubles was financial, something must be said about the country's economy. The period that runs roughly from 1730 to 1770 was one of prosperity and expansion. Industry grew. Between 1738 and 1789, production of coal increased 700 to 800 per cent, that of cast iron 72 per cent. Industrial heavyweights began to appear, like the textile manufactures of Mulhouse, the forges of Creusot, Oberkampf's textile printshops, Réveillon's wallpaper factory, and, greatest of all, the coal mines of Anzin, which turned out over 300,000 tons in 1790. With its 4,000 laborers, miners, and carters, Anzin was the biggest enterprise in France. New machines and processes were being developed —Jacquard's silkloom, Berthollet's chlorine bleaching method, Leblanc's artificial soda, Oberkampf's textile printing cylinder—which should remind us that the Industrial Revolution was quite at home in eighteenth-century France. Even criticism of industry and capital began to be heard and, in 1783, we find a Catholic moralist wondering: "Industry multiplies capital; but to whose profit? Of the artisans who contribute their industry? Their share, for the most part, is only labor, misery and degradation. The capital accumulated goes into the coffers of a small number of traders, fattened by the sweat of a multitude of workers who waste away in a somber workshop . . ."

But workshops were fewer than warehouses, and manufacturers fewer than merchants. The great fortunes of the eighteenth century were built on trade, not on industry—especially on colonial trade which enriched the Atlantic ports. Between the 1720's and the 1770's, French foreign trade figures quadrupled, and the noble mansions and public buildings of Nantes and of Bordeaux still bear witness to the profits it could bring. But this prosperity was at the mercy of a fragile credit structure. Reliance on gold meant dearth of credit. England had credit institutions, banks, and notes; France had not. Law's crash had turned the French away from such snares and delusions. Credit was available from the Crown, from great nobles like Orléans, from financiers whose resources came from taxes. Otherwise all enterprises had to be self-financed. This meant that French industry knew little flexibility: no gold, no business. When metal turned scarce, production dried up; so did goods, so did employment, in the cascade of disasters which would fall on the country when hard times returned in the 1770's.

Meanwhile, things went well. There was work for builders and artisans, there was more money for wages and, hence, for food and wine; crops sold well, rents from land increased, and living standards improved at least for some. Not for all since with prosperity there also went inflation. Even as the national wealth increased, individual buying power shrank in many cases; the poor could get poorer while the nation grew rich. And the poor bore the brunt of taxes, so that it was possible for the state to be poor as well, as long as its revenues were drawn from the poorest sections of a wealthy nation.

State revenues were high, higher than the British, but not high enough. All economists agreed that taxes must be rationalized, simplified, privileges and exemptions eliminated, indirect taxes which bore especially hard on the poorest pared down. But every move to introduce reforms met bitter opposition. How could courtiers put an end to waste from which they were the first to benefit, or magistrates correct injustices that fed their revenues? On whom could reformers lean? Royal authority rested on bureaucracy, and this had grown so utterly unwieldy as to clog all development and enterprise. Already in the seventeenth century Colbert complained that justice took 70,000 men to administer it and busied a million others with its pettifogging. By the eighteenth centry, one-third of the active population of a provincial center like Dijon was working in some office, and the King's finance minister could only guess at approximately how many people his services employed.

This civil feudality knew how to guard its rights and would not lose them without protest. The very bourgeoisie that called for changes was strong enough to hamper and prevent them, yet not strong enough to bring them about without convulsions that would unhinge the system as a whole. Aging regimes always face this problem: the impasse between reform and revolution. Original structures decay, support wanes, is lost, or is lacking altogether. The regime finds agony easier to bear than action, and any positive move seems to stir up the possibility of collapse. When the boat is rotten, it should not be rocked. The alternative is to do nothing and await an almost fatal end, or do something and precipitate it. Hence, would-be reformers are often rightly charged with an important part in the eventual catastrophe which they alone might possibly have averted.

Yet reformers did appear, because the need was even more evident than the danger. Rationalization and efficiency were the watchwords of the time. Why should not France put her house in order, abolish privileges, bring the privileged castes in line?

The nobles were changing, largely under the influence of English values and, some of them, in pursuit of opportunities for profit. But none of this meant the abandonment of their privileges. On the contrary. At the very time when new philosophies shed a lurid light on old privileges and abuses, these were taking on a new dynamic life. The nobiliar counteroffensive of the eighteenth century, on which we have touched already, would make the task of reform ever more difficult. Serfdom, often mentioned, was the least of nobiliar impositions. True, while Louis XVI abolished serfdom on crown lands in 1779, elsewhere it was only ended by the National Assembly decrees of 1789. But by that time only vestiges of serfdom had been left, no less irritating for that, but overshadowed by feudal and manorial dues, rents in money (*droits*), labor (*corvée*), and kind (tithes); by the obligation to grind corn in the lord's mill, bake it in the lord's oven, press grapes in the lord's winepress; by subjection to the lord's exclusive hunting rights and sometimes to his right to judge in his own manorial court.

It was such rights and rents and tithes which pressed so hard, the harder when we remember that the nobility, less than two and a half per cent of the nation, owned one-quarter of its land and one-third of its harvests, on which they paid no tax or hardly any. Nor did the clergy pay taxes on their lands and tithes. Fiscal injustice was the nub of the

Anne Robert Turgot, engraving by Francois Drouais.

French problem, and one on which reforming ministers would butt and fall again and again. They could let Parlements expel the Jesuits (1763) and throw the educational system into confusion; they could even free the internal grain trade as Turgot managed to do for a few years; but when they turned to the fiscal system, Parlements stood staunchly against them, raising a cry of liberty which the people echoed with simple-minded enthusiasm.

As a result of this, the French entered the American war in a sorry state, and came out of it looking sorrier still. What with inflation, the war cost France as much as the three other great eighteenth-century wars put together. The annual deficit, 37 million in 1774, had grown to 80 million in 1783 and 112 million in 1787. Merely the cost of handling the public debt accounted for half the annual state expenditure.

Anne Robert Turgot (1727–1781), greatest of the reforming ministers, had been defeated over the question of tax reform. His successors sought to temporize. If taxation could not be reformed, obviously money must be raised by loans. Jacques Necker (1732–1804), who followed Turgot, found loans at high interest until they dried up, turned to tax reform, and fell in his turn. The next finance minister, Charles de Calonne (1734–1802), having tried to govern on credit and exhausted it, came to the same conclusion as Turgot and Necker. But Calonne had a new idea. To outflank the opposition of the Parlement, he decided to convene an assembly of notables, picked by the King, in which he hoped his project would fare better. There is no policy without risks, remarks a contemporary French politician; but there are policies without luck. The notables (including Lafayette) met in 1787 and rejected Calonne's proposals. Only the Estates of the nation, the notables claimed, could declare new taxes; and, when the King turned to the Parlements, he got the same reply. Leaning on enlightened catchwords to defend antiquated structures, notables and magistrates, nobles and philosophers, appealed to "national rights" and "national representation." In 1788 the government gave in. The Estates-General would meet on May

1, 1789, and Frenchmen were free to present their ideas on the reforms to come. Freedom of the press had been permitted.

The political debate had been taking place against a steadily deteriorating economic background. The economic expansion of mid-century had increased population pressure, along with levels of social and economic expectation. In the depression of the 1770's and 1780's, taxes got slightly higher while taxpayers were least able to pay them. In the absence of an urban industrial alternative, the small owner or tenant in time of bad harvest and with more mouths to feed quickly consumed all the crop, had to borrow at high rates and to buy grain in the market. The same man as occasional laborer suffered from the decline in real wages during the price inflation.

Larger peasant owners and tenants were not necessarily hurt by bad harvests. If they still had a surplus to sell in the market, they profited from the very high prices. But the seigneurial dues which added to the small farmer's misery were a critical question to the larger ones, cutting into their profits and joining them to their neighbors in common hostility to aristocrats and cities and government. All cultivators came to resent dues, tithes, taxes, and to blame their troubles on them more than they would have done in better times.

The wine trade, too, had entered a depression which, between 1778 and 1791, would have serious effects. Eighteenth-century French viticulture fed over 2 million people—almost a tenth of the country's population—the very backbone of the small holders, more independent on the whole, more thoughtful, more articulate and argumentative than the mass of small peasants, a kind of bridge between agriculture and industry. Its troubles affected not only vintners and merchants, but the artisans who lived on their trade and worked for them—stave and barrel makers, carters, shippers, and many others—immediately or at one remove.

The financial crisis was aggravated by a seemingly endless series of economic disasters. The terrible winter of 1783–1784 brought things to a standstill for weeks, only to be followed by the worst floods of the century in 1784 and poor crops in 1784 and 1785. The agricultural depression affected industry. Cloth production alone fell by half between 1787 and 1789. This produced unemployment, which coincided with a rise in the price of bread, due to the poor harvest. A free trade treaty concluded with England in 1786, largely for the benefit of the vintners who hoped to sell their wares in that hard-drinking island, flooded the country with English goods and did not really make much difference to the wine trade. There were 30,000 unemployed in Lyons alone, many thousands out of work everywhere. Then came 1788 and a rotten harvest, the most wretched in eighty years, while the following winter was the worst since 1709, the sparrows themselves freezing in the trees. In Provence most vines and olive trees froze. Industrial inspectors were reporting 46,000 unemployed at Amiens, 25,000 in Lyons, 30,000 around Carcassonne, 10,000 in Rouen, many of them flocking to Paris to swell the figure of 80,000 unemployed which the capital claimed in December, 1788. Bread doubled in price in Paris, tripled in some provinces. Riots broke out, peasants and workers pillaged grain stores and bakers' shops, stopped grain transport, threatened their lords. Soon some forms of ration cards would be introduced by local municipalities to ensure that the poor got a minimum of bread.

Principles Take Arms

Meanwhile, elections to the Estates were setting the country by the ears. French intervention in America had been more than a fiscal catastrophe. It had gone against all the principles on which the monarchy rested, supporting rebels against their legitimate king and democratic and republican ideas against traditional authority. Of course, the Very Christian King had never scrupled about aiding his enemies' heretics while persecuting his own. But what could be done with impunity in the sixteenth and seventeenth centuries could not be done in the eighteenth without opening the gates to criticism at home. Intervention on the side of the colonists allowed expression of revolutionary and republican ideas which would soon turn from the majesty of the British crown to that of the French. First of all, in 1782, as a rehearsal of things to come, the republicans of Geneva had to be crushed by French intervention, and Genevan exiles, befriended by the "American party" in France, played a leading role in the agitation which destroyed the government that had first cast them out of their own city and then permitted them to live in France.

 Then came the announcement that criticisms and suggestions could be published freely; and a flood of pamphlets and periodicals followed. The first great issue to be settled was whether in the Assembly, which had not met since 1614, clergy, nobles, and the Third Estate would have equal representation or whether the Third, representing more than nine-tenths of the nation, should be granted more deputies. It might be mentioned at this point that, at best, the eventual deputies of the Third Estate represented the masses of the nation only at several removes. Of their 610 representatives at Versailles, one-quarter were lawyers, 5 per cent belonged to other professions, 13 per cent were bankers, merchants, or financiers, 7 to 9 per cent were countrymen, most of them landlords, not peasants. Still, they probably were and they certainly considered themselves representatives of "the people." They were closer to the masses in their daily lives and had the best opportunities of influencing and stirring them. Yet their wishes and—more important—their nuisance value were ignored. A decision that the Third Estate should have double the number of representatives allotted to the other orders was promptly nullified by the announcement that each estate would sit and vote separately. The numerical superiority of the Third, therefore, became a purely formal concession, precluding any effective expression of majority opinion. The possibility of real representative debate and decision had been held out, only to be withdrawn.

Again we see that hope is a dangerous factor in politics. It makes for dynamism, but also increases impatience and embitters disappointments. Now, the public debate on this issue took on ominous tones; and in a tract published in January, 1789, *What Is the Third Estate?* the Abbé Siéyès argued quite simply that the Third was the nation and the other estates nothing, since they played no useful role in society. This announcement of how the Third looked upon them, only confirmed the privileged in their determination not to yield an inch lest they lose a mile. Yet, the fact that Siéyès was a member of the clergy indicates that the first two orders were themselves far from monolithic.

The clergy in particular were split in many cases between the higher clergy—prelates, canons, abbots—nearly all of them of noble birth, and the secular priests, many of them poor and discontented. The French clergy were a small army. The country's 135 dioceses held 70,000 priests, 60,000 monks and nuns, some 3,000 higher clerics. The Church owned about 10 per cent of cultivable land, but incomes varied immensely between the 400,000 livres a year (about $800,000) of the prince bishops of Strasbourg, and the 7,000 livres a year of the Bishop of Vence —itself ten times the pay of an ordinary vicar. The sympathy of what we might call the clerical proletariat often lay with the Third Estate and, while in separate sessions they might succumb to the pressure of their

The first page of Abbé Siéyès' *What Is the Third Estate?*

QU'EST-CE QUE

LE TIERS-ETAT?

Le plan de cet Ecrit est assez simple. Nous avons trois questions à nous faire.

1°. Qu'est ce que le Tiers-Etat? Tout.

2°. Qu'a-t-il été jusqu'à présent dans l'ordre politique? Rien.

3°. Que demande-t-il? A y devenir quelque chose.

On verra si les réponses sont justes. Nous examinerons ensuite les moyens que l'on a essayés, & ceux que l'on doit prendre, afin que le Tiers-Etat devienne, en effet, quelque chose. Ainsi nous dirons:

4°. Ce que les Ministres ont tenté, & ce que les Privilégiés eux-mêmes proposent en sa faveur.

5°. Ce qu'on auroit dû faire.

6°. Enfin ce qui reste à faire au Tiers pour prendre la place qui lui est due.

A

superiors, if the Estates met jointly many of their votes could be expected to support the Third.

The nobles held together better. Yet, even among them, many who had learned the lessons of Montesquieu looked forward to the same opportunities for political action and distinction as their English counterparts, while a few—like Lafayette—drew their inspiration from America. Of the fifty-four men who presided over the Constituent Assembly between 1789 and 1791, thirty-three would be nobles; and several noblemen also presided over the Jacobin Club. Indeed, the more liberal among them were returned, like Mirabeau, as representatives of the Third Estate in their province.

Meanwhile, the Court havered. The King could not make up his mind. Most of his ministers, led by Necker, who had been restored to office as an earnest of good intentions, leaned toward the Third. The Queen, the King's brothers, and their friends worked against it. When the Estates opened in May, 1789, they were instructed to sit and vote separately. The Third refused to accept this, insisted on common sittings, and balloting by head and not by order. On June 10, the Third invited the other Estates to join it. On the 17th, joined by a few priests, it proclaimed itself the National Assembly. Three days later, locked out of their hall, the members betook themselves en masse to a nearby tennis court, there to take an oath never to separate before having established a constitution. The King could not intimidate the new "Commons," which were being joined by more recruits from clergy and nobility. Popular agitation was growing. On June 27 Louis approved the Assembly and invited the other orders to join it. The Third had won the first round.

But Louis was only trying to gain time while concentrating troops around Versailles and Paris, troops with whose backing he could impose his will. The troop movements in the country helped aggravate the political tension, persuaded the countryside and especially the cities that counterrevolution was afoot, that an aristocratic conspiracy was about to crush the Assembly. A strange crop of rumors spread everywhere, swift to alert villages and cities against nonexistent threats, feeding on the nervous tension caused by food shortages. It was the beginning of the "Great Fear" which would perturb the countryside throughout the summer. And it was in this tense atmosphere that the news of Necker's dismissal (intended to facilitate the reassertion of royal authority) on July 11 sparked an explosion. The word that the minister who symbolized reform had been dismissed set off rioting in Paris. The Paris electors, meeting at the Town Hall, set up a provisional municipal government (the Commune), and organized a citizen militia to be identified by its cockade in which the colors of Paris, red and blue, were joined to the royal white. But the militia had to have arms. Shopkeepers, craftsmen, artisans, soldiers from the regiments around Paris, set off in

The attack on the Bastille. It lasted two and a half hours. Versailles Museum.

search of arms, raided all arms depots, and, finally, on July 14, attacked the Bastille to obtain the powder stored there. The superannuated structure had long outlived its usefulness either as jail or fortress, but continued to loom over the populous quarters of Paris as a constant reminder of arbitrary imprisonments and royal might. The awful symbol of despotic power fell after a brief resistance and, after butchering the governor, three officers, and three soldiers, the jubilant crowd set free the prisoners of oppression: one nobleman imprisoned at the request of his family, two madmen, and four counterfeiters.

Liberté, Egalité, Fraternité

The Court was frightened, Necker was recalled, and the Assembly saved. On July 15 the governess of the Orléans children took her three charges, including the future King Louis-Philippe, to see the ruins of the "dreadful monument of despotism" and bless those tearing it down "whose vengeful hands seem to be those of Providence." On July 17 the King came to Paris to greet the new municipal council and to put on the new red-white-and-blue cockade. Friends of liberty throughout the world rejoiced. In far-off Königsberg, Professor Immanuel Kant missed his regular daily walk to stay at home and read the news about the fall of the Bastille. In the English Midlands, the chemist Joseph Priestley's sixteen-year-old brother burst in upon his friends waving his hat and shouting "Hurrah! Liberty, reason, brotherly love for ever! Down with kingcraft and priestcraft. The majesty of the People for ever! France is free, the Bastille is taken." The nineteen-year-old future poet laureate Wordsworth went to France, where he fell in love and therefore perhaps appreciated better

> . . . a time when Europe was rejoiced,
> France standing on the top of golden hours
> And human nature seeming born again . . .

No less enthusiastic, reverberations nearer home would be more concrete. Unrest spread through the provinces. The Revolution had triumphed. The Revolution must be defended. Aristocrats, bandits, Prussians, Englishmen, were out to crush it, to massacre the friends of liberty, rebuild worse and more terrible bastilles. It was harvest time, and awful rumors strained the far-strung nerves. In the east, they said, the Germans were advancing; in the southeast the armies of Savoy; in Brittany and Normandy it was the English who had landed; in the central region the King's brother was supposed to be marching with a large army from Bordeaux. Dust clouds could start a panic, as at Angoulême in July, where 20,000 gathered in order to oppose bandits who proved invisible. When the church bells summoned the peasants or the burghers and no enemy could be found in sight, the crowd frequently decided that "having found no enemies, they would go visit the nobles, and the priests who supported the nobles," set fire to castles, salt depots, and excise posts, tear up the feudal charters of their servitudes. Thus, the fear of aristocratic reprisal turned against aristocratic privileges. And meanwhile, out of panic and unrest, one city after another decided to set up a militia after the Paris pattern. Before July had passed the National Guard was born and, since this was a burgher guard, its representatives were loud in demanding an end to aristocratic privilege. The reforms of August would follow the fears of July. As Chateaubriand said later: "The patricians began the Revolution; the plebeians completed it."

Faced with a vast peasant revolt, the Assembly reacted with seemingly extreme reforms. On the night of August 4, burghers, priests, and nobles sacrificed the privileges that had set the countryside on fire, abolished the feudal regime, clerical tithes, and decreed fiscal equality.* Finally, on August 27, the Assembly, now known as the Constituent Assembly, voted the Declaration of the Rights of Man, which established freedom of opinion, of the press, of property "sacred and inviolable,"

---

* The measures of August were not as thorough as they seemed. Many rights were to have been redeemed by payments to their owners. But the peasants would have none of it, and they eventually got their way.

and equality of opportunity. Men "are born and remain free and equal in their rights"; one of these rights is the exercise of sovereignty which rests in the nation, no longer in the king and the Parlements, who can only represent it. The law is the expression of the general will, and law courts, no longer arbitrary, must administer the same law for all.

As in the case of American innovations, these moves reflected current philosophical ideas, the enthusiasm of some protagonists, and the pressures under which all labored. Though most of the innovations were more rhetorical than real, the illusions they created stemmed not only from the hopes nourished by the masses but from the self-delusions of their initiators too. In other words, many believed what they were doing.

So did the King, who refused to sanction this "creed of a new age," or the reforms decreed on August 4. Determined to resist, he called new troops to Versailles. But the army was disaffected. For the past few years it had been torn by internal dissensions over reform and promotion procedures. Commoner officers and noble officers distrusted one another. Meanwhile, in Paris food was running short and tempers shorter. On October 5 the market women of the capital, calling for bread, marched on Versailles. The National Guard followed. The King, the royal family, were compelled to accompany their captors back to the royal palace of the Tuileries, where they would be the prisoners of the patriots. The Constituent Assembly brought up the rear. Henceforth it would sit in the capital, its galleries open to the Parisian public.

It was success beyond anyone's wildest dreams. Between the meeting of the Estates-General in May and the King's return to the Tuileries in October, over a century after Louis XIV had moved the court from Paris to Versailles, the profoundest changes had taken place at extraordinary speed. The Revolution seemed accomplished. Yet it was only just beginning.

The End of the Monarchy

The Constituent Assembly was running the country now, with the people of Paris, the orators of the political clubs, the pamphleteers of the popular press, the demagogues and idealists, looking over its shoulder. The first thing to do was establish the nation's finances on a firm foundation. And the attempts to solve the financial problems out of which revolution had come would, in their turn, precipitate further revolution. The general opinion was that the best way of settling the country's deficit would be by selling the property of the church. Church property in 1790 was estimated to amount to some three billion livres, an immense

The March to Versailles, October 5, 1789.

treasure which could be taken over without offending the principle of property, since the Church theoretically did not *possess* its wealth, but only held it in trust for the faithful—that is, the nation which now stood in need of it. At a time when tax revenue had almost vanished and expenses grew apace, the mass of church property would provide security for a new paper money, the *assignats,* with which the state could pay its debts and which, in turn, could then be used by citizens to purchase portions of the new national property. Accordingly, in November, 1789, church property was nationalized. It seemed that the country's economy had been set on the road to recovery at last. But this was not to be, and from this perfectly rational measure, which a majority of the clergy seems to have accepted, dread consequences would flow: some were economic, others religious, all would affect political events.

The political changes had not improved economic conditions; on the contrary, crops were rotting in the fields, industry was in the doldrums, nobles and the rich were closing their houses and beginning to seek security in emigration, tradesmen were losing their customers, domestic servants by the thousands found themselves out of work.* As for the peasants, most of them felt that liberty must mean an end of all taxation; and, in fact, the administrative structure, severely shaken, was hardly equal to tax collection. The church lands themselves brought less than had been hoped. Their very mass may have spoiled the market and, while buyers with the necessary cash to buy them did very well, many were left unsold. Then, as need pressed, the government took to printing more *assignats.* The paper was supposed to have been de-

* One result of this was the appearance of public restaurants of quality, as opposed to cheap cookshops and taverns, now opened by chefs whose masters had fled the Revolution.

stroyed once it had been paid in for a piece of national property. Now it was reissued, along with more. Inflation, which had begun by spurring the economy, was ballooning and the *assignats* deflating in value. The deteriorating monetary crisis would have serious consequences before very long.

Having abolished tithes and nationalized church property, the Assembly became responsible for the upkeep of the clergy. If the state was to pay the salaries of clergy, it had to keep track of them. The Constituent Assembly was restructuring the country into new administrative divisions. The old provincial diversity against which the monarchy had struggled so long was now replaced by eighty-three departments (eventually eighty-five), each subdivided into districts, cantons, and communes. It would be logical for parishes to coincide with the new administrative arrangements. The Civil Constitution of the Clergy followed. Contemplative orders were suppressed as useless, as we saw happen under the "enlightened despotism" of Joseph II. Priests were to serve a social function. They would be paid, but would have to be elected by the local electoral assemblies. Like legislators, priests were representatives and servants of the people, and they were expected to take an oath of loyalty to the nation and to its constitution. This was going too far. In 1791 the Pope condemned the Constitution of the Clergy.

Not the Constitution itself but its extremities proved to be a blunder of the first magnitude, shattering national unity and setting patriotism and religion at loggerheads. The Assembly had wanted the National Church to be as much a bulwark of the new state as it had been of the monarchy. But the Papacy could not condone the democratic Erastianism of a national church whose officers were chosen by the people. Here was an extreme conclusion of Gallicanism when legislators pretended to subordinate the interests of religion to those of the state. Clergy and faithful were caught in the middle, between ecclesiastical authorities which rejected the right of secular ones to legislate in spiritual matters and a secular state demanding the right to adjust the church organization according to the nation's views and needs. Fewer than half the priests took the Constitutional oath, and few of those who did could carry out their office effectively. Religious schism menaced the stability of the new political order.

Louis XVI, in particular, felt that he could no longer reconcile his conscience to compliance with the demands of the new regime. At Easter in 1791 he tried to confess before a priest who had not taken the oath and he was prevented. This precipitated his decision to escape his warders. After an unsuccessful attempt to get away in June, 1791, the royal family was recaptured at Varennes, close to the eastern border. In this sense, the war, the Terror, and the end of the monarchy, may all be traced back to the religious problems which the Civil Constitution cre-

The distribution of *assignats*

ated. In August Louis's failure either to co-operate or to escape brought about the Declaration of Pillnitz, in which his brother-in-law, the emperor of Austria, and the king of Prussia invited all powers to help restore order in France.

The French Wars, 1792–1815

A successful revolution in the greatest of Europe's powers was bound to affect the continent and the world more than anything that happened in Holland, Geneva, or distant colonies overseas. Dynastic connections and self-interest led most crowned heads of Europe to support Louis XVI, a fellow monarch imperiled by his subjects. This embroiled them with the revolutionary enthusiasts whose creed threatened their thrones in principle, whose doings would shake them hard in practice.

Far more than the Americans with their *novus ordo seclorum*, French revolutionaries stood for a new order in society as well as state; and the hostility with which they felt themselves surrounded stimulated them into aggressiveness. War might have been avoided even so, for France's British competitors were in a pacific mood and rather pleased than not at her internal troubles. In February, 1792, Pitt, in the House of Commons, advised a reduction of naval estimates because "unquestionably there was never a time in the history of this country when, from the situation in Europe, we might more reasonably expect fifteen years of peace than we may at the present time." As a matter of fact, hostile armies had already begun to concentrate near the French border, not least an army of aristocratic *émigrés* led by the King's brothers, who threatened dire revenge against the rebels. This increased the revolutionary fever at home, and the patriotic appeals against the enemies of revolutionary liberty at home and abroad with whom the King and Queen became increasingly identified For his part, Emperor Leopold II wanted no trouble. There may well have been none had he not died in March, 1792. His successor, Francis II, would speak more sharply, trust in his big stick, and his method achieved at least one end: in April, 1792, France declared war on "the king of Bohemia and Hungary," a formula designed to show that the war was not against any nation, but one of peoples against kings.* The untried armies of the revolution, however, met with seeming catastrophe almost at once. Within weeks the French had been routed and Austro-Prussian forces were advancing on Paris. The soldiers streaming back raised the cry that they had been betrayed. The officers and the King, who sympathized with the reactionary invaders, were letting them down. The assembly voted emergency measures, and the King once more refused to approve them, thus confirming everyone's suspicions. At Louis's secret request, the Duke of Brunswick, commanding the advancing allies, launched a manifesto threatening that if any harm befell the royal family Paris would direly pay for it. The manifesto reached Paris on August 1 and produced exactly the opposite of the effect intended. A popular insurrection, fomented by the popular clubs and led by men like Danton and Robespierre, took the Tuileries by storm. The royal family was suspended from its functions, imprisoned, and new elections announced for a Convention (note the American inspiration) which would endow the nation with a new regime.

The military situation was growing worse. The border fortresses were falling. The fatherland was declared in danger, conscripts and volunteers hurried to the front. Fear of treason filled the air. What if the internal enemies in the Paris prisons should rise behind the army's back? The crowd invaded the prisons (September 2) and 1,368 helpless men and women were massacred—about half the inmates. The murderous new determination gained the army, which, in the rain and mud of the Argonne, at Valmy, on September 20, outfaced the Prussians and forced them to retreat. The nation in arms had triumphed, and now it would go over to the offensive. Before the year was over, Belgium had been overrun and French armies were advancing in the Rhineland, Savoy, and Nice. In Paris the new Convention, elected by universal suffrage while many moderates abstained, contained a strong contingent of republican "patriots." It had met on the day of Valmy. Two days later it proclaimed the Republic.

* The Assembly made very certain this would not lead to misunderstandings. It "adopted in advance all foreigners who, abjuring the cause of its enemies, will come to take their stand under its banners."

While tyrants trembled, the friends of liberty abroad exulted. It was up to France to extend to them a fraternal hand. "The French nation," Paris proclaimed, "will grant fraternity and aid to all peoples who want to recover their liberty." That was in November. In December, it announced that the French nation would treat as enemies countries which supported princes or privileged castes, while guaranteeing the independence of those establishing "free and popular government." Between November, 1792, and March, 1793, France annexed Savoy, Nice, Belgium, the Rhineland. In these territories the political regime was overthrown, the social order changed. Having declared war on both Britain and Holland in February, by March, 1793, France found herself at war with most of Europe. First Holland in 1795, then Italy in 1796, became satellite republics.

> And now, become oppressors in their turn
> Frenchmen had changed a war of self-defence
> For one of conquest, losing sight of all
> Which they had struggled for . . .

Their reception was necessarily mixed. Some people felt that "liberation" did indeed sweep away feudal rubbish of which they were better rid; and many benefited from the political and economic emancipation, the reorganization of laws and courts and administration, which followed in the wake of revolutionary conquests. Yet even liberals who welcomed the removal of old rulers, the demolition of outdated privileges and restrictions, were ambivalent in their reaction to invaders who proved both liberating and exacting. In the service of liberty, French armies plundered all they could lay their hands on. In the Rhenish Palatinate the locks were taken off doors and sent to France. Belgium was sucked almost dry. The treasure of Berne would serve to finance the Egyptian expedition. But propaganda continued to present the conflict as a social war: in Italy, in Ireland, in the Balkans, in Germany, where Baden and Würtemberg secularized Church property and abolished feudal rights. The French army included Polish and Irish, Italian and German units. War, like politics, appeared in a new light: an emancipating conflict, appealing to the unprivileged against the privileged and, sometimes, to the poor against the rich as well. A revolutionary conflict too, not only by intent but by its duration. For, while the parties altered, the fighting itself would continue—with only one brief interruption—to 1815.

A New Face for France

War was long and hard, and it would exercise its pressures close to home, more than it did abroad. The men who had declared it were known as

FRANCE IN REVOLUTION
1789–1793

- Areas under government control
- Areas dominated by Royalists and Girondists
- Areas of counter-revolutionary uprisings
- Territories annexed to France, 1791–1793
- ← Coalition offensives

NETHERLANDS

ENGLAND

HOLLAND

Rhine

HOLY

ROMAN

EMPIRE

BELGIUM

RHINELAND

Moselle

RHENISH PALATINATE

ENGLISH CHANNEL

Amiens

Rouen

Seine

Varennes

Meuse

× Valmy

Paris

Versailles

ENGLISH

Loire

FRANCE

Rhine

Berne

SWITZERLAND

VENDÉE

BAY OF
BISCAY

Saône

Lyons

SAVOY

ITALY

Angoulême

Rhône

Bordeaux

Garonne

Nice

Carcassonne

Marseilles

CORSICA

SPAIN

MEDITERRANEAN SEA

0   200 miles

Girondins, a group of lawyers, merchants, financiers, and intellectuals whose leading figures came from the area of Bordeaux: moderate in their republicanism, extreme in their nationalism, hoping that internal difficulties would disappear in the exaltation and community of war. They would be overtaken and borne down by more ardent republicans of the Mountain—so named from their location high up on the left of the Assembly. The Mountain drew its main support from the popular clubs which had sprung up in Paris, chiefly on the premises of

Bulloz

Marie Antoinette imprisoned at the Temple. Opposite: the beheading of Louis XVI.

abandoned convents, like that of the Dominicans—or Jacobins—or of the Franciscan gray friars—or Cordeliers. This is where its leading figures were recruited: powerful orators like Danton, in the Cordeliers, passionate doctrinaires like Louis de Saint-Just and Maximilien de Robespierre among the Jacobins.

Difficult questions faced the Convention. The Republic had been declared; what should become of the King? Many favored imprisonment. The Mountain called for death. Documents were discovered in the Tuileries proving the King's intelligence with the enemy and, in January, 1793, Louis XVI and his queen went to their execution. The King had betrayed the nation. The Queen was a foreign agent. They clattered toward the guillotine in open carts, and died with dignity beneath the roll of drums. The religious trouble was growing. After war had been declared, a proscription law outlawed priests who would not take the oath. Louis' refusal to sanction this had hastened his end. Thousands of priests fled the country. Many hid. Others preached sedition, resistance to a heathen regime. In the Vendée, over much of the west middle region, peasant rebellion broke out against the middle-class revolution.

Conditions of life were getting steadily worse. During the winter of 1792–1793 the laborer's daily wage hardly covered the price of one pound of bread, bakeries and butchers' shops were looted, queues began at four in the morning and service only at eleven. The *assignat* having lost more than half its value, peasants would not trade food for useless paper. The Convention, on the other hand, would not interfere with the free operation of the market. Popular discontent turned against the Girondists responsible for the war. In June, 1793, a new insurrection brought their arrest and execution. The Mountain took over. Its leaders had opposed the war, defended the interests of the poorer section of the

population: shopkeepers, artisans, small property owners, above all consumers of all sorts, prototypes of the *sans-culottes* who had abandoned the knee-breeches associated with the old regime for democratic trousers. The *sans-culottes* might be described as populists. They stood for a small-owners' society, where proletarians would be kept in their place but capitalists and privileged would be excluded. The leaders of the Mountain tried to carry out this somewhat confused ideal.

Economically reactionary, dreaming of a sort of Jeffersonian golden age, these people were politically revolutionary, calling for direct government and direct democracy. They always remained a minority in the country—a minority whom the necessities of war and economic crisis forced to impose conscription and taxation on the people they sought to rule. But conscription was a horrid novelty, and taxation was associated with the abuses of the old regime. Just as in the days of the Constituent Assembly, the people still felt that revolution was supposed to bring more freedom, not more encroachments and impositions. It is not surprising that the revolutionary rulers of France had to govern by terror, by coercion, enlisting on their side the nervous strain of the crisis situation that had brought them into power.

The Road to Terror

Power was exercised by special committees of the Convention, especially the Committee of Public Safety, dominated by the legendary figures of Robespierre and Saint-Just: an austere provincial lawyer and a reformed playboy with literary pretensions, hardly twenty-five years old. Under their rule, freedom of speech became the freedom to say the right thing; freedom of the press did not include the right to poison

529

public opinion. The public had to be educated by the right side, protected from corrupting views and voices. To such an end, most means were considered good.

Rousseau had attacked the theater as an immoral amusement which turned the minds of men from worthwhile preoccupations to lewd and antisocial diversions. The men of the Mountain admired Rousseau and felt that the theater could and should be used to instill civic virtue, glorify the community, honor the aged and deserving, spread the right social values. They were among the first to recognize the propagandistic possibilities of the stage. In a play like *The Republican Husband,* a man denounces his wife to the Revolutionary Committee and has her guillotined to great applause. In another play—*Last Judgment of Kings*—all the sovereigns of Europe (except for Louis XVI, who has just been executed) arrive in chains on a savage island. All are hungry, and they are thrown a piece of bread for which they scramble and fight. Pius VI throws his tiara at Catherine II, who hits him with her scepter and breaks his cross; the king of Spain loses his nose in the scramble. In the midst of this, a volcano erupts and destroys them all, thus settling the hash of monarchy for ever.

There were more sophisticated means of instilling the new ideas. In October, 1793, as fighting raged on the borders and civil war inside, a new calendar came into effect. It would last for twelve years, until January, 1806, and was meant to mark the opening of a new era: years of twelve months, months of three decades (ten days each), new names replacing the saints of the Gregorian calendar—plants, animals, agricultural implements, names culled from Greek and Roman history—the cycle of history and nature taking over from the traditional nomenclature.*

Even the pulpit was turned into the tribune of a new cult which worshiped Nature and the Supreme Being (unspecified), honored Humanity, its benefactors, and the French people. The pageantry of Reason replaced that of the Church in Notre Dame. Revealed religion gave way to natural religion, masses to Festivals of Reason. Statues represented Reason, actresses embodied her, garlands of flowers wreathed her, poems, hymns, speeches, and morality plays glorified her, massed choirs sang, and cannons boomed her praises.

Those who persisted in the old faith were hunted down, imprisoned, guillotined, shot, or, as at Nantes, "de-Christianized by immersion," that is, drowned in batches. The Jacobins were not deliberately against reli-

---

* Names like Gracchus and Publicola became common, and some enthusiastic Jacobins actually named their sons Conchgrass, Duck, or Dandelion, their daughters Cow, Carrot, or Rhubarb. In the words of Richard Cobb, "The roster of the Jacobin club read like a seed-catalogue." But the real significance of the calendar went beyond this. After struggling against all those wasteful feast days, it was a triumph to have only three holidays a month instead of four Sundays and umpteen saints' days. And what relief for industry! The Goddess Reason triumphed not only over the costly, useless clergy, but over idle workers too.

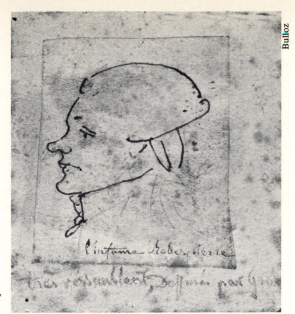

Robespierre, as drawn by
Antoine-Jean Gros.

gion. "Since my school days I have been a pretty poor Catholic," Robespierre told the Jacobin Club in 1794. "I am all the more attached to the moral and political ideas I have put before you. If God did not exist, we should have to invent him." And Hébert, a radical Jacobin speaking in the same tribune a few days later: "I advise priests to read the Scriptures. This moral tract seems to me excellent, and one must follow its maxims to be a perfect Jacobin. Christ seems to me the founder of popular clubs." But it was Christ and religion with a difference. The object of worship would no longer be God but society, not His will but Its values. Civic oaths, patriotic symbols, prophets and priests, martyrs, festivals, processions, altars of the fatherland and, of course, a creed—the rights of man and of citizen: these were the marks of a new religion, secular perhaps, but dedicated to the worship of a new reality with lasting effects: society, man, ultimately the collective self, directed by historical Providence and fulfilling—that is, directing—it in turn. "Only atheism is aristocratic," said Robespierre.

Revolutionary fervor has often been compared to religious enthusiasm. Burke, who saw "a revolution of doctrine and theoretic dogma" taking place in France, denounced its leaders as theologians and proselytizers. Tocqueville described it as a "religious revolution." And indeed the republicans themselves furnished grist for this mill, borrowing metaphors from ecclesiastical language, intoning civic invocations, reciting a republican creed, drawing up the republican civic Ten Commandments, crossing themselves in the name of Marat, and sanctifying the "holy Revolution" or the "holy guillotine." Apocalyptic, messianic, like all revolutions, the first great modern revolution necessarily borrowed the language that would suit it.

But that was only one aspect of it. "The eighteenth century had formed man for society," the Goncourt brothers would write. "The Revolution forms him for the state." A textbook, *The Elements of Republican Instruction*, contained the following dialogue between a student and a teacher:

—Who are you?
—I am a child of the fatherland.
—What are your riches?
—Liberty and equality.
—What do you contribute to society?
—A heart to love my country and arms to defend it!

And Saint-Just notes: "The child, the citizen, belong to the fatherland. Common instruction is necessary. Children belong to their mother till the age of five is she has fed them, and to the Republic thereafter, until death." This was total society, born of total crisis and trying desperately to solve its problems by any means at hand. "There are no citizens in the Republic but republicans," declared Saint-Just. "We must oppress the oppressors." Robespierre recommended "the despotism of liberty against the despotism of tyranny." Rigor was only used for the people's good. This was its justification. "Without virtue," said Robespierre, "terror is useless; without terror, virtue is powerless." Here, then, was the Terror, which one survivor later described as "a violent political crisis complicated by no less violent stomach crises."

Yet, as prices continued to rise, blood alone seemed able to assuage popular frustrations. The Revolution again was fighting for its life. The Committee of Public Safety, which called on the people to work, to go hungry, to furnish troops for campaigns on every front, including the Vendée and Toulon where royalist sympathizers had opened the port to the English, had to prove its determination, had to furnish an earnest example of what would befall the treacherous or the halfhearted. The guillotine gave proof. Between October, 1793, and July, 1794, 300,000 to 500,000 suspects were imprisoned, some 17,000 sent to their death. Heads, in the colorful phrase of one Jacobin, fell like tiles: thirty a day in Paris, in the last paroxysm of the Terror. Napoleon, who watched it all in the capital, summed up at Saint Helena: "No social revolution without terror. Every revolution is . . . a revolt which success and time legitimize, but in which terror is one inevitable phase."

Grim ruthlessness achieved its ends. The enemy was repelled, the rebels checked in the Vendée, Toulon recovered, prices regulated more stringently than under the old regime. Yet, if prices were regulated, it stood to reason that wages should be too. When Robespierre set a ceiling for wages, he deprived himself of the popular support which had backed him up. After the middle classes, cowering in terror, the artisan and worker supporters of the Mountain turned away from him.* Yet the

* Of the Terror's victims, 31 per cent proved to be workers, 28 per cent peasants.

guillotine worked on, though the emergency of invasion and civil war had passed. It was time for the surviving enemies of Robespierre to act— or shortly lose their own heads. In July, 1794, a coup sent Robespierre and his friends to the guillotine, silenced the popular clubs, brought back the survivors of the Girondins, replaced universal suffrage by a franchise founded on property qualifications, substituted bicameral legislation for the single assembly, and entrusted executive power to a Directory of five.

The Directory

The rule of the Directory was a time of victories abroad and hard times at home. At least the land question which had bedeviled the old regime and the early years of the revolution had been settled by the reforms of previous years, the mass of small landowning peasants was temporarily satisfied, and this ensured that they would pose no major problem. French peasantry, until the twentieth century, would play the role of a largely passive stabilizing force. The first proceeds of this came in the crushing of provincial insurrections.

But if the countryside was relatively quiet, Paris was not. The Directory sought but failed to settle itself firmly. Plots and counterplots, within and outside it, prevented this. Jacobins, monarchists, and sheer opportunists, grasped avidly for levers of power seemingly up for grabs. The image of these few years in the later 1890's remains colored by the brutal cynicism of the ruling clique. Too many of those who had survived the Terror felt what Napoleon described in a letter of 1793: "Among so many conflicting ideas, so many different perspectives, the honest man is confused and distressed . . . Since one has to take sides, it is just as well to choose the winning side, the side that loots, burns and devastates. Given the alternative, it is better to eat than to be eaten."

The victors of 1794 preferred to eat. They would do well and gradually entrench themselves in state and power. Cynical and practical, here was the new aristocracy; it had shed the optimism of the enlightenment and acquired the opportunism of experience. "Yesterday I went to the Chamber of Peers," remarked one of them in 1835. "We were only six when I arrived; we had all been in the National Assembly and we were all over eighty." They had survived the Terror. Henceforth, they would prevail and rule, if necessary by force of arms, calling in the army to suppress further insurrections; or, if not rule, at least they would profit.

The Revolution's Legacy

There were achievements also, and those of the Revolution of which the Directors were a part must be marked. France had been reorganized into "equal surfaces"—departments, which would "facilitate the exercise of [central] power" and whose capital city would never be more than a day's journey from any of its parts. The departments were given neutral names to help old provincial loyalties fade away. In 1790 the Civil Constitution of the Clergy gave each of them a bishop, and in 1800 Bonaparte would give them all a prefect—the secular agent of the central power. In all aspects of life a new uniformity was being introduced. Trade and industry had lacked any standard of measure.* A decree of 1793 would introduce meters, grams, liters, francs: a set of uniform abstractions divorced from man [foot], experience [rod or pole], tradition [bushel]. Here were products of intellectual concepts and of calculation, which took a long time to gain acceptance but which were destined to simplify and clarify business transactions, just like the new insistence on family surnames and individual (or Christian) names, or the new birth certificates and birth dates that replaced the old certificates of baptism.

Law replaced caprice, a mobile society replaced a static social order. If many of the new municipalities had officers who could not read or write, this was a proof of the new avenues of social promotion and effectiveness that opened under the new regime. Among Napoleon's marshals, Ney was the son of a cooper, Lefebvre the son of a miller, Murat the son of an innkeeper, Augereau the son of a mason, Lannes the son of a stable boy. And in the municipalities, after 1789, a National Guard appeared to drill and strut but, above all, to confirm the revolutionary right of citizens to bear arms—a concept first affirmed in the American Bill of Rights and one which would continue as a liberal ideal throughout the nineteenth century.**

War and revolution offered an extraordinary opportunity to youth. Some of the greatest figures of the Revolution and the Empire that followed were in their teens when the Bastille fell, many in their twenties like Saint-Just (1767–1794), Rouget de Lisle (1760–1836), who composed the "Marseillaise," Camille Desmoulins (1760–1794), or Chateaubriand (1768–1848), who fought in the emigré army. Danton was thirty when he was executed, Robespierre thirty-six; both left their mark in history. Hoche, a corporal in 1789, was an army commander in 1794 at the age of twenty-five. Most of Bonaparte's generals would find fame in their twenties, and Bonaparte himself seized supreme power when he was just thirty years old.

It may well be that, as the eighteenth was a century of growing population and hence of youth, the Revolution was an explosion of these forces. In 1789, only 24 per cent of France's population was over forty

---

* In England, by the 1760's, standard pounds, miles, and quarts had been more or less established for the kingdom as a whole.

** In 1848, in Rome and Milan, in Berlin and Vienna, one of the first popular demands was the right to organize such a body.

years old; 40 per cent were between twenty and forty, 36 per cent were under twenty. These mouths needed land, these hands needed work, these minds sought employment. In eastern and central Europe there was land at least; in England and Ireland emigration offered some escape. France had lost Canada, shed faith in Louisiana, her industrial revolution was not advanced enough to absorb surplus energies and population. Perhaps a political revolution, a great war of expansion, with the opportunities they brought, were needed to give all these men a chance . . . or eliminate them. And that was what happened. The *levée en masse* itself helped stabilize the new regime, transferring men from workshops to the ranks, from the streets to battlefields, from availability for civilian conflicts to more productive foreign ones.

The New Warfare

All this was closely connected with profound changes in the art of warfare. For the revolution ushered in, and its generals perfected, a style of warfare unknown to the eighteenth century, a scale of warfare that the world ignored until that time.

Eighteenth-century armies had been slowed down by cumbrous supply trains. As the century ended, improved economic conditions made more food and forage available, an advantage that revolutionary armies would enthusiastically seize. Formal and limited hostilities had first been abandoned overseas, where the American colonists ignored the milder European manners and treated war as total (as indeed it was), so that Sergeant Lamb in Dublin, remembering his campaigns in the War of American Independence, described the fighting there as "a sort of implacable ardor and revenge, which happily are a good deal unknown in the persecution of war in general."

The American War of Independence persuaded observers that willing soldiers were best. For Lafayette, only citizens could be expected to accept the hardships of military discipline and win. But citizen armies could not exist without political and social changes. Armies, as we have seen, included the most unproductive members of society: nobles as officers, tramps and unemployed in the ranks. Such troops did not prove reliable when facing revolutionary armies made of free men encouraged to heroics and initiative. But it was not really the heroics which won the wars of the Revolution so much as the new strategy and tactics, a military unorthodoxy that grew out of lack of orthodox training and means. The blitzkrieg which the French devised reflected the needs and the shortcomings of their ill-equipped and ill-supplied troops, which had to move fast to seize what they needed and which moved the faster for lack of the stores they sought. But this speed and unorthodoxy of maneuver became effective novelties, which allowed them to achieve decisive superiority at a given place at a critical moment.

The revolutionary armies did have one advantage from the first; and that was numbers. "Only numbers can annihilate," said Lord Nelson, and this was a novelty too: a double novelty, of aim and means. Most eighteenth-century battles were fought with armies of 40 and 50,000. Napoleon himself began his brilliant Italian campaigns with less than that. Ten years later, at Jena, he had nearly 200,000, and almost three times as many for his Russian campaign. His foes had to do as well, so that the allied troops in the Waterloo campaign of 1815 counted about a quarter million. These vast new masses of sometimes poorly trained recruits abandoned the old line-formation which needed well-drilled veterans to keep it up, for a mass column whose battering weight was much greater, but again, whose original source lay in the problems of lack of discipline and of time for drill.

The logic of the new mass armies would be formulated in the works of K. von Clausewitz (1780–1831), a Prussian officer who campaigned with the Russian Army against Napoleon in 1812 and who was present with the Prussians at the Battle of Waterloo. Writing in the 1820's, Clausewitz drew the lesson of experience when he emphasized the psychological factors which would henceforth have to be taken into account. He noted the triumph of spirit over mere form and matériel; he recognized the trend toward absolute and total war, which he described as "an act of violence pushed to its utmost bounds"; and he defined war as only a continuation of state policy by other means. No more limited conflicts were possible, said Clausewitz; war could no longer be the sport of kings now that national existence was at stake. "Since the time of Buonaparte, war, through being first on the one side, then again on the other, an affair of the whole nation, has assumed quite a new nature."

But if Bonaparte exploited its possibilities, the Revolution had created them. Being a movement of youth, the Revolution had all the violence, the color, the passion, and incoherence of youth, all its idealism and all its selfishness. Pompous, solemn, murderously destructive, the Revolution was also exuberant, generous, enthusiastic, naïvely confident in the principles it brandished—sometimes at the end of a pike. It brought not only carnage, but virtue, not only savagery but reconciliation, not only terror but fraternity.

Napoleon

In the 1750's the Corsicans had risen to assert their independence against their Genoese masters. Under the leadership of a remarkable man, Pasquale Paoli (1725–1807), who built schools, founded a university, asked Rousseau for a Constitution, and unsuccessfully tried to forge his supporters into a nation, Corsica held the Genoese at bay for over a dozen years. In 1768, the Genoese, tired of their useless efforts, sold the island to France and French troops defeated Paoli in May, 1769, driving him into exile. In August, 1769, the wife of one of Paoli's chief supporters in Ajaccio gave birth to a son who was christened Napoleone. The boy grew up there, speaking the Italian dialect, off-spring of a poor noble family in a poor, primitive land where the Middle Ages still endured, in clans, vendettas, and endless violence. In 1779, before he was ten years old, Napoleon was entered at the Royal Military Academy of Brienne, in Champagne, whence the short, skinny, serious lad was commissioned a second lieutenant in the artillery at the age of fifteen in 1784.

The opportunity to distinguish himself came in 1793 when, as a mere captain, he was charged first with the siege artillery and then with the siege plans of Toulon. He was successful, he was promoted, he hung around Paris—one more political general looking for pickings, escaped the purges of 1794, married Josephine de Beauharnais, discarded mistress of one of the Directors, lent a hand to suppress popular opposition to the Directors, was rewarded with the command of the army of Italy, and thereafter there was no stopping him. By 1798, having just won the victory of the Pyramids and having heard of the infidelity of his wife Josephine, he would write to his brother: "Greatness bores me; all my feelings are dried up. Glory is stale when one is twenty-nine; I have exhausted everything. . . . There is nothing left for me but to become really and completely selfish."

Even his failure served him. Off on a wild empire chase in Egypt (1798–1799), he was not involved in the scandals that besmirched the reputation of the regime. Incredibly, he managed to carry an expeditionary force across the Mediterranean, escaping British ambush and taking Malta on the way, to defeat the fierce but anachronistic Mameluke masters of Egypt, to overwhelm most of the Turkish troops in Syria. Yet, once the French Mediterranean fleet had been annihilated in the battle of the Nile (1798), the cause was lost. All Napoleon's ruthlessness and guile could not avail before Muslim hostility, the tenacity of Turkish troops holding out in the fortress of Acre, the ravages of plague, and the British blockade which cut off succor and supplies. Within a year Napoleon was sailing back to France, leaving his army to molder beneath the pyramids and finally to surrender. Those who survived would be repatriated when Egypt was recovered by the Ottomans a few years later.

The general himself went on to better things. His return to Paris found the Directory on its last legs; successive risings of the Left and Right had been suppressed, but no regime can erect *coups d'état* into a system of government. Siéyès, one of the Directors, was looking for a safe soldier to head yet one more coup. Bonaparte seemed ideal for the purpose, amenable yet crowned with laurels. In November, 1799, the coup took place. The Directory suppressed, was replaced by a Consulate. But the First Consul was General Bonaparte, and the rule of political adventurers gave way to that of a military adventurer. First Consul in

Napoleon's Coronation, by Jacques Louis David. The self-made emperor crowns himself. Versailles Museum.

1799, Consul for life in 1802, hereditary Emperor in 1804, Napoleon would give France a stable military dictatorship for nearly fifteen years, and modern Europe the most unsettling career of conquest that she had ever seen.

Clearly the heir of the enlightened despots, Napoleon appears as the greatest of them all. He was a creature of the Revolution, fated to affirm its gains, but no believer in its values, in the general will, in popular sovereignty, in government by assembly. Maybe he had believed in them once. But, as he said on his deathbed, "In my youth I had illusions; I got rid of them fast." He was immensely hard-working, toiling for as much as eighteen hours a day, dictating a prodigious number of orders, letters, and dispatches—some 80,000 in fifteen years of rule: an average of fifteen a day. He knew that he loved power and he knew that his going would be a relief to his subjects. "What will they say of me when I am gone? Ouf!" A voluble, lucid and captivating talker, slim, taut, little over five feet tall, dazzling when he wanted, he reveled in limitless ambition and egoism. What Napoleon believed in was competence, reason, the efficacy of an enlightened will backed by sound artillery. All this he would proceed to prove in great campaigns abroad and great decrees at home.

Finances, education, the roads, the army, all benefited by his meticulous soldier's mind. But two measures stand out among the others: the Concordat (1801) and the Civil Code (1804). Napoleon himself was indifferent to religion, ready to use or ignore it, as it suited him. But "religion is necessary for the people"; a religion which "must be in the hands of the government." Only agreement with the Pope could secure the stability of the regime, and agreement was secured at the same time as a broad amnesty reconciled most of the *émigrés* of the previous decade. The Concordat which healed the breach between the Church and the Revolution was one of Napoleon's great victories. The sale of Catholic Church property was accepted, and religious freedom was admitted by implication when the Concordat recognized Catholicism only as "the religion of the majority of Frenchmen." Bishops became prefects in violet robes, ruled by a minister of ecclesiastical affairs; and Napoleon would be able to declare that his power was based on three forces: "My gendarmes, my prefects, and my priests."

He spoke truly, and, in due course, a catechism, taught in every French Sunday school. included a revealing passage: "What are the duties of Christians towards the princes who govern them, and what, in particular, are our duties towards Napoleon I, our Emperor?" To which the answer was: "Christians owe to the princes who govern them, and we in particular owe to Napoleon I, our Emperor, love, respect, obedience, loyalty, military service and the taxes ordered for the preservation of his Empire and throne. . . . To honor and serve our Emperor is to honor and serve God himself."* He had made peace with the Church, but made it on his own terms. When his policy called for occupation of the papal states, he did not hesitate to do it. When the Pope tried to withstand him, he ordered his arrest.

What was a triumph for Napoleon was a deep change for the Church. Gallicanism came out of the Revolution broken, the Pope's prestige enhanced by persecution, the clergy detached from the old regime tradition turned back to Rome. When Napoleon was gone, the new church would be ultramontane—that is, its eyes would be directed across the Alps, where the authority of the Vatican ruled unchallenged except by the alien hostile forces of the new age, which only made it more unyielding. At the same time, the Church would become increasingly defensive—obsessed by the past, increasingly afraid of any novelty that might bring revolution back.

Next came the Civil Code. The monarchy had long sought to submit all its subjects to uniform laws. It was Napoleon who achieved this aim. Most of the Code he promulgated was concerned with property, which it sought to define and defend. Other provisions granted civil liberty and civil equality, except in the family, which was treated as a smaller state and just as despotically regulated. The father was master in the home, his wife (like his children) subject to his authoritarian power, unable to acquire property without his consent or, as a rule, to administer what she owned. Authoritarian, retrograde in many ways (as

* Quoted in E. E. Y. Hales, *Revolution and Papacy, 1769–1846* (London: 1960), p. 177.

with regard to the position of women), the Code reflected the ideals of a property-conscious society and the narrow morality of the Corsican upstart who ruled it. But it seems to have been ideally suited to the new century. Brief and clear, the Code firmly codified Revolutionary achievements, provided a long-needed unity of legislation, and furnished a model of civil law in the following hundred and fifty years, affecting much of Europe and America, even long after Napoleon's fall.

"What made the Revolution?" asked the new master: "Vanity. Vanity alone can put an end to it." The new regime would provide advancement, titles, even a new nobility. In the last forty years of the old regime the King had raised four hundred families to noble status, about ten a year. From 1808 to 1815, Napoleon created a new imperial nobility, often recruited from members of the old: 29 dukes, 44 counts, 1,468 barons, 1,289 knights—2,830 nobles in all, about one a day for eight years, over half of them soldiers, nearly half the remainder civil servants. Merchants, lawyers, doctors, professional men were no more recognized by the Empire than by the old regime. They would not come into their own for some time.

The furniture and decoration of this period reflected the new mood. Its shapes: solid, bulky, and four-square; its colors: dark for soberness, but with lots of gilt and rich materials from home industry; its symbols of power—eagles, thunderbolts, fasces, griffons, lions—or of victory—sphinxes, laurels, winged victories.

The symbols of victory and power were well-earned. Since his return from Egypt in 1799, Napoleon's armies had begun to inflict terrible defeats on all their enemies. But Napoleon had to go ever further to protect gains and borders to which his enemies would not resign themselves. In the end, he would go too far.

In Europe in his absence, the fortunes of war swayed back and forth across German and Italian territories. Whatever the force of France's Russian or Germanic foes, it had become clear in the process that Britain was the country to defeat. Indeed, the Egyptian enterprise itself had been intended to strike toward the main source of British wealth: India. That stroke had failed; and Napoleon, having made himself master of France, proceeded to restore the military situation on the continent. His swift strikes, his seemingly inevitable victories, achieved a brief interval of peace, first, with Austria (Treaty of Lunéville, 1801), then even with the British (Treaty of Amiens, 1802). Not peace, really, but a truce. The hero's popularity knew no bounds. But neither economically not strategically could France and Britain trust or abide each other. For Britain, Napoleon remained the man of revolution and of war, the upstart who would upset the balance of society and power. For Napoleon, the British stood in the way of his plans for European hegemony and, even more, for expansion overseas in the Americas and the Orient.

Britain was "perfidious Albion," and she seemed to prove it by being the first to reopen hostilities against France in 1803 and, then, by inciting one coalition after another to oppose Napoleon and by maintaining them with generous subsidies. Unable to strike at his unrelenting foe across the Channel, Napoleon used the troops he had assembled to invade England to defeat England's allies instead. In two years' hard, fast-moving fighting he shattered the Austro-Russian forces at Austerlitz in far-off Moravia (1805), destroyed the myth of the invincible Prussian army at Jena and Auerstedt (1806), pursued the Russians deep into East Prussia and beat them down at Friedland (1807). Then, in an interview at Tilsit on the river Niemen, he charmed Tsar Alexander into a friendly peace.

After the Treaty of Tilsit brought peace with Russia in 1807, only the stubborn British continued to hold out. Unable to defeat them, Napoleon could hope to choke off their commerce and bankrupt the state, so that it could no longer subsidize its allies. British power rested on British trade. The Royal Navy had long sought to blockade French-held Europe. To bankrupt the British and dry their source of power, Napoleon imposed his own counterblockade: the Continental System, meant to exclude British goods from European markets and to deny them the trading profits on which they ran their war.

The contest between blockading and counterblockading measures—British Orders-in-Council and Napoleonic decrees—led the British to bombard Copenhagen and seize the Danish fleet (1807), which they feared might be used against them; it led Napoleon to invade Spain in order to strike at Britain's Portuguese allies (1807). Both sides were led much further than they might have wished to go; and, while after 1808 the French became embroiled in a costly peninsular war, four years later the British would find themselves with an unwanted American war on their hands.

The meeting of Napoleon and Tsar Alexander I at Tilsit. Vanity and precaution placed the neutral no-man's-land on a raft.

H. Roger Viollet

The Continental System wreaked havoc with British trade and French privateering cut deep gaps in Britain's merchant fleet. But while Britain suffered, Europe suffered more. Smuggling flourished, prices soared, businessmen were ruined, Napoleon had to seize ever more territory in order to bring it within his system. "It is the English," he declared, "who force me to aggrandize myself unceasingly." It would be his anti-English measures, the cost of his occupation troops, the rigors of French administration and French demands, which turned his subjects and his associates against him. Spain in particular turned out a hornet's nest, providing the British with a long-awaited chance to fight the French on land as well as sea, encouraging even Francis of Austria to take up arms again—only to be swiftly and brilliantly defeated at Wagram (1809).

By 1810 Napoleon's realm stretched from Lübeck on the Baltic across the Alps to Genoa, and from the North Sea to Geneva. Europe, recast as it had not been for centuries, was gored all over by the marks of military engagements. Napoleon had littered central Europe with his victories, abolished the Holy Roman Empire (1806), reconstructed Germany and Italy, even revived a rump of Poland: the Grand Duchy of Warsaw (1807–1814).

France had despoiled all Europe of her treasures, bedecked herself with the art works and the gold of foreign palaces, drained toward her the wealth and raw materials needed for her wars, her industry, her display. Around her, a ring of satellites was ruled by the clan of Bonaparte: his brothers were kings of Westphalia, of Spain, of Holland (this last only until 1810, when it was annexed to France). His dashing brother-in-law, Murat, was king of Naples; another became Grand Duke of Tuscany; another, the Roman Prince Borghese, husband of the beautiful Pauline who has left us her image in Canova's marble statue, was prince of Guastalla. Napoleon's stepson was viceroy of Italy. There was a Bonaparte even in the papal *curia*: the Emperor's uncle, Cardinal Fesch. Beyond these territories, the hand of France lay heavy even where its garrisons did not stand guard, from the Mediterranean to the Vistula.

Having built an Empire, in 1810 Napoleon married an Emperor's daughter to secure the heir his first wife, Josephine, could not supply. Marie Louise of Austria was the conventional daughter of a conventional monarch, betrothed to the upstart who had just defeated her father—and not for the first time. Her husband's very divorce from Josephine was of dubious value, while he himself had just been excommunicated by the Pope. None of this prevented Marie Louise from doing her duty, which was to bear an heir. The heir, punctually born in 1811, was promptly styled king of Rome.

Yet the little heir found a crumbling heritage. War soon consumed what war had won. However strong they grew in Europe, the French

The Battle of Trafalgar, painting by Chambers. National Maritime Museum, Greenwich.

failed in their ventures overseas, whether they tried to carry revolution eastward to Egypt and Turkey or turned west to conquer Ireland or to attempt an English landing. Britain ruled the seas. Of this there was no doubt after the battle of the Nile and the destruction of the combined fleets of France and Spain at Trafalgar (1805). From their embattled island *entrepôt* the British watched for every opening. In the years following the French successes of 1807, they naturally lent aid to the Portuguese and Spanish opposition to the invading French.

Napoleon's own subjects began to turn against him. Dissatisfaction had been growing with the years. The imperial armies gobbled up conscripts: 60,000 a year until 1804, then over 200,000 a year, then over 250,000 every year. Desertions increased, so did self-mutilation and marriages which could exempt from military service, and grumbles from the peasants who lost the sons they needed on the land. The endless war with England, the Continental System, had proved increasingly costly. French ports lay ruined, empty, the economy dislocated, relations with allies and satellites were badly strained. Moreover, this policy hurt the middle classes in all countries, Napoleon's most obvious supporters, and persuaded them that the Corsican did not stand for enlightenment because he denied free trade, that he did not stand for equality because he set French interests above those of other countries, that—to sum things up—their interests and his did not coincide.

Except for Russia, all Europe lay in the great Emperor's thrall, but it was getting restive. Even with Russia relations were growing tense. Ruled by the grandson of the great Catherine—Alexander—Russia had followed an uncertain course. She had joined Austria against Napoleon, only to be soundly defeated with her Austrian allies at Austerlitz in 1805 and by herself at Eylau and Friedland two years later. After the Treaty of Tilsit, in 1807, on the other hand, she had changed sides and joined Napoleon against England. But the Frenchman's eastern ambitions and his Polish policies worried Alexander, while the Tsar's inability to comply with all of the blockading measures proposed against the British angered Napoleon. The Grand Duchy of Warsaw, incorporating territories Prussia and Austria had wrested from Poland, was a puppet of the French; that did not make it seem less of a threat to the Ukraine. The opening of Russian ports to neutral ships—that is, at one remove, to British goods—seemed a defiance and a challenge. Both sides prepared for war and war came in 1812. Victory in Russia would close the last gap in the Continental System, overcome the ominous giant on Europe's eastern border, open the way to the orient and to crushing stubborn Britain, all at one fell swoop.

In June, 1812, the *grande armée*, some 700,000 men, crossed the Niemen River into Russian territory. The French sought to bring the enemy to battle. The Russians avoided them, withdrawing faster than the enemy advanced, setting the towns, the crops, the countryside on fire; and what the Russians did not devastate, the horde of invaders would consume. In September, after one bloody encounter at Borodino, Napoleon was in the Kremlin. A few days later Moscow lay about him in ashes and ruins, three-quarters of it destroyed by fire. The Russian army remained elusive, French hopes of victory as usual seemed more elusive still, and the Tsar refused all of Napoleon's peace proposals. The French were in an impossible situation. With weather conditions growing worse, advance seemed impossible and retreat hazardous. Yet they must choose.

In October, winter already closing in, the retreat began. Weighed down with wounded and with loot, harassed by Cossacks and peasant guerrillas, the French were forced to move along the same route they had followed in the summer, amidst incredible devastation, in growing cold and snow, leaving behind them a long trail of arms, wagons, dead, and wounded. Soon the retreat became a rout, the rout a disaster. At the end of November, the ragged remnants of the grand army, hardly one-seventh of their original strength, reached Poland once again. Half a million men had died or been taken prisoner in the Russian plains. Space had defeated the armies no enemy had matched: space and the crushing blows of Russian winter.

The news of the defeat brought Europe up in arms. By December, rebellion was breaking out throughout the unquiet Empire. Napoleon raised fresh armies, fought new campaigns, which some consider the

Napoleon's Return from Russia, by Nicolas Charlet.

most brilliant of his whole career. But luck which had served him well and the balance of power he had so long ignored had veered against him.

At last, there were no more troops to be squeezed out of an exhausted land, the enemy whom the French had so often humbled now returned in force: the British, under Wellington, pressing up from Spain, and Russian, Prussian, and Austrian troops from the east and north. None would stand by the despot: not his wife, not his generals, not the people whom he had driven too hard. In April, 1814, the Emperor abdicated, receiving in return full sovereignty of the tiny isle of Elba, off the Italian coast.

But Elba proved too near to home: the fallen conqueror could see his victors quarreling over the spoils at Vienna, where they met in Congress in 1815; while in France the Bourbons who had been brought back in the enemy's baggage train and their *émigré* friends "who had learnt nothing and forgotten nothing" in twenty-five years of exile were stirring up old hatreds out of apathy. "I am not a man, but a historical figure," Napoleon once declared. A historical figure could not be left to molder on Elba's lava rocks. In March, 1815, with only a small detachment of his guard, he landed in the south of France. The troops sent to arrest him followed him instead. In three weeks the Emperor was back in Paris, promising peace again but awakening fears of war. For a hundred days, Europe teetered on the brink of a new batch of wars. But the Emperor had lost the magic touch, and the decisiveness of his past victories. The bickering allies, restored to unity, moved against him. Enthusiasm among the French waned before new conscription for another army. At Waterloo, in Flanders, the Duke of Wellington, strengthtened at the crucial moment by Prussian support, brought him to defeat. That was the end of Napoleon and of the French attempt to dominate Europe.

This time there would be no comfortable retreat in the Mediterranean. Unable to take refuge in the United States as he had hoped, forced to surrender to a blockading British warship, Napoleon would be sent to Saint Helena, a little island off the African coast in the South Atlantic, there to write his memoirs, bicker with the Governor, decay, and finally die of stomach cancer in 1821.

He had been right. In 1814, the great sigh that greeted his disappearance had been a sound of relief. It would take six years' hard work at Saint Helena and several more after his death to elaborate the gospel of his glory and recreate the Napoleonic legend which was to echo on throughout the years. Napoleon himself had said that geniuses are meteors destined to burn up while illuminating their century. The light which he cast was tinged with red.

Nationalism Confirmed

The revolution and the Napoleonic Empire had unleashed new forces and ushered in power struggles on a vast new scale. They had to be defeated by opposition on a similar scale: the masses of Spain and Russia, the vast resources of the British thalassocracy, the immense expanse of eastern Europe. Mass against mass, the greater won.

One other force had stimulated widespread opposition to the French, turning the campaigns of 1812–1815 into wars of liberation for many who had hitherto known only dynastic conflicts. That was nationalism: a sentiment for whose growth the French themselves were chiefly responsible, for modern nationalism is the child of the French Revolution. We might best describe it as an exacerbated form of patriotism, destined to affect first all of Europe and then the remaining world.

Love of the fatherland was nothing new, of course, in the eighteenth century any more than in the fifth century before Christ. Nor was suspicion of outsiders and foreigners identified with war, fear of invasion and rapine, or the greed and passions slaked at someone else's expense. However, as the century progressed, these simple sentiments had fed on historical studies of national origins and on theories then being formulated about the origins and structure of the state. As the state grew at the expense of particular provinces, interest groups, or institutions,

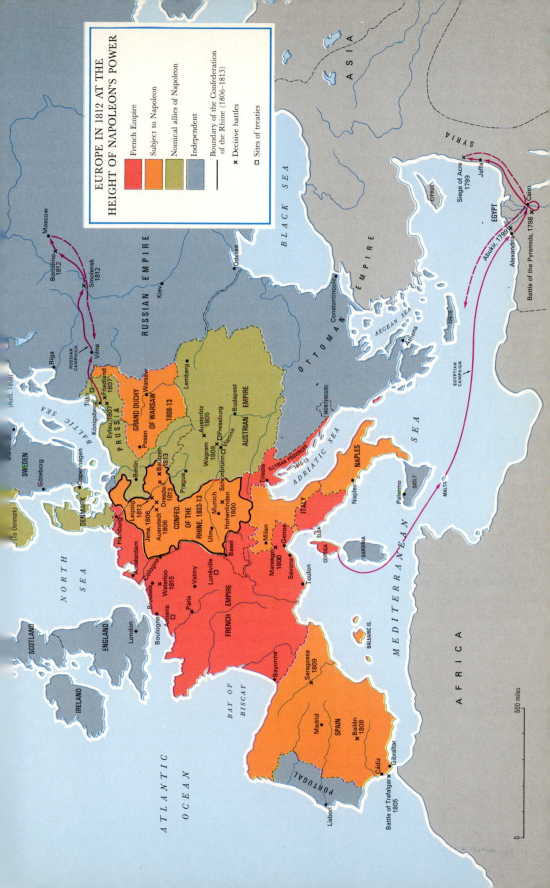

the local or factional pride that people took in belonging to a city, a county, or a gild, the special loyalty and attachment which they felt for them, became overshadowed by identification with greater entities: the state, and the nation that the state represented.

This happened first, as we might expect, in those societies where state sovereignty was most advanced and whose members had good reasons for identifying with it, to gain at least a vicarious share in its successes: that is, in countries like France and England. But the notion of a common and peculiar evolution accounting for the particular nature and institutions of a society spread elsewhere. The Germans, whose empire had lost all shred of sovereignty, dreamed of reviving bygone glories; Italians—very few to start with—also recalled a glorious past, well-past, and yearned to restore it.

Meanwhile, discussions of the fatherland became involved with arguments about the conditions which should prevail in it. Classical references, which came so naturally to eighteenth-century men, suggested the role of *virtue* without which nothing availed, the role of the *citizen,* his duties and his rights. Intellectuals, seeking to understand the peculiar personality of private individuals, turned to examine their historical origins, the common roots whence their society sprang. Trying to define the nation and the state, they reached revolutionary conclusions affecting all their individual members. The nation was more, they said, than a few men who ran affairs or held the helm of politics. The nation was the people. It followed that the people, all the people, should properly have a say in national affairs. "There is no fatherland under the yoke of despotism," wrote the *Encyclopedia*; and Montesquieu, who defined virtue as love of the fatherland, added "that is to say, the love of equality." All members of the nation, shoots off a common stem, were equal by that fact. They shared a particular language, tradition, culture; they had far more in common than anything that might differentiate or divide them; and their institutions should properly reflect this.

The men of 1789 never forgot this. "The nation," wrote the Abbé Siéyès in his pamphlet, *The Third Estate,* "exists before all things and is the origin of all things . . . its will is always the supreme law." It would become evident in due course that, practically speaking, the government of the people meant, as before, the government of the few, only endowed with immensely greater moral power since they now ruled in the nation's name and spoke for it. Individuals found themselves lonely and defenseless before a government that was supposed to represent them —a magnified, better, truer image of themselves—and to oppose which would be madness—a kind of suicide. Edmund Burke was not far off the mark therefore when he saw "individuality . . . left out of their scheme of government. The state is all in all." His conclusions were ominous, and experience has not proved him wrong: "Everything is referred to the production of force; afterwards, everything is trusted to the use of it.

It is military in its principle, in its maxims, in its spirit, and in all its movements. The state has dominion and conquest for its sole objects; dominion over minds by proselytism, over bodies by arms."

To put it differently, a total world view set out to bend first society and then the world to its philosophy, revealing the totalitarian possibilities of a well-meaning creed. The state, noted the German poet Hölderlin, became a hell just because man tried so desperately to turn it into a heaven. Burke had suggested that mass democracy may turn to tyranny. The evolution of the revolutionaries bore him out. Sovereignty, which had resided in the king alone, now rested in the nation; and those who wielded it knew none of the traditional limits the monarchy had had to recognize: none but the limits of power. The logical—that is, extreme—conclusions of this attitude would in due course be drawn by German philosophers like Fichte, for whom "the individual does not exist . . . the group alone exists, and it alone must be considered as existent." But first the point of view had to be spread, and it spread through Europe close on the heels of the conquering French.

When French patriotism degenerated into nationalism, neither liberating nor respectful of the national rights of others, it set off a reaction in its own image. The French had broadcast the notion of a new kind of sovereignty resting in the people and expressed in the nation state. Many had welcomed them as harbingers of liberty. Their occupation proved that you could buy liberty too dearly and that, indeed, the national self-expression of one people might have to be accomplished at the expense of others. Ideals, as usual, had turned into policies.

As patriot risings broke out against the French and their collaborators, nationalism reaped the whirlwind it had sown. French patriots had conquered Europe. They had also taught it the acute form of patriotism that turned against them. Obviously, after Waterloo Europe was vastly different from what it had been in 1789. The revolution had ransacked it from Seville to Moscow, leaving deep traces or a light sediment of change: social, economic, administrative, intellectual. Enlightened ideas had spread, national awareness had appeared and grown, a hoard of memories had been accumulated which played their part in policies to come. For half a century, international affairs would be dominated by fear of a new general war which, in the words of Chateaubriand, would have been the ruin of the social order. It follows that, in these years, not wars but revolutions would trouble the uneasy peace.

Chapter 12

THE PEACE OF
HUMPTY DUMPTY

Congresses and Alliances

With Napoleon defeated, his victors met in the capital of counterrevolution to settle the fate of Europe. The Congress of Vienna (1815) sought to re-establish the balance of power and the principles of legitimacy, both severely shaken by the events of the past quarter-century. But it was impossible to put legitimacy together again.

The chief French envoy to the conference, the Prince of Talleyrand, was symbolic of the changes that had taken place. A married ex-bishop, an aristocrat of proudest blood who served the Revolution, the Napoleonic Empire, and the restored Bourbon monarchy, a skeptic who knew his talents as thoroughly as he understood the weaknesses of other men, Talleyrand brought to Vienna, in his words, "the sacred principle of legitimacy" his master represented. Conquest did not make right for Napoleon, he argued. No more could it justify Napoleon's victors imposing their own will upon the map of Europe. Dynastic right and general recognition by all fellow states could alone legitimize a sovereign or a regime. Without this principle, Europe must head for ruin.

Such views, which clearly served the interests of Talleyrand's Bourbon masters—strong in dynastic claims but short on power—suited others less. The Tsar, especially, who had designs on Poland, and Prussia, desiring to expand her territories, would have preferred a more liberal approach to possible expropriation of some dynastic lands. If Talleyrand's views prevailed, it may be that this was a moment in time when arguments from principle could still obtain a hearing; it may be because the restoration leaned heavily on traditionalist applause of "legitimate monarchy."

More likely, it was because the Austrian chancellor, Prince Metternich, found virtue in the Frenchman's arguments from his own point of view.

Metternich has been identified with dynastic legitimacy. He was, in fact, a man of reason and order who believed that the nationalist and liberal currents set in motion by the Revolution could only upset order, not create it. The claims of nation states could hurt his master's multi-national empire as badly as the claims of liberty and equality could sap its foundations. Both must be stifled. Not that Metternich thought that they could be done away with. But they could be held in check by determinedly defending monarchy, aristocracy, and social hierarchy within each country; and by preventing international conflicts which could easily upset their hold upon the social body. If this could best be done by referring to dynastic legitimacy, or even divine right, the Austrian chancellor would appeal to them. Whatever best preserved national and international balance was good. Whatever would keep down radicals, Jacobins, who thought they could make and unmake regimes and constitutions, was better still.

In the end, the principle of legitimacy was theoretically vindicated, though only imperfectly applied. True, the Bourbons ruled in France once more, by grace of the Tsar and of Talleyrand. But old republics like Venice and Genoa never recovered their independence. The Holy Roman Empire could not be revived, nor did anybody want it back. The three clerical electorates which the French had secularized stayed so. Over three hundred German states remained in limbo. There was also talk about the balance of power; but the allies sought rather a concentration of power, first against the French whom they feared, then against the forces of revolution.

Their settlement was enshrined not at Vienna, but in the treaties of Paris (1814, 1815), whose main clauses drove France back to her borders of 1791 (thus leaving her some of the Revolution's gains) and surrounded her with guardians: the kingdom of the Netherlands, now including Belgium; Prussia, compensated on the Rhine for Polish territory incorporated in a Polish kingdom ruled by the Tsar;* Sardinia, which recovered Savoy and gained Genoa; Austria, which now dominated Italy from Lombardy and Venetia.

The Tsar made his contribution to the peace to come by drawing up a statement inspired by the "sublime truths" of religion and in which the "delegates of providence"—sovereigns by Divine Right, fathers but absolute fathers of their people—asserted their mutual support. Present-day historians, like certain observers of that day, think little of Tsar Alexander's invention. Yet it reflected and relied upon the growing attention focused on sentiment, and on a widespread international move-

---

* Her gains in north and west Germany changed the balance of Prussian population which had been one-third Slav and now became six-sevenths German, thus fitting her for a future role as leader of German nationalism.

The Congress of Vienna. Metternich stands at the left of the table with his hand apparently pointed toward Talleyrand, the third from the right behind the table, and Castlereagh, seated at the far right. Right: *Clemens von Metternich*, by Sir Thomas Lawrence.

ment that recoiled from soured politics to stress inner spiritual regeneration. Undogmatic, devotional, ecumenical, sentimental, the evangelical activities of eighteenth-century pietism had carried it from Moravia to colonial Georgia, from Britain to Russia. English Methodists had brought the Bible Society to Russia even as Napoleon was approaching Moscow; and Tsar Alexander was persuaded by them and by pietist friends around him that he was the chosen instrument of God.

It was not so farfetched to think that against the universal revolution one could lean on the pious enthusiasm of a universal "inner" church. Its romantic mysticism could appeal to vulgar commoners and sensitive aristocrats alike, spoiling both for more dangerous activities. Emotional religious commitments which, like English Methodism, did not set out to challenge the established churches, could compete with secular rationalism. Partly inspired by a vehement and eccentric missionary of the movement, the Baroness Julie de Krüdener, the Holy Alliance was a "Christian answer to the French Revolution." Its name derived from a passage in the Book of Daniel, its existence was dedicated to "the Most Holy and Indivisible Trinity." Its charter of 1815, which Metternich called a hollow and sonorous monument, and Goethe the best thing ever tried in the interest of humanity, would, in due course, be endorsed by all the sovereigns of Europe save the Pope, the king of England, and—rather naturally—the Sultan.

The essential purpose which the Holy Alliance was designed to serve—providing mutual support among heads of state against their own and others' revolutionaries—was given teeth and a machinery by the Quadruple Alliance of the victorious powers—Russia, Prussia, Austria, and Britain (1815)—which France joined in 1818. The war had been won by co-operation: only co-operation could preserve the peace. While revolution threatened, rulers did not doubt that it could be held in check as

A contemporary printing of the words and music to the *Marseillaise.*

long as no war diverted their attentions and their troops. To ensure great power co-operation, the signatories agreed to meet in frequent congresses where current problems could be discussed and joint action agreed upon. This was the Congress System. As long as it lasted, international peace could be accounted safe. It did not last for long.

The Revolution, uneasily buried, was far from dead. Beneath the surface of repression, police, and censorship, its believers were burrowing their shafts, meeting, talking, planning: secret societies and conspiracies flourished, especially in the backward and inefficient Mediterranean lands where the contrast between past glimpses of progress and the restored regimes seemed most striking. One such society, the *Carbonari* or charcoal burners, whose backbone seems to have consisted of anticlerical and antilegitimist veterans of Napoleon's armies and administration, spread from Italy to France and Spain. Other societies, some of them Masonic, most of them republican-minded, grouped intellectuals, professional men, sometimes even soldiers and artisans, who believed in popular sovereignty, representative rule, and constitutions, in places as far apart as Cadiz and St. Petersburg. Power, most of them argued, was in the hands of the privileged minority. A surprise attack by a determined handful of men should be enough to topple the oppressors and open the gates of freedom. That the masses lay supine did not discourage the enthusiastic few; and indeed, their risings, when they came, showed that in an age of minority government the struggle for power was still being conducted by small minorities.

The national ideal, suspected by the statesmen of the Restoration and alien to the structures they had set up in 1815, could not be denied.

From Scandinavia to the Balkans, from the Ukraine to Ireland, men dredged the past for languages abandoned by their fathers, collected folk tales and legends, compiled chronicles and dictionaries and song books. Poets sang and painters depicted the glories of the national past, idealized national heroes, hymned liberty and self-determination. A new musical particularism made its appearance, producing not only "German" and "Russian" opera, but national anthems too, so that the *Marseillaise* would soon be matched by a *Watch on the Rhine* and *Deutschland über alles*.

And, by a natural conjunction, those who exalted the nation praised the people too, the living mass from which the nation drew its strength and its dynamic energy. Democracy, it seemed, went hand in hand with nationalism: no wonder that the men of the Restoration feared the one as much as they feared the other and that, when he compiled his *History of Freedom* in 1862, Lord Acton chose to speak of nationalism as "the most attractive of subversive ideas and richest in promise of future power." By the time Acton wrote nationalism had proved its subversive possibilities. Nor had it waited long.

We shall note that 1820 and 1821 would see revolts and revolutions in Naples and Piedmont, Spain and Portugal, Greece and South America, which tested the machinery of the Congress allies and found it wanting. True, the Italian revolutions were soon suppressed and the Iberian revolutions also in due course—that in Spain being put down by French troops in 1823. But in the meantime the allies had split. The British had refused to let "peace and order" be re-established in Spain's revolted American colonies; and, while they would not prevent the Sultan from dealing with his obstreperous Greeks, they would not countenance foreign interventions in the Balkans which would either extend Russia's sphere of influence on the pretext of protecting fellow Christians or enhance Austria's position as protector of the Sultan.

Concord and Discords

In 1822, at the Congress of Verona, called to discuss the Greek and Spanish questions, and where French intervention in Spain was decided over the protests of the British foreign secretary, Canning, Metternich had invited Rossini to attend. The Imperial Chancellor neatly argued that, since Rossini was the god of harmony, he ought to be present at a meeting where harmony was so important. The composer came and provided five cantatas in honor of the Holy Alliance, including one of that very name whose words had to be rewritten three times to please a censorship which allowed no political references, including any men-

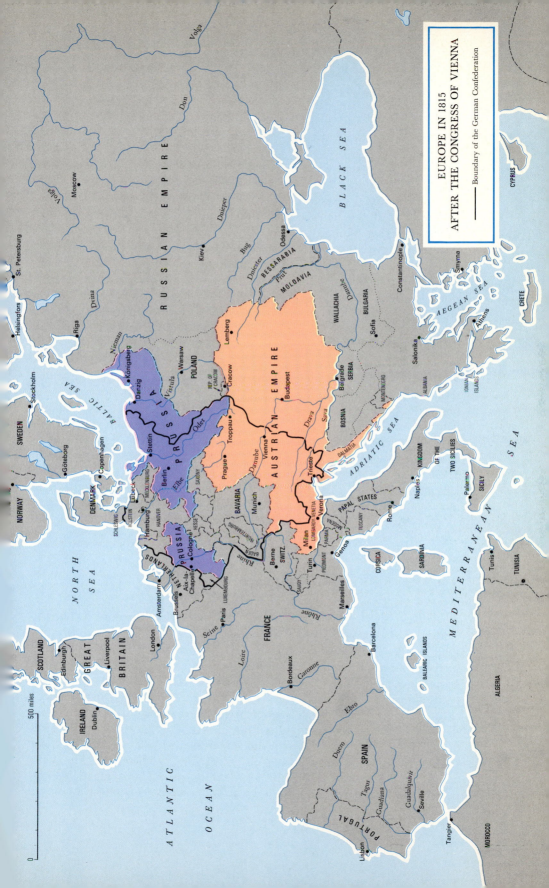

EUROPE IN 1815
AFTER THE CONGRESS OF VIENNA
—— Boundary of the German Confederation

Volga

Don

Moscow

Volga

St. Petersburg

Helsingfors

Stockholm

NORWAY

SWEDEN

Riga

Göteborg

Copenhagen

DENMARK

Dvina

RUSSIAN EMPIRE

Dnieper

Kiev

Bug

Dniester

Prut

BESSARABIA

MOLDAVIA

WALLACHIA

Danube

BULGARIA

Sofia

SERBIA

Belgrade

BOSNIA

MONTENEGRO

ALBANIA

IONIAN ISLANDS

Nieman

Königsberg

Danzig

Vistula

POLAND

Warsaw

REP. OF CRACOW

Cracow

Lemberg

AUSTRIAN EMPIRE

Budapest

Drava

Sava

Danube

Odessa

BLACK SEA

Constantinople

AEGEAN SEA

Smyrna

Athens

Salonika

CRETE

CYPRUS

PRUSSIA

Stettin

Berlin

MECKLENBURG

Lübeck

Hamburg

HANOVER

Oder

Elbe

SAXONY

Prague

Troppau

Vienna

Danube

Trieste

Verona

Milan

LOMBARDY-VENETIA

DALMATIA

ADRIATIC SEA

KINGDOM OF THE TWO SICILIES

Palermo

SICILY

Naples

PAPAL STATES

Rome

TUSCANY

MODENA

PARMA

Genoa

PIEDMONT

Turin

SARDINIA

CORSICA

BALTIC SEA

NORTH SEA

SCHLESWIG

HOLSTEIN

NETHERLANDS

Amsterdam

Brussels

Aix-la-Chapelle

Cologne

LUXEMBURG

PRUSSIA

HESSE

WÜRTTEMBERG

BADEN

BAVARIA

Munich

Rhine

Berne

SWITZ.

SAVOY

Marseilles

MEDITERRANEAN SEA

Rhône

FRANCE

Paris

Seine

Loire

Bordeaux

Garonne

Barcelona

BALEARIC ISLANDS

SCOTLAND

Edinburgh

Liverpool

GREAT BRITAIN

London

IRELAND

Dublin

ATLANTIC OCEAN

500 miles

0

Ebro

SPAIN

Duero

Tagus

Guadiana

Guadalquivir

Seville

PORTUGAL

Lisbon

Tangier

MOROCCO

ALGERIA

Tunis

TUNISIA

tion of "war" or "peace", and which could not be printed lest anybody understand anything. At a performance in the Roman arena of Verona the composer, as he tells us, conducted in fear of his life because the great statue of Concord beneath which he stood was insecure and threatened to topple over at any minute. That was the image of the Congress System.

By the following year, concord had collapsed. An alliance of great powers did not suit Britain's traditional policy of a balance of power based on national divisions. The Greek question gave Canning the opportunity to divide Russia and Austria, by arguing for intervention—which the Tsar wanted—but on lines which isolated Metternich and which led eventually to the establishmenf of Greek independence (1830) under the protection of Britain, France, and Russia. The Holy Alliance, split in 1822 by British dissidence, was shattered and international politics opened for maneuver once again. Henceforth, power groupings would reflect the difference in the evolution of the different powers: England and France faced Austria, Russia, and Prussia. This division, however, was far from constant: Austria and Russia were rivals in the Balkans, Austria and Prussia would become rivals in Germany, England and France could only co-operate as long as France accepted second place and did not let her expansionist interests challenge those of her jealous ally. Hence, England might co-operate with Russia against Austria in Greece, or with Austria against Russia when the latter's eastern ambitions grew too large; and Franco-English relations could be strained over Spain or Egypt, as they would be later over Napoleon III's Italian policies. Fundamentally, however, internal orientations affected foreign relations; and this could only be reinforced by the common fear of revolution felt by the autocratic rulers of the East.

The Restoration of France

The defeat of Napoleon was not the defeat of the Revolution, but the return of that Constitutional monarchy that had been swept away in 1792. Since Louis XVI's son and heir, Louis XVII (1793–1795), had died in prison, the throne went to the brothers of the executed king. Lazy, clever, selfish, and skeptical, Louis XVIII (1815–1824) wanted to be the king not of a party but of the whole of France. Yet, in the words of a contemporary, France housed "two peoples that differed in their memories, their habits and ideas and that could not understand each other. Two armies had fought one against the other, of which one celebrated as victories what the other deplored as defeats." The Constitutional Charter which Louis *granted* his people was meant to appease these dissensions. In some ways it heightened them. Resting on an electoral franchise determined by property qualification and by age, it added new divisions to those the Revolution had already created: not only between republicans and royalists, revolutionaries and *émigrés,* but now between supporters of a restricted franchise and those of a wider one, between young and old, rich and poor, set apart not only by wealth or age but by political definitions. A law which allowed men— provided that they paid sufficient taxes to qualify—to vote at thirty and run for office at forty, excluded the majority of grownups born after 1789, turned the political into a generational struggle with a vengeance, and went some way to explain the *mal du siècle* which affected young men avid for action and deprived of it.

All this would last not only through the reign of Louis's younger brother, Charles X (1824–1830)—a better man but a foolish ruler, a bigot rooted in a past he would not shed;* but through that of Louis Philippe (1830–1848), who only slightly altered the Charter and lowered the property qualification to double the electorate. There would be 300,000 electors in 1848, where there had been 90,000 in the 1820's, nearly 200,000 in the 1830's. An improvement, but only slightly so. There would, under Louis and Charles, be honest government, material order, and no financial finagling. There would even, at first, be relief among the young, like Lamartine and Victor Hugo, whom the heavy hand of the Emperor had stifled. But that did not last long, and disappeared entirely after the revolution of 1830, when young people were expected to know their place and innovators were accepted only when they were profitable or dead. Restlessness and growing agitation followed, at first among the propertied classes which felt they had votes but no political power, then, after 1830, when men of property came into their own, among the pettier bourgeoisie, coming up for their turn, and among the poorer classes squeezed hard by those in power. Behind it all there loomed a growing shadow, Bonapartism: the memory of Napoleon. First, in secret societies like the *Carbonari,* recruited among the students, soldiers, tradesmen, then, after 1830, becoming a kind of official cult with the return of Napoleon's remains in 1840, and an open threat (though not a serious one) with the attempted coups of the Emperor's nephew, Louis-Napoleon, in 1836 and 1840.

But Bonapartism remained for a long time only a latent force. Politics would be fought out between a Right and Left, each one divided into moderates and radicals. The King's opponents ran from the liberals— bourgeois and noble like Lafayette, future supporters of the Orléans monarchy—to Bonapartists and republicans. Among the King's supporters were the *ultras*—ultra-royalist—who referred to the arguments of Joseph de Maistre, for whom authority must finally rest on force and the executioner be acknowledged the foundation of the state, and of Bonald, for whom kings are made by God to govern men, so men must

---

* "There is only Monsieur de Lafayette and I who have not changed since 1789," he once declared.

obey kings and kings the Pope, who is God's first representative. Such extremities did not please the King or his more moderate supporters, who did not really like to hear the Archbishop of Paris refer to Christ as "the legitimate heir to the Judean throne." They felt that against the hostile bourgeoisie, the best policy was not to encourage those who wanted to re-establish a tighter parody of the old regime but to unite the ends against the middle: let the first class lean upon the last, let aristocracy gain popular support against the middle classes. This would not happen and the Revolution of 1830 was the revolt of middle classes kept out of politics against a crown which had not known how to secure the allegiance of its people.

A Restoration rests upon the revolution which it follows. Either it defines itself in contradiction to it, as the *ultras* wished, or else, as Louis proposed, it seeks to reconcile the order it represents with that evolved, evoked, by the revolution. In terms of personnel, a good few revolutionaries were integrated in the new regime.* But not enough of them and not for long. Under Charles X, the old nobility was largely in the saddle and Charles' last minister, the Duke of Polignac, believed he had been vouchsafed a special revelation from the Virgin Mary about his task. Only in 1830 did the men who had grown rich and influential after 1789 come into their own, and perhaps that is one reason why 1830 had to happen.

In terms of property a kind of settlement was managed. The question of national property—not that of the church but that seized by revolutionary governments from *émigrés*—threatened to rend the nation. Returning *émigrés* looked on their lost property as a hereditary and sacred right of which they had been deprived. Its buyers, peasants and bourgeoisie, felt that property was a social issue, defined by law and justified by labor and by action. A new capitalist class had arisen, whose fortunes were deeply involved in this matter. In Balzac's novel, old Grandet starts out as a master cooper on the eve of the Revolution, marries the daughter of a wealthy lumber merchant, uses her dowry and his savings to buy confiscated property, becomes a mayor and builds some fine roads to his farms which are assessed to pay low taxes, invests his capital in loans at usurious rates, discounts bills at frightful interest, buys a castle and the land of a local noble who has financial difficulties, puts some of his money in state annuities at 3 per cent and some in barrels, finally dies in 1827 leaving his daughter a multimillionaire. Grandet was only the image of real capitalist figures: farmers like the Thomassins of Pontoise, who under Louis XVI farmed 560 acres but owned only eight of them, who bought 185 more when national property was

---

* Chateaubriand has described Talleyrand's appearance in Louis XVIII's antechamber, when he saw "enter silently vice leaning on the arm of crime, Monsieur de Talleyrand walking supported by Monsieur Fouché; the infernal vision passed slowly before me . . ."

Liberty Leading the People, by Eugène Delacroix. For once the romantic image reflects contemporary romantic imagination.

being sold and 375 further acres in 1822; merchants like the Danse of Beauvais: tenant farmers in the sixteenth century, merchant dyers in the seventeenth century, important traders in the eighteenth century, ennobled magistrates under Louis XVI, great buyers of national land under the Revolution, magistrates and deputies under the July Monarchy; or, again, the Peugeots of Montbéliard, farmers in the fifteenth century, innkeepers in the seventeenth, millers in the eighteenth, who bought national goods, built a cotton mill in 1805, abandoned textiles for metal production in 1832, when they began to make swords, crinoline hoops, corset stays, and (appropriately) umbrella frames.

Such people had legally bought lands, some of which had lain neglected or ill-cultivated, and had worked them for twenty years. They were not going to let them be taken away from them and, if Louis XVIII had not guaranteed that sales of national property would be respected, he would never have been restored. However, the *émigrés* wanted compensation. National lands still left unsold were restored; but few were left and few benefited from this measure. Finally, in the 1820's, an indemnity was granted to the dispossessed—the *"milliard des émigrés"* at whose cost the Revolution was confirmed, the transfer of property accepted, and the notion that property was anything but a legal and social right (or fiction) denied forever.

But this important settlement which set property owners' minds at rest, contributed to the rising criticism of the regime. The millions of the *émigrés* was one more stick to beat the government with. Especially under Charles X, who tried to rule by principle rather than conciliation, tensions got worse. The power of the church was getting too obtrusive. Over three-quarters of the professors in royal colleges, nearly half the directors of communal schools, were in holy orders. Stringent ordinances threatened "blasphemy." Altogether, there were too many old men in power, or too many men representing old ideas. Should government represent the king, or the majority in the Chamber? The crown sought to assert its supremacy over the elected representatives of the nation. In 1830, the dispute came to a head. First, Polignac's government sought to muzzle the opposition press by new laws, but they were rejected by the Chamber of Peers. Paris illuminated for joy; and an observer remarked that, however bright the illumination, it would not be enough to enlighten the ministers. He was right, and the elections of 1830 returned a liberal majority which promised trouble. On July 26, Polignac published four ordinances dissolving the newly elected Chamber and altering press and election rules to the disadvantage of the liberals. The streets filled with barricades. "Three days sufficed to overturn one throne and make all others tremble." When they were over, the Bourbons had departed never to return and France had a new king: Louis-Philippe of the junior, Orléans, branch of the royal family.

After 1830

Monarchy New Style

The Charter was revised to affirm the principle of national sovereignty; the church was placed back on Napoleonic terms defining the Catholic creed, once more, only as that "of the majority of Frenchmen"; censorship and extraordinary courts were abolished; the age of electors and candidates to office was lowered; the monarch was called king no longer *of France,* but *of the French;* the white flag was replaced with the tricolor and the royal lilies with the Gallic rooster. Monarchy henceforth was a contract, which Louis-Philippe swore he would observe.

The echoes of the July Revolution were heard far afield. Even in Stockholm there was political unrest and a slump in trade. In Germany, many like the young poet Heinrich Heine had longed for something like it: "Lafayette, the tricolor, the *Marseillaise,* it intoxicates me!" Liberals stirred and rulers were frightened into concessions, constitutions, and press laws, which they would hasten to withdraw as soon as the revolutionary danger passed. In Italy, Parma, Modena, and Rome rose up against their antediluvian rulers. The Swiss cantons replaced the reactionary administration of local aristocracies with more liberal constitutions, ensuring equality before the law, rights of free expression, and asserting popular sovereignty. Far away, in Poland, a nationalist revolt sought to free the country from its Russian masters. All Europe stirred, moved by the French example, hoping for French aid. But no aid was forthcoming. The French were eager to reassure the other powers; and Louis-Philippe stood by while the Holy Alliance reasserted its hold from the Vistula to the Tiber.

Only in Belgium did a rising sparked by the news from France achieve its end. There, the settlement of 1815 had placed the southern provinces under the king of Holland whose rule, though economically advantageous, caused serious friction—especially on religious grounds. Belgian Catholics and liberals agreed that they wanted to be free from Holland and independent. On August 30, 1830, a performance of Auber's opera, *La Muette de Portici,* with its portrayal of Neapolitans rebelling against Spanish rule, set off rioting in Brussels which grew into a war of national liberation from the Dutch. In the case of Belgium, French and British interests coincided, support was forthcoming, and before the year was over an independent monarchy had been set up. The Belgian Constitution of 1831 would prove the most liberal in Europe, founded on popular sovereignty and guaranteeing all the revolutionary freedoms which seem quite commonplace today: of press and public meeting, worship and education.

Whether in Belgium or in France, the new style monarchy, while more liberal, remained a contract between men of property (or perhaps, explicitly became one). Louis-Philippe of France has been called the last of the enlightened despots, and he was certainly enlightened in terms of the eighteenth century which had formed him, along with the Revolution in whose armies he had served. Cultivated, avaricious, opportunistic, brave, the new king set out to portray the ideal citizen ruler, a bourgeois among bourgeois, a money man among plutocrats, a manager among a managerial oligarchy.

The French National Guard was revived, so that the middle class in arms could defend the new regime. It needed defending. 1830 had scared the bourgeoisie. The years that followed scared it more. The urban masses had made the Revolution only to be cheated of its benefits. Where aristocrats had ruled, the rich now took their place. Louis-Philippe's first prime minister was a banker, Laffitte; his greatest prime minister for half his reign was François Guizot, whose advice to youth was to become rich by work and savings in order to qualify for the vote.

Guizot defined the middle class as "a class which does not live on wages, which has in its life and thought freedom and leisure, which can devote a considerable part of its time to public affairs" and which is equally removed from past privileges and "from the class dedicated to manual trades." Those who lived on wages and by manual trades objected. France was beginning to feel the impact of industrial changes. Paris was still a city of craftsmen and artisans, manufacturers and home workers, but factories were beginning to spread. By 1840, 2,000 steam engines were in use; by 1847, 5,000. By 1850, 2,000 miles of railroad track had been laid down, and railroad. workers and mechanics would be noticeable on the barricades of 1848. Bread riots were being replaced by wage demands and strikes, while, behind the political publications of the middle classes, the voice of workers, of their organizations and publications, began to be heard.

The lot of industrial workers was not easy. The social dislocations and the misery that we have seen in England obtained in France as well. In the first decade of the reign the number of suicides increased 50 per cent, mostly among the poor. The number of foundlings, cared for in public institutions, had trebled between 1784 and 1830, and it continued to grow. Alcoholism was becoming a major social scourge. A long series of workers' risings speckled Paris and the provinces with blood; in eighteen years of rule there were seventeen attempts on the life of the King.

But the peasants were quiet. As long as the middle class put their trust in Louis-Philippe, the regime was safe. It had found its perfect representative in François Guizot (1787–1874), son of a protestant victim of the Terror, educated at Geneva, admirer of Bentham and Malthus and Adam Smith, translator of Gibbon and Shakespeare, cultivated, confident, austere, the very type of the *grand bourgeois* "grown rich by work and saving." Between 1840 and 1848 Guizot ruled France for the King and for his own kind, on the principle that the duty of government is to maintain social order. Tocqueville noted that the new, bourgeois rulers of France were "active, industrious, often dishonest, limited in outlook, rash at times through vanity or egoism, fearful by temperament, moderate in everything, except in a liking for prosperity and the mediocre." It looked as if that mediocrity and rule of the commonplace which Tocqueville had noted in his travels through the American democracy were spreading across the world. As for France herself, Louis-Philippe's government appeared "like a business company, all the operations of which were undertaken in view of the profit which would accrue to the shareholders."

When, in 1842, a slight electoral reform was proposed, Guizot opposed it: "All the great conquests are made, all the great interests are satisfied." Liberty had been won; order must now guarantee that liberty. Without order, there could be no freedom to act, to speak, to possess—especially to possess—when property was the ideal and reward of the age: "The goal and the reward of labor and probity, the most precious pledge of the spirit of order and stability," as the *Journal de Lille* would say on March 28, 1844. Stability was the watchword and, hence, resistance to change. This was a mistake. France's political system, as Fr. Bertier de Sauvigny has pointed out, was like a pyramid stood on its point, hence unstable. A broader base might well have reinforced it. While good times lasted the system endured. But around 1846, depression came, bad harvests, overproduction in industry, falling prices, collapse of rash railroad enterprises, a million men thrown out of work.

In their industrial struggles, the workers had learned to organize. Now

One of the national workshops under Louis Blanc. When few could read, newspapers were heard rather than scanned. But how much work was actually done there?

they were listening to political and social theories directed to their own political problems. There was François Raspail (1794–1878), a working doctor and researcher who helped found microchemistry and whom his contact with the poor persuaded that social reforms were more important than political ones; that if the rich would not help the poor, the poor must help themselves. Raspail advocated manhood suffrage, progressive taxes, and prison reform, as measures of social hygiene; and, he added, if need be, revolution too. There was Louis Blanc (1811–1882), who did not believe that self-help, the movements sponsored by Raspail, the co-operatives or collective organizations, could succeed by themselves and advocated state control of banks, railroads, insurance, and heavy industry, along with aid to labor. The best way for the state to aid the workers was by setting up co-operative social workshops. And these ideas Blanc set out in a book, *The Organization of Labor* (1839), which caught the workers' imagination. Last but not least there was Louis Auguste Blanqui (1805–1881), a professional revolutionist.* Tocqueville, when he saw him in 1848, found him to have the appearance of a moldy corpse which had passed its life in a sewer and had just left it. Blanqui was persuaded that the struggle for power between classes was unavoidable and could only be settled by an armed insurrection.

Uneasy Interlude

Belgium, Switzerland, and France apart, however, the revolutionary outbreaks of 1830 had been repressed by 1831 and the brief scare only reinforced the machinery of reaction. The crisis confirmed the fears and tightened the bonds of eastern autocrats threatened by events, and showed that the interests of autocracy were the same, whether in Warsaw or in Milan. Here was proof that Russia and Austria must stand together, confirmation for Metternich's view that their dissensions could only bring revolution in their train. But the new agreement between Rus-

* It was his pen that coined two potent concepts: Industrial Revolution and Dictatorship of the Proletariat.

sia and Austria raised the danger that they would set about solving the Turkish problem by themselves, much as the Polish problem had been solved before. What England wanted was to preserve the *status quo*, not have her continental rivals expand; and England's eastern policy would maintain this into the 1850's.

1830, said Victor Hugo, was a revolution that only went halfway. But, if the defeats or disappointments of 1830 held up the progress of revolution, they also confirmed it. To hold up is sometimes to uphold, and none could gainsay that in its crabbed and thrifty way the bourgeois monarchy of Louis Philippe fulfilled most of the dreams of 1789. So did the model constitutional government of Leopold in Belgium, a rule which soon made the Saxe-Coburg prince the mentor of constitutional-minded Europeans, not least of his English niece—Victoria.

By that time, constitutions were becoming quite familiar. Sweden had obtained one in 1809, Spain in 1812 (suppressed and re-established several times until it came to stay in the 1830's), Norway, Holland, Portugal, and a number of German states had proclaimed their own; and the 1830's would see more appear. But all representative institutions rested on a narrow franchise, and, constitution or no, the great contest of the 1830's and the forties would be between the idea that numbers are sovereign and the majority should rule, and the traditional concept of government by some kind of elite: of birth or money, property or talent. The difference between the autocratic monarchies of the east and the representative and constitutional ones of the west was immense, but it was a difference of degree. In both, political expression was legally restricted to a narrow section of society—40,000 Belgians out of 4 million, 300,000 Frenchmen out of 29 million, 620,000 Englishmen out of 16.5 million—between 1 and 3 per cent of the population. Only in the distant United States was there any approach to universal manhood suffrage. Only in Switzerland and France would this appear in 1848.

Yet these tiny groups of men who ruled by right of birth or money sought to hold the line against contenders pressing from below, and saw their problems largely in the light of squabbles with rival minority groups claiming access to political expression. Metternich knew better. Perhaps England could introduce partial change and then hold the line. No one else could afford to crack open a gate through which change was bound to rush in overwhelming force, a force the more destructive since it was more social than political. He wrote to his opposite number in France, Louis-Philippe's prime minister François Guizot, that the game of politics seemed inadequate to the needs of the time. He was right. Not political but social reforms were needed. Yet political reforms loomed so large in the mind of potential revolutionaries that when the revolution came again, in 1848, they thought of and sought for little else.

Chapter 13

THE BALANCE

OF THE POWERS

Spain

The eighteenth century was Spain's Indian summer, between the decay of the last Habsburgs and the ravages of war followed by political anarchy. Philip V (1700–1746) was no genius, but vastly superior to his Habsburg predecessors. He and his French advisers introduced Colbertian economic views and French administrative methods, fostered and protected new industries, did their best to remove at least some barriers to internal trade and some of the particularist privileges that hampered enterprise. With all their shortcomings, the first Bourbon kings gave Spain the best government since Philip II: economic recovery, industrial progress, technological innovation. Spain's population doubled to nearly 11 million, her army grew from 20,000 to 100,000, her fleet increased from 20 to 300 ships, her treasury advanced from bankruptcy to comfort. The late eighteenth century saw the American empire reach its greatest extent and prosperity, its population increasing with its riches, revenues rising sixfold in the century, while mines turned out half of the world's stock of precious metals. We should not forget that Mexico was still the major city of the western hemisphere and that Spanish San Francisco was being founded about the time when on the other coast the British colonists were asserting their independence.

Philip's eldest son, Ferdinand (1746–1759), continued his work. His reign ended on an unfortunate note when, in 1758, the death of his queen drove him from melancholy into depression. The King shut himself up, refused to shave or change his clothes, attacked the servants, tried to hang himself with the bed sheets or strangle himself with nap-

565

kins, and would in his lucid intervals talk only about his illness, which was being treated with ass's milk, quinine, white decoction of Sydenham, heartshorn jelly, along with fresh vipers and cordials for strength.

In 1759 Ferdinand died and was succeeded by his younger brother, Charles III (1759–1788), the very model of an eighteenth-century ruler, great hunter and devoted administrator. Royal manufactures were founded or encouraged, roads and canals were built, trading companies allowed to be set up on the Bay of Biscay and in Catalonia; economic and patriotic societies were founded to regild the tarnished honor of productive work. The Spanish upswing came most markedly in that last third of the eighteenth century when France was in the doldrums. Catalonia, where the cotton industry employed some 80,000 workers, was second only to England in its production and exports of cotton wares. An English traveler of the 1780's found Barcelona remarkably industrialized and booming. The province was a great exporter of wine and brandy—so great that the world price of brandy was practically set in Catalonia in the eighteenth century.

Yet these political and administrative changes seem to have affected society but little. The census of 1787 found one landowner among every thirty-five peasants: the north—Basques, Navarrese, Catalans—had many farmer-owners and so had the Huerta country of Valencia, though most of them were only dwarf smallholders. But elsewhere farmers starved, stifled by tithes and dues, on vast estates, half of them lying fallow. As late as 1840, when the French writer Théophile Gautier visited Spain and found it charming, there was no sense that either bourgeoisie or working class had really grown out of a century's travail.

The crown found its servants among hidalgos—that is, the petty gentry, sometimes almost commoners. The Spanish census of 1787 gave a figure of nearly 500,000 for the hidalgo and noble population, which might be compared with some 400,000 nobles in France, a country with more than twice the Spanish population. Many hidalgos, of course, were very poor; some were not distinguishable from commoners, especially where they could be found working as weavers, masons, or cowherds, or begging in the streets. In 1773, a royal rescript announced that hidalgos could engage in crafts without derogation. In 1783 the problem was attacked from the other end, and crafts like tanner, carpenter, smith, tailor, shoemaker, and several others were specifically declared to be honorable, so that those who engaged in them could hold noble rank or be elected to municipal office.

In Spain, as in Italy or in Russia, the struggle for political change was going to take place within the nobility not against it, between aristocracy based on land and lower groups based on government service. The professional classes played only a minor role and were ill-equipped to do better. Weak and ill-respected, lacking an economic base, they were forced to take double jobs. Schoolmasters, who were quite numerous, had to earn their living as gamekeepers or public letter-writers. At the other extreme of the social scale, the grandees, though quite useless, were much in evidence. Their strength lay in the lands they owned; and in the late eighteenth century four great families owned about one-third of all the cultivable land of Spain. The vast entailed *latifundia* were owned by absentees who lived at court or in the cities, *rentiers* who seldom improved and never sold their entailed domains. With so little land coming on the market, its price would be too high for would-be peasant or capitalist buyers. Short-term leases brought in high rents, but also discouraged improvements.

Innovation Blunted

New French currents found expression in the patriotic economic societies which sprang up in the provincial towns, sponsoring schools, agricultural innovation, scientific research, and publicizing their ideas in public debates and prize-giving speeches. But men who posed as *philosophes* when traveling in France remained good Catholics and quite traditionalist in Spain. The last sorcerer was handed over by the Inquisition to the secular arm to be burnt at Seville in 1781. The Inquisition would be definitely suppressed only in 1834. Some grandees brought up their children according to the precepts of Rousseau and engaged in scientific experiments, but new influences had but a shallow hold. Society remained lethargic, formal, and dull. "I do not conceive it possible for any great city to be duller and less agreable than Madrid," wrote the British ambassador, William Eden. At the very end of the century, the Duke of Arcos had 3,000 servants, paid little or nothing, ill-lodged and ill-fed, mostly to do nothing. The Duke of Medina-Celi spent 12,000 reals a day on the upkeep of his dependents. The Duchess of Benavente hired the Italian composer Luigi Boccherini to conduct her private orchestra at a thousand reals a month, bought Goya's *Los Caprichos* in 1799 for 1,500 reals, when that same year the average daily pay of workers in the capital was six or seven reals. One pound of old beef cost twelve reals, one pound of pork cost fifteen reals, one pound of bread cost three reals, one pound of chocolate cost five reals, one pound of sugar cost four reals. A shepherd earned a maximum of 160 reals a year, supplemented by two loaves of bread a day. An Andalusian day-laborer got three to four reals a day, when he was employed. The Spanish held that "there are more days than sausages," and indeed the staple food was often bread rubbed with garlic and dipped in oil, rye pancakes, along with onions, leeks, pimentos; and the diet got more Spartan the further south one went. The peasants used woden plows, the backbreaking sickle rather than the scythe, and threshed their grain with flails on earthen floors. Blast furnaces fed on wood. Wheat from Palencia, about 150 miles from the port of

Santander, cost twice as much in Cadiz as wheat shipped from France, where better roads facilitated transport. In the royal college of Madrid, in 1745, serious examination questions invited students to consider the causes and meaning of blood showers, and asked when bells should be rung to avert storm and hail. The French ambassador to Madrid summed up the Spain of 1759 as behind all other countries by at least two centuries.

On the industrial plane, production, even expanded, was insufficient to satisfy all needs. Even handkerchiefs (some with the portrait of famous matadors) came from Manchester. This meant that the demand for goods continued to be met from outside sources, especially in the Empire overseas, whose economy was rapidly expanding, and which looked ever more to British supplies to fill needs with which the home country could not cope. Eventually, this inability to supply the Empire, along with the insistence that its markets should still be subject to mercantilist controls, would lose Latin America altogether and, with it, precious revenues. But first the enlightened political and economic ideas which affected Spain in its higher reaches had to percolate into the colonies.

The standard-bearer of enlightenment was a monk and professor of theology, Benito Gerónimo Feyjóo y Montenegro (1676–1764), whose writings, published between 1726 and 1760 introduced Spaniards to all the ideas they had so long ignored. "The works of this man," wrote a contemporary, "produced a useful fermentation, they made us begin to doubt, they made known other books very different from those that were in the country, they aroused curiosity and opened to reason the door which had been closed by indolence and false knowledge . . . for they are in the hands of everyone." Orderly thought, logical progression, suspension of judgment until evidence brought an answer, concern for truth and public utility, were the new ideas and approaches that Feyjoo preached, subject always to the restraints and discipline of Christian faith. Philip, Ferdinand, Charles, all encouraged the spread of Feyjóo's works and Ortega y Gasset insists that, as a result, the eighteenth century would be the least Spanish of Spain's history.

But the new ideas were a thin veneer. The people stayed Spanish, that is, they stayed put, opposing all change. Inertia was their sole defense against an ever-hostile world, and a French visitor of 1782 found the peasants, above all others, abiding by "the absolute principle of always doing what had been done before and in exactly the same way." The ignorant peasant, the elegant officer, the son of a noble or a bourgeois, differed in style of life but seldom in line of thought: they all shared the same submission to authority, lack of private judgment or internal life, the same credulousness, superficiality, hidebound narrow-mindedness, fed on absurd romances and almanacs.

> He who reads Feyjóo
> And he who translates the French
> He who wears a frock coat
> Heretic!

was a refrain still hummed in the Madrid of early nineteenth century. The enlightened *afrancesados* were un-Spanish. On one hand we have acts without ideas, on the other, ideas without acts.

The church was probably the most democratic institution in the country, the greatest employer of labor, the greatest dispenser of charity, providing also a career open to the talented, so that a charcoal-burner's son could become the primate of Spain. But it would and could accept no ideas, rejected all liberal reforms, ruined their educational plans. The Spanish paradox was that liberals were elitist and unpopular, the church popular and obscurantist. Free trade in land and goods, which reformers advocated, suited the better-off but not the peasants or the poor. The poor looked to the church, on whose doles they depended. The life and property of cathedral towns turned around it; regular priests, close to the people, were poor and respected; the hierarchy was narrow-minded but strong. There would be no anticlericalism in Spain until the 1820's, and then this would be confined largely to the towns. Over one-third of the books and pamphlets published in 1784 and 1785 dealt with religious subjects; but religion, like the world, was still viewed in medieval terms. The French Dominicans who took refuge in Spain in the 1790's and were kindly received by their Spanish fellows could not help remarking that they had stepped out of eighteenth-century France into fourteenth-century Spain.

This was the country to which Charles IV (1788–1808) fell heir, and whose dimly enlightened rulers sealed it off so tight from events beyond the Pyrenees that a French priest seeking refuge in an Aragonese town at the end of 1792 found everyone in complete ignorance of the French Revolution.

Spain and the Modern World

Peace with France in 1795 allowed the spread of the disturbing news, but with little effect beyond the colonies of foreign merchants and artisans in places like Cadiz and Barcelona. A liberal "patriot" movement developed within the narrow limits of French influence. More important, a struggle for power was shaping up between the heir to the throne, Prince Ferdinand, and Manuel Godoy (1767–1851), his parents' favorite and ruling minister. In 1808, riots organized by Ferdinand's friends chased Godoy from power and forced the King to abdicate. Ferdinand VII succeeded to the throne, which he hoped to hold with

French support. Napoleon had other plans. He wanted the Spanish throne for his brother Joseph. Ferdinand was tricked and hustled into abdicating in his turn, and French occupation troops brought a new king whom his Spanish subjects lost no time in nicknaming *Pepe Botella* ("Joe the Bottle").

The French army had no difficulty in routing Spain's regular forces. But Napoleon's miscalculation turned the loutish Ferdinand into a symbol of national resistance. Friction with French occupation troops rubbed patriotic feelings raw, exacerbated native xenophobia, and precipitated an insurrection of the most popular kind—a rising in which liberal patriots found themselves thrown together with conservatives and army generals, while fierce priests led peasant guerrillas to fight for King and Christ. Resistance was backed by British support. Relentless guerrillas, well-adapted to the land, kept the occupant stretched out and tensed beyond his capacities. Only moderately effective, the guerrilla did nevertheless encourage Spanish patriotism and ease the task of Wellington's regular soldiers. It also left a heritage of lawlessness behind, reinforced revolutionary mentality, glorified violent political action, encouraged the tendency of military men to grab for power as and when they could.

While this went on, a representative assembly had found refuge at the extremity of the peninsula, in Cadiz, where, in 1812, it wrote a constitution for Spain which would enshrine the principles of the enlightenment: national unity, national sovereignty, equality before the law, proportional taxation, property rights—the very things that Joseph was trying to impose from his uneasy Madrid throne. But that was not what Spaniards died for. As Wellington insisted later, Spain "is the only country where two and two do not make four." The war the Spaniards fought, Napoleon thought, was a war of monks: and when in 1814 Ferdinand returned, the people shouted "Long live the absolute King!" "Down with the constitution!"

Ferdinand asked no better. He put an end to liberal experiments and reintroduced the despotism of yore. Spain was bankrupt. The restoration could neither reward the victors nor conciliate the vanquished. It lacked the means for either, let alone for both, as had happened in France. So the liberals lost their places, and the soldiers were ill-paid or not paid at all. American silver could solve the problems of the state, but the Hispanic American colonies were in turmoil and the bankrupt state could not summon up the power to lay its hands on the silver without which it remained insolvent and ineffective. The discontented army, assembled to suppress rebellion in the American colonies, made the revolution of 1820, revived the constitution of 1812, but lost its chance of popular support by clashing with the church, which disapproved equally of constitutions and revolutions. The French reappeared in Spain (1823), this time to liberate Ferdinand, who was practically a

The Execution of the Rioters, May 3, 1808, by Francisco Goya. On both sides, the savagery of despair. Prado, Madrid.

prisoner in his palace. Blessed by the church and cheered by the Spanish people, they crushed the liberals and the soldiers, who stood up no better to the guns of Louis XVIII than they had to those of Napoleon.

The King now proceeded to sow the seeds of future trouble by excluding his brother and heir, Don Carlos, from the succession in favor of his daughter Isabella (1833–1868). When Ferdinand died in 1833, he left behind him a foreign widow of doubtful reputation and a three-year-old heiress whom a section of the nation, persuaded that Don Carlos was the rightful heir, would not acknowledge. This ushered in a long succession conflict.

Don Carlos drew his support from the rural provinces of the north, where the church was strongest and provincial sentiment most intense. The Carlist rebellion became the struggle of the unadapted and inadaptable against the modern world, their primitive royalism opposing the centralist liberalism of Madrid. The conflict soon turned into a struggle between liberalism and reaction. Both the Queen-Regent, Maria Christina, and Don Carlos were absolutists, but Carlos's reliance on conservative provinces forced the Queen into an alliance with the liberals and the loyalist army.

In 1836, to finance the costly struggle, church property would be nationalized, anticlericalism become identified with progressivism: monasteries became factories, ministries, prisons, or barracks, or gave way to new streets and urban improvement schemes, while church lands were bought up by rich farmers and speculators. The press was freed, generals came to dominate politics by pronunciamento, power passed into the soldiers' hands and those of local bosses, many of whom could declare, as one general did on his deathbed, that he had no enemies to forgive because he had killed them all. Pending claims to direct power, the military became arbiters of politics, by providing or withholding protection for civilian governments. By 1839, Carlist guerrilla activity had collapsed into brigandage, and would continue as such into the 1860's, surviving chiefly as a loyalist, clerical, and reactionary tradition that could be revived in 1936.

Spain came out of the trial as a very inefficient but liberal and mercantile society. Entails had been abolished, the gild system abandoned in 1834, the *Mesta* in 1839; a real bourgeoisie was taking shape along with modern industry, even labor unrest was appearing in cities, along with middle-class radicalism, while Inquisition, censorship, and absolutism had passed away. Spain was still backward, still romantic, but open at last to the modern world.

Latin-American Independence

One other change that the nineteenth century brought was the loss of Spain's erstwhile empire in South America and the emancipation of most of her colonies.

Across the South Atlantic a vast empire had grown up in the two centuries since the *conquistadores,* with cities finer and wealthier by far than those of the mother countries, with presses, schools, universities, and riches which kept the finances of Spain and Portugal afloat. All this was realative, of course. Life for the whites throughout the Spanish Indies was probably better than for their counterparts in Spain; but society rested on the exploitation of native labor, made milder and more bearable only by the slackness and inefficiency of the exploiters.

Until mid-eighteenth century, neglect and fraud, corruption, petty tyranny, rapacious and unscrupulous administrators, produced backwardness and almost anarchy. Spanish officials battened on native-born *creoles,* the *creoles* on Indians and on mixed-breed *mestizos,* all of them part of a stiff dog-eat-dog heirarchy. An official report of 1749 did not mince its words: "The countries of the Indies, fertile, rich and flourishing, . . . governed by persons who often regard no interests but their own . . . are now reduced to such a condition . . . that justice has no authority and reason no power to make any stand against disorder and vice." One of the great bones of contention between France and Britain was the *asiento*—the right to supply the Spanish colonies with slaves—which Britain held until 1739 and France enjoyed on and off after the 1740's. But the Spanish government was always jealous of granting privileges which it wanted for its own Iberian subjects, and which the latter were seldom able to use properly. The colonists could not get supplies, manufactures, especially slaves, from Spanish sources; and Spain would not allow them to get them from others legally. Contraband flourished and, in the end, colonial protection collapsed under the battering of the smugglers. "Spain kept the cow, while Europe drank the milk."

Charles III tried to improve matters, appointing more efficient administrators and introducing some reforms, such as free trade among the different colonies of the Indies. As usual, the reforming measures came too late—when they were felt at all. A more efficient administration disturbed the *creoles* used to the bad old ways, and created the paradox of an absolute monarchy more liberal in some ways than the subjects it ruled—subjects who read Montesquieu and Voltaire, owned and maltreated slaves, claimed for themselves the rights they would not concede to others.

Visiting South America at the end of the eighteenth century, the German naturalist Alexander von Humboldt noted that "the most miserable European without education and without intellectual cultivation, thinks himself superior to the whites born in the new continent." As for the *creoles,* they thought of themselves as Americans, not Spaniards, and the reforms of Charles III, which included the formation of a colonial militia to improve defense, a militia in which *creoles* could satisfy ambitions frustrated elsewhere, increased their economic power and their yearning for the political rights which Spanish officials clutched so tightly. The Enlightenment was affecting both landed gentry and rising bourgeoisie; schools, periodicals, economic societies modeled after the Spanish ones, returning travelers and arriving officials, all spread ideas hostile to imperial restrictions and social humiliations. Even the economy which Empire free trade helped to flourish, created a demand for the international trade that was still prohibited.

The colonists became increasingly vocal in opposing the monopolistic policies of the old colonial system. They saw that in North America political emancipation had brought economic emancipation in its train. The thought that they too might follow the example of the northerners affected officers and landowners like the Venezuelans Francisco Miranda (1750?–1816) and Simón Bolívar (1783–1830), or the Argentine José San Martín (1778–1850), who read Rousseau, the physiocrats, and the *Encyclopedia.* In 1787, even a Brazilian whom Jefferson met in France dreamed and talked of obtaining United States support for Brazilian independence. When Charles III died in 1788, when fear of revolution hardened the heart and arteries of Spanish administration, when the old order reappeared, lethargic, venal, and oppressive, the newly awakened natives were bound to assert themselves.

All colonies depend on metropolitan—that is, home-country—arms for defense, on metropolitan goods which they cannot produce themselves or obtain elsewhere, on inertia and routine for allegiance, which will last as long as habit and lack of alternative persist. This arrangement, which had served Spain well enough, collapsed during the wars of the French Revolution. The war, beginning in 1796, cut off the colonists from the homeland, forcing the former to rely on themselves and on the foreign traders who had until then been dealt with only illegally. English and United States shipping sailed into the gap not to be dislodged again. Meanwhile, loyalty foundered before the problems which arose in Spain: should loyal Spaniards obey Ferdinand, or Joseph, or the dubious *junta* at Cadiz?

Risings and anarchy marked the years after 1808, until metropolitan rule could be restored again in 1815. But Ferdinand was paralyzed by new revolts at home and the *creoles* would not accept the restoration of the old monopolies. Brazil, whose population in 1800 equaled that of Portugal, had in 1808 welcomed the royal family fleeing before the armies of Napoleon. Rio had become a capital, in 1815 the capital of an autonomous kingdom, in 1821 that of an independent empire ruled by the son and heir of the Portuguese king. The Brazilian example proved infectious. The *creoles* too called for autonomy. They rose again in 1816, this time gaining the support of the local church which, after 1820, feared the effects of liberalism in Spain. The United States and Britain supported the insurgents, and their refusal to allow effective European intervention against them combined with Spain's own impotence meant that, by 1824, only Cuba and Puerto Rico would be left over from Spain's great American empire. Each of the several states that had sprung out of it had ports and cities to equip and build, agriculture to develop, armies to supply and train, all welcome openings to northern bankers, entrepreneurs, and shippers, first British, then French and German, at last also North Americans. A vast new market now lay open to the enterprise of the maritime trading powers.

Indeed, Spanish and Portuguese America would be the stage on which the modern variant of economic imperialism first appeared because colonial imperialism of the traditional kind would be excluded from them—at least for a long time—by the effects of President James Monroe's declaration of 1823. The American's gesture had been precipitated by specific events. The British Foreign Secretary, George Canning, at loggerheads with the Holy Allies and unwilling to see Ferdinand VII re-established in his American colonies, proposed an anti-interventionist Anglo-American declaration. President Monroe preferred to speak for the United States alone, and he was probably prompted as much by fears of Russian expansion along the north Pacific coast as by the plans of the Holy Alliance powers. His message warned all European powers against further colonial ventures in this hemisphere, and also against any attempt to interfere with the revolted Spanish colonies of the South.

Received with enthusiasm in the United States, his words fell rather

flat in Europe, where the British Navy was recognized as the real deterrent to interventionism. Yet, though it meant very little until mid-
century and beyond, the declaration was a momentous act. Reformulating
the isolationist doctrines George Washington had first expressed, it
marked the beginnings of a truly independent, American, diplomacy in
the hemisphere. Behind the shield of the Royal Navy, what became
known as the Monroe Doctrine allowed South Americans to fight one
another almost exclusively, without having to fear the Europeans too.
It also laid the ground for eventual northern domination when, late in
the nineteenth century, the doctrine ceased to be used to keep Europeans out and began rather to justify United States interventions and
annexations. But none of this was known in 1823; nor did George Canning suspect the future that would grow out of his initiative when he
boasted to the House of Commons that he had "called the New World
into existence to redress the balance of the old."

Italy

A Congeries of States

Twenty-odd dialects, a score of cities on every one of which the life
of a province turned, no roads worth the name, a congeries of states,
and a variety of regimes: royal in Savoy and Naples, republican in Venice, Genoa, and Lucca, papal in Rome, ducal in Tuscany and Parma,
Austrian in Milan and Lombardy—such was eighteenth-century Italy,
the garden of Europe, a mild, wild, sunny, fertile, poverty-stricken land
of splendid decaying cities, industrious and miserable populations, lively
and irrelevant cultural activity, where political divisions favored fascinating variety and petty tyranny, but scarcely any sense of Italy as
such.

The economy of the peninsula was backward and fragmented, its
population growing despite frequent food shortages. Agricultural productivity hovered near subsistence level; small markets and poor communications prevented real expansion. Improvement or reform on any
important scale were hamstrung by the wild variety of local currencies,
weights, measures, tolls, customs, civic privileges, feudal survivals, scler-
otic relics of medieval practice. Smuggling, brigandage, begging, and
domestic service were major industries, manufactures sluggish, illiteracy
widespread. The social pyramid here too rose on a mass of peasants, many
landless, some still serfs, fed on millet, maize, and beans, who could escape landless poverty in the countryside only to beg in cities or rob
in the hills. Next came the turbulent but largely unproductive urban

population, and finally the factious, fractious, decorative nobles at the top of the pile. It was these last who stoked the fires of cultural activity, lively but with little impact on everyday life until enlightened scholars and reformers turned to improving the public weal.

Even when reforms began, mostly in the north, superstition, intolerance, and crime seem to have held their own. The papal realm recorded 13,000 murders in the 1759–69 decade; Venice executed or sent to the galleys for life 73,000 men in the years from 1741 to 1762; Milan, Austrian since 1713, was violent and crowded. An ordinance of 1762 reveals the practice of breaking on the wheel, of cutting the murderer's hand off before his head, of dragging him to death behind a horse— the executioner's fee, in this case, to include the horse which the murderer was supposed to furnish.

It was in Milan and in Florence that prosperity and progress advanced with the century. The influence of Beccaria (see p. 652) was immense. In 1769 galleys were suppressed; in 1785 the penal code reformed; in 1789 torture abolished. All this in Milan but not in Rome, where, until the French occupation, violation of a convent sanctuary, kissing a woman in the street, or possession of a pistol were all punishable by death, as was the theft of a surplice or pretending to be a priest.

Rome was the artistic center of Eruope, drawing Goethe and Mozart, Canova and David, tourists avid for antiquities, Christians craving for its churches, priests in thousands, and beggars in tens of thousands. In a way, all of Rome lived on charity. Contemporaries estimated that a quarter of the population was made up of bureaucrats, who accounted for three-quarters of the class that did not beg. Probably more. In Rome, says Sismondi the historian, everybody wears a cassock, a livery, or rags. The popes avoided all reforms which might trouble the stability and quiet of the good people used to existing abuses. In the papal states, the line between peasants and brigands was a tenuous one, while the troops preying on both were simply privileged brigands making war on brigands who were not privileged.

Travelers found the cities filthy (rainstorms, wrote a visiting Dominican friar, are the brooms of Rome) and decayed. Cows were pastured in the Forum; people relieved themselves wherever they needed and could; garbage piles awaited removal by farmers' carts or, in Venice, barges. Houses showed little furniture, few carpets, and, except in the North, fewer fireplaces. Fire, the local people told Montesquieu in 1728, is unhealthy. Visiting Sicily in 1776, Roland, the future Girondin leader, found no beds in the common people's houses, only rush mats on which the people lay without undressing, so that "their *toilette* takes no longer than that of dogs: a shake and they are ready." On the other hand, music was everywhere and one traveler compared Italy to a tuning fork, with Naples holding the octave. With its half million people, its oranges and fig trees, its oils and saffrons, its vast port in a vaster bay, the palaces of its beggared nobles and the beggars of its sunny streets—a swarm of lazzaroni (idlers), strongest support of church and king and of an arbitrary disorder—Naples was heedlessly decaying amid its beauty. Reform or revolution, its poverty and its charm seemed to remain the same. Significantly, when in 1818 King Ferdinand IV of Naples abandoned his pigtail, he was the last of European sovereigns who had worn one. Court and city took this change in hair style as a revolutionary action, and briefly wondered whether the King had become a Jacobin.

In Florence, the last grotesque heirs of the Medici died out in the first half of the eighteenth century. Cosimo, hated by his people and by his heir, had been a senile bigot who even wanted to put breeches on a crucifix. The fifty-two-year-old son, Gian-Gastone, who succeeded him in 1723, was an indolent, benevolent, and bloated drunkard who ruled for fourteen years, mostly from his bed, which he had to have bestrewed with roses to stifle the smell that arose from it. The Peace of 1735 had settled the Polish succession by giving Tuscany to Francis of Lorraine; so, after 1737 when Gian-Gastone died at last, the duchy was governed by Austrians and Lorrainers, a definite improvement over earlier regimes, especially between 1745 and 1790 under the grand duke Leopold (later Emperor), a most enlightened ruler. Leopold took council with agronomists and economists, abolished the death penalty and torture, banned the Inquisition, centralized the administration, even prepared a constitution against whose publication Joseph II advised. In 1780, Tuscany enjoyed the most enlightened legislation in the world.

But the most fascinating tourist trap was Venice, with its 400 bridges, its 200,000 inhabitants, its carnivals that began at Christmas, its powerful corporation of gondoliers, its myriad painters—Canaletto, the Guardis, the Tiepolos, and many, many others—working to please the myriad tourists, all eager to take home a remainder of its beauty. Venetian painting seems to have produced the only original school in eighteenth-century Italy. Antonio Canal, known as Canaletto (1697–1768), was probably the master of *veduti* (views) for tourists, who even translated Venetian motifs to London and to Windsor when he visited England in 1756. Francesco Guardi (1712–1793) and his brothers introduced imagination, poetry, light, and shade into the straightforward paintings of their forerunners. Pietro Longhi (1702–1785) was the master of bourgeois realism, with much ironical social description, a favorite of his fellow citizens of the middle class.

The Venetian republic, to which the Peace of Karlowitz (1699) had restored some of her great territories, lost her last holdings in the eastern Mediterranean at Passarowitz in 1718. After the Turks, she now had Austria to fear, whose new free port at Trieste was draining trade and goods away from her moldering quays. With Mediterranean trade passing into French and English hands, and Italy increasingly dominated by Austria, the republic was but the timid shadow of her former

The Ducal Palace, Venice, by Francesco Guardi. Municipal Museum, Grenoble.

self, a survivor defended only by the reciprocal determination of France and Austria to maintain a balance of power. Unlike most parts of Europe, and of Italy too, the population of the city was diminishing, infant mortality rising, the numbers of the ruling class falling particularly fast, while its spirit became increasingly reactionary and unenterprising. The wool industry and the glass works decayed, the shipyards lay idle, the 12,000 silk workers of mid-century had been reduced to 379 by the eve of the Revolution, while beggars swelled from 445 in 1586 to 19,000 in 1760 and 23,000 in 1787. One-sixth of the population were mendicants, one-tenth were servants (12,819 in 1760), 3,776 were gondoliers, who were allowed free entry to theaters. In May, 1797, occupied by the French, the republic voted its own demise; and in October its French "liberators" would hand it over to Austria, as part of a larger bargain.

Somehow theaters seem the cathedrals of eighteenth-century Italy, vast prides of their communities and just as crucial to social life, with their boxes which were but the projection of a noble salon, containing armchairs, sofas, sometimes a gaming table. Each was equipped with curtains or with shutters so that the show should not interfere with conversation, sometimes even (as at La Scala) with a kitchenette for preparing snacks. The opera or theater nearly always provided gaming rooms. For common people, entrance was cheap—about one or 1.50 lire in Venice, half the price of hire for a gondola for the day—and consumption of plays immense. Carlo Goldoni, the Venetian playwright, wrote over 200 plays, some of them in eight days. There were more than twice as many public theaters in Venice as in Paris. And it was probably the opera, with its fantastic scenery, its escape from the real world into a brighter, calmer, make-believe one, that inspired the theatrical paintings of Tiepolo.

The enlightenment was advancing. In 1744 the dialogues of Galileo appeared with papal license, though prefaced by the sentence of the Holy Office (see p. 372) and Galileo's own retraction of his errors. In 1757 the Holy Office permitted the publication of books which revealed the movement of the earth. The *Encyclopedia,* too, did well in Italy. There were three reprints of the French language edition: in Lucca, in Livorno (with 1,200 subscribers), and in Padua, where the seminary press was used. In 1754, the first chair of political economy had been created—at the University of Naples, where, at that time, Charles ruled who would later become Charles III of Spain. Shortly, Beccaria would be named to a similar chair in Milan. Even in distant Savoy the feudal system was being liquidated to the benefit of the crown. "Everything is coming to life," exulted a Tuscan in the 1780's, "everything is becoming beautiful. New roads, new bridges, new canals, new buildings, new lands open to cultivation . . . everywhere unmistakable signs of movement and energy.'"

The long years of peace that stretched between 1748 and the irruption of French revolutionary armies in 1796 meant prosperity: not the brilliant creativity of the Renaissance, but the steady routines of crops and harvests, the growing bustle of tourism and trade, the renovations of enlightenment. "Water, clover, cows, cheese, money and music!" noted Arthur Young in Lombardy, during the autumn of 1789. "These are the combinations that string Italian nerves to enjoyment, and give lessons of government to Northern politicians."

There were shadows, too: dependence, lack of the initiative which provided the dynamic of change beyond the Alps, the rift between a few enlightened reformers at the top and the stubborn resistance to change among the masses, the conservative church opposing the secular endeavors of enlightened despots and civil servants, the ultimate precariousness of the uneasy balance maintained throughout the Italian peninsula and ready to topple over at the first hard shove. Then, with the 1790's, the shadows darkened, reformers sheered away, once-enlightened rulers began to see a Jacobin behind every bush and to apply the label even to the mildest liberals. The poet and playwright, Vittorio Alfieri (1749–1803), who had lived in Paris until 1792 and left, disgusted and afraid, to live in Florence, found his tragedies banned by the Pope and his steps followed by spies and by police. In Naples, in 1794, a man who had desecrated a church by crying *"Vive Paris! Vive la liberté!"* was condemned to be dragged by a horse, then hung, his tongue, hand, and head cut off, and all his goods confiscated. Simple curiosity about events in France became a motive for suspicion which could easily turn into persecution. Then came the French invasion, in 1796, and this brought not just a few dilettantes but all of Italy into physical contact with the new world outside. French armies carried the Revolution with them, recasting the map of the peninsula into a series of satellite republics.

The interior of La Scala. Museo Teatrale alla Scala, Milan.

But the Italian Jacobins who welcomed the French troops represented little beyond themselves. The new regimes had little more social foundation than in Spain. As late as 1811, only three and a half per cent of the populations of Napoleon's kingdom of Italy were occupied in commerce. In Rome, remarked Mme. de Staël, only the statues were republican. What could illiterate masses in cities or in the countryside make of the new calendar, the republican rhetoric, the military occupation? They were used to repression and taxes and exactions. Now they shuddered at sacrilege which laid impious hands on the Pope and sometimes on the churches. Yet thousands got administrative experience in the new bureaucracies sponsored by the French, and thousands more saw assemblies of Italians engaging in political debate. The experience would take long to become effective; but it would not be lost.

French occupation was costly; but it brought progress too. Secondary schools opened—even one for girls at Milan, a credit and mortgage system was introduced, a road and bridge corps founded, prefects appointed, heralding new administration and new laws. Serfdom with its servitudes, feudalism with its inequalities, were abolished; civic equality and the Napoleonic Code appeared; and, when the blockade closed in on the peninsula as on the rest of Europe, local industries developed in cottons, ironware, and sugar beets.

Restoration brought Austrian domination, but many of the reforms were retained. National sentiment was still limited, and national awareness too. The risings of 1820 and 1821 sought to win reforms of a local nature, not national unity. In twenty years this would change.

Nationalism Comes to Italy

The examples of European revolution, the ferment of ideas—romantic, patriotic, Bonapartist, national—would have their effect in Italy. The revolutions of 1820 had echoed Spanish events. The new and equally unsuccessful risings of 1830 in Modena, in Parma, in Bologna, echoed the Paris Revolution of that year. From one failure to another, Italian nationalism was learning to know itself, spreading from narrow groups of soldiers, businessmen, and old public servants of Napoleon's day, from secret societies like the *Carbonari,* to reach a wider audience with the writings of men like Sylvio Pellico, whose *Prisons* (1833) told of his imprisonment by the Austrians, or Leopardi, grandiloquently recreating ancient patriotism, or Alessandro Manzoni (1785–1873), the man perhaps most responsible, with his *Betrothed* (1827), for generalizing the Tuscan form of the Italian language and the sentiment of a shared Italian past. Beneath the inefficient tyranny of sloppy despots, yearnings for reassertion, for a revival, began to stir, manipulated from abroad by the correspondence and conspiracies of Giuseppe Mazzini, a strange and fascinating figure, stern, domineering, and doctrinaire. In the 1830's, the young Mazzini had had to flee the displeasure of the Piedmontese government, first to Marseilles where he founded his Young Italy Society (1831), then to Berne where he founded another society, Young Europe, then, at last to London. His organizations were less important than his creed, which was the need to unite all the divided energies of Italy toward a common end, the building of a third and independent Rome whose mission was to inspire the making of a new and better world. Each nation had its mission in the world; this was Italy's. In its pursuit, Mazzini never ceased to fight, and to make others fight, to realize his faith.

Meanwhile, the sovereign whose police Mazzini had to flee, Charles Albert of Piedmont (1831–1849), had visions of his own. After 1815 Charles Albert's cousin, Victor Emmanuel, had set himself to recreate the old regime, complete with pigtails, feudal dues, clerical and noble privileges, antiquated court costumes. But he was the only Italian ruler whose crown did not depend on Austrian support; and the heavy taxes levied to keep up an exaggerated army also maintained an independent Piedmontese policy. Thin, pale, gloomy, an introverted solitary man, Charles Albert was yet persuaded of his mission to free Italy, a dream confirmed by a visionary nun. Charles Albert's soon-known "secret" inspired Italians everywhere as they watched him in the late 1830's promote a statistical survey of his kingdom, promulgate a new civil code, sponsor a new history of Italy, create model farms, and project railroads which would link Genoa with north European trade. Piedmont seemed to stand for the modern age: free trade in goods and in ideas, education, railroads, and technology.

Then, in 1846, another national dream—Italian union beneath the primacy of the Pope—began to take shape as Pope Gregory XVI, whose government had been a byword for obscurantism and tyranny, died and in his place arose the bland appealing figure of Pius IX. Pius began his reign with an amnesty for political prisoners and exiles, continued it by introducing gaslights, railroads, and vaccination in his states, all of which Pope Gregory had held at bay. A customs union was concluded with Tuscany and Piedmont. The papacy seemed to be taking the lead in Italian unity. Kindly and well-meaning, Pio Nono did not quite know what he was doing. As one man said, liberal ideas filtered into his head like snow blowing in around the cracks in a closed window.

And yet the Pope was neither anti-Austrian nor constitution-minded, and the king of Piedmont had neither power nor prestige enough to free Italians from the Austrian yoke. Rebellion had to start within the Austrian realm itself. And it did. Lombardy under the Austrians, was the best-governed and the best-off of all Italian states, which is not saying much but still this was a hindrance to revolt. More children went to elementary school in Lombardy (68 per cent of the boys, 42 per cent of the girls), administration was cumbrous, slow, but honest; justice was surer and milder; taxes were heavy but not overwhelming, even though in 1847 Lombardy and Venice sent to Vienna three times as much as the French occupants had managed to squeeze in their time.

Jealous memories, sanguine hopes, a temper bred of centuries catering to occupants and tourists—a mixture of servility and scorn—were factors that the occupants underrated. Most advanced, the Venetians and the Milanese could also be the most rebellious. Their resentments, like their aspirations, carried them to the van of revolt, when it came.

The Germanies

> The dear old Holy Roman Reich:
> How does it hold together?

sing the carousers in Goethe's *Faust*. The end of the eighteenth century would see it fall apart at last. And yet the states which it had vaguely held together—396 of them, reorganized to 39 after 1806—were still united by language, memory, and secular habit, as well as by physical circumstance. Welcome or not, German was the common language from the Baltic to the Adriatic, from the Bohemian mountains to the North Sea; and even those who would reject it in the nineteenth century still used it as a *lingua franca,* still use it so today. Gladly or not, the trade of central Europe still had to pass along North German rivers or down Austrian waters to reach a sea. And the scattering of sovereign states, though long fascinated by French culture, by the prestige and sometimes by the power of Paris, revolved in the end about one of two native poles: Austria or Prussia.

The struggle for dominion in Germany would be waged between these powers and finally decided in the 1860's. Yet, in the eighteenth

Joseph II of Austria.

Austria must catch up with them, especially with Prussia, or grow ever weaker. By the time he finished, Jesuit property had been taken over and used to endow state schools at every level and in every province, where "useful, obedient and Christian citizens" should be trained. Textile and metal industries expanded. Austria won dominance in the Balkan trade. In Bohemia and in the Vienna suburbs factories almost doubled in number. State revenues, which also almost doubled in the decade after 1763, doubled again by 1788. The army was enlarged, reformed, improved, although its command remained mediocre, and thus condemned it to repeated defeats.

Joseph built hospitals, schools, orphanages, prisons, even new churches; his administration did a lot for the poor. But he cared for men as impersonal means, and men resented this. The end of the state lay not in its public works but in territorial expansion: the former were only the means of the latter. Religion, culture, economics, science, even liberty, were subordinated to power politics. It was the state that was considered sacred, Joseph its prophet and, in his mind, each civil servant cast as a missionary, living for its service. Devotion to the state was both a cult and a necessity. Files, spies, reports, and discipline were meant to bolster this sometimes lagging faith.

The two greatest problems, in Austria as everywhere, were poverty and privilege. "The peasant is miserable," reported Joseph: "the only human thing about him is his face and all he has is his bare life." In 1769, an official commission reporting on conditions in Bohemia went into greater detail. The villein labor to which peasants were constrained was tantamount to slavery. The serfs "become savage, brutish and work the lands they get only badly. They are rachitic, thin, covered with rags . . . in their rickety cabins, the parents lie on straw, the naked children on the edges of clay stoves; they never wash . . .

they have no doctor . . . whatever they own is at the mercy of their masters . . ." Savage punishments, beatings, torture, whose instruments stood on every market square or at the castle gate, kept them in check. Many serfs escaped to Prussia. The landowners chased away the Jews because they lent at smaller rates than they themselves would offer. Since taxes were paid only by serfs, the overtaxed masses could never become consumers for a market. The gentry, which could have furnished recruits for an urban class would not do so, preferring poverty to losing its noble prerogatives—freedom from taxes, from tithes, from duties. When Joseph II ordered a census and the numbering of houses, the nobles objected to this not only out of fear that it prefaced a general measure of taxation but out of sheer resentment that they and their houses could be counted on a par with common men.

Between 1765 and 1789, a series of measures seeking to transfer the fiscal burden to those who owned the land, while freeing the serfs who labored on it, set minimum limits for peasant holdings and maximum limits to what could be required of the serfs. In 1700, about 70 per cent of a serf's income went to the state, the landlords, and the church. Under the new system, with tithes abolished, 70 per cent of produce was left to the serf himself. Of the remainder, the state took 13 per cent, the landlord 17. In 1930, state taxes would take 22 per cent of a farmer's income. As this indicates, the reform projected at such an early date was too radical. The serfs welcomed it, but they could neither defend it nor adjust in time to what it meant. The landlords, faced with ruin, fought it tooth and nail. Eventually, the dogged opposition of the landowners, the central government's need for cash, and the peasant's unwillingness to rebel in his own cause, led to a land-tax settlement in 1792 which, while improving the status of the serf, really protected the interests of the proprietors. Until 1867 Bohemian nobles would continue to live off their peasants' hides.

Another reasonable scheme was to reform the government of Belgium. The Austrian Netherlands were a jungle of contradictions, confusion, administrative and legal chaos. Joseph II was prince of Brabant, Luxembourg, Limbourg, and Guelders, count of Flanders, Hainault, and Namur, suzerain of Malines, Stavelot, and Liège, governing each province separately, at least in theory. The architect of the state had his work cut out to turn this chaos toward his clear-cut ideals. But Joseph's reform attempts came down about his ears. In 1789, the Netherlands revolted. As in 1579, when they had reared at Philip II's taxes, they preferred tradition and its comforts to a more exacting efficiency, and only settled down after Joseph's death, their old ways restored. The home provinces also were in turmoil. Joseph's logic had to give in to facts.

Incapable of internal reform, Austria could not resign herself to the decline of its external power. But who could support reforms? Not the peasants, politically nonexistent; not the magnates, who resented the emancipation of serfs as an attaint against their position; not the gentry, which provided the stoutest defenders of anachronistic privileges that alone gave them a superiority over the bourgeoisie. Not the bourgeoisie, too weak, undeveloped, and heavily taxed to be of use or really friendly; not the clergy, which were disfavored, or the Protestants, who were tolerated but only just barely. No social, national, or religious groups could see the crown as its special ally, or find a particular interest in supporting its policy. Political reform should have been based on social reform. But the social structure had to evolve in time, and this is something that Joseph never gave it, nor felt he had himself. After Joseph, fear of revolution would stifle reform, as it did everywhere else, for a generation or two.

The Empire

Then, there was Germany: the Empire, a swarm of infinitesimal courts, based on anarchy abroad and oppression at home—in Westphalia, twenty-nine states within 484 square miles; in Swabia ninety states in 729 square miles. Germany, writes a noble chronicler at mid-century, "is full of dukes, three-quarters of whom are insane." They were certainly mad about hunting, as many German castles still testify today. In Würtemberg, the duke boasted of the 6,500 stags and 5,000 boars that he had killed in 1737 alone. Their manners and those of their subjects were to scale: forks appeared only toward the end of the eighteenth century, drunkenness was Gargantuan, amusement vicious or childish, animal fights a favorite show, bears against bulls, wild oxen, and mastiffs, boars against hounds. Every duke, margrave, or princeling wanted a court like that of Vienna, a castle like Versailles, with a swarm of attendants like Maria Theresa's which had 700 chamberlains, or the Bavarian court with 421. Frederick the Great, who had only sixty chamberlains, mocked at a margrave who kept eight of them, lodged them in a stable and fed them on black bread.

Most of these men were irresponsible autocrats, well-described by Frederick II. They "ruined themselves by reckless extravagance, misled by the illusion of their imagined greatness . . . The younger son of the younger son of an apanaged dynasty imagines he is of the same stamp as Louis XIV. He builds his Versailles, keeps his mistresses and has an 'army' at his beck and call—perhaps strong enough to fight an imaginary battle on the stage at Verona." Many had better than stage armies: they had soldiers for hire to England or Holland or France. The Hessians of the American war cost half a million pounds for 30,000 men, of whom only 17,500 returned.

Germany was an economic jigsaw. At the beginning of the nineteenth century the twelve greatest German towns taken together could still not match the population of London or Paris; eight- or nine-tenths of the inhabitants lived on the land, the rest in small provincial cities. Agriculture, still very backward, ignored the innovations of the west, its yields about half those of similar lands in England, the peasants a wretched lot, ignorant and depressed. In a letter of 1782, Goethe compares the peasants of Weimar—where they were better off than most— to plant lice who filled themselves on rose bushes only to be sucked dry by ants: "Things have gone so far . . . that more is consumed in a day at the top than can be produced in a day at the bottom . . ."

Voltaire had seen the rapacious and spendthrift courts, the exploited peasants, the slack and supine towns, and had predicted that Germany was doomed to eternal poverty. And it was true that those middle classes which were a source of energy and progress further west, appeared in central Europe as stagnant and submissive, very much the creatures of their petty princes. Given so little trade, a sluggish economic life (except in towns like Hamburg), the bourgeoisie were chiefly petty officials or artisans, catering to the rulers and all too dependent on their whims. Their social position reflected this and, in the early eighteenth century, the daughters of officials might well marry footmen or artisans or soldiers, while ministers of religion, physicians, or officials might marry some lady's maid, herself the daughter of a professional man. By the second half of the century, this was changing: members of the professions setting themselves off from the lower middle classes, a fact suggesting an improvement in their social—hence their economic—status.

In centers like Hamburg or Berlin, a small but prosperous and cultivated middle class welcomed the Enlightenment, furthered a cultural revival in which the Jews played an important part. Jews had long been tolerated in most of Germany, but could obtain residential rights only in exchange for heavy payments, were banned from gilds and corporations, hence from most crafts, and restricted largely to hawking, banking, or manufacture. They had to buy permits to own houses or move from town to town, paid heavy head taxes, had no political or civil rights. It might be said that orthodox Jews, in a sense, created their own ghetto: the religious observance of dietary regulations, holidays, and customs, prevented the orthodox Jew from entering military or civil service, complicated his legal affairs in which the oaths of Christian justice were unacceptable, and clashed with the laws and customs of surrounding society.

After the 1760's, a few rich bankers, intellectuals, and manufacturers left the orthodox Jewish communities and began to live like the enlightened middle class, trying to assimilate, joining reading clubs and opening their drawing rooms to a mixed, cosmopolitan, and often brilliant society. A series of governmental measures (Austria, 1782; Prussia, 1790) facilitated their assimilation; the French conquest in the 1790's and the Prussian reforms of 1812 finally vouchsafed Jews civic and political equality. The Frankfurt ghetto was abolished in 1824; restrictive regulations in the early 1830's. In return, the Jews contributed their minds and talents, their cosmopolitan inventiveness, and a loyalty which never failed the land that in the twentieth century would fail them.

Yet still the opportunities for enterprise were limited and it would seem that this bourgeoisie, teetering on the brink of some self-affirmation, found consolation in religious and cultural activities. Pietism flourished. Mystics preached an emotional faith, which Friedrich Klopstock's poetry reflected and which would reverberate in England when John Wesley was touched by the ideas of Moravian brethren. Not bourgeois only, but poor men, peasants, soldiers, wandering actors, adventurers, students, looked for salvation less in reasonable action than in chance, in luck, in miracles. As hope of social reforms waned, dreams of collective well-being turned into schemes of individual salvation, to a penchant for miraculous and catastrophic solutions that could turn Cinderellas into princesses and frogs into princes, the mentality that we call romantic and which can become revolutionary or reactionary for the sake of some heroic appeal. Coups, conspiracies, secret societies with exciting rites, or conversion to equally ritualistic and exalting religions—one way or another the new mentality abjured logical progression for gestures which would bring about some sudden change, public or private, but fundamentally unprepared. Not reforms but revolution, not work but inspiration, not thought but feeling, not Deism but illuminism, not medicine but magnetism, hypnotism, charlatanism.

Sickly, tense, nervous, ill or underfed, these people were prone to excitement and depression, fantasy and excess, their "romanticism" a hypertrophy of sensibilities sharpened by physical unbalance. Lotteries brought the rich men's gambling within the reach of all. Danzig, Moscow, Warsaw, Amsterdam, Vienna, Berlin, and St. Petersburg were fascinated by them. Get-rich-quick seemed better than get-rich-by-toil-and-saving. Love at first sight, or by a lightning revelation, better than anything. Destiny ruled. The theater provided an opportunity to play the parts which reality refused.

While the courts spoke French, read French, sponsored Parisian actors, and despised the vulgar Germans, the bourgeoisie found compensation in literary and dramatic descriptions of the vices and decadence of courts and nobility. Aristocrats were wicked, bourgeois were virtuous. Prurient fascination with noble license ran parallel with smug satisfaction that they, the bourgeois, were not like that—presumably for lack of opportunity. Plays taking this line flourished first and especially in the great bourgeois metropolis of Hamburg. The general strain of the domestic drama was personal, ethical, and private. Events and experience were seen as taking place not in the world but in the home and, better still, in the mind and heart where everyone was master. The German bourgeoisie combined a private rationalism and pietism, affirmed private morality and private life.

An illustration from *The Sorrows of Young Werther*, by Goethe.

Schiller's plays return over and over again to the individual's powerlessness before an unyielding society: the vain revolt in *The Robbers* (1781), the vain attempt in *Intrigue and Love* of lovers of different birth, different social status, to transcend the chasm that divides them, ending in suicide. Rebellious as a student, rebellious as a soldier, deserter from his duke's army, Friedrich von Schiller wrote his *Robbers* while chewing on potatoes that rotted in his drawer, attacked the routine and discipline that stifled all, the laws which could only hamstring real purity or greatness. Genius bred on liberty. The young men heard him. The young also shared the sense of oppression which Schiller expressed, the legacy of damping dullness, the smothering shallowness, the narrow limits of their little towns and courts and masters. They discovered nature, the world, themselves; they wandered, they rebelled; also, they waited.

How far can we see in this the protest of young men of humble birth (the philosopher Herder's parents had been very poor, the poet Klinger's mother was a washerwoman) against a society where their minds have glimpsed infinite horizons, and yet their fists beat impotently against closed doors? A rigid jigsaw of small states and minds evoked both the explosion of the *Storm and Stress* and the more lasting nostalgias of romantic escape. The German writers—some 3,000 in 1773, double that number by 1787—struggled for a public which would buy their works, and found it chiefly among the "uncorrupted middle class," for whose support they pleaded, against those alien influences and French philosophers who had been adopted by the Establishment. The *Storm and Stress* group took its name from a play of that name by Friedrich von Klinger (1775), inspired by the beginnings of the American War of Independence. For a brief moment, in the 1770's, it would represent the deliberate opposition of feeling to reason.

Such a philosophy had been formulated first by Johann George Hamann (1730–1788), the Magus of the North, as he was called. Man, argued Hamann, should act as a whole being, and not rely only on the reasoning part of himself. It is not reason which co-ordinates man's manifold faculties, but instinct and inspiration. The voice and will of nature are spontaneously expressed in feelings and in passions which produce not *thoughts* but *images*. Hence poetry, the most imagelike of our languages, is the most natural form of expression because it articulates these images and communicates their sense. This was the philosophy that J. G. Herder (1744–1803) would develop for his friends and disciples of the *Storm and Stress* circle, and which would provide one basis of romantic theory.

Yet *Storm and Stress* did not go very far. Its rebellious leaders grew up and did quite well in later life: Goethe became a minister, Herder a superintendent, Schiller a professor, Klinger a general in the Russian service. Meanwhile, the middle classes, which had begun by demanding freedom of thought and discussion, found that these did not necessarily bring about the acts that reasoning indicates. Reason needs an executive arm, and the French example suggested that this could be obtained only by political means. The middle classes therefore turned to political action, sought the right to take part in politics in order to carry out their ideas. Klopstock, Schiller, Goethe, welcomed the French Revolution, only to be discouraged by the Terror and to fall back on the possibilities of monarchic reforms, even if the monarchy continued absolute. Germany was not ready for a revolution. Only a very few young men, not afraid of violence, appreciated the possibilities revolution offered, and then the coming of Napoleon Bonaparte.

The Fate of the Germanies

In December, 1797, French troops occupied Mainz. Joseph von Görres (1776–1848), the future Catholic historian, considering the Empire dead, wrote its obituary: "Died at Ratisbon, on December 30, 1797 . . . aged 955 years, five months, twenty-eight days, . . . after complete exhaustion and apoplexy, fully conscious, and fortified by all the rites of the church, the Holy Roman Empire."

Görres was only a little premature. The French occupied the left bank of the Rhine, dissolved the ecclesiastical states, shared their lands and most of the free cities among the greater German princes, sixteen of whom would be grouped into the satellite Confederation of the Rhine (1806). The Empire vanished before Napoleon's will. When a German prince addressed the conqueror as if he were his peer, the self-made emperor replied "I am not your prince, I am your master!" Austria, defeated, had to contribute an archduchess to secure the master's dynasty. Prussia had decayed badly since Frederick's death. Rotten before ripe, Mirabeau had called it; and in 1806 the defeats of Jena and Auerstädt proved his point. As French troops marched into Berlin, its governor's proclamation instructed the people of the capital that "the first duty of citizens is to keep quiet."

They would not do so for long. What the romantic patriots of the 1770's and 1780's had not succeeded in doing, French occupation did. A patriotic publicist of the late eighteenth century had complained that Germans even had to swear in French because they had no adequate national oaths. In 1804 Madame de Staël had noticed that the Germans had no national spirit. This was no longer true by 1810 or so. French army boots seemed to stamp patriots out of the ground. Schiller was writing his plays about national liberation, the *Maid of Orléans* and *William Tell;* Hegel, Beethoven, Fichte, who began by welcoming French influence, now turned against it. Above all, a small group of Prussian statesmen adapted the lessons of the French Revolution, to forge a nation and instill it with a common purpose and a common civic pride.

The Treaty of Tilsit (1807) had reduced the Prussian kingdom to a third-rate power, deprived of half its territory and population, condemned to pay a crippling war indemnity. Within a few months, the King's edict of emancipation wrought a revolution from above, ending serfdom, feudal and caste privileges, granting the cities municipal self-government, even giving civil rights to Jews. Land reform turned the serfs into freeholders and, while Baron vom Stein and Karl August von Hardenberg were putting through civil reforms, generals Scharnhorst and Gneisenau were reforming the army and introducing general conscription, and Wilhelm von Humboldt forged a school system destined first to educate, then to regenerate a youth made keen and fit by the gymnastic societies sparked by Friedrich Ludwig Jahn. Gneisenau found himself wondering at the "infinite forces which slumber in the nation, undeveloped and unused." Around the University of Heidelberg, these forces were sought in folk tales, in legends, the *Nibelungen* saga was revived and adapted, the folk stirred up, the "true people of God," as Fichte called them, were taught that they could provide Europe with "a regenerating ferment." In February, 1813, the *levée en masse* would show that the French lessons had been well applied. A Prussia of five million turned out an army of 350,000, far more than Frederick had ever done.

Though it may not have been as pervasive as the patriots claimed, 1813 saw the beginnings of a really national movement in Germany. But victory was fated to bring disillusion. The landed aristocracy came back into its own, the patriotic student movements were suppressed, reform projects were stifled, local self-government suspended or abandoned, and all reforming politicians forced out of office. The French Revolution was the devil. Anything it had inspired was to be shunned—including the economic liberalism which had come in the wake of the French.

Yet, as in other lands, not everything the French did had been bad, or wasted. The Continental System, which ruined many merchants, also allowed German industrialists to develop, free for a while from English competition: cotton and woolen cloth, ironwares, sugar beet refineries, appeared and grew. The Industrial Revolution was slowly changing the face of Germany. As Theodore Hamerow has put it, the economy of stability was superseded by the economy of competition. Industry, mechanized production, began to spread across central Europe; linen, cotton, wool, silk manufactures sprang up; metallurgy grew. In the 1820's and 1830's familiar names began to appear: Krupp, Borsig, Stinnes, Mannesmann. Loans were being floated, money invested, joint-stock companies were being set up by the score. Railroads built after 1835, linked the industrial areas in the center with northern ports and created the largest railway network in Europe by 1850, which cut shipping costs by two-thirds and immensely spurred production.

The settlement of 1815 had given Prussia control of the main German coalfields in Westphalia and the Ruhr, and command of the chief commercial routes between east and west and north and south. These were the counters Prussia used, first to foster her own economic expansion by a discriminating tariff, then between 1828 and 1834 to establish her economic supremacy in north Germany by a customs union.* When Bavaria and Wurtemberg joined the Prussian customs union in 1834, the *Zollverein* offered a market of almost 34,000,000 people, an immense base for economic expansion and industrialization. August Hoffmann von Fallersleben, who had written *Deutschland, Deutschland über Alles,* rejoiced:

> Articles of home consumption,
> All our thanks are due to you!
> You have wrought without presumption
> What no intellect could do;
> You have made the German nation
> Stand united, hand in hand,
> More than the Confederation
> Ever did for Fatherland

Between 1815 and 1845 the German population would increase almost 40 per cent, the cities increasing nearly twice as fast as any country district. Factory workers also increased in numbers.**

---

* The great apostle of this union was Friedrich List (1789–1846), who had grown rich in the United States and returned home to preach what he had learned there: the fundamental importance of railroads and of tariffs.

** In Prussia 32,000 of them were children working up to sixteen hours a day. It was the news that the industrial districts could not meet the quota of conscripts because their physical fitness had been impaired by early work in the mills that alarmed the Prussian king and led to his order of 1839 prohibiting child labor under the age of nine and setting a work day of ten hours up to the age of sixteen. Prussia would be the first continental state to follow the English example, and this was followed in 1840 by Bavaria and Baden.

Yet factory labor accounted for scarcely 4 per cent of the population, while artisan and home industries employed three and four times as many. Hence, the decay of the old precapitalist system was sharply and widely felt. As local craft industries declined, artisan risings protesting against unemployment, hunger, and starvation wages speckled the decades between 1820 and 1848. The most famous of these was probably the 1844 insurrection in Silesia, which has been chronicled in Gerhart Hauptmann's play, *The Weavers*. The many thousands who earned their livelihoods from the linen industry were ruined by imported English yarn and cotton goods, with consequent mounting unemployment and shrinking wages. Revolt broke out against the factories, rioters sacked workshops and manufacturers' homes, subsided when looted food and wine had stilled their hunger, were crushed in blood by late-arriving troops, the ringleaders receiving heavy sentences and the survivors left worse off than before and far more bitter.

There was uneasiness on the land as well. Where the French Revolution had passed, serfs had become tenants, feudal lords had become landlords, servile obligations had been turned into rents, land became a commodity like any other. The peasants, freed from ancient servitudes, found themselves in a free economy where risks predominated over possibilities. Land hunger, loan and credit hunger, overpopulation, legislation which favored nobles over peasants, widespread dissatisfaction, boiled up in the spring of 1848 in great agrarian risings. Oppression had also meant custom and security, emancipation meant bewilderment in an unfamiliar world.

Where the lower classes yearned for better economic conditions, the middle classes longed for social and political improvements. The French Revolution suggested possibilities of emancipation, the war of liberation had caused great enthusiasm—not just against the foreigner, but for reforms which France had introduced or sparked and which the burghers approved as much as they resented French extortions and repressions. Social equality, political freedom were good, but they were lost with the Restoration. Students' clubs were nurseries of nationalism, and the professors provided fuel. Student meetings, agitation, propaganda, worried the defenders of order. Eventually a well-known writer, August von Kotzebue (1761–1819), was murdered by a student because he was an agent of the Tsar. This prompted a reaction and, by the Carlsbad Decrees of 1819, student societies were banned, professors were dismissed, and censorship tightened,* leading nationalists arrested, exiled, or, at least, closely watched. A general witch hunt drove liberalism underground.

This could not last. In 1830, Polish refugees passing through Germany stirred up enthusiasm on the way, and the sight of other nations rising for their rights encouraged Germans to think about their own.

* One Prussian official in the Rhineland censored an advertisement for a translation of Dante's *Divine Comedy,* arguing that divine things could not be comic.

The liberal tide began to flow again despite repression. When Jacob Burckhardt went to study in the Germany of the 1840's, he wrote back enthusiastically to his sister in Basel, thanking God that his mother-tongue was German: "What a people! What a wonderful youth! What a land—a paradise." Burckhardt would change his mind. The Germans not.

Meanwhile, more radical ideas also appeared: socialism, communism, discovered in Paris, funneled in by exiles and by publicists. The young editor of a radical newspaper forced into exile, described the revolutionary effects of capital on society and state, and prophesied the overthrow of the ruling class by workers. Marx and Engels' *Communist Manifesto* (1847) evoked as much echo as a dull thud, though brilliantly written and fated to a great future. It had little connection with conditions in Germany. As in eighteenth-century France, growing economic significance for the bourgeois paralleled political insignificance. Across the Rhine and the North Sea, bankers and manufacturers prospered and ruled. The educated middle class—lawyers, doctors, merchants—wanted as much and, to express their aspirations, they found liberalism, with its conjunction of enterprise and status, its affirmation of opportunity and its civic rewards, its rejection of the lower classes without property, its insistence on freedom of enterprise and gain. The peculiarly German concomitant to liberalism was the dream of a German union, which, it was argued, would provide the best scope for all this.

There were also radical democrats, equalitarian, calling for progressive income taxes, welfare legislation, economic and social reforms, sometimes republican, but never socialist, never communist, nothing but good bourgeois intellectuals. The Junkers and traditionalists, for their part, found a fine figurehead in the visionary King Frederick William IV, a man who, like Charles I in England, conceived the crown as the defender of the poor and weak against rapacious capital, of Christian charity and social justice against greedy immoral change. Enlightened absolutism based on the masses could win, said the romantic legitimists who gathered round him.

There was one man who knew that an alliance with the masses would not work, that the only hope of the old regime was to avoid all movement, lest it cause collapse. Klemens von Metternich (1773–1859) was the son-in-law of Kaunitz, and his heir. Born the same year as the future Louis-Philippe, speaking French better than German, Metternich was nineteen when the French invasion of his Rhineland home sent him off to Vienna to recoup his fortunes in the Habsburg service. Ambassador to Paris, then foreign minister, he promoted first Marie Louise's marriage, then the anti-Napoleonic coalitions. Just over forty and a prince in 1814, he would devote the next thirty-four years to the maintenance of that social and political peace without which his master's empire could not survive. His enemies called Metternich a butterfly; he himself preferred a comparison to spiders: "Their ugliness apart, the most charming little creatures, always busy, and arranging their houses with the greatest neatness in the world." Vain, sententious, shrewd,* and silly, certain that liberalism could lead only to Jacobinism, Metternich appears as the prototype of those conservatives who confuse moderate reformism with radical revolution, refuse all concessions, and, by sitting on the safety valve, cause the explosion which they dread.

Metternich's masters approved. "Peoples?" asked Emperor Francis of Austria: "What does that mean? I know only subjects." "The human race," declared an Austrian general, "begins with barons." Leopold II, enlightened and conciliatory, had died in 1792 after less than two years of rule. His son, Francis I (1792–1835), was a narrow reactionary, convinced of the virtues of immobility and of his right to rule by bureaucracy subjects whose only right was to obey. There was no cabinet at Vienna and, while all subjects could appeal to the Emperor directly, his decisions were never motivated, so that administrators could never tell why a project was sent back, hence did not know how it should be adjusted. Church and education were harnessed to produce high-minded religious and patriotic subjects; police and censorship were used to keep them so.

Victory in 1814 confirmed the policy and turned it into a system. When Francis died, the modern world moved into his lands. Francis had opposed railroads, industry, even (on moral grounds) the introduction of machinery. Ferdinand I (1835–1848) was a good-natured simpleton who reigned while others governed. A steamship company appeared in 1835, the first real railroad in 1839, modern industries began to be set up. Industry brought new wealth, but also new industrial problems which served to increase the force of pent-up discontents. Francis had been right. The national consciousness of the Empire's subjects was growing along with literacy and with communication. An Austrian poet summed up the situation in 1830: "The Hungarian hates the Bohemian, the Bohemian hates the German, and the Italian hates them all."

In the 1840's, inflation and hard times diminished the monolithic power which the Emperor's servants still tried to assert. Paternalistic absolutism stumbled into trouble: depression on top of oppression could only maintain itself by repression. The Prague papers, much freer than the Viennese, made great play with news of Irish miseries, which all their readers knew reflected the enslavement and the agrarian problems of Bohemia. In Austrian-dominated Italy, the scientific Congresses of patriotic societies discussed volcanoes in 1846, and the potato disease in 1847—the potato being the image of potato-eating Germans. In 1846 a Polish rising in Galicia was crushed when Vienna encouraged the Ruthenian peasants to rise against their Polish landlords. But other revolutions would not be dealt with so easily.

---

* He also proved himself a sagacious connoisseur when dividing up Europe: he kept 2 acres for himself—the vineyard of Johannisberg on the Rhine, whose vines grow the best hock in the world.

The Eastern Borderlands

Poland

The largest European country after Russia, Poland, was a republican monarchy, a democracy of the gentry, peopled by five nations—Poles and Lithuanians, Ruthenians, Jews and Germans—with as many religious beliefs. Orthodox and Catholic, Uniate and Protestant, detested one another and all despised the Jews. The land, greater than France, with only half its population, brought one-sixtieth of France's revenues. The King was poor, even though some of the magnates lived like little kings. The Lithuanian estates of a family like the Radziwills were as great as half of Ireland, the pomp and state they kept often eclipsed that of the King's court in Warsaw.

The Polish polity was in fact an anarchy, a neo-feudal arrangement in which gentry (*szlachta*) elected kings and sanctioned policy which could be vetoed by the least of its members. The Polish Diet operated on the principle of unanimity. Unanimity, real or enforced, had been the rule in most medieval assemblies. Dissenters might be threatened, shouted down, or forcibly silenced; but the ideal was maintained that a collective body (gild, corporation, chapter, or assembly) could have but one will and should act as one, with all concurring in its actions. Only with the sixteenth century did these ideals, with the consequent possibility of a veto nullifying action, give way to the vote of a majority. This may have reflected the rising individualism of the time, or the practical needs of states where legislation loomed larger than before. It certainly reflected a more differentiated view of a more obviously differentiated—hence modern—society. The principle of unanimity survived, however, in institutions like the Anglo-Saxon jury and, more particularly, where modernity itself lagged behind: in the Imperial Diet of Germany, and in Poland. If its survival reflected backwardness, it also ensured that it should continue.

Since the poor gentry were clients and cat's-paws of great magnate families, struggles between the magnates for supremacy and between foreign powers for predominance could hamstring any policy at all and usually did. "If this is liberty which one sees here," declared the British envoy to the Polish diet of 1733, "the Lord preserve us from such liberty. Here are what they call great and little nobility which are slaves to one another by turns. All goes in confusion and disorder."

A backward economy paralleled anachronistic institutions. Peasants were enserfed, oppressed, and largely landless. The production of grain in mid-eighteenth century seems to have been about one-third of what it had been in the seventeenth. Cities were ruined by the privileges of neighboring landlords who, free of taxes, could undercut local craftsmen and, free of customs dues, could import and sell all foreign goods they wanted. Merchants became their agents. Artisans took to the land to stay alive, leaving small crafts and trades to Jews. Forbidden to till the soil, the Jews became a surrogate and much resented middle class, representatives of the gentry, whom they served as stewards, farmers, or monopoly managers, collecting dues, selling liquor or hay. There were no urban professions, there was no urban culture, there is no mention of the earth moving around the sun until 1750, there are no schools worth speaking of until mid-eighteenth century. The Catholic hierarchy, intolerant of Protestants and Orthodox, seems to have been particularly obscurantist.

The 1697–1763 period, when a Saxon dynasty ruled the land, was a time of uneasy peace, when the prosperity of a few paralleled the misery of many, when magnates lived like kings, squires like benighted tyrants, and the masses much more like wild beasts. An Englishman, William Coxe, traveling from Cracow to Warsaw in the 1770's, found scattered wooden huts with no furniture, in which men and beasts shared space, and where even the most rudimentary tools seemed lacking. Servile, humble, begging, apathetic, the Polish peasants whom he compared with their proud Swiss counterparts were also natives of a poor liberty-loving country, but utterly different. The peasants opposed any reforms attempted; their inertia was as hard to budge as the selfishness of the nobles. Cracow gave the impression of a ruined city—half of its 16,000 population Jewish—and other cities seemed to have been built to scale, a mass of ruined palaces and miserable hovels.

In 1763, the death of the last Saxon king, Augustus III, who had himself succeeded to the throne by casting out the man the Diet had elected, Stanislas Leczinski—opened a fresh succession crisis, which was solved by Russo-Prussian pressure in the accession of a protégé of Catherine II: Stanislas Poniatowski. A man of the Enlightenment, Poniatowski had been imposed on Poland in order to avoid reforms which might turn the country into an effective power. His election was followed by a near-Russian protectorate, under the pretext that Russian troops were maintaining the liberties of the Orthodox subjects of the Polish crown. Some of the most important of Stanislas's opponents were arrested and deported to Russia.

Such methods, and French intrigues as well, encouraged a section of the nobility to form the Confederation of Bar, for the defense of Catholicism and Poland, and directed chiefly against the Russians. Fighting broke out in 1768, spread into a more general war between Russia and Turkey, and ended—as far as Poland was concerned—in the first partition (1772), in which Austria and Prussia received large slices of

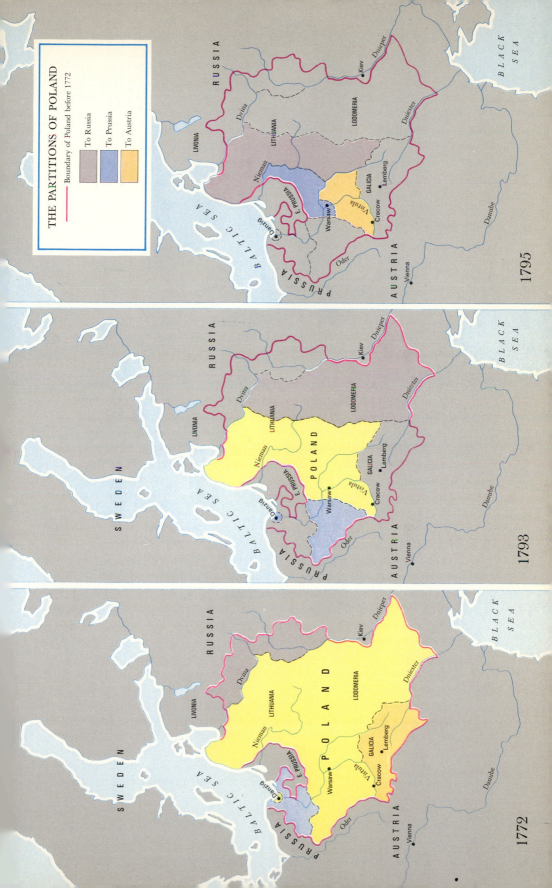

THE PARTITIONS OF POLAND

—— Boundary of Poland before 1772

To Russia
To Prussia
To Austria

1795

RUSSIA

BLACK SEA

Kiev
Dniepper
Dvina
Dniester
LIVONIA
LITHUANIA
LODOMERIA
Nieman
GALICIA
Lemberg
PRUSSIA
Vistula
Danzig
Warsaw
Cracow
BALTIC SEA
Oder
Danube
PRUSSIA
AUSTRIA
Vienna

1793

RUSSIA

BLACK SEA

Kiev
Dniepper
Dvina
Dniester
SWEDEN
LIVONIA
LITHUANIA
LODOMERIA
POLAND
Nieman
GALICIA
Lemberg
PRUSSIA
Vistula
Cracow
Danzig
Warsaw
BALTIC SEA
Oder
Danube
PRUSSIA
AUSTRIA
Vienna

1772

RUSSIA

BLACK SEA

Kiev
Dniepper
Dvina
Dniester
SWEDEN
LIVONIA
LITHUANIA
LODOMERIA
POLAND
Nieman
GALICIA
Lemberg
PRUSSIA
Vistula
Cracow
Danzig
Warsaw
BALTIC SEA
Oder
Danube
PRUSSIA
AUSTRIA
Vienna

Stanislas Poniatowski.

Polish territory in compensation for Russian gains in Turkey, while Russia herself annexed the eastern provinces of Poland, inhabited mostly by Orthodox Ukrainians. The kingdom had lost a third of its territory, but it had probably gained in homogeneity.

The crisis precipitated some much-needed reforms, both on the fiscal and the educational planes. King Stanislas placed a bust of George Washington in his study and, in 1791, while Russian and Austrian attention was directed elsewhere, a liberal constitution was proclaimed, reforming political institutions, improving the condition of the peasants, laying the basis for a modern state. The constitution, praised by men like Burke and the Emperor Leopold, appalled Russia and Prussia, who wanted Poland weak. In 1792, when Russia had once more concluded peace with Turkey and Prussian troops had turned back from Valmy, the second partition of Poland left the country with only a rump of some 4,000 square miles and just over four million population. When, under the menace of Russian and Prussian arms the partition treaty had been ratified, an insurrection broke out in the summer of 1794. Led by a butcher, a shoemaker, a Hungarian banker, above all by Thaddeus Kosciusco (1746–1817), a veteran of the American War of Independence, the Poles were crushed after a heroic struggle, and the third partition put an end to Poland as an independent state.

The coming of the French in 1806 brought a brief hope of revival, but the Grand Duchy of Warsaw which was set up from territories wrested from the Prussians turned out to be only a counter in Napoleon's games. After 1815, the Grand Duchy of Warsaw would be redivided, becoming the Grand Duchy of Posen under Prussian rule and the kingdom of Poland, which was joined to Russia by a common king. Pictures of Napoleon continued to hang in many manors, and the thought of this petty nobleman whom a military career had made immortal stirred the imagination of many petty nobles in Sarmatia too.

In the 1820's, Adam Mickiewicz, a follower of Schiller and of Byron, enhanced romantic patriotism, love of fatherland, nostalgic yearnings for past greatness, and fascinated the younger generations. Joachim Lelewel began to write about Polish history and glorify the Polish nation—a great lecturer, idol of the students and horror of the Russians, who turned him out of his history chair at the University of Vilna but did not prevent his election to the Diet as a deputy. Polish musicians were investigating national folk music, with notable effects on the young Frédéric Chopin, then studying in Warsaw and about to leave Poland for the west in 1830. Secret societies were spreading, despite attempts to suppress them and to control political and cultural activities.

In November, 1830, one of the many conspiracies about to be discovered precipitated a military coup that might have petered out had it not turned into a popular uprising, which the Polish army joined. A Diet deposed Nicholas I and elected a national government. But the peasants would not join the revolution, nor did they have much reason to do so. The peasants did not like the Russians, but they saw no profit in revolt: "As we have been up to now, so we shall be afterwards. Our misery will not change . . . Indeed, it will be better for the lords when they defeat the Russians. So let them fight them." Bravery was of no avail against political and social divisions. By August, 1831, Warsaw had fallen and the last Polish forces had been defeated, had surrendered, or had taken refuge in Prussian territory. Several thousands emigrated to the west, providing a source of revolutionary ferment in Italy, Germany, and France. Galicia and Posnania too, which languished under Austrian occupation, were stirred out of inertia into patriotism, and this would flare up briefly in 1846. But Poland was crushed for good and would not regain freedom until 1918.

Hungary

To the south of Poland, the kingdom of Hungary was of course a possession of the Habsburgs. The Peace of Karlowitz (1699), transferring old Hungarian lands from Ottoman to Habsburg rule, had been a Habsburg triumph but a tragedy for the Hungarians and Transylvanians whom Turkish defeat left at the mercy of a ruler far more determined to impose his will and faith than the Turks had ever been. Religious tolerance had been the rule in principalities where Catholic and Calvinist, Uniate and Lutheran had lived side by side since the Reformation. The Emperor Leopold I was determined to impose Catholicism, and also to deprive Hungarian nobles of their age-old right to elect their kings and offer armed resistance to those who sought to break their liberties. Long years of civil warfare followed, not ended until the reign of Charles VI, when the Peace of Szatmar (1711) settled the Habsburg rule in Hungary on a basis of compromise and tolerance, respecting the Magyars' essential liberties but making sure that the kingdom of St. Stephen would not become a noble anarchy like Poland.

The country, whose sixteenth-century population stood around four million, had been devastated by Turkish occupation in subsequent wars. In 1715, the population seems to have been about 1,700,000 in Hungary proper and another 800,000 in Transylvania. Moreover, of these, the Hungarians of the plains were the least numerous, while Serbs and Croats, Slovaks and Ruthenes, were, at least relatively, reinforced. After 1715, the empty spaces filled with colonists from the more sheltered parts of the kingdom, from the Romanian provinces, and from Germany and Austria. Nobility, too, which clung tenaciously to its privileges— especially to exemption from the tax—had been decimated and was refloated by newcomers from Germany, Italy, and Spain; and also by recruits among natives of lower birth who bought vacant estates. All these, however, soon became Magyarized or left, and Magyar nobility remained strongly Hungarian, where the Bohemian nobles were always Vienna-oriented, an alien group amidst downtrodden subjects.

The Hungarian nobles were the *nation;* and they were all those men economically and physically able to carry arms. The census of 1787 showed 75,000 noble families—one out of every five or six: far more than the 20,000-odd noble families that all of Prussia counted and comparable only to the Polish situation. In the country, where the bushel of wheat cost half a florin and the florin could buy 25–30 pounds of meat, the wealth of the great magnates was extraordinary. The yearly income of Prince Esterhazy, Haydn's patron, was more than 700,000 florins and his estates ran nearly seven million acres. Other family estates topped 100,000, while quite a few varied between 20,000 and 50,000 acres. The income of Count Czobor, who died in 1741, was about a million florins a year, and many nobles, while nowhere near as wealthy, could count on 50,000 or 60,000 a year. The brilliant costume which Prince Esterhazy wore in the Diet of 1847, with its pearl seams and diamond buttons, *shed* some 30,000 dollars' worth of jewels whenever he would wear it.

The eyes of people such as these were turned increasingly to Vienna, and this by a deliberate policy of the crown. "The proud Hungarians, who on their country estates were planning schemes of liberty, have been allured to the court or to town," wrote an eighteenth-century Swiss traveler. "By the grant of dignities, titles and offers of marriage and in other ways, every opportunity has been given them of spending their money in splendor, of contracting debts and of throwing themselves on the mercy of the sovereign when their [mortgaged] estates have been sequestrated . . . There is scarcely a single prominent family in Hungary which is free from debt . . . Having thus converted the most powerful part of the Hungarian nobility into spendthrifts, *débauchés* and cowards, the court has no longer occasion to fear a revolt."

But if this was true about the powerful and the rich who sought their honors and diversions in Vienna and at the Habsburg court, the lesser gentry clung to the soil, to their old privileges, and to the old ways. The magnates themselves valued their Magyar birthright too much to sell it for a mess of Austrian pottage. Relations remained good as long as Maria Theresa's restraining hand prevented serious infringement of traditional liberties. To Joseph II, however, the process of assimilation seemed to advance too slowly to satisfy his plans for administrative and cultural unity.

In 1774 Joseph abolished Latin as the official language of Hungary, changing the *lingua franca* of its many nations to German. Latin was the preserve of nobles and of lawyers, serfs could not understand it. The Emperor argued that no nation should be governed in a language it could not understand. Many Hungarian nationalists approved, but wanted the new national language to be Magyar. The gentry, however, opposed to the modern spirit and to the enlightened absolutism which German represented, did not want to abandon Latin. "As for commoners, who speak German, Serb or Walach, they can have no voice in affairs, for supreme Providence has designated them not to regulate the country's laws and control the sovereign, but only to respect them," wrote a Hungarian noble. One interesting aspect of this rebellious attachment to Latin appeared in 1799, when a brief rebellion brought echoes of the French Revolution to Hungary. The nobility burned the Imperial registers and decrees, while singing *La Marseillaise* and the sans-culotte song: *Ça Ira,* with their lyrics translated into Latin (*hoc ibit*). An odd encounter of Rousseau and freedom with these reactionary defenders of traditional privilege who would not dream of emancipating the people, and who, when they appealed to Liberty and Nature, thought only of themselves!

Although the aristocrats revolted against Josephism and called on Voltaire and Rousseau for arguments, they were ready enough to settle for withdrawal of the liberal experiments which they resented. As for the few middle-class "Jacobins," who actually wanted a social and political reform, they got no further than the gallows in 1795. The serfs were hungry, but they were weary too; the nobles were sated and quiescent. They would not really stir until the 1820's and then, once more, a move symbolic of reform would be the Diet's abandonment of Latin—not now for German, but for the Magyar tongue. Yet with her constitution, her county assemblies, and large "noble" class, Hungary was better prepared for political action than most countries outside England and France. With one person in fourteen classed as a noble, the electoral base compared favorably with England's one voter for every twenty-four inhabitants, or even the American one in eight, let alone the proportions in countries where only nobles enjoyed political rights, like Austria (one in 353), or Bohemia (one in 828).

During the 1820's and thirties, Count Stephen Széchenyi fostered the revival of Hungarian language and Hungarian pride, built the first bridge over the Danube in the capital, started the first steamboat services on it. Offspring of a great family, wealthy and cultivated, Széchenyi had traveled through the west, especially in England, and had come home convinced that his country was a "great fallow land," the masses degraded, the masters selfish and devoid of any social sense. In 1825, he offered a year's income from his estates to found a National Academy of Sciences, whose first task would be to purify and standardize the Magyar language. Thereafter, there was no stopping the fervent young men who scandalized their elders by calling for reform on every plane, an end to economic backwardness and social oppression. To the very extent that Hungary forged ahead, the need for self-affirmation became stronger, the possibilities of bearding the Austrians more tempting. And, as the danger of confrontation increased, so did the Magyars' relations with a west represented first by Vienna, but also by Milan and Paris.

By the 1830's Széchenyi's generation was being overtaken by a new more revolutionary one, incarnated in the brilliant journalist and orator Lajos Kossuth (1802–1894), inspired by French romantic radicalism to want not only traditional liberties and material progress, but democracy too, and justice for the peasant. Despite the misgivings of more moderate liberals disturbed by his egoism and ambition, despite pointed warnings from Széchenyi who feared that exacerbated tensions would come to no good, despite imprisonment, and despite Metternich's personal offer of a government post that might domesticate him, Kossuth drove on. For his growing following, the independence of Hungary became a necessary prelude to social progress. And, as the reform movement gathered momentum through the late thirties and the forties, nationalism became its major issue. Kossuth, its prophet, bent his efforts to increasing the national consciousness of his fellow Magyars.

Russia

Peter the Great's only son, Alexei, had been murdered by him or at his orders in 1719. When Peter died in 1725, Alexei's son, Peter II (1727–1730), was only nine years old, and his brief reign was soon cut short by smallpox. The realm was ruled by women—Peter's nieces: Anna (1730–1740) and, after a brief interval, Elizabeth (1741–1762)—by favorites and palace revolutionists. Elizabeth's heir, the son of the Duke of Holstein, married another German princess, Catherine of Anhalt-

Catherine the Great, painting by Lampi. Musée Jacquemart – André, Paris.

Zerbst. Peter III (1761–1762) ruled only long enough to save Frederick the Great from destruction by withdrawing Russian troops from the Seven Years' War, and to convince his officers and courtiers that their king was mad. In 1762, a palace revolution removed him from the throne on which it placed his wife. As Catherine II, she would rule for twenty-four years.

Catherine's first object was to free herself from the praetorian power which had raised her up. Soldiers and boyars had backed her *coup d'état.* The first part of her reign would be devoted to disciplining the army and the nobles, restoring the authority of the autocratic state. One instrument in this combat would be the enlightened ideas of the time, to which she referred for arguments against noble privilege and against the serfdom on which the fortunes of the nobles rested. To counteract the political ambitions of the nobles, Catherine began to talk about a code of laws that would improve the condition of other social classes. In 1768, commissioners were appointed from the more liberal nobles, the towns, and even peasants, to revise the laws; but they made haste slowly and nothing came of the scheme except an impressive set of *Grand Instructions,* soon translated and circulated throughout the West where they enhanced the enlightened Empress's reputation.

Meanwhile, the friction between crown and gentry, and the rumors of reform, stirred up the countryside. Russian society was a juncture of nobles who owed their privileges to service to the crown and peasant serfs who served their noble masters and the state. In 1762, Peter III had issued a *Charter of the Prerogatives of the Gentry,* exempting them from the basic obligation of service to the state. News of this act aroused the peasants' expectation of a second one, which would free them from servile obligations. When none appeared, the rumor spread that the gentry had conspired to suppress it; and this aroused rural unrest which, in the 1770's while Russia was deep in a Turkish war and the Empress and the nobles were at loggerheads, broke into a widespread peasant uprising whose leader, Emelyan Pugachev, claimed to be the murdered Tsar Peter III. Pugachev was captured and executed, but the social scare threw Empress and nobility together. The latter's privileges were confirmed, serfdom affirmed, and Catherine henceforth governed as the first landowner of her realm.

The realm was growing. Russian population, thirteen million in 1715, nineteen million in 1762, had practically doubled by 1800 and doubled once more by mid-nineteenth century. The birth rate was the highest in Europe; the infantile death rate twice that of France, three times that of Norway; life expectation about twenty-four. But there was land, and people bred, and moved, and bred some more. Russia's borders advanced in Asia and in Europe. The war with Turkey which ended in the Treaty of Kuchuk-Kainardji (1774), gave Russia a foothold on the Black Sea, with freedom of navigation on it and of passage through the Straits, while an obscure but useful clause gave Moscow a watching brief over the rights of the Orthodox subjects of the Porte. In 1783, Crimea and the Kuban were annexed to Russia. In 1792, the Peace of Iaşi brought all the Black Sea coast between the Bug and Dniester; * while by the partitions of Poland the Russian border came to stand on the Niemen and the Bug, far forward into Europe. It had pushed forward in the Caucasus as well, where Christian Georgia, a willing protectorate, would be annexed in 1801. During the nineteenth century, Russian expansion would take place mostly in Asia. In Europe, only three accessions were to come between Catherine's death and the reign of Stalin: Finland in 1809, Bessarabia in 1812, and Congress Poland after 1815.

The eighteenth century affirmed the rise of Russia. For the first time, in 1735, the end of the War of the Polish Succession saw a Russian army on the Neckar River. By 1815, Paris itself was occupied by Russian troops, and Alexander seemed the arbiter of all the powers. The army must have been the greatest national industry, a force which by the 1790's reached some 800,000 and gave employment to as many more. The equipment and supplies required by the army and navy, the resources which were needed to keep them up, seem to have been the central concern of the government. At Peter's death, 65 per cent of the Russian budget went to military expenses; as the economy grew more prosperous this proportion fell to 50 per cent in 1801 and 42 per cent by 1852. These remain impressive figures and they reflect the orientation of the land. They also reflect the fact, although less striking, that in this time, although the

* Odessa would be founded there in 1793; its population by 1814 numbered over 40,000.

500 miles

SWEDEN

Nystadt
Abo

WHITE
SEA

URAL MOUNTAINS

N. Dvina

Lake
Onega

KARELIA
Lake
Ladoga
Narva
St. Petersburg
ESTONIA
INGRIA
LIVONIA
Riga

BALTIC
SEA

W. Dvina

Moscow

Volga

Danzig
EAST
PRUSSIA

LITHUANIA

Nieman

Smolensk

POLAND

Warsaw

R U S S I A

Chernigov

Danube

Kiev
Poltava

Bug
Dniester

Don

Ural

Volga

HUNGARY

Azov

SEA OF
AZOV

CASPIAN SEA

Sevastopol

OTTOMAN

Küchük-Kainarji

BLACK SEA

E M P I R E

RUSSIAN EXPANSION IN EUROPE IN THE EIGHTEENTH CENTURY

THE RUSSIAN EMPIRE IN 1796

ALASKA

BRITAIN

GERMANY

Moscow

OTTOMAN

RUSSIA

Ural Mts.

SIBERIA

PERSIA

TURKESTAN

CHINA

JAPAN

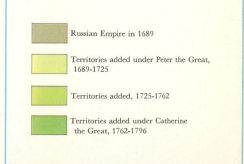

Russian Empire in 1689

Territories added under Peter the Great,
1689–1725

Territories added, 1725–1762

Territories added under Catherine
the Great, 1762–1796

country remained backward, its wealth increased.

So did its cultural activities. The service nobility made up of for-eigners and self-made men found its identity in foreign cultures, in the works published, the ideas mooted, in France, England, and Germany. The University of Moscow was founded in 1755. More books were being pub-lished, many of them translations. In 1726, just after Peter's death, seven books in all were printed in Russia. By the 1760's the annual average stood over one hundred.

Foreign trade augmented its turnover in real value four or five times between the middle and the end of the eighteenth century. Industry, still largely in the homes of peasant craftsmen catering to strictly local needs, expanded also. There had been roughly 200 or 300 factories in Peter's Russia; there would be ten times as many by 1800, 10,000 work-shops by mid-nineteenth century, employing a half million workers. Around 1800, Russian iron production was probably the highest in the world. Half of the Russian work force was unfree, however, their fur-naces burned charcoal and not coal, and Russian industry would lag behind the West for a good time longer.

An economist who spent some years as tutor of the future Tsar Nich-olas I observed in 1815 that Russia's lack of modern manufactures must be attributed to her failure to abolish serfdom. The evidence whether free labor is really more productive, remains inconclusive. But where the man was right was that, if serfs were freed without being given land, the human capital for industry would have been made available. And it is true that industrial expansion began in Russia after the 1860's, when there were no more serfs. Until then, manufactures drew on servile labor, furnished by landlords or by the state,* which still continued to be the *primum mobile* of enterprise.

Historian Max Beloff has compared the Russian nobles to the nine-teenth-century planter aristocracy of the American South: a similarly agrarian ruling class based on slave labor; prospering from the con-temporary rise in prices because demand for their produce rose; facing a similar rise in labor costs—that is, the price of serfs or prime field hands—while land itself was plentiful; similarly interested in consump-tion, rather than efficiency or improvement; and differing only in the Russians' readiness to obey the state, to whose patronage they always looked for aid. This last applied almost as well to the manufacturing classes. For, whereas in the West, freedom was the best spur to trade and industry, in eastern countries, and very much in Russia, the spur was tyranny, with the despotic initiative of the state fostering commercial and industrial enterprise. In the West, progress came mostly from individuals and led eventually to political emancipation; in the East progress

---

* When Catherine opened a state pawnshop at St. Petersburg to furnish credit facilities to her nobles, they pawned there mostly "souls"—peasant serfs—as the nobles of the neighboring lands would have done if their credit systems had been as advanced.

tended to come from above, depended on the central power and supported its growth. This was a trend that time would but confirm, and its concomitant was the tyranny just mentioned, a tyranny less noticed for being part of a secular order of things. "In Germany or France," noted Joseph II when visiting Catherine's Russia in 1787, "we would not even dare to try the sort of thing that finds no obstacle here. The master orders and the mass of slaves obeys. They are paid ill or not at all, and they do not even dare to grumble . . . The nobility, humbled, looks on the orders of a sovereign as on laws."

Peter had superimposed the artificial symmetry of Western-style Petersburg over the organic confusion of his land. Catherine erected monumental façades before its suffering, like the Potemkin villages * which her favorite built to simulate prosperity and progress where none existed.

Talk of reform continued until fears of revolution put a stop to it, turning the aged Catherine against the innovators whom she had tolerated and even encouraged at one time. Under Paul I (1796–1801) a beginning was made in limiting serfdom and restricting noble privileges, but it did not go far under that capricious despot. Then, in 1801, the great tradition of reform by murder was revived once more. A morose, unbalanced father was replaced by his mercurial and unstable son. Alexander I (1801–1825) was romantic and cynical, mystical and erratic. His reign swung from great reforming hopes to sour reaction. Serfs were not freed, but masters were allowed to give or sell them their freedom, and, most important, a law of 1801 allowed men of all classes to own land, thus recognizing the civil rights of other social groups besides the nobles.

Yet the French wars, the news from the rest of Europe, the spread of freemasonry and of the new ideas, made the peasants' freedom and their land the focus of political concern. By 1820, Russia had a score of Masonic lodges, with 1,600 members, among them generals, ministers, and even members of the imperial family. Secret societies wove a slender net between Petersburg, Moscow, and the army camps, wherein officers and aristocrats fascinated by the revolutionary experience, resentful that the Tsar refused his aid to the Orthodox subjects of the Turks, envious of the relatively liberal institutions granted to the population of his Polish kingdom, talked about reorganizing the country and its government, if need be by a *coup d'état*. They were mostly drawing-room conspirators, their plotting (as the poet Pushkin wrote) "idle chatter between cups of champagne," their sedition "just the fruit of boredom, of idleness—the pranks of grownup boys."

---

* The term refers to an invention attributed to Prince Grigori Potemkin (1739–1791). It is said that in 1787, wishing to conceal the shortcomings of his administration of the Ukraine, during Catherine's progress through the newly colonized South Russian steppes, he set up the prototype of stage sets: hollow shells of thriving villages filled with fake peasant-colonists, cattle, and trappings which could be shifted from place to place along her route.

And yet, in 1825, these plots emerged briefly from officers' messes and from drawing rooms to cause the Decembrist revolution; for Alexander's death opened an unusual succession crisis. The Tsar's apparent heir, the Grand Duke Constantine, had resigned his claim to the throne, following a morganatic marriage, in favor of his brother Nicholas. Yet the new order of succession had never been made public and, when Alexander died in December, 1825, Nicholas, in charge at Petersburg and eager to avoid a possible accusation of disloyalty, hastened to make all troops and ministers take their oath to Constantine as Tsar. Confusion followed when Constantine in Warsaw, where he was governor of the Polish kingdom, absolutely refused to accept the crown and every-body had to take a new oath to Nicholas. This was the opportunity for the disaffected officers, who tried to raise some of their ignorant troops for "Constantine and the Constitution." But the insurrection was put down very quickly and several hundred conspirators imprisoned, executed, or packed off to Siberia.

The reign of Nicholas I (1825–1855) was heavily marked by its inauspicious start. Police rule was intensified, all liberalism suppressed, constitutional reform sank out of sight. "One does not die here or breathe, except by permission of Imperial authority," noted a French visitor in 1839. The universities were placed under particular watch, and interest in foreign ideas exposed one to repression, as it would do the young Fedor Dostoevski, who was sent to Siberia in 1847 for belonging to a "socialistic" group.*

Determined to restore the "police" state of Peter, Tsar Nicholas appears as a reincarnation *à la mode* of dark and violent figures from the Russian past. He was irresolute, cruel, haunted by fear, driven by duty, deluded by superstition, and ready to believe that the fire which gutted the London House of Parliament in 1834 was God's punishment for the Reform Act of 1832. Yet, even under him, the country still advanced. It advanced in the Balkans, where Turkey for a while became its protégé. It advanced internally, as witness the first systematic code of laws compiled in 1832—some seventy years after the idea had been mooted under Catherine. Railways were appearing—the first near Petersburg completed in 1838—and Whistler's father would get to know the country in 1840 as a consulting engineer on the railroad which would link Moscow to Petersburg. Peter the Great had once complained that, although he found Turennes for war, he could never find a Sully for internal government. Neither did Nicholas and, when he died, his military regime was collapsing round him. But Russia would create her own Sullys to salve the scars her rulers' narrow-mindedness inflicted.

---

* The ideas entertained by Dostoevski and his friends were actually those of the French social utopian François Fourier (see p. 657). A quarter of a century later, the writer would depict Russian Fourierists in *The Possessed* (1871).

The Ottoman Empire

The Ottoman Empire was a creature of conquest, ruled by a kind of state of siege, its military machine in decline, its administration in chaos. The Sultan was also Caliph, commander of the faithful, religious head of Muslim communities from Caucasus to Gibraltar; but even there his authority was collapsing. Russia's success at Kuchuk-Kainardji contrasted with the destruction of the Turkish fleet, the incapacity of Turkish arms, the apparent disintegration of the Empire. North Africa had long been practically independent; in Cairo the Mamelukes—Circassian slaves—ruled a quasi-autonomous province; in Arabia the Wahhabite followers of a puritan prophet preached a return to Islamic orthodoxy (no saints, no coffee, no tobacco) and refused allegiance. In 1757, the Bedouin had attacked the great annual pilgrim caravan to Mecca and slaughtered 20,000, including one of the Sultan's sisters.

Constantinople, decimated by recurrent plagues, two-thirds razed by the great fire which swept it in 1782, was still queen of the Bosphorus, the Golden Horn still concentrating the trade of East and West. But there and in the Levant European merchants secured monopolies and concessions, while most of the Empire's business was in the hands of Greek or Armenian Christians. The Empire exported raw materials, imported finished goods; but the colonies of foreign merchants in its ports worked under special treaties (capitulations) which gave them privileged status, exempt from Turkish justice and from taxes, subject chiefly to their own consuls. Soon these capitulations would be extended to the clients and protégés of foreign powers, Jews or Christians. Since Muslim law prohibited usury, there were no banks, except in alien hands. And no universities, no secular higher education, no sciences, no intellectual life except of the most conservative and sterile sort. Mustafa III (1757–1774) assumed that Frederick the Great's successes were due to his superior astrologers. The first printed books in Turkish were authorized in 1727. By 1828, eighty titles had been published: The Turkish negotiators in 1791 thought that Gibraltar was a town in England, Spain a part of Africa, the Baltic a lake unsuitable for carrying large ships.

Against the opposition of reactionary landowners and religious leaders, Selim III (1789–1807) and his nephew Mahmud II (1808–1839) tried to reform and modernize their ramshackle holdings, rationalize taxation, build warships, improve the artillery. News of the French Revolution was spreading secular ideas, but mostly among Christians, increasingly attracted by dreams of emancipation, either in the Romanian principalities which were ruled by Greek princes from Fanar, the Greek quarter of Constantinople, or in the Balkan peninsula.

Selim had been deposed and murdered for his reforming pains. Mahmud survived but he did little better. He did abolish the last remains of feudal land tenure, forced landlords and rebellious pashas to obey, destroyed the janissaries (1826) who had long been an obstacle to government or discipline, set up a ministry of war and the beginnings of a modern army with European instructors, uniforms, and arms. A medical school was founded (1827) and the first Turkish newspaper (1831); but most of these reforms got scarcely off the ground and Mahmud's wars were almost uniformly unsuccessful. The end of Mahmud's reign saw Turkey's Balkan holdings disintegrating and his sixteen-year-old successor, Abdul Mejid, become a sort of ward of European powers now watching over a corpse in which stagnation ruled.

The Ottomans were used to fighting Austria and Russia in the Balkans. The new force which appeared in the nineteenth century was that of their own Orthodox subjects, who tried to assert their presence and their independent personality, first against their Muslim masters and then against the Austrians and Muscovites who wished to exploit them. The first instance of this occurred in Serbia, where the peasants rose in 1804 under the leadership of two illiterate pig-dealers—Kara George and Miloş Obrenovitch—against the plundering oppression of janissary occupying troops. What had begun as a local insurrection against a force which the Sultan liked little more than did his Christian subjects turned into a war of liberation in which the Serbs looked for help to Russia. This they did not get, and their revolt collapsed in 1812 only to start again in 1815 and to succeed in the 1820's in securing autonomy for the Serbs. In 1829, the Treaty of Adrianople recognized Obrenovitch (who had murdered his rival in the meantime) as hereditary prince of an autonomous principality, under the loose suzerainty of the Ottomans.

A more significant revolt had broken out, however, in the 1820's. The richest and best-educated men in the Ottoman Empire were Greeks: scions of the great families of Fanar, the Fanariotes, governed the Danubian provinces of present-day Romania; Greek merchants, sailors, traders, controlled much of the Near Eastern and the Black Sea trade; Greek priests and intellectuals wove a broad cultural web from Chios to Odessa, founded a university in the Ionian Islands, revived their literary heritage and memories of their ancient empire. Late eighteenth-century interest in Greek antiquities evoked much sympathy for the cause of their independence from "the stupid Muslim," as a French traveler put it in 1782, for a war of liberation which Goethe and Schiller extolled and which the young Hölderlin in his *Hyperion* (1792) described in anticipation. The *Marseillaise* was translated and adapted into Greek; two of Napoleon's marshals, Junot and Augereau, married Greek women; and Bonaparte himself encouraged the ambitions of Greek patriots. The appearance of Russians in the Ionian islands suggested even more obvious patrons for an Orthodox crusade. Greek colonies in Odessa and Trieste, Leghorn, Alexandria, and Marseilles kept in touch with the homeland and also with the currents of Enlightenment and Revolution.

All this suggested that the time had come for ancient glories to be resurrected, ideally in a new Balkan state which would be Orthodox in faith and Greek in language and administration. This seems to have been the aim of the *Philiké Hetairia,* a secret society organized at Odessa in 1814, which hoped to gain Russian support for a revival of the Byzantine Empire. In 1821, Alexander Ypsilanti, the son of a Fanariote hospodar (prince) of Moldavia, himself a Russian general and head of the *Hetairia,* tried to begin the general rising in the Romanian principalities. The Russian support he had banked on was not forthcoming, for Tsar Alexander refused help to all revolutions. He also hoped for Romanian support, but the Romanian landlords had no love for Greeks and a Romanian peasant rising, led by Tudor Vladimirescu, seemed to conflict with Ypsilanti's interests.* Ypsilanti stupidly forfeited all Romanian sympathies by murdering Vladimirescu and, defeated, was forced to take refuge in Austrian territory where he was promptly imprisoned.

Yet Ypsilanti's abortive rising had sparked revolt in the Morea, further South, and in the Greek islands, where the Turkish garrisons were soon isolated by a general uprising. The West, all of whose culture was rooted in Greek and Latin classics, rejoiced with Shelley:

> The world's great age begins anew,
> The golden years return,
> The earth doth like a snake renew,
> Her winter weeds outworn.
> Heaven smiles, and faiths and empires gleam
> Like wrecks of a dissolving dream.

The wrecks, at first, were more apparent than the dreams. Both sides went about their business with appalling cruelty, but the Greeks had superior public relations and the Turks had greater means for murder than their unruly subjects. In 1822, Turks slaughtered over 20,000 Greeks in Chios (an event which would inspire the great painting of Delacroix), and almost recaptured control of the peninsula. But the rebels commanded the sea, and the Turks had other troubles to contend with in Syria and in Persia. In 1824, the Sultan secured the intervention of Mohammed Ali, pasha of Egypt and its undisputed ruler since his massacre of all the Mameluk beys in 1811. Before long, the Egyptian

---

* As the historian C. M. Wodehouse remarks, for the Romanians, "liberation" meant liberation *from,* not *by,* the Fanariote Greeks.

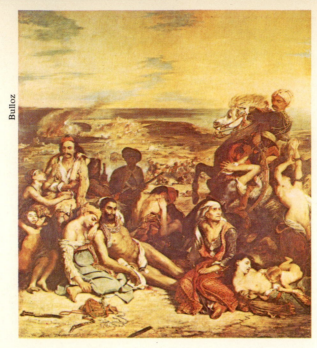

The Massacre of Chios, by Eugène Delacroix, Louvre, Paris.

army had devastated the Greek mainland and almost defeated the Greeks.

Then, in 1825, Tsar Alexander, reluctant to intervene, was replaced by Nicholas I, more interested in Balkan possibilities. Philhellene opinion was reviving under the impact of Egyptian atrocities. The Philhellenes were setting up thriving committees in Germany, England, France, and Switzerland; they were raising money, supplies, and volunteers, sending adventurers to help the rebels, and recruiting an international legion which soon saw action on Greek soil. The Greeks themselves organized a state, however anarchic. In 1827 they elected their first president, only to murder him a few years later. In 1827, too, the combined fleets of England, France, and Russia annihilated Turko-Egyptian forces in Navarino Bay. In 1828 the Egyptian troops left the country, and French troops landed to garrison the Peloponnessus and to afford a thin margin of security and order. In 1830 Greece was declared an independent kingdom, and two years later the younger son of the Bavarian king, who had been one of the most enthusiastic supporters of the Hellenic cause, was crowned as Otto I (1832–1862).

The new kingdom was very far from what Greek patriots had dreamed, or what Byron died for at Missolonghi. The history of its making reflects both the rivalries between the various subject peoples of the Ottomans, who ceased fighting the Turks only in order to fight one another, and the internal anarchy which the foundation of new states has never failed to cause. It also introduces one of the first of those irredentist problems which have plagued Europe ever since, threatening every peace arrangement with fresh attempts to win national territories remaining unredeemed.

But, however unsatisfactory its nature, it was a straw in the wind. Greek struggles were more *visible* than the Serb, and the Greeks actually achieved their independence. Further, their example stirred a new national consciousness among other subjects of the Ottomans: first the Romanians of Moldavia and Walachia, then the Bulgarians who had remained quiescent. The Treaty of Adrianople (1829) not only recognized the independence of Greece and the autonomy of Serbia, it brought the Romanian principalities into the Russian sphere. After 1821, the Romanians insisted on being ruled by native princes, not by Fanariote Greeks; and the Turks easily agreed. Between 1828 and 1834 Russian occupation of the Danubian provinces would see the elaboration of a protoconstitution there: the Organic Regulations of 1831. National consciousness was growing in Romania; and in 1835 the British Consul in Bucarest reported a rising popular desire for union under a prince who would be neither Russian nor Greek. This was not to come until thirty years later, but the process of emancipation had begun. The most underprivileged part of Europe was stirring to join the rest.

1848

Stirrings comparatively mild as yet in eastern Europe became positively eruptive once more in the west. From 1847 onward, bad harvests, famines, epidemics, all conspired to bring dissatisfactions to a head. Romantics, Socialists, Nationalists, bourgeois, workers, students, and peasants could all agree that things should change. For a brief moment the streams of discontent rush together, sweeping their disparate troops into assault against the ruling order, toppling established citadels, communing together in the feverish Mardi gras elation of revolution, only to fall apart in its chaotic aftermath. Revolutions are like carnivals, always followed by hangovers. Thus, at any rate, would 1848 appear when it was past. Only some remembered the festivities, and others the morning after.

Rising in Sicily in the first days of 1848, rebellion spread like wildfire through the Italian peninsula. The Venetians and the Milanese, when they heard the news from Sicily, made their own revolution, proclaimed their new republics, called to their aid Charles Albert and the Pope. Italy rose, the Austrians were thrown back, the country's unity seemed to have been reforged. That was in January. In February, Paris, ever the capital of revolution, exploded once again. The outbreak came, as usual, through a series of chance events. The opposition campaign for wider franchise had adopted the English method of political propaganda by banquets throughout the land. By early 1848, the government, concerned at their effect, tried to suppress them. A muddle round a last

The Revolution of 1848 in Paris.

great banquet, planned to be held in Paris in February that year, grew into a riot, the riot into an insurrection, the insurrection into the fall of Louis-Philippe and the proclamation of a Republic—second of that name.

In March, 1848, revolution struck fire in Vienna and Berlin, Prague and Budapest. In Vienna a student rising—almost a student lark—sufficed to topple the stiff, mindless regime. In Hungary, the news of revolution in Paris set off the revolution Kossuth had long nursed—a nonrevolutionary revolution to begin with, which soon exceeded the constitutional limits it had first respected. The speech that Kossuth made as soon as word from the Seine had reached the Tisa's banks, turned him into an international figure.

Master of the Hungarian Diet and of public opinion, Kossuth demanded an independent administration for the Hungarian kingdom, with separate army, government, and finance, as well as constitutions for the other Habsburg provinces. The Diet voted for this and also for a free press, a national guard, the abolition of feudal rights, and the taxation of nobles. Considering that the Diet was made up of noblemen, this was not doing badly.

In Berlin, news of events in Paris also encouraged the hopes of liberals, the fever of young men and businessmen and workers who hoped that the king of Prussia would give his kingdom a constitution at last and then unite Germany around it. Anarchy and good feelings reigned in these and in the other capitals of lesser German states.* National guards were founded, liberal governments were set up, assemblies gath-

* The only reactionary revolution came in Bavaria, where it was carried out against the artistic king and his liberal mistress: Lola Montez, darling of the radical students, horror of priests and conservatives, who had interfered in politics to get higher salaries for teachers and help install a Protestant prime minister. The King abdicated, Lola went into exile and eventually died in the United States; and Bavaria went back to its beery conservatism.

ered to write constitutions and plan for the future that was opening up.

The outbreak which the Holy Allies had feared and Metternich had striven to prevent had come at last. Louis Philippe had fled to England and Metternich and Guizot also took refuge across the Channel. The king of Prussia rode through his capital with a tricolor cockade in his hat; the imbecile Austrian emperor sanctioned a constitution; so did the Pope and the king of Sardinia, acclaimed as the hopes of a new liberal Italy. Czechs and Hungarians were asserting their autonomy; Germans and Italians were clamoring for national unity. The house that Metternich held up for the past thirty-four years collapsed in all its parts. England, which had never been a part of it, remained apart, avoiding revolution once again. While Europe writhed in the grip of new convulsions, the only barricade seen in London was one which Foreign Office clerks had built in their windows with bound volumes of *The Times,* to defend themselves against the Chartist violence that never came.

Yet, as glorious spring turned to dusty summer, the victors fell to quarreling away their spoils. In Italy, Charles Albert did not want a league under the Pope, and Pius IX liked war against Catholic Austria even less than he liked the revolution. The federal solution having failed, the only alternatives left were Mazzini's republic or a union under the house of Savoy. The latter seemed crushed with the Austrian victory of Custozza in July. The former fizzled out in the siege of Rome, eventually taken by French troops in 1849. Reaction triumphed, frequently atrocious, always stifling. Piedmont, which had tried to unite the peninsula in an Italian kingdom, survived only because the French would not allow it to be eliminated. Charles Albert abdicated, but his successor, Victor Emmanuel II, could hope to persevere. The Pope, thrown back by fear and principle to the reactionary camp, the monarchy of Savoy remained the only hope of Italian patriots.

The Hungarians, who had begun by asserting their rights against their Austrian masters, ended by trying to impose them on their own subjects. While liberal for Hungarians, the new regime's nationalism made Croats, Romanians, and Germans resent its attempts to impose the rule of Budapest and of the Hungarian language. They insisted on the rights of Magyar language and education against any other; and on the right of Magyars to rule all other races in the Magyar kingdom. In the new Diet, only Hungarian was accepted; in all higher schools Hungarian had to be taught, even where the local speech was different. Vienna did not fail to encourage the resentments this aroused.

Romantic nationalism had gained Croatia too, much of it imbibed during the French occupation of Dalmatia. It fed upon the work of historians and lexicographers who plumbed the depths of time for memories of medieval greatness overlaid by habit and oblivion. The Croat language, long forgotten among the educated, was revived and Magyar domination challenged. Croatian particularism, from which Vienna

had shied away during the thirties, now proved useful and the Habsburg government did not fail to invoke it against the nationalist pretensions of the rebels in Budapest. The Slovaks in the north, the Saxons
and the Romanians of Transylvania, also protested against the Magyar
tyranny and the decision of the Assembly in Budapest to incorporate
them, unconsulted, in a realm that showed so little regard for their
own national aspirations. But it would be the newly elected *Ban* (Governor) of Croatia, Colonel Joseph Jellačic, who first asserted the freedom of his province and then, after a long and weary struggle, helped
Russian troops reduce Hungary to submission.

Defeat was followed by repression, a brutal military occupation,
and the abolition of the country's secular autonomy. Hungary was administered by absolute bureaucrats backed by a newly recruited *gendarmerie*. Higher education was carried out in German, particularist
privileges eliminated. The poorer peasants, left in possession of their
freeholds, benefited; nobles and middle classes were hard-hit by loss of
land and ruinous taxation. Kossuth, from exile, called for emancipation, but this, when it came in the 1860's, came not through further
revolution but through conciliation.

Germany: Reaction Triumphant   The worst disillusions came in the
German lands. The liberals, unexpectedly bombarded into office by the
March revolution, dreamed of Parliamentary government and industrial development, of federal union opening rich vistas of political and
economic freedom, careers opened to talent and not just to birth,
riches available for investment. There were railroads to build, banks to
found, factories to create, fortunes to be made. But could these prospects secure and keep the support of those masses whose risings had
opened the gate of power, and without which the old order would sweep
them out again? The hard core of those masses were artisans, and
they wanted a return to just those gild regulations which the liberals
opposed, and the destruction of the machines which the liberals cherished. Peasant insurrection or industrial unrest threatened the property and order that stood highest on the list of liberal principles. By
April-May, the moderate liberals in power—lawyers, teachers, businessmen—had repressed any incipient revolution from below, and gathered
in Frankfurt to forge a constitution in which liberty and property, opposition and order, could recently combine. While the peasants clamored for rural reform, artisans for industrial regulation, and counter-
revolutionaries sulked or ranted, the liberals tried "to assure the middle
class a preponderant influence over the state," formulated a declaration of rights, a federal union based on manhood suffrage and economic unity, and finally, in March, 1849, a new constitution.

Meanwhile, small farmers, small artisans, workers without work,
peasants without land, gildsmen without gilds, strove only to survive.
Ideology meant nothing to them; food, work, security meant all. The

The opening of the Frankfurt Parliament,
May 18, 1848.

philosophical debates, the political struggles were of little interest to them except insofar as they advanced their cause, a cause which they hoped the old authorities would take to heart, then the liberals, then the patriarchal authoritarians of Bismarck's ilk. The men of Frankfurt had lost touch with their political supporters: dissatisfied artisans and handicraftsmen were rejected for the sake of free enterprise which they bitterly opposed, rustic support alienated by refusing to violate proprietary rights on behalf of the peasants.

During this time, reaction regained lost ground. The conservatives extolled particularism against federalism, men against machines, crafts against industrial anarchy and the money power, romantic loyalties against the liberal ideology. While the debate went on in Frankfurt, Vienna and Prague had been subdued by Austrian arms, Berlin had slunk back to obedience, one prince after another had recovered power either by force or, as in Prussia, by deals in which the peasants and the urban artisans got some of the things they wanted, like credit institutions and gild regulations in return for their support.

In March, 1848, Kossuth had called on "our beloved archduke Francis-Joseph," the Emperor's eighteen-year-old nephew, to support the aspirations of a free people. By December, while bitter war raged in Hungary, the Emperor Ferdinand abdicated in favor of Francis-Joseph, who would retain the throne until 1916. The new emperor's regard for a free people's aspirations was mirrored in the policies of the soldiers around him. The assembly was dissolved and the constitution abrogated. And still the Frankfurt Assembly talked on. By the time Parliament offered the imperial dignity to Frederick William IV, the king of Prussia was ready to reject what he called "the crown from the gutter." The Frankfurt Parliament melted away. A few scattered republican risings found little support and were quickly put down. The German

Confederation was restored and reaction triumphed, along with Austrian influence.

In 1848, says A. J. P. Taylor, "German history reached its turning point and failed to turn." Yet signposts for the new road had been laid down, the Germanies had been brought into the nineteenth-century world, the political problems raised in 1848 would be dealt with in the 1850's, and, even though German political developments took a different course than those that we can observe further west, their social and intellectual coloring would henceforth be the same.

France: The Most Singular Insurrection   In France, the King had fallen because he had served interests too narrow to afford a solid base, ignored the call for electoral reform which would have broadened it, and the demands for social reforms which were becoming louder. Political dissatisfaction and social distress combined in a familiar mixture and exploded as we might expect, but as no one at that particular time expected. Once the explosion had taken place, the tensions which had caused it still remained. Slavery was at last abolished in French overseas territories, and also flogging in the navy; public libraries were set up, agricultural schools in the countryside, even a university course for women, and government grants kept the theaters going by distributing free tickets to the poor. But, when it came down to essentials, there would be manhood suffrage, but there would not be work. There was little the Republic could do about this during a depression and less that contemporary economic ideas predisposed it to do. The middle class got the vote,* the workers were refused the right to work, and the vast majority of Frenchmen approved. So, in June, barricades arose for the second time that year, and the workers, thoroughly isolated both from their erstwhile middle-class allies and from a disapproving nation, fought alone, and lost, and were massacred. "It was not," Tocqueville recorded, "a political struggle, but a struggle of class against class, a sort of Servile War . . . the revolt of one whole section of the population against another;" and it was something new: "The most singular insurrection . . . in our history," a harbinger of things to come.

Americans in Europe at the time, who consistently rejoiced at popular successes and criticized the miserable conditions which lower classes at home in America escaped, doubted whether the revolutions could come to port with class divisions as intense and leaders as impractical as they were. European society was affected by a sickness that *America felix* had escaped. The Austrian assembly abolished the feudal system almost absent-mindedly before moving on to other things. The Germans, gathered in Frankfurt, talked more of unity than of reform. Mazzini told

* The Constitution of the Second Republic would amend manhood suffrage by requiring three years' residence in the same place, thus specifically excluding workers and the poor, who often changed their lodgings. Note that the formula "universal suffrage" gave no thought to women.

the tailors of Milan to wait when they asked for better pay and relief from Sunday work. In France, the republicans aggravated provincials and peasants by raising taxes partly intended to keep the workers quiet, but refused any hearing to the workers themselves. Meanwhile, the newly self-conscious nationalists were clashing with one another.

The theorists of nationalism had seen it as the foundation of widespread harmony and peace. Patriotism, wrote the French historian Jules Michelet, "is the necessary initiation for universal brotherhood." Mankind, cried Mazzini, dedicated apostle of Italian nationalism, "is an alliance of all nations to carry out their mission on earth in peace and love." But competing aspirations, however high-minded, foundered on the rocks of intransigence. Nationalism turned out to breed less harmony than divisions. In place after place, as Metternich had predicted, the veil which liberalism had cast over political revolts was torn down by radicalism in action.

Revolution had been defeated once again, partly by the dissensions that action had revealed, partly by the indifference or hostility of the majority toward a "revolution of the intellectuals," but largely by the surviving backbone of the Holy Alliance: the Tsar, the Emperor, and their armies, which, in the end, acted the part allotted to them in 1815. Reaction triumphed in Germany, in Italy, in Hungary, wherever Russia and Austria held sway. Hangings, whippings, stifling repression, marked the restoration of legitimate order. Police kept watch over the loyalty of teachers and civil servants everywhere. Even Froebel's *kindergarten* were suppressed as dangerous centers of socialism and atheism. Of those voices that could still be heard, only that of the British Foreign Secretary rose to condemn the brutality of military repression and to describe the Austrian troops as "the greatest brutes that ever called themselves by the undeserved name of civilized men."

The spate of revolutions which culminated in 1848 seemed to have had little effect on Europe, little indeed on the map of it: Serbia and Greece had come into existence, Spain and Portugal had lost great territories overseas, but, though in each case this stemmed out of rebellion, it had been achieved only as a result of intervention by some greater power. Not popular but power politics still reigned. Not revolutions but power struggles on traditional lines recast the map of Europe in the years following 1848. The next thirty years showed that not newfangled revolutions but old-fashioned wars would forge new Europe much in the image of that antiquated one it liked to reject as obsolete.

Withal, the revolutions had not failed as badly as it might appear. Russia and Turkey apart, the feudal autocracies which rode out the storms of 1789 did not survive the convulsions of 1848. The feudal system was dead, even in the most reactionary states which came out of the torment modernized: with forms of suffrage and assembly, new judicial, tax, and administrative structures. Social legislation had been used in Austria and in Prussia to splinter the revolutions and detach peasants, workers, or artisans from the political liberals. This legislation endured when the liberals had been defeated. Vast land reforms had been carried through, serfdom and legal servitude abolished, the conquests of 1789 carried forward to the rest of Europe. 1848, writes the French historian, Charles Pouthas, "brought about the end of a world, exhausted the ideology of 1789 by fulfilling it."

That *liberty* which had been one of the great slogans of 1789—one of those words that have more value, apparently, than sense—had been won; by some. The revolutionary Buonarotti derided it as no more than "the unlimited faculty to acquire." But many thinking men accepted the definition and thought that it was good. This was the point of view of those "higher and middling orders" which Macaulay, the historian, regarded as "the natural representatives of the human race" and which between 1830 and 1850 were finally taking over from the old regime.

Whether we attribute it to the political revolution or to the apolitical —industrial—revolution, the change cannot be ignored. This was when the black coat, symbol of bourgeois values, became the accepted garb of polite society despite original protests against men turning up in drawing rooms wearing "working dress." This was when the morality of Franklin's *Poor Richard,* with its respect for social utility and private enterprise, triumphed throughout the West. This was when moral values began to acquire a quantitative air reminiscent of industrial accountancy: a man's time is money, a man's word is as good as gold, a man's worth is evaluated in cash or credit, a man's happiness becomes the sum of an equation between pain and pleasure. The new society wanted to count, to measure, to know everything. Statistics, inquiries, reports, blue books of royal or parliamentary commissions, cascaded upon the century and upon an avid public. Unquiet, self-conscious, public opinion demanded them and fed its anxieties upon them. Curiosity, interest, replaced fear and suspicion of the census, of statistics, and inquiries. Facts, quantitative proofs, furnished the arguments of politicians and the color of the novels that the public read.

These people believed in progress: the progress which their predecessors promised and their heirs enjoyed. The "age of revolution" was the "age of improvement" too. About 1820 we find Walter Scott referring to the "improvement of national taste and delicacy." In 1848, Macaulay's *History of England* delighted in the fact that its story would fill all patriots with hope when they see how the history of England since 1688 "is eminently the story of physical, of moral, and of intellectual improvement." Even the least pleasing aspects of the new men stemmed from improving motives. Bourgeois snobbery was the new arrivals' desperate attempt to fit into the old society whose structures were still standing; hypocrisy insisted on some standards of morality and behavior; prudishness attempted to supplant the laxness and brutality of the older world; temperance campaigned against the plague of drunkenness which raised impassable barriers to social and political progress; "respectability" tried to attain and spread a new civilization, rather unrefined, better nevertheless than the gross brutality which ruled among the masses and especially over women, whom the new views protected with a kind of cosseting despotism; the gospel of earnestness and labor sought to make the most of new opportunities. The results could not be ignored: "Europe is racing towards democracy . . ." wrote Chateaubriand in 1834. "France and England like two enormous battering rams beat again and again upon the crumbling ramparts of the old society."

True, dreams of the future are sometimes an uneasy haven from present torments, as Condorcet indicated when he concluded his *Sketch for a Historical Picture of the Human Mind* (1794) with the admission that to contemplate the prospects of continuous improvement "is for him an asylum, in which the memory of his persecutors cannot pursue him." But there were concrete achievements to show, where there had been only dreams before. In 1816 Robert Owen could boast that in his mills at New Lanark 2,000 employees produced as much as the whole population of Scotland would have done sixty years before. "Wealth and speed are the things the world most admires . . ." wrote Goethe in a letter of 1825; "this is the century of clever minds, of practical men who grasp things easily . . ." What such minds and men achieved, no one has said better than two of their most typical representatives, the authors of the *Communist Manifesto,* writing in 1847.

[The bourgeoisie] has been the first to show what man's activity can bring about. It has accomplished wonders far surpassing Egyptian pyramids, Roman aqueducts and Gothic cathedrals: it has conducted expeditions that put in the shade all former Exoduses of nations and crusades. . . . The bourgeoisie, by the rapid improvement of all instruments of production, by the immensely facilitated means of communication, draws all, even the most barbarian, nations into civilization. . . . It creates a world after its own image. . . . It has created enormous cities, has greatly increased the urban population . . . and has thus rescued a considerable part of the population from the idiocy of rural life. . . . It has agglomerated population, centralized means of production, and has concentrated property in a few hands. . . . Political centralization [means] one nation, with one government, one code of laws, one national class interest, one frontier and one tariff.

The bourgeoisie, during its rule of scarce one hundred years, has created more massive and more colossal productive forces than have all preceding generations together. Subjection of Nature's forces to man, machinery, application of chemistry to industry and agriculture, steam navigation, railways, electric telegraphs, clearing of whole continents for cultivation, canalization of rivers, whole populations conjured out of the ground— what earlier centuries had even a presentiment that such productive forces slumbered in the lap of social labor?

Chapter 14

SENSE AND SENSIBILITY: THE ENLIGHTENMENT

Eighteenth-Century Science

The Applications of Science: Technology

"This is the enlightened century of philosophy . . . the age of enlightened reason . . . the philosophic century . . ." exulted the academicians of Tuscany in mid-eighteenth century.

Enlightenment meant knowledge and knowledge meant science, enthusiasm for the natural sciences especially, for experiments private and public, for courses which fashionable ladies and gentlemen crowded out, all cultivated people studying the mysteries of natural philosophy and worshiping at the shrine of scientists like Buffon or Franklin. Such widespread favor could be superficial, and often was, as when Joseph Addison praised the new science in the *Spectator* (No. 262 of 1711) because "it draws men's minds off from the bitterness of party and furnishes them with subjects of discourse that may be treated without warmth or passion . . ." The air pump, the quadrant, the barometer, could be "innocent amusements" diverting busy spirits from more disturbing activities.

That may have been a reason why many rulers sponsored the setting up of such a spate of scientific academies (Berlin, 1700; Uppsala, 1710; St. Petersburg, 1724; Stockholm, 1739; Copenhagen, 1743); but hardly the chief one. For the academies, once the select club and refuge of a cultivated elite, now turned to stimulate intellectual activity among the greatest possible number, to serving state and society and encouraging unity between them, to elaborating but also spreading knowledge. The sciences, explained an erudite Tuscan, were meant "not to exhibit ingenuity with useless pomp, but to be of service to navigation and manufacturing." Scientists had to be useful; techniques and application, once excluded from intellectual concern, became one of their primary interests: science had to be *applied*. The general laws of nature of the seventeenth century were brought to bear not only on the world as it was, but as it could be made to be: man could manipulate them for his benefit. He need not only admire his world—he could master and remake it.

Navigation and cartography offered a crucial instance of the truth of this. The problem of establishing longitudes still plagued the sailors. In 1750, Dutch and British maps placed the Newfoundland coast nine degrees from its true site; in 1741 Admiral Anson had wandered for a month looking for the island of Juan Fernández in the Pacific while eighty of his men died of scurvy; in 1763 a French ship bound for the Cape of Good Hope ended in Brazil; in 1775 a British ship bound for Gibraltar thought it was off Cape Finistère at the time when it was running aground near La Rochelle. In 1714 the British Parliament had offered £20,000 to anyone who could provide a solution to the longitude problem. By the 1760's and the seventies a chronometer helped provide one, and its inventor received at least half the prize money. If the device did not come into general use for one or two decades, that was no fault of the scientists bustling about their useful tasks.

This alliance between social and scientific progress comes out very clearly in the famous Lunar Society whose members began meeting around 1766 at Soho, in Birmingham, where Matthew Boulton's works provided the center for their original scientific-technological interests. Among the members were Boulton and James Watt, Samuel Galton, a manufacturer and chemist interested in optics and a fellow of the Royal Society, Dr. Joseph Priestley (1733–1804), the Unitarian minister who discovered oxygen and its role in supporting combustion. They would often by joined by John Wilkinson, the ironmaster who married Priestley's sister, by Josiah Wedgwood, whose work in chemistry revolutionized pottery techniques and glazing, and by the famous Dr. Erasmus Darwin living in nearby Lichfield. These men and their friends conducted experiments, reported on their findings, and their discussions of scientific topics soon moved on to the wider social and political questions that arose from them.

Men such as these moved easily and naturally between scientific inquiry, technological improvement, and civic affairs. For instance, with the population of Birmingham doubling between 1760 and 1800, radical problems of social hygiene arose. It was the Unitarian friends of Priestley and of Boulton who founded the municipal hospitals in Manchester and Birmingham, advanced projects for smoke abatement, town planning, and education. A man like the Liverpool banker William Roscoe, author of a then-famous *Life of Lorenzo de Medici* (1795), tried to turn Liverpool into the Venice of the north, founded its Society for the Encouragement of the Arts of Painting and Design (1773), organized the first public exhibition of paintings in the English provinces, fought for the abolition of the Test Acts and of slavery. As late as 1809, when the Lunar Society was no more, its radical membership blown apart by the storms of the French Revolution which most of them had welcomed, a visitor to Soho found that its influence survived "in a spirit of scientific curiosity and free inquiry, which even yet makes some stand against the combined forces of Methodism, Toryism and the love of gain."

We might look upon practical applications as a minor branch of scientific inquiry, in which curiosity and inventiveness used some possibilities suggested by research with sometimes quite remarkable results, but which stemmed rather from ingenuity than from creative thinking. In this category should probably be placed the balloons which thrilled late eighteenth-century crowds, beginning with the one the Montgolfier brothers sent up in 1783, by harnessing the properties of hydrogen. The first manned flight took place in the same year; then, in 1785, an American and a Frenchman flew across the Channel from west to east. The armies of the revolution would be equipped with balloon companies which they used for military observation. However, the great problem remained that of steering, and this was not solved until the late nineteenth century by the German, Ferdinand von Zeppelin. More practical, perhaps, was the visual semaphore system first introduced in France by Claude Chappe (1763–1805), who persuaded the revolutionary Committee of Public Safety to introduce his telegraph towers. These brought messages back to Paris in a fraction of the time that news had previously taken, and they remained in use well into mid-nineteenth century, until superseded by the electric telegraph.*

This latter probably came into existence to serve the spreading railroads' need for a warning system. The German astronomer and mathematical genius K. F. Gauss (1777–1855), who had at the age of ten worked out on his slate the principle of arithmetical progression, and who later became famous for his work on magnetism and optics, devised an electric wire which could carry coded messages between his observatory at Göttingen and his physics laboratory. Rejected by the German railways, Gauss's invention was taken up by the English, whence it would spread to other railway systems, was endowed with a code alphabet by Samuel Morse, and opened to public use in the late 1840's. By

---

* The Chappe telegraph took three minutes to convey a message from Paris to Calais (170 miles, 33 stations), eight minutes from Paris to Brest (375 miles, 54 stations), and twenty minutes from Paris to Toulon (667 miles, 100 stations).

Experience Aerostatique faite a Versailles le 19 Sept.bre 1783 en presence de leurs Majestes et de la famille Royale par M. de Montgolfier avec un Balon de 52 pieds d'hauteur sur 41 de Diametres Cette Superbe machine a fond d'asur avec le Chiffre du Roi pesant 900 livres. Ce balon a été enlevé avec toutes l'aplaudissement de tout les Spectateurs et a tombé dans le Bois de Vaucresson Carefour Marechal.

Montgolfier's balloon rises from the courtyard at Versailles, September 19, 1783.

1848, Siemens engineers were trying out a submarine cable in Kiel Harbor; and the following year news of the Frankfurt Parliament electing Frederick William IV as emperor of Germany was sent to Berlin by the first long-range electric telegraph wire in less than one hour.

There were numerous other inventions which contributed to changing our lives, like the first gaslights which appeared in London in 1803; the arc-lamp devised by Humphrey Davy in 1801; the canning method which Nicolas Appert provided to preserve the food for Napoleon's military and naval needs; the stethoscope invented by another Frenchman, the great physician René Laënnec, and first used in 1817; the printing presses capable of turning out 1,100 sheets an hour in 1814 and 8,000 by 1846, when the rotary press introduced a completely new dimension into printing; the sewing machine invented in France and perfected in the United States, which revolutionized clothes manufacture, making ready-made clothes possible and also the sweatshops; and the kindred American machine for the mass production of boots; not least, the humble sulfur match, which, invented in 1809, would come into general use in the 1820's and 30's.

Great advances were also made in medicine, greatest of them the innoculation against smallpox which Edward Jenner (1749–1823) perfected by a vaccine made from cowpox serum. Vaccinations began to be administered in the 1790's, were offered free of charge in France beginning with Napoleon, in England after 1840 (where they only became compulsory for infants in 1853), were gradually accepted everywhere, though some suggested that they went against destiny and Divine omnipotence. In the 1750's, Dr. James Lind had discovered the use of citrus juices (lime, lemon, orange) in preventing scurvy. His methods were introduced in the British Navy in the 1790's with staggering re-

H. Roger-Viollet

The Academy of Sciences at St. Petersburg, founded in 1724.

sults, cutting the casualty rate from sickness almost by three-quarters. Most interesting perhaps was the new enlightened interest in physical exercise and games, doctors and patriots both agreeing that gymnastics could build better bodies, train better soldiers, make better citizens.*

Last but not least, the harnessing of steam would provide a mobile and effective moving force to replace unreliable wind and water. The steam engine was invented in the 1680's or 1690's by Denis Papin (1647–1712?), a French Huguenot refugee, assistant to the Dutch scientist Christian Huyghens, who was fascinated by the possibility of propelling a boat by steam. It was improved, as we have noted earlier, by Thomas Savery and Thomas Newcomen of England, who at the turn of the seventeenth into the eighteenth century applied it to mine drainage pumps; and finally perfected by James Watt, a Scot who in the 1760's applied it to industrial use. A steam truck had been developed in France in 1770, but locomotives were first developed in England around 1800. A steam and paddle steamer was demonstrated at Lyons in 1783, but it would be in England and the United States that the new invention was successfully applied. We can do no better than quote Erasmus Darwin's ecstatic paean of 1789 to the steam engine's possibilities:

Soon shall thy arm, *unconquer'd steam!* afar
Drag the slow barge, or drive the rapid car;
Or on wide-waving wings expanded bear
The flying chariot through the fields of air.
—Fair crews triumphant, leaning from above,
Shall wave their handkerchiefs as they move;
Or warrior bands alarm the gaping crowd,
And armies shrink beneath the shadowy cloud.

* The relation between hygiene and enlightenment was sometimes very close: Botot, inventor of the mouthwash, was secretary to the revolutionary Director, Barras.

Philosophical Aspects of Science

However crucial, this technological branch was but a secondary aspect of the scientific revolution of the time. Science made little direct contribution to technology, beyond its point of view. It suggested system, order, method, logic. It contributed agronomy to agriculture and interchangeable parts to industry: precision, machine tools, accuracy of construction and production. But modern science was really something else. It was the heritage of the seventeenth century, when teleology had been displaced by mechanism, when the view that developments are to be traced to their ends was replaced by a relation to causes, and empirical observations were generalized into formal laws suggesting a general structure which could be checked by experiment and modified by fresh observation.

Modern science was power, and power was the understanding and control of motion. Newton had sought the force that moved planets according to Kepler's model, and had concluded that this force must be for each planet proportional to its size and in inverse proportion to the square of its distance from the sun. This attraction was exercised not only by the sun on its planets, but by all planets on those bodies that came within their own spheres—satellites like the moon, or simple objects. Here was the theory of universal gravitation, worked out with the help of a new mathematics, the infinitesimal calculus. This had been developed by Newton and by Leibniz, each working separately to find a way of simultaneously expressing a given state and how such a state varied in direction and intensity, that is, a method which would enable them to analyze continuous movement rather than stable states. Eighteenth-century mathematicians improved this method, while by mid-century astronomers verified Newton's findings. The researches and discov-

An early eighteenth-century laboratory.

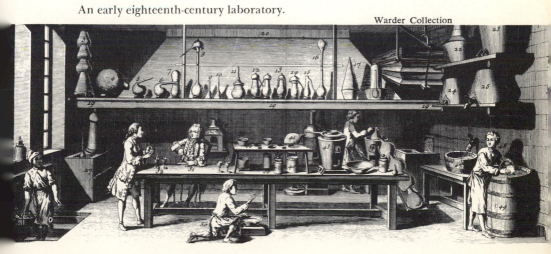

eries that this set off may be said to culminate with the publication of Laplace's *Exposition of the System of the World* (1796), in which a vast and changing universe appears in continuous evolution, full of galaxies, of suns, of stars, all of which take shape, burn, die, vanish, over an immense space and time.

Meanwhile, the search for power was the search for heat, for sources of kinetic energy and for its control. First, heat had to be measured. Galileo had invented the first primitive thermometer and Robert Boyle improved it. Fahrenheit, a meteorological instrument-maker from Danzig, worked out a scale for it (1724); Celsius, professor of Astronomy at Uppsala, built a more conventional one (1742), known as the centigrade; others were formulated. By 1780, nineteen scales were in use. The thermometer enabled Joseph Black (1728–1799), professor at Glasgow University, to differentiate between quantity and intensity of heat, between the latent heat of bodies and the specific heat of different bodies, and hence to infer the possibilities of their fusion and to control the steam arising out of this. And Black's labors permitted James Watt to perfect his engine.

But that was a side product. The main subject and object of these labors was really electricity. The possibility of producing quantities of electricity and storing it in condensers such as the Leyden jar (a glass bottle coated with tin foil), provided a marvelous toy, a source of canned lightning whose demonstration never ceased to fascinate. Louis XV roared with laughter to see a mile-long line of monks, all holding hands, leap up as one at being administered an electric shock. John Wesley was a confirmed believer in the curative power of such shocks. In 1748, Franklin and his friends killed a turkey by electric shock, roasted it on an electric spit over a fire lit by using the resources of the Leyden jar, and ate it while drinking the health of all famous electricians in electrified glasses, to the sound of the discharge of an electrical battery. "Electricity is universally allowed to be a very entertaining and surprising phenomenon," wrote Charles Burney in 1771, "but it has frequently been lamented that it has never yet, with much certainty, been applied to any useful purpose."

Burney was wrong. In 1752, Benjamin Franklin had drawn electricity from clouds by his famous kite and invented a lightning rod which George III would soon set up on Buckingham House. The first lightning rod in London appeared in 1762, in Italy in 1776, in Paris in 1782. By that year, Philadelphia had 400. The seventeenth-century philosopher Boileau had thought that thunder was the voice of God. Now lightning was explained and neutralized: divine ire had to find other means of expression. Then, in the 1780's, Luigi Galvani (1737–1798), professor of anatomy at Bologna, conducted experiments on frogs which convinced him that the animal's body was an organic Leyden jar: a holder and conductor of electricity. And Alessandro Volta (1745–1827), pro-

An illustration of Galvani's experiment on frogs.

fessor of physics at Como, found that electricity could affect the nerves, invented the electrical battery—an artificial producer of current—with which in 1800 water would be decomposed into its elements.

The new electrical current provided the means of analyzing bodies into their component parts; and chemistry in turn suggested that electricity might be measured, its quantity proportional to the mass of elements it isolates. In Copenhagen, Oerstedt discovered that magnets are activated by electricity too. The study of electromagnetics (on which the electrical telegraph would be based) was developed by Ampère and Faraday (the latter's work also permitting the conception of the dynamo), and its measurement suggested by the German, Gauss. This meant that electricity was now incorporated in mechanics, as astronomy had been the century before, and that it came within the empire of mathematics.

Soon, the same would happen to the universe. George Louis Leclerc, Count de Buffon (1707–1788), was himself something of a force of nature, with his love of pleasure, of money, of food, his speculations and his business enterprises, his peacock enjoyment of adulation in the *salons*. Yet he found time to publish thirty-two volumes of *Natural History* (1749–89), from which all spiritual activity was excluded and where natural history became simply the study of matter in motion: a system of laws of universal and necessary relations between observed facts. In 1749, Buffon's *Theory of the Earth,* and again in 1778 his *Ages of Nature,* outlined a theory in which the earth and other planets were parts of the sun's incandescent matter, torn off perhaps in some collision and progressively cooling while the sun (because of its mass) continued to burn. Buffon suggested the stages through which the earth had passed, the appearance of physical and animal life on it, the origin of fossils. He estimated the earth's age—some twelve times longer than that then approved by theology—and guessed the time it would take (93,000 years) before further cooling would again extinguish life on earth. Here was an audacious pattern, suggestive of evolution, based on geological and chemical experiments, and harbinger of modern geology and history— quite at variance with accepted dogmas and highly attractive to the educated reader, the more so because of the author's brilliant style.

Since it went counter to Genesis, *The Theory of the Earth* was condemned. Buffon submitted in word and persevered in deed, going on to suggest, at least by implication, that complex animals had developed from simpler organisms, which, in due course, became the organs of an evolving whole. This was the beginning of transformist doctrines—which Jean Baptiste Lamarck (1744–1829), tutor of Buffon's son, would formulate early in the nineteenth century.

The Swedish biologist Linnaeus, had classed man with the primates. Buffon had resigned himself to treating him as one of the animal species. In 1809, Lamarck's *Zoological Philosophy* suggested a theory of the evolution of species, the species varying according to the physical challenges they encounter and to which they respond or die. Here was the long-accepted notion of fixed, divinely created species challenged; and the debate this produced rose to a high point in 1830, so that Johann Peter Eckermann, expecting to find his friend Goethe preoccupied by news of the revolution in France, discovered him instead fascinated by "a far graver debate" going on there. Goethe was right: Lamarck's views may not have been correct, but they were far more revolutionary than their political counterparts. Nature, he said, is *the* great plastic force that makes, unmakes, remakes, animals and species. The physical environment changes; so do needs, so does behavior by willful action, and this becomes habit which eventually will affect the relevant organ, the whole organism, and ecology itself. Here was a voluntaristic and relativistic doctrine, appropriate, as we shall see, to the romantic age.

Already, Marie-Jean Condorcet in his *Historical Outline of the Progress of the Human Mind* (1794) had drawn his own conclusions from the science of his time and produced a theory of progress which sees man as indefinitely perfectible, confined only by the physical limitations of evolution. Condorcet's essay, completed on the run and on the brink of death, was an act of faith rather than a scientific argument; but it would link science and history with the romanticism of those who came after him.

In physics and also in chemistry—where it is hard for a layman to quite understand the dividing line—crucial developments were taking place. Here, too, the English seem to have held the experimental lead, while Frenchmen were the theoretical masters of their time.* Henry Cavendish (1731–1810) discovered inflammable air—that is, hydrogen; Joseph Priestley isolated and recognized seven new gases, among them oxygen and ammonia; while Daniel Rutherford (1749–1819) isolated "noxious air," or nitrogen. The experiments of Antoine Laurent Lavoisier (1743–1794) showed that air, fire, and water, which had been held

---

* Frenchmen published the first dictionary of chemistry in 1766, and the first dictionary of physics in 1781. The excellence of French chemists ensured that their side enjoyed the best gunpowder both in the American War of Independence and in the Revolutionary and Napoleonic Wars.

to be the basic elements, were actually compounds of other constituents: air being for instance a mixture of oxygen and nitrogen, water of hydrogen and oxygen. In 1789 Lavoisier's *Elementary Treatise of Chemistry* would do for that science what Newton's *Principia* had done for physics: provide the foundations for its study as a science, listing the elements, formulating the law of the indestructibility of matter. In 1791 Lavoisier could announce "the revolution in chemistry is accomplished." Three years later the other revolution, still advancing, would claim his head.

The revolution had taken place in more than chemistry. We have seen that for a great many people before 1800 science had been little more than a pastime or diversion. Now scientists became professionals, producing systematic treatises, instructing students, building a whole structure of teaching and communication which today we take for granted but which had never existed before. Experiment now became a structured procedure, conducted in established laboratories, with results reported in specialized periodicals. The French *Ecole Polytechnique,* founded in 1794, would, after 1806, be imitated throughout Germany, Switzerland, and Bohemia in *Technische Hochschulen* or technological institutes. When, in May, 1827, after twenty-five years of residence, Alexander von Humboldt left Paris for Berlin, it was an indication that the leadership in science and scientific research was shifting to Germany, where young men who had studied in Paris were now setting up their own laboratories and seminars, colleges, and specialized publications.

Science was no longer the preserve of a small elite. It had become a public concern. As scientific activity everywhere increased, discoveries would become cumulative and the progression which Malthus observed with so much dismay in the human race would be observed with mounting excitement in the scientific race: hopefully, the one making up for the other.

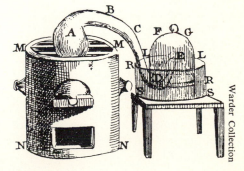

A contemporary illustration of the apparatus used by Lavoisier for the decomposition of air.

The Enlightenment and the *Philosophes*

At the end of the seventeenth century the first dictionary of the French Academy defined *philosophe* as one or all of these things: a student of the sciences, a wise man who lives a quiet life, a man who by free thought puts himself above the ordinary duties and obligations of civil life. The first of these definitions applies quite well to the protagonists of modern thought in eighteenth-century France, and the last applies in part, for *philosophes* though often emancipated, had a strong social conscience. The second definition, however, does not apply at all. Whether the philosophers were wise or not, they never lived or sought a quiet life.

What, then, were the *philosophes,* torchbearers of the eighteenth-century enlightenment? Many and different things but, chiefly, it would seem, rationalists determined to assess and teach the rights and powers of human intelligence. Pierre de Marivaux (1688–1763), the exquisite playwright of their age, has left us a working definition of what his generation meant by this. To philosophize, he says, is to render reason all its dignity, restore it to its rights, shake off the yoke of opinion and authority. This squares with the definition which Peter Gay, the most sympathetic American historian of the movement, has advanced in his book, *The Party of Humanity*: "The commitment to criticism, to humanity, to passion; the respect for the classical past coupled with a healthy self-confidence; stoic courage in the face of suffering; and irreverent humor . . ."

Decisive factors in shaping the doctrine of the *philosophes* were the science of Newton and the psychology of Locke. Newton taught that all nature is founded in universal law and can be mastered by the

Montesquieu, engraving by B. L. Henriquez. Opposite: Among the *philosophes* seated at the dining table are Voltaire with his hand raised, looking at d'Alembert in the left foreground. Diderot is seated on the left of Voltaire. Condorcet sits with his back to the reader in the center foreground. La Harpe is seated on Voltaire's immediate right.

human mind. Locke taught that "the faculty of reasoning seldom or never deceives those who trust in it"; and that men are reasonable beings, capable of using their own knowledge and intelligence for the promotion of their own happiness. So the *philosophes* believed that if you want to make men happy and perfect, all you had to do was to enlighten them. Enlighten about what? About themselves. "Sole judge of truth, in endless error hurled/The glory, jest and riddle of the world," men had to know themselves above all as social animals, understand the laws by which society lived and they in society, become historians and sociologists to know how they could live most fully and most reasonably. History was to provide the data for this, sociology interpret it, abstract reason analyze and conclude, argument persuade the world of the conclusions.

History as Sociology

Giovanni Battista Vico (1668–1744), who spent all of his life in his native Naples, appears as one of the founding fathers of sociology. His *New Science* (1725) explains how, within the human species, there are different societies, nations, formed according to peculiar circumstances, all of which must be studied in detail. Religion, law, government, ways of life and thought change under their own influence and that of other circumstances but, above all, according to superior cyclical laws which rule these evolutions. Among societies, peculiarities and uniformities may be found—statics and dynamics in social evolution, a sovereign law of eternal return. Appreciated only by a few friends, Vico himself was little known in his time; but a French traveler in Italy would read him and, through Charles de Secondat, Baron de Montesquieu (1689–1755), Vico affected the century.

639

In Montesquieu, sociology became the handmaiden of history—that is, of philosophy. The Frenchman observed, described, advanced from facts to laws and, thence, to principles. Examining the structure of societies, he would reveal their *laws,* that is, the principles on which they grow and work. His first and most popular book, *The Persian Letters* (1721), an ironic commentary on French society as seen through the eyes of two visiting Persians, placed all apparently fixed and unquestioned things, including monarchy, religion, and social values, in a relative and debatable light by comparing them with the institutions of Persia and Islam. His *Considerations on the Greatness of the Romans and on Their Decay* (1734) presented history as a tale of change, in which laws, institutions, and political power can be related to physical and economic circumstances and to social changes. At last, in 1748, his *Spirit of the Laws* sought to interpret the infinite diversity of laws and customs by which men ruled themselves; it deduced the principles of political institutions from their foundation in nature and historical circumstance and suggested the social implications of his conclusion that institutions were relative to circumstances and determined by them. Awareness of such determined laws would permit man, acting in consequence, adapting his social structures to their lessons, to move as freely in the social as in the physical world whose laws he had uncovered.

Liberty, said Montesquieu, is doing not what you want but what you ought to, and not being forced to do what you ought not. Liberty means freedom from arbitrary interference, from pressures that go contrary to the natural law which operates in a society just as it does in nature. But social laws, unlike their physical counterparts, differ from place to place. Some institutions are better suited here and others there, and laws should take this into consideration. Above all, though, laws must be not only good—that is, appropriate—but clear, and known, and properly applied, not subject to the arbitrary caprice of some prince.

This would become one of the first aims of the philosophers: "The finest right of humanity is to depend on the laws alone and not on the caprices of men," wrote Voltaire. "Liberty consists of depending on the laws alone. On this basis, a man is free today in Sweden, England, Holland, Switzerland, Geneva, Hamburg . . . A citizen of Amsterdam is a man; a citizen several degrees of longitude from there is a beast of burden." In this connection, it was important to limit the power of men, or groups of men, to interfere with laws. And Montesquieu's solution for control of power was that the legislative, executive, and judicial should never be concentrated in the same hands, but balanced one against the other as he thought was the case in England, social stability being based on continuous compromise and balance between competing interests.

Time was to show that Montesquieu's views had been too optimistic

CENTERS OF THE ENLIGHTENMENT

■ Cities with academies (with dates of founding)
● Birthplaces of writers and musicians

St. Petersburg (Sci. 1725)

Upsala (Sci. 1728)

Stockholm (Sci. 1741)

NORWAY

HOLBERG

SWEDEN

BALTIC SEA

RUSSIA

SCOTLAND
SMITH
Edinburgh (Sci. 1731)
BURNS
HUME

NORTH SEA

Copenhagen (Sci. 1743)

DENMARK

KANT

HERDER

IRELAND
Dublin (Sci. 1739)
BURKE
SWIFT

Liverpool
RICHARDSON

HARTLEY
ENGLAND
PAINE

London (Lit. and Arts 1766)

FIELDING
LOCKE

Hamburg

Warsaw

HOLBACH

Berlin (Sci. 1700, Lit. and Arts 1703)

POLAND

Göttingen (Sci. 1750)

Erfurt (Sci. 1754)

HANDEL

LESSING

Cracow

NETHERLANDS
Amsterdam
MANDEVILLE

Antwerp

Brussels

HOLY

ROMAN

BACH

BEETHOVEN
GOETHE

GLUCK

BENTHAM
BLACKSTONE
DEFOE
GIBBON
HOGARTH
POPE

CONDORCET

EMPIRE

AUSTRIA

HAYDN

D'ALEMBERT
HELVETIUS
QUESNAY
TURGOT
VOLTAIRE

Paris

SCHILLER

Munich (Sci. 1730)

Vienna (Lit. and Arts 1704)

HUNGARY

DIDEROT

MOZART

ATLANTIC

OCEAN

Dijon (Sci. 1740)
BUFFON

SWITZ.

FRANCE

Lyons

Geneva
ROUSSEAU

Milan
BECCARIA

Verona (Sci. 1780)

Venice

ADRIATIC SEA

Bordeaux
MONTESQUIEU

Turin (Sci. 1760)

Genoa

Toulouse (Sci. 1746)

Marseilles

Bologna (Sci. 1712)

FEYJÓO

ITALY

CORSICA

Rome

Madrid (Lit. and Arts 1713)

Barcelona

Naples
VICO

PORTUGAL

SARDINIA

SPAIN

Lisbon 1790)

Seville

Palermo

MEDITERRANEAN

SEA

SICILY

and his impression of the English system wrong. But his ideas, rational and progressive, suited the tendencies of a buoyant age and would provide not only the base of the politics of his fellow *philosophes* but the fundamental inspiration of the American Constitution of 1787, the French Constitutions of 1791 and 1795, and of the Prussian Law Code of 1792. Above all, though, there was the long-range influence of the historical image he presented. History drew attention to changes which had occurred in the past, suggested that the present was also subject to change, a part of history in which change comes about because of what men do. Change is inevitable, but men are the actors in it. What was true of the past must also be true of the present; and society, whose institutions and ideas had been shown to evolve with changing conditions, was also subject to the laws of change. From a mere chronicle of change, history thus became its inspiration.

The relativism of Montesquieu had to be reconciled with the ruling humanist tradition, which saw men and societies obeying the same universally valid laws. This was first attempted by those who argued, in the classic vein, that diversity and incoherence were only apparent. Alexander Pope, the English poet, advanced the argument in his *Essay on Man* (1732–1734):

> All Nature is but Art, unknown to thee;
> All Chance, Direction, which thou canst not see;
> All Discord, Harmony not understood;
> All partial Evil, universal Good;
> And, spite of Pride, in erring Reason's spite,
> One truth is clear, *Whatever is* is *right*.

Such a confident attitude—which so irritated Voltaire, whose *Candide* is directed against "the mania for pretending that all is well when all is ill"—saw universal harmony not only in nature, but in society too where "God and Nature link'd the gen'ral frame,/and bade Self-love and Social be the same." The great morality tale of this point of view was to be found in Bernard Mandeville's *Fable of the Bees* (1714), with its argument that even private vices become public benefits, that each bee pursuing her selfish interest contributed to the well-being of the hive, and that the introduction of moral notions could lead only to decline and ruin. "Luxury," wrote Mandeville

> Employed a million of the poor,
> And odious pride a million more.
> Envy itself, and vanity
> Were ministers of industry;
> Their darling folly, fickleness,
> In diet, furniture and dress,
> That strange ridiculous vice, was made
> The wiry wheel that turned the trade.

Montesquieu approved the argument and so did Voltaire, though many others, moved by the puritan sentiments that often accompany progressive views, disapproved of conspicuous consumption. It was Rousseau who formulated this latter view. Luxury, he said, feeds a hundred poor in our towns and kills one hundred thousand in the countryside. But

Voltaire dictating even as he gets out of bed, by Huber. Musée Carnavalet, Paris.

Rousseau was no *philosophe* and, for the moment, we should turn rather to the *philosophes'* greatest and most typical representative, Voltaire (1694–1778).

Voltaire

Conservative in his liberalism, critical in his acceptance of situations which could and should always be improved, Voltaire sought to repair the social structure, not destroy it; and to repair it before its faults led it to destroy itself. A creature of "fire and fickleness," as Byron described him, Voltaire was also a man of sense, and this proved at least as dangerous as his passion. Whenever Voltaire turned his mind to accepted ideas, the effects tended to be disintegrating: "The art of government consists in taking the greatest amount of money possible from a large portion of the citizenry to hand it over to another portion." "History is nothing more than the record of those who have availed themselves of the property of others." "Faith consists of believing what our reason cannot believe." Voltaire respected not battles and soldiers, but men and works who "prepared pure and lasting pleasures for men yet to be born. . . . *I call great men all those who have excelled in creating what is useful or agreeable.* The plunderers of provinces are merely heroes."

His was a modern mind, utilitarian, practical, concrete, preferring canals to courts and a beautiful painting to military glory, opportunistic in reformism as in private life. His program, like that of the *philosophes* in general, was secular, cosmopolitan, and humanitarian. *Candide,* which charges ruthlessly against the kind of optimistic world view that seems tantamount to resignation, is a vigorous and pessimistically cheerful work. The best way to put up with life, it says, is by practical action, not resignation or metaphysics. Cultivate your garden: positive action within your accessible ken is the best kind, and the one most likely to make the world work a little better. All this, told with great verve, set in the midst of improbable yet very concrete events, sparkled its way to immortality.

Yet Voltaire's works were not mere literary exercises or diversions, they were political pamphlets and "military machines" in a long campaign against social injustice and, above all, against the *Infâme,* the infamous fanaticisms and superstitions that helped perpetuate the existing mess. If these campaigns were bitter, we must remember the atmosphere of repression and constraint within which Voltaire and his fellows labored, the occasional violences which stood out the more in the midst of enlightenment and relative tolerance. In 1720 England, Voltaire could not get over the freedom of conscience that Englishmen enjoyed: "An Englishman, as freeman, goes to heaven by the road he likes." In France this was not so. Protestants were not officially tolerated there until 1787. Huguenot assemblies were dispersed, men sent to the galleys, women to life imprisonment, pastors to the gallows, as late as 1762. That was the year when the Calvinist Jean Calas was broken on the wheel at Toulouse, accused of having murdered his son (who had actually committed suicide) to keep him from turning Catholic. This was the origin of a great campaign, led by Voltaire, which three years later secured acknowledgment of the judicial crime committed against Calas and compensation for his family. Then, in 1766, an eighteen-year-old nobleman, the Chevalier de la Barre, was convicted of disrespectful behavior toward the Holy Sacrament and condemned to have his tongue cut out, his head cut off, and his remains burnt by the public executioner, together with Voltaire's *Philosophical Dictionary* (1764), which had contributed to his sacrilegious mood.

Repression and Subversion

Such were the kinds of thing that hung over the heads of *philosophes* and of all those who might express their skepticism in public. Their books were burnt by the public hangman as contrary to true religion and good morals, or simply condemned and banned. They risked imprisonment, sometimes brief, sometimes less so (Diderot spent four years in jail, another man died in prison); or exile, like Voltaire, who had to escape repeatedly. Many of their works could circulate only secretly and could be confiscated by police. Louis Mercier's *Sketches of Paris Life,* published in Amsterdam during the 1780's, leaves the impression of an atmosphere prefiguring certain twentieth-century regimes: "It is eleven at night or five in the morning; there is a knock on the door, the servant opens, your room fills with a squad of *myrmidons, . . .* resistance is superfluous; everything that you might use as a weapon is kept away from you and the ensign, who will not fail to brag about his bravery, takes even your inkstand for a pistol. Next day a neighbor, who has heard a noise about the house, asks what it could have been:—Nothing, just a man that the police arrested.—What has he done?—We do not know; he may have committed murder or sold a suspected pamphlet.—But, Sir, there is some difference between the two offenses.—That is possible; but he has been arrested." No wonder the writers of the age opposed political and religious tyranny alike, the *lettres de cachet* or the equally arbitrary condemnations on moral, theological, or political grounds of Sorbonne, Parlement, or royal censorship.

No wonder, too, that their exhortations sapped at the foundations of the established order. Criticism and irreverence chipped away at notions and institutions long accepted without question, rationalism and humanism proposed plausible alternatives to authorities and beliefs now every day denounced as arbitrary or superstitious. The *philosophes* were more than men of letters: they were embattled propagandists. Their ideas, widely publicized, flew across the world to spark or articulate devastating notions in the British and Spanish colonies of America as well as throughout Europe. The *Encyclopedia* they turned out was being read on the banks of the Vistula and of the Mississippi: Voltaire, Diderot, and lesser men as well, were honored guests even at royal courts. Despots like Frederick or Catherine, who were far from practicing what was preached in Paris, nevertheless realized the value of *philosophes* as publicity agents and the use that could be made of the rational approach which they proposed. *Philosophes* staffed the new academies of eastern Europe, supplied tutors for princes, and professors for distant universities. Their publications and their correspondence cast a wide web over the western world; and foreign visitors, converted in the salons of Paris, carried their message back to Milan and Naples and Madrid, to Philadelphia, Warsaw, Petersburg, and Stockholm. Not since the Reformation had so few men exerted so much influence so far in space and time.

"The fewer superstitions, the less fanaticism," declared Voltaire; "and the less fanaticism, the fewer calamities." It was true that religion, apparently, had spilled less blood than politics, but its crimes appeared more glaring because religion itself had been meant to curb them. The *philosophes* were not against religion as such, but they considered that it should be a private matter. A few were atheist or agnostic, but most of them were *deists* who believed that no church was necessary to worship God. Men had from primitive times worshiped God in a great many

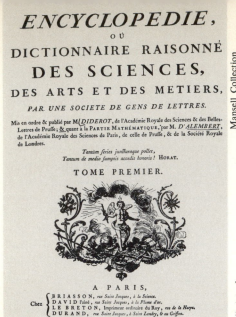

The title page from the first edition of Diderot's *Encyclopedia,* 1751. Opposite: an illustration from Diderot's *Encyclopedia,* depicting the manufacture of buttons.

ways, and out of this basic awareness and awe, this *natural religion,* all religions, including Christendom, had sprung. That being so, the claims of any one religion to exclusive truth or rights were quite unjustified, let alone any claims for state support or for the right to persecute those of a different mind. What the *philosophes* fought was therefore not religion but the "enthusiasm" which it seemed to sponsor, a kind of madness which they traced to fears or frustrations, and which they felt endangered the balance of a society or mind; and those organized institutions —church, Jesuits, Sorbonne—which appealed to such enthusiasm and to the ruling powers in order to stifle free discussion and reform.

For ages man lived in a state of bondage, the slave of an impossible and capricious nature and of his ignorance. Now material conditions appeared to lend themselves to his emancipation from institutional and spiritual bonds. Society was rapidly acquiring power over nature. It could acquire more. The church stood in the way. Of course, the whole of the eighteenth century was not passionately anti-Christian. Lutheran pietists, full of simple faith, ignored theology and found strength in God. Johann Sebastian Bach, who died in 1750, headed all his pages "S.D.G.": *Soli Deo Gloria* (To the Glory of the only God). Handel, in England, declared: "I should like to die on a Good Friday, in the hope of joining the good God, my sweet Lord and Savior on the day of his resurrection." His prayers were almost answered, and he died on Easter Saturday, 1759. But if pietism persisted and Methodism flourished, the liveliest representatives of their time justify the description of anti-Christian.

It may have been weariness of the high religious tension of the seventeenth century. It may have been an effect of the mood reflected in

Spinoza's attempt to quantify the moral universe (see p. 405). It may have been disgust at the excesses of religious mania—the persecutions, tortures, burnings, endless quibbles. It probably was in part the effect of the revocation of the Edict of Nantes, bringing all this home to the most industrious and articulate of communities, spreading it abroad by their exile and propaganda, or inoculating indifference on the heels of the conversions which it forced. Indifference could stem from the shock and horror of religious treason, of the forced abandonment of a faith for a conformism. Indifference, or hostility. There lay the seeds of a new attitude toward religion.

It was necessary to "change the general way of thinking," as Diderot hoped the *Encyclopedia* would do, to light up the great darkness that still obscured the world, to reveal reality and the possibilities that lay before man. The god of the deists was a constitutional god obeying his own natural laws, the principle of the nature that he himself had structured, forerunner of constitutional kings ruling according to the charters they vouchsafed or accepted. God or king, religion or legislation, their purpose was as self-evident as our forefathers proclaimed: the happiness of man, of a mankind most properly engaged in its pursuit.

Thus *la philosophie des lumières*—the philosophy of enlightenment—exalted light against obscurity, work against idleness, will against supineness, energy against indolence. But not all the enemies of the *philosophes* were indolent or supine; some of them were very active indeed! So, when the *philosophes* campaigned against error, against superstition, against the great pools of shadow which these evils cast around them and over the popular masses, they saw themselves battling the party of darkness, of obscurantism, of outworn and stupid but sturdy prejudice.

The Encyclopedia *and the* Salon

The heaviest gun of the Enlightenment was the *Encyclopedia* (1751–1780), whose thirty-odd volumes were turned out by 130 contributors under the editorship of Denis Diderot (1713–1784) and Jean d'Alembert (1717?–1783). The *Encyclopedia* could have taken as its slogan Francis Bacon's belief that knowledge is power. Rationalist, utilitarian, matter-of-fact, it sought to present the evidence of every subject treated, referred to experience, analyzed facts in terms of cause and effect, undermined old ideas and suggested new ones. The *Encyclopedia*, soon paralleled by the Edinburgh publication of the *Encyclopaedia Britannica* (1768–1771), offered its readers an immense survey of existing knowledge and, by its very existence, suggested more to come. But, despite its formidable influence,* revolution—Voltaire pointed out—could not be made by folio volumes selling at high prices. A vast propaganda machine was needed: newspapers, periodicals, and small cheap books, academies, philosophical societies, clubs, masonic lodges, even drawing rooms were launched, enlisted, mobilized to spread the light.

The eighteenth century is the century of the *salon,* the drawing room where taste and opinion are made by conversation, where reputations are established by word and wit. The cultural dominance of the court was passing to more intimate circles, the reign of wit replacing that of hierarchy and form. *Esprit* or wit, as Voltaire defined it, was simply ingenious reason operating in society, implying always more than it would say, using words as much to suggest as to articulate a feeling, a thought, a possibility. A social virtue, an art or pastime which needs a public more than most, relying on its echo in the partner's eyes to amplify and fulfill it, wit is superficial, evanescent, made for small company, light minds, quick hearts. Wit is not a guffaw but a smile; it is charm; it is a discreet sensuality and a convivial pleasure. Of the few.

In the salons we find an eloquence adapted to the age of Mozart and to the host of influential women who helped to make opinion and spread it abroad, women like Julie de Lespinasse, or Horace Walpole's friend, Madame du Deffand; or Necker's wife, in whose salon her daughter, the future Madame de Staël, sharpened her wits and her European education; or, greatest of all, Madame Geoffrin, whom Stanislas II of Poland called "Maman," the friend of Joseph II and of Catherine the Great, of whom it was said that she was one of the three empresses ruling Europe in the 1760's. In Madame Geoffrin's salon one could meet ambassadors like Kaunitz, Maria Theresa's future chancellor, artists and writers and foreign visitors: Hume, Wilkes, Beccaria, Garrick. It was a European institution, one of the most effective bases from which enlightened ideas spread.

Freemasonry

Another base, less charming but more widespread, was in the Masonic lodges which began to migrate from England in the 1720's, expounding and conveying their creed of humanity, brotherhood, and progress.

---

* La Tour's portrait of Madame de Pompadour shows the *Encyclopédie* and Montesquieu's *Esprit des Lois* beside her.

Reading at the Home of Madame Geoffrin, by Lemonnier. Musée des Beaux Arts.

The ideals of medieval Masonic corporations, adapted to eighteenth-century needs and seasoned by secrecy and symbolic rituals, caught the imagination of nobles and intellectuals all over Europe. Lodges appeared in Belgium (1721), Paris (1726), America and Russia (1731), Rome and Lisbon (1735), Copenhagen (1743). Montesquieu was introduced to the order in 1730 by Lord Chesterfield; the Prince of Wales, the future emperor—Francis of Lorraine, and Frederick II were all Masons. In 1738 the movement which bound members in a common fraternity, regardless of class or creed, was condemned by the Pope. But, although suspect, it was tolerated everywhere so that it grew and spread.

We have seen the influence of freemasonry in the 1825 Decembrist revolution in Russia. But the advance and effects of the Masons were most marked in France. By the 1770's lodges had been set up in army regiments and in the provinces; the movement which had begun as an aristocratic fantasy became an inspiration of the middle classes, fascinated by its social opportunities and its liberal, humanitarian philosophy, as well as by the ritual and hierarchy that created a parallel knighthood to that which survived from old. The Duc d'Orléans was its Grand Master, nobles and bourgeois mingled in its assemblies along with men like the Abbé Siéyès and the future Marshal Masséna. Many came, attracted by hope of witchcraft, magic, or occult wisdom; others in pursuit of virtue or of useful social connections. In the Paris lodge of the *Nine Sisters* one could find Voltaire, Franklin, the Dr. Guillotin, the sculptor Houdon, the painters Vernet and Greuze, John Paul Jones, and the future tutor of Tsar Alexander, the Swiss La Harpe. But elsewhere membership was more modest, including small rural bourgeoisie, non-commissioned officers of the army, lawyers, farmers, and even artisans. Masonry was equalitarian and, equally important, it got its adepts used to a structure of meetings, elections, and debates, which would provide good training for the maneuvers, discussions, and activities of the political assemblies of the new age.* The same was true of other societies, academies, lecture or reading groups—all of what Augustin Cochin, their historian, has described as *sociétés de pensée.*

Hostile to the official clerical establishment which disapproved of them and of their ideas, the Masons promoted secular schooling and devoted much attention to the educational questions which also preoccupied the *philosophes.* Enlightenment, after all, was largely a didactic campaign, predicated on the belief that men are rational beings capable of ever-greater advances to perfection, and that their minds can be formed by education. The mind, John Locke had written in his *Essay Concerning Human Understanding* (1690), which begins as a kind of blank, void of ideas, is furnished by experience. Experience contributes simple ideas, which the understanding learns to associate into more complex ones. Knowledge is founded in sensations, the action of external objects on the senses; man's mind is formed by his experiences, and these could be deliberately ordered and manipulated by education.

"Of all the men we meet with, nine parts of ten are what they are, good or evil, useful or not, by their education," wrote Locke in 1706. "I imagine the minds of children as easily turned this or that way, as water itself." Such statements implied equality, given an equal opportunity for training: "Men's happiness or misery is most part of their own making." When Shakespeare's Caesar had said as much, it had been *hubris*—undue pride; when Locke said it, it was common sense, which Helvétius echoed in 1758: "Goodness and humanity are not the work of nature, but only of education."

In 1749, David Hartley's *Observations On Man* carried the implications of Locke's sensationalism (the belief that nothing can appear in the mind which has not been channeled there by the senses) a step further. Ideas, Hartley said, arising from outside stimuli, tend to become associated in the mind. This means, on the one hand, the need to learn the laws governing such associations of ideas—that is, the psychological laws affecting the working of the mind—and, on the other, the need to manipulate the experience and education of children in order to provide the right impressions in the right order. At the time when the prevailing view still held that man was born with certain

---

* Of fifty-three future members of the National Assembly who took part in various deputations to the court in January and February, 1789, thirty-one were Masons. Among the deputies to the Estates General, half of the Third Estate, a third of the nobles, 10 per cent of the clergy are said to have been Masons. In many places the proportion of Masons among elected deputies was quite impressive: in one town of the Loire, four out of six.

innate ideas and instincts, the new doctrines insisted, as we can see, on habit and the acquired behavior, intellectually developed, inculcated by an education to which all men were open.

The point was further elaborated by Claude Adrian Helvétius (1715–1771) in his book *On the Mind* (1758). Children's qualities and thinking were made by education, argued Helvétius. Ultimately all children are much the same. How they evolve depends on the teacher who is responsible for developing their intellectual and their public spirit. Men are moved by self-love; the important thing is to use and direct their passions to the advantage of society and their own. Helvétius advocated teaching civics and social science. Society could be reformed by education but, clearly, education would only be reformed by a society that wanted such reforms. The Masons stood for the enlightenment that would facilitate reform and bring further enlightenment in its wake. The Jacobins were to take this up, along with Helvétius' pleas for practical training that might build up not only citizens but productive men.

Utilitarianism

This brings us to utilitarianism, the fundamental motive which seems to have inspired most of the philosophers of this age. Their analyses of man, of mind, of society, all aimed not at gratuitous enlightenment but at *use,* toward which all their efforts tended. Even the grandfather of the sect, old Bernard de Fontenelle (1657–1757)—the prettiest pedant in the world, as an enemy once called him—who had made his name with his *Entretiens* (conversations), in which a gallant astronomer initiates a charming marquise into the plurality of worlds (1686), while strolling in a starlit garden—even Fontenelle had devoted a whole treatise to happiness and concluded that happiness is "only a question of calculation."

Enlightened utilitarianism would even be reflected in the work of some eighteenth-century architects who strove to put up functional structures, eliminate ornaments which had lost their structural use, adapt furniture to the human body, and sometimes tried to express a building's purpose in its shape and decoration. This last led to some fascinating but awkward essays in expressive architecture, in which salt works were ornamented with stalactites of salt, offices for a river overseer planned in a kind of cylindrical funnel through which the river ran as through a turbine, and a monument to Newton was projected as a vast sphere speckled with tiny holes: stars lighting up the heavenly vault above the great man's tomb.

Literature, too, had its exaggerations. Thus, Julien de La Mettrie (1709–1751), a brilliant and eccentric doctor whom Frederick made a member of his Berlin Academy, published his *Man a Machine* in 1747. Man, argued La Mettrie, is nothing but an animal, made up of a number of springs, all set in motion by one another. This was the fictional figure of Hobbes carried to its logical conclusion. Ultimately, "man is a machine"—a modification of matter. Nature has created him to be happy, to do what comes naturally. Virtue is self-love; morality is self-interest; crime should be cured, not punished, by adjusting the mechanism. Helvétius said as much in greater detail, but turned self-love into a social purpose. Since "pleasure and pain are and will always be the only principle of human action," laws should take this into consideration and try to serve the needs of public utility—the interest of the greatest number.

Another philosopher, Baron d'Holbach (1723–1789), agreed: the end of society is utility, social utility must be gaged on the happiness of its members, and virtue is the furtherance of this end. The conclusion could only be that society should be organized for the welfare not of particular groups but of the greatest number of its individual members.

The first concrete results of such views came in the realm of law and law reform. The prevailing contemporary use of law was that it should be as terrifying as it was often ineffective. In progressive England alone, acts of 1722 and 1758 added some 350 capital offenses to the Statute Book. The law was not designed to deter from crime, but to avenge as harshly as it could those crimes which the forces of order were too ineffective to prevent. In 1764, Cesare Bonesana, Marquis of Beccaria, born in Milan in 1733 and educated in a Paris Jesuit college, a passionate reader of Montesquieu and of the other *philosophes,* would bring out a short analysis of the relation between crime and punishment: *Dei deletti e delle pene.* Soon translated into French, the little book caused a furor and inspired, first in intellectual circles and later everywhere, important penal reforms.

Beccaria's main idea was that, as in Gilbert and Sullivan, the punishment should fit the crime, and that it should not be exercised for vengeance's sake, to inflict suffering, but to prevent new crimes against society. "It is better to prevent crimes than to punish them. This is the fundamental principle of good legislation, which is the art of conducting men to the maximum of happiness and to the minimum of misery, if we may apply this mathematical expression to the good and evil of life." The object of legislation was "the greatest happiness of the greatest number." Society has an interest in keeping crime to a minimum, and "the true measure of an offense is the damage inflicted on society." If the criminal can be redeemed, so much the better; in any case "unnecessary and barbarous torments"—torture—are bad. As for punishments, they should be public so as to discourage others, prompt so that

AN

INQUIRY

INTO THE

Nature and Causes

OF THE

WEALTH OF NATIONS.

By ADAM SMITH, LL.D. and F.R.S.
Formerly Professor of Moral Philosophy in the University of GLASGOW.

IN TWO VOLUMES.
VOL. I.

LONDON:
PRINTED FOR W. STRAHAN; AND T. CADELL, IN THE STRAND.
MDCCLXXVI.

The title page from Adam Smith's
The Wealth of Nations.

the connection between crime and punishment is obvious, the lightest possible appropriate in the circumstances, proportionate to the crime, and fixed by law. Each of these commonplaces was a revolutionary demand in its time, and would reverberate through Europe as first Voltaire, then Jeremy Bentham, took them up.

In legal as in other matters we may take the *philosophe's* ideal, as Holbach voiced it, to be liberty, property, and security. Liberty to pursue one's own happiness without injuring others. Property being the advantages that each man could gain by his own labor and talent. Security to enjoy these in peace, under laws which prevented others from depriving one of them by using force or privilege. Such views would find fulfillment in the ideology of the young United States, of the Girondins in the National Assembly, and of the Orléanists who ruled in France after 1830. But the true heirs of the *philosophes* were the English utilitarians. And the seminal work in this tradition is Adam Smith's *Wealth of Nations* (1776), dedicated to developing Pope's remark that "true self-love and social are the same," by proving the harmony of economic interests in situations where free competition rules and where demand and supply are allowed to find their own levels.

Smith said many things in his essay which would be translated into French, German, Italian, Spanish, and Danish before 1800. He held that labor was the real standard of the value of a product, that the price of objects should be the price of the labor that had gone into them, and that this reward should go to the worker—the producer. He perceived that when a capitalist owns the instruments of production he lets the workers use them while keeping for himself a portion of the price; and that capitalist and worker struggle, each to appropriate a greater part of this price, thus giving rise to a class struggle. Smith admired all producers and refused to take sides in the struggle between classes, unlike some of his later readers, like the young Karl Marx. But most of those who read him paid little attention to such side issues. What they retained from Adam Smith was that wherever nature is left to herself, natural order must assert itself. Man will follow his tendency to improve his condition and, since every man is the best judge of his private interest, the conjunction of private interests was bound to tend toward the public good. *Laissez-faire, laissez passer:* an invisible hand guided the economy to equilibrium. Men should be left free, merely apprised of their dependence upon other men in the vast web of producers and consumers. Nature would do the rest.

This was exactly what progressive men wanted to hear and, in its implication, what the physiocrats were saying to the French (see p. 425). Freedom brought progress. But the argument could be conducted from another base, just as attractive to the modern mind: that of calculation; and this is what Bentham insisted on. The thing to remember about Jeremy Bentham (1748–1832) is that he was an eighteenth-century man, bred on a philosophical diet, fascinated by the reigning spirit of discovery, improvement, and exploration; persuaded that "knowledge is rapidly advancing towards perfection." Bentham would take the utilitarian principles of the *philosophes* for granted. The measure of right and wrong, his first work published in 1776 announces, is the greatest happiness of the greatest number. In 1779, his *Introduction to the Principles of Morals and Legislation* drew the appropriate conclusion: "Nature has placed mankind under the governance of two sovereign masters, *pain* and *pleasure*. It is for them alone to point out what we ought to do, as well as to determine what we shall do."

Laws, institutions, political and educational systems, were to reflect this search for satisfaction and for use. If God's will is eliminated from the political equation, only man's interest could be left, and that suggested a majoritarian calculus in which the satisfaction of the majority had to be the ultimate consideration. Should the majority have what they think they want—bread and circuses—or should they be taught what they ought to want, if need be by terror? There was the conundrum. One answer was provided by the argument that only those capable of rational thought should count in the political equation, and this was the utilitarian position in nineteenth-century England, and that of the Orléanists in France. The chief spokesman of the utilitarians, James Mill (1773–1836), tried to turn the closed society of merchants, landlords, and hereditary oligarchs into one open to those better qualified to govern in the general interest, that is, to the middle class—"that portion of our people to whom everything that is good among us may with certainty be traced." Here were the chosen people of utilitarianism: frugal, educated, enterprising, and productive. The problem was to secure them popular backing; and this, Mill suggested, might be done by education and universal suffrage. Bentham and Mill looked forward to a time when men would learn to connect social and selfish interests, so that they could act spontaneously as if the two coincided. Only the right education and the right political regime could bring this about and make the greatest-happiness principle an automatic reference point.

Meanwhile, social conditions were persuading some people that the best interests of *all* were not necessarily identical, that workers' interests were not necessarily the same as those of their employers and that, indeed, the very existence of a good many people was contrary to the interests of society as a whole. Before the eighteenth century closed, Thomas Malthus's *Essay on the Principle of Population* (1798) argued that—but for the intervention of famine, or disease, or war—population was bound to multiply beyond the means of subsistence. While mankind must increase in geometrical progression, the means of subsistence lag behind, increasing only in arithmetical progression. Misery is fatal and only ruthless countermeasures could prevent catastrophe. Education might intervene to restrict population growth. Unnecessary mouths, said Malthus, must be allowed no claim "to the smallest portion of food." They have no business to be here at all: "At nature's mighty feast there is no vacant cover for [them]."

That was the kind of view which made Coleridge fear the likelihood of being governed "by a contemptible democratical oligarchy of glib economists compared to which the worst form of aristocracy would be a blessing." But it also led Charles Darwin to his theory of natural selection, after reading the book of Malthus in 1838.

Since the 1790's were times of trouble and distress, Malthusian arguments caught on. The first national censuses, taken in 1801 and 1810, bore Malthus out by showing the population of England and Wales growing by a million and a quarter in ten years; experience suggested that industry could not use, or the fields feed, such masses. The radical political philosopher William Godwin (1756–1836) answered that misery was due not to overpopulation but to poor distribution of wealth, which was concentrated into few hands. In due course, Marx and Engels would also argue that this kind of theory treated the workers as just other animals. Actually, the masses were fed into the factories to turn out yarn, and more were being imported from Ireland to labor even at cheaper rates building thousands of miles of canals, roads, and docks, laying tracks and rails for railroads; and this, too, provided arguments against Malthusian strictures, which the workers themselves did not fail to take up.

By the second decade of the nineteenth century the great debate was on, and the workers joined in it, arguing against utilitarian economists and Scotch philosophers. The more poor there were—they argued—the fewer consumers there would be. Better wages would create more buyers, greater demand, further employment. Less child labor must mean more work for adults; shorter hours would allow less unemployment. Collectivism argued against competition, and competition won. In any case, reasoned their opponents, "scarcity . . . promotes industry." The worker "who can subsist on three days' work will be idle and drunken the remainder of the week . . . A reduction of wages . . . would be a national blessing." As early as 1771 we find Arthur Young declaring: "Everyone but an idiot knows that the lower classes must be kept poor, or that they will never be industrious."

The great thing about Robert Owen (1771–1858) is that he proved that humane methods did not reduce profit. Himself a graduate of the looms, Owen became the manager of textile mills at New Lanark in Scotland and braved bitter opposition to raise wages there and to reduce working hours from sixteen to ten and a half a day, abolishing all child labor under ten and making his factory village a model with decent quarters and free education. To everyone's surprise, productivity and profit went up, and his reform proposals could now expect a hearing. In his writings, Owen condemned child labor and the tendency to care more for inanimate machines than for human ones. Uncontrolled economic growth was creating a society where more and more people were being alienated or destroyed. Yet, like the utilitarians, Owen believed that if only ignorance were banished a society could exist where crime and poverty were cast out and health, intelligence, and happiness improved. "Train any population rationally and they will be rational," he argued.

Owen's pleas failed to impress the statesmen whom he tackled in 1818, at the Congress of Aix-La-Chapelle, but they had enough effect on Robert Peel to produce England's first Factory Act in 1819. They also inspired a long series of experiments designed to set up communities that we now call utopian, where property would be held in common and where the good life in co-operation would replace the catch-as-catch-can morals which presently ruled the world.

In 1825, Owen himself tried to set up a community in the United States at New Harmony, Indiana, which could serve as a showplace for his ideas, but, like most other such experiments, New Harmony collapsed. The division of labor and its reward caused too many problems, the strain of existence under a state of siege from society outside was too much to bear. But where utopia failed, compromise in the real world would work better. Owenism in England appealed to old traditions of mutual support and co-operation among working men in trades clubs, benefit and friendly societies. The English trade unionists referred to Owen and to an Owenite or Jeffersonian vision of a co-operative society of craftsmen and small holders. The Chartists (see

Robert Owen's textile mills at New Lanark.

p. 306 sought manhood suffrage, because through it manhood could be rehabilitated and workers gain some control over their own lives and labor. The idea that co-operation was better than competition, mutual aid superior to the profit motive, was a medieval notion not so far removed from what English workers still believed. It was tried out in practice, beginning on a small scale with the exchange of services among the members of voluntary associations, then going on to the marketing of their products, and it worked. By 1832, there were 500 co-operative associations in England, with 20,000 members; a hundred years later they would be a hundred times as numerous.

Strangely enough, this practical idealist is generally classed together with his French contemporaries, Fourier and Saint-Simon, partly because all three sought ways of creating a more harmonious social order and of integrating the oppressed into the world, not only of production, but of enjoyment too. Yet the two Frenchmen seem more in the utilitarian tradition of calculating the root of the good life, rather than building it. Charles Fourier (1772–1837) for one—who had directed the statistical office at Lyons during Napoleon's Hundred Days—was a true mathematical visionary, his writings full of figures, where evil was an equation, and so was good.

Fourier felt that the French Revolution had failed because, while plutocracy had taken the place of aristocracy, private interests still clashed with common interests, while general misery increased along with national wealth. The only remedy lay in *association*—a planned co-operation of people gathered in *phalansteries* where all would find something to do and all would be assured a basic minimum. Producers, said Fourier, are also consumers, and in *phalansteries* all members would be doing work suited to their abilities and inclination. Their education there would aim at developing their personality, not cast it in a set mold; and women, whom nurseries and other collective facilities would free from drudgery, could also work at what they pleased.

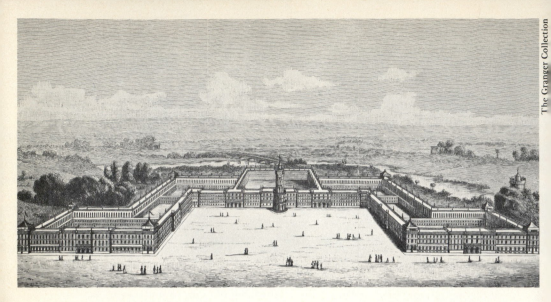

More influential in the long run was the thinking of Claude-Henri, Comte de Saint-Simon (1760–1825), a strange, brilliant eccentric who set out to formulate a philosophy appropriate to the new age which he could see beginning, and who proposed the reorganization of humanity not on the hit-or-miss basis which caused all revolutions and reforms to fail, but resting on a *positive science*—not on conjecture, but on verified facts.

Saint-Simon's attention turned increasingly toward industry, which alone could ensure universal peace and harmony when the government of men would have given place to the administration of things. He even edited a journal, *Industry,* which, financed by the banker Laffitte, bore as its slogan "All by industry, all for industry."

Modern society has one object only: production, industry. "A nation," says Saint-Simon, "is nothing but a great industrial enterprise." This means that it should be run not by useless politicians but by engineers, technicians, and scientists. The modern religion is labor. Wealth must go to ability, all producers must be reconciled in a rational, industrial order. After Saint-Simon's death, his disciples enshrined the doctrine in a manifesto that launched the well-known phrase: "From each according to his abilities, to each according to his needs!"

Soon, this would be described as *socialism,* a word already in current use in English Owenite publications. And, while many Saint-Simonians went on to apply their respect for industry by becoming rich and successful in the banking, business, and railroad enterprises of the 1850's and 60's, others, like Pierre Leroux, harked back to Jacobin memories of Gracchus Babeuf, who had called for community of property and for a society "where there should be neither rich nor poor," and who had lost his head for it in 1797. In 1847, Leroux's *League of the Just* would change its name to the *Communist League.* The future challenge to utilitarian liberalism had sprung from its very bosom.

Opposite: a design for a Phalanstery. The central portion was planned for public rooms; the wings were to house various workshops, with the noisiest placed at the extreme ends. Residents would live on the upper floors. Right: Le Comte de Saint-Simon.

The Metaphysical Philosophers

Liberalism, as we have seen, was based on a rationalist tradition according to which adjustment was possible between man and society, society and nature, on lines which could be rationally calculated or (in another view) expected to work out for the best. The link between man and the world was provided by the senses. Locke had furnished a plausible materialistic philosophy for an increasingly materialistic world. Yet, while Locke's sensationalism continued to be accepted, consciously or not, as the basis of most current arguments, it was being torn to shreds in the works of David Hume (1711–1776), who argued that, although ideas are born of sense impressions, our senses are very fallible instruments. The ideas which senses may convey often turn out to be phantoms risen out of error, or put together from figments of experience oddly juxtaposed by a fertile imagination. We could never know more than the appearance of things, said Hume, for that was all our mind was capable of grasping; causality is illusion, faith cannot be proved by reason. The only tenable position is one of skeptical relativism.

All this suggested that the "truths" and "rights" on which society rested, or might be made to rest, were no more than conventions, explicable by some prior development, but valid if at all only because society found them generally convenient, or chose to think them so. Man makes his own world, then he believes in it.

This idea would be carried further by Immanuel Kant (1724–1804). Our mind, the Königsberg professor argued in his *Critique of Pure Reason* (1781) and the *Critique of Practical Reason* (1788), does not re-

659

Immanuel Kant.

flect the image of things about it, as Locke and the sensationalists pretend. It molds its image of what may come its way on the basis of a kind of Platonic reality which it can never really know, but which has an existence in the mind before experience comes knocking at the door. Ideas, perhaps innate, perhaps conveyed by the society about us, color and shape every experience, every sensation, even our self-consciousness. We cannot know the world as it is, nor things as they are: we only know them through the deforming mirror of our understanding. Hence, science working with concrete realities is practically useful but cannot be harnessed in the service of metaphysics, of higher truths, whose scientific conception is impossible since reality is not equivalent to truth.

Kant claimed to have wrought a Copernican revolution of his own, by shifting the focus of philosophical inquiry from the traditional search for a truth to be found beyond a kind of existential veil to the relation between knowledge and man's mind—that is, the limits and possibilities of the latter, when tackling the mysteries of the world about us. The mind, as Kant conceived it, is a kind of explorer, testing the bounds and possibilities of perception, and pressing forward to the limits of perception in order to chart what can be known or practically inferred from what is known already. Yet, this must leave a vast margin of uncertainty. In the midst of a world which runs in terms of causalities and contingencies that we ignore, man can and must act *as if* he were free; and he is free because he thinks—as long as he thinks—that he is free.

But he is not alone. Man is surrounded by many other men, all at least endowed with the capacity to decide freely, and when he acts he takes them into consideration by acting only on such principles which he would be willing to turn into universal laws. The important thing is our estimate of the situation, and of the right way to act in it. No matter the nature or the results of our act, provided we honestly regard the act as right. If we think it is right, then it is right. Good will, said Kant, is innate; and reason shows how it might be applied.

Murder is bad; the murder of a tyrant, for example, is morally bad if undertaken in order to gain something, morally good if undertaken because considered just and right; and this is valid even if the murder should prove an error. This is the *categorical imperative* of Kant: to act on a maxim which you can wish to see become a universal law. The important thing is that men should act so that the free use of their will can coexist with that of other wills, according to a general law.

From utter relativism Kant was deducing the basis of new absolutes; creating an equalitarian assertion of a new freedom born of necessity, whereby each man must forge his law, a law which could be valid for every man just as Rousseau's General Will is taken to be. Here was a philosophical formula for translating thought to action, a bridge between speculation and practice, a shift from metaphysics toward the empirical fulfillment of self-made ideals which would mark the century to come.

Kant's work lies at the base of all the philosophical trends of the nineteenth century, and of a good deal in the twentieth century too. His relativism, which seemed to place decisions in the hands of every individual, could just as well reinforce the authority of the society whose partial product the individual was. This process can be seen in the evolution of Johann Gottlieb Fichte (1762–1814), who had begun as a democratic individualist, finding the source of all values in the conscience, refusing to accept social privileges or institutional rights which might prescribe morals or legislation. Such views led to Fichte's dismissal from his chair at the University of Jena, after which he moved to the Prussian capital, at Berlin. There, his thought turned from individual self-expression to those conditions which would permit it. The ideal state, which he described in *The Closed Commercial State* (1800), was one in which planning ensured the right to work, controls ensured fair shares for all, and tariffs stabilized the market, creating self-sufficiency. The humiliation of occupation by the French evoked his *Address to the German Nation,* a series of lectures delivered in the winter of 1807–1808, in which the philosopher fell back on ancient traditions whose inspiration could revive German self-confidence and create the kind of national spirit without which no social or political recovery was possible.

The extreme individualist ended as an extreme statist. Society was a unity and should be organized to function efficiently as a unified whole. Only the state could undertake such a task, which suggests among other things that individual life has no reality outside the transcendent meaning imparted to it by the agency of the state. There is no more sympathy for *laissez-faire* liberalism revolting against the autocratic state, but a very popular ideal of a paternalistic state devoted to the good of society as a whole and ruling its subjects with this good in mind—which necessarily meant the subjects' good as well—even if private property or interests had to give way before the general interest determined by the state.

Greater than Fichte, Georg Wilhelm Friedrich Hegel (1770–1831) would build his whole philosophy on contradicting Kant, in whom he found his source. Reality is not inaccessbile to our perception, argued Hegel; our own ideas forge reality. It is the movement of ideas that creates, that *is* reality. The ceaseless clash and combination of opposite ideas embodied in societies and institutions makes man progress beyond the possibilities of his present stage into one more advanced. The idea is the only thing that has a reality of its own; it is the absolute, which fulfills itself by the agency of the state—that state which alone can blend liberty and authority, the two poles and essentials of political life. Man is an abstraction which exists truly only in society, and society expresses itself truly only in the state: a state which embodies history— the worldly expression of God—and is therefore completely sovereign and also the only vehicle of liberty for its subjects.

Hegel's state was not, like that of Adam Smith, a structure which had been devised to protect the property and activities of men. It was an organic growth whose roots went deeper than classes or individuals, whose rights rode higher than those of its members, whose purpose was defined by history and to whose self-affirmation private interest or morality were irrelevant. The state was self-defining, sovereign, morally autonomous; its subjects existed through and by it, and its history alone could judge it.

But if the state, as Hegel saw it, is history in action, the history is largely one that has already taken place. The basis of Hegel's teaching seems to have been a sense that the era of great deeds was over, the time of meditation and interpretation had been reached—a time of philosophy which comes into her own when a civilization has grown old and an epoch is drawing to a close. This inclination to set an end to the historical development which he had sketched, to the rich dialectical process in which opposing forces ceaselessly resolve into new advances, in its turn evoked the criticism of Karl Marx.

Georg Wilhelm Hegel lecturing in 1828.

Karl Marx.

Marx (1818–1883) proceeded to take over Hegel's dialectic method in order to account for a reality which changes by encountering opposite ideas, and turned Hegelian idealism into a materialism which could explain social relations in terms of man's changing needs and means. It is not man's consciousness that determines his way of life, said Marx, but his way of life that determines his consciousness. Man creates God, ideas, ideals, to match his needs or, more correctly, the needs of the economically dominant class at a given time. Since in all ages different social groups struggle for the possession of the means of production, history is a record of their struggles—of class war. The latest act in this drama has been the conflict between the feudal and the bourgeois class. Now the latter, having won not only the political but the economic struggle, has to face the very creation of its economy, the proletariat which can only free itself by destroying the class and the economic structure that enslave it. Destroy capitalism, said Marx; destroy the state that serves it (as it must always serve the master class), free the proletariat, allow mankind at last to blossom out in a classless society.

Marx had gone far beyond the limits of Hegel's argument. He had suggested a rich and diversified interpretation of historical change, only to end like Hegel in a static situation. The interesting thing is that, for him as for his master, the basic fiction on which their philosophy stands comes not at the beginning (as with the mythical concept of a state of nature) but at the end. Here was a new teleology, reflecting an age that believed in progress. Out of the skeptical criticism of existing laws, new laws had come to be deduced, new necessities asserted; out of the relativism which tried to come to terms with its own limitations in a private morality for each individual man, great thinkers had built new massive systems which justified the authority of collective bodies: classes, states. With wry historical irony, skepticism drifted into dogmatism and laws built on relativity turned out as constraining as the divine or natural precepts they had replaced.

The Traditionalists

Amidst these critical currents, tradition and religion retained their votaries. Indeed, while fascinated by highly articulate philosophies and systems which would become so influential in our time, we are liable to forget that most men remained religious, most men did not think to question the habits and beliefs on which their lives were based, and that—whether affirmative or critical—conservative theories too were being formulated which still subsist in our own day.

The eighteenth century had shaken religion badly. The upper classes had lost their religious faith and kept up only the forms of religion, for the sake of social convenience and perhaps also, as Voltaire implied, of order. But they missed something to believe in, and sought it avidly in mesmerism and occultism, and masonic lodges, and in the tear-drenched sentimentalism associated with Rousseau. A religion of humanity replaced the religions of God, a religion of humanity which in the last analysis turned into a religion of self. Worse still, in respectable eyes, such beliefs implied that man must be the measure of all things, and opened the door to egalitarian reforms which, as the Revolution proved, could threaten the very existence of their upper-class believers.

By that time it was becoming evident that philosophy and science—Kant and Laplace—produced an interpretation of the universe which explained its order in purely physical terms. Without meaning to, Galileo had begun to replace God with nature and Descartes to turn him into mathematics or, rather, into the creator of those mathematical possibilities Descartes enjoyed so much; so that, as Bertrand Russell has put it: "No God, no geometry; but geometry is delicious, therefore God must exist." But if, for Descartes, God—in whom he profoundly believed—was simply the creator of matter and motion, once given which everything else follows; if, for Newton, God was just the designer and maintenance man of the universal clockwork—the "intelligent agent . . . very well skilled in mechanics and geometry"; then an explanation of how matter and motion could have come about might render Him inessential, especially in the particular guise which organized religion offered. Deists remained, but their deism, just like religious ritual, would seem increasingly irrelevant to the functioning of the mechanical universe.

Although it took time for this to be acknowledged, the new alternatives were both subjective ones: faith or denial. And yet it seemed, as Napoleon said, that society could not exist without religion. When we have made this world unbearable to men, the least that we can do is promise them another. The early nineteenth century saw the revival of religious faith and of religious institutions. Sentiment found solace in the aesthetic qualities, the beauties of religious worship, so that with Chauteaubriand men wept and they believed. Hope found fulfillment in the pietism of enthusiasts like Madame de Krüdener, who prayed with Tsar Alexander in his tent and promised that regeneration would surely come through repentance. The poor found exaltation or escape in revivalist meetings, the well-intentioned found in the Christian spirit a vital inspiration of practical reform, lastly the men of order saw in the church—in all the churches—a strong support of order that they could not do without.

This last was put most forcefully by the philosophers of the Restoration, a term probably suggested by *The Restoration of Political Science,* which the Bernese patrician Karl Ludwig von Haller published in 1816, advocating a return to feudal and corporatist traditions, and to religion as the only trustworthy basis and instrument of political power.* But Haller was only one, one of the less important, among the many who sought order, stability, rest, after twenty years of agitation and disorder. Such men aspired to stability in the midst of change, and became prophets of the past in an age which yearned toward the future. Instead of a renaissance, they offered a restoration. They rejected their time or, at least, tried to freeze it, rejected the city, suspected social mobility, fell back on rural reality, on the soil, the family, on stable property, a stiff hierarchy in home and state.

To secure this last on the most enduring possible foundation they brought in God, enlisting religion in the service of conservatism. We have seen how Methodism in England turned its devotees from public to personal reform. German Pietists, likewise, damned the Enlightenment and considered the French Revolution to be the Beast of the Apocalypse. But Protestantism, however orthodox, nursed a spirit of free inquiry that threatened established values. Only the Catholic Church offered serious guarantees of authority without which there could be no enduring order. A romantic Frenchman, Félicité de Lamennais (1782–1854), condemned the spirit of free inquiry that had inspired Luther. "There can be no peace for the mind," he wrote in 1817, "except when it is sure of possessing the truth." Not individual opinions but the theocratic authority of the Middle Ages restored could furnish such assurance, only the Catholic religion could ensure it. In Belgium and Austria, in Prussia and Bavaria, theocratic ideas, theological justifications for legitimacy, obedience and hierarchy, led to conversions and religious activity.

* Haller himself converted to Catholicism in 1820 for political reasons.

But the clearest formulation of such views was found in France.

In 1820, Louis de Bonald (1754–1840) would see his work as showing the intimate alliance of religion and political truths. Even superstition, said Joseph de Maistre (1753–1821), was but a vanguard of religion. And when, in 1832, the French university curriculum enjoined professors of philosophy to teach the existence of God and the immortality of the soul, people such as these protested against the introduction of rational argument, of any argument at all, where only authority should reign. There should be no debate; not even the seeds of one. Proving the existence of God, declared Bonald, was to abolish faith.

Yet, though the Catholic Church, like most of the other churches, firmly ranged itself on the side of reaction, it would be split by a liberal minority that called for the freedom of conscience which the Vatican denounced. The oppression of Catholic Irishmen by Protestant Englishmen, the complaints of Catholic Belgians against the Calvinist Dutch, above all the Polish rising of 1830, reminded Catholics that some tyrannies denied the liberties of the church as well as many others. In France especially a liberal group arose. Lamennais's romantic radicalism could lead as easily to populism as to reaction. His newspaper, *Avenir,* founded in 1830, argued for freedom of education, of press and association, for more elections and a broader electorate, for the separation of church and state. In 1832 the encyclical *Mirari Vos,* condemning freedom of conscience and of the press, crushed his incipient crusade. At the same time a papal brief addressed to the Polish bishops implicitly condemned the rising of Catholic Poles against their Orthodox Russian masters. Yet Lamennais's friend, the Count of Montalembert, translated Mickiewicz's passionate plea to God to save Poland from her Orthodox oppressors (1833), and this in turn inspired Lamennais to write his *Words of a Believer* (1834), which preached radical social ideas in biblical language, and which the Pope condemned, unwilling to accept a distinction between spiritual obedience and temporal freedom.

Lamennais had begun by looking to the church for salvation from the state; he would end by turning to the people for salvation from both. Condemned by the Pope, Lamennais would in turn condemn him and leave the church to devote the rest of his life to social struggles. Within a few years, his *Modern Slavery* (1839) outlined the antagonism between proletarian workers and masters of capital and denounced the latter. The foundations of Christian socialism were being laid.

Religion could evidently be turned against the existing order as well as to its support. The most reliable philosopher of conservatism would not be drawn from the ranks of the religious faithful, but from eighteenth-century rationalism. Edmund Burke (1729–1797), who had justified revolution in America because men have the right to resist oppression, condemned it in France for a similar reason: because it did not bring liberty for all, but the supremacy of a group which, brutally setting history aside, upset the delicate balance of society. Burke's *Reflections on the Revolution in France,* translated into French by Louis XVI himself, earned him a medal from the king of Poland, the praise of his own king, and the hatred of the Whigs whom he had helped lead during the American conflict and whom he now abandoned in revulsion against the anarchy across the Channel.

To Burke, all society was a historical product: a partnership between the dead, the living, and those yet to be born, the result of long evolution and experience, its laws and institutions forged by trial and error and not to be lightly—let alone violently—altered. In the American Revolution, as in 1688, historical evolution had used force to press ahead on its established path. In 1789 it had been thrust aside by men who would ignore it for some theoretical scheme which they were ready to impose by force at great cost to society. Burke's anger was an honorable one: he hated suffering in India or in Ireland, as much as he did in France. But, as Thomas Paine reminded his readers in the *Rights of Man,* Burke pitied the plumage and forgot the dying bird. Against Burke, Paine "contended for the rights of the living" against "the manuscript-assumed authority of the dead." Each generation could redefine its rights, reform its government. Not government by precedent but government by people—by the people—that is, by the majority "framing their own laws," as Wordsworth sang in 1793, was what the new recipe recommended.

Yet such a doctrine introduced a principle of endless instability that no society, Burke contended, could accept and survive. There is virtue in lasting institutions, in social constraints which avoid a far worse anarchy, in religion as a great social institution and supporter of traditional values, even in prejudice, which, Burke explained, "renders a man's virtue his habit." What Burke did not like about radical agitation was that it removed the Emperor's clothes and showed him naked, shivering and imperfect: "all the decent drapery of life . . . rudely torn off." This is just what radicals have always found so exhilarating. A great truth—the rights of men, of nations, of workers—once revealed had set them free, first to shout and then to hit out. And that is just what made bystanders uneasy—even those whom the radicals proposed to emancipate—and drove them to agree with Burke and rush to replace all that decent drapery without which life, presumably, would be just too awful to bear, too fearful to behold.

But Burke could offer more: he could suggest a way to reconcile history—that is, change—with stability by insisting that past advances removed the need for serious future ones. Above all, his argument that political institutions should conform to the political traditions of their particular society combined relativism and tradition in a pragmatic way which would provide the basis of modern conservatism.

Chapter 15

SENSE AND SENSIBILITY: THE ROMANTIC REACTION

It is practically impossible to define romanticism, while the attitude which we currently describe as "romantic" is a part of human make-up scarcely confined to any given time. Yet, since the romantic movement played a crucial part throughout the nineteenth century, it is essential to give an account of it. Germaine de Staël (1766–1817), whose book *On Germany* (1810) revealed romantic art to the international public, thought its "originality" lay in being "modern, national, popular, grown from the soil, from religion and the prevailing social institutions." This puts its finger on some crucial characteristics—the predominance of the particular over the universal, the popular over the elitist, the sentimental over the rational, the original over the conventional, the modern over the classical—and it suggests that, in effect, romanticism is the diametrical opposite of the classical spirit, the culmination of a revolt against classicism, but also against the enlightened rationalism which reigned over the eighteenth century.

The more or less enlightened society of the old regime could be both charming and revolting. It was an urbane world which, much of the

668

The Swing, by J.-H. Fragonard. Wallace Collection, London.

time, seems to have been dedicated to keeping life at bay, excluding pain and age by refusing to admit them, arming against the slings and arrows of outrageous fortune in a gilded carapace of amenity: courteous and cool. Enthusiasm was excluded. An eighteenth-century gravestone praising the virtue of the deceased tells us that she had been "pious without passion." Of course, passion survived; indeed all the passions, but harnessed by manners, by a conscious effort to put on a good face. This made a gracious life for those who could afford it, and leaves behind a glow of charm and taste. It also carried risks: artifice can become habit, coolness degenerate into callousness, hollow formality come to fill all life. Keeping the heart out of things, behind the fence of manners, would lead in due course to wearing the heart on the sleeve, an attitude more trivial and less dignified. One thing is striking: when these men and women do not charm, they chill. And those they chilled rejected them as and when they could, them and their manners and their values, their taste and their approach to life. Herein, as we shall see in due course, lies one important aspect of romanticism.

But there was more to it. To the great rationalistic current which culminates in the Enlightenment, the great search for order and efficiency which plays such a large part in modern history, there is a parallel tradition—and one as strong although not always evident—which from ancient days has championed Dionysius against Apollo, passion and inspiration against method and discipline, content and color against form and line. We have seen this expressed in the mysticism of the Counter-Reformation and in the wild flamboyance of some of the baroque. We meet it again under different aspects in rococo and in romanticism. And, if the Enlightenment was first a French creation, it might be said that romanticism was English—perhaps German: the reaction of rival cultures against the predominance of the French.

Paris in the eighteenth century, and to some extent in the nineteenth, was the cultural center of Europe; and even movements which opposed it tended to advance only when taken up by the metropolis. It is in the eighteenth century that the French language takes the place of Latin for good, as the international idiom all cultured people understand. Voltaire, arriving in Berlin in 1750, heard not a word of German spoken at the Court of Frederick the Great. A Scot traveling through Germany twenty years later found French the only language of fashionable people, whose children learned it before their mother tongue. The transactions and the publications of the academies of Berlin and Petersburg appeared in French, Frederick the Great, Catherine, Leibniz wrote in that tongue, Gibbon published his first work in the French language even though in London (*Essais sur l'Etude de la Littérature*, 1761). Many other books by Dutch, Italian, German, or English authors were first published in French in order to reach a wider public, many ideas and fashions, even Anglomania were spread by such French writers as would take them up, and English or Italian works were often translated into other languages from French translations of their originals. "Europe is a state composed of several provinces," had noted Montesquieu; a state whose capital was in Paris. And it would be in France, in the early years of the eighteenth century, that the rococo style was born, a native reaction against the rigors of an older day.

Rococo

The death of Louis XIV in 1715 ushered in a revolt which had long been brewing against the stateliness and the restraints of the previous reign. With the Regency, and even more under Louis XV, imagination, grace, and comfort took over, attempting to create a world upon which crude life impinged as little as it could. Furniture grew softer and less massive, Turkish sofas appeared that one could lounge upon discarding earlier stiffness in the bearing, lightness and gaiety brightened ladies' dresses and even the fripperies of fashionable men. Ponderous grandeur was no longer admired. Humor, elegance, brightness, intimacy,

Designs for three chairs, by Thomas Chippendale.

were what the new fashions sought. The pupils of François Boucher (1703–1770), who was the favorite painter of Madame de Pompadour, are said to have thrown bread pellets at paintings of the days of Louis XIV; and if the story is apocryphal it is certainly in character, for lack of reverence was still another feature of the moment.

If baroque aimed to astonish and impress, then rococo was meant to delight and charm. How well it succeeded one may tell by looking at the paintings, furnishings, decorations produced in France and Italy roughly between the twenties and the sixties of the eighteenth century and culminating in the days of Madame de Pompadour. Enchanted wistfulness with Watteau, enchanted exuberance with Boucher, enchanted theater in Tiepolo, enchanted mirages in the Guardis, enchanted flippancy in Fragonard: always enchantment, color, freedom, and delight.

Rococo and romanticism are closely connected, appropriately enough in gardens, where so much of the activity of both seems to have taken place. The word *romantic* was first used in England, early in the eighteenth century, to describe new style gardens, picturesque places that favored reveries and rambles, unlike the orderly alleys of the French style that seemed more like open-air drawing rooms. Shadow and mystery had been excluded from the straight beds and disciplined concourse of classical parks, like those around Versailles. Now, whimsical twists, irregularities, the unexpected, would be reintroduced—partly by way of a growing fad for exotic things. *Chinoiseries* and *Turqueries* marked the first fashionable appearance of that taste for the outlandish so characteristic of the romantic age. Rococo was fanciful. The news that in the imperial gardens of Peking there "reigns a fine disorder, an antisymmetry" reinforced this. The vaporous, apparently frivolous lines of Eastern art fitted the contemporary protest against old formality, lent themselves to bizarre illusions on porcelain and fans and screens and garden walks.

"Gaiety, magnificence, the rude Gothic or the Chinese unmeaning style, are the study of our modern architects, while Grecian and Roman

Jean-Jacques Rousseau, by La Tour.

purity and simplicity are neglected," complained an English architect in 1755. The effect of this could be seen in the tremendously popular designs of "household furniture in the Gothic-Chinese and modern taste" of Thomas Chippendale (1754), where lacquer, gilt, and caprice blended Chinese and gothic in fantastically decorative ways. Pagodas now sprang up beside Grecian templets. Fragile asymmetrical constructions replaced the straight and solid lines of classicism. "Without doors, from the seats of our dukes to the shops of our haberdashers, all is Chinese," wrote the London *World* in December, 1756. "And in most places within . . . Raphael and Titian give place to the more pleasing masters of Surat and Japan."

It was on these artificial props that the rococo fed its pretty fancies. But fancy could find nourishment nearer home. The *philosophes* cherished not only reason but nature, not only thought but feeling. They were convinced that the source of wholesome, vigorous sense lay in sentiment; and this could easily degenerate into sentimentality. Thus, Diderot's plea to painters: "Touch me, thrill me, startle me, make me cry and shudder"; and his admiration for Greuze's soapy attempts to sentimentalize and moralize painting.

Rousseau

The master of this trend came from one of those borderlands which characteristically felt the full impact of French cultural dominance and yet reacted against it. Jean-Jacques Rousseau (1712–1778) came from Geneva, most French of un-French cities, to Paris of which he disapproved and which he exploited to the full. The opening words of his novel *Émile* reflect the conclusion which he drew from this: "Nature has created man happy and good, but society depraves him and makes him miserable." Against the dangers of a corrupt and corrupting world the only refuge is to be found in nature, the only hope in the common people. Rousseau alone had criticized Mandeville's *Fable of the Bees,* and the educator who brings up Émile would exhort his charge: "Respect your species, remember that it is composed essentially of the masses of common people and that, if all the kings and philosophers were taken away, they would not be missed and things would go on just the same." Against the reefs of a tormented and tormenting world, the only refuge is in our feelings, in our hearts: "We are small as far as our lights go, but we are great through our feelings." "True worship is worship of the heart." And though our hearts may be corrupt already, it is still possible to put our hopes in those of children, if they are well brought up. So Rousseau wrote the great educational novel of the eighteenth century, *Émile*.

The educational ideas that *Émile* expressed were quite revolutionary: that child psychology is different from that of adults and that a child's view of the external world differs from his teacher's; that children's minds develop through various stages and that educational experiences should accommodate themselves to this; that experience is better than books and that children must learn to think for themselves, not be stuffed with other people's precepts; that education is for living not for profession or vocation. In all these points *Émile* became, in the words of a Danish philosopher, the Magna Carta of all children, the inspiration of the great educational reformers like Pestalozzi, Montessori, and Froebel. More immediately, it was taken as a treatise on the original goodness of human nature.

If *Émile* offered a recipe for man, the *Social Contract,* also published in 1762, offered one for man in society, a counter-political science in contrast to that expounded by contemporary *philosophes,* based on a counter-psychology of man and nature. For Rousseau, the state of nature knew no laws and no morality, no notions of good and evil. Original man was happy and perhaps even good because he did not know what being happy or good meant; he followed his instincts in the solitary, unthinking life he led. Society turned man from a beast following its appetites into a more or less reasoning being, but one depraved because society was depraved and because the values he could learn from it were not only unnatural but deformed. Nature endows man with the capacity to be good, but *men* live in society, and society will not permit them to be good. Hence men are miserable and nasty. The problem is to reconcile them with society, and Rousseau approached this by suggesting not how men should be improved but how society should be mended: a revolutionary difference between him and many others, and which would turn him into the great denouncer of social evils, an anti-sociologist whose *Social Contract* submitted a recipe for the abolition of social conflict in the unanimity of the general will.

Montesquieu had already observed that a man's freedom does not consist of license to do all he wants, but of not being subject to another's will. In a society of social contract, each individual giving up his independence becomes subject not to any other individual but to that impersonal entity, the community, whose will he can obey quite freely because in doing so he obeys simply a general will as impersonal as a law of nature. You can submit to the law of gravity without a particular feeling of constraint; you can accept the general will in the same way, as you would the impositions of your own body. Having given up the capacity to satisfy physical appetites with no regard for anybody else, you are emancipated from the animal impulses which you once obeyed, and you become a civic, thinking being, free to enjoy the higher freedom of moral liberty as a member of the collective body you have joined, a member of the sovereign people—whose will carried out by the state is really the true higher will of each.

It is fairly clear that such an argument reflects profound alienation and a desperate attempt to resolve it. But Rousseau's success—especially with contemporaries—suggests that his case was not an isolated one. As the traditional social order broke up and familiar bonds, the accepted framework of life, were loosened, as society shifted toward anonymity and mass, the question began to pose itself: when is a mass of individuals more than a mere mass—a real, political, and social entity? This was the question Rousseau asked, the question of the modern world in which social disintegration, personal disquiet, social alienation, suggest an emphasis of roots, of nature, of some kind of organic belonging. With Rousseau, the unbalanced modern individual enters the lists of history: sensitive, anguished, raw, and self-pitying, fascinated by his own quirks and feelings, and ready to exhibit them to all; seeking escape from this exacerbated self-obsessed individualism in some kind of *whole,* the lost limb redeemed in organic salvation.

Political philosophers had long attempted to find a balance between private and public, man and state. Rousseau looked not for balance but for integration. In his vision the clash between individual and society is abolished as the individual merges with all others, surrenders his rights to the community, where all is one and one is all. When the self becomes collective, freedom becomes the will of all, a supreme law which none dare to gainsay without challenging their own self, transcended in the community. Whoever refuses to obey "shall be forced by all the body, which only means that he will be forced to be free." One more vindication of tyranny in the name of freedom, of terror in the name of love, pleas which the human mind has been so fertile in devising. In 1793, when the liberal ideas of emancipation seemed to have run their course, the Revolution could turn to this for arguments why the general must always have precedence over the particular and, if need be, even exterminate it. A mystic, an exile, and a neurotic, unwittingly provided the recipes for the totalitarian, organic, integral nationalism of the nineteenth and twentieth centuries.

The Precursors

If Rousseau carried his views to the most logical and hence most extreme conclusions, the tendencies that he expressed were, on a more moderate level, those of his age. Reason and sentiment, the return to nature, the cult of simplicity, touched all contemporary society as they touched the arts. The intertwined currents of rationality and sentimentalism preaching a return to nature can be noticed in contemporary music. Franz Joseph Haydn (1732–1809), probably the inventor of the modern symphony, produced one called *The Philosopher* (No. 22 in E flat major of 1764). In his string quartets Goethe could recognize the intelligible "conversation of four sensible people." But Christoph Willibald Gluck's *Orfeo* (1762) has arias like popular ballads which delighted Herder, the folklorist, and many other operas of the time eschewed the grandeur of the lyrical tragedies that Louis XIV admired. The tradition of Lully and Rameau was forsaken for harmony and melody and simple tunes reminiscent of folk songs. The subjects of operas also changed. If Mozart's apparently frivolous works (1756–1791) still mirror noble society in never-never land, Pergolesi's *La Serva Padrona* and Rousseau's own *Devin du Village* are about the doings of simple people in places far removed from the drawing rooms that furnished their audience.

It may well be, of course, that this was only another form of exoticism, a game of leaving one's own element, like the fake farms and stables with which Marie Antoinette played, like the pet lambs which ladies in bright satins led about on ribbons. And the exotic existed in time as well as space. Early eighteenth-century England discovered the titillating possibilities of historical ruins as well as history. Edward Young's formidably successful *Night Thoughts on Life, Death and Immortality* was

Horace Walpole's country house at Strawberry Hill. Built in 1747, it was a model of gothic eclecticism.

written in the 1740's; but in 1726 already another English poet, David Mallet, could make great play with tombs and ruins, skulls and bones, moss and solitude:

> All is dread Silence here, and undisturb'd
> Save what the Wind sighs and the wailing Owl
> Screams solitary to the mournful Moon
> Glimmering her western Ray through yonder Isle,
> Where the sad Spirit walks with shadowy Foot
> His wonted Round or lingers o'er this grave.

What Kenneth Clark describes as a love for dramatized decay would affect first literature, then painting. By 1739, an English traveler at the Grande Chartreuse was writing of cliffs, precipices, torrents, as "pregnant with religion and poetry." Then, in 1764, Horace Walpole published *The Castle of Otranto: A Gothic Story,* which matched contemporary romanticism and set off a whole wave of gothic romances. From graveyards to dungeons, gloom, mystery, and horror thrilled the readers, but also stimulated imagination and, perhaps, chivalry. The Gothic Middle Ages became fashionable, and so did all their trappings: churches and houses began to be built in the gothic style, and Horace Walpole again led the field when he remodeled his country house at Strawberry Hill in the 1750's.* By 1772, young Goethe would expatiate on Strasbourg Cathedral: "It rises like a most sublime wide-arching Tree of God which, with a thousand boughs, a million twigs, tells forth to the neighborhood the glory of God." God, nature, and the Middle Ages, all at one. And the aesthetic medievalism which led to the building of fake cloisters like Fonthill Abbey (1796) also brought recruits into the Catholic fold, beginning with the herald of French romanticism, René de Chateaubriand.

The taste for medievalism could go a long way. But the way was generally eclectic, for lovers of the bizarre sought it in all quarters. Thus in the 1780's a Duke of Würtemberg built a dream castle for his favorite in whose park there stood a temple of Flora, a temple of Vesta, a large pyramid, a funerary monument dedicated to Nero, and an ancient prison. His mistress could wander past sham ruins of arches and broken columns, leading a lamb on a ribbon. The park was filled with evocative scenes: a monk tolling a bell, prisoners rattling their chains in dungeons, shepherds sounding their horns, a hermit praying before the empty tomb destined for the Duke himself. In 1793, while revolution raged across the Rhine, the Margrave of Hesse-Cassel built the first *château troubadour* in his park of Wilhelmshöhe. Nor did the revolution bring only ill to England. In the 1790's the Duke of Bridgewater was one of the most

---

* When the houses of Parliament burned down in 1834, nothing seemed more natural than to lodge the defenders of "our old Gothic constitution" beneath arches suitable to a free people.

The Oath of the Horatii, by J. L. David. Louvre, Paris.

generous hosts to emigrant French ecclesiastics. Several score of monks were put up on his country estate, where chapels and lodgings were built in the gothic style, with the sole obligation that on certain days a bell tolled and all had to walk around in the habit of their order, breviary in hand, to create a suggestive sight that the Duke could point out to his guests. Much more picturesque, their host would remark, than sheep or deer! Medievalism was in the air, and even the Cadiz *cortes* of 1812 argued the case of a constitution inspired by the Enlightenment and by revolutionary France by referring to medieval Spanish precedents.

The ancient world, too, about which so much contemporary education turned, was being brought back to life. Herculaneum was excavated in 1738 and Pompeii discovered ten years later, although excavations there did not begin until the 1760's. These and other ruins were being illustrated in books and lithographs that caught the public fancy. One of their most important generators was a Venetian architect who had settled in Rome—Giambattista Piranesi (1720–1778), whose etchings of Roman antiquities exercized vast influence, not only by popularizing Roman sights but by their romantic quality. The romantic inspiration is particularly evident in his series *The Prisons*—which, though imaginary, actually inspired some real jails, like London's Newgate Prison, built in the 1770's. In 1764, J. J. Winckelmann (1717–1768), son of a German cobbler, fascinated by antiquity, published the first *History of Ancient Art,* which treated the subject in the context of the social and religious life of the societies that had produced it. Winckelmann idealized and glorified the "noble simplicity" and "calm grandeur" of the Greeks. This fitted the preoccupations of contemporary *philosophes,* and it became proper to condemn those arts that spurred moral decay, titillated

An etching by Piranesi. Collection of Mr. and Mrs. Barry S. Brook.

the senses, and undermined the vigor of society. Luxury, it seemed, led to moral decline and art was one of the corrupting agents. It could equally well be an agent of revival, and, by mid-eighteenth century, Diderot and his friends were appealing to painters and sculptors to turn their hand to nobler themes that would elevate the soul and inspire the mind.

There is a paradoxical quality about the fact that, just when the early stirring of romanticism began to assert subjectivity, sentiment, and relativism, the classical revival seemed to affirm the opposite: a fundamental external reality, independent of man or history, and which the artist sought to express in the great Palladian structures of early eighteenth-century England, or the neoclassic style of the century's second half. The fact is that Greece and Rome inspired the romantics as much as the Middle Ages would; and the mingled inspiration is very obvious in the engraving of Piranesi or the paintings of Hubert Robert, where ancient grandeur is always qualified by a strong dash of the picturesque. The prints that revealed the ruins made the most of local color—ivy, natives, camels (when appropriate—for instance in Palmyra), and stage effects that fall just short of the theatrical. Then, around 1775 simplicity and purity would triumph briefly, and romanticism was sent back to gardens, there to bide its time while Rome and Greece preached moral virtue, service to the state, and devotion to duty. Louis XVI bought David's *Oath of the Horatii*—the great painting success of the decade—a trade trend which the stirring revolutionary years and the imperial ambitions of Napoleon would only stimulate.

Yet sensibility also marched on. Suicides and swoons became increasingly fashionable; deep feelings were indispensable. "Alas!" sighed Madame de Staël's nine-year-old daughter, "they think me happy and I have abysses in my heart!" And a lady who had just seen a horror play: "What a pretty show! I was taken ill three times!" Tears were ever on the verge of welling, and that prose was deemed best that brought them most. Napoleon, whose favorite poet was Ossian—that "mist of the imagination" as Lamartine described him—confessed that he could never read a minor trashy book, *The Trials of Sentiment,* without crying.

The truth is that these people were eclectic, like their age. But the taste for sentiment and sensibility, the attention paid to personal character and psychological analysis, led to re-emphasis of the individual, insistence on individual faces, on portraits, on intimacy. From the nostalgic reverie of gardens there was but a step into the evocative alleys of romantic parks where one could find at will the melancholy, unquiet echoes of inner unease or the inner peace to be derived from nature.

Here, in the new role of nature and its new importance, we find another herald of romanticism. As the eighteenth century ended, men talked less about clocks and more about trees. Mechanics became less important than organic ideas. Rousseau had called for man in his natural genuineness. Rousseau's influence produced a radical change in taste, a novel appreciation of natural beauty, wildness, forests, fields. To seventeenth-century travelers the Alps had been "huge monstruous excrescences of nature." In mid-eighteenth century, Voltaire's niece had shunned his charming but rather isolated château of Cirey in Lorraine as "a lonely place terrifying to humanity . . . in a country where there is nothing to see but mountains and uncultivated lands." Half a century later, mountains and uncultivated lands had become a landscape which cultured people had learned to see and like, so that even the author of *An Essay on the Management of Hogs* could turn away from a field of turnips to expatiate on the beauty of a distant prospect. The same was true of those humble themes in which, as Wordsworth had it, "the passions of men are incorporated with the beautiful and permanent forms of nature."

Romanticism

All these tendencies—to nature, naturalness, simpler or humbler themes, to mystery, history, and sentiment, to a rejection of the rules and order more generally accepted all around—would come together first in Germany in the wake of Lessing, of Herder, and of Kant. The first, a playwright and dramatic critic, insisted in his *Laocoön* (1776) that the task of art was not to copy from some classic model but to create, to add a new world to the real one from which it starts. The second, an unclerical Lutheran minister, spoke much like Rousseau of "human feelings flowing from a full heart." The artist, said Herder, tries to communicate "the obscure and ineffable forces" in his soul. For Kant, beauty was subjective, an ideal each man must devise for himself. There could be no more universal standards, no more academic art with its set rules.

Of course, none of this meant that standards and rules disappeared. It did mean that they would be challenged in the name of values more indefinite but no less strongly held. *Subjective* values—a term that first appears in dictionaries about 1812—now faced, clashed, and competed with the objective world. And out of this romanticism was born.

Born out of battle, there hangs about romanticism an aura of rebellion which is very strong: Byron, Shelley, Schiller turn with great violence against the world, against society and values which they will not accept. Schiller's play, *The Robbers* (1781) contrasts two brothers: the calculating and conformist representative of existing society, and the decent, generous youth driven to outlawry by dint of being honest. Goethe's *The Sorrows of Young Werther* (1774) which so marked the age were due at least in part to his rejection by, and of, unjust society. And the group which first embodied so many of these values has gone down in history under the label *Sturm und Drang,* meaning storm and stress. We have already seen (pp. 594–595) the role it played, if briefly, in Germany's political awakening.

There is, or there should be, a kind of psychopathology of romanticism. The stress and fever that sear so many works must have affected artists quite literally, burnt up many among them: Novalis, Shelley, Keats, Bonington, died before thirty; Schubert at thirty-one; Bellini and Géricault at thirty-three; Hölderlin, Lenau, Schumann, Poe went mad. Lermontov, Pushkin, Évariste Galois were killed in duels; Kleist, Chatterton, Nerval committed suicide. Others died of hunger, of consumption, of strange, peculiar illnesses and accidents. The crisis of a changing world seems to have been reflected in these stormy lives, in consciousness tormented by, revolting against the present, yearning for vanished Edens, golden ages, or the lost imaginary innocence of childhood. If the essence of classicism lies in stability, repose to be found in order, romanticism is movement, yearning, the endless search for what is not to be.

This is how the German romantic Friedrich Schlegel (1772–1829) describes himself: "An aimless love burnt in him and consumed him . . . without aim and without occupation, he roamed midst men and things . . . all could attract him, nothing could satisfy him. . . . His unsatisfied desire made him ever more savage; despairing of the spiritual, he became sensual, began to do foolish things to challenge destiny. He could well see the precipice before him, but felt it wasn't worth it to slow down . . ." It does not seem surprising that such men turned to death or to a suicide which forced the pace of death, supreme escape from the world with which they could not cope.

But not all died, of course; and then escape had to be found elsewhere: in the theater, for example, where the artificial world of illusion could

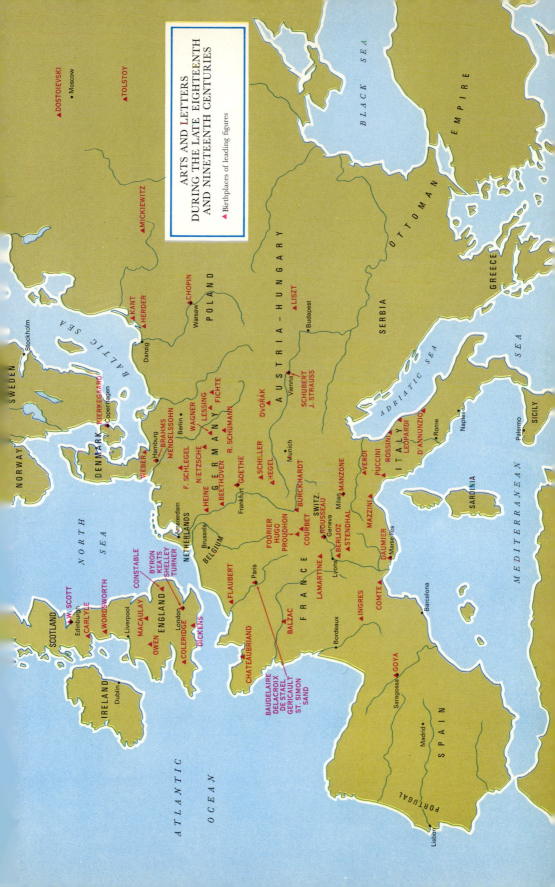

ARTS AND LETTERS
DURING THE LATE EIGHTEENTH
AND NINETEENTH CENTURIES
▲ Birthplaces of leading figures

▲DOSTOIEVSKI
• Moscow
▲TOLSTOY

BLACK SEA

OTTOMAN EMPIRE

GREECE

▲MICKIEWITZ

SWEDEN
• Stockholm

NORWAY

BALTIC SEA

▲KANT
▲HERDER

DENMARK
▲KIERKEGAARD
• Copenhagen

▲CHOPIN
• Warsaw

POLAND

AUSTRIA–HUNGARY

SERBIA

• Budapest

▲LISZT

• Vienna

ADRIATIC SEA

ITALY

SARDINIA

SICILY
• Palermo

SEA

• Danzig

▲WEBER
▲BRAHMS
MENDELSSOHN
• Hamburg

WAGNER
▲FICHTE
▲LESSING

F. SCHLEGEL
▲HEINE
▲NIETZSCHE
▲BEETHOVEN
R. SCHUMANN

GERMANY

▲SCHILLER
▲HEGEL

GOETHE
• Frankfurt

• Munich

BURCKHARDT

DVOŘÁK

SCHUBERT
J. STRAUSS

VERDI
▲PUCCINI
▲ROSSINI
LEOPARDI
D'ANNUNZIO

• Rome
• Naples

MAZZINI

NORTH SEA

Amsterdam

NETHERLANDS
Brussels
BELGIUM

FOURIER
HUGO
PROUDHON

COURBET

SWITZ.
ROUSSEAU
• Geneva
Milan MANZONE

BERLIOZ
STENDHAL
DAUMIER
• Marseilles

ATLANTIC OCEAN

MACAULAY

BYRON
KEATS
SHELLEY
TURNER

CONSTABLE

W. SCOTT
• Edinburgh
▲CARLYLE
▲WORDSWORTH
• Liverpool
OWEN
ENGLAND
• London
▲COLERIDGE
DICKENS

▲FLAUBERT
• Paris

FRANCE

LAMARTINE

BALZAC

CHATEAUBRIAND

BAUDELAIRE
DELACROIX
DE STAEL
GERICAULT
ST. SIMON
SAND

• Bordeaux

SCOTLAND

IRELAND
• Dublin

• Lyons

INGRES

COMTE

• Barcelona

GOYA
• Saragossa

SPAIN
• Madrid

PORTUGAL
• Lisbon

MEDITERRANEAN SEA

Frederic Chopin, by Eugène Delacroix. Louvre, Paris.

make up for everyday disillusion, where a *coup de théâtre,* an unexpected twist, could always unravel impossible situations. In space which steam was laying open, broadening the horizons of travel but also of fantasy: the golden east, the misty isles, the frozen somber north, different worlds and climates, especially those like the Spanish or the Arab lands that still lived in the past, all the mysterious and prestigious places on which romantic reveries could feed. In time, especially times that seemed most picturesque, spiritually alive, nationally—hence personally—significant. "Night of the Middle Ages, maybe!" wrote Schlegel: "but it was a night resplendent with stars!" Above all, in music, which alone can express the inexpressible, carry vast passions on its slender wings.

Music becomes a kind of poem, a kind of painting, evoking nature and feeling as no other art can do. In Karl Maria von Weber's *Freischütz* (1820) the forces of nature become symbols of good and evil, the music seeks to capture the sound and soul of the landscape, the sighing of the wind, the murmuring of forest trees. Ten years later, Felix Mendelssohn's *Fingal's Cave* would be greeted as landscape painting in sound. The tone poem is a romantic invention, and the tone painting too. Before the painters learned to catch the moment in a dab of color, the composers learned to ride with it through time, stirring emotions which otherwise would be crushed under the weight of words: anguish or reverie in Chopin, introspection in Schumann, explosive lyricism in Berlioz, heroic exaltation in Weber and in Wagner; and always, always color, brimming over into the other arts which music can inspire and musical terms—analogies—supply.

Music had remained one of the least prestigious arts until the first representatives of romanticism became concerned with expressing feeling and dream rather than action and thought. "All music which depicts nothing is nothing but noise," d'Alembert had said, and his contemporaries found the art diverting when it did not try to do more than that. What music can do supremely well, however, is to express those things words cannot express, passions and sentiments that can hardly be depicted in rational terms. These were the very things romantics cared about, for whom rational activities could neither plumb nor express essentials, and for whom music—the limitless language of the unconscious and the unknown—was the idiom above all others.

The nineteenth century—especially its beginning—would be the age of the *virtuoso,* musical incarnation of romantic individualism, whose self-expression was facilitated by the piano's triumph over the more tinkly clavichord. There were virtuosos of the violin, like Kreutzer for whom Beethoven wrote the *Kreutzer Sonata* (and who never condescended to play it), or Paganini; and even virtuosos of brass instruments, like Sax, inventor of the saxophone. But the greatest lions were pianist-composers like Chopin and Liszt who, when they performed, evoked shrieks, faints, hysteria among their admirers, fits which Heinrich Heine attributed to "musical cantharides." The heroine of one of Stendhal's novels, living in a provincial town, missed only one thing from Paris: the music "which had the power of increasing in surprising fashion the intensity of her spells of reverie." A generation later, the wife of a Paris publisher spoke in a similar vein: "It is a terrible thing to hear Chopin: bourgeois life seems pretty tedious on the morrow . . . the ideal discourages real life."

Perhaps that was the intention. Certainly, as Baudelaire explained, the romantic artist set out to "create a suggestive magic, containing at the same time object and subject, the world outside the artist and the artist himself." If romanticism is a way of feeling, romantic art is the communication of that feeling as forcefully and as directly as it can be done. That was one reason why the theater of men like Victor Hugo and Alfred de Musset rebelled against the bulbous, convoluted "noble" style whose pompous monuments in prose and verse were turning early-nineteenth-century literature and theater into elusive puzzles.* Now, poetry on stage and page became, as Hugo called it, "a sonorous echo" of its author and of his sentiments, an echo that everyone could hear and feel.

Painting underwent a similar evolution. The art historian Marcel Brion has pointed out that an age of revolutions and great wars developed a new, more dramatic vision, new ways of feeling and of communicating feelings, a new interest in the tragic and unusual aspects of life, in tension, suffering, madness, darkness, death—as can be found in the paintings and engravings of Francisco Goya (1746–1828) or in the work of a much younger man, the Frenchman Théodore Géricault (1791–1824)

---

* Thus, in the poetry of a much-appreciated author of that day—Jacques Delille (1738–1813), an umbrella would be apostrophized: "Precious and supple structure of that ilk/That joins the arts of whalebones and of silk!" while a pig became "Cold celibate ill-suited for pleasure/Unwilling martyr to a table's measure."

The Raft of the Medusa, by Théodore Géricault. Louvre, Paris.

whose painting *The Raft of the Medusa* was based on interviews with survivors from a shipwreck and endless sketches of sickness and of corpses.

Since the Renaissance, painting had operated in the realm of measurable things and conformed to the rules of measure, with perspective, proportion, and form to govern its compositions. Now it would quit this ponderable ground for the realm of suggestion and suggestiveness, where what counts are moods and sentiments, not visible things but the intimate, the secret, the sensed. Not form but color, not realism but imagination, not tranquility but movement, would henceforth dominate; and the romantic artist led the way in the great nineteenth-century break out of reality into fantasy. It had been possible, the classic artists thought, to reproduce things objectively. Romantics disagreed. And were it possible, they said, it would not be nearly so interesting as the poetic vision of one given man—provided that he has a vision to impart.

Goethe contrasted and sought to reconcile *Dichtung und Wahrheit*— Truth and Poetry—implying that they are two different things. Art is a dream or, rather, its evocation, the resonance of a secret vision which hopes to evoke an echo in some beholder's soul. The images which the artist handles reach out to pluck the senses, not the mind. The painter pursuing "the suggestive magic" tries to combine color, light, and shade in such a way "that they go straight to the heart." These are the words of Eugène Delacroix (1798–1863), and one can see them come to life in the man's paintings. The work of Delacroix mirrors most of the concerns and passions of his time: the romantic fascination with suggestive heroes like Dr. Faustus or Hamlet and with Byronic characters, with the Middle Ages in his historical paintings, with the exotic and colorful and wild in his Moroccan and his hunting scenes, with philhellenism in his *Massacre of Chios,* with revolution in the famous *Liberty Leading the People* and *The Barricade,* finally the characteristic romantic yearning for the impossible in his last great fresco of Jacob's struggle with the angel. Movement, color, passion, vivid intensity and tragic vision, made Delacroix the greatest painter of his time.

The tide of fantasy and of imagination which we can see at its flood in Delacroix must not make us overlook a parallel directness and simplicity. The romantics looked around them with their eyes wide open; and their revolt stemmed from the things they saw: hypocrisy, injustice, ugliness, against which they fulminated—shouting so loud because most people would not lend an ear. Southey denounced the way in which "men and beasts are considered mainly as machines;" and Coleridge pointed out that "national wealth . . . is national only in statistical tables," and asked that "even for patriotic purposes no person should be treated as a thing." Hugo described "that people which works and suffers" and which no one, after his *Misérables,* could any more ignore. The growing interest in historical sources, in sagas, folk songs, ballads, spawned the historical novels of Walter Scott and the historical chronicles of Augustin Thierry (at one time personal secretary of Saint-Simon).

Colorful, heroic, lyrical, resurrecting a romantic version of the national past, such works could not fail to draw attention to the people, the folk, fount of national energy, generous, laborious, pure, from whose depths alone regeneration was to be expected, and yet oppressed, degraded, driven to destruction by forces which, in weakening the people, weakened the nation too. In 1820, Augustin Thierry had called for a history not of kings and heroes but of citizens and subjects: of the people. In 1837 Thomas Carlyle's *French Revolution* provided such a book, where events in street and workshops and before the hearth were in the foreground of the action. At last, in 1846, Jules Michelet's *The People* raised a paean to their essential role.

One can refer to a romantic populism, deeply connected with their interest in the nation and in national sources; or a romantic nationalism, arising out of their historical self-consciousness. It may not be far-fetched to see in this a logical outcome of that relativism which the eighteenth century did not exactly discover but at least made public. The great romantic exercise is history, the chronicle of change and its continuous proof, vulgar or academic, vicariously exciting and frequently unsettling—in opera, in painting, in literature, even in philosophy where, for Kant and Hegel, consciousness develops in time. History is, like music, the art of time and change. It now became the great exponent of those diversities of experience which lie behind the variety they stress: variety of regions and of nations, languages and traditions, folklores and laws, justifying not only present differences but future change as well, a promise to some and a threat to others.

New Public and New Culture

Education

By the eighteenth century, the traditional seats of learning had become quiet harbors for fossils of a former age. Despite occasional flashes of life, the older German and Italian universities were decaying; the Sorbonne in Paris was the Gibraltar of anachronism; Oxford and Cambridge, the homes of "ignorance in stilts" as Cowper, the poet, called it. Gibbon records his recollection of mid-eighteenth-century Oxford: "I spent fourteen months at Magdalen College; they proved the fourteen months the most idle and unprofitable of my whole life." The Fellows were "decent easy men, who supinely enjoyed the gifts of the founders . . . From the toil of reading, or thinking, or writing, they had absolved their consciences."

True, while the old universities decayed, new colleges were being founded in America and new universities in Europe, designed to carry forward the spirit of Enlightenment: Yale (1701), Göttingen (1734), St. Petersburg (1747), Moscow (1755); while at Halle and Leipzig teaching methods were reformed under the influence of a disciple of Leibniz, Christian Wolff (1679–1754), professor of mathematics and physics, which were the typical sciences of the modern age. The new curricula, still strongly based in classics, now also emphasized mathematics and philosophy, learning by thinking as well as by mere rote. But change came only slowly. Göttingen provided understanding and a home for scientific studies, but it remained exceptional for quite a while. At Innsbruck, in 1740, the university refused to set up a professorship in botany and chemistry, which could be studied quite well in apothecary shops; at Erlangen the professor of chemistry had to set up his own laboratory at home, in order to provide the practical instruction his university spurned.

At last, in 1810, the Leibniz-Wolff tradition would find embodiment in the University of Berlin, whose courses were designed not just to pass on knowledge but to develop the student's mind, train him for life, prepare a grounding from which he could develop any specialization he might later need. Above all, Berlin held out the ideal of a school where students were free to pursue learning and teachers to impart it as they thought best. Unfortunately, this was easier said than done; especially since the university was dependent on the state and on its vagaries.

Meanwhile, through most of the eighteenth century, men interested in the new ideas were pursuing them in academies, clubs, and coffeehouses, rather than in schools. In Britain, while universities ossified and the upper classes turned to the local vicar or to private tutors, the middle classes found the most useful education in the Dissenting Academies founded in the provinces to train nonconformist ministers and to give laymen "some knowledge . . . in the more useful branches of literature, and to lead them to an early acquaintance with and just concern for the true principles of religion and liberty." Clearly, religious and political dissent were bound to combine. It was in the Dissenting Academies in the 1760's that history and English literature were first treated as regular academic disciplines, along with natural history, science, and living languages. The Scottish universities also, close-linked with civic life, heeded the changing world which the richly endowed colleges of Oxford and Cambridge could afford to ignore. Professors applied their knowledge to worldly needs, sought to solve the problems of the linen industry or, like Adam Smith, professor of moral philosophy in the University of Glasgow, analyzed industrial civilization, labor, and production in lectures which would furnish the basis for his *Wealth of Nations.*

At last, in 1828, the influence of Scotland, of Berlin, of Jefferson's new University of Virginia (1819), which offered a wide curriculum and a liberal education, led to the foundation of University College, London, designed to serve "the middling rich," as its sponsors (Bentham, Priestley, Mill—himself an Edinburgh graduate), put it, who were aspiring to a more modern world and a more modern education.* Opposed by the establishment as the "Godless college," part of the philosophical radicals' campaign to "overthrow altar and throne," University College was only officially recognized in 1846 as part of the new University of London, alongside King's College, which had been founded in opposition to it

---

* Indeed, aspiring to be educated at all; for Jews, Catholics, and Dissenters were still at this time excluded from Oxford and Cambridge.

University College, London, as it appeared in the early nineteenth century.

by friends of King and church. Meanwhile, Durham University had also been founded, and a college for Wales as well—St. David's, Lampeter.

At lower levels, too, changes had taken place. The lower schools had long concentrated on inculcating knowledge by rote learning. Since children were held to be weak in judgment, it was thought best to fill them with facts rather than understanding until they went to college. In the late sixteenth and in the seventeenth century, a number of educational reformers had moved away from this insistence on memory and appealed to the students' intelligence. Jesuit educators and Protestant grammarians came to think that learning was best related to reality, lectures enlivened by example and anecdote, rules placed in the context of their application, with examples drawn from literature and life. Texts were still learned by heart, but they were also explained; classical authors were still parsed but they were also illuminated by connecting them with the experience of the students; mathematics and natural sciences were considered increasingly relevant.

The eighteenth century brought further reforms. If, as the philosophers thought, man is what he makes of his experience, the way to make him better is to expose him to better experiences. *Émile* had argued that children should be allowed to develop freely, and learn as much as possible from experience. A Swiss teacher, Johann Heinrich Pestalozzi (1746–1827), set up an experimental school to apply these theories, educate children for life rather than pump them full of knowledge, turn out not trained puppets and regurgitators of set formulae but good citizens, whose freedom from constraint would also free them from the rebelliousness arising from repression. In 1837 an admirer of Pestalozzi, the Prussian Friedrich Froebel (1782–1852), would pioneer the education of smaller children, and found the first Kindergarten. A German follower of Rousseau, Johann Basedow (1724?–1790), attempted to put his views in practice in the 1770's in an experimental college founded at Dessau. His *Philantropinum* was coeducational, residential, and progressive, abandoning wigs and awkward clothes for sensible garb and country walks and river bathing, trying to teach *real* things—languages, sciences, skills—in lively fashion. *Realschulen* spread through Germany as far as Russia and, leaving their mark on German upper schools whose excellence the nineteenth century admired, helped to make Germany "the classic land of barracks and of schools."

All this, of course, served only the upper classes and "the middling rich." Enlightened men, who talked a great deal about education, were chiefly interested in universities and secondary schools. Voltaire, who wanted education to enlarge the middle class, did not wish it to change the common people who, if educated, would not want to carry out the difficult and unpleasant labors that someone must perform. Napoleon created a grandiose public education system, but one which stressed discipline and higher education—the lower classes being better off without much learning. By 1814 France boasted 36 *lycées* with 9,000 inmates, largely the sons of middle- and upper-class families, whose day began and ended to the sound of a drum. But there were fewer village schools than under the old regime. The career open to all talents was evidently still some way off. The Austrian Empire had free and compulsory education, with probably the worst-paid teachers anywhere but nevertheless providing a great opportunity for bright farmers' sons in lands where, to get married, men had to show an elementary-school certificate; and high schools took the better elementary graduates tuition-free, letting the parents pay their board in kind. Many students at Vienna University, too, were poor and attended free, living on a pittance. The nobles had tutors at home or went to a special nobles' academy for the army and the diplomatic corps called the *Theresianum*.

But, really, outside a few countries like Austria and Denmark, the problem of the illiterate masses was hardly being touched. In France a royal ordinance of 1816 enjoined every commune to educate all children. But it did not work. In 1821 France boasted 28,000 primary schools, in 1829, 30,000; but of the 39,000 communes in the country nearly half had no primary school at all and of a hundred conscripts only forty-two were found able to read; among twenty-five million adults fifteen million could not read. Nevertheless, the number of those who could read and write was steadily increasing. In the hundred years before the Revolution, it had grown by 18 per cent for men and 13 per cent for women, and it would grow better than twice as fast in the three-score years that followed. Education had always been the concern of Christian churches, and where these existed, priests, monks, and nuns continued to furnish a majority of teachers. But teachers were scarce, perhaps because they were so ill-paid, and various schemes attempted to make up for it: in Sunday schools, launched in the eighteenth century by Robert Raikes of Gloucester; or in the monitorial system devised by Joseph Lancaster (1778–1838), which used more advanced students to drill the younger ones in the rudiments of reading, writing, and arithmetic, thus enabling large numbers to be trained in economical fashion.

But education for the poor was looked on with suspicion. The Sunday School Union, founded in 1785, argued that Sunday schools would produce "orderly and decent comportment." Their critics rejoined that education would refine and innervate, disqualifying its recipients "for the duties of a humble station." Pioneers like Hannah More, the "Bishop in petticoats" of the Clapham Sect (see p. 498), had to reassure themselves and the propertied classes that their little charges were not being brought up to be Jacobins. They certainly ran little risk of it under Miss More's tutelage where, as she wrote in 1801, "they learn on weekdays such coarse work as may fit them to be servants. I allow of no writing for the poor."

Actually, education would have advanced faster if it had not got caught up in endless and bitter religious arguments. In England the Royal Lancasterian Association of 1810 had to be matched by a National Society for the Education of the Poor in the Principles of the Established Church in 1811. In other countries, too, clergy and anticlericals, church and chapel, tugged at the schools and students until learning itself fell out.

Yet, even so, more poor learned how to read. In the 1780's and 90's already, corresponding societies were gathering together artisans, laborers, small tradesmen, who wanted to spread knowledge among their own kind: "To enlighten the people, to show the people the reason, the ground of all their complaints and sufferings." The workers taught themselves in their own adult and infant Sunday schools, which taught not only reading and writing, but also hatred "of our corrupt and tyrannical rulers." They taught themselves at home, using nearly 120,000 copies of Cobbett's *Grammar of the English Language* between 1818 and 1833. Many remained ignorant, like the arrested English rebels who thought a provisional government was one to give them more provisions, or the pitmen who thought universal suffrage meant a kind of suffering in common. Nevertheless, some two out of three workingmen in England could read in some fashion, although fewer could write. Many bought and more read pamphlets and papers like Cobbett's *Twopenny Register,* which sold 40- to 60,000 copies a week, or the *Black Dwarf,* which sold 12- or 13,000. By 1840 French workers had their own newspaper, written and run by workmen like themselves and called *The Workshop.* A broader literate public was appearing. True, literacy and education, advancing fast among the middle classes and skilled artisans, were forging ahead more slowly in the lower classes, painfully slowly in the countryside; but the scale of the new reading public was incomparably greater than it had ever been, and this reflected on the trades which provided its supplies.

The Writing Trade

Traditionally writers, like artists, had always depended on the support of patrons drawn from the church, the court, or the nobility. Art by itself did not nourish its man, unless a patron helped him. Ben Jonson had complained that poetry beggared him, and many could say as much. By mid-seventeenth century opportunities appeared to gain security by entering public service. John Milton was Latin Secretary under the Commonwealth, Andrew Marvel gave up a post as private tutor to become Milton's assistant, Dryden was secretary of Cromwell's chamberlain, Pepys entered the civil service before the Restoration and continued in it until 1688. Thereafter, English literary men did even better: Matthew Prior was appointed ambassador; Addison became secretary of state and married the dowager Countess of Warwick; Steele became a member of

Parliament, and so did Sheridan and a dozen others. Pope of course held court at Twickenham:

> Above a patron, though I condescend
> Sometimes to call a minister my friend.

In eighteenth-century France, as we may guess, the prestige of literary figures was also growing. Ocean-going ships were being named for Rousseau, Voltaire, and d'Alembert; and a contemporary observer could declare that three qualifications were needed for social success: birth, wealth, and literary talent. The second qualification was new enough as a social factor; the third was a revolutionary novelty. Yet, probably, the estimate of literary talent was not unconnected with whatever wealth its success could bring.

With illiteracy shrinking, the reading public grew and so did the size of editions of new books. Authors gradually freed themselves from private patronage, first in England, where successful authors could earn really large sums, then in France, and slowly gained economic independence. Milton received £10 for *Paradise Lost;* Matthew Prior, who died fifty years after Milton, got 4,000 guineas for his collected poems. The revenues of most continued to be modest, and men like Diderot still depended on help from generous patrons like Catherine the Great, while Rousseau who tried his best to stay independent by copying sheets of music or herborizing, had to accept the aid of his well-meaning friends.

Part of the problem lay in pirated editions, which made money for publishers but brought the authors nothing. This did not come to an end in France until the Revolution, which, in 1793, brought a Conventional decree vesting control of all writings, compositions, and works of art in their creators for their lifetime. The property of playwrights in their plays, which had been pirated just as often, had been established in 1791 by the Constituent Assembly.

Another difficulty was simply that books were costly, and many people got theirs from lending libraries and reading rooms which flourished everywhere. We have a picture of such a library in Paris of the 1780's, whose author sensibly observes that the most worn books are those in greatest demand: "Those works which describe the manners, which are simple, naïve, and touching, which are not affected or arrogant and use no academic jargon, these are the ones that people come to get from all quarters of the town . . ." And "there are works which cause such a ferment that the book dealer is forced to cut the volume in three to answer the eagerness of the numerous readers; and then you pay not by the day, but by the hour . . ." In Germany around 1780 circulating libraries catered to craftsmen and soldiers, as well as to the better-off. By 1806, a German journalist noted that reading, once the preserve of scholars, had become a general habit, "even of the lower classes, not only in the towns but in the country too."

Among the things found in reading rooms were papers and periodicals, whose number also increased so that they, and the works of reference and popularization now in great demand, furnished an important source of income to struggling authors. Dictionaries, encyclopedias, grammars, would pay the rent; reviews and articles in a journal could bring in something too; but popular fame could be acquired most quickly with a successful play. The broadening interest in literature, the greater numbers of the literate, were reflected in the theater-going public. After mid-eighteenth century this grew to include not only the cultivated middle class—lawyers and school-masters, writers and members of the liberal professions—but footmen and barbers, porters and shop assistants, the livelier representatives of the lower classes who had presumably picked up a taste for plays and literature in their employers' houses and in reading rooms.

Hack work of every kind could still be supplemented by pensions, sinecures, and grants from official sources. But the strongest support for professional writers, their best source of employment, came from the growing press. Newspapers and periodicals seem to arise from old-fashioned almanacs and calendars, which became biannual in the sixteenth century, for sale at fairs, and then monthly or even weekly in the seventeenth century, as numerous cities began to publish bulletins of news. Such publications appeared first in the great Italian cities of the sixteenth century, where professional newsmen provided selected subscribers with regular newsletters based on information gathered in local inns, banks, and antechambers.

From a subscription business, the bulletins became an open trade, beginning to be sold in the city streets. In Rome their producers were called *novellanti* (newsmen) or *menanti* (drivers or leaders) because, as the Venetian ambassador explained, "They lead opinion." They were already attacked for being liars with no respect for the authorities or God, and in 1629 Ben Jonson's play *The Staple of News* satirized their exploitation of public credulity. By that date the press had aroused two of its constant concomitants: official repression on the part of governments suspicious or resentful of its influence, official patronage from similar sources eager to gain publicity for their ends.

Where the Inquisition did not undertake the task, the state controlled booksellers and printers (often the same men), trying to limit their numbers in order to facilitate surveillance. In mid-seventeenth-century France, salaried royal censors were appointed to carry this out independent of the Sorbonne and parlements. A century later there were four-score of them and by 1789 they numbered 178. Between 1667 and 1676, the number of printer-booksellers in Paris fell from 84 to 36: still more than the 20 printers authorized in London. There, after 1660, rigid censorship had been re-established and only one government

An ad appearing in the first issue of the *Illustrated London News,* May 14, 1842.

news-sheet was allowed to appear. Any other, as the editor of the government publication explained, "makes the multitude too familiar with the actions and councils of their superiors."

This remained the crux of the matter even when censorship disappeared in the 1690's and England joined those rare lands like Holland where the press was relatively free. The problem of keeping the news from the multitude was solved by stamp duties which raised prices, kept circulation low, and made the press dependent on handouts and subsidies. These the political parties and especially the government managed either directly or indirectly by taking out advertisements in friendly papers or buying large numbers of their copies for free distribution.

Daily papers were beginning to appear: the first in London in 1702. Paris and Philadelphia followed in 1777 and 1783 respectively. But daily newspapers depended on a concentrated buying public which only some big cities could provide, and on possibilities of regular distribution, and these were not available throughout most of Europe until postal services improved with the nineteenth century. Periodicals were more successful, like Defoe's *Review* (in which *Robinson Crusoe* provided the first serial novel) or Addison and Steele's *Tatler* (1709) and *Spectator* (1711), or the *Mercure de France* (1798), providing literary, political, and social comments; or then, again, like the *Monthly Gentlemen's Magazine* (1731), accounts of Parliamentary debates disguised as reports from Lilliput. Beside these, a myriad of pamphlets and flysheets would spring up written for plain folk who could read and pay their penny, and out of which many a workman's child would be taught to read. Despite all the attempts to muzzle it, the English press enjoyed increasing freedom. This would come on the continent but slowly, even the Revolution opening the gates only briefly before Napoleon slammed them shut again, not to reopen for several decades.

But even while the free press languished, the popular press grew, enjoying the advantages of new technology. Paper from rags was dear and growing scarcer. In the late eighteenth century, its manufacture from wood pulp had been proved possible and large-scale manufacture began by the time of the Restoration. Printing processes were revolutionized when, in 1814, the London *Times* introduced printing machines—devised by a German, Koenig—which printed 1,100 sheets an hour, eventually increased to 7,000. Koenig's machines were soon installed in Paris and Berlin. Other technical advances permitted the publication of illustrated papers (the *Illustrated London News* in 1842, *l'Illustration* of Paris in 1843), which appealed to many families not interested in the political, literary, commercial, or society news of the regular periodicals. Illustrations could also mean satire and caricature, which were much in vogue in the 1830's and 1840's; especially the political and social satire of weeklies like *Charivari* founded in 1832 and much in demand for the drawings of Daumier and Gavarni, of *Punch* founded in 1841, or the *Fliegende Blätter* (1844).

The French electoral law of 1831 doubled the number of electors; the British reform of 1832 introduced the petty bourgeoisie to political life; primary schools were spreading skills and disciplines in Prussia and Switzerland, England and France. A new reading public was growing, which the press attempted to attract. But taxes and production costs still put the papers beyond the reach of poorer men. In the late 1830's, Émile de Girardin cut the cost in half by relying on publicity; and the 38,000 subscribers of his *Siècle* almost equaled the combined sales of all the London dailies, which came to 40,000 in 1829. In 1833 the *New York Sun* had launched the daily at two cents, which gave it by 1835 greater sales than the London *Times.* That year Gordon Bennett published the *Morning Herald,* triumph of popular sensationalism, which printed 33,000 copies in 1849. Freed of stifling duties only in the 1850's, the London press would take longer to grow. The penny press was born in 1855 with the *Daily Telegraph,* selling at the equivalent of the *Sun's* two cents or the *Siècle*'s subscription price. By 1855, the *Times,* which printed 17,000 twenty years before, was selling 60,000.

Interestingly, the attraction of popular papers differed in different lands. In France, sales went up through serials on whose adventures the public hung. Balzac, George Sand, Alexandre Dumas, brought thousands of subscribers to the papers; above all was Eugène Sue, whose serials were devoured by tens of thousands. His *Mysteries of Paris* would be translated and then copied by many German papers eager to attract new readers, to such an extent that thirty-six varieties of *Mysteries* were published in Germany in 1844 alone. Indifferent to politics, the European reader could be caught by love and adventure stories. The Americans cared little for literature, even of the most vulgar kind. The *Sun* or *Herald* offered a diet of human interest stories, "true facts," crimes, city news, and family tragedies. With all their differences, newspapers now appealed no longer to a small elite but to all those who could read. The unrefined public which they tapped was wooed with rough, attractive fare fitted for simple minds and simple people; and this is what it has remained since then.

Publicity is to business what steam is to machines, said Lord Macaulay. It certainly was that to newspapers, which had to provide ever more pages at an ever smaller price. Production costs could not be covered by income from sales without increasing the price and thus reducing sales; the answer to this was found in advertising income, which could cover the deficits. And advertising became one of the great forces which maintained and influenced the press.

Better roads, then better railroads, meant that newspapers could be carried and sold over a wider area. They also meant, along with the new electric telegraph, that news could travel further and faster. In November, 1847, Queen Victoria's speech at the opening of Parliament was telegraphed in full. The great newspapers set up correspondents and messenger services all over the world. News agencies were founded, first in Paris by Garnier and Charles Havas in 1832,* then by Julius Reuter, who settled in London in 1851 having learned his trade with Havas, and by Bernhard Wolff in Berlin.

Men still contended that all this paper was only devoted to telling public lies in private causes. Many felt what a Balzac character expressed: "All newspapers are cowardly, hypocritical, infamous, lying, murderous; they will kill ideas, systems, men, and flourish on it." Perhaps. But the same could have been said just as easily about mankind. For better or for worse, a great new social force had taken shape.

The Public Arts

The interaction between a changing public and its purveyors which is so evident in the written word also appears in other fields. Despite a diversity of tastes that henceforth increased diversity of forms up to the eclecticism of the twentieth century, music—like painting, literature, and architecture—proceeded to reflect the subordination of classical lines to the pictorial element, the anecdote or the subjective feeling dear to the romantics. To begin with, opera particularly, with its vast productions, remained in the eighteenth century a luxury of the rich, especially of the courts and narrow cultivated circles of refined connoisseurs for whose expert delight servant-composers labored. Public performances appear more like leftovers from the royal board, unless they are organized for some special festivity or religious occasion, such as the concerts of religious music that one could hear at Christmas or in Lent. As the eighteenth century drew on, however, more and more cities set up permanent

---

* In 1840, Havas scooped the news market by organizing a carrier-pigeon service between Paris, London, and Brussels. America got its first news agency when the Associated Press was set up in New York in 1856.

C. W. Gluck and His Wife. Historisches Museum der Stadt Wien.

music societies with concert halls of their own, and musicians found that they had a choice between hiring themselves out to private patrons or to a less-exalted public and one whose expectations were quite different.

Both Johann Sebastian Bach (1685–1750) and George Frederick Handel (1685–1759) may be said to have written music for the select, their tonal architecture directly related to emotional, philosophical, and mystical values, their musical dramas full of psychological characterization expressed in melody. This, along with a lot of picturesque ornament and design and an architectural magnificence dear to their age, made for a rich kind of stateliness that can be compared with the dresses, the wigs, and buildings of their day. Then, in middle life, Handel turned from writing operas for the entertainment of his royal and aristocratic patrons to oratorios for a soulful and unsubtle middle class: "What the English like is something they can beat time to," Handel told Gluck. He gave them the vigorous, unsubtle, and often-rollicking oratorios which many could sing and all, even Philistines, can still enjoy. Frivolous or mythological themes had been abandoned for Biblical ones; a rich, capricious public for a sober, solid one. The same might be said of Franz Joseph Haydn, whose sparkling classsicism in the service of the great magnate family of Esterhazy shifted into a more accessible, less rigorous key in the London symphonies he wrote in the 1780's.

In the second half of the eighteenth century, the rococo which had begun in exuberance and fantasy was drying into vulgar sentimentalism. The change can be seen in painting between Boucher and Greuze. In music, the same drift from frivolity to simplicity meant that more complex earlier forms were abandoned for melodic effects that would please a less refined public, more interested in melody and tonal color than in structural elegance.

However, the eighteenth century was also the age of enlightened philosophers who were, as we know, much interested in music, in its reform, in its return (like society's) to "nature" under the example of antiquity. Their great musical ally and exponent was C. W. Gluck (1714–1787), who had begun by writing operas in the Italian manner, or smaller ones full of rococo charm. In 1762, with *Orfeus and Eurydice,* Gluck abandoned this ornamented manner for a more sober style aimed at the sort of antique purity which Lessing's *Laocoön* had recommended. His clarity and logic, the correspondence of words and sounds in the tunes he wrote, reflected the philosophy of the encyclopedists and the plastic ideals of Greek art. Maria Luigi Cherubini (1760–1842) continued the heroic opera style of Gluck, which he adapted to the revolutionary spirit of the 1790's. Cherubini dealt realistically with people—with *the* people—now being taken seriously for the first time, with violent death, and fear, and rescue from danger, and relief at escaping them, along with the concomitant joy.

As the Revolution habituated people to crowd participation in hymns and ceremonies, often propagandistic, opera too became increasingly grand. Soon, the emotional expressionism which Gluck played down, the use of instrumental tone color, the adaptation of heroism to patriotic rather than classical themes, would appear in the operas of Karl Maria von Weber (1786–1826), whose *Freischütz* in 1820 revealed the triumph of national sentiment along with the possibilities of romantic opera.* Weber was the director of the "German" opera at Dresden, in which Wagner's adoptive father sang the tenor roles; and when in 1844 Weber's body was brought back from London where he had died to be reinterred at Dresden, it would be Richard Wagner (1813–1883), then the conductor of the city opera, who composed the funeral march for the occasion. By that time Wagner, who scored his first successes with *Rienzi* (1842) and *The Flying Dutchman* (1843), was refusing to make any concessions to the public taste; and his *Tannhauser* (1845), with its long recitatives, was not very well received. Increasingly disgusted with the Philistines who did not appreciate the complex web of sound in which he tried to weave the heretofore-distinct elements of the operatic pattern, Wagner drifted into radical politics, ended up on the barricades of 1849, and had to flee Dresden to exile and to fame.

We notice here how quickly the artist working for a patron had become first a caterer to the public and then a creator looking to himself alone, if need be at odds with conservative music publishers and slow-moving public taste. Beethoven had already seen himself not as a mere

---

* Similar patriotic concerns, combined with respect for the national past, led to the rediscovery of idioms quite different from the composers' own. It was romantic musicologists who revived the works of Palestrina, Protestant church music, and old Dutch music; it would be Felix Mendelssohn who discovered and first performed in Berlin (1829) Bach's *St. Matthew Passion.*

entertainer, but as the priest and officiant of a new cult (especially in the *Ninth Symphony,* first performed in 1824), whose ideas music carried better than words could do. The late quartets of Beethoven or the songs of Schubert were the beginning of a new tradition, which Gustav Mahler articulated at a later time when claiming that he composed not for his contemporaries but for posterity.

And yet, of course, no artist however stubborn can escape his time. Some do not wish to do so. Thus, Rossini's *William Tell,* first produced at the Paris Opera in August, 1829, was a deliberate appeal to current nationalistic ideas, a fact which nowise affected Rossini's credit at the Court of Charles X. In the next few years, the inclusion of his opera in the repertory of other European theaters posed significant problems: in Milan, the Austrian censorship had the Swiss patriot turned into a Scotsman—William Wallace—and Austrians to Englishmen. In Rome, papal censorship turned William Tell into Rudolph of Sterling and filled the lyrics with pious references. In Prussia, William Tell became Andreas Hoffer, a hero of the Tyrolean insurrection against Napoleon's French; in Russia, he became Charles the Bold of Burgundy. In Vienna alone of all reactionary capitals Rossini's libretto was left unmauled, the public shouting "Long live the Habsburgs!" after every performance, thus reassuring a lenient government. Yet, even Rossini, who lived for nearly two-score years after *William Tell* had triumphed, wrote scarcely anything thereafter, a strange self-censorship which may be explained by the words he wrote a friend shortly before his death: "This art of music which is based solely on sentiment and ideals, cannot escape the influence of the times we live in, and the sentiment and ideals of the present day are wholly concerned with steam, rapine and barricades."

The story of the theater is somewhat similar. Much seventeenth-century drama had been either stilted and unreal, or else licentious: abetting cynicism, adultery, and deception to such an extent that in 1719 a reforming chaplain conclusively demonstrated that the plays of his time offended a minimum of 1,400 Bible texts. Then came John Gay's *Beggar's Opera* (1728) and George Lillo's *London Merchant,* which ushered real life onto the distant stage. Gay's play took London by storm, running for sixty-three days—a record at the time. Everyone assumed that Gay's rogue-hero, MacHeath, was a portrait of Walpole and delighted in a social satire whose protagonists were footpads, fences, and prostitutes. Lillo's play allowed a middle-class hero—and an apprentice at that—to glory in the kind of tragic ending which had hitherto been reserved exclusively for nobles. Both represented "vulgar" subjects with humor and vitality, using a language which sounded forceful—at least by its novelty.

All this time stage lighting, scenery, stage effects, were improving: dividing the stage from the audience more effectively and thus perfecting the possibilities of illusion, allowing the theater to become more realistic and, in a sense, less theatrical. This lent itself increasingly to social satire,

The first page of *The Beggar's Opera,* by John Gay.

such as the comedies which Sheridan or Beaumarchais provided, or to plays of manners which paralleled the novels of the time. Since sober people still abstained from the theater during most of the eighteenth century, or were deprived of its pleasures by lack of means, the latter mode was more apparent in books than in plays and it is there that we most clearly see the change in mood that marks the 1740's. Frivolousness and cynicism retreated; virtue and sentiment, prudence and morality, must now serve the sentiments, the conscience, the prurience of a new kind of public.

It was for these people who suspected elegance, distrusted the other classes, and indulged their own emotions that Samuel Richardson (1689–1761), a printer's devil who eventually married his master's widow, began to write the model letters from which readers could learn style and manners. By 1740, the letter-writing manual had become *Pamela, Or Virtue Rewarded,* the prototype of a thousand romances in which the prudent poor girl gets the seducer in the end. Then, after *Pamela,* came *Clarissa Harlowe,* which Alfred de Musset considered the first novel in the world and which was avidly read by men like Goethe and Diderot. After that, there was no stopping the cult of broken hearts, of pathos, and moralizing.

But *Pamela* evoked a counterblast in *Shamela,* where Henry Fielding (1707–1754) exposed those hypocrisies that Richardson glorified. Fielding abandoned the rather primitive letter-writing convention for a straightforward and exuberant narrative that makes him the real

father of the English novel. Fortunately, his technical skill was complemented by wit and by sympathetic knowledge of human nature. In works
like *Joseph Andrews* (1742) and *Tom Jones* (1749), Fielding's shrewd
and forthright humor sketched out a world whose humanity goes far beyond the platitudes of Richardson, and proved that self-delusion need
not necessarily set the pattern of modern fiction.

The plastic arts, too, underwent similar changes, built up new structures adapted to different social conditions, adopted themes suited to
new attitudes, and methods devised to reach a broader public. There
had been no museums, no galleries, no exhibitions, before the seventeenth century. To see real paintings, usually, one had to gain admittance to private collections; to sell them one had to hang them in a
tavern or attract buyers to one's home—a more likely method of getting
an order from a rich patron. In France alone there existed since Louis
XIV the Academy of Fine Arts with its drawing school, its scholarships for study abroad, its annual exhibition: the *salon*. In England, the
first public exhibition dates back only to 1760, the Royal Academy
of Art to 1768.

The growing prosperity of the middle classes meant a new art public,
unversed or uninterested in mythological themes but rather, like the
seventeenth-century Dutch, in more familiar subjects. And so, perhaps
by way of England, the great materialistic tradition of the Dutch came
back into its own, the intimacy of everyday scenes, the pleasures of family life, the solid quality of humble objects, lived again in the canvases
of Pietro Longhi, of Sir Henry Raeburn and of Sir Joshua Reynolds,
above all in the work of Jean Baptiste Chardin (1699–1779), the
most concrete and dignified observer of reality. Yet intimate realism
could drift into sentimentalism, as it did with Greuze, or into academ-
icism, which preached the use of ideal forms to express moral sentiments.
Thus, Reynolds painted *The Triumph of Truth* (1774), in which a
professor refutes Hume, Gibbon, and Voltaire, and other edifying painters limned every sort of virtue to the edification of respectable art patrons.
The man who built a bridge between the solemn and expensive horrors
committed in academies and cheaper but equally moralistic products for
a more general public was William Hogarth (1697–1764).

Hogarth appealed to middle-class tastes and pockets against the tyranny
of aristocratic patrons and connoisseurs. He turned his paintings into
prints, put the prints up for subscription and lottery, demonstrated
that artists, like writers, could find an alternative source of income, found
that engravings could be pirated in a way that paintings were unlikely
to be, and, to defend his property, fought for and obtained legal protection for the result of artistic invention—a copyright law, Hogarth's
Act. Against the tyranny of fashionable taste, Hogarth set out to prove
that pictures can be legible, reviving a cartoon technique that anyone
could follow without classical references; and the crudeness which put

Marriage à la Mode: The Contract, by William Hogarth. National Gallery, London.

off the elegant attracted the common people, who gaped and commented at his works exhibited in shop windows.

Hogarth's work inspired many of the great English novelists—especially Fielding—and it has left us with the richest picture book of his age. Thereafter, images multiplied, first by the invention of lithography in Germany (1798), which greatly simplified reproduction and permitted the illustration of books, periodicals, and the printing of separate pictures like Daumier's; and then in 1839 by the photograph, soon to be perfected by two Frenchmen—Niepce and Daguerre. The arrival of color and decoration for walls which had for centuries stayed bare might well have outweighed the shoddy wares they spread.

True, the appearance of a new mass public meant on the whole the triumph of the senses over the mind, of vulgarity over refinement, of show over taste. It was just because Paris had a large theater-and opera-going public that its plays and operas were so often third-rate, seeking the level of that larger public to which they must appeal, that Dumas triumphed on the boulevards and Donizetti, Bellini, Auber on the musical stage, that Rossini was preferred to Mozart and Meyerbeer to Berlioz, that Wagner was laughed off the stage for refusing to place a ballet where dandies late from dinner could enjoy it. Music like art was an amusement, a decoration.

Yet other things became available. There was, increasingly a *choice*—a choice for more and more people. The theater based on box office remained sporadic or uncertain, the literature grew florid and diffuse, painting conformist and all too often dreary. Yet the vogue of amateur theatricals, like that of chamber music, like that of water colors, could spread to bourgeois homes. Once the preserve and practice of the very few, the arts were becoming public before they became popular.

With few exceptions, the seventeenth-century art public had still been restricted to the court and church, the very noble or the very rich. By the nineteenth century, municipal theaters, opera houses, and museums were making art available to the middling classes: first steps in a process leading from Molière's *Bourgeois Gentilhomme* to H. G. Wells' Mr. Kipps, the little clerk avid for culture, which he considers a part and perhaps a path of social promotion.

As the nineteenth century opened, most poets, artists, writers, stemmed from upper reaches of society. The age of private enterprise was also the age of private incomes and, in their shade, creativeness—which sometimes wilted—also put forth astonishing blooms. Ingres and Delacroix, at logger-heads about the way to paint, were free to wield their brushes as they pleased: both greatly. Gustave Flaubert (1821–1880) would never have developed his literary talent without the solid family fortune on which he lived. Nor would Charles Baudelaire (1821–1867), whom we shall meet again, who bore his poems while squandering his father's legacy.

Yet, by the 1840's already, many aspiring artists were of humbler extraction: offspring of tanners, artisans, small shopkeepers, minor employees. Henri Murger (1822–1861), who in 1845 began to sketch their world in his *Scenes of Bohemian Life,* was the son of a janitor who doubled as a tailor; the father of Champfleury, founder of the realist school in French literature, was a provincial town-hall clerk; Courbet, the painter, was of peasant origin. A private income was no longer a necessity. In the arts, as in contemporary commerce, a greater public, a wider market, afforded more variety and greater options: in style, but in content too; for the buyer, but for the purveyor as well, free(r) to pursue inspiration, fantasy, or profit, to react against fashions and conditions or to accept them. And all of this reflected a diversified world where opportunity and insecurity went hand in hand.

PART IV

The Age of Masses

1848 to the Present

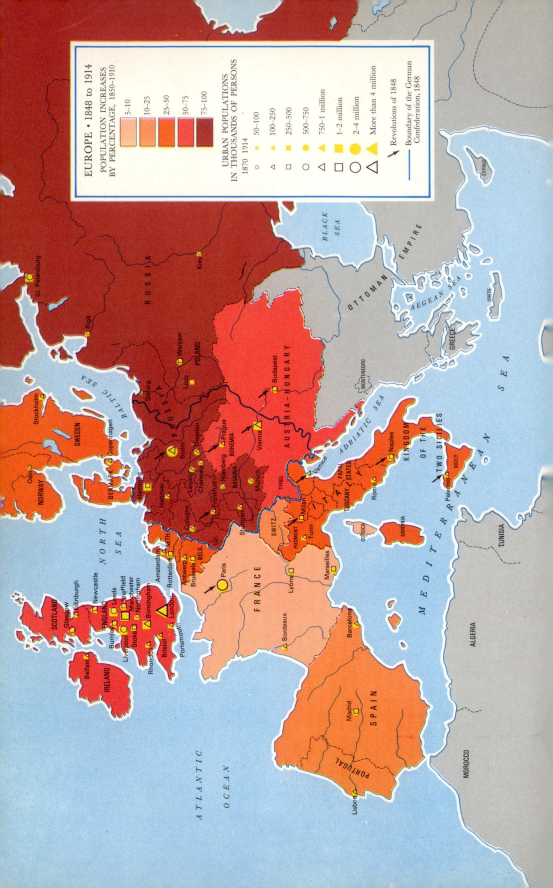

EUROPE · 1848 to 1914
POPULATION INCREASES
BY PERCENTAGE, 1850–1910

5–10
10–25
25–50
50–75
75–100

URBAN POPULATIONS
IN THOUSANDS OF PERSONS

1870 1914
50–100
100–250
250–500
500–750
750–1 million
1–2 million
2–4 million
More than 4 million

Revolutions of 1848

Boundary of the German
Confederation, 1848

NORTH SEA

BALTIC SEA

ATLANTIC OCEAN

BLACK SEA

AEGEAN SEA

ADRIATIC SEA

MEDITERRANEAN SEA

RUSSIA

PRUSSIA

POLAND

AUSTRIA-HUNGARY

OTTOMAN EMPIRE

GREECE

FRANCE

SPAIN

PORTUGAL

SWEDEN

NORWAY

DENMARK

SCOTLAND

ENGLAND

IRELAND

BOHEMIA

BAVARIA

TYROL

SWITZ.

PIEDMONT

PAPAL STATES

TUSCANY

KINGDOM OF THE TWO SICILIES

SARDINIA

CORSICA

SICILY

CRETE

CYPRUS

MONTENEGRO

NETH.

BELG.

LUX.

MOROCCO

ALGERIA

TUNISIA

St. Petersburg
Riga
Kiev
Warsaw
Lodz
Danzig
Budapest
Copenhagen
Stockholm
Oslo
Hamburg
Berlin
Dresden
Prague
Vienna
Leipzig
Hanover
Nürnberg
Chemnitz
Frankfurt
Munich
Stuttgart
Cologne
Amsterdam
Rotterdam
Antwerp
Brussels
Paris
Lyons
Bordeaux
Marseilles
Barcelona
Madrid
Lisbon
Glasgow
Edinburgh
Newcastle
Leeds
Sheffield
Manchester
Liverpool
Burnley
Stoke
Nottingham
Birmingham
London
Bristol
Rhondda
Portsmouth
Belfast
Milan
Turin
Venice
Rome
Naples
Palermo

The End of European Hegemony

No PERIOD, certainly none in the six centuries or so covered by this book, shows a more impressive internal coherence than the interval between the revolutions of 1848 and the aftermath of the Second World War. There is something of Greek tragedy about this hundred years: the rise of the tragic hero, his self-confidence and pride akin to the *hubris* the Greeks always warned against, the prophecies of doom ignored, the lengthy catalog of errors, the final crash, and the humiliation leading to some extent to self-exposure and, perhaps, to greater understanding. There is even a sequel, a *coda* of fresh liveliness which marks the end but also a beginning—just of what it is hard as yet to say.

The hero of all this is Europe: a smallish peninsula at the western end of Asia whose power, wealth, and historical significance we have watched increasing since the fourteenth century, an increase whose internal dynamic became greater all the time but never at the pace or on the scale that the late nineteenth century witnessed. As the century closed, Europe dominated the world: its wealth, its science, and its guns ruled it from end to end. Where they did not, those of its offspring did. Yet already, at the peak of its power, signs of an ebb were showing. Confusion grew. Values and self-confidence, which had seemed like the motor and mirror of its dynamism, crumbled away. There was mounting awareness of mighty challenges sprung out of its own energies in semi-European powers: Russia, the United States. All this brought talk of decadence. There was no decadence; but it would come and would accelerate, as the forces Europe had made and which made Europe in their turn—national states, democracy, industrial and military power—having reforged the world, turned in upon themselves, devouring one another. The process culminates in the weary, murderous thirty years' war that began in 1914; and Germany—itself a creation of the late nineteenth century—incarnated Europe's *hubris*. To reassert Europe once more, Germany united it by conquest and sought to claim that world power which all felt to be slipping out of Europe's hands. Then Germany fell, and Europe conquered (or liberated) by American and Russian arms, fell with it. Whatever the eventual recovery—and it would be impressive—the age of European supremacy was ended.

Here, then, is one of the great themes of the coming pages: world dominion briefly achieved and lost. But there are others. Foremost, the phenomena to which the title of this part refers: the unprecedented growth of population, the increasing concentration of people in cities, and the involvement of more and more of them in national affairs.

Between 1850 and 1950 roughly a quarter of the world's population lived in Europe. But, if the proportion stayed about the same, absolute numbers rose from 266 million in 1850 to 400 million in 1900 and nearly 600 million in the 1950's. The problems and possibilities such numbers represented were crucial in Europe's dominant world role and also in the struggles waged for supremacy in Europe. We shall see in Chapter XVI how Europe's human resources changed the face of the world. The great migrations, the great invasions of the fourth century which toppled the Roman Empire and altered the face of the West, involved a few hundred thousand souls. Between 1846 and 1924 some sixty million Europeans left Europe. They—and those who stayed behind—would write the history of the world.

Meanwhile, the changing demographic picture within Europe itself altered the balance of power which generally inclines, like God, to the side of the big battalions. And battalions had to get bigger as war came to consume not thousands but millions and its accounting grew ever more costly. The older European powers—England and France—would be challenged by more populous Germany; and Germany would be overborne in turn by still more populous nations cast on continental scales.

Other millions moved about within Europe, from country to country, or from country to town, reflecting the human concentration in large cities, which by 1900 would shelter a majority of the population of industrial nations. And cities spawned more cities; for, paradoxically, the flight of urban dwellers out of the great centers in search of relief created new resorts destined for urban development in their turn: Brighton, Nice, Miami, Chamonix, or Darjeeling. Chapter XX will show the social developments all this evoked, the way people lived and thought in their new circumstances.

The concentration, the new weight and altered conditions of great masses, affected ideology too, and politics. Despite their failures, the movements and the revolutions of 1848 affirmed or confirmed the importance of new classes and, above all others, of the *bourgeoisie*. Except for Russia, 1848 was the last of the great string of political revolutions which, since the 1780's, had put an end to the privileged order of the old regime. Now that the old hierarchies were abolished, advancing industrial revolution would create new social classes based on fresh kinds of wealth and different functions. The middle of the nineteenth century saw the triumphant assertion of this process which culminated as the twentieth century began. Here too, however, forebodings were in order. Just as European expansion created the competitors who brought it to an end, so the industrial base of bourgeois supremacy created the economic and social groups which challenged its power and slowly wore it down: the men and women who dug its mines, ran its factories, drove its ships and trains and trucks, staffed its offices and shops, increasingly diversified, increasingly ready to claim a share of the wealth that bourgeois initiative had engendered but workers' sweat had watered.

The revolutions of 1848 shed a crude light on the new class conflicts and men were not slow to draw conclusions: as the *bourgeoisie* had wrested power from the old orders, so workers would have to win it in their turn. What happened was rather different: more and more workers came to live like bourgeois and to think like them, the vague term "middle classes" (usually in the plural) came to describe an increasing proportion of modern societies, and political action—no longer the preserve of a narrow group—eventually exhausted the bourgeois monopoly of wealth and hence of power.

This did not happen without difficulty. Most men regard the change of existing conditions as catastrophic; and those who liked things as they were put up a stout resistance against those who did not. The great battles in this struggle were fought out (to the west of Russia) in the quarter-century preceding 1914. Some of the most striking achievements were won in the 1930's. But the embourgeoization of the proletariat, and the narrowing gap in income and living standards between the poorest wage earner and the best paid, were not achieved on a mass basis until after the Second World War. By then, bourgeois supremacy was no more; nor could one clearly say what a bourgeois was or was not. The term had lost its meaning and it is doubtful whether the class definitions of the nineteenth century apply to its grandchildren of the mid-twentieth. Certainly the close relation between personal wealth and power, or even social status, so characteristic of the bourgeois age, has been worn down if not eliminated now that power in its various aspects lies in the hands of managers rather than of owners.

Which brings us to another crucial change. An important aspect of the century after 1848 is the predominance of politics, that is, the public discussion of affairs of state or of society; and of politicians, men whose lives are devoted to this task. With few exceptions, politics had been the preserve of very small social groups, carrying on most debates or disputes in private, over what amounted to personal opinions or interests. There had been moments when, as in the Wilkes affair or the French Revolution, the debate was carried to a wider public and an attempt made to enlist broad sections of society in support of a cause no longer essentially private. But not until 1848 do we see such attempts sustained in time and progressively elaborated toward the kind of political action with which we are familiar, because not until 1848 did really large sections of the public have a say in politics.

After 1848 the masses entered politics and politicians adjusted their activities to the new situation, elaborating parties, doctrines, national networks, permanent organizations, public meetings, a whole new strategy suited to an increasingly numerous and self-assertive electorate. In England there were 650,000 electors after 1832, over 4.5 million after 1884. In France, 241,000 in 1847, 10 million in 1852. In the Prussian lands after 1867, in all of Germany after 1871, universal male suffrage obtained. Gradually, as the old century ended, as a new one began, other countries followed suit. But the machinery of representative government had been devised for a restricted public, educated, reasonable, able to debate or consider arguments concerning its interests. Adjustment to the immensely vaster scale of manhood—let alone universal—suffrage inevitably meant maladjustment. The need to mobilize the greatest possible number of votes from a disparate public meant that political platforms would be as general as possible, avoiding concrete issues as far as could be done and the most awkward most of all, appealing whenever they could to sentiment and passion rather than to mind. Such methods, inherent in the machinery which democracy had inherited from oligarchy, were soon recognized as manipulative and dishonest, a fragile front for the old-fashioned pursuit of interest and power. Politicians were denounced and political institutions pilloried for their failures; but would-be reformers tinkered with the mechanism instead of replacing it.

The war of 1914 and its after-effects accented the failure of representative institutions. When national survival was at stake, public and politicians placed their policies in the hands of providential leaders at the head of governments and armies; of managers who could operate vast supply, planning, or financial services. Then, as the free market economy of the 1920's (what was left of it) disintegrated, so did free market politics. The Soviet government in Russia, the Fascists in Italy, and the Nazis in Germany, experimented with new structures of representative government. All, in different ways, tried to cope with the mass nature of politics by getting closer to the groundroots in soviets, or gilds, or corporations, by "educating" and indoctrinating the citizenry to issues and necessities that faced them, by treating the masses *as* masses rather than as collections of many separate and rational individuals.

While none of these experiments proved successful, they did underscore the disintegration of traditional democratic politics. And, while the defeat of fascism left Europe apparently divided between contending political structures, these now look upon government less as the embodiment of an ideal program or doctrine than as administration and management. Political contests which once opposed different philosophies of how life should be lived and how things should be done now take place between rival teams of managers and efficiency experts, each claiming that they can achieve the common end faster or more economically. The problem of scale and effect—of making people feel that they really have more than a consumer's share of what is being done to them or planned for them—remains unsolved. Lincoln's well-known formula reflected the aspirations of the political age, even to its totalitarian climax which tried to reconcile the sovereignty of the general will with that of a national state. Apparently it failed. Government of the people by some people, even if it is for far more people, remains the rule.

Another thing that failed was the sovereign national state operating in a world of sovereign national states; a magnified reflection of the other nineteenth-century political ideal, the free individual operating in a world of free individuals. There have never been completely sovereign national states or completely free individuals, but both existed as ideal concepts and as legal notions most forcefully expressed during this period. Both were seen to be impractical at the time of their greatest apparent success. The free individual was nibbled away by society; the sovereign state triumphed in 1918 only to reveal its insufficiencies. The outbreak of the Second World War was the ransom of its failures, its ending an indication that something else was taking shape. Quite what, we do not know.

To sum up, then, the story that unfolds after mid-nineteenth century is one of affirmation and disintegration: a class structure in which the bourgeoisie plays the predominant role develops and exhausts itself, a political structure designed for a restrictive leadership is stretched to fit a mass electorate and collapses, democracy is realized on a scale that turns it toward technocracy or totalitarianism, modern states affirm their independence only to learn that it is an illusion. Even the most extreme affirmation of the notion of national independence, war with another state, stresses interdependence. What A. J. P. Taylor has called "the struggle for mastery in Europe" had to be settled by two world wars. One thing that both wars had in common was that, beginning as conflicts over fairly clear issues, they ended in utterly unexpected ways: the first changing the map of Europe, and the second its place in the world.

Chapter 16

INTERNATIONAL PERSPECTIVES

The Age of Steam and Gold

Beneath the surface of the conventional account that lists wars, revolutions, governments and laws, a current runs (closer and closer to the surface in modern times) which is that of economic life; a current whose flux affects moods, attitudes, and actions. Just as the economic recessions of the fifteenth century stirred up the disquiet of the "waning middle ages," so the economic expansion of mid-eighteenth century spurred the sanguine enlightenment, and the fresh recession of 1817–1852 played its part in the romantic pessimisms and the social troubles of those years. The economic fluctuations of the period may similarly be reflected in the optimism of 1850–1880, the self-doubt of the so-called *fin-de-siècle*, the aggressive recovery of the decade before 1914, and the tense tone of the postwar years. This is a rough and superficial index. It can easily lead one into error, for prosperous periods knew momentary setbacks and some countries advanced while others experienced recessions or marked time. Furthermore, periods of recession like the 1880's and the 1890's brought comfort to certain classes and dismay to others. A general survey can register only the most general trends and, generally speaking, the economic curve that we can follow until 1914 is an ascendant one.

"Railroads and gold mines are the two secrets of Europe's commercial and industrial prosperity," wrote a French review in 1865. Certainly the transport revolution of the 1850's and 60's played a major part not only in the economic but in the political history of Europe. Between 1850 and 1914 railroads multiplied thirty times, European mileage increasing from 35,000 to one million kilometers. There was a close relation be-

709

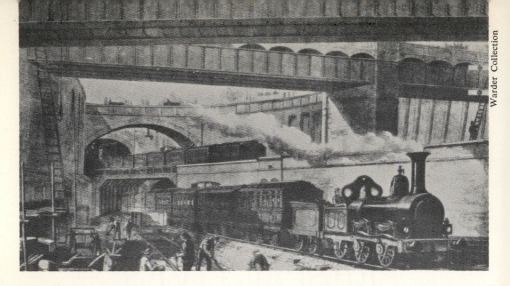

tween prosperity and the density of the rail network: Britain, Germany and France averaging about 13 kilometers of rail per 100 square kilometers of territory, while Austria showed 8, Italy 6, Spain less than 3, and Russia—despite heroic efforts in building 74,000 kilometers—only 0.32. Railroads were the first expression of the mass age and its first great agents as well, shifting greater numbers and quantities than any means of locomotion before them, facilitating the mobility of persons and of goods, eventually their mobilization too. In 1880 French railroads carried 18 million persons and 4.5 million tons of goods; by 1913 they were carrying 547 million persons and 173 million tons of goods. By that time, 6 billion travelers a year were journeying on the railways of Germany, Britain, and France. The economies of such countries received an extraordinary impetus, their social structures were affected by the armies of employees enlisted in the upkeep and administration of great networks, their national administration expanded to keep up with new needs, their armies learned to take advantage of new possibilities.

Railroads integrated nations as nothing else had done, linking distant provinces, developing truly national economies where there had been parochial ones, orienting the flow of travelers and goods along their line of passage, stamping new cities out of the ground (as along the great American and Siberian railways), or animating old ones.* Railroad networks imposed the primacy of the capital where they began and ended, advanced cohesion in newly forming nations, breathed new life into continental areas heretofore cut off from economic activity. Before rails advanced into the great land masses of the world, power which went with the riches of trade, of productivity depending on easy access to raw materials and to shipping points, accompanied maritime activity. Wealth and power nested on the shores of the Mediterranean, the Atlantic, or the Baltic Sea. Continental countries—central and eastern Eur-

* While French population grew 9 per cent in fifty years, that of towns along the Paris-Nice railway line doubled.

Opposite: a complex London railroad crossing in the 1860s. Right: digging for gold in South Africa.

ope, even the United States—found it hard to compete with the wealth and enterprise of the maritime powers. Railroads permitted the settlement, equipment, and exploitation of vast continental zones in North and South America, Russia, Africa, and China. Thus, a great European invention which began by affirming and expanding European supremacy, would end by strengthening other continents against Europe.

Before the twentieth century made this evident, the advantages of steam were there for the reaping. Europe was following England into the "cotton millenium" and steam power, in George Eliot's words, had "driven on every wheel double pace and the wheel of fortune along with them." But coal alone was not enough to stoke the fires of fortune. Another fuel was needed: gold. And gold was running short, hampering exchanges, trade, expansion; its dearth contributing to the hunger of the hungry forties.

Between 1848 and 1851, gold discoveries in California and Australia provided (as the London *Times* put it) "an electric impulse to our entire business world," and moved the future Lord Shaftesbury to wonder in his diary whether this was not "God's chosen way to fulfill his commandment and replenish the earth." In twenty years, between 1850 and 1870, as much gold was added to the world's stocks as in the previous 350 years, stimulating the economy, raising prices and production, quadrupling profits between 1851 and 1873. In the late 1890's fresh supplies from South Africa and western Canada ended the recession of the 1870's and 80's by pumping more resources into the economy. More gold, more paper money backed by it, more money circulating, higher prices, consumers buying more, producers and merchants making, stocking, and selling more, employing more workers, willing to grant higher wages, stimulating greater buying power. This was (and still remains) the mechanism of expansion and inflation. By 1904 the world gold stock was four times greater than it had been in 1885. Its index figure, taking the year 1500 as 1, stood at 45 in 1800, 1,000 in 1860, 2,800 in 1914.

711

His way eased by gold and steam, modern industrial man began to install himself in the climate of change and mobility which the previous half century had ushered in. Change became a part of life and of experience in politics, in society, in economic activity. The world adjusted to this too: legislation took note of industrial workers and their needs; municipal government organized or reorganized the great encampments of transient slum dwellers (transient largely between land and death) into something more stable and even more comfortable in its dreariness; some of the rising prosperity began to spill over into the working classes, improving their standards of living and their expectation of life.

We shall see that the improvements were relative. Surveys taken in England early in the twentieth century showed one-third to a quarter of the population still miserably poor, depending on earnings "insufficient to obtain the minimum necessities for the maintenance of mere physical efficiency." By this definition over one-third of the people of London, over one-quarter of the people of York, lived in poverty. One Englishman in five died in a workhouse and was buried in a pauper's grave. One baby out of every six born in the working classes died before a year, one out of every two grew up underfed, underdeveloped, sickly, and poor. That was the richest country in the world.

Yet this must be seen in the perspective of a mid-twentieth century where the richest country in the world admits that one-fifth of its population still lives at or below the margin of subsistence. And certainly a fitter image of the period may be found in the great London International Exhibition of 1851 that ushered it in, and in the Crystal Palace that symbolized its excitement and ingenuity. One million square feet of glass, 33,000 columns, 2,300 girders, all prefabricated and most interchangeable, 100,000 exhibits by 14,000 exhibitors, 6 million visitors, proclaimed the triumphs and the expectations of the age. The bad old days before 1848 were left behind, part of another era. The Crystal Palace proposed "a new starting point, from which all nations will be able to direct their further exertions."

And, true enough, Europe now forged itself anew. Railroads, roads, utilities, machinery, spread and multiplied throughout the West, even in North Italy and northwestern Spain. Then, in a second phase, beginning in the 1870's, western Europe, having built itself, set out to equip and develop the rest of the world and also the more backward parts of its own continent. Mines, oil wells, plantations, bridges, canals, power plants, port installations, tramways, banks, lighthouses and docks, gasworks and sewers, carried European industrial civilization throughout the world, to Constantinople and Nagasaki, Romanian oil fields, Bolivian mines, and Asian estates. Between 1870 and 1914 British foreign investment tripled; between 1880 and 1914 French foreign investment followed suit. From the 1840's to the eve of war the value of

THE GROWTH OF RAILROADS
IN EUROPE · 1850–1914

Representative railroads in 1850
Increases to 1914

Trackage per square kilometer (1914)

0–2 kilometers
2–4 kilometers
4–10 kilometers
More than ten kilometers

Boundaries in 1914

Place names visible on map:

Moscow, Kiev, RUSSIA, Warsaw, Stockholm, SWEDEN, Oslo, NORWAY, BALTIC SEA, NORTH SEA, Copenhagen, DENMARK, Berlin, GERMANY, Amsterdam, NETH., Brussels, BELG., LUX., London, ENGLAND, SCOTLAND, Glasgow, IRELAND, Dublin, Paris, FRANCE, Marseilles, Barcelona, SPAIN, Madrid, PORTUGAL, Lisbon, SWITZ., Milan, ITALY, Rome, CORSICA, SARDINIA, SICILY, Vienna, AUSTRIA-HUNGARY, Budapest, Belgrade, SERBIA, MONTENEGRO, ALBANIA, RUMANIA, Bucharest, BULGARIA, Sofia, GREECE, Athens, Constantinople, OTTOMAN EMPIRE, BLACK SEA, AEGEAN SEA, ADRIATIC SEA, MEDITERRANEAN SEA, ATLANTIC OCEAN

The Crystal Palace at the London International Exhibition of 1851.

world trade increased thirteen or fourteen times and Europe carved out a major share of it. England, of course, remained the greatest trader in Europe and the world but, significantly, by 1913 Germany replaced France in second place, her 13 per cent of world trade challenging the 17 per cent of Britain.

Such competitive jockeying reminds us that national rivalries were reflected in economic competition, and that the latter had its share in egging nations one against the other. Economic liberalism had set out to free economic life from political motives. By the late nineteenth century it had enlisted politics to serve particular interests. Soon, political interests would come to manipulate economic activities, to the limits of control, planning, and economic autarchy. Political and economic liberalism crumbled together, the proponents of the one being often the first to pick at the other. Yet capital was international. Coal and iron companies operated across the Franco-German, Franco-Belgian, Belgian-German borders, owned mines and factories in all countries. Russia's Putilov works were dependent on German companies like Krupp and French ones like Schneider, which, like England's Vickers, sold their arms to everybody; Belgian capital helped to build the Paris subway; two-thirds of the hotels on the French Riviera were owned by foreign capital.

The dominant trend of the prewar years was toward exchange not autarchy, expansion not retrenchment. Europe overflowed with people, capital, goods, techniques, ideas, ways of thought and action. These poured into the other continents and in due course trickled back, bringing subtle alterations in thought and taste, obvious contributions to the table and warehouse and treasury of the West. The captive world enmeshed its captors in a network of political and economic interests, the industries of one dependent on the materials of another, the markets of one swallowing the products of another, the profits or labor of one depending on the prosperity and activities of another. By 1914, Britain, France, and Germany among them accounted for seven-tenths of the world's productive capacity, for 83 per cent of all the world's foreign investments (compared with 5 per cent for the United States). They were the center of world economy, of its money market and international trade. The east European countries were their economic colonies, so were most countries overseas. Russia, Britain, and France ruled over half the world, over one-third of mankind. The foreign territories owned by Britain were one hundred and forty times greater than the home country, France's twenty times greater, Belgium's eighty times greater, Holland's sixty times greater.

Yet hindsight points out some crucial indices of relative decline. Europe accounted for 75 per cent of the world's trade in 1800, 66 per cent in 1900, 58 per cent in 1913. By 1938 this had become 52 per cent. Her share of goods produced throughout the world was also falling, and some began to look uneasily at a trend whose acceleration they forecast as continents and countries that Europe had equipped began to claim a part of the profits and possibilities of trade.

Politics for the Masses

Never has the world known such a political age—such widespread politicization—as in the last hundred years or so. The notion of political debate had arisen in the ancient Greek city states, when rulers and restricted ruling groups based on traditional authorities were replaced by oligarchic factions that sought wider support in their disputes. It only reappeared when similar circumstances made it relevant in the urban politics that flourished between the thirteenth and the sixteenth centuries, to wane again before the reappearance of patrician or monarchic rule. With few exceptions like the Netherlands, it was not until the nineteenth century that the notion revived that social and economic life offers alternatives, that one can *choose* among different courses, among different kinds of institutions, that debate directed to such objects is more than academic. As long as the appointed round of life had seemed everlasting and the structure within which it unfolded perpetual (for memories were short and alterations were soon regarded as part of an unchanging destiny), the realm of choice was limited and petty. Men (a very few) disputed over *interests* far more than *policies,* issues of finite scope within the ineluctable infinity of fate.

Only new men—individuals who carried their destinies in their hands not in their birth—could challenge such a view. Part of the rise of the bourgeoisie was its belief that the structure and course of society could be changed. Men are not fixed once and for all. They are not only free to choose, they are condemned to have to choose. Whether they choose or not, they are still choosing—the *status quo* or an alternative—even if they are only choosing not to choose. As men claimed power or a say in it not by some immemorial and unchallenged right, but by argument (which goes with choice) and reasoning (which goes with argument) and force (if only the force of numbers, often brought in to settle arguments), the shape of modern politics was rounded out by theoretical constructs which placed immediate issues in a broader context, defined or rationalized the values in whose name men strove, proposed new models of reality against the old that were being rejected or at least contested.

The tensions that these arguments and struggles generated brought ever more men within the scope of politics. Even the "revolutionary" politics of early nineteenth century had been played out among restricted numbers. By mid-century this began to change, echoes of the restricted contest awoke new batches of contenders, the scale of politics spread out to include all members of the nation, the issues and effects of political disputes were seen to be so vast that one ignored them only at one's peril. Masses acquired political relevancy, and politics became a struggle relevant to every one of their members.

But if the politics of masses affected nations, the beliefs that lent them inspiration cut across national boundaries. Liberalism, socialism, or reaction could unite men whom the accidents of birth or geography divided, persuading them that class, conviction, or historical neccessity gave them more in common than a passport could. And this, in turn, provided a significant factor in the history of the time; for the political attitudes of ordinary men and women began to weigh on national and international affairs.

Basic political attitudes can be found in Plato's Athens, where conservatives stood for a social order rooted in hereditary privileges and castes, in agriculture, frugality, and the simple life, suspecting trade, novelties, foreigners, and everything that might be responsible for change. Opposed to them, the partisans of change and movement rejected anachronisms, inclined to democracy or tyranny, welcomed modern life, favored the merchants, developed the fleet, relied on foreign trade to increase the private and public riches. Before such widespread contrasting attitudes can be made meaningful to the modern world, the shape that they took needs more definition.

Liberalism

The first partisans of movement in more recent times were the liberals— description less of a party than of a point of view, a climate of opinion. The term "liberal" had long been used with reference to education or

John Stuart Mill.

else to generosity. Its political application began in Spain, during the revolutions of the 1820's, and took some time to live down the pejorative connotations that attached to it as they had done to words like "Whig" or "Tory." Then it came to mean a political attitude associated with national assertion, free institutions, constitutions, individualism; an economic doctrine that said the state should keep out of economic activities, leaving them to free enterprise; and a philosophical position supporting freedom of thought and of expression, humanity and tolerance. In places such as England, Germany, and Belgium, Liberal parties also appeared whose programs included some, though not all of these propositions, parties that represented a middle-class elite competing with land-owning interests and with the aristocracy of the old regime, but as opposed to the masses as they were to the restrictions and the privileges of birth.

The finest expression of liberal ideals at mid-century is to be found in John Stuart Mill's essay *On Liberty* (1859). Mill's idea of liberty was that men should be free to make of themselves what they want and can, live their own life, do as they please, as long as they do not interfere with others, develop their personalities to the fullest extent compatible with the interests and development of their fellow men. The idea was excellent. Its fulfillment posed almost every social problem men had faced over the ages. Just as an example, advocates of *laissez faire* objected to public education on the grounds that men were responsible for the upbringing of their children, not those of others; refused public subsidies to cultural activities since art, an industry like any other, should learn to make a profit; opposed conscription because soldiers should be hired at the going market rate like other laborers; and argued that any limitation of working hours or conditions interfered with the personal liberty of the worker. One man's freedom was another man's restriction, one man's logic another man's poison.

All this lent weight to conservative criticisms of bourgeois liberals with their pious economic slogans and their selfish political restrictions.

It was individualistic liberalism, said the conservatives, whose *laissez faire* created the proletariat, introduced change, questioned religion and hence destroyed resignation, creating social unrest. Materialist motives must be replaced by old-fashioned charity, human relations restored to the personal plane, change banished by stability, discipline, patience, and hope of a better world not in the realm of reform or science fiction but of God.

Yet the liberal logic that could lead to illiberal conclusions was equally capable of radical developments, witness the work published in the same year as the essay *On Liberty*: Samuel Smiles' *Self Help*. In less than half a century *Self Help* would sell a quarter of a million copies, more than the sales of the great novels of its time; it would be translated into French, German, Dutch and Danish, Italian and Japanese, Turkish, Arabic, and several Indian languages; while quotations from it were inscribed on the walls of the Khedive's palace in Cairo. Its creed, that God helps those that help themselves, was appropriate to a mobile, dynamic society where it was no longer a crime to educate a child beyond his station, and where every man could hope to rise by his own perseverance.

Interestingly enough, Smiles had started as a radical in the 1840's and his lectures, from which the book was put together, were directed at the working class whose education and social promotion were very near his heart. What he preached was self-improvement through education and work, thrift and determination, a recipe that made sense in times when prosperity created opportunities for all and inflation did not whittle savings. It reflected an awareness (strong in the nineteenth century, weak in ours) that the ultimate radicalism is not expressed in a combination of dependence and interference, but in individualism. As Richard Cobden, the free-trader, wrote to Smiles in 1853: "Depend upon it, there is a spice of despotism at the bottom of all this intervention by combined bodies in the concerns of individuals . . ." There was and is, and most societies seem to oscillate between despotism and interference at one extreme, injustice and inequality at another. This was the quandary that Mill faced but could not overcome in his essay *On Liberty*.

Yet, as Smiles grew old, his advice grew less relevant. Industry was getting larger and less competitive; social promotion came to depend more on the education received in youth than on initiative and self-help when adult. Thrift itself began to be attacked by economists who argued that savings made for underemployment and checked economic development. Finally, the wheel came full circle. Smiles had come to self-help when radical experience convinced him that collective action could only fumble in the dark as long as individuals rotted in poverty and ignorance. By the 1870's men like Mill himself had qualified their view of liberty. Men could not become or be themselves without the opportunities that society alone was able to provide. Real individualism and self-fulfillment needed a collective springboard. Samuel Smiles was turned upon his head. "The social problem of the future," noted Mill in his *Autobiography* (1873), "we considered to be, how to unite the greatest individual liberty of action, with a common ownership of the raw materials of the globe, and an equal participation in all the benefits of combined labor."

An answer to this question would be formulated by T. H. Green (and other "Oxford idealists") in his *Lectures on the Principles of Political Obligation* (1879–1880): "Human development in its richest diversity" can only exist if the state provides the opportunities for it. The freedom of the individual can be endangered if economic evolution is allowed to act without hindrance. The common good may be served by state intervention to free the individual, by providing him education, sanitation, housing, credit, opportunities to work, security in illness or old age. In 1881, Gladstone's Land Act provided security and opportunity for Irish farmers. After 1883 Bismarck's insurance acts provided greater security for German workers. As theoretical liberalism turned into social liberalism, the last two decades of the nineteenth century would see a spate of social legislation all over Europe, the beginning of the welfare state.

Old-fashioned liberal entrepreneurs, like the Scotch-American ironmaster and millionaire Andrew Carnegie, still regarded the world as an unregulated free-for-all and rich men like themselves as benevolent oligarchs, responsible for improving their community. Yet when Carnegie's *Gospel of Wealth* appeared in 1889, liberalism had undergone a sea change. Mill, Green, and the Fabian group that derived from them articulated the change of mind and heart that led liberals from individualism (asserted against privileged oppression of one kind) to collectivism (asserted against privileged exclusivism of another kind). The evolution in the way they viewed the situation was reflected in their doctrines. The long gradual infiltration that brought about capitalist supremacy in the developed world would now be followed, said the Fabians, by socialism: transforming capitalism by stages into something that conforms still better with the requirements of the new economic and industrial order.

The social liberals and the Fabians were not alone in their perception that the world had changed. Both Bismarck and Louis Napoleon believed that prosperity could replace liberty, that strong government could reconcile economic and social antagonisms, educate and discipline both entrepreneurs and wage earners. For Louis Napoleon "The day of class rule is over, the day of mass rule has begun. The masses must be organized so that they can formulate their will, and disciplined so that they can be instructed and enlightened as to their own interests." This splendid formulation of democratic authoritarianism had only one weakness: its aims would be achieved not by authoritarians but by their opponents —the socialists. At least until the twentieth century.

The political debate which had been reserved largely to the educated, the wealthy, and wellborn, was being taken up (as we have seen) by interlocutors representing portions of society which had little voice and less say until that time; above all by the urban workers. This meant that the factors in debate would change, its tone would rise, and its implications would become more serious for all participants. The terms of the debate still reflected the two dominant views of earlier days. The evolutionary, moving with the times and relying on the changes time would bring; and the revolutionary, rejecting any possibility of adjustment, putting its trust only in violent change. But the participants altered. Gradually, Liberal parties attained most of their ends and lost their sense of purpose, declining into sectarianism or concern with preserving what they had won. They became conservative in fact if not in name, and conservative sentiments now preserved or developed many achievements of the liberal era. The new parties of change were those of labor or of nationalism, less revolutionary to the extent that reform anticipated discontent, more so to the extent that force sought to suppress it. All were more conscious of divisions—national or social—than their predecessors who believed in unity; all paid more attention to struggle than to reconciliation, which had been their predecessors' hope. In these ways, too, they seem to have reflected the modern character of their age, the more so since of the two major movements of the Left one amplified the individualistic tendencies of waning liberalism and the other the scientific obsessions of the day. And the seminal thinkers behind each, P. J. Proudhon (1809–1865) and Karl Marx (1818–1883) hailed respectively from France and Germany.

Anarchism

The anarchism that we associate with Proudhon's name was almost a logical projection of Samuel Smiles' *Self Help*. Printer by trade, Proudhon believed that workmen of his kind could count only on themselves, on their own efforts and associations to improve their lot, gain a just return for their labor, demolish economic inequalities, abolish the private property which, he said, is nothing but theft—the appropriation by one man of the plus-value created by the work of others.* The universal suffrage dear to democrats cannot provide a true reflection of a country's nature, for all democracy leads to centralism and authoritarian government. Only the removal of all the things that trammel individual liberty can lead to freedom and this can never be done from above. State,

* The French novelist, Anatole France, makes one of his characters, Monsieur Bergeret, ponder that the essence of social justice rests on the fact that while theft is wicked, its gains are sacred.

P. J. Proudhon, by Gustave Courbet. Petit Palais, Florence

army, police are all part of the repressive organism set up to protect the
property of the few who exploit the efforts of the many. Whoever controls this machinery, the exploitation will continue even though the
hands switching the levers of power may change. So, said Proudhon,
only their destruction—dismantling the governmental machinery, suppressing the state—can emancipate the society of the future so that there
could be a loose federation of small, free communities working under no
constraint. Democracy—the rule of the people—shall be replaced by
demopedy—education of the people. Politically anarchist, organization-
ally Proudhon was a syndicalist, advocating the independent action of
workmen grouped in their professional associations, uninvolved with
politicians who always in the end will let them down and sell out to some
new oppressive government. Ultimately, Proudhon was a moralist, aiming at a *just* society, one where the collapse of bourgeois injustice would
permit the evolution of a "new man," no longer exploited, asserting
his dignity in Saint-Simonian terms as worker and producer.

Proudhon's disciples followed similar lines. Their criticism—not only
of society, but of the tendency reformers have to become oppressors
in their turn—is cogent. Mikhail Bakunin (1814–1876), a volcanic dino-
saur of a man, appears as a survivor from another age, the seeming embodiment of anarchism. Liberty was the be-all and end-all of Bakunin's
philosophy, but a liberty admitting neither property nor competition, neither exploitation nor *laissez faire.* Opposed to any society
based on coercion, insisting on free groups where no coercive authority
balks the individual or thwarts the associations he may freely join,
Bakunin's revolutionary gospel looked forward not to the capture of
the state but to its abolition. Not revolutionary organization, but the
revolutionary instincts of workers and peasants voluntarily grouped in *ad
hoc* associations, would overthrow the old society and recreate a new.

The important thing was to get on with it; for as Bakunin saw it, there was no time to lose. Unless anarchism were established right away, the industrial revolution would come and prevent it.

Bakunin—who had fled his aristocratic Russian home, fought in the revolutions of 1848, survived long years of jail and of Siberian exile to escape and fight again—moved through the Europe of the 1860's as an incarnation of revolt, founding secret societies wherever he went, preaching and plotting revolution and helping to found the First International Workingmen's Association in 1864. A greater theorist, Prince Peter Kropotkin (1842–1921), agreed with him that we could dispense with the coercive armor of society and state because men's social nature produces social behavior spontaneously. Men, argued Kropotkin, himself a distinguished geographer and ethnologist, incline to work together without being forced to it. They will do so in pursuit of common aims, like other animals and savages. Civilized men are as naturally bent to co-operation and gregariousness as they are to struggle and competition. Society should reflect not the survival of the fittest but "mutual aid," which was the title of his major study published in 1902.

The arguments of anarchism, superficially so attractive, collapsed before the contact of reality. Its social and psychological criticisms were forceful, but they denied the possibility of any organization that would carry them out. The anarchists' ideals made their political action ineffective. Ready to blast society to pieces, they could envisage no workable alternative to the order they found wanting. They faced their greatest problems in more advanced industrial societies in which the limited local structures and voluntary associations that anarchism recognized were overlaid by means of transport and production which only wider organization and co-ordination could keep up. An Andalusian or a Calabrian peasant need not care about railroads or power stations; an English, French, or German worker did. And the more economically developed countries showed relatively little interest in anarchism.

In these latter countries, anarchism was also adversely affected by growing trade union and labor organizations whose scale and practices went counter to its views but which achieved evident gains for labor. In countries like Russia and Spain, where governments kept the social opposition from expression, it was more effective. In others, like France and Italy, where unions were backward and fragmented and the revolutionary tradition strong, a compromise anarchism took shape, incorporating some of its techniques, like direct action and the general strike, in *syndicalism:* separate unions, ignoring politics and parliament, carrying on their fight on purely professional grounds by sheer industrial warfare. Generally though, where anarchism did not somehow compromise with political socialism, its most forceful expression came in isolated acts of violence. Direct action translated into terrorism brought a long string of murders and attempted murders: attempts to kill the Kaiser, the kings of Italy and Spain, assassination of two American presidents (Garfield in 1881, McKinley, 1901), of an emperor (Alexander II of Russia, 1881), an empress (Elizabeth of Austria, 1898), a king (Umberto of Italy, 1900), a president of the French Republic (Carnot, 1894), and countless other political figures.

When in 1910 Kropotkin wrote the article on anarchism for the eleventh edition of the *Encyclopaedia Britannica,* he pointedly denied that such "propaganda by the deed" was its inseparable essence. Everybody uses violence, he wrote, "in proportion as their open action is obstructed by repression and exceptional laws render them outlaws." There was much truth in that. But it was equally true that, in proportion as their appeal was slipping in freer societies like France, the anarchists also used the means which Alfred Nobel's invention of dynamite (1868) had put to hand. The year 1892 alone would see over a thousand dynamitings in Europe, over five hundred in the United States. France, in the 1890's one of the freest societies in Europe, was harshly struck by anarchist outrages directed as often against cafés as against banks or the Chamber of Deputies. Desperation can stem as much from depression as from repression. The anarchists were losing ground, and knew it, not to oppression but to the modern world. When in 1898 an international governmental conference met at Rome to concert means of combating them, most of the special measures there envisaged were actually directed against a more serious threat to the established order and to anarchism alike: the growing power of the socialists.

Socialism

As all discussions of anarchism start with Proudhon, so all discussions of modern socialism begin, perhaps unfairly, with Karl Marx. Where Proudhon insists on the particular, Marx looks to the general. Proudhon was a moralist who believed in justice for the individual. Marx was a moralist who believed in scientific laws, sought their expression in human society and economy, described a historical mechanism which explained the rise and predicted the fall of capitalist society.

The model Marx proposes is a sociology based on economics, that is, on the belief that the structure of production, the economic structure of society, is the basis of its legal and political institutions, of its culture, of its morals, of its self-consciousness. "The means of production of material life determines in general the social, political and intellectual process of life." Hence Marx's studies of the framework of production on which different classes rise, dominate, and challenge one another; and his theory of class struggle—not a new invention, but now presented as part of a process of historical evolution in which the latest victor, the bourgeois, was meeting a new challenger, the industrial proletarian, whom present exploitation only steeled for victory to come. Since the class structure at any given time changes with the forces and structure of economic production, the class struggle of modern industrial society was bound to end in the victory of the proletariat and in its dictatorship, which (since no other class would be left to contend for power in its turn) would usher in a classless society in which class struggle was impossible for lack of classes and the repressive state edifice therefore could be dispensed with.

There is greatness in Marx's historical models, and a splendid instrument of social analysis: a structure of hypothesis into which almost every historical phenomenon can be fitted. But in the end his utopia is not very different from that of Proudhon, whom he detested. The really important thing about Marx (apart from the lessons historians have learned from him) is his contribution in persuading the workers that they had a collective personality, and in holding out the "scientifically demonstrated" hope of a better world based on the fact that the very economic forces on which the capitalist world was thriving were working against that world and against its capitalist masters. Professor Tawney once remarked that he did not need Marx to tell him that capitalists exploited workers. Yet Marx provided more than an economic explanation: a trumpet call, the text for a thousand sermons and the inspiration for effective action.

One might say at once that Marxist thought took time to make its way. The *Communist Manifesto,* ignored in 1848, remained a rare pamphlet for connoiseurs until reprinted in 1872, and became a best seller only in the 1890's with the rise of social democratic parties in the West. The first volume of *Das Kapital* appeared in 1867. A Russian translation was published in 1872 and did quite well since the censors did not think it worth suppressing.* As late as 1879, when the English wife of the heir to the German throne read it and inquired about the author, she was informed that "it will not be he who, whether he wishes it or not, will turn the world upside down."

The Princess's informant was mistaken, not only because Marx's theories fitted important needs of a rising class but because they fitted the preconceptions of the modern mind. Marxist relativism attacked belief in absolute values. Values, said Marx, are relative to their time and place. Slavery, serfdom, capitalism were all progressive innovations in their time and could only be criticized when they became obsolete

---

* The censors had suppressed a Russian translation of the *Communist Manifesto* in the 1860's. Its first English translation dates from 1886. *Kapital* was translated into French in 1875 and into English in 1887. A new Russian version of the *Manifesto,* with an introduction by Marx, appeared in 1882, a year before his death. The 1870's had convinced him that there was no hope of early revolution in the West; now he was finding more followers in Russia and beginning to think that perhaps conditions for social revolution there were better than elsewhere.

and hampered further development. That was why Marx and Engels *
attacked capitalism, not because it was absolutely or inherently bad, but
because in turn it had become corrupted. Such relativism came close to
the evolving scientific attitudes of the day which regarded all truths as
only approximate at best, all involving contradictions to be revealed and
resolved in time. Hence Marx and Engels' scientific theories appealed to
scientists. Their dialectic analyzed history and social development in
terms not of abstract *ideas* but of events and *things,* used concepts like
force and motion familiar to the natural sciences, which, Engels pointed
out, were naturally dialectical because they studied the movement and
the interaction of bodies no more static or independent than men and
societies. Dialectics, too, was a science: "the science," Engels said, "of
the general laws of motion and development of nature, human society
and thought."

This coincidence in approach and language was as important to the
fortunes of Marxism as the coincidence of liberalism and the Enlightenment had been a century before. Intellectuals are the clergy of modern
times: during the eighteenth century and much of the nineteenth their
values and perceptions coincided with those of the bourgeoisie.
Through most of the twentieth they would largely coincide not with
those of the working class but with its interpreters, first and foremost
Karl Marx.

As has been said already, socialism progressed slowly, Marxism even
more so. After 1848, "political reaction and economic recovery advanced
hand in hand to destroy what was left of the revolutionary movement
in the leading countries." ** When the first Socialist International was
set up in London in 1864, as the International Workingmen's Association, its founders were British and French trade unionists joined by a
number of exiles like Marx, Engels, Mazzini, and Bakunin. The followers
of Owen, Proudhon, Blanqui, and Marx could join behind the slogan
"Proletarians of all lands, unite!" They did not stay united long and the
history of the First International is a long account of feuds, intrigues,
and scissions.

The first workers' mass movement appeared in Germany in the
1860's, the work of a brilliant, dynamic Silesian Jew, Ferdinand Lassalle
(1825–1864). Before he died in a duel at the age of thirty-nine, Lassalle
had founded a vast organization whose first demand was for manhood
suffrage. Where Marxists tended to side with the progressive sections
of the middle class against the aristocratic and autocratic state, arguing
that they would turn against the bourgeoisie when this had performed

* Friedrich Engels (1820–1895): Marx's closest collaborator, son of a prosperous German manufacturer and himself manager of one of his father's mills, in Manchester,
until he retired at forty-nine to devote himself to writing, study, and the criticism of
the class of men he represented.
* G. D. H. Cole, *A History of Socialist Thought,* vol 2.(London: 1953), p. 3.

its historic task of displacing its anachronistic rivals, Lassallians preferred a workers' alliance with the state against the bourgeoisie, and Lassalle himself put much faith in Bismarck. The state (as Fichte had preached) should be the instrument of the people's good. Once workers had the vote, the state's policy would reflect their wishes. They would be given credit to set up their own enterprises and, free of their capitalist employers, would henceforth enjoy all the benefits of their productivity, not just the tiny share they now received in wages.

As a matter of fact, Bismarck seems to have borrowed some of Lassalle's ideas when he introduced manhood suffrage first in the North German Confederation (1867), then in the German Reich (1871). But he borrowed them only to nullify them and, when this was realized, the Lassallians merged with the Marxist Social Democrats (1875) led by Wilhelm Liebknecht (1826–1900) and August Bebel (1840–1913). By that time the French working-class movement had been destroyed in the hopeless Paris Commune (1871), which left the leadership of Western socialism to the Germans. German Social Democracy thus became the model and ideological leader of the string of Marxist parties about to be set up.* Its Marxism became orthodox doctrine throughout the renascent labor movement and the accepted doctrine of the Second International which the Socialist parties joined (1889–1914) and which asserted its reviving influence by the international demonstrations of May 1, 1890: the first labor day.

The Second International was an altogether more visible body than the First and its member parties soon won a significant place in the political structure of their countries. With the beginning of the twentieth century, French Socialists were playing an important role in various governmental coalitions, the young British Labor Party began to reveal itself as an electoral force, new franchise laws in Austria enabled Austrian Social Democrats to elect 87 delegates to the *Reichsrat.*** On the eve of the First World War, Italian Socialists had 79 deputies in the Chamber, French Socialists 103, the Germans—with over a third of the votes cast— were the most numerous party in the *Reichstag.* Even in the United States the Socialist Eugene Debs who had garnered 100,000 votes in the presidential election of 1900, could win ten times as many in the election of 1912.

All this had been achieved by hard organizational work; and the organization that spelled success, also (as the Anarchists predicted) spelled eventual decay. Mass movements are the modern answer to the weakness of individual men facing the power of rich and influential adversaries. But, born to serve as armies of democracy, they often developed undemocratic traits inherent in their structure. It was a pioneer student of Ger-

* Denmark and Spain, 1879; France, 1882; Britain, 1884; Belgium, 1885; Norway, 1887; Austria and Switzerland, 1888; Holland and Sweden, 1889; Italy, 1892.
** Their anti-semitic Christian Socialist opponents had 96 seats.

man Social Democracy, Robert Michels, who pointed out as early as 1910 that "the masses" are the weakest members of society, that they can be effective only when organized, and that organization generates its own conservatism, its own oligarchic power structure, which subjects the membership to a new authority the better to fight the old. The bigger the organization, the bigger its leaders' power and the less the democracy in whose name it was built. These perceptions of 1910 were verified first in the history of Social Democratic parties and of the bigger trade unions, then in that of Communist and Fascist parties, eventually in the better organized political parties everywhere.

Leaving aside the undemocratic tendencies of mass movements, their very need to triumph on the electoral plane—that is, to attract a majority of voters—meant that they had to bend principle for the sake of practice, devise a compromise that would satisfy their militants' beliefs without frightening off potential supporters. For Socialists began to realize that a workers' party could not gain majority power by workers' support alone. The number of industrial workers was growing, but the proportion of white-collar workers was increasing too: in 1866 France counted ten commercial employees to 240 other workers, by 1914, 120 to 240: the proportion had changed from 1:24 to 1:2. It would change even more after the war. G. D. H. Cole contrasts the acuteness with which Marx observed capitalist developments around mid-nineteenth century against the lack of realism with which he appraised events thereafter. The creation of a new petty bourgeoisie recruited among managerial and administrative employees, the growth of a new middle class consisting not only of *rentiers* but of technicians and managers, the new labor skills taking the place of disappearing ones, the improving standard of living of more and more workers, the growing number of small investors, all contradicted Marx's predictions that petty capitalists would be superseded by large-scale production.

The Socialists, as one of their leaders put it in the *Social Democratic Catechism* of 1893, were "a revolutionary party, but not a party that makes revolutions." They would gain power by legal means, win a majority of the popular vote, a majority of seats in parliament, then change society by passing laws. Class warfare would be organized, it would be peaceful, it would be less and less class-conscious or warlike. Like extras in a chorus line, the Socialists sang "We march! We march!" and never moved beyond the footlights. They tried to reconcile revolutionary language and reformist activities, the former camouflaging the latter and confusing issues: preventing co-operation with natural allies among middle-class reformists, giving the increasingly conservative Social Democratic movements a good radical conscience and permitting them to evade real issues like the supremacy of Junkers and soldiers in Germany, or the lack of mass support in Germany or France for any real revolutionary policy.

Here was a sit-tight policy that became increasingly apparent and from which different people drew different conclusions: some, like the Frenchman Georges Sorel, whose *Crisis of Socialism* appeared in 1898, tried to enlist revolutionary syndicalism in a revision of Marxist theory which would revive the revolutionary tenor of the movement. The necessity of a revolution, not just to improve existing conditions, but to destroy the existing order and replace it with a better one, was being lost from sight. Reformists and temporizers were forwarding the corruption of the very class from which salvation could still come. They believed that the proletariat could be integrated in a society that was rotten to the core. They accepted the scientistic optimism of the *bourgeoisie* and the pragmatism that Sorel denounced as "the last stage of bourgeois thought": a philosophy for *parvenus* in a cynical world.

Attacking *The Illusions of Progress* (1908), Sorel argued that the working class must build its own civilization *against* existing society, assert its values against the parliamentary reformists who sought to integrate it in a decaying world. Here was a morality and a world-view strongly affected by Proudhon.

An essay published the same year, entitled *Reflections on Violence,* reiterated and developed the theme. The proletariat, if it chose to, could act upon the world around it rather than let the world mold it to its will. The proletariat could be shaken out of the lethargy into which reformist sops had cast it by the effect of *myths,* which Sorel defined as "the constructions of an indeterminate future in time," and which, he said, could provide a means of acting on the present, hence of preparing a revolution, if they incorporated the strongest tendencies (albeit unconscious) of the people, party, or class they were destined to affect. Here was one reflection of an age increasingly aware that dreams are relevant, and that dreams held in common are a tremendous lever in shaping, hastening, or simply revealing the future. And the dream—the revolutionary myth Sorel proposed, his great remedy against apathy and reformism—was the general strike, a method much discussed in the mid-nineteenth century as a way of stopping war by paralyzing the society. In the 1890's the notion was revived as a weapon of social war, paralyzing bourgeois society, leading to civil war and revolution. Strikes, even general strikes, argued Sorel, might not get far. But, even if they failed, they would stir up political consciousness among the previously apathetic masses, make both workers and bourgeois aware of their divisions and rival interests, heighten the revolutionary tension between them. As it turned out, the general strike was used rather to fight political battles * than to exacerbate the social situation.

A diametrically different, far more important theory was the revision-

* By the Belgians and the Swedes to win manhood suffrage or by Dutch labor to oppose a Strike Law, in the Russian Revolution of 1905, and in Germany to put down the Kapp putsch of 1920.

ism of Eduard Bernstein (1850–1932), who attacked the catastrophic views of more orthodox Marxists. Bernstein, who had been much influenced by the Fabians, noted that Social Democracy was progressing not (as Marx predicted) in the midst of worsening misery but within growing prosperity, which made the bourgeoisie itself more amenable to ethical arguments of social justice. Prosperity and democracy together could reform the social order without revolution. As for the Socialists, they should bend their efforts not toward an impossible and improbable revolutionary ideal, but toward obtaining greater parliamentary representation, strengthening the unions, furthering public ownership at the local level (municipal socialism, quite advanced in Britain, was forging ahead in Germany and Austria), enlisting bourgeois support for progressive reforms leading toward more efficient and just social organization. Bernstein's book, *Evolutionary Socialism* (1899), argued that socialism would come as the result of piecemeal changes, not in gigantic reforms initiated only after the attainment of political power. If Socialists took advantage of opportunities for action as they came along, socialism could gradually evolve out of a capitalist society. Such Fabian views of cumulative change, though close to the practice of French and English Socialists, were unacceptable to orthodox Marxists. Bernstein was made to toe the line and continental socialism, following the Germans, continued to puff up in splendidly ineffective isolation.

The Catastrophic Heroes

The isolation of Socialists refers, of course, to potential friends; rivals it had enough. The origin of these rival forces, like that of Socialism itself, is to be found in the nineteenth century, when optimistic doctrines of progress founded on reason were met by counter doctrines inspired by unreason, or, by values to which reason bore little relevance. Among the representatives of these views Thomas Carlyle is often mentioned ("a Lear who never came in from the storm," an English reviewer once called him): prophet of will, forcefulness, and heroic genius, always insisting that instinct and imagination would provide the answers which his contemporaries sought in logical progression. But the great prophet of this camp was Friedrich Nietzsche (1844–1900), a German intellectual whose aphoristic philosophy would deeply mark the generations of the twentieth century.

Profoundly moral in an amoral world, Nietzsche had to recreate a structure of morality. Deeply religious in a godless world, he had to become God. Obsessed by death, he had to create an immortality of his own. The undertaking drove him to madness, which he himself described as "the mask of a deadly and too self-assured wisdom." "It is not doubt," he wrote, "but certainty that makes us mad." Of course, his certainties were answering the pressure of his doubts.

Friedrich Nietzsche.

Like all philosophers but more than most Nietzsche has lent himself to misinterpretation. The briefest account of what he had to say risks being misleading. What is said here reflects at most the kind of notions that contemporaries derived from reading his works (which they began to do around 1890) and even more from echoes caught at second hand from those who had read them.

Nietzsche reacted against the ruling determinism (which Darwin and Marx accepted and bolstered further) by asserting the primacy of human will over rational intelligence too apt to be affected by ambient pressures. Rejecting the human anthills piled up by modern industry and education, he insisted on the suppression of a mythical equality, the need for self-differentiation, "the creation of all powerful beings." What the world needed was not fat conformists but creative individuals superior to their circumstances, whose will and vision could transcend existing values and forge new ones. This insistence on personality and will in an age of growing conformity fascinated not only intellectuals—Gabriele D'Annunzio, the poet, George Bernard Shaw, Thomas Mann, and Richard Strauss—but popular publicists for whom the vulgarized version of Superman became a convenient theme.

The dramatic tension of works oscillating between dream and nightmare was enhanced because they expressed the fundamental instability and the insecurities of a fast-changing *fin de siècle* world in catastrophic terms. Many appreciated Nietzsche's criticism of the pretentious, false, and stodgy bourgeois values which he lashed with inspired moralism. Many responded to his appeal for vital and heroic living. One may well ask how far the sentimental and brutal world that Nietzsche tore apart was from the brutal sentimentalism of his admirers; one can point out that the false wings of his Superman, the pretentious philosophy of his followers, the inflated rhetoric of his *Thus Spake Zarathustra* were very close to those they excoriated. The fact remains that in the "era of the common man" most leading figures in thought and literature were in the opposition, arguing for Superman with Nietzsche and with Shaw, for the elite with Lenin, for detached, heroic individuals with Malraux, Mann, and H. G. Wells, André Breton, T. S. Eliot, D'Annunzio, Proust, Yeats, and Marinetti.

The new interest in nobility of character may have been an attempt to compensate for the disappearance of nobility of birth, fulfilling society's need to replace a lost authority by another whose ethical pretentions did not prevent its being modeled on an ideal image of the knightly nobleman. Knights, heroes, and heroics were a constant theme and inspiration to an age whose standards of behavior, rapidly changing, gave an impression that values were declining, creating a sense of need for new codes and orders, preferably reassuring new editions of the old. Besides, democracy itself called for outstanding individuals.* The modern hero is himself the product of a mass society, all of whose members are small, inconsequential, and eager to surpass their mediocrity by projecting their image of an ideal on one man after another. Aristocracies have few heroes, and those are often designated by birth or function. In democracies heroes are a necessity. Nietzsche articulated this need at a high level. Some of his disciples expressed it on a considerably lower plane.

It was the paradoxical fate of Nietzschean ideas to be devalued and demeaned by adaptation to the very mass conditions he detested. Proud elitists of the ending nineteenth century came to the conclusion that they could best be themselves as part of the particular society in which they had their roots, their land, and their dead. They fled the mass and came full circle back into the nation, affirming which (they said) they best affirmed themselves. We can see now that at a time when old authorities were waning and decaying, when even God was discovered to be dead (Nietzsche announced it in 1882), the nation could appear a living authority, its history and tradition endowing patriots with the sense of identity they felt was missing, and faith in it providing a religion that tapped new sources of social energy for national revival and self-assertion.

In 1864, the French historian Jules Michelet had penned one of the fundamental expressions of the populist nationalism of those days, his essay *The People*. The people, said Michelet, embodies the momentous myth of the spontaneous dynamic force of a historical creation naturally oriented to justice and collective freedom. Men are good. The People is good. There is no need to fear it. A nation revives its strength by plunging back into its refreshing, revivifying waves. The mass age would find a creed to its measure by learning to worship itself. Here were spirits with which one communed by instinct, not by reason. Here was an

* This is what President Grévy of France did not understand when he visited the annual painting exhibition during the 1880's. "No great painting this year," said the Director of the exhibition to him, "but a good average." "A good average—just what a democracy ought to have!" answered Grévy. Quoted in Gordon Wright, *France in Modern Times* (Chicago: 1960), p. 297.

inspiration that one expressed less in words than in primeval gestures, in violence, in action. Here, too, at last, was a political idiom that one could oppose to effete democracy, corrupting Socialism, all the socially divisive policies of reason.

Against Socialist notions of class struggle, Nationalists asserted the organic unity of the nation. For the rest, the most radical among them could sound remarkably like Socialists, opposing the decadent, hypocritical bourgeoisie, big business and big labor for their soullessness, the money powers that exploited the defenseless poor, calling for a social and a spiritual revolution that would regenerate and purify the whole community. The major difference between the nationalism that flourished in the early 1800's and that which revived as political force at the century's end, was that the latter had shed its liberalism and, while retaining certain leftist aspects as can be seen above, was also shedding its leftist associations.

Populist but antidemocratic, authoritarian, activist, and generally young, the new Nationalists applied current notions about the survival of the fittest (which the Marxists interpreted in terms of class) to the struggle between nations, consciously or unconsciously refocusing aggressions on the external plane. They also enlisted romanticism in the service of their cause, developing what would become two principal traits of mass politics in the twentieth century: the organization of paramilitary bands of toughs to sell their newspapers, terrorize opponents, and dominate the streets; and the paranoid style of politics (as Raymond Carr has called it). The latter, which saw society threatened by secret, subtle, and powerful conspiracies among its "foreign" elements—atheists, Masons, Protestants (or Catholics), Jews, Marxists, or even intellectual eggheads—had long been a specialty of conservatives and reactionaries. Now it became a political staple, particularly effective among the half-educated and those (increasingly numerous) who felt their way of life threatened in some respect.

One cannot tell to what extent the nationalist leaders were sincere in the fears they professed for national welfare threatened by subterranean enemies. One thing is sure: obsession with alien conspiracies deflected their sights from social problems which also, they claimed, concerned them. And the greatest of these derivatives was anti-Semitism: the Socialism of fools as it has been called.

Anti-Semitism: An Aberration

The Jewish lot in Europe has always been affected by paranoid visions. The intolerance manifested against the Jews—rising, at least in theory, from their guilt for the death of Jesus and their constant refusal to recognize his divinity—was basically connected with a tendency men show everywhere to suspect outsiders, particularly in times of strain when everyone seeks a scapegoat for his troubles. The strangers in our midst become obscurely and mysteriously connected with all the evil coming from outside, whether invasion, drought, or epidemic. In societies like the Christian, where social identification was closely connected with religious practice, the Jews were the most obvious, the most identifiable, and omnipresent aliens. When they did not conform to the society they lived in, they were considered unassimilable and possibly ill-intentioned. They must be kept at a distance, relegated to functions others would not undertake. When they turned in upon themselves, in their ghettoes or conventicles, they became even more suspect; when they converted, on the other hand, they must denounce their sometime-fellows and put flesh on the horrid skeleton of popular fancy to prove their own good faith.

In the course of the nineteenth century, the secular restrictions directed against Jews and stemming from religious prejudice were gradually removed. The emancipations witnessed in the major Western countries before 1848 followed more tardily elsewhere. Jews were confined to ghettoes in Piedmont until 1848, in Rome until 1870, excluded from Spain until 1869, lived only on sufferance in several Swiss cantons until the 1860's. By then, however, such holdouts were exceptional in the West. Given equal rights, Jewish communities prospered remarkably, took advantage of opportunities for education and enterprise, produced some considerable intellectuals, financiers, and entrepreneurs— notably the Rothschilds of Frankfurt, the Saint-Simonian Pereire brothers in Paris, or Bismarck's banker, Gerson Bleichröder, "the Rothschild of Berlin" and the first Prussian Jew to become a hereditary nobleman without conversion. They would soon figure prominently in political life, providing Britain with a Prime Minister in Benjamin Disraeli, France with a number of distinguished figures, and Socialist movements everywhere with an important section of their leadership.

In 1860, leading Jewish personalities had founded the *Alliance Israélite Universelle,* to protect and advance the interests of their people —as they did, for instance, soon after its founding by securing Napoleon III's intervention to improve the lot of Jews in the Romanian principalities. Jewish numbers also were increasing. Some three million around 1830, they stood around seven million forty years later. Between two-thirds and three-quarters of these lived in the so-called *Pale* of Russia and Poland, once, long ago, a refuge from persecutions elsewhere but now an immense ghetto stretching along the western borders of the Russian Empire. There Jews lived in separate Yiddish-speaking communities, subject to medieval restrictions and victims of destructive pogroms, in which popular dissatisfaction could be vented not against the government and the great but against more helpless objects.

Eager to escape their onerous condition and settle where opportunities and freedom were both greater, thousands of Jews left the Russian Pale, hundreds of thousands in the second half of the century, especially after the unsuccessful Polish rising against Russia in 1863 and 1864, and again after a great spate of pogroms that followed the Tsar's murder in 1881. Those who could made their way toward the Western countries or America. But most settled in the first freer lands they reached: Germany, Romania, the territories of the Habsburg Empire. Their coming in great numbers revived or emphasized the old prejudices against aliens, while blending with resentments of a more modern kind. In a time of change which many feared and resented, Jews appeared as the most visible agents of change: bankers, traders, journalists, carriers of a cosmopolitan culture and market economy. "Down with Rothschild! Down with Jews!" wrote a French nationalist leader, Maurice Barrès in 1890: "It's the formula which summarizes the resentments of those who have not enough against those who have too much."

Poor Jews frightened the rich and competed with the native workers; wealthy Jews competed with the native rich and were resented by the poor; successful Jews were thought to have succeeded at the expense of natives; unsuccessful Jews were resented when they cost money for relief; assimilated Jews were identified with their fellows of more recent coming who dressed, spoke, and behaved so strangely. All became the object of bitter, anti-Semitic campaigns that spread from the more backward Eastern countries—Russia, Romania, Hungary, Austria, Germany —in the 1870's as far as France in the late 1880's. Christian Social parties trying to build up a clientele among the peasants, the laborers, the lower middle classes of central Europe, found anti-Semitism a useful talking point directing social tensions not toward property owners but against the ill-assimilated immigrants. Above all, the new Nationalists saw them as the principal source of national weakness, an alien host exploiting and corrupting the race in whose midst it settled.

Contemporary fascination with the notion of "races," identified with "Peoples," directed Nationalist attention to racial purity in which they saw a factor of national strength. The Jews, they argued, marrying only among themselves, were the purest of European peoples and hence most likely to dominate all others; and they unveiled a vast conspiracy (shaped only in their minds) whereby the "Jewish race" engaged in a ruthless struggle against other races, kept itself pure while using every means at its disposal—the ruin wrought by its financiers, the social disruption of the political movements it manipulated, the moral and intellectual pressures of democratic or Marxist doctrines, the blood pollution of mixed marriages—to weaken its opponents. No matter what Jews did it could be held against them for they were judged guilty before trial began. At the turn of the century, a French liberal pacifist like Romain Rolland could persuade himself that Jews were "a national danger": at worst because they destroyed the Fatherland, at best in wanting to replace it by a wider community.

Notions such as these enabled Nationalists to ignore the real nature of social evils which they criticized and to concentrate their fire upon irrelevancies. Just as medieval epidemics were blamed on spirits, witches, or the Devil rather than on hunger, dirt or rats, so now real social evils were blamed on fantasies which the Jew embodied. While this prevented the identification of real evils, let alone their cure, it also maintained the notion of basic national unity, so that German or French exploiters were merely misguided tools, German or French Socialist workers ill-advised followers of conspirators outside the national body.

Such ideas were far more socially disruptive than the fantastic conspiracies that they pretended to reveal. Sensible men rejected them and they did not make a serious impact except where societies at the end of their tether adhered to them as a last resort.* They would come into their own with the Great War and the new conditions war created.

Europe and the World Overseas

Europe Explodes

Not coal or oil but men are the basic fuel of history, the energizing and explosive factor of its movement. No part of the world has tapped so much of this human fuel as Europe in the past two centuries; none had the resources Europe seemed to have. In the Stone Age, about 10,000 years ago, the total population of the world did not come up to 20 million. In 1800 it probably topped 900 million, which more than doubled by 1930 and trebled by 1960. Until quite recently, Europeans and their descendants led in this accelerated race to increase and multiply. Between 1800 and 1930 "whites" or "Caucasians" increased in number from 200 to 700 million: that is, from one-fifth to over one-third of mankind.** The great reservoir of manpower lay in Europe, whose population increased by 30 million between 1850 and 1870 and by another 100 million between 1870 and 1900, at which time it numbered some 400 million: about a quarter of mankind.

Between 1851 and 1960, about 60 million people left Europe for Siberia, other parts of Asia, or other countries overseas. Over a third of these went between 1870 and 1900, the flow increasing thereafter until it reached its peak before the First World War when, between 1909 and 1914, about a million and a half immigrants were spilling out of Europe

---

* Or, one might add, as in Russia, where governments in similar straits appealed to them to excuse their bungling.

** By 1960, with 860 or 870 million, their proportion of the world's 2,700 million population would once again be lower.

every year.* By 1900, Europeans had settled the Americas, Australia, New Zealand, Siberia, the Caucasus, and South Africa. More thinly and less solidly in some cases than in others, but in every case sufficiently to generate further expansion from the settlements themselves. Population seemed to grow at compound interest: the 10,000-odd French people who had first settled Canada in the seventeenth century had, by the twentieth, become five million (not all, of course, descendants of the original settlers); the new self-governing colony of Victoria in Australia boasted a population of 97,000 in 1850, a million in 1875—Melbourne alone, its capital, was a great city of over half a million when Queen Victoria died. European languages had penetrated everywhere, taken over the Americas and the Pacific, provided the major means of communication between myriad peoples in Africa and India, or the base of new mixed languages chiefly derived from English (*pidgin*), while new mixed religions inspired by Christian variants sprang up from China to Haiti, from Congo to Brazil.

Europeans had always traveled, traded, conquered, settled. The nineteenth-century acceleration of this process came when steam helped them to push up river valleys, repeating rifles gave them a murderous superiority over opponents, modern medicine provided immunity against tropical fevers. The natural obstacles and diseases which had once held them back were being eliminated. So, to a great extent, were the human ones. In 1849 Carlyle eulogized the law of force and cunning in *The Nigger Question*.** A little later, the English prophet of muscular Christianity, Charles Kingsley, asked whether Christian values applied to "beasts" like the Dyaks of Borneo. "Sacrifice of human life?" he asked their intercessors: "First prove that it is *human* life." Such feelings were widespread among invaders to whom superior technological equipment suggested a kind of righteous racism soon reinforced by Darwin's theories.

The white invaders shot or poisoned natives who hampered them, particularly in the Americas and the Pacific. In California as late as the 1870's Sunday shooting parties were organized against the Indians; and American atrocities are said by experts to compare only with the brutality which Russians exhibited in Siberia and Alaska. More murderous than weapons were the diseases which invaders carried, against which they themselves were immunized by habit, but which burned like wildfire through peoples unprepared for them. By 1876 the native population of Tasmania was extinct, the number of U.S. Indians diminished by three-fourths, that of New Zealand Maoris by four-fifths, and the aborigines of Australia, hunted like wild beasts, seemed to be dying out.

This was about to change. Much of the destruction, wrought un-

---

* The flow thinned to less than half that figure in the 1920's and to about 130,000 a year in the 1930's; it would rise again to half a million a year in 1946–1960.
** Soon answered by J. S. Mill's *The Negro Question* in 1850.

The Last of England, by Ford Madox Brown. The City Museum and Art Gallery, Birmingham, England.

wittingly, was a by-product of individual enterprise careless of anything except immediate profits or private satisfaction, changing the ecology of great regions, destroying native ways of life when they did not decimate the natives.* In due course, as in the industrial revolution, the more destructive aspects of private enterprise would incite the public conscience to intervene, while its more stimulating aspects benefited survivors or descendants of the sufferers themselves.

Bare figures tell the tale of a world in which the touch of Europe both opened scars and healed them. Epidemics were harnessed, famines circumscribed, food circulated farther, health improved. Today, the Maoris of New Zealand, the Indians of South America, have recovered their numbers of preinvasion days. The 800 million inhabitants of Asia in 1914 do not equal the population of today's China alone. This is some indication of our role in breaking the natural balance between soil and water on one hand and the number of mouths to feed on the other. Most suggestive is the case of Egypt, which probably supported some 7 million people in the days of its ancient greatness. By Napoleon's day this had shrunk to less than 3 million. It then began to rise: 5 million in 1850, over twice as many in 1900, about 30 million in the 1960's, it holds out the fearsome prospect of coming close to 75 million in the

*As we can find in *Moby Dick,* the mid-nineteenth century saw whales disappear from the Northern Hemisphere and whalers turning toward the Antarctic. By 1900 the buffalo, basis of the economy and livelihood of the American Plains Indians, was practically exterminated thanks to the repeating rifle. Buffalo would survive thereafter only in zoos and game preserves. Men exploited the whole world and whole species disappeared, hunted to extinction for a moment's profit before game preserves or artificial breeding (seals, ostriches) intervened.

year 2000 with no idea of how such numbers will find nourishment and livelihood.

Imperialism

Demography and technology provide the concrete background of modern imperialism, a reflection of the dynamics affecting European peoples and their offspring for several centuries and culminating as the nineteenth century ended in the vastest colonial expansion that the world has seen. During the two score years before 1914 the Western nations took to themselves the greatest part of the remaining world.* Much has been said and written about the economic factors behind this process which Lenin described as part of the final—monopoly—stage of capitalism. In fact, economic motives, which had their share in white expansion, need not have led to modern colonialism. As recent experience shows, capital could achieve its ends more profitably under different conditions. Egypt, before the French and British took it over, was already (in a British statesman's words) "an earthly paradise for all who had money to lend at usurious rates of interest or third-rate goods of which they wished to dispose at first-rate prices."

Throughout the colonial period, the economic involvement of imperial countries in their own empires was and remained relatively small. In 1914 Britain had not quite 13 per cent of its total foreign investments in its own colonial empire; France had less than 5 per cent; the Germans less than that. There was more German money invested in British colonies than in their own. To many, as to Benjamin Disraeli, the "wretched colonies" remained "a millstone around our necks." In 1913, German colonial trade amounted to half of 1 per cent of German total trade, while colonial deficits cost German taxpayers over a billion marks. Investors much preferred developed areas to backward ones, which meant that most Western capital stayed at home or went—like 70 per cent of Britain's foreign investments—to independent countries in temperate climates.

Industrial nations are always one another's best customers. The French put their money in Europe and in the Ottoman Empire, the British placed more loans in the United States than in any other country, the United States invested more in Canada than Britons did. Companies existed which made vast profits from colonial enterprises, but they never had sufficient influence or power seriously to affect national policy. This was achieved in part by national vanity and excess energy, in part by demagogues and dreamers who reflected these, providing them with purpose and direction. The true imperialist was really a dreamer, burning to

---

* As an example, in 1875 Europeans held 11 per cent of Africa; in 1902 they held 90 per cent. During that time one-tenth of the world's population and one-fifth of its land had come under their rule.

turn the fiction of today into the reality of tomorrow, to conquer Egypt or China, tame the Sahara, plumb the mysteries of the Congo, join Berlin to Baghdad or the Cape to Cairo, link the Mediterranean and the Indian Ocean. Before they lay on the green baize tables of diplomatic conferences or financial board rooms, the maps of men like these had sprung from the *Thousand and One Nights*. It is significant that the many-faceted movement of expansion remains embodied in what has been called the scramble for Africa, poorest and least profitable of the continents, yet redolent with challenges which sparked their own response.

Africa   We have already seen that antislavery forces played an important role in encouraging African trade. There would be as many missionaries in Africa, Asia, and the Pacific as there were soldiers, most of the time and, until 1900, probably more. Trade was closely bound with missionary fervor, a fervor both cultural and Christian, both religious and secular. There was a great task of exploration, which mapped most of Africa between the 1840's and the 1880's,* but also of "alleviating human suffering" by bringing medicine, hospitals and popular education to the natives, as David Livingstone (1813–1873) insisted.

The hope that the explorer Speke expressed in 1855 "of raising his fellow men in the scale of civilization" was explicitly voiced by David Livingstone in his account of *Missionary Travels and Researches in South Africa* (London: 1857). Livingstone expected that, by promoting commerce, Europeans would end the slave trade,** "introduce the Negro family into the body of corporate nations," and bring "a much larger diffusion of the blessings of civilization." He was right in thinking that the economic activity would be more effective than "efforts exclusively spiritual and educational"; but he did not make enough allowance for exploitation and for greed, nor for the sheer destruction wrought by the appearance of this tougher civilization in the midst of traditional societies which it would smash to smithereens. Self-satisfied dynamism, viewing the values it brought as supreme, spared little thought for those which it displaced. What counted—as King Leopold II, one of the greatest colonial entrepreneurs, told the International Colonial Conference meeting at Berlin in 1885—was that "the most intelligent of our youth demand wider horizons on which to expend their abounding energy, our working population will derive from the virgin regions of Africa new sources of energy and render more in exchange."

By then the scramble for territories had already started, set rolling by adventurers fascinated by the possibilities of lands which they surveyed. It acquired momentum under the pressure of public opinion

---

* The sources of the Nile were found in the 1850's and 60's, and the Congo Basin mapped in the 1870's, Mount Kenya and Kilimanjaro discovered in the 80's.
** In East Africa, largely in Arab hands.

dazzled by vainglorious chauvinism. National pride prompted governments to seek compensation for one anothers' advances, national interest furnished them with arguments—the strongest of these being that territories acquired by others were lost to national trade. When the powers began to back their traders and investors, commerce turned into territorial claims and these spread from the coasts over the interior like great patches of oil. Shortly they would find, as a British prime minister put it, that the appetite had grown with eating. The division of Africa was manufactured in Europe and decided as if the land were empty, open to the decisions of European diplomats who projected upon it the ambitions and the bargains of another continent. Africa itself was still little known, the maps inaccurate, the frontiers often traced along lines of latitude and longitude for lack of more detailed information, their reality slight on the ground and long meaningless to peoples whose destinies had been bandied about European Cabinets and Conferences.

It is well to remember that the alternative to colonial expansion by one power was not freedom for a territory (whatever that might mean), but colonial expansion by another power. The undeveloped, unorganized parts of the world were going to be developed, organized, exploited, and dominated by some nation that would take advantage of the opportunities, respond to the challenges, they offered. The only question was which nation it was to be. The dynamic of imperialism was negative: trade may or may not have followed the flag (more often it was the other way around), but where one flag went the trade of others was largely excluded. So, dreams and pride were followed and borne on by policy and interest. But behind it all lay the burning vision of a few men like Pierre Savorgnan de Brazza or like Cecil Rhodes, the notorious King of Diamonds whom a French diplomat described as "a force cast in an idea." "One is facing more than a business man, an instrument of government or of a company; here is the passionate, violent, audacious, indefatigable agent of British expansion . . . ," manifest destiny personified in a heroic figure who complained that he could not reach the stars, declaring "I would annex the planets if I could."

For men like Rhodes, or the French General Lyautey who pacified Morocco, the joy lay less in acquisition than in action. In Africa, Siberia, or Southeast Asia, the great proconsuls of the time found a kind of *tabula rasa* on which their will and character could leave its mark. Perhaps that was the loudest call of empire for men who fulfilled themselves by pushing ever further without a direct object for their deeds. They managed to communicate their will and vision, appropriate to an expansive age, to a large part of the general public which gained not profits but vicarious satisfaction from what they did and from seeing maps on which the national possessions loomed increasingly large. Imperialists like these could have cited Cromwell: "He goeth furthest who knows not whither he is going." The costs of colonial

COLONIZATION IN AFRICA
TO 1914

Dependent states:

- British
- French
- Belgian
- Portuguese
- Spanish
- Italian
- German
- Independent states

enterprise were larger than the profits: in 1885 a French politician pointed out that for every Frenchman then settled in Algeria four men had died and two soldiers stood on guard. Why, asked Lord Kimberley, who had found both a fortune and a title in the goldfields of South Africa, why dispute for "barren deserts of places where white men cannot live, dotted with thinly scattered tribes who cannot be made to work." Nevertheless, as Beatrice Webb noted in her *Diary*, imperialist sentiment was "in the air!—all classes drunk with sight-seeing and hysterical loyalty."

If the material profits were dubious, the psychic revenue seems to

THE RHODES COLOSSUS
STRIDING FROM CAPE TOWN TO CAIRO.

Cecil Rhodes. Left: a contemporary cartoon from *Punch*.

have weighted the balance. Frenchmen, Belgians, Germans, Britishers, argued that their "conquest of virgin nature and heathen races" was a "peaceful crusade," bringing millions "into the Empire of civilization" helping them to "raise themselves bit by bit towards our level." Western superiority implied a moral responsibility to

> Take up the white man's burden
> Send forth the best ye breed—
> Go bind your sons to exile
> To serve your captive's need;
> To wait in heavy harness
> On fluttered folk and wild—
> Your new-caught, sullen peoples,
> Half devil and half child. . . .

The white man's burden, as Kipling formulated it, was heavy. On the other hand, willingness to shoulder it could be construed as evidence of superiority, avoidance of the responsibility as a sign of weakness, perhaps of decadence. "All great nations in the fullness of their strength have desired to set their mark upon barbarian lands . . ." argued the German historian Treitschke in 1887. "Those who take no share in this great rivalry will play a pitiable part in time to come. The colonizing impulse has become a vital question for a great nation." Conversely, the very act of self-assertion might be expected to improve a nation's forces and morale. To many French nationalists before 1914 North African expansion was an important factor of the Nationalist revival they wished to bring about, Moroccan territory—often described as *le Far West* of France—would be the cradle of a new race of energetic self-confident patriots, the source of soldiers whose aid would be essential in struggles yet to come.*

Not only social energies but also social peace could be expected from the imperial harvest: social and demographic pressures would be eased by emigration, without the nation being impoverished by the loss of its men settling in foreign lands. The passions of the working classes might be directed toward common enterprises that would contribute employment, opportunities, and benefits more difficult to wrest from the possessing classes at home. "If you want to avoid civil war," argued Cecil Rhodes, "you must become Imperialists." Many were convinced like those Italian politicians who, in the 1890's, beset by public scandals and frightened by social agitation, thought to find a diversion in colonial enterprise . . . and found only defeat.

Others did far better. Thus, in the 1870's, the exploration of the Congo Basin was undertaken by an international association sponsored by Leopold II of Belgium and devoted to opening the Dark Continent to civilization. In 1885, a Congo Free State was recognized as independent, under the sovereignty of Leopold who undertook to suppress the slave trade, protect missionaries and explorers, and open his territories to international commerce. In fact, while the Arab slave trade was indeed suppressed, the Congolese were chained to more efficient slavery by being forced to labor on land and in the mines.** Their tribal lands were taken and all resistance was brutally suppressed. What had begun as a progressive enterprise turned into a ferocious pursuit of minerals, ivory, and rubber in which the worst atrocities were lost from sight before the indifference or ignorance of the public.

A few of those who knew tried to tell the world. In 1899 the Polish-born Joseph Conrad wrote *Heart of Darkness* to denounce (he told his publisher) the "criminality of inefficiency and pure selfishness when tackling the civilizing work in Africa." In Conrad's pages, even the hero —a once-liberal, progressive scholar, preparing a thesis on the eradication of barbaric customs—ended by scrawling his conclusion across it: "Exterminate the brutes." Perhaps it took a Pole to sympathize with the paradox of civilized people surrounded by barbarism, of subjects oppressed by superior power. In 1904, at last, the revelation of Congolese abuses set off an international agitation which ended in 1908 with the transfer of the Free State to Belgium, whose colony it became.

By then the Boer War (1899–1902) had brought the whole imperial issue into question by opposing a seventeenth-century farmers' republic founded on slavery and small enterprise to the twentieth-century

---

* Other Nationalists, on the contrary, condemned colonial enterprises as dangerous distractions from the "blue line of the Vosges" where the main task of *Revanche* against the Germans awaited patriots.

** The Kaffirs of Mozambique still, apparently, maintain that monkeys refuse to speak for fear that if they do they will be put to work.

imperialist dreams of Rhodes, founded on mining interests and economic progress. The Dutch-descended Boers had fled the Cape to remain independent from the British. The modern age caught up with them when gold and diamonds were discovered on their ranches. Now the rural society for which they stood, reactionary and static, had to withstand far less the imperial ambitions of Great Britain than the demands of industrial society and capital. Kruger, the Boers' leader, was a puritan farmer who thought the world was flat and all worthwhile knowledge lay in the Bible. Rhodes was a visionary millionaire who pursued money for the power it brought and power for the great things that could be done with it—especially controlling the world through an Anglo-American union. Both inspired utter loyalty in their followers, for there was meaning as well as meanness in their visions. Inevitably (or so it seemed), anachronistic Transvaal succumbed before the British Empire. Less inevitably, it only did so after a long and desperate resistance in which the British troops suffered serious reverses and the British ego far more serious ones. The Boer War showed the British how isolated they were, and suggested an alteration of their diplomacy which led first to the Japanese Alliance and later to Entente with France and Russia. Equally important, it spurred soul-searching almost as profound as that which their defeat by the American colonies had suggested and accelerated important changes in the imperial structure.

For over half a century the stated goal of Britain's colonial policy had been responsible self-government for its component parts. Australia had been granted this in the 1850's, the British North America Act of 1867 set up a united Dominion of Canada with its own federal government and legislatures, the Cape colony was founded in 1872 and New Zealand in 1876. All, it will be noted, were white settler colonies where home rule was meant to prevent the disaffection which lost the American empire. In 1907, within a few years of the Boers' defeat, these colonies became dominions, and were joined within two years by a self-governing South Africa. A few men perceived that emancipation of white settlers would prevent that of native peoples—especially of Africans whose safeguard had prompted so much of nineteenth-century colonial enterprise. A look at Irish policies and problems would have shown what later decolonization would make obvious: that one man's freedom was to be achieved at another's expense. But comparative judgments of this sort did not begin to be made until mid-twentieth century.

India   The great showcase in which the possibilities and failures of colonial government were displayed was India, since the late eighteenth century crux of the British Empire. There the East India Company subjected to increasing parliamentary control lost first its monopoly of trade, then its commercial functions, and, finally, its governing power. This

An illustration from a contemporary book, *Campaign in India,* depicting an attack by the Bengal Lancers on the mutineers of 1857–58.

final change occurred in 1857, when the great Indian mutiny burst out of the varied discontents of change, caste and religious grievances, peasant dissatisfaction with foreign innovations, to shake the very core of British power. Reforms and interventions—abolition of suttee, in which a widow would throw herself on her husband's funeral pyre, and infanticide, efforts to emancipate women, disregard of the caste system, missionary challenges to Hindu religion, educational threats to Hindu and Muslim orthodoxy—provoked revolt directed less against the foreign presence than against the accelerated westernization of the past few years. If the trouble first broke out in the army, it was because there alone were Indians organized in any numbers. Beginning in 1857, fighting raged over North and Central India; European men, women, and children were massacred, battles were fought in temperatures as high as 110° in the shade, and more combatants on both sides died of sickness and heat than were killed in battle. By 1859 the mutiny had been put down largely with the help of loyal Indian units, the East India Company abolished, and reform accelerated to allow for the participation of more Indians in the magistracy, the executive, and the legislative branch of a government of India now run from London and controlled by the British Parliament.

In many respects, the sources of the great rebellion misnamed a mutiny may be found in the inevitable consequences of alien rule, however well-meaning. Yet Jawaharlal Nehru has drawn attention to the fact that one of the Hindustani words which soon became a part of the English language was "loot." Continued trade which was the origin of the British presence meant that, when the native administration failed, the

British must step in. The Moguls were no more than an expensive sham. They finally disappeared in 1856. Meanwhile, the peninsula was governed, administered, taxed, defended by the British. Indian economy was subordinated to British interests and British policy in turn was deeply affected by India's needs. India's security dictated the British orientation toward Russia, Persia, and Afghanistan, toward China, Burma, and Southeast Asia; it suggested the necessity of Egypt—finally occupied in 1882—and the significance of the Cape; dictated the occupation of coaling stations for the steam-driven iron ships which in the late nineteenth century came to defend the Empire.

Under British rule, religious murders were gradually suppressed, bandits thinned out and outlaws hunted down, telegraphs and railroads built, irrigation sponsored so that there were fewer famines.* Public works and public administration meant an educated class trained in Western ways. How could the British, asked Lord Macaulay, subsidize education according to native beliefs, use public funds to teach children an astronomy that would throw an English girls' school into fits of laughter, a history of kings 30 feet tall and reigns 30,000 years long, a geography where seas ran with honey or butter? A new Western-educated class grew up which absorbed English values to the point of reacting against England from which it had learned nationalism and a sense of its own tradition. Nineteenth-century Europeans had discovered Indian culture, Sanskrit literature, Buddhism, and the historical achievements of the Hindus. The westernized Indian, torn between his school and home, between fascination with the British Raj and frustration at the lack of opportunity to use his education, clutched at European admiration of his country's past for a tradition that he could take pride in, and on whose basis he could assert himself.

Crushed, the rebellion of 1857 left an enduring legacy of bitterness, enlarged the gulf between Indians and their occupiers, making the latter feel more insecure and the former more resentful. Attempts to govern India in an Indian way were now abandoned. The British were trustees whom providence set over the continent, not answerable to the people's will as in Australia or in Canada but only to their own sense of right and wrong. The Indians should have freedom too, like others, but only when they were fit for it. That time seemed far off, as the coronation of Queen Victoria in 1876 as Empress of India indicated.

The Indians would, of course, be ruled for their own welfare. As things turned out, they would see little reason to believe this. The British were concerned more with stability than with development, more with order than with reform. They concentrated on good administration and honest justice—which benefited most those who could afford it; on sanitation—which helped the population soar beyond the economic

---

* By 1940 nearly 33 million acres, one-fifth of the peninsula's cultivable area, were under irrigation.

potential of the country; on cash crops like tea or jute—which enriched planters, not the natives. Over one-third of the Indian peasants had no land; all were deep in debts whose interests (as high as 100–200 per cent) might take up four-fifths of a family's annual income. Old handicrafts and village industries collapsed before the influx of machine-made goods, and native industry was very slow in making an appearance. When it did start it produced the familiar horrors of industrial revolution magnified by the extreme poverty of the land. Child mortality among the working classes of Bombay was more than one in two. Life expectation, twenty-three years in 1911, would rise to twenty-seven years in 1931 and thirty-two years in 1955.

Still, the growth of local representative institutions continued, leading to demands for provincial and national self-government. In 1885 the Indian National Congress (established with official sponsorship) provided a forum in which the native middle classes could militate against the occupants. But, having succeeded in creating an Anglicized upper and middle class, the British now refused the moderate reforms these classes were demanding. The British, said the Viceroy in 1905, must govern the peninsula "as if . . . forever."

The Far East   We have noted the tendency for Europe to form and inspire the men and societies that would, in due course, become its challengers and competitors. Nowhere was this as true as in one Asian country which never lost its independence: Japan. For two centuries the islands had kept themselves tightly secluded against disturbing influence from the outside. This isolation collapsed before the guns of American warships appearing before Yedo (modern Tokyo) in 1853. Within ten years Japan shed her feudal garments and set out to oppose Western power by learning its secrets and adapting them to her needs. "Rich country, strong army," became the slogan of modernization, of the awareness that only productivity can finance military strength, that only military strength can defend riches, and that both—at that time—depended on skills and knowledge that could only be garnered from the West.

In 1868 the Emperor's "Charter oath" declared that "Knowledge shall be sought all over the world." It was; and it was put to use. Teacher training colleges were established in 1872. By 1886, 46 per cent, by 1896, 61 per cent, by 1906, 95 per cent of school-age children were receiving an elementary education. An industrial structure was built up. Cheap and shoddy foreign manufactures were countered by cheap and shoddy Japanese goods which the Japanese could turn out as shoddily and more cheaply than anybody else until it became good business to improve quality, when they demonstrated that they could do that too. But there was nothing cheap or shoddy about the military equipment or the military training in which they invested much of their resources and their

Prisoners of the Boxer Rebellion being held in Tientsin.

energy. Within a lifetime of 1853 the results of their will and enterprise would be seen in the defeat of a European power by the new might of modernized Japan.

The greatest of Asian powers, China, had also secluded herself from outside intrusion. But her masters lacked the Japanese capacity for decisive action. Except for Macao, which had been granted to the Portuguese in 1557 for services they rendered against pirates, foreign trade had been confined to the port of Canton alone. The foreign merchants trading at Canton operated under onerous restrictions, but their business was too profitable for them not to accept the rules set by the Chinese. Trouble came only in 1839 as a result of friction between the local Chinese authorities and the British. The latter wanted to sell their Indian opium; the former tried to enforce the imperial ban against it and quash all contraband. The right of Indian opium to the Chinese market was enforced by British battleships. In 1842 the Treaty of Nanking marked China's inability to withstand them and opened a long period of national disintegration before Western encroachments. Through the door which the British blasted open came other foreigners: French, Germans, Americans, and Russians, extorting more and more concessions, settlements, bases, extraterritorial rights, and picking off the frontier provinces of the Empire.

As the weakness of the imperial government became more evident, revolutionary movements and societies began to organize, some seeking national salvation in reaction and others in Japanese-style westernization. There were sporadic insurrections, but the imperial government maintained itself—partly with foreign help. In 1894 a crisis occurred when China stumbled into war over Korea not with a Western power but with her smaller neighbors in Japan, only to be disgracefully defeated. The shame of this defeat intensified the debate between westernizers and traditionalists. It also persuaded the imperial government to modernize the country's structure and these timid beginnings of reform stirred up a wild reaction, rising to fanatical heights iń the Boxer Rebellion of 1900, which had to be put down by foreign intervention.* China became a kind of common colony of the foreign powers which controlled her ports, her customs authorities, almost her government. More and more students who wanted to learn how to reassert national independence against the foreigner went to Japan to study.

It would be Japan, as we shall shortly see, which reasserted Asia's will to independence and to imperial power.

The Intrepid Americans

The United States is a good if exceptional example of a colonial country which freed itself first from foreign rule, then from dependence on foreign capital, to become in turn a colonial and imperial power.**

When the constitution had been signed, the United States owed European creditors some 60 million dollars. From such small beginnings American borrowers made their country the world's greatest debtor by 1914, owing 6.5 billion dollars to a variety of European investors.† By that time the Union was a great world power. It had eliminated the native enemy and competitor of the invading settlers by killing the Indians, pushing them across its borders and herding the rest into reservations. It had broken the economic power of the slave-owning aristocracy in a great civil war (1860–1865) which liberated the slaves, opened the continent to settlement and speculation, and freed American industry of a conservative rival.

Encouraged by the vast demands created by the equipment of a continent with a growing population, protected by tariffs which the defeated South would not have let grow so high, fed by the cheap labor hordes of immigrants provided, industry grew apace. By 1889 the Eiffel Tower in Paris would be equipped with American elevators. By 1900 the United States claimed the industrial leadership of the world, which it would lead into a second Industrial Revolution that would be sped no longer by steam, but by oil and electric power.

Meanwhile, advancing across the continent which they would make their own, Americans expropriated or bought out not only their old British masters and other colonial powers like France, Spain, and Russia, not only the native Indians, but also neighbors like the Mexicans.

---

* The "Boxers" were members of village militias and patriotic societies organized to defend the country against foreigners. "Righteous Harmony Bands (or Fists)," they believed themselves invulnerable to bullets, murdered Christians and missionaries, and beseiged the foreigners in Peking until defeated by an international relief force.

** Such an evolution, far from being unusual, frequently appears in history. The story of ancient Rome, of the Parthian Empire, or of early medieval England may serve as examples of it, no less than those of sixteenth-seventeenth-century Sweden or of Russia. But such comparisons may appear less relevant than modern instances of similar developments in Australia or South Africa.

† Even the 11 million dollars needed to buy Louisiana from Napoleon had been advanced largely by English, Dutch, and French bankers.

Between 1850 and 1900 the population more than trebled, rising from 23 to 76 million, exports grew tenfold; one-third of the world's industrial power, 41 per cent of its railway mileage, lay within the borders of the United States. It was time, men like Cecil Rhodes insisted, that the United States shoulder the white man's burden; and it was to them that Kipling directed his appeal to that effect. Mark Twain answered Kipling in a little note the New York *Herald* printed on December 30, 1900, and which purported to be a salutation from the nineteenth century to the twentieth: "I bring you the stately matron named Christendom, returning bedraggled, besmirched and dishonored from pirate raids in Kiao-chou, Manchuria, South Africa and the Philippines, with her soul full of meanness, her pocket full of boodle and her mouth full of pious hypocrisies. Give her soap and a towel, but hide the looking glass."

In 1898 U.S. imperialism would cut its teeth on a suitably dilapidated foe: Spain. When the war ended, the United States found herself with a colonial empire on her hands: the Philippines, which were to be granted independence at the earliest possible moment and got it in 1946; Puerto Rico, which was annexed as a dependency in 1899; and Cuba. The Cubans had fought hard for independence and this they officially secured in 1902, when American troops evacuated the island. But the United States kept a base at Guantánamo (on a ninety-nine-year lease) and retained intervention rights which they exercised when circumstances appeared to call for it. The revolutionary ideal of a free, democratic republic foundered on the alliance of Cuban oligarchs and American interests. Cuba subjected its economy to a single crop—sugar, its sovereignty to American oversight, and its domestic politics to a succession of strong men.

The North Americans were taking the lead in inter-American affairs where Spain and later Britain had held sway. The Monroe Doctrine would be interpreted not only to keep others out, but to force or insinuate Americans in. Since 1889 Pan-American conferences held out prospects of close friendly relations which were belied by U.S. policies and by South American realities and desires. Most South Americans were closer in sympathy and culture to western Europe than to the Protestant power to the north. Many on the east coast found Europe more accessible than their own neighbors, let alone than the United States. In any case, Pan-Americanism was regarded as an instrument of political and economic penetration wielded by the superior power whose activities did little to belie the thought.

To face its new imperial responsibilities in both Atlantic and Pacific, the United States took a strong interest in plans for joining the two oceans by a canal that would allow its fleet to pass at will from one ocean to the other. The most convenient place for the canal was across the Isthmus of Panama, in Colombian territory. But Colombia was uncooperative in conceding what the Americans felt were safeguards necessary for the security of their canal. In 1903, revolt conveniently broke out in Panama province. United States forces intervened to restore order while preventing the Colombians from doing the job themselves. A Republic of Panama was swiftly organized, and hastened to sign a treaty recognizing U.S. sovereignty over the Canal Zone itself.

It soon appeared that the demands of the Monroe Doctrine called for armed intervention and occupation (to forestall European interference) whenever the United States judged fit: in Cuba in 1906–1909, in Nicaragua in 1912–1933, in Mexico in 1914 and 1916, in Haiti in 1915–1934, in San Domingo in 1916–1924. Clear indication that, with the best intentions, no great power can abandon its interest in the econmic and political space it dominates.

The Uneasy Balance: Europe 1848–1914

It was against this background that diplomats and politicians went through their complicated motions, any account of which is bound to be schematic and selective. Historians have interpreted the events of this period as the fulfillment of a historical trend toward national unity and independence, progressively advancing through the events of 1859 (Italy's war for unity), 1866 (Austro-Prussian War), 1871 (Franco-Prussian War), all the way to 1918. Or, again, in terms of England's steadfast attempt to maintain a balance of power in Europe, and that of other countries to incline the balance in their favor. They have talked about the rivalry of Germany and France as a secular enmity rising to a climax between 1870 and 1940; or, more convincingly, about the progressive narrowing of the possibilities for international maneuver as Europe's debatable lands, which had long served as a kind of safety valve for great power ambitions (in the manner of the American frontier), were pared down by the appearance of new sovereign states, first in the center and then in the east of Europe. Every one of these theories provides some foundation for a general interpretation. But it is possible to include them in an argument which divides the time since 1848 into a short spell of twenty years or less dominated by France, followed by a longer period of German hegemony ending in 1944 or 1945. During this time Germany exhibited the same aggressiveness that her predecessors—Spain and France—had shown in the days of their ascendancy.

One can relate Germany's new energy to demographic changes by which France, still except for Russia the most populous country in the Europe of 1851, was soon outstripped by Germany as her population tripled in the course of the nineteenth century. About equivalent to French population in 1871, it would be 55 per cent greater in 1914.

POPULATION IN MILLIONS, 1851-1951

	BRITAIN w/out Ireland	GERMANY	FRANCE	ITALY	RUSSIA w/out Asia
1851	22.6	35.9	35.7	25	57.2
1901	38.7	56.3	38.9	32.4	103.4
1951	50.6	68	42	46.5	150

And, while there were more Germans, they were also younger, hence more active and more readily available for productive work or military service. By the eve of the First World War persons over sixty numbered 126 per 1,000 in France, only 78 per 1,000 in Germany. By 1940 the same age group accounted for 127 Germans in every 1,000, but for 135 English and 150 French per 1,000.

War in Crimea

At any rate, before the unification of Germany, France continued to be the most populous advanced country in Europe, and its policy, in the hands of the great Napoleon's nephew, Louis Napoleon (1848–1870), was dedicated to undoing the verdicts of 1815: reaffirming French supremacy, furthering the national aspirations which the victors of 1815 had scotched, dividing the Holy Alliance which Russian intervention in 1849 had reasserted. The first opportunity to carry out these intentions came when Russian ambitions in the Black Sea area began to alarm both Austria—fearful of her rival's expansion in the Balkans—and Britain, concerned for the security of India and its Middle Eastern approaches. Ottoman attempts to reform their ramshackle empire disturbed both their Christian subjects and Russian hopes for an early Ottoman collapse. In 1853, a Russian ultimatum demanded a watching brief over the interests of all non-Latin Christians in the Sultan's lands. When this was refused, Russian troops occupied Moldavia and Walachia, and the Russian navy moved toward the Bosphorus, destroying a Turkish fleet and convincing Britain that only intervention could keep Russia out of Constantinople. The clash of two obscurantist empires became a struggle between the interests of Western liberalism and the autocratic imperialism of the Tsar. "In this instance," noted Karl Marx, "the interest of revolutionary democracy and England go hand in hand." Indeed, only a few years after 1848 and 1849, many who cared little for the balance of power which Russian actions threatened, looked on the Tsar as a tyrant, and on his power as the chief obstacle to European freedom.

Thus, when war broke out in 1854, Russia was isolated. While Britain and France sought to put their naval power to use by besieging Sebastopol in the Crimea, Russia's main naval base in the Black Sea,

Interior of fortress guarding Sebastopol after evacuation by Russians.

Austria—but recently saved by tsarist intervention in Hungary—maintained a hostile neutrality. Piedmont, eager to curry Franco-British
favor, provided an expeditionary corps in 1855. Only Prussia showed
sympathy for a neighbor whose friendship she might someday need. For
two years the Crimean War dragged on: messy, costly, and largely inconclusive in a military sense. Short of equipment, supplies, and food;
led by brave, squabbling, incompetent generals; the troops on all sides
suffered incredibly from cold, dysentery, cholera, and typhus. Characteristically, what we remember of the Crimean War are the charge of
the Light Brigade—a body of British cavalry sent by a series of mistakes
to attack impregnable Russian guns and destroyed in the process; and
the work of the British nurse, Florence Nightingale, to ease the lot of the
sick and wounded. Over 10 per cent of the French troops, over one-third
of the British, perhaps half a million Russians, died—far more from sickness than in battle.

All sides were glad to conclude peace in 1856 after Sebastopol had fallen. The treaty signed in Paris in that year gave the Ottomans a respite
from Russian pressure, transferred Bessarabia from Russia to Moldavia,
replaced the Romanian principalities under Turkish suzerainty and
neutralized the Black Sea: a humiliation Russia cast off in 1871. The great
loser of the war would be Austria. The house that Metternich had built
had finally collapsed. The failure of the Austro-Russian entente born
in Napoleon's time opened the way to the advance of Prussia, which
could take place only at Habsburg expense. It also opened the way to
Italian unification, likewise achievable only against Vienna's interest.

The Habsburgs Humbled

With Russia eliminated for a generation, Austria weakened by Russian
hostility, Britain more interested in peace and overseas affairs, Napoleon

III seemed to become the arbiter of Europe. The Treaty of Paris had been signed with a quill torn from an eagle in the Tuileries Gardens. For the next decade he would use his power to implement the nationalist ideas of his youth, when he had dreamed of "tyranny dethroned" and nations free at last to give themselves the institutions they desired.

Under the impulse of their ambitious premier, Camillo Cavour (1810–1861), the Piedmontese had joined in the Crimean War chiefly to assert their existence and their future claims to Anglo-French support. They would be the first to benefit from Napoleon's tendency to enlist his good intentions to the greater glory of France. In the summer of 1858 Cavour and the French emperor met at Plombières, a spa in eastern France, and there agreed how to provoke a war with Austria which would advance the course of Italian unity. It was, however, less the plot hatched by the two conspirators than Austrian blunders in threatening Piedmont that led to the outbreak of the war they wanted in April, 1859.

The Austrians' timid generalship led to their defeat in a series of engagements—greatest among them the battles of Magenta and Solferino, both fought in June—and their total loss of Lombardy. Soon after this, Napoleon III, appalled by the carnage of the battles he had witnessed, entered into secret negotiations with the Austrians, concluding in the Armistice of Villafranca (July, 1859), prologue of a compromise peace that threatened to cheat Cavour of the gains he banked on. Yet, Villafranca proved unenforceable and Austrian defeat permitted the Piedmontese to annex not only Lombardy but other states that had risen to the call of national liberation: Tuscany, Parma, Modena, and Emilia.

In the end, neither Cavour nor Napoleon got quite what he had hoped for. The former was disappointed of Venice, left in Austrian hands. The latter had not expected his Italian enterprise to snowball as it did when, in 1860, spurred by Garibaldi's expedition, the double annexation of Naples and the papal states created a Kingdom of Italy up to the gates of Rome. He consoled himself with Savoy and Nice, which Piedmont ceded to France in exchange for her support of Cavour's enterprises.

French diplomacy also promoted the Romanian cause. In 1856, the Peace of Paris had stripped Russia of the right to interfere in the Danubian principalities, and returned these to the Ottoman realm with a promise of "independent and national administration" within it. Before three years had passed, Napoleon's support enabled Moldavia and Walachia to unite under a common ruler. By 1862 the two principalities had merged into a new political entity: Romania. By 1866 they had acquired a prince of the house of Hohenzollern: Carol I, who brought them independence in 1877 and the consecration of a royal crown in 1881.

Napoleon had humbled the Habsburgs; he had advanced the interests of the Prussian Hohenzollerns, Vienna's traditional opponents, generally regarded as representatives of nationalism and progress in Germany. He would have liked to aid the Poles when they rose against their Russian masters in 1863, but neither Britain nor Prussia would co-operate. The British saw no reason to advance French power which had become too great already; the Prussians—aware of their own Polish subjects—were sympathetic to the Russians. In any case, they had better fish to fry: German national aspirations were expressed in 1864 at the expense of the Danes. Austrian and Prussian troops campaigned together to wrest the Duchies of Schleswig and Holstein from the Danish crown and Napoleon, peeved by British coolness over Poland, refused in turn to support their gestures on the Danes' behalf.

But Prussian ambitions went far beyond limited enterprises. Since 1862 Prussia's first minister had been Otto von Bismarck, a Prussian patriot and brilliant opportunist. Differences over the newly occupied duchies furnished the pretext for a break with Austria, skillful diplomacy afforded the opportunity to challenge her on favorable terms. Napoleon was sympathetic, so were the Russians. An alliance with Italy which was promised Venetia forced a split in Austria's forces; and English sympathies for Italy ensured Britain's benevolent neutrality. Above all, the Prussian army and the Prussian railroads brought swift victory. Helmuth von Moltke (1800–1891), Chief of the General Staff, who had already distinguished himself in the war against the Danes, used his country's new railroad network to concentrate his troops against the lumbering, ill-equipped, Austrians. In July, 1866, the battle of Sadowa (Königgrätz) in Bohemia foreshadowed the shape of the century to come, altering not only the map of Europe but its balance of power. After Sadowa, Austria was excluded from Germany. Prussia, her own territories vastly increased, forced most of her partners of the Zollverein into political federation too.

Prussia now dominated a North German confederation whose resources in man- and industrial-power matched those of France. The achievement of complete unity, by incorporating those German states like Bavaria which still maintained their independence, was only a matter of time. It was precipitated by Napoleon III's desperate attempt to rescue something from the ruins of his policy. He could not stand by while a dangerous rival rose without trying to obtain some gain that would serve French interests or at least salve their pride. Belgium, Luxembourg, the Rhineland, were all considered as possible consolation prizes. But Bismarck refused to co-operate, and other European powers were indifferent or hostile. French diplomacy sought allies, but Austria was suspicious and undecided; the Italian friendship foundered on the rock of Rome, which Catholic opinion obliged Napoleon to defend for the Pope against the Italian will to regain the nation's obvious capital. "Rather the Prussians in Paris than the Italians in Rome," declared Empress Eugénie, ignoring that the one would open the way to the others.

Franco-German tension grew, both sides increasingly persuaded that a showdown was inevitable. It came in 1870, when the Spaniards, desperately seeking a candidate for the throne from which they had removed a queen, persuaded a Hohenzollern prince (brother of the one ruling in Romania) to accept it. It came, too, during the summertime, when all who could were taking waters at some fashionable spa. The permanent secretary of the British Foreign Office had just remarked that he had never known such a lull in foreign affairs. The French prime minister, speaking in the Chamber, found that the peace of Europe had never been so stable. Then, the news of a Hohenzollern prince about to become king of Spain revived the Habsburg situation of long ago, the possibility of a two-front war for France, the certainty of a new diplomatic humiliation. Tempers boiled and did not simmer down even when the Hohenzollern renounced his candidacy.

Paris might have remained content with a diplomatic success. The war party, encouraged by Empress Eugénie, sought more. The king of Prussia, head of the Hohenzollern clan, must make amends to salve French tempers. Approached by the French Ambassador while holidaying at Ems and asked for an assurance that the Hohenzollern candidature would never be renewed, the old gentleman refused to entertain the suggestion. The cable he sent to Bismarck, with an account of his courteous refusal to discuss the matter further, was edited by his chancellor in such a way as to turn the defeat of Bismarck's policy into a snub inflicted on the French. Broadcast in the Prussian press, then in the French, sensationalized, exaggerated, the Ems telegram inflamed tempers in both countries to the point where all reason was abandoned. Belligerent Paris mobs abetted by a belligerent Chamber carried France to the war Bismarck later claimed he had always wanted in order to realize "the construction of a united Germany."

The Franco-Prussian War

In 1854 already, British public opinion had driven a divided government into hostilities with Russia "in defence of the right," and welcomed with Tennyson "the blood-red blossom of war with a heart of fire." Now, French public opinion—or what passed for it—would do the same for France, and with direr results. And so the French, the Spanish issue determined in their favor, nevertheless went to war with Prussia (July, 1870)—went to war and lost.

The first result of war declared was that the states of southern Germany, long suspicious of Prussian aggrandizement, joined their fellow Germans against the aggressive French. The next was that the superiority of Prussian staff work under Moltke's direction, and the greater efficiency of Prussian mobilization, railroads, and supply system, enabled them to concentrate long before French reservists could rejoin their units.

Outnumbered by nearly two to one on the battleground, outgeneraled, outfought, the French were pressed back in Lorraine, their main armies divided, their chief force under Marshal MacMahon surrounded at Sedan near the Belgian border, and shelled into surrender.

Within seven weeks of the declaration of war, the Emperor—who had accompanied MacMahon—was a captive in German hands (September 2), the Empire was no more (September 4). Another three weeks and Paris was besieged, to starve throughout the winter until an armistice (January, 1871) opened talks of peace. In May, 1871, the Treaty of Frankfurt showed that French supremacy in Europe was at an end. The French would pay a war indemnity calculated to match that which Napoleon had imposed on Prussia in 1807, and German troops would occupy eastern France until the indemnity had been paid. More important, France lost Alsace and much of the neighboring province of Lorraine to the new German Empire which had been proclaimed during the siege of Paris in the Hall of Mirrors at Versailles. The war had achieved the unity of Germany, north and south. It had been the king of Bavaria who, at Bismarck's urging* had hailed William I of Prussia as first emperor of the new German Reich.

A German Empire then; and a French Republic—third of the name— confirmed the great reversal begun in 1866. The greatest significance of the war, however, lay in the issue of Alsace-Lorraine which it raised between Germany and France and which, in Woodrow Wilson's judgment, "unsettled the peace of the world for fifty years." The defeat of the second empire need not have sowed lasting hostility between Germany and the French Republic. Loss of national territory was bound to turn occasional conflict into historical enmity, persuade both countries that the other was its "secular" foe, and create the preconditions for further conflict. Bismarck probably felt that Alsace-Lorraine would be the cement of German unity. For the present, he was not far wrong, but in the long run he built on quicksand.

Bismarck's Europe

Within a ridiculously short space of time and through three swift, successful wars, Bismarck's dream had been achieved and Germany, now Prussia's Empire, rose over Europe, a mass over 40 million strong. The problem now, as Bismarck saw it, was to stabilize the situation. Germany was sated and wanted no further change. Henceforth, Bismarck's great abilities were bent on preventing change in Europe, for any major conflict could result in a modification of Germany's favorable situation. His first concern was the isolation of France, so that the new republic could not pursue her plans of revenge. His second, rising out of this, would

* And his promises of Prussian subsidies for the Bavarian's vast artistic and architectural projects in and around Munich.

be to keep Russia and Austria from clashing over the Balkan spoils of
decaying Turkey. The danger of this happening was stressed in the mid-
seventies when a Bosnian rebellion against the Turks was followed by
the intervention of Serbia and Montenegro and then in 1877 by that of
Romania and the Russians. Hard fighting in Bulgaria and the trans-
Caucasus ended in Russian victory by 1878. But the treaty which the
victors imposed on Turkey suited neither Austria nor Britain, and a new
settlement had to be negotiated at Berlin while Bismarck acted as ar-
bitrator between the contending parties. Russia recovered Bessarabia;
Serbia, Montenegro, and Romania were recognized as independent kingdoms; Bulgaria—considered too much under Russia's thumb—remained a
vassal principality of the Turks.* Last but not least, great power balance
was maintained when Austrian troops received the right to occupy Bosnia and Herzegovina, where the revolt had started three years before.

There is no good reason why so much fuss was made over the Balkans,
except that the area provided the last debatable land in Europe. Bismarck, who held that they weren't worth the sacrifice of even one Prussian
grenadier, had the right idea; but he could not persuade the Austrian soldiers or the foreign investors or the international meddlers to keep out
of the thieves' kitchen. Neither Balkan wars nor Turkish collapse need
have proved an international tragedy if the powers could have divided
their loot amiably as they had done with Poland, instead of grudging
everyone else's gains except their own. There was nothing wrong, there
was nothing new, about international anarchy until it became rigid. Bismarck's purpose was to keep it fluid. Lord Salisbury described Bismarck's
diplomacy as "employing his neighbors to pull out each other's teeth." It
would seem rather as if he bent his energies on persuading them to
sheath their claws or at least, if not, to use their teeth and claws on lesser
antagonists whose straits would not precipitate a European war.

The base of his diplomacy would be the Austrian alliance. Once they
had been excluded from Germany, it was in Prussia's interest to keep
the Habsburgs friendly and to moderate Balkan ambitions which their
defeat in Germany was bound to spur but which, if pressed too far,
risked upsetting the uneasy balance. To do this, Bismarck calculated,
he would make Vienna feel secure by German guarantees of her existence. In 1879, the Dual Alliance assured the Habsburgs of German support in case of a Russian attack. The treaty, concluded for five years but
regularly renewed until both partners' collapse in 1918, became the keystone of German diplomacy. Yet Russian friendship had to be maintained. So Bismarck encouraged Russia to turn eastward, where her ambitions would not challenge those of Austria and where, furthermore,
her expansionist policies would make Britain uneasy, thus hopefully
moving that power to rely increasingly on German support. Italy, too,

---

* The southern part would only join the north in 1886. The country became an
independent kingdom in 1908.

had to be prevented from disturbing Austria. This was done by encouraging her to join the Austro-German camp in what became the Triple Alliance of 1882, and to spend her energy in Africa where she would clash with France. France, lastly, must have her eyes diverted from Alsace-Lorraine. She was encouraged to seek compensation overseas, where, in her turn, she clashed with Britain and with Italy, powers which otherwise might be too amical toward her.

All this worked well enough while Bismarck, at the helm of the state, steered it through the shoals of trouble. By 1890, when a young emperor, William II, decided to "drop the pilot," it was beginning to fail, less under political than under economic pressures. The free trade policies which much of western Europe had adopted during the prosperous sixties succumbed to criticism from sectional interests when times got worse in the mid-seventies. Developing industries demanded protection; so did the farmers threatened by a flood of grain from Russia and the New World. In the United States alone 400 million acres were brought under cultivation between 1860 and 1900. Yet it was not so much new lands being put to plow, as the new railroads, which, in the United States were tapping the wheat fields of the Great Plains and in Russia bringing grain to the Black Sea and Baltic ports. Their effect had been delayed first by the Crimean War interrupting Russian trade during the fifties, then by the American Civil War interfering with United States exports in the sixties. But then, in the seventies and eighties, reduced transport costs more than halved the price of grain shipped to European ports. As a result, tariffs began to rise in the United States and Russia, Germany and France. Between 1879 and 1893 every Western country except Britain, Holland, and Belgium built ever higher walls around itself. With tariffs there went friction, and one such issue hammered in the wedge between Russia and Germany, the latter's agricultural producers doing all they could to keep out cheap grain from Russia's Polish and Ukrainian wheat fields.

Economic differences between Germany and Russia were compounded by renewed friction over Russia's Balkan activities. In 1886 and 1887 Bulgaria provided the occasion of new strains which almost led to war. They were resolved, but in the process, as part of German pressure on St. Petersburg, Russian bonds had been excluded from the Berlin stock market. Russia could not develop her resources or maintain great power status without capital. Hard put for this and unlikely to get what she wanted in hostile London, she turned to France, which had money to lend and every interest in lending it if, by doing so, she could detach Russia from her German friendship. Within a few years (1891–1894), the two countries were allies, though odd ones for the Russians remained friendly to Germany and hostile chiefly to Austria and Turkey, while the French (holding most of the Turkish state debt) were cool to Russia's Balkan plans and hostile to Germany. Russia and France

Bismarck.

could agree only on common enmity to England, whose overseas enterprises clashed with the ambitions entertained in Paris and Moscow, and this posed no threat to German interests as yet.

Yet Bismarck's ingenious structure was not at the end of its troubles. For, encouraged by hints from Berlin, the French had been pressing forward in Africa, where Franco-British rivalry in a dozen places climaxed at Fashoda in 1898, when a British army pushing up the Nile met a small French mission installed there after a year-long 3,000-mile march to claim the upper Nile for France. The soldiers faced one another while the diplomatic crisis spun itself out in Europe. It soon became clear that France could not fight a power which, unassailable in its island, could use her fleet to pick off French colonies one by one. She not only gave in on Fashoda but, drawing the conclusions of her failure, decided that understanding would be more profitable than contest. The outstanding issue between Britain and France was Egypt, which Britain had taken over by default but very much to French chagrin.* France, which held Algeria and Tunis, coveted Morocco. Perhaps the French could concede the British rights to a country that did not belong to them but which they already held, if Britain looked with favor on the idea of France acquiring a country which did not belong to her but that she would like to hold. In 1902, the German ambassador in London reported a long conversation between the French ambassador and a leading British minister of which he overheard two words: "Morocco" and "Egypt." His government reassured him. It was as unlikely that France and Britain would draw together as that Britain and

* Egypt, still formally a Turkish dominion until 1914, gained strategic significance after the opening of the Suez Canal in 1869 gave it control of a crucial route to India and the Far East. Though the Canal had been a French enterprise, Britain acquired a controlling portion of the shares in 1875 and followed this up seven years later with military occupation of the country—a *temporary* measure which ended only in 1956. The Canal and the Middle Eastern base Egypt provided remained the crux of Franco-British rivalry for over a generation following the 1870's.

Russia would resolve their differences. Two years later the *Entente Cordiale* had come into being; three years more and the differences between Britain and Russia had been resolved as well.

Bismarck's successes were coming home to roost. Launched on a course of eastward expansion, the Russians were not doing things by halves: in Persia, in central Asia, in China, Manchuria, and Korea, they pushed forward, threatening British interests in the Middle East, in India, and in the Far East too.

A short story by Rudyard Kipling, written in 1891, features an unpleasant Russian cavalryman visiting a British regiment in India, all of whose officers, like their Russian guest, are convinced that there would soon be an Anglo-Russian war for India.* There is no understanding turn-of-the-century politics without remembering this widely held assumption.

The British became increasingly uncomfortable. They had reveled in their splendid isolation: now they found it lonely and looked for support. The only power that could effectively aid them was Germany. But Germany, as Bismarck said, had no intention of pulling British chestnuts out of the fire. Moreover—staunchly though Bismarck had resisted the notion of colonial expansion—business and shipping interests and above all the impetus and vainglory of national pride, had propelled him into the colonial field as well, and his successors looked upon the British as rivals. They, like the French, had drawn the moral of Fashoda and decided that a colonial empire needed a fleet to protect it—a fleet which could hurt its probable rival badly even if it could not hope to match it. In building such a fleet the Germans posed a serious threat to British security and even more to British pockets; for, faced with the German naval building program, the British had to keep ahead whatever the cost. This did not help the fraying friendship between English and Germans or calm British nerves.

Only one power at the beginning of the twentieth century felt just as threatened by Russia's advance as Britain, and this was an unknown quantity, risen out of limbo to dubious prominence: Japan. Japan, too, looked for support in Berlin against Russia, and failed to get it. In 1902 Britain and Japan gambled on each other's support. Clearly, the treaty they signed that year was directed against Russia; but there was danger that Russia's ally—France—might be dragged in somehow. And it was partly to forestall this eventuality that the Franco-British *Entente* of 1904 was concluded at the time when Japan, her flank secured, set about liquidating the Russian danger. A sudden night attack sank a good

---

* The opening of Kipling's tale is particularly interesting: "Let it be clearly understood that the Russian is a delightful person till he tucks in his shirt. As an Oriental, he is charming. It is only when he insists upon being treated as the most easterly of western peoples instead of the most westerly of easterns, that he becomes a racial anomaly, extremely difficult to handle. . . ."

Theodore Roosevelt at Portsmouth
with (*left to right*) Witte, Rosen,
Komura, and Takahira.

part of the Russian Far East fleet moored in Port Arthur, a sudden
land invasion rolled the Russian armies back through Manchuria, and the
heavy fighting that dragged through 1904 and 1905 only confirmed these
first defeats. By 1905 a Russian relief fleet had been annihilated in its
turn, and the naval fortress at Port Arthur forced to surrender. The
peace, eventually signed in 1906 at Portsmouth, New Hampshire, under
the aegis of President Theodore Roosevelt, settled Russian evacuation of
Manchuria, transferred Russian leases of Chinese territory (especially
Port Arthur) to Japan, and determined Japanese preponderance in Korea.
Russia would advance no farther in the Far East, where the sun of a
new power was arising. Soon, Russian diplomatic interests swung back
to their other pole: the Balkans. Not before, however, they had settled
their differences with England in an agreement of 1907 which focused
on Persia but intimated more. After 1907 the Triple Alliance faced a
Triple Entente joining France, Russia, and Britain.

Triple Alliance and Triple Entente

Yet both these groupings were exceedingly fragile. England's chief concern was to keep out of war. France's rival was Germany: she had no
quarrel with Austria. Russia's rival was Austria: she had no quarrel
with Germany. Germany felt threatened by France and made Britain
feel threatened. Austria's interests lay southeastward. As for Italian
interests, they lay in Austria; and, indeed, Italy detached herself progressively from her allies, once she had resolved her conflicts with France
by an agreement in which the French recognized Italian interests in
Libya (then a Turkish possession) in return for Italian recognition
of French interests in Morocco (then a more or less independent state).

Africa and the Balkans would be the two weak points of European
peace, the focus of the long series of prewar crises whose cumulation

built up a situation in which the outbreak of war came to be taken for granted and only its occasion remained in question. While the powers jockeyed for place, international tensions magnified the growing sense of insecurity that marked the opening years of our century—an insecurity even stronger on the social and intellectual than on the military plane—turning people toward symbols of stability and lasting order: armies, navies, flags, and discipline. The multicolored elegance of uniforms at a time when gold braid, plumed helmets, and garb of every hue and shade were still the norm delighted the crowd. So did military tattoos and torchlight processions reinstituted shortly before the war to catch civilian fancy. So did the massive self-confidence of officer corps in which many could see the last surviving instance of traditional authority.

But there was more to armies than braid and pretty fancies. After 1866 and 1870, conscription, universal military service, militarized Europe from Belgium to the Balkans. War was seen to depend as much on transport as on armaments, especially on railroad networks able to move troops and matériel swiftly from one point to another. Strategic railways added a costly burden to national budgets, and one which does not usually appear in armaments statistics. But modern war was also waged with modern weapons, their range ten times greater under Napoleon III than in his uncle's day, forty times greater in 1900 than in 1800, vastly more deadly and vastly more efficient. When the American Civil War broke out, Colt had given mankind his repeater revolver. Soon Doctor Gatling produced his "labor-saving device for warfare," capable of firing first two hundred then twelve hundred rounds a minute. By 1889 the modern machine gun was perfected, capable of incredibly murderous rates of fire. But these and other martial splendors involved crippling costs, the higher because modern war materials have a rapid rate of obsolescence. Between 1875 and 1914 armament expenses doubled in France, tripled in Germany and Britain. One-third of Russia's budget went into armaments. In France, 1.5 billion was allotted to the army and navy compared to 330 millions for educational purposes. Every shell of a battleship cost the yearly salary of a public employee. This at a time when, unlike any previous period, the state had also to face the costs of burgeoning public education, social security, and social welfare.

For the age of mass production replaced highly trained professional soldiers by mass armies which were like the mass products of industry—cheaper and more numerous but, like machine-made goods, not quite the same as in professional days. Mass armies meant educational and medical services for the masses that would serve in them, to make them fitter, more literate, more technically efficient and also more uniform. If all members of the population were subject to conscription it mattered that they should be fit, that they should be loyal, that they should speak and understand one and the same language. This played a major role in the social revolution of our time. But, having so to speak nationalized the masses, the politicians found they had to count with them, heed the resentments, the prejudices, and antagonisms which they had helped create by education and by propaganda. Doctor Frankenstein had made public opinion and public opinion henceforth was a monster to take into account.

Public opinion fed on crises and was exacerbated by them. There was a host of minor incidents, border troubles, and flare-ups which heightened tension, filled the air with threats and counterthreats, sharpened the sense of insecurity and mutual suspicion. The British had given the French a free hand in Morocco in return for French recognition of their position in Egypt. Now, as France edged forward, the Germans also sought a *quid pro quo*. Their heavy-handed methods created serious crises in 1905 (Tangier) and 1911 (Agadir), gained them little, but persuaded the French that Germany was bent on war. She was not: she was only clumsy. Balkan affairs would show that she was not alone in this respect.

In the Balkans, the national aspirations of small newborn states threatened what was left of Turkey's realm in Europe. They also endangered the multinational empire of the Habsburgs. In 1908, the imprudent schemes of a Russian foreign minister with an eye on Constantinople failed, but enabled Austria to annex the provinces of Bosnia and Herzegovina which Austrian troops had occupied since 1878. This proved a serious setback to Russian prestige; one whose repetition St. Petersburg would not permit. But Serbia, remembering the increase that wise alliances and fortunate campaigns had brought Piedmont, still dreamed of a great South Slav kingdom; and her ambitions cast a shadow over the newly annexed provinces, and over Croatia too. The stronger Serbia became, the greater her attraction for the Slav subjects of Austrians and Magyars. In 1912 and 1913 this danger grew acute, through a conjunction of African and Balkan issues.

The French, determined to secure North Africa from Tunis to the Atlantic, had promised compensation not only to the British, but to the Italians too. As usual, it was to be carved out of somebody else's territories: in this case, those of the Ottomans. When, in 1911, France openly declared her protectorate over Morocco, Italy was free to raise her claims: Italian troops attacked the Turks in Libya and occupied Tripoli. The Turks resisted with determination and the fighting drew out. Meanwhile, Turkish problems provided a chance which the Balkan Christians were quick to seize. They had several times—but unsuccessfully—tried to defeat the Ottomans and deliver those Orthodox Christians still remaining under Turkish rule. In 1912—with the main Ottoman forces fighting the Italians—Serbia, Bulgaria, Greece, and Montenegro attacked and defeated their old Muslim masters. But their troubles were only just beginning. Bulgaria also saw visions of a great South Slav kingdom, only led by her; and in this she was encouraged

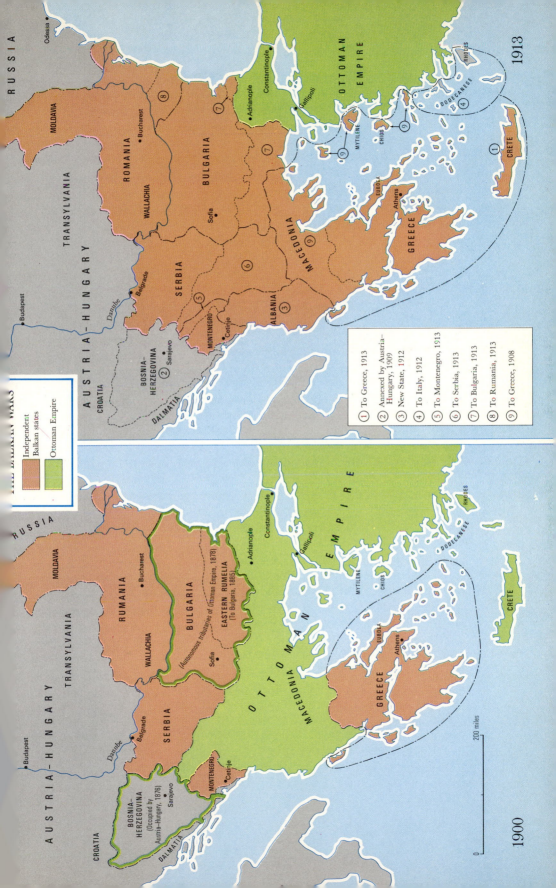

THE BALKAN WARS

Legend
- Independent Balkan states
- Ottoman Empire

① To Greece, 1913
② Annexed by Austria–Hungary, 1909
③ New State, 1912
④ To Italy, 1912
⑤ To Montenegro, 1913
⑥ To Serbia, 1913
⑦ To Bulgaria, 1913
⑧ To Rumania, 1913
⑨ To Greece, 1908

Map 1913

RUSSIA
Odessa
MOLDAVIA
• Bucharest
ROMANIA
TRANSYLVANIA
WALLACHIA
BULGARIA
• Sofia
AUSTRIA–HUNGARY
• Budapest
Danube
SERBIA
• Belgrade
MONTENEGRO
• Cetinje
BOSNIA–HERZEGOVINA
Sarajevo
CROATIA
DALMATIA
ALBANIA
MACEDONIA
• Adrianople
Constantinople
Gallipoli
OTTOMAN EMPIRE
RHODES
DODECANESE
MYTILENE
CHIOS
EUBOEA
Athens •
GREECE
CRETE
1913

Map 1900

RUSSIA
MOLDAVIA
• Bucharest
RUMANIA
TRANSYLVANIA
WALLACHIA
BULGARIA
• Sofia
EASTERN RUMELIA
(Autonomous tributaries of Ottoman Empire, 1878)
(To Bulgaria, 1885)
AUSTRIA–HUNGARY
• Budapest
Danube
SERBIA
• Belgrade
MONTENEGRO
• Cetinje
BOSNIA–HERZEGOVINA
(Occupied by Austria–Hungary, 1878)
Sarajevo
CROATIA
DALMATIA
MACEDONIA
• Adrianople
Constantinople
Gallipoli
O T T O M A N   E M P I R E
RHODES
DODECANESE
MYTILENE
CHIOS
EUBOEA
Athens •
GREECE
CRETE
0   200 miles
1900

by the Austrians who wished to balance the growing influence of Belgrade. By 1913, the victors had fallen out over the spoils. Serbs, Greeks, and Montenegrins, joined by Romania, fell upon the Bulgarians whose ambitions threatened all of them. Thus, by the end of 1913, not just the Turks but the Bulgarians also, became the losers of the Second Balkan War. And these remote conflicts involved great interests: for Serbia's victory redounded to the prestige of her patron, Russia, and increased the insecurity felt in Vienna.

There, some politicians and many soldiers were becoming persuaded that the national agitation and the anti-Habsburg conspiracies which grew in intensity with the excitement of the Balkan Wars were a serious danger to the security of the monarchy. They could only be suppressed by suppressing Serbia and turning her into a province or a satellite of the Habsburg empire. Such an undertaking must mean war. And an Austrian attack on Serbia would not take place in a vacuum. The Russians could not stand by and see their Slav brethren beaten down. If they intervened to defend them, they would set in motion the machinery of rival alliances, with Germany bound to aid Austria and France Russia. Yet—whatever speculations might be pursued in Vienna—Austria was in no position to start a major war. For one thing, the Magyars had no wish to incorporate still more Slavs into a realm where they were already too numerous for their taste. Budapest opposed a warlike policy. More important, the Germans held their Austrian allies on a leash, and only when they slipped it did war become a threat.

In any case, Austro-Serbian friction was only one of many conflicts that diplomacy and compromise had settled in the past. Why should they fail this time? As it turned out, it seems that war came when enough men believed that it would come and, most particularly, when certain men in Germany became convinced that the sooner it came the better.

Discussions of the war of 1914 and of the lesser conflicts that preceded it have tended to attribute them to imperial rivalries and economic interests. But the first never led to full-scale conflict between European powers (which preferred weaker prey), and the second operated on the whole *against* a settlement by arms (peace is more profitable than war). True, wars raise prices, create profitable scarcities, make fortunes for brokers negotiating loans and manufacturers selling supplies. But economic arguments against war went deeper. Russia was Germany's greatest source of supplies, Britain was Germany's best customer. The French were more interested in trade with Austria than in fighting her. British financial circles were strongly opposed to any intervention in continental conflicts. War increased taxes for the rich and took the peasants' sons for military service, it disrupted business, it hurt government credit, it strengthened the military whom the workers detested and the middle class distrusted. The arguments for war, therefore,

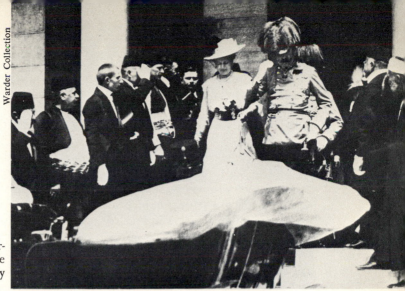

Archduke Francis Ferdinand and his wife shortly before they were assassinated.

found more solid ground in sentiments of national pride, concern for the safety of the nation's soil, love of excitement and of sensation, even calculations that defeat might open the gates of revolution. All these were reinforced by recurrent crises, by the mounting uncertainty that hurt trade and fretted tempers, by a growing feeling that, if there was to be war, it had better come and be done with.

But arguments and even feelings do not make war or unmake it. Men decide, who have the power to decide and the means to act. When, in June, 1914, Archduke Francis Ferdinand—heir of the old Emperor Francis Joseph—and his wife were clumsily murdered in Bosnian Sarajevo and Austrian resentments against Belgrade where the murder had been prepared welled into bitter hatred, there was nothing that made war inevitable except the will of those who wanted it to take place. These men now sat in Vienna and Berlin.

The constant threat that Serbia's existence and ambitions posed to the fissile Empire seemed to have materialized at Sarajevo. Vienna was determined that the Serbs should be brought to heel, their challenge eliminated once and for all. Encouragement came from the leaders of the German General Staff and from the Kaiser himself. The Austrians felt their position getting ever weaker as nationalism threatened the monarchy with disintegration. The Germans felt at the peak of military preparedness. In a few years their competitors might gain on them or even, if Russia ever marshaled its latent strength, overtake them. But soldiers, in those days, did not decide on wars; they only fought them. The trouble was that Germany lacked other effective institutions with power to decide. The German people spoke with many contradictory voices: it had a representative assembly—the Reichstag—but the assembly had neither authority nor effective powers. Since 1890, the Chancellor had been a creature of the Emperor; since 1908, when he had disgraced himself in an interview to an English paper, the Emperor had lost much of his own political authority. Hence crucial decisions were made by action rather than deliberation; gestures and intrigues committed the German Empire to its course, and the actors found themselves in charge by default, writing their script as they went along.

The Germans promised to back Austria to the hilt against the Serbs. The Austrians sent the Serbs an impossible ultimatum which the Serbs all but accepted to everyone's surprise. The Austrians, set on war, seized on one slight demur to declare it. The Russians, unable to stand by and see their protégés destroyed, mobilized against Austria, were told that this would bring Germany into war against them on Austria's side, and nevertheless went on. The Germans set their own war plans in motion. The French, who still hoped they might escape a war, had to be forced to fight; for German war plans envisaged a two-front war beginning with a knockout blow at France, after which the giant in the east could be dispatched at leisure. The essence of the plan was an attack on France, passing through (neutral) Belgium. This was one act England would not condone. Her ultimatum, demanding German evacuation of Belgian territory, referring to the little kingdom's neutrality guaranteed by Germany since 1839, exasperated the German chancellor: "Just for a scrap of paper, Great Britain is going to make war upon a kindred nation," he remarked bitterly to the British Ambassador. So, having hesitated to help France, Britain came in to help itself by helping Belgium. And in London, while crowds cheered around Buckingham Palace, the Foreign Secretary, Sir Edward Grey, looking out of a window at the gas lights being lit in the street below, remarked to a friend: "The lamps are going out all over Europe; we shall not see them lit again in our lifetime."

By August 4, 1914, a great part of Europe had gone to war. One thing which had played little part in it was the alliance structure. The Austro-German Alliance, designed to hold Austria in check, had actually dragged Berlin into a Balkan quarrel, not so much by the workings of the treaty as by the unconsidered gestures of Berlin. Russia had no obligation to intervene on Serbia's side, France hoped to escape her obligation to join Russia, England felt no obligation at all to fight for Serbia,* and, as for Italy, the Triple Alliance bothered her not at all.

Thus all the participants joined in with a perfectly good conscience, each able to tell himself he had never wanted war. Both Austria and Serbia believed that they were fighting for survival; the Russians believed that honor and Slav solidarity commanded their intervention on Serbia's behalf, which only German meddling had turned into gen-

---

* Just before war broke out London's *Punch* commented:
> Well, if I must, I shall have to fight
> For the love of a bounding Balkanite;
> But O what a tactless choice of time,
> When the bathing season is at its prime!
> And how I should hate to miss my chance
> Of wallowing off the coast of France!

EUROPE ON THE EVE OF WORLD WAR I

Nations of the Triple Entente   Nations of the Triple Alliance

St. Petersburg

Moscow

R U S S I A

B A L T I C   S E A

Stockholm

Copenhagen

Brest–Litovsk

Warsaw

Vistula

Oder

Tisa

Jassy

ROMANIA

B L A C K   S E A

Constantinople

O T T O M A N   E M P I R E

Smyrna

(Italian)

Bucharest

Danube

BULGARIA

Sofia

SERBIA

Belgrade

Sarajevo

MONTENEGRO

ALBANIA

GREECE

Athens

A E G E A N   S E A

NORWAY

N O R T H   S E A

DENMARK

Hamburg

Berlin

Elbe

G E R M A N Y

Weser

Prague

Danube

Munich

A U S T R I A – H U N G A R Y

Budapest

Vienna

Drave

Save

A D R I A T I C   S E A

I T A L Y

Rome

Po

SICILY

M E D I T E R R A N E A N   S E A

Rhine

NETHERLANDS

Amsterdam

Brussels

BELGIUM

LUX.

SWITZ.

CORSICA

SARDINIA

TUNIS

TUNISIA (Fr.)

A T L A N T I C   O C E A N

G R E A T   B R I T A I N

Aberdeen

Manchester

London

IRELAND

Dublin

F R A N C E

Seine

Paris

Versailles

Geneva

Rhone

Marseilles

Loire

Bordeaux

Barcelona

Ebro

S P A I N

Madrid

ALGERIA (Fr.)

Algiers

Gibraltar

ER RIF (Span.)

MOROCCO (Fr.)

Tagus

PORTUGAL

Lisbon

500 miles

eral war. The Germans, sharply aware of the hostility their clumsy aggressiveness had itself created, feared encirclement and the isolation that an Austrian defeat would bring. The French felt they had been forced to fight and fought in a good cause, for national integrity and for Alsace-Lorraine. The British, whatever triggered their intervention, followed a secular policy: "We have always fought for the balance of power," wrote the *Times* of August 4. "We are fighting for it today."

War 1914–1918

Between 1871 and 1914 there had been no national wars in Europe outside the restricted cockpit of the Balkans. For over forty years the West had enjoyed peace and growing prosperity, a period of time to which the twentieth century would wistfully look back and which it would invest with all the charms of a lost golden age. How true this was for people living then we shall see in later chapters. Yet peace itself, undoubtedly maintained, was shaken constantly by crises which never allowed fears of war to fade. Peace did not mean peacefulness, and those who grew up in the last third of the nineteenth century never felt that war was far away. Then, with the new century, tensions increased. Crisis followed crisis, inuring public opinion to the thought of war, sharpening national tempers and the expectation of an inevitable clash. Many young men, ignorant of warfare, longed for its thrills and glories. Many older men saw in it an opportunity for fulfillment or revenge. The social and political conflicts, sharpened by the rise of workers' parties or by nationalist claims, were setting nerves on edge and suggesting to some that the consensus which a war could bring would solve insoluble problems, to others that war might accelerate the fulfillment of their revolutionary hopes.

The outbreak of war pricked the growing tensions and brought relief from political and social struggles. All could express themselves now, if only briefly, by turning their hostilities against external foes. The German chancellor rejoiced about "this wonderful spirit, which welds the hearts of the German people into an unprecedented unity . . . As if by magic, the barriers have fallen which . . . separated the sectors of the people from each other . . . It is a liberation and a blessing that at last all this trash has been swept away, that only the individual person counts, one equal to the other, one stretching his hand to the other for a single, holy goal." This temper would pass, but the memory of it survived: the memory of exaltation, of fraternity, and of what could be done with people in such a mood.

Indeed, for a good many men—especially those employed in offices and shops, in dead-end, unexciting jobs—the war must have appeared as a relief from a pointless round, a holiday from routine, a doorway to excitement and usefulness. Military service can bring not only release from responsibility, but a sense of purpose which the whole apparatus of organized opinion labors to maintain. All this imparted an extraordinary glow to the war's beginning, an enthusiasm soon lost, forgotten, as Europe floundered forward in its blood but which is worth remembering as part of the explanation of many modern wars.

Young Frenchmen in red trousers and blue coats attacked in close formation behind their white-gloved officers with drawn swords and fluttering plumes and banners. Germans went forward with military bands playing immediately behind the fighting troops. All fell like flies. "I adore war" wrote Julian Grenfell to the *Times*. "I have never been so well and so happy . . . the fighting excitement vitalizes everything . . ." "It is all a terrible tragedy," Rupert Brooke, the poet, wrote home, "and yet in its details it is great fun. And—apart from the tragedy— I've never felt happier or better." The tragedy itself could be transcended: a twenty-six-year-old lieutenant wrote to his parents about what he called the happiest moment of his life, under heavy shelling, surrounded by wounded men: "We were all just on the brink of the next world. Suddenly everything seemed to become clear, and one no longer saw through a glass darkly; one felt certain about what one hardly understood at all. And fear and nerves and egoism all vanished in the joy of just being there. I am not mad, and I will one day try to explain it to you." He did not live to do so; and the mood itself withered away as "the fresh and joyous" war of August dragged out into the weary misery of winter.

Strategy and Slaughter

For the swift war everyone expected soon turned into something else, and the conflict which had begun with four months of movement ended in four static years of trench warfare. As we have seen, the German plan hinged on a hard drive through Belgium, violating her neutrality for the sake of a break through the French flank which would roll up the French armies in short order and enable German divisions to turn about and defeat the slow-moving Russians. Burning and destroying, the German Right Wing swung through Belgium, brutally discouraging opposition, ravaging villages, executing civilian hostages, reducing cities like Louvain with its unique medieval library, to flames, massacring 678 civilians at Dinant—including a three-week old child.

But the great German blow against France was held just short of Paris on the Marne, in early September: a long, confused struggle through the fog of broken-down communications, in which divisions marched toward the sound of the cannon, and which saw the first tactical use of motorized infantry when a brigade rushed out of Paris in requisitioned taxicabs and buses, to reinforce the hard-pressed French.

Having held the first German attack, the French and British counter-attacked with no decisive results; and the fighting turned into a series of attempts to outflank each other, moving progressively closer to the Channel coast: a race for the coast whose prize would be the Channel ports by which British reinforcements and supplies could enter France. Marching and countermarching for days on end, with only three or four hours' sleep in twenty-four, the soldiers of both armies staggered along in a daze, seeing mirages, and sometimes dropping in their tracks, fast asleep. Retreating troops were sometimes forced through sheer fatigue to stand and fight, as the British did at Le Cateau (they won). Suplies ran out, especially those of the advancing Germans, buoyed by a sense of victory but often hungry and frequently slowed down for want of silly things like horseshoe nails that could immobilize whole cavalry and artillery divisions. But courage and enthusiasm, in these early days, never flagged. In October, 1914, the first battle of Ypres caused such losses in the German reserve divisions—almost all young students—that the Germans dubbed it "the massacre of the innocents": *das kindermord von Ypern*. Despite such sacrifices, the Germans lost the race though they stabilized their lines across a good part of northern France and most of Belgium. By November, 1914, the two sides faced one another from parallel lines of trenches and fortifications running from the Swiss border to the English Channel.

If the Allies had managed to contain the German thrust, it was in part thanks to the Russians whose desperate offensives had drawn off German reserves at the height of battle. Ill-armed and ill-prepared for modern war, Russia relied on manpower. By 1917, one Russian in three would be called up to be thrust into battle, sometimes without a weapon, often without ammunition, and generally without serious artillery support. Where the war in the west turned static, that in eastern Europe surged over immense distances, while great infantry battles, now forgotten, were won or lost in hand-to-hand fighting where bayonets counted more than firepower. Things had changed little since Napoleon had passed through the plains and marshes of Poland and the Ukraine. Roads were few, dusty and choking in summer, quagmires in the rain, traps for wheeled transport, misery for marching men. The Russians, under pressure from their allies to attack while still unready, suffered heavy losses—nearly four million men in the first year alone—replaced by untrained and often unarmed draftees, expected to pick up experience, like a rifle, on the front itself.

Such sacrifices, effective enough against the Austrian armies, availed little against the modern equipment and superior generalship of the Germans, but probably saved the French and British from irresistible pressures. And, while the Russians grimly fought on despite immense

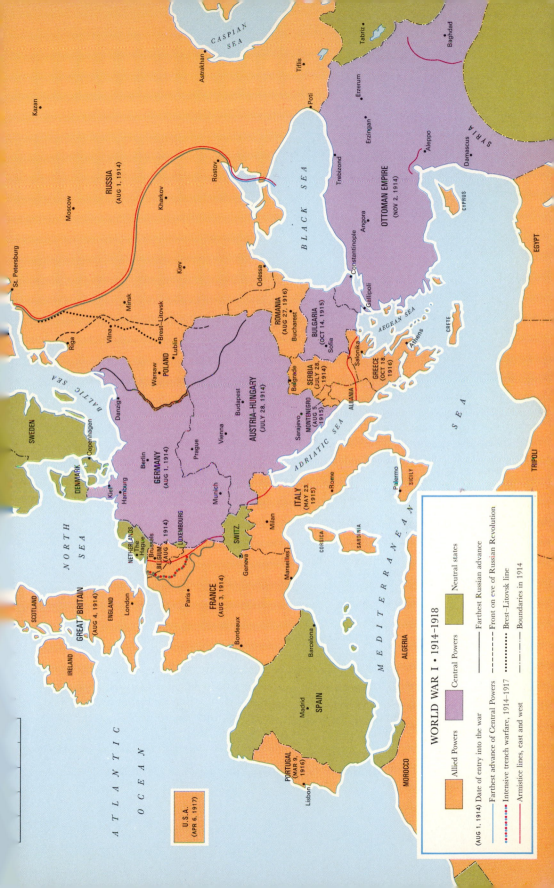

CASPIAN SEA

Astrakhan

Kazan

RUSSIA
(AUG 1, 1914)

Moscow

Rostov

Kharkov

Kiev

St. Petersburg

Minsk

Riga

Vilna

Brest-Litovsk

Lublin

Warsaw

POLAND

Danzig

BALTIC SEA

SWEDEN

Copenhagen

Kiel

DENMARK

Hamburg

Berlin

GERMANY
(AUG 1, 1914)

Prague

Munich

Vienna

AUSTRIA-HUNGARY
(JULY 28, 1914)

Budapest

Odessa

BLACK SEA

Tabriz

Baghdad

Tiflis

Erzerum

Erzingan

Aleppo

SYRIA

Damascus

Poti

Trebizond

OTTOMAN EMPIRE
(NOV 2, 1914)

Angora

Constantinople

Gallipoli

CYPRUS

EGYPT

AEGEAN SEA

CRETE

Athens

Salonika

GREECE
(OCT 18, 1916)

ALBANIA

MONTENEGRO
(AUG 5, 1915)

Sarajevo

SERBIA
(JULY 28, 1914)

Belgrade

BULGARIA
(OCT 14, 1915)

Sofia

Bucharest

ROMANIA
(AUG 27, 1916)

ADRIATIC SEA

Rome

ITALY
(MAY 23, 1915)

Milan

Genoa

SWITZ.

Marseilles

CORSICA

SARDINIA

SICILY

Palermo

TRIPOLI

MEDITERRANEAN SEA

ALGERIA

MOROCCO

SPAIN

Madrid

Barcelona

PORTUGAL
(MAR 9, 1916)

Lisbon

FRANCE
(AUG 3, 1914)

Paris

Bordeaux

Geneva

LUXEMBOURG

BELGIUM
(AUG 4, 1914)

Brussels

NETHERLANDS

The Hague

NORTH SEA

GREAT BRITAIN
(AUG 4, 1914)

SCOTLAND

ENGLAND

London

IRELAND

ATLANTIC OCEAN

U.S.A.
(APR 6, 1917)

WORLD WAR I · 1914–1918

Allied Powers	Neutral states
Central Powers	

(AUG 1, 1914) Date of entry into the war

——— Farthest advance of Central Powers

——— Farthest Russian advance

- - - - Front on eve of Russian Revolution

•••••• Intensive trench warfare, 1914–1917

•••••• Brest-Litovsk line

——— Armistice lines, east and west

——— Boundaries in 1914

Trench warfare.

costs in life and territory, the war of movement in the west became a gigantic slugging match. Machine guns and barbed wire turned it into mutual siege and, under siege conditions, old methods and primitive armories were revived: bayonets cut into saws or taped to broom handles turned into spears, coshes, knuckle-dusters, jam-tin bombs, mines and countermines, mortars, grenades, flame throwers, finally armor and helmets.* Stretching for some 450 miles, the western front was a lunar expanse scarred with trenches, with their smell of stagnant mud, latrine buckets, rotting sandbags, disinfectant, lime, and stale sweat, stretching amidst muddy fields and tangles of barbed wire, flooded in rain, freezing in winter, ceaselessly shelled and sniped and raided, treeless, birdless, and with no wildlife besides rats, lice, and fleas, where the thick square ration bisquits were often used for fuel, where soldiers were expected to last four or five months, sergeants and junior officers half that time, and where men who considered themselves under suspended sentence of death prayed for the flesh wounds that would save their lives.

Even within this great sausage machine—as its own victims called it because it was firmly screwed into place while one fed living beings in at one end, to have them churned out as corpses at the other— even there none of these horrors could hide the fact that, as a combatant reported home, "the most terrible part of war is still man." Yet individual man was most likely to be lost from sight behind the plans, the maps, and statistics of those who used him. The best military thought on the eve of war insisted on the superiority of moral over material factors, of quality over quantity, of movement over firepower, of bayonets and the offensive spirit. This nonsense would be shattered in the charges of the first few weeks; but its victims did not live to point out the fact, and so the generals kept their prestige and the power to send more masses to their slaughter.

With very few exceptions, the military leaders on all sides (Haig

---

* Envy of the Germans, first to be equipped with capacious steel helmets, led to their being dubbed "jerries."

leading the English, Moltke and Falkenhayn the Germans, Joffre, Pétain, and Foch the French) showed an extraordinary lack of imagination and enterprise. Strategy gave way to tactics, and this last seems to have consisted largely of massive blows in which even surprise was soon sacrificed to vast artillery bombardments and what counted was the weight of matériel and men. Ingenuity was contributed by civilians like the British Secretary of the Navy, Winston Churchill, who suggested combined operations to outflank the Germans in Belgium or open the Dardanelles; but such suggestions were only reluctantly taken up by the soldiers and steadfastly bungled.* What counted was steadiness under fire, which generals like Joffre and Pétain had in plenty.

With the western front settling into siege conditions, the strategy of the Central Powers should have been to hold there while trying to knock Russia out of the fight. Two great generals, Hindenburg and Ludendorff, had already inflicted serious defeats upon them. Instead, both the Germans and the Allies continued to feed hundreds of thousands into offensives which netted little except corpses. "Corpses, corpses, corpses," noted a German writer serving in Flanders: "streams of wounded . . . everything becomes senseless, a lunacy . . . a negation of all civilization, killing all belief in the capacity of mankind and men for progress . . ." The greatest of these holocausts took place at Verdun, which the Germans planned to use as a vast slaughterhouse that "would bleed France white of all able-bodied men," and where the fighting raged murderously from February to December, 1916, slaying over 600,000 evenly divided between the two sides. The French, under General Pétain, held their own and the German commander Falkenhayn was replaced by the Ludendorff-Hindenburg team which for the next two years commanded not only the German army but increasingly Germany as a whole. Meanwhile, on the river Somme, a great Allied offensive proved even costlier than Verdun, especially for the British who lost 400,000 men —twice as many as the Germans who gave practically no ground. Both Verdun and the Somme were important more for their symbolic value than for their results: the one proving the French nation's will to fight, the other that of the British, whom German propaganda accused of fighting only to the last Frenchman. But they were costly tokens of determination, and if they improved home-front morale, they did not do so well for the morale of troops increasingly skeptical about the uses of such slaughter.

Deadlocked in the west but unwilling to admit it, both sides also tried to divert the enemy's resources and to increase their own by opening other fronts or drawing other combatants into war: Turkey (1914) and Bulgaria (1915) on the German side; Italy (1915) and Romania

* Thus, in 1915, Allied attack on the Black Sea straits foundered at Gallipoli, while Turks honed their martial ardor by massacring three-quarters of a million Armenians, and the poet Rupert Brooke, yearning to sail to Constantinople with the conquering British fleet, died of blood poisoning on the Greek island of Skiros.

Supplies backing up the last German offensive at the Somme Front, April 1918.

(1916—just in time to ease the pressure on Verdun) on the Allied side.* The Allies missed their chance of active Greek support because the Russians feared Greek designs on Constantinople, which they wanted for themselves. Thus, Greek willingness to join in the war against Turkey was rejected in 1915 on the direct intervention of the Tsar. Thereafter, the Greeks lost interest in a conflict from which they could expect no clear gains. Hard pressed to abandon neutrality for commitment on the Allied side, they were gradually forced into belligerence by 1917, especially after Russia left the war.

The superior mobility of British sea power brought little direct profit when combined operations against the Belgian coast or the Dardanelles ended in failure. It did permit German colonies to be picked off and to establish a blockade of the Central Powers, while ensuring massive shipments of food and supplies from overseas, especially from the United States.

The Eastern Front

The first decisive break appeared in the east, where fortunes had fluctuated from the first in the far more mobile fighting. For three years, the Russian armies, abominably equipped though they were, put up a solid show, did well against the Austrians, less well against the Germans, gave ground but still held their own. Then, in 1917, riots that began with the sacking of bakers' shops turned into revolution. By the autumn the Russian front had dissolved, the soldiers "voting with

* One might add Portugal, on whom Germany declared war in 1916 for seizure of German ships in Lisbon harbor, and which sent a small expeditionary force to the western front.

their feet" against continuation of the war. A great deal has now been written about the Russian Revolution and the Allied opposition to it. It is important to realize that even while a revolution in March, 1917, forced the Tsar's abdication and another in November brought the Bolsheviks to power, the "Ten Days That Shook the World" really did not. The world had its eyes fixed elsewhere: on the long stretch of mud, shell holes, and barbed wire across northern France where the Allies faced the Germans; on the gray-green waters of the North Atlantic which had become the graveyard of thousands of sailors and hundreds of thousands of tons of shipping; on the banks, factories, and training camps of the United States; on the great struggle between the Western powers and Germany. In this context, what happened in Russia was a distraction, relevant only in terms of the effect it could have on the war, and Allied hostility to Bolsheviks stemmed less from fear of their revolution than from the belief that it was "made in Germany," that Lenin & Co. were German agents, and that their power in Russia must be destroyed as part of the war effort.

We know that they were not destroyed. But if the Allies were mistaken in some of their judgments they were right in considering Bolshevik victory a disaster for their side. Russia's new masters, determined to end hostilities, accepted German conditions at Brest-Litovsk. The Romanians, driven into a corner, their capital occupied, also sued for peace. It seemed as if the Central Powers might win the war; and the treaties of Bucharest and Brest-Litovsk, imposed in the spring of 1918, provided an indication of the kind of peace which they had in mind. Romania, Poland, the Ukraine, and the Baltic states became satellites of Germany. Russia lost 26 per cent of her population, 27 per cent of her arable land, a quarter of her railroad mileage, a third of her textile and three-quarters of her iron industries, and had to pay a large war indemnity to her victorious foes. None could know that all this would come to nothing. For six tense months, Romanian grain and oil, Ukrainian wheat and coal, replenished the resources of the Germans, while divisions withdrawn from the eastern front stiffened their potential in the west. After four years of blockade and war, the German army on the western front was twice the size it had been in 1914.

The Bitter End

The Allies, on the contrary, were weakening. While German supplies improved, theirs fell, along with the means to buy more of them from the United States. The winter of 1916–17 was the worst Europe had known since 1880. At the end of April 1917, Senegalese infantry on the western front were so numb with cold that their French officers had to load their rifles for them. And 1917 as a whole was the most bitter time that the Allies had to endure. A devastating German submarine campaign briefly faced Britain with starvation; the Italian front came dangerously near collapse; French troops mutinied all along the line, refusing to go uselessly to slaughter. Drastic steps were taken to cope with the situation, reinforcements rushed to Italy, the Allied commander-in-chief, Joffre, replaced by the more aggressive Foch, command on the western front entrusted to Pétain who had made his name at Verdun and who now enhanced it by husbanding the lives of troops under his command. Cold, methodical and taciturn, he was a defensive fighter, sparing of his men and sparing in his moods. The English Cabinet had been restructured in 1916 under a strong popular liberal, David Lloyd George. Now an old Jacobin took the helm of France: Georges Clemenceau, who, said Keynes, "had one illusion—France; and one disillusion—mankind, including Frenchmen." Clemenceau remembered France's defeat in 1871 and was determined that it should not recur.

Equally important, Germany's submarine campaign at last brought the United States into war on the Allied side where ideology and investments already ranged them.* While American troops would be of little help until 1918, American factories and banks were better than the Ukraine. In spring 1918, when the Germans launched their last offensive, seven million soldiers faced one another in Flanders and northern France, about equally divided between the two sides. Under the leadership of Foch, the Allied lines strained, cracked, but held. By summer 1918, the Allies had taken the offensive. The long siege had ended. Turkey and Austro-Hungary were breaking, Allied troops moved forward on every front, the German military leaders, defeated, asked for an armistice. The war was over.

* A tremendous propaganda campaign had been waged to win U.S. support. In New England, a contemporary remembers attending a great meeting sponsored by the local church during the winter of 1916–17: "A speaker demanded that the Kaiser, when captured, be boiled in oil, and the entire audience stood on chairs to scream its hysterical approval."

Imperial War Museum

Signing the Brest-Litovsk Treaty, the German representative, von Kuhlman, on the left and the Russian, Count Czernin, on the right, March 3, 1918.

Chapter 17

NATIONAL COUNTERPOINT: INTERNAL AFFAIRS, 1848-1918

The thoughtful traveler who crosses the swift border between France and Spain, or flies from the brisk atmosphere of Stockholm into the strangely preserved anachronisms of Leningrad, knows that the changed environment is both contemporary and alien. Even when he does not have to adjust his watch, the world he walks into lives on a different time: its smells, its food, its rate of movement, its scale of values, its code of behavior, its processes and practices have a life of their own, similar to others across national borders and yet true to some distinctive experience. Even if all such factors cannot be noticed here, some of them must be, for they illuminate national characteristics and national history. Different national traditions, conditions, institutions, produced men and societies which—while sharing the common fate of other Europeans—lived out their lives each in specific ways.

A general treatment of the great lines of history leaves little room for particulars. The impact of industrial and technological advances, the development of political institutions, the evolution and expression of ideological currents, differ from place to place, and such differences are best understood in terms of more limited traditions. A general account of

779

industrial changes that turns on England and on France casts little light on the peculiar fate of countries that industrialization affected less or later. The effects of the First World War, cataclysmic in central Europe, were felt quite differently and less in England, hardly at all in neutral countries like Spain. The ideas of socialism took on different shapes, created different institutions, in Germany, England, or France.

The following sections illustrate how the general trends we have been examining worked themselves out in particular terms, how movements and events already sketched above affected different members of the patchwork: Europe.

In some respects the same events seem to recur in country after country; but with a difference. What matters is this modified framework, the diverse circumstances, creating in the end dissimilar situations, so that industrialization (for example) proceeds in Germany with a distinct tempo and evokes quite different effects than in France or England. Each story told below, then, is a tale apart, yet part of a greater whole as well. Each provides the counterpoint of the great central theme and interweaves with tales of other parts, each emphasizing some particular aspect of the *ensemble*.

One fact should become clear as one reads on: that events which had great effect on one country passed others by, so that wars, especially wars —great favorites for beginning or ending chapters—made little impact beyond belligerent lands. Thus, during the Crimean War, Russia continued to pay interest on its foreign loans to enemies as well as to neutrals; and the war of 1870–1871, crucial for Germany and France mattered far less in London, Moscow, Vienna. Even in France, people lived on as they had done before, as most would still do after 1914. In other words, great political crises may be no more than marginal to the economic trends, to the everyday realities, more direly affected by inflation in the early twenties, by Depression after 1929, than by victory in war or even by defeat. True, after the holocaust of 1914–1918, the lives of the defeated were altered more radically than those of men and women on the winning side but probably not as thoroughly or to the same extent as they were to be in the 1940's.

At any rate, what counts in all these sections is not a country's international role but her internal travail and evolution; the latter hopefully casting some light on the former that we already know. Nevertheless, given the long sweep of time each of these sections covers, one remark may be in order. This volume is predicated on the belief that the years between 1848 and 1945 have a particular unity that overrides the different crises cutting across it like great crevasses in the 1890's, in 1917–1920, or again after 1929. Despite the fact that the national histories that follow run only to the First World War—1917, 1918, or 1920—it is well to remember that this is a matter of convenience. From 1848 to 1945, continuity matters more than particular changes. And some changes came, or failed to come, with little regard for climactic dates. "It was in 1915," wrote D. H. Lawrence, "the old world ended." But Lawrence himself retained a maid much longer than that, suggesting that some essential aspects of the old world persisted.

Britain

Seen from the present the history of the United Kingdom is one of comfortable decline. For an observer of 1850 it could look like a spectacular rise, at least up to a point. It may be possible to reconcile these views with the suggestion that relative decline set in around the end of the nineteenth century and that it became absolute in the 1930's with the rise of much greater powers. Certainly the last part of the nineteenth century would see the highest point of British influence. "With steam and Bible," as a historian of the great exhibition of 1851 put it, the British covered the world. The country's shipping tonnage, which doubled in the quarter century before 1850, increased five times in the next score years. By that time—1870—two-thirds of the world's ocean-going tonnage flew the British flag. Britain led the world in coal and iron, trade, and investments overseas; and it led Europe in real income, which grew 30 per cent between 1851 and 1878 and somewhat less thereafter until the end of the century, despite a continued increase in the population, which also rose at an unheard-of rate.

But Britain's economic supremacy shrank back eventually before the changes that her own investments and inventions wrought elsewhere. Her share of world trade, one-fifth in 1880, had fallen to 14 per cent by the eve of war. Yet she remained the largest trading nation and the London money market reigned supreme, still clearing deals half a world away. In 1894, Peking's war indemnity to Tokyo was paid through the Bank of England; a generation later, London still acted as the chief banker of her European allies. Yet, by 1914, British industry, though outwardly thriving, was slipping behind its competitors because it failed to modernize. Reluctance to try new things, to sacrifice textile machinery working well enough for the more efficient sort installed by American firms, to introduce modern equipment in mines and mills and foundries relying on plentiful cheap labor, was a kind of prodigality for which modern nations have to pay in the end. In the decade after 1900 the Germans doubled their steel output, the Americans increased theirs 150 per cent, the British only 20 per cent. In chemicals and dyestuffs Britain was far behind the Germans, in the electrical industry behind the Germans and Americans, in the automobile industry behind America and France. The reckoning would come during the First World War and after. Until then, the exuberance of expansion persuaded most Britons of their superiority. They were, as Thomas Arnold put it, "one of the chosen peoples of history," carrying out—explained Charles Kingsley— "the glorious work which God seems to have laid on the English race, to replenish the earth and subdue it."

Britain (whose safety, thought Lord Shaftesbury, was "the special care of Providence") dominated the world as it ruled the waves; the world whose clearinghouse it had become, its greatest shipper and carrier, banker and supplier:

> Pride in their port, defiance in their eye,
> We see the Lords of humankind go by.

The Lords of humankind believed in free trade and self-help, smugly ignoring those who were not free to help themselves. They also believed in representative institutions like their own.

> Where freedom broadens slowly down
> From precedent to precedent,

especially by rational debate based on a common moral code. Truth was "a question of the reconciling and combining of opposites." It was to be attained, argued John Stuart Mill's essay *On Liberty*, "Only by the collision of adverse opinions." Yet, Asa Briggs remarks, debate of this kind was only possible because very few people joined in it. Free interchange of ideas took place, but its scope was limited to agreed bounds, to restricted circles, and to private rather than public circumstances.

A system such as this carried no further than the limits of the deferential society that practiced it. Its own reforms reduced its potential by introducing more participants in the debate and whittling down the possibility that particular decisions would meet with general acceptance. The second Reform Bill of 1867 gave the vote to urban laborers; the third Reform Bill (1884) to most of the rural laboring classes, with Conservative majorities passing both.* But, even after 1885, residential, economic, or educational qualifications gave half a million Englishmen more than one vote, so that a university graduate who also ran a business in the City of London voted three times: once at home, once for his university, and once in the city. Democracy was a relative term; deference—the habit which takes respect for social superiors for granted— toward the upper classes still lived on. In the most advanced industrial country in the world the badge of the ruling class continued to be the ownership of land, as long as it was owned in great quantities. In 1873, four-fifths of the United Kingdom was owned by less than 7,000 persons and, though the wealth of the landed classes in relation to the

---

* It is interesting that the strongest opposition to electoral reform came not from the aristocracy or even from the rich but from intellectuals who opposed mass rule in the name of education and intelligence.

other classes was declining, the aristocracy—based on land—increased in strength and confidence at least until the 1880's.

Withal, Britain in mid-century was a middle-class nation and, though the term is impossible to define except as what the society itself considered middle-classness, it would appear that the category numbered about 3 millions in 1851 (one-tenth of the population) and over 5 million in 1867. Along with the "upper classes," almost a quarter of the nation lived in a way that was not that of the "lower classes," thinking of itself as "gentle" and "respectable." This group was obviously growing, prospering, abandoning the thrift and sobriety on which it had risen for conspicuous and competitive consumption which publicized their rise and announced another age.

The major moral values of this dominant class were drawn from religious belief. An evangelical conscience survived the Evangelical movement: keen awareness of rewards and punishments in the hereafter, bearing them in mind in prayer and church attendance, basic honesty (also good for trade), and self-improvement. This waned very slowly.* Far into the twentieth century inertia maintained what conscience once imposed, and sometimes for the better. The social aspects of the evangelical conscience were bolstered by the spread of education. The Reform Bill of 1867 persuaded the politicians that "now we must educate our masters"; and free compulsory elementary education was the result of this. At another level, the new civil service built up by reformers rested on probity even more than business did, and the new English public (that is, private) schools tried to turn out decent, loyal, upright men. The mores of the English were to be those of gentlemen, their values those of the public schools; and useless gentlemen, gradually excluded from the public service as patronage gave way to selective recruitment, were to be replaced by useful gentlemen in every aspect of national life. Greater moral and political awareness (however relative) played its part in further political reforms: the secret ballot introduced in 1872 and the Corrupt Practices Act of 1883, which, limiting election costs, made possible really representative government not based on influence or bribery.

The Crown and the Parties

As suggested by its lasting label, the spirit of Victorian England found an appropriate symbol in its monarch's personality. Emotional, loyal, obstinate, endowed with little intelligence but much common sense and many good intentions, Queen Victoria (1837–1901) was once de-

* The worst horrors of the English Sunday began to give way at the turn of the century, under the impact of the Prince of Wales's weekend parties and Sunday festivities. But the religious orientation had already veered. In 1870 there were more than twice as many books on religion published in England as works of fiction; sixteen years later novels far outnumbered religious works.

Queen Victoria (1) surrounded by her royal relatives. They are (2) her daughter Victoria, wife of the German Kaiser Frederick III, (3) her grandson, Wilhelm II, (4) Czar Nicholas II, and (5) his wife, Alexandra, (6) her son, the Prince of Wales and future King Edward VII of England, (7) the Crown Princess, and (9) her son, Duke Alfred of Coburg.

scribed by Bismarck as "a jolly little body." But Bismarck also added: "What a woman! One could do business with her!" Her most Victorian aspects grew under the influence of the short-lived husband (1840–1861) whom she never ceased to worship: Prince Albert of Saxe-Coburg-Gotha, an earnest, conscientious German intellectual of liberal leanings, devoted to music, art, and progress, endowed with statesmanlike abilities. The Crown, however, had very limited powers. With the appearance of party government, executive duties had fallen into the hands of the Cabinet. By 1867, when Walter Bagehot published his popular account of the English Constitution, the rights of the sovereign could accurately be defined as "the right to be consulted, the right to encourage and the right to warn." Within a system in which until today the monarch has a say in who the prime minister should be, the influence of the Crown never disappeared. But the real power henceforth lay with the political parties, characteristically in this period born from clubs: the Conservative Carlton Club founded in 1832, the National Union of Conservative and Unionist Associations (1867), the Liberal Reform Club founded in 1836, and the National Liberal Federation (1877), finally and much later the Labour Party founded in 1900.

During the last half of the nineteenth century the political scene would be dominated by their leaders, chief among them Benjamin Disraeli (1804–1881): the brilliant, charming, resourceful son of a Jewish man of letters, for thirty-three years Conservative leader in the House of Commons, and who died Lord Beaconsfield; and William Ewart Gladstone (1809–1898): the formidable son of a Liverpool merchant, who held his first government office at twenty-five and would be four times

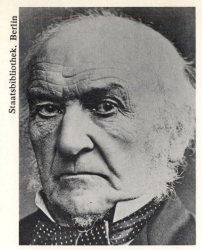

William Gladstone. Right: Benjamin Disraeli.

Liberal prime minister between 1868 and 1894 for a total of almost fourteen years.

The rivalry between Conservatives and Liberals was incarnated in the emulation of their two great parliamentary leaders, both of them reformers and both in a sense trying to see who could initiate more reforms. The Electoral Reform Bill of 1867 was due to Disraeli's determination to "dish the Whigs"; Gladstone's Franchise Bill of 1884 extended the franchise practically to manhood suffrage; Disraeli's administrations were responsible for legislation on public health, artisan dwellings, conditions in the merchant navy; Gladstone's for educational and civil service reform, army reorganization, and the first measures to fix employers' liability in industrial accidents. Yet Disraeli's name would remain attached above all to Britain's new imperial policy, facilitated by his acquisition of a controlling interest in the Suez Canal (1875) and the assumption by Queen Victoria of the title of Empress of India (1876). And Gladstone's reputation would be colored, as we shall shortly see, by his Irish policy and his insistence on Irish Home Rule, which would break up his party by driving some of the liveliest Liberals into the dissidence of Unionism.

This long excursion should not be taken to mean that Conservatism and Liberalism were the only political movements; simply the most important. Social and political reform found its champions rather outside these parties. Radicalism was embodied in Charles Bradlaugh (1833–1891): a convinced republican, atheist, and Malthusian, who fought against the established Church, against the blasphemy laws, against the requirement to take oaths on the Bible, and against restrictions on birth control propaganda.* Social idealism found advocates in men like

* This last with Annie Besant (1847–1933), later a Fabian leader. Elected to the House of Commons in 1881, Bradlaugh refused to take the oath necessary for being seated, was expelled, was re-elected and expelled again in 1881, 1882, 1884, and 1885, finally winning his point and being allowed to *affirm* instead of swearing. In 1888 a law to this effect made affirmation legal in the courts.

John Ruskin (1819–1900) and William Morris (1834–1896), who were less radicals than reactionaries on aesthetic and moralistic grounds. In *Unto This Last* (1862), Ruskin denounced the selfishness of current economic views and the decay of popular arts and artistic feelings. Men should be reintegrated into society, purpose and execution reintegrated into things they made, as they had been joined (thought Ruskin) during the Middle Ages. The good life could be restored by curing the alienation caused by industrial production, turning the worker back into a craftsman, re-establishing social and creative identity. Morris, the younger man, carried these views further.

Artist, craftsman, and poet, William Morris was shocked by the drudgery and wretchedness of most workers, not only poor but condemned to toil at jobs which provided no satisfaction, no pride, no pleasure. Eliminate exploitation and profit-making, give people a chance to serve ideals not masters, educate them to the point where this becomes a real possibility: Morris disliked the depersonalization of producers and of objects in mass production. They should be "a joy to make and joy to the user." Social equality, social fellowship, social craftsmanship could bring social salvation. How they were to come about (except by education) Morris did not say, though he did say it should not be by violence. That was his Socialism, close to Anarchism, hoping that, once men had found a better way of life, the state would wither away of its own accord.

In 1883, Morris joined the Democratic Federation founded by Henry Hyndman (1842–1921), who called for public ownership of land and capital.* But, though their ideas found an eager audience, the movements of Morris, Hyndman, and even the Independent Labor Party (ILP) founded in 1893, never pulled much weight. Much greater influence would be exercised by the Fabian Society, founded in 1884 by middle-class intellectuals committed to Socialism but also to its achievement in a gradual manner, as their label—furnished by the name of the great Roman temporizer—implied. The founders of the Society were mostly in their twenties—George Bernard Shaw (1856–1950), Sidney Webb (1859–1947), Beatrice Webb (1858–1943), Graham Wallas

---

* The two men soon split, the one setting up his own Socialist league, the other a Marxist Social Democratic Federation.

Warder Collection

Intellectuals in politics: Sidney and Beatrice Webb.

(1858–1932), H. G. Wells (1866–1946)—and they had many years in which to leave their mark on England. But the *Fabian Essays in Socialism* that they published in 1889 showed their philosophy to be in the classical English tradition: not Marxist but utilitarian, not revolutionary but evolutionist. They all believed that economic developments rendered Socialism inevitable (though what was Socialism each one defined in his own way). But it would come by an evolution which was already well advanced and which democratic pressure would push further. Someone had to show the electorate how to accelerate the process, how they could manage their own affairs dispensing with their capitalist masters, and this was the purpose of the Fabians. The intellectual power of the little group, its activity and its wide connections, ensured that British reform would, in effect, take place on the lines they advocated, that British Labor would be not Marxist but revisionist, that the political coloring of all the British parties in years to come would be tempered by the Fabian outlook.

In another sense the Fabian philosophy was simply the reflection of a tradition which rendered revolution irrelevant. Reform, often sluggish, never quite ceased after 1832. It received an unexpected boost from the Crimean War, which, said Nathaniel Hawthorne, gave England "a vast impulse toward democracy." The mess of the war splashed off on its leaders: soldiers were brave enough but officers were incompetent, administrators chaotic and ineffective. Roused public opinion suggested that great administrators' and contractors, men who managed factories, railroads, and shipping lines, might do better than politicians. Charles Dickens wrote *Little Dorritt* (1857), lampooning the Circumlocution Office and the useless breed of Barnacles in it. Associations sprang up throughout the country calling for military and administrative reform. A bill was introduced opening the Civil Service to competitive examinations. None of this brought concrete changes for over a decade, but the agitation helped clear the atmosphere.

The third quarter of the century was in any case a time of social progress advancing on a flood of prosperity. Then, when recession and unemployment in the 1880's made economic progress seem less infinite, a wave of trade union agitation and the concurrent rise of labor movements shifted the radicals from liberalism to socialism, and the workers from support of Liberals to support of a party of their own: Labour. Between 1885 and 1890 union membership tripled, no longer restricted to the aristocracy of skilled workers but drawing on poorer, less skilled groups who needed bargaining agents. A ferment of working-class activity began, expressed in strikes and industrial unrest. The greatest social troubles come not when the poor are very very poor but when their condition is improving, and when a little luck can help to accelerate the trend.* At least, this was what happened in England where

* The improvement, like everything else, was relative: in 1912 there were 280,000 inmates in workhouses and, by Salvation Army estimates, some 10 per cent of Britain's population lived on the brink of starvation or actually died of it. Shaw's *Major Barbara* (1905) is predicated on this.

the prewar years saw a spate of social legislation inspired by Fabian reports, sponsored by Liberal governments, and copied from Bismarck's measures of the 1880's.

With all their shortcomings, the Housing and Town Planning Act of 1909 and the National Insurance Act of 1911 were the prelude of English legislation in these realms. A flamboyant Welsh lawyer, David Lloyd George (1863–1945), fought to get the money for these limited measures and, in the process, abridged the power of the House of Lords. Meanwhile, Britain was prey to a general political and ideological ferment. All repressed groups—workers, women, and colonial peoples—were astir. Militant suffragism harried ministers and destroyed property; militant labor created industrial unrest; worst of all, in Ireland, Catholics and Protestants seemed on the brink of civil war.

Ireland

> Ireland never was contented
> Say ye so, ye are demented . . .

So runs the song; and it seems an accurate account of conditions since 1848 or, indeed, before then. The island colony had recovered slowly from the great famine and losses of mid-century. In 1858 a secret society called the Fenian Brotherhood (from the Gaelic *Fianna:* soldiers) was founded there and in the United States to organize rebellion in Ireland and an attack on Canada from the United States. In 1865 a wave of arrests broke the organization's back in Ireland and the rising, when it came in 1867 along with action in England where jails were attacked and prisoners released, was soon put down. Marx had hoped that an Irish insurrection might help spark a wider social revolution. As it happened, it sparked soul-searching and eventual rebellion within the English Liberal Party.

The Liberal leader William Gladstone saw the pacification of Ireland as his mission, tried unsuccessfully to achieve it by compromises between what he thought was good for the Irish and what Parliament could be persuaded to vote, split his party on the issue of Home Rule for Ireland (1886), and sent the Liberal unionists into co-operation with the Conservatives. Gladstone finally carried Irish Home Rule in 1893, and this was followed by a lull really broken only by new home rule disputes after 1912. The trouble now came less from the Catholic Irish than from Protestant Ulstermen in the North, who feared that they would be submerged by Catholic majorities in a self-governing island. A bitter struggle raged around this issue until it was overtaken by the war and the disputed measure suspended *sine die.* In 1916 an Irish Republican rebellion broke out in Dublin and was put

English troops raiding a Sinn Fein party printing office in Dublin during the Irish Rebellion.

down. A more serious rising occurred in 1919, and Irish "troubles" unfolded like a prototype of later colonial wars of liberation in which terror, murder, and guerrilla warfare conducted by an activist minority eventually wears down the alien occupiers already doubtful of their moral right and even more of the profit involved in hanging on. In 1921–22 the nagging sore was settled by partition. An Anglo-Irish Treaty separated six northern Protestant counties from the rest, giving home rule to the Irish Free State, which became a dominion of the Commonwealth,* and making Ulster a largely self-governing part of the United Kingdom of Great Britain and Northern Ireland. Ireland would pose no more internal problems for the next fifty years.** But there were enough other problems to keep the British busy.

France

If England suggests that too much stability and too little friction may be a problem, France presents the alternative: a society constant in its instability, fervent in its divisions, whose members look upon their compatriots as their fiercest competitors, where perhaps men hate their neighbors even more than they hate themselves, where—as if deliberately —a great nation applies itself to proving Rousseau wrong and Hobbes correct.

The history of France since the great Revolution had marked the

* "The settlement was followed by southern civil war between the intransigent supporters of United Ireland and the moderates content with what they had. In 1932 under Eamon de Valera, Eire proclaimed itself a republic, whose independence Britain recognized in 1937, as it did in 1948 its independence from the Commonwealth.

** Even when the late 1960's saw Ulster reedit the civil conflicts that once ripped all Ireland apart, these troubles no longer affected English politics directly.

A contemporary drawing of Napoleon III on horseback.

failure of every attempt to reconcile the nation to any one regime. Lacking the English notion of a loyal opposition and gradual reform, the French viewed politics as sheer struggle for power, defeat in which could mean exclusion (or self-exclusion) from national affairs. There was little in their experience to suggest other solutions. The legacy of 1848, like that of previous revolutions, was bitter. The rebels of June had been blasted out of their barricades—2,000 or 3,000 killed, 12,000 arrested, the Republic made safe for property, and class hatred established on solid foundations of mutual fear. General Cavaignac, the hero of the bourgeoisie, became military dictator. There would be no more national workshops, no more social reform. A new constitution balanced legislative and executive power—a parliament and a president, both popularly elected—but did not say how they could be reconciled. The first president would solve the problem. In the presidential election of December, 1848, the poet Lamartine received 17,000 votes, Cavaignac a million and a half, and Louis Napoleon (1808–1873) five and a half million.

A New Napoleon

The new president was forty years old. Son of Louis Bonaparte, king of Holland, and of Josephine's daughter, Hortense, he had grown up in Bavaria and in Switzerland with a Jacobin tutor who was the son of one of Robespierre's most devoted friends. In 1830, Louis joined in the Italian struggles for liberty and narrowly escaped being arrested. In 1832, Napoleon's son, the duke of Reichstadt, died in Vienna and Louis became his uncle's political heir. Two unsuccessful attempts to claim his heritage had netted an imprisonment for six years in a lonely fortress, escape from which in 1846 took him to America and then to

London, where he remained until the revolution of 1848 allowed him to return home legally.

Louis's character was a mass of contradictions, a little like a many-faceted stone that sparkles differently according to the light. Sensitive and taciturn, kindhearted and ruthless, idealistic and skeptical, apathetic and dynamic, a loyal friend, a cynical intriguer, this was the mass of apparent contradictions who came to be known as Napoleon III. For the moment he was only the president of France's Second Republic, although elected by almost three-fourths of the votes that had been cast. Louis had campaigned as representative of order and security to reassure the respectable, promising amnesty to Socialists, freedom of schooling to Catholics, "revival of credit, resurrection of labor, protection of religion, family and property." But it had been his name which brought in the votes. "The Napoleonic cause," he once said, "goes to the soul." Presumably, he knew the soul was a more effective political motor than the mind. Veterans whose ears and noses had frozen in Russia, peasants who hung the Emperor's image on their cottage walls, men who recognized this name when they knew no other, followed the magic of a memory.

Now, Louis Napoleon faced the competition of a legislature dominated by conservative interests and remembered that in 1852 his term would end and the Constitution did not permit his re-election. In his first years he played along with the legislature, signing their bills to reform education in a Catholic direction, to restrict the suffrage and deprive one-third of Frenchmen of a vote, to whittle down freedom of the press and of political assembly. Perhaps he hoped that, in return, the Constitution would be revised allowing him to succeed himself; perhaps he was only giving the legislators rope to hang themselves in the public's eyes. At last, in December, 1851, when it was clear that he would get nothing legally, he seized power by a military coup, imprisoned his opponents, dissolved the Assembly, restored universal suffrage, and had his actions ratified by a plebiscite in which 7.5 million voted *yes* and 650,000 *no*. The country was weary of instability, the wealthy feared unrest, the workers detested the bourgeois who had put them down in 1848 more than they did Louis Napoleon, the peasants wanted security for their harvests. A new constitution made him chief of state with a legislative assembly subject to him. Within a year, nearly 8 million people voted *yes* in one more plebiscite (only 250,000 voted *no*). He was now Emperor Napoleon III.

The French historian and economist Ernest Labrousse suggests that Napoleon came to power because nineteenth-century men faced with twentieth-century problems of moving from agricultural to industrial conditions while living in an eighteenth-century society panicked, and looked for a providential man. They certainly found a very twentieth-century solution which enlisted nationalism, socialism, and a widespread sense of insecurity, in the service of personal power.

Napoleon dreamt of a state both authoritarian and socialistic, which would take over from the incompetent bourgeois regime disintegrating around him—the faster for his help. He had no precise political orientation. His team grouped Orleanists like his half brother, Charles de Morny,* who looked on the masses with a kind of utilitarian paternalism, well-intentioned but suspicious of them; and democratic socialists like his cousin, Prince Jerome Napoleon. As he once expressed it: "The Empress is legitimist, my Cousin is republican, Morny is Orleanist, I am a socialist; the only Bonapartist is Persigny and he is mad." **

But if Napoleon III was no Bonapartist, he was certainly heir of other doctrines, not least those of Saint-Simon (see p. 658). Throughout Louis Philippe's reign the Saint-Simonians had repeated that, having come to power in alliance with the people, the middle classes must meet their allies' material needs by developing education, credit, means of communication, and opportunities for employment, or lose their power. The middle classes failed to heed this. The years 1848 and after proved that the Saint-Simonians had been right. Louis Napoleon profited by the lesson. He has been called a Saint-Simon on horseback and, in effect, his regime was a great time for producers and speculators, entrepreneurs, engineers, and financiers, many of Jewish or Protestant origin and many of them disciples of Saint-Simon, graduates of the Polytechnic School, adepts of industrial civilization. The regime fulfilled their creed. This was when the French industrial revolution really got its start in industry and coal mining, the rise of department stores and credit enterprises whose chronicles we can find in the novels of Émile Zola. Even the free-trade treaty signed with England in 1860 reflected the personal initiative of the Emperor, convinced by Saint-Simonian arguments; and the alliance of competence and money was sanctioned by the influential philosopher, Ernest Renan, suggesting an elite ruling by its skill and reason; and by the founding of a school to train this elite: the School of Moral and Political Sciences created by a Saint-Simonian, Boutmy.

Between 1847 and 1867 foreign trade trebled, urban population grew from a quarter to a third of the country's total, ironworks like Le Creusot which turned out 18,000 tons a year in 1847 were producing seven times as much twenty years later. The French economy passed from the artisan to the industrial plane, although new factories still lived side by side with workshops and home industries. The value of industrial production doubled, that of trade quadrupled, so did the number of shops using steam engines, while the horsepower in them grew fivefold. New banks

---

* "A consummate politician with all the daring of a gambler," Morny (1811–1865) was an aristocratic adventurer with flair for profit, talent for political maneuver, and incredible lust for pleasure. He burned himself out too soon to help Napoleon III in the difficult years of transition to a liberal Empire, dying just in time to be regretted by all, "even by his wife."

** Persigny was Napoleon's devoted friend and minister.

A contemporary engraving showing the reconstruction of Paris.

mobilized capital, pulling small savings into investment and speculation. The railroad network grew from 3,600 to 18,000 kilometers and railroad personnel from about 30,000 to about 140,000. Living standards improved and the Second Empire would see consumption of wheat rising 20 per cent, sugar 50 per cent, potatoes 80 per cent, wine 200 per cent, coffee 300 per cent.

Great public works helped spread prosperity. The greatest of them all, the reconstruction of Paris under the leadership of an Alsatian Prefect, G. E. Haussmann (1809–1891), produced the fortune of many a speculator and also the city that we know today with its impressive vistas, its wealth of squares and parks, adequate water supply, and sanitary sewers. Haussmann and his aides did not only seek to increase security, lessen the chance of revolution and of barricades; they appreciated the majesty of straight, broad avenues, the disappearance of the maze of alleys where crime and insurrection bred or sheltered, the new physical barriers that amplified and clarified social ones. Poorer people who could not afford high rents in the new central quarters migrated into suburbs. The distance between bourgeoisie and workers, who once had lived in the same buildings and the same parts of town, grew; and one effect was that both parties began to nourish fantastic or exaggerated notions about the other's way of life. Thus even the best intentions could have unexpected results and the ambiguous nature of the regime appeared in everything it did.

Napoleon III sought to reconcile the revolutionary appeal to universal suffrage with the stability of hereditary succession, the Napoleonic tradition of expansion with support of national self-determination, populist sympathies and economic development, political power and liberal tendencies. This worked well enough for a while. Universal suffrage provided the dynasty with a solid base of peasant loyalty, successful campaigns brought glory and a feeling of achievement, economic expansion gave prosperity to the *bourgeoisie* and left some over for the working class, a subtle political game gave all parties something that would please them. Then, in the late 1860's, things began to go wrong. The workers were stirring. The discipline that factories imposed reduced working hours but also the absenteeism that had lightened the workers' load. *Saint Monday,* which many workers worshipped by staying away from work lost its faithful; and even the "shorter" twelve-hour working day often drew out to fourteen, when one counted meals and machine cleaning. There were worse restrictions on the workers' freedom: all employees had to carry the *livret,* a certificate which marked dates and places of employment, along with possible comments, introduced in 1746, suppressed in 1791, re-established by Napoleon in 1803, somewhat forgotten during the July Monarchy, to be reaffirmed by a law of 1854 and only abolished in 1890. Even the workers' better pay was only relative, for, while real wages rose by about 28 per cent between 1850 and 1870, employers' profits increased fourfold.

Artisans, doing badly as their crafts declined, hollered for help; skilled workers did well, but wanted to do better. A French miner's pay went up 30 per cent between 1852 and 1870; the dividends paid to owners of mining stock tripled. Workers' housing in the industrial north was as bad in the 60's as it had been in the 40's. Even the new houses lacked light, sanitation, let alone adequate space. Pregnant girls were unable to tell magistrates whether their father or their brother had put them in the family way. And while far more salaries at the end of the Empire allowed a decent life provided the wage earner was childless, the employers' growing fortunes ostentatiously stressed the contrast between them and the poor wages of their personnel.

Napoleon had confiscated most of the property of the Orléans family, allotting the considerable proceeds to credit unions, mortgage banks, workers' housing, and a retirement fund for destitute parish priests. Honest government pawnshops had replaced usurers; earnest attempts had been made to curb alcoholism; Sunday rest had been introduced in government offices and enterprises. After an early period of repression, workers' self-help received much encouragement, co-operatives were subsidized and supported; and it was Napoleon's initiative in sending a large worker delegation to the London Exhibition of 1851 that led to the foundation of the First International. But the attempt to reconcile the workers failed. Strikes, legalized after 1864, were still looked upon by employers as rebellion, and government officials often protected blacklegs as well as property, prefects and judges being less impressed by the distress of the strikers than by the ingratitude they showed to their employers. When freedom of assembly and of the press were granted in 1868, they released a flood of criticism and opposition. Concessions only spurred demands for more concessions. In the plebiscite of 1870, while seven and a half million approved the liberal orientation of the Empire, one and a half million showed their opposition not to liberalism but to its inefficiency: the urban workers had passed into the opposition camp.

Yet many had reason to be satisfied. France was growing richer and its wealth was being more widely distributed. Without the tax burden being raised, revenue from taxes increased from 42 to 57 francs per inhabitant between 1851 and 1861. In 1849, 730,000 persons had 97 million francs in savings bank deposits; in 1869, 2.5 million had eight times as much.* Investments grew and turned increasingly from land to stocks, to the kind of deals best carried out with someone else's money, until (in the words of a novelist) the Stock Exchange became for this generation what the cathedral had been for the Middle Ages, and the habit of investment or speculation spread to the lowest classes—with Ferdinand de Lesseps of the Suez Company being told by a cab driver: "I am one of your stockholders." To have money invested in stocks and a *rente*—a yearly income from them—became the crux of comfort and every Frenchman's aim: what an estate or office had been under the old regime. In 1800 the sum of annuity interest paid out in the country was 713 million francs; in 1870 it was 12 billion, and 36 billion in 1895. In this last year, state bonds alone accounted for 80 billion owned by 3 million bondholders, while almost 9 million persons had savings accounts totaling over 4,000 billion francs.

The history of the French middle class in the nineteenth century will not be written or its economics understood until we have a history of that crucial figure: the *rentier*. The *rentier* was not always retired on his savings. Ideally he or she had never had to work. The hero of Flaubert's *Sentimental Education* (1869) is such a person. Frédéric Moreau had dreamed great dreams of conquering Paris before he found out the figure of his yearly income—the equivalent of a paltry 600 dollars (far more than an industrial worker or servant earned). On this, he could only envisage vegetating in his provincial home, going to Church with his mother, playing cards, brooding on his frustrations. Then he inherited a fortune from an uncle,** revived, returned to Paris expecting to become at least a minister, and, finally, ended up as the coupon-clipper he had started. Never in all his ups and downs, however, did Frédéric envisage taking a job and really working at it. The rewards of labor were too small to justify the effort when one could stay alive by other means: and this perpetuated a situation in which millions were immobilized by private revenues. For some like Manet, Degas, Proust, or the young Léon Blum, this meant that they were free to direct their creative talents as they pleased, and literature, art, politics, scholarship all benefited

---

* This would remain a French characteristic, at least until the First World War: 13 per cent of the national revenue was salted away in savings under the Second Empire, nearly as much in 1910.

** Not merely a literary device, inheritance was a major factor in the aspirations and the realities of nineteenth-century life, when very few indeed could envisage comfort on what they earned alone.

from it. But for the few set free to do something creative, there was a mass of useless consumers living in cautious comfort, contributing to the country's stability but hardly to her wealth.

The End of French Supremacy

The security of such people would be only briefly shaken by the collapse of Napoleon's foreign policy. The Emperor had re-established a kind of French supremacy in Europe. Wars in the Crimea (1854–1856) and in Italy (1859) had affirmed the power of French arms, humbled first Russia and then Austria. But Napoleon had to spare the feelings of the Catholic party and he was forced to do this by protecting the Pope's hold on Rome at the expense of Italian friendship. Then, business and conservative interests plunged France into a weary conflict overseas. In Mexico, intense unrest had risen to chaotic proportions. In the thirty years after 1827, executive office changed hands forty-seven times. In the mid-50's revolt by the reformist forces eventually resulted in a civil war, with the Liberals led by the Zapotec Indian, Benito Juárez (1806–1872), opposed by conservatives and by the Catholic Church. In 1861, Britain, Spain, and France sent troops to Vera Cruz to extort payment of the sums which the bankrupt Mexican Republic owed to its European creditors. Mexican conservatives welcomed the intervention, which they hoped would help restore their interests. The United States, engaged in civil war, was unable to assert the Monroe Doctrine but did its best to discourage the powers' trespassing on what she regarded as her domain. The British and the Spaniards finally withdrew, but the French were persuaded to stay on. To many Mexicans their help was the only hope of countering U.S. pressure which had been far more costly over the years than any European interference. Egged on by his empress, Napoleon now hatched the dream of a Mexican Empire which would defend the Catholic Latin cause against Anglo-Saxon Protestantism and persuaded a brother of the Austrian emperor, Archduke Maximilian, to accept its crown (1836–1866). But nothing availed against the Republican forces of Juárez, nor was there time to wear them down. In 1865 the United States was free again to aid Juárez. In 1866 the French expeditionary corps had to be withdrawn under this pressure and that of events in Europe. Maximilian's ramshackle realm collapsed and Maximilian, who refused to flee, was captured and executed at Querétaro.

Worse than the Mexican debacle: Napoleon's German schemes were going wrong. He had hoped to keep Germany divided, while providing all possible satisfaction to German national sentiments. After 1866 a new and dangerous power had to be taken into account, partly as a result of his miscalculation; and in 1870 the crisis came to a head. By that time, more than a third of French foreign investments were concentrated in Spain. When the Spaniards offered their throne to a German prince, the prospect of a Hohenzollern on the Spanish throne compounded the economic and political danger.

Meanwhile, the Empire seemed threatened from within—partly by the political tremors which the regime's liberalization started, partly by the failing power of Louis Napoleon, ever more frequently disabled by the dreadful pains of the gallstones which would finally kill him in 1873. Historians have spoken of growing disaffection. This is true: in the elections of 1869 opposition candidates attracted almost 45 per cent of the votes cast. Yet in the plebiscite of May, 1870, better than seven Frenchmen out of every nine endorsed the Empire's policies. Twenty years' rule had made no dent in the support Napoleon could count on. Not the opposition but the Court threatened the dynasty. As the Emperor weakened, the influence of Empress Eugénie (1826–1920) grew. The beautiful, pious daughter of a Frenchified Spanish grandee, Eugénie was cosmopolitan, haughty, supremely elegant, a dyed-in-the-wool reactionary worshiping at the shrine of Marie Antoinette. Her enemies who had begun by finding the marriage futile, ended by considering it fatal to the Empire. That is what it proved.

Eugénie and her friends had pressed to keep French troops in Rome and send others to Mexico. Now, their obstinacy turned a quest for diplomatic success into military disaster. In July, 1870, the Hohenzollern candidature to the Spanish throne became a handle to the humiliation of Prussia. Under French pressure, William of Prussia intervened to make his Hohenzollern nephew withdraw his acceptance of the Spanish crown, but the war party in the Tuileries were not content with that. When the old Prussian king refused to be pressed too far, Eugénie's bellicose friends steered France into a war for which the country was ill-prepared and which, to the world's surprise, her generals quickly bungled. In a few weeks, the superior generalship of the Germans defeated the main armies of the French and, on September 2, 1870, Napoleon III was a prisoner at Sedan. Two days later a Third Republic had been proclaimed in Paris and Eugénie, deserted by all but her American dentist, was on her way to England.

The Third Republic

But the new Republican government had to admit defeat in its turn. The hastily organized levies could not long withstand the well-trained German armies and Paris, after a nineteen-weeks' siege during which it was reduced to near starvation, had to capitulate. Peace talks had prepared an armistice in January, 1871, but Bismarck would conclude peace only with a properly elected government. In February, with German troops occupying a large part of the country, elections were held, turning largely on the issue of peace or war. Sentiment for peace worked against the

Leader of the Third Republic, Adolphe Thiers (hand outstretched), and his Council of Ministers, 1872.

Republicans who, under the leadership of Léon Gambetta (1838–1882), favored continued resistance. The war was blamed on the Bonapartists, its continuation on Gambetta, who had escaped beleaguered Paris in a balloon to organize resistance in the provinces. The new Assembly counted 400 Monarchists, mostly provincial gentlemen who had kept away from the discredited Empire, and only 150 Republicans. It was this conservative and pacific majority, under the leadership of a seventy-four-year-old survivor of the July Monarchy, Adolphe Thiers (1797–1877), which ratified the German peace terms: loss of Alsace-Lorraine, a war indemnity of 5 billion francs, and German occupation of eastern France pending the payment. It would soon face a serious internal crisis.

Paris with its host of workers, artisans, students, drifters, and assorted intellectuals, had always been a radical powder keg. The siege bore hard on its population and, at one time, a radical and socialist rising to set up a Commune in the tradition of 1792 had been put down by force. Nerves frayed by suffering and tension were wound to fury by the peace terms. It is hard to tell whether the loss of Alsace-Lorraine caused greater indignation than the brief Prussian occupation of the capital. Then came the news that the reactionary Assembly, gathered at Bordeaux, had decided it would not return to Paris but settle at Versailles, where it would be out of reach of the disturbances the city mob might breed. Along with this came a decree that rents and bills, on which a moratorium had been placed during the siege, must be paid at once. Unable to meet overdue bills at short notice, many shopkeepers and householders were faced with ruin. The city seethed with anger, while many of the wealthier citizens who had left the city in search of better air, diet, or security as soon as the siege was lifted, were missing to counterbalance the rebellious mood. At this point, in mid-March, 1871, a government attempt to seize the artillery of the National Guard (bought by public subscription) set off an insurrection. While Thiers withdrew his troops and government to Versailles, the Commune ruled in Paris during ten further weeks of siege, and social war raged between the insurrectionists and the Versaillese, who only recaptured the city at the end of May.

Between March and May, the *Communards* barked loudly but bit little. They talked of decentralization, separation of Church and State, abolition of the standing army to be replaced by the National Guard, but had no clear-cut program beyond their pent-up frustrations. There was no unity among the Commune's leaders—most of them very young —who ranged from Jacobins to followers of Proudhon or Blanqui or Marx, some of them manual workers, some journalists or soldiers, but almost all, whatever their doctrine, earnest humanitarians.

While the Versaillese shot rebel prisoners out of hand, the Commune hardly killed a prisoner or hostage until the end, when, in the midst of chaos, individuals took the law into their own hands. Marx, watching from London, would criticize the Communards for doing little to destroy the fundamental institutions of the order which they challenged. Indeed, their most radical measures were to prohibit night work in the bakeries and, under the guidance of Courbet, the painter, to topple over the great column in the Place Vendôme on which the first Napoleon's statue stood. The financial executives of the Commune respected the deposits in the Bank of France, kept scrupulous accounts, and maintained an orthodox financial policy. None of this moderation stood them in good stead when they were beaten. Humiliated by the Prussians, the upper classes took out their terrors and resentments on revolutionary Paris, carrying fire and sword through its streets, executing 20,000 and deporting more, turning an unsuccessful popular rising into a lasting symbol and a memory. The actual performance of the Commune came to be less significant than the myth it left to later propagandists of a first attempt to set up a Communist state.

Thiers and the Assembly were now free to make France safe for conservatism. The country was liberated from the Germans when, in 1873, Thiers paid off the war indemnity eighteen months ahead of schedule and did it without increasing taxes, preferring to have recourse to loans. It

Hostages put to death during the Paris Commune.

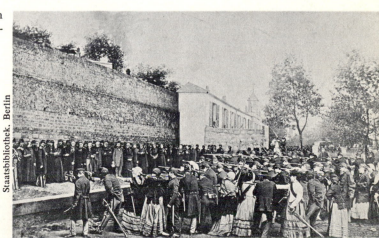

Staatsbibliothek. Berlin

A contemporary engraving of Paris burning during the Commune.

could not be freed as easily of the democratic danger. Manhood suffrage could not be abandoned, but the Chamber of Deputies which it selected was balanced by a Senate designed as the Grand Council of the country's communes, made up by indirect election from electoral colleges where every municipality—whether Paris with its millions or a large village with only a few hundred—had an equal vote. The highly conservative Senate served as a check on the direct democracy of the Chamber; and this became important when in a few years the Monarchist hopes of 1871 were ruined and the Republicans forged ahead once more.

The Monarchist majority was actually divided between supporters of the Bourbons and those of the Orléans. Each side preferred a Republic to the triumph of its rivals until a settlement was reached by which the Comte de Chambord, Charles X's grandson, was recognized by his Orléanist cousins as Henry V (1820–1883) and he, having no children, tacitly accepted the Orléans princes as his heirs. Royalist hopes were raised and, in 1875, France was endowed with a Republican constitution that could be adapted to a monarchy by giving the head of state powers greater than those of many European kings, and which, as it was to turn out, would not be used by the eleven presidents that spanned the course of the Third Republic. In 1873 Thiers was replaced by one of Napoleon III's better soldiers: Marshal MacMahon, who was expected to cede his place to the Bourbon pretender at the first opportunity. But restoration plans foundered on Henry V's refusal to accept the tricolor flag and, by 1877, MacMahon had to contend with a Republican majority in the Chamber. His unsuccessful attempt to go against them, by dissolving the Chamber he did not like, failed and ensured that no other president would dissolve an elected assembly and that, in other words, the legislative power would be predominant over the executive.

After 1879, when MacMahon resigned in disgust, France was governed by moderate Republicans; but memories of every other political allegiance survived so that the nation was endlessly divided by rival creeds. While things went well and the economy remained prosperous, this did not matter much. Under strain, the usual recriminations of political parties were colored by the tendency to question fundamental institutions, to recognize as good Frenchmen only those who held the right political views, and to exclude all others from the national community. France had known so many constitutions, so many dynasties, so many loyalties and political doctrines in less than a hundred years, that no political institution seemed stable or enduring. Even the most patriotic Frenchmen kept their strongest loyalties for the family and for the abstract concept of a fatherland with which the state or government were identified but little. Hence the paradoxical contrast of an unusually stable society with equally unstable politics.*

The Heart and the Pocketbook

Despite serious recessions, the years to 1914 were quite prosperous. The great depression that affected Europe in the late 70's, the 80's, and the early 90's, hit France far less than more developed and hence more vulnerable countries. The serious difficulties of agriculture were largely remedied by protective tariffs which permitted farmers to vegetate without fear of competition. But the static penalties of protection were lost from sight behind its advantages. Between 1870 and 1914 industrial output tripled, the national income doubled, real wages in industry went up 50 per cent. In 1870 a third of the peasantry was still illiterate. By 1914 illiteracy had been wiped out. Schools, trains, bicycles, newspapers, all spread political awareness through the land. France was a country of small men content to be independent on small profits and a German proverb described the good life as living like God in France.

Population shifted from agriculture to industry, but it did so more slowly than in neighboring countries. In 1914, 44 per cent of the population still made a living out of agriculture. Many of these consumed a good part of their produce, bought as little as they could, kept out of the market economy as far as they were able, putting little money into circulation and investing their savings in safe quarters: mainly state bonds, foreign or French, least productive from the viewpoint of capital expansion.

Industry lagged, partly for lack of capital, partly from lack of raw materials—above all, coal. French coal deposits were few, awkwardly situated, costly to exploit. A ton of coal cost about one-third more in France than in Germany or England. Furthermore, in the territories lost to Germany in 1870, the Republic had also forfeited her main iron-ore deposits. Developed in 1878, the Gilchrist-Thomas process of turning mineral ore to steel made available Lorraine deposits which were too mixed with phosphorus to have been used in earlier converters. Great ironworks arose in French Lorraine, but none were so important as those developed on the German side. In any case, the coal for their furnaces

* The Third Republic enjoyed forty-two different governments between 1881 and 1914, forty-odd more between the wars.

came mostly from the Rhineland and the Saar. French heavy industry, dependent on German fuel, was tied to German industry and limited by it.

Given the role of coal (and steel) in modern war, industrial inferiority was translated into political weakness whose effects continued evident as late as the defeat of 1940. Its economic effects were felt more quickly, for a modern economy depends on the heavy sector whose relative backwardness and high production costs slowed down the pace of French economic progress until mid-twentieth century.

Another fuel was also in short supply: industrial manpower. New arrivals from the land preferred small businesses to factories. Between 1866 and 1906, the number of industrial workers increased by a quarter, that of tradesmen by two-thirds. It was France which now became a nation of shopkeepers. "The Frenchmen work for the few, but we for the millions," declared an English manufacturer. French industry was caught in its tradition of catering for luxury trades. Buyers of perfumes and dresses, glass or leatherware, jewelry and fine wines were more constant in their means and even in their tastes than the new popular buying public, which was tempting in its possibilities but frightening in its capricious changes and in the fluctuations of its revenues.

More important, perhaps, were the Frenchman's reluctance to invest money in industry when he could get equal or greater revenues from state loans, and his historical tendency to retire from business, withdrawing his capital when he could no longer personally control it and placing it in *rentes,* in real estate, or, simply, in the coffers of some bank. Between 1850 and 1914 a third or a half of French savings were lent or invested abroad—even more than Britain's. French loans and investments in Russia amounted to 16 billion francs in the thirty years before the war. There and elsewhere French investors would lose a large part of their money in 1918. Reluctance to invest in industry made for a leisurely pace of life but had unfortunate consequences. Some of the century's great discoveries in medicine, physics, hydroelectrics, and cinema were made in France, but their use was slight and slow. It was the work of French engineers that brought the first cargo of refrigerated Argentine meat to Le Havre in 1878, but French investors would not provide the capital to follow up the success and the inventors turned to Britain. In 1914, of nine great dyestuff factories in France, five were German, one Swiss, and 87 per cent of colorants used in France came from Germany, which boasted 30,000 chemists, fifteen times more than France. Inventive enough, France lagged in industrial application and its productivity lagged behind that of other powers.

So did its population. At the beginning of the eighteenth century more than one-third of Europeans were subjects of Louis XIV. Toward 1850 the French accounted for 14 per cent of the continent's population, by 1913 only for 9 per cent. The rate of population increase, probably the weakest in Europe, was six or seven times less than that of France's nearest neighbors. For every four children born in the 1860's there would be only three on the eve of war. By then, the annual excess of births over deaths for every 10,000 inhabitants was about two. It had been 67 under Charles X. If the nation's numbers were stagnating, its body, too, was getting older, with all the immobilism, retrenchment, and defensiveness that this implies. In 1851, for every 1,000 people 361 had been under 20; in 1911 only 126. By 1945 there would be two old people for every seven adults, twice the proportion found in contemporary Russia . . . or in eighteenth-century France! While Britain, Germany, Italy poured out emigrants, France now became an immigrant's haven drawing the surplus of Spain, Italy, and eastern Europe: by 1881 a million foreigners, by 1914 three million, were taking up the slack in her population.

All this had repercussions on the political scene. The early years of the Republic had been marked by struggles between Conservatives and Progressives, which, by the 1880's, the latter won. The educational opportunities that they now created brought all the middle classes into political life, giving them every chance to assert themselves at the political level. The proportion of the population in the professional classes and in public service was growing faster than any other class except the tradesmen and, hence, more and more people felt that they had a stake in society. But the society they liked and wanted to keep expanded only slowly and could ill afford to find resources that would improve the lot of those who did not get a fair share of its benefits. The farmers, shopkeepers, small tradesmen, doctors, lawyers, *rentiers,* who formed the backbone of the political Left so long as this concerned itself with issues like secular education or the separation of Church and State (finally achieved in 1905), turned Rightward when the issues became social; and unions, labor laws, income tax, threatened their pockets. If the hearts of the great French middle classes remained on the Left, their pocketbook was on the Right and the politics of the past century reflect the tension between these two poles. The tension would be resolved in a swing which, by the 1930's, had shifted a majority of the population to the Right. They remained radical in theory but security-minded in practice, patriotic in spirit but pacific in fact, appreciative of revolutionary-sounding rhetoric but favoring revolutionary leaders who proposed to lead them backwards, out of danger and especially away from the threat of change.

The threat of change was represented by the working-class movements beginning to revive during the 1880's,* a constellation of contending factions that mirrored every kind of tendency. By the end of the century France harbored six Socialist parties, two major union organizations,

* The Communard prisoners were amnestied in 1880; the first Marxist-Socialist party founded by Jules Guesde in 1882, the unions given legal status in 1884.

and several anarchist groups. Compared with the German Socialists all were puny: five out of six workers were not unionized, the political parties were small, and relations between them and the unions were made more difficult by the philosophy of syndicalism. This rejected politics because they split workers into factions and favored industrial action by trade unions, which would be the instruments first of social struggle and then of management by the producers themselves. In 1895, partly out of labor exchanges which the syndicalists had established to help themselves, a confederation of labor (CGT) was finally organized and, a few years later, in 1905, under pressure from the Socialist International, a unified socialist party was also founded (SFIO).

The SFIO's leader, until his murder in 1914, would be Jean Jaurès. Orator, humanist, statesman, Jaurès had started out as a professor of philosophy. He ended as the conscience and the inspiration of the movement he sought to organize. Jaurès saw that, having overthrown the hierarchies and the faith which gave cohesion to the old regime, his generation had to find fresh social cement, a new inspiration, which, he proposed, lay in social justice and equality. "You have stilled the old song which had lulled mankind," he told the Chamber. In its stead Jaurès offered not a lullaby but a march. He knew that in a country where the middle classes were growing fast while the industrial proletariat hardly increased at all, no social revolution could succeed without middle-class support. For a moment, he believed that this would come out of the Dreyfus Affair.

Right, Left, and the Dreyfus Affair

In 1894 a Jewish officer, Captain Alfred Dreyfus, had been accused of selling military secrets to the Germans and condemned by a court martial to life imprisonment on Devil's Island, off the South American coast. By 1897 a growing number of people, alerted by Dreyfus' family and his few friends, had become aware that the court had judged on the basis of secret evidence, some of which turned out to have been forged. They called for a review of the case. The army leaders refused to admit that an error could have been committed, eventually arguing that even an injustice could not warrant the harm done to their authority by the revisionist campaign. By 1898 the case had become an affair, had turned from a particular issue of alleged injustice to a contest between national security (the honor of the army) and individual freedom.

One of the most interesting things about the Dreyfus affair is the thought that it would be so utterly unlikely to occur today: not because there are no possibilities of injustice, but because they make so much less of a stir. What mattered in France, however, was that the case polarized the fissiparous country into two political camps: on one side the partisans of order and tradition, the Church, the army, nationalists, and

Captain Alfred Dreyfus.

conservatives *; on the other the radical middle class and the workers, who had drifted apart on economic issues, now reunited by a principle that radicals like Clemenceau and socialists like Jaurès could both agree on: justice.

In 1899, Dreyfus, found guilty for a second time "with mitigating circumstances," was pardoned by the President of the Republic after France had briefly edged on civil war. No one had really won; and the disillusion of idealists on either side increased the national inclination to political skepticism. But the affair had precipitated an important change. The Left, especially the left-wing intelligentsia, which for a century had maintained the Jacobin nationalism of revolutionary tradition, had spent several years fighting the general staff, the army, militarism, and nationalism. It now jettisoned its Jacobin heritage for the internationalism, antimilitarism, and pacifism of socialism, while the Right, which had been pacifistic and rather internationalist through most of the century turned toward nationalism. Instead of providing a bridge between the workers and the middle class, the Dreyfus affair and its consequences thus built one on which the "radical" but patriotic middle classes could join the conservatives: a common nationalism beneath whose shield their opposition to social reform henceforth sheltered.

The right-wing radicalism of new style nationalism had been developing partly in connection with demagogic calls for anti-German *revanche,* partly in reaction against the corruption and incapacity of Parliament. In 1888 and 1889 it had been incarnated briefly in the figure of a handsome officer on a black charger who became the darling of the radical masses for his patriotism and populism. But General Boulanger was a flash in the pan. Triumphantly elected to Parliament from Paris in January, 1889, he already had his future behind him. Instead of seizing power, as his friends expected, he temporized, missed his chance,

* These categories are general. There were, of course, conservatives, Catholics, and even soldiers on the Dreyfus side and plenty of the middle class against him.

and fled the country. It was revealed that he had bid for Radical support and received subsidies from the Monarchists. The alliance of the ends against the middle, of those dissatisfied with Parliament and those who rejected the Republic, proved popular and electorally effective. It might have worked but for Republican determination to wreck it by all available means. Boulanger was convicted of a treason he had never dreamed, his movement's electoral progress stopped, and the general committed suicide shortly afterward. Boulanger's legacy was the antiparliamentary, populist, and authoritarian language which his youngest and most idealistic supporters inherited and which Maurice Barrès forged into the doctrine of a new nationalism. This blossomed forth during the Dreyfus affair and played a great part during the prewar years in persuading France that a conflict was inevitable. One of its offshoots would be a refurbished monarchism, whose prophet, Charles Maurras, argued that France could only be herself under a king and that true nationalism and royalism were one. Another was a school of military thinking which insisted on the offensive spirit, believed that the coming war would be won not by matériel but by bravery, and sent many thousands to unnecessary death charging machine guns with swords and bayonets in the opening weeks of fighting.

The men who believed that democratic and parliamentary institutions could not carry France through danger were proved wrong in the war. It was the steadiness of her conscripts in the trenches and the determination of an old Jacobin radical—Georges Clemenceau (1841–1929) —that enabled her to win it. But they would get their chance when the war was over.

Germany

In Germany, the years before 1864 or 1866 were, according to Bismarck, "a time when nothing happened." Enough happened, however, to make possible the events of 1866, a first fulfillment of the unitary aspirations that had gone down to failure in 1849. The most important of these happenings were in Prussia.

Prussia's king, Frederick William IV (1840–1861), was a vain, romantic addlepate. Loyal to the Habsburgs for traditional reasons and to Prussia for dynastic reasons, he could not accept the sovereignty of the people, nor any paper constitution coming between his country and the purposes of the Almighty embodied in himself. Fascinated by possibilities of greatness, Frederick William could not grasp them when they came to him from the hands of "bakers and butchers." He refused the German crown the liberal Assembly of Frankfurt proffered, while yearning for one from his fellow princes. His disappointment in this expectation, like the liberals' disappointment in their expectations of him, put an end to the dreams of 1848. Liberals and radicals were emigrating, conservatism and provincialism spread over the land.

A brief attempt by Prussian conservatives to assert Prussian supremacy in a union of states in North and Central Germany was soon defeated by the superior diplomacy of the Austrians. In 1850, the agreement of Olmütz, in which the former recognized the primacy of the latter, sealed Prussia's humiliation. The German Confederation carried on in the invertebrate terms of 1815. Yet Austria took no advantage of her opportunities, remaining outside the *Zollverein,* which Prussia continued to dominate. While German industry forged forward, Austrian economic development suffered from the Crimean and Italian wars. Investment, speculation, profits, took people's minds off 1848. "The German nation is sick of principles and doctrines," wrote the educator Julius Froebel in 1859: "What it wants is Power, Power, Power!"

This would be given it at last by Prussia. Frederick William's unbalanced mind had given way to madness and his sixty-one-year-old brother William ruled as regent (1857–1861) and then as king (1861–1888). Frugal, direct, hard-working, William I had, as his brother said, all the characteristics of a sergeant major. Among them was an overwhelming devotion to the Prussian army. It was the Prussian Diet's unwillingness to provide credits for the army reforms which he contemplated that brought about a constitutional crisis in 1862 and set William looking for a man who could put the reforms through against the Diet. He found him in Otto von Bismarck (1815–1898). Son of a middle-class mother and a Junker, Bismarck combined the intelligence of the one and the self-assurance of the other. They must have been difficult to reconcile, for Bismarck was throughout his life doubt-ridden and neurotic, facts he concealed behind a massive facade of confidence and increasingly imperious authority.

The new prime minister stated his point of view at once, before the finance committee of the Liberal-dominated Diet: "The great questions of our time will not be decided by speeches and majorities—that was the error of 1848—but by blood and iron." He forthwith demonstrated his determination by ignoring the Diet's votes, putting through the contested military reforms despite it, collecting taxes and duties which the Diet had refused to sanction, and managing quite well since times were prosperous and the yield of tax revenue was rising. The Diet had no legal means to prevent his actions and it was powerless to oppose him. But Bismarck knew that the first sign of failure would mean perdition. He operated, so to speak, on short-term credit. He had to show successes fast or else his king and, not least, he himself would be in serious trouble.

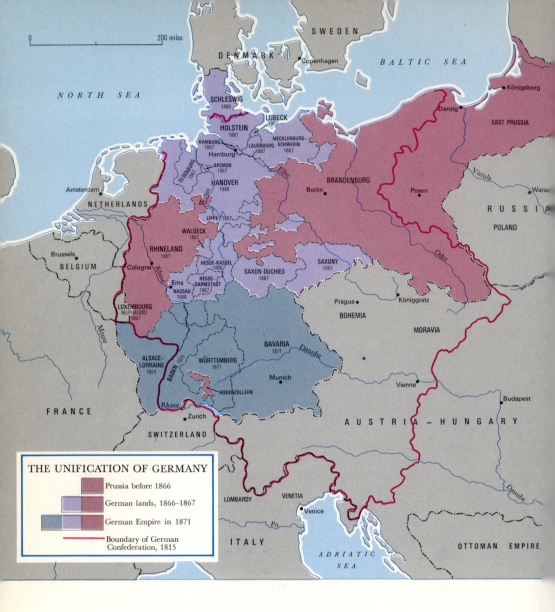

THE UNIFICATION OF GERMANY

Prussia before 1866

German lands, 1866–1867

German Empire in 1871

Boundary of German
Confederation, 1815

And he meant to show successes very fast, above all in defeating Austria
and fulfilling the national dreams of the Liberals.

Bismarck gained Russian friendship by supporting her against her
Polish rebels in 1863. Then a controversy over the succession to the
Duchies of Schleswig and Holstein and over Schleswig's union with Den-
mark led to war with Denmark in 1864, Schleswig and Holstein's in-
corporation in Germany, and their occupation by Austro-Prussian forces.
Bismarck's policy now aimed at eliminating Austria from North Ger-

Kaiser William I.

many and annexing the two duchies. When Austria proved unwilling, he concluded a military alliance with Italy, which was promised Venetia, and nonplussed the Liberals by supporting a new constitution based on universal suffrage for North Germany. A three-week summer war in 1866 sufficed to defeat Austria and exclude her from the rest of Germany, annex Hanover, Hesse, Frankfurt, and Schleswig-Holstein to Prussia, and form the North German Confederation. Then, four years later, the Franco-Prussian war, this time six months long (1870–1871), completed the unity which Bismarck many years before had described contemptuously as "the German swindle," and capped it with an Imperial constitution that at first sight fulfilled the liberals' dearest dreams, and yet maintained the supremacy of Prussia for which Bismarck labored.

A German Character?

In 1871 no country in Europe had a lower house elected by manhood suffrage as the new Reich did. But its Reichstag could not initiate legislation, could not enforce its will, and had no control over government policy. It was, a Socialist once described it, the fig leaf of absolutism. Real power lay in the hands of the chancellor, who was also prime minister of Prussia, and in the old emperor-army alliance—the emperor appointing all imperial officials including the chancellor, and the army supporting him unhesitatingly as long as the interests of the landed officer corps were defended by him. They were defended well: by 1906, all of the Guard regiments counted only one officer of bourgeois origin and he would be transferred to the General Staff in 1907. Until the war, officers remained the very cream of society: "After God the Father comes the cavalry officer, then his mount, then nothing, nothing, still nothing, then the infantry officer. Very far behind come the civilians: first the reserve officers and at last . . . the remainder."

Officer was almost identical with Junker, by now symbolic figure of a ruling military caste of feudal landowners whose estates, originally conquered from other races, had been more recently wrested from the peasants at whose expense they had been put together. During the nineteenth century, while many peasants became landless laborers, the Junkers' power increased, especially in East Prussia, where farms over 250 acres took up almost half the arable land—four or five times as much as in the rest of Germany. Most Junkers were small and medium landowners, lacking the metropolitan and national experience which made greater aristocrats aware of the new world of coal and steam and iron, lacking the margin, too, which could make greater men envisage compromise—the sacrifice of something to save something else. The Junkers felt they could not afford to abandon anything: poor, they scrabbled for more; fearful, they stonewalled against all change except that which might profit them; short of capital, they could not modernize, increase productivity and profits. They were caught in a vicious circle from which they expected the state to save them by protection, subsidies, or both. Their pressure groups supported governments which supported them, opposed and upset those that did not. Since they furnished the greater part of high administrators and army officers, their influence, which went far beyond mere votes, lay heavy on the Wilhelmian Reich before 1914 and on the Weimar Republic after 1918.* This was the class that furnished the backbone of the army and thus fulfilled an indispensable role.

As it had been for Prussia, the army was the bond of the disparate new empire. The vicarious pride it instilled, the order it ensured, the industrial profits it secured, all helped toward social and national unity. So did universal military service. The conscript learned to be faithful, brave, obedient, his standards of duty and honor focused not just on one dynasty but upon Germany as a whole. He also developed a readiness to accept blows from above and pass them on below when the occasion offered, a sadomasochism which would become a latent national characteristic prompt to reveal itself.

As for the Liberals, territorial unification and economic expansion meant that the content of their creed ran out as fast as the profits were raked in. The essence of German liberalism had been unification. When it was offered to them on a plate in 1866, Liberals quickly abandoned parliamentary principles and constitutional quibbles, gave Bismarck the indemnity bill he requested for having collected taxes without

---

* Twenty-one out of thirty-five Prussian district presidents before 1914 were titled; 90 per cent or more of upper ranks in the services were so too.

parliamentary sanction, legalized all the transgressions they heretofore condemned, and conceded that not they but the government should henceforth make German policy.

All this had momentous effects on the German people. One has to ponder that the new German empire covered over 200,000 square miles in the center of Europe, bound by more iron rails than any of its neighbors and turning out more coal than France and Belgium together, eventually more iron and steel than the United Kingdom. It was ridiculous, William II said in 1911 when told that Germany wanted to dominate central Europe: "We simply *are* central Europe . . ." Here was the sense of destiny and power that audiences found in the works of Wagner, all rooted in the notion of a chosen people, a young, pure Germany imposing her will on herself and others, carrier of a heavy fate, fulfiller of a mission. Yet German unity had in all a very short existence: seventy-four years, forty-seven of them in the Empire, fifteen under the Weimar Constitution, twelve in the Third Reich. There was an exaltation about such temporality, but also restlessness and fever. Unlike some nations that need think little about their being, the Germans never settled down or took themselves for granted. Anguished, self-questioning, uneasy, the German self was torn between mountebanks and nihilists.

Bismarck's successes rehearsed the same tale as those of Frederick the Great. They seemed to prove that discipline and determination could work miracles, achieve the apparently impossible. Will, courage, toughness, and self-sacrifice became the German ideals: qualities which, while valuable, demand a great deal of tension and repression, accompanied by fear of failure which must be compensated by rigor and overacting. The German was no more brutal or ruthless or brave than anybody else; but, being taught that he had to be all these things, he became a prey to conflicts and rigidities that other Europeans did not have to suffer, part of a mental climate whose price would be paid in the twentieth century. Other-directed and seeking security in discipline and obedience, the German tends equally to be self-absorbed to the point of ignoring any other point of view. His lack of self-confidence is counterbalanced by a strong wish to have his own way.

In 1862, when Bismarck refused to respect the Constitution and talked about blood and iron, one Liberal lawyer warned him to remember what he presented as a fundamental German characteristic: "the belief in a firm moral and legal order as the last and decisive factor in the history of states." If this belief prevailed in 1862, after Bismarck it would be no more. As long as the country had been poor and weak, it put its trust in principles. What else could it do? Success taught it other values, as it had done the French in their days of power. But so did failure: failure before Bismarck's strength, which convinced many Germans that he was justified in asserting that might is right and that "whoever has the power . . . acts according to his views." Bismarck's autocracy relegated the middle classes into economic rather than political activity, broke the beginnings of their self-reliance, and, at the same time, by a familiar process, encouraged them to identify with the triumphant autocratic state. Parliament was no place for men to shine: the ambitious went into business, the independent into lonely rebellion and angry sulks, the masses were left to apolitical loyalty, Philistinism and conformity.

The Political Spectrum

These are generalities. Politics are more specific and Bismarck was a politician above all. The king of Prussia and his army were patriots for Prussia and for the Hohenzollern dynasty. If they envisaged German unity it was as an accretion or conquest around Prussian territories, not as the middle-class revolutionaries of 1848 had hoped to establish it, regardless of the dynasties or of Prussia. Bismarck produced a German empire which gave the Liberals unity and the Prussians dominion; and based it on the alliance of these two forces, which worked well enough as long as he was there to manage it. But middle-class Nationalists and Prussian patriots had more differences than they had things in common. The first were liberal, the others authoritarian and conservative. Nationalists were opposed to particularists. Against them there arose first the Center Party, chiefly Catholic but grouping all opponents of the new regime—priests opposed to Prussian Protestantism, aristocrats who preferred Vienna to Berlin, provincial opponents of Hohenzollern centralism like the Hanoverians annexed in 1866, workers and peasants —especially Catholic and Polish ones—ranged against the big business supporters of the Empire, all of whom opposed Bismarck's middle-class allies; and the Social Democratic labor movement, growing rapidly in the 1870's. Bismarck managed to play Catholics and Socialists against each other, while keeping his original allies in hand.

The Catholics were not only by definition opponents of the Protestant Prussians, they were predestined allies for Catholic Austria and France, Germany's defeated enemies and chief rivals. Against them one could muster both Prussian Conservatives as Prussian patriots and the liberal middle class as German Nationalists. In 1871, Bismarck began the so-called *Kulturkampf,* restricting the political activities of the clergy, their supervision of schools, and their authority over Catholic laymen, banning first the Jesuits, then foreign or foreign-educated clerics, and finally most of the religious orders. By 1876, every Prussian bishop was in prison or in exile. This lasted until 1878, when need for support against Social Democrats and Liberals led to a gradual relaxation of the siege. Relations with Vienna had solidly turned to fair, the

Third Republic in France was becoming increasingly anticlerical, the Church itself was militantly opposed to socialism. A *rapprochement* with the Catholics took place at the expense of Social Democrats, who now received the brunt of the Chancellor's fire. Beginning in 1878 a series of anti-Socialist laws dissolved the party and the structure of Social Democracy and kept them underground, even though individual Socialist candidates continued to be elected to the Reichstag. Between 1878 and 1890 Germany had no Socialist party. The only antibourgeois movements left in the open were Christian Social ones, which moved even further to the right as Socialist competition revived after 1890.

While he muzzled the workers with one hand, Bismarck tried to content them with another. Between 1884 and 1889 gigantic welfare schemes, the first of their kind in the modern world, provided health, accident, and disability insurance, pensions for widows, orphans, and the aged, giving workers greater security and better living conditions. Germany could afford it. She was undergoing an economic explosion from which she emerged by the turn of the century as Europe's most advanced industrial economy, challenging England's primacy with a more modern and enterprising industry and a far superior educational system. Between 1870 and 1914 German population grew from 40 to almost 70 million; national income rose faster than that of other European powers, and so did living standards. The new generations consumed twice as much meat and beer, three times as much sugar, ten times as much rice, fifty times as much cocoa and tropical fruits, a hundred times as much coffee (all per head) as in mid-nineteenth century.

At that time, agriculture had still been the major occupation. In the early 1890's the number of persons employed in industry passed that of those employed in agriculture. By 1907 industry employed nearly twice as many as did farming, and the scale of industry grew like the small steel business that Alfred Krupp had founded with four workers in 1826 and which in 1887 counted 20,000. In heavy industry, chemicals, dyestuffs, and electrical products, Germany stood supreme. Native tradition suggested the planned use of relatively meager resources and state support for industrial enterprise—but also for education and for culture. Around 1900, Germany was the musical center of the world, boasting some 120 opera houses, scores of symphony orchestras, hundreds of choral and chamber music societies. None could gainsay the prestige of her schools and laboratories, her music and her art, her scholars and her soldiers, her *Kultur* and her superior technology and methods. Her

The Krupp steel mills in 1876.

Kaiser William II on the far left, and Archduke Francis Ferdinand, center foreground, with other members of a hunting party.

material primacy in Europe could be compared with that of France a hundred years before: her army intake was double that of the French Republic, her population, her productivity, her resources could not be matched. It was Germany's turn to grasp for European mastery as France had done, and her struggle for this would not end until 1945.

Yet behind all this there lay a serious lack of balance. The German middle classes never developed the self-confidence, the values, the capacity for criticism and self-criticism which would permit them to seize political power or, when entrusted with it, to exercise it. They accepted the ideals of the establishment which kept them out, they bowed to the values in the name of which they were excluded from power. This was reflected even in literature and art, whose outstanding task, declared the Kaiser, was "to foster the ideal." In the 70's and 80's, when English, French, and Scandinavian writers explored society and current spiritual problems, the Germans continued to write in a conventional way, detached from the surrounding world, idealistic, romantic, and conformist. When in the 1890's rebellion in art and music did appear, it tended to combine social and apocalyptic notes, as if no other conjunction could bring change. Anguished and messianic, the German art of the turn of the century reflected the despair of men imprisoned in structures so rigid that thoughts of escape turned from concrete possibilities to fantasy, a foretaste of the tendencies exhibited by the existentialism of Husserl between the wars: the more cosmic for being less concrete.

This lack of balance was reflected also in the personality of the new Kaiser, William II (1888–1918). Born in 1859, the same year as the *Origin of Species,* a withered arm gave the Emperor a lack of balance more evident in character than in physique. William invited adjectives and seems to have justified them all: restless, impulsive, vain, abstemious and flamboyant, humorous and magniloquent, given to playacting and to fantasies, he embodied some of the best and the worst traits of his race. His typically truculent mustaches just as typically

"Dropping the Pilot," a cartoon in *Punch* at the time of Bismarck's resignation.

masked the sensitive features in front of which they raised their aggressive points. Torn between his admiration for England and his pride in Prussia, affected by ancestral insanities and by modern tensions, he strove to live up to a grandiose image for which he lacked the stature and the means.

"The Kaiser," muttered Bismarck, "is like a balloon. If you don't hold fast to the string, you never know where he'll be off." The first to be off, in the circumstances, was Bismarck himself, nagged into resignation by 1890. The great chancellor retired to the hotel near Hamburg that he had turned into a country house, carting along with him his collection of 13,000 bottles.* German foreign policy passed into the hands of Friedrich von Holstein, whose name survives in the veal cutlet which he was first to surmount with a fried egg; and of a series of chancellors the best of whom, Bernhard von Bülow (1849–1929), has been described as "nothing but plaster beneath the shiny paint."

The political spectrum was no more promising: everywhere a little scratch revealed the plaster close beneath the paint. German Liberals were not liberal, they were capitalists: industrialists, bankers, big businessmen. They were against the landowning interests that constituted the backbone of Prussian policy and against agricultural protection, but for Prussia's aggressive imperialism, for expansion and colonialism and militarism, not any kind of parliamentary liberalism or democracy that the term evokes.

Liberal democracy, with all the humanism and all the indecision this implies, became the preserve of Social Democrats. We have seen already that the revolutionary slogans of the Socialists masked a reformist spirit. Their theories which relegated revolution to the morrow of electoral victory also prevented them from exploiting the reformism which they practiced. Dazzled by numbers, fascinated by their organization, fuddled by their own verbiage, the Social Democrats made the worst of all

* All full.

worlds in imperial Germany, as they would do after 1919 in Weimar. Allowed to operate freely after Bismarck's fall, they won ever greater proportions of the Reichstag vote: 20 per cent in 1890, 30 per cent in 1903, one-third of all votes cast in 1912, nearly twice as many as the next strongest party, the Catholic Center. Such gains made them overoptimistic. Their power was illusion; their impotence was real. For one thing, they had not fought for their successes but cashed in like all others on the gifts of Bismarck. They had never, like the French, the Belgians, or the British, struggled to obtain the suffrage or social legislation. With no tradition of combat, they could as easily lose what they had easily gained. For another thing, only a coalition could produce a majority in the Reichstag and, while coalitions sometimes helped win elections, their occasional allies of the National Liberal Party tended to back away toward the Conservative alliance that they much preferred. The professional men, shopkeepers, and salaried employees who might be briefly persuaded to co-operate with Socialists always sheered off as soon as they heard the bugle calls of imperialism.

Just as patriotic as other Germans, the Socialists were hampered by their internationalist and pacifistic doctrine. Nationalism was a realm in which they could not match the competition; and nationalism in Germany was trumps. In the 1890's, a Pan-German League had been founded to assert the rights of the Master Race to colonies, and gather in all sons of the German race. They talked a plausible line. Between 1871 and 1881, 800,000 Germans left their country. Far more had left over the century as a whole. The population was growing, and patriots felt that if Germany had colonies for her men to settle there would also be greater demand for her goods, and hence more jobs to keep prospective immigrants home. In 1842 the king of Prussia had refused an offer to buy California from Mexico. A little later a chance to settle independent Texas had been missed when Texas joined the United States. Most Germans did not want colonies—their attentions were engaged nearer home. Bismarck agreed. Overseas trade could be advanced without costly acquisitions or the internal and international friction that went with them. A brief change of mind in the 1880's led to the annexation of territories in Africa and the Pacific, but they were largely leftovers, arid, disappointing, and, by 1914, held no more than 25,000 Germans including officials and troops. Still, the shipping interests, the banks and iron industry that fed them, and the navy too, supported a policy whose rewards must have been more psychic than concrete.

The Pan-German League was a middle-class organization of teachers, businessmen, and lawyers out to forget their pettiness in their country's, greatness, their personal frustrations in Germany's success. Action, vigor, determination, regardless of anyone who stood in the way (including Germany's own real interests), was what they wanted. While they always remained a lunatic fringe, their rabid national chauvinism inevitably affected the mind of Germany, the more so since even more

Solid citizens for pride and profit: a meeting of the *Deutsche Gesell-schaft,* businessmen affiliated with the Pan-German League.

moderate men spoke in similar accents. For the sociologist, Max Weber, Germany could have done without unification "if it was to be the end and not the beginning of a policy of German world power." And in 1897, Friedrich Naumann, a leader of the Progressive Liberal party which sometimes allied with the Social Democrats, published his *National-Social Catechism,* in which nationalism was defined as the effort of the German people to spread their influence over the whole globe.

Lastly, the Reichstag had only limited powers.* It could not dismiss unrepresentative ministries any more than the Prussian Diet could in 1862, or control policy. This went to such lengths that in 1914 the Reichstag had no knowledge of how diplomatic negotiations were progressing between the murder of Archduke Francis Ferdinand and the outbreak of war. Parliament and party leaders kept up with events by reading the papers. There was no parliamentary system, as we know it, in Germany before 1918. Nor did the Reichstag have a say in the internal affairs of the separate states, each with its own kind of representative assembly. In Prussia, greatest of German states, representatives to the Diet were elected by a cumbrous indirect voting system heavily weighted in the Junkers' favor. In Saxony in 1896, where a much wider franchise had obtained until then, a system similar to Prussia's was introduced especially to thwart the Social Democrats. The peaceful conquest of political power became less likely every year. The Social Demo-

* Just how limited would appear from the incidents that took place at Saverne in Alsace during the winter of 1913. There, friction between locals and officers of the garrison culminated in demonstrations against the officers' behavior. The garrison commander, feeling the civilian authorities were not carrying out their functions, ordered his soldiers to seize a number of the demonstrators and shut them up in the barracks, a move far exceeding his powers and suggesting that high-handed military action could always trample on civilian rights. In the Reichstag debates where this scandal was brought up, the army defended its own, the government stuck by the army, and, while a large majority condemned the government position (293 to 54), a court martial held immediately after vindicated the colonel responsible and showed that the Reichstag and the majority of the nation were powerless against the officer corps and the Prussian system.

crats would never admit this. But their demands for truly representative government and a fair franchise at all levels remained unfulfilled until 1918.

From Bismarck's day to 1914 no German government had a secure majority in the Reichstag. All had to rely on a series of coalitions and combinations with anti-Socialist parties. The Social Democrats, strongest of the parties, could have used this situation to achieve measures they favored by opportunistic alliances with opposition parties, most of which also wanted more constitutional government, ministerial responsibility, and the liberalization of state machinery. But Social Democrats were wedded to the view that they must not co-operate with bourgeois parties but wait for their collapse, never adding to the power of the state (for example, by nationalization) until they themselves could take it over. Thus, while urban and working classes grew, the legal framework of society did not alter. Now that the middle classes had accepted the political order along with prosperity, it was the turn of the workers to be antimilitarist, critical, and internationalist. Concessions could have won their support for the established order, but neither the privileged aristocracy nor the profit-making employers would really make concessions, and those who did propose them were powerless. Germany stuck in a political deadlock, where the executive would not introduce the legislation the Reichstag wanted and the Reichstag, unable to initiate legislation of its own, would not accept that of the executive.

Then, in 1908, the London *Daily Telegraph* published an interview in which the Kaiser protested his friendship with England while revealing alleged sympathies for her during the Boer War. This caused a tremendous uproar in Germany and a serious political crisis from which the Kaiser came out much diminished, having promised in future to respect his "constitutional obligations." Since these remained as unclear as ever, the effect of the incident was to remove yet one more source of authority, however imperfect, and leave Germany more than ever in constitutional chaos.

After 1908, the Kaiser had no real authority, nor did the chancellors who existed through him, nor did the parties which had no effective avenue of expression, nor did the Reichstag which had no hold on power. Not even the services were of one mind: the sailors opposed England, the soldiers opposed France, and their pacifist or progressive opponents opposed Russia. Policy oscillated according to the chance of events and, in the end, Germany stumbled into war less because she knew what she wanted than because she did not know what that was.

The Nemesis of Power

The Germans, the best of whom could carry out a particular task supremely well, were incapable of deciding on a direction or a context; and this also prevented them from agreeing on precise war aims. The soldiers who, by default, had brought them into war were allowed to continue fighting (which they did very well) without precise direction, aim, or limit to their endeavors. The vacancy of authority which permitted the drift to war prolonged the drifting through it.

On the home front, things got steadily worse. Enthusiasm or resignation among virtually all sectors of the population made light of deprivations that for the poorer classes came close to famine. And only the soldiers' decision that they could do no more put an end to the fighting and presented the civilians with a revolution ready-made. In 1918 authority changed hands largely by default. The Kaiser abdicated. A republic was proclaimed. But even when the autocracy was revealed as an empty suit of armor, the reins of power were not grasped by conscious claimants, as in Russia, but gingerly placed into civilian hands by soldiers concerned to cut the army's losses. Once again, German institutions and German liberties increased without exertion, as a gift from above.

There had been mutiny at the end of October, 1918, when the fleet at Kiel had received orders to put to sea for a last forlorn battle, and there had been voices raised calling for the Emperor's abdication. Revolt had spread and "Soviets" had been founded here and there, while in Bavaria, always autonomist, an independent Republic under a Socialist, Kurt Eisner, was proclaimed. During the war, while the unions and the Social Democratic party fully supported the war effort, a very small opposition movement on the party's extreme Left had gradually grown under the leadership of Karl Liebknecht (1871–1919) and Rosa Luxemburg, sturdily antimilitarist, pacifist, and unwilling to exchange their revolutionary ends for patriotic ones as most of their fellow Social Democrats had done. Liebknecht and Luxemburg believed that workers should organize for revolt not collaboration, and that they held a stout weapon in the general strike which should be used to overthrow the existing order. In other words, they held to the original party doctrine; and in this they were at odds with the moderate leaders of Social Democracy.

In 1917, stimulated by revolution in Russia, by growing famine among the poor at home, and by disgust with the continuing, increasingly useless slaughter, this group left the party and set up the Spartacus League, named after the leader of the greatest Roman slave rebellion, which called for a revolution to end the war and seize power for the workers. The year 1918 gave them the chance to put their views in practice, views which were shared by revolutionary groups in other parts of the country. It soon became clear, however, that the extreme Left had a very small following even among the workers, most of whom supported the majority Social Democrats when they did not prefer the Catholic Center. It also became clear that Germany was not ready for revolution, that the Socialist-Center coalition which ran the first republican government under Friedrich Ebert (1871–1925), who had led the pro-war Socialists in the Reichstag, refused to countenance disorder, and that the army would not stand for it.

The Prussian military aristocracy which had run the army had largely been mowed down on the battlefields. But the power of the army and the professionals that managed it endured. It had been General Erich Ludendorff (1865–1937) who forced the Kaiser into abdication and permitted the proclamation of a republic; and Friedrich Ebert had greeted the troops returning from the front with the assurance that they remained undefeated. Ebert understood quite well that, without the army, extremists might take over. He kept in close communication with the Chief of Staff, while encouraging the formation of auxiliary "Free Corps" of national veterans and students which would be free to operate where the regular army was checked by the victorious allies. When the Spartacists, hoping to drag a reluctant people into revolution, rose in Berlin, they were crushed and their leaders murdered. Other Communist risings —such as that in Bavaria—were similarly dealt with. The new regime, like past ones, would be founded on an alliance between the army and the state, the former tolerating the activities of the latter as long as its interests and its existence were preserved.

Italy

Eight different states, a score of dialects unintelligible to outsiders, local traditions ranging from the French-oriented culture of Piedmont and the progressive tendencies of Lombardy to the clerical corruption of the papal states and the backward feudalism of Sicily: such was the Italian peninsula in 1849. Charles Albert of Sardinia-Piedmont had disgraced himself in Lombardy, the Pope's wonted liberalism had turned to despotism under the guard of a French expeditionary force, municipal rivalries had proved stronger than national sentiments. Charles Albert had declared: *"Italia farà da sé."* In fact, she could not go it alone. Charles Albert having abdicated, his son Victor Emmanuel II returned to a conservative policy and to entente with Austria (until one with France could be obtained). Even defeated, his country remained the symbol of Italian hopes, the only state preserving the red, white, and green flag and a vestige of constitutional government. In the capable hands of Massimo d'Azeglio and Camillo Cavour, rationalism, anticlericalism, and cautious reforms marked its government.

Piedmont and Unity

Son of a nobleman who had married a Swiss Protestant, strongly influenced by English parliamentary ideas and by the moderate liberalism

Camillo Cavour. Right: Victor Emmanuel II, known for various motives as "the father of his people."

of Louis Philippe's bourgeois monarchy in France, tireless improver and modernizer, Cavour became the motor of Italian unification. The Agricultural Societies, banks, railroads that he promoted, the newspaper he published—*Il Risorgimento* (The Resurgence), even the Whist Club that he founded in Turin, endowed Piedmont with the framework of a modern state. All became pillars of nationalist activity. As Victor Emmanuel's premier from 1852 to his death in 1861, Cavour reorganized finance, spurred railroad construction, encouraged agrarian credit and co-operatives, improved the army and his country's standing in the world. Shrewd, moderate, persevering, aware of the disproportion between the ends that he pursued and Piedmont's means, Cavour had to contend with patriots less patient than himself, with the republican followers of Mazzini whose ideas of Italian unity did not include the Crown, and, above all, with the brave and bellicose Giuseppe Garibaldi (1807–1882), a charismatic and uncontrollable leader who had learned the trade of arms as soldier of fortune in South America. After twelve years of guerrilla warfare in Brazil and Uruguay, Garibaldi returned to his native Nice in 1848.* Thereafter, he would act as a patriotic firebrand, his rashness often landing him in trouble and sometimes cutting across Cavour's more deliberate plans.

Each in his way, Cavour the schemer and statesman, Garibaldi the impassioned demagogue, contributed to the rise and unification of their land. But it was not Piedmont's slowly recovered strength that made Italian unity. French support brought it Lombardy in 1859, British support allowed Central Italy to choose annexation to it in 1860, and, that same year, Garibaldi's genius and initiative contributed Naples, Sicily, and the opportunity to annex most of the Papal states. The first *Italian* parliament met in Turin in 1861 and Cavour, whose diplomacy

---

* French at the time of his birth, Nice was part of the Kingdom of Piedmont from 1815 to 1860, when it was returned to France together with Savoy after a plebiscite to which Piedmont consented in return for Napoleon III's acceptance of the accession of the central Italian states to Victor Emmanuel's crown.

Giuseppe Garibaldi.

had been behind the lightning expansion, died·six months later. But there was more to come. In 1866 the Prussian victory at Sadowa brought the lands of Venice. In 1870, the French troops guarding Rome for the Pope were withdrawn at last and Victor Emmanuel's men marched into their longed-for capital. Italy stood united, when twelve years before she had still been a geographical expression of the textbooks: but united neither by the popular initiative that Mazzini hoped for, nor by the valor of its own arms, and, still, united only in the most formal sense.

The long peninsula was quartered by the Apennines and broken up into further segments by its hills. What nature had put asunder railways bound together again: but at the price of debts and taxes. The sovereign states now became *prefectures,* too often governed by officials from Piedmont so that their inhabitants sometimes felt less free when ruled by fellow Italians than when the Austrians had been there. Southerners especially exchanged their retrograde and inefficient Bourbon kings for an oppressive colonial administration that taxed peasants more heavily than the Bourbons had and drove them to desperate rebellion in the 60's and to chronic banditry for a long time after.

From the nineteenth century into the twentieth two nations endured side by side. In both there was unemployment, underemployment, hunger, and malnutrition; but the southern part was poorer, worse fed and housed, more illiterate, more malarial, more *African.* In Sicily and Calabria the feudal world survived on great estates and among brutalized peasants who sometimes rose like storms out of despair.

Divided We Stand

Rent by regional, historical, and cultural differences—between north and south, country and town, growing industry and small-scale production, between Anarchists, Socialists, Syndicalists, Republicans, Mazzinians, Monarchists, Liberals, and Conservatives—the kingdom was hurt by one division, still more profound. For threescore years after 1870 the Pope refused to accept the occupation of his city, Rome, or recognize the existence of the Italian state. Regarding himself a prisoner in the Vatican, he rejected the overtures of the government and in a firm decree (*Non Expedit*) forbade all Catholics to vote in elections or take a part in national affairs. The government reacted: if the Pope rejected Cavour's principle of a free Church in a free state, the state would apply it unilaterally—the freer for the political absence of the Catholics. Inevitably, official policy became more anticlerical than it would have been. Tithes were abolished; Church charities were taken over by the state, thus shifting the influence that came from the control of alms and doles from priests and friars to secular officials; secular education spread and inculcated the anticlerical views of the regime.

Still, Italy remained a very Catholic country. Even anticlericals were often married in Church and had their children baptized there. Soon disendowed foundations were endowed once more and, in the last twenty years of the nineteenth century, the number of monks and friars increased, while that of nuns almost doubled. By 1904 the Catholics were back in politics to support moderate policies against the Socialists and, the following year, a Papal encyclical withdrew the *Non Expedit* of 1871. Meanwhile, however, the combination of a kind of administrative colonialism in large parts of the country and of the internal emigration of the Catholics had dug a ditch between the popular masses and a government nominally representative, but viewed most often as an alien and oppressive power wielded by men somehow unrelated to those who paid for their caprices.

In fact, part of the heavy taxes went for necessities of a modern state which were not evident to a great many people and yet essential for its growth, like communications. When the Kingdom of Naples had become part of Italy, 1,621 of its 1,848 villages had no roads at all. Until roads were built they would never, even in the slightest way, become a part of the new national and economic unit being forged around them. The opening of the Suez Canal, coinciding with unification, improved the economic situation by placing the peninsula on the now reopened trade routes to the East. Rice, sugarbeets, and orchards prospered in the north where the possibilities of hydroelectric power began to be put to use. But roads, and rails, and power projects cost money; so did schools and teachers, however pitifully few; so did the army.* And there was little basis for a sense that most of those who paid for all these things had any share in them. Until 1882, while total population stood over

---

* Between 1901 and 1921 about 2.4 per cent of the country's budget was devoted to education and fine arts; between 20 and 30 per cent to the army and navy.

28 million, about half a million men had votes. Then, until 1912, by which time the population had grown to 35 million, there were 2 million voters. The franchise was kept narrow by tax and literacy requirements. It was only in 1912 that most workers and peasants got the vote; and the first elections under manhood suffrage were held in 1913. Thus politics remained the plaything of a limited class, rather alike to that which profited from the July Monarchy in France from which Cavour had drawn his inspiration, while the industrial workers and, in some parts, the rural proletariat struggled for better conditions and greater legal rights.

Ultimately, the country's problems arose out of economic imbalance. Italy lacked the natural resources on which Britain, Germany, and France built their industries. Where at the turn of the century one Frenchman in three, one Englishman in twelve, got his living from the land, three out of every five Italians drew their living from it, a few more than in Japan at the same time. Even in 1921 more than twice as many Italians worked in agriculture as in industry; and this continued to be true until the mid-1950's. The development of Italian industry was much slower than that of other countries to which industrial expansion also came late: Sweden, or Russia, or Japan. The country developed labor and revolutionary organizations even before the industrial substructure was productive enough to furnish some of the things that labor asked for; and labor unrest probably held back some of the developments that could have taken place. Industrial expansion bogged down in wrangling and strife, while the invertebrate character of Italian politics prevented both effective reforms (as in Britain) and effective repression (as in Russia or Japan).

The country's economy crept forward where its neighbors' rushed. Wages never caught up with prices. The condition of laboring people improved, but so slowly that they fell ever farther behind their contemporaries in other Western countries. This relative stagnation and the resentments born of fear, want, and insecurity meant chronic turmoil. Prolonged, violent, and generally futile labor struggles created a climate in which the classes watched one another like cats and dogs, in which no moderate unions could survive, and labor identified with the politics of revolution, while industrialists and landowners placed their hopes in repressive reaction.

In the 1890's a Socialist party was organized, not unconnected with the popular unrest and the irrelevance of parliamentary cliques. Nationalist groups sprang up in the early years of the twentieth century, and a Nationalist party was formed in 1910. But while the Socialists hoped to solve the country's problems by revolution, the Nationalists tended to look for relief in overseas expansion, colonial settlements that could ease the population problem and help the economy—quite how, they did not say. The African wars this brought were marked by humiliating failures, the worst being the defeat Italian troops suffered in 1896 at Adowa, at Ethiopian hands. Labor opposition, violence, disorder had now become endemic. In 1900 an anarchist workman (who had returned from America) killed King Umberto I (1878–1900). His heir, Victor Emmanuel III (1900–1946), promised reform, permitted unions to operate legally, but only precipitated a wave of strikes and walkouts accompanied by shootings and violence. There was too much pent-up misery for peaceful evolution, the trumpery parliament helped little, and a contemporary recession worsened economic conflicts.

The negative experiences of this time inspired a number of reactions: the historical idealism which Benedetto Croce formulated against the materialism and the self-satisfaction of the bourgeoisie; the romantic Nietzschean rebellions of poets like D'Annunzio and Marinetti disgusted with the sham and mediocrity they witnessed all around; the elitist political theories of social philosophers like Gaetano Mosca and Vilfredo Pareto cutting through the cant of pretended democracy and the pretenses of political hypocrisy. On the political stage, meanwhile, Socialist militancy grew more intense as the government entered the Libyan war; and their antimilitarist campaigns popularized the youngest and most dynamic among Socialist leaders: Benito Mussolini—son of a Socialist blacksmith and of an elementary-school teacher—named for the father of Mexican independence, Benito Juárez, himself teacher and journalist, fiery, erratic, grandiloquent, and forceful.

Every military campaign consumed resources the country could ill afford, to very little profit. This seemed particularly true when European war broke out in 1914 with Italy happily neutral. Neutrality was what most Italians wanted to maintain, but there were also cries for intervention. France and Britain played on irredentist sentiment for the still-unredeemed territories in Habsburg hands, in the Trento to the north of Venice and at the head of the Adriatic, around Trieste. Mussolini now emerged as a leading advocate of intervention, breaking with his Socialist comrades and founding a Nationalist newspaper, probably with Allied funds. While propaganda tried to rouse the martial ardor of a pacific country, behind the scenes frenzied bargaining went on: the Italians were demanding exorbitant compensation from the Austrians for Austria's expansion at Serbian expense. The Germans, eager to keep Italy neutral, urged their Austrian allies to give in. The Western allies, on the other hand, were ready to offer more for Italian intervention, since none of it would be at their own expense; and they needed her help. But Vienna made up its mind too slowly: a few days before it accepted Italy's demands, the secret treaty of London had been signed, promising Italy, among other territories, Trentino, Trieste, and much of the Dalmatian coast. In May, 1915, Italy had been maneuvered into war. She would have done better had she remained neutral.

Spain

The political reality of a country where universal suffrage had been imposed on a backward society, where electors were ignorant and apathetic, where local patriotism had more meaning than national and national issues no meaning at all, was *caciquismo*—the feudal regime of local bosses protecting their clients and their particular regions and "delivering" them in turn at the polls. "Politics ran like an express train, through the desolate townships and villages of Spain, stopping only at election times."* The rest of the time it was a case of charity and jobbery.

Of course, elections counted little. With a small electorate, nearly half of it made up of state and municipal employees or pensioners, electoral fraud was standard and the opposition often abstained from the machine-dominated polls, leaving elections in the hands of governmental parties and showing them up for the mockery they were. What really counted was the occasional intervention of the army: ill-paid when paid and recurrently discontented. Privates regarded service as a kind of serfdom, the junior ranks as ill-rewarded drudgery. "Nothing is more common," reported the London *Times* in August, 1847, "than to see Spanish officers . . . begging alms in the streets of Madrid after having in vain tried to earn a livelihood as servants in hotels." An officer's only hope of comfort lay in a rank or a political prebend to be achieved by insurrectionary gestures that shook things up and propelled him faster than the endless promotion schedule would have done. So politics was permanent sedition in which the discontent of the military joined with that of a faction out of power to make a pronunciamento—that is, a rebellion by mutiny. Yet political power achieved by insurrection invited further mutinies which could bring others into power in their turn; settling political issues by rebellion made rebellion the key issue of politics and other working compromises the less likely.

For the past century and more, every Spanish regime has lived and died in function of the army: created, tolerated, or upset by it. Republics or monarchies, *juntas, córtes,* and cabinets rose and fell, came and went; rebellions broke out, pronunciamentos were attempted; the constant fact remained that without the army nothing could keep going or be done. Under the surface of political chaos constantly brooded the fear or hope of social and political revolution. The rebellious tendencies of the Carlists clinging fiercely to tradition and church, the millenial dreams of Anarchists, republicanism under the Monarchy, monarchism under the Republic: stability was the rarest commodity in Spain.** As for the

* Raymond Carr, *Spain 1808–1939* (Oxford: 1966), p. 369.
** The two most relatively stable periods have been 1874–1898 and the years since 1939.

simple people, they projected their yearnings and their hopes to escape poverty on bandits, bullfighters, and generals risen from the ranks. But primitive rebellions paralleled loyalties and conservatism just as primitive and just as fierce. Latent or active, revolution and reaction were the two poles of Spanish politics.

There was a third factor in the political game: the Court, which tried to hold the balance between political machines and the army. The Court meant Ferdinand's widow Maria Christina, and then her daughter Isabella (1833–1868), declared of age in 1843 when she was only thirteen years old. Maria Christina had secretly married a shop-keeper's son and had as much trouble concealing her repeated pregnancies as her speculations and ventures into the Cuban slave trade. Isabella, an obese, devout, ill-educated girl, was also torn between her sexual proclivities and her religious guilt, eventually succumbing to scandal and political failure like her mother, after a reign marked by reactionary laws and bloody insurrections.

In 1868 one more such insurrection presided over by General Prim deposed Isabella, established manhood suffrage and constitutional government, and began the search for a new monarch which would set off the Franco-Prussian War. The brief reign of Amadeo, son of the king of Italy (1870–1873), ended in abdication and was succeeded by a republic also of two years' duration, which enjoyed four presidents—one of them a Socialist who held office for one day. Prim had been murdered in 1870 and, in the absence of any dominant figure, the Republic was a spell of civil war between Carlists, Anarchists, assorted Republicans and the supporters of Isabella or, rather, of her son Alfonso XII (1874–1885). In the last days of 1874, the latter (who had just come of age) was proclaimed king by a generals' *junta*. The suffrage was limited once again but, on the whole, Alfonso's ten-year reign enjoyed prosperity. When Alfonso died in 1885 the country once again had an infant king, Alfonso XIII (1886–1931), who reigned under his mother's regency. This time the politicians avoided instability by a tacit agreement to share power in alternating liberal and conservative governments. In 1890, a liberal cabinet reintroduced manhood suffrage, which merely reinforced the *cacique* system of electoral management, now master of rigging lists and intimidating voters.

By that time, economic development in the northern cities was beginning to create labor unrest. Representative government was evidently a farce, the parliamentary system discredited, and the underprivileged were driven to violent extremes—particularly anarchism, which, in the rural regions, meant chiefly land redistribution but which appeared everywhere as a violent idealistic reaction against a confused, unjust disorder perpetuating itself by corruption and force. Since the Catholic Church was allied with the possessing classes, the opposition parties became violently anticlerical and none more so than the Republicans and

Spanish and Belgian Royal Families. Standing, from left to right, are Prince Leopold of Belgium, King Albert of Belgium, Alfonso XIII of Spain, and Prince Charles of Belgium. Seated in front are Queen Beatrice of Spain and Queen Elizabeth of Belgium.

Anarchists. Anticlericalism was almost a precondition of liberalism in countries where the Church appeared an obstacle to every kind of progress. But it saddled progressive parties not only with a stubborn foe but with a dangerous canker; for it became an easy substitute for reform, driving other issues from the center of progressive preoccupations. Time was to show that persecuting priests and burning churches was no substitute for concrete social measures, although it often proved (like anti-Semitism elsewhere) a convenient way of channeling popular passions.

While radicals concentrated their energies on the clergy, conservatives were looking overseas. In Cuba, a ten-year long revolt had been ended in 1878 by a convention in which the mother country promised liberal reforms. Some such reforms were partly initiated. Notably, slavery was finally abolished in 1886. But Spain these days was incapable of fair administration. Unrest broke out again, encouraged by the United States, which looked upon the island with economic and strategic interest. By 1897, when a liberal government offered the Cubans something like autonomy, the Cuban leaders had decided that they would only be satisfied with independence. Unwilling to abandon an island it could not afford to keep, jingo opinion called for war at first against the Cubans and then against the United States (1898), whose own jingoes succeeded in forcing a conflict which most sensible men hoped to avoid. The war went disastrously for Spain. She was decisively defeated, losing not only her last American dominions (San Domingo, Cuba, and Puerto Rico) but also the Philippines. It was no consolation to the Spanish that defeat rid them of a colonial drain with which the United States would now be saddled. In any case, soldiers and jingoes would seek no less costly compensation in the colonial possessions that were left, especially in nearby Morocco, which became the particular preserve of the army and the chief terrain where promotion might be gained or mutiny hatched.

Spain remained caught in a familiar dilemma, her economy typical of backward lands whose population grows faster than their productivity. As long as the vast majority of Spanish people, living on the land, remained in misery, purchasing power was lacking to back industrial expansion on any serious scale. As late as 1936 more than half the Spaniards still wrung their living from agriculture; in 1956, 47 per cent.* Economic and political backwardness could be overcome only with resources that progress and reform could bring, but progress and reform would affect powerful interests vested in keeping things as they were. Additional revenues could be found only by estate and income taxes, which the political situation and the ruling mentality rendered out of the question; and the imperial ambitions of the military meant an army and a navy ** too big for available means, yet useless for any purpose except employing several tens of thousands and cowing the rest.

Spain was still a congeries of provinces uneasily held together with little sense of a national or cultural community. In 1904, when the aspiring young Pablo Picasso left Barcelona to affirm himself on a broader canvas, it was not to Madrid that he went but to Paris. By then, though two-thirds of the population over seven was still illiterate, a limited cultural renaissance was going on. In 1870, no Spanish scientist had known how to use a microscope. About that time a group of professors expelled from their chairs for their liberal ideas set up the Free Institute of Education, which became the center of secular education and of an intellectual revival. Inevitably the effects of the Institute were as limited in scope as those of the enlightened *afrancesados* a century earlier. But it helped breed the "generation of 1898"—social critics and enlighteners like Miguel de Unamuno, José Ortega y Gasset, and Ramiro de Maeztu, who tried to regenerate society by a heroic appeal to cultural patriotism (*Hispanidad*). Strongly affected by Nietzsche and George Bernard Shaw, these men rejected the crude materialism of the ruling bourgeoisie along with the vulgar masses and the shabbiness of democratic politics against which they affirmed their impossibly exalted ideas. But the shabbiness of Spanish politics, like the sobriety of the Spanish people, stemmed not from taste but from necessity. Policy and apathy had made a poor country even poorer. Food, quarters, equipment were comparable to what existed in southern Italy or the Balkans; the countryside hardly saw a bicycle before the 1930's; motor cars belonged only to the few and rich.

The Spanish death rate had been nearly twice the European average. With the end of the nineteenth century this was curtailed. By 1940 life expectancy for those who lived beyond the age of one was fifty-two

* In 1956, 42 per cent of the national income came from agriculture compared with 66 per cent in 1913. This figure should be compared to India's 50 per cent, and contrasted to 10 per cent in France or 17 per cent in Italy in 1960.

** After 1898 Spain was left with over a hundred admirals and no capital ships.

José Ortega y Gasset.

for men and fifty-nine for women: about the same as half a century before in France. Population grew from 18 to 24 million by 1930, faster thereafter. Those who could went to the cities or to America. Twentieth-century towns became what their nineteenth-century counterparts had been in France and England: vast refugee camps, half their population made up of laborers who had left the land to find casual work or unemployment in the city. Needs outran possibilities in a manner characteristic of such situations, outskirts turning to slums, electricity lighting populations which still got their water from inadequate pumps. Municipal government continued to be primitive and wretched. As late as the 1920's Madrid could collect only one-third of the town's refuse, leaving the rest to scavengers and the sewerless outer suburbs to death rates double those elsewhere.

Trotsky once pointed out that workers are fashioned by their masters and masters get the kind of workers they deserve. The violence of a country's social struggles mirrors the violence of the oppression out of which they grow. In Spain, the attempts of industrial workers and rural laborers to set up unions and associations were looked upon as insults to employers, somewhat akin to servile revolts, and were repressed as such. This attitude on the part of employers and officials tended to produce the revolts it had been meant to stifle. There ensued a dialogue of repression and reprisal in which each side felt certain that *it* stood for right and its opponents for wrong and provocation.

Social unrest was intensified by particularist stirrings in the Basque provinces of the northwest and in Catalonia. After 1893 a powerful Catalan nationalist movement sprang up, particularly important not only for reflecting a traditional resentment of Castilian rule but because Catalonia was Spain's richest and most advanced province and Barcelona the country's economic capital. In 1909 serious defeats in Morocco forced the government to find reinforcements by calling up the Catalan reservists. This set off a general strike in Barcelona, followed by bloody riots in which convents were set on fire, monks and priests were killed in what had become part of the ritual of Spanish insurrections. Following this "bloody week" a well-known anticlerical radical, Francisco Ferrer (1859–1909), was arrested, tried, and shot. Ferrer had been in England at the time of the rising and bore no responsibility for the massacres that marked it. But he was the founder of the "modern school" movement and a leading rationalist. His secular enterprises threatened the educational monopoly of the Catholic Church and aroused its violent hostility, while the schools he launched threatened the political monopoly of the ruling classes. A brief liberal reaction that followed Ferrer's death soon crumbled before the opposition of the King, and Spain was left to traverse the war years once more in conservative hands.

Russia

"A strange superstition prevails among the Russians," wrote the American minister to St. Petersburg in 1853, "that they are destined to conquer the world." Less than a century later, the idea seemed far from strange. It is the purpose of this section to span the interval between the time when it appeared humorous and that when to many it became a frightening likelihood.

Up to 1917, Russia remained formally the same monarchy that Catherine the Great had ruled. The Tsar was the father of his people, an irresponsible autocrat. Ministers answered to him alone and none—at least in theory—could gainsay his will. Mid-nineteenth century found Russia under the rule of the same Nicholas I (1825–1855) who smothered the Decembrists. It was under his rule that a French traveler compared the Empire to a military camp living in a state of siege, that Marx gained his impression of a looming barbaric power whose reactionary masters, allied with equally reactionary Prussia, threatened to overwhelm the progressive West. But Nicholas died under the impact of defeat in the Crimea, and for a while the threat discerned by Marx hung fire. Nicholas had three successors: Alexander II (1855–1881), oscillating not unlike his namesake between good intentions and disillusioned failure, was finally murdered after fifteen years of unsuccessful attempts on his life; Alexander III (1881–1894), more reactionary than his predecessor, a conscientious autocrat devoid of ability or imagination; and Nicholas II (1894–1917), stubborn, weak, and foolish, a naïve traditionalist without capacity or decisiveness to maintain the autocracy he stood for.

The accession of Alexander II seemed to usher in a liberal period. Rigid censorship regulations were relaxed, education was reformed, a new enlightened generation trained in new model schools, above all a beginning made in the burning question of "baptized property": the peasants. In 1861 private serfdom was abolished, some 20 million serfs granted civil rights. They could own property, move about, engage in business, marry or go to court as free persons, which was a great advance. Great but limited, for all kinds of legal, economic, and social discriminations remained, or were now raised against them. Thus, the reform raised serious problems, for relative freedom which did not carry with it the means to stay alive was bound to cause more troubles than it solved. The new free men lost part of the land which they had tilled as serfs and had to pay for that which they could keep. The sense of grievance arising out of this erupted in widespread agrarian troubles in the 60's and the disillusion of 1861 marked Russian politics until 1917. Conspiracy and agitation never ceased again.

Still, Alexander's reign saw quite material changes: local government assemblies (*Zemstvos*) were set up; a new judicial system was introduced, based on a surprisingly independent judiciary operating in open courts, frequently with juries * ; the army was reformed and based on universal military service; vast areas of land changed hands. About a third of noble lands passed into the hands of capitalists or richer peasants more interested in production for the market; perhaps as much was bought from the poorer peasants affected by taxation and by their need of cash to redeem themselves from serfdom.

None of this altered a basic situation of very limited liberties and even more limited facilities for leading a decent life. For the *mujik,* so went the proverb, God was too high and the Tsar too far. Judging by the mortality rate, said to have risen from about 24 per 1,000 at the beginning of the century to 35 per 1,000 in 1880 (though in Russia such statistics are even less reliable than elsewhere), emancipation did not improve the lot of most. As the 1870's ended, about half the peasantry owned enough land to keep body and soul together. As population kept growing,** more of the peasantry fell below the subsistence level. Even well-to-do farmers like Leon Trotsky's parents lost four out of eight children, used few candles and less soap. Lesser people found even tea a luxury.† Famines remained current until late nineteenth century; malnutrition, degeneracy, and illiteracy were commonplace. In 1894, school attendance figures were 24 per 1,000 in Russia as compared to 140 per 1,000 in Sweden or 172 per 1,000 in Germany. After the turn of the century, while some peasants—the *kulaks*—grew

---

* In 1878 a young girl, Vera Zasulich, shot the governor general of St. Petersburg in reprisal for the corporal punishment of a political prisoner, and was tried and acquitted by a jury. As a result the government abolished jury trial in political cases.

** Despite heavy mortality it grew over 50 per cent between 1860 and 1897, when it stood around 125 million, one-third of these landless poor.

† The Russian word for "tip" is "for tea."

more prosperous, the immense majority continued poor and deep in debt. Even the not so poor carried a heavy burden of debt and taxes which forced them to sell all the grain they could, grain which they would otherwise have consumed themselves, thus providing the exports that made Russia the granary of Europe, a granary where most denizens never ate their fill, but which did give Russia a favorable trade balance, kept the ruble steady and allowed high interest payments on foreign debts.

Reform and Revolution

On the political side, after hopes of more reforms had died in the middle sixties politically minded Russians had to be revolutionaries, for they had no other form of action left. Even expressing their thoughts was a revolutionary act, thus ensuring that few Russians would be politically active, but that those who were would be revolutionary. They had to operate underground, in a kind of vacuum, and were driven to extreme ideas and activities. The only hope of ever changing a system far harsher than the mitigated autocracies of Habsburg and Hohenzollern lay in revolution. The choice lay between a policy of immediate revolution and its preparation for a more distant future by social and educational propaganda. Both these avenues were treated by the state as equally subversive.

Three major tendencies can be noticed among the small, but determined and often violent, opposition groups. The first might by styled Populists, in that they followed Alexander Herzen's advice of 1861, "Go to the people" (*Narod*), seeking both strength and purpose among the peasant masses. Their prophet was Nikolai Chernyshevsky (1828–1889), who believed that Russia could avoid the industrial capitalism that was defacing the West and create a free, democratic society based on peasant producers. Translations of the social novel he had written in prison, *What Is To Be Done?* (1862), influenced opponents of industrialism and centralization all over Europe, inspired *Narodniks* to shy away from politics and parties toward the wretched, oppressed, illiterate bulk of the nation who had to be civilized and led to the point where they could help themselves. But the masses they wanted to help were indifferent or hostile. Populism, like socialism in one revolutionary's words, "bounced off the people like peas from a wall." Reformers could establish no contact with the masses of the Russian people, whom they so desperately wished to help. The young idealists who "went to the people" evoked no response except suspicion and resentment. The government had no difficulty in rousing the dross of cities and countryside against Jews, as against those forces of change the Jews were made to symbolize. Pogroms diverted resentments, frustrations, hatreds from the system to the scapegoat. Russians, like everybody else, found no difficulty in believing that people who were pursued and persecuted must be guilty of *something*. For awhile the threatening revolution would, as Plehve—the minister who permitted the greatest pogroms—put it, be drowned in Jewish blood.

The Populists, caught in a cruel dilemma of ends and means, reacted to these experiences with a contemptuous determination that ignorant men would have to be forced to be free; or else with utopian visions in which the state, captured and transformed, became the protector of the masses, shepherding them to liberty and self-realization. In due course, they organized themselves into the Social Revolutionary Party. This stood for land reform, more land for peasants, co-operative enterprises, village revival, and believed that such things could only follow political revolution.

Meanwhile, many disillusioned or impatient Narodniks had turned toward the less peaceable alternative of nihilism, a term spread by another novel of 1862: Turgenev's *Fathers and Sons,* one of whose characters—the revolutionary Bazarov—rejected all existing social values *in order to think them out afresh*. Many of Bazarov's admirers (most of them students) went only as far as the rejection. Individual emancipation, they believed, could only be achieved by exploding all the values of society, destroying bourgeois morality and the institutions that perpetuated it. Social nihilism soon turned to politics. Violence, terror, would blast the way through to peace and order, humanity and tolerance. "History is terribly slow," said one, "it must be pushed forward." In 1881 it was, with the murder of Alexander II, one among the many of their terrorist enterprises.

The third revolutionary formation was the Social Democrats, whose principal figure was Georgy Plekhanov (1857–1918), chief interpreter of Marxism to the Russians and of Russian Social Democracy to the West. The Marxists, as we might expect, placed their hopes in the development of urban industries and of an industrial proletariat rapidly growing toward the end of the nineteenth century. They were the least important of revolutionary groups and significant only in view of their later effect on Russia and the world. We have seen already that, in 1903, Russian Social Democracy split on the issue of who should join and who should lead the party. Lenin wanted a tight, disciplined group made up of dedicated militants, ruled from the center, and one in which the intellectuals, who dominated the Social Democrats as they did every other Russian movement, would be balanced by proletarians and subject to "proletarian discipline." Lenin's opponents envisaged a mass party, open to anyone it could attract, watering down its program if need be for the sake of inclusiveness and unity. The clash between elitism and mass, between centralism and compromise, was resolved when Lenin got his way in the party Congress and his opponents broke off to form a new party—the Menshevik or minority faction of the Social Democrats—leaving the original organization to the majority Bolsheviks.

Alexander III invested the energies of the state equally in economic development and in political repression. Aided by his old tutor, the Procurator of the Holy Synod, K. P. Pobyedonostzev, an antediluvian strong man devoted to the Middle Ages, the Tsar ran a tight ship. Religion, police, censorship, Russification policies for minorities, anti-Semitism to furnish do-it-yourself circuses for lack of bread, marked a regime sustained by foreign loans, ravaged by famines, seared by land hunger, misery, and painful adjustments to incipient industrial revolution.

Russia's great problem (and one well known to developing countries in mid-twentieth century) was that her rapid population growth was not matched by any comparable expansion of agricultural productivity or of alternative openings in industry. Rural poverty limited the domestic market and offered no outlets to industry; without outlets, industry could not grow and absorb the surplus rural population; the peasants remained underemployed, industrial progress slow. Beginning in the 1880's—and especially after the accession of Nicholas II—desperate attempts were made under the aegis of two vigorous ministers—Sergei Witte (1849–1915) and Piotr Stolypin (1863–1911)—to foster economic development, force-feeding industry and mobilizing peasants by putting agriculture on a money basis and encouraging the farmers to own their land or leave it for settlement in colonial Siberia and the Caucasus, or for the towns. Rural credit for the one alternative, foreign capital for the other would, it was hoped, raise the country into the modern age. For the moment it only threw it into worse confusion. To the cacophony of political grievances and calls for reform, economic and social arguments were added and the relative success of Witte's industrial policy and Stolypin's land reforms increased the stresses and the maladjustments . . . or simply awareness of them.

The sound of axes chopping down the cherry orchards was advancing.* Railroads pushed their steel tentacles in all directions: 1,000 miles in 1860, they stretched 14,000 miles in 1880, twice that in 1900, almost doubling again by the eve of war. To feed them, coal, iron, and steel production rose vertiginously; so did exploitation of the men, women, and children recruited to turn them out.** The number of urban workers doubled and doubled again between 1865 and 1900, growing faster than the population of the country or even that of the expanding cities. In other words, the worker proportion of the urban popula-

---

* "The time has come, an avalanche is descending upon us, a great wholesome storm is brewing, approaching, almost here, about to sweep idleness, indifference, prejudice against work and foul *ennui* out of our society. I shall work, and 25 or 30 years from now, everyone will be working too." Chekhov, *The Three Sisters*, 1900.

** The Donetz steel industry began in 1869, with blast furnaces built by English and Welsh steel workers led by John Hughes whose name lived on until 1940, when the city of Hughesovska (Yusovska) became Stalino. In 1903, two brothers from Lancashire, brought the cotton industry to Moscow. One of them would also found the first Russian football team, the Morozovtsi, who retained the national championship until 1914.

tion was increasing and their place in cities becoming established, as the floating casual workers of yore—just up from the land and likely to drift back to it—became the hereditary factory hands of the new industrial landscape.

The average monthly salary of a male industrial worker was 14–15 rubles a month, that of a woman about 10 rubles. While skilled workers could hope to take home two or three times as much, sums such as these compared badly with the pay of a lady's maid, who could expect 15 rubles a month* in addition to her clothes and keep: some 180 rubles a year, compared to the 600–700 rubles a year of a ballerina, or the 700–800 rubles of a second lieutenant in the army. Hardly up from serfdom, Russia's industrial proletariat were merely serfs of a different sort, re-enacting the sufferings and tragedies of Western industrial revolution but with fewer traditional defenses than existed further west: no unions, no right to organize or strike, no parliaments to intercede for them, no respectable public opinion to which they could appeal.

"A Short, Victorious War"

Then, in 1900 industrial growth, which had been advancing at a great rate during the past decade, ran out of breath. Depression aggravated the workers' lot and that of the people in the countryside who had to pay heavier taxes—that is, hand over a larger share of their crops so that the government could pay for railways, imports, and equipment just at the time when their growing numbers asked for food. The government, ever in fear of insurrection, banked on "a short victorious war that would stem the tide of revolution." The venue for it would be the Far East, where the Treaty of Peking (1860) had consolidated Russia's position on the Pacific shore. Since then her influence, spreading in Manchuria, had been strengthened by the acquisition of Port Arthur in North Korea

---

* Same as the price of a box for one show at the Bolshoi Theatre. We might remember that the pay of a ballerina at the same theater was 50–60 rubles a month, that of a priest 60 rubles a *year*, that of police spies 20–50 rubles a month.

Warder Collection

The locomotive of a Trans-Siberian railroad train laden with tourists during the early 20th century.

and the building of the great Trans-Siberian railway, finished in 1903. Now she met opposition from Britain, whose interests in central Asia she imperiled, and from Japan whose ambitions in Korea rivaled hers. Instead of coming to terms with them at China's expense, Russia blundered forward to a clash with Japan, hoping that war would dam the revolutionary pressures rising at home. The war (1904–1905) was uniformly disastrous and culminated in the brisk destruction of Russia's Baltic fleet, which had sailed round the world to founder at Tsushima (1905).* It discredited the regime and set the tide of revolution, which it had been meant to stem, running even faster.

Revolution rose in the end directly from another government initiative designed to deflect it. The new industrial proletariat had sporadically organized itself to improve its lot. A spate of strikes in the last years of the nineteenth century had precipitated passage of a Factory Act (largely unenforced) limiting the workday to eleven and a half hours. Police and government were not especially sympathetic to employers, most of whom represented foreign investors, many of whom favored constitutional reform, and whose interests often clashed with those of Tsarist autocracy. But they did want to control the explosive forces of the workers. So, the police inspired "tame" unions, which were allowed to voice some real grievance provided they did not come under Socialist or revolutionary control and which sparked great industrial strikes in 1902. In 1903, the mildly liberal policy of Witte was abandoned for the reactionary plans of Viacheslav Plehve, who tried to divert unrest into anti-Semitic channels and, finally, into war.**

Under the impact of defeats suffered in the war with Japan, the feeling grew among sections of the population which revolutionary propaganda had not touched before that drastic reforms were needed. Conscription, taxes, the economic and social dislocation, first of war itself, then of defeat in it, widened the unrest. One Sunday in January, 1905, some 150,000 persons led by a priest, Gapon, whose labor union had been subsidized by the St. Petersburg police, marched to the Winter Palace singing hymns and carrying icons and pictures of Nicholas II, to whom they wanted to present a petition asking for constitutional reform, land settlement, and redress of economic grievances. The great, unarmed crowd, full of women and children, was met with gunfire and there were hundreds of casualties. The Grand Duke Sergius, governor of Moscow, would be assassinated shortly after in partial retribution. Meanwhile, great strikes broke out in Petersburg and spread to other cities, venting the grievances which the massacre of "bloody Sunday" exacerbated

---

* On its way to Korea, the Baltic fleet took some English fishing vessels encountered in the North Sea for Japanese destroyers and opened fire with dire results. The future King George V would comment: "All I can say is they must have been drunk or else their nerves must be in such a state that they are not fit to go to sea in Men of War." He was probably right on both counts.

** Plehve died in 1904, murdered in a plot stage-managed by a Jewish agent whom his own police had planted in the Social Revolutionary terrorist organization.

Bloody Sunday, January 22, 1905.

and the general opposition to the war.

The agitation which had begun among the poor soon gained the middle classes. Liberal elements had long struggled for a hearing in the *zemstvos*, the local government bodies, in rural areas, where certain landowners, officials, and economists argued in favor of agrarian changes, credit banks, and assistance to the more prosperous and enterprising peasants. Now these formed a party—the Constitutional Democrats or *Cadets* led by Pavel Milyukov (1859–1943)—calling for constitutional government and greater power for local government bodies like the *zemstvos*. Middle-class agitation relayed rural and industrial troubles from Warsaw to Baku, a naval mutiny at Odessa in which the conscript crew of the battleship *Potemkin* mutinied in sympathy with the local strikers, and fresh pogroms encouraged by the police and carried out by the reactionary *Black Hundreds*. The Social Revolutionaries led the peasants in attacking landlords, the Social Democrats (while squabbling between Bolsheviks and Mensheviks) tried to work with the Soviets. These had grown up as strike committees grouping union and factory representatives, which became local executive authorities and spurred industrial revolt in the cities. The army could not be trusted.

In October, 1905, the Tsar, who had been ready to flee, promised constitutional government, a legislative assembly—the Duma—and franchise for peasants and middle classes. This split the middle-class reformers while the revolutionary movement was wearing thin. Strikes began to die down, fresh military and naval mutinies were crushed, the Soviets were put down, sometimes after heavy fighting. By December, 1905, reaction was back in the saddle. The promised reforms were watered down, indirect elections gave preponderance to the landlords and the rich, there would be no ministerial responsibility, the Duma's decisions were subject to the Tsar's approval. Even so, the strongest party in the Duma remained the liberal Cadets, not the reactionaries. In mid-1906 the new assembly had to be dissolved and the more repressive regime took up where it had left off in 1905. Governmental agrarian reform and a large French loan bolstering finances improved the situation of the regime even while courts-martial terrorized the revolution underground. Despite this, a new Duma in 1906 turned out even more radical than its predecessor, but just as hopeless. Dissolved, its leading radicals arrested or hunted into exile, it was succeeded by a third assembly, elected on a franchise revised to ensure reactionary success and which became a government rubber stamp. Jew-baiting revived. Land reform went ahead. Foreign investment in industry, reassured by restored stability, grew. Where 1905 had counted about three million strikers, by 1909 only 64,000 dared to take such a step. By that time the number of active underground revolutionaries stood around 10,000—less than a tenth of what it had been in the revolutionary year. Revolution had been beaten down.

It seemed that Russia had turned the cape of her troubles. A prosperous peasant class was taking shape, agricultural productivity increasing and diversifying, industry speeding up again—by 1914 per capita income was comparable to that in Italy. Social mobility was greater than anything in living memory. So was the middle class. Urban population had trebled in the past fifty years to some twenty million, one-sixth of it industrial workers now. Important industrial concentrations had risen in the Ukraine, around the two capitals and on the oil-rich Caspian shores at and near Baku. The horsepower of steam engines had soared, the educational budget had increased sixfold between 1894 and 1914.

Russia was still very backward when compared to the West: there were two and a half times as many wooden plows as iron ones, fifty times as many wooden harrows as iron ones. One-third of the peasants had no land, one-third of the farms had neither cattle nor farming instruments, average yields per acre were half those in France, a third those in Germany or Denmark. Rents and taxes were heavy and growing heavier. In all essentials of industrialization Russia was an underdeveloped land, its production of iron (per head of population) one-seventh of Germany's, one-eleventh of the United States'; of coal one-fourteenth of Germany's, one-twenty-sixth of the United States'. Even the expanded armaments industry could only turn out a little over three million rifles between 1914 and 1917 for the fifteen million men in uniform. Still, Russia could take pride in its advance. Then came 1914, and war again.

Russian policies in the Balkans continued tendencies at least as old as Peter the Great. But the slow, opportunistic moves of earlier Tsars had been rationalized into a new nationalism for popular consumption. In the last third of the nineteenth century, Pan-Slav doctrines had adapted current Darwinism to the needs of the Russian struggle less for existence than for supremacy. In 1871, Nicholas Danilevski's *Russia and Europe* argued Russia's mission to unite all Slavs whatever their creed or nationality, if need be by force. The struggle for existence raged among nations as it did among species. Russia could only survive by delivering her fellow Slavs from the foreign yoke, founding a Slav empire which, free of Western influences, would "overthrow decadent Roman-German civilization." Pan-Slav literature looked beyond Eastern Europe to Constantinople and the Near East. Constantinople—Tsarigrad—was a constant aim and symbol of the struggle it postulated. War was envisaged not only with Turkey but with Austria—Russia's rival for Turkey's spoils and the oppressor of other fellow Slavs: Czechs, Poles, and Serbs. The echo of such ideas drove Russia into war with Turkey in 1877. It kept up constant pressure, especially on behalf of the Southern Slavs. It would have been very difficult—especially after the humiliation of Japanese defeat—for Russia to stand by in 1914 and see the Serbs annihilated by Austria. And so it went to war.

The End of the Tsars

Ill-prepared and inefficient, Russian armies nevertheless played a major role in war. Their first offensive in 1914 probably saved the Marne and Paris; another in 1916 played a similar role at the time of Verdun and helped bring Romania into the war. But the costs were immense. The first year's fighting alone saw four million casualties. The troubles of a half-industrialized country fighting a modern war against a great industrial power were magnified by corruption, profiteering, disaffection, and incompetence. Men died, went barefoot or unarmed, so that some contractor should make millions; Petrograd (the capital's name had been Russified in 1914) went hungry while the court jeweler, Fabergé, boasted that business had never been so good. The winter of 1915–1916 was outstanding for casualties, diamonds, and extraordinary ladies' gowns. Men went about muttering that "everybody steals, and Christ himself would steal if his hands were not nailed to the cross." Industrial wages almost doubled, but prices nearly tripled, while essentials rose even more: bread 500 per cent, butter 830 per cent, shoes and clothes 400–600 per cent. By January, 1917, the cost of living was seven times what it had been when the war broke out.

Not even this would have brought disaster had there been a Peter or a Catherine at the helm. But the Tsar, Nicholas II, as the Kaiser once told a British foreign secretary, was only fit to live in a country house and raise turnips; while most of his family of grand dukes knew little besides how to make the fortune of champagne merchants. For a long time, Sir Bernard Pares has written, "the Russian ministers were selected by an ignorant, blind and hysterical woman on the test of their subservience to an ignorant, fantastic and debauched adventurer."

Grigori Rasputin, an illiterate, licentious, self-styled holy man from Siberia, had managed—probably by hypnotic power—to stem the Tsarevitch's deadly hemophilia and thus gained vast influence at court, where the Empress regarded him as her family's "holy friend." His influence and that of allegedly pro-German ministers led to talk of treason in high places, eventually to his assassination in an aristocratic plot in the

Tsar Nicholas II and his family.

last days of 1916. The war was going badly, morale was very low, and it is possible that a palace revolution would have broken out had not strikes, riots, and mutinies in the capital forestalled it in March, 1917. Within a week the Tsar had abdicated and formal authority passed into the hands of the Provisional Government, headed by Prince Lvov (head of the liberal *Zemstvo* Union) and joined by men like the Cadet leader Milyukov and the Socialist Alexander Kerensky.

Pending the election of a Constituent Assembly, the Provisional Government tried to carry on the military operations, promulgate social reforms and civil liberties, manage a major revolution in the midst of a major war. It could not be done. The great mass of the Russian people looked for two things from the revolution: peace and land. Most of the middle class, the intellectuals and officers, considered these popular aims secondary to the pursuit of war, fulfillment of Russia's obligations to her allies and the eventual conquests (especially of Constantinople) to be reaped from victory. The two points of view could not be reconciled and this was proclaimed widely in the Soviets, which had been set up in the wake of revolution according to the example of 1905.

Representing the soldiers and workers who had made the revolution, elected and controlled by factories and army units, the Soviets had much more effective and immediate influence than the government, whose authority rested on very little. But the rivalry between Soviets and Provisional Government did not mean that the former wished to overthrow the latter. They only wanted to goad it forward. In the view of the Socialists and the Social Revolutionaries who led most Soviets, the government representing the Duma and the upper middle classes should carry through the revolution, just as its French forebears of 1789 had done. Unless this happened and the capitalist revolution was achieved, the proletarian revolution would have no base to rise on according to the historical analogies they accepted. There followed a brief paradoxical struggle between the bourgeois moderates, whom the Soviets cast for revolutionary roles but who rejected this, and the Socialists, including the Bolsheviks, determined if need be to make the revolution for the *bourgeoisie,* then settle down to wait until capitalist developments opened the further way to socialism. This changed only when in April, thanks to German funds and German permission to cross their territory on his way home, Lenin steamed into Petrograd's Finland Station.

The sealed railway car in which the German government permitted Lenin and his Bolshevik companions to return home from their Swiss exile, has become the modern equivalent of the Trojan horse. There can be little doubt that such an unusual gesture was sparked by hope that revolutionary activity in Russia would redound to Germany's benefit. As for Lenin, he was quite prepared to take advantage of any opportunity to hasten the march of a revolution which was getting bogged down in theoretical considerations and revisionism.

Lenin had seen at once that the theoretical process could be accelerated, the bourgeois revolution skipped, if workers, peasants, and soldiers could carry out a socialist revolution of their own and establish the dictatorship of the proletariat without further ado. The analytical theory of Marx was adapted to the "objective situation" of the moment in a new kind of revolutionary strategy we now call Leninism: one which Lenin had found in Marx himself. One of the last things Marx had written was a preface for the new Russian translation of the *Communist Manifesto,* published in 1882; and, there, the old contemner of that barbarous land changed sides. Impressed by the immense changes that had taken place in Russia since 1848 when the Tsar was the chief reactionary of Europe, impressed by the rapid advance of industrialization and capitalism, Marx wondered if Russia might avoid some of the stages of capitalist development that western Europe had known and make her revolution, achieve a socialist structure, on the basis of "Russian peasant communism." Half the Russian land was already held in common in village communes. "Russia constitutes the advance guard of the European revolutionary movement . . . If the Russian revolution becomes a signal for the working class revolution in the West, so that the two revolutions complement each other, the existing communal property in Russia can become the starting point for a communistic evolution."

Lenin now grasped that economic backwardness and political anarchy could be used as springboards to propel his tiny group to power. He admitted that Russia was not ready for socialism; but Europe beyond it was. War had made Europe ripe for revolution. The Russians, having given the example of overthrowing a rotten old regime and grasping power, could hope that proletarians of other countries would soon follow their lead. When this happened, socialist governments in industrially advanced countries—particularly Germany—would provide the base and motor

Lenin addressing Moscow crowds. Trotsky stands to the right of the platform.

of true Marxist revolution and the possibility of carrying it out in Russia itself. Using these arguments and grasping every opportunity to apply them, Lenin raised the Bolsheviks in a few months from a few thousand underground conspirators to become first the masters of the Soviet network and then the rulers of some 150,000,000 people, no more than a quarter of whom endorsed them in elections to the Constitutional Assembly at the end of 1917—the last free elections to take place in Russia.

Lenin's first move was to reverse the previous policy of his fellows by calling for "all power to the Soviets." This meant in effect that the Soviets, which already controlled far more effective strength than the Provisional Government, should be given formal power too. He then advanced a program calling for an immediate end to war, immediate seizure of land by peasants, immediate control of industry by workers. While the Soviets argued about this (with Lenin strongly supported by Trotsky, who had arrived from America in May), the government and the Duma argued over war aims. A last Russian offensive collapsed in June, precipitating another workers' rising in Petrograd, which the government suppressed, arresting a great many Soviet and Bolshevik leaders, including Trotsky. Lenin went into hiding to escape arrest.

Nevertheless, Soviet pressure had driven the Provisional Government steadily to the Left. Partisans of patriotic war to the end, like Milyukov, had left the government in May. Now, in July, 1917, Prince Lvov resigned and the moderate Socialist Kerensky became prime minister, holding the fort against the peace for which the country yearned. But Kerensky's position depended on the support of officers who rejected all the ideals he stood for. In September one of these, General Kornilov, under the pretext of liberating the government from Soviet pressure, advanced on Petrograd. The incipient counterrevolution was broken only when Kerensky enlisted the support of the Soviets (advised by Trotsky from his prison cell); and now the Bolsheviks were on the move

Russian soldiers join Bolsheviks in front of the Winter Palace during the 1917 Revolution in Russia.

again. Within a few weeks they felt strong enough to remove Kerensky. Their leaders released or returned from hiding, they established their headquarters in a girls' academy whence they began world revolution by overthrowing the Provisional Government on November 6 (October 24) 1917.* Kerensky fled and subsequently went into exile. The Girondist phase of the revolution had passed. The Mountain was in power.

The following day the Second All-Russian Congress of Soviets opened in Petrograd and attendants cheered the newly elected president of the new Council of People's Commissars, Vladimir Lenin. An American enthusiast has left us a description of Lenin on this occasion: "A short, stocky figure, with a big head set down in his shoulders, bald and bulging. Little eyes, a snubbish nose, wide generous mouth and heavy chin . . . Dressed in shabby clothes, his trousers much too long for him. Unimpressive to be the idol of the mob, loved and revered as perhaps few leaders in history have been . . ." ** Within three weeks, elections for a constitutional assembly brought less than half the country's 90 million electors to the polls. Over half of those who voted, voted for the Social Revolutionary heirs of the Populists, a party chiefly identified with the rural population. Bolsheviks got about a quarter of the votes cast and half as many deputies as the Social Revolutionaries. The Constituent Assembly met in January, 1918, and was dispersed at once. The Bolshevik government brooked no opposition. By then, opposition was rife all around it.

The first thing Lenin's government did was to open negotiations with the Germans for a peace "without annexations or reparations." The peace they were finally forced to sign at Brest-Litovsk abandoned one-third

* Russia having retained the Julian Calendar when most of Europe adopted the new Gregorian style, its dates were thirteen days behind those of the West until 1918, when the Soviet government abandoned the old style for the new.

* John Reed, *Ten Days that Shook the World* (New York: 1960 edition), p. 170.

of Russia's arable land and population, four-fifths of its coal, one-half of its industry. Nor was anyone sure that the Bolshevik government could retain the rest. "White" opponents supported by the Allies, allied expeditionary forces—British, French, American, Japanese, and even a Czech contingent—, eventually when Germany collapsed German, Polish, Ukrainian, Finnish, and Baltic armies, operated in every corner of the Russian Empire. In July, 1918, the imperial family were murdered *en masse* in the cellar of a house far away in the Urals and their bodies burned. Their deaths did not end White resistance. By August, 1918, about twenty governments were operating on Russian soil, and none could have predicted which one of them would last.

The Habsburg Empire

The Austrian Lands

After 1848, as after 1815, the major concern of the Habsburgs was that they should last. The symbol of survival was Francis Joseph (1848–1916), who once described himself to Theodore Roosevelt as the last European monarch of the old school. Sober, austere, pious, and conscientious, he went meticulously through his long, ceremonious life. Francis Joseph lacked all spark of originality or brilliance and he was probably not very intelligent; but his characteristics were well suited to keeping his uneasy crown from being upset.* In retrospect his reign appears in a tragic light: his son committing suicide, his next heir murdered, his Empress going mad and being murdered too, his brother executed in Mexico, his wars all lost, his power in decline. But in a reign that spanned sixty-eight years, itself part of a dynastic history ten times longer, these were but sorry incidents of a vast design.

It may have looked at first as if the power of the Crown could be reestablished. The Liberal Constitution of March, 1848, was revoked in 1851. Four years later, a concordat assigned great privileges and powers to the Catholic Church, restoring its property and its hold on education. Most of the peasants were satisfied by their emancipation, which weakened the nobility but not the Crown; Germans and Czechs found opportunities in the growing bureaucracy of the Empire; the Poles were pleased with what amounted to home rule in Galicia; the army en-

---

* That this devoted man repressed something all his life appears in his one impulsive act, his marriage to his cousin of Bavaria. Empress Elizabeth seems to have been a kind of elf, tall for the part but beautiful and dreamy, who stifled in the stuffy, conventional Vienna court, loved the livelier Hungarians (who loved her in return), and who broke down after her eldest son's death in 1889. Her madness ended in absurd assassination by an Italian Anarchist in 1898.

sured order. 1848 had shown that the Habsburg realm rested on its army. "Austria reposes in your camp," the poet Grillparzer told Field Marshal Radetzky: "We are but scattered fragments." The army was the base and cement of monarchy; and when the army lost the monarchy was shaken. First after 1859, then after 1866, constitutional government advanced through the gaps which defeat had torn in the absolutist structure. Concessions had to be made, especially in Hungary; and the *Ausgleich* (compromise) of 1867 brought a settlement which lasted fifty years.

Hungary became once more an independent kingdom, its crown joined to Austria's by the common monarch. Except for military, financial, and foreign affairs, each state had separate governments and separate citizenship as well. Each was a medley of many nations.* During the discussions of 1867, the Austrian premier had told the Hungarians: "You look after your barbarians and we'll look after ours." By 1914, of the 51 million subjects of the dual monarchy 30 million lived under Austrian rule. Of these only one-third were Germans, almost one-fourth Czech and Slovak, some 17 per cent were Poles, and there were sizable minorities of Ruthenians, Slovenes, Croats, and Italians. Most of these lived on the land, working on large estates or drawing a meager living from dwarf holdings. In the 1870's, agricultural workers whose wages had doubled since 1848 labored from dawn till dusk for 12–18 cents a day and women for less. Conditions gradually grew better, but they never approached those further west.

After her defeat by Prussia in 1866, Austria set out to modernize her institutions and, above all, the army. Universal military service was introduced, compulsory elementary education was decreed on paper, jury trial became common in the courts, freedom of religious belief and unbelief was at last established, and the last legal restrictions on Jews were removed. During the 1880's and the 90's electoral reforms broadened the franchise to include Jews, peasants, urban middle classes, and even many members of the working class. Almost inevitably, the more liberal orientation, however relative, brought friction with the Church. In 1870, when the doctrine of papal infallibility was promulgated, the Concordat of 1855 was denounced and state policy turned back to Josephism. The Catholic Church of Austria, a foreigner explained in 1915, is less a state church than an ecclesiastical state department, working like the army, the police, or the civil service to support the government's interests.

But if the Church became a kind of state department, Catholic influence played a major part in politics where Christian Socialist movements

* In 1880 Austro-Hungary counted 9 million Germans, 6 million Magyars, 17 or 18 million Slavs, 3.5 million Romanians and Italians. In 1910: 12 million Germans, 10 million Magyars, 8.5 million Czechs and Slovaks, 7 million South Slavs, 5 million Poles, 4 million Ukrainians and Ruthenians, 3 million Romanians, three-quarters of a million Italians.

among the poor rivaled the Socialists and spread a potent anti-Semitic miasma particularly among the peasants and the petty bourgeoisie. The great protagonist of Christian Socialism would be Karl Lueger, who, as mayor of Vienna from 1896 until his death in 1910, made the capital "the best administered city" of his time and "the most socialized," with all transport and utilities in municipal hands and stringent control over city planning. Hitler, who lived in Vienna at this time, learned his lessons from Lueger's party, which was both national and social and which skillfully used anti-Semitism to channel the more radical instincts and resentments of its followers toward a select, "alien" group, thus protecting fundamental conservative interests by equating big business only with the Jews.

Nationalisms vs. Unity   Lueger hoped to preserve Austrian cohesion, but, while phenomenally successful, he could not fight against the nationalisms which strained against the Empire. The Austrian Germans felt no more attachment to the Habsburgs than the other nations did. Many looked forward to national fulfillment in a greater Germany; many accepted the Empire only as a matter of custom and convenience; but at least they knew they were the ruling race. The Czechs on the other hand had no such consolation. Industrially they were the most advanced of the Habsburg peoples. The Czech aristocracy had every interest in upholding the union with Austria on which their own privileges were based but, as the century ended, industrial and economic development created middle and working classes which formed the base of a more widespread and militant nationalism than that which had been crushed in 1848. After 1868 Emil Skoda's ironworks at Pilsen had grown into a vast metallurgical complex; while in Moravia Thomas Bata used American manufacturing methods to build the largest shoe and leather works in Europe. By the end of the nineteenth century, with nearly half the monarchy's railroad mileage, Bohemia was its industrial center, providing half its textiles, beer, and sugar, one-third of its paper, and one-fourth of Austria's revenues.

The nationalism of 1848 had not been really popular or democratic; but in the 1880's a liberal democratic Young Czech movement sprang up, recruited among intellectuals and the middle classes. It demanded home rule similar to that which the Hungarians enjoyed, and soon came to dominate Czech politics. Its leader, Thomas Masaryk (1850–1937), had worked his way through the University of Vienna and been appointed professor of philosophy at Prague, where he opposed French and English thought to German influence but also stressed the rich native tradition to which the majesty of the Bohemian capital bore a living witness. A national theater opened in 1881, could draw on the works of native poets like Jan Neruda and composers like Bedřich Smetana (1824–1884), Anton Dvořák (1841–1904), and Leoš Janáček (1854–1928),

Thomas Masaryk, father of modern Czechoslovakia.

all inspired by national history, folk poetry, and folk music. What counted even more was the *Sokol* athletic movement, combining gymnastics and patriotism as Jahn had done in Germany in Napoleon's time. By 1914 the Sokols had over 130,000 members: the militants and cadres of Czech patriotism.

The Southern Slavs were more backward in national awareness. The Croats were subjects of the Hungarian Crown but in Bosnia, occupied since 1878, the Austrians too ruled a sizable Slav population. The Bosnians did well under Austrian rule. Between 1878 and 1906 their numbers grew by half, industry, roads, and railroads were created, schooling and order improved, revenues rose. Yet nearly half of the population followed rather their orthodox faith than their interests and looked to Serbia not Austria for fulfillment. It would be the growth of Pan-Serbian agitation that helped to decide Austria's annexation of Bosnia and Herzegovina in 1908. But this only envenomed the situation and led, as we know, to war.

In 1906 and 1907, the reverberations of Russian revolution persuaded the government in Vienna to grant manhood suffrage or something very close. Part of the purpose of the reform was to enlist a large body of new uninstructed voters and thus upset the pressures of the privileged classes which were becoming increasingly critical of the regime. In fact, the Franchise Law was so structured that it emphasized the national separateness of Habsburg subjects at the expense of unitary parties like Liberals or Socialists. There was no escaping the effects of nationalism. Even the Jewish community, whose important social and economic functions made it the scapegoat of Christian Socialism, was inspired by its difficult position to a nationalism of its own. It was a Viennese journalist, Theodor Herzl, who, having tried and rejected both assimilation and socialism, formulated a political Zionism aiming at a Jewish homeland in Turkish Palestine.* By 1907, four Zionists sat in the Austrian Parliament. The same tendencies can be seen at work in the Socialist Party. Founded in the 1880's by the Viennese psychiatrist, Dr. Victor Adler (1852–1918),

* *The Jewish State* (1896).

the Socialist Party called itself the Little International, for it reflected current nationalist strains, each major national group insisting on its own organization, more national than socialist much of the time.

Twilight in Vienna   The sense of disintegration all this created was echoed in the works produced in Austria at this time, brilliant, vivid, subtle, and ironic, but haunted by transience and melancholy, as in the plays of Arthur Schnitzler (1862–1931) and Hugo von Hofmannsthal (1874–1929).* Like life, art insisted on the combination of irony and pathos: poetic and grotesque experience went together. The Emperor asserted a tranquil genius for mediocrity, the Court and government remained oases of talentless stuffiness amidst the talent crowded in a brilliant city. Yet if the results of official nullity were serious they were never grave; for gravity was not an Austrian characteristic, let alone a Viennese, and the surface splendors of the Empire concealed its feebleness.

Nothing could be further from the dreary grandeur of the imperial court than the liveliness of the imperial capital, handsome with new avenues and buildings, fat with pastries and cookshops, gay with the light wine of its hillsides, lounging in its cafés, twirling to the waltzes of its garden-orchestras, bursting with intellectual and artistic activity. The schools and thinking-shops of Vienna were the focus of southeastern Europe; the medical work done there was world famous and, in their shadow, disapproved by the professional establishment, Sigmund Freud (1856–1939) spun the analytical system which, by the eve of war, was beginning to affect European thought.

Some of the great Viennese composers reflected their awareness of Freud's discoveries and also of the crisis within which they lived. The tormented, contradictory music of Gustav Mahler (1860–1911), who directed the Vienna Opera from 1897 to 1907, reflects a consciousness of internal anguish, confessing the failure of modern man, compensating external decline by private greatness affirmed in works of gigantic scope, a last romantic attempt to escape from civilization to nature, god, and self-destruction. A cooler expression of similar sentiments appears in the works of Arnold Schönberg (1874–1951), expressionist like the German painters of his time, dissolving classical forms in harsher, unfamiliar tonalities. In 1911 Schönberg dedicated his revolutionary *Treatise on Harmony* to Mahler, in whom he recognized the most audacious and modern of German musicians. Schönberg's *Pierrot Lunaire* (1912), now a classic of the twelve-tone scale, followed upon other compositions that have been described as "musical psychoanalysis . . . in an unreal world of morbidity and hysteria." Here was one reaction of sensitive spirits to a Vienna where the end of a century foreshadowed the end of

* Schnitzler is best known in the West for his sardonic *La Ronde;* Hofmannsthal for *Everyman* and the wistfully brilliant libretto he wrote for Richard Strauss's *Rosenkavalier.*

a whole way of life.

But the music of Schönberg was appreciated by only a small circle, and even that of Mahler was less well known than the waltzes and operettas of Johann Strauss or the clever scores of his namesake, Richard Strauss, whose *Rosenkavalier* triumphed in 1911. The typical Viennese *genre* was the operetta, dedicated to the glorification of wine, women and song, like Franz Lehar's *Merry Widow* (1905). Its light music, bubbly humor, frothy plots, unreal, erotic, evanescent situations that bankers and shop assistants could enjoy together set the hallmark of those halcyon days, "the very breath of it transforming facts and the bludgeonings of fate into something light as eiderdown, as thought itself." Robert Musil, the author of these words, used them to describe another aspect of the Viennese character. His *Man Without Qualities,* written in the 1930's, recaptured the dominant mood of imperial Vienna: live while you can, gently, pleasurably, aware that the sun is setting and that, while the afterglow is golden, night may fall at any time.

However, in the declining empire, the light was as yet far from gone. Against the fissile tendencies of its different peoples and the forebodings of its intellectuals there stood tradition, habit, inertia, dynastic loyalty, fear of alternatives; but also more positive reasons. The Empire was the largest free trade area in Europe after Russia, more advanced, more economically integrated, better administered, better equipped with industrial and commercial facilities than its eastern neighbor. Dynastic patriotism and material reasons were the twin pillars of the Habsburg realm. But the first was fragile and the second could, if circumstances changed, turn against the Empire's preservation. In 1918, defeat meant disintegration. The Emperor Charles I (1916–1918) abdicated on Armistice Day. The Polish, Czech, Hungarian, and South Slav provinces split apart and German Austria was left, the unwieldy rump of a once great empire, forbidden to join the German Republic as most Austrians wanted and forced to learn to live uneasily by itself.

The Hungarian Lands

The Magyar revolution of 1848 aroused immense enthusiasm but also vast dissensions; not only Croats and Romanians but many Magyars too objected to the brand of democratic nationalism put forward by their leader: Lajos Kossuth. In the end, Kossuth was brought down not just by Russian troops but by the opposition of an aristocracy that preferred foreign rule to native democracy, and of the Romanians and Slavs who preferred Habsburgs to Hungarians. After the defeat of 1849, Hungarians, deprived of their autonomous institutions, were governed by imperial bureaucrats. Then, by the *Ausgleich* of 1867, they recovered their historical rights and more: the Habsburgs, emperors in Vienna, were kings in Budapest. The army of the monarchy was federal, but Hungary had its own territorial forces, its own parliament and government and budget, an electoral system even more backward than that in Austria, and its own subject peoples.

The kingdom of Hungary included Slovakia, Carpatho-Ruthenia, Transylvania, Croatia, and Slavonia. Ten million Magyars, three million Romanians and as many Slavs, two and one-half million Slovaks and Ruthenians, two million Germans. Over these lands in which they constituted less than half the population, Magyars ruled. Croatians had home rule since 1848 but, aside from them, 95 per cent of the deputies in the Hungarian Parliament were Magyars. This was achieved in part by electoral manipulation designed to ensure Magyar supremacy over the crazy quilt of their subject nations, in part by a determined program of Magyarization, which, applied in all schools beginning with kindergarten, affected almost all the middle class. Budapest, which had been largely a German city in 1848, was four-fifths Magyar by 1900. Anyone could become a Magyar by assimilation and many twentieth-century Hungarian nationalists were of German, Slav, Jewish, or even Armenian descent.

In a country where four-fifths of the rural population was illiterate, electoral arrangements based on property and educational qualifications meant that about 6 per cent of the population was eligible to vote. The lower classes could never challenge their masters effectively, either on national or on social issues. The latter were gaining importance as industry developed. By 1900, 13 per cent of the active population was in mines or in industry, in conditions better than those on land but nevertheless quite shocking.* Like the enlightened Nationalities Act of 1868, with the extensive rights it promised to minorities, most labor legislation remained a dead letter. When in the 1890's unions (legalized in 1872) sought to better hours and wages, a so-called "slavery law" (1898) suppressed all strikes and labor agitation, while making rural workers subject to compulsory labor. Here as in Austria, to fight the growth of socialism and radical agitation, Social Catholic parties used anti-Semitism to channel the hostility of the poor against the Jews.

By 1900 the Jewish population, less than 1 per cent a hundred years before, had grown to some 5 per cent of Hungary's population. Concentrated in the towns, their wealth and influence appeared out of all proportion to their numbers. In Budapest, where about a quarter of the residents were Jewish, nearly half the doctors, over 45 per cent of lawyers, over 42 per cent of journalists, over one-fourth of those engaged in "literature and arts," better than 1 in 10 of teachers and professors were Jews. So were a large proportion of radical and Social Democratic leaders. The Jews, of all Hungarians, had been most enthusiastic in accepting Magyar culture and their contribution to it was extremely high. For that very reason, so were the resentments they accumulated, just as they did

---

* The first Factory Laws in 1872 had fixed the maximum work day at 16 hours. Samuel Gompers, the American labor leader, visiting Budapest in 1909, found skilled workers earning less than 80 cents a day, women less than 40 cents, miners who worked 21 hours a day 60 cents.

in the German lands to the west and north. Resentments founded on competition and on prejudice were fed by a constant influx from the East, which took the inhabitants of the Russian *Pale* in stages first to Romania, Bohemia, Bukovina, and Hungary, then on to Vienna, Berlin, and cities further west, the more acclimated, skilled, or enterprising leading the migration westward, constantly replaced by unadapted migrants. This process, which has not yet been studied, probably played an important role in the anti-Semitism of east and central European countries, where culturally assimilated Jews were constantly identified with numerous unassimilated aliens who presented an easy target for their enemies' calumnies.

Yet even anti-semitic parties shared in the rising radical mood that marked the beginning of the twentieth century when the news of the Russian Revolution of 1905 disturbed all eastern Europe, causing widespread agrarian uprisings from the Black Sea to the Baltic and setting off fresh agitation for reform. But the electoral reforms that Francis Joseph granted in his Austrian dominions would have upset Magyar supremacy in the Hungarian lands. Even the radical nationalists opposed them on this ground and nothing came of successive efforts to introduce manhood suffrage bills but growing agitation, disturbances, and friction between various nationalities. Francis Joseph, at loggerheads with Budapest over the federal army, for which he wanted more Hungarian recruits and in which the Hungarians wanted to substitute their language for German, exploited the suffrage issue to get his way and, while the Empire finally got a stronger common army, its Hungarian part never got the vote. Many of its people were not going to get it until after the Second World War.

Eastern Europe

The lands of the great belt between Germany and Russia have much in common. From Black Sea and Aegean to the Baltic lay agricultural countries, most of the peasants farming for subsistence only, living on plots too small for comfort let alone for profit, constantly subdivided, using primitive cultivation methods, bowed down under a burden of debt (for they had no credit) and taxation (left mostly to them by the wealthier classes). Except in Poland and Romania, where large estates exported their crops, only a few regions produced cash crops like pigs or tobacco. Except in Romania where oil was discovered in the 1850's and exploited after 1900, industry was negligible: mostly handicrafts. In Poland, by the 1920's, only some 10 per cent of the population would be employed in mining, factories, or transport; no more in other countries, generally less. Everywhere living standards were low, illiteracy astronomic, underemployment maintained by meager industrial development, and industrial wages depressed by the endless supply of unskilled labor drifting to the towns. Emigration appeared as the poor peasants' only hope.

Avenues for social promotion existed. The sons of wealthier peasants could rise in the world if they went to school, found a career in the armed forces, state administration, law, teaching, or politics, eventually joining the middle class. This was more true in Greece, Serbia, or Bulgaria, where peasants owned their land, than in Poland or Romania, where a landed aristocracy created greater problems. But everywhere the dearth of opportunities meant that underemployment on the land would be reflected in an underemployed middle class, desperately scrambling for a limited number of places and leaving a residue of disgruntled men who placed their hopes in political preferment or political change, while their social position and their education made them more interested in national self-assertion than in social change.

Above all this there loomed the antagonism of Slav and German, continued hostility to Turkey in the south, and the political rivalries of the contending nations. Most of the inhabitants of the area were Slavs. But while patriots in Slovakia or Croatia were enthralled by the maps in nineteenth-century ethnographic studies which showed how far Slavdom spread, the Slav world was divided among four religions, a dozen nationalities, and even more ambitions. Slovaks and Czechs, Croats and Serbs, Serbs and Bulgarians, Russians and Poles, Poles and Ukrainians, Ukrainians and Russians: their aspirations clashed. To the Poles the Russians were Asiatics, the Ukrainians serfs; to the Croats the Serbs were barbarians; to the Serbs the Bulgars were brutish enemies. These were the basic facts upon which the politics of the region would be founded.

North of the Carpathians, national aspirations had to contend with foreign domination. Bohemia was ruled from Vienna, Slovakia and Transylvania governed from Budapest, the Baltic lands from St. Petersburg. The ancient Polish kingdom had become the restive colony of its greater neighbors: in the south, Galicia was a Habsburg province, Posen or Posnania in the west had been annexed by Prussia, the kingdom of Poland and Lithuania lay under Russian rule. After the abortive Galician rising of 1846 Poland lay quiescent. The fireworks of 1848 attracted attention but raised no effective echo. Partition was creating different conditions in the different portions of the land. The Galician Poles probably did best, since after 1867 they were left to rule the Ruthenian masses in exchange for political support in the Vienna *Reichsrat*. The Prussians tried to Germanize their subjects and settle German farmers on Posnanian lands. But the Russians were the most successful in their policy of destroying Polish linguistic and cultural consciousness.

In 1863 as in 1830 a national insurrection failed, less because of Russian might than because of internal factions and the deep divisions between aristocrats and peasants. Fighting between "Red" Poles and "Whites" (those who wanted and those who opposed social and land reform) killed more people than the returning Russians would execute. In 1864 the Tsar's decree rewarded the peasants for remaining quiet by freeing them from serfdom, thus giving them what the White wing of Polish nationalists had refused. The emancipation of the serfs reduced the power of the nobles and eased the economic way of peasant farmers, who could advance themselves if they abandoned Polish for Russian and co-operated with the occupants.

Not everybody was attracted by the prospect. Thousands of political refugees were followed in the decades to come by nearly two million Polish migrants to the United States, Canada, Brazil (where in the state of Paraná in 1900 a quarter of the population was Polish), and Germany, where wages in Silesia and Westphalia were 50 per cent higher than at home. It was not the exiles or the rebels who kept up the hopes and the unity of their land despite police censorship and hostile officials, but the poets. Poets, novelists, intellectuals in the universities, nursed memories of past greatness and hopes of recovering independence. As the nineteenth century ended, Mickiewicz found an heir in Henryk Sienkiewicz, preaching the hopeful faith of early Christians in adversity (*Quo Vadis?*) and the eventual triumph of Polish knighthood in works like *Pan Wolodyjowski*. But Polish nationalism had to contend with the attractions of the occupiers, with opposition between democrats and the reactionaries who dreamed of a restored Poland ruling its subject races, and with divisions between Russian, Prussian, and Austrian Poles, each of whom looked to another power as sponsor of their plans.

The southern peoples were, in some ways, more fortunate—at least politically. Ottoman rule was easier to shake off. Greece achieved independence in 1830. Serbia had enjoyed autonomy since 1829. In 1878, the Congress of Berlin recognized her independence and that of Romania whose principalities—Moldavia and Walachia—emancipated from Russia by the Crimean War, had managed to unite in a Romanian state (1861). Bulgaria, her autonomy accepted after 1878, followed the same course as Romania, growing under Russia's aegis before it emancipated itself from their protectorate. By the 1880's "the Balkans"—a cultural label rather than a geographical term—had achieved independence, even though Bulgaria only acquired it formally in 1908 and though, in practice, all were the client states of greater powers.

All would be ruled by men who started out as revolutionaries to attain a national independence and, in some cases social changes too; and who, once they gained their end, became in their turn oppressors. In Romania, union, then independence, had been achieved by the landowner class and it was they and their urban allies who ran affairs under a liberal constitution (1866) which covered a multitude of sins. Rack renting— squeezing everything the farmers would bear and then some—and ruthless taxation kept the mass of peasants poor and backward. The beginnings of industrialization only increased the gap between their misery and rising prices, their subsistence economy and the rising productivity of the large estates, the isolation of the villagers and the Western-oriented culture of the educated. Only taxpayers voted and the poorest taxpayers were vouchsafed little in direct representation. After 1905 echoes of Russian and Polish risings articulated grievances, set off first a spate of pogroms, then a tide of peasant risings in 1907 which were crushed in blood, leaving behind them the memory of 10,000 dead.

Social unrest, however, could often be shuffled off into external conflicts: irredentist campaigns against Hungary in Romania, against Austria in Serbia, against the Turks in Bulgaria and Greece, clamored that the redemption of national minorities under a foreign yoke would somehow solve the problems of the miserable masses at home. War in 1912 and 1913 brought defeat first to Turkey, then to the Bulgarians who had turned upon their Christian allies, and territorial gains to Greeks, Serbians, and Romanians. Success made it harder to control the passions of nationalists whose greed grew with success or of politicians in Vienna who feared that a greater Serbia would eventually challenge their hold on the Southern Slavs. This combination of alarm and ambition exploded in 1914 when preventive war arose out of Austrian apprehension of the Serbs and other countries followed their greed, fear, or hatred into hostilities.

Turkey

Perhaps the people of this area which proved most successful in negotiating the transition to modern nationhood was that from which such advances could be least expected. As every schoolbook tells us, the Ottoman Empire of the nineteenth century was the sick man of Europe—sicker by far than Austrians or Russians, for it was caught in an impossible quandary. To match their rivals, the Ottomans had to reform their institutions. But, while standing pat meant that their power crumbled and fell a little lower all the time, reform could lead to its disintegration and the cure might kill the sickness and the sick man both.

Islamic tradition counseled against change: "The worst things," went a saying attributed to the Prophet, "are those that are novelties. Every novelty is an innovation, every innovation is an error, and every error leads to hell fire." The Ottomans had always borrowed from the West things fitting their needs—at first mostly for war, like guns and ships, then for peace as well (such as a fire brigade, first organized in Istanbul by a French convert in 1720). But the basic sense of superiority over barbarian unbelievers, reinforced by the successes of the past and ossified into stubborn indifference, continued until the French Revolution provided ideas untainted by Christian associations, secular notions that Mohammedans could consider without danger to their religious beliefs. As the nineteenth century advanced, Western material culture, Western political and social ideas, affected the society, the politics, the aspirations of Islam in new and revolutionary ways. They sapped old authorities and suggested new ones in government, society, and law, introducing a long struggle to reorganize and reform, sowing dragon's teeth of nationalism and rationalism in the exhausted fields of Islam. The power of the West which Ottomans were learning at their increasing cost seemed somehow associated with western constitutions and parliamentary institutions, with Western patriotic and liberal ideas. If the West where such ideas and institutions ruled was strong, perhaps the Ottoman state could profit by their adoption.

The first to be adopted were the most obvious things in areas where the Empire was immediately deficient. Mahmud II (1808–1839) tried to build a modern professional army, but never perceived the need for corresponding modernization in the economic and social spheres to help bear the costs. Over the years, other novelties were introduced. In 1831 the first newspaper in Turkish had been founded. By mid-century this official gazette was supplemented by private newspapers and also by official censorship, prohibiting all mention of troublesome or touchy subjects.* A postal system was founded in 1834 and became the chief factor in the building of a post-road network. In 1855, during the Crimean War, the French and British laid the first telegraph lines that would become a powerful instrument of central government. The first railroad appeared in 1856 and, while as late as 1913 the Ottoman Empire still had a smaller mileage than Belgium, the first train from Vienna reached Constantinople in 1888. All this immeasurably strengthened administrative centralization.

But the institution most closely identified with Westernization and reform remained the army. It had been in its realm that the deficiencies of the traditional structure were felt most sharply. It would be from its ranks that impulses for further change would come. The new model regular army of the nineteenth century was the embodiment of the "new order." It would be its harbinger as the century advanced. All innovations were connected with military needs: either directly with equipment and training, or indirectly with the administrative structure without which there could be no adequate revenue, conscription, or control. New educational institutions were meant to prepare competent officers: a medical school opened at Istanbul in 1827 trained doctors for the army while civilian ones were still turned out by traditional institutions; an imperial music school (1831), boasting Donizetti Pasha (brother of the composer) among its instructors, provided bandsmen for the army;

* Thus, regicide could never be reported; so that the Empress Elizabeth of Austria died of pneumonia, President Sadi-Carnot of France of apoplexy, President McKinley of anthrax, and, when the King and Queen of Serbia were murdered in 1903, Turkish readers were told they had both died of indigestion.

a school of military sciences (1834) was modeled after the French military academy of Saint Cyr; finally, after 1838, very slowly, grammar schools appeared to supply a modernized civil service. But the crux of training for government and public affairs lay in the young men who, beginning in the 1830's, were sent to receive their education or improve it abroad, learn Western languages and acquire Western ideas, chiefly in Paris but also in other Western capitals.

Among these men the kernel of reformist opposition began to take shape. Inspired by Western experience and especially by the positivism of August Comte, they opposed constructive Turkish virtues to the anarchic fanaticism of Arabs, and proposed to merge the disparate nations of the Empire into one common fatherland. This "Young Turk" opposition came to the fore during the reign of Abdul-Hamid II (1876–1909), who did his best to keep the Empire afloat—though only barely—by playing on the divisions of the great powers. To crush unrest among his Christian subjects, Abdul Hamid attempted to revive Muslim religious passions, stifling Bulgarian, Cretan, and Armenian insurrections by mass murder and extraordinary atrocities unmatched in scale until the 1940's. The Young Turks, who had placed the Comtean slogan "Order and Progress" on the masthead of their clandestine publication and chosen for themselves the title "Union and Progress," * were distressed to see the country so barbarous, but more distressed still at Hamid's policy of retrenchment, police rule, censorship, and not the slightest hint of any real reform that might compensate for the brutality of police repression. Their propaganda spread among the administration and the army. In 1908 it triumphed. Many army officers were disgusted with the inefficiency of a government that kept them from using the skills it had taught them, and, worse still, starved the army of credits, equipment, and pay. The government seemed to reject Ottoman traditions but offered nothing in their place. The Young Turk officers rebelled in the name of modernity: national patriotism, political freedom, constitutional government. Their mutiny quickly spread, the Sultan was forced to yield, and constitutional government dominated by the Committee of Union and Progress was installed.

But the constitutional revolution and the nationalist regime were badly hit by losses in territory and prestige as Bulgaria declared its independence, Austria annexed Bosnia and Herzegovina, Crete joined Greece, and home conditions failed to improve. Ottoman nationalists, the new men tried, as the British Ambassador put it, a policy of "pounding the non-Turkish elements in a Turkish mortar." It did not work. Nor did their increasingly terroristic government. As rebels became oppressors they sparked new rebels where they themselves had risen: in the army. In 1912, the impact of the Italian war brought a new officer rebellion. The Committee of Union and Progress could only maintain itself in power by a virtual military dictatorship which ruled until 1918.

*The Union and Progress Committee included a Christian and a Jew.

Chapter 18

THE WORLD
FROM WAR TO WAR

Peace?

When the Great World War was ended, all agreed that there had been
—there could be—no other like it. The world could never again bear
such a toll. Over 8 million Europeans, perhaps 10 million people in all,
had died on the battlefields *: 2 or 3 million Russians, 2 million Germans, 1.5 million Frenchmen, three-quarters of a million from the United
Kingdom. Germany and France had each sacrificed some 16 per cent of
their male population. The 300,000 Serb dead were 9 per cent of the
country's population, a loss whose equivalent in terms of the present
American population would come to some 15 million of this country's
adult males. The figures are uncertain, yet so astronomical that several
hundred thousand seem irrelevant. Of 74 million men who had been
mobilized during the war, about 10 million died in battle; almost as
many were taken prisoner, of whom some 10 per cent died in captivity;
millions more—perhaps three times the number of the dead—were
wounded, many of them crippled for life. Finally, in 1918–19, a vast
influenza epidemic swept through a cold, hungry, weakened world,
killing about twice as many people as the war had done.

Such immense exploits cost money: England alone had spent 44 billion dollars on the war—more than all British capital invested in all the
industrial and financial undertakings of the United Kingdom. War costs
swallowed 22 per cent of Germany's national wealth, 26 per cent of that
of Italy, 30 per cent of that of the French. France had lost half its gold
reserves, Italy six-sevenths of the gold it had.

* C. R. Cruttwell, *A History of the Great War* (London: 1936), p. 630, puts the number of killed at 13 million.

Here was the ransom of the mass national wars whose ideology the French revolutionaries had been first to conceive. Since then, the inventions and industrial achievements of the nineteenth century had amplified all possibilities and these meant not only objects and facilities in unprecedented quantities, but techniques too: logistics, the modern version of the ancient art of getting there firstest with the mostest. The American Civil War had been the first modern war. Between 1860 and 1870 soldiers had learned to mobilize great masses of matériel and men in contests where victory depended on superior industry and communications. War, Clausewitz had long before explained, was "an act of violence pushed to its furthest limits." There was no way of winning such a war "without great bloodshed." Modern warfare would be "absolute"—that is, total. But Clausewitz's readers never envisaged the war into which they blundered: one in which all human and technical resources were enlisted in the fighting and affected by it, in which the scale of the contest dwarfed the contenders and its needs obscured all other considerations.*

Such tremendous efforts could only be kept up by involving the whole nation morally and emotionally in the struggle. War aims formulated in economic or political terms, a piece of land, a diplomatic success, could not warrant the sacrifices demanded. A moral cause alone could hope to justify the senseless immorality of extended murder. God, Justice, Right, became the prize of war and tremendous efforts were made to persuade each side that it was right and just, the others wrong and wicked. War was thus turned from concrete aims into a trial by combat; public opinion was persuaded by the miseries and propaganda of four years to look upon the enemy as guilty, upon victory as an opportunity not only for material gains but for meting out punishment.

When the war was over, the first great cry was that the guilty men be punished, the Kaiser hanged, the enemy be made to pay for the destruction which he inflicted, "squeezed until the pips squeaked," as one English politician put it. Northern France and parts of Belgium lay in

* When asked why he wanted to annex so much Baltic territory, Hindenburg replied: "For the maneuvering of my left wing in the next war."

Northern France in ruins.

ruins. The former alone counted 300,000 houses, 8,000 factories and mines, 52,000 kilometers of roads, 6,000 kilometers of rails destroyed, over 7,-000,000 acres of arable land ravaged and lost to cultivation. Nor could it be forgotten that (whoever had begun the war) the Germans would never consent to end it and to make a peace "with no annexations or indemnities." The kind of peace they favored had been demonstrated at Bucharest and Brest-Litovsk. It is in this perspective that the treaties which the Allies imposed on their defeated foes * have to be considered.

Seeds of Trouble

The victors received their rewards: France in the return of Alsace and Lorraine; Belgium in two small chunks of German territory; Britain in the destruction of the German fleet; Italy in the recovery of the still-unredeemed *irredenta* in the Austrian Trentino, and portions of the Adriatic's eastern shores; France, Britain, and Italy in shares of the German and Turkish empires overseas. Serbia became the center of new-born Yugoslavia—the greater South Slav kingdom of her dreams. Romania doubled in size, acquiring Transylvania from Hungary, Bessarabia from Russia, and portions of Austrian and Bulgarian territory. New republics sprang up in Czechoslovakia, Poland, and four Baltic states. Only the United States got nothing. Crucial in victory, dominant in peacemaking, Americans thought to achieve justice and reaped muddle and disillusion. President Wilson, the high pontiff of Versailles debates, preserved the Rhineland for Germany by offering to guarantee French security jointly with the British; attempted to reconcile Yugoslav and Italian demands in the Adriatic; tried to defend and apply the principle of nationalities and self-determination; above all, sought to establish the noble notion of a League of Nations which would preserve peace, apply a juster and more effective international law, train lions to lie down with lambs and lambs to operate as full-blown sheep. Such excellent intentions did not prevent a failure which must be attributed first and foremost to the circumstances in which the treaties of peace were formulated by the victors, imposed on the vanquished, and finally applied on a catch-as-catch-can basis.

"We had to let this war occur," Max Weber, German sociologist and patriot, explained in 1914, "in order to have our say in deciding the future of the earth." The future of the earth looked glum indeed in 1918, with Soviet republics rising or threatening in Budapest, in Munich, and, briefly, in Berlin; with revolutions or nationalist wars flaring in every borderland from Finland to Asia Minor. Even in Switzerland, where Lenin's Zurich exile had left its mark on local Socialists, a general strike

* The German treaty signed at Versailles in June, 1919, the treaty with Austria signed at Saint Germain in September, 1919, the treaty of Neuilly with Bulgaria in November, 1919, and that with Hungary at Trianon in June, 1920.

EUROPE AFTER THE
TREATY OF VERSAILLES

— · — · — 1914 boundaries

New independent nations

Zone of Allied occupation

———— 1926 boundaries

WHITE SEA

FINLAND

Murmansk

NORWAY

SWEDEN

Helsinki

Petrograd

Oslo

Stockholm

ESTONIA

LATVIA

Moscow

LITHUANIA

BALTIC SEA

DENMARK

Copenhagen

Memel

U. S. S. R.

NORTH SEA

DANZIG
(Free state)

Danzig

(GERMANY)

GREAT
BRITAIN

Hamburg

London

The Hague

NETHERLANDS

Berlin

Warsaw

Brest–Litovsk

BELGIUM

Brussels

GERMANY

POLAND

Kiev

LUX.

SAAR

Prague

Cracow

Lemberg

Versailles

Paris

ALSACE–
LORRAINE

CZECHOSLOVAKIA

FRANCE

Munich

Vienna

Lyons

SWITZERLAND

AUSTRIA

Budapest

BESSARABIA

Geneva

HUNGARY

MOLDAVIA

Milan

Trieste

ROMANIA

Marseilles

Venice

Fiume

YUGOSLAVIA

Bucharest

Barcelona

ITALY

ADRIATIC SEA

Belgrade

WALLACHIA

*BLACK
SEA*

CORSICA

Sarajevo

Rome

BULGARIA

SARDINIA

Naples

Sofia

Constantinople

ALBANIA

GREECE

*AEGEAN
SEA*

TURKEY

MEDITERRANEAN SEA

SICILY

Athens

ALGERIA

Tunis

MALTA
(Br.)

CRETE

TUNISIA

0   500 miles

in November, 1918, was meant as a preliminary to social revolution. This was the background of the peace conference which one member of the British delegation described as a "riot in a parrot house", and Winston Churchill as "a turbulent collision of embarrassed demagogues." All those present looked anxiously over their shoulders at the reactions of the home electorate, of the press, and of political opponents ready to exploit any apparent weakness on their part.

Whatever the final treaty may have been, one thing is certain: it was democratic, with all the rancor, the shortsightedness, and the incoherence but also the good intentions and high hopes that tend to color popular politics. The treaty has been criticized for its harshness, for its weakness, for its unrealism, for its lack of idealism. Yet it was a fair compromise and might have worked had statesmanship made it work. The real point about it, as about any treaty, is that it was a compromise whose virtues or weaknesses would come out in its application. And it was to be the latter that triumphed. "Peace," quipped Clemenceau, "is only war pursued by other means."

We must remember that, on the whole, the peace largely confirmed the results of war and could have done otherwise only at the cost of further war. Nothing else could have deprived Poles, Czechs, Romanians, and Serbs of the territories they had occupied from their fallen foes and, clearly, having proclaimed that national self-determination was one of their first aims, neither France nor Britain, let alone the United States, would fight to prevent its expression. Beyond Alsace-Lorraine restored to France and the territories wrested from Poland in the eighteenth century, Germany herself lost very little: some chunks of land to provide the Poles with access to the sea and some more in Upper Silesia to assuage their hunger for industry and coal. The Saar was placed under French administration for fifteen years, the produce of its coal mines to count as partial repayment of French losses, but a plebiscite would then determine what its future was to be and few doubted that this future would be German. Germany had, of course, been deprived of her territories overseas, but it is hard to tell whether this was a blow to national interests or merely national pride.

The great losers lay in the east, where a string of newborn or newgrown nations marked the disintegration of three multinational empires. From Finland to Bessarabia, the borderlands Russia had gained since Peter the Great detached themselves; Austria and Hungary became small independent states, poorer, weaker, and less populous than the new Czechoslovakia, Romania, and Yugoslavia that rose around them; Turkey, which suffered few further losses in Europe, was shorn of its Arabian Empire now shared between the British and the French. From the ethnic point of view, the new arrangements were less unjust and more consistent than those which they replaced. Yet we shall see that they were not just or consistent enough to last; and perhaps it was in the nature of things that they could never be so.

Now German, Russian, and Ukrainian minorities lay under Polish rule; German and Hungarian under Czech; Hungarian, Ukrainian, German, and Bulgarian under Romanian; Hungarian and Bulgarian under Yugoslav; German and Slav under Italian. The national triumph was a lopsided one. Over a third of the population in Czechoslovakia, a little less than a third in Poland, a quarter in Romania, were minorities; and for a long time better than half the population of Yugoslavia was in the same situation while Serbs lorded it over Croats and Slovenes. Multinational empires were now succeeded by multinational states almost as checkered, almost as uneasy, but far less powerful and hence less able to maintain themselves. The obvious means of doing so was by the victors closing ranks against the nations which they had despoiled. But a consistent policy on these lines was prevented by the contentions of the victor states themselves. Poland was at loggerheads with Czechs and Lithuanians, Italy with Yugoslavs and Greeks. The aftermath of war was marked by squabbling and crises between former allies whose future security depended on co-operation. Most publicized among these was the friction between Yugoslavia and Italy over Austro-Hungarian lands along the Adriatic, where the old city ports were Italian-speaking, the countryside was Slav. The port of Fiume, chief bone of contention at this time, was occupied for a year by the black-shirted bands of a romantic and highly demagogic Italian poet and war hero, Gabriele D'Annunzio, and finally left to Italy (while the hinterland went to Yugoslavia), not without an enduring rift between the two countries.

Italian claims, indeed, were as vast as their war record had been meager.* Perhaps as compensation for a dispiriting war which they had entered in answer to Allied entreaties and survived only thanks to Allied aid, Italian policy sought a hegemony over southeastern Europe and the eastern Mediterranean which the country's resources scarcely justified. Disappointment over ambitions gone sour made the Italians the first revisionists of the treaties to which they had put their signature, and led them to support Hungarian and Bulgarian claims against their Balkan neighbors.

Perhaps more important than some of the things done at Paris were certain things that were left undone. Thus, Russia, ignored in all the treaties, still figured there somewhat like Banquo's ghost, its ominous revolution which all dreaded inspiring an attempt to build along its borders an "isolation belt" that would prevent its spreading. But there were still the Germans, some 60 million of them, to whom the principle of self-determination was denied when the small Austrian rump of the old Habsburg Empire was not allowed to join the new German Republic risen from defeat, when 3 million Austrian Germans in Bohemia were incorporated in the new Czech state, when the German city of Danzig

* However, they had held a difficult mountainous front and suffered heavy casualties.

was forced to be Free rather than German in order to serve the interests of the Poles. Had these groups joined Germany, as great majorities among them wished, the country would have come out of the war stronger by far than it had entered it. Even so, Germany lay in the midst of Europe, greater and more populous than any of its neighbors, apt at any time to try to reverse the verdict of defeat. The French, who had only two-thirds of Germany's population, were well aware of the danger this presented—first of all to Germany's eastern neighbors, eventually to themselves—and tried to diminish it, particularly by detaching the highly developed Rhineland and making it autonomous. This France's allies did not permit to happen, nor in all likelihood did the Rhinelanders want it to. Instead, the treaty's terms demilitarized the Rhineland, giving the French a margin of security on their border where Germany could neither build fortifications nor station troops; and imposed stringent disarmament conditions on the beaten Germans, cutting down their forces to where they presented no serious threat to their neighbors.

War Debts and Reparations

The British, of course, as soon as the war was ended and their own safety ensured by the elimination of the German fleet, approached European problems in terms of a balance that did not want France too strong or Germany too weakened. But the deciding voice through 1919 was that of the United States, or rather of its president, Woodrow Wilson, a man whose high ideals deeply affected the making of the peace. American intervention had probably saved the Allies from defeat, American help had certainly won the war. During the cold, hungry, miserable postwar period, some 35 million tons of American supplies, freely distributed, brought relief to many parts of Europe. The Allies knew that they owed not only gratitude, but some 10 billion dollars: weighty arguments on the American side. What counted even more than the wealth and power which Wilson represented were the hopes he bore of a just settlement followed by a reconciliation and a lasting peace, hopes which millions throughout Europe shared. Yet justice looked far different according to one's stance: Italians and Yugoslavs, Germans, Poles, or Frenchmen, Romanians and Hungarians, differed fundamentally on what justice was. The statesmen who thrashed things out in Paris— Wilson among them—could only compromise between ideals and interests. The peace they put together was imperfect. Its only hope of lasting even as it stood (and many thought imperfect peace better than a war) was that Americans who had contributed to its making should help maintain it. They did not.

Americans, inclined by historical experience and the vocabulary of their politics to see complex questions in the simplest terms, had been encouraged to believe that power and good will could straighten out a

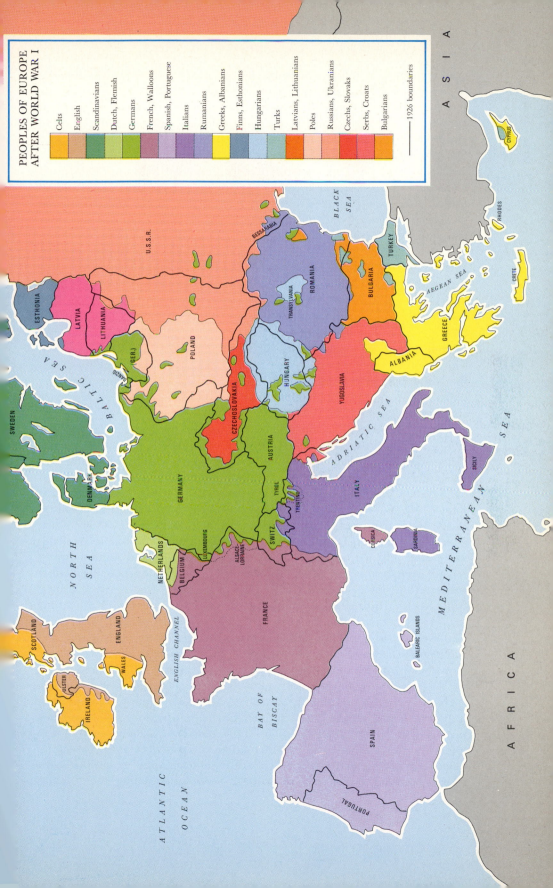

PEOPLES OF EUROPE AFTER WORLD WAR I

- Celts
- English
- Scandinavians
- Dutch, Flemish
- Germans
- French, Walloons
- Spanish, Portuguese
- Italians
- Rumanians
- Greeks, Albanians
- Finns, Esthonians
- Hungarians
- Turks
- Latvians, Lithuanians
- Poles
- Russians, Ukranians
- Czechs, Slovaks
- Serbs, Croats
- Bulgarians
- —— 1926 boundaries

ASIA

AFRICA

U.S.S.R.

BLACK SEA

BESSARABIA

TURKEY

AEGEAN SEA

RHODES

CRETE

CYPRUS

ESTHONIA

LATVIA

LITHUANIA

DANZIG

(GER.)

POLAND

ROMANIA

TRANSYLVANIA

BULGARIA

GREECE

ALBANIA

HUNGARY

YUGOSLAVIA

CZECHOSLOVAKIA

AUSTRIA

SWEDEN

BALTIC SEA

DENMARK

GERMANY

TYROL

TRENTINO

SWITZ.

ADRIATIC SEA

ITALY

CORSICA

SARDINIA

MEDITERRANEAN SEA

SICILY

NETHERLANDS

BELGIUM

LUXEMBOURG

ALSACE-LORRAINE

NORTH SEA

ENGLISH CHANNEL

FRANCE

BALEARIC ISLANDS

ATLANTIC OCEAN

BAY OF BISCAY

SPAIN

PORTUGAL

SCOTLAND

ENGLAND

WALES

ULSTER

IRELAND

web entangled through the centuries. Wilson's influence at Versailles prevented power politics from running riot, but failed to write utopia into treaty terms. Meanwhile, internal political developments discredited even what had been achieved, defeated Wilson's policies, withdrew the United States from a Europe which failed to carry out their hopes and had instead confirmed secular prejudices against a bad old world that most Americans or their ancestors had fled and left behind. The United States had joined the war to make the world safe for democracy and to protect their investments. The world refused the former and threatened the latter. Americans cast off from the world or tried to do so, and their first step was to reject the peace. Having elicited great concessions from their allies, partly by military guarantees such as the one Wilson and the British offered to the French, the United States flounced out of their undertakings, leaving Europeans to pick up the pieces and retaining mostly the right to criticize. The League of Nations which Wilson had conceived and that the United States never joined was left to operate as best it could. The British refused to stand by France alone when the United States no longer acknowledged the guarantees Wilson had shortly promised. France was left to look after her own security. which she could only ensure (or so her leaders thought) by keeping Germany down. "This isn't peace," commented Marshal Foch. "It is an armistice for twenty years."

There was one thing the United States retained and that was the power of the purse. A major issue at Versailles had been the reparations that Germany should pay her victors, particularly to Belgium and to France, large parts of whose territories had been devastated, often deliberately, by German acts. The sum of reparation payments was finally fixed not in terms of concrete possibilities but of political pressures in the victor countries, at the astronomical figure of $32,500,000,000, a bill expected to be paid in forty-two annuities between 1921 and 1963, pending whose payment portions of German territory would remain under Allied occupation and other portions (like the coal-producing Ruhr) subject to it in case of default. The reparation issue proved a long canker eating through the twenties, clear evidence to many of rancorous injustice—especially on the part of the French who pressed it furthest. Yet France was spending half her yearly budget on reconstruction and war pensions. No wonder she was intent on reparations and bitter about her war debts. Moreover, deprived of their allies' support and faced with a renascent giant—one of whose first acts, they feared, would be to threaten them—some French could see salvation (however temporary) only in a nagging policy that drained Germany of resources, slowed her recovery, and maintained it weak. This policy was abandoned in the later twenties, though not before creating vast resentment in Germany, where the government, ready to cut off its nose to spite its face, precipitated ruinous inflation in the postwar years, threatening the foundations of society and the state for the sake of its anti-French measures.

There was one broader problem that better relations themselves were not enough to solve. For the crux of reparations lay in the war debts which the Allies had contracted to the United States. As long as they were held to payments on these, the Allies could not afford to do without payments to them from Germany. Nor did it seem just that the defeated Germans, who were responsible for the war, should have their debts remitted while the winners were condemned to pay theirs to their own rich ally. The matter was extremely complicated, with the French and many other European countries owing Britain almost as much as Britain owed the United States; and Britain repeatedly proposed the general remission of all war debts among allies, along with serious scaling down of German reparations, suggestions which the United States would not entertain. Instead, complicated arrangements were made whereby the German war debt was indeed scaled down (Dawes Plan, 1924); and American banks lent money to Germany which, in a sense, was used to pay reparations to America's European allies who could then pay their United States creditors. There must have been simpler ways of doing it.*

The Twenty Years' Armistice

War, Trotsky once said, is the locomotive of history. The war of 1914–1918 had pulled Europe and the rest of the world a long way from their starting place. One of the greatest changes which had taken place was that in the role and position of the state. Gradual advance, gradual increase in the functions that the state performed has been a constant part of modern trends, particularly so in the quarter century before 1914 when large numbers of people brandishing new votes made politics hinge on satisfying mass demands. Now, this process took on a new and faster pace.

The state had already been called in to police safety, not only against crime but against undue exploitation. Factory laws appeared in the 1830's and 1840's. By mid-century Britain enforced its regulations by inspection. The first state inspectors appeared in Prussia in the 1850's, in the United States after 1866, in France in 1883. Meanwhile, the greatest mass of workers on land, in shops and offices, domestic servants or outworkers, were not yet touched by new regulations. Universal male

---

* Between 1924 and 1929 Germany paid 8 billion gold marks—2 billion dollars—half of it to France, one-fifth to Britain. In 1930 the Young Plan revised reparation debts to a new lower figure payable in fifty-nine installments ending in 1988. The plan went into operation in 1930 when the Depression was about to make it meaningless and Germany paid very little after that, while the last Allied occupation troops left Germany in June of 1930.

suffrage, established or approximated in France, Germany, and Switzerland in the 1870's, in Britain in the 1880's, in Belgium, Holland, and Norway in the 1890's, eventually in Sweden (1907), Austria (1907), Italy (1912), gradually created a new political clientele increasingly concerned with government services and placing an ever heavier burden on them.

Budgets, once kept as low as possible, began to expand in answer to the masses' demand for security. Workers' insurance schemes were introduced almost everywhere in the last twenty years of the nineteenth century. In 1909 a young English politician could sum up democratic politics in the word "insurance." Whether the result of social pressures or of government attempts to head them off, the first steps toward the collectivist spending policies which marked twentieth-century economics were being taken. The state was intervening in everybody's private life and activities, regulating industry and conditions of labor, fixing minimum wage rates, running public utilities, supervising sanitation and education, controlling wealth and redistributing it by graduated income and capital taxes and death duties.

But planning, social security, a fairer distribution of incomes, preventive medicine and national health policies, social services, all made the greatest advances during the war, when all states needed to elicit collective sacrifices by promising collective gains. Nor was collective compensation the only motive force. Even more important were the demands of a struggle which one could survive only by harnessing all energy and resources to its pursuit. Production and distribution had to be planned, supplies rationed, prices controlled, manpower directed, the whole economy co-ordinated. This was achieved first in Germany, where businessmen like Walther Rathenau (who had learned economic generalship in his father's giant electrical corporation) ran the country's economy, and the General Staff ran the country: its officers distinguishing themselves not as heroes but as experts and managers in uniform, owing their places less to privilege than to competence and intellectual achievement, masters of planning and of calculation, manipulating men, machines, transport, propaganda, and espionage in a manner and on a scale unknown by earlier soldiers. Soon, warfare came to be regarded less as a collision between armies than as a contest between collective economies. Most belligerent countries set up ministries of armaments and munitions, shipping and labor. Those that did not do so collapsed, like the Russians, or came very near it, like Italy. And, while most of these structures would be dismantled after the war, they would soon be revived piecemeal.

Structured or not, however, there was no going back on the swelling attributions of the state. The British, most reluctant to encroach on the prerogatives of privacy, reflected the glacier-like inevitability of the trend. In 1850, the British government spent 12 per cent of the gross national product and only 3 per cent more than that half a century later. In 1914, despite a new social legislation and heavy expenditure on defense costs, Britishers spent more on drink than on *all* their government expenditures. By 1918, this had changed. The government had become a dominant force of national economy, spending over half the national income. By 1944, a generation later, it spent nearly three-quarters of it and controlled two-thirds of Britain's labor force.

Big government and big industry went hand in hand or, rather, side by side. As industry developed, so did its need for capital. Beginning in the 1850's and the 60's, joint stock companies and limited liability mobilized investment by encouraging anonymous and irresponsible shareholders who left management to others. In the 1860's the cotton crisis set off by the American Civil War hit small manufacturers, forced bigger ones to install costly new machinery (such as for Indian cotton), led to a concentration of the textile industry throughout the West, just as the effects of the Zollverein in Germany and of the Franco-British Free Trade Treaty of 1860 worked in the same direction. The concentration of industry also meant concentration of industrial labor, growing class consciousness and organization; and in France, for instance, the *Comité des Forges,* grouping the largest iron and steel masters, was set up in the same year, 1864, as the International Workers' Association. The recession of the 1880's saw the further elimination of smaller enterprises and the growth of trusts set up to monopolize production or distribution,* cartels set up to control associated and subsidiary industries catering to a group of firms, and *agreements* between rival producers to share out the market and fix prices or fares or freight rates affecting their products. "The day of combination is here to stay," mused John D. Rockefeller. "Individualism is gone never to return."

Competition in action tended to kill competition in fact, and those whom this hurt appealed to the state for help. Government intervention, government control were invoked by the very advocates of the free trade which free competition restricted. In the United States, the Sherman Anti-Trust Act of 1890 enforced competition by law and penalized its logical conclusions. The state would regulate enterprise and lay down rules as to how business could properly be conducted.

Up to a point. "The thrusts," opined Mr. Dooley, "are heejous monsthers—on wan hand I would stamp them under fut; on th'other hand, not so fast." A few years before the war, 1 per cent of American enterprises employed a third of the labor force and turned out 43 per cent of all manufactured products. At the same time in Germany 1 per cent of enterprises employed two-fifths of the labor force and used three-fourths of the power. This concentration of industry and labor continued after the war, unions continued to grow, the largest trusts in

---

* The first trust was Rockefeller's Standard Oil Corporation in 1882; the first international trust was Nobel's Dynamite Trust in 1886.

Germany were formed in these years, and large-scale concentration pressed even further in countries like Italy and Russia. Here was the firm base and the raw material of the new economic order in which industrial capitalism became state capitalism; in which, indeed, business and industry on one side, public administration on the other, vied with each other, the former regarding the latter not only as a source of costly interference in its affairs, its production, and labor expenses, but also as a dangerous competitor for lawyers, administrators, accountants, and experts, raising their wages or tempting them with holidays, greater security, or more relaxed conditions of work.

Planned economies stemmed not from socialist ideas but out of the great industrial concentrations which first planned and regulated production and trade on a vast scale. From trusts that controlled an immense proportion of a country's manufacturing capital, to the assistance lent them by government, to the shift of economic planning from private to public offices, the transition took place almost insensibly, speeded up by the industrial mobilization of the war and precipitated by the crises of the 1930's and the forties, to be dealt with in the following pages. From control by a few capitalists to control by a few bureaucrats there was but a step, once business and politics had interpenetrated. When national and international economic structures broke down, there would be no withstanding the demand for deliberate planning to replace the free self-adjusting ideas of the nineteenth century. Politics were called into play to redress the balance of economics.

By that time, experience was beginning to suggest that economy was manipulable, like men, not ruled by unchangeable natural laws with which one could not tamper. Government, like economics, was seen less as a free market than as an organized structure that was best run by experts. In 1942 the economist Joseph Schumpeter concluded that controlled planning was the least evil for coping with our problems. In the same year James Burnham's *Managerial Revolution* predicted the decline of the liberal economy and its replacement by state capitalism managed by technicians and technocrats. A second great war had precipitated the conclusions of the first.

The End of Liberalism

All this would be confirmed by the catastrophic tremors and quakes that rocked the economy of the world in the 1920's and thirties to bring much of it crashing down. However traumatic the war itself had been, millions had gone through it as through an incident, had preserved their way of life with only a few scars, and meant to treat it as a parenthesis after which things could be taken up where they had been left off. Young men, like Max Ernst, the painter, "died on the first of August 1914 and returned to life on the 11th of November 1918." And it is true that, whereas for some countries the war brought radical change, in others it could be viewed as a passing disturbance whose end permitted life to go on as before—permitted, that is, a conscious attempt such as we find in Aldous Huxley's early novels to recapture and recreate the past, not move with the times.

This sleeping-beauty view of life was bound to go awry. Thomas Mann was more correct when, in his 1924 foreword to *The Magic Mountain,* he spoke of the novel's taking place "in the long ago, in the old days, the days of the world before the Great War . . ." That this was long ago and far away would seem much clearer to a central European than to a Westerner. All combatants had financed war costs largely out of loans, all had to pay for it when war came to an end in higher prices (they had, for instance, risen 250 per cent in France and Italy between 1913 and 1920) and inflated currency. In France, where reconstruction was also financed by loans (supposed to be repaid from reparations) and where the public debt was nine times larger in 1921 than in 1914, the franc, five to the dollar before the war fell as low as fifty in 1926. Soon thereafter it was stabilized at twenty-five, a fifth of its prewar value. This was a hard blow for savers, *rentiers,* creditors, pensioners, small businessmen having to replenish stocks at ever higher costs, and wage earners wearily pursuing mounting prices.

Much worse was the plight of the defeated countries whose currencies practically collapsed or had the hard task of adjusting to new borders, and where productivity proved highest among the printers grinding out new and worthless bills. In Austria prices rose to 4,000 times their prewar level, in Hungary they multiplied 23,000 times, in Poland 2,500,000 times, in Russia 4,000,000,000 times, in Germany a thousand *billion* times. Housewives took baskets of money to market and returned with small loaves of bread. In November, 1923, the German mark stood 4,200,000,000,000 to the dollar and when the Poles introduced their new currency, the zloty, in 1924, it was exchanged for nearly 2,000,000 of the paper marks that were in use till then. Before currencies had been stabilized—in Austria 1922, in Germany 1923, in Hungary 1924, in Britain 1925 (idiotically at prewar parity with the dollar, thus sacrificing industry and employment to banking interests), in France 1926 (more wisely, well below the prewar level, thus facilitating exports and eventually delaying the effects of the world slump), in Italy 1927—millions had been ruined. Not merely hurt, as in France or England, but ruined utterly, their way of life smashed and with it much of the old stability of which they, with their small savings and possessions, were an essential part.

Something else and something more profound had also passed away.

The industrial center of gravity of the world, long settled on the Atlantic's eastern shores, had shifted to North America. By 1913, the United States produced one-third of the world's manufactures: almost as much as Germany, France, and Britain together. Fifteen years later she would produce two-fifths. The war encouraged further industrial development in the United States and also in countries like India and Japan which had been cut off from their normal sources and had learned to shift for themselves. Meanwhile, European economy had been focused on profitless murder, capital equipment worn or destroyed, currency disorganized, foreign assets much reduced. European countries, once creditors, were now debtors of the United States, which had become in turn the greatest creditor in the world.

Not only industry expanded during the war. Production of foodstuffs and raw materials, too, had advanced all over the world—even in regions where production costs were normally too high for a competitive market. Once the war was over, once shortages had been filled and European production recovered, capacity exceeded demand, surpluses began to accumulate, and agricultural producers found themselves in difficulties. Farmers had contracted debts in good years which they couldn't settle in the bad. Coal mines found themselves in similar difficulties as new sources of power were developed (gas, hydroelectricity) and consumers learned to economize on solid fuel. Producers caught in wage/price squeezes tried to increase their output only to depress prices further. Industry, which expanded capacity and increased output by 20 per cent in the decade since 1914, was in a quandary. Industrial production increased more rapidly than the production of raw materials and basic foodstuffs, but the population of the areas producing raw materials increased more rapidly than that of industrial areas, while the wealth of the latter grew faster. Industrial producers required relatively smaller quantities of foodstuffs, primary producers wanted more industrial products but could only pay for them if the industrial areas bought more of their stuffs, which they did not, or did only at reduced prices. Between 1919 and 1928 the price of wheat fell by half, of corn by four-fifths, of rice by three-eighths, of cotton by two-fifths. In 1927 the revenue of American farmers, a quarter of the country's population, was half that of 1919. So the countries and peoples that wanted to buy available goods could not afford to do so, demand for them fell and cut even further the purchases that primary producers could afford to make, until the demand for industrial goods began to fall in turn. One man's difficulties created others: the farmers' problems meant fewer buyers, less demand, a further shrinking market. Sporadic unemployment had been part of the business cycle that went from boom to slump throughout the nineteenth century. Now unemployment became endemic. After 1921 there were never less than one million unemployed in Britain, twice as many in the United States. At the height of renewed prosperity in 1927 and 1928 Germany had one and a half million unemployed. Costly to city or

Inflation in postwar Germany. Small firms prepare to meet payrolls with bags containing 4½ million marks each.

state, unemployment would be a demoralizing experience for workers and work-seekers, an increasing number of whom never found a regular job at all.

This was the vicious spiral behind the spurious upswing of the latter twenties when, with agriculture in difficulties and industrial profits falling, stocks continued to advance perhaps because there was no other direction left for loose money to take. The precarious structure of international credit, founded on receding realities, needed only a push to topple over. In October, 1929, the great stock market crash on Wall Street removed the credit with which American investors had propped up the finances of central Europe. In 1931 attempts to shore up the German and the Austrian economy in an Austro-German Customs Union collapsed before Franco-British opposition and, with them, the greatest of Austrian banks went into bankruptcy, dragging down a long train of other banks and institutions. The United States proposed a year's moratorium on all international debt payments while the financial situation straightened out. But solvency was no greater in 1932 when, as a matter of fact, the crisis reached its peak. Since 1929, industrial production in the United States and Germany had been halved, and wholesale prices had fallen 37 per cent in the United States, 28 per cent in the United Kingdom. Worst hit were those countries whose economy rested on primary products. In January, 1933, rubber prices were 13 per cent of what they had been three years before, silk 28 per cent, wool 22 per cent, copper 29 per cent, cotton 34 per cent, coffee and rice 41 per cent, wheat 42 per cent, sugar 50 per cent, timber 55 per cent. In other words, the rubber planter got 13 cents where he had got a dollar a few years before, and the farmer 42 cents.

Catastrophe for primary producers spelled some mitigation for those who fed these raw materials through their factories, such as the English whose real incomes fell relatively little.* Even so, unemployment soared:

* Indeed, the incidence of the Depression was uneven. Britain, though hard hit, benefited from low raw material prices. France, less industrially advanced than her neighbors, enjoyed a balanced economy and the advantages of a cheap currency at least for

in March, 1932, nearly 3 million Britishers, 5.5 million Germans, 13.5 million Americans, were out of work. The hope that international payments might resume when the year's moratorium ended proved vain. America's debtors proposed abolishing reparations altogether in return for a settlement with their creditors; but the Americans would not accept. With Germany freed of her obligations, the debtors now refused to be held to theirs, and defaulted on their debts. Reparations were at an end, and so were normal financial relations between the powers.

Men had become persuaded that free competition and free markets would not work. The economy had to be regulated in peace just as in war. Economic liberalism was being jettisoned even in its American fortress. In 1931 the Harriman Committee of the United States Chamber of Commerce called for "a national program of production and distribution" and for a national council to co-ordinate the country's economic problems. In 1932 a German "moderate" declared that the "times of laissez-faire, laissez-passer and unlimited individualism" were past. It was time now for the state to intervene by deflationary measures to restrict credit, control prices and wages, regulate or nationalize private enterprise, devalue currency, control exchange and supplies, subsidize crucial enterprises or undertake new ones, reabsorb the unemployed or keep them on the dole, regulate independent economic activity, investment, and production, secure recovery on autarchic lines of national self-sufficiency. Abandoned internally, the free market with its jungle laws of survival was acknowledged only in the international free-for-all wherein every country sought to save itself by every means at hand.

The notion of property as an absolute right, freedom of contract, integrity of salaries, had all been shaken during the century. Now society's right to interfere with owner and employer was generally acknowledged. Municipal or state governments henceforth fixed rents, wages, prices, arbitrated settlements, set wages no longer governed by considerations of supply and demand alone, and supplemented them by allowances, insurances, and pensions. "Money," which had been looked on as a basic value, was now recognized as "nothing more than a means of facilitating the production and exchange of goods and services." Of course, people had always known this, but they had preferred what-

---

a while. The French counted 10,000 unemployed in 1929—equivalent to nothing—and still welcomed immigrant labor. By 1932 the unemployment figure had tripled but was still one-thousandth of the unemployment rate across the Channel. Hundreds of thousands of foreign workers had been expelled to protect the welfare of French labor. By 1935 France acknowledged half a million unemployed and, although this receded only slowly, French unemployment figures were never as high as elsewhere. In the United States, certain financiers did not suffer as much as others. Andrew Mellon acquired twenty-one paintings from the Hermitage Museum in St. Petersburg for about 7 million dollars in 1930—indicating Russia's shortage of exchange but also the capacity of *some* American millionaires to raise a lot of cash in the depths of the Depression.

ever served as money to have some intrinsic value and had acted as if the gold and silver coins they used really had such value. When coins were replaced with paper, gold reserves were kept as backing for the currency. By the 1920's and 30's, however, men realized that what really counted was the possibility of exchanging currency for something of the value it was supposed to represent, of having it accepted as "money"—that is, a token of exchange at its face value—and that what counted in maintaining this possibility was not the gold reserve but confidence that fair exchange was a real possibility.

The sacred international gold standard, which assumed that currency was convertible into gold and that credit and debit balances in international trade could be settled out of national gold stocks, was suspended and exchange rates were now arbitrarily set at artificial levels. Finally, the brilliant English economist J. M. Keynes eased the survival of a capitalism adjusted to changed challenges and conditions by arguing that attention must shift from distribution to production, from private to public scales, from shortage of consumption and demand to means of reviving them by coaxing savings into investment, by increasing the money in circulation, redistributing revenues, creating fresh demands, and breathing new life into the economy.

The first to adopt means similar to those Keynes suggested were the societies in direst straits. Russia, Germany, Italy, Japan tried to secure outlets for their products by means of bilateral agreements negotiated by state agencies which were in a good position to deal for vast quantities and exact the most favorable conditions, especially from the small producers of eastern Europe and Latin America, taking a vast proportion of their exports and, in the process, turning them into economic satellites. The most explicit in this policy and the most successful were the Germans. Between 1934 and 1938 the German exports to Bulgaria rose from 22 to 58 per cent, to Yugoslavia from 16 to 50 per cent, to Turkey from 15 to 51 per cent, to Hungary from 20 to 48 per cent; and these countries' exports to Germany from 30 to 63 per cent for Bulgaria, from 8 to 50 per cent for Yugoslavia, from 13 to 48 per cent for Turkey, from 12 to 50 per cent for Hungary. In other words, over half these countries' foreign trade came to be with Germany alone.

We have already seen how industrial concentration facilitated the exercise of state power. The latter almost presupposed still more concentration, which the Depression furthered by sending the weaker to the wall. In the United States in 1929 out of half a million companies, 500 made half the total profits, 20,000 companies accounted for nearly nine-tenths of profits. Now necessity accelerated developments which had already taken place in the world's leading producer—the United States. By 1935, eighteen great firms controlled two-thirds of British iron and steel production, and great trusts controlled the chemical, tobacco, and auto industries. In Italy fewer than 1 per cent of the country's enterprises owned more than half of the industrial capital. In Japan fourteen trusts controlled two-thirds of the investment capital and three-fourths of the bank deposits. In Germany less than 200 firms owned two-thirds of the investment capital.

Under the pressure of necessity, technical efficiency also increased. In 1938, the industrial output per man hours was half as great again in England than in 1913, twice as great in the United States. Thus, even as recovery began, new hands were joining the labor pool while industry had learned how to raise the volume of production with fewer employees. In those countries where the economy was least organized and activity still free, chronic unemployment survived to the end of peace, a constant factor of uneasiness and social guilt. Recovery was relative in any case. By 1936 international trade stood well below its level of 1929. Two years later European trade figures were still only 40 per cent of those of 1929.

Even so, most people in the West were better off on the eve of the Second World War than they had been on the eve of the First. They would have been better still had not many countries organized for war rather than for prosperity. War production did, however, mean that national economic structures had less to change in shifting from a peace to a war economy in 1939, particularly in Russia, Germany, Italy, and Japan, but also in other countries where planning and intervention during the thirties simplified rationing and control during the forties. This was the economic background against which the film of the twenty years' armistice unrolled, the setting for the rise of great pseudoreligions offering panaceas for Europe's worldly ills.

A Revolutionary Left: Communism

The first and perhaps greatest of twentieth-century creeds was an offshoot of late-nineteenth-century Socialism. It would be formulated by Vladimir Ilyich Ulyanov (1870–1924), better known as Lenin. Born at Simbirsk on the Volga, the son of a college principal who later became the director of elementary education throughout the province and whose position made him a member of the nobility, Lenin grew up in the subversive atmosphere that teachers' families notoriously generate. All of the Ulyanov children were revolutionary and in 1887 the eldest son, involved in an abortive plot to kill the Tsar, was executed. Vladimir himself, expelled from the university for his political activities, was finally permitted to secure a law degree and practiced law and Marxism side by side until he was arrested and exiled to Siberia. Released in 1900, he escaped to Geneva and founded a periodical: *Iskra* (The Spark), which, printed on cigarette paper, was smuggled into Russia to spread the Marxist gospel there.

Lenin's Russian experience gave him little sympathy for revisionism or for conventional mass movements, both of whose possibilities he doubted. In a long pamphlet of 1902, entitled *What Is To Be Done?* he gave his recipe for political action based on "a small, compact core consisting of reliable, experienced and hardened workers . . . connected by all the rules of strict secrecy with the organizations of revolutionaries." Though the recipe was given in a tactical context, its implications went against the democratic bent and tradition of the International, rejoining certain subversive arguments which had been heard among reactionaries and anarchists, doubting the capacity of majorities to help themselves and even to see clearly what would help them.

When in the last third of the nineteenth century revolutionaries discovered that universal suffrage was less a weapon for radical reform than a tool of autocracy and reaction (as Napoleon III and Bismarck knew), they began to think that only a conscious minority could be trusted to advance the cause of revolution, carrying the masses along. Representative democracy traded on the votes of fools. Utilitarian liberals had long thought so. Lenin agreed with them. In 1903, the second Russian Social Democratic Congress agreed on the necessity of socialist revolution and of the dictatorship of the proletariat, but divided over the nature of the party which would bring these about. Was it to be a mass party patterned on the West, or the disciplined, dedicated elite of professional revolutionaries that Lenin thought fitted Russian conditions better? Lenin's argument won the day, the tiny party split into majoritarians (Bolshevik) and minoritarians (Menshevik), and Trotsky, who belonged to neither faction, predicted what Lenin's model of revolutionary militancy implied: the party would be dominated by its organization, the organization by its central committee, and the central committee in the end by a dictator.

For the moment, none of this mattered very much and few paid great attention to the disputes of a small and exotic party. Yet Lenin's chance would shortly arise out of the war the Socialists had not been able to prevent despite repeated invocations. It would come because, when Russia collapsed into revolution, Lenin alone saw how the transition from autocracy to socialism could be telescoped by Bolshevik revolution. But also because social democracy had discredited itself during the war, almost all its leaders unable or unwilling to stand up either for peace or for revolution, their patriotism greater in the end than their revolutionary principles.

The victory of Bolshevism in Russia, enthusing millions of Socialists abroad, posed an awkward challenge to Socialist leaders. Communist centralism was incompatible with the parliamentary socialism of most

Western parties accustomed to working with a mass electorate interested in local questions and immediate gains, and utterly unready to give up the gains achieved over a generation of parliamentary action in order to pursue a will-o'-the-wisp of revolution in the Russians' wake. The Russians, on the other hand, followed Lenin in demanding that fellow parties shed their parliamentary-style leaders and policies, and acknowledge the supremacy of the Third International which they had set up in Moscow (1919).

After 1921, Socialist parties everywhere split on this issue between national-reformists ready to collaborate with other political parties on gradual reforms and democratic government and Communists dedicated to the pure, hard line of class war and revolution. This meant, in effect, that the Left was weakened afresh by its divisions: the Communists long remaining small though dynamic groups, never strong enough to make their revolution and heavily dependent on Moscow aid; the Socialists fated to ineffective compromises unlikely to secure the reforms they hoped for. From France to Scandinavia (and in Italy too, until suppressed in 1926), Socialist or Labor parties made a strong showing in elections, but never strong enough to let them take office unhampered by bourgeois allies.

Socialist parties were showing signs of staleness. Their leaders seemed conformist and increasingly aged—especially when compared to those of their revolutionary competitors. Their membership—increasingly middle-aged as the young, impatient, took their energy elsewhere—became more middle-class, as the industrial workers drifted into Communist ranks to be replaced by teachers, white-collar workers, and other partisans of moderate reform. Participation in governmental coalitions gave Socialists "governmental" habits of compromise, designed less to achieve particular measures than to remain in power. They were then further compromised by failure to answer the challenge of depression.

In moments of crisis when sacrifices are in order the essence of power is the capacity to impose these sacrifices on others than oneself and one's friends. This is the stake of the political game—a very important stake, as politics of the 1930's would show—and one which the Socialists lost when they proved unable to initiate any original measure that would not hurt the poorest citizens first. Caught in the maelstrom of the Great Depression, Labor and Socialist parties never managed to re-think their programs, foundered to disgrace along with other parties, or were suppressed as in eastern and central Europe. The only Socialist party which applied original methods was the Swedish, which, after 1932, went in for deficit spending, public works, and major investments in ways similar to those recommended by Keynes and thus curtailed unemployment, setting off economic recovery.

Rare were the labor leaders who formulated other possibilities. Some tried to reconcile autarchic retrenchment and economic revival, socialism with ambient nationalism: among them Oswald Mosley in England and Henri de Man in Belgium. The latter's *Beyond Marxism* (1927) voiced conclusions suggested by the experience of the Germans whom he had learned to know: the force of national feelings, the use of state machinery in controlling the capitalism of trusts and monopolies, to give workers a chance to build a stake in society, own property in it, become bourgeois too. Nationalization—part of the basic program of Socialist parties—was necessary only in crucial sectors like banking, transport, heavy industry; for the remainder, state *control* would be as effective as state *ownership*. De Man's ideas, which made their way into France during the thirties, were first applied by Fascists and by Nazis, before becoming the general practice of Western capitalism. Tarred with the Fascist brush, however, they horrified Socialists as did various attempts to blend socialism and nationalism. Socialist parties clung to the good old doctrine as they had done before the First World War and persuaded all who looked for fresh answers to their pressing problems that they would have to look elsewhere.

Increasingly, such people looked to Communism, less for its similar doctrines than for its certitudes. Socialism had taken on too much of the pessimistic, timid coloring of the society to which it had adjusted. Zealous, active, fanatically persuaded that their cause was right, Communists attracted a good many people who were dissatisfied with things as they were and more interested in change and action than in the precise nature of either, so that a number of them eventually turned to Nazism or to Fascism. True that in Russia—showplace of the creed—the dictatorship of the proletariat soon turned into dictatorship over the proletariat. The ruling Bolshevik Party, vanguard of working-class revolution, was a centralized authoritarian organization, a cross between teacher and policeman, a more efficient, more technocratic, more bureaucratized version of its heavily organized predecessors. But Russia was only a beginning, one could reason. Besides, it was far away and more impressive as a distant beacon of hope than as actual fact, while all around the tide of reaction rose.

Reaction reared against machines, against individualism, against science and alienating rationalism, against the technological advances causing unemployment, against the class struggle, against mechanization and mass production (glorifying gilds, artisans, and peasants). The optimist philosophy of progress was jettisoned all along the line. Those who did not like this had almost no choice but to join the Marxist camp. Once again, the intellectual appeal of a hopeful creed of change mobilized intellectuals increasingly convinced that the social order responsible for so much misery and injustice could not be maintained.

Socialism, as all could see, hampered the functioning of the profit system without doing anything to change it. Communism, even if unable to replace it with a better system, at least promised its destruction. Intellectuals and artists who had engaged in anarchic and detached rebellions during the postwar years—W. H. Auden, John Dos Passos, Louis Aragon, André Malraux, Fernand Léger, Pablo Picasso, and many others— went over to commitment. In the Soviet Union, wrote Malraux in 1935, the writer was no longer alienated from industrial society; Soviet writers were one with their civilization. No wonder Westerners sought to follow suit! The economic interpretation was as one-sided and as unconvincing as any other creed. But it was psychologically satisfying. It provided the key to the impenetrable confusions of history, a plausible, clear, well-structured pattern of interpretation, suited to the materialistic mentality of our age. A materialistic idealism: what more could one ask? It need not be true, only convincing: simple, certain, prophetic. Besides, it seemed to offer the only hope in a world increasingly dominated by other, darker forces and ideologies.

A Radical Right: Fascism

We have traced to late nineteenth century the ominous rise of notions that can be described as catastrophic in more ways than one. Insecurity and discontent would help them soar from insignificant beginnings to overwhelming force, especially as they provided an alternative to hopes (or dangers) on the Left.

War introduced habits and practices that we today associate with social revolution: regimentation, propaganda, state control of vast sectors of economy and life, rule by decree, the fixing of prices and wages, requisition or confiscation of certain private property or even people, limitless expenditure and limitless waste, the argument that money and property must be at the service of a society many of whose members were laying down their lives for it, the implied rights of fighters and workers whose sacrifices must be repaid by recognition, a heroic or dramatic approach to public affairs increasingly viewed in totalitarian fashion so that the sacrifice of private opposition or private values to a public consensus became the acme of morality, faith in the tonic value of action— forceful and prompt rather than appropriate or even effective. Men had been told that criticism was treason, had learned that patriotism justified the end and, with it, the means. The infallibility of leaders pounded into nations to improve morale gave followers a good conscience and the vast relief of sharing in a righteous but risky game played recklessly. The dictatorial figures of the next decades had only to perfect what their predecessors had begun.

Leichenbegängnis, by George Grosz. Staatsgalerie, Stuttgart.

This was one kind of change. But there were others. Fortune or ruin, death or survival, were now seen once again (after the brief interval of a century or so when man had thought himself the master of his future) as the result of chance. The strongest and most skillful were not necessarily those who survived the fighting. The thriftiest did not come through inflation better than the shiftless kind. Men who had worked and saved all their lives saw their income (from pensions, stocks, or bonds) fall or disappear. No wonder the following generations lost interest in saving, even when they had the chance. Consumption was better than loss or devaluation; immediate gratification safer than any deferred prospects.

A major effect of this, thought a sensitive observer, was "loss of all confidence in justice as one of the principles which regulate the course of human life." Once belief in causality was replaced by faith in Providence, reward and retribution, cause and effect, became anachronistic concepts. One expression of this trend was the reliance on chance and random experience that we find in much contemporary art and literature. Another was a tremendous loss of faith in previously respected authorities: age, public bodies, political institutions, tainted with the lies which they had told, with wartime propaganda,* and, above all, with failure. Rulers of defeated countries paid for their failure by being overthrown; but the institutions of the victors were just as compromised.

The parliamentary system had long been under fire from reactionary quarters. As the nineteenth century ended, other critics began to express themselves. Universal suffrage, remarked Tolstoy, was no more than a method whereby prisoners elect their prison guards. Its representatives had, as the title of a book expressed it, "the cult of incompetence and the horror of responsibility"; and parliaments were only a haven for a multitude of parties and politicians squabbling over access to the public trough. This was what the dreams of 1848 had come to by 1900, the snows of hope melting to grubby slush in the light of experience. After the war, men who had experienced the lies and hypocrisies of their governments, had seen parliamentarians betraying their ideals and profiteers prospering by it while their fellows died,** retained no faith in what a young French Socialist convert to communism described as "the uncertain regime of the popular will surprised every four years in its sleep."

The opportunity for revolutions of the Right and Left was excellent and, facing the critics of the radical Left, a radical Right arose, reformulating the nationalist aspirations of the prewar years in the more favorable circumstances of the 1920's. Nationalists had two advantages which they had lacked before: the revolutionary menace now embodied into

---

* The French called it brain-stuffing (*bourrage de crâne*).
** As in the famous *Punch* cartoon that shows a small boy inquiring of his porcine parent: "Father, who did you do in the Great War?"

actual practice, which predisposed many sensible people to back the most forceful opponents of communism, and the aftermath of war and economic depression, which turned many more individuals into potential recruits. Many demobilized soldiers missed the comradeship of the trenches and looked for some alternative to the struggles of civilian life. Workmen torn out of their regular routines, women and adolescents mobilized for war service and being ordered back to shop or scullery or school, yearned for a stronger purpose. Finally, crisis—apparent or real—shook the enduring structures of established order and persuaded a good many people that salvation lay in action—even if only action for action's sake. Apart from communism, which many of them rejected, existing political movements offered little choice: the Liberals ever less liberal, the Radicals ever less radical, Conservatives merely conserving, and Socialists ever more the party of the middle-aged middle class.

This was the opportunity and source of fascism, which combined (in theory at least) the methods and appeals of national and social action, proposing to replace democratic and parliamentary institutions by a dictatorial one-party state and the free economy of liberal competition by one organized and planned on *corporative* lines: the virulent fulfillment of modern nationalism. Beginning as small bands of loud-mouthed hooligans, the Fascists gained in appeal and numbers in those societies where the relation between political power and the expression of the popular will was either absent or seemed least evident, and where belief in the capacity of individuals to express their interests or opinions was most restricted. Out of the Italian turmoil of the early 1920's the first of fascist movements grasped at power under the leadership of Benito Mussolini. It concealed, even from many followers, a fumbling kind of conventional politics beneath the guise of radical-seeming gestures, in the service of a disciplined mass movement (no more alienation) endowed with a supreme leader who claimed exclusive possession of political truth (no more individual responsibility), and exclusive power to assert it (no more squabbling parties).* Here was a new kind of security, a new kind of fulfillment, that would be expressed most fully in the national socialism of Adolf Hitler (1889–1945). Where Mussolini practiced action for action's sake, Hitler preached action for the sake of doctrine. The fascism of Mussolini was a brutally pragmatic opportunism. Hitler's Nazism attempted to play out a gigantic fantasy that proved as enthralling to millions as it proved murderous to more. Hitler's fantasy was racist. It used possibilities inherent in nationalism but which need not necessarily be developed, as the Italian experience showed, where racism was only a foreign and ill-accepted import. For

---

* Fascists did not attract hooligans only, but idealists too, interested in developing the collectivistic and populist aspects of its romantic nationalism. In Italy and elsewhere, fascist-type movements often recruited in circles similar to those of the radical left: disaffected syndicalists, students eager for action, intellectuals searching for a faith still undiscredited.

Hitler and Mussolini parade through the Brandenberg Gate in Berlin, 1937.

Hitler racism was essential: scheme of a giant combat between good and evil, the former embodied by the Germans—core of the blond Aryan race—the latter by the Jews, incarnation of dark Semites. Baseless in fact, this myth which Hitler and many followers accepted as Holy Writ served a moral and dynamic purpose: the one enabling the Nazi Party to justify all means by the inspiring end, the other by furnishing ideological impetus and unifying force.

In Hitler, turn-of-the-century nationalism reached a logical conclusion, before it foundered on the blood of millions sacrificed on the altars of a maniac faith. But we may remember that many other trends were accomplished in his one-party state. There was the dominant power of the state itself, whose powers, we have noted, had been growing all along and paradoxically so under the impact of democracy. Once the state became truly democratic (and liberal reforms seemed to hold out such a prospect), then there was no further need to restrict its powers. If only large-scale intervention could increase efficiency and improve society (as T. H. Green believed), then state bureaucracy was more important than laissez-faire tradition; if patriotism overrode particular loyalties, then the national state could claim far greater rights than the older oligarchic and particularistic structure. In any case, new nations, formed, as Karl Marx put it, "by the simple addition of like entities, much as a sack of potatoes consists of a lot of potatoes huddled into a sack," lent themselves to little else. The political opinions and influence of such people, whose identities are unexpressed and not clearly perceived, tend to operate in favor of some executive which runs society from above—democracy making for autocracy. Already in the seventeenth century Hobbes had spoken of the state as a "mortall God." The twentieth century would prove both terms where earlier times applied only the latter.

SCOTLAND
IRELAND
ENGLAND
London
NORWAY
Oslo
SWEDEN
Stockholm
DENMARK
NETHERLANDS
Amsterdam
Hamburg
Brussels
BELGIUM
LUX.
Paris
FRANCE
GERMANY
Weimar
Berlin
Nuremburg
Prague
Munich
CZECHOSLOVAKIA
SWITZ.
Geneva
Locarno
Vienna
AUSTRIA
ITALY
CORSICA
SARDINIA
Rome
SPAIN
FINLAND
Helsinki
ESTONIA
LATVIA
Memel
LITHUANIA
Danzig
E. PRUSSIA
Warsaw
POLAND

NORTH
SEA
BALTIC SEA
Leningrad
Moscow

UNION OF SOVIET SOCIALIST REPUBLICS

HUNGARY
Budapest
ROMANIA
Belgrade
YUGOSLAVIA
Bucharest
BULGARIA
Sofia
ALBANIA
GREECE
Athens
Istanbul
SICILY
CRETE
TURKEY
ADRIATIC SEA
AEGEAN SEA

BLACK SEA
CASPIAN SEA

MEDITERRANEAN SEA
CYPRUS
SYRIA
IRAQ
IRAN
Tripoli
Benghazi
LIBYA
PALESTINE
Cairo
SUEZ CANAL
TRANS-JORDAN
EGYPT
PERSIAN GULF
SAUDI ARABIA
TUNISIA

FRENCH WEST
AFRICA

FRENCH EQUATORIAL
AFRICA

ANGLO-EGYPTIAN
SUDAN

RED SEA

ERITREA
YEMEN
ADEN
Aden
FR. SOMALILAND
BRITISH SOMALILAND

CAMEROON
Addis–Ababa
ETHIOPIA
ITALIAN SOMALILAND
UGANDA
KENYA

0   500   1000 miles

THE GROWTH OF THE
NAZI AND FASCIST POWERS

Areas of Axis control, August 1939

The trend toward the rule by experts, the talk about "a conscious minority" manipulating the levers of power was a part of this. Talk of the good society in progressive circles at the turn of the century suggested not only Nietzschean supermen like those half humorously set forth in some of the plays of George Bernard Shaw, or H. G. Wells's dedicated samurai, half boy scouts and half knights, but also eugenics, selective breeding, euthanasia, the elimination of weak, useless, or criminal elements from society. All these Hitler carried out or tried to, though with a heavier hand than Shaw or Wells would have liked to see.

Finally, Hitler's politics were as popular with his people as those of democratic politicians and perhaps more so: a kind of fulfillment of popular representation. If Michelet's version of "the people" showed it sane and just, other observers sang another tune. The people, wrote the Intendant of Marseilles to Colbert in 1667, is "a hundred-headed beast that wants to be led without knowing where it is going." Two centuries later the first analytical observer of the masses, the French sociologist Gustave Le Bon found that the *crowd* was worse in character and conduct, more violent, less reasonable, less decent certainly, than its average member. The character of a crowd is set by its lowest common denominator. So, often, is that of modern mass society. Swayed by rumors, catchwords, appeals which would leave the average individual cold or revolted, the crowd turns into a mob, doing or condoning things that no sensible individual by himself would accept.

Such crowds had existed in other ages. But now they had become a political factor, an electoral mob, endowed with sovereignty and armed with votes, capable of letting their crowdlike proclivities run riot or having them enlisted for witch hunts and wars presented by some showman as a great crusade. José Ortega y Gasset's *Revolt of the Masses,* published in 1930, noted not only the essential novelty of the mass age itself, but its tendency to treat violence—the direct action of Syndicalists, Anarchists, Sorelians, Fascists, and Nazis—as the supreme means of action and expression. It is easier to understand this when we remember that the vocabulary of politics changes as interlocutors change. Separate individuals speak the language of reason. Individuals in the mass are most effectively swayed by primeval noises, react most readily in terms of their common animality. That most people are not so most of the time is a tribute to the immense changes that have taken place not only in society but in human character since the Stone Age. But the voices of sanity, proportion, decency, and restraint whisper in public while others bellow coarser appeals. Hitler rightly sensed this and used his perception with masterly force to ride the whirlwind which he conjured up to its—and his—appointed doom.

The Day of the Dictators

We have seen that the Bolshevik revolution almost reversed the course of the First World War and, for some years thereafter, appeared to threaten the rest of Europe with social war. The determination of Bolshevik leaders to leave the war brought allied support for their political enemies: the White or anti-Bolshevik forces. This continued even when the German war was ended, for by that time all powers in the West felt their stability and their interests threatened not only by Bolshevik policies inside Russia but by "red" revolutionary propaganda outside. There seemed to be no possible compromise between a regime convinced that its survival depended on the cause of world revolution and regimes at whose expense such revolution had to be achieved.

In any case, Russia was difficult of access and the news that trickled out made its experience sound less like that of 1789 or 1793 than like that of the Congo or Indonesia today. Bolsheviks were criminals at home, subversives abroad, best represented by the image of the man with a knife between his teeth. Not surprisingly, their neighbors feared their contagion and the Western powers lent support to White forces which for several years attempted to resist and defeat the Red revolution. This was also why the peace treaties excluded the Russians whose public image placed them outside the counsels of the civilized world—hopefully, as a temporary aberration. Clemenceau refused to let Soviet representatives set foot on French territory. Wilson and Lloyd George, who would have liked to deal with the Soviets as a *de facto* government, could convince neither their allies nor majority opinion in their own countries. Between 1917 and 1920 the tides of undecided warfare that surged along the confines of central Europe, the spate of revolutions and revolutionary strikes that broke out from the Arctic to the Mediterranean, sharpened awareness of the Bolshevik danger.*

At first, the real barrier against Bolshevism was envisaged in the long string of succession states between the Baltic and the Black Sea that were supposed to provide a so-called *cordon sanitaire,* or quarantine belt, which—since the new Russia could not be stifled—would contain and seclude it. Time proved the barrier to be a flimsy one, too dependent on the support of its Western patrons and on the acquiescence of the Germans. As this became increasingly apparent, the diplomacy

---

* Arno F. Mayer, *Politics and Diplomacy of Peacemaking: Containment and Counterrevolution at Versailles, 1918–1919* (1968), argues convincingly that the main unstated object of the peacemakers was not to establish self-determination and to make the world safe for democracy, or even to humble Germany, but to preserve the world from Bolshevism and to isolate Red Russia.

of the Western countries tended to look to Germany as the only really reliable barrier against Bolshevism, a fact which greatly restricted the Westerners' possibilities of diplomatic maneuver. This worked in favor of the Germans, suggesting an argument destined for a long run: that undue harshness shown to the Germans would throw them into the arms of Bolshevism. The German peace treaties were somewhat mitigated by this consideration and so was their application, especially as regards reparations. "Ordinary common prudence," explained Lloyd George in 1922, "demands that Germany should be treated decently in order to save her from Communism."

To begin with, however, the most striking aspect of postwar diplomacy was the disunion of the victors concerning how Germany should be treated: the French taking a hard line toward their impenitent neighbors, the British showing a more conciliatory attitude. Hoping to construct a rampart against both Germany and Russia, France turned to the successor states of eastern Europe—Poland, Czechoslovakia, Romania, Yugoslavia—equally aware of the dangers that a resurgence of the defeated camp could represent. Soon, a series of alliances linked these countries with one another and with France. Unfortunately, while France depended on her allies to strengthen her position, they in turn relied on her to affirm theirs, creating not a real force but a conjunction of weaknesses destined to give way before serious pressure. On the other hand, Russia and Germany, determined to make up lost ground, drifted together. In 1922, an international economic conference held at Genoa and designed to lighten the burden of reparations offered an opportunity for representatives of Russia and Germany to meet in nearby Rapallo, settle their economic differences, and sign a pact of friendship that shocked the other powers and ensured the collapse of the larger conference.

Britain and France reacted in opposite ways to the Treaty of Rapallo. The French, angered by German defiance, became more insistent on Germany's fulfillment of her obligations. When in 1923 Berlin defaulted on the schedule of its reparation payments, French troops were sent to occupy the Ruhr, vital center of German mining and industry. The occupation was answered by a general strike and this in turn brought about the collapse of German economy: there was soaring inflation, political confusion, social disruption on a vast scale as millions lost their savings and investments. The international repercussions of this crisis which soon affected the economies of other countries persuaded even the French to make concessions. The British, whom Rapallo had strengthened in the resolve that only kindness could keep Berlin and Moscow from moving even closer together, were glad to help mend the German predicament. In 1924, reparation schedules were revised and foreign loans provided by an international commission headed by an American banker, Charles Dawes; and this was followed in 1925 by a political agreement that guaranteed existing boundaries in the west.

The Treaty of Locarno, which settled outstanding disputes between Germany and her western neighbors, enlisting Britain and Italy as guarantors, seemed to open a more peaceful era of collaboration between the powers whose quarrels had marked the last six years. In 1926, Germany entered the League of Nations; in 1928 twenty-three nations signed a pact in Paris abjuring the use of aggressive war; in 1929 reparations were further scaled down by another commission headed by yet another American financier, Owen D. Young; and the last Allied occupation troops left German soil the following year. But Locarno settled some disputes only to let others fester: notably the question of Germany's eastern frontiers, deliberately left out of account because unacceptable to Berlin as they stood. The possibility of raising this issue (although one that, according to the treaty's terms, could only be settled by peaceful means) provided a potential threat to the French alliance system, but also an expression of the—tacit—hope that German expansion, should it begin once more, would be directed eastwards, reinforcing her assigned role as champion of Europe against Bolshevism.

Thus, to a great extent, European relations between the wars were affected by fear of Soviet Russia; and this raises the question how such fear can be explained. Why these precautions? What was the challenge of this revolution that stirred and alarmed great countries and great masses of people?

Louis Fischer, who went to Europe as a very young free-lance reporter just after the war, describes Bolshevism both as a protest and a hope: a protest against the old world and the old men who had made the war and spoiled the peace; a hope, as he put it, not of a better present but of a brighter future. Even when they merely presented old appeals dressed up in fresh slogans, this promise of a brighter future proved terribly important against the background of a dreary present. The Communists could point to a promised land which really existed, and this gave their talk of reshaping Europe a special power and effectiveness. Especially since, as Fischer points out, if Europe had needed no reshaping, it would not have been so worried.

That was the crux of the matter. The war had plunged Europe into a revolutionary situation. It revealed the incapacity, the impotence of the existing system and of the men who ran it to deal with the problems that they themselves created. It is possible that there would have been revolutionary outbreaks even without the Russian example. But the Russian example was there to act as an inspiration and the revolutionary situation created by war, economic collapse, and political confusion was compounded by the revolutionary lead of Moscow. Thus, those who feared the overthrow of their established order and the subversion of their way of life were justified in dreading the new revolutionary power arising in the east and doing everything to hamper or to tame it. Not because they disapproved of Soviet terror and dictatorship, but because they disapproved of the ends to which these methods were directed.

That fear of Bolshevism was more than suspicion and condemnation of the dictatorship and loss of political liberties in Russia can be seen from the fact that the democracies found dictatorship and its implications easier to accept when this respected property and used its force to maintain the familiar order rather than upset it. Between the wars, as David Thomson put it, "It seemed that democracy had merely made the world safe for dictatorship." In 1918 four empires fell, and all but the German fell to pieces. All had been dynastic, oligarchic, multinational, authoritarian structures. All were succeeded by very different entities—national republics or monarchies (except for the federated Soviet Union), popular or populist at least in outer guise, yet soon to evolve more toward authoritarian government. With the single exception of Czechoslovakia, the succession states were backward societies, largely illiterate, politically inexperienced, ignoring how to make multi-party government work when suddenly endowed with universal suffrage.

Representative party government in the West was the creation of small, self-conscious groups that ruled somewhat inert apathetic masses until these last developed a political consciousness. In most of the new countries (or in old ones like Portugal, Spain, and Turkey) where little political consciousness and less experience in democratic politics existed, a mass electorate and an authoritarian-minded political class could only coexist by dint of manipulation, which critics called corruption and, finally, by forcefully imposing the dictatorial rule of a man or faction. Thus, very soon, for widely differing reasons. countries as far divided in their tendencies as Hungary and Russia, Turkey and Italy, rejected liberal government for dictatorship: Hungary in 1919, Turkey 1920, Spain 1923, Italy 1925, Portugal, Poland, and Lithuania 1926, Yugoslavia 1929, Germany, Austria, and Estonia 1933, Bulgaria and Latvia in 1934, Greece in 1936 or earlier, Romania in 1938. This does not in all probability exhaust the list but gives an idea of its variety. The only thing all dictatorships had in common was a determined anticommunism. Some, as in Romania, were royal dictatorships of an old-fashioned authoritarian kind or, as in Hungary, almost the same thing without a king. Some, as in Spain during the 1920's, reflected a strong man's rule using personal prestige and military power to impose the will of one faction and exclude all others. Such regimes did not abolish parliament or representative institutions but rather circumvented them and pulled their teeth. More determinedly reactionary regimes appeared in Portugal and Austria, where dictatorships based on the Catholic Church, the army, and the police attempted to launch "new states" firmly anti-parliamentary and antidemocratic.

Mussolini

The most original dictatorship, however, established itself in Italy between 1922 and 1925 when the King backed the government of a former Socialist leader turned nationalist—Benito Mussolini—and the one-party rule which he imposed. Mussolini's Fascists had grown out of the national resentments of Versailles and the social fears of postwar readjustments. Yet they were more than mere reactionary bands. Pretending to defend society against "Red revolution" they also touted a revolution of their own against the dreary and corrupt established order, its exploitation and its compromises, its worn old men and its corrupting ways. Nationalist and populist, they used revolutionary language against the revolutionaries, attractive to those who wanted change (especially the young) but also to those who feared the greater change that the Reds might wreak. To the young they promised action, to the old, order; to the exploited they promised justice, to investors, stability; to the restless they spoke of change, to the replete and fearful, of tradition; to the ambitious they offered an avenue of social promotion, to the patriotic they hymned national greatness and unity. This last, indeed, was their most specific disagreement with the Left, to whose concept of class struggle they opposed one of class reconciliation and common interests within the organic body of the nation. Spottily formulated, slowly articulated, capable of being most things to most men, Fascism crudely joined the two great concerns of modern times—the national and the social—in a social nationalism whose influence carried far.

When this motif has been perfected in the national socialism of Adolf Hitler, and after Hitler had come to power in Germany in 1933, variants of what we might call fascism appeared in every country's politics, though nowhere as luxuriantly as in Italy and Germany. Fascist-type parties appeared in every land from Finland to Switzerland and Britain. They would grow strongest where government was weak, social and economic problems great, the traditional structures of society threatened or collapsing. Where an effective conservative or authoritarian government maintained itself in power, as in Hungary, fascism got no grip. Where social and economic problems did not overwhelm the system, as in France or England, or where they were solved with a will, as in the United States, the Fascist movements remained embryonic, often competing with more conventional reactionary or conservative groups. Where, as in Germany, the foundations of life seemed to give way beneath the feet of millions who lost their jobs, their savings, and their self-respect, coming to feel that anything was better than the present, the revolutionary and millenial note of Fascist politics could reach the masses, their violent language and methods promised forceful ac-

tion, while all the time their reference to nation and tradition con-
ciliated the ruling classes.

Just as anti-Bolshevism reconciled the victors of 1918 to spare and
humor Germany, so it prompted the partisans of established order to
spare and humor fascism, and then to favor it. In each of these
cases things eventually went wrong, for fascism proved both revolutionary and destructive. At first, however, it merely seemed the most
forceful and efficient of the modern creeds, a useful ally against Bolshevism and most impressive in the apparent order and unity it created
by eliminating those opportunities for free expression which tend to
make democratic societies such a jumble of contending voices.

Fascist dictatorships also made an impressive show of force. Their
rulers knew what they wanted and went about it with a dramatic will.
Among the first to adopt the doctrines of economic relativity and
control, they were the first outside Soviet Russia to absorb the suppurating unemployment that dragged down morale as much as prosperity. Before the apparent "triumph of. their will" the democracies
seemed limp and decadent. In a sense they were, for the advanced democracies were also most advanced in the decline of that demographic curve
whose rise in past centuries had marked their own rise in the world. The
twenties and especially the thirties saw birth rates falling in all countries, particularly in northern and western Europe where, despite a compensating fall in death rates, the population growth slowed down from
12 per cent in England of the 1890's to 4.5 per cent forty years later, from
13 per cent in Switzerland to 4 per cent, from 2 per cent in France to
less than 1 per cent, whereas in Germany the fall over the same period
went only from 14 to 9 per cent and in Italy from 10 to 9 per cent.

The Malthusian tendency of attributing unemployment to overpopulation and favoring birth control was oddly rare outside Britain. Other
countries were more concerned about the gun and factory fodder they
were losing, and staged campaigns to raise the birth rate by family allowances, loans, preferential treatment for large families; and none
was more successful than the Italian Fascists and the German Nazis,
both of whom succeeded in raising birth rates far above what they
had been at their accession. In France and England meanwhile, the proportion of older people in the population increased. In England, where
in 1901 32 per cent had been below fourteen and 20 per cent had
been over forty, by 1940 21 per cent were below fourteen and 32 per
cent over forty. France of the 1930's was the country where there were
more old and fewer young people than anywhere else in the world. This
kind of shift implied adjustments in economic structure which aging
populations are ill fitted to make, and suggested that the growing number of aged would have to be maintained by a shrinking active population. In the military sphere a deficiency of manpower meant a reluctance

The tunnels of the
Maginot Line.

to engage it, well reflected in the defensive strategy whose massive symbol
stretched from the Swiss to the Belgian border in the gun-bristling fortifications of the Maginot Line. Determined to husband her diminishing
manpower, France entrenched herself behind a long wall of concrete
which, expected to ensure her safety, merely certified her impotence.
Military immobility meant diplomatic inertia. The fortifications became
a ghetto from which the French watched the destruction of their eastern
allies before they permitted their own.

The greater proportion of older people also hinted at growing conservatism, failure of initiative, slow and hesitant reactions, fumbling
policies. Those conditions which had made for dynamism in the eighteenth and nineteenth centuries were now to be found in the Fascist
and Communist dictatorships, which assumed the aggressive stance given
up by their aging rivals; and the politics of the 1930's reflect this change.

Hitler

Although he impressed his contemporaries—not least Hitler—Mussolini
was not in a good position to make a mark on the world. The country
which he ruled did not afford him a sufficient base. Only a great power
could provide that and Italy never had the resources to become one.

Germany did. In Adolf Hitler she found a maniac leader who combined incoherent vulgarity and delusive obsessions with insights that cut through the conventions of national politics like a hot knife through butter. Hitler meant to reverse the verdict of 1918, redeem Germany's honor, and establish her unchallenged dominance over all of Europe, perhaps all the world. He proclaimed not only his mission but also his intentions in far greater detail than any politician before or since; and reaped the profits of his candor in the enthusiasm of his followers and the skeptical disbelief of foreigners unable to accept the scale or implications of what he ingenuously proposed. Yet Hitler achieved much of what he set out to do, partly because many of the gains he sought on the international plane were at the points where the peacemakers at Versailles had failed to reconcile principle and practice, leaving their heirs a strong feeling of guilt.

Hitler's demand that Germans be allowed to join their homeland and German territories be reunited to the Reich sounded plausible—the more plausible perhaps for the thought that Germany satisfied would rally to the cause of peace, that German claims denied would lead to war, a war in which either Germany won anyway or else she fell and, with her, the last solid barrier against Bolshevism. This was the rationale of appeasement which in practice, writes A. J. P. Taylor, "meant endorsing the claims of the stronger and then making out that these claims were just." It also meant throwing your friends to the wolves in the hope that the wolves would be sated before they got to you. Evidently, governments based on popular approval found it harder to face the prospect of war than those who could force their decisions on their subjects. At the same time, not only the "democracies" but the "Fascists" too based their policies on a wide range of popular approval. We might note that—more than ever before and perhaps since—the foreign policies of Britain, France, and Germany between the wars mirrored the opinions and the wishes of majorities. Democratic politics got the representatives and the results that they deserved.

Thus, Europe labored out of the Depression years into hard times of recurrent crisis on the political stage, a half decade of anarchy which partly reflected the post-operative shock of the Great Depression. "There never was a war in all history easier to prevent by timely action . . . without the firing of a single shot . . ." Churchill would recollect in 1946. "But no one would listen and one by one we were all sucked into the awful world war."

The first sort of timely action envisaged by the politicians of the West had been the enlistment of Mussolini in a common anti-German front. This might have worked (whether it *should* have worked is another matter) had not the British public in 1935 refused to sacrifice principle to policy. Mussolini wanted Ethiopia as an imperial sop. Aggression

was immoral; no more immoral, though, than the aggressions whose results created the French and British empires. Yet, public opinion would
not stand for it and the politicians who heeded their public fell between
two stools: unwilling to use force against Italian aggression, they let
it happen while making ineffective gestures to prevent it, thus ensuring their own inefficacy while driving Mussolini into Hitler's arms.

The Axis and the Allies

In May, 1936, Italian troops occupied Addis Ababa. A few weeks before,
something far more important had occurred, as crucial as the battle of
Sadowa seventy years before: German troops had reoccupied the Rhineland, a territory which they were bound not only by the Versailles Treaty
but by freely signed agreements (Locarno, 1925) to leave demilitarized.
It had been Clemenceau who pointed out that as long as the Rhineland
remained demilitarized Germany could not move against the Czechs'
Bohemian bastion. Once allowed to fortify it, she was free to challenge
all European arrangements. Clemenceau was right. The year 1936 liberated Hitler from fear of a French invasion should he become obstreperous. Now he could turn against his eastern neighbors—who were
also France's allies—without fear that French retaliation might overrun a rich, unfortified portion of his land. Nor did he need to fear any
Italian demonstration on his flank, for Italy was now his ally as a direct
result of the Ethiopian war, which had left Mussolini with no alternative
allies. Announced on November 1, 1936, the Rome-Berlin Axis sharply
challenged the sleepy London-Paris tandem.

Another war, this one a civil war in Spain, would tie the Axis allies
even closer. Spain had been a republic since 1931, oscillating between
left- and right-wing government, prey to repeated risings and disorders,
teetering on the brink of worse disorders still. Early in 1936, general
elections returned a coalition of left-wing parties combined in a Popular
Front whose policies encouraged military revolt that summer. Spain had
a long tradition of pronunciamentos and that of 1936 might have been
one more had not determined resistance by workers and students turned
the half-successful military coup into prolonged struggle. This soon took
on the coloring of social war, with Europe's Catholic and right-wing
forces supporting the military insurgents under General Francisco
Franco, and the Left, from liberals to Communists, supporting Spain's
legal government. The latter's obvious support would come from France
and Britain, democratic countries, in the first of which moreover a
similar Popular Front also ruled. Its fate was sealed when, determined
to keep out of trouble, the British government put pressure on the French
to deny the Spanish government their aid. Instead, the two democracies
bravely launched a policy of nonintervention which prevented aid from

reaching the republican camp while placing no obstacle in the way of German and Italian help to Franco's "nationalists."

As a result of such democratic self-denial, the levers of governmental power in Spain gradually passed to the most determined anti-Fascists, mostly Communists; and Soviet aid convinced conservatives in the democracies that they were right in favoring the nationalist cause. The civil war dragged on to 1939, focusing most of the feelings and sympathies of the liberal public on both sides of the Atlantic. It seemed symbolic that in this first confrontation between Fascism and what appeared to be the forces of freedom or, at least, of popular government, the latter should be left to fight and lose alone while governments in which the liberal world set its hopes withdrew their skirts from danger. In fact the situation was deceptive, for neither side really stood for freedom; and Franco, who readily accepted Fascist help, was not himself a Fascist but an authoritarian conservative of ancient stamp. This did not alter the fact that, while the Fascist powers effectively helped their friends, the democracies let theirs down.

Nothing went so far to reinforce this view as the events of 1938, when the defeat of the Republicans in Spain became a foregone conclusion and when Nazi aggression was carried out with impunity with Italy's aid and British benediction. Italy had helped maintain Austria's independence. Now that Italy was Hitler's friend, Austria became Hitler's prey. In the spring of 1938 he plucked it. Few could gainsay the right of a German population to join their brethren in the German Reich. The more so since Austrians, by and large, welcomed *Anschluss* (that is, union with Germany), and many, at their worst, outdistanced German Nazis in their fanaticism. And, Vienna taken, the argument of national self-determination would be used to claim back some three million Germans, onetime Austrians or Saxons, who lived within the borders of Bohemia.

Czechoslovakia was France's ally: a solid, stable country, a real democracy, whose army, behind strong fortifications supplied by the gigantic Skoda armament works, could offer serious resistance to the Germans, especially if backed by fellow democracies in the West. But France's government was most reluctant, and any readiness on its part to back the Czechs was sapped by British pressure. Britain was bound—as much by interest as by treaty—to help the French in case of war, and Neville Chamberlain, the British prime minister, was utterly unwilling to lay down British lives "because of a quarrel in a far away country between people of whom we know nothing." Then there was Russia. Hitler's pretext for marching into the Rhineland in 1936 had been a Franco-Soviet Pact which seemed to revive the Franco-Russian Alliance of 1894. Now, Russia offered help to Czechoslovakia in the name of collective security. But she had no more common border with the Czechs than had the

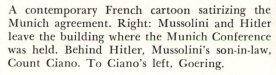

A contemporary French cartoon satirizing the Munich agreement. Right: Mussolini and Hitler leave the building where the Munich Conference was held. Behind Hitler, Mussolini's son-in-law, Count Ciano. To Ciano's left, Goering.

French; and Czechoslovakia's neighbors were more concerned about their own security from Russia than about facilitating any aid to the Czechs. In any case, the thought of help from Russia, if not underrated, was quite enough to spur Chamberlain and the French foreign secretary, Georges Bonnet, even further in seeking to accommodate Hitler without war. If Chamberlain had no heart for war, Bonnet did not have guts for it; while Daladier, the French prime minister, a veteran of the trenches and an old schoolteacher, shared the shamefaced reluctance of his fellow Frenchmen to face the horror of warfare once again.

The predicament was solved at a quadripartite meeting called at Mussolini's behest and held in Munich in September, 1938. There, Daladier and Chamberlain conceded on behalf of the Czechs all Hitler's claims to the Bohemian borderland. The Russians had been totally and significantly ignored, the Czechs treated as objects in a trade, whose fate mattered but little. Hitler and his acolytes triumphed once again. The vainglorious vulgarity that we perceive so well in retrospect about the Nazis only sets in relief the weak, vapid, well-meaning mediocrity of Western leadership, whose bad faith concealed both cowardice and guilt. Hitler considered his Western interlocutors nonentities, and Daladier must have agreed with him when the Paris crowds greeted him on his return from Munich not with rotten vegetables but with flowers. Chamberlain had no such doubts. He knew that his abdication represented, as A. J. P. Taylor recently wrote with a straight face "a triumph for all that was best and most enlightened in British life." So did the crowds that gave him a hero's welcome on his return from Munich.

Chamberlain would awake when, within six months of Munich and of Hitler's declaration to him that the Sudetenland was his last territorial demand in Europe, Nazi troops occupied the rump of the country he had helped dispatch, leaving some pickings to Poland and Hungary, glad at this time to act as jackals to the German wolf. It appears that Chamberlain honestly hoped that a fair settlement on ethnic lines would still Hitler's appetite. If so, it seems strange that, riled by Hitler's breaking his personal word to him, Chamberlain chose to deny the Germans the right to Danzig, and to certain territories within the Polish border to which they had as good a right as to the Sudeten regions. But he did, and reacted to German occupation of Bohemia by guaranteeing all Polish territory against attack. This created several problems. In the first place, the French were as reluctant to go to war for Danzig as the British had been to fight for the Czechs. In the second place, the Franco-German border now consisted of two giant lines of fortifications which made any effective intervention from the west most doubtful, and suggested that help for Poland could only come from the east. But the Poles, remembering past experience, rejected Russian help. As arrogantly confident as they were ill prepared, the colonels who ruled Poland thought they could hold the Germans by themselves.

The French and British made somewhat half-hearted efforts to persuade them to accept Russian aid, and equally half-hearted efforts to negotiate a pact with Russia. They only succeeded in persuading Stalin that Russian security lay in a pact with Hitler. It seemed as if the Western powers, equally afraid of Communists and of Nazis, wished the two to fight each other. Certainly some Western newspapers hinted as much. But the Russians would not pull capitalist chestnuts out of the fire. They could make a more profitable deal with the Germans, dividing the lands between them rather than fighting over them. In August, 1939, with a Nazi propaganda storm over Danzig at its height, the news of the German-Soviet Pact burst on the world. It seemed as if, once again, Hitler would achieve his aim without war. Who could withstand him now? Who would? "Our enemies are little worms," he told his generals on August 26, 1939. "I saw them at Munich." He had good reason for his judgment. And it seemed borne out by a letter which the London *Daily Telegraph* carried on September 1, 1939, from Lord Alfred Douglas, delighted that Britain could avoid "the odious predicament" of alliance with Russia now that Russia and Germany had allied instead, and relieved that "there would be no war."

The first of September was the day the Germans invaded Poland. Forty-eight hours later Europe was at war. The worm had turned at last. Awkwardly, reluctantly, not knowing quite what to do, perhaps at the wrong moment, perhaps in the wrong cause, it had perceived that it must stand and fight for it had no choice. There is something ironic about the way in which those men whom we describe as statesmen will disavow the most reasonable statements of their predecessors. Bismarck had declared that the Balkans were not worth the bones of a single Pomeranian grenadier and his successors staked the empire Bismarck built upon a Balkan issue. In 1925 the British foreign secretary, Austen Chamberlain, deliberately echoed Bismarck: "For the Polish Corridor no British government ever will or ever can risk the bones of a British grenadier." His younger brother was to prove him wrong—though right in the event, like Bismarck.

The Second World War

Defeat in Europe

German troops attacked Poland on September 1, 1939. Britain declared war on Germany at noon on September 3 and France followed suit a few hours later. But the action, unlike a quarter of a century before, was in the east. Impotent and circumspect behind the Maginot Line, the Western allies watched Poland overrun by Germans, invaded by the Rus-

German tanks sweep into Poland.   Warder Collection

sians, and, before the month had ended, partitioned for a fourth time between its greater neighbors. In mid-September Harold Nicolson dined with a conservative minister and noted in his diary: "At heart he is longing to get out of it . . . any reference to Russian assistance makes him wince and at one moment he sighed deeply and said, 'You see, whether we win or lose, it will be the end of everything we stand for.' By 'we' he means obviously the capitalist classes."

Quite a few men in France as much as Britain felt that their countries were at war with the wrong enemy. They suffered, one might say, from a counter-idealism so acute that they forgot where their national interests lay, remembering only their deep prejudices against Bolshevism. That Germany threatened their national existence seemed less significant than the danger which the Soviets constituted for a world order they confused with their personal interest. It would take a dyed-in-the-wool Tory like Churchill to see his country's immediate interest clearly, detached from personal predilections, and to understand, as some great predecessors had, that one concludes alliances to serve not taste but interest and that one makes war to win. But before Churchill came to power, Britain and her ally indulged a mealier mood. The war along the western front trod water while Hitler bade his time and, further east the Russians sought to enlarge their defensive *glacis*. Having advanced up to the Curzon Line in September,* during October they secured military privileges in the Baltic states,** and in November sought to obtain similar rights from ·Finland. When the Finns refused, war broke out— a war which at once aroused the enthusiasm of the Western world and offered it an opportunity to escape the uneasy situation which the French called *la drôle de guerre* (the phony war). Unable to make real war against the Germans, the French and British now proposed to make war against the Russians too. Some may have hoped that before long they and the Germans could be reconciled against the predestined enemy. They were disappointed when March, 1940, brought a Russo-Finnish treaty that gave the Soviets more than they had asked at first—specifically more ground between their second city, Leningrad, and the border.

Thereafter, events moved fast. In April, 1940, German forces invaded Denmark and Norway, making short shrift of the local armies and of the improvised expeditions that France and Britain sent to help. In May they struck at France through Holland and Belgium, turning the flank

---

* Suggested in 1920 by the then British foreign secretary as a means of settling the Russo-Polish conflict, the Curzon Line left the Ukrainian provinces east of the Bug River in Soviet territory. Though ignored by the Poles, this line provided a rough border between Orthodox Ukrainian peoples and the Catholic Polish-speaking population further west.

** Estonia, Latvia, and Lithuania would be occupied in June of 1940.

A street scene during the bombing of London.

of the Maginot Line, using their aviation to clear the way for armored columns which broke through all opposition. Four days from the attack's beginning the Dutch army had capitulated; the Belgians held out for sixteen. Swiftly, mercilessly, the British Expeditionary Force in France, cut off from its allies, its flank exposed by the Belgians' fall, was forced on to the coast. The first days of June saw an extraordinary feat: 215,000 British and 120,000 French troops evacuated from the Channel beaches, chiefly near Dunkirk. Meanwhile, the Germans raced on. They were in Paris on June 13. The fleeing French reconstituted their government, placing at its head Henri Philippe Pétain, the hero of Verdun, who asked the Germans for an armistice (June 16). The armistice was signed on June 22 at Compiègne, in the same railroad carriage where twenty-two years before the Germans, too, had signed armistice terms. Forty-two days had passed since the campaign's beginning. Hitler could think that the war was over.

So did most of the French. Meeting at Vichy, the parliament of the Third Republic handed full powers to Pétain as head of a state more than half of which lay under German occupation. The capital of the unoccupied zone was in Vichy itself, a spa for sufferers from liver ailments. The ancient enmity for Britain reappeared, fed by deep resentment when—fearful that the French fleet would end in German hands—the British attempted its destruction and the subversion of French colonies. Men like Pierre Laval, an astute parliamentary figure, felt that France's hope lay in developing better relations with the Nazis. The war,

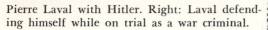

Pierre Laval with Hitler. Right: Laval defending himself while on trial as a war criminal.

he thought, would soon be over and favorable terms could only be secured if France collaborated with her occupants. Few dissented: among them an unknown brigadier, Charles de Gaulle, whom the British helped to set up a national committee of Free French in London to continue the fight against the Germans. Britain's new prime minister also disagreed. For Winston Churchill, who had succeeded Chamberlain in May, following the Norwegian fiasco and on the eve of the German offensive in the west, Britain "had only begun to fight."

Most of Britain's military equipment had been left behind at Dunkirk. Fresh arms and supplies were secured from the United States, naval and air bases in Britain's Atlantic possessions exchanged for American destroyers to patrol the sea lanes. The Royal Air Force, however, had been saved and, while Britain rearmed, it beat off the constant air strikes which were supposed to usher in German invasion. Between August and October, 1940, many British cities had been torn and burned, civilian casualties stood at tens of thousands, 14,000 had died in London alone. But nearly 2,400 German planes had been brought down against only a third that many lost to the R.A.F. The courage of the latter's fighter pilots, the spirit of the British people, and the radar network which provided early warning of the enemy's approach, had won the Battle of Britain: in General von Rundstedt's opinion, the crucial battle of the war. By October, 1940, the direct German threat had been fought down; but very heavy raids continued on every part of the country, and particularly on London, until May, 1941, when the German air force had to turn its face toward the east. The Battle of Britain was the first German defeat: as in the 1800's the conquerors of the Continent could not cross the Channel and finally turned eastward to seek a solution to their perplexity. As in those years but more so, the unconquered island remained a lonely fortress base at the enemy's rear from which the final assault against him could be mounted. As in those years too, the overweening conqueror would break his teeth on Russia, the stubborn resistance of her peoples, and the no less stubborn immensity of her space.

While Germany was conquering the west, Russia had recovered the territories lost by the Tsarist empire in the Baltic, Poland, and Bessarabia. Her demand for this last from Romania—whose rulers had counted on a French alliance rendered quite worthless by the French defeat—set off a spree of claims on the territories that country had acquired from Bulgaria in 1913 and Hungary in 1919. Cut down in size by almost half, Romania gave herself a military dictator and joined the Axis in search of self-protection. So did her Hungarian and Bulgarian enemies.

Yet Germany's Balkan flank floundered in a situation that Mussolini had created out of sheer folly. When war had started in 1939, Italy had not been prepared to join it. Both sides were glad to see her neutral: the Allies to have one less enemy, the Germans for the supplies that could be channeled through her. In June, 1940, however, Mussolini could not resist the spoils of France then being overrun. He declared war on the Allies and Italian troops did miserably in the Alps before the French fighting ended. That same autumn, with German power spreading through the Balkans, Mussolini sought compensation against Greece. He had no reason to attack that country except the desire to gain some cheap glory while Germany was triumphing all along the line; but he found that his troops did no better there than against the French. Across the Mediterranean, in Africa, the British overran his colonies. No attack on Russia could begin without the Balkan flank secured. The Germans intervened, which meant that first they must subdue the Yugoslavs who refused them passage into Greece. Within a few weeks the Balkans had been won. By the end of April, 1941, German writ ran to the Aegean Sea. It would have run still further had not the British managed to secure Iraq and to prevent the Vichy French governors of Syria and Lebanon from handing their air bases over to the Germans.

Now Germany was free to attack Russia, despite frantic attempts on Stalin's part to avoid a showdown. And when, in June 1941, German, Finnish, Hungarian, Italian, and Romanian troops opened hostilities on a front that ran 2,000 miles, Churchill at last found a reluctant ally, but one that would fight ruthlessly to the end.

A blow-by-blow account of a great war would be impossible in this context. Slowly, what had begun as a European contest drew in the remaining world. Russia had attempted to stay outside it and could not. The United States, increasingly aware that British defeat menaced her own survival, was drawn into taking a more active part in the defense of sea lanes which were the island's lifeline. American forces landed in Danish Greenland, Dutch New Guinea, and in Iceland. America, too, however, sought to avoid open warfare and might have done so had not Japan, Germany's ally but careful for her part to avoid war with Russia, tried to use the opportunity to gain dominion over the Pacific.

The World at War

The Japanese had waged war since 1931 to win and keep control of China. After the fall of France they had obtained the right to occupy Indochina and they controlled Thailand as well. They coveted the resources which lay in the colonial territories of the other powers that Germany had defeated, but knew the United States would not stand by and see them taken. They must annihilate America's power to withstand them, and they went far toward doing so when, on December 7, 1941, they unexpectedly attacked Hawaii and the Philippines, destroying much of the U.S. Pacific fleet in Pearl Harbor. Within six months, the Japanese tide had swelled as far as India's borders and the Aleutians, engulfing British, Dutch, French, and American territories in its wake.

Now the lines were drawn: on one side aggressor powers which had conquered immense areas of the world and meant to conquer more; on the other Britain, the United States, and Russia with their allies, a disparate group forced to hang together if only to avoid hanging separately.* War spread its wings over all continents: a new kind of war, not only in its scale but in its limitless implications. For, if Japan and Italy visualized gigantic gains from their aggressions, Germany hoped that hers would bring her dominion of the world.** Considering the means that the twentieth century could furnish for control and conquest, the

---

* Hindsight suggests that, once the United States had been drawn in, the war's result was a foregone conclusion. Not counting the areas occupied by their enemies, the Allies had over three times the national income, almost four times the industrial power, almost double the population of the three Axis countries.

** As the SS song went:

> If the whole world lies in ruins
> What the devil do we care?
> We march on still,
> For today Germany is ours
> And tomorrow the whole world!

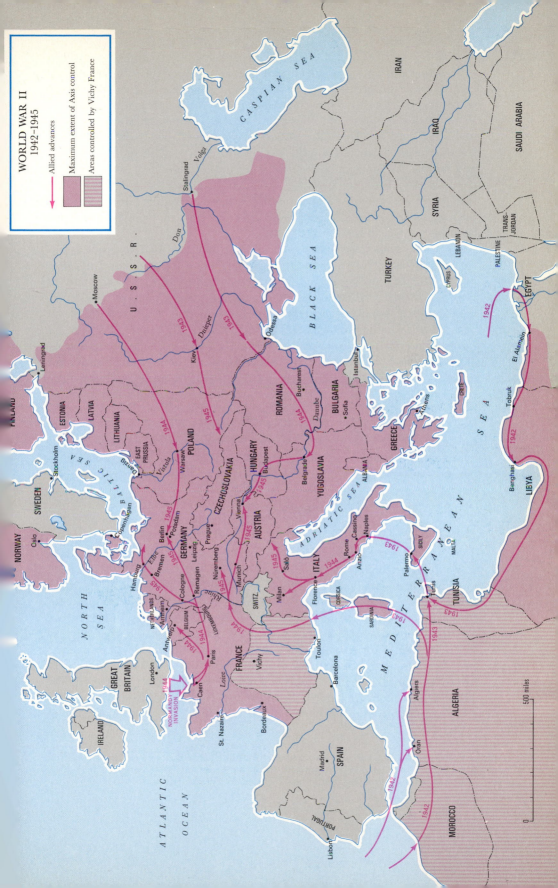

WORLD WAR II
1942–1945

Allied advances
Maximum extent of Axis control
Areas controlled by Vichy France

NORWAY
SWEDEN
Oslo
Stockholm
FINLAND
Leningrad
ESTONIA
LATVIA
LITHUANIA
Copenhagen
Danzig
EAST PRUSSIA
BALTIC SEA
NORTH SEA
GREAT BRITAIN
London
IRELAND
Hamburg
Bremen
Berlin
Potsdam
Leipzig
GERMANY
Cologne
Remagen
Elbe
Rhine
NETHERLANDS
Antwerp
Amhem
BELGIUM
LUXEMBOURG
Nuremberg
Munich
Prague
CZECHOSLOVAKIA
Vienna
AUSTRIA
SWITZ.
Caen
NORMANDY INVASION
Paris
Loire
FRANCE
Vichy
Bordeaux
St. Nazaire
ATLANTIC OCEAN
Lisbon
Madrid
SPAIN
PORTUGAL
Barcelona
Toulon
Milan
Salò
Florence
CORSICA
SARDINIA
Rome
Cassino
Anzio
Naples
ITALY
Palermo
SICILY
MALTA
TUNISIA
Tunis
Oran
Algiers
ALGERIA
MOROCCO
MEDITERRANEAN SEA
ADRIATIC SEA
Moscow
U.S.S.R.
Don
Volga
Stalingrad
Dnieper
Kiev
Odessa
Danube
Vistula
Warsaw
POLAND
Budapest
HUNGARY
Belgrade
YUGOSLAVIA
ALBANIA
ROMANIA
Bucharest
BULGARIA
Sofia
GREECE
Athens
CRETE
BLACK SEA
Istanbul
TURKEY
CASPIAN SEA
IRAN
IRAQ
SYRIA
LEBANON
CYPRUS
PALESTINE
TRANS-JORDAN
SAUDI ARABIA
EGYPT
El Alamein
Tobruk
Benghasi
LIBYA

1942
1943
1944
1945

500 miles

proposition was a tenable one, and no price too great for its achievement.

The really dreadful thing about such a conquest was that not only its process but also its achievement promised only slavery, terror, and destruction for millions and scores of millions. More consciously and deliberately than any previous conqueror, and even than their own allies, the Germans meant to establish the supremacy of their master race and sacrifice all other nations to their needs, exterminating some peoples, condemning others to lingering destruction, ruling and exploiting all, the basic differences among non-Germans ranging from servants through cattle, to even lower beings like the Jews or Gypsies, whose extermination was to cleanse the world.

War was again transformed into trial by combat, but its implications were sometimes worse for noncombatants than for the men at arms. From Java to the Japanese concentration camps of California and to central Europe, civilians of every age and sex were penned up, humiliated, treated as potential enemies or burdens that were expendable at best. Everywhere, great herds of prisoners were driven to more or less forced labor for their conquerors.* But the Germans added to this a refinement which only monomania could suggest: torture and murder for millions, on which an important part of their resources and organization were lavished to the extent of diverting them from the war effort itself. Much of all this went on in darkness—in night and fog as the Germans characteristically dubbed their extermination plans. At the front of the stage, in the fierce light of battle, lay the tides and eddies of a war in which the Axis powers that grasped at victory in 1941, were slowly pressed back thereafter as their enemies marshaled and organized their strength.

Allied Victory

The tide of battle turned in 1942 when the Americans began to leap-frog forward through the Pacific islands; an Anglo-American force invaded French North Africa clearing that continent of Germans and Italians, providing the base of the Free French state and a jumping-off ground for invading Europe; and Russia held the Germans on the Volga before forcing them back in 1943. The year 1943 opened with the great victory of Stalingrad which marked the turn of the Russian tide, when twenty-two German divisions cut off in the ruins of that Volga city were forced to capitulate. Then, as the Russians rolled slowly westward, the Allies began advancing north through the Italian peninsula. Mussolini fell, escaping to head a make-believe Fascist state in the shadow of

---

* German forced labor policies provided resistance movements in occupied countries with recruits, most of whom would have preferred to stay at home but who, after 1942, preferred outlawry to slave labor in heavily bombed German factories.

the Alps, while Italy signed an armistice and became a battleground in her turn. All over Europe partisan bands went into action, often led and organized by Communists but armed and supplied by the Allies whose air bombardments were pounding German cities into ruins, preparing the ground for invasion in the west.

This came on D-Day: June 6, 1944. The greatest amphibious operation of all time, commanded by General Dwight D. Eisenhower, brought into play all the experience and planning skill the Allied Command had gained in North Africa, Italy, and in scattered landing operations on the European coast. Ten thousand planes, 4,000 ships to ferry troops and supplies, 80 warships to guard the armada and use their heavy guns to flatten a way for the assault, artificial harbors to provide port facilities, eventually an underwater pipeline from England to the coast of France, contributed to success. Within a week of D-Day, over 300,000 British, Canadian, and U.S. troops had landed on Normandy beaches. By mid-August their numbers stood well over 2 million, backed up by 4 million tons of supplies carried in nearly half a million vehicles. By the end of August Paris had been freed. By September Allied forces stood on the Rhine. They would not cross it until March, 1945, and would face some of their bitterest fighting in the interval. But the war was being won.

In the east the Russians, having delivered their own country, pursued the Germans into Hungary, Romania, and the Balkans. The Germans fought desperately, the more so since Nazi propaganda made the most of the Allied demand for an unconditional surrender. Russian, American, and British troops converged through lunar landscapes that merciless retaliation bombing had brought about, made more dramatic by the progressive liberation of German death and torture camps. The last

The D-Day invasion of France as seen from an Allied landing craft.

Warder Collection

few months of war brought the Götterdämmerung, the twilight of the Nazi gods, which Hitler, the Wagnerian, always envisaged as the only alternative to victory.* Hitler and some of his close lieutenants committed suicide just before final defeat which unconditional surrender acknowledged on May 7, 1945. Their country lay in ruins all about them. Three hundred and fifteen tons of explosives had been dropped on Germany for every ton she had dropped on Britain. Over three million Germans were dead, more than twice as many maimed. Around Germany, all of Europe lay crippled and devastated by her mad grab for power and by the consequences it had brought about.

Japan, too, was being fast defeated. In July, 1945, the Allied leaders meeting at Potsdam to decide the fate of Germany and the future conduct of the war invited the Mikado to surrender. There was no reply. On August 6, the port of Hiroshima and three days later that of Nagasaki were destroyed by atomic bombs. Within a few days Japan followed her late allies to surrender.

There has been much discussion about the decision to use the atom bomb at all. But six years of desperate destruction had forged a mentality and attitudes difficult to recapture in a time of relative peace. From the Caspian to Glasgow, from Sidney to the Aleutians, men had learned the language of terror, had yearned for retaliation, had come to think of the enemy as purely evil—which he often was. In the kingdom of war destruction was coin of the realm, destruction sometimes for destruction's sake, as when England's cathedral cities were ruined or when, in one night of February, 1945, one of Europe's most beautiful old cities—Dresden—was wiped out by Allied bombardment from the air and at least 120,000 people with it (possibly twice as many): more victims than would die at Hiroshima. In winter and spring of 1945, as tens of thousands died in Germany's blazing townships, the British and their allies had reason to fear that murderous German rockets falling on their cities would soon be equipped with atomic warheads which the enemy would not hesitate to use. Japan, too, even before the 200,000 dead of the atomic raids, had suffered considerable civilian losses and stood to suffer more. The accountancy of horror becomes meaningless: enough to note that fear, suffering, hatred had made men brutes. Europe appeared "a rubble heap, a charnel house, a breeding

* All possibility of any other end was defeated by the failure of a desperate plot to murder Hitler at his headquarters on July 20, 1944. Hitler escaped with a light concussion and almost all conspirators were brutally executed. Most of them had been Christian Conservatives and German patriots, senior officers or civil servants, diplomats or clergymen, who envisaged a compromise peace that would allow Germany to keep some of Hitler's conquests without Hitler. Their success might have allowed Germany to collapse in the Italian fashion. Their failure meant that she would fight to the finish.

Few buildings stand in Hiroshima after the atomic bomb.

ground of pestilence and hate," as Churchill still described her two years later. Nor was there any hope as there had been in 1918; and that proved an advantage, for there were no illusions this time to embitter men. Hope rose like a mist over the ruins, and men scarcely spared a glance for it.

"The end of the war is simply the end of this war," noted Jean-Paul Sartre in 1945. "The future is not committed: we don't believe anymore in the end of wars . . . but one has to bet. The dying war leaves man naked, without illusions, abandoned to his own forces, having learned at last that he can count only on himself."

Chapter 19

NATIONAL COUNTERPOINT: INTERNAL AFFAIRS SINCE 1918

The internal affairs of the individual countries unfolded at different rates and in different ways. We return now to look at each of the countries, taking them up in the aftermath of the First World War and carrying them to the present day. In all this, 1945 stands as a great watershed. The quarter century since 1945, during which particular national developments are less significant than *European* politics as such and Europe itself can be treated adequately only as part of the wider world, will be surveyed in Chapter 21.

If the march-past begins this time with Russia—perhaps least European or representative of the great powers—this is in order to establish from the start *the* great event of the twentieth century: a revolution of world consequence yet of peculiarly Russian coloring; a movement that saw itself as the fulfillment of a long tradition which placed 1917 after 1776, 1789, 1848, and 1871, yet that unraveled in a quite different way; finally, an event (and the society it created) in terms of which the men and politics of our century have largely defined themselves.

Germany follows. If Russian history stays stubbornly marginal to common European experience, that of Germany is central and, in this

910

period, crucial. Where England and France dominated the culture and politics of Europe during previous centuries, Germany grasps the lead late in the nineteenth century, grimly maintains it despite her setbacks, becomes the last power to assert (or attempt asserting) European supremacy in a wider world.

Italy, too, makes a brief gesture in the same direction, rasher but just as catastrophic in its ending. Like Germany, Italy is a newcomer among the *nations,* born in the nineteenth century out of diplomatic maneuvers and a few swift wars, a heterogeneous coagulation of states, each boasting a tradition older and more enduring than that of the new nation-state, united by the will of a minority, kept united by determined dreams as much as by interest or habit. Like Germany, too, Italy feels at a disadvantage for having entered the world scene too late as a unified nation, and tries to make up for it by acting in haste. Impatient and sometimes violent self-assertion marks its international stance; patchy, sporadic, and uneven activity provides the hallmark of internal policies.

None of these three nations—Russia, Germany, Italy—has a tradition of liberal institutions developing in time. All represent first the authoritarian, then the totalitarian forms that would be one European answer to the problems of mass democracy.

France and Britain follow: older nations that had led the field in the nineteenth century, almost imperceptibly giving way thereafter until the trend accelerates and the Second World War, at last, reveals decline in the most brutal light. Different as they are, the atmosphere and institutions of the United Kingdom and of France represent another possible response to the emancipation of the masses, while, on the other hand, their political fortunes illustrate the connection (more evident, more urgent today than it has ever been before) between productivity and power.

The other countries that are mentioned had their hour of glory some time before, or never had it at all. They struggle not for dominion but simply for survival or for recognition. Their significance is incidental, like Spain's—arena of a civil war transformed into the first armed encounter between Fascists and their foes; like Austria—rump of the Habsburg empire whose clumsy attempts at self-preservation set off the First World War; like the vast and varied area from Baltic to Aegean that furnished the last debatable lands of Europe and its unfailing powderkeg. Most of the time such countries do not decide, they just endure. At certain moments, though, some desperate or foolhardy gesture may turn a pawn into a pivotal figure—as in 1914 and again in 1939.

The second great war of the century precipitated the ruin which the first began, putting an end not only to an epoch but to a way of life. As with the swordsman who thought his opponent's blow had missed him until he shook his head,* the world supremacy of Europe, the

---

* It fell off.

social supremacy of the upper classes, the commercial or diplomatic initiative of heretofore sovereign exchanges and marketplaces, all collapsed at once.

Each of the following sections sketches not only the collapse but the recovery that followed. The interesting aspect of the post-1945 years, however, is that what was done in them was done no longer in terms of European initiatives, models, aspirations, but of foreign ones. Economic recovery, the shaping of new alliances, the abandoning of colonial aspirations, the patching up of political and financial crises, allowed for an extra-European factor. This was new.

So was the mass fulfillment of what, until that time, had been premonitions: mass politics, mass markets, mass education, mass access to culture (and concomitant mass indifference to it). Hitler had failed to conquer Europe. But he succeeded in pushing her over the brink of a nineteenth century that had persisted beyond its time. Those institutions that continued to subsist did so under suspended sentence. And we shall see in Chapter 21 that even the greatest political invention of the modern age, the national state, was to be called in question.

Russia

In the midst of chaos the Bolsheviks had hammered together an administrative structure, while the ruthless leadership of Leon Trotsky forged a Red Army more successful than the tsarist one. They had not only to reconquer but to re-educate a whole nation, as their French predecessors had had to do; and they accepted the precept Saint-Just had formulated that "what makes a republic is the total destruction of those opposed to it." In 1920, one of the Commissars, Zinoviev, admitted that he and his fellows had never expected they would have "to resort to so much terror or find our hands so bloodstained." Terror was supplemented by conscription of wealth, direction of labor, food levies, wages paid in kind when money lost all value. For three years the Bolsheviks fought for dear life over a ravaged country where men stumbled through famine and terror, not knowing whence their death would come.* War communism was a disaster, but it pulled them through. By 1920 Russia turned out 5 per cent of the steel, 6 per cent of the textiles, about half of the grain produced before the war. Transport had broken down, consumer goods were impossible to find, 7 million had died since 1917, 5 million or more would die of famine in the Great

---

* In 1918 the Suprematist painter Ivan Puni (Jean Pougny) glued an empty plate to a canvas—the first provocative statement of hunger at a time when war and revolution made hunger a matter of fact.

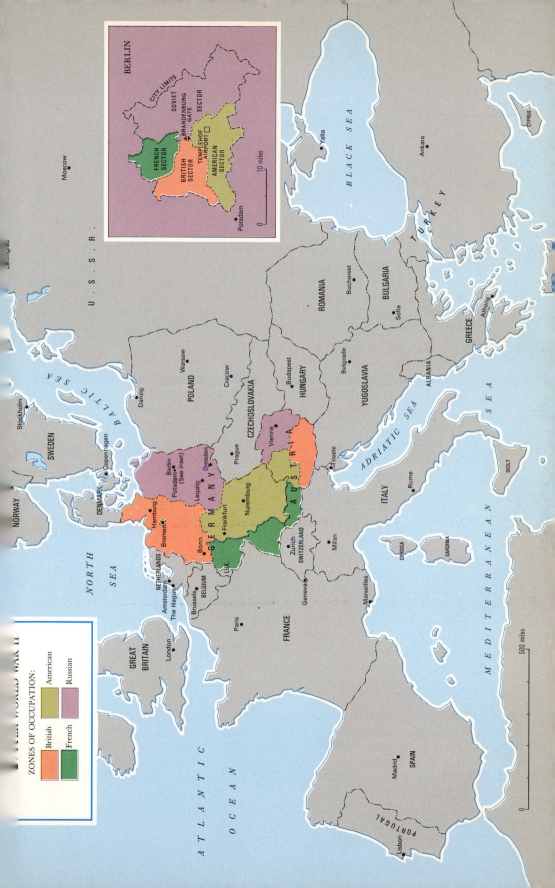

BERLIN

CITY LIMITS

SOVIET
SECTOR

BRANDENBURG
GATE

FRENCH
SECTOR

BRITISH
SECTOR

TEMPLEHOF
AIRPORT

AMERICAN
SECTOR

10 miles

0

Potsdam

Moscow

U. S. S. R.

BLACK SEA

Yalta

Ankara

TURKEY

ROMANIA

Bucharest

BULGARIA

Sofia

GREECE

Athens

CYPRUS

NORWAY

SWEDEN

Stockholm

BALTIC SEA

Danzig

POLAND

Warsaw

Cracow

CZECHOSLOVAKIA

Prague

Vienna

AUSTRIA

HUNGARY

Budapest

Belgrade

YUGOSLAVIA

ALBANIA

ADRIATIC SEA

Trieste

Rome

ITALY

SARDINIA

CORSICA

SICILY

MEDITERRANEAN SEA

DENMARK

Copenhagen

Berlin

Potsdam
(See inset)

Leipzig

Dresden

GERMANY

Hamburg

Bremen

Bonn

Frankfurt

Nuremburg

LUX.

Zurich

SWITZERLAND

Milan

Geneva

NORTH SEA

NETHERLANDS

Amsterdam

The Hague

Brussels

BELGIUM

Marseilles

Paris

FRANCE

GREAT
BRITAIN

London

ATLANTIC OCEAN

SPAIN

Madrid

PORTUGAL

Lisbon

500 miles

0

ZONES OF OCCUPATION:

British   American

French   Russian

Drought of 1921 and the following winter. Seven years of chaos since 1914 had taken some 28 million lives. But Bolshevism was firmly in the saddle. In 1920 the last serious threat to the new regime—a Polish attempt to conquer the Ukraine—had been repulsed to the gates of Warsaw; and, though that penetration was followed by defeat, an armistice with Poland was concluded in the fall. The last White forces were ousted before the year had ended. Peace returned: a peace of exhaustion.

The Bolshevik revolution had succeeded at first because it promised what an immense majority of Russians wanted: peace and land; then, because the tightly organized and well-directed Bolsheviks faced no real institutional opposition and their enemies never really united against them; lastly because in the civil war the peasantry was on their side. But now the peasantry was restive and the sympathetic revolutions the Bolsheviks had hoped for in other lands were burned out or crushed. Soviet Russia, devastated by civil war, was left to make its way alone. Then, in March, 1921, the sailors of the naval base at Kronstadt, outside Petrograd, who had helped the Bolsheviks into power, took arms against them calling for "a third revolution," for Soviets not dominated exclusively by Bolsheviks—the kind of Soviets the October Revolution had envisaged, without dictatorship, coercion, or bureaucracy. The mutiny was put down but it forced the Communist Party (as the Bolsheviks had renamed themselves in 1918) to a new course designed to provide the country with a respite and the party dictatorship with a safety valve of wan prosperity.

The New Economic Policy (NEP, 1921–1927) sponsored by Lenin was in the economic sphere a kind of Bolshevik Thermidor, only self-executed, nearly suspending the advance of revolution by temporary concessions to what Marx had once described as rural idiocy. To reconcile the peasants and encourage them to provide more food for the starving towns, grain levies and requisitions were replaced by a limited grain tax, inspiring farmers to plant more and make a profit, re-creating a class of *kulaks*—richer and more productive peasants—and ending in a general upswing that affected both industry and trade. Within a year or two, three-fourths of the country's retail trade was in private hands. While the strategic heights of the economy continued to be controlled by the state, NEP men played an increasingly important role as middlemen, traders, retailers, and even manufacturers of consumer goods.

Determined attempts were also made to re-establish relations with other countries, attract capital and technicians from outside, revive exchanges without which the Russian economy panted for oxygen. Russia's greatest hope in this direction lay in German resentment of Versailles and Germany's readiness to grasp at any straw to further her revenge. In 1922, the Treaty of Rapallo, settling outstanding differences between Germany and Russia, marked the co-operation of the two "pariah nations" as Lloyd George called them. But this itself harked back to earlier trade relations, to a common hostility to Poland, and to certain secret agreements concluded in 1921 whereby German armament factories were set up in Russia, German advisers helped to train the Red Army, and German credit speeded the country's industrialization.

Behind the relatively liberal façade of NEP, party power grew. The more concessions the Bolsheviks made, the less criticism they tolerated, for the more criticism was likely to be effective. This was the period when the tolerated remnants of open opposition—Social Revolutionaries or Mensheviks—were finally "liquidated": a term which, in those days, meant that they were forced into the Communist Party, into exile, into silence. This was also when the Soviet system was finally structured into two parallel hierarchies. On the one hand, the Soviets, their All-Russian Congress, its Central Executive Committee, and the small, ultimately effective Council of Peoples' Commissars. On the other hand, the great structure of the Communist Party whose members staffed most government posts, a state within the state, with its own professional party men—the *apparatchiki*. As we have seen happen in other cases, the bigger the party organization, the less influence individual members had in it and the more power fell to the men running the central office: ultimately the general secretary of the party committee, after 1922 a Georgian, Joseph Stalin (1879–1953).

Stalin: A Man of Steel

A lonely, harsh and self-sufficient man, Stalin was one of the few Bolshevik leaders who did not really know the West. Trained in a hard school, he had left an Orthodox seminary for the dangerous life of an underground organizer, occasionally spiced with banditry to replenish party coffers, and paid the penalties of his grim, gray devotion in prison and Siberian exile. Commissar for National Minorities after the November Revolution, he was accounted a figure of the second class, less brilliant than Trotsky or Bukharin, less articulate than Zinoviev, less learned or

Warder Collection

Joseph Stalin and party officials in the late 1920's.

intelligent than any. Experience showed him to be cruel, vindictive, unscrupulous, cunning, intolerant, and ruthless; a great manipulator and a very great ruler in the Russian tradition.

It was in 1922 that the first of a series of strokes forced Lenin gradually to give up the reins of power and ushered in the struggle for succession which began in real earnest after Lenin's death in 1924. The chief apparent claimant for succession was Trotsky, the organizer of Red victory in the civil war and Lenin's personal lieutenant. Great orator and organizer, capable of inspiring devotion and hatred, moody, remarkably bad at intrigue and compromise, vain, headstrong, intolerant, un-cooperative, Trotsky was a devoted Socialist, an inspired theorist, a fine writer, but too aware of his superiorities to work well in harness with anyone he did not respect as he respected Lenin.

Between 1924 and 1927 the succession struggle rent the party, first between Stalin and Trotsky, then between Stalin and the men who had been his allies against Trotsky. The arguments exchanged in these debates are in a sense irrelevant, for men changed their arguments as they changed their sides and, finally, when he had won, even before Trotsky had been sent off into exile in 1929, Stalin was going to adopt most of his rival's case. There was one fundamental issue, however, in which Stalin triumphed. Dissidents, frequently associated with Trotsky, had asked for the possibility of free discussion *within* the party before decisions were made, though never disputing the necessity for discipline thereafter. Stalin had argued for the monolithic domination of all from the party's center. His point of view marked Russia and the party for a generation and, indeed, for more.

Stalin also got the better of the debate between the partisans of continued world-wide revolutionary endeavor and those who, like himself, felt that they had underestimated the resilience of the capitalist system and overestimated the revolutionary will or power of the Western workers. Unable to rely on the kind of aid Lenin had hoped for, Russia had to resign herself to build socialism in one country. This did not mean forever. The rise of fascist movements—especially after 1929—was taken as the last desperate attempt of the capitalist order to halt inevitable decline by using force. In time, capitalism was bound to break under the accumulated weight of its own contradictions and socialism would then inherit the earth. It was up to Communist parties to accelerate this coming and, world revolution once deferred, such parties became largely the instruments of Russian policy. But it was up to Russia to avoid the dangers of its own contradictions which had, by the late 1920's, created serious economic quandaries.

Under the market economy of the NEP, greater agricultural production could be had only by offering the peasants consumer goods that they could buy with their profits. Consumer goods could be provided in adequate quantities only by sacrificing the investment in heavy equipment and industry, without which Russia would remain a tributary of the West. In any case, the fragmented structure of peasant holdings was inefficient. Only large-scale cultivation could provide the surpluses that would feed the country and its expanding economy. And this, the theory went, could only be achieved by taking away from individual peasants the plots of land won in the revolution itself. The choice the Communist Party faced was whether to drift toward a modified capitalism, or take drastic action to turn a backward agricultural economy into an industrial power by ruthlessly cutting consumption and comforts in order to plow all capital back into industrial growth. Each alternative was fraught with danger: the way of facility would spell the doom of a Communist party which had denied the reasons of its being by jettisoning principle; the other was a gamble against the wishes of most Russian people, demanding gigantic exertions—the sacrifice of the present for a postulated future. Yet there was never really any choice. As Stalin said in a speech he made in 1931: "We are fifty or a hundred years behind the advanced countries. We must make good this lag in ten years. Either we do it, or they crush us." If Communism was to survive and prove itself in Russia, "socialism in one country" was the only alternative. And that country was one whose historical tradition had always disregarded the human cost of any enterprise. Now, Communist doctrine encouraged the leadership to disregard the sufferings of all but proletarians. And who the proletarians were, they alone defined. Costs counted little. Final accounts would anyway be balanced in the books of historical inevitability. What counted were not individuals but classes, not entities but collectivities, not the present but the future alone.

In 1928 NEP was discarded for a new socialist offensive designed to build up heavy industry and collectivize the land, according to objectives set out in a series of five-year plans. The military verbiage of battle was appropriate, for casualties were catastrophic on all fronts. An American engineer who helped to build the great ironworks of Magnitogorsk compared the losses of the enterprise to those in the battle of the Marne. In the countryside things were still worse. The *kulaks* and others who stood out against forcible collectivization were murdered or left to starve. Stubborn resistance by the peasants was fought with terror and mass deportation. Collectivization created chaos, shortages and famine led to bitterness and unrest, evoking further repression. Between 1928 and 1933 the number of horses and cattle in the Soviet Union decreased by more than half, that of sheep and pigs by two-thirds. By that time, however, that is in 1933, four-fifths of peasant households, two-thirds of the country's grain lands, were organized in collective farms. State farms held a further tenth of the land and a million workers. Supplies of grain and foodstuffs began to increase again, and there was no more fear that the cities would go hungry. When the first Five-Year Plan reached fulfillment, ahead of schedule in 1932, Russia had become the third industrial producer of the world. Between 1929 and 1939 its productivity increased 400 per cent. The thought that she had more ground to gain and that productivity per head remained lower than in the West could not obscure the fact that she was now, with the United States and Germany, the greatest industrial power in the world.

Many of the ideals of the original revolution had been sacrificed to the achievement of the Plan. A more intense dictatorship of the proletariat went along with the reassertion of lower middle-class morality, increasingly enforced against all the socially disturbing experiments of the past decade: free love, divorce, abortion, progressive education, abstract art, expressionist poetry. Even equal wages were banned, dismissed as petty bourgeois by the petty bourgeois who were busily replacing the dictatorship of the proletariat with their own. The slogan "From each according to his abilities, to each according to his needs" was rewritten to replace "needs" with "labor." Equality, branded a petty bourgeois notion, had to give way to true socialist competition; and this was prompted by incentives like piece rates and selective wages, social recognition for the hardest workers, medals, privileges, larger rations of food and better lodgings for heroes of labor, like the miner Stakhanov, who was able to do the work of nine men in one day.

It was certainly a kind of progress when heroism was connected with activities linked with construction rather than destruction; and when battle losses were incurred in building dams and steel works rather than waging war. But the costs were great. Along with the freedom of business and agricultural enterprise, freedom of labor was also stifled and labor unions became an arm of the state. Along with the discipline of the Communist Party, its control of private and public life and culture was immeasurably tightened. Lenin's huge tomb in Moscow began to look as if it were, in Isaac Deutscher's words, "only the pedestal for his successor"—but also the repository of doomed hopes for the freer society Lenin had envisaged.

Stalin's dictatorship grew, finding its justification in the dangers that increased as the international situation changed after 1932. The threat of hostile capitalist states, abated in the twenties, grew more acute after the rise of fascism. Just as the Nazis rose in reaction to the Communist menace, so the worst excesses of Stalinism followed their coming to power in Germany, Nazism and Communism reflecting each other like deforming mirror images. The USSR considered itself in a state of siege, threatened by enemies outside and treachery within. After 1934, the second Five-Year Plan (1933–1937), destined to provide some of the consumer goods (shoes, clothes) and lodgings that were so badly lacking, had to be revised in view of the Nazi danger. The tightening of a tension already hard to bear seems to have aggravated the internal strains and played a part in the great purges by which, between 1936 and 1938, Stalin eliminated critics and potential critics of his rule. Probably half or more of men and women holding key positions in industry, army, and every sector of society were ousted, deported, or killed. Two-thirds of the diplomatic corps and over two-thirds of the Communist Party Central Committee were liquidated; over half the membership of the Party were expelled. In the Red Army alone, during 1937 and 1938, the *Yezhovchina* (so named after the Secret Police head who was in due course killed himself) eliminated 3 out of 5 marshals, 13 out of 15 army commanders, 110 out of 195 division commanders and all the commanders of military districts. A fine bag!

In this light, the Western powers' reluctance to ally with Russia becomes more understandable. But it is well to look at Russian policy in Communist perspective too. As they saw it, revolution had to learn to live in a largely hostile capitalist world, to adjust its diplomacy to the standards obtaining outside Russia and its aims to isolation. Socialism in one country was possible at great cost; living alone was not. After 1921 the diplomacy of the Soviet Union was dedicated to lessening isolation and defending its regime. The Treaty of Rapallo in 1922 inaugurated a more forthcoming phase based on Russo-German collaboration. Nonaggression pacts were signed with whoever would subscribe to them. When Germany turned reactionary, Moscow was led to gradual adjustment toward the West, while trying to maintain good relations even with the Nazis until 1934 when Hitler concluded a German-Polish nonaggression pact, putting an end to the Rapallo policy. A few months later the Soviet Union joined the League of Nations, reopened formal relations with the United States, concluded mutual assistance pacts with France and Czechoslovakia (1935), tried to put teeth into the League, initiated the Popular Front policy of co-operation with anyone who opposed Fascism. But collective security failed before Franco-British appeasement, and their reluctance to co-operate with a Communist regime just involved in the great purges. So Stalin turned back toward Rapallo, fulfilling its promise, after repeated snubs from the democracies, in the German-Soviet pact of August, 1939, which brought its fruits in fresh partition of Poland, reannexation of the Baltic lands and Bessarabia, the gain of Finnish territories designed to protect Leningrad. Ready enough to supply Germany, afford her bases, support her abroad, and even hand over to Nazi revenge German and other Communists who had taken refuge in Russia, Stalin was not prepared to concede her domination in the Balkans and to turn eastward as Hitler wanted. Romania, Bulgaria, and Turkey he would not admit as parts of the German sphere. Friction over rival greeds convinced Hitler that war must come —the sooner the better. The 22nd of June, 1941, marked the end of an era and Russia was to emerge from war a great power at last.

A great power, but in a sorry state. Russian military casualties seem to have been around 10 million but some 18 million men and women had died in all and the demographic effects of these losses were still being felt in the 1960's. A quarter of all the nation's property had been destroyed: 17,000 towns, 70,000 villages, 31,000 factories, 84,000 schools, 40,000 miles of railroads, 45,000,000 horses and pigs and cattle. All was to do again. But Stalin also faced another problem. War had loosened the firm Communist structure, given more influence to the soldiers, introduced a disrupting contact with the West, threatened the rigid authority of the regime and the dominion of the party. Previous wars had brought reform or revolution. If either was to be avoided this time, Communist power must not be relaxed but consolidated; and Stalin knew only one way of doing this: by force. The Soviet Union would be subjected to a fresh repression, as murderous and brutal as the purges of the 1930's and which only ended with Stalin's death in 1953.*

Whereas after the revolution the country had taken nearly a decade to reattain its prewar production level, after 1945 this was done in four years. Russia rebuilt and simultaneously rearmed, exploding the first of its atomic bombs in 1949. The great difference now lay in the substructure of specialists and skilled men, administrators, technicians, engineers, and workers who had been lacking in the 1920's and whom the great training and educational efforts of the 1930's and 40's built up in numbers adequate to support and rebuild a great modern economy. By 1955 the population had grown beyond 200 million chiefly in the large cities,** while the industrial center shifted eastward to the Ural Mountains and beyond. The productivity now doubled every twelve years —a phenomenal rate of growth when kept up. Today, productivity per inhabitant is comparable to that of the West European countries behind which Russia had lagged so long. Indeed, by 1950 the Soviet Union ranked as the second industrial power in the world.

Russia After Stalin

Stalin's death was followed by an intricate power struggle in which personalities and factions engaged in shadowy battles for control of the state. After the elimination of Lavrenti Beria, head of the Secret Police † and of a passing figure, G. M. Malenkov, power was progressively assumed by the Ukrainian-born master of the party machine, Nikita S. Khrushchev (b. 1894). Khrushchev is best remembered for his great speech of 1956 before the Twentieth Congress of the Communist Party, with its bitter denunciations of the dead dictator and of the "personality cult" which had grown up around him. Equally crucial, Khrush-

---

* De Gaulle, who saw Stalin at the end of the war, noted the "shadowy charm" of the figure he recognized as a great Tsar. The shadows would be more in evidence than the charm in the last years of Stalin's bloody greatness.

** Characteristically, 6 per cent of Russia's population lives in two-thirds of the territory, 6 per cent of the country's territory accommodates half the population.

† When Beria was arrested and executed in the summer of 1953, subscribers to the *Great Soviet Encyclopedia* were ordered to cut out the article devoted to him, remit it to the authorities, and replace it with a description of the Bering Sea.

Nikita Khrushchev in what became a characteristic pose.

chev attempted to heal some of the wounds that Stalinist excesses had left behind, releasing a good many of the political prisoners, unclamping the stifling regime of censorship and terror, increasing the availability of consumer goods, mending bridges broken with Tito and even with the West, with whom he envisaged a relationship of "peaceful co-existence" that allowed for competition and subversion but stopped short of open war.

In 1964, Khrushchev was forced into retirement by younger and more businesslike politicians: notably Leonid Brezhnev, his second in command of the Party Secretariat, and Nicolai Kosygin, chairman of the crucial State Planning Commission. Even more than their predecessors, the new rulers of a society where masters still endure though there are no more slaves insisted on the collective nature of the political leadership. They seem to represent the institutionalization of a revolution long past for the majority of their subjects, a government of bureaucrats and technicians interested more in internal efficiency and external power than in the proletarian insurrections to which they still pay homage on the first of May.

The Soviet Union was still behind the United States, which it longed to overtake. In the 1960's, whereas 12 per cent of America's active population worked in agriculture, some 45 per cent of Soviet citizens did so. And, while collectivized agriculture had increased over-all production, it had not kept up with the growing population *or* with its expanding needs.* But Soviet society is now modern, disposing of an army of researchers, scientists, technicians, and engineers. It still lacks the possibilities of free enterprise in its most fundamental sense of research, interpretation, decision, and initiative; and it is not sure that the abundance which modern means permit and to which Russians, like every-

---

* In 1969, the Third *Kolkhoze* (collective farms) Congress, first in thirty-four years, enlarged the area of land each farmer can work for his own account from about a half acre to one and one-half acres. The measure was explained by the fact that over half the eggs and vegetables, over a third of the meat, sold on the internal markets of the U.S.S.R. are produced on these plots.

body else aspire, will be attained without it. Not only literature, scholarship, and the arts, but economics, too, are hamstrung by survivals of the Stalin age—perhaps, in the first place, by survivors guarding vested interests by repression. Lenin had defined socialism as "the power of the Soviets plus electrification." Russia has the latter, but the former is only a memory. Today, the ideology that inspired the years of revolution has long run down from dynamism to dogma. Yet the ruling Communist Party cannot dispense with it, for it provides the authority of its continued rule. Nor is it sure that an anachronistic faith cannot maintain itself and exercise a strong influence within societies which could do well without it. It was Marx who said that a people that oppresses another could not be a free people. But perhaps few peoples really care for freedom. Especially those who have never known it.

Meanwhile, the immensity of what has been achieved remains impressive. The great grandsons of serfs, the grandsons of illiterate peasants, are now sophisticated writers, scientists, and organizers. Literacy, industrialization, urbanization, emancipation from the hold of foreign capital, have turned a primitive, backward people into civilized men who can control and marshal their energies and resources to constructive ends. All this was done at immense human and material cost. While there is no compensation for human suffering, one may reflect that similar though less deliberate suffering elsewhere had produced far less.

Germany

The Weimar Republic

In January, 1919, as the Spartacists were put down by the army, Liebknecht and Luxemburg arrested and killed, a National Assembly gathered at Weimar under army guard to write a constitution. Germany now became a federal republic in which most states survived as separate units but the old privileges were replaced by universal suffrage and proportional representation. This last encouraged fractionalism and the survival of political factions at a time when unity should have been paramount. It removed all possibility of real majority government, ensuring that power would be exercised by coalitions and hence remain unstable and weak. As the republic which it consecrated was being inaugurated in the Weimar state theater, fly sheets fluttered down from the gallery nominating a mentally deranged poet for its first president. The Assembly elected Ebert, son of a tailor, himself a saddler by trade, to the presidency; and Ebert, as he had proved, embodied the traditional German spirit by now solidly established in the lower middle class.

The Weimar Republic lived out its short span under this contradictory aegis of a conventional spirit backed by the army and operating in the midst of Dadaist confusion. Its governments never quite accepted the terms of peace.* And the country never quite accepted its governments. Social Democrats, who had won one-third of the voters in prewar elections, won nearly half in the elections of 1919. But they were weakened by internal divisions and, after the formation of a Communist party, could never hope for a majority again. In 1921 Social Democrats were down to 20 per cent of a poll where Communists figured for almost 13 per cent; in 1928 the Social Democratic share was 30 per cent and the Communists' 10. Meanwhile, first the Catholic Center, then the Moderates increased in influence as the Reichstag (under the effect of proportional representation) divided into groups maneuvering for office in various coalitions. Seventeen coalition governments held office between 1920 and 1930: all of them—whether Socialists shared in them or not—of a conservative hue. In 1925 President Ebert died and the Left's weakness became more apparent: the Socialists by themselves received far less support than the Nationalist candidates. A hastily patched up coalition in which the Socialists supported a center candidate for a second turn was defeated when the right-wing parties put up the greatest military hero of the war, Marshal Paul von Hindenburg (1847–1934). The Centrist would have been elected had not almost two million Communist votes gone to a Communist leader. But in the eyes of the extreme Left there was no real difference between the Centrists and Hindenburg, and very little more between the Socialists and the Center.

That this had come about was partly due to the Socialists themselves. As usual, their moderate instincts clashed with their professions and thus prevented any consistent action on their part. The Left could see that the sympathies of men in power went toward Nationalists, not toward the workers. In March, 1920, the Free Corps which Socialists had helped create turned against the government, forcing it to flee Berlin. This was the Kapp putsch, named after the minor functionary whom the rebels hoped to make head of the state. The putsch was put down only by a general strike forcing its collapse. Then the restored coalition government used army units (which had neither supported Kapp nor moved against their Free Corps comrades) to put down workers who seemed too sanguine over their brief triumph, while military rebels went unpunished. A few months before, after the Red Republic in Bavaria had been crushed, 2,209 persons had been sentenced to long terms of prison or to death. Now the courts handed out one sentence only, and that for "honorary confinement."

Meanwhile, the determination of all German governments not to fulfill the reparation clauses of the Versailles treaty, stiffened by a Nationalist terrorist campaign in which several hundred insufficiently patriotic politicians were murdered,* was bringing dire results. Reparation demands, though excessive, were not impossible to meet pending an agreement. Between 1933 and 1939 Hitler would spend seven times more a year on rearmament than his predecessors were asked to spend on reparations and did not. But, to finance payments, the tax structure would have to be seriously reformed and this the country's rulers would not do. Not only would it hit the rich too hard (as they were hit already in Great Britain), but it would imply their readiness to come to terms by showing that they could fulfill them. They preferred to default and take the consequences. In January, 1923, French and Belgian troops, claiming that Germany would not fulfill her obligations, occupied the Ruhr, center of German industry and major source of the Republic's revenues. The German government called for passive resistance and found support among all sections of the public. But the economic ruin that ensued set off serious troubles. "Red" governments appeared in Saxony and Thuringia, a separatist movement in the Rhineland, a monarchist movement in Bavaria followed by an attempted putsch led by General Erich Ludendorff and by Adolf Hitler, obscure leader of an even obscurer National Socialist German Workers' party. All failed, but all stressed the straits of the Republic.

Nine months of economic struggle came to an end when a new government headed by Gustav Stresemann (1878–1929) concluded that the country could not survive without the raw material, markets, and capital of the West, came to terms with the French, and secured American and British help in exchange for "fulfillment" in the future. Stresemann and Hjalmar Schacht, head of the Reichsbank, stabilized the situation and quickly secured a new agreement on the reparation proposals. Between 1924 and 1931 over 35 billion marks poured into Germany in foreign loans and investments, mostly from the United States. In the same period Germany paid the Allies 21 billion marks in reparations.

The second half of the 1920's was a time of prosperity for Germany and for Europe. But the scars of past years were hard to heal. We know that antireparation tactics had involved unlimited inflation of the currency, the mark. At the height of the Ruhr struggle, the mark became meaningless, prices were quoted in billions, debts and savings wiped out, *rentiers* and pensioners ruined, middle and professional classes largely displaced. All internal debts were wiped out by inflation and this meant that the great bankers and industrialists emerged from it more powerful than ever. Contractual obligations collapsed. So, in their wake, did social conduct and the sense of moral obligation which is no more than a habit learned by experience and just as easily unlearned by

* Among them in 1922 Walther Rathenau, chief organizer of Germany's economic war effort, guilty of being Jewish.

Warder Collection

The aging leader of the Weimar Republic, Hindenburg, followed by Hitler, Goering, and other Nazi Party members.

same. The harvest of the inflation of 1923–1924, aggravated and fulfilled by the fresh crisis of 1929–1933, was reaped within the decade. In 1929, England was almost as hard hit as Germany, and the United States harder; but German stabilizers had been injured five years before by their own policy and four years of prosperity had not brought enough recovery to restore them. The Depression meant utter catastrophe for millions. Within two years salaries fell by half, production by two-thirds, the number of unemployed rose six- and sevenfold, 80 per cent of the Germans were what contemporary estimates call "proletarianized." By 1932, the middle-class backbone of society had been broken, and great masses of once law-abiding workers were set in motion, looking for some change where any change seemed better than none.

The Thousand-Year Reich

Dictatorship appeared the only solution and the providential man who offered to bring salvation was the same Adolf Hitler whose putsch had failed in Munich in 1923. Hitler had used his brief and comfortable stay in prison to write a book—*Mein Kampf*—about his life, his theories, and plans: a hodgepodge of the national, social, and racial doctrines which flourished in Germany and Austria since the nineteenth century. His National Socialist movement advanced only slowly during the years of prosperity but, as the thirties opened, despair turned the masses toward apocalyptic doctrines of which his own was the most extreme. It looked as if Germany was splitting down the middle, between the radical Right and Left; and funds from industrialists and bankers seeking defenders against the Reds poured into Nazi coffers, nourished the party's propaganda, equipped its brown- and black-shirted storm troopers. The Nazis, who had polled 800,000 votes in the national elections of 1928, won 6.5 million two years later, 14 million in July, 1932. With 230 seats compared to 12 in 1928, they were now the largest party in the Reichstag.

Hitler as absolute ruler reviews his passing troops.

In the new elections of November the Nazi poll fell by 2 million votes. But by that time all other combinations and permutations had been exhausted and two months later, in January, 1933, Hitler became Chancellor, heading a coalition government of Nationalists and Nazis. In the elections of February, 1933, over 17 million Germans voted for Nazi candidates. The Hitler coalition could now boast what no German government had known: a clear parliamentary majority.

The new Reichstag voted a bill which practically abrogated the Weimar Constitution and which permitted the government to pass laws without parliamentary endorsement. Only Social Democrats voted against the bill, though even they were ready to endorse the government's assertive foreign policy and were repaid by dissolution in June, 1933—as were the Nazis' Nationalist allies. The Nationalist leaders, who had entertained some hope of manipulating the inexperienced Nazis, were soon shuffled out of the way and Nationalist troops absorbed in the NSDAP * by a government which did not mind drastic actions. The Communists were banned, the Social Democrats broken, the unions taken over and incorporated in a Nazi labor front, the separate state governments abolished and the states totally integrated in the Reich, united under a central administration for the first time in German history. Brown-shirted Nazi storm troops (SA) and black-uniformed SS elite corps supplemented police in a campaign of unlimited violence against all opponents. May Day was converted into a Nazi labor festival, industrial and employer interests thoroughly subordinated to the party. By July, 1933, Hitler could declare all parties dissolved and Germany a one-party state.

But if Germany was subordinated to the party, the party must be subordinate to Hitler. The SA was the organization of the more radical party militants: its members and its leadership were hard to keep in line. Their rowdiness and radicalism threatened to compromise Hitler's more gradual plans and his maneuvers. In 1934 the power of the SA

* National Socialist German Workers' Party.

was destroyed in a few bloody days when most of its leadership were massacred. Hitler was now absolute in Germany.

The Nazis were not hampered by many economic preconceptions. Advised by Hjalmar Schacht, they were quite ready to apply whatever means they might consider necessary to refloat the economy, controlling both labor and employers. The state became Germany's greatest banker, controlling two-thirds of banking capital, directing the most important sections of industry and press, introducing social reforms, using the structure of capitalist economy as the instrument of its policies. The profit motive remained the essential motor of production, but its direction was henceforth in public hands and managers themselves fulfilled a public function. Private enterprises, regarded as public trusts, were taken over, controlled at second hand, or left to operate freely, as expediency might dictate. Hitler had come to power just as the economic crisis was beginning to subside. His economic policies accelerated recovery, priming the economic pump and stimulating business. Rearmament, public works, loans and subsidies to private enterprises, began to absorb unemployment before the year was out and made for full employment by 1936. By that time industrial production had returned to the high-water mark of 1929. By 1939 it was 33 per cent higher, more than double what it had been when Hitler came to power. Labor was controlled to keep wages down, and prices were controlled to make wages acceptable. The deficit spending that had been rejected for economic reasons was enthusiastically accepted for military and patriotic ones. No one really had to choose between guns and butter: guns meant butter (or at least margarine) for far more people than had enjoyed any before. Foreign trade was managed by way of exchange controls, import and export licenses, bilateral agreements with other countries. German conquests after 1939 simply set the seal on what these economic policies had begun, completing the economic integration of a Europe focused on German needs.

Such marked success was bound to make the Nazis very popular. All Germans (except Jews and political opponents who were mercilessly persecuted) lived better, felt better, prouder, more at ease in the new society of the Nazis. Even intellectuals came to terms with it. With few exceptions most of them had opposed or ignored the Weimar Republic: too dull, too conformist, too decadent. On this Expressionists, Realists, and Idealists, Right and Left, Communists and Nazis, could agree: the Republic was not a cause fit for a man's commitment. The greatest German intellectuals—men like the historian Friedrich Meinecke, the economist Werner Sombart, Thomas Mann, and the sociologist Max Weber—distrusted democracy, which they thought ill suited to German character and tradition, preferring a regime in which the people would be represented by an elite . . . like them. Even the president elected by a direct vote (an Americanism advocated by Max Weber) was

Victims of Belsen, one of Hitler's concentration camps for "political" prisoners.

not meant to reflect the opinions of the electorate but the call of collective will, a national spirit close to that which Rousseau had once imagined. Election was a kind of mystery and German intellectuals were its muddled prophets. No wonder that they found Weimar disappointing and the Third Reich which Hitler introduced much closer to their ideals, reinforcing the notion that social problems must be resolved from above.

Another German intellectual ideal fulfilled in the Third Reich was that heroic and virile concept which we find in certain works of Wagner or some youth movements of the time that dreamed of purity, of a new order, and of a providential leader who would show the way.* All this made for a tendency to purify the horrid democratic society by turning inward to secret male societies from which women (weak, corrupt, corrupting) were excluded; to suck up vitality from primitive sources and to recognize it (again) in that figure with which romantic tradition from Hegel to Wagner and Nietzsche had filled their dreams: the providential leader. Thus, many intellectuals welcomed Hitler and extolled his Nationalist revolution, pointing to Goethe and Schiller as the first National Socialists. Others, like Erich Kästner, author of brilliant, satirical children's stories, chose internal emigration, opting out while living on as best they could. Others again, like Thomas Mann, escaped abroad. But there was little danger that an active opposition should arise from this quarter.

In effect, after the first few months, Hitler met little opposition from any quarter, which must have strengthened his faith in his own star. It may even be that his fervent anti-Semitism was a device for creating

---

* There was a lot of this in the works of Stefan George (1868–1933), whose poems glowed with dreams of heroism and of the apocalypse. George would be quoted by Nazis and anti-Nazis, by SS, and by Count Stauffenberg, who placed the bomb that missed Hitler in July, 1944. Here is a typical passage from a poem he wrote after 1918:

> When these Generals will have purged the shame
> Cast from their necks the convict's chains
> Nothing but honor craving in their bellies
> Then, on the fields of death, in the endless tombs
> Will burst the bloody light and on the clouds
> Will pass the roaring armies, the fields
> Shall bellow in the third assault, the supreme dread
> When the dead return!

opponents where none existed, legislating a menace by decree in order to create and preserve that tension and struggle without which a dictatorship may prosper but a Fascist-type movement decays. Hitler had some notions of Darwin and of the struggle for existence. "Life," he once said, "is only preserved because other living things perish through struggle." The life of Germany, the life of the Nazi Party could only be ensured, like that of Aztec gods, by dint of war and blood and human sacrifice. The temples of the Nazis stood not in Munich or at Nürnberg, but in more desolate, blood-soaked places: at Dachau, at Belsen, and at Oranienburg. It is not so surprising that the concentration camp at Buchenwald should have been built around Goethe's favorite oak tree.

The Nazis and Their Prey

The crux of the Nazi regime was not its brutality (which never formed the basis of its power) but its delusions and its self-delusions. For Hitler proved that myths could be managed and stage-managed to convert a whole nation into a gigantic make-believe; and that this make-believe can create concrete results in morale, production, power, and wealth. He dipped into his own and his peers' unconscious, pulled out collective fantasies, and then proceeded to enact them, thus lending his enterprises an extraordinary force. For just as the greedy, murderous adventurers who went crusading into the Levant, the Indies, or America disguised themselves as Christian knights, so Hitler's troops and torturers put on the armor of Wagnerian heroes: Siegfried, Parsifal. We all reach back to find justification and disguise in the dressing rooms of national history; and Hitler's hordes found a martial storeroom from which they issued forth to take or break the world.

That was when the fantasies proved their power and their danger. To the Nazis the Jews were submen, bacillae, creatures of darkness, destructive and vile, a mirror reflection quite obviously of themselves. If Jews were not destroyed, they would destroy the best and highest parts of mankind and enslave the rest: just what the Nazis did propose to do. They must be massacred and those people whom they had most affected must be exterminated too, or, at least, decimated like the Russians of whom the intention was to kill 30 million, though only 20 million died in the end. Before the German millennium, then, the Jews had to be exterminated; and the war in which Germany engaged was above all meant to wipe them out, achieve that final solution of the Jewish problem which, by the summer of 1944, was having 12,000, 15,000, 22,000 Jews a day gassed, processed and cremated in Auschwitz camp alone. "The central issue of this war" repeated the Propaganda Ministry, "is the breaking of Jewish world domination." *

* That the world domination of half-witted fantasies remains unbroken was attested in Jerusalem in 1961 when Adolf Eichmann, a major cog in the extermination process, explained its failure by the fact that Hitler himself was but a puppet of "the Satanic international high finance of the Western World."

Jews, but not only Jews: men, women, children of every land and creed were scourged, tormented, delivered over to dread, degradation, death. But death itself is easy; dying, long and hard. The camps were not devoted to mere extermination, but to humiliation, torture, to the fulfillment of the guards and the dehumanization of their inmates. Hundreds and thousands were made to choke on dirt, to beg for sustenance or life or mercy seldom granted, to prey on each other—slaves tormenting slaves, mothers biting on their children's rations to gain a brief reprieve, man turning wolf to man and worse on an unheard-of scale.

What none would do to animals was done to human beings. They were drowned in cesspools, torn to pieces by dogs, strung on barbed wire, or by their fingers, or by their legs head down, raped, shot, whipped, hanged, starved to death, beaten to death, trampled to death, kicked to death, stoned to death, punched to death, frozen to death, run over by trucks or tractors, used as guinea pigs, maimed, injected with murderous drugs, castrated, sterilized, amputated, asphyxiated, electrocuted, poisoned, machine-gunned, gassed, thrown down quarries, or into pits or wells or ditches or hastily dug trenches or well prepared mass graves, or herded into ovens; but only when they had been stripped of everything, not just their personality, their dignity, their human respect, but all material things, the shabby, slender masks that we hold up toward the world: their chattels collected for the Reich's winter relief, earrings and wedding bands torn off, the gold in their teeth pried out for the Reich treasury, their hair swept into appropriate containers, their fat rendered down for grease or soap, their ashes for fertilizer.

Those who took part in this were ordinary men and women. Ordinary people who, willing or unwilling, did or helped to do these things, denouncing and arresting and marshaling and guarding and sentencing and employing and invoicing and shipping and storing; those who threw the switches for the long trains to pass, the stinking sealed long trains of cattle cars whose carriages built for eight horses or forty men held a hundred and two hundred prisoners, their refuse and their vermin, their thirst and hunger, their wailing and their fears; and all the people who stood and watched the trains go by loaded with dread; and those who read the letters from the eastern front or from the Polish occupied territories telling of these things; and those who wore the jewelry of the victims, sometimes their clothes, and knew or at least suspected what they wore; or stood and watched the great barbed wire enclosures bobbed with looming towers, saw the convoys arrive, saw the smoke rise, smelled its peculiar stench; all those who knew or guessed but did not wish to know; thousands and tens of thousands, hundreds of thousands who can still remember all these things: those who still remember them and those who have driven most of these memories out of their waking life. Many still survive, living ordinary lives, doing ordinary things in shops and factories and banks and offices and ministries and barracks and in courts of justice, bringing up ordinary children; bringing them up perhaps to think as they think themselves that all this is no more than history: dead, irrelevant, like the millions of shadowy ghosts they turned into statistics.

To Hitler, for whom God did not exist, conscience was a Jewish invention, suffering was irrelevant; only will mattered and the Providence which had assigned his mission, in whose pursuit he went his way "with the assurance of a sleepwalker." Nothing was impossible, neither the defeat of France nor the utter extermination of his enemies.* For the sake of racial principles he even sacrificed military and psychological advantages. This was what carried him first to victory, then to utter defeat. All the time the people he fascinated kept their belief in the miracles to which Hitler, like Bismarck, had accustomed them. Accepting the searing hardships of the home front, rejecting and reproving any stirring of opposition, they maintained the deadly conviction that Hitler's myths were real. After Stalingrad, German propaganda was constantly referring to the death of the Russian empress which had saved Frederick II from defeat and Prussia from division in 1762 (see p. 474). But no miraculous deaths and no miraculous weapons could intervene this time. The spirits Hitler raised now turned against him, as demons sometimes turn on witches who invoke them. In the midst of the Europe she had wasted from the Urals to the Pyrenees, Germany lay in ruins—the ruins of her dream.

Germany Partitioned

In 1945, what Hitler had described as the thousand-year Reich was divided into four zones of occupation. In the west, south, and southeast its borders returned to where they had been in 1937. In the northeast, the Russians annexed a portion of East Prussia, including the old Hohenzollern capital of Königsberg, and unilaterally endowed the Poles with all German regions east of the Oder and the western Neisse.** Meeting at Potsdam the Allies had agreed that Germany would be treated "as a single economic unit." But four-power management did not last; the Russians, remembering the devastation of their own country, treated the Germans as they had treated them: without mercy. The Westerners were more concerned about conditions in their occupation zones. Eighty

---

* In Treblinka alone, over a period of twelve months in 1942 and 1943, 800,000 Jews entered and forty survived the war. It was possible to kill 24,000 persons between 7 A.M. and 1:15 P.M. with a staff of forty SS and several hundred Ukrainians.

** The issue of Germany's eastern borders turns on whether Polish writ should run as far as the eastern Neisse, or to the western Neisse, some 200 miles beyond. In 1970, agreement between Bonn and Warsaw seemed to confirm the *status quo*.

German children trying to salvage food from garbage cans, 1946.

cities had been partly or wholly destroyed, 600,000 civilian lives lost (ten times as many as were killed in Britain), 800,000 others maimed. A great many Germans had fled the cities that were being bombed to rubble or the advancing armies on both fronts; millions had been expelled from their homes in Czech or Polish territory. In the winter of 1946, 100,000 died of cold and hunger in Hamburg alone; in Cologne only one child in ten was of normal weight; everywhere men, women, and children lived on charity, black marketing, and prostitution, or else starved. The British and American occupiers who had been spared the experience of German occupation could not endure this prospect. They sought to set the wheels of the economy in motion and bring the people back to life again.

Soon, however, another factor entered the equation. As relations between East and West got worse, each side began to treat *its* Germans less as defeated fiends than as potential partners, handing them ever more authority over their own affairs while Cold War tension grew. The Soviet zone was given a German Communist administration. In the West, municipal government provided a base for the rebirth of national politics. Enjoying a good deal of local autonomy, the great German cities had always been the training ground of great administrators and, sometimes, of national politicians. The greatest of these would reveal himself in the Rhineland at this time. Konrad Adenauer (1876–1967) had been a Cologne municipal official since 1906, its mayor since 1917, deputy to the Prussian *Landtag* in Weimar days, and speaker of that Assembly from 1928 to 1933. Dismissed by the Nazis in 1933, reinstated in 1945 by the Americans only to be hustled out by an unfriendly British general a few months later, the authoritarian old gentleman turned from local to national politics, became leader of the newly founded Christian-Democratic Party (1948) and, in 1949, federal chancellor of the first autonomous German government—a post he retained until his reluctant retirement in 1963.

But while *Der Alte* (the old one), as he came to be known, was cast for a crucial part in the spectacular recovery of his country in the

1950's, German personalities were of secondary consequence in the decisions of the middle forties. It would be economic considerations that led to the progressive integration of the British, American, and French zones of occupation. By 1948, East and West Germany had separate currencies, governments, and economies: the Democratic Republic of Germany in the East, the Federal German Republic in the West—soon to be integrated into the economies of their respective camps, "good Germans" to their friends if not to one another.

What other Germans, after all, were left? The leading figures of the Nazi regime, tried by an Inter-Allied Military Tribunal at Nürnberg in 1945–1946 had been condemned to death (eleven cases) or to varying sentences of imprisonment. The denazification process decided by the Allies, never very thoroughly applied, affected mostly the pettier officials, those who could not hide, bribe, argue their way out or work their passage to forgiveness. Of the greatest criminals, many went underground or escaped abroad. Nor would it have been possible to do a thorough job of denazification without almost eliminating a generation that the war had already decimated.

It was natural that the men who sought to rebuild a devastated land should pay less attention to retribution than to reconstruction. Many of these men belonged to the pre-1914 generation when both Adenauer and Kurt Schumacher, who came out of a concentration camp to reconstitute the Socialist party, had begun their careers; and what they sought to restore were the virtues (and to some extent the system) of those good old days. Instead of awakening new forces they appealed to old ones: discipline, hard work, economy, respect for authority, the bourgeois virtues proved their worth even to the Social Democrats, who quietly abandoned all traces of Socialism. By the mid-1960's, far from remembering the doctrines of class warfare, Socialists had joined the Christian-Democrats in a governmental coalition; by 1969 they had replaced them as the ruling party, their leader Willy Brandt, a long-time opponent of Nazism, becoming federal chancellor.

The Federal Republic, restored to international sovereignty in 1954, had by that time recovered and multiplied the economic power which it once enjoyed. This "German miracle," as it has been called, turns out on examination to be less miraculous than it might appear. If Germany was in ruins, its industrial plant was not. Only 10 to 20 per cent of it had been put out of action and, as soon as the economy began to turn, the machines did too. As in 1923 and in 1930, financial collapse left the industrialists free of debts and the country practically free of reparations. As in the later twenties, billions of dollars in gifts and loans aided recovery. West Germany had no army and colonies to waste her money on, the sums paid for the upkeep of foreign occupation troops were almost all spent on her territory and, after 1955, her own defense expenses were lower even than the military budget of Belgium or Italy.

The Federal Republic was overcrowded. By 1970, some 60 million people lived where not quite 40 million had lived in 1949. But it could draw on a cheap, hard-working labor force, their numbers keeping down wages and hence production costs, while their demands stimulated the economy. The aid that society provided to veterans and poor was small and taxes low. Profits were plowed back into business. The large-scale industrial combines that the Allies broke up soon reformed, regaining their hold on the German market. By 1950, industrial production—in 1946 one-third of 1936—had returned to prewar figures. By 1961 the Germans were importing foreign workers to feed their factories. The standard of living rose steadily: cigarettes, which for years had replaced currency, returned to their proper use—burning; motorcycles and cars replaced bicycles; people ate fewer potatoes and more cakes, and Germany was the most valued European ally of the United States.

Here was some justification for the Russians' fears. For, while the division had come increasingly to be accepted, Communists knew that the dynamism of the great power refurbished between Rhine and Elbe might once again be turned toward its traditional frontiers in the east.

Temporary creation *par excellence,* governed from the non-capital of Bonn, once a sleepy little university town on the Rhine, the Republic's origins condemned it to run after its own definition. Adenauer thought he had found it in his dreams of a Carolingian Europe, united by common faith, from within which his part of Germany, rebuilt and consolidated, could exercise a magnetic attraction on the forsaken east. Yet this resulted only in the self-definition of an eastern rival which became the more resolute and the more conscious of its own originality the more the Federal Republic established its own. Unwilling to pay the price of the last war (that is, to accept its existing frontiers), or that of possible unification (that is, neutralization), Bonn's Germany took refuge in the good feeling that—with its free political parties (except for the banned Communists), its federal institutions, its democratic (and rather unusable) army, its parliament, and its respect for traditional virtues—it was quite unlike the Prussian-style Communist society of the GDR. But whatever its moral arguments, its best alibi rested in economic prosperity.

As the 1970's opened, the attempts of Socialist Chancellor Brandt to improve relations with Germany's eastern neighbors had eased some of the tensions, but, in a manner of speaking, the tension itself that German power generated had become a vested interest—for German nationalists and irreconcilable Communists, like those still ruling in East Berlin. The attractions of a friendly Germany might prove as dangerous, in their eyes at least, as the arms of an embattled one. It looked as if, at any rate for some time, the politics of Europe would continue to revolve around the fears of all Germany's neighbors and their anxious hope that Germany should learn to be herself not at somebody else's expense.

Italy

The 1914 war, which was highly unpopular and remarkably unsuccessful, had brought economic ruin to Italy along with formal victory. At Paris, Italian negotiators seeking to secure the payment promised in 1915 found President Wilson hostile to the secret treaty of London and its anti-Slav implications. The other powers deferred little to an ally which had been more a burden than a help. The grandiose hopes of London turned to dust: "only" some 1,000 square miles of territory, one for every 700 Italians who had died for them and scarcely worth the price. Meanwhile, the country lay in the grip of scarcity, soaring prices, and inflation. Prices in 1919 were 266 per cent higher than in 1913 (twice as much as England), the lira only a fraction of its prewar value. This stirred up fresh industrial agitation, demands for higher wages to meet the higher prices, strikes in the countryside as well as in the cities, while disaffected soldiers refused to march against the strikers. Employers, dreading the prospect of red revolution, resenting the cost of the subsidy with which the government kept down the price of bread and moderated misery and tempers, began to look toward the black-shirted bands of veterans and students which Mussolini was organizing into *fasci*.

In 1919, the nationalist poet D'Annunzio, now a war hero, led a free corps of legionaries to occupy the Istrian city of Fiume, disputed between Italians and Yugoslavs.* None dared dislodge him until 1920; and then the city was left to Italy. Lawless violence seemed to work well in the postwar world. In 1920 when the bread subsidy was cut, workers' demands for wages—more desperate than ever—led to industrial lockouts and these, in turn, to the occupation of many factories by the workers. Before the masterly inactivity of the government a near revolutionary situation simmered down into a settlement which settled nothing except that the revolutionary tide was on the wane. So was the star of D'Anunzio, who had been tossed out of Fiume ** without fighting. His failure, like the failure of the strikes, reinforced the Fascists who were busy harping on the danger—now past—of Bolshevik revolution. The "respectable" classes, landowners, employers, officers, state officials, were more inclined than ever to subsidize and support the patriotic hoodlums of the *fasci*. An influx of disillusioned followers of D'Annunzio strengthened Fascist ranks, and also their tendency to uncompromising violence coupled with heroic posturing.

* The Berlin Dadaists sent D'Annunzio a telegram hailing "capture of Fiume Dadaistic master stroke. If Allies protest telephone Club Dada Berlin."
** By his own government, at Allied insistence.

Since before the war the political situation had altered. Universal suffrage had turned the parliament into a more representative assembly, though hardly a more effective one. The Socialists had won nearly one-third of the seats in the elections of 1919. Then, Communist secession weakened the whole Left and in the elections of 1921 Communists and Socialists together garnered fewer votes than two years before. Their competition came from the Catholic Popular Party, appealing both to confessional loyalties and to the peasant masses eager for reform. After the beginning of the century most Catholics had entered political life as supporters of the right-wing parties. But a few of them formed a democratic wing whose sympathies went to small farmers and landless laborers against extortionate landlords and harsh authorities. In 1918 this tendency led to the organization of the Popular Party which, under the leadership of a Sicilian priest, Don Luigi Sturzo, supported peasant ownership, land and tax reform. Impressed by the possibility which Sturzo demonstrated of keeping peasants and workers out of Marxist clutches, the Vatican granted him its halfhearted blessing. The only way for the parties that stood for change to be effective would have been a united front. But while a coalition of Socialists and Populars made sense, it fell down under the weight of doctrine. The Socialists, aware of their unreadiness for revolution, adhered to it nevertheless, thus forfeiting the possibility of more moderate reforms. The Populars, who had been sanctioned specifically to bar the road to Marxism, could not cooperate with a violently anticlerical and revolutionary Left.

Meanwhile, the old parties, bypassed by new ones, sought to play the Nationalist game as loudly as the Right and bid for popular support against the revolutionaries. Mussolini's Fascists hesitated between radicalism and nationalism until they realized that the two could be reconciled in action. They proved their nationalism by beating up Socialists and Unionists, their radicalism by their brutal methods; they benefited from the support of the authorities and from their own determined tactics which terrorized opponents into silence or broke them down. And, as is usual in such circumstances, supporters flew to the aid of victory by joining them in droves when they had proved the stronger. As the domestic chaos grew, so did the uncertainty of the Left. It had preached violence, but hesitated to practice it or lost when it tried. Its opponents, more determined, garnered the fruits of its mistakes. In October, 1922, after the simulacrum of a march on Rome, the King offered the premiership to Mussolini rather than use the army to disperse his bands. By grace of Victor Emmanuel, Italy had a government which really meant to exercise power. But it moved slowly at first.

Il Duce

The Cabinet was a Fascist-Nationalist coalition, supported by the Populars whom pressures from the Vatican had pushed toward the Right,

Mussolini and his fascist followers march in Rome.

while eliminating Sturzo from their leadership. The most important measure passed at this stage was an electoral law according to which the party or coalition gaining the most votes—even if only a minority of the total—was allotted two-thirds of seats in Parliament. In the elections of 1924 the Fascist-Nationalist coalition got more votes than their other rivals and hence the parliamentary majority it needed. When the Socialist deputy Giacomo Matteotti denounced the intimidations and electoral frauds by which this majority was gained, he was promptly murdered by fascist bullies. A few years later the affair would have been hushed up. In 1924, vestiges of older decencies troubled public opinion and lent force to the protests of the parliamentary opposition. However, when unable to obtain retribution the opposition walked out of the chamber, thus leaving the field open to Mussolini. In 1925, after some hesitation, he declared them excluded from Parliament, suppressed all opposition parties, amnestied Matteotti's murderers, and installed a Fascist dictatorship at last.

Compared with the total grip of Communist or Nazi power, Mussolini's fascism appears a primitive affair. But it was the first to eliminate parliamentary institutions, subvert popular government, and proclaim the one-party state; and that, in the early 1920's, was impressive. Its structured organization, its disciplined, uniformed party, the way in which it swept laws and liberties away with impunity, and the histrionics with which it replaced them, made a great impression all around, not least on Adolf Hitler.

The leftist tendencies of many Fascists received a sop in the corporativism on which the Fascist state was founded. The corporative state was Mussolini's alternative to both capitalism and communism. It drew the collectivist conclusions of nationalist socialism, but also of a much older tradition. On the one hand, individual interests were subordinated to those of the nation; on the other, labor was proclaimed to be a social duty, as medieval theologians had taught: a part of the social good. Drawing on the Catholic doctrine that social classes are not opposed but interdependent, and on the anarcho-syndicalist idea that workers should control production, corporativism proposed to reconcile different economic and professional groups in corporative assemblies that faced and resolved the concrete issues concerning them, self-governing bodies of organized workers and employers, bypassing class conflict and co-operating to direct the country's economy.

All this, quite plausible in theory, became in practice a façade for authoritarian governments, dousing rather than eliminating class antagonisms and severely limiting the independence both of capital and labor. What Italy got, beyond the vast bureaucratic structure that corporativism called for, was a quarter of a century of industrial peace which soon brought consumption and production back to prewar levels. It also got labor tribunals to arbitrate individual grievances and collective disputes, a body of civil servants trained in labor relations and collective bargaining, protective legislation for industrial and agricultural laborers, social services, national insurance, and welfare organizations, holidays with pay, educational and recreational facilities, and a great many benefits which, largely symbolic in the prewar years, would be put to good use after the war.

In this, as in other respects, Mussolini set an example which other nationalist dictators followed in Austria and Portugal, Spain and Vichy France. Many of his measures were empty gestures. They nevertheless helped restore order and self-confidence where they did not exist before. There were some real advances: begging was suppressed, crime reduced, dirt, disease, and illiteracy pushed back, a measure of efficiency introduced into public life. While tourists praised the trains that ran on time and the new splendors of the Roman Forum, statisticians could note that a static society was getting underway under the impetus of educational opportunities: of children between five and fifteen, one in two had gone to elementary school in 1921; nine in ten would be going in 1941. During that period high-school attendance had doubled and university attendance tripled. But Mussolini's greatest contribution to politics was in the realm of constructive deception. Idle hands and minds, energies that could not be constructively employed in backward or stagnant economies, had long caused trouble and disorder. Now they were turned to marching and parading, solaced by public displays of power and purpose, salved with a vicarious self-importance. They were no less useless than they had been before; but they were harnessed and disciplined.

The coincidence of Fascist and Catholic thinking that we have seen in corporativism was not fortuitous. Conservative and authoritarian, Pope Pius XI (1922–1939) had served as *nuncio* in Poland in the difficult years before 1921 when the Bolshevik tide threatened Warsaw and perhaps the rest of Europe. He saw Fascism as a useful counter to godless Bolshevism and welcomed Mussolini as "the man of Providence" only a little after Matteotti's murder. In 1929, several years of negotiations resulted in the Lateran Treaties, which settled old feuds and granted the Church a privileged position in the state. The 108 acres of Vatican

City were recognized as an independent state, and a concordat reversed the policies of fourscore years. Until the late 1930's, when a struggle for control of youth organizations and educational policies brought Church and Fascist state to loggerheads, their entente overshadowed occasional squabbles, giving Mussolini the firm base he needed; and nuns marched past him escorting little boys in uniform giving the Fascist salute.

Against this happy background the Fascists sought to regenerate Italy by harnessing labor and employers, subordinating the unions to themselves and capital to the Chamber of Corporations, persuading a skeptical public that the strenuous life was best and that the glory of ancient Rome could someday be recaptured by its distant heirs. Here, as in Germany and Russia, we hear the vocabulary of struggle: Mussolini proclaimed the battle for wheat, the battle for coal, the battle for the lira, and, maddest of all in Italy, the battle for births (including a tax on bachelors and medals for the most productive mothers). In schools and universities, as in the state administration, loyalty oaths were imposed on all personnel; censorship in the press, secret police, special courts, completed the panoply of dictatorship by now so familiar but then still strange and, to some, exciting. But the regime's great battles ended in muddle and, soon, most Italians took refuge in cynicism. They had no long experience with representative government behind them and no particular sense that Mussolini's rule was worse than what they had before. But apathy would be replaced by growing disillusion. The glories of imperial Rome were pursued in war: first in Ethiopia (1935–1936), then in Spain (1936–1939), eventually in the annexation of Albania (1939). War expenses bore heavily on currency and on taxes, made for devaluation of the lira, levies on precious metals and on capital, heavier intakes of conscripts for the army. After 1938, the introduction of anti-Semitic measures on the Nazi pattern in a country which had no anti-Semitic tradition and few Jews, stressed the growing artificiality of Fascist notions.

New War and New Disasters

When the Second World War broke out Italy once more had the possibility of remaining neutral, and once more chose war, gratuitously and dangerously, largely for glory's sake. However, when we say "Italy" we must remember that most Italians had no more choice in their country's policies than Frenchmen had two centuries before. Italians did their ruler's bidding: the only difference was that Italy, perhaps wrongly, was considered a "freer" Western country and its people identified with their country's deeds—both by the myths of Fascism and those of national sovereignty.

The war was a disaster. By attacking France in June, 1940, Mussolini had hoped for spoils of victory without any effort or pain. His forces, unprepared for any serious fighting, did badly against the French in their short alpine campaign, worse against the Greeks in 1940–41, and could not even establish a firm hold on the Croat-Dalmatian kingdom which the Germans allotted them from the remains of Yugoslavia. By spring, 1943, the only Italians left in Africa were prisoners of war. By summer Sicily had been lost as well, and the Fascist regime had toppled over as easily as it had risen twenty-one years before. The King now hoped—and so did most Italians—that Italy would be allowed to leave the war. Instead, the armistice concluded with the Allies in September meant that the peninsula became a battleground subject to extraordinary devastation as Allied troops fought their way north with painful slowness. Not for another year was Rome free of the Germans. Not until 1945 was the country north of Florence liberated and Mussolini—who had briefly ruled as German puppet master of a rump Fascist republic—killed by partisans.

By the time peace came, to the monstrous ruin of Italian cities was added the misery of all the populace. The harvest was half what was needed to provide supplies, industrial production less than a quarter of that before the war, unemployment had soared beyond statistics. The country was flooded with worthless currency; supplies, fertilizers, and machinery lacking; the economic dislocation seemed total. Italy, like Germany, was a disaster area. The political dislocation was to scale. Political parties, suppressed for twenty years, fumbled their way into being during the years after 1943. By 1945, three major parties vied for the support of their countrymen: Communists, Socialists, and Christian Democrats. The latter, a new version of the Populars whom the Vatican had sacrificed to Fascism in the twenties, effectively governed the country until the 1960's. The royal house, discredited by its hypocrisies, was jettisoned soon after the war had ended.* In 1946 Italy became a republic. The kingdom of Italy, born in 1861, had lasted eighty-five years. Its disappear-

* The voting pattern reflected the peninsula's sharp split between north and south. All the northern provinces and Rome voted for the republic; all the south and the islands voted for the monarchy.

Mussolini and his mistress, killed by partisans.

ance and the recovery that followed showed that, in that time, Italy had joined the ranks of modern nations.

Italy Modernized

Within three years the economic destruction had been repaired, within fifteen national income, though still only half that of Germany or France, had risen to double the figure of 1938. The beginnings of land reform gave 100,000 families nearly three million acres whose production increased almost fourfold. Less than a third of the population now lives in rural areas, while backward Southerners have moved into the factories of the north. Meat consumption, always a suggestive indicator of well-being, is going up so fast that productivity cannot keep up with it. The country's economic growth (about 6 per cent a year between 1950 and 1960, compared with 4.5 per cent for Western Europe as a whole) allowed modernization, full employment, improved social security and public health. Italy had become an industrial nation.

The "miracle," as in Germany, was not entirely miraculous. Nationalism and militarism had consumed between 25 and 40 per cent of the country's wealth. These costly indulgences abandoned, the nation's energy and resources could turn to economic growth. Anticommunists, who had invested in fascism to ward off revolution, now invested in prosperity. Nationalists who had been fascinated by martial glory learned to expect more from production indexes. Ordinary people were glad to have jobs, houses, plumbing, and a modicum of comfort rather than colonies and parades. Population had doubled, but it no longer presented a threat to stability: rather a promise of further dynamism. What was more important, life expectancy doubled too—thirty-five years in 1880, sixty-five in 1950—even while the fertility rates had been cut in half. What had been a largely illiterate and provincial people was now better schooled (8 per cent illiteracy in 1962), accustomed to a national outlook and to the ways of the modern world.

Yet, as elsewhere, these advances created new difficulties. Italy's greatest problem remains the deep division between the more advanced and the underdeveloped regions. In the Mezzogiorno (the portion of the peninsula roughly south of Rome) and the islands, years of effort have improved conditions, but too slowly for populations that have at least learned impatience from modernity. A riot like that which caused two deaths at Battipaglia, near Salerno, in April, 1969, reflects the crisis of industrialization in progress. In 1951, Battipaglia had a population of 15,000; double that number in 1969. Marshes had been drained, industries brought in. But these very changes—the restructuring of land-holdings, the modernization of industrial and business enterprises—which give work and hope to some, have displaced others. Instead of 15,000 underemployed and hopeless people the population had come to number some 3,000 unemployed, and many more who were simply impatient for better conditions: no longer peasants, but not yet an industrial proletariat. The problems have changed but they are, if anything, more pressing, more explosive. The divorce between the good words of politicians, the good intentions of a public opinion fundamentally indifferent, and the realities of sagging enterprise, unemployment, emigration (northward), and economic colonization by the more advanced sections of the country, resented as intolerable, helps recruit rioters and create an explosive situation.

Democracy is being sought beyond the anachronistic structures and the authoritarian bureaucratism of state employees. But the channels of reform are clogging. Since 1962, the Socialists have joined the Catholics in governmental coalition, the Communists are resolutely reformist, the extraparliamentary opposition hampers reform in universities and administrative structures where reform is badly needed and provides a convenient alibi for reactionaries who reject all change. Few of the numerous dissatisfied join the small bands of Left or Right extremists, but all provide kindling for their fires. In 1969, some observers considered Italy to be in a prerevolutionary situation; but Italians, experienced in political acrobatics, hoped that expanding possibilities would catch up with the expectations they had sparked.

France

France had come out of the First World War victorious but badly weakened: of all Western nations, she had suffered the highest losses in proportion to her population—eight million had been mobilized, five million killed or wounded. Two out of every ten young men had died,* another three had been somehow disabled. Industrial production was 60 per cent less than prewar and the franc worth about one-fifth of what it had been. The tax structure was uncertain, with income taxes— introduced only in 1916—providing less than a quarter of total revenues between the wars. The public wanted high prices for its products and low living costs—high wages, shorter working hours, yet higher productivity and lower taxes. These inconsistencies passed unobserved for some years. Governments, subsisting on loans, had to reconcile lenders, not frighten them with talk of taxes or devaluation. This made for recurrent economic crises, more easily settled in the 1920's while the economy still flourished, but presenting insoluble difficulties when France's economic weakness caught up with her at last.

We have already seen that France remained an agricultural country far

---

* Among those of military age, the figure was near one in three.

longer than her neighbors. Urban population only equaled rural in 1928; in 1939 it stood at 53 per cent, only slightly above numbers in the countryside, much of it in sleepy burgs which were urban in name only. This meant that the Depression came late to France; but also that it stayed longer. While other countries devalued their currencies to give their goods a better chance on the international market, pressure from the saving public prevented such a measure until fall 1936, when it was too little and too late to help an antiquated and undercapitalized industry. French policy reflecting the will of the majority, struggled to maintain the old social and economic structures, to keep going hundreds of thousands of shops and factories whose high operating costs would have ruined them in a free market but which, while tolerated, enabled greater firms to make high profts by keeping their own prices unnaturally high. What triumphed in France was not efficiency but conservatism, dedicated to keeping alive enterprises which would succumb under competition or be abandoned in a planned society. Modern democracy could afford neither the ruthlessness of *laisser-faire* nor that of dictatorship. It was bound to founder.

Divisions and Defeat

The contradictions of French economics reappeared in French politics between the wars. As in other countries, the Socialists—who had long furnished recruits for ministerial posts—now became a governmental party, following in the footsteps of the Radicals. Their policy, like that of the Radicals, inclined toward an understanding with Germany which the Right rejected until the middle 30's when everything turned about, the Left arguing for resistance (though not for the necessary armaments), the Right for better relations *and* armaments but against the taxes that would make them possible. No party could gain a majority in parliament, no coalition could long maintain itself. There had been sixty-four cabinets between 1870 and 1920; there would be another forty-three by 1940: more than two a year. It is not surprising that in March, 1936, when Hitler reoccupied the Rhineland, and in March, 1938, when he marched into Austria, French policy was in the hands of weak caretaker governments, holding the fort between crises and ill-equipped for decisive action.

Such a record encouraged the appearance of right radical leagues, combining prewar nationalist ideas with the methods and inspiration of the Fascists. Their violent criticism of parliament was self-fulfilling, discrediting the discredited Republic even more. But, while creating trouble, the leagues never made a revolution, for their supporters wanted not radical change but more stability. The torch of revolution had passed to the Communists, in whom, as Robert Wohl has put it, French workers and intellectuals saw not the totalitarian tendencies of Moscow

Léon Blum at a meeting of the national council of the Socialist party, 1936.

"but their own revolution, the one they had failed to make in 1919–20," the one which they would always fail to make. After the rise of Hitler, Communist policy, previously hostile to any *entente* with "Social Fascists" immediately to the right, endorsed the notion of a Popular Front that would unite Radicals, Socialists, and Communists against the conservatives and reactionaries who had long held the upper hand. In the 1936 elections the Popular Front won a victory which brought a left-wing government to power, headed by the Socialist Léon Blum.

The uneasy coalition soon foundered under the strain of internal divisions and the difficulties of foreign policy. It gave way to more moderate cabinets whose fate was to stumble uneasily to war. Before it died, however, after a year of power, Blum's Popular Front coalition had passed a series of social measures which, while they hampered the production of armaments for the coming war, did at last lead the working class into the twentieth century: the forty-hour week, higher wages, compulsory arbitration, paid holidays, and the nationalization of certain industries. By 1938, though fewer French homes had electricity, indoor sanitation, running water, or any other comforts than those in Germany or Britain, most of the poorer Frenchmen lived better, ate better, and dressed better than they had done a decade or two before. But Frenchmen were even more disunited. The failure of the Popular Front, combined with the international situation, stressed the discord between workers and employers, revived the agitation of the leagues and of the Communist Party, and further strained relations between Frenchmen.

France entered the second war divided against herself. Yet it was not her divisions but the incompetence of her generals (and allies) that ensured defeat within five weeks of the German offensive of 1940.* But it was the conservatives who feared social revolution who induced the government of Marshal Pétain to conclude an armistice which left the country at Germany's mercy.

* In this, the Communists, bound by the German-Soviet Pact, had done their best to help by defeatist propaganda and sabotage. After June, 1941, they would become the backbone of resistance.

Pétain was eighty-four years old in 1940 and his government, at **Vichy,** reflected the fact. Its slogan, "Labor, Family, Fatherland," went back to an earlier age to which it hoped to return the country, making it once again an agricultural economy endowed with gilds and corporations, educated in religious faith and bourgeois virtues. It was too late for that. France became the stake of a struggle between the Germans and the Allies in which each camp had its French supporters: on one side more or less enthusiastic collaborators with the Nazis, on the other the Resistance —Communists, patriots, democrats, all finally (if temporarily) embodied in Charles de Gaulle's Free French. "You think too much about the French," Pétain's aide-de-camp told him in 1942, "and not enough about France." The reverse was true of the lanky brigadier who had escaped from his surrendering land in June, 1940, to continue the fight from London and from France's overseas territories. Upon his figure there would eventually concentrate the hopes of Resistance fighters recruited from all prewar factions, few and isolated at first, more numerous after 1942, armed and equipped from London which they supplied with valuable information.

For most resisters, getting rid of the Germans was only a step toward a complete national renovation. Purged in the fires of suffering, the country would at least have shed the rotten old order and its dis-credited representatives, would be ready for new economic and political structures that could realize the democratic ideals to which prewar in-stitutions had only paid lip service. The ideology of the resistance com-bined humanism and collectivism in a vague revolutionary synthesis, too uncertain to provide a common program but sufficient to provide a common hope. The hope and the credit of it were going to be captured by politicians: Communists, Gaullists, even prewar ones. Before that, however, they sufficed to recruit impressive numbers to the underground. Resistance brought repression which in turn fed the flames of resistance even more. Two hundred thousand French men and women were de-ported to Germany, four out of five fated to die there; twenty thousand were shot by the occupying forces, aided at times by French militiamen. Despite—or perhaps because of—this, by the time Allied forces landed in Normandy, tens of thousands of armed, organized resisters were in a po-sition to give real help, harassing enemy troops and hampering their movements by sabotage and guerrilla activity.

Yet, whatever their heroism, in the end the country's fate was decided not by Frenchmen but by the fortunes of other people's wars in which they played only the part they were permitted. France was liberated in 1944 to the accompaniment of purges that killed between 40,000 and 80,000 persons who had collaborated with the Germans or were suspected of having done so, while twice as many were imprisoned or otherwise penalized. It was no longer a great power. The first challenge of peace was that it must learn to live with this new fact.

The Fourth Republic

Simply speaking, French politics under the Fourth Republic (1944–1958) were the parliamentary politics of the past rendered chaotic by the problems of the present. A parliament elected by proportional representation could not be made to work—the more so when a quarter of the electorate elected Communists who unbalanced it still further. It followed that France was run less by squabbling politicians and impermanent governments than by permanent civil servants whose freedom and initiative were all the greater for the impotence of the country's elected representatives. The Fourth Republic would boast twenty-five cabinets with an average life of six months. Even the most determined premiers, like the Radical Pierre Mendès-France (June, 1954–February, 1955), whose decisiveness extricated France from Indochina and began to ease her out of North Africa, left less of a mark than great administrators like Jean Monnet, architect of European union. This is what made for a situation often described as one of great stability below an anarchic surface.

The greatest positive contribution of this period was to turn another legacy of the war days into reality: the idea of European union, which German propaganda had exploited for its own ends, became the redeeming dream of the Resistance leaders. The war had demonstrated that industrial and political power were one. But Europeans could hope for neither without organization, concentration, and co-operation across national borders. France and Germany must learn to cooperate. Whatever their divisions, they had more in common than each had with other powers that had not shared what they had gone through. This was the only way in which Europe could hope to play the major world role to which its component parts no longer could aspire separately. It would be Frenchmen like Monnet and Foreign Minister Robert Schuman who launched the plans from which European integration arose; it would be France which drew the most important profits from them.

But such advances were less apparent than the problems the Fourth Republic faced. Liberation coincided with the reversal of the demographic trend of a century and more. In the ten years following the war French population increased about 10 per cent, by over four million: a tide of youth which continues to rise today (though more slowly) so that soon one Frenchman in two will be under thirty-two. Expanding economy and expanding population upset the stagnant balance of several decades, encouraged economic growth and social mobility, created great demands for housing, schooling, and mass-produced consumer goods, but also new tensions, inflation, dissatisfactions, all aggravated by psychological crisis. France, we have said, was no longer a great power. But she had fallen in the world so suddenly that many Frenchmen could not accept the thought, especially when challenged by the population of their colonies, asking for freedom in their turn. The cost of warfare in Indochina (Vietnam) and then Algeria increased inflation; and failure increased instability. A million French settlers in Algeria prevented negotiation with Nationalist Algerian rebels. France was stretched on the rack of a colonial war which threatened to turn into a civil one (1954–1962).

De Gaulle and a New France

The Republic and its political masters could neither tame their rebels nor free themselves from them. They would be replaced by a man who could do both: Charles de Gaulle (1890–1970), who cared for France more than for any party, for France's anxious glory more than for its possessions. An actor and a poet with a sense of history, de Gaulle descended from a long line of men who had served the state. Inspired by Barrès and Maurras, he had made a religion of his fatherland. Here was a seventeenth-century figure, born in the nineteenth to serve the twentieth. Too authoritarian and unbending for democratic politics, the General, who had become head of state at the liberation, had resigned in 1946. Since then he had survived as a great memory and a disrupting influence. In 1958 he returned to head a new government, to extract France from its Algerian anthill and from further colonial entanglements. The Fourth Republic collapsed under its confusions to be succeeded by a Fifth built on the economic edifice of the previous decade.

Thus the Fourth Republic proved both a dismal failure and a startling success. Years of political instability and running inflation hid from sight great advances in power production and the modernization of key industries. In 1958 the Fifth Republic inherited an economy whose dynamism, ignored by a public fascinated by political hassles, surprised everybody. Its task would be to secure the stable conditions in which an ever-growing section of the population could concentrate on the exhausting but increasingly satisfying pursuit of money.

As for de Gaulle, he concentrated on the state. A sound, or sounder economic structure; the final settlement of the suppurating Algerian conflict in 1962 and the resettlement of nearly a million refugees; a wary entente with Germany, preferred to more powerful allies; the classic ideas of balance of power applied in improved relations with Russia—all these permitted a more independent foreign policy, a firmer tone with the United States. The General shared his countrymen's resentment of overweening allies, their reluctance to go in too deep with one side and lose all touch with the other. Above all he wanted to preserve his country's freedom of maneuver, prevent her from becoming the vassal of more powerful friends, place her in a dominant position within the limited European sphere which could still be hers, and reassert her influence wherever the French language carried. Given peace, good management, and luck, the policy worked well enough, providing the prestige and the recognition which France had long been denied, securing a greater apparent independence than France's European allies enjoyed.

The year 1968 would show up the fragility of a bid for power resting on shaky foundations. In May, pressure of numbers, insufficient facilities, anachronistic structures, led to serious explosions within the great centralized nationwide structure of the University. Briefly but unforgettably, a generation which never knew what it was like to be occupied by the Germans set about showing the country what being occupied by the French was like. Parallel to this, inflation led to lasting and widespread strikes in spring, and the settlements that followed the strikes encouraged further inflation and migration of capital, threatening the stability of the franc by fall of that year. The General's insistence that France could go it alone had to be toned down as nationalistic pride gave way to anxiety and disturbance.

Visiting Romania in May, 1968, de Gaulle had hailed "the healthy wind rising from one end of the continent to the other," and reaffirmed the need of reuniting Europe from the Atlantic.to the Urals, with no iron curtain in between. Now, hardening Soviet policy seemed to refurbish the iron curtain; Russian occupation of Czechoslovakia made nonsense of the thaw he hoped for, embarrassing the Franco-Russian *rapprochement* that French foreign policy had leaned on; the drain of dollars and of gold reserves after the events of May put paid to aggressive independence asserted against the United States; the rising winds blew little good to France, less to her president.

Gaullism—the policy, or lack of policy, of the General's varied but numerous followers—united authoritarian progressivism and liberal (that is, conservative) opportunism in uneasy harness. Governmental authority and stability, greater than France had known for a century, seemed to produce only piecemeal initiatives and spasmodic improvements. Little had been done to prepare the succession of a man who, like all great men, believed himself irreplaceable and therefore did not bother with what might follow his passing. Hampered in part by anti-European parochialism, economic momentum was running down. Financially, France was well off despite the run on its money. But unemployment and productivity gave cause for concern, labor and white-collar workers clamored for a greater share of national wealth, and so did students and peasants. France suffered the acute discomfort that goes with growth and change. Men with one foot in traditional society and another in the modern world showed the strain of such schizophrenic conditions. Shopkeepers rebelled against the pressure of large stores spreading at last throughout the provinces and the fiscal burdens of a costly state; peasants rioted against the competition of large-scale farms and the costs of modernization; everyone felt the difficulty of adjusting the mentalities of one age to the techniques of another.

There was little a government could do about problems of that nature. But de Gaulle always regarded politics as a personal affair. Eager to reassert his authority, he insisted on a referendum which was in effect a plebiscite: that is, a request for a confidence vote. But confidence was lacking. Some of the great barons of the regime, like ex-Premier Georges Pompidou, gave only halfhearted support. The Jewish community, mortified by the General's brutal break with Israel and support of the Arab cause, opposed him. The partisans of order feared he had lost his grip, the partisans of change doubted he could adjust to the new world around. De Gaulle's foreign policies raised fears of French isolation, his internal ones raised prices and taxes both. Above all, de Gaulle had ruled too long: longer than anyone since Napoleon III. He was getting old, clinging too hard to office. The disorder he had replaced forgotten, many judged his order the more harshly, dismissed it more easily.

In April, 1969, not quite eleven years after he had grasped political power, the General was out of it by the will of that people to which he had always turned for confirmation. But the majority that had united to turn him out was a conglomerate of many trends, ranging from extreme Right to extreme Left, and quite incapable of offering an alternative when de Gaulle resigned his office. Parliament retained a strong Gaullist majority held together by common interest in administrative efficiency, political effectiveness, and the perquisites of power. Whether under new president, Georges Pompidou, or another, Gaullism without de Gaulle seemed the fate of France for some time to come.

Britain

Victory in 1918 had proved a costly bauble. Three-quarter million dead, one and a half million wounded, the domestic and foreign debt ten times greater than in 1914, revenue from foreign investments cut by almost half, workers and veterans clamoring for social reform, taxpayers for lower taxes, these were some of the facts confronting a government torn every which way. In 1920 the French ambassador to London told Winston Churchill: "In the twenty years I have been here I have witnessed an English revolution more profound and searching than the French Revolution itself. The governing class has been almost entirely deprived of political power and to a very large extent of their property and estates; and this has been accomplished almost imperceptibly and without the loss of a single life."* By 1937 5.6 per cent of the national income had been redistributed from rich to poor. In 1939 there were 7,000 people in England with net incomes after taxes of $30,000 or more. In 1949 there would be seventy.

All this was in part the work of the Lloyd George budget of 1911, with its heavier taxes and its death duties, especially for higher income brackets. It was even more the result of war and the greater equality induced by shortages, rationing, wage rises, and the shrinking number of domestic servants. The war effort absorbed both men and women who were reluctant thereafter to reassume their servitude. The number of domestic servants in 1920 was half that of 1914; it would continue to fall, and particularly after 1940. But, though even the lowest wages were now above starvation level, A. J. P. Taylor reminds us that in 1920 1 per cent of the population still owned two-thirds of the national wealth while 0.1 per cent owned one-third of the nation's wealth **—the changes England underwent in the First World War were far from the catastrophic character of the 1940's. As England entered the 1920's democracy was still limited by institutions, custom, and deference; plural voting continued to 1945; women over thirty received the vote in 1917, those over twenty-one only in 1938; the same classes kept their hold on the levers of power. In a period when Conservatives ruled most of the time, two-fifths of the members of Parliament belonged to families with a hereditary title, and a quarter of them between 1918 and 1939 had been educated at Eton or Harrow.

Still, the Labor Party, which had never got more than half a million votes before the war, was emerging as the main opponent of the Tories. The Liberals, having exhausted their program in 1911, crumbled away as their chief vote-getter, Lloyd George, shifted toward a "national"—that is, conservative—platform. In 1918, while Lloyd George's national coalition got five and a half million votes, Labor got two and a half million and the Independent Liberals only a million and a half. In 1922, though the Conservatives stayed well ahead, Labor doubled its poll and more than doubled its seats in Parliament. In 1924, with Liberal support, Labor would form the government (though only for ten months). A cabinet in which the Home Secretary had been an ironworker, the Chancellor of the Exchequer a former clerk, and the Prime Minister, Ramsay MacDonald, the illegitimate son of a domestic servant: this had the

---

* W. S. Churchill, *My Early Years* (London: 1947), p. 90.

** "Even this was an improvement on pre-war when 88% owned nothing." A. J. P. Taylor, *English History 1914–45* (Oxford: 1965), p. 171.

A scene during the general strike in London. Police escort wagons attempting to make deliveries in spite of the protests of strikers.

value of a symbol. But it did not last and, under the Conservative government that succeeded, Labor agitation grew apace. An attempt at a general strike in 1926 was soon defeated; but the general elections of 1929 brought a Labor majority to Parliament and a fresh Labor government, installed that year, had to bear the brunt of the Great Depression. Labor governments have seldom been lucky. After 1929 unemployment soared, made worse by the drastic economies which were the only policy the government could think of,* and the Labor Cabinet was soon succeeded by a national coalition and then by Conservatives.

Over one man in five was unemployed and many of an age to work had no idea what steady work was like. But they received the dole—unemployment insurance payments—and need not starve, just lose their self-respect. The government would not consider the investment policy that the economist John Maynard Keynes proposed to refloat the economy, but it was willing to pay to keep the unemployed from despair. It seemed to men like the Conservative Chancellor of the Exchequer Neville Chamberlain (Prime Minister 1937–40) that it cost four times as much to put a man to work as to keep him out of it. So, many stood idle on the dole and what they might produce, or earn, or spend had they been employed, never came into existence to provide work for others. Yet this policy meant that the British masses were spared the wretchedness that drove the Germans to radical lengths. Theirs was a quieter dejection and one that was partly remedied as the economy slowly recovered. By 1937 unemployment was "only" 12 per cent; and by 1939 preparation for war created full employment. But men remembered the bad years between the wars, the general strike, the dole, the unemployment. Such memories would emerge in 1945 in a determination not to have these things happen again even at the cost of restrictive union practices which increased costs and lowered productivity.

* Only Sir Oswald Mosley, a junior member of the Labor Cabinet, fought for a bolder policy supported by the left-wing—Lansbury, Strachey, Bevin. Mosley resigned from the government, was narrowly defeated at the Labor Party Conference, resigned from the party in 1931 and set up The New Party, which soon turned into the British Fascist Party, destined for historical oblivion.

Winston Churchill during a wartime visit to the Western Front. In the foreground, Marshal Montgomery.

Increasingly England turned in upon herself. Economically and spiritually she lived on capital, her old dynamic wasted. In 1936, as German troops reoccupied the Rhineland, as Popular Front governments appeared in France and Spain and civil war broke out in the latter, none of these events captured the popular imagination or the attention of politicians so much as the issue whether the new forty-one-year old king might marry a commoner who was both American and divorced. Since Victoria, Edward VII (1901–1910) and George V (1910–1936) had ruled over the kingdom. Neither mattered much politically, any more than Edward VIII or his successors were to do. But the private affairs of a monarch are just as fascinating as those of a film star and lend themselves to more acute moralistic considerations. In December, 1936, Edward VIII abdicated and his younger brother succeeded him as George VI (1936–1952). Such were the things that mattered.

With leaders whose chief concern was to keep spending down—as their electors wanted—no positive position was possible in international affairs. The Labor opposition, pacifist on principle, called for resistance to Fascism but opposed rearmament. The Conservative majority, more consistent, preferred a combination of economies and appeasement. In 1933 an event showed the way the wind was blowing among the cream of the nation's youth. A debate in the Oxford University Union ended in victory for the motion that students would *not* "fight for king and country." Why should they when Wilsonian aspirations had stumbled to apparent failure, when war had failed to end war or save the world for democracy, when peace had built no homes fit for heroes to live in, when their elders had shown their incapacity to lead and their fellows their unwillingness to die?* Even more characteristic was the Peace Ballot, an enterprise of the League of Nations Union, whose results were announced in June, 1935. Almost all who answered, and they num-

---

* Within a very few years most of the motion's supporters would be in uniform, fighting and dying as bravely as their forebears.

bered close to twelve million, voted in favor of the League of Nations, disarmament, and economic sanctions against aggression. Far smaller numbers envisaged military measures to deter aggression. Fewer still would pay for the armaments without which no forceful measures would be possible. Here was the cue for what we call appeasement: a policy which, setting aside its moral aspects, was largely a refusal to pay the costs of strength, a choice between armaments and certain social measures (Chamberlain was a great municipal reformer), and a refusal to choose between irreconcilable principles as the Left insisted stubbornly on both disarmament and anti-Fascism and the Right just as blindly on economy and security.

Only a small group of men around Winston Churchill (1874–1965) opposed the weak and vacillating policy this made for, calling for the re-armament without which there could be no firm, consistent policy. But they were excluded from the seats of power in favor of more sensible politicians. It was only when the Germans had invaded Holland and Belgium that Neville Chamberlain resigned and was succeeded by Winston Churchill. Churchill's old-fashioned pride in Britain and his belief in his country's destiny, the very fact that his mind was naturally closed to certain possibilities while open to every consideration and combination that might bring victory, made him an ideal leader in a desperate situation. Today we cannot recreate the loneliness of England's stand, without resources, friends or—really—any reasonable hope, while one after the other European countries fell to German arms. For a year, for two, the situation got steadily worse while only unreasoning confidence counseled resistance. Protected by the Channel, by the R.A.F., and by the confidence that Churchill fanned, the United Kingdom was able to hold out and to emerge victorious from the conflict.

The Search for Stability

Not only victorious, but ruined. Not only ruined, but more of a social whole than it had ever been. During the war, the bloodless revolution had advanced with giant steps throughout a people mobilized for life-or-death resistance. The vast experience of wartime rationing proved that physical fitness and productive efficiency were related and that well-fed workers meant more regular timekeeping, greater output, lower absentee-ism and sickness rates. Planning and direction of industry and labor had been almost total and had contributed to victory; they were now enlisted to rebuild the country. Taxes which had soared to finance war expenses were turned toward a vast social and economic revolution. This was the program of the Labor government which, in July 1945, won a tremendous electoral victory, defeating Churchill's Conservatives because they refused to acknowledge that things had changed and the need to change them more radically still.

But Labor faced a gigantic task. Britain had lost half her merchant tonnage and almost all remaining revenues from abroad. Industrial production, totally concentrated on armaments, had to be reconverted to a peaceful use. Fifty million people, crowded into an island a little bigger than New England, had to find the exports to pay for the raw materials and the food almost all of which came in from abroad. The Labor government tried to achieve recovery and social security side by side, and it went far in both directions, with the aid of heavier taxation, American aid, and an austerity program which extended wartime rationing and weary working hours until 1950. Banking, transport, key utilities and industries were nationalized; education and national health insurance extended to provide opportunities and security for all. When in 1951 a Conservative government succeeded Labor, it would do little, in effect, to reverse the socialization of the national economy.

But, somehow, the country seemed to have lost the sap which had coursed so briskly through it during several centuries. In a way, Britain found herself in a situation similar to that of France twenty-five years before: she had fulfilled her aspirations, she had exhausted her resources, she wanted to preserve her rank in the world, she felt her security depended less on her own power than on her allies', she hoped to preserve a *status quo* rapidly slipping into revolutionary changes, she sought to shut herself off from the irritating influences of the outside world; but, unable to face the costs of power, unwilling to pay its price, she did not know how to react coherently to her crumbling international status. The effort the country exerted during the war exhausted its last resources. Worse, perhaps, its victory in 1945 and its position through the following decade as the only excombatant who had not somehow been overrun, devastated, and humiliated, encouraged the persistent illusion of great power status now that she was no more than America's tarnished second.

Britain had come out of the war a very little power still shouldering the burdens and world responsibilities of the great power she had been, still nursing the belief that she dominated Europe and cherishing the antiquated ways *despite* which she survived. She could not face the prospect of political or economic equality with her neighbors on the continent, or of close co-operation with them, preferring her special relationship with the United States (more interested in Germany) and with the Commonwealth (more interested in the United States).

When the European Common Market was set up Britain kept out of it. As a result, though still the greatest trading nation in Europe, Britain lagged terribly behind her continental rivals in economic growth, productivity, exports, wealth, and dynamism. In 1950 she produced 10.3 per cent of the world's steel and built 37.7 per cent of its ships. By 1961 these figures had fallen to 6.1 per cent and 14.8 percent respectively. The change from Labor to Conservative government in 1951, from

Conservative to Labor in 1964, made little difference to a nation oscillating with remarkable cheerfulness between comfort and crisis. National revenue growing more slowly than that of any Western country (11 per cent against 23 percent in the Common Market), lagging industrial productivity (up 30 per cent between 1953 and 1962, as compared to 100 per cent in West Germany and 90 per cent in France), too many imports chasing too few exports with consequent balance-of-payments crises and devaluations of the pound sterling, withdrawal from outpost after outpost of Empire marked by some last imperialist hurrahs (notably at Suez in 1956), withal complacency, armaments and colonies draining funds needed at home: Britain's story in the last decade is one of dreary stagnation turning in the mid-60's to exuberant decadence.

While the economy declined, the nation furnished the deer park of Europe, a happy hunting ground for tourists, the Venice of the twentieth century. It is possible that economic stagnation and the freedom and public decency the country still enjoys go together; that the kind of government which would increase economic growth would also cut into public liberties; that the many institutions whose interests are vested in the present situation can only be set aside by something like a dictatorship; and that a dictatorship might suppress liberties without necessarily putting an end to stagnation. England, whose political and social institutions may be too advanced, too developed, to permit adjustment to the challenges of the present, poses one of the great conundrums of our day: is stability the greatest danger of modern society?

Spain

Spain's policy of neutrality throughout the First World War allowed Spanish industry to develop further and, with it, social tensions and the influence of Socialists and Anarchists. The movement for the autonomy of Catalonia, where much of this industrial growth took place, also advanced and broke into mutiny and separatist revolt in 1923 on the occasion of one more disaster in Morocco. This was met by a military coup establishing the dictatorship of a general supported by King Alfonso: Miguel Primo de Rivera, who, with French help, settled the Moroccan conflict while suppressing free press, free courts, free institutions, and the liberal opposition at home.

Primo's dictatorship, which lasted from 1923 to 1930 saw a desperate and partly successful effort to modernize the economy, increase production and improve the conditions of the working classes. Roads and dams were built, rural electrification schemes developed, industry protected, railways modernized, rivers used for hydraulic power. Order helped the work and prosperity lasted until it collapsed with the world depression. But the military factions were getting restive and students and intellectuals soon stirred again. Primo, discouraged and ill, resigned in 1930. His fall was shortly followed by that of the king who had backed him and who now shared his discredit. In 1931, municipal elections resulted in overwhelming victory for the Republicans who called for Alfonso's abdication. The King left Spain and a republic was bloodlessly installed, accepted by the soldiers who would attack it within a few years.

But Spain was too divided for anything to hold it together except force. Extreme Right and Left both rejected the bourgeois republic from the beginning; army and property owners soon turned against it when military expenses were pared down and land reform plans threatened large estates. The basic break, as in the French revolution, came on the religious question. The Republicans, wanting to separate Church and State and to diminish clerical privileges, shocked the "respectable" Catholic middle classes. These could not stomach such atheistic and Jacobin measures or the government's incapacity to prevent sporadic attacks on churches, convents, and convent schools attended by their offspring. Eager to do the right thing but not to do too much, to reform but not alarm, to advance but not disturb, the Republicans discontented their critics, disappointed their supporters, and frightened the rich and respectable without weakening them. The recipe was made for trouble, and trouble came in 1936 when a coalition of center and left-wing parties—the Popular Front—won the elections. Coalition governments can seldom act with firmness. In Spain's troubled situation, the triumph of the Popular Front only accentuated internal divisions without imposing order. Soon, the debate passed from *córtes* into streets, and the resulting anarchy called forth the traditional pronunciamento.

Only this time when the military conspirators, led by General Francisco Franco (b. 1892), revolted, the government held its own in some of the major cities, particularly Barcelona and Madrid. A new political factor had arisen: the organized, class-conscious workers, unwilling to allow political decisions to be made without them. The insurgency controlled most of the army and the air force. The government, supported by the parties of the Left, organized forces of its own. What had begun as one more classic coup, which had gone wrong because neither side was strong enough to gain a quick decision, now turned into a conflict of ideologies, with foreign powers intervening on both sides and the outcome decided finally by the more effective foreign aid. The Republicans and their allies of the Left fought bravely but they were starved of help, internally divided by profound dissensions between the partners of the Popular Front, and were progressively driven back. Little help came from abroad. The United States, dreading all foreign

Warder Collection

Left: Nationalist troops move through Madrid, November 1936. Franco and one of his generals dining during the Spanish Revolution.

entanglements, drew back its skirts from the horrid conflict. The Popular Front government in neighboring France, hamstrung by internal dissensions, was powerless to give effective help. The British, eager to appease the Axis, launched a nonintervention policy which only they and the French observed. Mexico and Soviet Russia sent some aid, but never enough to be effective. Meanwhile, Fascists and National-Socialists recognized their own. Franco's Nationalists, with strong support from Germans and Italians, pressed steadily forward.

The Legacy of Civil War

The Spanish civil war was more than an opportunity for Communists and Fascists to confront each other and for the Axis powers to try out their weapons at other men's expense. It was, for thinking people throughout the West, the traumatic experience that made their quandary clear, the quandary created by the persistent failure of the democratic powers to live up to their responsibilities, to face fascism and oppose it with a positive gesture or idea of their own. The year 1936 was in many ways a turning point. In March the Germans had finally revealed their aggressive intentions, in May the Popular Front in France had won the elections there, in July Franco's insurrection had broken out in Spain, in November the Rome-Berlin Axis had been openly proclaimed and it had recognized a protégé in Franco. Here, at a time of great popular hopes and fears, the contradictory forces and ideas of the past decade came to a head in a conflict between what looked like popular democracy and constitutional government on one side and the old order represented by its most classic symbols on the other. It was not quite like that, but that was how it looked to Hemingway, Malraux, and Brecht, and Orwell and Picasso, who saw open cities like Guernica ruthlessly bombed or shelled into ruins from the sea, and who exulted to see themselves at last fighting side by side with workers and peasants for democracy and against the Fascism that their own governments were too weak to face.

While over 10,000 Germans and seven times that number of Italians

Guernica, by Pablo Picasso. On extended loan by the artist to the Museum of Modern Art, New York.

supported Franco,* thousands of volunteers from all over Europe and America flocked to the International Brigades on the government's side. Many of them were refugees from Fascism, many were ordinary men— students, workers, intellectuals—who saw in Spain the secular plight of democracy and social justice assailed by brutal force. Some came to look on communism as the only political system that would stand up to it, but some learned a different lesson. Just because the Spanish war was the peak of a social commitment into which Western intellectuals could enter unhampered by the considerations that arose in the case of a national war, it provided not only a challenge but a touchstone of political purity, on which many intellectuals swung back from idealism to deception, from commitment to detachment and skepticism.

On the Left men like Stephen Spender or George Orwell, on the Right convinced Catholics and Royalists like Georges Bernanos, discovered that reconciling liberty and justice with modern warfare and political maneuvers was more difficult than they had ever thought: that there are not two sides but many, or one only in which all massacre, all suffer, and all are finally united in the death and the human condition that Bernanos depicted in his terrifying book *The Great Graveyards under the Moon* (1937), or Spender in the poem where

> Clean silence drops at night when a little walk
> Divides the sleeping armies, each
> Huddled in linen woven by remote hands.
> When the machines are stilled, a common suffering
> Whitens the air with breath and makes both one
> As though these enemies slept in each other's arms.

---

* Weapons were even more important than men. German and Italian tanks, planes, and guns, along with the specialists to man them, proved decisive in the end.

The political game on either side was not as clear or simple as had been imagined. Both sides wreaked destruction, took hostages, imprisoned suspects, raped, and murdered; both stifled the idealists in their own camp to serve what they conceived to be political or military efficiency. The Communists sacrificed all hope of social revolution on the Republican side to reassure the middle classes in Spain and abroad. The calculation failed: the workers were discouraged and the bourgeois hardly reassured. Franco eliminated and imprisoned his more radical supporters as being too disturbing for the conservatives he wooed. But the ideals of the Right—order, church, and the preservation of property—could reconcile themselves more easily to this state of affairs than those of the Left. Many liberals discovered with dismay that the faults they knew and criticized at home, the injustice or bad faith of their own governments, existed also in the "popular" and "democratic" regimes of Spain or Russia.

There was little reason, or so it seemed, to place faith in democracy's power to withstand evil; but there was not much hope in communism either. Protected by Soviet Russia—the only major power to aid the Republicans—the Communist Party, small and weak in 1936, came to dominate the Left, purging its armies and counsels of all who would not toe the party line. The purges in Spain echoed those then decimating Russia. Acquaintance with all the dirt and treachery of politics broke some of the last illusions of social and political-minded intellectuals. The year 1936 had been a time of hope in danger. The years that followed saw exasperation turning to despair. Many shared the feeling Orwell described in *Homage to Catalonia* that volunteers like him had become "pawns in an enormous political game."

"There is no use any longer," concluded Stephen Spender, "in taking sides with those politicians who seem a little nearer to the truth than the others." They might be just a little nearer, but they were almost as far away. So, many poets, thinkers, artists, who had briefly descended into the marketplace and onto the battlefield, beat a retreat. These were the years of the "God that failed." * Years of disillusion but of clarification too, when erstwhile Socialists, Liberals, and even Fascists decided that in the end, when all the words had been spoken and all the gestures made, what counted was "the decency of human beings" (Orwell), "man's dignity" (Silone), his "self-possession" (Malraux), his self-respect (Bernanos).

But such soul-searching, though important for Western thought and self-awareness, was for the few as yet. For the Spaniards there was suffering and devastation. When in the spring of 1939 Madrid at last surrendered and the United States recognized Franco's new regime a week before his adhesion to the German-Italian-Japanese Anti-Comintern Pact, some 700,000 lives had been lost in battle, some 50,000 more in air

* A book of that name, edited by Richard Crossman, was published in 1958.

raids, executions, and simple straightforward murders. Hundreds of thousands escaped to foreign exile. Catholicism was back in seventeenth-century garments, its control over schools and minds restored and supported by an official censorship which Raymond Carr tells us was designed to crush "pornography, Marxism, and dissolvent Liberalism." Nearly a million prisoners languished in Franco's jails. Many have died, many were released, some remain there still. The country had peace at last: a time to lick its wounds and to recover.

The convalescence has been slow. Spain became a monarchy again, but the pretender waited in exile while Franco ruled.* Despite misconceptions, Spain is not a Fascist country. Its native Fascist movement, the *Falange,* never very strong, had been domesticated by Franco, who turned it into a tame militia, never allowing it to do more than suited his policy. Franco was part of an older Spanish tradition: an authoritarian conservative, paternalistic and patriotic. He kept his country out of the Second World War ** and navigated the rapids of the peace until his steadfast anticommunism won American favor. Deprived of free institutions, almost thirty years of peace have given Spain the modest beginnings of prosperity. There have been significant efforts to reconcile a divided people, but extremes of wealth and poverty have not been eliminated and every step toward a more liberal regime tends to be followed by two steps back toward repression. There is no knowing whether Spain after Franco will break into civil war again. What she will make of herself and of her future remains to be seen.

Austria

Of seven and one-half million Austrians, over two million lived in postwar Vienna, which was given the status of a separate province in the New Republic. Most of the rest lived on the land or in small towns, provincial, backward, and strongly influenced by the Catholic Church. Between the provinces and the cosmopolitan modern capital a deep divide developed. After 1920, "red Vienna" run by Social Democrats stood in permanent opposition to the rest of the country governed by clerical governments reflecting rural opinion, reactionary and poor. In Vienna the Socialists followed in Lueger's footsteps, developing an impressive program of municipal socialism and public works. But Vienna, like the whole country, had lost its economic hinterland and was eco-

* Before dying in 1941, Alfonso XIII had designated his son, Don Juan, to succeed him. But the real pretender, since 1954, has been the latter's eldest son, Don Juan Carlos, born 1938, now officially designated as Franco's successor.

** Yet German soldiers were garrisoned on Spanish soil and British aircraft that strayed beyond the *campo neutral* separating Gibraltar from Spain were shot down by anti-aircraft guns built in bunkers facing the Rock.

nomically unbalanced. Austrian welfare now hung on foreign loans. When foreign credit was withdrawn in 1929, the economy began to crumble, sought to save itself by concluding a Customs Union with Germany (1931), which international intervention prevented, and collapsed into political as well as financial chaos.

By then the country was astir with paramilitary formations: the Socialist *Schutzbund* in the major towns, the Christian Socialist *Heimwehr* patronized by landlords in the countryside, and, everywhere, the burgeoning brown shirts of the Nazis. Heimwehr and Schutzbund had clashed for several years, with the Socialists losing ground as Catholic governments supported the Heimwehr against them. The Depression accelerated their decline. In 1932, a Christian Socialist Cabinet under Engelbert Dollfuss sought to stabilize the situation. In 1933, challenged by growing Nazi agitation which Hitler's rise to power in Germany encouraged, Dollfuss suspended parliamentary government, dissolved the Nazi Party, and established a dictatorship which the Socialists tried to challenge in 1934 only to be crushed. Within a few months Dollfuss himself had been murdered in a clumsy Nazi coup whose perpetrators were routed and executed by the Heimwehr. Authority now passed to Dollfuss's close collaborator Kurt Schuschnigg, who, for the next few years, maintained Austrian independence with the support of Italy.

Schuschnigg's corporative state, backed by all conservative elements and placed directly under the authority of God, allowed for no elections or plebiscites. It held little attraction for the young, the nationalists, and the unemployed, who, now that the Left had been eliminated, leaned increasingly toward the Nazis, still banned but increasingly influential. In 1937, the conclusion of the Rome-Berlin Axis removed Schuschnigg's Italian backing against Germany, just at the time when Hitler was making ready to forestall a possible restoration of the Habsburgs. In March, 1938, while drawing closer to Czechoslovakia and to France, Schuschnigg tried to call a plebiscite on the question of Austrian independence, was faced with a German ultimatum to resign, did so under menace of invasion, and National Socialists took the country over. The postponed plebiscite, now administered by Nazis, produced a vote of 99.75 per cent in favor of union with Germany; and Austria was incorporated into the Reich where she remained until 1945.

The country which enthusiastically welcomed Hitler and which accounted for about 8 per cent of the Third Reich's population, furnished a higher proportion of Nazis—one in every ten—than Germany. Among the murderers of the SS one in three were Austrians; among their Jewish victims almost half were killed by Austrians. Eichmann, who shipped thousands to their death, was an Austrian; so was Gestapo Chief Ernst Kaltenbrunner, and so, of course, was Hitler. Nazism was particularly lively in this lovely country and it has remained so since the war, when political power has been shared between Catholics and Socialists while Nazi survivors control the balance between the two camps.

Hungary

Hungary came out of the First World War still a semifeudal country. In October, 1918, the kingdom had broken off from Austria and signed a separate armistice. In November a republic was proclaimed under the presidency of the liberal count Michael Karolyi, who hoped to conclude peace on the basis of new national policies and thoroughgoing land reforms. As subject nations broke away, the possibility of such policies succeeding vanished. Socialist and Communist agitation spread before Karolyi could introduce his land reforms and democratic franchise. In March, 1919, Karolyi resigned rather than evacuate the areas which the Allies destined for Romanian occupation, and a dictatorship of the proletariat was set up almost by default. Its chief, Béla Kun, blundered badly when he announced that his government would not distribute land but nationalize it, thus forfeiting the support of peasants who lost interest in the conflict. Romanian troops marched into Hungary, occupied Budapest, ousted the Kun regime, and cleared the way for a reactionary takeover.

There was little Wilsonian self-determination about the peace which Hungary signed at Trianon (1920). Hungary lost three-fourths of her former territories and two-thirds of her former population. About three million Magyar-speaking persons now lived in Czech, Romanian, and Yugoslav territory. One injustice had replaced another, an even more virulent irredentism succeeded the national irredentisms of before the war.

Devastated by war, civil war, invasion, red and white terror, plundered by Romanians and amputated by the peace, the country would now be ruled by men who had led the anti-Bolshevik forces in the days of Kun. The republic, associated with revolution, was abolished; the kingdom of St. Stephen was re-established, but not for a Habsburg any longer. The kingdom without a king was to be ruled by an admiral without a fleet: its regent would be Miklos Horthy (1868–1957), erstwhile commander of the Imperial Navy in the Adriatic.

Impoverished by war, hard hit by inflation and by the loss of savings invested in the bonds of the vanished Empire, the middle class was also overcrowded by an influx of refugees from the successor states, embittered by the loss of posts, businesses, and homes. It would prove fertile ground for archconservatism rivaled only by movements of the radical Right. Revisionism became the touchstone of Hungarian politics. Even the

Socialists were Magyar irredentists. This meant that talk of agrarian or electoral reform could always be submerged by cries for the recovery of the *irredenta*. Three million landless peasants out of a population of eight million were of less importance than three million Magyars under the foreign yoke, suffering rather less than their present oppressors had suffered under that of Magyars.

When modest recovery in the later 20's stumbled into depression, the country turned from conservatism to racist protofascism, orienting itself ever more firmly toward the revisionist alliance first of Rome and later of Berlin. Anti-Semitic measures took people's minds off more material issues, while native National Socialists called for land reform and social legislation to bring relief to the industrial and agrarian proletariat. In the absence of a radical Left the extreme Right assumed the radical role which conditions in Western countries often obscured or made secondary. But Horthy was firmly in the saddle and his more conservative authoritarianism seemed to pay off when in 1939 Hungary reacquired Ruthenia from the Czechoslovakia Hitler had dismembered, in 1940 Transylvania from Romania (by Hitler's award), and in 1941 some of the territories that Yugoslavia lost.

This last act meant war with the West and in due course with Russia, collapse in 1944, and occupation by the Russian troops. It also meant that, by co-operation with the Germans, several hundred thousand Jews were deported and exterminated. The peace treaties of 1947 restored the borders set at Trianon, with the exception of some Transylvanian districts and small further losses to the Czechs. By that time the country was run by a "workers' bloc" of Communists and Social Democrats. By 1948 the Communists had taken over entirely, the economic system began to be Sovietized, and collectivization of the land was introduced. In 1956, national revolution indicated the force of the resistance. Revolt grew out of intellectual circles, their unrest spreading to the students and workers of Budapest and to the peasants who promptly began to divide the lands that had been gobbled into collective farms. The explosion that began in late spring was symptomatic of unrest that has since surfaced in other satellites (see below, pp. 968–972). The manner in which the West stood by while Soviet tanks mastered the rebels proved that it would not dispute Russian domination over the sphere of influence they had been tacitly conceded. The Hungarians, like their neighbors, continued to be treated as pawns in the political games of greater powers.

Nevertheless, revolution crushed, a milder regime appears to cause less frustration. Hungary, like most of her East European neighbors, was never quite free in the Western sense of the term. It is hard to say whether she is less free now than in the 1930's.

Eastern Europe

After 1918, out of the defeat and disintegration of the eastern empires the map of this whole region was recast. Estonia, Latvia, Lithuania were no longer Russian provinces but independent states. Poland was a republic, uniting the portions which its partitioning neighbors had carved out of it in the past 146 years. The ancient kingdom of Bohemia and Moravia now took new shape in a Czechoslovak republic. Romania doubled in size with territories acquired from Russia (Bessarabia), Hungary (Transylvania), Austria (Bukovina), and Bulgaria (Dobruja). The South Slavs were united around Serbia in a Yugoslav kingdom including not only Austro-Hungarian spoils but also part of Bulgarian Macedonia and the small principality of Montenegro.

Here was a treasury of future trouble not only between victors and vanquished, but among the successor states themselves. Whether regarded on ethical or ethnic lines the state of Eastern Europe was uneasy. The Poles held the corridor between East and West Prussia and parts of Silesia which the Germans thought were theirs. They held a large chunk of Ukraine, well beyond the ethnic line Lord Curzon had suggested in 1919 as a roughly fair border between them and Russia, which meant additional friction between the Catholic majority and the six million Ukrainians and White Russians who were either Orthodox or Uniate. They also held the city of Vilna, which they had seized from Lithuania. The Czechs held Teschen, useful for its coal and iron, coveted by the Poles. Lithuania had seized the German port of Memel for an outlet to the sea; and German Danzig, severed from Germany under a League of Nations commissioner, stood as a free city within Polish borders. There were three million Germans in Czech territory, Hungarians and Ruthenians in Slovakia, Hungarians and Germans in Transylvania, Ruthenians in Bukovina, Ukrainians and Russians in Bessarabia, Turks and Bulgarians in Dobruja.

Yugoslavia had the most serious national problems internally, her politics between the wars bedeviled by struggle between Serb Centralists and other nationalities led by the Croats, who wanted a federalist state allowing greater provincial autonomy. The clash between Croats and Serbs made parliamentary government impossible and eventually led to King Alexander's coup in 1929, abolishing the constitution and taking power into his own hands—a royal dictatorship only slightly modified when Alexander was murdered by a Croat terrorist in 1934. The Croats would secure autonomy in their own province in 1939 and then, again, after 1945. But every country had similar troubles: the Czechs plagued by their increasingly obstreperous Germans, the Bulgarians by Macedonian terrorists who demanded independence, dominated their part of the countryside, collected their own taxes, and set up their own courts.

All countries, above all, feared the rise of communism or its arrival on Soviet bayonets. Economic conditions were certainly propitious—a breeding ground for dissatisfaction, and irredentist problems were aggravated by economic backwardness. Three-quarters of the population of the area drew its meager living from the land. After the war there had been much talk of land redistribution and great domains had been dispatched or nibbled at in varying degrees. But large estates were few south of the Danube and, to the north, Hungary and Poland left most of them untouched. Only in Romania, where in 1920 sixty-three landowners still held one-third of all cultivated land, was a real effort made to gain over the peasant veterans. By 1925, about 6 million acres had been distributed to 700,000 families. Within a few years agricultural statistics showed that—with far more land under wheat than before the war —production for the market had diminished by a vast amount. This provided opponents of small peasant properties with impressive arguments against continuing the process. They forgot that the first thing the peasants did was eat a little better and bring less food to market. In any case, while they were given land, the farmers had neither capital for seed, fertilizer, and equipment, nor credit facilities. The old masters or new ones were soon back in the saddle, renting them seed, tools or money at usurious rates, which left the small owners almost as poor and backward as they had been before. In 1939, production per acre in Romania and Yugoslavia was less than a third that in Denmark, infant mortality three or four times that in western Europe.*

Ailing Nations

Industrialization, as far as it took place, was often divorced from local possibilities and needs, concerned with national prestige and armaments, regional rivalries, and an impossible desire to be self-sufficient. Industrial development was so slight that, everywhere but in Bohemia, less than one man in ten could find work in factories, mines, or transports. By 1939, Poland—rather more advanced than most of her southern neighbors—was less productive than its three separate fragments had been in 1914, with average output per worker about one-third that to be found in Italy, one-sixth that in Germany, and one-thirteenth of North American rates. In any case, industrially, these countries were colonies of foreign trusts and banks. In Romania, Poland, Yugoslavia—wherever mineral resources could not be developed without foreign capital—alien

---

* In Romania infant mortality in 1940 was 188 per 1,000: comparable to the French rate a century before and higher than that of contemporary India.

companies controlled the more important half of industry.

While foreigners and their agents dominated the economy, governments controlled their peoples. An illiterate peasantry, a miserable proletariat, provided no basis and little support for democratic government. In the Hungarian countryside and in the Yugoslav kingdom after 1931, voting was open, the secret ballot unknown. Equally open everywhere were intimidation, violence, and electoral fraud. Police and hooligan bands kept opponents from the polls, imprisoned or beat up unwanted rivals, and made quite sure that peasants voted as local bosses or the gentry wished. Sooner or later political instability in every country was "solved" by coups, which were generally directed by soldiers like Jozef Pilsudski in Poland and Joannis Metaxas in Greece, or by kings like Alexander in Yugoslavia and Carol in Romania. Everywhere except in Czechoslovakia embryo democracy gave way to government by cliques or colonels, militaristic, authoritarian, inefficient, and yet supported by large sections of the property-owning classes.

Peasant parties were either powerless or, in other cases, ineffective. The Communists were outlawed everywhere, the Socialists an insignificant minority of middle-class intellectuals. Sometimes university students provided the only opposition, going to the peasants or the workers, braving the police, often in the wake of their professors. In the absence of any organized Left, students and such other radicals as existed often took up National Socialist positions, drawing the collectivist conclusions of their patriotism and founding movements of the radical Right as violent as the tone of local politics. Such movements, always in conjunction with anti-Semitism, arose in every country; the most notorious being the Romanian Iron Guard, a militant Christian populism which attracted impressive numbers of intellectuals, workers, and poor peasants. But though the Iron Guard briefly attained power in 1940, when in the wake of grave territorial losses the king (Carol II) was forced to abdicate, it could not maintain itself any more than any of the others. In Romania, as in Hungary and elsewhere, conservative authoritarians controlling the armed services held on to power and were confirmed in it even by the Germans who preferred order to social revolution. It would be the conservatives, not the fascists, who joined Germany against Soviet Russia and who, in due course, lost.

Realignments

After the war was over, East European countries were either annexed or occupied by Russia, or else became its satellites. It made no difference whether, like Poland or Yugoslavia, they had fought against the Germans or, like the others, with them against Russia. The three Baltic states, which the Soviets took over in 1940 and lost again in 1941, were reoccupied a few years later. Poland, which had enjoyed a generation of independence between 1918 and 1939, emerged from the war a Russian vassal, amputated of her eastern provinces but enlarged toward the west at Germany's expense. The Oder-Neisse line of her new German border remained up to 1970 a bone of contention with Germany, ensuring Poland's reliance on Russian support against a possible revision. Eastern Germany, Hungary, Romania, Yugoslavia, Bulgaria, and Albania—some hundred million people—also depended on Russia's will. In 1948, the last free country of the area—Czechoslovakia—toppled into the Russian camp as a result of a coup executed by local Communists backed up by Soviet pressure.

Czechoslovakia excepted, all these lands faced gigantic problems. Almost one-third of Poland's prewar population were dead: murdered, executed, or killed in combat. More than half her buildings were in ruins, some towns almost wholly destroyed, three-quarters of the railways out of use, half the bridges blown up, vast patches of cultivable land sown with mines. On a less catastrophic scale the same conditions existed everywhere else. Inflation was rampant, dislocation rife. Of the millions of Jews who had inhabited Europe's eastern borderlands few survived except in Romania: only a few thousand out of two million Polish Jews, scarcely a few hundred of the thousands south of the Danube. National elites, never very numerous, had been decimated by warfare, exile, and the deliberate policies of the occupants—German or Russian. Cultured or not, here were peoples caught, torn between East and West, most of them speaking an Eastern language while using a Western alphabet; living an Eastern life while, in many cases, they worshiped in Western churches; belonging to an Eastern bloc but looking westward whence they had drawn their culture before they were dismembered; ambivalent, unquiet, confused, and frequently heroic to the point of anachronism.

However much resented, the territorial changes imposed by the Soviets meant that all these countries, once a national jigsaw, enjoyed greater homogeneity. Wartime devastation in some, Communist pressure in all, made for industrial development and land reform, redistributed populations internally, changed the proportion of urban to rural dwellers. In 1945, urban population still accounted for less than a quarter of the country's population in Romania and Yugoslavia, less than half in Poland and Hungary. Now, at last, it changed in favor of the cities. More schools, more electricity, more industrial power, vast capital investments painfully squeezed out of poor economies, provided the equipment first for recovery and then for growth. By 1950, in most places, industrial production was double that of 1938, and illiteracy shrinking fast. Starting from misery and chaos, the Communist countries of Eastern Europe have maintained a high rate of growth, about 6 or 7 per cent every year, higher on the whole than the average for Western Europe and North America.*

* Significantly, this applies to the more backward countries which had more ground to cover. Czech growth rates consistently lagged behind those of their neighbors and

The Fate of Popular Democracies

The most interesting fate was that of Yugoslavia. Self-liberated by Marshal Tito's forces, the Yugoslavs organized a federal state, redistributed land, and nationalized industry. Completely devastated by the war which had cost the life of one peasant in ten and caused losses equivalent to four years' national income, the country set out to rebuild itself, broke with the Cominform in 1948, secured Western credits one year later, traded with the West and, eventually, with her Eastern neighbors too, developed an orginal Communist order which tried to associate the masses to the socialism it sought to build, replaced collectives by cooperatives and mitigated Communist dictatorship. The Yugoslavs showed their Communist comrades that socialism was capable of development in other ways than Moscow envisaged, that even a poor country could aspire to political independence and integrity. The last few years suggest that, given time and freedom, some of their neighbors would try to follow this trail, though they might not succeed.

The year 1956 would furnish illustration of this point in the twin risings that shook Poland and Hungary: "spring in October," as Warsaw radio put it when, for one brief exultant moment, it seemed as if liberation had really been achieved—from the occupying Russians, but also from the despotic, stultifying official bureaucracies that personified not the dictatorship of the proletariat but its stupefaction.

The great changes of the later forties—land reform, expropriation of private property, forced collectivization, impetuous industrialization, mass education—had been imposed from outside but widely approved. As late as the mid-fifties a popular Polish poet still hailed the days "when Communism was the supreme poetry and effort of every day, and poetry the road to Communism, life for Communism." Yet gradually, through the excesses of senile Stalinism, as their bureaucracies hardened into corruption and brutal paranoia, the Communist regimes came to devour their subjects, and, first among them, their most devoted sons. A generation that had grown up under socialism began to feel that it was forced to live a travesty of the ideas taught in the schools, ever-repeated by party mandarins but honored rather in the breach than the observance.

Between June and October 1956 in Poland, June and December 1956 in Hungary, petitions, speeches, demonstrations, strikes, degenerating into large-scale violence affirmed Socialist hopes against the harsh reality of Communist regimes. First the rebelliousness, then the rebel-

---

Czech national output actually fell in the 1960's. Communism, apparently appropriate for backward countries determined to lift themselves by their bootstraps into the modern world, seems less useful in a developed economy. Furthermore, Italian productivity has risen faster during the 1950's and sixties than that of almost all East European countries.

Hungarian freedom fighters in Budapest, 1956.

lion of factory workers, miners, students, journalists, and intellectuals brandished the principles of Marxism itself. "This state of policemen and bureaucrats must go," proclaimed the Hungarian writer Tibor Déry, an old Communist himself, to the enthusiastic approval of the young Communists of the Petöfi Circle. Such rebels referred to the Yugoslav experience, appealed to the nationalist and anti-Russian traditions, but remembered above all the ideals professed by the very regimes that they attacked. They failed. The Russians were too near. In Hungary there was fighting, bloodshed, brutal repression. In Poland (perhaps because of the Hungarian lesson) there was compromise, ending in the gradual elimination of would-be reformists by other reformists (like Wladislas Gomulka), shrewder and readier to work with Moscow. In Warsaw as in Budapest, October's spring did not last for long.

Among the results of these events—apart from 200,000 Hungarian refugees—there would be a muddy and uncertain thaw, greater discretion on the Russians' part in the exercise of their dominion, some patchy and hesitant relaxation in the party's grip, but no weakening of the Communist hold on Eastern Europe. In his analysis of the institutionalization of what had been a revolutionary movement, *The New Class* (1957), the Montenegrin Milovan Djilas drew the conclusions of the whole experience: "International Communism . . . at one time the task of revolutionaries, . . .became the common ground of Communist bureaucracies, fighting one another on national considerations." This would be still more clearly demonstrated a dozen years later when one more spring blossomed only to wither in yet another Communist capital: Prague.

Among the popular democracies of Eastern Europe, Czechoslovakia was the most modern, boasting the longest acquaintance with democracy and industrialism. Its decline since the Communist takeover in 1948 illustrated the deadening effects dogmatic Communism could have on advanced economies, and the slight chances of even *Communist* opposition to Soviet imperialism. In 1968, the Czech economy was still the fifth in Europe for coal production per head, the fourth for steel, the sixth for cement. But would-be Czech reformers, like the economist Ota Sik, were pointing out that emphasis on productivity in purely quantitative terms ignored consumer needs. The country's great industrial machine was engaged in production for production's sake, a race against ever-higher production norms that paid no heed to demand or quality, contributing nothing to the life of the Czechs themselves.

The ruling fascination with sheer output and statistics allowed machines to grow prematurely old, and turned production records into fakes. Where American metallurgy needed 272 pounds of steel to turn out 1,000 dollars' worth, the same job in Bohemia took 870 pounds of steel. In 1938, building a home had taken an average of 1,392 working hours; thirty years later it took 330 hours more. The atomic power station of Trnava, begun in 1958, still stood unfinished ten years later. In the United States a power station of the same potential would generally be finished in three years and a half. Czech productivity per head is 20 per cent higher than in France, yet Czech economists estimate French living standards to be well over twice as high as theirs: six times higher for engineers, double for factory workers. Something was surely wrong.

Just as important, Czech students and intellectuals in their turn were starting to react against the stifling regime to which they were subjected. It hardly seemed to them that the communism, socialism, and democracy they believed in need be expressed only in equality of dreariness and oppression. Under their impulse, with the support of factory workers and mere men-in-the-street, the Czech Communist Party went through an internal revolution, replacing its long-time Stalinist masters with new men, just as Communist but younger and more liberal minded. From January to August, 1968, "the spring of Prague" excited the hopes of Czechs and Slovaks, the sympathy of the world, the fear and the reproof of uneasy neighbors in Poland, Hungary, and East Germany.

While Moscow stayed its hand, it briefly seemed as if Communist regimes responding to the popular will could really become dictatorships of the proletariat, carrying out policies that found as much support in the trade unions and the Communist Party as in the countryside, the universities, and the national press. Supported by a great surge of national enthusiasm, guided by free discussion as it went along, the (communist) government proceeded with plans to modernize the economy, liberalize institutions, expand trade beyond the limited scope of the Communist bloc, permit a cooped-up people to travel abroad rather than merely flee. Such goings-on could not be tolerated long. In August, 1968, at long last, the country was invaded by a Communist force of 650,000 men, greater than the American armies at that time in Vietnam.* Passive resistance petered out before this overwhelming force and, on October 16, 1968, a treaty signed in Moscow legalized the country's occupa-

---

* On September 9, 1968, most Czech newspapers featured the words of Russian Army Marshal Gretchko, condemning the United States for "wishing to stifle by force of arms the love of a people for its liberty and independence."

Russian tanks enter Prague,
August, 1968.

tion by the Russians for an indeterminate length of time. Czechoslovakia, in its turn, ceased to be one of the rare European countries permitted to "edify its socialism" in the absence of the Red Army.

Moscow had energetically affirmed what is now known as the doctrine of limited sovereignty: the sovereignty of their satellites, its limits set by Moscow's appreciation of the superior interests of international communism. In 1968 as in 1956, these interests had been threatened by the liberal evolution of a neighboring Communist regime whose unforeseeable outcome might endanger the authority of dictatorship in Russia itself as well as the security of Russia's borders. As a Soviet spokesman explained,* "bourgeois" democratic liberties are a good thing in capitalist society, but bad in socialist society "for they are inevitably used by the remains of exploiting classes against the workers' interests." In actual practice, the men who crushed attempts at liberalization within their sphere acted in the tradition of the authoritarian rulers, feudal lords, and great bourgeois they once displaced, regarding the slightest reform as prelude to disintegration and trusting their fortune and their privileges only to the army and police.

What conclusions can one draw from such experience? It seems to follow that a Communist regime demands the lasting maintenance of censorship, of constraints, of the internal cold war that the Communist ideal once hoped to do away with. A revolution, said one Czech intellectual, makes sense only if it produces a better system than the one it overthrows. Communist revolutions, at least in Eastern Europe, seem to produce neither freedom nor well-being, their fragility turns attempts at self-expression into a menace and the criticism even of their own militants into subversion.

Nevertheless, even as Russian satellites, the Eastern Europeans continue to affirm their national personalities. Yugoslavia, of course, carries on the experiment on which it embarked in the mid-1940's. Romania carries on a subtler campaign of national emancipation, affirming her independence from the COMECON—the common market of the Soviet bloc—and doing her best to establish diplomatic and trade relations with

* *Le Monde,* Paris, September 20, 1968.

non-Communist countries, including France, West Germany, and Israel. The economic and industrial reforms that Ota Sik suggested, and that the Czechs tried in 1968, were introduced in Hungary as early as 1966 and Sik's writings are still used in courses at the University of Budapest. Since Hungary discreetly introduced her liberal reforms, industrial productivity has gone up by 30 to 50 per cent, trade balances have become more favorable, wages and prices have remained stable. One may expect other Communist satellites to imitate her methods. The collaborationist rulers of occupied Czechoslovakia themselves are sometimes anti-Stalinists, as concerned to get the Russians out of their land as they are to keep their clique in power. The 650,000 Russian and East German soldiers sent to do away with dangers symbolized above all by a free press can be taken as much for a promise as for a threat. Spring, after all, is a recurring phenomenon.

Turkey

Despite divisions and defeats, the years of the Young Turks saw many positive changes. Modernization proceeded, middle-class education got a serious start. A gendarmerie was created to keep the army out of politics, a measure of land reform begun, municipal reform brought drains and even garbagemen to cities like Constantinople. But the new men were unable to solve the basic problem of an Ottoman nation hard put to enlist the loyalties of its subject peoples. They had sought to apply nationalistic doctrines evolved in culturally homogeneous nations to an empire not only multinational and multiracial but multireligious too. Could Muslims and non-Muslims live as equals, when the Muslim faith said no? Were they, indeed, to identify themselves as Muslims or, above all, as Turks? These were almost insoluble questions until the nationalists realized that they could best imitate Western nationalism not by trying to copy Western models but by being themselves.. The turn from Ottoman hangovers to Turkish nationalism was facilitated when defeat in 1918 brought final collapse of the anachronistic Empire and loss of its non-Turkish territories.

Allied with the Central Powers, Turkish troops had fought stoutly on several fronts, beaten off an attempted allied landing at Gallipoli, and even forced a British army to surrender in Iraq. But—though they put on as good a show as their Russian enemies and kept it up longer than the Russians—the strain proved too much for the farflung realm which lacked the administrative and industrial substructure for a modern war. As Germany and Austria weakened, as French and Greek troops drove the Bulgarians back from the Aegean coast, the Turkish front crumbled

Mustapha Kemal
(Ataturk) at the
window of his per-
sonal train car.

before British armies driving north from Mesopotamia and Palestine.
Soon, English, French, Greek, and Italian troops were occupying the
country which seemed to have disintegrated completely. Then, in the
highlands of Anatolia, Turkish nationalism regathered its forces under the leadership of the country's only victorious general: Mustafa
Kemal (1881–1938)—the future Ataturk. The stubborn courage of the
Turkish troops, the generalship of Kemal (already responsible for Turkish success at Gallipoli), supplemented dissensions among the victors
who quarreled over spoils. British, French, and Italians withdrew, leaving the Greeks, who dreamed of a new Byzantium, to face the Turks
alone. By 1922 the Greeks had been defeated and, in 1923, the Treaty
of Lausanne set the borders of the new Turkish nation where they
stand today.*

The great losses of Ottoman dominions in Asia were compensated
by the national revival which, in a few years, had shaken off all traces of
foreign domination. Turkey was now a republic, the Ottoman dynasty
was banished, the capital was no longer in cosmopolitan Constantinople
(renamed Istanbul) but in Anatolian Ankara; Kemal was president.
His dictatorship would be nationalist, secular, and progressive, breaking with the past and modernizing the country as fast as it could bear—in
many cases faster. The Gregorian calendar was introduced, the twenty-
four hour clock, Western dress; the fez and the veil were driven to oblivion, religious law was abandoned and religious courts replaced by the
Swiss civil code, polygamy was excluded, and equal rights were introduced for all religions, the Latin alphabet replaced the Arabic, women
were given the right to vote, surnames and weekly holidays were introduced and titles abolished. Before his death in 1938, Ataturk, the most
beneficial of dictators, had not only remade his country but dragged it
grudgingly, reluctantly, into the twentieth century.

Such measures were slow to take effect. Literacy, about 10 per cent

---

* The Treaty of Lausanne acknowledged Turkey's hold of eastern Thrace up to the
Maritsa Line, leaving better than one million Greeks in Turkish territory and half that
many Turks in Greek areas. The problem was solved by a vast exchange and resettlement of populations which, after the first difficulties, allowed the Greco-Turkish rift to
heal until the recent Cyprus troubles.

in the 1920's, was only 35 per cent in 1950. But, where in 1926 there were six times as many wooden plows as iron, today the wooden plow has disappeared and agricultural production rides forward into the age of tractors and combines. Still poor, backward, overpopulated for its underdeveloped resources, Turkey is nevertheless the most advanced and stable of Islamic nations, and this must be attributed to Ataturk's policies.

A crucial component of these policies was the reassertion of an independent state, establishing good relations with the neighbors who had been the Empire's subjects or its enemies. Relations with Communist Russia remained distant but not unfriendly, for Turkey, well aware of the territorial ambitions of her ancient rival, had no particular fear of Communist doctrines and no great fear of the Soviets until their power and expansionism revived. It seemed more urgent to keep southeastern Europe outside the scope of the power struggle developing in the 1930's. Toward this end Turkish diplomacy created the Balkan Entente of 1934, from which Albania and Bulgaria were kept by Italian pressure but which Romania, Greece, and Yugoslavia joined. If the Entente did not succeed in keeping war out of the Balkans, Kemal's heirs at least kept Turkey itself out of the war. Professor Bernard Lewis quotes a Turkish saying during the Second World War: "What we would really like would be for the Germans to destroy Russia and for the Allies to destroy Germany. Then we would feel safe."

Torn between sympathy for the Allies, traditional fear of Russia, and even greater fear of costly involvement, the Turks maintained a difficult neutrality until February, 1945, when, like other neutrals, they declared war on Germany in order to join the United Nations conference. The end of war meant new concerns for safety, however, for the German threat had been replaced by that of Russia, now an expansionist power once again, particularly dangerous since Communist propaganda could hope to get a hold on the half-educated masses of a partly secularized land. Reluctantly, the Turkish government abandoned its nonalignment policy, accepting American aid and, in due course, American military bases.

Partly as a result of these new orientations the ruling dictatorship relaxed its hold. In 1950 the country's first free and fair elections brought the opposition Democrats into power after twenty-seven years of rule by Kemal's Republican People's Party. Events would show that political democracy was not so easy to maintain and that the ultimate decisions still rested with the army. A two-party system and a hesitant advance toward freer political activity have marked the last few years. On the other hand, freedom of expression (however relative) has allowed reaction against the forced march into the twentieth century to assert itself. Turkey exports emigrant laborers to the West, and very little else. The country is declining once again into traditional torpor, a return that suggests that—like certain wines—Western political institutions travel badly and that, perhaps, Western views on the virtues of productivity, efficiency, or, even, simply work, find it hard to take root in unfamiliar ground.

The United States: A Special Case

If anyone doubted that the United States was one of the world's great powers, they could not continue to doubt it after the First World War. American supplies and loans had been decisive in the survival of the Allies, American intervention in the defeat of the Central Powers, American diplomacy in the drafting of the peace treaties, American internal policy in abandoning Europe to its own devices. President Wilson was a great reformer but a tactless, single-minded man. His failure in political maneuver, his zealous prickliness, ensured defeat first in Congress and then in national elections. The crusading policies he represented were voted down, business as usual voted back again in a succession of conservative presidents who believed with Calvin Coolidge that "the business of the United States is business," not costly meddling in world politics. This meant that the foreign policy of one of the world's great powers affected international affairs between the wars chiefly by abstention—or, more correctly, by continuous attempts to keep out of things.

The United States, like King Canute, made resolute moves to order back the tide of modern life. It curbed the flow of immigrants ("America must be kept American": Coolidge), smiled on the Ku Klux Klan with its "white, gentile, Protestant" membership, legislated against the teaching of evolution in schools, prohibited (by the 18th Amendment to the Constitution, 1919–1933) "the manufacture, sale or transportation of intoxicating liquors," and did its best to design legislation meant, as one historian has described it, to keep the country out of the war of 1914.

The war had bitten deeply into European investments. By 1918 the 6.5 billion of 1914 had been cut by half. The United States was now the world's greatest creditor, having lent nearly 2 billion to her allies in 1917–1919 and invested another 9 billion in Europe in 1919 alone. But the political mentality with which she approached the postwar world had been developed in the debtor era and reflected the defensiveness of mortgaged farmers, developing industries, and debt-ridden utility companies. Here lay the rationale of protection which wrecked all possibilities of sensible arrangements by which the outer world could have bought U.S. industrial products and settled accounts by exporting its crops and less sophisticated goods.

Yet, if Americans did not wish to buy, they were quite willing to invest. After the First World War (and especially after the Second), American capital supplanted European as the dominant economic power south of the Rio Grande, seeking to organize the vast region according to the needs of American industry. About one-third of the capital invested in Latin America comes from the United States, with which a great proportion of the continent's foreign trade is conducted (90 per cent of Mexican imports, 75 per cent of Mexican exports). In Cuba (1930) American sugar companies owned one-fifth of the land surface, two-thirds of the sugar refineries. while most of the remainder depended on U.S. credits. In Central America, the United Fruit Company owned more land than the whole of Belgium, operated most of the railroads, employed armies of laborers, and dominated national production. In Venezuela, where 17 per cent of the world's oil is produced, American companies controlled its exploitation.

Franklin Roosevelt's Good Neighbor Policy, restraint in intervening, tactful diplomacy, improved relations between the Northern and Southern Hemisphere until, in 1945, all American nations signed the Act of Chapultepec, which, in effect, discarded the unilateral use of the Monroe Doctrine in favor of a regional security system within the United Nations. But latent hostility persisted and the U.S. tendency to intervene when its interests were threatened persisted too. The supremacy that soon became clear in the U.S.'s back yard would take longer elsewhere, but would be as firmly asserted. Until the late 1920's, the resources that the European economy needed to rebuild itself came in good part from American banks. Then, a speculative boom based on security prices inflated beyond any reasonable expectation of earnings, stanched and reversed the flow. In 1928 American capital which had sought profits from European (especially German) investments began to find that it could make a better profit right at home. In 1929 the precarious credit structure on which the boom was based collapsed, and American investors had to scramble for any liquid funds they could get their hands on, recalling short-term loans and, of course, investing no more. The consequent economic depression made payment of Allied war debts even more difficult, at the very time when America's own problems made her even more determined to fend off products which could have paid the interest. "The debts of the outside world to us are ropes about their necks, by means of which we pull them towards us," declared the president of Chase National Bank in 1930. "Our trade restrictions are pitchforks pressed against their bodies, by means of which we hold them off."

Except for Finland, all of America's debtors defaulted on their debts; upon which Congress took steps to see that such a situation would not recur again, by prohibiting all defaulting nations from floating loans or securities in the United States (Johnson Act, 1934). But prevention was even more important than revenge. The United States must not again, at any price, become involved in the profitless conflicts of the outer world. A Gallup Poll showed that 70 per cent of Americans thought it had been a mistake to enter the Great War. In the summer of 1935, while

Mussolini made it clear he was about to break the peace, Congress adopted the first of a series of neutrality measures prohibiting credits, loans, export of arms or implements of war to belligerents, and making very clear American unwillingness ever again to become entangled in a foreign conflict—including, said an act of 1937, the kind of civil war then raging in Spain.

What had been made between 1934 and 1937 had to be unmade as best as President Roosevelt could in 1940, when German victory in Europe indicated that American security could not be cut off from world affairs. The U.S. aided Britain (Lend-Lease) and extended aid to Russia when she was attacked. But the Germans, remembering their earlier mistake, stayed their hand. It was the Japanese who forced it. The Japanese trying to conquer China, felt that only U.S. support permitted it to hold out against them. The United States refused to curb their aid to China or make concessions to Japanese needs. On December 7, 1941, the Pacific fleet at Pearl Harbor and the air force base at Manila were destroyed from the air and, within a few days, the United States, unprepared for the actions her politics precipitated, found herself at war with Japan and with Japan's German and Italian allies.

This time, victory found the United States quite willing to face her responsibilities throughout a world in which she now towered as the richest, strongest power. Unfortunately, as an opponent of German colonial policy once remarked, "World politics is for a nation what megalomania is for an individual." General de Gaulle complained about President Roosevelt's "will to power cloaking itself in idealism"; and this would be increasingly felt about Roosevelt's country after Roosevelt's death, as the will to power began to wear through the ideals. Ignorance, benevolence, self-interest, good intentions, a rough-and-ready naïveté, and the readiness to believe that arms could solve problems which wealth could not cure, characterized American politics into the 1960's.

There was nothing particularly wicked about this, only a giant's fumbling joy in his force and natural confidence in his own judgment. The United States is only the latest inheritor of an imperial role which others before her have handled with alternative presumption and dismay under the suspicious, wary, or hostile eyes of the other powers. The natural expression of power, riches, and abounding energies is never really matched by wisdom or foresight to everyone's satisfaction. It only becomes significant when its results affect not only a restricted area but the world itself, and this is truer today than it ever was.

Chapter 20

THE MATERIAL
REVOLUTION

Technology and Production

In 1776 when Adam Smith wanted to demonstrate the wonders of modern mass production he used the example of ten workers producing 48,000 needles a day. A hundred years later a machine turned out 180 needles a minute, so the ten workers would have produced 2 million needles a day. The textile worker who turned out 9,600 yards of cotton in a thirteen-hour work day in 1840 was turning out 300,000 yards in ten hours in 1880. Cyrus McCormick's Harvester allowed one American farmer to harvest seventeen acres in the time that one European scythed through one.

The marvels of eighteenth-century technology were dwarfed by the nineteenth century, as these in turn were due to be left behind by the twentieth. The high priest of this acceleration was the engineer, whom Tennyson hymned in his *Mechanophilus*.

> Now first we stand and understand,
> And sunder false and true,
> And handle boldly with the hand,
> And see and shape and do.
>
> Dash back that ocean with a pier,
> Strow yonder mountain flat,
> A railway there, a tunnel here,
> Mix me this Zone with that!

978

The engineer's product was the machine, turning out more machines, ever more precise, ever more interchangeable, ever more productive.

Without specialized machine tools there could be no mass production of goods on a modern scale, without the high precision of their construction there could be no mass production of machines themselves, no replaceable parts, none of the fine and complex web of industry that we associate with the modern age. Improved machines allowed their own materials to be turned out in greater quantities and at lower prices. Coal —"the modern philosopher's stone," whose gas was used for light, whose tars went into benzine and anilines, whose elements could be used, like picrates for explosives and which itself provided fuel for power, heat, and locomotion—was being mined in greater quantities: 90 million tons in 1850 (ten times the total of sixty years before), 1 billion in 1900, 1.5 billion in 1950. Iron: 5 million tons in 1850, 44 million in 1900, 130 million in 1950.* In 1875 Sidney Gilchrist Thomas discovered a process for refining phosphoric iron ores, thus making available great deposits of previously useless ores like the *minette* of Lorraine just acquired by Germany. And, just as England had been responsible for the avalanche of cheap iron that covered the nineteenth century, so it would be an English engineer, Henry Bessemer, whose converter (1856–1858) turned hitherto rare steel into a democratic commodity, not only six or seven times more resistant than iron but now accessible in price. From 1825 to 1866 the price of iron had fallen by two-thirds. In the next fifteen years steel followed suit, and in America, where technological expertise was most advanced and production highest, the price of steel rails fell 90 per cent between 1875 and 1898.

Mass production, of course, depends on mass consumption. The most striking evidence of the machines' success at the everyday level was the increased availability of consumer goods of the most ordinary kind— soap, chocolate, cheap paper, or beef extract—none of which had been so ordinary in earlier days. The lead pencil, developed in the eighteenth century, was only mass-produced after the 1850's. So was newsprint (15

---

* In terms of volume, nine-tenths of all the world's mining—not just coal or iron— would be carried out after 1800.

A mechanized bakery. A dog-powered tread-mill outside the building operates the kneading machines illustrated here.

cents a pound in 1867, half that price fifteen years later). Pens with steel nibs, used in the first half of the century in lieu of quills, also became cheaper: 2 dollars a gross in 1830, 12 cents a gross in 1861. Fountain pens, appearing in the 1830's, became generally available in the 1880's, at the same time as inexpensive watches. Very costly portable cameras were metamorphosed by 1900 into the Brownie box camera which anyone could buy for 5 shillings or a dollar.*

In 1850 Isaac M. Singer marketed the first practical sewing machine, providing a great spur to ready-made clothing, whose value in production doubled within the decade. By 1880 boot and shoe manufacturers had applied similar machines to their needs, reducing the cost of sewing them some twenty-seven times. At first, home seamstresses could not afford to buy sewing machines and lost a lot of trade, while workshops, prisons, and convents that installed them competed with home dressmakers.** By the 1860's sewing machines began appearing in private homes, first in the United States, then throughout the world. Another humble engine which had a great impact was the velocipede: "Machine equipped with two, three or four wheels, activated by the feet and which permits one to move faster than a horse." The original high-wheeled bicycles with solid rubber tires were soon replaced by modern types with pneumatic tires and proper brakes. In the 1890's a bicycle was still a middle-class article, costing in France about 500 francs or $100—equivalent to two months of a lieutenant's pay. By 1900, at a third of this price, it had become accessible even to workers.

On its own humble level the bicycle was an invention as revolutionary as the automobile, opening distance to persons who had seldom gone far beyond their homes for lack of individual means of locomotion. Village swains could get on their bicycles on Sundays to court girls who lived in another valley, five or ten miles away. Women, long restricted in their movements, could mount their pedaled steeds and leave the chaperone behind. Physical mobility was the symbol of social and economic mobility, the prelude of more. By 1900, a million bicycles were being turned out in the United States.

This was the period when machines began to invade the home and office: carpet sweepers, washing machines, telephones, all in the 1870's, electric bells in 1880, electric fans, vacuum cleaners, and phonographs (invented by Thomas Edison in 1878) in the 1890's, refrigerators after 1900. The house, no longer a mere shelter as it had been until then, became a comfort, a machine for use and pleasure as very few of our ancestors could enjoy or imagine. White transparent window glass, a conquest of the seventeenth century which must have made an immense

* In 1884, Pope Leo XIII, who liked photography, had one of the Vatican galleries embellished with frescoes of religion blessing the arts, including Photography with her attendant cherub holding a large camera.

** Incidentally, this explains the hostility of many workers in European countries to the competition of convents and charity workshops.

A patent office illustration for an early motorized vacuum cleaner.

difference to domestic comfort, was still lacking in most peasant houses by 1800, when shutters, boards, or other means closed the scarce openings. By 1900 the poorest could enjoy it. Running water, central heating, electric light, the facilities offered by modern utilities, not to speak of air conditioning, were all conquests of the last century which may have affected our lives more than the airplane or the cyclotron.

Most of the new inventions depended not on steam but on electric power: not least electric light, made possible partly by Edison's invention of the incandescent lamp in 1879. While gas light continued to light streets and homes well into the twentieth century, the 1880's would see public and private buildings lit by electric light and electric traction motorizing first streetcars, then underground railways. The Chicago World's Fair of 1893 included the exhibition of a model electric kitchen: the shape of things to come, but not at once.

In 1886, Monsieur de Goncourt visited an American lawyer in Paris to sign a contract concerning one of his plays and reported that "the act was printed on a little piano." The typewriter had become a commercial possibility in the 1870's. It would soon be joined by calculating machines, cash registers, and tabulators—ancestors of the first modern computer, which IBM developed in 1943. Soon the question would arise of reconciling men and machines, fitting them one to the other, designing machines for the best results, training their users to use them to the best advantage. The notion would be first applied to adjust workmen as thoroughly as possible to the potentials and needs of their machine. Around 1900, an engineer, Frederick Taylor, raised the efficiency of coal shovelers by analyzing their movements and cutting out all unnecessary ones; another engineer, F. B. Gilbreth, did the same for bricklayers by reducing stooping and arranging their tools in a more practical way. Taylor initiated "time and motion studies," first at Bethlehem Steel, then elsewhere, to determine the standard time of each workman's task and to increase the productivity of workers. By 1907 Taylor's methods were applied by men like Henry Ford, who introduced a moving assembly line to turn out his Model T, cutting assembly time from 14 hours to 93 minutes per car. Europeans, who denounced Taylorism for turning the workman into a cretinized automaton, were not long in learning the lessons of "scientific management" when they found that it worked, and that in plants where it was applied the production index soared even while, as in the case of Ford, the wages could be higher for fewer hours of work.

New Links, New Trails

Alfred Marshall, the economist, remarked in 1890 that "the dominant economic fact of our age is the development not of manufacturing but of transport industries." The greatest of these in Marshall's day was still the railroads—the first great web in which nineteenth-century man organized his space and eventually, as we shall see, his time. "All railways," asserted a member of the British Parliament in 1844, "are public frauds and private robberies." But he was a lonely holdout. Forty-five thousand miles in 1860, 450,000 in 1895, 700,000 in 1910, steel rails spread their tentacles over the world. Great tunnels through the Swiss and Austrian Alps (Mont Cénis in 1871, Saint Gotthard 1882, Arlberg 1884, Simplon 1906) linked France and Italy, Germany and Italy, Switzerland and Austria, facilitating exchanges between North and South, East and West, and making Switzerland the turntable of Europe.

Charles Dickens, visiting America in the 1840's, already reports passenger cars with corridors and sleeping arrangements. G. M. Pullman's first sleepers appeared in the early 60's, his dining car in 1867. Europe was slower: sleeping cars appeared on trains in 1883 and dining cars in 1884, at the same time as great international expresses like the Orient Express, whose luxuries caught the popular imagination. But local passenger services were even more important. Cheap workmen's fares, "to

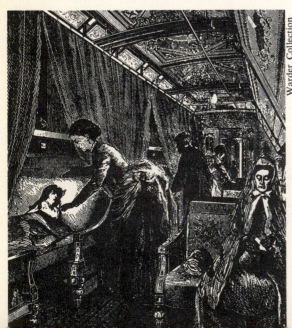

Warder Collection

A contemporary illustration of one of the first Pullman sleepers.

encourage the migration of the working classes into suburbs" and relieve housing congestion in the center, came in during the 60's and the 70's. Elevated and underground railways, appearing in the 1860's, extended the urban area and created new residential districts. Tramways, which have been called the gondolas of the people, also cut the time workers needed to get to work while helping bring new areas like public parks and sports grounds within their reach.

The trains wore down distinct regional cultures based on isolation and a large measure of self-sufficiency, fused separate regions divided as much by different rates of change as by cultural divisions, broke down local markets. The introduction of rail freight cut shipping costs by half to three-fourths in the earliest days and, shortly, far more than that. In 1817 it cost $140 to ship a ton of freight from Pittsburgh to Philadelphia; seventy years later $3 or less. In Nigeria, in 1926, a man could still choose between porters, trucks, and rail in cost proportions of 15 to 6 to 1. In remote regions where the high cost of porterage had made only the shipment of very costly goods (ivory, gold) economic, railroads—however expensive to build and operate—revolutionized the carriage of bulk freight. Where the trains went, local building materials were supplanted by cheaper bricks and slates, later by cement. The trains, which facilitated migration and hence cosmopolitanism, also facilitated the tendency to industrial concentration and specialization, accelerated the growing uniformity of the economic and cultural landscape. Rails turned the states they bound together into nations—Germany, Italy, the United States, Canada, Russia, India—with common concerns and a common center of gravity.

Timetables played their part in standardizing time itself, which had long differed from place to place. On England's Great Western Railway a timetable of July 30, 1841, indicates in a footnote that "London time is about 4 minutes earlier than Reading time, 7½ minutes before Cirencester, 14 minutes before Bridgewater." Engineers and travelers had to make their own adjustments until, in the early 1850's, the telegraph allowed time signals to be sent from London with which all stations could synchronize. From that point on, "railway time" spread from station into village, town, and hinterland, gradually bringing London time—that is Greenwich Standard Time—to every place.* No wonder that colonial powers, which wanted to assert their control over the vast spaces they possessed and harness their potential to their needs, built railroads like the Russian Trans-Siberian or the British over India, which by 1940 still had more railway mileage than all the rest of Asia. No wonder either that, with over a third of the world's railroads in North America and another third in Europe, the Western world outstripped all other areas in wealth and in cohesion.* *

* With the exception of holdouts like Christ Church Cathedral in Oxford, whose clock still clings to local time.
** By 1920, total African and Asian mileage was less than a third that of the United States.

Technology was advancing on the seas as well, forging new links between the continents. In 1620 the *Mayflower* had taken 66 days to cross the Atlantic. In 1776 news of the Declaration of Independence took 44 days to reach Europe. Mid-nineteenth-century packets were taking 21 days, the fastest clippers 14 days or so, iron steamships 9 or 10. The 1930's would cut the length of passage to 4 days. But steam took a long time supplanting sail, and the world's steam tonnage only caught up with that of sailing ships in 1893. The real advantage of steamships was that, no longer dependent on wind, they could hold a schedule which sailing ships could not be sure of doing. But for a long time fuel problems made them relatively uneconomic until, in the 1860's, new screw propellers replaced paddle wheels and new compound engines, demanding less fuel, left more space for cargo. This was when rates on bulk freight began to fall, and export of wheat, meats, and minerals to soar, turning the whole world into one great marketplace.

A great spur to overseas trade came with the invention of refrigeration. Ice cut from lakes and rivers, preserved in ice houses, exported all over the world in special storage tanks, had been for some time a minor American industry. American home consumption in 1876 had been more than 2 million tons, and the industry employed 10,000 men and 4,000 horses. Artificial ice began to be manufactured in the 1860's, mechanical refrigerators for the house in 1900, but not in mass production until the 1920's. The first refrigerated steamers sailed to Europe in 1877 carrying frozen mutton. In 1883 the first modern packing plant was set up near Buenos Aires. By that time refrigerated shipments of fruit and dairy products, as well as meat, were coming not only from America but from New Zealand and Australia.

The real breakthrough came when the Suez Canal, opened in 1869 (with Verdi's *Aida* written especially for its inauguration), cut the distance between Europe and China by 3,000 miles. In 1862 the journey from Marseilles to Bombay had taken 26 days; in 1872 Jules Verne's Phileas Fogg took 18 days from his London club (and 80 days to go around the world). Ten years after the opening of the Suez Canal, freight rates between Europe and India had fallen to a quarter of their previous cost. Other canals followed: in 1893 the Corinth Canal that Nero had dreamed of digging linked the Aegean and the Ionian Seas; in 1895 the Kiel Canal shortened the distance between the North Sea and the Baltic; in 1914 the Panama Canal joined the Atlantic and Pacific Oceans. The dreams of the Saint-Simonians had been realized. The volume of international trade grew fiftyfold between 1800 and 1900.

By then the internal combustion engine was replacing steam in ships as on the land. Worked on throughout the 1860's and the 70's by men in Germany, Austria, and Italy, the internal combustion engine and the carburetor were first patented by Gottlieb Daimler in 1885. His automobile inspired other engineers, like René Panhard and Armand Peugeot in France, Karl Bentz in Germany, R. E. Olds, J. W. Packard, and the Dodge brothers in the United States to build models of their own. Rudolf Diesel—a German born in Paris—would develop his oil injection engine in 1893. Horses and carriages—dust on hedgerows and on roadside grass in summer, mud that stuck carriages in winter, click of horses' hooves and clatter of wheels over paving, smell of horse manure—still dominated the railway age: coach and cab, berlin, barouche, daumont and Landau and phaeton and coupe, rolled and rattled over country lanes and through city streets. By 1900, however, some 4,000 autos were running over city cobbles or country ruts, exhilarating to their drivers, a dangerous nuisance to everybody else. By 1914 there were two million of them, and they could reach speeds as high as 50 m.p.h.

The auto industry stimulated other enterprises: tarred roads which made auto movement possible ended the dust problem of the early days, the rubber industry which had developed pneumatic tires for bicycles (1885) now found a growing market in automobiles (Dunlop pneumatic tires, 1900) and increased demand for its raw materials from South America, India, and Southeast Asia; manufacturers of steel, glass, plastics, electrical accessories, and machine tools all profited. So did newly motorized bandits. But the greatest beneficiary was the petroleum industry, which had appeared in the 1850's to supply paraffin and kerosene for lamps and stoves, petroleum as a lubricant, and oil for ship's boilers.

Oil, preferably derived from sperm whales, began by being used mostly for lubrication and to fuel oil lamps. When in mid-century whales began to run out, interest shifted to mineral sources meagerly tapped in France and England, the United States, and eastern Europe. Romania produced crude petroleum in 1857, but the first commercial production of it came in Pennsylvania at the end of that decade. Soon other countries were following suit, especially Russia, whose oil fields

Warder Collection

Victoria Embankment in London during the early 1900's.

The Wright Brothers' first flight at Kitty Hawk, North Carolina. Opposite: a Fokker F-32, one of the most popular early commercial planes, which accommodated 32 passengers.

National Archives

around Baku in the Caucasus produced more crude oil than Americans did by the beginning of our century. Though still mostly used for lighting and lubrication, world crude oil production rose from half a million barrels in 1860 to 400 million in 1914. By then it was being used to feed the growing appetite of cars, ships, trains, and even airplanes. By 1962 the world production of crude oil would be over a billion tons a year * and the United States (since 1902 the leading producer) accounted for almost a third of it.

The internal combustion engine increased mobility and opportunities even more than trains. Regular motor omnibuses began to run in London in 1904 and 1916 saw the last horsedrawn bus. Motor taxis were replacing hansom cabs; in 1912 a hansom was placed in a London museum. In 1911 the London Fire Brigade abandoned horses for internal combustion engines. Motor buses provided the poor with the first real opportunity for day trips to seacoasts or countryside that most had never seen before, and stressed the opportunity to escape from towns to suburban living. So did cars which supplemented commuter transport, creating the tentacular suburban spreads characteristic of the twentieth century, new settlements "composed," as A. J. P. Taylor puts it, "of little more than individual motor cars come to rest." The effects were revolutionary. Most of the children in John Steinbeck's *Cannery Row* (1944) were, as he says, "conceived in Model T Fords and not a few were born in them. The theory of the Anglo-Saxon home became so warped that it never quite recovered." The automobile could also be highly destructive. Today, 200,000 people die and 5 million are maimed yearly in road accidents: more in all, so far, than all the casualties of both world wars.

Sea and land transportation were not alone affected: the internal combustion engine also made possible the control of flight. We have seen that balloons, born before the French Revolution and put to use in its wars, had caught the popular fancy. But their use was strictly limited by steerage problems. During the siege of Paris in 1870, when balloons provided the only means of communication with the outside world, carrying 2.5 million letters, 400 pigeons, 102 passengers, and 2 dogs, of 66 balloons launched from Paris only 58 landed safely. The rest ended in

* In 1956, at the time of the Suez crisis, the non-Communist world consumed 690 million tons of oil turned out by an industry with assets of 38 billion dollars. By the Middle East War of 1967 both these figures had doubled, and they are expected to double again by 1980.

Prussian territory, out at sea, in Holland, Munich, and one even in Norway some 2,000 miles away.*

In 1900 a retired German cavalry general, Count Ferdinand von Zeppelin, conceived and built the first heavier-than-air dirigible airship, almost concurrently with the first powered, sustained, and controlled flight of an airplane made by the Wright brothers at Kitty Hawk, North Carolina (1903). Airships would carry over 20,000 persons before 1914 and render great services during the First World War; but their advantages were less than the dangerous flammability of the gases in their skin, and they were ultimately abandoned in favor of the airplane, whose development proved incredibly swift. In 1909 a Frenchman, Louis Blériot, flew the English Channel. The First World War gave aircraft a great impetus, confirming high expectations of their more murderous possibilities. The 1920's would see airplanes entering into general use, the building of airports serving the cities, the first nonstop flight from New York to Paris,** the development of air mail and of passenger transport. By 1933 the airplane had cut Phileas Fogg's record of sixty years before by nine-tenths, circling the world in less than eight days. However, the routines we take for granted today are very recent. In 1946, the Dutch National airline KLM established the first regular flights between Europe and New York; in 1947 Pan American began scheduled round-the-world flights. Where air travel had logged 8 billion passenger kilometers in 1945, it counted 275 billion in 1967, not including Russia and China.

There was yet a faster means of communication: telegraphy. In 1860, messages were still relayed by the same means as Caesar used. While stagecoaches still took three weeks from St. Joseph, Missouri, to San Francisco, the pony express proved that it could carry urgent dispatches in half that time. Within one year the transcontinental telegraph had put it out of business by taking only seconds for the job. The telegraph was not new in 1861. The new development of the mid-nineteenth century was its extension, in part by underwater cables which linked Europe to England in 1851, to the United States in 1866, to India in 1870, to Australia in

---

* Pigeons supplemented balloons in carrying letters for which a microfilm process was developed. Every pigeon carried six tiny films, each containing 5,000 letters. While the Prussians used hawks against the pigeons, Krupp developed a special anti-aircraft gun to check the air lift.

** By Colonel Charles Lindbergh in 1927. Two Englishmen had made the first crossing of the Atlantic from Newfoundland to Ireland in 1919.

1871. "They have killed their father Time," wrote Rudyard Kipling of *Deep Sea Cables:*

> . . . Hush! Men talk today o'er the waste of the ultimate slime,
> and a new Word runs between: whispering, "Let us be one!"

Ocean cables set up a novel and extraordinary link between different continents. An urgent message from London or Paris to New York could not be answered in less than three weeks before 1866; one to India in less than two months before 1870; one to Australia in less than four months before 1872. After those days they took minutes.* The result was a revolution in trade, diplomacy, and news-gathering of every kind. The price of commodities and grain, the evolution of a political situation, could be followed hour by hour rather than after laborious delays. Orders could be placed, commodities bought, ships redirected—and this was further facilitated by the use of radio telegraphy. G. Marconi sent the first radio message in 1894, his first trans-Atlantic signal in 1901. In 1900 Emil Rathenau, president of the great German electrical trust of AEG, set up the first radio aerial on the roof of his Berlin building, and within a few years radio contact had been established with Germany and the world. By then, ships at sea could get radio messages, the importance of which was publicized when the "unsinkable" *Titanic* sank in 1912.**

Improved communications meant that every kind of postal service grew apace: gummed stamps and the penny post had multiplied the number of letters sent in England to over half a billion a year by 1860. The Germans, who in 1840 dispatched 1.5 letters per inhabitant, were sending about 60 per inhabitant yearly in 1900. The U.S. Post Office sold 1.5 million stamps in 1850, 4 billion in 1900, six times as many in 1960. Europeans, who sent 9 million telegrams in 1898, were sending nearly 400 million before the First World War. There were 12 million telephones in 1908, 171 million in 1964 (nearly half of them in the United States). Materially the world was contracting, its separate parts being pulled closer to one another, the great trade fairs of the Middle

---

* Shortly the cables would also be used for telephones: a London-Paris telephone line opened in 1891.

** Radar, which uses a directional radio impulse to find the range and bearing of aircraft, ships, or other moving objects, and television were further developments of the discovery of how to transmit sound waves by electrical impulses. The first ship equipped with radar appeared in 1938, the first transmission of television signals was made in 1927, the first commercial television program was broadcast in the late 1930's after the Olympic Games held in Berlin in 1936 had been televised. Meanwhile, electronic research developed tubes capable of emitting ever shorter waves. After 1932, electronic optics developed electronic microscopes (capable of distinguishing to 1/100,000 of a millimeter), telescopes (which can work 120 times as rapidly as their predecessors), spectrographs, photoelectric cells (electric eyes) used in sound film, radar, and TV. Norbert Wiener developed cybernetics based on the analogy between electronics and the human brain.

Ages replaced by a spate of international exhibitions, the international rivalries overlaid by international agreements: to treat wounded and medical personnel decently in war (1864), standardize weights and measures (1875), establish a world postal union (1878), protect works of literature and art by copyright (1886), settle conflicts by international arbitration (1907), or, if unsettled, fight them out according to accepted rules (1907).

Industrial Progress and its Problems

The world of 1900 was more complicated than it had ever been. Men —even enemies—had to co-operate in order to function. All this resulted from technological changes taking place gradually but with increasing acceleration. On the European continent and in North America the years to 1870 or so saw only the beginnings of industrial revolution: the basic accumulation of equipment, the growth and reinvestment of capital, the rapid rise of population and its migration from country to towns, the increasing supply of consumer goods and, more slowly, of agricultural products. After 1871, the application of electricity in industry and the rise of industry in central Europe ushered in a second industrial revolution, marked by an immense development of synthetic products, dyestuffs, cosmetics, insecticides, drugs, plastics, synthetic rubber or fabrics, but, above all, by a shift in the source of industrial power from steam to internal combustion and diesel, from coal to oil and electricity. This meant that the balance of economic power shifted from the older industrial countries to new ones which adjusted more rapidly (Germany and Japan) or which enjoyed richer sources of new power (the United States and Russia) , and the balance of industry shifted from railways to automobiles and tractors and trucks and airplanes.

The new industrial revolution was backed by the spread of machinery to the land, and the consequent rise in agricultural production and fall in food prices. While the population stabilized, removing the pressure of new mouths, the living and consumption standards of the popular masses, which had been little improved or adversely affected by the first industrial stages, bettered markedly despite—and sometimes because of—the brutal break of the First World War. The depression which began in 1929 masked the technological developments that would accelerate economic progress, bring new and basic changes in the ways and standards of all whom they affected—largely beginning around 1950. A second century of technological progress opened, whose crux seems to be its—painful—spread to vast areas which have remained in an earlier stage of economic development. Obviously, India or China live in conditions similar to those obtaining in the days of Frederick the Great and, while the majority of English or French people are just gaining the comforts which most Americans of the late 1930's took for granted, the economic level of Spain or Greece today is better compared with that of Bismarck's Europe.

Historically, this too is a new situation precipitated only in the last two centuries. In 1700, at least as regards essentials—that is, food—all the world's peoples faced similar circumstances. By 1800 this was no longer so even in Europe; by 1900 the differences were startling. It now looks as if the closing of the gap, which we have observed first within industrial societies, then within the area of their influence, will be the chief purpose and, it is hoped, the main effect of future technological developments. The crux of these lies in productivity; for it is interesting to note that whereas the indispensable raw material of the first industrial revolution was human, after 1913 not manpower but machine power accounted for increased production. Tractors, reapers, and other gear turned farmers into mechanics and agricultural labor into something performed largely by machines. In Russia 90 per cent of the sowing is now done by tractors, in the United States more than that. Cows are now milked and products processed by machines. The armaments industry is almost wholly automated. Where once twenty-three men produced 900 grenades per hour, now only two are needed. In the grenade factory at Rockford, Illinois, "no human hand touches the product from the time when blocks of steel enter the manufacturing process to the time when the finished weapons have been packed." In Ford's automated plant at Cleveland, forty-one men do the work that three times that number accomplished under the conveyor belt system. In the phonograph recording industry, five times as many records are turned out every day by four operators instead of 250 in the 1930's. Between 1880 and 1953 the productivity of men at work in an average European industry had doubled. It doubled again between 1953 and 1962, achieving as much progress in nine years as had been logged in the preceding seventy.

Such progress in turn creates serious problems, for modern industrial economy is eating into the resources on which it has been built. As the nineteenth century ended, the annual paper consumption of a successful Paris daily chewed up the equivalent of a 25,000-acre forest. The United States used more metals and mineral fuels since World War I than the whole world has used through all its history up to 1914. Shortages which develop as more advanced societies consume ever more of the world's raw materials cause the cost of supplies to rise, even in the case of industrial water of which it takes 20 cubic meters to refine a ton of petroleum or sugar, 150 cubic meters (some 250 tons) to make one ton of steel. The need of water per head of population has grown fifty times in as many years. Before 1914 water consumption was about 20 pints a day for every member of mankind. Today the figure stands around 800 pints.

We are outgrowing our usable resources. People can eat just so much.

But they aspire to ever higher living—that is, consumption—standards in manufactured goods and, there, supplies are being reduced to the point where rising costs may curtail their use.

Consumption of energy has soared in the past century, eating up in one year the fossil fuels accumulated over several centuries. The world's consumption of energy, 12 million kilowatt-calories per inhabitant in 1953, had risen to 20 million by 1968. Sooner or later coal, oil, and gas reserves will be exhausted. Humanity is trying to devise ways of tapping alternative sources of energy—solar or atomic. This last, if properly harnessed, holds out extraordinary possibilities. Thus in 1954 U.S. power plants generated 410 billion kilowatt-hours. If the nuclear fusion reaction now used in bombs could be manipulated as a source of controlled energy, a single cubic mile of sea water would yield five times as much. While such developments remain in the realm of fantasy, six years after Hiroshima the first EBR-1 reactor was generating electricity from nuclear power and, by 1966, twenty-one nuclear power plants had been ordered by public utility companies in the United States, the rest of the world following along behind.

But while we know that there are alternative sources of power and that man-made materials can be, and are being, fashioned to replace those that we exhaust, basic natural resources are being lost, polluted, or dangerously mutated. The earth's atmosphere is vast but not limitless. In time, it can become saturated with the toxins that we send up in it, just as the world's waters are beginning to be poisoned. And, while serious changes take place in the air and waters that surround us, the ground beneath our feet shifts under the weight of great masses of water gathered behind our dams, trembles at the nuclear blasts set off in its bowels, imbibes the noxious fallout of above-ground explosions, staggers and sometimes gives way before our assaults. Sooner or later there is retribution and, usually, though the fathers ate the grapes it is the children's teeth that are set on edge. On October 21, 1966, 144 inhabitants of the village of Aberfan in Wales, among them 116 children, died crushed by the sudden slide of a mountain of mining refuse. Accumulated in a century or more, the great mound—720 feet, one million tons—long loomed over the village before it fell on it, treated with the indifference

An atomic power plant under construction in Scotland.

Warder Collection

of habit: a manmade volcano ready to erupt but, unlike a volcano, the creation of man's indifference to the results of his own handiwork.

Imponderable things are also being lost, whose disappearance statistics do not mention. "Cultural treasures" are destroyed by the world that worships them and destroyed the faster the richer the society: the mosaics of Ravenna, the sculptures of the Acropolis, shaken to pieces by passing planes; the paintings of Lascaux and of the Catacombs defaced by tourist scribbles; acres of frescoes ready to fall off their walls because of the tremors of passing traffic; gardens of castles in the Loire Valley decaying because neighboring factories deprive them of water; stones rotting and disintegrating under the chemicals in the air around them; the pines of Rome dying from too much hydrocarbon and Venice itself threatened by the waves of its vaporettos.

Problems of this order are far from insoluble. The social investments they suggest—not just the schools, hospitals, and highways we now take for granted, but relief of asphyxiated cities, of threatened countryside, of torn or eroded lands, protection of natural and artistic resources, the battle against pollution of water and air—could easily play the role of economic motor that defense now plays in many developed economies. Only time will show whether the immense potential we have begun to tap on every level will be applied to make life better or put an end to it.

Medicine and Hygiene

Medicine has always been a field in which art and science meet, but imagination had long prevailed over precision. As the nineteenth century opened, the practice of medicine in the West had only recently freed itself from earlier "harmonies" which related metals, humors, elements, and passions with the signs of the zodiac. Diagnostics no longer took account of the position of the stars, prescriptions no longer included pounded toad or the excrement of cats, academic considerations ignored the symbolic relation between bodily functions and the planets. Medicine could now turn from affirmation to observation, from observation to definition and experiment, from experiment to application on a quantitative and scientific plane.

There were certain drawbacks. Since its birth medicine had reflected the common culture of the educated, had been pursued as a kind of dialogue between patient and physician, both speaking a similar language and sharing much the same basic knowledge. Medicine was an aspect of philosophy, a kind of applied psychology or science in which the bodies of men, their pathology, their biology, intruded only slowly and late. In Restoration France, Balzac's Country Doctor still had to guess a patient's trouble from his account of it. Soon thereafter doctors began to use clinical thermometers to examine patients, to put their

ear or their stethoscope on back and chest to hear the sound of heart
and lungs, to draw their own conclusions. Thereafter, the gap between
the patient and his impressions and the doctor and his diagnosis grew
to a point where communication broke down almost entirely: the patient reified by the technical competence of the doctor. Men became
cases, the sick man disappeared behind his sickness.

But, if the sick became increasingly *objects* of their doctors' care,
sickness and pain were effectively pressed back. The first medical revolution had come with a vaccine early in the nineteenth century. Some 60
million persons had been killed by smallpox during the eighteenth century. In the nineteenth, wherever vaccine was adopted, mortality from
smallpox became negligible.* The great medical breakthroughs were
still to come: antiseptics and anesthetics lie at the basis of the modern
world as much as steam. There were great delays between their discovery
and their application. Chloroform, found in 1831, was first used as an
anesthetic in Edinburgh in 1847 (American surgeons had started using
ether in 1844); carbolic acid, discovered in 1834, was used as an
antiseptic after 1865. Part of the delay stemmed from superstition, as
when relief of pain in childbirth by unnatural means was opposed on
religious grounds even after Queen Victoria accepted chloroform in 1853
for the birth of Prince Leopold. More stemmed from inertia and ignorance in the medical profession. As late as 1868, doctors still treated
hepatitis complicated by serious lung infection by using leeches, cupping,
and lancing to "draw off the bad blood"—a method compared to which
the scapulars and holy water that Catholics recommended might prove
less murderous.

Florence Nightingale's *Notes on Hospitals* (1859) opens with a revealing phrase: "It may seem a strange principle," she writes, "to enu-
merate as the very first requirement in a hospital that it should do the
sick no harm." In practice, mortality in hospitals was higher than outside, because elementary sanitary precautions were ignored and, when the
nineteenth century ended, 50 per cent of hospitalized cases still died of infections caught in the hospital. One of the few positive results of the
Crimean War was Florence Nightingale's campaign to establish nursing as
a profession. But, even as trained nurses trickled into wards and, eventually, into the countryside as well, better ventilation, greater cleanliness,
improved food and drainage, could have saved thousands. Their virtues
would not be seriously considered until the 1880's, or still later when the
magic evoked in Thomas Mann's *Magic Mountain* began to be tapped,
and tubercular patients were sent to sanatoria chiefly to get lots of pure
fresh air.

While hospitals could remedy the woeful lack of nursing personnel and

---

* During the war of 1870–71, in the German army, where vaccination was compulsory,
297 died of smallpox; in the French army, where vaccination was not compulsory,
23,400 died of smallpox.

Florence Nightingale.

provide their patients with real nurses' care after the 1870's, they could not triumph over the conditions in which they operated until their basic environment was changed. The drains and sewers of the larger cities were well described by the London woman who, when asked if her house had drains, answered, "No thank God, Sir, we have none of them foul stinking things here!" In London in 1849, when over 14,000 persons died of cholera, sewers poured more than nine million cubic feet of muck and sludge into the Thames, whence came the city's water described by *The Spectator* as "a more or less concentrated solution of native guano." Legislation began to remedy the situation in the 50's but river windows of the House of Commons remained steadfastly closed and in 1858 there was serious talk of moving Parliament away from the unbearable stench of the river.

A great campaign for better drains in the 1870's gradually drove back typhoid fever, headaches, sore throats, and nausea, along with rotten pipes, damp, dankness, rats, and unsanitary drains. It was only thus that the soaring death rate of all cities could be lowered. Public drains called for private plumbing. If he could not be a prince, declared the future Edward VII who nearly died of typhoid fever in 1871, he would wish to be a plumber. And, on his humble level, the plumber appears as very much the guardian angel of late nineteenth-century hygiene. Plumbers made possible "public conveniences," which, first installed in the Crystal Palace (1851), helped diminish what the *Official Report* of the Exhibition called "the sufferings which must be endured by all, but more especially by females, on account of the want of them." Plumbers, installing running water in private dwellings, also made possible bathing, first in hip baths—which were recommended as "very beneficial in various forms of cholera, colic, liver complaints, diarrhea and disordered conditions" —then in tubs and bathrooms. In the 1880's one out of six urban residents in North America could boast a bathtub and, by that time, the possibilities of thorough washing had been supplemented by the greater availability of soap, which only became accessible to the poorer classes in the last thirty or forty years of the century.*

Against this slowly brightening backdrop the progress of medicine took place. In the 1860's and 70's Pasteur in France, Lister in Scotland, Koch in Germany established that diseases caused by microbes can be fended off by inoculation and asepsis. Where these were applied, legislated, and enforced as in England, the death rate which had hovered around 22 per 1,000 since 1840 fell to 18 in 1890 and 15 in the 1900's, and average life expectation grew by 10 years. In Russia where little was done on these lines, the death rate in 1890 was still 35 per 1,000. Meanwhile, mortality was being forced back in other quarters. In the early eighties German researchers identified the bacilli of typhoid, diphtheria, and cholera; in 1894 the French that of the plague; in 1898 the Japanese that of tetanus. Before the century ended the Caesarian operation had been developed, forceps gave gynecologist or midwife a better chance of delivering the baby, an artificial incubator which Pasteur developed preserved infants prematurely born, and baby foods improved the prospects of the infant's health. German researchers like Robert Koch and Paul Ehrlich, employing aniline dyes to identify bacteria, suggested the possibility of chemotherapy, using chemical agents to kill noxious microscopic organisms without hurting body tissues. Ehrlich dreamed of a "magic bullet," discovered Salvarsan in 1909, and laid the groundwork for later sulfa drugs and antibiotics. Medicine was now aided by biochemistry, discovering vitamins whose absence from our diet causes deficiency diseases: scurvy, rickets, pellagra; and hormones: adrenaline (isolated 1901), insulin (1922) for diabetes, cortisone (1936) for arthritis. In 1910, the discovery of different groups of blood made blood transfusions safe, while surgical possibilities increased with the development of machines for artificial respiration.

The results of all this are recorded in dry statistics. Between 1870 and 1905 England saw deaths from typhoid fever reduced by nearly seven-eighths, from tuberculosis by more than half. In Italy where in 1887, 836 per million had died of typhoid, 595 of malaria, 534 of smallpox, 115 of pellagra, twenty years later these figures had been reduced to 225, 125, 13, and 48.

During the twentieth century even greater advances would be made—greater it has been said than in all the ages since the world began. Biological and physiological discoveries, psychopathology, modern surgery

* Toilet products remained luxuries. Artificial hair dressing (as opposed to bear grease) appeared in 1793 with Rowland's Macassar Oil, to be mentioned in Byron's *Don Juan* and Lewis Carroll's *Through the Looking Glass,* and survives in the term "anti-macassar." Cutthroat razors appeared in the fifteenth century, special shaving soap in the seventeenth century. Razor strops date from the eighteenth century and the first safety models from the same time; but private shaving remained exceptional until K. C. Gillette's invention of the nineteenth century, which passed very quickly from an exorbitant five dollars to ten cents. Modern toothbrushes appeared in the nineteenth century, until which time mouth wash was used to supplement a cloth or a sponge with which the teeth were wiped.

and anesthesia, endocrinology, serums, sulfamides, hormones, antibiotics, preventive methods, equipment and research, all made giant strides. Sulfa drugs after 1935, antibiotics in the 1940's (beginning with penicillin in 1941) reduced infectious illness—typhus, typhoid, tuberculosis, cholera, syphilis. Surgery and prosthetics have surged forward, as has the use of physical agents—radioactivity, electric waves, sound waves, etc.

In 1835, a French expert had written that to find a hundred men fit for military service one needs 135 conscripts of the middle and upper classes, or else 343 of the poorer classes. At Mulhouse in Alsace, at about that time, life expectation for offspring of the rich was twenty-eight, for those of textile workers one year and three months. Among the latter, for every 100 births, 30 died in the first month, 20 in the following nine; only 27 reached the age of ten, 17 got to twenty, 6 got to forty, one sometimes lived to sixty. This level of 500 deaths per 1,000 matches the worst plague years of the eighteenth century. The difference in death rates between rich and poor persisted into the twentieth century, but much attenuated; so that the poor in France today have a life expectancy of over fifty.

Given the high mortality of—say—the year 1700, out of 1,000 living babies only 475 could be expected to reach the age of twenty, when a person begins to think and act independently. Of these, only two-thirds would see their fortieth birthday, only one-third their sixtieth. Today, 960 out of 1,000 are likely to complete their studies and can look forward to forty or fifty years during which they may contribute to society as well as enrich their own lives. The social gain that derives from this is immense, contributing, in effect, to the other sources of capital accumulation from which we benefit.

Some of the most remarkable improvements have come after 1930, when state intervention brought the masses (most of whom hardly saw dentist or doctor unless they were gravely ill) within the scope of medical and social care. Infant mortality, 142 per 1,000 in the United Kingdom in 1900 was 31 per 1,000 in 1950; in Sweden it was 21 per 1,000. Yet, even so, in 1958 about one-third of Britain's buildings were still bathless, nearly 50 per cent in some poorer quarters. In Western Germany, a few years ago, 200 homes in one town were found to have 125 TV sets and 3 baths. Even in the United States, while 42,400,000 (84 per cent) of the nation's homes had TV, a million fewer had bathtubs. When Stalin died in 1953 with the most modern medical equipment in his room, his doctors were still prescribing cupping. In France in 1950, about 12 per cent of national revenue went to consumption of alcoholic beverages, 4 or 5 per cent to the country's medical needs—which did not prevent the cost of the latter being attacked harder than that of the former.

It is true that medicine has become much more costly and that its very advances make life itself more costly: keeping people alive who without it would die of illness or of age. Old-age pensions, better hygiene and food, prolonged life, raise the porportion of aged to adults in the community, impose heavy social costs, affect activity, enterprise, attitudes, politics, and public life. Improved drugs mean that men live longer, that the sick suffer longer, that the unfit survive to procreate, to spread infections, or, simply, to be an added burden on society. The wonders of medicine are its hazards too.

Once upon a time, circumstances favored the survival and multiplication of those who were stronger, fitter, or better adapted to the world's demands. Now, society intervenes to help the weak and the ill-adapted —not necessarily to lead better lives, but—at least to survive. Genetic laws which worked in favor of the strong are being reversed as prudence, skill, and initiative are enlisted rather in preventing conception than in ensuring it. The most advanced societies may have evolved a process of natural selection in reverse.

But, if survival presents problems in the most advanced countries, it has catastrophic effects in backward ones. In India, whose population growth rate only passed that of Europe in 1921, the 300 million-odd inhabitants of the century's beginning have, by today, increased by almost two-thirds. Latin-American population has practically doubled in fifty years. These abrupt changes, not compensated by a parallel productivity of either food or goods, threaten dire consequences and create the explosive situation with which the second half of the twentieth century must learn to cope.

Science and Thought

Evolution

In 1859, Charles Darwin (1809–1882), son of the poet-doctor-member of the Lunar Society, published the results of many years of work in a book entitled *The Origin of Species,* in which it was suggested that living organisms, including men and other animals, had come into existence not as a result of special creation but by a process of evolution and natural selection. The work was but a stage in the long process of inquiry and definition which we have seen proceeding in earlier years (pp. 635–637). Its impact was the greater because the ground had been prepared for it and because, while it threatened many preconceptions of the day, it fitted many others.

By 1859 time had been recognized as a crucial factor in history as much as in astronomy: now first geology, then biology followed suit.

The notion of evolutionary growth had become commonplace in a society which believed in progress because it actually saw progress taking place. It became shocking when applied to Bible and to man, denying the literal truth of one and the special dignity of the other. Tennyson asked if really man

> Who trusted God was love indeed
> And love creation's final law—
> Tho' nature, red in tooth and claw
> With ravine, shriek'd against his Creed—

was just another animal fated to die like them. Not God but apes, not apes but sperm, not sperm but slime, here lay the ancestry of man: from dust to dust was more than a formula, and all of wisdom was but chemistry. This was hard to take.

But a dynamic world could not hold out long for static theories. Darwin's hypothesis was better suited to minds prepared by Malthus and by their own grim struggles to glory in natural selection when they could no longer boast of privileged creation. Even Fabians saw social change and reform as an accumulation of minute variations eventually and inevitably changing the face of society. And Oswald Spengler, in his *Decline of the West* (1918), would use the biological analogy for life and death of civilizations and cultures which behaved like living organisms in their passage from birth to death.

The very dismay that many felt before the crumbling of the old authorities; the sense that

> . . . We are here as on a darkling plain
> Swept with confused alarms of struggle and flight
> Where ignorant armies clash by night. . . .

reinforced a fresh will to believe and to obey new gods and new authorities. Where should these be found but in the science which had denounced the old? Even in 1848, the French philosopher Ernest Renan had seen that "Science is a religion; science alone leads man to resolve the eternal problems of which his nature imperiously calls for a solution." Twenty years later Renan's beliefs had penetrated the popular mind in the guise of scientism. Dazzled by the technical applications of scientific discoveries, public opinion was converted to a creed of science, progress, and the future of humanity, all borne out by steam, internal combustion, and electricity, by medical advances and inventions of every sort.

The Cult of Science

Science fascinated everybody. History, politics, economics became social sciences; philosophy became a moral science. It was still very hard to tell just what science was and what was scientific. Many had recourse to pseudo-sciences like phrenology: a method of telling the personality and ability of a person by examining the bumps on their skulls;* and pseudo-faiths of a mystic nature: spiritualism, table rapping, crystal ball gazing, medium experiments, and the like. Table turning and the evocation of spirits from another world fascinated high society from Victor Hugo to Empress Eugénie, a very superstitious lady. Perhaps these were the late nineteenth century's substitute for a near-exploded faith: new superstitions to replace the old. The healing work of magic and of faith was also carried on by patent medicines providing spells and love potions for their aficionados, fairy tales for commercials, and immense profits for their manufacturers without doing too much harm. Though dandruff, baldness, or halitosis persist, men and women often feel better if they think they should be feeling better and, within limits, that is worth the price.

One thing, however, seemed increasingly apparent: God, who had been banished from laboratories could now be dispensed with in an outer world which traced its origins to other sources. In 1865 a French medical student called Georges Clemenceau, obtained a doctorate with a thesis entitled *The Generation of Anatomical Elements.* which indicated the biological irrelevance of God. The issue was more clearly stated shortly after by one of Darwin's strongest advocates: Ernest Haeckel (1834–1919). "The cell," declared the German biologist, "consists of matter called protoplasm, composed chiefly of carbon, with an admixture of hydrogen, nitrogen, and sulfa. These component parts, properly united, produce the soul and the body of the animated world, and suitably nursed become man. With this single argument the mystery of the universe is explained, the deity annulled and a new era of infinite knowledge ushered in."

Many popular prophets busied themselves explaining how infinite the possibilities of knowledge and control now were. For Victor Hugo, the progress of chemistry revived the dreams of ancient alchemists. By the twentieth century chemistry would actually realize Doctor Faustus' dreams and transmute mercury into gold. For the growing number of science-fiction writers—Jules Verne (1828–1905), Arthur Conan Doyle (1859–1930), H. G. Wells—science suggested new possibilities: flying to the moon, sailing under the sea, navigating in time, rounding the world in the ridiculously short space of eighty days, making war with flying ships, rockets, or land cruisers (tanks), eventually destroying cities and perhaps the world. Nothing was beyond human ingenuity: not even man himself.

"All human facts, moral and physical, being bound up with causes and subject to laws," wrote Hippolyte Taine in 1870, "It follows that

---

* Prince Albert took phrenology very seriously, and had the royal children undergo periodical examinations.

Charles Darwin, by John Collier.
National Portrait Gallery, London.

all works of man, art, religion, philosophy, literature, moral, political
or social phenomena, are but the results of general causes that must be
determined by scientific methods." Scientific methods meant above all
measurement for those who believed that progress would eventually connect all knowledge in one great integrated science, based on mathematics
and able to account for man and cosmos and life and even God. A
French chemist, Marcelin Berthelot, good friend of the philosopher Renan, affirmed: "Science is the benefactor of humanity . . . under her impulse, modern civilization marches with ever faster step." Science eased
labor, created human brotherhood, " a new conception of human destiny,
directed by the fundamental notions of universal solidarity between
all nations." The methods of the natural sciences used in pursuit of
the laws determining human behavior suggested a mechanistic view of
life and man, in which all actions are determined by previous actions, in
which we could calculate destiny out of the mass and motions of particles in the universe, in which (thought men like Taine) brains secreted
thought much as the liver secretes bile.

Science and Society

The first great formulator of this point of view, prophet of nineteenth-
century positivism, had been Auguste Comte (1798–1857), appropriately
a teacher of mathematics at the Paris Polytechnic School. Comte's approach applied scientific methods not only to nature but to society as
well, where history provided the laboratory of man's social experiments,
a laboratory whence observation could extract the basis of a correct
social morality. For Comte history passed through stages, each colored
by the way in which men explained and handled phenomena about

them: the first *theological* stage was largely animistic, the second— *metaphysical*—still preferred abstractions to realities, the third and last was the *positive,* examining phenomena in relation to all other phenomena and in connection with general laws.

Auguste Comte offered a great vision of inevitable progress, humanity moving onward and upward past successive barriers of ignorance and superstition to the positive truths of science. Scientific methods could and would reveal the laws of social organization and individual behavior, laws which magicians and priests still hid from sight. The task was twofold: discover and formulate these laws by "the exact study of facts and things" (Zola); assert them against obsolete metaphysical survivals from the past. Because of its anticlerical overtones, positivism would become a fighting creed in those societies where liberalism came up most forcefully against the church: in Turkey and in Catholic countries like Italy, France, Mexico, and Brazil. And Freemasonry, which had developed to improve the world of man, took up this task like a crusade.

Clearly, the wonders achieved by scientific methods in the realm of nature could and should be repeated in the social sphere. A science of society would parallel the sciences of nature. Comte had sought to do this by his kind of historical psychology that focused on the experience and the mind of man. An alternative notion was proposed by Social Darwinists like Herbert Spencer (1820–1903), who saw society passing from a military and despotic to an industrial and democratic phase, condemned state interference with the struggle for survival, and preached a robust individualism that appealed especially to the more successful members of the middle class. Society, said Darwinists like Spencer, cannot safely ignore the principle of natural selection by artificially nurturing and preserving those of its members who cannot take care of themselves. "The poverty of the incapable, the distresses that come upon the imprudent, the starvation of the idle, and those shoulderings aside of the weak by the strong which leave so many in shallows and miseries are the decrees of a large, far-seeing benevolence." Millionaires were also a product of natural selection. So were states—"the organized control of the minority over the majority," as an Austrian sociologist described them— resulting from a conflict between social groups in which one group, superior in intelligence and ability, hence fittest to rule, had triumphed.

Here was an approach which allowed for variations. Karl Marx was also an admirer of Darwin. In 1867 Marx had wanted to dedicate the first volume of *Das Kapital* to Darwin, who declined the honor. In 1883, speaking at Marx's funeral, Engels stressed the connection: "Just as Darwin discovered the law of development of organic nature, so Marx discovered the law of development of human history." For both, change came through conflict: class war being the social counterpart of the struggle for existence and survival. But Marx despised the psychological intellectualism of Comte and regarded the optimistic vitalism of Spencer as superficial. His science rested on economic development and on the classes which this forged, classes whose struggle and self-affirmation were the solid substance of history. Hegel had seen history as the fulfillment of abstract ideas embodied in the state. Marx would see it as the conflict of very concrete interests and forces embodied in social classes.

Unfortunately, his observations were founded on an early stage of British industrial development, when the working people were indeed turned into a vast undifferentiated mass. Hence Marx's classes were monolithic, not prone as they have proved to ever greater differentiation. He saw economic development increasingly depersonalizing the individual, battering him into his class like a gigantic power hammer, opposing impersonal mass and impersonal capital. And even as developments, first in Britain and then in other industrially advanced countries, were contradicting Marx's conclusions, other countries just entering the industrial race seemed to prove him right, winning him votaries in underdeveloped areas while the developed ones moved toward revisionism. The Marxist analysis which fitted the England of the 1840's, fitted the Germany of the 70's and 80's, the France of the 90's, the Russia of prewar years. Here was a materialist philosophy for materialistic times, a religion of inevitable progress for a progressive age.

From Determinism to Relativism

Marx's death in 1883 marked the beginning of a great reaction in which the clear, determined, progressive universe of positivism crumbled away under a bombardment of new discoveries and of their implications. Nineteenth-century rationalism was founded on Newtonian mechanics operating in a world of matter which was conceived as continuous and permanent. The world was made up of chemical elements, and elements of atoms; but in between, completing the continuum, lay an invisible ether which rendered motion possible by displacement of matter in space. In 1887 a series of experiments conducted in Chicago by Michelson and Morley emptied the Newtonian universe of its invisible ether stuffing, and left people wondering what was there instead. In 1895 the German Karl Roentgen discovered X rays which could traverse apparently solid matter. Within a few years the work of the Curies in France, of Rutherford in England, revealed the instability and disintegration of radioactive atoms. Atoms which had been believed to be the firm, indivisible base of the material world, could split, releasing a quantity of energy in the process.

The idea of continuity had been fundamental to classic theories of light, energy, and matter. Now, Max Planck (1858–1947) suggested that when bodies emit light they actually radiate energy, pulsating in infinitesimal measures, or *quanta*, proportional to the frequency of the

Warder Collection

Warder Collection

Albert Einstein broadcasting a warning on the terrors of the hydrogen bomb. Right: Max Planck.

radiation. All energy is ultimately quantified: emitted not in rays but in this discontinuous radiation.* One after the other, the solid notions which paved the floor of science seemed to melt away. A new physics suggested new hypotheses about the structure of the universe, of matter, of perception. The mechanical principles of Newton, the mathematical determinism of the past 300 years, were being rewritten into a new relativism.

In 1905, the theory of relativity which Albert Einstein (1879–1955) formulated suggested that neither time nor space were absolutes. Time has not the absolute character we imagine, but passes at different speeds according to whether the observer stands still or moves at great speed. This fact suggests that space also is a relative notion. Albert Einstein's studies of accelerated movements, discovering that the mass of a body varies with its speed, led to the formulation of the general relativity theory (1915) asserting the equation of energy and mass ($e=mc^2$). A body radiates energy at the expense of its mass, and matter is itself a form of energy. Matter could turn into energy; and the basic component of matter—the atom, a tiny compound of compressed energy—could turn into light, or into heat, or both. The atom was not solid, but made up of electrons revolving around a kernel; and these electrons, said the Dane Niels Bohr, could jump from one atom to another, emitting energy as they did. Indeed, the jumps—the transmutation of matter and the release of energy incidental to it—could be set off by bombarding atoms with radioactive rays. In 1932, the first cyclotron was built to accelerate this bombardment. It was also found that in the case of atoms of certain elements like uranium, their disintegration was accompanied by a chain reaction—the emission of neutrons causing the split of further atoms emitting yet more neutrons—and that such splits were accompanied by the intense emission of energy. This was the basis of the 400-pound bomb

* In 1923 Louis de Broglie provided a fresh notion of continuity by arguing that the little particles of light or matter are part of the propagation of a wave, and thus created undulatory mechanics.

which on August 6, 1945, destroyed Hiroshima.

Many years passed between the 1880's when this process started and the 1940's when it seemed to culminate. But, as its implications trickled into public consciousness, the mechanical universe began to crumble and, with it, an element of psychological security. A good expression of the traditional view of how the world was ordered can be found in Ecclesiastes I, 4–9:

> One generation passeth away and another generation cometh: but the earth abideth forever. The sun also ariseth and the sun goeth down and hasteth to his place where he arose. The world goes towards the South and turneth about unto the North; it whirleth about continually; and the world returneth again according to his circuits. All the rivers run into the sea; yet the sea is not full: unto the place whence the rivers come thither they return again. All things are full of labor; man cannot utter it: the eye is not satisfied with seeing nor the ear filled with hearing. The thing that hath been, it is that which shall be; and that which is done is that which shall be done: and there is no new thing under the sun.

There was no basic change in this world view when the seventeenth century established the laws of permanence in a moving world. Matter, space, and movement were all constant, and even the laws which Newton postulated were only constants to be discovered, not changes to be traced. Time, space, and movement were absolute quantities. If logic suggested that this might not always be so, God was there to correct accidents and make sure His grand machine worked as it should. The discoveries of the nineteenth century would throw a wrench of doubt into the works. The world was made of matter. But over great areas of space, such as the sky, this matter is invisible. Newton had postulated that the space across which forces of gravity operate was filled with ether, a compound of infinitesimal particles. We have seen that in 1887 Michelson proved that ether does not exist. Physics was at a loss. The material universe collapsed. Not immediately or in all its parts, but in the sense that "exact science" acknowledged an element of unpredictability about its calculations and that this element was enhanced by the work of Planck, Einstein, and Bohr, until exactness became an approach rather than a fact, and relativity replaced absolutism as the dominant of modern scientific thought.

After Einstein, neither time nor distance were absolute values any more. After Planck, measurements were understood to be affected by sensations. After Paul Langevin (1872–1946), matter and energy became identical. The world today is neither set nor stable. Space or distance may alter with density. Hence the world may well expand as its mass rarefies. In this variable universe, compound of solid laws, Newtonian survivals and relativism, only mathematical representation independent of the observer retains objective meaning. Experience reveals only the relative. Only concepts may permit an objective view, founded on experience maybe but transcending it.

This was more disturbing than evolution in which natural philosophers believed long before Darwin: it contradicted evolution by painting a nature proceeding not in a continuous line but in bounds, discontinuous and perhaps dialectical as well. Worse still in some respects, the realities Einstein and Planck revealed were expressible only in mathematical symbols and abstract formulae. It may well be that abstraction "is the normal and fruitful course of the scientific spirit," as a philosopher of science has recently asserted, but the evolution from more or less visual geometry toward the complete abstraction of mathematical equations removed it from the ken even of cultivated persons. Science, which had been part of educated men's equipment, became an arcane field for initiates, its mysteries and its revelations all the more disturbing for their inaccessibility.

While the debate as to the meaning of their theories divided physicists, its echoes shattered large panes of the optimistic rationalism that had grown up around them. Scientism, having battered down religion, had affirmed that it carried the keys to truth. Now it had to admit what most scientists had known all along: that "formulae are not true; they are useful," and to insist that science did not really explain the nature of things but only their relations. The philosophers of science offered little comfort. G. E. Moore's *Principia Ethica* and Bertrand Russell's *Principles of Mathematics* (both published in 1903) argued essentially that men perceived not objects as wholes, not things in themselves, but shapes, colors, images, as real in dreams or hallucinations as in waking sensation. Things *are* because we see them so, as Berkeley had once said; and the world is no more than an infinity of particular perceptions. Science thus became "a system of relations," scientific certainty became probability, and ordinary men were left panting for a faith that would reassure, a system that would reorder their disordered world.

It seemed as if Prometheus had overreached himself. Science was to have made man autonomous. The doubts its progress raised made him querulous. A French Catholic critic, Charles Brunetière, proclaimed "the failure of science"; a neo-Marxist like Georges Sorel denounced the illusions of progress; human science, affirmed Pope Leo XIII in 1902, cannot "quench the thirst for truth, for divinity, for infinity, which devours us." That was not what human science had set out to do. To the extent that its advocates had claimed too much, their dogmatic scientism was breaking down, making way for a new irrationalism less favorable to reason than to faith. The mysticism of Leo Tolstoy or Rabindranath Tagore, the philosophies of action like those of William James and Georges Sorel, and those of intuition like that of Henri Bergson, who suggested that real continuity lies only in our consciousness; the phenomenology of Edmund Husserl, arguing that reality cannot be

William James.   Henri Bergson.

shown by rational explanation or evidence but through some structural intuition; the relativism of existential philosophy which recognizes no objective truths; the theology of Karl Barth and Karl Jaspers calling for acts of faith based on no rational certainty, as an escape from the unstructured absurdity of the material world: all spring in one way or another from this collapse of the house that Galileo, Descartes, and Newton built.

Rationalism Qualified

The first great philosophy of action was what William James (1842–1910) formulated as pragmatism. James realized that men need to believe more than they actually know, or can hope to know. You cannot act only on knowledge that can be proved rationally, because then you would act very little. You must act on beliefs, justified by need or practice. "An idea is true because it is useful; it is useful because it is true." In any case, said Bergson (1859–1941), intellect distorts reality, which only intuition can grasp. The will, responding to the needs of the struggle for existence, suggests the aspects or interpretations of reality that it most needs. Bergson's early work dates back to 1889; but his most revolutionary book was published in 1907: *Creative Evolution.* In it and in his exceedingly popular lectures at the Collège de France, Bergson reacted against the reigning rationalism and demolished it with reference to the new indeterminacies that scientific discoveries suggested. Bergson appealed from materialism and rationalism to those vital forces which drive us and which alone can reveal us to ourselves, rehabilitating intuition against the excesses of reason, pointing out the force of instinct, of chance, the superiority of metaphysical over merely physical truth.

Verbiage? But expressed in a fascinating, deceptively clear style which came as a relief after the Germanic obscurities of so much nineteenth-century philosophy. Above all, verbiage which—when science was going through a revolutionary change—reflected the anti-rationalist reaction of its time: a reaction very evident in literature and politics, as in the Catholic revival—not only that of the masses drawn to new devotions and pilgrimages, but that of poets like Charles Péguy and Paul Claudel, philosophers like Jacques Maritain, painters like Georges Rouault, musicians like Georges Auric, César Franck, and Vincent D'Indy, whose *Schola Cantorum* dates back to 1896. Like his contemporary, Sigmund Freud, Bergson set obscure forces in motion simply by plumbing them. The eloquent philosophy of freedom, which he drew from the collapse of scientism, became the inspiration of an anti-intellectual offensive that rejected the works of reason as distortions of living experience and obstacles to intuitive perception. Reality lay not in the mind and in its apprehensions but in a "life force" that intuition tapped and that will alone expressed in acts and gestures. Living reality could not be encompassed by logical formulae: "All that is vital is anti-rational," declared Miguel de Unamuno, one of the intellectual leaders of twentieth-century Spain.

But, in denying reason, the anti-intellectual intellectuals were denying the characteristic equipment of man himself; were admitting that, after all, man is not free to be free. They ushered in the time of disillusion for the few, who would eventually communicate their disillusion to the many; the time when man begins to think of himself as an incidental occurrence and of mankind as a passing phase of a perpetually changing world. The mood of such intellectual circles was well summed up in a statement of the Italian philosopher Benedetto Croce:

> We no longer believe . . . like the Greeks, in happiness of life on earth; we no longer believe, like the Christians, in happiness in an other-worldly life; we no longer believe, like the optimistic philosophers of the last century, in a happy future for the human race . . . we no longer believe in anything of that, and what we have alone retained is the consciousness of ourselves.

Soon this last, too, came under fire. The war of 1914–1918 emphasized and broadcast the conviction that men were playthings of "other" forces before which their consciousness, let alone their will, was powerless. And yet some of the most obvious of these "other" forces were the work of men. In this connection, the general public now discovered the work of Sigmund Freud, whose basic research into hidden emotional energies and their effect on man's conscious acts had been completed just before the war, but who spoke most clearly to the postwar mood. Freud's psychoanalytical approach formulated for the individual what Marx had formulated for society half a century earlier: a theory which sees men moved by forces of which they are unconscious, their culture, morals, institutions, beliefs shaped by interests and repressions they ignore, and the discovery of this situation as the first step toward liberation.

Philosophers, sociologists, and anthropologists took similar lines to Freud's—the social scientists proceeding to analyze the subterranean currents that make societies, men, and cultures be what they are, and change as they do. But the first and most striking of these revelations, dissolving the solid structures of the psychological universe much as the physicists had destroyed those of theirs, came from the psychoanalysts. Freud's speculations on dreams and the unconscious, Carl Jung's ideas of the collective unconscious and inferiority complexes, Alfred Adler's theories of compensation, and Erik Erikson's identification of an identity crisis, were so many revelations battering at established attitudes and constraints, from logical reasoning to sex, from women's inferiority to parental superiority and paternalism in industry or politics. That the new techniques were revolutionary soon became clear—at least to insurrectionists like Trotsky, who hoped to synthesize the work of Marx and Freud, and to Béla Kun who, during the Hungarian revolution of 1918, set up in Budapest the first institute for the training of psychoanalysts. To analysts like Wilhelm Reich, who joined the German young Communists, material and sexual misery appeared as one. And the revolutionary implications of psychoanalytical ideas were just as clear to great reactionaries like Stalin and Hitler, both of whom condemned Reich's essay of 1932, *The Sexual Struggle of Youth*.

Realism Under Fire

As established notions of reality crumbled away, the arts followed the reaction against nineteenth-century realism and rationalism, abandoning space or scale, perspective or harmony as artificial conventions, in favor of self-made rules or models in a new relative world which all could reconstruct according to their vision. Abstract artists like Jean Arp, Alexander Calder, and Piet Mondrian deliberately referred to science which shows no ultimately established nature and suggests that solid appearances conceal a mobile reality. The work of Piet Mondrian (1872–1944), for instance, reflects the impact of the world around him, insisting first on mass and absence of detail, later on the increasing abstraction that can be observed in his *Composition in White, Black and Red*. A work like his *Broadway Boogie-Woogie* reminds one that a Frenchman of the same generation, the painter-architect Le Corbusier, once described Manhattan as hot jazz in stone. Thus, nonfigurative artists set out to evoke things and create them rather than reproduce them. The new mood was expressed by writers as varied as James Joyce (*Ulysses,* 1922), Sinclair Lewis (*Babbitt,* 1922), T. S. Eliot (*The Waste Land,* 1922), all of whom denounced the futility of life, of man and of society. In 1924 the *Surrealist Manifesto* articulated this "refusal of traditional humanism" with its institutions and its ways of thought and feeling, and announced the foundation of an Office of Surrealist Re-

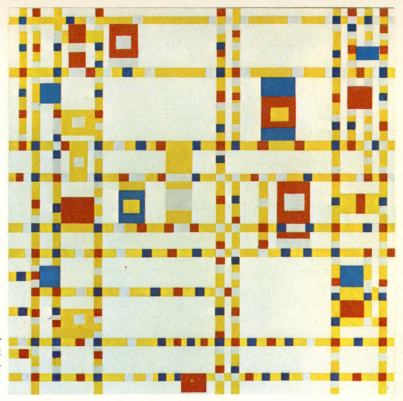

*Broadway Boogie-
Woogie,* by Piet
Mondrian. Muse-
um of Modern
Art, New York.

search concerned with the question of how sincerity could be recaptured
by escape from the "deforming influence of reason."

Surrealism, after all, was not surprising, in an age that made Oedipus
complexes available to all and when, in the words of an English
moralist, "even typists knew that they were not fond of apples for
nothing." But there was more to it. Less than five centuries after European sailors looking for Asia found America in their way and went
beyond it to circumnavigate the world, their descendants would set
foot on the moon. The acceleration of scientific knowledge and techniques was not only frightening or exhilarating: it soon became overwhelming. Ninety-three per cent of all the full-time scientists who
ever lived are alive today. But, while the world's population doubles
every thirty-five years, the mass of science and technology doubles twice
as fast and its demands are beginning to nudge the limits of our resources in money and mind. The results of the cumulative scientific
knowledge whose rate of increase has been doubling every decade for the
past three hundred years have placed culture in what has been called a
state of permanent mobilization. Unwilling to live in a continuous
cultural crisis, some persons have reacted exactly as they would react
when personal tensions and crises grow too great, by taking refuge in
defiant stolidity or exaggerated irrationalism. But even the well-intentioned become uneasy, find it increasingly hard to tell just who or what
they are supposed to be, and what they are supposed to do. Such issues

Jean-Paul Sartre, photographed in front of his portrait by Picasso.

seldom arose for earlier generations conditioned by habits and customs that rapid change has rattled to pieces in the modern West. But contemporary men—the static individual faced with a dynamic society, the private individual condemned to public solitude, the singular individual offered only techniques and laws applicable to masses—are disconcerted. They are driven to define themselves as members of bodies which seem to them endowed with more solid contours than their own personality: a church, a party, a movement, an ideology.

It would be in this context that Jean-Paul Sartre formulated the challenge of his existential philosophy: man's choice between letting himself become what others see in him—the image of a false and abstract notion: Jew, Negro, waiter, bourgeois, traitor, thief—and choosing a role which he himself defines and acts out with all its implications. Condemned to freedom and to loneliness, both absurd and both absolute, Sartrean man finds that his condition can be transcended by himself alone as he endows life, events, above all himself, with a meaning that he weaves like a spider out of his own resources. Looking around at a world in which he finds neither norms nor faith, Sartre rejects despair for an affirmation arising precisely from despair, leading to choice, to action, and to the creation of one's own destiny.

Against this last assertion of free will, the "new philosophy" of structuralism, connected with the French anthropologist Claude Lévi-Strauss and anthro-analyst Michel Foucault, approaches man as one more source of data for computers. Three-quarters of a century after Nietzsche's "God is dead," Foucault declares that man is dead as a subject, as a whole being. The man of "humanism" and of the humanities is no longer a fit subject for literature or drama, or of knowledge for philosophers. He is dis-integrated into series, gestures, moments, fitted into abstractions to which living individuals are marginal if not irrelevant factors. Structuralism is an attempt to classify societies and cultural systems, decode their particular myths, languages, and structures, produce (as it were) an entomology of men: an exact, descriptive, comparative, and analytical science directed not at the way in which men live but at the structures in which their lives are cast, not at the way societies change but at the way they are ordered. If we believe the structuralists, a whole conception of man, of the world, of human being and relations, is coming to an end.

Meanwhile, the professional scientists have carried on their work and science has recaptured the belief in reason which most scientists never lost. Those who proclaimed their failure had no share in, and little understanding of, scientific life. As the world settled uneasily to relativity, the religion of science waned along with the impossible notions of perfection that its supporters and detractors had entertained. Today, critics of science attack it not because it has failed to explain the world but because it has played and plays such an essential part in the making of it. Science and technology are rejected to the extent that the modern world seems frightening: not only by its wars, which scientific discovery has made more destructive, but by the threat of dehumanization, of technological enslavement it holds out. Unfortunately, those who doubt man's capacity and future have little better to propose than a recapitulation of his past.

Religion

If the nineteenth century was not an age of faith, it was at least an age of conformity. Christian values were basic social currency, Christian morals were the foundation of ethics and of socially acceptable behavior. Even cultivated liberals in the 1890's "did not see how an *atheist* could at bottom be an honest man." Church attendance was a mark of respectability in the middle classes and above, churches and chapels were built and restored, crowded every Sunday, bookshelves filled with sermons, devotional literature, and religious tracts. In England and Wales, in 1851, out of a population slightly below 18 million, 4.5 million went to church on Sunday morning, 3 million in the afternoon, 3 million in the evening. But the same religious census that produced these figures (not less impressive if we realize that in many cases the same persons went several times a day) revealed great deserts of paganism in the cities, where fewer than one in ten attended church on Sunday. No wonder that Florence Nightingale, who knew something about the urban population from her nursing work, told Cardinal Manning that "the most thinking and conscientious of the artisans have no religion at all," the most intelligent of urban workers have "almost entirely gone over to atheism" and would only look at a book about religion if "it were *against* the Bible." No wonder either if some sermons had a defensive shrillness. Even before Darwin, authority was threatened, orthodoxy shaken, most intellectuals qualified their faith or doubted altogether.

Orthodoxy Challenged

Skepticism had long sapped the foundations of religious belief, and critical studies rejected a literal reading of the Bible. In 1835 a disciple of Hegel, D. F. Strauss, had published *A Life of Jesus,* treating Christ as a human being so impressive that messianic and miraculous myths crystallized around him. In 1863, Renan's *Life of Jesus* abandoned Hegelian mythology for a purely historical interpretation: Jesus was a very great man, but a man nevertheless. When, before publication, Renan expounded these views at the Collège de France, his lectures there had to be suspended; not because of official prejudice (the Minister of Education agreed with him) but because public and students objected in "noisy demonstrations." As always, it was less the upper than the middle classes that resented novelty. The Bible was still considered to be an authoritative historical account of ultimate truths: the age of the world, the process of creation, the fall, these could not be denied. But geology with its awkward fossils and strata, history with its distressing chronologies, physics and biology with their uniform laws of nature were sapping it. Philosophies of science (like that which Comte proposed) claimed that what could not be proved by scientific methods was not true knowledge.

Darwin's work made it impossible to ignore biological evolution. His theory that not only primates but man too evolved from lower forms of life in a great struggle for existence struck fatal blows to Genesis, to traditional doctrines of the Creation and the Fall. If there was no creation then there was no fall, and if there was no fall then there was no original sin. The origin of man was like that of other species, and his character was not revealed in the Bible but in a Hobbesian history of struggle. "The principle of natural selection is absolutely incompatible with the word of God," wrote the Bishop of Oxford. A powerful argument but one which, when the principle came to be admitted, would turn against the word of God. The debate was bitter: "Leave me my ancestors in Paradise and I will allow you yours in the zoological gardens," pleaded one defender of traditional beliefs.

The Darwinian controversy was spiced by publications like *Essays and Reviews,* in which well-known members of the Church of England, such as Benjamin Jowett, master of Balliol, and a future archbishop of Canterbury, Frederick Temple, argued for the right of free discussion within the Church and suggested that the Bible account of Genesis might be regarded as a Hebrew myth. The greatest arguments raged around the suggestion of Bishop Colenso of Natal that logistical considerations rendered the story of Noah's Ark incredible. Temple and Huxley, Colenso and Darwin, were all put in the same basket and their daring to question the literal reading of the scriptures castigated: "Revelation neither invokes human science to confirm its truths, nor does it challenge human science to disturb them. It does not stoop to notice science at all. . . ." * That was telling them. But it was not enough. By 1872 Winwood Reade's *Martyrdom of Man* concluded with a paean to the coming age when purgatory-earth would become paradise, freed from hunger, disease, hard labor, with wide-ranging men mastering nature, becoming "manufacturers of worlds. Man then will become perfect; he will then be a creator; he will therefore be what the vulgar worship as a God."

Protestantism had claimed that *its* theology rested on reason. Now reasonable doubts pecked at its foundations; moral laws were seen to rest on blind faith and social utility.** Protestantism would never recover from the blow. Rome did better. It had always limited the province of reason. Now it opted out of the modern world, thus minimizing its impact but also that of its own creed, exchanging reasonableness for obscurantism.

The Church

Shocked by his experiences of 1848, Pius IX (who held the papal throne longer than any other pope) would spend the last thirty years of his reign as a confirmed reactionary, treating all liberals as revolutionaries, all revolutionaries as devils, and liberal Catholics as simple traitors. Liberal Catholic groups in France, England, and Germany were censured in 1864 when the encyclical *Quanta Cura* was accompanied by a *Syllabus* of "the principal errors of our times," including Bible societies, communism, freedom of conscience, of discussion, of the press, religious toleration, rationalism, naturalism, socialism, Freemasonry, separation of Church and State, and condemning above all the proposition that the Pope "can and should reconcile himself to and come to terms with progress, liberalism and recent civilization." No reconciliation or agreement was possible with them.

The Pope had opted for the Middle Ages, and his opponents were delighted to see their worst predictions confirmed. The General Council of the Catholic Church which met in 1869–70 confirmed them further, by proclaiming the dogma of papal infallibility to the discomfiture of

* J. R. Young, *Modern Scepticism* (1865), quoted in James Laver, *The Age of Optimism* (London: 1966), p. 129.

** Even the arguments of the religious suggested as much. Reviews of Darwin's *Descent of Man* in 1871 criticized an author who revealed "his zoological conclusions to the general public at a moment when the sky of Paris was red with the incendiary flames of the Commune." Darwin endangered faith, faith bolstered patience, obedience, and duty, its crumbling could only mean dire danger for society: radicalism, free-thinking, social revolution.

Pope Leo XIII.

liberal Catholics. The day after this decree had been voted in the midst of a thunderstorm, war broke out between France and Prussia. Within a few weeks French troops, which had protected papal power since 1849, were withdrawn from Rome and, by September, 1870, Italian troops occupied the city. The temporal power of the papacy was ended, the kingdom of Italy—at last united—had recovered its ancient capital. But the impression Pio Nono left on Catholicism was only emphasized. Despite reforming popes and active social movements, the image of Catholicism allied to reaction persisted into the twentieth century.

It seemed that there could be no conciliation between a totalitarian Church and a state not only indifferent to its claims but nursing totalitarian ambitions of its own. Nor, apparently, could there be conciliation between the anachronistic cultural concepts formulated in the *Syllabus* and the technical civilization of the modern world. This was the point of the *Kulturkampf*, a point significantly formulated by a famous pathologist, Doctor Rudolf Virchow, in the Prussian Chamber. In 1878, Leo XIII's encyclical *Quod Apostolici Muneris,* which condemned socialism, communism, and nihilism as deadly plagues "tainting society to its very core and bringing it to a state of extreme peril," reinforced the censures of the *Syllabus*. This would have wide effects.* Christian Socialists had to abandon their label and any identification with socialism; the radical Christianity of Lamennais was discredited again; socialist movements were confirmed in their hostility to religion in general and Catholicism in particular. On the other hand, the condemnation of tendencies and ideas reproved in all respectable quarters was not a barrier but a bridge between the Vatican and large parts of conservative society. An encyclical of 1888, *Libertas,* denied that the Church "looks unfavorably on *most* modern political systems and rejects *all* the discoveries of

---

* When in 1880 an eminent Dominican preaching in a fashionable Paris Church urged the reconciliation of Church and modern society, he was denounced by his congregation and banished to Corsica. Both sides in France agreed: you had to be either a Christian or a Republican.

contemporary genius." Leo XIII (1878–1903) supported the reconcili- ation of French Catholicism to the Third Republic and, eventually, the participation of Catholics in Italian politics, permitted after his death but in his spirit. He tried to come to terms with moderate political movements and with modern learning, opened the Vatican Archives to scholars, encouraged the revival of Thomistic studies which tried to reconcile science and theology, faith and reason. Most interesting to many, in 1891, his encyclical *Rerum Novarum* set out a social doctrine in which the ideologies of revolution and class war were challenged by reassertion of original Christian principles on which a practical social policy could be based.

Rerum Novarum condemned capitalist exploitation of human beings as if they were just another commodity, and declared that the state had a right and a duty to legislate against economic oppression and find rem- edies to social needs. Catholics now need no longer opt out of their age. They could form Christian unions, fight for social justice, appeal to workers, work with and for them; and though in its beginnings, before 1914, the echoes of *Rerum Novarum* touched only narrow circles, its principles prepared more widespread and effective action after the First—and especially after the Second—World War.

But even Leo reacted violently when the climate that he helped create encouraged Catholics to apply critical methods to the Bible or go too far in their advocacy of social reform. The modernist movement, which tried to reconcile modern scholarship and traditional tenets, was reaching dangerous conclusions in the work of men like Alfred Loisy (1857–1940) and George Tyrell (1861–1909). Dogma, they suggested, is not an unvarying truth but something that grows and changes with the times. Revelation is not an unchanging formula, but a living experi- ence. Leo XIII's successor, Pius X (1903–1914), would not accept such notions. In 1907, the modernist movement was suppressed by papal pronouncement (*Pascendi*), modern velleities broken, and tight conform- ism reimposed. A kind of fatality hovered over the great institution which, based on dogma and authority, could only liberalize itself at the expense of the cement that bound it. Allied so often with those who were rich and mighty like itself, the Church over and over had to suppress movements for social justice among its own faithful.*

The quandary affected all churches in some degree, during an age which no longer took their authority for granted. Atheism, by its very denial of God, seemed to take Him seriously. Agnosticism—the term itself

---

* This did not prevent confessional parties and trade unions, both Catholic and Protestant, from mobilizing quite a bit of working-class support in Holland, Belgium, France, Italy, and Germany, thus splitting workers without bringing them any com- pensating influence. Such confessional parties and unions were controlled by conserva- tive personalities or interest groups connected with the Church hierarchy, who would have the last word in policies which, in the last resort, tended to conservatism. This was shown in the case of the worker priests in France, a hopeful experiment of the 1940's disowned in the 1950's after numerous complaints from employers' organizations.

coined only in 1869—affirmed only doubt. This could make God irrelevant. Their supernatural authority increasingly questioned, the churches had to justify their existence on the same ground as any social institution. They found this ever more hard to do. "We'll not refute you: we'll explain you," had said John Morley. Christian apologists spluttered but failed to explain themselves, to adjust theology to new knowledge and currents of ideas, or to meet their challenge. Religion, already identified with political reaction, became identified with intellectual reaction and sterility as well, with opposition to modern science and education, with pietistic revivalism akin to superstition. When Gambetta proclaimed "Clericalism, there is the enemy!" he spoke for more than French republicans, in so far as the clergy, which refused to allow religious concerns to rest in private spheres, too often hampered social activities and progress. Politics competed with religion by suggesting another form of hope.

Dechristianization

By 1939, when the *Times Literary Supplement* reviewed T. S. Eliot's *Idea of a Christian Society,* written between Munich and the invasion of Poland, it had to remark that intelligent men seldom admit even the possibility that Christianity "is a system of truth from which flow inexhaustible principles in metaphysics, ethics and politics." Hardly anyone would have doubted the thought half a century earlier—at least not in public. But the half century had seen great changes. The dechristianization of Western Europe advanced with rationalism and even with irrationalism, as the latter grew more eclectic. Devotion and piety were relinquished to the simple mind. The number of religious ordinations fell as the rewards of a clerical vocation shrank in proportion to other opportunities—in the liberal professions for the middle class, in teaching, government service, and trade unions for the poorer—and the social authority of priests and ministers was diluted by the competition of other professional classes. The number of parishes without a priest increased nearly fourfold in France in the half century before 1900, and further still in the twentieth century. In Portugal, by 1930, the Archdiocese of Lisbon had only 320 priests for one and one-half million people. Priests were less educated, their sermons less inspiring, so were church art and music; people went less to church as other amusements became available. Country weekends among the upper classes, religious doubts among the middle classes, the rise of the labor movement, refusal or inability to find a penny for the collection plate among the urban and especially the rural poor, diminished church attendance. Greater material possibilities on earth meant less need for solace in the hereafter. On the other hand, Christian charity was called into question.

The political and national commitments of churches—priests taking sides with a particular party or blessing their nation's arms—discredited religion. Above all, alternatives now offered for the many services— social and psychological—which the Church alone had offered in the past.

Every civilization, Victor Hugo said, begins in theology and ends in democracy. While the evolution did not seem very clear, current experience convinced a great many that theology and democracy were mutually exclusive. The process of dechristianization was as other-directed as religious conformity had been in the past. People had gone to Church with and like their neighbors; when enough of them stopped going, whole neighborhoods fell away. People had enjoyed the comforts of belief. Now they enjoyed the comforts of indifference. A great deal is written—even today—about the pangs of loneliness without a God, nothing about the relief and release of getting rid of the jealous, frowning Lord, terrible in his wrath and holding out more hell than heaven, the problems of continual self-examination and emotional fear, the growing problems too of intellectual doubt, of reconciling religion and science. Agnosticism or atheism could be pragmatically justified. To a great many they brought release, relief, and new hope: "the daring which goes forth into the sunshine and under the stars, to study and enjoy, without leave asked or fear of penalty." So noted Harriet Martineau in her *Autobiography* (II, p. 56), while Tennyson in his "Despair" reflected

And we broke away from the Christ, our human brother and friend,
For He spoke, or it seemed that He spoke, of a Hell without help, without end.

Everywhere religious practice declined and conformity became increasingly occasional. In London, by 1902, only about two out of eleven residents went to Church on Sunday. In central France, the proportion of children left unbaptized rose from 2 per cent in 1899 to 40 per cent in 1914; that of civil marriages increased from 14 to 60 per cent. Men went to church far less than women, workers far less than the middle classes, young people less than the old. In Spain, in 1933, most cities were pagan and only 5 per cent of parishioners went to Easter Mass. In Italy, the number of communicants fell by half between 1938 and 1948. Today, in Belgium about a quarter of Catholics go to Mass, in West Germany about 50 per cent, but only half that in cities; in France between 20 per cent in middle-class and 5 per cent in working-class parishes. In Austria, where 86 per cent of the population is Catholic, only 20 per cent of the population goes to church. The same is true of Protestants. About 5 per cent of England's population, 20 per cent of Scotland's, belongs to any church at all. In the United States less than half the grownups surveyed declared that they belonged to a church of any kind.

Pope John XXIII.

Theology for Today

Yet through the centuries the message of the Scriptures has provided ground for radical criticisms of the way life in society is lived. Of recent years, in Europe as in Latin America, clergy and laymen jostled by the world around them have insisted once again that religious beliefs are related to contemporary problems. The "revolution" revealed in the papacy of John XXIII (1958–1963), and in the Vatican Council that met in 1962 at his behest, had been going on unnoticed for a long time, individual Christians questioning the established order in its injustices and their churches in their conservative orientation: a slow, unspectacular process, but leading in our day to the presence of more progressive personalities in positions of authority within the hierarchies of their churches and to the progress of an ecumenical movement devoted to the collaboration and union of divided Christians.* This evolution is particularly noticeable in the ranks of the Roman Church, whose members—Young Catholics, Syndicalist Catholics, Worker Priests, prelates, and laymen—are often found in the van of social rebellion (as in France, Italy, Spain, and Latin America), making a point which had been long forgotten: that, as the title of a recent book affirms, *God Is Not Conservative.* * *

The word *religion* comes from a Latin term meaning "to bind" and, if the mystic bond is that between man and God, the social bond is that

---

* Under the rule of Paul VI, the Church applied the brakes on its progress into the twentieth century, while its membership urged it forward. The Pope resisted pressure to allow the marriage of priests; less reasonably, the Vatican opposed attempts to legalize divorce and the sale of contraceptives in Italy, thus reviving the image of a Roman Catholicism determined to beat back even the most moderate reforms.

** A tract circulating in Lisbon in May, 1969, and reproduced in the Paris *Monde* of May 13, 1969, p. 11, states: "Reward to those furnishing information leading to the capture of a certain Jesus Christ, accused of sedition and conspiracy against the established order. Frequents workers, homeless persons and vagrants, dangerous professional agitator."

between men who share a common faith and, hence, a common set of values. With the religion of the West decaying, disgruntled men and women inevitably sought reassurance in substitute bonds and systems of identification: on the religious plane the mass of sects and churchlets which would begin to swarm late in the nineteenth century,* on the political plane a common worship of certain great abstractions—people or nation, proletariat or race—whose destiny could lend an eschatological meaning to their times and lives. "When people cease to believe in God," remarked G. K. Chesterton, "they don't believe in nothing, but—what's far worse—in anything." Fascisms and communisms are also great religious movements of our time to which individuals could give the loyalty and veneration they once accorded an established church, in which they could find the total revelation, dogma, and reassurance that another kind of worship provided their ancestors. Creed, since the Reformation polycentric, became polymorphous too, and the cultural divisions of Western society were reflected in the diversity of its beliefs.

While institutional Christianity decayed, the spiritual quest of many was offered answers tempered by new experiences. Lonely individuals, faced with the responsibility of choice without authorities to guide them, could not be satisfied either by traditional forms or by the liberal theology in which "a God without wrath brought men without sin into a kingdom without judgment through the ministrations of a Christ without a cross." ** Domesticated, institutionalized, its hair combed, its teeth filed, its claws trimmed, its brightness tarnished, Christianity had been tamed into a social custom, the resplendence of its original madness dulled down to bearable proportions, the logic of its peculiar folly—the folly of the cross—abandoned for that of everyday reason and compromise, the paradox and scandal on which Paul of Tarsus throve rendered irrelevant. This was the sense of the message that the new theologians refurbished.

The answer to man's religious problems did not lie in a theology where sin and salvation, good and evil, were happily reconciled in a harmonious transition from darkness to self-knowledge. This feeling had led Søren Kierkegaard (1813–1855) to turn violently against the theological counterpart of the optimistic rationalism of his day. Majority rule was a snare ("Truth is always in the minority") and "sciencemongery" a delusion. The human personality could not be explained or manipulated in mechanistic terms. Kierkegaard's vision stressed not

---

* This is not to mention the growing mass of private enterprise catering to popular superstition. "There will come a time," wrote Voltaire, "when all people will have discovered the roguery of all astrologers." Today there are a thousand professional astrologers in Paris alone, some 50,000 in all of France, counting seers, card, coffee, and crystal ball gazers; There is a union of 120,000 occultists in Italy; 60 per cent of French people read astrology forecasts regularly; German businessmen consult astrologers (as did Hitler), and one English astrologer counts among her regular clients fifty British and forty-nine foreign firms.

** Richard Niebuhr, *The Kingdom of God in America*.

gradual transition but moral struggle. Only hard, abrupt decisions could deliver men from sin. The way to salvation could not be taught or reasoned. There was, there is, no intellectual proof of Christianity or of any other ultimate truth. Faith is an act of will, not of understanding. A conventional, respectable, established Church is a hollow fake, for the truth it promises cannot be found in its pews but only in the night of man's own soul, "through fear and trembling."

Ignored in his own time, Kierkegaard was rediscovered when confidence in reason, convention, conciliation, hit rock bottom and much of Europe lived in fear and trembling. After the First World War, Kierkegaard became a patron saint of existential philosophy and of the theology of crisis, both of which stressed the view that ultimate truth cannot be accepted from outside, but only apprehended by living it out in a total existence. Under the pen of men like Karl Barth and Karl Jaspers, the gospels turned into "special delivery letters to the 20th century." Men were challenged to jettison easy routine and acceptance in favor of free choice. Faith, they were told, cannot be reached by any human road: "It is a leap in the void. And it is possible for all only because it is equally impossible for all."

An absurd world had found a theology in its own image.

The Way They Lived

The Countryside

Most people's lives reflect their work: its circumstances and its wages. In this respect, one of the greatest changes of this period lies in the shrinking of the portion of the population making its living on the land. In 1900, only the nations of North and Western Europe could show less than half the active population employed in agriculture. By 1950, less than four in ten of all active Europeans (two in ten in the north and west) worked on the land. The peasant of the old regime "dressed all in canvas like a windmill," as the saying went, was disappearing. Peasants were still, as ever, dissatisfied, embittered, rapacious, hopeful, clinging to every bit of earth and greedy for more, humble and assertive, submissive and tough. But they were learning to fill in official forms, to use new foods and buy their trousers in the markets, to ignore older authorities and to respect new ones. Rural conditions were still much worse than urban ones, agricultural laborers still the worst paid of all salaried workers, untaught, unwashed, and unenterprising.

As in many countries of Southern Europe today, the rustic cottages, the pretty countryside romantic to outsiders, hid abject poverty and chronic want for most peasants at least as late as 1914. An English union ballad described the laborer tramping

> . . . Off to his work while townfolk were abed,
> With nothing in his belly but a slice or two of bread;
> He dined upon potatoes and he never dreamed of meat
> Except a lump of bacon fat sometime by way of treat . . .

The peasant's staple diet into the 1870's consisted of broth, potatoes, and bread, and remained almost wholly meatless except for diseased meat, or game snared despite the severe laws against poaching. Fresh air and, where it existed, sunshine did not make up for insanitary lodgings and shortage of water. Nostalgic references to horse-and-buggy days forget that manure in the home, yard, or village street is no less nauseous and insanitary for being natural.

Rural living was distinguished less by health and good cheer than by rudimentary education, limited horizons, and a high incidence of illegitimate births. "Fornication and adultery, incest and murder, abortion and poisoning—all the tangled annals of the poor—this is "Our Village" at work, this is Christian and happy England," remarked the *Saturday Review* of March 3, 1857. No wonder that those who could went to the towns much as rivers run into the sea. Not into the small provincial towns, though, which held out little opportunity and little enough change, where there was no excitement except the feuds and gossip of a narrow world, where there was no variety except for seasons, and ageing. They went into the cities, where there was employment and life and growth. By 1930 about one-fifth of people in the world dwelt there, while most of the rest lived in conditions much closer to those of ancient Romans or Egyptians than to those of Kentish or Midwestern farmers. And, since it was mostly the young who left, over the years small towns and villages became places where the retired and the old predominated, leftovers of a slower-changing world whose ways increasingly contrasted with those of the modern city.

The Cities

In 1801, Europe boasted twenty-one cities with populations over 100,-000; in 1900, 147. Where less than 2 per cent of Europeans had lived in cities over 100,000, now the proportion was 15 per cent and higher than that in the Atlantic West. The population of Paris doubled, that of Berlin quadrupled in the last half of the century. In 1837, the year of Queen Victoria's accession, only six British cities had more than 100,000 inhabitants. By the century's end there were twenty-four. By then, 15 per cent of Englishmen and Welshmen lived in London, one Scotsman in five lived in Glasgow. Human groups seemed to exercise a magnetic force proportionate to their mass.

The cities grew like coral reefs, ramparts giving way to broad new boulevards, roads, rails, and aqueducts reaching out for food—and even more for water, which had to come over great distances to satisfy a level of consumption that seemed almost to double decade by decade. The urban reefs spread outward in irregular accretions, with bits of blighted country in between, swallowing up what had been isolated villages (Montmartre, Passy, Kensington, Islington), allowing new slums to rise in formerly elegant quarters, turning undeveloped land on the outskirts into suburbs, some—similar to medieval *faubourgs*—sheltering the shanties of those who could not find room within the city, others accommodating the flight from smoke and noise, the quest for new amenities like fresh air. "I am alien to what is coming, to what is here already," grumbled Goncourt in his *Journal* (November, 1860), "like these new boulevards with no turnings, with no adventure of perspective, implacable in their straightness, which retain nothing of the world of Balzac, which make one think of some American Babylon of the future."

The high pressure of city life, its nervous rhythm and hurry, evoked particular comment. Oscar Wilde, lecturing in New York in 1882, found its inhabitants all "in a hurry to catch a train;" and an American doctor coined the term "neurasthenia" to describe a malady arising typically out of the noisy, crowded city streets. Cities frightened the beholder and they thrilled him. Jefferson had called them "ulcers on the body politic." Rousseau believed that they corrupted. "Men," he insisted, "are not made to be crowded together in anthills." A popular mid-nineteenth-century novelist thought that they were "the results of the Fall." Cities were rough, dirty, dangerous, dissolute. They were overcrowded. Some parts of Liverpool had a density of 1,200 persons to the acre; some suburbs of London, six and ten persons to a room. Planning and rebuilding, inspired by the work of Haussmann in Paris, fascinated civic

Mansell Collection

Glasgow tenements during the mid-19th century.

reformers as far apart as British Birmingham and Chicago, Brussels and Barcelona. But rebuilding created difficulties of its own:

> Who builds? Who builds? Alas, ye poor!
> If London day by day "improves,"
> Where shall ye find a friendly door,
> When every day a home removes?

The masses added new dimensions to old fears of frightening mobs. "The population is hourly increasing in breadth and strength," noted a Victorian. "It is an aggregate of masses, our conceptions of which clothe themselves in terms which express something portentous and fearful." They intrigued and titillated romantic imaginations spurred by ignorance of depths, dark and unrevealed as the unknown wastes of Africa and Asia to which they were often compared. In 1890, General Booth of the Salvation Army published *In Darkest England,* comparing the slums of London with the regions which Stanley had just penetrated. Another author had just remarked that the same sun which never set on the Empire never rose on the dark alleys of London's East End. T. H. Huxley, Darwin's champion, compared Polynesian savages and London slum dwellers. It is hard to say how far all this reflected ignorance of how the other half lived, even more than any real parallels. The new masses seemed to pose a special threat to the politics of personal influence which had developed on quite a different scale, and many expected (as many hoped) that they would soon use their strength of numbers to secure radical—or even socialist—ends.

The Working Classes

How did these people live? What did they do? Their clothes, their food, their living quarters and outward surroundings improved in mid-nineteenth century and after. But the intensity of their working effort, the strain during working hours, the stress of urban living itself, the time spent getting to and from work also increased. Women were generally paid half a man's wages even for doing the same job. And a woman usually had to work to supplement her husband's pay. Insecurity was the watchword of the worker's life, at the mercy of accident, illness, depression, unemployment. True, savings banks flourished, but so did grogshops. The workman felt the need for protection and sought it in unions and associations, harking back to old traditions but also to present habits of a collective life not only in the workshop but in the pub, or bar, or coffee shop that offered refuge from cold, uncomfortable, ill-lit lodgings; warmth, company, the opportunity to read a paper or to discuss current events and common concerns. Unions were born in pubs but grew in didactic enterprises like the French Ligue de l'Enseignement or the English Workers' Institute. Education was the workers' major weapon of self-help; organization was another.

Among the more frugal and industrious of the skilled workers in mines, shops, and factories, who could pay cash for what they bought and even save a little, the Cooperative Movement prospered. In England, where it had begun in the 1840's, 1914 saw it reach a membership near 4 million and an annual turnover of over 500 million dollars. The same skilled workmen, afraid of being swamped by the unqualified masses, launched the first trade unions in the 1850's and 60's. There seems to have been a certain consensus in liberal societies that unions were justified. "Our only chance," declared a workman in a mid-nineteenth century English novel, "is binding men together in one common interest; and if some are cowards and some are fools, they must come along and join the great march whose strength is numbers." Thomas Hughes, who was not only the creator of that model of Anglo-Saxon enterprise—Tom Brown—but also a member of Parliament, agreed: "Under a system which professes the right or rather the duty of all men peacefully to pursue their own interests for themselves, unionism appears to us the exact correlative of competition."

Unions achieved legal recognition in France between 1864 and 1884, in Belgium in 1866, in Austria and Britain after 1870, in Spain after 1881, in Germany in 1890, in Russia after 1906. First in Germany, then in Britain and in a number of other countries, the unions became vast enterprises running a variety of insurance systems, administering large treasuries, and augmenting property in buildings, hospitals, recreation centers, eventually even investments in industrial or trading companies. Their members, and especially their managers, were thoroughly identified with the existing system; their officials, accountants, and bureaucrats were little different from those of the companies with which they bargained within the framework of the existing—capitalist—order.

As we may imagine, the basic attitude of such bodies was apolitical. Most of their members were neither socialist nor Marxist, and they kept out of politics whenever they could. Two factors forced them into political action. The first was the struggle to gain recognition for themselves and for characteristic activities like picketing and strikes. This could only be achieved by legislation which came in response to political pressure at the polls or in the streets. The second factor was that the makeup of labor and of industry were both changing. During the prosperous years of the mid-nineteenth century, workers who shared the general feeling that technical progress, material improvements, and better living standards all went hand in hand, accepted the ruling faith in progress even for themselves. Experience apparently confirmed this. Visibly, workers could become managers, shopkeepers, manufacturers, and even millionaires. In 1872, 80 per cent of masters had begun as workmen, 15 per cent were the sons of workingmen. But this was the last generation to stem from the working class. Economic conditions which permitted such social and economic promotion began to alter, economic expansion lagged, relations between patrons and workers grew rarer, education and capital needed for success rose to a higher order, the worker felt he would not get the chance his predecessors enjoyed. Industrial expansion was mobilizing a different kind of workman in ever greater numbers—less skilled, less secure, more aware of the gap between his earnings and those of his employers. The concentration and growth of industry were separating worker and master, the latter increasingly distant from his employees, the masters becoming an invisible presence in the Board room, with whom relations could only be in class terms, far from the old personal ties however hostile these may occasionally have been.

In this changing context, the mass unions were well adapted to mediate between the increasingly distant and hostile parties. They did their work well: their first aim, and that of the Second International founded in 1889, was to cut working hours. These, which were patterned after those of agricultural labor, beginning at dawn and ending at dusk, amounted to 3,500 or 4,000 hours a year—12 hours or more a day for 6 days a week. The agitation to reduce the work week to 60 hours had brought its first results in the United States, where the 60-hour week was introduced in the 1860's. The new International made its demonstrations so impressive (the May Day was launched in 1890 as the first of them) that Kaiser Wilhelm II called an international conference that year to consider possible labor legislation * and by 1900 the 60-hour week was almost general. It fell to 48 or 50 hours after World War I, and lower still between the 1930's and the 1950's. As a result, most twentieth-century workers enjoyed far greater leisure than their ancestors. The average sixty-five-year-old man retiring in 1900 had worked about 220,000 hours of his life; the average Western workman of our day at retirement will have worked 100,000 hours or less.

Real wages were improving (70–90 per cent between 1866 and 1936). Conditions of life and labor were getting better. There were many poor, but even the poorest were consumers now. They bought pins and buttons, tea or candles. The remainder simply bought more. In other words, vast numbers of people appeared, most of whom had never existed (numerically) in previous centuries, most of the remainder of whom had never existed as consumers of anything but basic foodstuffs— millions and millions of consumers of manufactured products whose very existence created the demand which gave them the jobs, hence the wages, hence the means to carry out their consumer's function.

Higher wages did not only keep up with higher prices but also with increased expectations. Bread consumption remained steady while that of meat, wine, and beer went up. In the 1850's and 60's, 61 per cent of

* *Rerum Novarum* was another response to the agitation for social reform.

Pit boys at the Derbyshire coal
mines in the early 1900's.

the French working-class budget still went for food. But the poor were
beginning to actually buy clothing—though still generally secondhand
—instead of relying only on charity. Soon living standards improved:
fewer children, fewer married women, went out to work; working hours
were reduced; real wages edged up as prices of consumer goods went
down; so did the size of the average family, falling from five or six
to four in the last decades of the ninteenth century. The very poor
were still very poor, but there were fewer of them. Meanwhile, more and
more were being reconciled to a society in which conditions of life and
work were notably improving, life expectation going up, elementary
education provided for every working child. In the 1880's English
workers began to take holiday trips like their social superiors. Manners,
behavior, public safety improved; streets were cleaner, better lit and
paved, safer at night; there were more parks, better drains and sewers,
more stringent inspections of working conditions, food purity, weights
and measures: all of which made life better for a lot of people, quite
apart from wages.

More, the income gap between rich and poor was narrowing. A textile
worker of the Second Empire had to work 15 days for a good pair of
boots, which his descendant earns today in as many hours. A Berlin
dressmaker around 1900 put in 7 hours' work to buy a pound of beef,
seven times more than her granddaughter today. A suit which would take
a well-paid miner 12 days' work to buy before 1900 could be acquired
with one day's wages today. The bicycle which cost a Frenchman the
equivalent of 100 work days in 1900, cost only 10 in 1938. In 1900 the
inner tube of a bicycle cost 40 hours' work: today only 2 hours.*

* It is interesting to glance at the relative cost of various products, not in time but
space, in the 1950's, and to note, incidentally, that costs in what economists call tertiary
or service categories differ little: one pair of shoes costs 7 hours' work in Chicago, 15 in
Paris, 54 in Moscow; one pound of bread costs 7 minutes' work in Chicago, 15 minutes
in Paris, 25 minutes in Moscow; however, a seat at the opera costs 8 hours' work in
Chicago and Paris and 7 hours' in Moscow, while a medical consultation costs the
equivalent of 5 hours' work in each of these cities.

This closing of the income gap between rich and poor has been one of the greatest changes of the past century. Economists like Jean Fourastié have calculated that in 1800 the income of a senior judge was fifty times that of his janitor; in 1950 it was only four or five times greater, while the proportion of the hours they worked respectively (2,000 a year for the one, 3,000 or 3,500 for the other) has changed considerably. Comparing the salaries of a higher public servant and those of an industrial worker, the ratio alters from 55:1 in 1800, to 13:1 in 1900, and 7:1 in 1960. Of course, what matters is buying power; and everybody knows that if the workman's mean hourly wage has increased a thousandfold since the day of Louis XIV, so have prices. But not all prices have gone up in the same proportion: the price of mirrors, for instance, proportionate to hourly wages has been immensely reduced, while that of personal services has not. In 1700 a mirror six feet square cost relatively as much as a Cadillac does today. At that time, and until the beginning of the nineteenth century, half or more of a working-class family budget might go for bread alone. By 1831, only a quarter of such budgets went for bread. By mid-twentieth century bread figured for only 3 per cent in a French worker's budget and for 1 per cent in a New Yorker's, while in both cases nine-tenths of food expenses now go for things which made rare or no appearances on working-class tables a hundred years ago: meat, fruit, milk, and fresh vegetables.

The large proportion of expenses which food took up is now devoted to new comforts, like refrigerator or washing machine, auto or television. The very *standard* of living has utterly changed from times when comfort meant sufficient heat, when clothes and lodging accounted for a tiny proportion of the budget and meager household equipment for even less. The level of what we regard as a minimum has soared to include far more things, and men's capacity of paying for these things has improved too—though proportionally more so among the former underprivileged. Thus, while between 1830 and 1960 the nominal income of a French factory hand increased from 60 to 64,000 (index points), that of a colonel or an office manager went up just half that much: from 60 to 32,000. And, while such a salary in 1950 stood for 2,250 working hours a year, its counterpart in 1831 had to be earned in 3,600 hours.

But class differentials, if smaller, clearly subsist. Thus, in pre-1914 years, while a French miner came to earn 20 per cent more, his employer's profits doubled. On the eve of that war in Britain, 5 per cent of the population owned 85 per cent of the national wealth. To the extent that wealth and well-being increase, that of the wealthy increases faster. In 1954, in Paris, infant mortality for children of unskilled workers was more than double that of the children of the managerial staff; and four times as high for children of laborers as for the children of doctors or lawyers.

Food (and Drink)

Nothing can illustrate the improvements that have taken place so well as changes in food habits.

In 1842, many poor townspeople lived entirely on potatoes and porridge, eking these out with rotten vegetables and vegetable refuse. Consumption of tea increased so much partly because many people could not get milk and looked to the tea for warmth. After 1860, things improved, but bread remained the mainstay until the end of the century. Toast is probably an English invention, made to disguise the taste of stale bread. In 1864, the typical Lancashire worker's diet consisted mainly of bread, oatmeal, bacon, perhaps a little butter, treacle, tea, and coffee. Skilled workmen did better, getting butter and Sunday meat. When fuel was dear and weariness overwhelming, most people could afford only two or three hot meals a week; and these were cooked on an open fire or baked in a brick oven. Closed ranges began to show up in middle-class kitchens in the 1860's, and domestic gas ovens, which appeared about the same time, only came into general use at the end of the century. They were for a long time out of reach of poor people, who could not afford their price and that of cooking utensils. What with inadequate water supplies, limited means, and little time, no wonder cookshops flourished.

So did drink shops. In 1860 there was one for every seventy French men, women, and children. Even in the London of 1900, one house in seventy-seven was a public house. A third to a quarter of a working-class family's income seems to have gone for drink—a welcome argument for those who attributed the poverty of the poor to their own improvidence. But drink, like gambling, is typical of a search for satisfaction or relief not otherwise available to people with no reason to believe that gratification may be deferred. Also, more simply, poor working people could seldom find snacks or meals elsewhere than in taverns. It would be the awareness of this fact among temperance workers, shocked first of all by the large number of drunken children, that produced concrete results (first in England after the 1850's) in chains of cafés, refreshment houses, and temperance restaurants, where one could order food or nonalcoholic beverages at very moderate prices.*

The temperance movement was only one reflection of a growing, sometimes muddled but ultimately effective, awareness of social problems—prison abuses, juvenile delinquency, prostitution, and alcoholism. The awareness was emphasized by the crusading propaganda carried out

* The temperance movement also sparked the foundation, in 1880, of the first temperance music hall, which—situated in a popular quarter of London—would become the Old Vic Theatre.

A British institution and the gathering place of the whole neighborhood: the pub.

in books and pamphlets. There were those meant for children, some selling by the million, all fully equipped with dramatic conversations and death scenes, but well informed about the condition of the destitute, especially the young, which were graphically described. There were books for grownups: the accounts and surveys appreciated by the age, and novels like those of Charles Dickens. Today we find much of their tone pathetic and rather overdone. But as a later critic, the novelist George Gissing, pointed out: "such pathos is called 'cheap' . . . In Dickens's day the lives, the happiness of children were very cheap indeed and . . . he had his purpose in insisting on their claims to attention." The same might be said about the sordidness that seems to overflow from the naturalistic novels of the 1870's and after. They, too, like the pathos of their predecessors, had a social purpose and achieved it.

By the 1880's a social conscience had become fashionable. The American Society for Prevention of Cruelty to Animals had obtained conviction of a parent who starved and beat his child, by claiming that the child was an animal in distress. In 1884, the London Society for Prevention of Cruelty to Children was founded. In the same year the *Oxford English Dictionary*, which had defined the word "slumming" as "frequenting slums for discreditable purposes," added a new variant: "to visit slums for charitable or philanthropic purposes, or out of curiosity, especially as a fashionable pursuit." Middle-class intellectuals and idealists were going to the people, beginning to work and teach in the slums of Paris and London, as the Narodniks were trying to do in the Russian countryside.*

After the 1880's a new recession prompted a new look at conditions of working-class life. The facts produced by contemporary surveys suggested that poverty was not due to improvidence or sin as had been com-

---

* Yet neither rich nor poor questioned the assumption that they were different races, each fated to a different place in the world. Equality was an idea entertained only by those above the poverty line, not below it.

fortably supposed, and placed in relief the sufferings of the very old and the very young—the latter could hardly be charged with improvidence, except in being born. The Young Men's Christian Association, which had been founded in 1844, was now followed by the YWCA, set up in 1877 as a prayer union for young girls. Then, in 1883, came the Boys' Brigade, designed to teach poor boys "drill, physical exercises, punctuality, cleanliness and obedience to command." * More important perhaps, the social conscience found a wide open field in the realm of food and drink, where fraud, adulteration, and exploitation abounded. When the controls, inspections, and regulations of the bad old days before Adam Smith had been removed, competition became a vicious spiral in which little men survived only by undercutting their fellows, overworking their employees, deteriorating their wares, and defrauding their customers. One Liverpool firm even took out a patent in 1851 for a machine which could compress chicory into the shape of coffee beans, to cheat the buyer. Manufacturers, brewers, vintners, wholesalers, retailers, all set out to press back the limits of private enterprise. The public—especially the ignorant and poor—paid. Chronic gastritis, characteristic of the nineteenth-century urban populations, was only one result of a diet containing alum, plaster of Paris, lead, mineral dyes, and any number of poisons introduced in search of profit and under the cover of a vast conspiracy of silence.

First Englishmen, then Americans, then others, began to be informed that their breakfast sausage was a mess of spiced and flavored putrid meat, their coffee grains were mixed with dried blobs of horses' blood from the knacker's yard, the cream on which they smacked their lips was thickened with calves' brains, their sweets bore poisonous decorations, their infusions were for a good part sweepings, their tea gum and dust, their bread loaves only partly wheat, and all their food a major carrier of disease and dirt. The campaign against this and the legislation it set off achieved many improvements in the quality of food. Commercialism now intervened to show that it was profitable to sell pure foods—if at a higher price—and, by the 1880's, increasingly effective laws made adulteration dangerous and unprofitable. Packaged foods (tea, sugar, flour) appeared as a first result of some manufacturers' determination to see their products reach the consumer in a pure state. Breakfast foods, probably first developed in the United States to provide pure food for Seventh Day Adventists waiting for a second coming, began to appear in Europe. Infantile mortality fell, partly as a result of movements to supply unadulterated milk free to poor mothers. France, then England and

---

* This soon had a membership in the tens of thousands and helped to inspire boy scouting, which appeared around 1907, making its appeal to the middle classes. The poor could not afford to join, since scouts had to read, write, and own a small sum in savings, while the uniform cost too much for children whose only clothes were hand-me-downs.

Holland, established milk dispensaries, followed by health visitors and infant welfare centers. Milk *was* getting purer and its consumption rising. But it was still relatively expensive, and figures for 1902 show that while middle-class English families consumed six pints per head per week, the lower middle-class consumed four, artisans less than two, and laborers less than one pint.

The best will in the world could not furnish food where there was none, or no means to get it. Prosperity and technology worked hand in hand to provide these. Substitutes like margarine, invented by a Frenchman, developed by the Americans and the Dutch, became an important part of working-class diet. A vast increase in processed foods made ready-made eating possible. The difficulty of transporting meat was tackled first by salting and drying, then by canning, always with highly unappetizing results. Canning processes had been invented and used during the Napoleonic wars. The California gold rush, the Crimean War, and the Civil War in America had provided them with a further impetus. Prejudices against canning still persisted; and British sailors, referring to a woman who had been cut into small pieces in a famous murder case of 1867, called their canned meat "Sweet Fanny Adams," an expression that survived until the First World War. Then, in the 1880's, the problems of refrigeration were solved, introducing really cheap imported meat and, also, adding fresh fish to the salted or pickled herring to which the working classes had been restricted until then. One has to remember how narrow the margin is between the slaughter of an animal and its putrefaction, the picking of a fruit and its rotting, the milking of a cow and the milk's turning, the freshness of butter and its rancidness, to get a sense of what the world gained from refrigeration.

We have already seen that, as incomes generally rose, a smaller proportion of them was spent on food. In England of 1885, while the working classes spent three-fourths of their earnings on food and drink, the middle classes spent 44 per cent. At the same time, as they became better able to choose—that is, afford—more people shifted from dark bread to white, from bread, potatoes, and other fillers to meat, from carbohydrates to proteins, from make-dos to luxuries: tea, coffee, cocoa, chocolate, sugar, eggs, jams. In all, to more variety and better nutrition. The consumption of food increased with the buying power of the masses: between 1890 and 1914 the consumption of wheat doubled in Belgium, trebled in Germany. The average Englishman who had eaten 6 pounds of sugar a year in 1800 was eating 80 pounds in 1900, the Frenchman had been promoted from 4 to 46. Sugar consumption seems, incidentally, to provide a very accurate reflection of industrial prosperity. Its spread among the poorer classes and the comparative figures of average consumption in the early 1880's per head of population range themselves in a hierarchical table of industrial and social advances at that time:

Spain	5.1 lbs. per head per year
Italy	7.6 lbs. per head per year
Russia	7.7 lbs. per head per year
Austria	13.2 lbs. per head per year
Germany	15.0 lbs. per head per year
France	22.6 lbs. per head per year
Denmark	38.0 lbs. per head per year
Great Britain	68.8 lbs. per head per year

Nevertheless, although conditions had been steadily improving throughout the century, for millions of men and women the wartime rations of the First World War were far better than anything that they had known before. During the Boer War, army recruiters lowered the minimum height to five feet, and still had to reject two men in every five for physical deficiencies. In Leeds (1902) half the children in the poorer quarters had rickets; in Britain as a whole (1904) one-third of all children "were undernourished in the sense that they actually went hungry," and the average height of boys at private schools was 5 inches greater than that of boys at council (or public) schools. 1906 and 1907 brought school meals, medical and dental treatment, infant welfare clinics, followed by old-age pensions (1908), health and unemployment insurance (1911). Poverty and disease could only be tackled on the public level: a fact which Communists and National Socialists recognized, but which the free economies accepted only after 1940 when shortages were turned to dietary improvements and rationing was deliberately used to change the health and habits of the popular masses.

Today, almost all of Europe has sufficient food. Dietitians tell us that the average daily ration of a normal population ranges between 2,700 and 2,800 calories. This range has by now been attained even in poor countries like Italy or Greece—although statistical averages do not show how much overconsumption in certain quarters balances the hunger of other men. Even so, counting all of Europe, all of Soviet Russia, the United States, and the white dominions of the British Empire, this accounts at most for half the population of the world. The other half still lives, hungry or undernourished, in the conditions Europe left behind with Louis XIV. There are perhaps a few hundred thousand people among the scores of millions of the West who eat as little and as badly as the average man of Asia's 700 or 800 million. Until this disparity has been effaced, their hunger must influence not only the conscience but the stability of the world.

The Bourgeoisie

If the outstanding characteristic of the past century has been the rise and assertion of the masses, the most articulate and constructive roles would still be played by the *bourgeoisie,* however general or misleading the term: people living in cities as a rule but who, particularly, do not derive their living from manual labor, whether they be landowners, *rentiers*, clerks, bankers, manufacturers, shopkeepers and employees, lawyers, or veterinarians. The *bourgeoisie* allows for subdivisions—high, medium, petty—among those who have a fortune, those who are building one, and those who have no hope (and perhaps no ambition either) of ever attaining it. But it does set itself apart from those who work with their hands in industry or on the land, and also from those who derive their status specifically from birth: the landed aristocracy.

The latter's social significance diminished to the point of irrelevance halfway through this period. Over most of Europe their wealth, the revenues of their estates and of the property they held in and around the fast developing cities, enabled the aristocracy to retain social and economic predominance until 1900 or 1918. The horse and carriage, the notion of gentleman derived from landed values, remained symbols of social standing into the twentieth century. But the majority among the nobility—pompous, shallow, narrow-minded and ignorant—looked increasingly like an anachronistic polyp on the body politic. Hunting and gambling seem to have been their greatest passions and while the latter ruined only the players, the former caused vast hecatombs whose results can still be viewed by wondering tourists in the eerie stuffed-corpse-lined chambers of some hunting lodges and castles.* But the trend of the age toward investment and management rather than pomp and circumstance emphasized wealth as the base of status rather than birth. Aristocracy was being pressed back by plutocracy, and rich aristocrats simply melted in it. It was also being sapped by bureaucracy and specialization.

Society was becoming increasingly complicated, requiring and recruiting immense numbers of men to make it run. Between 1880 and 1910, in Germany alone, the number of postal and railway employees increased from 245,000 to 700,000. New professions, new pursuits appeared: policemen, sanitary inspectors, medical officers, permanent professional officials, colonial and other civil servants. There and in teaching, science, and technology, amateurs were steadily replaced by specialists; and the new structure called for educated men to run it. Men of background and breeding were preferred, of course, but there were not enough of them. A wider elite was taking shape, appealing to capacity —as when the British Civil Service began to be recruited by competitive examinations—and sometimes forming it by scholarships and grants. The hierarchies of money and of social function would gradually eliminate the hierarchy of birth.** On the other hand, the industrial condition

---

* Between 1867 and 1900 a keen but not exceptional hunter of his day, Lord Ripon, slaughtered 142,343 pheasant, 97,759 partridge, 56,460 grouse, 29,858 rabbit, 27,686 hare, 97 wild pig, 19 sambur, 12 buffalo, 11 tiger, and 2 rhinoceros: nearly 30 lives a day for 33 years.

** However, as this happened, the importance of decorations and titles also grew: in England, elevation to or promotion within the peerage; in France appointment to some order, especially the Legion of Honor; in Germany and Austria not only ennoblement

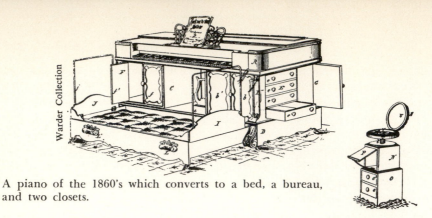

A piano of the 1860's which converts to a bed, a bureau, and two closets.

out of which they grew also reduced the distance between classes, offering all the same increasingly showy, shoddy goods, creating a common taste for the fashionable and the superficial, which most men could increasingly indulge. Mass production laid the groundwork for a new mass age: refining the people, vulgarizing their masters, imparting to both a certain identity of tastes and manners even while it differentiated their material situations.

This can be seen quite plainly in their homes and dress. Perhaps the most widely recognized form of self-expression the last century knew was spending money.* The bourgeoisie, General de Gaulle once remarked "is wealth: the consciousness of having it, or the desire to acquire it." Conspicuous consumption became a badge of rank, as it had been a responsibility of rank in earlier days. Objects poured forth to fill once empty rooms and cupboards, parlors became teeming hoards of loot both from the past and from the farthest corners of the earth, as mixed and crowded as purse and ingenuity could achieve. Men and things responded exuberantly to the possibilities held out by the new machines: in furniture, spring upholstery made possible by cheap metal springs was an immense advance in comfort but a failure in looks. In decoration, design gave way to mass-produced adornments to satisfy an ever-growing number of uneducated customers. The ingenuity of ornament turned into a kind of game where every object concealed its function in an alien shape: embroidered spittoons, antler hatstands, stuffed bears to hold umbrellas, doilies concealing tables, flowers opening to embrace toothpicks, gothic bookcases, baroque tubs: the more machines could multiply ornaments, the uglier ornaments seemed to be. This was the essence of the "home, sweet home"—the song of which name became almost the anthem of English-speaking countries in the nineteenth century.

but, even more, honorary and other ranks in the civil service; these rewarded political utility as much as they did service to the state. Differentiating labels would be as rife in the modern world as in the old.

* The decree appointing Giuseppe Verdi a senator in 1875 spoke first of the amount of tax which the composer paid and only second of his services to music. The order, which shocked some music lovers, was highly indicative of the contemporary and especially Italian atmosphere.

But homes are relatively private; and people outside their homes were most easily set apart by dress. Until the 1880's, men of the "respectable" classes—although less and less differentiated among themselves by their dark, drab clothes—were easily identified by the frock coats and top hats which they wore, it seems, on all occasions.* Thereafter, with the spread of ready-made wear, workmen abandoned their smocks and corduroys and men began to shift toward the modern practice of dressing differently for different activities—sports, labor, lounging, or formal wear occasions.

They could afford to do so, for they retained a formidable agent of conspicuous consumption in their womenfolk. The clothes that wives and daughters wore would testify to the wealth of their more drably garbed husbands and fathers. The well-upholstered shapes of womankind answered the well-upholstered furniture in the parlors, in the same spirit: showing off. But here the problems involved led to sartorial escalation.

Women's fashion magazines, appearing early in the nineteenth century, had brought information to circles which would never otherwise have had it, so that even tradesmen's daughters could wear the same costume as their betters. Cheap textiles contributed to this, and one contemporary complained that "while expensive silks were worn they could not be attained by persons of small means, but when a few shillings could purchase a muslin gown quite in the fashion every woman could command one. . . ." As ready-mades and patterns encroached on society, *ladies* preserved their prerogatives by extravagance. Fashionable glamour became increasingly expensive, out of the reach of smaller purses. The dimension of clothes came to indicate social importance, the latter increasing with the diameter of the crinoline or the bulge of the bustle.

Fashions were the more exclusive the more useless they rendered their wearer. It was a long cry from the ladies' dresses of the beginning of the century when a young girl at a London ball could ask her partner: "Pray, Sir, do not tread on my dress and tear it, for as you can see I have nothing on underneath." Now women's bodies were swaddled like Chinese ladies' feet, and with the same debilitating results. As late as the 1870's, a girl asking her mother what "abdomen" meant was told that no lady needs to know about something only found among the lower orders. No wonder that women who did not know about abdomens—let alone other parts—suffered gastric troubles, acidosis, various results of poor diet, tight lacing, and general bad hygiene.

Wasp waists, corsets, bustles, crinolines were said "to restrain the impulses of one sex while arousing those of the other." "The crinoline," wrote a guide to etiquette in the 1870's, "is an ever present monitor indirectly bidding its wearer to exercise self-restraint; it is evidence of a well-disciplined mind and well-regulated feeling." But, if tight

* Millais' portrait of Ruskin shows him on a mountain walk in black frock coat and top hat (1854); much later Lord Salisbury went rabbit shooting in the same garb.

A group of women tram conductors in Edinburgh. Right: a woman chimney-sweep in London.

lacing meant that no woman so bound could stoop to conquer, no more could she stoop to dust. Burdened by 20 yards of heavy material, cut and deformed by steel-hard stays,* trammeled and hamstrung by a wealth of lace, fancies, and trimmings, the late-nineteenth-century woman of fashion was a triumph of artifice, the walking Christmas tree of her menfolk's thrift. Now it was time for her emancipation.

Women

The story of the emancipation of women is seldom mentioned in the same breath as that of other submerged groups, like workers or colonial peoples. Yet it should be. For, sometime at the turn of the nineteenth into the twentieth century, a process started which, by today, is well on the way to liberating half the human race. There was a great deal more than clothes from which women had to be liberated. Existing legislation tended to treat them as objects or, at least, as subjects of their masters' will. They were chattels of their fathers, transferred eventually to a husband's rule. In a novel of 1897, a father who breaks off his daughter's engagement is asked what she thinks. "She's got nowt to think," he answers, "I'm her father, I think for her." Marx denounced bourgeois marriage as prostitution, in which a woman sold her body for her keep. Tennyson slashed at "the woman markets of the West/where our Caucasians let themselves be sold." It certainly looks as if the love match that we more or less take for granted was almost a nineteenth-century invention; and that the widespread tendency of young people

* A letter from a schoolgirl, published in *The Englishwoman's Domestic Magazine* in the mid-sixties, mentions that at her boarding school stays are compulsory, sealed up by a mistress on Monday morning, removed on Saturday for one hour "for the purposes of ablution." The result: a 23-inch waist at fifteen was reduced to 13 inches by seventeen. Sleeping in tight-laced stays, remarks one mother, "carries no hardship beyond an occasional fainting fit."

to marry without dowry, contract, or marriage settlement only came in much later, with full employment and social security. As for spinsters, "devoured by little black relations just like fleas," many of them were simply murdered slowly by families that turned them into maids of all work.

All this applies in practice to the middle classes rather than the poor, to whom material considerations and contracts remained irrelevant. But, while among the poor the woman remained a workhorse, among the better off she was condemned to triviality. The bourgeois helpmate was rendered futile by domestic help, the active woman stultified by respectability. The ideal of nineteenth-century womanhood was sensitive, delicate, and useless: for what greater luxury could a man afford? She sighed, fainted, suffered from the vapors, dissolved into tears at the slightest provocation. Although some, like Florence Nightingale, ate like horses and lived to be ninety, many, like Flaubert's Madame Bovary, lived mostly in a dream world, unfit for anything but fantasies.

Emancipation came partly with the opportunities that the economy offered to the poor, partly with the self-assertion of the better off. The economic and educational issue here was crucial. In most European countries high-school education for girls became available only in the 1880's and 90's. Opportunities for independent work were slight. Respectable women took work at home in secret (sewing, embroidery, copying), taught music or languages at minimal fees. No woman could expect to live on her own earnings: prostitution or marriage were her only hope. One other opportunity lay in domestic service, which constituted the second largest occupation in England in 1851 and still employed one and a half million before the First World War, when the *Ladies' Home Journal* rightly but unbelievably predicted "we are gradually coming to the abolishment of a permanent serving class in our homes."

In the 1880's, telephonists, secretaries, and woman office clerks appeared. Between 1890 and 1900 the proportion of female clerks rose from 8 to 18 per cent; by 1911 one-third of all clerks were women. In England, women—even fashionable women—could now run shops (milliners, dressmakers), become professional photographers, doctors (212 in 1901), dentists (140 in 1901), or accountants. Erstwhile maids and cooks found that factories offered more freedom and sometimes better pay. The post office, the schools, opened their doors to cheap female labor.

Women were becoming more independent, using the trams and the omnibuses launched in 1870, setting up committees, turning toward higher education, asking for the vote. The first women's colleges in the United States date back to the 1830's, in England to the 1870's; the first teachers' training colleges in France to the 1880's. Women's dress was also becoming simpler, more practical, if only relatively and slowly. Until the appearance of the reticule in the 1890's, women had only a hidden pocket *under* the skirt. The reticule, forerunner of the handbag, permitted money, keys, card case, and purse—eventually cigarettes and cosmetics—to be carried in comfort and used without embarrassment. About the same time, knickers began to replace petticoats, lightening the load of material that women had to carry, eventually permitting shorter skirts and greater freedom of movement. The tailor-made dress with its efficient look reflected the new mood with its assertion of equality and emancipation. So did the safety bicycle, which freed women from their chaperones and encouraged the emancipating trend. One sometimes thinks of Ibsen's Nora slamming her way out of the *Doll's House* (1879) and riding off into a broader life mounted, quite likely, on a bicycle.

Women were going in for sports, playing golf, tennis, hockey, and, in England, cricket. They dueled or went in for Greco-Roman wrestling. They jettisoned social constraints to take on a new, slender, fluid shape, that of the hermaphrodite dear to the aestheticism of the 1880's and nineties. One of the literary heroes of the day * is smitten by a Miss Urania, a circus acrobat: "And as he admired her suppleness and strength, he could see an artificial change of sex taking place in her." This kind of allusiveness (with its picture of women becoming more masculine) was somewhat premature. Nevertheless, by 1900, women, still tightly bound by their garments and hobbled by their skirts, were striking out in ever new directions. Tearooms were offering them a respectable public meeting place unescorted by husband or brother; hotel dining rooms saw the first cigarettes being lit, perhaps in London's *Savoy* in 1896; ** powder compacts began to come out in public places; suffragettes (whom *Punch* wanted to call *Insuffrabelles*) were fighting for the vote which they would get in England in 1917.

The feminists set out to secure not advantages but equality: the recognition that a woman's sex was no reason for subjection, no mark of inferiority. They had achieved successes, attained greater legal independence, seen divorce laws enacted, but all by the "generosity" of the males. They would be satisfied only by equal rights, and these they would obtain by fair means and by foul. By 1914, women had voting rights in New Zealand (1893), Australia (1902), Finland (1907), Norway (1913), and in eleven Western states of North America. After the war they were enfranchised—though sometimes with reservations—in Soviet Russia, Germany, and all West European countries except for France (1945), Italy (1946), Belgium (1948), Spain (where they got the vote under the Republican Constitution of 1931 and lost it with Franco), Portugal, and Switzerland. By 1924 the first woman was holding office as cabinet minister (in Denmark). In 1950, except for Switzerland, Portugal, and Spain, women had the vote in all European countries. Their influence made the electorate more conservative but also more interested

---

* Des Esseintes in J. K. Huysmans' novel *Against the Grain* (1884).
** In 1864, three young ladies had been arrested for smoking in the Tuileries Gardens.

in social security, family allowances, pensions, health schemes, and public education: trends which connect with modern politics.

The greatest single factor in the emancipation of women, however, was not the vote but birth control. The most common form of birth control in all ages has been abortion, always widespread, nearly always illegal. But in the eighteenth century, when mortality rates were falling, the better off—finding that the greater number of surviving children created problems—began to have recourse to contraceptive methods. Once the fatality of death was placed in question, the fatality of birth could be questioned too. Now that survival was no longer subject *only* to chance, the notion of family planning became possible. At the same time, greater interest in individual children, greater concern for their welfare and character, encouraged parents to limit families.

A diversity of factors spread these practices beyond the upper classes. In the French countryside, the provisions of the Napoleonic Code which stipulated that land must be divided among all heirs, discouraged large families if a workable holding was to be held together. In industrial societies Thomas Malthus argued that excessive numbers make for misery and, in his wake, there came the first deliberate propaganda for birth control.* But theoretical arguments were less convincing than experience. In the second half of the nineteenth century, the spread of child labor laws and compulsory education were turning the children of the poor from a potential source of profit into a burden, those of the rich into a luxury. Surveys of working-class families found that their circumstances were more strained in proportion to their size. Middle-class families, struggling to keep up appearances, found that the cost of educating children accounted for about one-fourth of their budget. Cheap servants were getting harder to find, large apartments were expensive.** Tutors, dancing, drawing, language and music lessons could be a sound investment but proved a heavy charge. Greater expectations of comfort provided an added inducement for family planning, while the decline of religious authority, the spreading capacity to plan ahead, the availability of contraceptive devices and information about them, all contributed to a declining birth rate in the more advanced nations of the West.

Middle- and upper-class families now shrank from twelve or seven to two or three children, and their staff, houses, and stables shrank with them. Between 1851 and 1950 birth rates per 1,000 fell from 34 to 16 in England and Germany, from 32 to 16 in Sweden, from 48 to 26 in Russia. The greatest drop came in the twentieth century when really effective contraceptive devices became available, and when the more

---

* James Mill wrote an article about it in the *Encyclopaedia Britannica* of 1818, recommending chastity and abstinence. The labor leader Francis Place, more realistic, recommended contraception.

** The Victorian precept that children should be seen and not heard reflects the defensive needs of adults at a time when the average family had five or six children and *kept them in the house.*

backward countries joined the others. Between 1905 and 1950 the Italian birth rate fell from 32 to 19, Spanish and Greek from 34 to 20, Hungarian from 36 to 21. Given the choice, more and more people were limiting their families or avoiding children altogether, to the benefit of their living standards and of their independence. They were still, mostly, members of the social groups best able or most inclined to take advantage of such opportunities. It turned out that the more skilled and prosperous had fewer children, the poorer and less educated had relatively more. Contraception furthered the survival of the unfittest. It also, very likely, in its imperfect stage between the 1880's and the 1940's, caused frustrations which might have been reflected in the nerves and temper of widening sections of the population of the West. But it did a great deal to better the lot of women, to turn them into free or *freer* agents, to introduce a great element of choice into their lives.

So did the possibility of divorce which, like family planning, introduced an element of deliberation in what has been called the successive polygamy of earlier days, when high mortality rates made for frequent remarriages of widowers and widows.*

Of course, greater choice was paralleled like everything else by less security. The family, kept together by the economic dependency of almost all its members, broke asunder: "The young men and women of our day are parting fast from their parents and each other," declared an English novelist as early as 1851. Neither men nor women have found it easy to adjust to a situation in which true equality of the sexes, at least in advanced societies, becomes really feasible. But it is possible to imagine that, just as the emancipation of the working class has mobilized vast new energies for social use, so the probability of women finding other purposes in life than childbearing and rearing, another fulfillment than the strictly biological, will enrich the world rather than impoverish it.

The Victorians

As the twentieth century grows ever more complex and insecure, the nineteenth appears ever more attractive, a haven of security and straightforward situations. In the last decades of the twentieth century many have begun to look somewhat wistfully toward a period which their parents and grandparents emphatically rejected. This epoch, best de-

---

* Such mortality may have been spurred by the fact that, until the liberalization of divorce procedures, chiefly after 1920, divorce was so hard to come by that poisoning of spouse was probably the shortest way out of unhappy marriages. Poisoning was one of the most frequent marital crimes, and mid-nineteenth-century legislation like the English Arsenic Act, took cognizance of the temptation.

scribed by the term "Victorian," runs roughly from the middle to the end of the nineteenth century and does not concern only England, from whose sovereign it derives its name, but most of the middle and upper classes of Europe, which seem to have borrowed its values and mentality. It is in this sense that we use it here.

Today, the term "Victorian" begins to acquire all the rather hazy aura that we associate with the good old days, *la belle époque,* which ended in the First World War. It had not been so to many of its more thoughtful contemporaries. H. G. Wells thought it a slovenly and wasteful age. For Leslie Stephen (1832–1904), who fathered the *Dictionary of National Biography* and also Virginia Woolf, nobody would ever want to revive what its biographer, Lytton Strachey, later called its "slow funereal barbarism." In fact, as always, it was all things to all men, and curiously like our own time. It was not a contemporary commentator but a country doctor who, in a book of 1860, denounced the unbearable social pressures under which his patients labored: "The craving lust for gold, the restless goading of ambition, and the insatiable yearnings for display, these march hand in hand with an unscrupulous and reckless luxury and with new, artificial and intolerable anxieties, in the wear and tear of which the human machine prematurely breaks down."

"We live sadly too fast," complained social commentators of the 1860's in articles with titles like "The Sad Intensity of Modern Life." A scheme was mooted to erect a statue to Worry in the city of London. Worry can never have been absent from the city of London or anywhere else; but anxiety, insecurity, fear of failure and of the morrow (as well as hope), must have taken very concrete forms in an age when limited liability was mostly lacking until mid-century, and bankruptcy meant not only ruin and the likelihood of jail, but loss of social status: coming down in the world and sinking to the dread condition of the poor. Hence the pace of life and business constantly on the run, the rising incidence of heart disease after 1850, the discovery of "neurasthenia," the new interest in nervous disorders—not only in Victorian London, where Beatrice Webb found people with "no roots in neighborhood, in vocation, in creed, or for that matter in race," but in every other city where the same situation prevailed. Hence the self-analysis and introspection which, complained an observer in 1868, were being "pushed to the verge of monomania." Hence the "ennui and depression" which Matthew Arnold in his inaugural lecture at Oxford in 1856 found to characterize contemporary literature and, obviously, people too. Frustration, discontent, hopelessness recurred under the pens of undergraduates and men of letters in the 1850's as they had done in the 1820's, as they would do in the 1920's and 1960's.

> For what wears the life of mortal men?
> 'Tis that from change to change their being rolls;

> 'Tis that repeated shocks, again, again
> Exhaust the energy of strongest souls . . .
>
> Like children bathing on the shore,
> Buried a wave beneath,
> The second wave succeeds, before
> We have had time to breathe.*

They reeled under "a thousand facts and notions, which they know not how to classify, pouring in on them like a flood."* * "They hear so much said," noted J. S. Mill in his diary on January 13, 1854, "or find that so much can be said about everything, that they feel no assurance of the truth of anything." Perhaps this is why home was so sweet: a symbol of stability, a world enclosed, secured, that one could hope to encompass and to dominate. Perhaps this is why the activity of men was so feverish: work could keep doubts at bay. While they worked, they need not think or worry; after they had worked, they were too tired for it. A modern student of the Victorian frame of mind, Walter Houghton, attributes the immense productivity of many "Victorian" writers to "their frantic need to bury their doubts and anxieties" beneath an equally frantic activity.

The hold of traditional values and beliefs declined. The classes which traditionally forged these values or endorsed them—clergy and aristocracy—also declined. Bereaved of authority, men were thrown back on themselves to make the best of their own judgment. Those who could not, must refer to others: to political prophets, to literary and intellectual figures like Carlyle or Tolstoy, or simply to one of the periodicals which now began to "teach the multitude of men what to think and what to say" (1850).

Here were the antitoxins. Convention, conformity, the pressure of public opinion, acquired a new importance as other cohesive or stabilizing forces wore away. Mrs. Grundy, born in a play of 1798, had become a power half a century later. People who had cast off the tyranny of kings bent 'neath that of their neighbors. Men were free, but not of public opinion: "It exacts obedience to itself," wrote Walter Bagehot, "It requires us to think other men's thoughts, to speak other men's words, to follow other men's habits." Ambitious men and women, climbing or trying to climb into new spheres, unsure of what obtained and seeking to conform, would naturally look around and do as others do. As for the others, most of them, they were unsure too. In 1845, to quote him once again, Matthew Arnold deplored their "want of independence of mind, the shutting their eyes and professing to believe what they do not, the running blindly in herds, for fear of some obscure danger and horror if they go alone. . . ."

* Matthew Arnold, *The Scholar-Gipsy* (1853).
* * Charles Kingsley, *Yeast* (1851).

And so society became a lot of people, uncertainly looking to one another for reassurance or a lead, and duty became "complying with whate'er is expected here." All this conformity, pretension, and evasion only increased the tension between head and heart, between emancipation and dependence. Repressed sensuality turned to greed, either for food or objects; faith, doubt, tension, dissolved into sentiment and were superficially resolved in it; sentiment turned to sentimentality, to tears, to supersensitivity, and vapors; duty turned sour in hypocrisy. Much of the smugness, dogmatism, and self-assurance that we detect in the Victorian temper masked self-doubt, bewilderment, and even skepticism. In reading men like Carlyle or Ruskin, Nietzsche or Tolstoy, one gets a feeling that the more they doubted the more passionately they insisted that they *knew*, the more insecure they felt the more positive they acted (with respect to God, Society, Truth, or Beauty), the more shaken they might be the more inflexible their views on religion, morals, or reform became. All stood at Armageddon and battled for the Lord. The issues seemed to warrant such a stand: God, Society, the Nature of the World and Reality were at stake. No wonder that arguments tended to be dogmatic and the debaters rigid.

The great barrage of criticism, of critical analysis, of doubt, of private judgment, to which the social and the private conscience were subjected stirred up inevitable reaction. High-flown idealism, anti-intellectualism, irrationalism, bear harsh witness to the relentless intellectual and rationalist offensive which upset and endangered most people's peace of mind. Threatened by arguments like those of John Stuart Mill asserting liberty against conformity, like those of Darwin and the Darwinists against orthodoxy, a great many people reacted like Ulysses among the deadly Sirens. Like him they bound themselves to a dogmatic mast to withstand the temptations of unbelief or, like his crew, stopped up their ears with wax.

The differences among educated people encouraged the uneducated to think that they might be as right as any, even if they thought not at all. If every authority was being contradicted by some other authority, then what authority was left, how could one discriminate between them, why should one try? The open mind became an empty mind or, rather, one in which contending notions and ideas clashed, rattled, and jangled with only the vaguest attempt at reconciliation or at synthesis. This became known as reaching one's own conclusions. Self-educated, half-educated people ignored the lengths and depths to which real study and thought could go, the true value of evidence. Shallow judgments were good enough for them. The possible contribution of books began to be underrated. Everyone ignored what had been done or said. Limited and indiscriminate learning, encouraged by the limitations of the publicists, critics, journalists on whose work it fed, produced a bumptious, insensitive (or possibly oversensitive) mentality: that of our own day.

The Modern Age

By the time Queen Victoria died, society had been democratized willy-nilly by the continuous change that turned traditional privilege, estate, or even heritage into fluid and transitory things. Men were no longer defined by birth or status but free to become what they could, and what passing opportunity offered. They were individuals and had to assert that individuality by rational means, because routine and tradition could no longer be trusted to cope with situations as they arose. Democratic, individualistic, and rationalistic, this society was also the counterpart of all these things: increasingly specialized, class-conscious, and elitist, ever more conformist, conventional, and other-directed, less and less likely to follow rational arguments under the pressure of mass emotions and mass appeals.

Almost all the changes that are connected with the postwar years had germinated in the decade preceding 1914: the reluctant but final acceptance of parvenus in high society, the emancipation of workers and of women, the stirrings of irrationalism in philosophy and politics and art, the expanding scale of politics and the contracting scale of family life. Even the local color of the 1920's—jazz, cocktails, looser clothes —made its appearance in the prewar years, along with the mad "abandoned" dances of the modern age: first the Boston, then the Turkey Trot and the Bunny Hug, finally "the terrible Tango."

Drugs also became fashionable at this time. They had been common enough, not only for poets seeking new sensations, but for invalids and housewives seeking relief. It almost appears, if the term be allowed, that in a nineteenth century where no (or few) laws regulated the activities of pharmacists, drugs were a drug on the market. Cordials containing morphia, physics laced with laudanum, sedatives prepared with opium, alleviated the pains of the incurable, quieted squealing children, or soothed the nerves of their harassed mothers and nurses. Then their significance began to be realized, and from commonplace they became wicked—hence titillating. Paul Poiret in *My First Fifty Years* claims that in Paris "opium dens were in full blast everywhere"; and London's *Punch* (July 12, 1911) showed two ladies talking at a garden party: "If it were only chloral; or even morphia. But Laudanum, my dear— Laudanum is so frightfully middle class."

Too little liberty in the nineteenth century brewed up too much license in the twentieth. Or maybe just enough. For most people most of the time prefer to seem better than they are, not worse; and conformity, less strenuous than cynicism, provides a better conscience. Hence the frantic wildness and self-assertion of the postwar years were on the whole the franchise of the few, more people lived like Babbitt than like Gatsby. So the revolt and glumness of the 1920's, which have left their mark on the collective memory, were only representative in a minor key. The bitterness of the articulate partly reflected resentments among the upper and middle classes whose comforts were shrinking; the fact that, as A. J. P. Taylor reminds us, more lawyers and doctors and professors now had to do their own dishwashing, the fact that—while class consciousness persisted—economic, sartorial, and educational differences between the classes were becoming smaller.

Zip fasteners, first manufactured in the United States in 1917, made their contribution to simpler dresses and to their emancipation from hooks and maids. Artificial silks and other fabrics made both stockings and dresses cheaper and inspired the poet to sing

> Whenas in silk my Julia goes
> That nothing to the silkworm owes,
> But is compact of cellulose;
>
> Then, when I note the moderate fee
> Charged for the same by Jules and Cie,
> O, how that cheapness taketh me!

Clothes becoming simpler could be easily copied at home or in ready-made models. Upper- and middle-class people worked in shops and offices, like everybody else; workers went hiking and eventually traveling abroad wearing clothes very similar to their "betters"; elegance was no longer ornate but simple and casual like a Chanel suit; understatement became fashionable. Cruises, which had begun before 1914 for people who could not quite afford their own steam yachts, became popular for inexpensive middle-class holidays, before being enlisted for the workers by Nazis and Communists. Standards of comfort also differed less, as fewer families kept servants or sent their children to private schools, as more families ate and lived better, and hoped that their offspring might obtain not only secondary but higher education.

The middle class was expanding but, even as it did, its status was shrinking with its income, bitten into by death duties and higher direct taxes, which before 1914 had accounted for a negligible proportion of budgets but which would thereafter constitute between 10 and 20 per cent of total expenses. There were other factors too: before 1914 the difference between comfort and straitened circumstances often lay in a source of private revenue: income from dowries, inheritances, land, rents, or interest which could provide all or most of a middle-class family budget, and generally provided a portion of it. The role and proportion of such unearned income shrinks as the twentieth century advances, that of salaries or other returns on work done rises fast. An engineer or lawyer, half of whose income might, before 1914, have come from his wife's dowry or his own inherited wealth, would get only a quarter or a third of his income from such sources by the 1930's, less in postwar years. In other words, earned income takes over from unearned: another equalizing factor when one considers that most great fortunes are inherited.

Inflation also played a most important part in the disappearance of savings. It was becoming increasingly apparent that, while enterprise could still make money, prudence and thrift no longer could. When money kept its worth a lifetime through, not only members of the middle class but even workers could save their way to retirement. After the 1920's this was no longer true. No wage earner could henceforth feel secure by his thrift alone. This meant that unemployment, sickness, and age became community problems whose cost further cut down the income of the rich, whose benefits supplemented the income of the poor, and whose effects narrowed the economic gap between the classes further.

All this was relative but still significant. The average consumer is a myth. But even the destitute and the poor in the hard years of the 1930's were less destitute, less poor than they would have been even a generation before. They drank two pints of milk a week when the rich drank five, they ate one or two eggs a week when the rich ate four, but these themselves were things regarded as luxuries by their forebears. Overcrowding and malnutrition continued to exist even in industrialized countries, but they were being pressed back. Above all, the standards by which they were defined were rising. The miseries of the nineteenth century had disappeared outside the undeveloped countries of the South and East. In 1939, A. J. P. Taylor reminds us, half the population of England never left home even for a single night. But holiday travel— a middle-class habit in the nineteenth century—caught on in countries where the 1930's brought holidays with pay—day trips for some, holiday camps for others, and cruises. By mid-century, the novelty of one generation was treated by another as a natural right.

Buying on the installment plan, introduced in the 1930's, generalized in the 1950's, gave poorer people a chance to obtain things whose price they could never scrape up at once—household goods, automobiles, and even homes—and the increased demand thus tapped when things really got going in the 1950's stimulated production in its turn. Even the modern cult of slimness, the increasingly obsessive concern with weight, reflected a new well-being in which all could eat their fill and then some. By 1939, the working classes were better fed, housed, and clothed than their parents. A generation later this could be said of all. And workers of one kind or another accounted now for most of society.

The Public and its Servants

Sports and Entertainment

The equalization of the classes becomes particularly visible in the great public sectors of sport, entertainment, and education. Sport for a long time had been a preserve of the rich, who could afford it and who had time for it.* Tourneys and hunting had provided substitutes for the fighting and warfare of earlier days. Physical satisfaction, the sense of danger and adventure, had been channeled into less destructive directions. Team sports played similar roles in debrutalizing the masses, filling their leisure time, and offering opportunities for distinction with less regard to class (or race) than might reign otherwise.

The first of these sports was football (soccer); which English schoolmasters of the nineteenth century came to encourage as an antidote to immorality and a lesson in discipline. Eager to keep their charges from drinking, poaching, gambling, teachers saw a valuable substitute in limited mayhem on the playing field, and then began to think that games could inculcate positive virtues too: team spirit, a sense of loyalty, co-operation, and self-sacrifice—all the things exalted in Kipling's novels, like *Stalky and Co.,* the moral virtues that Sir John Squire sings in his poem *The Rugger Match*:

> A selfless flinging of the self in the fray,
> Strength, compassion, control, the obeying of laws,
> Victory and a struggle against defeat.

But all this was still for the rich, until the Factory Act of 1847 prohibited the employment of women and children on Saturday afternoons. Soon the men were freed too. Here was a new weekly holiday to be filled, and one of the major contenders for filling it was football. In the 1860's the rules of Association and of Rugby football were stabilized, in 1871 the Football Cup competition was established, by 1905 England could boast 10,000 member clubs, one in almost every English village. More and more working-class clubs appeared which, by the 1880's had come to dominate the game. Along with the clubs, the number of watchers rapidly increased. Socially select clubs could draw only on a small public. Popular clubs attracted a much larger audience. By the mid-80's attendance figures at important matches ran in tens of thousands (the Cup Final of 1901 drew over 110,000). Generations of football watchers

* Under the Tudors, the lower classes were supposed to stick to useful sports like archery, while gentry could indulge in bowls or tennis.

grew up who lacked room to play the game themselves, but had little else to do in their free time. Men began to be paid to play, and 1885 saw professionalism recognized as a fact and regulated. Games, no longer played only by amateurs for their own sake, became mass entertainments, masterfully handled for profit by skillful athletes and their managers.*

Thus, while the unprofitable pursuits like hunting and tennis remained mere games, football was the first to serve the needs of the industrial society in which it grew, itself becoming an industry and a business. By 1950, 86 million in Britain alone watched football matches through the year.* * Every week more than 6 million paid for their tickets, while 7 million played the football pools which have become one of the largest industries in Europe—employing over 100,000 people in England alone. The only greater entertainment and source of revenues was cinema, which (to take the same British statistics for 1950) had sixteen times more viewers and twelve times more revenues than football, serving nearly one and a half billion patrons and making gross receipts of some 300 million dollars.

The cinema was born of two inventions: that of photography and that of celluloid, which permitted the making of film strips whose rapid projection gave the beholder the illusion of a moving image. The first public projection seems to have taken place in Paris in 1895. Very soon the process was being imitated all over the world, and some of the films' great classics were made before 1914. After 1927, the appearance of sound and the need for large capital investment this created ensured the industry's domination by banks and by a few large concerns which turned it, as Erich von Stroheim put it, into a giant sausage machine. Nevertheless, films offered better entertainment than either church or tavern. They also offered pleasures that men and women could enjoy together —unlike the sports or the carousing that had separated them. A century ago, the greatest entertainment centers of the world—London, Paris— catered to no more than two or three thousand persons nightly. Today, tens of thousands sit in cinemas and millions watch television everywhere, any night of the week.

Technology, a German philosopher once suggested, is simply a trick designed to arrange the world so that we do not have to experience it, but only reproduce various experiences. The cinema is one of our liveliest art forms. It also became our greatest step toward the industrialization of dreams. In its darkened temples men and women grasp at real life substitutes, find an escape valve from dreary existence, experience vicarious enjoyment of power, beauty, and riches beyond their grasp.

* English experience was repeated on the continent only after 1920 or so, partly because working hours were longer and were effectively limited only much later, but partly too because sports were regarded as a prerogative of the ruling classes, training their scions to meet the rising challenges of democracy.

** That same year 50 million attended greyhound races, 12 million speedway races, 5 million cricket matches.

They also learn how unknown classes and distant peoples live. Which means that the cinema suggested new desirabilities and standards, first in the West, then all over the world, spreading its stereotypes across class or national barriers.

Education and Popular Culture

More stereotypes would grow from education. For the romantic humanist, education had been the great liberating and creative force by which man discovers his true nature and thereby gains his freedom. "The powerful travail of self on self," as Michelet had called it, made "every man his own Prometheus." This lyrical vision would be paralleled by a more utilitarian one. Man, said the sociologists of the modern age, is not the work of nature but of society. His shape changes according to society's intentions, particularly the pressure of deliberate education designed to turn out citizens in its own image.

The image that the nineteenth century conceived was that of disciplined, useful, patriotic citizens. The educational structures set up on the continent in Napoleon's wake treated adolescents much like soldiers, put them in uniforms, trained them to perform a socially useful function as rationally and obediently as they could. This tendency went furthest in the German schools and, after 1871, the French—claiming that the Prussian victory was due above all to Prussian schoolmasters—set out to imitate them. But Prussian schoolmasters had not been active only in *gymnasia*: they had taught the common people, among whom illiteracy had been pressed far back. Here, too, there was work to be done; here, too, the basic arguments were utilitarian. It was not only that a man who could read, write, count, would make a better workman or soldier. He would also be a better citizen: indeed, become the citizen he wasn't. Adam Smith already had pointed out that, while the division of labor is the source of "universal opulence," it makes the laborer "as stupid and ignorant as it is possible for a human creature to become." Laborers were being turned into productive animals at the expense of their human and civic qualities, just when their growing numbers and concentration made such developments dangerous. Education could prevent this. State investment in it would protect the masses from "the delusions of enthusiasm and superstition which, among ignorant nations, frequently occasion the most dreadful disorders," make them more apt to think, less open to seditions and factious arguments, "less apt to be misled into any wanton or unnecessary opposition to the measures of government."

Malthus, too, had felt that education would make the common people "bear with patience the evils which they suffer," and realize "the folly and inefficacy of turbulence." By 1848, the Chartists were complaining that men moved by these motives "would educate us not, as you sometimes pretend, to fit us for the exercise of political rights, but to make us indifferent to these rights." There must have been less consciousness and more good intentions about educational ventures than the suspicious thought. There was the simple hope of improving man and life by mechanical means. There was the dream of a richer life achieved by the mobilization of social potential which had long lain dormant. There was the simple yearning to increase the dignity and capacities of human beings. There was belief in progress, of which knowledge was seen as an intrinsic part. And there was, ultimately, a real and wide-felt need to adapt the newly significant masses to life in newly created national states: not only in the nineteenth-century creations like Belgium and Italy, the German Empire, or the French Republic, but in older societies turning into nations: Norway, Denmark, Holland, and even Spain.

This was the task of free, compulsory elementary education, which had become general in most Western countries by 1900, and of its carriers, the schoolteachers. Secular public schools which taught not only reading, writing, and counting, but morals and civic sense, were a major instrument in developing patriotism, spreading common notions and a common language, ousting religion from its near monopoly of popular education, and opening new avenues for rising in the world.

The first to benefit were the teachers themselves. In the 1870's and 80's teaching became a promising occupation for the bright, ambitious sons and daughters of workmen or peasants whose horizons had been limited heretofore by domestic service or a clerical career. Teachers were ill-paid, but they enjoyed prestige and social status. They were particularly influential in small villages and towns, where the intellectual credit and strategic position of the teacher challenged older authorities like landlord or priest. Their sons, with an even better education, became professional men, entered the civil service and the universities. A vast proportion of twentieth-century professors and intellectuals are sons of elementary teachers; and teachers traditionally play a role in democratic politics quite disproportionate to their numbers. Thus, under the Third and Fourth Republics in France, while only one Frenchman in 3,000 or more was a teacher, one deputy in every twenty or so had at some time taught.

Education made a crucial contribution to the social mobility which we have seen increasing in our time. Educational opportunities meant social and economic opportunities. Professional and technical schools proliferated. More high schools were created and scholarships opened them to poorer students too. Thousands whose parents never learned to read could now at least *aspire* to higher education. Evening and correspondence courses reached out to many who had had to miss, or drop out

Boys in the Cloisters of the Blue-coat School in England.

of, school. Free public libraries encouraged study and reading. By 1914 among French conscripts, one-fourth of whom could not read or write in 1863, the illiteracy rate was only 2 per cent. In 1880 one in six Frenchmen, one in three Frenchwomen, could not sign their marriage license. By 1939 the figures would be about one out of 120. By 1950 the estimated adult literacy rate in North and Western Europe was 99 per cent, in the Soviet Union 90 per cent, in the European South 80 per cent.

The only Western country that lagged for a long time in this process was the United Kingdom, which lacked an elementary or secondary network comparable to those in France or Germany, let alone adequate systems of industrial or technical education. In 1903, while Germany led Europe in the number and quality of its 22 universities, Britain had only 13, receiving two-thirds less public aid than German ones.* This was in part the reflection of a public in which plain men took pride in successes achieved by uninstructed common sense and lack of study. They knew their opinion to be as good as anybody else's, despised teachers and theorists because they were not men of action, insisted that "those who can, do!" Reading, thinking, talking were not necessities but ornaments, more suitable for women and for idle men. Education made sense as long as it had a practical application, but studies which were not clearly or immediately useful only distracted men from the main object of life which was to earn money, amass property, get on in life. The British upper classes were accommodated in private schools, where they were taught the classics, sports, and leadership. Little was done for others until the twentieth century. The price of such neglect was paid by British industry, which fell behind its competitors in equipment, inventiveness, and the trained skills of its available work force.

But even in England, as education improved with the new century

* At that time, Italy counted 21 universities, France 15, and the United States 134.

and the population of secondary and grammar schools went up, its effects were being felt. By 1913, more than twice as many books were being published than a decade before, more than twice as many were being borrowed from public libraries. Then, as now, the favorite reading of workers and the lower middle class tended toward crime stories, sentimental romances, popular novels quite forgotten today, moralistic or political pamphlets. Only exceptional men went further; and it has been claimed, perhaps with justice, that the educational process which, it was hoped, would widen their horizons, merely equipped them for conformity.

The twentieth century, which saw the triumph of formal education, would also witness reading and writing becoming increasingly irrelevant and twenty-year olds who forgot the unused skills with which they had left school at fourteen. Recent French surveys show a frightening number of conscripts who have *forgotten* how to read or write. Nevertheless, by 1960 the least schooled of European countries, Portugal, had a higher proportion of schoool-age children sitting in its schools than any African, Asian, or Latin American country.* At the same time, however, means of communication had become increasingly verbal and visual. Telephone, radio, motion pictures, and, in due course, television, escaped the limits and disciplines of writing while abandoning its lasting power. As Gide noted in his *Journal*: "How many fine letters lost in talks over the telephone. . . ."

Ideally, modern education sought to inculcate awareness of our limits, permit men to discover the liberating quality of intellectual activity, the capacity to be most fully themselves, taking pride in human talents which alone permit the affirmation and organization that are specifically human. What it produced, only too often, were simplification and vulgarization: charlatans masquerading as experts, and experts learning to talk as charlatans. Already in the 1880's Nietzsche was complaining that, far from enabling man to become richer and greater, education was "essentially the means of ruining the exceptions for the good of the rule. Higher education: essentially the means of directing taste against the exceptions for the good of the mediocre."

Learning itself, people complained, was being killed by *degrees,* used to turn out cogs for the wheels of the social machine, standardized products with standardized minds for an increasingly standardized way of life. How true this is we simply do not know. But there is no need for quantity to stamp out either quality or independence. If a majority of the products of modern education are more conformist and mediocre than it had been hoped, a majority of mankind has always been this way. A larger proportion of the world being educated must mean that a large proportion of the educated will show signs of conformism and mediocrity. It also means, however, that many more—though not necessarily a ma-

* Forty to 60 per cent of Portuguese and Mexican children of school age go to school; 25 to 30 per cent in Latin America; less than 20 per cent in Africa and Asia.

William Randolph Hearst

jority—discover possibilities which had remained unsuspected both in themselves and in the outside world. And that, as long as Western man continues to be curious, must be counted as clear gain.

The Popular Press

The most impressive and sometimes depressing monument to mass education was the popular press. Newspapers that wished to sell more than a few thousand copies had to catch the eyes of those whom George Gissing in his *New Grub Street* (1891) called the quarter-educated: "The young men and women who can just read but are incapable of sustained attention." Throughout the 1880's men sought a formula that catered to a public which knew how to read, but little else. The American "yellow press" had found it: scandal, rumor, trivialities, "revelations," issues picked to the extent that they helped circulation, stirring sensation or public interest. Here was the stuff of life or, at least, the stuffing. The name of William Randolph Hearst (1863–1951) had come to represent low but profitable journalistic standards. Lurid illustrations, glaring headlines, sensationalism, and jingoism built up unprecedented sales— over a million and a half a day for his *New York Journal* in 1896.

That year, Alfred Harmsworth's *Daily Mail* introduced the formula to England. It worked. By 1901 the sales of the *Daily Mail* had risen to a million copies a day. The paper, which an English politician described as written by office boys for office boys, was rather by and for the semi-educated. Women, servants, tradesmen, all those who—outside their particular concern—retained the minds and tastes of twelve-year olds, bought it, read it, liked it. Bright, bitsy, predigested, the *Daily Mail* and the numerous progeny it spawned throughout the rest of Europe assumed that serious news or interpretation would bore a public whose attention span was very short indeed.

By 1900, rotary presses, type-setting machines, the linotype turned out the printed pabulum of the masses. The expense of such equipment for mass production was very great. This meant that more than ever a newspaper cost more than it could earn. A sheet which sold for a penny in the street would bring its publisher only two-thirds of that and probably cost a penny and a quarter to turn out. The gap between the moderate price without which there could not be large sales and the high costs of production was filled by advertising. Publicity had also grown with the buying public and, as the nature of customers changed and simplified, it had created a fresh art style expressed in posters and eventually in print.* The publicists, like the newspapers, had to catch attention in a flash, make an impression which would help their product. To this purpose they created a visual universe which has taught the twentieth-century world to experience most things—from washing machines to sex—less through the rational mind than through the eye.

Essentially, most publications depend on subsidies and cater to subsidizers. Since newspapers wanted all the advertising they could get, they too found that they had to cater to the widest public. Most of the advertisers were (at least relatively) politically neutral, and they objected to any orientation that might alienate possible buyers. Distinct political views became increasingly rare. The press became an industry like any other and, like all other industries, increasingly concentrated under the ownership of powerful financiers or groups.

With brand-name goods being sold from one end of the country to another, national advertising increased in scope and scale. The national press that carried it gained ground at the expense of local papers and of the smaller, uncompetitive sheets. As more and more publications were swallowed or scuttled, variety of opinion notably decreased. In Britain between 1920 and 1945 half the morning papers, a quarter of the evening papers disappeared. In France, which had 238 dailies in 1939, 1953 saw only 164. In the United States in 1955 fourteen men controlled 25 per cent of daily sales. The need to cut costs, to please the many and displease only few, made for standardized agency fare, widely syndicated and reproduced, the reign of comic strips and of innocuous, vapid stuffing for heads that asked no better, supplementing the vast periodical industry that turns out women's weeklies and cheap sentiments, vicarious sensation or conformist thrills.

Literature and the Arts

Artists and writers are less "the unacknowledged legislators of the world," as Shelley had it, than its mirrors (perhaps deforming mirrors), reveal-

---

* Just over a century old, the publicity poster is, like the film, an integral part of the modern world, which would be very bare and very different without it. Designed to make a brief, sharp appeal, posters were first to accustom the general public to a shorthand and synthesis of image and of message, familiarizing it with elliptic modern art styles it would never have accepted otherwise.

ing aspects of a time, suggesting possibilities and perspectives which, without them, might well remain unnoticed. When there is a direct relation between artists and their public—that is, when the number and choice of both are still restricted—the work of art reflects the taste and the ideas of its time; or, rather, of that small elite in which cultural life is concentrated. The moment this limited balance breaks, when the elite is paralleled or supplanted by a wider public, this changes. Potential opportunities encourage some men to strike out on their own. This means that some among them—those who, like Rembrandt, Blake, Van Gogh, or Cézanne, persistently ignored the demands of society around them for the sake of a personal quest or vision—become heretics and rebels, departing from convention and risking misery. This situation, exceptional before the eighteenth century, became the norm in the nineteenth when a restricted market for works of literature, music, or art became an open marketplace where everyone could vie for public favor. In a hundred years, the once limited aristocratic public grew in number and proportion as the middle classes grew, until by the twentieth century all of society became potential patrons. This immeasurably increased the opportunities of all artists. But it also meant (as we have already seen in the romantic era) a definite break between the art tradesmen catering to current tastes and the independents who pursued a vision of their own.

The new art patrons of the nineteenth century were rich but hardworking—enjoying little of the leisure their clerical and aristocratic predecessors had enjoyed. For men of little time and little taste, art had to speak loud and fast, offering striking effects and reassurance of a good money's worth: plenty of paint, of effect, of anecdote, or ornament. Weary men did not want to think. They wanted to escape their hard, ugly world and find a substitute paradise in a painting or book, or to relax listening to undemanding music. All these would be appreciated for the soft glow they could bring, rather like a good meal, the entertainment or the reassurance that they might provide.*

It follows that the great painters, novelists, often musicians also, whom we today remember, found very little favor in their time. Their appeal was always restricted, while the popular artists and best sellers are nearly all forgotten today or looked at only for their period flavor. In all the arts, the contemporary period stands out by the "divorce between what is officially and socially successful and what is aesthetically good." This was the age when many concert societies were founded to react against bad public taste, when anti-exhibitions rebelled against academic conformity, when public protests kept the impressionists out of French museums and forced Edvard Munch to withdraw his paintings from a Berlin exhibi-

---

* They would also, at least in theory, have to preach the moral lessons respectable people respected in public and sometimes in private too: "The art that doesn't serve to ennoble and purify and help us in our lifelong struggle with sin and evil," wrote *Christian Remembrances* of April, 1854, "however beautiful, however serene and majestic, is false and poor and contemptible."

tion, when both Flaubert and Baudelaire would be condemned in court. Hence, the present section deals in large part with *unrepresentative* works and figures.

Realism and Naturalism

A great deal of nineteenth-century art, for instance, reflected the contemporary interest in accuracy, the yearning for scientific objectivity, the progressive tendency to edify and reform. With Honoré de Balzac (1799–1850) the romantic searchlight moved from the rural landscape to the urban, and from high society to middle and lower classes. Part of the romantic thrill had always been the exploration of unknown regions, which the novelist revealed to a curious public. This was now complemented by a documentary approach, as novels rivaled contemporary reports and blue books, producing studies of society in the making and of its reefs and shoals, documents reflecting change in time or political pamphlets about conditions that must be .changed. Balzac had led the way in shifting the novel from private life onto a social stage, insisting on the growing role of *things,* of money, and of a society in which man himself (and woman even more) became a negotiable object. Friedrich Engels would remark that he had learned more from Balzac "than from all the works of the historians, economists and professional statisticians put together."

Society novels became social novels. Dickens' introduction to *Oliver Twist* (1841) proposed a "service to society" by offering not descriptions of picturesque scenes but of the "cold, wet, shelterless streets of London." This was the particular effect of mid-century positivism. The people who are generally labeled realists (Flaubert, Courbet) or naturalists (Zola) followed the same course, trying to abandon the last bits of lyricism and color and to describe actions and things as objectively and precisely as they could. Like scientific researchers, they set out to observe and note their observations. Human beings, they and their interpreters reasoned, are feeling, thinking bodies, provided with organs, moved by passions, feelings, ideas, and needs. Their fate and their behavior are determined by natural laws—heredity, environment, causality. It is up to the novelist or playwright to study these elements as a psychologist or a pathologist would; and try to represent them in reality.

This is what Gustave Flaubert (1821–1880) did in his novel *Madame Bovary* (1857): a kind of documentary of small-town life and ways in mid-nineteenth-century France, which shows pretentious, petty people, living on some small income, gorging themselves on commonplaces and on platitudes. Although Flaubert is often labeled a realist, *precisionist* might be a better term for this meticulous stylist who reacted against romantic passion and expressiveness by tying a cannonball to his quill. Perhaps the most realistic thing about Flaubert's novel is the romanti-

Bulloz

Honoré de Balzac,
by Auguste Rodin.
Right: Gustave
Flaubert.

cism of his characters. On the one hand ideas *about* life, on the other
hand life itself. On one hand books, education, prejudices, and on the
other reality. There is no reconciling the two, either for Madame Bovary
or for the idealistic hero of *A Sentimental Education* (1869): both disintegrate rather than take shape under the battering of experience and
of time. Where the romantics had painted a lost generation of fallen
angels and fiery rebels, that of the realists had a flaccid cast, less strong,
less cultivated, and more hopeless.

Some painters also turned to characters and scenes from everyday life,
which they depicted in all reality or, as contemporaries claimed, in all
vulgarity. In the late 1840's the painters of the "school of Barbizon" (a
village not far from Paris) escaped from the artificial light and scenery
of the studio to paint simple, familiar landscapes in the open air. Camille
Corot (1796–1875), insisting that "nature must be interpreted art-
lessly," produced fresh, spontaneous pictures still filled with the light
of limpid afternoons. J. F. Millet (1814–1875) glorified farmers and laborers to such an extent that he was accused of being a socialist. Less sentimental, more brutally realist, Gustave Courbet (1819–1877) rejected all
idealization. He painted priests with red noses, prostitutes, vigorous
ugly workers, the face of people plain. His letterhead proclaimed "Gustave Courbet, Master Painter, without ideals and without religion." No
wonder that Napoleon III's Minister of Fine Arts saw realism as
"democratic painting"; and he was right, for Courbet would become the
Fine Arts Commissar of the Paris Commune.

Men like Courbet and like the naturalists who came after him reacted,
of course, against the monumental fantasies of the established order. But
their purpose was fundamentally ethical. The object of their rebellion
may be seen by a quotation from an English novel of 1851,* in which
a painter who has just painted a gamekeeper in the fashionable heroic
style of the day is asked by an artless girl: "Why have you been so un-

* Kingsley's *Yeast,* Chapter 3.

The Gleaners, by Millet. Louvre, Paris.

faithful to your original? Why have you, like all artists, been trying to soften and refine on your model?"—"Because my dear lady, we are bound to see everything in its ideal—not as it is, but as it ought to be, and will be, when the vices of this pitiful world are exploded." This dialogue illuminates the character of Podsnap in Dickens' *Our Mutual Friend* (1864), who does not want to know, discuss, or admit anything that spoils his comfort: poverty, injustice, faults in the system or society.

Here the subversive character of naturalism becomes clear; not only in aesthetics but in politics too. The plays of the Norwegian Henrik Ibsen (1828–1906) showed the social possibilities of modern theater, exploring all the themes that preoccupied society in this time: the limitations and potentialities of man (*Peer Gynt,* 1867); feminine emancipation (*A Doll's House,* 1879); heredity and syphilis (*Ghosts,* 1881); social hypocrisy (*An Enemy of the People,* 1882); artistic integrity (*The Master Builder,* 1892). In France, the great exponent of the naturalist creed was Émile Zola (1840–1902). His novels and especially the twenty-volume cycle of *The Rougon-Macquart* published between 1871 and 1893, followed the fortunes of a family right through the Second Empire. Zola's works, in which heredity and environment, the taints and corruption of society and human beings, helped to reveal each other, shocked the public with their insistence on sex and violence, their subversive pounding at ignorance, prudery, and evasions.

Even more deliberately revolutionary would be the Germans, to whom naturalism came late. Gerhart Hauptmann's play *The Weavers* (1892), which has no human hero, dwells rather on the inarticulate tragedy of

The Port of La Rochelle, by Corot. Louvre, Paris.

a wretched Silesian village where all—workers, rebels, and exploiters —are playthings of mechanisms they can neither master nor comprehend. Here was a prediction of the new mass age, passing from the particular to the general, and of a literature of impotence that our century knows well. This last found its first expression in Russia, where contact between the cultivated classes and reality was slight and ineffectual, and where control over one's fate seemed far more faltering than in the West. The plays and stories of Anton Chekhov (1860–1904) mirror the futility, the isolation, and the boredom of Russian living (*The Three Sisters,* 1900); the impossibility of communication (*The Sea Gull,* 1898, *Uncle Vanya,* 1898); the decline of the landowning family whose cherry orchard is sold to be cut down (*Cherry Orchard,* 1904). They all expressed an attitude which the turn of the century saw spreading: creeping despair about man's ability to manage his affairs, expressed more stridently in the works of men like August Strindberg (1849–1912) and in a conciliatory vein by Leo Tolstoy (1828–1910), perhaps the greatest novelist of modern days (*War and Peace,* 1869; *Anna Karenina,* 1877). Tolstoy's answer to the human predicament was to reject the constricting scale and absurdity of society and history, seeking salvation in homely happiness— the goodness and naturalness of simple lives.

Whatever the variety of solutions they proposed, many such works carried an aesthetic radicalism just as shocking to a public used to the lies and evasions of academic art as the socialism which some artists espoused. The artist's political opinions did not really matter. Daumier, Courbet, Pissarro, Morris were for revolution; Degas, a reactionary; Flau-

1059

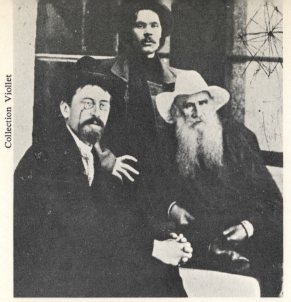

Chekhov, Gorki, and Tolstoy.

bert and Monet solid bourgeois; and many others indifferent to politics. What mattered was that, in opposing truth to falsity, artists attacked the basis of convention. Anna Karenina, Madame Bovary, Courbet's lascivious women, Manet's Olympia in her disturbing nakedness, were all unorthodox, all challenged visual, social, or literary patterns, and thus threatened stability. A selfish, acquisitive society wanted reassurance not reminders, its conscience salved not stirred. Ends should be happy, and horrors swathed in sentiment as bees neutralize disconcerting foreign bodies by covering them with wax. Flaubert, Zola, and even Tolstoy were too sad, too harsh, for a sad, harsh world. No wonder they were greeted with hostility. No wonder that they were slow to find success.* No wonder a Russian minister of education once remarked that he would only be able to sleep soundly when there was no longer any literature at all.

The strange detachment that we sense in Chekhov and in Tolstoy mirrored the intellectual situation of societies in which theology and science clashed and deadlocked. Deprived of a clear, authoritative reality or truth, many artists, like other people, denied any responsibility to a superior truth, turned toward "beauty" or their perception of it. If life was meaningless, a moment's beauty could be fixed by art. In 1842, the young Karl Marx, writing in the Rhenish *Gazette* on freedom of the press, had already affirmed that "the writer doesn't look on his works as a *means*. They are ends in themselves. . . ." Paul Cézanne (1839–1906)

---

* Millet had to sell his drawings to buy shoes, Auguste Renoir's family went without food, Claude Monet had to stop painting for lack of money to buy paints. All of them sold their pictures at ridiculous prices. Millet's *Angelus* sold by him in 1859 for $360 was bought by a millionaire in 1881 for $320,000. In the late 1870's Monet's paintings were selling for less than 200 francs: about 40 dollars. In 1884 the contents of Monet's studio were sold by his executor. Among them *Olympia* fetched $2,000, *Le Bar aux Folies Bergères* $1,170, *La Servante de Bocks* $500, *Le Balcon* $500. By 1924 they were going to sell at prices a thousand times greater.

agreed: "Painting," he said, "is its own end." It was not supposed to represent an anecdote, a moral lesson, a conversation piece, a historical or religious memory. The subject, treated for its own sake (whether a patch of light, a flower, or a hunk of beef) became autonomous. This was the point of view of those who practiced "art for art's sake."

Impressionism

First, and today most familiar, among these are the impressionists who, like naturalist writers, refused to paint "noble" subjects, preferred the commonplace. The academic art of the day combined photographic exactness and arbitrary subjects. After the 1870's, persuaded that photographs provided a more exact reproduction of reality and that the world held as much beauty as the imagination, painters turned away from a pursuit in which they were outmatched by cameras: from form to color, to light, and to suggestion. They let their eyes roam freely and sought to catch the moment on the wing. The canvases that Pissarro, Monet, Renoir, turned out shimmered with light and color but were considered vulgar because they failed to provide the idealized pictures which the public had been used to. The things impressionists painted were neither clear nor detailed. They did not look finished or conform to the "law of appearances," complained the critic Ruskin comparing them with the grotesque pictures of the Chinese that lacked all linear or aerial perspective. Their subjects, too, were vulgar: streets, suburban scenes, railroad stations—an urban landscape now incorporated in the domain of art. To the impressionists, industry had a magic of its own: cotton and iron garbed and encoiled the world. Their distant adventures and mysterious destinations suggested romance to color-hungry producers in the livid North. Why not, then, the same treatment for cityscapes which held the excitement and mystery of frenzied movement, belching smoke, hazy steam, thickets of chimneys, cliffs of houses, the color and bustle of endlessly drifting crowds?

But patrons would not buy them because, as one explained, "When you have daughters, you have to have a solid-looking house." And when, in 1877, Renoir asked his friend Gambetta for a helpful article about the Impressionist Exhibition of that year: "It would be impossible," the editor told him, "It would be scandalous! Don't you realize that you are revolutionaries?"

Abstract Art

Yet it would shortly seem that naturalists and impressionists were the last accessible—understandable—artists of an age whose search for novelty and expression turned ever to new sources and new idioms, abandoning the material for the abstract, the objective for the subjective, the descrip-

Émile Zola, portrait by Manet which includes a miniature reproduction of the artist's painting, *Olympia.* Louvre, Paris.

tive for the evocative, leaving behind narrative, form, melody, representation, for symbol and allusion. Impressionists and naturalists had made the world their own and glorified it. Even their criticisms implied acceptance, suggested the potential of goodness and beauty in the world. Henceforth the tendency would be to retreat into the self and into art which can make life livable, but on the most personal plane alone. "The artist should not even glance at nature," declared the visionary painter Rodolphe Bresdin (1825–1885), a favorite of Odilon Redon, Gustave Moreau, and J. K. Huysmans: "He has everything within himself." He can plumb reality with the help of drugs and of the visions they entail, of alcohol, of strange evocative cults, like Satanism, of the exploration of dreams, mental maladies and alienation.

This was the mood of Aestheticism, Decadence, Symbolism, Art for Art's Sake—different labels for a common flight from and rejection of the world, which found its patron saint in Charles Baudelaire (1821–1867). Once experience had been valued for its fruits. Now it would be valued for itself, like Art. What counted, counseled the Oxford Aestheticist Walter Pater (1839–1894), was "to catch at any exquisite passion . . . stirring of the senses, strange dyes, strange colors and curious odors, or work of the artist's hands, or the face of a friend," anything that might set the spirit roaming for a moment. The world was full of mysterious analogies, harmonies, connections: colors, shapes, sounds related to each other and to states of mind. Man was a wanderer through "a forest

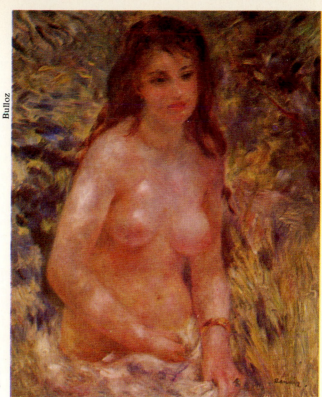

A Young Woman in the Sun,
by Renoir. Jeu de Paume,
Paris.

of symbols," each one an intimation of a great many things if he could
but perceive them.

Science seemed to be turning from objects to sensations, from the
stable to the relative, from the whole to the parts. The world was an
illusion: senses provided the only reality. Where there was no coherence, the part must be greater than the whole, and immediate sensation counted more than any possible significance. It was up to the poet
and painter to transmute the beautiful into its possibilities, increasingly
musical, increasingly abstract; to create Harmonies, Symphonies, Noc-
turnes, as James Whistler (1834–1903) called his paintings; to explore
the possibilities of optics and sensation (Georges Seurat 1859–1891; Paul
Signac 1863–1935), discover the emotions that shapes and colors can
evoke (Paul Gauguin 1848–1903), search for the geometrical symbolism
underlying nature (Paul Cézanne); reveal the magic possibilities of
words, when statements lost their meaning (Stéphane Mallarmé 1842–
1898, Arthur Rimbaud (1854–1891); or do in tone what painters did on
canvas: use pure colors to produce delicate, luminous sounds (Claude
Debussy 1862–1918).*

* Debussy, a friend of Mallarmé and of the symbolists, tried not only to conciliate
literature and music but to express contemporary scientific tendencies in a new musical
technique. Works like *Pelléas et Mélisande* (1902) or *La Mer* (1905) introduced the use
of whole scales, new harmonies and dissonances, helped suggest the rhythm and tonality
of Igor Stravinsky (b. 1882: *The Firebird* 1910, *The Rites of Spring* 1913), and prepared
us for the musical expression that we know today.

The classic or traditional style, image, or melody corresponded to a stable, orderly universe in which thought and expression were tamed and disciplined. The chaotic universe we discern around us calls for an equivalent reflection that we can recognize in Joyce and Schönberg, Cézanne or Mathieu, dismantling erstwhile structures into an intuitive chaos analogous to that around us. In modern science, statistics take the place of laws and working probabilities take the place of absolute certainties. Art can no longer imitate a nature that physics reveals in movement, biology in evolution, psychology in depth, philosophy in process of becoming. What art does now is to follow the new ways of nature, the elasticity of space, the deformability of forms, the possibilities which the new probability theories open up. Paul Klee (1879–1940) looks through a microscope and draws his strange subjects from histological slides. Vasili Kandinsky (1866–1944) paints the geometry of diatomic algae. Franz Marc (1880–1916) declares "Instead of contemplating the world, we x-ray it." Arnold Schönberg rejects traditional tonality and the chromatic scale, the composer's hand, in favor of new forms suggested by mathematics. Melody is jettisoned in favor of logical constructions: the twelve-tone scale, serial music, obey external laws. Like Cézanne, Henry James (*The Turn of the Screw*, 1898) is fascinated by the "multiplicity of the aspects of vision."

Color bites into forms; things pulse and vibrate; shapes disarticulate like syntax. And, just as the rational Renaissance setting out to encompass the world had produced both double-entry bookkeeping and perspective, so the increasingly hurried and abstract modern world of speed and symbols would see the generalization of shorthand in business and in art along with the increasing abstraction of both. "Do not copy too much from nature," advised Gauguin. "Art is an abstraction. Draw it from nature while dreaming before it." It was the dream that counted, not the nature: nature that was bent and twisted to the haunting dream whose intensity could sometimes end in madness, as with Vincent Van Gogh (1853–1890). Like the symbolists, Van Gogh appreciated the symbolism of movement and of color. The flame that burned him licks over his canvas, whirls in the branches of his trees, convulses his skies, glows in the harsh tones of his oils.

The Arts of Anarchy

Unnoticed behind the politics of pre-1914 Europe, the movements of the future were taking shape in deliberate attacks on established structures and categories. The influence of Cézanne was prompting Georges Braque and Pablo Picasso to the distortions and simplifications of modern cubism. Categories began to mix and mingle. In 1910 the Russian composer Alexander Scriabin included projections of colored lights in the performance of his symphony *Prometheus;* in 1911 (probably)

Picasso (or Braque) first introduced newsprint and wallpaper into an oil painting; in 1917 Erik Satie would introduce a typewriter into the orchestra; in 1918 Guillaume Apollinaire's typographic venture, *Calligrammes,* began the association of the poetic and the graphic image. Why not? Metal and string, sand and wood, could henceforth be incorporated in a painting just as a shotgun or a vacuum cleaner could play its part in a musical composition, or a waterfall in the design of a millionaire's living room. Incongruity in art articulated the incongruous and complex world whose categories and hierarchies commingled in collapse.

The art of the impressionists had been contemplative. The language of twentieth-century art would be critical, exasperated and tormented by the great cities that the poet R. M. Rilke damned, where "unsatisfied men labor to live and die not knowing why they've suffered." The "infernal chaos of rhythms and images" about us echoed in art and music which grimaced back at a grimacing world: *The Cry* of Edvard Munch (1893), the "Howling Wave" of Alban Berg's opera *Wozzeck* (1921), *The Cabinet of Doctor Caligari* (1919) with its dissonance, its shadows, its equivocal madness, reflecting its time and rejecting it, prophesying the rise of fascisms, violence, and irrationality. The years before the war had seen a last attempt to reconcile art and the modern world. The futurists were affected by the revival of aggressive and nationalistic sentiments in a young generation excited by the political friction of its time and tired of the rationalism of its teachers. They saw modernity breaking through old forms, everything in motion, turning on wheels and axles, beating with pistons and hammers, whirling with propellers, running with tramcars and railway engines, flashing with lights, roaring with crowds and with cannon. They tried to substitute this sense of masses and of movement, of action and of power to the static techniques of the day, by exploiting the audio-visual possibilities of the phonograph and the film. Their painting (like the contemporary world) subordinated form to motion, attempting to capture the simultaneous quality of films and affecting future surrealists like Marcel Duchamp (*Nude Descending a Staircase,* 1911).*

The war of 1914 put an end to thoughts of conciliation. The futurist influence endured in its most violent aspects, in its advocacy of action for action's sake, dissonance, and motion. All these were now intensified by the war. German Expressionism, for instance, formulated well before the war, rose to frenetic rebellion and rejection when it ended. So did Dada, likewise born out of prewar experiments but even more out of the fire and blood of war. To the murderous absurdity perpetrated or

---

* Much twentieth-century music seems to derive from futuristic *bruitism* (noises) devised as artistic provocation by Futurists in pre-1914 years. Luigi Russolo had built a noise organ (1911) which could produce distracting sounds. Edgard Varèse incorporated these sounds into his music, while Bunuel and Dali used them in the sound track of their film *L'Age d'Or* (1930).

Nude Descending a Staircase, by Marcel Duchamp. Philadelphia Museum of Art: Louise and Walter Arensberg Collection.

abetted by the respectable public, Dadaists answered with harmless but shocking absurdities of their own. Society was led by criminals and lunatic muddlers. The Bible in one hand, a cleaver in the other, generals and politicians were driving mankind to perdition with their claptrap of reason, patriotism, and logical purpose. If the most sensible and responsible men devoted themselves to destruction and mayhem, the only answer lay in salvation through nonsense. Developed in wartime Switzerland by a Romanian, Tristan Tzara, an Alsatian, Hans Arp, and a German, Hugo Ball, Dada was nihilistic, opposing art, coherent creativity, and, above all things, reason.* It simply held all existing values up to ridicule, and Dada groups appeared in Germany and France even before New York discovered it in Marcel Duchamp's contribution to the Independent Show of 1917: a plain marble urinal entitled *Foun-*

* The *Cabaret Voltaire* where Dada was born in 1916 stood at number 1 of the Spiegelgasse in Zurich; Lenin lived across the street at number 12. The police were more suspicious of the Dadaists then of the "quiet, studious Russians": Lenin, Radek, and Zinoviev.

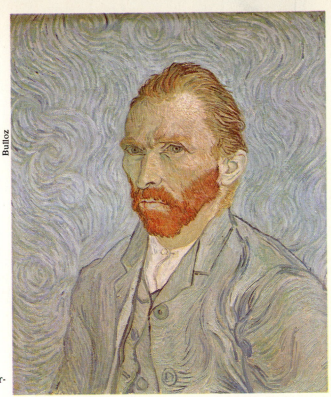

Vincent Van Gogh, a self-portrait. Jeu de Paume, Paris.

tain. But, since it was destructive and nonsensical, Dada could neither last nor create. It would give way to an offspring whose members wanted to build as well as to destroy: surrealism.

Like Dada, surrealism was founded by angry, unknown young men: André Breton (1896–1966), Jean Cocteau (1889–1963), Louis Aragon (b. 1897), Paul Éluard (1895–1952), most of whom had been involved with Dadaist demonstrations. Like Dadaists, surrealists rejected cultural norms, conventions, commonplaces of society for spontaneity, immediate experience, subjective impulses and fantasies. Like Dada, they subjected the world around them to a semantic bombardment under which order, meaning, and perspective disintegrated, revealing the inherent absurdity of life. But, unlike Dada, surrealism was hopeful as well as destructive. Surrealists believed in "truth" and the possibility of attaining it with a key furnished by André Breton, himself an analyst: they set out to apply the lessons of Freudian psychoanalysis in art, by the use of automatic writing, of free association, of methods designed to break through the crust of convention and illusion to the reality of the unconscious mind. The method, which certainly had a reinvigorating effect on art, did not as the surrealists hoped affect society and the public mind in any particular way, since it was—like most original concepts—good only for elites.

The free association surrealists proposed depended on the wealth and the variety of the practitioner's imagination and was then extended

1067

Jean Cocteau with one of his ceramic pieces, "Three Eyes."

to depend on, or to appeal to, the same capacities in beholder or listener. The drawback of the method was that, since most people are quite limited, free association was little freer than habitual or conditioned association; and little wider either. In most cases, after the first shock wore off, it was seen that one narrow, conventional mode merely succeeded another. While those who *could* appealed to interior riches and broke into original patterns and connections (like Breton or Max Ernst), most would-be surrealists expressed themselves even better as their forms became more organized (e.g. the American poet Ezra Pound or the Spaniard Salvador Dali).

Nevertheless, surrealism did see itself as a revolutionary movement, out "to change life" (culled from Rimbaud) and "to transform the world" (culled from Marx), which meant that a number of its adherents eager to smash the old bourgeois values entered revolutionary politics. Some (Aragon, Éluard) joined the Communist Party, some Trotskyist groups, some tended to anarchism (Dali, Cocteau), some went through all these stages before being adopted by the Establishment and the art dealers (Dali, Cocteau, Joan Miró), emphasizing the paradox of the last twenty to thirty years in which the avant-garde is swallowed by public taste before it has had time to get far ahead. Nowadays publicity lights up "arts" like fashions, in a situation where everything goes and in which the survival of avant-garde artists is based on the support of businessmen who sell them and the appreciation of rich connoisseurs who buy them.

The Meaning of Modernity

Art and literature, which had once described man in his greatness, began to seek him in his privacy, perhaps because great deeds are so often bloody and blood has become once more, along with violence on every kind of scale, a commonplace of everyday experience. Display gave place to introspection, confession to analysis, concrete things melted into abstractions, wholes dissolved into parts, experience turned to fragmented sensations, like a vast puzzle disintegrates into its components in some surrealist cartoon that leaves us with an impression of shapes, colors, moods, but with no stable, tangible image. Painters abandoned the imitation of nature for what E. H. Gombrich * calls "a man-made construction, a colored canvas." From illusion to painting deliberately man-made constructs on canvas, from content to configuration: planes, textures, lights, and shades, assembled first according to the creator's will and later according to chance, would take the place of narrative or message. No more illusion. No more perspective. No more the artifice of the image that brings together the disparate multiplicity of what we witness. Instead, the artist's act and the beholder's reactions exist in separate worlds.

Victorian society believed in order and so did the philosophers, the writers, and the artists who sprang from it. Today, neither society nor the men and works that reflect it conceive of order as more than something arbitrary, imposed from outside. The art of the future, Strindberg had prophesied, "will, like nature, leave a lot more to chance." Chance meant the end of choice and of discrimination. The reign of randomness was translated from the laboratory to the studio and, hence, to the eye and mind of the beholder. How indiscriminate taste has become can be seen from the recent fortunes of nonfigurative art, moving from one simplification to another, toward ever greater abstraction: from the first compositions of Kandinsky in 1910, divorcing color and form from the world of nature, through the reconstructed Cubism of Mondrian in the 1920's, to the calligraphic abstractions of Tobey, Hartung, or Soulages in the 1950's. Object and subject have been so manipulated in the past eighty years that they have finally vanished altogether in works which seem the very essence of art for art's sake. And in the last stages of rebellion, nonfigurative art returns to the realism it had abandoned. Sculptors take over all the offal and waste of industry, enlist the flotsam and wreckage of an object-bound world. Painters now imitate real materials or use them in their compositions. Finally, neo-realists like Bazaine insist on the intrinsic abstraction of *all* painting, since it merely uses objects as starting points of "the plastic invention." There is no point, they say, in nonfigurative art, since even the figurative is abstract.

Certainly, labels become irrelevant when faced with action painting, minimal painting, primary structures, pop, op, mec, or cynetic art, and happenings, all of which seek less to express anything than plunge men into a "situation" where they can play at being free and take a passing

* In his great work *Art and Illusion* (New York, 1960).

cure of nonconformism. Derivative, repetitious, romantic, vulgar, this is an art for amusement parks and fair grounds, occasionally amusing for that very reason. The question arises whether crushed cars are sculpture, whether programmed silence or noise are music, and so on. The only answer possible is the one given by Stravinsky,* that "it is still generally thought of as art if it is shown in a gallery, and as music if it takes place in premises traditionally associated with concerts; which is hardly an answer, but in the absence of identifying rules and conventions, and at a time when an aesthetic object may be anything at all, the limits of art are not only not air-tight but indefinable."

One wonders whether the highly individualistic tradition of Western art is not giving way beneath the pressures of modernity: the burden of research, of learning, of discovery, of creation, has become too much for individuals, has been passed to teams—of scientific researchers, of artists, or of scholars. Even musical composition becomes corporate, even the work of art—once the expression of a single genius—turns toward mixed media put together by several cooks. All this stresses and enhances the gulf which opened in the nineteenth century between intellectuals and society, between intellectual and artistic life and the remainder of an increasingly fractured existence. Music, literature, or painting appeal to initiates, and their obscure idioms widen the gulf between their adepts and the rest, even though within two generations they have permeated western cultural fabrics, become the commonplaces of a consciousness divided between beliefs it has retained in science and in progress and the contemporary philosophy of relativism and doubt.

Contrasting with the plastic arts, the great *writing* of the twentieth century would be social and, hence, political and ideological. We have seen that the novel turned from individual psychology and restricted games played within the limits of a social group to description of social

* *New York Review of Books,* June 1, 1967.

W. H. Auden

problems, culminating in the great crusading works of naturalism. But even most of these presupposed a change of heart, of mind, of luck, of opportunity, rather than of the social order. After the First World War this changed radically. Thomas Mann's hero, Hans Castorp, descends from his Magic Mountain into the battered plains of war and politics, Dada turns to surrealism and surrealism to revolution, the detached observers of an earlier day—delineators of men and society in decay and isolation—decide that only political action can change society, and that they must take sides in the political battle.

Surrealist fantasies were enlisted to articulate *The Waste Land,* in which more men than T. S. Eliot found themselves:

> A heap of broken images, where the sun beats,
> And the dead tree gives no shelter, the cricket no relief,
> And the dry stone no sound of water . . .
> Hooded hordes swarming . . .
> Falling towers
> Jerusalem Athens Alexandria
> Vienna London
> Unreal.

The nightmares of 1925 became the realities of the 30's, when the works of W. H. Auden (b. 1907) crept and seethed with secret conspiracies, hidden guerrillas, dangerous frontiers, industrial ruins, in which events to come were outlined with prophetic lunacy: "A preliminary bombardment of obscene telephone messages for not more than two hours, destroys the morale already weakened by predictions of defeat made by wireless controlled crows and pack cards. Shock troops equipped with wire cutters, spanners and stink bombs penetrating the houses by infiltration silence all alarm clocks, screw down the bathroom taps, and remove plugs and paper from the lavatories. . . ."

Depression, fascism, Nazism, purges, concentration camps, defeat, betrayal, the collapse of one world, the need to build another, echoed through the 30's and the 40's: Malraux, Silone, Brecht, Koestler, Steinbeck, Hemingway, Orwell, culminating in Sartre and Camus. Statements of failure all—failure of synthesis or communication (Eliot, Pound), failure of decency or faith (Malraux, Orwell), failure of man and society (Camus, Auden), failure of logic and coherence (Sartre, Breton), failure of trust or will (Silone, Koestler)—and yet, illogically, statements of a new commitment, hopes renewed, the necessity of decision when all alternatives fail, the ultimate assertion with Albert Camus that—isolated in an alien world, meaningless, unless he introduces meaning into it— man can and must assert himself. Sisyphus, condemned everlastingly to roll his rock to the mountain's top only to see it roll down again, finds that "the struggle itself towards the heights is enough to fill a man's heart. One must imagine Sisyphus happy."

Chapter 21

THE LATEST AGE:
1945 TO THE PRESENT

The Ebb of Empire

The year 1945 was the end of a period and also of a way of life. The war had shaken the earth like a great earthquake and nothing after it would be the same again. The age of European dominance was over. The supremacy of European countries, based as much on prestige as it had been on power, could not survive the blow it had received. Great colonial empires, sapped in earlier years by declining confidence among the masters and ever more strident appeals to the liberal doctrines which the masters taught, would quickly fall to pieces when the economic and military power that had won and held them disappeared. The confidence that made Europeans shoulder the white man's burden uninvited, long before the concept itself was formulated, broke down. The war had shown that the seats of power now lay outside strictly European limits, above all within her two great offspring—the Soviet Union and the United States—and that the new power conflict would be reflected in their rivalries.

A New China

Indeed, the effect of these rivalries would be to raise up a third and further rival and one whose titles as a non-European power could not be gainsaid. No greater proof could be demanded that European empire was on the ebb than the revival of the great Far Eastern power which, having long withstood Western cajolements and pressures, had crashed down at the turn of the century. A more powerful dissolvent than Western guns, the nationalist ideas the West brought to China or that China borrowed from the West, had put an end to the last imperial dynasty, and to Chinese unity for half a century.

The imperial unity of China went back to the days of the Roman Empire and beyond. But since 1644 a foreign dynasty of conquerors from Manchuria ruled in Peking. The nationalist movement, led by foreign-educated students, attacked the corrupt and reactionary Manchus as instruments of the foreigners and of national decadence. In 1908 both the Emperor and his mother (who had kept him imprisoned over the past decade) died suddenly, leaving the throne to an infant. The central administration now disintegrated completely, local warlords setting themselves up as independent rulers in various provinces. In 1911 a republican revolution broke out, led by Sun Yat-sen (1866–1925), a peasant's son, converted to Christianity and trained as a surgeon by missionaries, who would devote his life to revolutionary activity. In 1911 Sun became president of a newly proclaimed republic and the revolutionary society he had founded in the 1890's became the National-ist Party, or *Kuomintang*. The Kuomintang stood for opposition to the foreigners and the Manchus, and for three positive principles: national-ity, democracy, and a livelihood for all. The program was easier to form-ulate than to apply. For several years, the Republicans were but one more faction struggling against various warlords to control the central government in Peking to which the foreigners remitted revenues from the international customs they controlled.

Then came the First World War and, though Sun joined the Allies, Japan pulled greater weight in their councils. While Western powers were otherwise engaged, the war years saw Japan enforce her supremacy

Sun Yat-sen, leader of the Kuomintang, surrounded by his military staff.

over China's ports. As a result, the Chinese nationalists turned to Moscow. The Communists had a simple view of colonialism which Lenin formulated in 1916. According to this, imperialism was simply the highest stage of capitalism. Industrially developed countries were plundering backward ones, growing fat on their exploitation, avoiding the collapse which contradictions inherent to the capitalist system would otherwise bring about, keeping up living standards at home by securing cheap raw materials and easy markets in colonies. The Western workers who benefited from this were themselves accomplices of capitalist imperialism. Hence Communists supported national or independence movements in all colonial territories, and attempted to emancipate weak or backward countries from great power domination, as they did in China.

With Russian help, the Kuomintang was reorganized on Soviet lines. In 1926, its Bolshevik-trained army, led by Sun's political heir, Chiang Kai-shek, imposed itself at last. Central authority over the provincial warlords was reasserted, Western tutelage cast off and, shortly after, the Communists themselves were murdered or expelled. But China was not to know peace or independence quite so easily. In 1931 she had to face Japanese aggression, designed to bring a new order to Asia in which a Japanese-dominated "co-prosperity sphere" would give Japan an even greater empire than that which the West had dominated not long before. Long years of warfare, during which the Japanese occupied large parts of North and Eastern China, ended only with Japanese defeat in 1945, but their elimination did not put an end to war.

Not all Communists had been destroyed in Chiang's great purge. Some who survived, having barely escaped annihilation by flight into the far north of China, reorganized their forces by enlisting the peasants to their cause. Led by Chiang's classmate Mao Tse-tung, another product of Soviet tutelage, and with little or no support from Moscow, which (rightly) suspected the orthodoxy of their Marxism, they devised a new revolutionary strategy based not on the urban proletariat but on the rural disinherited. Wherever they went, the Communists made war on landlords and usurers, gave land to the smaller peasants, allowed them a say in local government, defended them against exactions and pillage. Unlike other soldiery China had ever known, the Red Army behaved correctly toward civilians. Such tactics, along with superior discipline and training, enabled the Communists to attract recruits and gain the sympathy of most intellectuals and nationalist democrats disgusted with the corruption, nepotism, and inefficiency of the Kuomintang dictatorship and its subordination to foreigners (chiefly Americans) who furnished its arms and money.

The Kuomintang had never established its authority over the whole of China. While attempting a number of reforms (undertaken partly in order to please his foreign friends), Chiang never managed to extirpate

EAST ASIA TODAY

Communist

Non-communist

0   1000 miles

the wide-ranging corruption of the administration he controlled, let alone the brutal anachronisms surviving in the quasi-independent fiefs of warlords who paid him only the vaguest homage. Great armies marched under Kuomintang banners; but they were ill-trained, often ill-armed, and their loyalty was as uncertain as their pay. Unable to hold the countryside against the Red guerrillas, the Kuomintang gradually lost the cities too. In 1949 Chiang's two remaining strongholds fell—

U.S. Army

Warder Collection

the capital. Peking, in the north and the great port of Canton in the south—and the dictator was forced to take refuge on Taiwan (Formosa), an island colony whose attempt to achieve independence he had crushed only shortly before. The mainland remained in the hands of the Communist "People's Republic of China." Since then, the Communist attempt to reorganize and industrialize the country, using its human resources as basic capital, has subjected China to the agonies which Russia had to face thirty years before, revealed the possible pattern of an original kind of national revolution, and alarmed the world at the prospect of the resurgence of a major power in Asia, a power now vying with Russia for leadership of the Communist camp.

India

The great Japanese imperial venture, while it crashed down in 1945, had weakened the Western hold on Asian lands beyond repair. One of the first casualties had been Britain's Indian Empire. The British certainty that they were in India to stay, their willingness to give the upper classes education but refuse them responsibility, allow them liberty but not effectiveness, made the worst of a bad situation. If ruthlessness could have kept the Indians down, indifference could have left them alone when they ceased to be profitable. Imperial inertia radicalized the moderates and opened the way to more extreme groups, especially to the leadership of Mohandas Gandhi (1869–1948). This seditious saint, as Churchill called him, who opposed every form of alien "progress"— machines, speed, urban growth and the increasing drift away from land, tradition, and religion—advocated the development of village industries (particularly handloom weaving), the vitalizing virtues of goat's milk, the political uses of nonviolence and civil disobedience.* After

* Between the wars, an American newspaper would write of him as "the only figure of world importance operating practically naked."

Opposite: Chiang Kai-shek, leader of the Nationalist Chinese and Mao Tse-tung at a desk in his cave headquarters during the Communist take-over of 1948. Right: Mohandas Gandhi and his political heir, Jawaharlal Nehru.

1907, Gandhi's *Satyagraha* campaign of passive resistance furnished a base for the increasingly revolutionary agitation of the National Congress. The struggle between India and Britain was further complicated by a rift between the Hindu and Muslim communities, each after 1906 endowed with separate electorates, each growing increasingly aware of cultural differences, until only partition or civil war could settle their divisions.

There would be Indian soldiers in Flanders in 1914, twenty-four centuries after Indian archers opposed Greeks at Plataea in 479 B.C.—their first appearance on a European battlefield. But the end of the First Great War only saw national agitation grow worse, and the communal rift grow wider. The Second World War made it clear that Britain would be unable to hold on to India much longer. Not that most Englishmen wanted to do so.

Partition and civil war followed in 1947, when predominantly Hindu India, Muslim Pakistan, and the island of Ceylon severally received their independence. The British had taken over a war-torn, miserable, and divided land. They left it torn by war and by communal strife, marked by inequities and disillusion. In 1948, Gandhi was murdered by a Hindu nationalist and the subcontinent's chances of peaceful evolution diminished still further.

In the new India most people are still underfed and hungry, misery is still a way of life, 2 per cent of the population drain half the national revenues. An educated middle class finds no opportunities to employ its limited talents. A superstitious populace finds no relief in the administrative structure inherited from the British. One thing the foreigner could not achieve was to reform the religious and caste system which

Ho Chi Minh.

contributes to the country's inability to cope with its own problems—especially soaring birth rates and lack of initiative. Nearly two centuries after the battle of Plassey, India is equipped with the administrative structure the British have left, with modern laws and railroads, ports and industries, but with less than 1 per cent of its 300 million working in industry and 80 per cent or more of its population dependent on the backward agrarian economy Britain had maintained.

Southeast Asia

Far beyond India and far more than there, Southeast Asian nationalists had welcomed the Japanese co-prosperity sphere. Despite its racialist militarism, Japanese occupation seemed preferable to Western imperialism. To opponents of European and American colonial power in Manchukuo, India, Indochina, Malaya, Burma, Indonesia, or the Philippines, Japan appeared (however briefly) as a friend because she opposed the whites who had too long dominated Asian affairs. After Japan had been defeated, any national government seemed (and still seems) better than the most enlightened colonial administration. Nor were the old colonial powers in a position to hold out against such feelings. The immense Dutch empire in Indonesia, harking back 300 years and incorporating myriad islands—some 735,000 square miles of land stretching out for nearly 3,000 miles—acquired independence in 1949. The Philippines had reached independence in 1946; Burma, conquered piecemeal between 1824 and 1886, gained independence at the same time as India in 1947. Malaya, which took longer to achieve independence, became a British dominion ten years later.

The greatest problems arose in Indochina. In 1885 China had recognized French supremacy there and the provinces of Tonkin, Annam, Laos, and Cambodia had become part of the French colonial empire soon thereafter. There as elsewhere colonization ruined village economies and communal institutions, favored usurers who alone could provide money to pay taxes at 10 per cent a month, turned farmers into tenant laborers and sharecroppers. Japanese occupation followed by collapse of French authority encouraged the proclamation of independence in 1945 by Emperor Bao Dai and the king of Cambodia, while nationalists, chief among them the Communist Vietminh led by Ho Chi Minh, fought both the French and the Japanese. The Japanese defeat allowed the setting up of an independent government which resisted French attempts to re-establish their rule in the colony. Guerrilla war led the French to try to restore the former collaborationist Bao Dai, but this failed. The Vietminh were everywhere, the French and their collaborators restricted to the towns. The battle of Dien Bien Phu in 1954 determined the end of a war unpopular in France; and the Geneva Agreements of that year, while paying lip service to eventual unification, patched up a compromise peace that left the north to the Vietminh and the south to a "representative" regime surviving only with American aid. Since then, both parts have been the prey of civil war which threatens to leave both devastated, a war moreover which has come to involve half a million U.S. troops and the diplomatic or military intervention of a score of other nations.

It is unclear whether China, preoccupied with her own revolution, has any serious designs on Southeast Asia, an area which the automobile revolution, emphasizing oil, tin, and rubber, has made the richest in the world in relation to its size. It would seem rather that most of the countries of this region cherish traditional particularisms of their own. But it would not be surprising if China, like Japan, expressed the self-confidence of economic upsurge and national revival in imperialist aspirations. If it did, it would only be doing what we have seen the Western powers do in their time of energy and expansion. But one may pause to think how little this phase has lasted,* how soon the conquering countries lost their energy and their political hold, how quickly they learned that the most effective means of domination lay not in fleets and armies but in subtler relations.

The Middle East

One region that illustrates both these points is that between the Tigris and the Nile, stage of kaleidoscopic changes for a quarter of a century.

The discovery of oil fields in Persia, Iraq, and Arabia had turned the backward Middle East into a focus of power politics, the prize of struggles to control an area that became crucial after 1913 when the

---

* Germany's colonial period ran from 1884 to 1917, Italy's from 1885 to 1941, that of the United States from 1898 to 1947. Of the old colonial powers, Portugal and Spain still hold certain African territories, Holland retains only the island of Curaçao in the Caribbean, France and Britain retain small parcels of the vast empires they accumulated during centuries. In the past twenty-five years over fifty new states have sprung from these colonies.

British Admiralty decided to convert its ships from coal to oil. In one generation the Middle East passed from the Biblical age of asses and camels into the age of trucks, buses, and refineries. By developing communications and stirring up the population, technology replaced the community of Islam with national aspirations learned from the West. Egyptian and Turkish nationalisms had appeared before 1914, proportionate to Western influences. After the Great War, during which the Allies had competed for Arab support against their Ottoman rulers, Arab states were set up in which nationalist politics directed against French and British domination were always sure of a following: the more extreme the better. The combination of unlimited aspirations and limited capacity to fulfill them provided a constantly explosive fuel for the region's politics.

In 1944, the Arab League joined together the Arab states of the Middle East in uneasy pursuit of common objectives. The first of these was to get rid of foreigners. The old colonial powers, whose determined pupils they had been, had lost their force and, what was worse, their self-confidence. The French sourly withdrew from Syria and Lebanon in 1945, the British reluctantly and gradually were pressed out of the region by 1956.* As they went, chaos and disunion too often took their place.

There could be little community between a rich paternalism like the sheik of Kuwait's and the fly-ridden savagery of Iraq, the prosperous cosmopolitanism of Lebanon and the isolated puritanism of Saudi Arabia, the national-socialism of Damascus ideologues who leaned on Moscow and the medieval court at Riadh, relying on tribal loyalties and oil revenues. Cairo and Baghdad have traditionally been rival poles of attraction in Islam, not allies. Syria fears the possible domination of Egypt, Lebanon apprehends Syrian greed, Jordan—torn between native Bedouin and rebellious Palestine refugees—subsists by an effort of her sovereign's will. Egypt itself—the leading power of the region, by dint of numbers and by the personality of its former president, Gamal Abdel Nasser (1918–1970) —is hardly an "Arab" power. Though Muslim in their majority, Egyptians never considered themselves to be Arabs before the 1930's.

Confusion was compounded by conflict in Palestine, between Jews and Arabs: long, bitter, and apparently inextricable. It had begun when, in the course of the First World War, the British government sought Jewish support by holding out the hope of a national home in Palestine—then a Turkish province. Influenced as much by Old Testament memories as by the needs of war, the Balfour Declaration of 1917 thus promised the Jews a homeland that Britain did not own, and which it only came to control by right of conquest.

This fulfilled a long-standing aspiration of the Jews, one which the

* With the exception of Aden, which was only evacuated in December, 1967, when the area was incorporated into a newly independent South Yemen Republic.

Warder Collection

Nehru with Egyptian leader Gamal Abdel Nasser.

Zionist movement had articulated late in the nineteenth century and
had begun to carry out in the colonization of Palestine even under Turkish rule, so that the Jewish population of that province, 24,000 in 1882,
stood at 85,000 in 1914. But it clashed with promises other British emissaries had made to the Arabs, whose risings contributed to Turkish
defeats.

Serious trouble might still have been avoided if immigration to Zion
had not been spurred by flight from a Europe darkened by Nazi persecution in Germany and rising anti-Semitism elsewhere. 150,000 in
1927, the Jewish population of Palestine had trebled by the thirties' end.
The competition between modern methods which the Jews employed
and the traditional methods of the Arab population, the friction of
rival nationalisms, each of which came to regard the other as the beach-
head of alien culture, made trouble inevitable or, at least, predictable.
Threatened in their homeland, the Arabs reacted with wild, sometimes
blind, violence: riots, arson, murder. The British authorities were caught
between Arabs who blamed them for letting in Jews and Jews who
blamed them for not admitting more. The Arabs spoke of their rights
in what was still their country. The Jews of life and death, only alternatives seemingly open in Hitler's Europe. Between 1944 and 1948, terror
and counter-terror competed in a now-familiar crescendo, nationalist
terrorism turning increasingly against the British occupants against
whose prohibitions of illegal immigration was being pursued. *Mutatis mu-
tandis,* the activities of terrorist groups like the Stern Gang or the Irgun
Zvai Leumi did not differ greatly from the crimes their Palestinian Arab
foes were to perpetrate twenty years later. Against the British in Ireland, against the Germans in France, soon against the French in Algeria,
patriots demonstrated that—however much conditions might differ—
the terrorism of small, scattered bands could dent the inertia of the majority and harry an occupying power into recruiting enemies by repression.

Jewish nationalists found widespread support in a world horrified by
Nazi crimes and eager to help Jewish survivors in search of shelter find
that shelter in Palestine, rather than elsewhere. The debt that Europe

owed the Jews, much aggravated by common responsibilities in Hitlerite horrors, would be paid at someone else's cost, creating an unending source of resentment and conflict. One could count the establishment of Israel as an independent republic in 1948 as a clear gain, were it not for the rancors that fester on, for the hatreds that still rage unabated.

Three wars, in 1948, 1956, and 1967, have opposed Israel and its Arab neighbors, each an Arab defeat, none an Israeli victory beyond the battlefield, all falling far short of a solution to the region's problems. Israel is too strong for her enemies; the Arabs are too numerous for their foes. A detailed account of their struggles would be irrelevant, for facts have little hold on this head-on encounter of the rival rights (and wrongs). Only some things are certain: that the new state of Israel will not be eliminated short of annihilation; that the economic and the human drains of war threaten the stability of every Arab state; and that the needs of warfare increase the contestants' dependence on alien powers which alone can subsidize and arm them.

In 1956, a last attempt to reassert the traditional imperial influence ended less with a bang than a whimper, when a joint Franco-British invasion force had to leave Egypt under the threat of United Nations sanctions. Yet more illuminating than the humiliation were the conditions of their failure. For the Franco-British expedition against Suez harked back to glorious days when denunciation of a contract or failure to pay a debt by some small state would bring French or British gunboats to Greece, Egypt, or Mexico, to enforce the interests of their subjects. In this case, President Nasser, angered by refusal of Anglo-American aid for the building of Egypt's high dam at Aswan, had prematurely abolished the Suez Canal Company's ninety-nine-year lease. The interests involved were slight. The costs of the canal had long been paid off; revenues were now sheer profit, but they would end in 1968 in any case. Nationalization was only twelve years ahead of the contract's expiration. What was at stake was not profit, but a state of mind. And clearly, in Paris and in London this state of mind was muddled. For what appeared as a Franco-British initiative was a by-product of the struggle between Washington and Moscow for influence in Egypt, of Egypt's efforts to arm itself against Israel, of Israel's attempts to seize the initiative against Egypt. The combined operation that was launched from Cyprus against Nasser's troops reflected less what France or Britain wanted than what others had done or wished to do.* It ended ingloriously when Washington and Moscow forced them to halt and remove their troops from Egypt. And the only ones to benefit were the Israelis, whose forces had

---

* The Americans sought to recruit Egypt for a regional defense pact directed against Russia, the Russians to keep it from any such alignment; the Egyptians wanted arms against Israel, Israel wanted an end to Egypt's blockade of her crucial Red Sea port at Eilat. When the United States refused Egypt the arms it wanted, Egypt got them from Communist sources, thus raising Washington's ire and making it withdraw its promise of support for Aswan, a project which Moscow quickly undertook.

THE MIDDLE EAST

Territory occupied
by Israel, 1967

100 miles

DAMASCUS
SYRIA
Amman
Beirut
LEBANON
Haifa
Tel Aviv
Jerusalem
Gaza
Port Said
SUEZ CANAL
Suez
Cairo
JORDAN
ISRAEL
DEAD SEA
Aqaba
Eilat
GULF OF AQABA
SAUDI ARABIA
SINAI PENINSULA
EGYPT
RED SEA
MEDITERRANEAN SEA
Nile

U.S.S.R.
AFGHANISTAN
WEST PAKISTAN
INDIA
Indus
IRAN
Teheran
CASPIAN SEA
Baku
TURKEY
Ankara
GREECE
Athens
CRETE
AEGEAN SEA
CYPRUS
Nicosia
MEDITERRANEAN SEA
SYRIA
Beirut
LEBANON
Damascus
Amman
Tel Aviv
ISRAEL
JORDAN
SUEZ CANAL
SEE INSET
Cairo
Alexandria
U.A.R. (EGYPT)
LIBYA
Tigris
Euphrates
Baghdad
IRAQ
KUWAIT
PERSIAN GULF
QATAR
TRUCIAL STATES
MUSCAT AND OMAN
ARABIAN SEA
SAUDI ARABIA
Riyadh
Mecca
RED SEA
Luxor
Aswan
Nile
Khartoum
SUDAN
Port Sudan
ERITREA
ETHIOPIA
YEMEN
SOUTHERN YEMEN
Aden
FRENCH SOMALILAND
Djibouti
SOMALI REPUBLIC

500 miles

Israeli troops move to the Egyptian border during the 1948 war.

performed with their usual brio, and who had succeeded in opening the way to their vital port at Eilat.

But the withdrawal of the Europeans, which the Suez fiasco symbolized, left the area free for the confrontation of the Soviet Union and the United States. Riven by internal dissensions, torn by external temptations, the Middle East could not stand by itself, could certainly not learn to act as an independent entity. New imperial interests moved in to replace the old. Nature abhors a vacuum of power.

Dependent Independence

It is clearly possible to control other countries by economic influence rather than by conquests, by use of loans or investments which would affect their policies, by the penetration of industrial methods and products which shatter native economies frequently already in decay and keep them as the lenders' vassals until they rebuild their own power or break away by revolution or war. Actual practice is more complex.

As communications were shrinking the world, and trade tying its disparate parts together, the need of industrial nations to interfere with those less developed increased—if only because without their products and their markets (but especially the former) the industry was liable to run down. On the other hand, more backward countries—Turkey or China, Egypt or Peru—could only hope to match their exploiters in wealth and power by developing capital and skills which they could only secure by enlisting Western aid: that is, by facilitating even greater foreign meddling in, and control of, their affairs. The West could not be kept out without Western techniques, and these could not be acquired without bringing in the West. This was a quandary. But while, as we have seen, such changes meant social and cultural revolution for the adjusting economy, they need not always mean political subjection. Even a poor country like Algeria today can limit the influence of foreign investors if it wills; even a capital-poor country like the United States of the nineteenth century can develop its equipment and resources almost wholly on a flood of foreign loans, and yet maintain its political and diplomatic independence. A country sufficiently determined could adapt its borrowings to its peculiar needs as did Japan, could expropriate foreign capital as did Mexican revolutionaries or Russian Bolsheviks, could assimilate it by bankruptcies as did the United States, could try to do without it almost altogether as does Communist China, or rely on it utterly and yet control it as Israel does today.

What has been called economic colonialism is seldom the result of economic conquest and much more often that of a native default: the failure to develop possibilities which may be realized and yet ignored, not for lack of means but because those who have the means have no wish to use them in the public good. Foreign capital is thus attracted to do things that national capital does not care to do.

In this connection we should do well to remember the words of John Stuart Mill, like his father before him an official of the East India Company: "One people," wrote Mill, "may keep another for its own use, a place to make money in, a human cattle farm to be worked for the profit of its own inhabitants," but not for that of the subjects. Whatever motives moved the empire builders, Mill's words proved terribly true in Asia as elsewhere. But everywhere, as in India, Europe trained the leaders and inspired the ideologies that would first challenge and then displace its power.

The Protean Conflict

On the night when the Japanese had attacked Pearl Harbor, General de Gaulle, then head of the Free French Committee in beleaguered London, had rejoiced. "The war is now definitely won." As for the future, he went on to predict two phases: Germany restored by the Allies and a great war between Russia and America. The first proved true within half a dozen years. The second was only avoided by dint of mutual fear.

Only a few men could be so clear-sighted. The exuberance and the needs of combat fought in common toned down the differences between reluctant partners whom Hitler turned to allies. Most of the American people, like the British, impressed by Russian sufferings and valiance, could not conceive that they and the Soviets need ever again be foes. In 1942, to General Douglas MacArthur as to his countrymen, "the hopes of civilization" appeared to "rest on the worthy banners of the courageous Russian army." Men like President Franklin Delano Roosevelt and his chief advisor, Harry Hopkins, seem to have felt that the United States and Russia had more in common in some ways than either had with more old-fashioned countries maintaining social hierarchies at home and colonies abroad. Men like Churchill, Roosevelt felt, desperately clutching at the past, would attempt to reimpose the anachronistic values of another world, reinstall royalist or conservative regimes, restore imperial structures. Against such aims Russia and the

United States could co-operate, all the better if Russia's legitimate concerns for her security and welfare were satisfied. Even Americans who did not think this way seem to have held that the successful conduct of the war came before any consideration of postwar policies. Until the end, American leaders like the commander of the Allied armies in Europe, General Dwight D. Eisenhower, regarded military victory as prior to and distinct from political decisions, which meant that American policy was to win the war and hope for the best thereafter.

This is not to say that the British, the Americans, and their allies gave no thought to the world which they hoped to build once peace had come. The Allied leaders—Churchill, Roosevelt, Stalin, joined sometimes by leading figures and representatives of friendly countries—met frequently for talks and conferences which would define war aims and postwar actions. One of the concrete results of such talks was the foundation of the United Nations, set up on American initiative to replace the defunct League of Nations in which Roosevelt had lost all faith.

The League of Nations had not lived up to its supporters' expectations. It had provided a platform for the lesser nations and a meeting ground for members, accustoming statesmen to continuous negotiations and playing a useful part in its nonpolitical organizations for health, labor, or drug limitation on the international plane. But it had shown that peace could only be maintained with the co-operation of the greatest powers, whose support it lacked. Only co-operation could defeat Fascism; only continued co-operation could maintain peace. Roosevelt proposed to abandon his country's policy of isolation and, with the support of his greatest allies, provide the basic structure of a world where democracy would prevail and aggression be suppressed once for all. The United Nations, whose declaration was signed shortly after Pearl Harbor (1942) and which came into being three years later, was endowed with a Security Council of six nonpermanent members and five permanent ones (the Soviet Union, the United States, Britain, France, and China), who could only act in unanimity against aggression (hence the veto);* and a General Assembly in which, despite Stalin's objections to giving little countries (like Albania) which he despised the same rights as those of the greater powers, every member nation had an equal vote. The United Nations would, in due course, become less the peacekeeping agency of Roosevelt's dream than a forum of international affairs. But it was hardly, then or in retrospect, more than a hopeful gesture toward a better peace, a sop ceded to Roosevelt by the Russians who were preoccupied by far more concrete things.

In any case the wartime and postwar conferences, conducted in haste and under pressure, aimed rather at agreement on common formulas than at definitions which would clarify and settle the differences be-

---

* In 1966 the Security Council of the U.N. was enlarged to fifteen, and the Big Power veto abandoned.

A meeting of the
United Nations Se-
curity Council.

tween the parties present. While all agreed that the new world should
be democratic and that the peoples of liberated Europe were entitled
to self-determination, no one quite knew or perhaps wished to know
what such terms implied. Peoples, democracy, self-determination, had
different meanings for each party. For Communists, in any case, words
and gestures had no intrinsic meaning, only a dialectic value arising
out of the aims and realities of a given moment and passing away with
it. This was something Roosevelt would learn too late. But if the Russians
were the most ruthless both in fact and doctrine, the Americans and
British also bent ideals to particular ends: in Greece, where in 1944 a
Communist rising was suppressed by the British army; in Yugoslavia,
where Churchill backed the Communist Tito against both Germans and
pro-British royalists, only to find him assert his independence of British
plans as he would later of the Russians too; in Poland, where "compromise" allowed the Russians a government which would be at their
beck and call; and everywhere that great power decisions settled the
fate of peoples without real reference to their wish.

While the Americans were chiefly interested in somewhat abstract
notions of international security and justice, the Russians understood
only the politics of power. Like their allies, the Russians were determined that Germany, once vanquished, should never rise again. But they
also nourished the thought for themselves of a protective rampart
against any revived threat to their security. In other words, they wanted
to control Eastern Europe, partly because its states affected the security
of their borders (Finland, Poland, Romania), partly because they were
traditional protégés (Bulgaria, Yugoslavia), partly because they lay
athwart strategic routes toward Germany (Hungary, Czechoslovakia).
Moreover, by 1945, all these states between the Greek and Finnish
borders were occupied by Russian troops and the temptation of "what
we have we hold" was very great. "This war is not like those of the
past," Stalin told Tito in 1945, "Whoever occupies a territory imposes
his own social system upon it. Everybody imposes his system as far as his
army can advance."

Yet unilateral decisions could not hold without some consent of the
other powers; and these were bound by principles and treaties to quite a

different set of views. The independence of Poland in particular, for whose sake the war had started, could not be easily abandoned. Churchill himself in 1944 had agreed with Stalin on their respective East European zones of influence, a deal in which most of the countries along Russia's borders became in effect Russian satellites, while Greece became a protégé of Britain. But even Churchill fought hard to let the Poles choose their own government as they wished. This was a point which the Russians—having killed, arrested, or otherwise eliminated most of that country's non-Communist leadership—never would concede. The first years following the war were marked by desperate and unsuccessful attempts by the Western powers to prevent Eastern Europe and especially Poland from falling entirely into Russian hands. By 1948 their failure and Russia's establishment of its effective hold upon this region determined the complete breakdown of the wartime alliance and its division into hostile camps.

The roots of this division went back to the great conferences of Teheran (1943) and Yalta (1945) in which the leaders of the Allied powers bargained for the world. Yalta is a good case of the dangers of leaving such large decisions to the debate of a few powerful but fallible individuals.* Here, Roosevelt's rather naïve expectation that he could hold the balance between British imperialism and Soviet Communism, reconciling the Russians to the "one world" he had in view,** in which lions would work with lambs in the United Nations, came up against the grim realism of Stalin. The future of Germany was settled and its division into Allied zones of occupation confirmed; it was agreed that Russian intervention against the Japanese would take place shortly after the end of hostilities in Europe; but no agreement could be reached on Poland, which Stalin regarded as an avenue through which the Germans might again attack Russia. There was little opposition to his proposal that Poland's eastern border should be approximately on the Curzon Line, while she received compensation in the west at Germany's expense, but no settlement as to his determination that the Polish government must be in hands on which he could rely. Indeed, the most striking thing about the outcome of the talks at Yalta, as at every other summit conference, is not what was decided but what was left undecided.

Perhaps this is easier to understand if one bears in mind the brutal changes and the multitude of problems that faced the victorious peacemakers. As Winston Churchill told the House of Commons on his return from Yalta: "We are now entering a world of imponderables, and

---

* Of the major participants at Yalta, Churchill was, according to the American Secretary of State, Stettinius, going through his menopause; Roosevelt, very ill, maintained only a brittle contact with life; his chief adviser, Harry Hopkins, was dying of cancer; only Stalin was in fine fettle.

** A term coined by his unsuccessful Republican rival in the presidential election of 1940: Wendell Willkie.

Big Three representatives—Stalin, Roosevelt, and Churchill—dine at Livadia Palace during the Yalta Conference. In the left foreground is Secretary of State Edward Stettinius, and to the right of Churchill is Soviet Foreign Minister Molotov.

Warder Collection

at every stage occasions for self-questioning arise. It is a mistake to look too far ahead. Only one link in the chain of destiny can be handled at a time."

But such self-questioning seems to have been limited to the West. For, as soon as the conference had ended, the Russians took steps to collect on the half-concessions which they had managed to secure. Within a few weeks, their hold on Bulgaria, Romania, and Poland was affirmed, despite the protests of their Western allies. It would be solidly established in the next two years, as not only national leaders but also Communists whose complete devotion Stalin doubted were eliminated one by one. As Marx had prophesied in the New York *Tribune* of April 12, 1853, the western borders of the Soviet Empire now stretched "from Stettin to Trieste." Along them, declared Winston Churchill in a great speech at Fulton, Missouri, in March 1946, an iron curtain cut off the peoples of the East from freedom.

Yet, as it had been during the war itself, the crux and focus of international tensions and great power rivalries was Germany. There, the occupation zones hardened into a division of the country between the western part under British, French, and American occupation, and the eastern, where the Russians established the rule of local Communists everywhere but in the provinces beyond the Oder and Neisse rivers, which were handed over to Polish administration. By 1948, friction between the occupants on economic and political questions (reparations, monetary reform, the fate of Berlin) led to a confrontation focused on the old capital which was under their joint administration. The Allied position in Berlin, a hundred miles within Communist territory, marked the city out as a permanent sore, and one which the Russians could scratch whenever they wished. Angered by unilateral Allied currency reform in the West, the Russians sought to close their access to Berlin. Cut off by land, the Westerners survived by means of a giant airlift: 300,000 flights and over 2,000,000 tons of supplies between July, 1948, and May, 1949.

But Berlin, like Poland, Greece, or Turkey, was only one point where friction turned to crisis, where constant Communist probing had to be withstood. Here was an unheard-of situation: neither peace nor war but a world-wide struggle in which every possible weapon was used short of a frontal attack that would lead to major conflict. Local wars, insurrections, political and ideological infiltration and subversion, propaganda by every available means, political and economic pressures, added up to what the American Bernard Baruch described in a speech of 1947 as the "Cold War."

The Lagging Unification of Europe

The Cold War was a conflict which the impoverished survivors of Western European power were in no position to maintain. Only the United States could face Russia in defense of areas as yet free from Communist rule. In 1947, President Harry S Truman announced American military aid to Greece and Turkey then under heavy pressure from the Communists. Then, in February, 1948, a Communist coup took over Czechoslovakia, the last country in Eastern Europe to preserve its recovered independence. The democratic government in Prague was sympathetic to the Soviet Union which had opposed the betrayal of Munich, and had done its best to function as a kind of bridge between East and West. The native Communist Party was numerous and Soviet prestige high, but public sentiment favored social democracy rather than proletarian dictatorship. Nor did the Communists have the excuse of oppressive government or social injustice, since the country's institutions and her industrial structure were among the most progressive in Europe. But in the struggle between East and West there was no room for neutrality. Moscow had no use for an uncommitted neighbor or for a government that did not reflect the wishes of the local party. Backed by the presence of Soviet troops at the border, armed Communist militia took over the country. Czechoslovakia was part of Russia's defensive pattern; she became, for twenty years at least, the most docile of Stalin's satellites.

Her rape, followed in short order by the blockade of Berlin, made 1948 a very nervous year. Soviet armies could have overrun Western Europe with little opposition from existing European or American forces, and the Soviet Union was seen as a serious threat to independence and free institutions everywhere. Nor could the Europeans be sure that the distant United States would use her atom bombs to defend them. It was as a first step in their own defense that Britain, France, and the Benelux countries signed a fifty-year defensive treaty in March, 1948. Within a year, with North American encouragement, this grew into a wider alliance including the original five, the United States, Canada, Denmark, Iceland, Italy, Norway, and Portugal all of which signed the North Atlantic Treaty in April, 1949. Greece and Turkey would join in 1952. The expenses of the North Atlantic Treaty Organization (NATO) were largely borne by the United States, but its structure took some time to crystallize. Then, in 1950, the conflict feared in Europe broke out at the other end of the world with the invasion of South Korea by the Russian-trained troops of her sister state in the North.

Annexed by Japan in 1910, the Koreans had never given up their struggle for national independence. In 1945, they had proclaimed a People's Republic that surprised all the allies, who had envisaged a long-term trusteeship that would prepare the peninsula for self-government. Russian occupation of the country north of the 38th parallel and American occupation south of it had resulted in rival regimes: Communist in the north and National-Conservative in the south. Attempts to unify the peninsula under a single government naturally failed and the equally oppressive and unrepresentative rulers of the two sections faced the familiar alternative of turning temporary division into permanence or modifying it by force. When the North Koreans took the initiative in the latter, the United States was able to enlist United Nations opinion in favor of defending the *status quo*. The common "police action" decided upon lasted three years and cost some three million casualties among the military and civilian populations involved, including 140,000 Americans, the U.S. having contributed the largest contingent of the U.N. Expeditionary Force.

Peace negotiations begun in 1951 ended in 1953 in an armistice that has been uneasily maintained ever since. But the fears excited by the conflict, the passions aroused by Chinese intervention on the North Korean side, the difficulty of fighting the kind of limited war of containment that General Douglas MacArthur (for a time commander of the U. N. forces) denounced as "a war without victory," seemed to bring world conflict very near. At the same time, the outbreak of the war in 1950, with the demands it made on American resources and the additional strain it imposed on Europeans contributing their share to the Korean enterprise, had spurred the NATO powers into fresh initiatives. Most particularly, the pressing danger argued for greater manpower that could only be contributed by a (West) Germany rearmed and integrated into the military alliance of her victors. Prolonged negotiations for an all-European army having collapsed in 1954 before the objections first of the British, then of the French, Germany entered NATO and the Western alliance system as a full-fledged member in 1955.

In 1969, members of the Atlantic Alliance celebrating its twentieth anniversary could pride themselves that the fear of Russian aggressiveness which presided over NATO's foundation had given way to a more relaxed attitude; and certainly compared to 1949 both Eastern and Western camps seek to avoid tension and to encourage appeasement in

Europe. Yet, if it has kept the peace, the Alliance has hardly preserved the freedom of the nations it was also designed to protect: neither that of member states like Portugal or Greece, nor that of the Czechs whose loss of liberty in 1948 precipitated the Alliance in the first place.

But, even to achieve very limited successes, military aid was not the only way. The Communists did best where economic and social dislocation on a major scale wore down the middle class and discontented labor, creating social grievances that they could utilize. The anti-Communists had to make war on poverty, unemployment, and hunger. In June, 1947, the U.S. Secretary of State, General George C. Marshall, announced a new policy: "directed not against any country or doctrine but against hunger, poverty, desperation and chaos. Its purpose should be revival of a working economy. . . ."

The Marshall Plan worked. The actual financial aid which it provided was somewhat less than the American aid that Europe had received up to the time it started.* But previous aid had been distributed haphazardly; the new aid would be coordinated by the Europeans themselves. Indeed, the greatest function of the Marshall Plan was to promote European co-operation in the establishment of a common recovery program (1948), which, by 1951, brought industrial output back to prewar levels.

Within a series of international agreements ** Western Europe tried to leave behind the conflicts of national claims and ambitions which had shaped and scarred it over the past century and a half, and moved toward political and economic integration managed by supranational institutions. It is unlikely that this would have developed without the original American initiative; or, one would think, without the stubborn policy of Stalin, who was determined to keep his part of Europe out of it. The advance of West European integration and of Communist policy developed in a kind of counterpoint. Marshall aid itself a counter to Communist progression; a tightening of Stalinist reins on Eastern satellites in answer to it culminating in the abolition of Czech independence in 1948; the struggle over Berlin in that same year encouraging the creation of a North Atlantic security pact; the outbreak of the Korean War in 1950 speeding the emancipation of West Germany, whose manpower and resources could not be spared and leading to the recognition of a sovereign Federal Republic in West Germany in 1952 and of the rival Democratic Republic (GDR) in the East. This German resurgence, in turn, suggested the pooling of coal and steel resources of Belgium, Holland, Luxembourg, France, and Germany in the Euro-

---

* U.S. aid to Europe before the Marshall Plan amounted to about 17 billion dollars; Marshall aid provided approximately 11 billion dollars: a quarter to Britain, a fifth to France, 11 per cent to West Germany, 10 per cent to Italy.

** Organization for European Economic Cooperation (OEEC) 1948; European Coal and Steel Community (ECSC) 1951, European Economic Community (EEC) 1957, European Free Trade Area (EFTA) 1959, and many others.

pean Coal and Steel Community, which restrains German economic activity in a freely negotiated settlement. Finally, there would develop out of this a European Economic Community (1957), establishing a common market with common tariffs, ensuring the free movement of capital, labor, and goods, and working out common social and economic policies.

If the challenges of recovery and the aid of the United States played important parts in this process, a significant and unexpected force working for European integration was to be found in the Vatican. Remembering the days before the sixteenth century when national divisions counted less than the bonds of widely shared religion and culture, the Catholic Church looked with sympathy upon ideas of European union mooted with particular urgency since the First World War. It so happened that the late 1940's saw Christian-Democratic (that is, Catholic) parties and leaders in dominant positions, notably in Germany, where Konrad Adenauer remained in power from 1949 to 1963; Italy, where Alcide de Gasperi held the premiership from 1945 until his death in 1953; and France, where Robert Schuman was a constant member and sometimes head of successive cabinets from 1946 into the early 1950's.* These men and their supporters realized that if Europe did not somehow unite, its energies, unable to express themselves effectively, would curdle into the same old parochialism and lead to the resurgence of national rivalries which had already cost it dear. Paradoxically enough, the promoters of this initiative—the most progressive that Europe had known in centuries—were old men: Adenauer, born in 1876, de Gasperi, born in 1881, Schuman, born in 1886; they had all grown up at a time when nationalisms had not yet hardened into myth, had been formed in a Catholic bourgeois tradition where common interests and beliefs counted for more than passports.

The first move in this direction would take place in 1948, year of the Communist coup in Prague and of the Berlin blockade, when arguments for European unity carried particular conviction. A thousand delegates, twelve ex-premiers, forty ex-cabinet ministers, belonging to nineteen European countries, presided over by Winston Churchill, who had made himself the unexpected champion of a United States of Europe, gathered in the Hague and called for new unitary institutions. Governments responded promptly, the French and Belgians taking the initiative, the British hanging back. In a series of official committees, the hopes of 1948 were pared down to purely consultative institutions: there would be no federal union, no European government. But on May 5, 1949, the Council of Europe was set up "to ensure a closer union of its members," originally Belgium, Denmark, France, Ireland, Italy, Luxembourg, Holland, Norway, Sweden and the United Kingdom. Twenty years later,

---

* All came from border zones: Schuman and Adenauer from opposite sides of a Rhine which has traditionally served more as a highway than a border, de Gasperi from the Trentino; all were especially aware that frontiers of the modern kind were a new invention, artificial sunderers of normal relationships.

Jean Monnet.

the original ten had become eighteen, including all non-Communist European nations except for Finland, Portugal, and Spain. The Council's structure could be used to advance political integration when Europeans were ready for it, while committing them to nothing for the present.

Meanwhile, European ideas were to be carried into action by a less public figure: the Frenchman, Jean Monnet (b. 1888). Monnet had made his career as a supranational technocrat and administrator, first in the League of Nations, then in the commissions that negotiated economic agreement with Britain and the United States. It was he who, in 1940, as his country was being overrun by German armies, invented the proposal fruitlessly advanced by Winston Churchill that France and Britain should be fused in one, with a common citizenship for their peoples. Now he felt that the reconstruction of Europe offered an opportunity to restructure national into international institutions, beginning with economic integration but leading to political union. He proposed that this should begin where interdependence was already most evident, in a supranational authority controlling the continent's great coal-producing areas in the Saar and Ruhr and regulating the coal, iron, and steel industries of the West. Adenauer and Schuman agreed; Italy, Belgium, Holland, and Luxembourg followed suit; only the British held out.

There were many reasons for London's attitude: among them, suspicion of an initiative launched by politicians who were not only Catholic (hence tarred by historical memories with the brush of reaction) but overt supporters of capitalism and free enterprise. As a member of the British Cabinet later explained, the Labor Government "were determined not to allow interference by a European Committee with our full employment policy, our social services, our nationalized industries, or our national planning." No Socialist Party, stated a Labor pamphlet, "could accept a system by which important fields of national policy were surrendered to a supra-national European representative authority, since such an authority would have a permanent anti-Socialist majority and would arouse the hostility of the European workers." British Conservatives agreed for reasons of their own. For Churchill, speaking in the House of Commons, Britain "could not be an ordinary member of a federal union limited to Europe" and excluding the Commonwealth and the United States. And future Conservative Prime Minister, Harold Macmillan, asserted: "One thing is certain and we may as well face it. Our people will not hand over to any supra-national Authority the right to close down our pits or our steel-works."

Insularity, pride, selfishness, understandable concern for specific orientations that were ideological and sentimental as much as economic kept Britain out; and their expressions deserve attention because they are human, natural, representative, and typical of how one day's certainties may become another's rue. At any rate, in the 1950's Britain produced half the coal and a third of the steel of Europe so that its refusal to join the proposed Authority was a serious blow. The European Coal and Steel Community (ECSC) proceeded nevertheless, its High Authority (virtually autonomous in its particular realm) fixing prices, determining production, controlling investments and imports, closing down uneconomic mines, removing internal tariffs and setting external ones as it saw fit among the six members of the Community.

It is a classic rule that unification provides a vaster market and opportunities, not only for trade but for supranational planning on a more economic scale. Monnet hoped to extend the economic harmonization worked out within ECSC to the rest of the economy of the six original partners and to work out supranational institutions on a political level that would integrate them and Europe as a whole. The European Economic Community (EEC), generally identified as the Common Market, should have been the vehicle of this new advance and did, to some extent, play this role. But Britain, concerned for her Commonwealth ties and her privileged position in relation to the United States, still unwilling to subject her policy to authorities other than national ones, remained outside the EEC until too late, organizing a rival organization: the European Free Trade Association. Then, after 1958, as the Common Market forged steadily ahead, General de Gaulle turned French policy away from further integration. Europe, he insisted, existed only as a coalition of nations united at the governmental level, but jealously retaining their separate political identities. The Council of Europe had first been watered down by the British; now it was opposed by the French, who saw to it that the meetings of the Council of Ministers and of the annual Assembly of member nations at Strasbourg should remain purely verbal affairs, lacking power or effects upon national governments.

L'Europe des patries which de Gaulle imposed upon his partners set back the prospects of thorough economic—let alone political—union transcending national boundaries by a decade. At the same time, when—in 1963—Britain, chastened by her economic difficulties, sought to join the Common Market, France's negative vote prevented her admis-

Representatives of the European Common Market countries after one of their first meetings.

sion. The Council of the EEC must vote unanimously on questions such as admission of new or associate members. There were concrete reasons that made British entry into the European Economic Community difficult to negotiate: Britain's past record and her extra-European orientation raised suspicions as to her real intentions, above all the island kingdom's reluctance to give up the domestic subsidies and the cheap food imports from the Commonwealth which permitted low food prices and, hence, relatively lower wages, thus indirectly subsidizing industrial exports. But General de Gaulle's veto prevented the question from being decided on its merits. His fall from power in 1969 reopened the possibility of negotiations, without removing the obstacles in the way of Britain's admission. The major problems now were no longer in the agricultural field, but in that of currency and balance of payments. Members of the Common Market had reason to fear the weakness of the pound sterling, a currency with interests and vagaries of little profit to the Six. Yet the changing factors—from agriculture to currency—suggest that when objections of principle are removed, the problems to be solved fall in the realm of those everyday issues that all economies constantly face; experience indicates that, in or out of the EEC Club, the fates of sterling, franc, dollar, and mark are inextricably entwined; and one imagines the admission of Britain and her European Free Trade Association partners to a growing European Community to be henceforth a matter of time and perseverance.

Meanwhile, EEC and EFTA have continued to co-operate within the Organization for European Economic Cooperation, established in 1948. By 1960 their consumption, their productivity, the level of their living standards, had doubled compared to prewar days. Western Europe, with only 3 per cent of the land and 10 per cent of the population of the world, had 20 per cent of its food, 25 per cent of its total output, 40 per cent of its trade. One can see that the eighteen members of the OEEC, if they were really united, would be the most powerful economic unit in the world today. But also the most vulnerable: dependent on foreign trade, on raw materials, on continued peace, above all on adjustment and response to the challenges that face it.

From Cold War to Coexistence

The Cold War redefined and restricted the meaning of the West as that part of the world where Soviet writ did not run—thus including Turkey but not Czechoslovakia, Spain and Portugal but not Finland, Australia but not India, eventually Japan and Formosa but not Cuba. The social and political structures of these "Western" nations varied widely; but in all the capitalist system had been and was being steadily modified. In most of them, either between the wars or after 1945, a certain degree of nationalization had taken place. Railroads, industries like steel or armaments or aviation, mines, public transport, utilities, banks, insurance companies, tobacco companies, match manufactures, automobiles—all or some of these were taken under state control, either as public corporations or in some other way. War, Marx once said, is the forcing house of democracy. The Cold War was that too. And, while the Western world moved ever further from the capitalist model Marx and Lenin described, the Soviet world has moved closer to the kind of old regime it professes to replace, complete with intellectual slavery, terror, and power hunger.

By the 1950's, each side had come to regard the other as an incarnation of evil and itself as the champion of justice and truth. In the nineteenth century Tocqueville had seen the future world divided between Americans and Russians, one party standing for liberty and the other for servitude. But now the almost pathological hostility between the rival camps rose to fantastic heights. It was sharpened by common terror of the weapons which a new war might bring into use. War, which had been temporarily excluded from the everyday experience of nineteenth-century men, now became a way of life as in the Middle Ages and, more: a total threat. The United States in 1952, the Soviet Union in 1953, possessed hydrogen bombs. By 1957, the Soviet ICBM which could lift an earth satellite into orbit could also carry atomic missiles to the United States.

Historical events seem to reproduce the relationship of thunder and lightning. The happening itself is a flash soon lost in darkness. But the thunder reverberates, carries on the news of it amplified to monstrous proportions. If lightning burns and scorches, it is thunder that brings fear. People knew that the power of the two bombs dropped on Hiroshima and Nagasaki was equal to two-thirds of all bombs dropped on Germany in the course of the whole war. The first hydrogen bomb tested in 1952, equaled two hundred of the earliest atom bombs; and its three megatons would be dwarfed ten years later by the Russians'

60-megaton bomb, which enlarged the destructive area of atomic power from a single city to a whole region or country. Men also knew that atomic radiation, spreading far beyond a given target, could prove more deadly than any given bomb. They knew, in fact, that a major war could easily mean the end of the human race. And such prospects of Armageddon were matter-of-factly envisaged both by U.S. Defense Secretary Robert S. McNamara describing U.S. forces in 1963 as "large enough to insure the destruction, singly or in combination, of the Soviet Union, Communist China, and the Communist satellites as national societies . . ." and by the deputy commander of Soviet missile forces answering that his rockets could "raze all industrial and administrative targets and political centers of the United States," and "completely destroy the countries on whose territories American bases are situated." Others took the likelihood of destruction with less calm. Europeans in particular tended increasingly to place their hope in a possible "third force," detached from either side, and, at least in private, to call a plague on both their houses. Still, there was little that they could do but wish: the third force that might have modified the balance of terror or escaped from it could arise only out of a united Europe, and Europe was far from that.

It seemed as if the unrelenting conflict had become an established fact of life and that Europe must learn to live ever divided in two parts. Neither side, however, was as monolithic as appearance might suggest. After Stalin's death in 1953, a series of succession struggles in Russia ended, as we have seen, in the temporary victory of Nikita Khrushchev, who expressed a widespread revulsion against the rigidities of Stalinism. He would pursue a policy of coexistence, theoretically based on the certainty of eventual Communist victory but practically inspired by the balance of atomic terror.

The relative easing of international tensions was reflected in 1955 by two events: Russia's signature of a peace treaty with Austria and the withdrawal of Soviet troops from that country; and the concurrent establishment of the Warsaw Pact, which linked Moscow and her vassals in an alliance ostensibly directed against NATO but in effect permitting the continued presence of Russian troops on the territories of neighboring countries. Russian occupation of eastern Austria had justified the maintenance of garrisons in Hungary and Romania, "to guard lines of communication." Once the Warsaw Pact provided an alternative excuse for this, peace with Austria could be concluded, neutralizing the country and reassuring Marshal Tito, to whose heresies the new Russian leaders reconciled themselves, admitting that there could be different roads to socialism.

It would soon appear that liberty in this respect varied in proportion to a country's proximity to Soviet borders and to the Kremlin's estimate of its own interests. In 1956, Khrushchev's denunciation of Stalin's capricious tyranny and paranoiac murderousness before the 20th Congress of the Communist Party weakened the infallible authority of Moscow and opened the way to a new polycentrism, expressed that very year in national revolts in Poland and Hungary but, more importantly, by greater practical independence from Moscow throughout the Communist world. Crushed in Hungary, settled by intimidation and compromise in Poland, both rebellions would bear fruit: an easing of pressure on peasants, intellectuals, and the Catholic Church; increased production of consumer goods; a relaxation of the tension and oppression that had gripped these countries for a decade.

Tito's stand against Stalin was followed within a few years by the victory of communism in China. After 1956, the Communist governments of Poland, Hungary, and then Romania, while maintaining close relations with the Soviet Union, set themselves to gain the popular acceptance that would provide support in case of conflict with Moscow, relaxing some constraints and placing great emphasis on national sentiment and independence. By the later 1960's, while Communist governments ruled over a billion people in fourteen states, there would be almost as many brands of communism as there were national parties, and rival centers for differing tendencies: Moscow, Peking, Belgrade, Havana.

This meant that, in effect, the Soviet Union's pressure on Western Europe relaxed after a last flare-up of trouble over Germany. There, the Federal Republic proved too attractive to citizens of the Eastern zone who were passing in frightening numbers to the West, particularly by using the facilities offered by the joint occupation of Berlin. Formally ruled by the four Allied commanders, incorporated in neither zone, the old capital functioned as two separate entities—East and West—joined by a multitude of practical bonds and, crucially, by freedom of movement; which meant that many Berliners lived in one sector of the city and worked or walked in another. Taking advantage of this, some 4,000 East Germans a week, almost a quarter of a million yearly, had been choosing the greater freedom and comfort of the West. In the late fifties, a future British cabinet minister remarked to East German economists that if he were in their position, watching their human and financial resources seeping to the West, he would build a wall. His sally would shortly come true. By July, 1961, the emigration, which had risen to over 10,000 a week, threatened to drain the GDR of its youngest, most skilled, and enterprising inhabitants. Hence the sealing off of their last escape route by building the famous Berlin wall, separating the Soviet sector from the remainder of the city in contravention of the agreements that had maintained Berlin under the joint control of the four occupying powers.

Quickly prolonged by impassable obstacles sealing off the whole border between East and West Germany, this measure cut the manpower drain and turned the German Democratic Republic into an economically

The Berlin Wall. Right: Walter Ulbricht.

viable state. Since 1961, West Berlin has been languishing. The East Germans, on the other hand, now look upon their existence as a permanent fact rather than a temporary arrangement pending reunification. Under the leadership of a dour old Stalinist, Walter Ulbricht, they are pressing forward with long-range economic plans they had not been able to undertake in the earlier period. Thus, with the wall, the German problem was for the time being settled; not, as Russia had wanted, by Germany's subjection but by its division into rival states, each one a key component of its alliance system, each one viewed by its allies with mingled respect and fear.

Eastern Germany had once been the Reich's granary. But the regions richest in grain as in minerals lie in the territories forfeited to Poland; and the chief wealth of Ulbricht's realm (as, for that matter, of the Federal Republic) is its high standard of technical training and administrative skill. Technical and higher education is more modern and accessible than in the West, less restricted by considerations of .means and class (though far more so. of course, by ideological considerations). Living standards are still well below those of the West, but opportunities for personal distinction and reward are fast increasing and the defection rate is much lower even when opportunity occurs. The GDR has become a leading producer and exporter of machine tools, optical goods, office and railroad equipment, its industrial output second only to Russia's among Socialist countries. By 1963, beneath the dictatorship of its Stalinist rulers the ripples of intellectual and moral discussion were spreading as they did both east and west of an increasingly porous Iron Curtain. The new academic, technological, and managerial elite sought for a road not back to capitalism but to "a humanized and more democratic form of Socialism." Pending a mutation that may be long in coming, the country and its ruling party, no longer simple instruments of Soviet policy, becomes an ever more assertive member of its bloc. In 1968, Ulbricht appeared as the chief advocate of a tough line against the liberalizing Czechs, and his troops furnished the Soviet Army's chief support in Czechoslovakia's occupation.

The Federal Republic, meanwhile, has grown into the world's third greatest economic power, its army the most numerous contingent in NATO, its currency dominating those of its European allies. Bonn's foreign policy, long oriented toward the reunification of German territories, was expressed in what became known as the Hallstein Doctrine, from the foreign minister who enunciated it in 1955: refusing to recognize the existence of the GDR and to maintain relations with any government that did recognize it (with the exception of the Soviet Union). Recently, however, the Doctrine has begun to be quietly discarded. In 1967, diplomatic relations were established with Romania, which naturally recognizes the fellow regime of the GDR. With the accession of the Social Democrats to power in 1969, and the opening of direct talks between the two Germanies in 1970, it is probable that other exceptions will whittle down the rule.

Adenauer's Germany had been one of the most enthusiastic supporters of European Union and the Common Market, looking to them for opportunities of self-realization and vicarious greatness denied to a defeated and still-suspected land. By the 1960's, discouraged by French opposition to political integration on a European scale, the Federal Republic has shown a tendency to go it alone or seek its support in Washington. Its industrial enterprises prefer American to European alliances, its politicians often do so too. Denied the armaments in which she once sought her power, West Germany finds herself once again the dominant force in Western Europe and proud of her success. In the process, she is slowly abandoning hopes of a reunificaton rendered ever less likely as the temporary structures of the two Germanies harden into a semblance of permanence. The signature in 1968 of the Nuclear Non-Proliferation Treaty (designed to maintain Russo-American predominance by denying nuclear weapons to other powers) also consolidated the European *status quo* and the division of Germany by maintaining the country under a measure of international control and keeping it out of the nuclear club. One of the great international issues of the postwar age, the German question needs to be settled afresh every few years. For the moment, with the land divided and (relatively) unarmed, its neighbors can take advantage of the undoubted contributions Germans can make to the prosperity of the continent.

The fact that this also applies to members of the Soviet bloc, where —in Poland and Hungary, Czechoslovakia and Romania—German capital is invested and jointly operated factories are built, indicates that after the wall, paradoxically enough, the division of Europe became not more but less clear and tangible, tourism and trade between East and West increased, traditional links eliminated in 1945 were re-established, so that in 1965 there were ten times as many tourists, twice as many trade exchanges, between its two parts as there had been four years before. Relations are often easier where limits are clearly drawn; but these limits themselves are slowly giving way to the reassertion of national interests and local tendencies within each bloc and across its borders.

In a world where one year's records are tomorrow's anachronisms, one year's crises are next year's good old days, exchanges between the two camps were growing. The level of industrial development seems more important than ideological coloring and, as the economies of Eastern Europe advanced, their integration with those of their Western neighbors became more difficult to avoid. Joint enterprises—Italo-Russian, Franco-Romanian, German-Polish—linked the interests of capitalist and noncapitalist countries. In the Soviet Union a new (or newly articulate) economic school, associated with the name of Professor E. Liberman of Kharkov, argued successfully for the introduction of the profit system into state enterprises, greater managerial initiative, attention to consumer demand rather than norms set by the State Planning Commission and other planning enterprises that still employ some ten million persons. In the German Democratic Republic managers were paid by results and workers' wages geared to the profits of their enterprise. Romanians and Russians were invited to lend their savings to the state at 4 per cent interest. In 1968, the Secretary of the Central Committee of the Hungarian Workers' Party declared: "Profit is the only true indication of what an enterprise is worth." "We know that bourgeois liberties are partial, often false or truncated," declared a Russian student to the correspondent of a foreign newspaper: "But give them us all the same!"

The admission that the Communist world could counter the superior attractions of the West only by force was followed in 1962 by the further admission that such force as the Communists had would not (at least for the moment) be used in a nuclear conflict. In October, 1962, the great race for strategic superiority between Americans and Russians culminated in Khrushchev's attempt to place missiles in Cuba and his surrender to an American ultimatum.

The origins of the crisis went back to 1956 when a young Havana lawyer, Fidel Castro, began a guerrilla campaign against the Cuban dictator Fulgencio Batista. By 1959 Batista had been expelled from Havana and Castro embarked on the more difficult campaign to modernize Cuba, give it a viable economy, and free it from dependence on foreign business interests. Under the pressure of native anti-Americanism and of American suspicions of his own national-socialist inclinations, Castro's revolution—originally idealistic and middle-class—quickly turned toward the extreme Left. Concrete disputes over agrarian reforms that affected powerful U.S. corporations merged with ideological differences, and Castro was driven to seek support from native Communists and lean ever

Fidel Castro.

more heavily on ideological revolutionaries like his old guerrilla companion, the Argentinian Ernesto (Che) Guevara.

Before long, Cuba became a base for armed revolutionary attacks on other Latin American dictatorships (notably Nicaragua and the Dominican Republic), and for virulent propaganda against other conservative-reactionary regimes, its activities a serious source of concern to the United States. In 1960, the nationalization of American-owned properties * and trade agreements with the Soviet bloc intended to free Cuba (and especially its mammoth sugar industry) from dependence on the U.S. market, added fuel to the fire. Unhelpful but conciliatory to begin with, the Americans became ever more intransigent. Communism in Latin America, declared the State Department, was not negotiable. The Cuban example could endanger more important American interests in other parts of the Southern hemisphere. Arms and training facilities were made available to Cuban refugees planning to dislodge Castro. Then, in 1961, economic warfare turned to open fighting when an American-supported expedition attempted to land in the Bay of Pigs on the island's coast only to be repulsed with heavy losses.

It was in the wake of this that Cuba had taken the final steps to enter the Communist camp, acquiring Soviet arms and persuading the Russians to place nuclear missiles on the island as a credible deterrent to the aggressive intentions evidenced by their mainland neighbors. The United States could not tolerate the presence of these missiles only miles from its territory. Challenged by President John F. Kennedy, Khrushchev backed down and removed them (possibly in exchange for a secret understanding that Cuba would not be invaded). Nuclear war had been very close but, the crisis settled, the air was clearer for the mutual (if tacit) admission that one great power would tread very lightly or not at all in areas vital to the other. Before long, American

* With the compensation values to be assessed on the basis of the figures the companies themselves had provided in the past for their tax returns!

missile bases near the Soviet border (rendered out of date by the development of longer-range weapons) were also being abandoned. Other steps followed in the same direction. By 1963, Americans, British, and Russians could sign an agreement banning nuclear tests in the open, symbol of their appeased relations and of the fact that the participants considered survival more important than competition. Equally significant, that same year a special "hot line" provided a direct link between the Kremlin and the White House, both equally eager to avoid fatal errors of judgment by keeping in contact.

Since that time, the polycentrism that we noted in Communist politics has spread to both camps and—as we saw—to fields other than doctrine. The French, also a nuclear power, and the Chinese, who exploded an atom bomb in 1964 and a hydrogen bomb in 1967, refused to sign the nuclear test ban. The treaty, which was less an effective gesture than the indication of a change in mood, calmed some fears while verifying others. The Nuclear Non-Proliferation Treaty of 1968, again refused by China and by France (along with other not-yet-atomic nations) seemed to confirm the common interests of Moscow and Washington in restricting the membership of their exclusive "club." The Cold War, once clear and definite, was becoming vaguer if not less dangerous; and it appears that, once again, the Soviet Union and the United States have more in common than each has with its fresh potential enemy in Asia.

Polycentrist tendencies themselves were to receive a brutal rebuff in 1968, when Czech attempts to liberalize one of the longest-lived Stalinist regimes in Europe and broaden the scope of their economic activities at home and abroad were crushed by invasion and occupation. Six hundred thousand Russian, Polish, Bulgarian, Hungarian, and East German soldiers reasserted Moscow's tenuous hold on its uncertain vassals; their impunity proved the unwillingness of the Western allies to intervene in the "internal" affairs of the rival bloc. It was within the latter that reactions to the aggression proved the divisions among Communists themselves. Romanians and Yugoslavs held off, while showing all the sympathy they dared for the oppressed Czechs; Hungarians and Poles continued their relatively independent economic activities, while lending a loyal hand to their Russian allies. The members of the Warsaw Pact were far from the "mere purveyors of raw materials" that Peking Radio accusingly described. Within the limits of discretion, each followed its own interests, getting the most for itself out of its neighbor's discomfiture.

The Czech invasion confirmed the non-Communist Left and wide sections of the Communist world in their suspicion of the Russian oligarchy and of its good faith. To Milovan Djilas, sometime vice-president of Communist Yugoslavia, it proved the abandonment of ideological dynamism for imperialist interests. To the Communists of Peking it demonstrated the re-establishment of a "bourgeois dictatorship" appealing to Socialist dogma for private ends. In Peking the Soviet government is officially regarded as counter-revolutionary: "a new Tsar" oppressing the peoples of Europe and its own subjects too, "social-imperialist, social-fascist, colonialist and aggressive." The conclusions that the Chinese and their supporters draw from this are far-reaching. Premier Chou En-lai has described (September 30, 1968) how "American imperialism and Soviet revisionism struggle and collaborate in a vain attempt to delimit their zones of influence and redivide the world."

The new situation suggests the possibility of tactics in which the policy of "peaceful coexistence" for which Peking long reproached Moscow may now be wielded by the Chinese to divide their two chief enemies. To China, Russia is not only a foreign enemy and a rival for colonial possessions that run the whole length of the two powers' Asian frontiers. She is also and above all the symbol of a great revisionist menace—a revisionism that slumbers apparently even in the best of Communists and against which China's cultural revolution was launched in 1966–68 to prevent the bureaucratization and embourgeoization of its own revolution. Russia is therefore an internal as well as external danger, more threatening than the American representatives of an alien system. No longer able to carry the banner of ideological cold war, long overtaken by radicals more revolutionary than its own leaders, Russia is condemned to seek some kind of *entente* with its recent rivals in order to face more pressing challenges elsewhere.

All this has accelerated another phenomenon: the tendency for Communist parties in Western countries, such as Italy and France, to become less revolutionary and to take up the stance of a responsible opposition following the parliamentary road to socialism. Socialist parties, of course, had participated in governments since the First World War. By the late 1960's, in Belgium, Germany, and Italy, coalition governments of Christian-Democrats and Socialists reflected the increasing similarity of majority parties that differed about the degree and tempo of reform, not about the principle of reform itself. One result of this has been the appearance of an extraparliamentary opposition, representing the active minority disillusioned with existing parties and particularly embarrassing to the Communists who see themselves overbidden by "adventurist and anarchic leftists." The latter have done their best to contest the established order and its reformist machinery, precipitating the long series of disturbances which have marked 1968 and 1969 and which the Italians describe as *maggio strisciante,* or "creeping May," from the French riots of May, 1968.

Too weak for effective revolution, the pressure of the leftist forces has nevertheless encouraged an acceleration of reform (which leftists reject), for instance in many universities, and—more important—a rethinking of the programs and responsibilities of left-wing parties, including Communists no longer regarded as the revolutionary, liberating force they once appeared to be.

All in all, the internal and external power blocs first precipitated in the late 1940's by the conflict between the U.S. and the U.S.S.R. have both hardened and weakened. Their appearance reflected the exhaustion of a Europe which had been unable to free itself from Nazism by its own forces, and the weakness of governments unable to maintain themselves without the aid or protection of powers one of which was only half-European, while the other was not European at all. The division of Europe naturally ran along the demarcation line between their rival occupation troops and reflected not only the balance of power but the aspirations of Moscow and Washington to dominate the world. Today it rests on a common incapacity to provide for its own security in the nuclear era by setting up a confederation sufficiently strong to be a nuclear power in its own right.

The Atlantic Treaty of 1949 had sought "a just and lasting peace founded on appropriate guarantees" for the security of its members. The signers of the Warsaw Pact of 1955 had claimed as much, adding that they would be glad to abolish their treaty as soon as a system of European security could be set up. Thus, the negotiations envisaged by both sides in 1969 to achieve a real *détente* in Europe have a common aim. There is no reason why a working settlement should not be achieved. The soaring recovery of the 1950's could not have been foreseen in 1948, nor the progressive emancipation of Eastern European countries in 1956. In this perspective, the union of Western—and perhaps of Eastern Europe too—seems far from impossible.

This is perhaps the best indication of the hazards of history written too soon after events. For, while the sense and proportion of things that happened long ago seem clear in adequate perspective, those of the events of yesterday remain obscure. Things which loom large seen from nearby appear in quite another light when time has placed them in a vaster complex. This is, really, why the present chapter has been more narrative than interpretative or, at least, why the former can be provided more easily than the latter. For interpretation, like Athena's owl, only takes its flight when the dust of the past has settled.

The Third World

One of the great novelties of the postwar era has been the appearance and progressive self-assertion of a "third world" born of the dissolution of erstwhile colonial empires. At least fifty new republics have joined the ranks of the United Nations since 1945. By 1970, the only colonial empires left to Europe were those of Russia and of Portugal. The physical holdings of France or Britain are scarcely worth mention, let alone comparison with those of countries like China, Brazil, South Africa, Indonesia or, even, the Sudan. Europe's age of territorial imperialism seems to be over and that, itself, is a remarkable change. But—leaving aside new variants of colonialism and domination—the colonial enterprises of the past have left their mark behind them. Today, as in the nineteenth century, the impact of harder, better-armed cultures remains as evident as it appears unavoidable. Whether they came, as they still come, to heal, teach, order, or exploit, the Europeans were bound to revolutionize (when they did not destroy) the societies, peoples, cultures that they touched.

Benevolent, indifferent, or selfish, some actions can have dire effects if based on an inappropriate estimate of what is good. Condensed milk for babies, solid meals for starving men, cold water for the overheated, can hurt or kill. Similarly, so can constitutions and other alien imports, like a determined desire to introduce efficiency. European technology always brings with it European ideas of much broader scope. You cannot introduce machines and factories without implicit concepts of what man can or should do; or social services without attendant ideas about what man needs and what man is. One materialism ushers in another, one ideology elbows out another and imposes itself, even when its importers are basically defensive or hostile.

To take only one example, European ideas concerning property proved as much a dissolvent as European arms and techniques. When land, like any other object, was treated as private, separate pieces of property subject to sale or transfer or mortgage by one particular owner, then different forms of land tenure were torn to shreds and, with them, the societies, crafts, and tribes which had evolved quite different structures. Like land, labor too had to be brought in line with European concepts and European needs. Money wages, open markets, regular hours, above all the notion of work as a value rather than as a demeaning necessity, replaced older forms of labor organization—sometimes forcibly. Barter or subsistence were replaced by money, self-sufficiency by exchange, tens of millions who had seldom or never used currency were initiated into its delights or pressured by taxes and other obligations into cash-producing activities. Efficiency replaced haphazardness, secularization replaced traditional magic observances, laws and administration replaced custom, incorruptibility replaced compromise and convention, impersonality replaced face-to-face relationships.

Some of this was an improvement; all was upsetting. In Asia, Africa, America, one society after another was affected by alien concepts generally applied with little understanding of the historical conditions behind existing institutions and the stability provided by existing practices. Men who knew what they wanted and who subordinated their activities to their ends, triumphed over societies whose members subordinated their actions to their habits. Weapons counted in this, but states of mind counted even more. Men who had operated time out of mind as parts of the customary cultures were introduced to the possibilities and insecurities of change. They became subjects and, faced with their new masters' formidable power, sought refuge in migration, in idleness, in religions that provided an excuse for evasion, before finally turning from religion to politics as a substitute for hope. But the colonial process is not as simple as it is often painted, and it does not operate in one direction alone. The occupier does not simply rule the occupied, he haunts him, fascinates him, infiltrates his consciousness and his life, takes hold of him inside and out. Yet the process works both ways and, in this kind of coupling, it is hard to tell after a time which of the parties has sucked the other's blood, which has contaminated the other, which (in the precise sense of the terms) is oppressor and which oppressed.

All this indicates the possibility that technological society did not destroy values but rather suggested new ones. Contract replaced tradition, the free-moving, free-wheeling individual replaced the static family or tribe, democracy with all its drawbacks and opportunities replaced the stable hierarchies of status and of birth. Changing legal structures transformed society and social attitudes, technological innovations turned congeries of provinces into countries, spread modern skills, suggested the revival of native industry and enterprise in a new guise and on a new scale. The implications of these changes—equality before law and politics, for instance—are making themselves felt even in nontechnological societies; and so are those arising from the technologically induced shrinkage of a world more truly and more uncomfortably *one* than ever in its history.

Nothing illustrates this better than the principal quandary of our world, which is the disparity between the advanced European and Europoid countries and all others, the imbalance between the industrialized "West" and the agrarian remainder of the world. It must have become clear in chapter after chapter that the greatest distinction between our society and previous ones lies in the quantitative factor. In the first place there are simply more men. More human beings were being born between 1870 and 1914 than between Adam and Newton. But material commodities have increased too: not only their use, but the volume of their production. During the last four centuries the volume of coal production increased 3,000 times, that of iron production 4,000 times, that of glass 5,000 times. And yet we know that this applies in practice only to limited sections of the human race. We know that time has not unreeled at the same rate for men in every country—as it seemed to do, generally speaking, until 100 or 200 years ago, when most men everywhere still lived approximately in similar circumstances. Today, a glance across the world reveals extraordinary differences which neither Herodotus nor Marco Polo would have encountered: differences more on a scale of time than space. Thus, one can say that life in Britain or France today is similar to that which the United States knew in the 1930's; that life in Spain or Turkey has striking analogies to that of France in the 1860's; that life in India or Sumatra continues in conditions not very different from those of Peter the Great or Louis XIV. The number of doctors per inhabitant is very revealing in this connection. The progression runs from one for 700 in the United States, to one for 1,400 in France and Germany, one for 3,000 in Poland, one for 4,500 in Egypt, one for 10,000 in Iraq, one for 50,000 in Indonesia; and it varies within the countries themselves according to local wealth. The practical reflection of this can be seen in the fact that where life expectancy in the mid-twentieth century was 67 years in Canada, 70 in Holland, 58 in Japan (where it had been 48 in 1930), it was 44 in Egypt and 32 in India. Where three out of four Dutch babies can expect to live to 60, only one out of two Indian babies can. In other words, a uniformity of techniques and values leaves room in some respects for a much wider diversity of evolutionary stages.

Behind this lies the fact that, while all the world advances, its most advanced areas advance the fastest. Asia, Africa, Latin America, are increasing their production, but not nearly as much as Europe and North America, which have less than 30 per cent of the world's population and produce 80 per cent of its income. In 1962, Asia, with more than half the world's population, had 3 per cent of its motor vehicles; Africa and Latin America, with more than one-third of the world's land, had 7 per cent of its surfaced roads. The amount of world trade has increased tremendously, about sevenfold in the last fifty years—most of it since the last war. But in 1960 Europe and North America still accounted for two-thirds of it and Western Europe for two-fifths. Indeed, the post-war recovery of Europe (including Russia) becomes clear when one considers that its share of world trade—46 per cent in 1937, 33 per cent in 1947—was 53 per cent by 1960. Despite the appearance of non-European trading powers like Japan, Canada, and the United States, Europe continues to consume the greatest share of the surplus foods and raw materials of the world and to provide the leading exporters of manufactured goods, just as she had done in 1900.

The great change which has taken place since then is that, whereas in the earlier period manufactures were mostly exchanged against primary products from more backward countries, today the mass of exchanges takes place between the industrial nations themselves. Europe, which took three-fourths of the world's raw materials in 1913, only took half of them in 1953. This suggests that primary producers in Asia, Africa, and South America, with their rubber and oil and tin, do less trade and do it on worse terms than before because demand for their products is shrinking, or is only maintained by artificial means. A country like Ghana produced more cocoa in 1964 than in 1954 but earned less than half what she had earned a decade before. In effect, nonindustrial economies, no

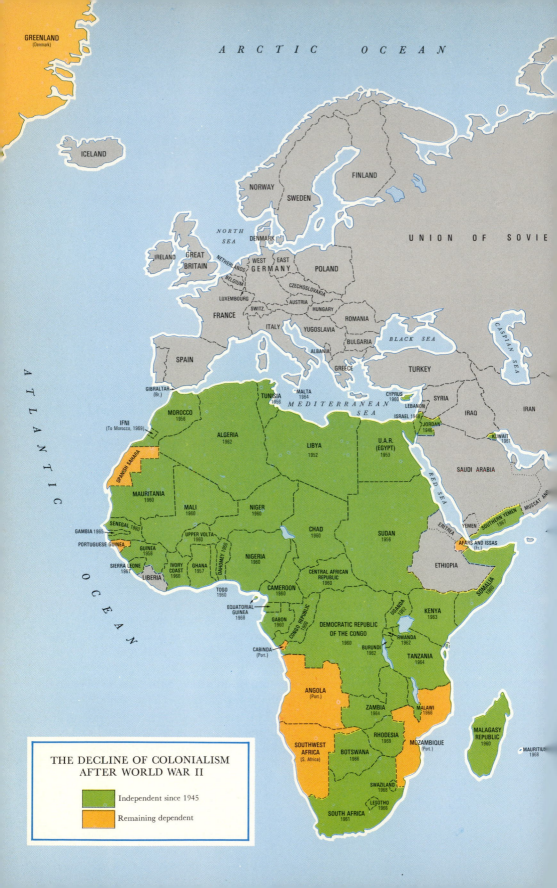

ARCTIC OCEAN

GREENLAND
(Denmark)

ICELAND

NORWAY
SWEDEN
FINLAND

UNION OF SOVIE

NORTH SEA

IRELAND
GREAT BRITAIN

DENMARK

NETHERLANDS
WEST EAST
GERMANY
POLAND
BELGIUM
LUXEMBOURG
CZECHOSLOVAKIA
FRANCE
SWITZ.
AUSTRIA HUNGARY
ROMANIA
ITALY
YUGOSLAVIA
BULGARIA
BLACK SEA
ALBANIA
CASPIAN SEA

SPAIN
GREECE
TURKEY
IRAN

ATLANTIC OCEAN

GIBRALTAR
(Br.)

IFNI
(To Morocco, 1969)

TUNISIA
1956

MALTA
1964

MEDITERRANEAN SEA

CYPRUS
1960

SYRIA
LEBANON
ISRAEL 1948
JORDAN
1946

IRAQ

MOROCCO
1956

ALGERIA
1962

LIBYA
1952

U.A.R.
(EGYPT)
1953

KUWAIT
1961

SAUDI ARABIA

SPANISH SAHARA

MAURITANIA
1960

MALI
1960

NIGER
1960

CHAD
1960

SUDAN
1956

RED SEA

ERITREA

YEMEN
SOUTHERN YEMEN
1967

MUSCAT AN

GAMBIA 1965
SENEGAL 1960
PORTUGUESE GUINEA
GUINEA
1958
SIERRA LEONE
1961
LIBERIA

UPPER VOLTA
1960

IVORY
COAST
1960
GHANA
1957

DAHOMEY 1960

NIGERIA
1960

CENTRAL AFRICAN
REPUBLIC
1960

AFARS AND ISSAS
(Fr.)

ETHIOPIA

SOMALIA
1960

TOGO
1960

EQUATORIAL
GUINEA
1968

CAMEROON
1960

GABON
1960

CONGO REPUBLIC 1960

CABINDA
(Port.)

DEMOCRATIC REPUBLIC
OF THE CONGO
1960

UGANDA
1962

KENYA
1963

RWANDA
1962
BURUNDI
1962

TANZANIA
1964

ANGOLA
(Port.)

ZAMBIA
1964

MALAWI
1966

MALAGASY
REPUBLIC
1960

MAURITIUS
1968

SOUTHWEST
AFRICA
(S. Africa)

BOTSWANA
1966

RHODESIA
1969

MOZAMBIQUE
(Port.)

SWAZILAND
1968

LESOTHO
1966

SOUTH AFRICA
1961

THE DECLINE OF COLONIALISM
AFTER WORLD WAR II

Independent since 1945

Remaining dependent

WESTERN HEMISPHERE

GULF OF MEXICO

ATLANTIC OCEAN

BAHAMAS (Br.)

CUBA

HAITI

PUERTO RICO (U.S.)

BR. VIRGIN IS.

ST. MARTIN (Neth. and Fr.)

DOMINICAN REP.

JAMAICA 1962

U.S. VIRGIN IS.

ST. KITTS (Br.)

GUADELOUPE (Fr.)

BRITISH HONDURAS

HONDURAS

CARIBBEAN SEA

MARTINIQUE (Fr.)

BARBADOS 1966

NETHERLANDS ANTILLES

BRITISH WINDWARDS

NICARAGUA

COSTA RICA

CANAL ZONE (U.S.)

PANAMA

TRINIDAD AND TOBAGO 1962

PACIFIC OCEAN

COLOMBIA

VENEZUELA

GUYANA 1966

SURINAM (Neth.)

FR. GUIANA

OCIALIST REPUBLICS

U.S.S.R.

MONGOLIA 1947

N. KOREA 1948

S. KOREA 1948

JAPAN

GHANISTAN

CHINA

WEST PAKISTAN 1947

NEPAL

E. PAK. 1946

PACIFIC OCEAN

INDIA 1647

BURMA 1948

LAOS 1954

N. VIETNAM 1954

HONG KONG (Br.)

TAIWAN

IAN EA

BAY OF BENGAL

THAILAND

S. VIETNAM 1954

PHILIPPINES 1946

CAMBODIA 1953

REPUBLIC OF MALDIVES 1965

CEYLON 1948

BRUNEI (Br.)

NDIAN OCEAN

MALAYSIA 1963

SINGAPORE 1965

NEW GUINEA (Aust.)

PAPUA (Aust.)

INDONESIA 1948

TIMOR (Port.)

AUSTRALIA

longer limited or self-sufficient, have become even more unstable than the industrial economies on which they depend; especially so when they have focused on a single product, as in the case of Mauritius, 99 per cent of whose exports is sugar; Bolivia, 97 per cent of whose exports is tin; Liberia, 95 per cent of whose exports is rubber; Egypt, 87 per cent of whose exports is cotton; Colombia, 86 per cent of whose exports is coffee; Ghana, 85 per cent of whose exports is cocoa; Ceylon, 85 per cent of whose exports is tea. All in all, over a score of countries still depend on a single product for over half of their export trade and lead a precarious existence, teetering on the brink of catastrophe with every oscillation of world commodity prices.

Meanwhile, the inflationary effects of incipient industrialization and urbanization affect backward states much more than more developed ones. The cost of living index is a highly artificial but nevertheless suggestive indicator of this. It shows that, while between 1958 and 1968 the cost of living went up from 100 to 110 in the United States, 119 in Germany, 122 in Britain, 131 in Italy, and 133 in France, it rose to 149 in India, 202 in Ghana, 250 in Yugoslavia, 879 in Argentina, and 2,260 in Brazil, all countries where anachronism and modernization are at odds.

Inflation is only one aspect of economies caught between soaring demand and insufficient supply, a demand created not only by higher expectations but by the human avalanche which modern sanitation has released upon these countries—that is, by overpopulation. The traditional world of limited resources, such as that which Western Europe left behind after 1848, balanced demand and supply by dint of high mortality rates. These have now been pressed back with the result that in most parts of the world far more people stay alive than can be adequately fed.

History, said Voltaire, is only a pack of tricks that we play on the dead. How far, one may ask, is it a pack of tricks the dead play on us and of which we become aware as one hidden mine or firecracker after another goes off unexpectedly? At any rate, in the realm of overpopulation, many have tried to warn that we are advancing through a mine field. In 1933, a noted Australian scientist reporting to the Rockefeller Foundation on the results of campaigns against malaria, pellagra, and hookworm, remarked that "in 10 years the Foundation would be spending more money in dealing with the results of its successes than in dealing with disease itself." It took less than a decade for his prediction to prove correct.

Lower death rates in countries with high fertility rates, the introduction of industrial sanitation techniques in countries with an agricultural mentality and a lagging technology, meant that demographic changes which took centuries in the West were carried through in less than a decade in certain Asian or South American countries, far faster than the population could adjust to the conditions thus created. The continents least able to bear it find their population rising fastest. Asia, with 50 per cent of the world's population, has 11 per cent of its revenues; North America, with 7 per cent of the world's population, has 45 per cent of its revenues. In Ceylon, for instance, when DDT wiped out malaria after the Second World War, the death rate was almost halved in seven years (1945–52). This compounded a population explosion already set off by the control of other diseases so that the population of Ceylon, which had been growing about five per 1,000 at the end of the nineteenth century, was increasing at the rate of nearly 3 per cent by 1950. The population of many countries grows at an even faster rate: North Vietnam's at 3.6 per cent, the Philippines' at 3.7 per cent, Mexico's at 3.8 per cent, Venezuela's at 4 per cent. At 2 per cent a population doubles every 35 years, at 3.5 per cent every 20 years, at 4 per cent every 15 years. India, with a population nudging 550 million, is expected to double her numbers to over a billion within 25 years.

Men have multiplied for 200,000 years to reach the present three billion mark, but short of catastrophe they will double that in forty years. It was pointed out in 1967 that one human being in two once lived under Western rule, one in three lives in a Communist regime, one in four is Chinese, and two in three are short of food. Yet these hostile or demanding masses, which are no longer powerless or silent, which grow because of our medical advances, which ferment because of our transistors, cannot afford our comforts, our cars, our nourishment. Discontent can spread more rapidly than prosperity. As Nehru once remarked, "What is new in India is not misery, but the consciousness the Indian people has of it today and its impatience to be free of it." Yet, while an American farmer can feed forty-four persons, a Frenchman twelve, a Russian five, the average producer in an undeveloped country can generally feed only himself, at best one other person. It takes fifteen Indian cows to give as much milk as one American cow, seven acres of Vietnamese ricepaddy to harvest the same quantities as those produced by one acre in Australia.

Two-thirds of mankind are hungry all the time: which is why, when traveling in underdeveloped countries, one has the impression that people are always eating something. Undernourishment makes for the "apathetic" character of so many peoples, which needs to be stimulated with drugs, alcohol, or spices, the weak constitutions that leave them at the mercy of epidemics or contagious diseases, and the difficulty of extracting hard and sustained work from them. There is little reason to think that the hungry countries whose population by 2000 A.D. will be over 5 billion (four-fifths of the total foreseen for the whole earth) can be modernized fast enough to keep them from becoming a miserable, suffering, and explosive sore. The greater the population, the less likely their living standard is to improve. The less the living standard improves, the less chance there is of lowering the birth rate. The greater the population pressure on available resources, the fewer resources can be spared to increase productivity, to better living conditions, and to create possibilities and attitudes conducive to limiting the population.

All this has lent itself to much debate. One side argues that population is not outstripping resources, that the latter are simply being mismanaged by those who control them. The 27 million people in northeast Brazil would not suffer from hunger if the region's agronomical possibilities were rationally developed. Millions of Indians would not be left to starve or vegetate if dams controlled water, if one grain out of four was not left to be eaten by rats, monkeys, or sacred cows, if a fertilizer industry existed. Another side answers that the fault rests with lack of international solidarity, with failure to accept that everyman's death diminishes *me*. It does not explain, however, how such solidarity can be reconciled with national sovereignty and with its vagaries: preferring to invest resources in armaments, prestige schemes, heavy industry, or let them scatter in popular but unproductive directions, or again to serve vested interests, avoid needed reforms, let the rich become richer and the poor vegetate.

Overpopulation, of course, is a relative affair which comes down to the capacity to organize the population productively. Every West European country today supports a population which would have been unthinkable in the age of Malthus—let alone before him. It is possible to increase food production—as Israel has shown by raising its own by nearly 9 per cent a year for the past fifteen years. The area of the world's cultivated lands can be tripled, productivity greatly intensified, new aliments tapped in the seas and in laboratories. A fuller, more balanced diet might even cut down the demographic flood. Recent experiments suggest that hungry societies whose diet is deficient in proteins may be particularly prolific, while protein-rich diets reduce the fertility rate. It is possible also to bring the birth rate down to compensate the lower death rate, as Japan has shown since the war. It is possible to enlist science in solving the problems of subsistence, production, and population. But capital and technology depend on human attitudes and decisions. The goods and services men want, the price they are prepared to pay for them, the sacrifices to which they will consent, reflect their abstract and social values. Production and consumption answer not only hunger, but needs and formulas that change with every culture, so that the hungry and backward countries of the world challenge the industrialized West to aid them while accusing it of ignoring or destroying their peculiar culture and their values.

Between 1950 and 1963 the fifteen industrialized countries of the Organization for Economic Cooperation and Development contributed some 50 billion dollars in gifts and loans to less-developed countries. But a Danish report (*Le Monde,* October 6-7, 1968) indicates that in 1959 countries of the third world spent a total of 19 billion dollars on armaments (which are all imported, since none produces its own) while, during the same period they received from abroad only 4 billion in loans and subsidies to increase living standards. Though more recent figures are lacking, everything suggests that this disproportion has grown greater in the last decade. Once again, political decisions command material possibilities; cultural and ideological orientation affects and directs the uses of the means at a society's command; and, from this point of view, the most dramatic angles are oft, alas, obtuse.

It is quite possible that such dire prospects will melt away before developments that we no more suspect than Malthus could foresee the solution of the problems of his time. It is equally possible that populations will be limited by traditional means—famine, war, plagues, and self-destruction—and that the same great factors which set off the demographic avalanche may actually intervene to break it up. Historians are only the prophets of the past. The future, perhaps fortunately, remains obscure. "The wird bloweth where it listeth and Thou hearest the sound thereof, but canst not tell whence it cometh and whither it goeth." (John 3:8).

The Revolt of Youth

Another revolutionary development of the postwar era would be the changed social role of young people, a group whose significance we have seen growing over the past 150 years, but who had never done more than walk on the stage in obedience to the injunction that they were more properly seen than heard. The demographic explosion of the postwar years turned under-25's into near-majorities of their national populations, while prosperity afforded them unusual opportunities for self-definition and independence. Most important perhaps, where in earlier times the immense majority of young people, forced to work from an early age, merged into the surrounding adult world, today an ever-greater proportion of them was condemned or privileged to the relatively irresponsible isolation of higher education. Between 30 and 45 per cent of their age group in the United States, 15 or 20 per cent in the U.S.S.R., students accounted for 10 to 15 per cent of their coevals in other parts of the West, where they had seldom reached 1 per cent at the turn of the century and little more than that in 1940.

The growth of student numbers created a special "class," consuming high proportions of the national budget, responsible for a good part of the national market, a class which sociologists had not envisaged and whose particular originality lay in its constant renewal. By the late 1960's it was impossible to ignore the rise of a generation which had not known the war nor, often, the hard times that followed; for whom Hitler and Stalin were names and the past increasingly irrelevant in the light of a kaleidoscopic present.

Youth is the personification of permanent revolution, hardly significant when it lacks autonomy and self-consciousness, highly significant when it has both. Traditionally, the rebellion of youth had expressed itself in sporadic gestures of violence and nonconformity. In the postwar society, these were found increasingly impossible or unsatisfactory. Heresy is meaningful only against dogma, nonconformity against conformism; and these have lost their hold on a West that has abandoned the rigid standards and conventions of the past. Only in the bosom of Communist parties and extremist sects, last bastions of conservative conventions, can real heretics indulge their vocation and pay some kind of price. Elsewhere, tolerance eases their lot, indifference makes them irrelevant, generalization conventional. Their would-be unconventionality frustrated, their natural turbulence repressed in an increasingly orderly society, some young people began to break out in unexpectedly violent forms of nonconformism—provos in Holland, hippies in the United States, drug-taking—whose common basis was a rejection of the surrounding society.

The year 1968 would see this tension explode into rebellion all over Europe and all over the world. In Warsaw and Madrid, in Belgrade and Paris, in Prague and in Berlin (as in Rio, Tunis, and Tokyo), serious troubles threatened and sometimes shook men and regimes in power. Their origin was novel, for they broke out in times not of penury but of prosperity, and they reflected less economic grievances than ideological ones. In every case, their dynamo lay in the universities, in every case their original militants were students and intellectuals, most often very young.

The University: An Incubator

This youthful insurrection marked the gradual emancipation of another portion of society claiming its rights after workers and women had established theirs. The universities, tremendously expanded in the years since 1950, their population greater than ever before, played the role that factories had played in nineteenth-century working-class history. They concentrated young people, gave them a sense of difference from surrounding society, the confidence of numbers, and a base of operations.

Parisian policemen armed with helmets and shields against the rebelling students, May, 1968.

H. Roger-Viollet

Schools, but above all universities, taught the values the community claimed to respect and the techniques which society needed in order to operate and to expand. They also analyzed the communities in whose midst they rose, revealed how these failed to live up to their own principles, suggested values higher than those by whose application or whose breach they thrived. In itself, this was nothing new. Long before Socrates, thinking men must have threatened the routines and acceptances of their time. Thomas Hobbes, himself no mean iconoclast, found that "the core of rebellion [against his Stuart patrons] are the universities." Men, he suggested, are only too inclined to think well of their wits.* Once educated, they imagine they can run the country. Drawing the practical conclusions that many statesmen followed in centuries to come, one of Charles II's advisers suggested halving university admissions and cutting school intakes too.

Despite such views—sometimes put into practice—most twentieth-century universities continued to furnish a sanctuary for critics and heretics, a repository for every sort of idea, a kind of privileged haven and debating ground. This was particularly true in Western Europe and North America in the years after 1945 and, though far from affecting all students or all teachers, it had its effect both within and without university walls—though never as sharply evident as in 1968.

The revolt of youth against authority is, of course, a revolt against paternalism at every level, against the very notion of adult civilization and of adulthood itself. The demands voiced for abolition of examinations, for instance, reject not only an established test of social selection, but—as a writer in the Paris *Monde* put it in May, 1968—"the capital initiation rite of modern society," the rite of passage into "the adult's adulterated universe." What this manner of rebel seems to want is a kind of permanent adolescence not very different from the permanent revolution that Trotsky preached.

Revolt of youth against age, rejection of the old for new, has flourished particularly since the romantic tide of the nineteenth century. It has

* One hundred years later, Diderot's views on the university were no different: "That's where they teach the art of speaking before the art of thinking," he said, "that of expressing oneself well before having any ideas to express."

been alimented by disillusionment in the wake of revolutions (after 1815 or 1848) or of wars (1918, 1945) expected to usher in better days, and by the "modern" feeling that the old dates very quickly and that change is somehow good for its own sake. At the same time, prosperity and full employment diminished the dependency of young people on their elders, released ever more of them for longer periods of study or leisure, turned adolescence from a purgatory into an enjoyable condition, and one whose prolongation appears both feasible and desirable.

Sustained revolutionary action has ever been the province of the uncommitted: those who have not yet been integrated in society, who do not have to earn a living or cannot, who have not taken up or have been refused entry to a career. The reservoir of such people, once full of vagrants, unemployed, or social rejects, came to be found among the growing numbers of the young whose irresponsibility and uncommitment society or parents prolonged by their subsidies, and whose idealism was little diverted by concern for necessities of life.

Idealistic youth found plenty to criticize. "The international of the twenty-year olds," declared an Italian weekly in 1968, "shares the same ideological masters, brandishes the same flags, holds to the same ideas. They are disillusioned by a democracy often only formal, and they reject a socialism suspicious of intelligence." Democratic ideals, praised in both capitalist and communist countries, appear little in evidence as they look around them. Postwar European economies are planned and directed. Whether in Germany or France or Britain, half or more than half of capital investments are financed by the state. Created by revolution or imposed by conquest in the case of Communists, established or attempted by fiat in the Fascist dictatorships between the wars, collectivism now springs from the needs of large industrial units and corporations, from the calculations of modern industrial states, establishing everywhere its managers, its bureaucrats, and its planners. Like the modern industrial state, the organized parties of the Left have developed bureaucratic structures that both paralyze and conserve them. The power of the people gives way to the power of an elusive oligarchy.

The new industrial state, writes the American economist J. K. Galbraith in a book of that title, turns us into the servants of the machine we created. Economic objectives replace all other aspirations, and the ultimate question becomes what a man does to increase the gross national product. "If you own something," proclaims the advertising of a German bank, "you are something." It is such attitudes and such effects that the rebels spurn—forgetting that they had been quite typical of other societies too—and that they rise against. Petrels of a longed-for storm, they condemn the continued exploitation of the working classes, of underdeveloped countries, of outcast races, imperialist wars abroad or social injustice at home, but, above all, what they regard as an impersonal and inhuman power, a welfare state in which quantitative satisfactions stifle qualitative needs.

Many who felt this way found their justification in the works of a German philosopher who had taken refuge in the United States from Nazi persecution: Herbert Marcuse. Born in 1898, Marcuse's chief references are drawn, very appropriately, from the two main authorities of our time: Marx and Freud. For Freud, the history of man had always been the history of man's repressions, the tale of aimless animal drives transmuted into societal instincts, of the pleasure principle blindly seeking satisfaction transmuted into the reality principle. The drive for immediate personal gratification, Freud had taught, is culturally destructive. Sublimated, it creates civilization, art, a working and productive society.

For Marcuse, the impressive results of this process in the West have created an increasingly unsatisfactory situation. Man is in a position to achieve what Marcuse calls "the rational organization of the realm of necessity." But he lets himself be taken over by his means. Technology itself has taken on the appearance of a new necessity. "The instruments of productivity and progress, organized into a totalitarian system, determine not only the actual but also the possible utilizations." In his most explicit attack on this state of affairs, *One Dimensional Man,* Marcuse avers that "advanced industrial society is approaching the stage when continued progress would demand the radical subversion of the prevailing direction and organization of progress." Once agents of hopeful change, science, technology, democratic institutions, political emancipation, have turned into stabilizers. "The status quo defies all transcendence," digests all digressions, assimilates alternatives, contains all change but that which suits its limited ends, discourages those internal oppositions and criticisms which made for a healthy dialectic, in favor of a one-dimensional society with room only for one-dimensional men. Capital and labor, *bourgeoisie* and proletariat, Establishment and opposition, even the United States and Soviet Russia, no longer clash as agents of historical transformation; unhealthy fat has stifled the dialectic. As opposites are unified and qualitative change counteracted by common interest in preserving and improving what already exists, even affluence, freedom, tolerance, become the vehicles of a totalitarian universe where opposition, criticism, life itself are killed by kindness but killed nevertheless.*

Only sheer and total negation of the administered good life—the good in it as well as the bad—can counter the deadening forces, break through the illusions of advanced industrial society, reject the rules of a game rigged from the start, reopen the possibilities of real change, for better or for worse.

Fortunately, our technological successes, while stifling in their effects, have created the preconditions for abandoning or rejecting the restraints that made them possible, the repressions without which our conquest of nature (including our own) could not have been carried out. "The continued rule of the performance principle as the reality principle . . . has

* The quotations are from *One Dimensional Man* (1954), pp. 235, 255, 16, 17.

perhaps created the preconditions for a qualitatively different, non-repressive reality principle."* The struggle for existence no longer calls for a repressive organization of the instincts. Contemplation, enjoyment, acceptance of what the world has to offer, could now replace struggle and constraint. Repression and renunciation are presently being justified no longer by objective needs but for their own sake. They could be abandoned, and freedom, fantasy, transcendence, allowed to reign instead.

Not surprisingly, such views appealed to young intellectuals, to students, to all those who in every generation cannot but find fault with their world and time, and who will strive to replace it with something that is not just better but ultimately good.** Affluent heirs of an opulent culture, glutted with the wealth of their collective past, they proposed to reject it now for more sober fare, which, on examination, bears within it many ingredients of the past—not least romanticism—but unacknowledged.

The University: A Target

But if the universities appeared as breeding grounds of criticism and revolt, they soon became its targets.

> I turn my eyes to the Schools and Universities of Europe,
> Works of many Wheels I view, wheel without wheel, with cogs tyrannic
> Moving by compulsion each other: not as those in Eden, which
> Wheel within Wheel in freedom revolve in harmony and peace.

What William Blake had viewed better than a century and a half ago still seemed as real to his visionary successors, and to many who were not visionary at all. Numbers overwhelming facilities, classes overflowing lecture halls, professors invested with enormous authority, wielding autocratic powers over students they ignore, absentee teachers indifferent to their charges, courses irrelevant to subjects—let alone to life or work. Slow to change their ways, highly elitist and hierarchized, European universities suffered from institutional rigidity and from a kind of self-imposed isolation from the world around. In 1966, an academic conference held in France called them the last refuge of feudalism in Western Europe. Yet, as they sought to modernize themselves and follow in the footsteps of American universities, it was found that the "adjusted" university turned into a "knowledge factory," chiefly devoted to producing the "useful" knowledge required by society, industry, the military, to training its managers and indoctrinating its members.

The old schools of humanistic learning and culture have become mul-

---

* Herbert Marcuse, *Eros and Civilization* (1955), p. 129.
** Neither they nor Marcuse, however, could explain how the gifts of high productivity could be enjoyed while ignoring the discipline and restraints which maintain that productivity.

tiversities, dedicated to teaching not minorities but majorities, geared to mass production and mass consumption, increasingly structured, bureaucratized, and impersonal, like the rest of the world. Their academic staffs, in turn, have become the clerks of the modern world, furnishing its basic wisdom, the authority for its actions, the advice for its leaders. And, critics complain, just as the clergy had become the tamed, institutionalized servants of religious and secular institutions, so today university faculties have turned into just another kind of civil service: a bureaucracy of the intellect has succeeded a bureaucracy of the spirit.

In fact, things are more complicated. Universities are caught between growing demand for university education and growing reluctance of taxpayers to foot the costs this entailed; between the number of their students and the number of openings available to them on graduation; between growing expectations of students from faculty and growing preoccupations of a faculty increasingly involved in the surrounding world.

In Europe and elsewhere, universities displease the many they cannot accommodate and some of those who, having been accepted, are sent out with degrees but with no place to use them. And those who do not resent being ill-adapted to society's needs fear that they will become too well adapted to the one-dimensional standards of bureaucracy and technology. In other words, some want the university to adapt itself to modern life, while others blame it for being too well adjusted, reject the life it trains for as repressed, repressive, sordid, and mean, seek not integration into adult society but escape from its corrupting embrace, denounce in the same breath rotten liberals and "Stalinist blackguards." "The path of excess leads to wisdom," asserts a French student sticker. It would certainly lead to agitation throughout 1967, and particularly in 1968, when Europe's universities suddenly boiled over.

The trouble had started in 1967 at the Free University of Berlin, where students and a few of the younger faculty attacked inadequate and anachronistic structures particularly out of place in the most modern of German academic institutions. It spread to Italy in the winter, where students took a leaf out of the syndicalist notebook to occupy the faculties in great sit-in strikes; and to Spain, where the University of Madrid was officially closed for part of the academic year. It would culminate in France in the spring of 1968, where student revolt precipitated the strike of nearly ten million workers, clerks, and civil servants, and seemed about to topple the Fifth Republic. A generation which had known no war devised mini-conflicts to its measure by building barricades as symbolic as they were anachronistic. But, as Alexis de Tocqueville, the most perceptive observer of the revolution of 1848 once remarked, "in a rebellion as in a novel, the most difficult part to invent is the end."

Very soon, students realized that the changes they sought within the university structure had to be related to broader changes within the state itself. The teaching methods and the academic obstacle course which they critized, reflected the authoritarianism and the class barriers of surrounding society; the institutions of representative democracy outside the university gates were reproduced by student representative bodies, just as irrelevant to student realities, just as far removed from the needs of their electorate, just as absorbed in sterile political-party games.

Thus, from parochial claims, student movements progressed to a criticism of the university's function in society and then to criticism of society itself. In Berkeley, Paris, or Berlin they rejected the consumer society. In Madrid, Prague, and Belgrade they refused the yoke of police and censorship. In Warsaw and Moscow they criticized regimes which seem to organize production for penury. The points they raised were different; the dissatisfaction, the refusal, the same. Alienated by economic mechanisms that lead them to consume what they do not want, or by political mechanisms that force them to think and do what they do not want, they condemned both. They condemned the structures which, they fear, will swallow and use them, along with the institution that provides both a temporary refuge from the world outside and a conditioning agent for it. "We believe that the university is an essential element supporting society. We are convinced that the sole way of solving the problems at all levels is to take part in the destruction of the system" (*Le Monde,* May 29, 1968). Turning in the easiest direction first, they sawed off the branch on which they sat, smashed the bed of Procrustes, as the first gesture of rebellion against a fate they would not accept.

The fate which they rejected was not theirs alone, but that of the oppressed everywhere. "We think that the struggle of French workers and students is one with that of the peoples of Latin America," declared an Argentine admirer of the revolutionary guerrilla leader Che Guevara. Wherever possible, students connected their aspirations with those of black men, of the North Vietnamese, of the agricultural and industrial proletariat. The latter, long cast in the role of a progressive force, would be crucial to their ambitions . . . and their miscalculations. In Italy and Spain, in Germany and in France—where the greatest and most publicized outburst of spring, 1968, snowballed into near civil war—student rebels supported labor claims or, more often, spurred them on, striving to unite student and labor action.

The "revolution of 1968" was directed less against the consumer society (to which workers seek admittance and from which students profit) than against organized society, highly structured and bureaucratized both in East and West, in capitalist and socialist countries. Yet structures and administrations which flatten men also fatten them. Industrial societies cannot operate or expand without them. Their rejection by a utopian or anarchist Left is almost the counterpart of their rejection by a reactionary Right dreaming of a return to nature, of bygone nonexistent ages of happy peasants and artisans.

Che Guevara shortly before his death.

Furthermore, if student claims were largely ideological, those of labor remained steadfastly utilitarian. The students opposed both university and society, the workers sought material gains within the existing system. If the former were revolutionary, the latter were not.* The seeds of the "revolution's" failure lay in its irreconcilable aims, in the inner contradictions of a movement that sought to change men and had to use them as they were, which rejected industrial society but not the advantages it offered, which scorned the Communists and the unions as too conservative but could supply no alternative organization, and no slogans beyond those of romantic self-indulgence: "It is forbidden to forbid"; "The duty of every revolutionary is to make the revolution"; "Imagination has seized power"; or "Be realistic, demand the impossible."

The failure of such efforts in the West appeared to show that the conjunction between labor and youth was spurious. It indicated also that these—like other—fighters for a better world were more impressed by action than by thought. Paradoxical in intellectuals (or would-be intellectuals), this was reminiscent of other modern movements that preach and sometimes practice action for action's sake. And, indeed, those who affirm the primacy of action over thought make an important point. Reflection slows you down, often paralyzes. A search for motives, an examination of alternatives, a balancing of factors and of possible effects, prevents the decisive act. Action, on the other hand, carries its meaning (and reassurance) with it. Hence, Goethe's Doctor Faustus replaces *word* with *deed* in the old wisdom: "In the beginning was the act." Explanations and a search for meanings only too often hamper. Our activists have learned Faust's lesson, and that of the world around.

There was another lesson in the spring of revolution, if one looked hard enough. For the first time since 1848,** the actions of a few students had precipitated major changes in the political scene. The United States, France, Czechoslovakia, bore witness to the possibility that a few determined wills could sensibly affect the course of history. This would, in

* Moreover, from a worker's perspective, the students rioting in universities were like mice rioting in a cheese. And left extremism achieved the paradoxical result of enacting in reverse the class war that it preached, when lower-class police and gendarmes (and factory workers) turned on the privileged revolutionaries of the "upper" or educated classes.

** With the exception of 1956, when the Hungarian revolution also grew out of student and intellectual circles.

due course, color existing interpretations of political action and its possibilities. To understand just how, we must retrace our steps and recapitulate the fortunes of the revolutionary idea in the modern world.

The model of revolution that Karl Marx designed suggested that the most advanced nations would develop a technology and means of production so collectivized that workers would be able to take them over, eliminate private ownership, and, turning private property to public ends, turn productive processes to social ends. Lenin's success in Russia and the failure of communism in Germany and Italy suggested a variant model, according to which revolution could only succeed in technologically backward societies, where the government's means of defense could not operate and the causes of general dissatisfaction could be harnessed to social-revolutionary ends.

The experience of France in 1968, though limited, went far to revalidate Marx's original version. Where managers have taken over, where production depends on technocrats and society on bureaucrats, where private property has been depersonalized and the small property owner turned into a wage earner, corporate and state collectivization may be turned into a political fact by spontaneous revolution. The revolutionary struggle of a conscious minority may yet spread awareness of real democracy and turn formal democracy into real democracy, formal socialism into real socialism. This could apply as easily to Russia as to France. The depersonalized rule of privileged bureaucrats and managers who monopolize public force and public power, enjoying economic and social privileges at the people's expense, could be shown up for the fake it is and wrested from them in a great explosion of popular will.

Thus the theory. But now the theory referred to an experience. And if the experience seemed disillusioning, it would not discourage the revolutionaries bred in the ever-replenished reservoir of youth. As J. M. Keynes once noted of his own early years, youth is "an age when our beliefs influenced our behavior, a characteristic of the young which it is easy for the middle-aged to forget."

An Interim Report

If every man is not yet, or not quite, his own historian (as Carl Becker suggested), every age is: rewriting, reinterpreting history to fit its needs. That simply means that men, as always, turn to the past—as they do to the world around them—for answers to the questions that concern them here and now. The peculiar needs and formulas that change with every culture provide the sieve that retains experience, or lets it run through and down the drain. As the culture alters, so does the sense it seeks and finds in cultures and experiences of the past.

The twentieth century has proved an age of speed, an age in which the rate of physical movement which we have come to take for granted is paralleled by the acceleration of history and of change itself, the rapidly growing distance between us and the past, the realization that the experience of our grandparents may have been closer to that of Cardinal Mazarin than to our own. The universe has grown smaller but also larger. Larger because it was realized that the world is part of a galactic universe about 100,000 light years in diameter, itself but one of 100 million or so galaxies of about the same size, the nearest of them about 500 million light years away. The order of magnitude involved in this appears from the term "light year" itself, invented to cope with these astronomical distances and denoting the space which light, traveling at 186,000 miles per second, covers in one year.

In the last hundred years cultural changes such as these have come thick and fast, faster than man has ever known before. Under their bombardment the questions men have asked of history have altered too until, in certain cases, the history of a generation or of a decade has come to seem irrelevant to the next—let alone to peoples somewhere else. In this respect, all that the historian may hope to do is to record a passing point of view as honestly and as thoughtfully as he knows how: not to provide a chronicle of facts or cut a slice out of the pie of Truth, but to suggest plausible interpretations to his time and indicate to others who come later how his own age mirrored itself in its past.

This has now been done. For better or for worse the story of the last 600 years, beginning in the days when Europe became conscious of its forces and of itself, ending when its power to control the world collapsed, has been told. From where we stand it seems to be a whole, comprising (as we see it) a beginning, a middle, and—in 1945—an end. What follows after is not so much past as process: things still becoming, impossible to envision in perspective, to record in more than the most passing shape. A history of Europe written in the 1950's could only conclude with its decline and fall. A similar history written ten years later can dwell not only on fall but on recovery. And it is hard to tell what yet one more decade will add, but easy to insist that these things too will justify no more than mere conjecture.

The politics of Europe now, its trade, its industry, are part of the pattern of the world. This too is changing rapidly. Ten years ago it could be seen and told in terms of the great rivalry of the United States and the Soviet Union. Now this polar pattern shifts, as the forces of other continents come into play, as the dilemmas and hostilities that we have known in our small corner of the world are reproduced with world significance elsewhere. All we can say with any certainty is that where, once, the struggles and rivalries of European powers echoed through the world, today they have been relegated to provincial states. France, Britain, Germany, may still go to war. But general war can only rise from decisions arrived at somewhere else.

Yet, paradoxically, the end of Western Europe's dominion of the world comes at a moment when the whole world has come to bear its mark. Attitudes, values, techniques, even ways of life, evolved in a few cities at the Western end of the Eurasian land mass prevail everywhere, even among their foes. And the superpowers, whether in Asia, in America, or in Eastern Europe, run on ideas and on a dynamism which Western men taught or imposed not so long ago.

The great peculiarity of European culture is that it developed the belief that fate "rests not in our stars but in our selves," that men, not superhuman powers, are a crucial part of their own destiny and that of others. The story of the last six centuries is the evolution and the assertion (sometimes in brutal, overweening, murderous ways) of humanism: respect for man and for his capacity to make himself great, forge his own destiny, free himself, and assert his personality on the world around. The price of such ambition is, sometimes, success. This, as Prometheus discovered, carries its discomforts. Most notable among them has been the need to adjust our lives and minds to the conditions that technological progress has created, the problems of abundance rather than scarcity and, possibly, of leisure rather than toil.

As long as human productivity remained constant—that is, as far back as recorded history goes—wealth that went beyond the most modest limits could arise only from the exploitation and deprivation of others. The great novelty of our times is that it is possible to enrich *all* members of a given society by successive improvements in the techniques, the instruments, and the organization of labor, that the wealth thus produced can furnish the means of yet further developments, and that this process can be both rapid and indefinite. Of course, this does not happen everywhere or affect everybody, but the phenomenon is sufficiently widespread to have a serious impact on modern mentalities and practices. What St. Paul and Karl Marx once cited as a law of nature—the obligation or the right to work—is being mitigated, affected by the social virtues of consumption, disrupting the value systems of societies and men conditioned by the experience of ages. Free time becomes a problem: in literature, in the films of Fellini and Antonioni, in the discourse of politicians and social critics. Education, once designed to teach skills, is being redesigned in part to train men and women for leisure.

But, while the material reality in industrially developed societies changes, old-established attitudes persist—not least the belief in the virtue of toil ("He who works prays"). Like anesthetics or contraceptives, material plenty seems to go counter to the higher will of nature. Taking man out from the rule of necessity appears a kind of blasphemy, not only against God who ordered us to make our living by the sweat of our brow, but against the wisdom of centuries that connected virtue with effort, with suffering, and repression of the instincts. As misery decreased, as famines and plagues disappeared, as material well-being spread, moralists and social critics thought they discerned the ebbing of faith and higher values too. Material abundance brought spiritual decadence. Bread and bathrooms for all wore down the tragic sense of life. Comfort made placid. In 1966, Michael Harrington's *Accidental Century* analyzed the reactions to this aspect of modernity, all the way from Dostoevski and Nietzsche to Ortega y Gasset and T. S. Eliot. Harrington quotes Robinson Jeffers' attack on "the new abundance:"

> Blind war compared to this kind of life
> Has nobility, famine has dignity.

Here was a kind of fat boy's revolt: an elitism of the sated. With plague and famine no longer endemic in the West, those who were spared them could afford to think them a spiritual advantage, regret the loss of moral fiber that went with great trials, consider the ages when they still endured to have been more vital and fine than ours. And even though over most of the world hunger persisted, and even when men proved that terror and tragedy had hardly relaxed their grip, poets and thinkers continued to feel that the society they lived in was barren and the lives they lived in it absurd. That was in part, at least, because they had the energy and leisure to spend on critical thought. In part because they knew that many lacked their advantages, hence felt embarrassed and guilt-ridden about the false peace and comfort permitting some to write or appreciate art while others suffered and died. In part, however, also because—as more men came to die in bed rather than through some irrational catastrophe—a certain tension had gone out of life. Man has gone far toward mastering the irrationality of nature. He is still prey to irrationalities of his own.

Even without this, the problems he must face suffice to make him uneasy. The speed of jets and rockets is reproduced in the speed of social and technological change: the gap between the evolution and the application of scientific theories narrows, the time span shortens between laboratory, factory, and general use, the results of technological progress are in all hands within years where once they could have taken centuries, are enjoyed quickly and widely, cast off just as quickly, replaced by fresh triumphs of skill and imagination fated like them to early obsolescence. Our mental equipment, like that of our daily lives, grows out of date before we have time to die. Education for living is not the once-for-all training that it used to be, but an awkward, never-ending readjustment to social and material activities on a stage where the scenery, the rules, even the language of the play, are in constant motion.

Our cities, the core of our civilization, alter. The modern metropolis is a place whose scale makes it different in kind from those the past world knew. Ancient Rome had a million inhabitants, but they could still walk from one part of the city to another, or out into the countryside. Today, even a car may take hours to achieve such a feat. By the end of the century, most people of the world may live in still vaster metropolitan complexes, ranging from 10 to 20 million and covering areas wider than those that appall us now.

The modern industrial system changes too. Industry has come a long way from the free enterprise to which it pays lip service, dominated by tremendous corporations dedicated to planning their activities and organizing relations between one another, between themselves and government, themselves and organized labor, rather like states in international affairs. Union contracts eliminate the uncertainties of the free labor market. Government intervention eliminates fears of collapsing demand. Publicity and market research eliminate uncertainty and condition the consumers. Planning restricts the free play of the economy to safe limits, that is, narrow ones. Problems like those of transport, communications, or urban land development cannot be left to individual initiative: road traffic or air traffic, for example, *have* to be planned on a very large scale. The development of backward areas or social groups will not occur by itself: industry, for instance, tends to locate where markets and facilities are most developed, and incentives have to be artificially provided to encourage it to settle somewhere else.

In such a situation, where scale introduces a difference of kind rather than degree, the whole tends to overshadow the part in ways that a world where everything was man-size could hardly have imagined. The tendency toward abstraction that we can see in economics and arts, in the nature of our currency, the shape of furniture, or the issues of political debate, appears in every other aspect of a life in which nations or classes take precedence over their individual members, entities or concepts tend to be more real and certainly more important than people, statistics take the place of a reality that outruns our capacity to grasp it. In other words, means become ends at every level, taking on a life of their own until even wars and revolutions count more than any purpose which they may be held to serve. The impersonality of abstractions helps to explain the facility of modern mass murder, itself a simpler and less obtrusive operation than leaving people workless or letting them starve to death.

Within this world, once-solid institutions are giving way. Society, which briefly visualized itself as a community of people similar in attitudes and values and objectives, has had to accept itself as a much looser conjunction of people with common habits and rules but whose relations are close rather because they live together than because of a deliberate and sustained choice: conscripts in the same company rather than partners in a marriage. The atoms of social reality, on which society's superstructure rose, disintegrate in the reactors of social and economic change. Family, age, experience, knowledge itself, crumble into apparent irrelevance. Thus, we have seen that the old, through most of history, had an important function. They had survived, hence were a rarity; also a source of wisdom (knowledge, memory) not otherwise available, and possibly of power—controlling property or authority for which others had to wait their turn. Today their survival is hardly an achievement, more a burden; their knowledge is available to all and, anyway, out-dated: property and authority spread far more widely. The old are more distinguished by their needs than by their contributions.

Similarly, the family household in which most people lived was also the basic social unit of production. People had to work together in order to survive. No wonder they stayed together. The young were the insurance of the old, the old at times the reassurance of the young. In modern urban society this is no longer so. The family consumes but it does not produce: it has lost a sense of necessity, it has lost its focus and it is fast disappearing except as a way station to emancipation. Even the ancient rites of breaking bread together, perpetuated in the family meal, decay and wane. Families that had eaten from a common dish first learned to dine round a common table, before even this commensality declined to snacks, to meals taken on the run, and the communal ceremony turned to the bare gesture of feeding.

Along with unifying facts or rituals there also wanes the old sense of individual responsibility, affected by the eruption of chance into a world of will, of self into a world of social duty. Politics, which was the luxury of an elite, has become the condition of men's lives, the arena where fundamental decisions are taken in societies where everything has to be decided afresh all the time. Even so, most groups and individuals are indifferent to politics until dissatisfaction brings them into it; political activity is chiefly the expression of sectional or fractional dissatisfactions. This can mean that politics serves as a safety valve and echo chamber of social tensions, a valve that some regimes know how to turn on and off, while diverting outward the tension it alleviates or easing it by the judicious use of bread and circuses.

Responsibility to God, then to the city or the state, are gone as comprehensible and accepted choices (at least for most men). There are more duties but fewer responsibilities. First adults, then adolescents, have drawn the conclusions of a situation in which they find themselves, affluent but ineffective, able to assert themselves largely in games, illusions, fantasies, while real decisions are made beyond their ken. The modern world is, by contemporary definition, a place where not production but services are economically predominant. Of all these the most important are those that furnish packaged irresponsibility: entertainment, drugs, alcohol, the vehicles of vicarious experience and of escape from reality—that is, from morality, which is about how to come to terms with reality, not abandon it.

The tensions of this kind of living have lent themselves to a great deal of talk, either in sorrow or in anger, while its advantages have attracted far less comment. It is a fact that what has been called the open society in which we live is an unstable, impermanent succession of situations and arrangements that make many men terribly uneasy. Perhaps because they know that the competition on which it is based means elimination, that the competence which is its norm means selection, that the specialization which is its core means eventual obsolescence. More likely, though, because they do not know their place in a world where the very notion of a "place" is either transitory or anachronistic. Once upon a time the effective unit of production and of action was, by our standards, very small: the family or clan. It could not easily be larger, since large groups could not be fed or moved or controlled with any ease, so that cities or armies were small, and self-assertion or defense did not require great numbers. This changed, as means of communication improved and possibilities of organized production and control improved with them. The scale of states grew, nation states appeared, regional structures lost their independence, and men forfeited the power to operate within the accessible confines of small-scale hierarchies. They found some reassurance in transferring their ideological allegiance to the nation which now superseded kinship as a means of identification. Irrelevant in the mass, men discovered vicarious relevance for themselves as members of the nation which was the effective working unit of a larger world and, within it, of various groups linked by more or less abstract ideologies, like political parties. The more impotent people felt as individuals, the more they stressed their importance as members of a group. Now that the nation is being superseded by supranational entities, while the scale of politico-economic effectiveness increases, men have to adjust again, adopt some other notion that will alleviate their impotence and give them meaning.

Technology has outrun the world's ability to cope with its advances. Much of mankind reacts with a nostalgia often amounting to aggressive longing for what is past and lost. This easily leads to falsification; to pretending that what is, is not, because we wish it different; to the substitution of delusive meanings for a straightforward look at what lies around.* The crackpot creeds that flourish in our day are evidence of the helplessness that many feel about the possibility of acting sensibly in a world where, like little children, they find effectiveness far beyond their grasp. They may well represent attempts to adjust to new situations, nets to catch men and organize them in some way, at a level they find comprehensible and at which they can feel effective. There is a tension here between the demands of growing scale which call for commensurate ideologies and those of individuals dwarfed and dismayed by the process. On one hand a tendency to the particularism in which reality remains accessible if, sometimes, unreal; on the other the need to transcend the sense of helplessness and borrow power from identification with a yet wider solidarity.

---

* It also leads to a running fight between two rival cultures, rather than an attempt to reconcile them and come to terms with their implications. Or to the kind of bitter detachment that a contemporary of Jonathan Swift expressed nearly 250 years ago: "For my part," wrote Lady Mary Wortley Montagu, "as it is my establish'd Opinion that this Globe of ours is no better than a Holland Cheese and the Walkers about in it Mites, I possess my Mind in patience, let what will happen, and should feel tolerably easy though a great Rat came and eat halfe of it up."

The problem modern people face is not lack of freedom, for they are freer of their biological trammels than ever in the history of mankind. The problem is how to apply their power and their knowledge without abandoning or denying the very capacities that increased them so. This brings us back, however reluctantly, to politics, which are, as Napoleon once said to Goethe, the fatality and also the tragedy of our time, because they reveal in the most public and dramatic fashion the fatal gap between what one wishes, what one says, what one does, and what eventually happens.

There is—there has always been—something strange about the way we look at history. We live on the conquests of our mind, yet gaze fascinated upon the glamorous catastrophes produced by our passions. Out of the past, we cherish less the constructive than the destructive: wars, murder, mayhem, the battered abysses on whose rim we still teeter today. Lord Macaulay remarked that times which are exciting to write about are not good to live in. We are in a position to confirm this. Surgeons have learned to replace vital organs; biologists synthesize life artificially in test tubes and prepare to affect the genes which control our physique and, perhaps, our personality; bioculture can affect not only environment, but life: manipulate it and preserve it. It cannot govern it. Nothing fails like success.

Yet, as Einstein once said: "The most extraordinary thing is that the world certainly has a meaning." Perhaps that meaning is the one with which we endow it: like the Indian sage who had the gods whose images watched over the sacrificial tables of the temples replaced by mirrors. Thus, man's suggestions are more important than his certainties and his questions mean far more than the answers he may hazard. But even the value of questions—like that of sincerity—lies not in themselves (as some seem to believe), but in what they may reveal.

It is reassuring and convenient to pretend that, in the end, nothing really changes very much except appearances. Human nature remains much the same. Soviet Russia carries on the work and methods of Tsarist Russia, as the Fifth French Republic continues the evolution of the Fourth. And yet, in fact, after evolution or revolution, reconstruction or stabilization, nothing is quite the same, nothing is quite finished, nothing is quite set. The social changes that we mark with suspicion or with satisfaction bear in themselves further awarenesses, dissatisfactions, claims, and emancipations. The dialectic of history does not consent to halt, nor lend itself to more than limited foresight—let alone prophecy. The only thing that one can say for sure is that however fair the moment, no Doctor Faustus can stay its passing. That men will go on being born, suffering, and dying. And that this—men, the things they do, they think, they feel and say—will be the stuff of history as long as there are men and as long as they continue to invent themselves.

E quindi uscimmo a riveder le stelle.

GENEALOGICAL
TABLES

THE FRENCH SUCCESSION

Louis IX
1226–70
St. Louis

Philip III
The Bold
1270–85

Robert
m. heiress of Bourbon

Philip IV
The Fair
1285–1314

Charles IV
1322–28
*Last
Capetian king*

Charles
COUNT OF VALOIS

Louis X
1314–16

Philip V
1316–22
*m. Jeanne of
Burgundy*

Philip VI
1328–50
Founder of Valois line

Isabella=Edward II
OF ENGLAND

Edward III
OF ENGLAND

John of Gaunt
DUKE OF LANCASTER

Henry IV
OF ENGLAND

Henry V=Catherine
OF ENGLAND

Henry VI
KING OF ENGLAND
AND FRANCE

John II
1350–64

Charles V
1364–80

Charles VI
1380–1422

Louis
DUKE OF ORLÉANS

Charles VII
1422–61

Charles
DUKE OF ORLÉANS

Louis XI
1461–83

Louis XII
1498–1515
m. (2) Anne of Brittany

Charles VIII
1483–98
m. Anne of Brittany

Anne
m. Duke of Bourbon

Jeanne (1)

John
of ANGOULÊME

Charles
of ANGOULÊME

Francis I
1515–47

Henry II
1547–59

Catherine de Medici=

Francis
DUKE OF
ALENÇON
AND ANJOU

Elizabeth
m. Philip II of Spain

Francis II
1559–60
*m. Mary Stuart
of Scotland*

Charles IX
1560–74

Henry III
1574–89
DUKE OF ANJOU
Last Valois king

Margaret
m. King of Navarre

Jeanne = Anthony
QUEEN OF   DUKE OF
NAVARRE   VENDÔME

Margaret (1) = Henry IV = (2) Marie de Medici
1589–1610
HENRY OF NAVARRE
*First king of
House of Bourbon*

Louis XIII
1610–43

Philip the Bold
DUKE OF BURGUNDY

John the Fearless

Philip the Good

Charles the Bold

Maximilian I=Mary
EMPEROR
House of Habsburg

THE FRENCH SUCCESSION · 1610–1848
(House of Bourbon)

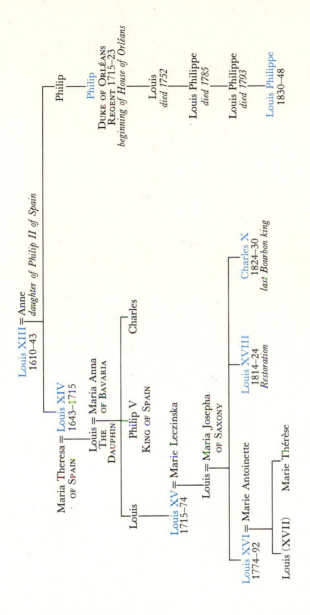

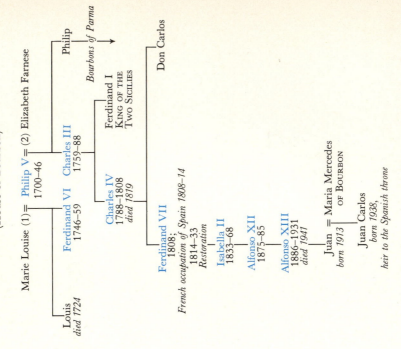

Marie Louise (1) = Philip V = (2) Elizabeth Farnese
1700–46

Louis
died 1724

Ferdinand VI
1746–59

Charles III
1759–88

Philip

Bourbons of Parma

Charles IV
1788–1808
died 1819

Ferdinand I
King of the
Two Sicilies

Don Carlos

Ferdinand VII
1808;
French occupation of Spain 1808–14
1814–33
Restoration

Isabella II
1833–68

Alfonso XII
1875–85

Alfonso XIII
1886–1931
died 1941

Juan = Maria Mercedes
born 1913   of Bourbon

Juan Carlos
*born 1938,
heir to the Spanish throne*

THE SPANISH SUCCESSION • 1479–1746

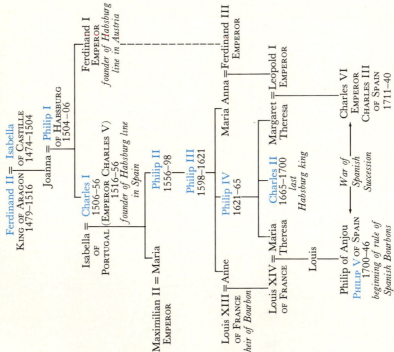

Ferdinand II = Isabella
King of Aragon | of Castille
1479–1516 | 1474–1504

Joanna = Philip I
        of Habsburg
        1504–06

Ferdinand I
Emperor
*founder of Habsburg
line in Austria*

Isabella = Charles I
of   1506–56
Portugal (Emperor Charles V)
           1516–56
           *founder of Habsburg line
           in Spain*

Maximilian II = Maria
Emperor

Philip II
1556–98

Philip III
1598–1621

Maria Anna = Ferdinand III
             Emperor

Philip IV
1621–65

Margaret = Leopold I
Theresa   Emperor

Charles II
1665–1700
*last
Habsburg king*

Louis XIII = Anne
of France
heir of Bourbon

Louis XIV = Maria
of France   Theresa

Louis

Charles VI
Emperor
Charles III
of Spain
1711–40

*War of
Spanish
Succession*

Philip of Anjou
Philip V of Spain
1700–46
*beginning of rule of
Spanish Bourbons*

THE ENGLISH SUCCESSION • 1327–1509

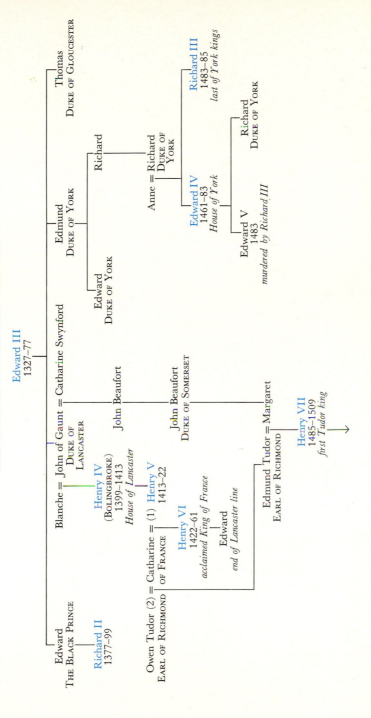

Edward III
1327–77

Edward
THE BLACK PRINCE

Richard II
1377–99

Blanche = John of Gaunt = Catharine Swynford
DUKE OF
LANCASTER

Henry IV
(BOLINGBROKE)
1399–1413
House of Lancaster

Owen Tudor (2) = Catharine = (1) Henry V
EARL OF RICHMOND   OF FRANCE   1413–22

Henry VI
1422–61
acclaimed King of France

Edward
end of Lancaster line

John Beaufort

John Beaufort
DUKE OF SOMERSET

Edmund Tudor = Margaret
EARL OF RICHMOND

Henry VII
1485–1509
first Tudor king

Edmund
DUKE OF YORK

Richard

Anne = Richard
DUKE OF
YORK

Edward
DUKE OF YORK

Edward IV
1461–83
House of York

Edward V
1483
murdered by Richard III

Richard
DUKE OF YORK

Richard III
1483–85
last of York kings

Thomas
DUKE OF GLOUCESTER

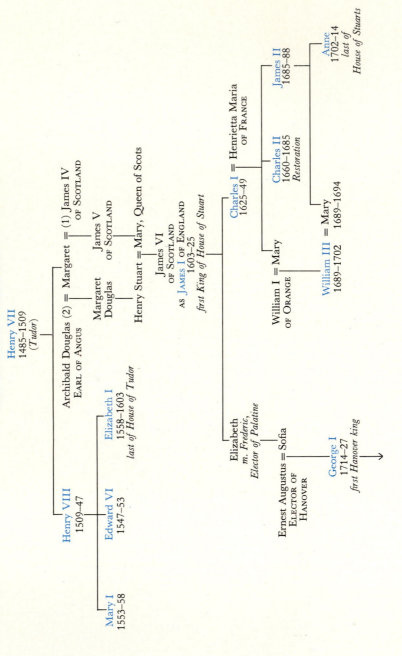

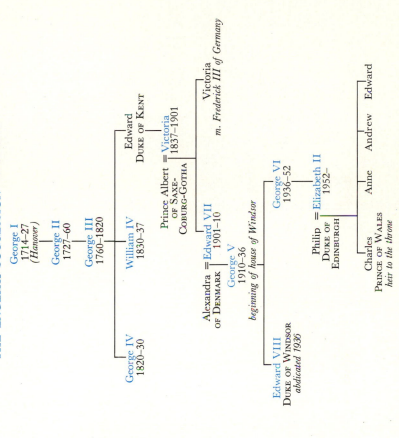

THE ENGLISH SUCCESSION • 1714–1971

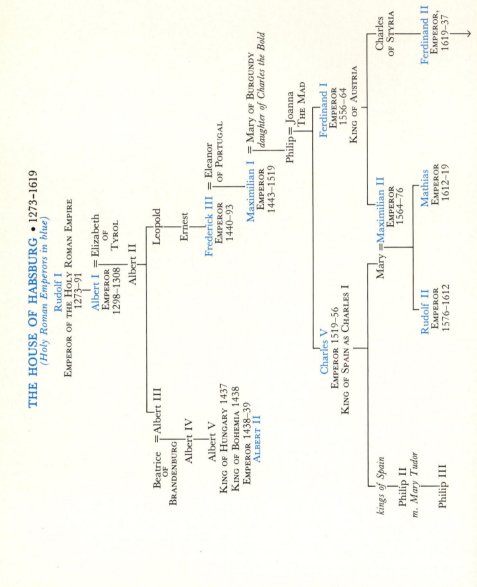

THE HOUSE OF HABSBURG • 1273–1619
(Holy Roman Emperors in blue)

Rudolf I
EMPEROR OF THE HOLY ROMAN EMPIRE
1273–91

Albert I = Elizabeth
EMPEROR   OF
1298–1308   TYROL

Albert II

Leopold

Ernest

Frederick III = Eleanor
EMPEROR   OF PORTUGAL
1440–93

Maximilian I = Mary OF BURGUNDY
EMPEROR   *daughter of Charles the Bold*
1443–1519

Philip = Joanna
         THE MAD

Beatrice = Albert III
OF
BRANDENBURG

Albert IV

Albert V
KING OF HUNGARY 1437
KING OF BOHEMIA 1438
EMPEROR 1438–39
ALBERT II

Charles V
EMPEROR 1519–56
KING OF SPAIN AS CHARLES I

Ferdinand I
EMPEROR
1556–64
KING OF AUSTRIA

Charles
OF STYRIA

Ferdinand II
EMPEROR,
1619–37

Mary = Maximilian II
          EMPEROR
          1564–76

Rudolf II
EMPEROR
1576–1612

Mathias
EMPEROR
1612–19

kings of Spain

Philip II
m. Mary Tudor

Philip III

THE HOUSE OF HABSBURG • 1619–1918
(Holy Roman Emperors in blue)

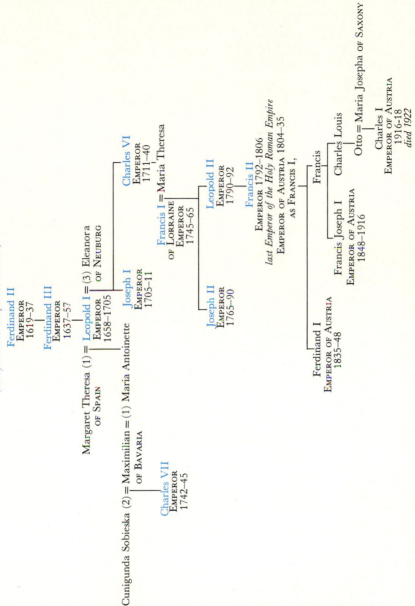

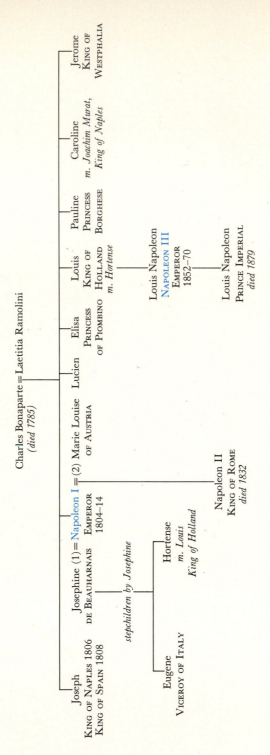

THE HOUSE OF BONAPARTE

Charles Bonaparte = Laetitia Ramolini
(died 1785)

Joseph
KING OF NAPLES 1806
KING OF SPAIN 1808

Josephine (1) = Napoleon I = (2) Marie Louise
DE BEAUHARNAIS   EMPEROR   OF AUSTRIA
1804–14

Lucien

Elisa
PRINCESS
OF PIOMBINO

Louis
KING OF
HOLLAND
m. Hortense

Pauline
PRINCESS
BORGHESE

Caroline
*m. Joachim Murat,
King of Naples*

Jerome
KING OF
WESTPHALIA

stepchildren by Josephine

Eugene
VICEROY OF ITALY

Hortense
*m. Louis
King of Holland*

Napoleon II
KING OF ROME
died 1832

Louis Napoleon
NAPOLEON III
EMPEROR
1852–70

Louis Napoleon
PRINCE IMPERIAL
died 1879

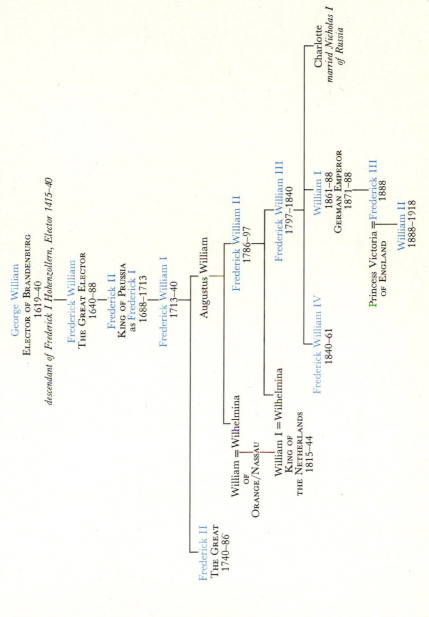

THE HOUSE OF HOHENZOLLERN • 1619–1918

George William
ELECTOR OF BRANDENBURG
1619–40
descendant of Frederick I Hohenzollern, Elector 1415–40

Frederick William
THE GREAT ELECTOR
1640–88

Frederick II
KING OF PRUSSIA
as Frederick I
1688–1713

Frederick William I
1713–40

Frederick II
THE GREAT
1740–86

Augustus William

William = Wilhelmina
OF
ORANGE/NASSAU

Frederick William II
1786–97

William I = Wilhelmina
KING OF
THE NETHERLANDS
1815–44

Frederick William III
1797–1840

Frederick William IV
1840–61

William I
1861–88
GERMAN EMPEROR
1871–88

Charlotte
married Nicholas I
of Russia

Princess Victoria = Frederick III
OF ENGLAND   1888

William II
1888–1918

RUSSIAN TSARS · 1462–1917

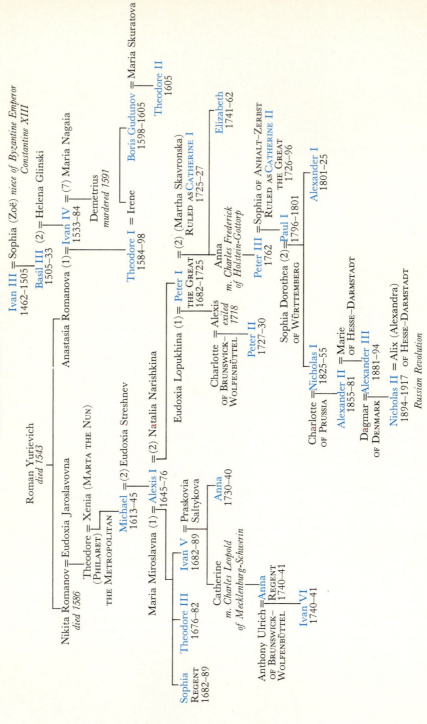

BIBLIOGRAPHY

General works

It would be useless to list all the good books concerned with the general problems of European history. The few that follow provide sound points of relevance and suggestions for further study. An asterisk (*) indicates that the book is available in paperback.

*Carlo Cipolla, *Economic History of World Population* (1962) (Penguin) and B. H. Slicher van Bath, *Agrarian History of Western Europe, A.D. 500–1850* (1963) are excellent accounts of economic history. See also Shepard B. Clough and C. W. Cole, *Economic History of Europe*, 3rd ed. (1952). *John U. Nef has given us a good general survey in *Western Civilization Since the Renaissance: Peace, War, Industry and the Arts* (1963) (Harper Torchbook) and a fresh point of view in his essay *War and Human Progress* (1950) (Norton). Since the present book is much concerned with intellectual history, the following works may prove useful: Bertrand Russell, *History of Western Philosophy and Its Connection with Political and Social Circumstances from the Earliest Times to the Present Day* (1945); Franklin L. Baumer, ed., *Main Currents of Western Thought*, rev. ed. (1964); *Jacob Bronowski and Bruce Mazlish, *The Western Intellectual Tradition: From Leonardo to Hegel* (1960) (Harper Torchbook); Crane Brinton, *Ideas and Men: The Story of Western Thought* (1963); and Hugo Leichtentritt, *Music, History, and Ideas* (1950). Political ideas may be explored further through George Sabine's classic, *History of Political Theory* (1937) and John Bowle, *Western Political Thought: An Historical Introduction from the Origins to Rousseau* (1948). In the realm of the plastic arts, *Arnold Hauser's *Social History of Art*, 4 vols. (1951) (Vintage) is a suggestive reflection of the dialectical materialist approach, best read in conjunction with the critique of E. H. Gombrich, in his *Meditations on a Hobby Horse and Other Essays* (1963). The latter's *Story of Art* (1956) (Praeger) is probably the best existing treatment of art history in a social and intellectual context. On a simpler level there is a good revised edition of William Fleming, *Arts and Ideas* (1966).

Certain series maintain a high standard of excellence. One may turn to them with confidence for basic facts or thought-provoking interpretation. Thus *The New Cambridge Modern History*, most of whose fourteen volumes are already in print, while hardly a bedside book, is convenient, informative, and readily accessible. So is the Cambridge Economic History of Europe, whose sixth volume, in two parts, edited by H. J. Habakkuk with M. M. Postan (1965), is entitled *The Industrial Revolutions and After*. Although a trifle dated and still incomplete, the volumes of the Rise of Modern Europe series, edited by William L. Langer, are learned, readable, and provide handy bibliographies. *The

1145

Norton History of Modern Europe series, Felix Gilbert, General Editor, 6 vols. (1970) also maintains a high standard of excellence. The best sources of bibliographical information are the two Clio series published by the Presses Universitaires de France: the older in the 1930's (revised after the Second World War); the new—Nouvelle Clio—in the 1960's, comprising more volumes and much up-to-date data and discussion of work in progress.

The French publishing house of Albin Michel publishes two series inspired by the school of Annales, which has done more than any other to enrich the study of history in the past half-century: L'Evolution de l'Humanité, founded by Henri Berr, and Destin du Monde, directed first by Lucien Febvre and after his death by Fernand Braudel. The volumes of the latter are sumptuously illustrated, as are those in the Histoire Générale de la Civilisation, directed by Maurice Crouzet, and the less expensive volumes of the History of European Civilization, edited by Geoffrey Barraclough. Lastly, an impressive series—Arts, Idées, Histoire—published by the Swiss publisher Skira, sets out to link art and architecture to the tendencies and atmosphere of particular epochs.

When all is said and done, historical narrative or interpretation cannot by itself come as close to reality as the documentations of the time, which may be found in many good collections of readings but, above all, in contemporary works like *Chaucer's *Canterbury Tales,* *Cervantes' *Don Quixote,* *Grimmelshausen's *Simplicissimus,* *Goethe's *Werther,* *Stendhal's *The Red and the Black,* *Flaubert's *Sentimental Education,* *R. M. du Gard's *Jean Barois,* or *Simone de Beauvoir's *The Mandarins.* Each in its own way recaptures and reflects attitudes, problems, and atmosphere peculiar to its own place and time. There are many similar works: too many to list but generally revealing, the most accessible dating from the last two hundred years, when novelists began to hold up more or less distorting mirrors to society.

Novelists have also contributed imaginative reconstructions of historical situations, and some of these reveal far more than any textbook. *Helen Waddell's *Peter Abelard* (1933) (Compass) or *H. F. M. Prescott's *Man on a Donkey* (1952) (Ballantine; Collier) are splendid reconstructions of the living past by important scholars. More straightforwardly combining use and enjoyment are the works of men like Alfred Duggan, Maurice Denon, and C. S. Forester. Unfortunately, some of the great practitioners of the art have concentrated on portions of history preceding the period we are studying, but Mary Renault, Robert Graves, Marguerite Yourcenar, and Frans G. Bengtsson can be read with pleasure and profit, whatever their immediate relevance.

PART I

Europe in the Middle Ages

A History of Europe from the Invasions to the XVIth Century (1955) (Anchor), written by the Belgian historian Henri Pirenne, remains one of the best general interpretations of early European history. For the Middle Ages, most reliable are Robert Fawtier, *L'Europe occidentale de 1270 à 1328* (1940) and *The Capetian Kings of France: Monarchy and Nation, 987–1328* (1960) (St. Martin's). L. Halphen, *L'Essor de l'Europe* (1932) is one of the best accounts of economic, social, and political changes during the eleventh to thirteenth centuries. A brilliant English-language evocation of the same period may be found in *R. W. Southern, *The Making of the Middle Ages* (1953) (Yale). For a more general survey see R. Trevor Davies, *A History of Medieval Europe* (1962), and especially Robert Lopez, *The Birth of Europe* (1967), a fascinating and original book. One of the best interpretations of the last medieval centuries is to be found in *Johan Huizinga, *Waning of the Middle Ages* (1967) (Anchor). *Edward P. Cheyney, *The Dawn of a New Era, 1200–1453* (1936) (Harper Torchbook); Wallace K. Ferguson, *Europe in Transition: 1300–1520* (1963); and *Denys Hay, *The Medieval Centuries,* 2nd ed. (1964) (Barnes & Noble) are all excellent brief treatments. For social and institutional history Marc Bloch, *Feudal Society* (1962) (Phoenix) and *Land and Work in Medieval Europe* (1967) (Harper Torchbook) are fundamental; so is the older book of *Pierre Boissonade, *Life and Work in Medieval Europe: The Evolution of the Medieval Economy from the Fifth to the Fifteenth Century* (1927) (Harper Torchbook). But no student should miss the writings of Marc Bloch, preferably in the original French. A solid general survey of the problems facing the central authority and of the process of centralization may be found in *Charles Petit-Dutaillis, *The Feudal Monarchy in France and England: from the Tenth to the Thirteenth Century* (1964) (Harper Torchbook); for the everyday life of medieval people see *Armando Sapori, *The Italian Merchant in the Middle Ages* (1970) (Norton); G. Cohen, *Scènes de la vie en France au Moyen Age* (1950); and *Eileen Power's classic, *Medieval People,* 10th ed. (1924) (Barnes & Noble); most of the works of *George G. Coulton (for example, *Medieval Panorama,* (1938) (Cambridge); and the writings of *Helen Waddell, especially her wonderful novel *Peter Abelard* (1933) (Compass). Further bibliographical suggestions can be found in R. Trevor Davies, *Medieval European History: A Selected Bibliography, 395–1500* (1963).

The Renaissance

First published in 1860, *Jacob Burckhardt's *The Civilization of the Renaissance in Italy* (Harper Torchbook) still represents one of the most interesting approaches, not only for Italy but for Europe in general. For more recent points of view, see *The Penguin Book of the Renaissance,* edited by J. H. Plumb, (1964) (*The Horizon Book of the Renaissance* is the 1961 edition of the 1964 Penguin); *Peter Burke, *The Renaissance* (1964) (Barnes & Noble); and *Margaret Aston, *The Fifteenth Century* (1968) (Harcourt, Brace & World). One of the best general accounts of Renaissance culture and civilization is to be found in G. Laini, *Rinascimento Europeo* (1965). The social history of the time receives attention in *Alfred von Martin, *Sociology of the Renaissance* (1944) (Harper Torchbook) and *Iris Origo, *The Merchant of Prato* (1963) (Peregrine), a fascinating account of a fourteenth-century Tuscan merchant, based on his own papers. Some contradictory aspects of the Renaissance and the most important interpretations proposed by historians are discussed by *Denys Hay in *The Italian Renaissance in Its Historical Background* (1962) (Cambridge) and *The Renaissance Debate* (1965) (Holt, Rinehart & Winston); *Eugene F. Rice, Jr., *The Foundations of Early Modern Europe, 1460–1559* (1970) (Norton). *K. H. Dannenfeldt, *The Renaissance: Medieval or Modern?* (1959) (Heath); *George C. E. Sellery, *The Renaissance: Its Nature and Origins* (1950) (Wisconsin); and Wallace K. Ferguson, *The Renaissance in Historical Thought: Five Centuries of Interpretation* (1948). For a picture of daily life, most interesting and suggestive are A. Lefranc, *La vie quotidienne au temps de la Renaissance* (1938); Jean Lucas-Dubreton, *Daily Life in Florence in the Time of the Medici* (1961); and *Eric R. Chamberlain, *Everyday Life in Renaissance Times* (1965) (Capricorn). Nor should one forget *Garrett Mattingly, *Renaissance Diplomacy* (1955) (Penguin), which throws its own light on a particular aspect of the period.

Economics Among the great number of general books dealing with late medieval and modern European economic history the following works are suggested:

J. W. Thompson, *Economic and Social History of Europe in the Late Middle Ages, 1300–1530* (1931); Frederick L. Nussbaum, *A History of the Economic Institutions of Modern Europe* (1933); Heinrich E. Friedlander and Jacob Oser, *Economic History of Modern Europe* (1953); Jacques Heers, *L'Occident au XIVᵉ et XVᵉ siècles: Aspects économiques et sociaux* (1963); and, above all, Eli F. Heckscher, *Mercantilism*, 2nd ed., 2 vols. (1955). For agricultural life, the outstanding work is Marc Bloch's *French Rural History* (1966), whose full text is to be found in *Les Caractères originaux de l'histoire rurale française* (1931). N. S. B. Gras, *Business and Capitalism: An Introduction to Business History* (1939) and *Maurice Dobb, *Studies in the Development of Capitalism,* rev. ed. (1964) (International) would be useful to those interested in general interpretation of the rise of capitalism, and an excellent description of its beginnings can be found in Richard Ehrenberg, *Capital and Finance in the Age of the Renaissance* (1963). See also Carlo Cipolla, *Money, Prices and Civilization in the Mediterranean World, Vth to XVIIth Century* (1956). Jakob Strieder, *Jacob Fugger the Rich* (1931); Ernst Hering, *Die Fugger* (1942) and *The Fugger News-letters, 1568–1605*, 2 vols. (1924–1925); and *Raymond de Roover, *The Rise and Decline of the Medici Bank, 1397–1494* (1963) (Norton) are serious analyses of the rise of the new class. Pierre Jeannin, *Les Marchands au XVIᵉ siècle* (1957) provides a more colorful picture of the process, while Frederic C. Lane, *Andrea Barbarigo, Merchant of Venice, (1418–1449)* (1944) has given us the solid biography of a merchant astride two ages. For a general history of commerce and its impact upon social and economic structures, see Laurence B. Packard, *The Commercial Revolution, 1400–1776* (1927). For a more limited but revealing picture, *Medieval Trade in the Mediterranean World,* Robert S. Lopez and I. W. Raymond, eds. (1955) (Norton) and K. Pagel, *Die Hanse* (1963).

The Great Discoveries   John H. Parry, *Europe and a Wider World, 1415–1715* (1949) is a brief survey written by an expert. Albert Bettex, *The Discovery of the World* (1960) and J. A. Grenville and G. J. Fuller, *The Coming of the Europeans: A History of European Discovery and Settlement, 1415–1775* (1962) are other good general accounts. For the first period and its influence upon the general development of Europe, see Charles A. Jullien, *Les Voyages de découverte et les premiers établissements (XVᵉ–XVIᵉ siècles)* (1948); *Boies Penrose, *Travel and Discovery in the Renaissance, 1420–1620* (1952) (Atheneum); and *John H. Parry, *The Age of Reconnaissance* (1963) (Mentor). Also, *Charles E. Nowell, *The Great Discoveries and the First Colonial Empires* (1954) (Cornell). A first-rate book on Columbus himself is S. E. Morison, *Admiral of the Ocean Sea* (1942).

Italy   Excellent general works on medieval Italian history have been written by G. Volpe, *Medio Evo Italiano* (1961) and F. Cognasso, *L'Italia nel Rinascimento* (1965); Jean Luchaire, *Les Sociétés italiennes du XIIIᵉ au XVᵉ siècle* (1954) is a sound interpretation of Italian history by one of the most serious French historians. See also Valeri Nino, *L'Italia nell'eta dei principati, dal 1343 al 1516* (1949) and Lacy Collison-Morley, *The Story of the Sforzas* (1934).

Will Durant, *The Renaissance: A History of Civilization in Italy from 1304 to 1576* (1953) and *Federico Chabod, *Machiavelli and the Renaissance* (1960) (Harper Torchbook) are lively surveys of Italian society during the late Middle Ages and the Renaissance. *Studies in Italian Medieval History,* Philip Grierson and J. B. Ward-Perkins, eds., (1957) also deserves examination.

On diplomatic history see Ramolo Quazza, *Preponderanza spagnuola, 1559–1700* (1950) and *Garrett Mattingly, *Renaissance Diplomacy* (1955) (Penguin).

Two excellent studies of local societies are David J. Herlihy, *Pisa in the Early Renaissance* (1958) and Lauro Martines, *The Social World of the Florentine Humanists* (1963).

Humanism   There are many good books on humanism. There are useful general surveys in *Renaissance Culture: A New Sense of Order,* Julian Mates and Eugene Cantelupe, eds. (1966); *Frederick B. Artz, *Renaissance Humanism 1300–1550* (1966) (Kent State); André Chastel, *The Age of Humanism: Europe, 1480–1530* (1963); and *Myron P. Gilmore, *The World of Humanism, 1453– 1517* (1952) (Harper Torchbook). *Paul O. Kristeller's *Renaissance Thought: The Classic, Scholastic, and Humanistic Strains* (1961) (Harper Torchbook) is one of the best interpretations of Renaissance intellectual life. For Italy in particular, most interesting are Eugenio Garin, *Italian Humanism: Philosophy and Civic Life in the Renaissance* (1966); Roberto Weiss, *The Spread of Italian Humanism* (1964) and the classic work of *Hans Baron, especially his *Crisis of the Early Italian Renaissance,* 2 vols. (1955) (Princeton) and also "Secularization of Wisdom and Political Humanism in the Renaissance," *Journal of the History of Ideas* XXI (1960). The characteristic traits of French humanism (as well as its late blooming) stand out in Augustin Renaudet, *Préréforme et humanisme à Paris pendant les premières guerres d'Italie* (1916); those of German humanism are discussed in Lewis W. Spitz, *The Religious Renaissance of the German Humanists* (1963). For the influence of humanism outside Western Europe, the best account is J. Irmsher, *Renaissance und Humanismus in Mittel und Osteuropa* (1962).

Apart from these general interpretations, many books deal with more specific aspects. Concerning the role of antiquity in the appearance and development of Renaissance and humanism, interesting points of view are found in *Robert R. Bolgar, *The Classical Heritage and Its Beneficiaries: From the Carolingian Age to the End of the Renaissance* (1954) (Harper Torchbook) and *Gilbert Highet, *The Classical Tradition: Greek and Roman Influences on Western Literature* (1949) (Oxford). A good philosophical interpretation of Renaissance mentality is *The Renaissance Image of Man and the World* (1968), edited by Bernard O'Kelly; while the best account of political ideas is still John W. Allen, *Political Thought in the Sixteenth Century,* 3rd ed. (1958) (Barnes & Noble).

There is a huge number of biographies of Renaissance thinkers and humanists. A good essay, dealing also with the medieval background of their thought, is *Paul O. Kristeller, *Eight Philosophers of the Italian Renaissance* (1964) (Stanford). Morris G. Bishop, *Petrarch and His World* (1964); A. Renaudet, *Machiavel* (1954); Felix Gilbert, *Machiavelli and Guicciardini: Politics and History in Sixteenth Century Florence* (1965); Friedrich Meinecke, *Machiavellism: The Doctrine of Raison d'Etat and Its Place in Modern History* (1957) go beyond the men themselves, to trace the fate and influence of their work and ideas. For Erasmus, the best portraits are in *Johan Huizinga, *Erasmus* (Harper Torchbook), written in 1924 and translated over a quarter of a century later, and *Margaret M. Phillips, *Erasmus and the Northern Renaissance* (1950) (Collier), but a good general interpretation can still be found in Preserved Smith, *Erasmus: A Study of his Life, Ideals, and Place in History* (1923). A particular aspect of his intellectual activities is treated in A. Renaudet, *Erasme et l'Italie* (1954). *Jack H. Hexter, *More's Utopia: The Biography of an Idea* (1952) (Harper Torchbook) is the best account of the life and thought of the great English humanist. See also *Raymond W. Chambers, *Thomas More* (1958) (Michigan) and, above all, More's own *Utopia* (especially in 1955 revised Everyman Edition).

The history of education has received relatively little attention. But see *William H. Woodward, *Studies in Education During the Age of the Renaissance, 1400–1600* (1906) (Teachers College) and *Vittorino da Feltre and Other Humanist Educators* (1905) (Teachers College), as well as Asztrik L. Gabriel, *Student Life in Ave Maria College, Medieval Paris* (1955).

Renaissance Science   For a general introduction see *Herbert Butterfield, *The Origins of Modern Science, 1300–1800,* rev. ed. (1962) (Free Press); Marie Boas,

The Scientific Renaissance 1450–1630 (1962); *Alistair C. Crombie, *Medieval and Early Modern Science,* 2nd rev. ed., 2 vols. (1959) (Anchor) and *Augustine to Galileo: The History of Science* (1952); and Kingston Derry and Trevor I. Williams, *A Short History of Technology* (1961). The social transformations wrought by the development of science and technology are emphasized by *Lynn White, Jr., *Medieval Technology and Social Change* (1962) (Oxford). For the period of the Renaissance itself, most interesting are Bertrand Gille, *The Renaissance Engineers* (1966); William P. D. Wightman, *Science and the Renaissance* (1962); *Thomas S. Kuhn, *The Copernican Revolution* (1957) (Vintage) and U. Forti, *Storia della technica dal Medioevio al Rinascimento* (1957). *George Sarton, *Six Wings: Men of Science in the Renaissance* (1957) (Meridian) and V. P. Zuboo, *Leonardo da Vinci* (1968) provide more biographical details. More encompassing is *A History of Technology* (edited by Charles J. Singer, Alfred R. Hall, Trevor I. Williams), Vol. I (1954).

Renaissance Art   One of the better general accounts is Frederick B. Artz, *From the Renaissance to Romanticism: Trends in Style in Art, Literature, and Music, 1300–1830* (1962) (Phoenix). A suggestive discussion of the philosophical meaning of Renaissance art is A. Tenenti's *La Vie et la mort à travers l'art du XVIe siècle* (1952). Rudolf Wittkover, *Architectural Principles in the Age of Humanism,* 3rd ed. (1962) links architectural and philosophical ideas; while Frederick Antal's *Florentine Painting and Its Social Background* (1948) attempts to link the evolution of artistic and social life, the attitudes of artists and patrons. André Chastel, *The Golden Age of the Renaissance, Italy 1460–1500* (1965); *Bernard Berenson, *The Italian Painters of the Renaissance* (1959) (Meridian; Praeger); and *Mary McCarthy, *The Stones of Florence* (1959) (Harcourt, Brace & World) are suggested for Italian art. James Lees-Milne has treated the North in *The Tudor Renaissance* (1951). For music one can refer to *Alec Harman's *Medieval and Early Renaissance Music* (1958) (Schoken) or to Gustave Reese's scholarly *Music in the Renaissance,* rev. ed. (1959).

New Capitalism   Some relevant works have already been indicated in the section regarding the economy; somewhat dated, Henri E. Sée, *Modern Capitalism: Its Origins and Evolution,* 2nd ed. (1931) provides useful supplementary reading. Benjamin N. Nelson, *The Idea of Usury* (1949) discusses the ideological and sociological roots of the prohibition of usury. For the controversial problem of the role of Protestantism in the rise of capitalism, see *Max Weber's seminal discussion, *The Protestant Ethic and the Spirit of Capitalism* (1930) (Scribner); *R. H. Tawney, *Religion and the Rise of Capitalism* (1926) (Mentor); and H. Barge, *Luther und der Fruhkapitalismus* (1951). Developments in northern Europe may be approached through *Violet Barbour, *Capitalism in Amsterdam in the Seventeenth Century* (1950) (Michigan).

Printers and Books   One of the best introductions to the history of printing presses and books is Lucien Febvre and H. J. Martin, *L'Apparition du livre* (1958), which covers the fifteenth and sixteenth centuries. For the same period see George P. Winship, *Printing in the Fifteenth Century* (1940). There are many works on Gutenberg; among the older: Otto W. Fuhrman, *The 500th Anniversary of the Invention of Printing* (1937); Douglas C. McMurtrie and Don Farran, *Wings for Words: The Story of Johann Gutenberg and His Invention of Printing* (1940); and D. C. McMurtrie, *The Invention of Printing* (1942). For more recent interpretations, emphasizing the social and economic aspects of the invention of the press, see J. Guignard, *Gutenberg et son oeuvre* (1960) and Victor Scholdered, *Johann Gutenberg, the Inventor of Printing* (1964). An excellent account of the history of the book during the Renaissance is Ernst P. Goldschmidt, *The Printed Book of the Renaissance* (1950).

Northern Renaissance One of the best short general surveys of the Renaissance outside Italy is *Margaret M. Phillips, *Erasmus and the Northern Renaissance* (1950) (Collier). For France, the outstanding work is Georges Duby and Robert Mandrou, *A History of French Civilization* (1964), the first volume analyzing the Middle Ages, the second running from the seventeenth century to the present. Jean Babelon, *La Civilisation française de la Renaissance* is also suggested. Older but still useful are the studies of Arthur A. Tilley, *The Dawn of the French Renaissance* (1918) and *Studies in the French Renaissance* (1922). *Emile Mâle, *Religious Art from the Twelfth to the Eighteenth Century* (1949) (Farrar, Straus & Giroux) and Anthony Blunt, *Art and Architecture in France, 1500–1700* (1957) should be consulted for the history of French art.

For Germany, F. Leitschuh, *Studien und Quellen zur deutschen Kunstgeschichte des XV–XVI Jahrhunderts* (1912) is still useful. German art can be approached through studies of Dürer's life and works, such as Richard F. Heath, *Albrecht Dürer, 1471–1528* (1929); *Wili Kurth, ed., *The Complete Woodcuts of Albrecht Dürer* (1946) (Dover); or Walter Conway, *Writings of A. Dürer* (1958). Essential, however, is Erwin Panofsky, *The Life and Art of Albrecht Dürer* (1955).

Among the great number of studies regarding English cultural achievements during the Renaissance, the most useful would be William Johnstone, *Creative Art in Britain: From the Earliest Times to the Present* (1950) and Mary D. Anderson, *Drama and Imagery in English Medieval Churches* (1964). Otto Pächt, *The Rise of Pictorial Narrative in Twelfth-Century England* (1962) is an excellent survey of the origins of modern English art.

For Spain, Oskar F. L. Hagen, *Patterns and Principles of Spanish Art* (1936) and George Kubler and Martin Soria, *Art and Architecture in Spain and Portugal and Their American Dominions, 1500 to 1800* (1959) are suggested.

France Robert Mandrou, *Introduction à la France moderne. Essai de psychologie historique, 1500–1640* (1961) is strongly recommended. Franklin C. Palm, *The Establishment of French Absolutism, 1574–1610* (1928); Pierre Champion, *Louis XI* (1929); Charles Terrasse, *François Ier, le roi et le règne* (1945); and *John E. Neale, *The Age of Catherine de Medici* (1963) (Harper Torchbook) are important for understanding the process of centralization and the establishment of the political structures of modern France. For the social and political unrest of the sixteenth century and the outbreak of the religious wars, see Franklin C. Palm, *Calvinism and the Religious Wars* (1932); A. Lévis-Mirepoix, *Les Guerres de religion* (1950); and Robert M. Kingdon, *Geneva and the Coming of the Wars of Religion in France, 1555–1563* (1956). For the general European background of the religious wars and the involvement of England and Spain, see J. H. M. Salmon, *The French Religious Wars in English Political Thought* (1959); J. W. Thompson, *The Wars of Religion in France, 1559–1576: The Huguenots, Catherine de Medici, Philip II* (1958); and *Garrett Mattingly's beautiful and lucid *Catherine of Aragon* (1941) (Vintage).

England Economic and social history should be approached in the works already mentioned in connection with economic and social history. For more specific interpretations, see *G. M. Trevelyan, *English Social History from Chaucer to Queen Victoria* (1944) (McKay) and *Geoffrey Baskerville, *English Monks and the Suppression of the Monasteries* (1937) (Hillary). *S. T. Bindoff, *Tudor England* (1952) (Penguin) is an excellent survey. More details are to be found in John D. Mackie, *The Earlier Tudors, 1485–1558* (1952) and *Conyers Read, *The Tudors: Personalities and Practical Politics in the 16th Century* (1936) (Norton). For the reign of Henry VIII, see *Albert F. Pollard, *Henry VIII* (1905) (Harper Torchbook) and *Francis Hackett, *Henry the Eighth* (1929) (Liveright). For Elizabeth's life and reign, *John E. Neale, *Queen Elizabeth* (1934) (Anchor); A. L. Rowse and G. B. Harrison, *Queen Elizabeth and her*

Subjects (1935); and A. L. Rowse, *The England of Elizabeth: The Structure of Society* (1951) (Macmillan) are the best accounts. *Geoffrey R. Elton, *The Tudor Revolution in Government* (1953) (Cambridge) analyzes some interesting institutional aspects. *Raymond W. Chambers, *Thomas More* (1958) (Michigan) is not only the description of the life and ideas of the great English humanist but also an excellent description of English society.

Spain   For the rise of Spain and the unification of the country, J. Calmette, *La Formation de l'unité espagnole* (1946) and Jean H. Mariéjol, *The Spain of Ferdinand and Isabella* (1961) are the best introductions. *J. H. Elliott, *Imperial Spain, 1469–1716* (1964) (Mentor); *R. Trevor Davies, *The Golden Century of Spain, 1501–1621* (1958) (Harper Torchbook); and Bohdan Chudoba, *Spain and the Empire, 1519–1643* (1952) are suggested for the period of Spanish hegemony in Europe. The problems of the colonial empire are discussed by John H. Parrry, *The Spanish Seaborne Empire* (1966). Interesting interpretations and more details about the period of Philip II will be found in M. Devèze, *L'Espagne et l'empire espagnol sous Philippe II*, 2 vols. (1965). A good general introduction to the problems of Spanish society during the sixteenth century is A. M. Fernandez, *Economia, sociedad y corona* (1963). An earlier period is treated in *Spanish Life in the Late Middle Ages* (edited by Kenneth R. Scholberg, 1966). For the history of the Inquisition see *Cecil Roth, *The Spanish Inquisition* (1954) (Norton); for the peninsula's agricultural history Julius Klein, *The Mesta* (1920); and for the great enterprise of Philip II see *Garrett Mattingly, *Armáda* (1959) (Sentry).

The Germanies   Paul Frischauer, *Imperial Crown: The Story of the Rise and Fall of the Holy Roman and the Austrian Empires* (1939) is an excellent general survey. So is Hajo Holborn, *A History of Modern Germany*, vol. I: *The Reformation* (1964). The reign of Charles V could be approached through *Karl Brandi, *The Emperor Charles V* (1939) (Humanities). A lively description of a great late-medieval city appears in *Gerald Strauss, *Nuremberg in the Sixteenth Century* (1966) (Wiley).

The Turks   Roger B. Merriman, *Suleiman the Magnificent, 1520–1566* (1944); Sydney N. Fisher, *The Foreign Relations of Turkey, 1481–1542* (1948); A. Tambora, *Gli stati italiani, l'Europa e il problema turco dopo Lepante* (1961); and the brief account by Paul Wittek, *The Rise of the Ottoman Empire* (1958) are excellent introductions to the beginnings of the Eastern Question. A serious work of institutional history is W. E. D. Allen, *Problems of Turkish Power in the 16th Century* (1963). For the Balkans see Nicholae Iorga, *Histoire des états balkaniques* (1924) and Leften S. Stavrianos, *The Balkans since 1453* (1958).

Mercantilism   For an excellent introduction, see Eli F. Heckscher, *Mercantilism*, 2 vols. (1956); for a very brief but clear survey, Charles Wilson, *Mercantilism* (1958) and John W. Horrocks, *A Short History of Mercantilism* (1925). Laurence B. Packard, *The Commercial Revolution, 1400–1776* (1927) and E. Silberner, *La Guerre dans la pensée économique du 16ᵉ au 18ᵉ siècle* (1939) have a more general character.

Religion in the Fifteenth and Sixteenth Centuries   For general accounts of European history during the Reformation, see G. R. Elton, *Reformation Europe, 1517–1559* (1964), concise and clear; S. Harrison Thomson, *Europe in Renaissance and Reformation* (1963) and A. G. Dickens, *Reformation and Society in Sixteenth Century Europe* (1966) (Harcourt, Brace & World), brief, up-to-date, and beautifully illustrated. A good short survey is *George Morse, *The Reformation*, rev. ed. (1963).

As for the humanistic aspects of reform, *E. Harris Harbison, *The Christian Scholar in the Age of the Reformation* (1956) (Scribner) provides the soundest introduction; William E. Campbell, *Erasmus, Tyndale and More* (1949) and M. Gershat, *Melachton neben Luther* (1965) are important for understanding the mentality of some of the most important humanists.

The following works are also suggested: Jan Herben, *Huss and His Followers* (1926): Harold J. Grimm, *The Reformation Era, 1500–1650* (1965); J. Delumeau, *Naissance et affirmation de la Réforme* (1965); *Owen Chadwick, *The Reformation* (1964) (Penguin); *H. Daniel-Rops, *The Protestant Reformation* (1961) (Image); *Roland H. Bainton, *The Reformation of the Sixteenth Century* (1963) (Beacon); *Norman Sykes, *The Crisis of the Reformation* (1967) (Norton); and (liveliest and most readable) Vivian H. H. Green, *Renaissance and Reformation* (1952). Differing interpretations of social and economic aspects are presented by *Lewis W. Spitz, *The Reformation: Material or Spiritual?* (1962) (Heath) and *Kyle C. Sessions, ed., *Reformation and Authority: The Meaning of the Peasant's Revolt* (1968) (Heath). An intriguing approach may be found in Guy E. Swanson, *Religion and Regime: A Sociological Account of the Reformation* (1967). *Norman R. C. Cohn, *The Pursuit of the Millennium: A History of Popular Religious and Social Movements from the 11th to the 16th Century* (1957) (Harper Torchbook) should not be missed, any more than the seminal writings of Lucien Febvre, particularly his essays collected in *Au Coeur religieux du XVIe siècle* (1951) and his great work, *Le problème de l'incroyance au XVIe siècle: La Religion de Rabelais* (1941).

The English Reformation can be approached through *A. G. Dickens, *The English Reformation* (1964) (Schocken) and *Frederick M. Powicke, *The Reformation in England* (1941) (Oxford). For the beginning of the movement see William A. Clebsch, *England's Earliest Protestants, 1520–1535* (1964) and, better still, Kenneth B. McFarlane, *John Wycliffe and the Beginnings of English Nonconformity* (1952). An excellent account, especially for the reign of Henry VIII, is *Ernest G. Rupp, *Studies in the Making of the English Protestant Tradition* (1948) (Cambridge).

Luther General histories of the Reformation aside, the life and ideas of its founder can be approached through more detailed works, most of them biographies. Among the most recent: John M. Todd, *Martin Luther: A Biographical Study* (1964); *Vivian H. H. Green, *Luther and the Reformation* (1964) (Capricorn); James Mackinnon, *Luther and the Reformation* (1962); Ernest G. Schwiebert, *Luther and His Times* (1950); and *Roland H. Bainton, *Here I Stand: A Life of Martin Luther* (1950) (Apex; Mentor). The best concise treatment is still Lucien Febvre, *Martin Luther: A Destiny* (1930). For a less classical interpretation see *Erik H. Erikson, *Young Man Luther: A Study in Psychoanalysis and History* (1958) (Norton).

Calvin *John T. McNeill, *The History and Character of Calvinism* (1954) (Oxford) is an excellent general survey, while *E. W. Monter, *Calvin's Geneva* (1961) (Wiley) concerns itself less with the creed than with its incidence in a specific community. Among the huge number of biographies, the following are useful: Kilian McDonnell, *John Calvin, the Church, and the Eucharist* (1967); Gervase E. Duffield, ed., *John Calvin* (1966); and Jean Cadier, *The Man God Mastered: A Brief Biography of John Calvin* (1961). See also *André Bieler, *The Social Humanism of Calvin* (1964) (John Knox) and W. Walker, *John Calvin* (1906), not yet superseded by more recent works.

The Catholic Reformation Many aspects of the Counter-Reformation are discussed in the works regarding the Reformation and its leaders. For a more detailed interpretation one may consult L. Willaert, *Après le concile de Trente: la restauration catholique, 1563–1648* (1960); Pierre Janelle, *The Catholic Reformation* (1963); *Edward M. Burns, *The Counter Reformation* (1964); and, best of all, *A. G. Dickens, *The Counter Reformation* (1969).

PART II

Early Modern Europe

Fernand Braudel's *Civilisation matérielle et capitalisme, XVᵉ–XVIIIᵉ siècles*, Vol. I (1967) and *La Méditerranée et le monde méditerranéen à l'époque de Philippe II*, rev. ed. (1966), and Pierre Chaunu's *La Civilisation de l'Europe classique* (1967) are among the outstanding introductions to modern European history. One of the foremost examples of a more traditional approach, with all its virtues, is in Roland Mousnier, *Les XVIᵉ et XVIIᵉ siècles* (1965). An excellent work, *Europe in the Sixteenth Century* (1968) is by H. G. Koenigsberger and G. L. Mosse. Less profound but still useful are *George N. Clark, *The Seventeenth Century* (1929) (Oxford); Leonard W. Cowie, *Seventeenth-Century Europe* (1960); and David Maland, *Europe in the Seventeenth Century* (1966). For a briefer survey, see *Richard S. Dunn, *The Age of Religious Wars, 1559–1689* (1970) (Norton).

Society in the Sixteenth and Seventeenth Centuries There has been a great deal of argument around the theme of class consciousness and class struggle in the early modern period. In *Narodnie Vostaniie Vo Francii, 1623–1648* (1948), Boris Porchnev claims to find it in rural as well as urban France. His work, available in German and French translations, has been answered, among others, by Robert Mandrou in *Classes et luttes de classes en France au début du XVIIᵉ siècle* (1965) and by Roland Mousnier in *Fureurs paysannes* (1967). This topic may be pursued by consulting works like Gaston Roupnel's influential *La Ville et la campagne au XVIIᵉ siècle* (1922), republished in 1956, or Mary Purcell's *The World of Monsieur Vincent* (1963). Two great works of recent date have thrown new light on the life of ordinary men: J. LeRoy-Ladurie, *Paysans du Languedoc*, 2 vols. (1967), a masterpiece on all aspects of peasant life in southwestern France from the fifteenth to the eighteenth century, and Pierre Goubert, *Beauvais et le Beauvaisis de 1600 à 1730* (1958), a pioneer and detailed study of life in all its aspects in a region of northwestern France. Before adults, and illuminating their ways, there come children: *Philippe Ariès, *Centuries of Childhood: A Social History of Family Life* (1962) (Vintage) tells the story of changing attitudes toward them. For other aspects of society and life, see Robert Baldick, *The Duel* (1965); Louis B. Wright, *Middle Class Culture in Elizabethan England* (1935); H. R. Trevor-Roper, **European Witch-Craze of the Sixteenth and Seventeenth Centuries and Other Essays* (1969) (Harper Torchbook); and Alan Macfarlane, *Witchcraft in Tudor and Stuart England* (1970).

The King See John N. Figgis, *The Divine Right of Kings* (1922); Francis D. Wormuth, *The Royal Prerogative, 1603–1649: A Study in English Political and Constitutional Ideas* (1939); E. Stehleder, *Absolutismus und Aufklärung, 1648–1789* (1964); *Max Beloff, *The Age of Absolutism, 1660–1815* (1954) (Harper Torchbook).

The Reformed Church and the Counter-Reformation See H. Daniel-Rops, *The Church in the Seventeenth Century* (1963), followed by his *The Church in* *the Eighteenth Century* (1964)—both are excellent general accounts. Straightforward and readable: *Gerald R. Cragg, *The Church and the Age of Reason, 1648–1789* (1960) (Penguin); K. Eder, *Die Geschichte der Kirche im Zeitalter des konfessionallen Absolutismus, 1555–1648* (1949); and Pierre Janelle, *The Catholic Reformation* (1949). For the Jesuits, see Paul Dudson's biography, *St. Ignatius of Loyola* (1949), *James Brodrick, *Origins of the Jesuits* (1940) (Longmans) by a Catholic; and Heinrich Boehmer, *The Jesuits* (1928) by a Protestant. For developments inside the Protestant Church see *Robert W. Green, ed., *Protestantism and Capitalism: The Weber Thesis and Its Critics* (1959) (Heath) and H. R. Trevor-Roper, "Religion, Reformation and Social Change," in *Historical Studies,* IV, 1963.

The Struggles for Empire

See W. J. James, *Habsburg and Bourbon, 1494–1789* (1955) for an excellent description of the diplomatic and military struggle between France and Austria, and of its impact upon European history. *Garrett Mattingly's *Armada* (1959) (Sentry) combines good history and good reading. *Trevor H. Aston, ed., *Crisis in Europe* (1965) (Anchor) and G. C. Argan, *L'Europe des capitales* (1964) are also suggested. The Thirty Years' War should be approached mainly through *C. V. Wedgwood's *The Thirty Years War* (1938) (Anchor) or the more recent *S. H. Steinberg, *The Thirty Years' War* (1967) (Norton). For a readable biography of one of its major figures see Francis Watson, *Wallenstein* (1938); for living detail see Hans Jakob Grimmelshausen, *Simplicissimus* (1669). The period of French hegemony has been treated by M. Moorman, *William III and the Defence of Holland* 1930); A. Saint-Léger, *La Prépondérance française: Louis XIV* (1935); and Louis André, *Louis XIV et l'Europe* (1950).

The impact of wars upon economic and social life are discussed by several excellent historians, among them, Earl J. Hamilton, *War and Prices in Spain, 1651–1800* (1947); F. Redlich, *De Praeda Militari: Looting and Booty, 1500–1815* (1956); Charles W. C. Oman, *A History of the Art of War in the Sixteenth Century* (1937); and Herbert W. Richmond, *The Navy as an Instrument of Policy, 1558–1727* (1953).

Italy   Henry B. Cotterill's *Italy from Dante to Tasso, 1300–1600* (1919) is still a good general introductory work; see also Lacy Collison-Morley, *Italy after the Renaissance: Decadence and Display in the Seventeenth Century* (1931). Incredibly detailed and a monument of scholarship is J. Delumeau, *Vie économique et sociale à Rome dans la seconde moitié du 16e siècle* (1957). For the period of Spanish domination see F. Nicolini, *Aspetti della vita italo-spagnuola nel cinque e seicento* (1934), and R. Quazza, *Preponderanza spagnuola, 1559–1700* (1950). Good descriptions of contemporary life and customs may be culled from Wilfrid Blunt, *Sebastiano, the Adventures of an Italian Priest* (1956), the account of the journey of a young Italian priest from Bologna to Rome and back in 1664–1665.

Spain   Some of the basic works regarding Spanish history during the sixteenth century have been mentioned in the bibliography of Part I: *J. H. Elliott, *Imperial Spain, 1469–1716* (1964) (Mentor); *R. Trevor Davies, *The Golden Century of Spain, 1501–1621* (1937) (Harper Torchbook); Bohdan Chudoba, *Spain and the Empire, 1519–1643* (1952). One may add John Lynch, *Spain under the Habsburgs* (1964). The problems of Spanish decadence are discussed in R. Trevor Davies, *Spain in Decline, 1621–1700* (1957) (St. Martin's) and in J. H. Elliott's splendid dissertation *The Revolt of the Catalans: A Study in the Decline of Spain (1598–1640)* (1963). Cecil J. Cadoux, *Philip of Spain and the Nether-*

lands (1947), and H. G. Koenigsberger, *The Government of Sicily under Philip II of Spain* (1952) help one to understand the relationships of Spain with her European possessions. A very good description of Spanish life and society is M. Defourneaux, *La Vie quotidienne en Espagne au siècle d'or* (1964).

The Netherlands   Pieter Geyl's books are the best accounts of the Netherlands' history during the sixteenth to seventeenth centuries; see especially, **The Revolt of the Netherlands, 1555–1609* (1962) (Barnes & Noble) and *The Netherlands in the Seventeenth Century,* 2 vols. (1961–1964). George Masselman, *The Cradle of Colonialism* (1963) and Charles R. Boxer, *The Dutch Seaborne Empire, 1600–1800* (1965) outline the problems and achievements of Dutch colonial expansionism. More details regarding the very important seventeenth century are found in Ernst H. Kossmann, *In Praise of the Dutch Republic: Some 17th Century Attitudes* (1963) and *Violet Barbour, *Capitalism in Amsterdam in the Seventeenth Century* (1959) (Michigan). For the biography of one outstanding political figure see *C. V. Wedgwood, *William the Silent* (1944) (Norton). P. Zumthor, *La Vie quotidienne en Hollande au temps de Rembrandt* (1959)], Jakob Rosenberg, *Rembrandt* (2 vols. 1948), and J. J. M. Timmers, *A History of Dutch Life and Art* (1959) are also suggested.

France   There are several important problems regarding French history in early modern times. A good approach for institutional history is to be found in Franklin C. Palm, *The Establishment of French Absolutism, 1574–1610* (1928). The reign of Henry IV can be examined through M. Andrieux, *Henri IV dans ses années pacifiques* (1954) and M. Reinhard, *Henri IV ou la France sauvée* (1943). Excellent is Roland Mousnier, *L'Assassinat d'Henri IV* (1964). More intimate and intellectual aspects of the same period are touched on in Samuel Putnam, *Marguerite of Navarre* (1935) and *John E. Neale, *The Age of Catherine de Medici* (1944) (Harper Torchbook). V. Tapié, *La France de Louis XIII et de Richelieu* (1967) is the best description of the problems facing the monarchy of the Bourbons during the first half of the seventeenth century. For the life and activity of one of the most outstanding French politicians of that time see Orest A. Ranum, *Richelieu and the Councillors of Louis XIII* (1963) and *Carl Jacob Burckhardt, *Richelieu: His Rise to Power,* rev. ed. (1964) (Vintage). The social and political unrest of French society, especially the nobility, is reflected in Paul R. Doolin, *The Fronde* (1935) and Ernst H. Kossmann, *La Fronde* (1954).

For French history during the long reign of Louis XIV, one of the most readable works is still Pierre Gaxotte, *La France de Louis XIV* (1946), written from a royalist point of view. Sounder are Pierre Goubert, *Louis XIV et vingt millions de français* (1967); *Maurice P. Ashley, *Louis XIV and the Greatness of France* (1948) (Free Press); *Laurence B. Packard, *The Age of Louis Fourteenth* (1938) (Holt, Rinehart & Winston); *John B. Wolf, *Louis XIV* (1968) (Norton). Louis André's *Louis XIV et l'Europe* (1950), already cited, is excellent for the problems of foreign policy. Internal policy is extensively discussed by J. Saint-Germain, *Les Financiers sous Louis XIV* (1950); *Lionel Rothkrug, *Opposition to Louis XIV: The Political and Social Origins of the French Enlightenment* (1965) (Princeton); Warren C. Scoville, *The Persecution of the Huguenots and French Economic Development, 1680–1720* (1960); and Eleanor C. Lodge, *Sully, Colbert and Turgot: A Chapter in French Economic History* (1930). One of the greatest scandals and at the same time one of the crucial issues of Louis XIV's early reign is treated by Georges Mongrédien, *L'Affaire Foucquet* (1956). The well-known collection of La Vie quotidienne has published several interesting works on everyday life in France during the early modern times: Philippe Erlanger, *La vie quotidienne sous Henri IV* (1958); Emile Magne, *La vie quotidienne au temps de Louis XIII* (1942); and Georges

Mongrédien, *La vie quotidienne sous Louis XIV* (1948) are the most reliable. See also A. J. Grant, *The Huguenots* (1934) and S. L. England, *The Massacre of St. Bartholomew* (1938).

England H. R. Trevor-Roper's *The Gentry, 1540–1640* (1953) is brilliant social history, useful for the understanding of various aspects of English society at the beginning of its modern development. It is well to read this in conjunction with J. H. Hexter's incisive "Storm over the Gentry," in *Encounter,* May, 1958. For a good general account see D. P. Adams, *Tudors and Stuarts, 1485–1714* (1962) and *John S. Millward, *The Sixteenth Century* (1961) (Fernhill). There are more details regarding Tudor times in G. R. Elton, *England under the Tudors* (1960); John B. Black, *The Reign of Elizabeth, 1558–1603* (1936); Godfrey Davies, *The Early Stuarts 1603–1660* (1937); and George N. Clark, *The Later Stuarts, 1600–1714* (1934). But the greatest contribution to the history of seventeenth-century England has been *Lawrence Stone's monumental *Crisis of the Aristocracy, 1558–1641* (1965) (Oxford). The half-century preceding the English revolution could be approached through *Maurice P. Ashley, *England in the Seventeenth Century* (1960) (Penguin) and Sidney R. Brett, *The Stuart Century: 1603–1714* (1961). *G. P. V. Akrigg, *Jacobean Pageant: Or, The Court of King James I* (1962) (Atheneum) and Eric Linklater, *Ben Jonson and King James* (1931) sketch in the background. Gerald E. Aylmer, *The Struggle for Constitution, 1603–1689: England in the 17th Century* (1963) is more interested in the institutional aspects of politics. For comparative history see *J. R. Jones, *Britain and Europe in the Seventeenth Century* (1966) (Norton). The important period of English revolution should be approached first through the excellent works of C. V. Wedgwood: *The King's Peace, 1637–1641* (1955) (Collier), *The King's War 1641–1647* (1959), and *Oliver Cromwell* (1956). See *Christopher Hill, *The Century of Revolution, 1603–1714* (1967) (Norton). For the early stages of the rebellion, the best book is J. H. Hexter's brilliant *Reign of King Pym* (1941). Although old, John Morley's *O. Cromwell* (1900) and G. M. Young's *Charles I and Cromwell* (1935) are still useful. More recent are two books by Maurice P. Ashley: *Cromwell's Generals* (1955) and *The Greatness of Oliver Cromwell* (1958) (Collier). For the reign of Charles II and the "Glorious Revolution," see Arthur Bryant, *King Charles II* (1949) and more especially *G. M. Trevelyan's *The English Revolution, 1688–1689* (1939) (Oxford), but also Arthur Bryant, *Samuel Pepys,* 3 vols. (1939–1944), based on one of the liveliest diaries in English—see *The Diary of Samuel Pepys,* edited by R. Latham and W. Matthews, vols. 1–3 (1970). For other aspects of English life, see James E. Gillespie, *The Influence of Oversea Expansion on England to 1700* (1920); *Michael L. Walzer, *The Revolution of the Saints: A Study in the Origins of Radical Politics* (1965) (Atheneum); and *C. V. Wedgwood, *Poetry and Politics under the Stuarts* (1960) (Michigan).

The Baltic W. Reinhard's *Baltische Geschichte* (1954) provides a good introduction. Interesting points of view are expressed by Oscar Halecki, *Borderlands of Western Civilization* (1952). The best introduction to Polish history is Stanislaw Arnold and Marian Zychowski, *Outline History of Poland* (1962). *Oscar Halecki, *A History of Poland* (1966) (Regnery) is sound; William F. Reddaway, ed., *The Cambridge History of Poland* is also sound but dull. The first volume of the latter (1951) ends in 1696, while the second (1941) carries the story to 1935.

Scandinavian history is somewhat better served by Stanley M. Toyne, *The Scandinavians in History* (1948); Karen Larsen, *A History of Norway* (1948); Ingvar Andersson, *A History of Sweden* (1956) and Stewart Oakley, *Short History of Sweden* (1966). Above all, students may turn to a splendid biography which illuminates the crucial period of Swedish history: Michael Roberts, *Gustavus Adolphus: A History of Sweden, 1611–1632*, 2 vols. (1953–1958). The romantic life of Charles XII and the beginning of Swedish political setbacks are described by O. Haintz, *König Karl XII von Schweden* (1958) and Frans G. Bengtsson, *The Life of Charles XII, King of Sweden* (1960).

Russia   The best recent general history of Russia is Nicholas Riasanovsky's *History of Russia* (1963). Also recommended is *Bernard Pares, *History of Russia,* rev. ed. (1953); (1965) (Vintage). One of the best economic and social histories of the country is *Jerome Blum's *Lord and Peasant in Russia: From the 9th to the 19th Century* (1961) (Atheneum). The process of unification and the growth of Moscow appear in Stephen Graham, *Ivan the Terrible: Life of Ivan IV of Russia* (1933); Harold Lamb, *The March of Muscovy: Ivan the Terrible and the Growth of the Russian Empire, 1400–1648* (1948); and J. L. I. Fennell, *Ivan the Great of Moscow* (1962). For the beginning of the Romanov dynasty see William A. Gerhardi, *The Romanovs* (1939), and P. Pascal, *Avvakum et les débuts du Raskol: La crise religieuse du 17ᵉ siècle en Russie* (1938). Moving to a later period, Harold Lamb, *The City and the Tsar: Peter the Great and the Move to the West, 1648–1762* (1948); Constantin de Grunwald, *Peter the Great* (1956); and *B. H. Sumner, *Peter the Great and the Emergence of Russia* (1965) (Collier) describe the modernization of Russia and its emergence as a big power. For a readable and exciting interpretation of Russian culture: James H. Billington, *The Icon and the Axe* (1966).

The Ottoman Empire   For general accounts of Turkish history see Richard F. Peters, *The Story of the Turks from Empire to Democracy* (1959) and Stanley Lane-Poole, *Turkey* (1966). Some internal aspects are discussed by W. E. D. Allen, *Problems of Turkish Power in the 16th Century* (1963), while the foreign policy and the international relations of the empire are described in Dorothy M. Vaughan, *Europe and the Turk: A Pattern of Alliances, 1350–1700* (1954). For the peoples under Turkish domination, see R. W. Seton-Watson, *A History of the Roumanians* (1934); Nicholae Iorga, *A History of Roumania* (1926); Walter A. Heurtley, *A Short History of Greece* (1965); *Stephen Clissold, ed., *A Short History of Yugoslavia* (1966) (Cambridge); Mercia Macdermott, *A History of Bulgaria, 1393–1885* (1962); Charles and Barbara Jelavich, *The Balkans* (1965); and *Traian Stoianovich, *A Study in Balkan Civilization* (1967) (Knopf).

The Holy Roman Empire   Besides Hajo Holborn's new *History of Modern Germany* (1959), one can consult Gerhard Schilfert, *Deutschland von 1648 bis 1789* (1962). Of all German states, Prussia has received the most attention. See especially Francis L. Carsten, **The Origins of Prussia* (1954) (Oxford) and *Princes and Parliaments in Germany: From the 15th to the 18th Century* (1959); Hans Schoeps, *Preussen: Geschichte eines Staates* (1966); C. Edmund Maurice, *The Life of Frederick William, the Great Elector of Brandenburg* (1926) or— better—Ferdinand Schevill, *The Great Elector* (1947). Military and diplomatic history have been well served by *Gordon Craig, *Politics of the Prussian Army, 1640–1945* (1955) (Oxford), and—more immediate to this period—Nicholas Henderson, *Prince Eugen of Savoy* (1965) and Paul Frischauer, *Prince Eugene, 1663– 1736: A Man and a Hundred Years of History* (1934).

Early Modern Culture

*Paul Hazard, *The European Mind: The Critical Years (1680–1715)* (1953) (Meridian) is a splendid account of the change in intellectual mood which prepared Western Europe for "Enlightenment." Preserved Smith, *A History of Modern Culture, 1543–1776,* 2 vols. (1930–1934) (Collier) and John H. Randall,

The Making of the Modern Mind, rev. ed. (1940) are also good. *Frederick B. Artz, *From the Renaissance to Romanticism: Trends in Style in Art, Literature and Music, 1300–1830* (1962) (Phoenix) is a swift, convenient, inevitably superficial survey. *Basil Willey, *The Seventeenth Century Background* (1934) (Anchor) examines the thought of the age in relation to religion and poetry. John U. Nef, *Cultural Foundations of Industrial Civilization* (1958) is slender and thought-provoking. *Frederick L. Nussbaum, *The Triumph of Science and Reason, 1660–1685* (1953) (Harper Torchbook) provides some thoughtful chapters and handy bibliography. More recent, but also more extensive, Pierre Barrière, *La Vie intellectuelle en France du XVIe siècle à l'époque contemporaine* (1961) is excellent for reference, and Robert Mandrou, *De la Culture populaire aux 17e et 18e siècles* (1964) explores a little-known subject: the readings of the masses.

Language and Writing   A start can be made with any of the following: *Arthur S. Diamond, *The History and Origin of Language* (1959) (Citadel); J. Fevrier, *Histoire de l'écriture* (1959); and M. Aquirre, *La escritura en el mundo* (1961). For more details and more specific aspects of the period covered in this volume see Samuel A. Tannenbaum, *The Handwriting of the Renaissance* (1930); G. Harnois, *Les Théories du langage en France de 1660 à 1821* (1928); A. Pagliaro, *La dottrina linguistica di G. B. Vico* (1959); K. Apel, *Die Idee der Sprache in der Tradition des Humanismus von Dante bi Vico* (1963); and especially Merton W. Bloomfield and L. D. Newmark, *A Linguistic Introduction to the History of English* (1963).

Literature   Imbrie Buffum, *Studies in the Baroque from Montaigne to Rotrou* (1957) may serve as a general introduction. H. Candwell, *Introduction to French Classicism* (1951) and Jean-Jacques Demorest, ed., *Studies in Seventeenth-Century French Literature* (1962) should be used for French literature. For England, see Helen C. White, *Seventeenth-Century Verse and Prose,* 2 vols. (1951), and for an earlier period, E. M. W. Tillyard, *The Elizabethan World Picture* (1950), while *Basil Willey, *The Seventeenth Century Background* (1934) (Anchor) shows how science affected writers and thinkers. The golden age of Spanish culture can be approached through *Angel Flores, ed., *Masterpieces of the Spanish Golden Age* (1957) (Holt, Rinehart & Winston); González López, *Historia de la literatura española* (1962); and *Otis Green, *Spain and the Western Tradition: The Castilian Mind in Literature from El Cid to Calderón* (1963) (Wisconsin).

For Germany see Solomon Liptzin, *Historical Survey of German Literature* (1936); Archer Taylor, *Problems in German Literary History of the Fifteenth and Sixteenth Centuries* (1939); and the short but stimulating essay of Leonard W. Forster, *The Temper of Seventeenth Century German Literature* (1952).

Art   René Huyghe, ed., *L'Art et l'homme* (1961) is sound on facts and brilliant on general interpretation; for the centuries discussed in this part see the third volume. For general references see especially Eugenio D'Ors, *Du Baroque* (1935); Carl J. Friedrich, *The Age of the Baroque, 1610–1660* (1952); J. Pijoan y Soteras, *Arte barroco en Francia, Italia y Alemania, siglos XVII y XVIII* (1963); *Victor L. Tapié, *The Age of Grandeur: Baroque Art and Architecture* (1960) (Praeger). Marcel Reymond, *De Michel-Ange à Tiépolo* (1912), though old, is still useful. For regional studies see Rudolf Wittkover, *Art and Architecture in Italy, 1600–1750* (1958); Horst Gerson and E. H. Kuile, *Art and Architecture in Belgium, 1600 to 1800* (1960); and Eberhard Hempel, *Baroque Art and Architecture in Central Europe* (1965).

Very interesting: Emile Mâle's *L'Art religieux de la fin du 16e siècle, du 17e siècle et du 18e siècle* (1951) and Henri Lavedan's first volume of *L'Histoire de l'urbanisme* (1959). For the history of music see Manfred F. Bukofzer, *Music in the Baroque Era, from Monteverdi to Bach* (1947); *Edward J. Dent, *Opera*

(1949) (Penguin); Alec Robertson and D. W. Stevens, eds., *The Pelican History of Music*, Vol. II: *Renaissance and Baroque* (1964) (Penguin); and *Marc Pincherle, *Vivaldi: Genius of the Baroque* (1957) (Norton), a good biography of the great Venetian composer.

Science   There are many excellent works on this topic: Abraham Wolf et al., *A History of Science, Technology, and Philosophy in the 16th and 17th Centuries* (1935); *Alfred R. Hall, *The Scientific Revolution, 1500–1800* (1954) (Beacon); *Alistair C. Crombie, *Medieval and Early Modern Science,* 2nd rev. ed., 2 vols. (1959) (Anchor); *Herbert Butterfield, *The Origins of Modern Science, 1300–1800,* rev. ed. (1962) (Free Press); and the third volume of *A History of Technology,* edited by Alfred R. Hall and Trevor I. Williams (1957) are the most useful. A variety of points of view expressed on the occasion of an international conference at Royaumont in 1957 have been published in *La science au 16e siècle* (1960).

For more specific aspects, see George N. Clark, *Science and Social Welfare in the Age of Newton,* 2nd ed. (1949); Martha Ornstein, *The Role of Scientific Societies in the Seventeenth Century* (1938); and S. F. Mason; "The Scientific Revolution and the Protestant Reformation," in *Annals of Science,* Vol. 9, Nos. 1–2, 1953. The impact of science on literature is traced in *Margaret Nicolson, *Science and the Imagination* (1956). The foundation of the Royal Society and the atmosphere surrounding it are reflected in Dorothy Stimson, *Scientists and Amateurs* (1968) and in Robert K. Merton's scholarly *Science, Technology and Society in Seventeenth Century England* (1970). * Edwin A. Burtt, *Metaphysical Foundations of Modern Physical Science* (1925) (Anchor) discusses the scientific thinking of Copernicus, Galileo, Newton, and their contemporaries. In this context, three other works stand out: Charles C. Gillispie, *The Edge of Objectivity* (1960) traces scientific advances since Galileo; *George de Santillana, *The Crime of Galileo* (1955) (Phoenix); and *Arthur Koestler's more popular *The Sleepwalkers: A History of Man's Changing Vision of the Universe* (1959) (Grosset & Dunlap).

Philosophy   For the general background one may refer to *Jacob Bronowski and Bruce Mazlish, *The Western Intellectual Tradition: From Leonardo to Hegel* (1960) (Harper Torchbook); Etienne H. Gilson and Thomas D. Langan, *Modern Philosophy: Descartes to Kant* (1963); *Alexandre Koyré, *From the Closed World to the Infinite Universe* (1958) (Johns Hopkins); and *Stuart Hampshire, *The Age of Reason: The 17th Century Philosophers* (1956) (Mentor).

More specific works: Sydney H. Mellone, *The Dawn of Modern Thought: Descartes, Spinoza, Leibniz* (1930); *Richard H. Popkin, *The History of Scepticism from Erasmus to Descartes* (1961) (Harper Torchbook); James Iverach, *Descartes, Spinoza and the New Philosophy* (1904); *Stanley V. Keeling, *Descartes* (1934) (Oxford); Leon Roth, *Descartes: Discourse on Method* (1937); Albert Balz, *Descartes and the Modern Mind* (1952); Roger H. Soltau, *Pascal: The Man and the Message* (1927); Morris G. Bishop, *Pascal: The Life of Genius* (1936); and Harvey Robinson, *Bayle the Sceptic* (1931). Richard H. Popkin has also edited a volume of selections from *Pierre Bayle, *Historical and Critical Dictionary* (1966) (Bobbs-Merrill), with a splendid introduction and extensive bibliography.

Science and Religion   The following works are suggested: Richard S. Westfall, *Science and Religion in Seventeenth-Century England* (1958); Franklin L. Baumer, *Religion and the Rise of Scepticism* (1960); *John Dillenberger, *Protestant Thought and Natural Science* (1960) (Abingdon); Charles E. Raven, *Natural Religion and Christian Theology* (1953); very good, Paul R. Anderson's *Science in Defense of Liberal Religion: A Study of Henry More's Attempt to Link*

Seventeenth Century Religion with Science (1933). See also Frank S. Taylor, *Galileo and the Freedom of Thought* (1938).

Political Thought   See Pierre Mesnard, *L'Essor de la philosophie politique au XVI*^e *siècle* (1951); *John W. Allen, *A History of Political Thought in the Six-teenth Century* (1928) (Barnes & Noble), already cited; John N. Figgis, *Studies of Political Thought from Gerson to Grotius, 1414–1625* (1923); Bernice Hamil-ton, *Political Thought in Sixteenth-Century Spain: A Study of the Political Ideas of Vitoria, De Soto, Suárez and Molina* (1963); and Otto F. Gierke, *Natural Law and the Theory of Society, 1500 to 1800* (1934). More specifically, the best modern version of *John Hobbes's *Leviathan* is that edited by Michael Oakeshott (1966) (Collier), preceded by an excellent introduction. There is an equally good edition of John Locke's *Second Treatise of Civil Government* (1946) by John W. Gough, and a conveniently abridged edition of his *Essay Concerning Human Understanding* (1950) by A. S. Pringle-Pattison. Maurice Cranston has given us a reliable life of the philosopher: *John Locke: A Biography* (1957); Stuart Hampshire is equally good on *Spinoza* (1951). For Hobbes, however, two nineteenth-century lives still hold the field: by George C. Robert-son (1886) and *Leslie Stephen (1904) (Michigan).

PART III

An Age of Revolution

For general information regarding European history during the eighteenth century the following works are recommended: Albert Sorel, *Europe under the Old Regime* (1947); *Walter L. Dorn, *Competition for Empire, 1740–1763* (1940) (Harper); *Leo Gershoy, *From Despotism to Revolution, 1763–1789* (1944) (Harper); *Matthew S. Anderson, *Eighteenth-Century Europe, 1713–1789* (1966) (Oxford); *Leonard Krieger, *Kings and Philosophers, 1689–1789* (1970) (Nor-ton); and *Charles Breunig, *The Age of Revolution and Reaction, 1789–1850* (1970) (Norton). The diplomatic problems of this period are discussed briefly in Arthur H. Buffinton, *The Second Hundred Years War, 1689–1815* (1929) and at greater length in Robert B. Mowat, *A History of European Diplomacy 1451–1789* (1928) and Arthur Hassall, *The Balance of Power, 1715–89*, 5th ed. (1960).

The world-wide revolutionary tendencies and implications of the age have been traced by *R. R. Palmer in his *Age of the Democratic Revolution, 1760–1800*, 2 vols. (1959–1964) (Princeton). *J. Christopher Herold, ed., *The Horizon Book of the Age of Napoleon* (1963) (Dell) teases both eye and mind. The Congress of Vienna and its aftermath may be followed in *Harold G. Nicolson, *Congress of Vienna: A Study in Allied Unity, 1812–1822* (1946) (Compass); *Guglielmo Ferrero, *The Reconstruction of Europe: Talleyrand and the Con-gress of Vienna, 1814–1815* (1941) (Norton); G. de Bertier de Sauvigny, ed., *France and the European Alliance, 1816–1821* (1958); Hans G. Schenk, *The Aftermath of the Napoleonic Wars* (1947); and *L. C. B. Seaman, *From Vienna to Versailles* (1956) (Harper). For the period after 1789 see *E. J. Hobsbawm, *The Age of Revolution: Europe from 1789 to 1848* (1969) (Mentor); Irene Col-lins, *The Age of Progress: A Survey of European History from 1789 to 1870* (1964); *Jacques Droz, *Europe Between Revolutions, 1815–1848* (1968) (Harper Torchbook); and *J. L. Talmon, *Romanticism and Revolt* (1967) (Harcourt, Brace & World)—this last highly speculative. George T. Romani's study, *The*

Neapolitan Revolution of 1820–1821 (1950) shows the reasons for its failure which can be applied to other contemporary rebellions. *Benedetto Croce's *History of Europe in the Nineteenth Century* (Harcourt, Brace & World) (1933) remains an interesting interpretation of the period, although the information is a bit dated. *Frederick B. Artz, *Reaction and Revolution, 1815–1832* (1935) (Harper); *Arthur J. May, *The Age of Metternich, 1814–1848,* rev. ed. (1964) (Holt, Rinehart & Winston); and John W. Dodds, *The Age of Paradox: A Biography of England 1841–1851* (1952) deal with various aspects of European history during the first half of the nineteenth century. As far as diplomacy is concerned, René Albrecht-Carrié's *A Diplomatic History of Europe since the Congress of Vienna* (1958) is still the best work.

For the revolutions of 1848 see François Fejto, ed., *The Opening of an Era: 1848* (1950); Priscilla Robertson, *The Revolutions of 1848, A Social History* (1952) (Princeton); *Lewis B. Namier, *1848: The Revolution of the Intellectuals* (1946) (Anchor); Reuben J. Rath, *The Viennese Revolution of 1848* (1957); Joseph Redlich, *Emperor Francis Joseph of Austria* (1929); Jerome Blum, *Noble Landowners and Agriculture in Austria, 1815–1848* (1948); *Cecil B. Woodham-Smith, *The Great Hunger: Ireland, 1845–1849* (1963) (Signet); and E. E. Y. Hales, *Pio Nono* (1954).

The World and Its Horizons

Industrial Revolution A general survey has been given by *T. S. Ashton, *The Industrial Revolution, 1760–1830* (1948) (Oxford) and *Paul Mantoux, *The Industrial Revolution in the Eighteenth Century* (1937) (Harper Torchbook). For particular aspects see William O. Henderson, *Britain and Industrial Europe, 1750–1870* (1954) and *Philip A. M. Taylor, ed., *The Industrial Revolution in Britain: Triumph or Disaster?* (1958) (Heath). E. E. Lampard, *Industrial Revolution: Interpretations and Perspectives* (1957) is brief but illuminating; *W. W. Rostow, *The Stages of Economic Growth* (1960) (Cambridge) is controversial but suggestive. See also *John H. Clapham, *The Economic Development of France and Germany, 1815–1914,* 4th ed. (1937) (Cambridge); Abbott P. Usher, *A History of Mechanical Inventions,* rev. ed. (1954); and Arthur L. Dunham, *The Industrial Revolution in France* (1955).

Agricultural Revolution For agrarian changes, see N. S. B. Gras, *A History of Agriculture in Europe and America,* 2nd ed. (1940) and M. Augé-Laribé, *La Révolution Agricole* (1955). There are many works on the general economic history of this period. Among the more useful are Witt Bowden, Michael Karpovich, and Abbott P. Usher, *An Economic History of Europe since 1750* (1937); A. Philip, *Histoire des faits économiques et sociaux de 1800 à nos jours* (1964); Rondo E. Cameron, *France and the Economic Development of Europe, 1800–1914* (1961); *Carlo Cipolla, *The Economic History of World Population, 1750–1918* (1962) (Penguin); *Karl Polanyi, *The Great Transformation, 1750–1918* (1957) (Beacon); and Daniel T. Jack, *Studies in Economic Warfare, 1789–1815* (1941).

Society and Societies The history of social classes could be approached through M. C. Buer's *Health, Wealth and Population in the Early Days of the Industrial Revolution* (1968). For the nobility see especially *Albert Goodwin, *The European Nobility in the Eighteenth Century* (1953) (Harper Torchbook); Esmé C. Wingfield-Stratford, *The Squire and His Relations* (1956); *Franklin L. Ford, *Robe and Sword: The Regrouping of the French Aristocracy after Louis XIV* (1953) (Harper Torchbook); Robert Forster, *The Nobility of Toulouse in the Eighteenth Century* (1960); and M. Reinhard, "Elite et noblesse dans le seconde moitié du 18e siècle," in *Revue d'histoire moderne et contemporaine,* Vol. III, January, 1957. *Elinor G. Barber, *The Bourgeoisie in 18th Century France* (1955) (Princeton) is excellent. *Gwyn A. Williams, *Artisans and Sans-Culottes* (1969) (Norton) compares the working classes in eighteenth-century Britain and France, while Duncan Bythell, *The Handloom Weavers: A Study of the English Cotton Industry During the Industrial Revolution* (1969) is the most recent study of those whom the new technology displaced. Among the accounts of working-class life, *Edward P. Thompson, *The Making of the English Working Class* (1964) (Vintage) and L. Chevalier, *Classes laborieuses et classes dangereuses à Paris pendant la première moitié du 19e siècle* (1958) are the best, but they should be complemented by contemporary pictures of life in the industrial revolution: *Friedrich Engels' classic *Condition of the Working Class in England in 1844* (1845) (Stanford); *Mrs. Gaskell's *Mary Barton* (1848) (Norton); or *Victor Hugo's *Les Misérables* (1862) (several editions).

Slavery has been extensively studied by Gaston Martin, *Histoire de l'esclavage dans les colonies françaises* (1948) and Hugh A. Wyndham, *The Atlantic and Slavery* (1935), while Eric E. Williams, *Capitalism and Slavery* (1944) presents the case for the prosecution. For some of the other problems treated in this chapter, see R. Priouret, *La Franc-maçonnerie sous les Lys* (1953); George N. Clark, *Science and Social Welfare in the Age of Newton,* 2nd ed. (1949); and R. H. Shryock, *The Development of Modern Medicine* (1947).

Enlightened Despotism See *Geoffrey Bruun, *The Enlightened Despots,* 2nd ed. (1967) (Holt, Rinehart & Winston); *Roger Wines, ed., *Enlightened Despotism* (1967) (Heath); John G. Galiardo, *Enlightened Despotism* (1967); and Fritz Hartung's fine pamphlet, *Enlightened Despotism* (1964). For more detailed studies: Franco Valsecchi, *L'Assolutismo illuminato in Austria e in Lombardia* (1931) and Helen P. Liebel, *Enlightened Bureaucracy Versus Enlightened Despotism in Baden, 1750–1792* (1965).

Internal and Constitutional Changes

England English political history could be approached through the readable works of J. H. Plumb, one of the greatest interpreters of eighteenth-century England: *England in the Eighteenth Century* (1950) (Penguin), *Chatham* (1953), *The First Four Georges* (1956) (Wiley), *Sir Robert Walpole* (1956); and Erich Eyck, *Pitt versus Fox: Father and Son, 1735–1806* (1950). *Ian R. Christie, *Crisis of Empire* (1966) (Norton) is an illuminating summary of events between the 1750's and the 1780's, with excellent bibliographical notes. Social history is well served by Dorothy Marshall, *English People in the Eighteenth Century* (1956) and *M. Dorothy George, *London Life in the XVIIIth Century* (1925) (Capricorn). Sound information and interesting points of view may be found also in Derek Jarrett, *Britain, 1688–1815* (1965); Denis G. Richards, *Britain 1714–1851* (1961); *Asa Briggs, *The Age of Improvement* (1959) (Harper Torchbook); and Stanley E. Ayling, *The Georgian Century: 1714–1837* (1966).

The nineteenth century is covered more extensively in Ernest L. Woodward, *The Age of Reform, 1815–1870* (1938); David Thomson, *England in the Nineteenth Century (1815–1914)* (1964); and John W. Derry, *Reaction and Reform, 1793–1868* (1963). Social and political changes of the nineteenth century may be followed in the writings of John L. and Barbara Hammond: *The Village Labourer, 1760–1832* (1920), *The Town Labourer, 1760–1832* (1917) (Anchor), *The Skilled Labourer, 1760–1832* (1919), *The Bleak Age* (1934); in M. C. Buer's *Health, Wealth and Population in the Early Days of the Industrial Revolution* (1968); and in *Edward P. Thompson's vigorous and fascinating *The Making of the English Working Class* (1964) (Vintage). See also *Peter Laslett, *The World We Have Lost* (1966) (Scribner) and Reginald J. White, *Waterloo to Peterloo*

(1957). Among the best biographies: John Osborne, *William Cobbett* (1966); Michael S. Packe, *The Life of John Stuart Mill* (1954); G. D. H. Cole, *Life of Robert Owen* (1930); and John L. and Barbara Hammond, *Lord Shaftesbury*, 4th ed. (1936).

Imperial ventures are treated in *Charles E. Carrington, *The British Overseas* (1950) (Cambridge); Leland H. Jenks, *The Migration of British Capital to 1875* (1927); and Alfred L. Burt, *The Evolution of the British Empire and Commonwealth from the American Revolution* (1956).

The United States It is not the purpose of this book to analyze the history of the United States—only its connections with Europe. In this context, one may consult *Michael Kraus, *The Atlantic Civilization* (1949) (Cornell); *John R. Alden, *The American Revolution, 1775–1783* (1954) (Harper Torchbook); *Clinton L. Rossiter, *Seedtime of the Republic: The Origin of the American Tradition of Political Liberty* (1953) (Harcourt, Brace & World); *Edmund S. Morgan, *Birth of the Republic 1763–89* (1956) (University of Chicago); *Carl L. Becker, *The Declaration of Independence: A Study in the History of Political Ideas* (1922) (Vintage)—all readable and authoritative. The relation of American events to the mind and politics of Europe appears in *Lewis B. Namier, *England in the Age of the American Revolution* (1930) (St. Martin's); Herbert Butterfield, *George III, Lord North, and the People, 1779–80* (1949); Charles R. Ritcheson, *British Politics and the American Revolution* (1954); Werner Start, *America: Ideal and Reality: The United States of 1776 in Contemporary European Philosophy* (1947); *Durand Echeverria, *Mirage in the West: A History of the French Image of American Society to 1815* (1957) (Princeton); Lewis R. Gottschalk, *The Place of the American Revolution in the Causal Pattern of the French Revolution* (1948). See also *Charles M. Wiltse, *The New Nation, 1800–1845* (1961) (Hill & Wang); John Dos Passos, *The Shackles of Power: 3 Jeffersonian Decades* (1966); and *Russell B. Nye, *The Cultural Life of the New Nation, 1776–1830* (1960) (Harper Torchbook).

France Paul A. Gagnon, *France since 1789* (1964); Gordon Wright, *France in Modern Times* (1960); and John Lough, *An Introduction to Eighteenth Century France* (1960) are clear, knowledgeable surveys providing handy bibliographies. C. E. Labrousse, *La Crise de l'économie française à la fin de l'ancien régime et au début de la révolution* (1944) remains the fountainhead of most recent works on that subject. Diverse aspects of the old regime are treated in Henri E. Sée, *Economic and Social Conditions in France during the Eighteenth Century* (1927); *Elinor G. Barber, *The Bourgeoisie in 18th Century France* (1955) (Princeton); John McManners, *French Ecclesiastical Society under the Ancient Regime* (1961); Douglas Dakin, *Turgot and the Ancien Régime in France* (1939); E. Faure, *La Disgrace de Turgot* (1961); E. G. Leonard, *Mon village sous Louis XV, d'après les mémoires d'un paysan* (1941) and *Le Protestant français* (1953); and Herbert Luthy, *La Banque protestante en France*, 2 vols. (1959–1961).

Three of the most revealing works, however, are the contemporary account of *Arthur Young, *Travels in France during the Years 1787, 1788, 1789* (many editions) (Anchor); *Alexis de Tocqueville's classic *The Old Regime and the French Revolution* (Anchor), written over a century ago; and *Georges Lefebvre's wonderfully compact and perceptive *Coming of the French Revolution, 1789* (1947) (Princeton).

On the revolution itself, the best account remains that of Georges Lefebvre, *The French Revolution*, 2 vols. (1961–64). *R. R. Palmer, *Twelve Who Ruled* (1941) (Atheneum) provides illuminating biographical studies. See also *Crane Brinton's comparative *The Anatomy of Revolution* (1938) (Vintage); George F. E. Rudé, *The Crowd in the French Revolution* (1959); A. Soboul, *The Parisian*

Sans-Culottes and the French Revolution, 1793–4 (1964); J. M. Thompson, *Robespierre* (1936) or, briefer, **Robespierre and the French Revolution* (1953) (Collier); *J. L. Talmon's controversial but suggestive *Origins of Totalitarian Democracy* (1952) (Norton); and Jacques L. Godechot, *France and the Atlantic Revolution of the Eighteenth Century, 1770–1799* (1965). In *The Vendée* (1964) (Wiley) *Charles H. Tilly has undertaken a sociological study of the counter-revolution of 1793. See also *Alfred Cobban, *The Social Interpretation of the French Revolution* (1964) (Cambridge) and **Aspects of the French Revolution* (1968) (Norton).

For Napoleon and the Napoleonic era, see F. M. H. Markham, *Napoleon* (1964); a good survey, *Geoffrey Brunn, *Europe and the French Imperium, 1799–1814* (1938) (Harper Torchbook); and J. Christopher Herold, *Bonaparte in Egypt* (1962). The changing aspects of the Napoleonic myth are analyzed in *Pieter Geyl, *Napoleon: For and Against* (1949) (Yale). The changing aspects of life in *Crane Brinton's *The Lives of Talleyrand* (1936) (Norton).

The years after 1815 should be tackled first in G. de Bertier de Sauvigny, *The Restoration* (1967). Other evaluations may be found in Douglas W. J. Johnson, *Guizot* (1963). Stanley Mellon, *The Political Uses of History* (1958); Frank E. Manuel, *The New World of Henri Saint-Simon* (1956) (Notre Dame); John P. Plamenatz, *The Revolutionary Movement in France, 1815–71* (1952); T. E. B. Howard, *Citizen-King: The Life of Louis-Philippe, King of the French* (1961); and (fascinating for the revolutions of 1848) *The Recollections of Alexis de Tocqueville* (1948), edited by Jacob P. Mayer.

Spain   *Harold V. Livermore, *A History of Spain* (1968) (Minerva); Rafael Altamira, *A History of Spain, from the Beginnings to the Present Day* (1949); and Salvador de Madariaga, *Spain* (1958) are convenient general surveys. For the eighteenth century, the basic works are J. Sarrailh, *L'Espagne éclairée de la seconde moitié du 18ᵉ siècle* (1954) and (in English) *Richard Herr, *The Eighteenth-Century Revolution in Spain* (1958) (Princeton). See also A. Ramos Oliveira, *Politics, Economics and Men of Modern Spain, 1808–1946* (1948) and Gabriel H. Lovett, *Napoleon and the Birth of Modern Spain* (1965).

Italy   *René Albrecht-Carrié, *Italy from Napoleon to Mussolini* (1950) (Columbia) and *Arthur J. Whyte, *The Evolution of Modern Italy, 1715–1920* (1944) (Norton) are useful general works. The eighteenth century could be approached through O. Barrié, *L'Italia nell'Ottocento* (1964) and the very good collection of lectures given at the Italian Institute in London in 1957–1958, published under the title *Art and Ideas in 18th Century Italy* (1960). For the nineteenth century and especially for the Risorgimento, see C. Giardini, *Il Risorgimento Italiano, 1796–1861* (1958) and Kent R. Greenfield, *Economics and Liberalism in the Risorgimento,* rev. ed. (1965). The history and the role of the church are discussed by E. E. Y. Hales, *Revolution and Papacy, 1769–1846* (1960) and *Pio Nono* (1954). For the intellectual history of Italy see G. Maugain, *L'Evolution intellectuelle de l'Italie de 1657 à 1750* (1909). More detailed aspects are to be found in H. M. M. Acton, *The Last Medici,* rev. ed. (1959), *The Bourbons of Naples (1734–1825)* (1957) and *The Last Bourbons of Naples (1825–1861)* (1962); George T. Romani, *The Neapolitan Revolution of 1820–1821* (1950); A. J. P. Taylor, *The Italian Problem in European Diplomacy, 1847–1849* (1934); and the first volume of Bolton King, *A History of Italian Unity* (1923).

The Germanies   For Prussia, see *Walter H. Bruford, *Germany in the Eighteenth Century* (1935) (Cambridge); *Gordon A. Craig, *The Politics of the Prussian Army* (1955) (Oxford); *Sidney B. Fay, *The Rise of Brandenburg-Prussia to 1786* (1937) (Holt, Rinehart & Winston); and William F. Reddaway,

Frederick the Great and the Rise of Prussia (1904). Pierre Gaxotte's biography *Frederick the Great* (1942) is highly readable, if biased. Essential for eighteenth-century Prussia is H. Brunschwig, *La Crise de l'état prussien à la fin du 18ᵉ siècle et la génèse de la mentalité romantique* (1947), which links the history of institutions with that of political and social thought; and *Hans W. Rosenberg, *Bureaucracy, Aristocracy and Autocracy* (1958) (Beacon). See also Robert R. Ergang, *The Potsdam Führer, Frederick William I, Father of Prussian Militarism* (1941) and Peter Paret, *Yorck and the Era of Prussian Reform* (1966).

The Austrian empire has been chronicled in Paul Frischauer, *The Imperial Crown* (1939) and *A. J. P. Taylor, *The Habsburg Monarchy, 1809–1918* (1949) (Harper Torchbook). For the eighteenth century one may consult Heinrich Kretschmayr, *Maria Theresa* (1925); George P. Gooch, *Maria Theresa, and Other Studies* (1951); Saul K. Padover, *The Revolutionary Emperor: Joseph the Second, 1741–1790* (1934); and François Fejtö; *Un Habsbourg Révolutionnaire, Joseph II: Portrait d'un despote éclairé,* (1953)—all excellent. For the history of the peoples which were part of the empire, see William E. Wright, *Serf, Seigneur, and Sovereign* (1966) on the agrarian problems and reforms of Bohemia; Henrick Marczali, *Hungary in the Eighteenth Century* (1910), an old work but still unreplaced; Carlile A. Macartney, *Hungary: A Short History* (1962); Robert J. Kerner, *Bohemia in the Eighteenth Century* (1932); and R. W. Seton-Watson, *A History of the Czechs and Slovaks* (1943).

The ideas and politics of the early nineteenth century are well treated in *Theodore S. Hamerow, *Restoration, Revolution, Reaction: Economics and Politics in Germany, 1815–1871* (1958) (Princeton); J. G. Legge, *Rhyme and Revolution in Germany 1813–1850* (1918); *Arthur J. May, *The Age of Metternich, 1814–1848* (1933) (Holt, Rinehart & Winston); and Richard H. Thomas, *Liberalism, Nationalism and the German Intellectuals, 1822–1847* (1952).

The Eastern Borderlands Stanislaw Arnold and Marian Zychowski, *Outline History of Poland* (1962) and William F. Reddaway, ed., *The Cambridge History of Poland,* 2 vols. (1941, 1951) are sound general works. For the eighteenth century and certain less-known aspects of the Enlightenment, see J. Fabre, *Stranislas-Auguste Poniatowski et l'Europe des lumières* (1952). For the partitions of Poland, see Robert H. Lord, *The Second Partition of Poland* (1915) and Herbert H. Kaplan, *The First Partition of Poland* (1962). The later period is covered in William J. Rose, *The Rise of Polish Democracy* (1944) and R. F. Leslie, *Polish Politics and the Revolution of November 1830* (1956). Later developments are treated in R. W. Seton-Watson, *The Historian as a Political Force in Central Europe* (1922). For Hungary, see the references for the Austrian empire in the preceding section on the Germanies.

Russia For general narratives see the works of Bernard Pares and N. Riasanovsky. The reign of Peter the Great should be approached through B. H. Sumner's *Peter the Great and the Emergence of Russia* (1951) (Collier) and *Peter the Great and the Ottoman Empire* (1950). *Marc Raeff's *Peter the Great: Reformer or Revolutionary?* (1963) (Heath) reviews the controversial aspects of the reign of the creator of modern Russia. For his successors, see George P. Gooch, *Catherine the Great and Other Studies* (1954); Gladys S. Thompson, *Catherine the Great and the Expansion of Russia* (1950); Ian Grey, *Catherine the Great* (1962); and Constantin de Grunwald, *Tsar Nicholas I* (1955). Already cited, James H. Billington, *The Icon and the Axe* (1966) and *Jerome Blum, *Lord and Peasant in Russia* (1961) (Atheneum) are basic for cultural and agrarian history respectively. Hans Rogger, *National Consciousness in Eighteenth-Century Russia* (1960) traces the relationship of westernization and national feelings. Leonid I. Strakhovsky sketches an uncertain personality in *Alexander I of Russia* (1947). Mikhail

O. Zetlin's *The Decembrists* (1958) goes beyond the unsuccessful rising to the general unrest affecting Russian society at the beginning of the nineteenth century. See also R. Portal, *L'Oural au 18ᵉ siècle* (1950), useful for the origins of Russian industrial development; Robert J. Kerner, *The Urge to the Sea* (1942); and Frank A. Golder, *Russian Expansion on the Pacific, 1641–1850* (1914).

The Ottoman Empire   A general bibliography for the empire and the countries controlled by the Turks has already been given. One should add some works regarding the beginning of the process of modernization and the impact of the West upon the southeast part of Europe. Useful remarks and bibliography may be found in the book edited by Charles and Barbara Jelavich, *The Balkans in Transition* (1963). One may also consult Wesley M. Gewehr, *The Rise of Nationalism in the Balkans, 1800–1930* (1931) and R. W. Seton-Watson, *The Rise of Nationality in the Balkans* (1917). *Bernard Lewis, *The Emergence of Modern Turkey* (1961) (Oxford) and H. A. R. Gibb and Harold Bowen, *Islamic Society and the West*, 2 vols. (1950–1957) are basic. J. A. R. Marriott, *The Eastern Question*, 4th ed. (1940) surveys Ottoman decline and its effects on the international plane. The Turkish point of view has been presented by Halide Edib Adivar, *Conflict of East and West in Turkey* (1935). For one of the most important events of the early nineteenth century, affecting not only the Balkans but all Europe, see C. M. Woodhouse, *The Greek War of Independence* (1952).

Sense and Sensibility

Science and Technology   For general surveys regarding the role of science and technology in modern civilization, see *Alfred R. Hall, *The Scientific Revolution, 1500–1800* (1954) (Beacon); Abraham Wolf, *A History of Science, Technology and Philosophy in the Eighteenth Century*, 2 vols. (1961); Charles J. Singer, Alfred R. Hall, and Trevor I. Williams, eds., *A History of Technology*, Vol. IV (1958); *Lewis Mumford, *Technics and Civilization* (1963) (Harcourt, Brace & World); Archibald and Nan Clow, *The Chemical Revolution* (1952); L. T. C. Rolt, *The Aeronauts: A History of Ballooning, 1783–1903* (1966). Stimulating: *Charles C. Gillispie, *The Edge of Objectivity* (1960) (Princeton) and G. Bachelard, *La Formation de l'esprit scientifique* (1960). *Charles C. Gillispie's *Genesis and Geology* (1951) (Harper Torchbook) is excellent for the impact of scientific discoveries upon religious belief in the decades before Darwin. For the impact of Darwinism itself see *Loren C. Eiseley, *Darwin's Century* (1958) (Anchor) and *Gertrude Himmelfarb, *Darwin and the Darwinian Revolution* (1968) (Norton).

The Enlightenment and the *Philosophes*   Good introductions to the general history of ideas and thought during the period are found in *Paul Hazard, *European Thought in the Eighteenth Century* (1954) (Meridian); Gerald R. Cragg, *Reason and Authority in the Eighteenth Century* (1964); and Lester G. Crocker, *An Age of Crisis: Man and World in 18th Century Thought* (1959). For the Enlightenment, see *Peter Gay, *The Enlightenment: An Interpretation* —Vol. I, *The Rise of Modern Paganism* (1966) (Vintage) and Vol. II, *The Science of Freedom* (1969), and *The Party of Humanity: Essays in the French Enlightenment* (1963) and *E. Cassirer, *The Philosophy of the Enlightenment* (1955) (Beacon, Princeton), all basic. René Mauzi, *L'Idée du bonheur au XVIIIᵉ siècle* (1960) is heavy going but worthwhile for the serious student. *Carl L. Becker, *The Heavenly City of the Eighteenth-Century Philosophers* (1932) (Yale) should not be missed—delightful reading, best followed by a look at Raymond O. Rockwood, ed., *Carl Becker's Heavenly City Revisited* (1958). Other general works: *Frank E. Manual, *The Age of Reason* (1951) (Cornell); A. Bruno, *Car-

tesio e l'illuminismo (1949); Geoffrey Clive, *The Romantic Enlightenment* (1960); and Louis I. Bredvold, *The Brave New World of the Enlightenment* (1961). For the old discussion concerning the impact of enlightened thought upon the French Revolution, see Alfred Cobban, *In Search of Humanity: The Role of the Enlightenment in Modern History* (1960) and *William F. Church, ed., *The Influence of the Enlightenment on the French Revolution: Creative, Disastrous or Non-existent* (1964) (Heath). Other suggested works: Eric W. Cochrane, *Tradition and Enlightenment in the Tuscan Academies, 1690–1800* (1961); M. Fubini, ed., *La Cultura iluministica in Italia* (1957); George M. Addy, *The Enlightenment in the University of Salamanca* (1966); and Henry Higgs, *The Physiocrats* (1952).

Among the best biographies: Robert Shackleton, *Montesquieu* (1961); *Henry N. Brailsford, *Voltaire* (1935) (Oxford); and *Peter Gay, *Voltaire's Politics* (1959) (Vintage); Lester G. Crocker, *The Embattled Philosopher: A Biography of Denis Diderot* (1954); *Frank E. Manuel, *The Prophets of Paris* (1962) (Harper Torchbook) for Turgot, Condorcet, Saint-Simon, Fourier, and Comte; Jacob S. Schapiro, *Condorcet and the Rise of Liberalism* (1934); J. Christopher Herold, *Mistress to an Age* (1958), a splendidly readable biography of Madame de Staël; Richard Friedenthal, *Goethe: His Life and Times* (1965); Henry N. Brailsford, *Shelley, Godwin, and Their Circle* (1969); and Michael S. Packe, *The Life of John Stuart Mill* (1954). More revealing than any biography are the autobiographies of *Edward Gibbon (1961) (Meridian) and *John Stuart Mill (several editions).

Other Philosophies   For ideas and systems of thought other than those of the Enlightenment, see *Robert L. Heilbroner, *The Worldly Philosophers*, rev. ed. (1967) (Clarion); Godfrey E. Elton, *The Revolutionary Idea in France, 1789–1871* (1969); Simon Maccoby, *English Radicalism:1786–1832* (1956); *Guido de Ruggiero, *The History of European Liberalism* (1927) (Beacon); Harold J. Laski, *The Rise of Liberalism* (1936); *Harry K. Girvetz, *The Evolution of Liberalism* (1963) (Collier); Donald G. Rohr, *The Origins of Social Liberalism in Germany* (1963); and Leonard Krieger, *The German Idea of Freedom* (1957).

Utilitarianism, at least in its British aspects, is well treated in Leslie Stephen, *The English Utilitarians*, 3 vols. (1900); John P. Plamenatz, *Mill's Utilitarianism: Reprinted with a Study of the English Utilitarians* (1949); and *Elie Halévy, *The Growth of Philosophical Radicalism* (1955) (Beacon). The best Owen biography is Margaret I. Cole, *Robert Owen of New Lanark* (1953). A good short introduction, *Hegel* (1883) is by Edward Caird. For the evolution of historical ideas, see Sherman B. Barnes and Alfred A. Skerpan, *Historiography Under the Impact of Rationalism and Revolution* (1952).

Good analyses of European conservatism and of traditionalist thought are to be found in *Peter Viereck, *Conservatism Revisited: The Revolt Against Revolt, 1815–1949* (1949) (Free Press); John Morley, *Edmund Burke* (1924); Alfred Cobban, *Edmund Burke and the Revolt Against the Eighteenth Century* (1929); and Ernest L. Woodward, *Three Studies in European Conservatism: Metternich, Guizot, the Catholic Church in the 19th Century* (1963). See also *Michel Foucault, *Madness and Civilization: A History of Insanity in the Age of Reason* (1965) (Mentor); J. L. Talmon, *Political Messianism: The Romantic Phase* (1960); *Alexander R. Vidler, *The Church in an Age of Revolution* (1961) (Penguin); and Kathleen Heasman, *Evangelicals in Action* (1962).

The Romantic Reaction

Rococo   The Rococo could be approached through the following works: A. Schönberger and H. Soehmer, *The Rococo Age: Art and Civilization of the 18th Century* (1960); A. Anger, *Literarisches Rokoko* (1962); and *Michael Levey,

Rococo to Revolution: Major Trends in 18th Century Painting (1966) (Praeger). The vogue of Asia, and particularly of China, is discussed by H. Cordier, *La Chine en France au 18ᵉ siècle* (1910) and William W. Appleton, *A Cycle of Cathay: The Chinese Vogue in England During the Seventeenth and Eighteenth Centuries* (1951).

Rousseau For Rousseau, the best English work is Frederick C. Green, *Jean-Jacques Rousseau* (1955). See also Alfred Cobban, *Rousseau and the Modern State* (1934); and *Ernst Cassirer, *The Question of Jean-Jacques Rousseau* (1954) (Indiana) and *Rousseau, Kant, Goethe* (1945).

Romanticism For Romanticism see *Jacques Barzun's *Classic, Romantic and Modern* (1961) (Anchor), a new edition of his earlier *Romanticism and the Modern Ego* (1943); *Kenneth Clark, *The Gothic Revival* (1950) (Penguin); P. Moreau, *Le Romantisme* (1957); *M. H. Abrams, *The Mirror and the Lamp: Romantic Theory and the Critical Tradition* (1953) (Norton). David O. Evans, *Social Romanticism in France, 1830–1848* (1969) and *Hans Kohn, *The Mind of Germany* (1960) (Harper Torchbook) help one to understand the relationship between Romantic ideas and political commitments. For different aspects of Romantic theory see E. Newton, *Romantic Rebellion* (1962); Allen F. Casebier, *The Historical Conception of Romanticism* (1964); Theodore H. von Laue, *Leopold Ranke, The Formative Years* (1950); J. Fabre, *Lumière et romantisme: énergie et nostalgie de Rousseau à Mickiewicz* (1963); J. Bousquet, *Les thèmes du rêve dans la littérature romantique* (1964); and *Kathleen M. Tillotson, *Novels of the Eighteen-Forties* (1954) (Oxford). The Romantic background can be found in *Eugen Weber, ed., *Paths to the Present* (1960) (Dodd, Mead).

Nationalism *Hans Kohn, *The Idea of Nationalism: A Study of its Origins and Background* (1961) (Collier) is the best beginning, along with *Boyd C. Shafer, *Nationalism: Myth and Reality* (1955) (Harcourt, Brace)—clear and succint. See also E. H. Carr, *Nationalism and After* (1945) and the older work by C. J. Hayes, *The Historical Evolution of Modern Nationalism* (1931). For an extensive bibliography see Karl W. Deutsch, *Interdisciplinary Bibliography on Nationalism* (1955).

New Public and New Culture

*George Rudé, *The Crowd in History* (1964) (Wiley); A. Brulé, *Les Gens de lettres au 18ᵉ siècle* (1929); and M. Glotz and M. Maire, *Les salons du 18ᵉ siècle* (1949) all help one to understand the problems discussed in this chapter.

Education Robert F. Butts, *A Cultural History of Western Education,* 2nd ed. (1955); William Boyd, *The History of Western Education,* 8th ed. (1966); and Brian Simon, *Studies in the History of Education, 1780–1870* (1960) are all dependable works. So is John W. Adamson's older *Short History of Education* (1920). For the history of pedagogical ideas see G. Snyders, *La Pédagogie en France au 17ᵉ et 18ᵉ siècles* (1965); Frederick Mayer, *A History of Educational Thought* (1960); and W. A. C. Stewart and W. P. McCann, *The Educational Innovators, 1750–1880,* 2 vols. (1967). A. Babeau, *L'Ecole de village pendant la Révolution* (1885) and E. Philip Trapp, *The School Teacher* (1957) are recommended for the problems regarding education in rural areas. Hugh M. Pollard, *Pioneers of Popular Education, 1760–1850* (1956) is also useful.

The Writing Trade Convenient for reference are Alfred Hessel, *A History of Libraries* (1950); Elmer D. Johnson, *A History of Libraries in the Western World* (1965); Herman J. Vleeschauer, *History of the Library Since the French Revolu-*

tion (1965); Irene Collins, *The Government and the Newspaper Press in France, 1814–1881* (1959); and G. Weill, *Le Journal: origines, évolution et rôle de la presse périodique* (1934). For writers themselves see the works of Arthur S. Collins, *The Profession of Letters* (1929) and *Authorship in the Days of Johnson* (1929); James Hepburn, *The Author's Empty Purse and the Rise of the Literary Agent* (1968); Robert J. Cruikshank, *Charles Dickens and Early Victorian England* (1950); and Monica Stirling, *The Wild Swan: A Life of Hans Christian Andersen* (1965).

The Public Arts   Francis D. Klingender, *Art and the Industrial Revolution* (1947) discusses the impact of social realities on art and artists. Of the innumerable books on various aspects of European art during the eighteenth and nineteenth centuries, the following are among the most useful: *Michael Levey, *Rococo to Revolution* (1966) (Praeger); Marcel Brion, *Romantic Art* (1960); *Eric Newton, *The Romantic Rebellion* (1963) (Schocken); E. de Kayser, *L'Occident romantique, 1789–1850* (1965); and J. Starobinski, *L'Invention de la liberté, 1700–1789* (1964).

David Ewen, ed., *From Bach to Stravinsky* (1933) is an excellent general work. See also Alfred Einstein, *Music in the Romantic Era* (1947) and J. Chantavoine and J. Godefroy-Demombynes, *Le Romantisme dans la musique européenne* (1955); or for an introduction to musical ideas, Donald N. Ferguson, *A History of Musical Thought*, 2nd ed. (1948). *Alfred Einstein, *Mozart, His Character, His Work* (1945) (Oxford) is an excellent biography of the great composer; Francis Toye, *Rossini* (1963) is a splendidly readable introduction to the world of Italian opera; while *Jacques Barzun, *Berlioz and the Romantic Century*, 3rd ed. (1969) (Meridian) illuminates the whole Romantic period through the life of its most representative composer.

Fiction   The best and pleasantest way of entering into the life and problems of a given time is through its literature. The eighteenth and early nineteenth centuries offer us a new vehicle for this purpose: the novel. The shady life of Louis XV's France is reflected in *Abbé Prévost, *Manon Lescaut* (1731) (several editions); the questing, moralizing skepticism of the Enlightenment in *Denis Diderot's *Rameau's Nephew,* written in the 1760's and best tackled in Jacques Barzun's edition of 1956 (Bobbs-Merrill); the amoralism of late eighteenth-century society in *Pierre Choderlos de Laclos's *Liaisons dangereuses* (1782) (Signet); the sentimentalism blowing out of Germany in *Johann Wolfgang von Goethe's *The Sorrows of Young Werther* (1774) (several editions), and the Romantic world-view even better in his *Wilhelm Meister* (1796) (Collier).

However, a new society was taking shape and sparking a new kind of social novel, less fantastic and closer to life. After the turn of the century, contemporary reality is mirrored in the works of *Jane Austen—*Pride and Prejudice* (1813) (several editions), *Emma* (1816) (several editions)—and especially in those of two great Frenchmen, Stendhal and Balzac. Stendhal (the pen-name of Marie Henri Beyle), writing mostly in the 1830's, has left us three masterful accounts: *The Red and the Black* (1831) (several editions), of the frustrated yearnings and rebellious stirrings of the post-1815 generation; *The Charterhouse of Parma* (1839) (Signet, Penguin), of antediluvian institutions and youthful idealism in anachronistic Italy; and (unfinished) *Lucien Leuwen* (New Directions), about the 1830's themselves. His contemporary, Honoré de Balzac, survived him; but some of Balzac's most revealing novels (*Lost Illusions*, *Eugénie Grandet*, *Père Goriot*) were also written in the thirties. They give us the richest and truest picture of life and values of those days.

PART IV

The Age of Masses

For a general approach see N. Ponente, *Les Structures du monde moderne, 1850–1900* (1965). Quincy Howe, *A World History of Our Own Times,* 3 vols. (1953); and Frank P. Chambers, *This Age of Conflict,* 3rd ed. (1962). Concerning population and population movements, see M. Reinhardt, *Histoire de la population mondiale de 1700 à 1948* (1949); Alexander M. Carr-Saunders, *World Population* (1936); Julius Isaac, *Economics of Migration* (1947); Donald R. Taft and Richard Robbins, *International Migrations* (1955). Specifically concerning the role of the masses, see Henry P. Fairchild, *People: The Quantity and Quality of Population* (1939); Robert E. Dickinson, *The West European City* (1951); Gustave le Bon, *The Crowd,* new ed. (1925); *José Ortega y Gasset, *The Revolt of the Masses* (1932) (Norton); and William L. O'Neill, ed., *Echoes of Revolt: The Masses, 1911–1917* (1966). *Peter N. Stearns, *European Society in Upheaval: Social History since 1800* (1967) (Macmillan) is the first attempt to provide students with a synthesis of the subject. Another crucial connection is treated in *Carlo M. Cipolla, *Literacy and Development in the West* (1969) (Pelican).

The International Scene Most of the problems included in this chapter will be discussed in detail in later sections. Nevertheless, for a very general survey, one can turn either to the relevant volumes of the New Cambridge Modern History (X, XI, XII, and especially the last, edited by David Thomson, *The Era of Violence, 1898–1945* (1960); to A. J. P. Taylor, *The Struggle for Mastery in Europe, 1848–1918* (1955); or to *Felix Gilbert, *The End of the European Era, 1890 to the Present* (1970) (Norton).

For the economic aspects of the international scene, there are several excellent works: among them William Ashworth, *A Short History of the International Economy Since 1850,* 2nd ed. (1962); Michael Tracy, *Agriculture in Western Europe* (1964); M. Lévy-Leboyer, *Les Banques européennes et l'industrialisation internationale dans la première moitié du 19e siècle* (1964); *Herbert Feis, *Europe, the World's Banker, 1870–1914* (1930) (Norton); *C. P. Kindleberger, *Economic Growth in France and Britain, 1851–1950* (1964) (Clarion); and Eugene Staley, *War and the Private Investor* (1935). *Lewis Mumford, *Technics and Civilization* (1934) (Harcourt, Brace & World); Ludwig F. Haber, *The Chemical Industry During the Nineteenth Century* (1958); Walter Henry Green Armytage, *A Social History of Engineering* (revised 1961); and N. G. B. Pounds and W. N. Parker, *Coal and Steel in Western Europe* (1957) are also suggested, along with *John H. Clapham, *The Economic Development of France and Germany, 1815–1914,* 4th ed. (1935) (Cambridge) and Gustav Stolper, *German Economy, 1870–1940* (1940).

Politics for Masses

Liberalism Harold Laski's works, especially *The Rise of Liberalism* (1936), are basic. Also good, *Guido de Ruggiero, *The History of European Liberalism* (1959) (Beacon); John H. Hollowell, *The Decline of Liberalism as an Ideology* (1943); and Harry K. Girvetz, *The Evolution of Liberalism,* rev. ed. (1963). For liberal perspectives see the optimistic book of Joseph Grimond, *The Liberal Challenge* (1964).

Anarchism   This should be first approached through the general work of G. D. H. Cole, *Socialist Thought: Marxism and Anarchism, 1850–1890* (1954). Among specific works devoted to the subject see *James Joll, *The Anarchists* (1965) (Grosset & Dunlap); *George Woodcock, *Anarchism* (1962) (Meridian); R. Gaucher, *Les terroristes* (1965); *E. J. Hobsbawm, *Primitive Rebels* (1959) (Norton); and Jean Maitron's vast *Histoire du mouvement anarchiste en France* (1955). Good biographies of the founders of the movement are D. W. Brogan, *Proudhon* (1936); George Woodcock, *William Godwin* (1946) and *Pierre-Joseph Proudhon* (1956); E. H. Carr, *Michael Bakunin* (1937); G. P. Maksimov, ed., *The Political Philosophy of Bakunin* (1953); and *Peter Kropotkin, *Memoirs of a Revolutionist* (1899) (Dover).

Socialism   The basic work on socialism is G. D. H. Cole, *A History of Socialist Thought,* 4 vols. (1953–1956). Among others: *Norman I. Mackenzie, *Socialism: A Short History* (1950) (Harper & Row); Carl Landauer, *European Socialism,* 2 vols. 1959); and *Alexander Gray, *The Socialist Tradition: Moses to Lenin* (1946) (Harper Torchbook). *Edmund Wilson, *To the Finland Station* (1946) (Anchor) is the clearest and most readable discussion in English of "the revolutionary tradition in Europe and the rise of Socialism," but *George Lichtheim, *The Origins of Socialism* (1969) (Praeger)—less discursive and more scholarly—is almost as readable and more tightly argued. For national aspects see Henry M. Pelling, *A History of British Trade Unionism* (1963); Val R. Lorwin, *The French Labor Movement* (1955); Harvey Goldberg, *The Life of J. Jaurès* (1962); *George Lichtheim, *Marxism: An Historical and Critical Study* (1961) (Praeger); and *Peter Gay's account of revisionism in *The Dilemma of Democratic Socialism* (1952) (Collier).

The Catastrophic Heroes   The theoretical backgrounds of Nazism and fascism are discussed in *Peter Viereck, *Metapolitics, from the Romantics to Hitler* (1941) (Capricorn), *Ernst Nolte, *Three Faces of Fascism* (1966) (Mentor); Franz Neumann, *Behemoth: The Structure and Practice of National Socialism, 1933–1944* (1944) (Harper Torchbook); * George L. Mosse, *The Crisis of German Ideology: Intellectual Origins of the Third Reich* (1964) (Grosset & Dunlap). See also Louis L. Snyder, *German Nationalism: The Tragedy of a People* (1952); Michael Curtis, *Three Against the Third Republic: Sorel, Barrès and Maurras* (1959); and Eugen Weber, *The Nationalist Revival in France, 1905–1914* (1959). For the intellectual history of the past fourscore years, a stimulating introduction may be sought in two works by H. Stuart Hughes, *Consciousness and Society: The Reorientation of European Social Thought 1890–1930* (1958) (Vintage) and *The Obstructed Path: French Social Thought in the Years of Desperation, 1930–1960* (1969) (Harper Torchbook), and in *Gerhard Masur, *Prophets of Yesterday* (1961) (Harper & Row).

Anti-Semitism   For a general outline: Leon Poliakov's *The History of Anti-Semitism,* 4 vols. (1965); *Norman R. C. Cohn, *Warrant for Genocide* (1967) (Harper Torchbook); James W. Parkes, *The Emergence of the Jewish Problem, 1878–1939* (1946); and Koppel S. Pinson, ed., *Essays on Antisemitism* (1946). Works concerning individual countries include Paul W. Massing, *Rehearsal for Destruction: A Study of Political Anti-Semitism in Imperial Germany* (1949); Robert F. Byrnes, *Antisemitism in Modern France,* 3 vols. (1950); and *Peter Pulzer, *The Rise of Political Anti-Semitism in Germany and Austria* (1964) (Wiley). On some of the causes of anti-Semitism, see Nathan W. Ackerman and Marie Jahoda, *Anti-Semitism and Emotional Disorder* (1950); Rudolph M. Loewenstein, *Christians and Jews* (1951); Peretz F. Bernstein, *Jew-Hate as a*

Social Problem (1951); Jules Isaac, *The Teaching of Contempt: Christian Roots* of Anti-Semitism (1940).

Europe and the World Overseas

Europe Explodes Herbert Feis, *Europe, the World's Banker, 1870–1914* (1930) (Norton) is still very good on Europe's role in the development of the world. The colonial problem should be approached through the following works: René Maunier, *The Sociology of Colonies: An Introduction to the Study of Race Contact,* 2 vols. (1949); Mary E. Townsend, *European Colonial Expansion Since 1871* (1941); Heinrich A. Wieschoff, *Colonial Policies in Africa* (1944); John T. Pratt, *The Expansion of Europe into the Far East* (1947); Christopher Hollis, *Italy in Africa* (1941); *Archibald P. Thornton, *The Imperial Idea and Its Enemies: A Study in British Power* (1959) (Anchor); John F. Cady, *The Roots of French Imperialism in Eastern Asia* (1954); and *David S. Landes' brilliant *Bankers and Pashas: International Finance and Economic Imperialism in Egypt* (1958) (Harper Torchbook). See also the special issue "Colonialism and Colonization in World History" of the *Journal of Economic History*, XXI, No. 4, December, 1961, and the works of A. Grenfell Price: *The Western Invasions of the Pacific and Its Continents: A Study of Moving Frontiers and Changing Landscapes, 1513–1958* (1963) and *The Importance of Disease in History* (1964).

Imperialism William L. Strauss, *Joseph Chamberlain and the Theory of Imperialism* (1942) is still a good theoretical introduction, while William L. Langer, *The Diplomacy of Imperialism, 1890–1902*, 2 vols. (1935) provides practical exemplification of what imperialism was. For the same period see C. J. Lowe, *The Reluctant Imperialists*, Vol. I (1969); John Atkinson Hobson, *Imperialism: A Study* (1902), pioneer of the economic interpretation, *V. I. Lenin, *Imperialism, the Highest Stage of Capitalism* (1939) (China Books); *Joseph A. Schumpeter, *Imperialism and Social Classes* (1919) (Meridian); Earle M. Winslow, *The Pattern of Imperialism* (1948); Archibald P. Thornton, *The Imperial Idea and Its Enemies: A Study in British Power* (1959); and Richard Koebner and Helmut D. Schmidt, *Imperialism* (1964). For the reaction of the colonized, see *Frantz Fanon, *The Wretched of the Earth* (1965) (Grove).

India Percival Griffiths, *The British Impact on India* (1952) is good on the problem of contacts between different types of civilizations. *Stanley A. Wolpert, *India* (1965) (Spectrum) provides the best brief introduction. Thomas W. Wallbank, *India: A Survey of the Heritage and Growth of Indian National-ism* (1948); Charles F. Andrews and Girija Mukerji, *The Rise and Growth of the Congress in India* (1938); and *Percival Spear, *India, Pakistan and the West*, 4th ed. (1967) (Oxford) are also recommended.

The Far East Good introductions may be found in Cora A. Du Bois, *Social Forces in Southeast Asia* (1959); Maurice Zinkin, *Asia and the West,* new rev. ed. (1953); Jan Romein, *The Asian Century: A History of Modern Nationalism in Asia* (1962); and Paul H. Clyde, *The Far East: A History of the Impact of the West on Eastern Asia*, 2nd ed. (1952). The role of the West is discussed also by G. B. Sansom, *The Western World and Japan*, and Edwin O. Reischauer, *The United States and Japan*, rev. ed. (1957). Brian Harrison, *South-east Asia: A Short History* (1954) should be used for that area of the continent. China is best approached through *Kenneth S. Latourette, *A History of Modern China* (1954) (Penguin); S. H. Tang, *Communist China Today: Domestic and Foreign*

Policies, 2nd ed. (1961); and *John K. Fairbank, *The United States and China,* rev. and enl. (1958) (Compass). For two illuminating biographies, see Emily Hahn, *Chiang Kai-shek: An Unauthorized Biography* (1955) and *Benjamin I. Schwartz, *Chinese Communism and the Rise of Mao* (1951) (Harper Torchbook).

Europe 1848–1914   For the second half of the nineteenth century there are good general accounts in Robert C. Binkley, *Realism and Nationalism, 1852–1871* (1935); *Norman Rich, *The Age of Nationalism and Reform* (1970) (Norton); and *C. J. H. Hayes, *A Generation of Materialism, 1871–1900* (1941) (Harper & Row). The Crimean War provides the background for *Cecil Wood-ham Smith, *The Reason Why: An Exposé of the Charge of the Light Brigade* (1953) (Dutton), an exposé also of the incompetence of those responsible for the conflict. *Michael Howard has written a good account of *The Franco-Prussian War* (1961) (Collier). See also Edgar Holt, *The Boer War* (1958); Heinrich A. Wieschoff, *Colonial Policies in Africa* (1944); *Erich Eyck, *Bismarck and the German Empire* (1950) (Norton); and William L. Langer's massive studies of diplomatic history, *European Alliances and Alignments, 1871–1890* (1931) (Vintage) and *The Diplomacy of Imperialism, 1890–1902,* 2 vols. (1935). Finally, ample and useful, Oron J. Hale, *The Great Illusion, 1900–1914* (1971).

War, 1914–1918   *Barbara Tuchman, *The Proud Tower: A Portrait of the World Before the War, 1890–1914* (1966) (Bantam) and **The Guns of August* (1962) (Dell) are readable accounts of the years when war clouds gathered, and of 1914, when they burst. Among the myriad studies of the war's origins, the most accessible is Nicholas Mansergh, *The Coming of the First World War* (1949). For the German and French views, well stated, see Erich Branden-burg, *From Bismarck to the World War* (1927) and Pierre Renouvin, *The Immediate Origins of the War* (1928). On the fighting itself, *Cyril B. Falls, *The Great War* (1959) (Capricorn) and Hanson W. Baldwin, *World War I: An Outline History* (1962) (Grove) are both sound general surveys. For the position and role of the United States, see *Ernest R. May, *The World War and American Isolation, 1914–1917* (1959). (Quadrangle). Other aspects of those years are treated in Frank P. Chambers, *The War Behind the War* (1939); *Arthur Marwick, *The Deluge* (1966) (Norton)—both on civilian society— *Alistair Horne, *The Price of Glory: Verdun, 1916* (1963) Harper & Row); and Bernard Bergonzi, *Heroes' Twilight* (1966), a study of the literature of the war.

Peace   H. W. V. Temperley's *History of the Peace Conference of Paris,* 6 vols. (1920–1924) is a mine of information but without a general theoretical view; Thomas A. Bailey, *Wilson and the Peacemakers* (1947) focuses on the U.S. role in the peace conference; *Harold G. Nicolson, *Peacemaking, 1919* (1939) (Grosset & Dunlap) is a handy brief account by a British participant. Thomas Jones's biography *Lloyd George* (1951) provides information on another dominant figure of the conference. The economic debate on the wisdom of the peace terms is best followed in John Maynard Keynes, *The Economic Consequences of the Peace* (1920), a brilliant criticism, and *Etienne Mantoux, *The Carthaginian Peace: or The Economic Consequences of Mr. Keynes* (1946) (University of Pittsburgh), an attack upon it. The role and the destiny of the smaller nations at the conference table should be approached through Stephen Bonsal, *Suitors and Suppliants: The Little Nations at Versailles* (1946). Paul Birdsall, *Versailles—Twenty Years After* (1941) is a stimulating appraisal of the far-reaching effects of the peace settlements.

The Twenty Years' Armistice   *A. J. P. Taylor's *From Sarajevo to Potsdam* (1966) (Harcourt, Brace & World) is brief and readable. See also the general works of M. Baumont, *La faillite de la paix 1918–1939* (1945); *E. H. Carr, *The Twenty Years' Crisis,* 2nd ed. (1946) (Harper Torchbook); and Ephraim Lipson, *Europe, 1914–1939,* 7th ed. (1957); and the satirical social history by *Robert Graves and Alan Hodge, *The Long Week-end* (1941) (Norton). The hopes and the failure of the League of Nations are well described by F. P. Walters, *History of the League of Nations,* 2 vols. (1960). *John Kenneth Galbraith, *The Great Crash, 1929* (1955) (Sentry) helps one to understand the troubled events which led to the rise of Nazism and the Second World War. The period preceding this last is analyzed by *John Wheeler-Bennet, *Munich: Prologue to Tragedy* (1948) (Compass) and in two collections of essays by Lewis B. Namier: *Diplomatic Prelude, 1938–1939* (1948) and *Europe in Decay: A Study in Disintegration, 1936–1940* (1950).

The End of Liberalism *Elizabeth Wiskemann, *Europe of the Dictators, 1914–1945* (1966) (Harper Torchbook) is factual and useful. See also Alfred Cobban, *Dictatorship: Its History and Theory* (1939); G. W. F. Hallgarten, *Why Dictators?* (1954); and Carl J. Friedrich and Zbigniew K. Brzezinski, *Totalitarian Dictatorship and Autocracy* 2nd rev. ed. (1956). *Erich Fromm, *Escape from Freedom* (1941) (Aron) argues that modern man, unable to bear the burden of freedom and self-definition, desires to escape into irresponsible mass movements. *Barrington Moore, Jr., *The Social Origins of Dictatorship and Democracy* (1966) (Beacon) attempts a comparative study of the process of modernization in different countries, suggesting why this led to fascism, communism, or democracy.

Communism The practical aspects of communism, especially in Russia, will be discussed in another chapter. For a theoretical interpretation see *G. D. H. Cole, *The Meaning of Marxism* (1964) (University of Michigan); *Alfred Meyer, *Marxism: The Unity of the Theory and Practice* (1954) (University of Michigan) and *Marxism Since the Communist Manifesto* (1961) (Service Center for Teachers of History). There is a good life of Marx by *Isaiah Berlin, *Karl Marx* (1939) (Oxford), while *Franz Mehring's sympathetic *Karl Marx: The Story of His Life* (1957) (University of Michigan) is very thought-provoking.
    See also *Massimo Salvadori, *The Rise of Modern Communism,* rev. ed. (1963) (Holt, Rinehart & Winston); Kermit E. McKenzie, *Comintern and World Revolution* (1964); and R. N. C. Hunt, *Theory and Practice of Communism* (1950). *Hugh Seton-Watson, *From Lenin to Khrushchev: The History of World Communism,* 2nd ed. (1960) (Praeger) is a sound, readable survey.

Fascism Some of the relevant works are listed under national rubrics. But studies of the fascist phenomenon as such have increased in number during the 1960's. Works like *Franz Neumann, *Behemoth: The Structure and Practice of National Socialism* (1942) (Harper and Torchbook) and *Hannah Arendt, *The Origins of Totalitarianism,* 2nd enl. ed. (1958) (Meridian) are basic. *Ernst Nolte, *The Three Faces of Fascism* (1966) (Mentor) is a philosophical discussion of the Fascist syndrome. *Eugen Weber, *Varieties of Fascism* (1964) (Van Nostrand, Reinhold), and *Hans Rogger and Eugen Weber, eds., *The European Right* (1965) (University of California) describe the variety of a many-faceted phenomenon and its relations with traditional Left and Right.

World War II *A. J. P. Taylor's controversial *Origins of the Second World War* (1962) (Premier) is strongly recommended but should be read critically. Further, on the causes of war see Cyril B. Falls, *The Second World War,* 3rd ed. rev. (1950); and especially *Lionel Kochan, *The Struggle for Germany,*

1914–1945 (1963) (Harper Torchbook). Herbert C. O'Neill, *A Short History of the Second World War* (1950) and J. F. C. Fuller, *The Second World War, 1939–45* (1949) are comprehensive general works. The most readable and effective account of the whole war, however one-sided, remains *Winston Churchill, *The Second World War*, 6 vols. (1949–1952) (Bantam). Jon Kimche, *The Unfought Battle* (1968) deals with the phony war of 1939–1940; *M. L. B. Bloch, *Strange Defeat* (1949) (Norton) is a moving analysis of France's surrender in 1940. *Alexander Werth, *France, 1940–1955* (1956) (Beacon) and *Robert Aron, *The Vichy Regime 1940–45* (1958) (Beacon) provide good accounts of subsequent events there. The broader scene is well covered in *Chester Wilmot, *The Struggle for Europe* (1952) (Harper); *Herbert Feis, *Churchill, Roosevelt, Stalin* (1957) (Princeton); *Gordon Wright, *The Ordeal of Total War, 1939–1945* (1968) (Harper Torchbook); and *R. J. C. Butow, *Japan's Decision to Surrender* (1967) (Stanford).

Internal and Constitutional Affairs

Russia An excellent survey is *Lionel Kochan, *The Making of Modern Russia* (1962) (Penguin). For the pre-Soviet period see the survey of Mikhail M. Kapovich, *Imperial Russia, 1801–1917* (1932); *Bernard Pares, *The Fall of the Russian Monarchy* (1939); *Hugh Seton-Watson, *The Decline of Imperial Russia, 1855–1914* (1952) (Praeger); and Thomas C. Masaryk's old but valid *The Spirit of Russia*, 2 vols. (1919). Further, Launcelot A. Owen, *The Russian Peasant Movement, 1906–1917* (1937); *Franco Venturi, *Roots of Revolution* (1960) (Grosset & Dunlap); Werner E. Mosse, *Alexander II and the Modernization of Russia,* (1966) (Collier). For the Revolution and the Communist Regime, see *John Reed, *Ten Days that Shook the World* (1919) (several editions); *Bertram D. Wolfe, *Three Who Made a Revolution* [*Lenin, Trotsky, Stalin*], 4th rev. ed. (1964) (Delta); E. H. Carr, *A History of Soviet Russia, 1917–1926* (1950–1952); Leon Trotsky's own account, *History of the Russian Revolution* (1932) and his autobiography, *My Life* (1930); and the vivid biographies of Stalin (Oxford) and Trotsky (Vintage) by *Isaac Deutscher. Estimates of achievements and further outlook are to be found in Walter Laqueur, *The Fate of the Revolution: Interpretations of Soviet History* (1967); *Isaac Deutscher, *The Unfinished Revolution: Russia 1917–1967* (1967) (Oxford); and the essays *The Impact of the Russian Revolution, 1917–1967: The Influence of Bolshevism on the World Outside Russia*, issued under the auspices of the Royal Institute of International Affairs (1967) (Oxford). For institutional history see John Hazard, *The Soviet System of Government*, rev. ed. (1960). * George F. Kennan, *Russia and the West under Lenin and Stalin* (1961) (Mentor). Franz Borkenau, *The Communist International* (1938) and *European Communism* (1953); and Robert D. Warth, *Soviet Russia in World Politics* (1963) will be useful for international issues.

Germany Ernst Kohn-Bramstedt, *Aristocracy and the Middle Classes in Germany, 1830–1900* (1937) provides a fine introduction to social history. For the making of imperial Germany see *Michael Howard, *The Franco-Prussian War* (1961) (Collier) and the following biographies of Bismarck: *Erich Eyck, *Bismarck and the German Empire* (1950) (Norton) and Otto Pflanze, *Bismarck and the Development of Germany: The Period of Unification, 1815–1871* (1963). William H. Dawson, *The German Empire, 1867–1914* (1919) is still a readable survey, to be complemented by *J. Alden Nichols, *Germany after Bismarck* (1958) (Norton) and Alexander Gerschenkron, *Bread and Democracy in Germany* (1943). For the period immediately preceding the First World War, Michael Balfour, *The Kaiser and His Times* (1964) is the best English biography of William II. *Carl E. Schorske, *German Social*

Democracy, 1905–1917 (1955) (Wiley); Peter Gay, *The Dilemma of Democratic Socialism: Edouard Bernstein's Challenge to Marx* (1952) (Collier); and Mary E. Townsend, *The Rise and Fall of Germany's Colonial Empire, 1844–1918* (1930) discuss various aspects of the prewar years, while *Fritz Fischer, *Germany's Aims in the First World War* (1967) (Norton) illuminates the coming of the war itself and its ends.

*Richard Grunberger, *Germany, 1918–1945* (1964) (Harper & Row) and *Erich Eyck, *A History of the Weimar Republic,* 2 vols. (1963) (Atheneum), one brief, the other detailed, and *S. William Halperin, *Germany Tried Democracy* (1946) (Norton) are recommended for the times following the collapse of 1918.

For the collapse of the Republic and the rise of National Socialism, see *George L. Mosse, *The Crisis of German Ideology* (1964) (Grosset & Dunlap); *Fritz R. Stern, *The Politics of Cultural Despair* (1961) (Anchor); *Robert G. L. Waite, *Vanguard of Nazism: The Free Corps Movement in Postwar Germany, 1918–1923* (1952) (Norton); John W. Wheeler-Bennett, *Wooden Titan: Hindenburg in Twenty Years of German History, 1914–1934* (1936); Klaus W. Epstein, *Matthias Erzberger and the Dilemma of German Democracy* (1959); and *Gordon A. Craig, *The Politics of the Prussian Army, 1640–1945* (1955) (Oxford), already cited. Also good are Walter Z. Laqueur, *Young Germany: A History of the Germany Youth Movement* (1962); *Klemens von Klemperer, *Germany's New Conservatism* (1957); (Princeton); A. Mendelssohn, *The War and German Society* (1937); *Siegfried C. Kracauer, *From Caligari to Hitler: A Psychological History of the German Film* (1947) (Princeton).

William Sheridan Allen has described the gradual aspect of *The Nazi Seizure of Power* (1955) as it affected a small German town. The years of the Third Reich may be approached through *William L. Shirer's popular *Rise and Fall of the Third Reich* (1960) (Crest; Simon & Schuster); Konrad Heiden's *History of National Socialism* (1935); *Franz Neumann's *Behemoth* (1942) (Harper Torchbook), already cited; or the collective study cited by M. Baumont, J. H. E. Fried and Edmond Vermeil, *The Third Reich* (1955). The destructive aspects of Nazism are revealed in E. Crankshaw, *Gestapo* (1956) and *Eugen Kogon, *The Theory and Practice of Hell* (1950) (Medallion); its more positive side in *David Schoenbaum, *Hitler's Social Revolution* (1966) (Anchor). The best biography of Hitler is *A. L. C. Bullock, *Hitler, a Study in Tyranny,* rev. ed. (1964) (Harper Torchbook), while his end and that of the regime are vividly sketched in *H. R. Trevor-Roper, *The Last Days of Hitler* (1947) (Collier).

The postwar period is examined in Henry C. Wallich, *Mainsprings of the German Revival* (1955); Edgar Alexander, *Adenauer and the New Germany* (1957); and Grant S. McLellan, ed., *The Two Germanies* (1959).

Italy Good general surveys are to be found in Denis Mack Smith, *Italy: A Modern History* (1959), and (from the economic aspect) Shepard B. Clough, *The Economic History of Modern Italy* (1964) and Maurice F. Neufeld, *Italy: School for Awakening Countries* (1961). G. M. Trevelyan, *Garibaldi and the Thousand* (1909); Denis Mack Smith, *Garibaldi* (1956); Raymond Grew, *A Sterner Plan for Italian Unity* (1963); John A. Thayer, *Italy and the Great War: Politics and Culture, 1870–1915* (1964) carry the story through to the rise of fascism. Renzo di Felice's great history of Mussolini's Italy, *Mussolini il Fascisto* (1968), has, in its second volume, reached the end of the 1920's. The best English biography of Mussolini is by Ivone A. Kirkpatrick: *Mussolini: A Study of a Demagogue* (1964). His regime should be approached through the works of Federico Chabod, *A History of Italian Fascism* (1963); and Richard A. Webster, *The Cross and the Fasces: Christian Democracy and Fascism in Italy* (1960); Roman Dombrowski, *Mussolini: Twilight and Fall* (1956); and Dante L. Germino, *The Italian Fascist Party in Power* (1959). For the foreign policy of

Fascist Italy see Elizabeth Wiskemann, *The Rome-Berlin Axis* (1949). Muriel Grindrod, *The Rebuilding of Italy: Politics and Economics, 1945–1955* (1956) and *A. J. White, *The Evolution of Modern Italy* (1965) (Norton) deal with the postwar period. A stimulating overview of recent historical orientations can be found in Leo Valiani, *L'Historiographie de l'Italie contemporaine* (1968).

France   Edward M. Earle, ed., *Modern France* (1951) is still one of the best introductions to most aspects of French life, thought, and politics. Also excellent are J. E. C. Bodley's old *France* (1898); Gordon Wright, *France in Modern Times: 1760 to the Present* (1960); *John C. Cairns, *France* (1966) (Spectrum), a brief, wise, readable essay; and *Stanley Hoffmann, ed., *In Search of France* (1963) (Harper Torchbook). Good works on Napoleon III and his times: George P. Gooch, *The Second Empire* (1960); *James M. Thompson, *Louis Napoleon and the Second Empire* (1955) (Norton); Theodore Zeldin, *The Political System of Napoleon III* (1958); Albert J. Guérard, *Napoléon III* (1943). For a recent assessment, see Theodore Zeldin, *Emile Ollivier and the Liberal Empire of Napoleon III* (1963); while the watershed of 1870 is described in *Roger L. Williams, *The French Revolution of 1870–1871* (1969) (Norton).

Two important works are René Rémond, *The Right Wing in France* (1966) and Paul M. de La Gorce, *The French Army* (1963). Guy P. Chapman, *The Third Republic of France: The First Phase, 1871–1894* (1963) is excellent, as is the brief illuminating essay of *David Thomson, *Democracy in France Since 1870*, 4th ed. (1964) (Oxford). The best account of the Dreyfus crisis is by Douglas Johnson, *France and the Dreyfus Affair* (1966). The years between the wars are somberly depicted in Alexander Werth, *The Twilight of France, 1933–1940* (1942); their economic aspect in A. Sauvy, *Historie économique de la France entre les deux guerres*, 2 vols. (1965/67). The politics of the first half of this century are reflected in *Eugen Weber, *Action Française* (1962) (Stanford) and in several good biographical studies: Harvey Goldberg, *The Life of Jean Jaurès* (1962); Joel Colton, *Léon Blum* (1966); P. Miguel, *Poincaré* (1961); Rudolph Binion, *Defeated Leaders* (1960). War and its aftermath are reflected in *Robert Aron, *The Vichy Regime* (1958) (Beacon); *Alexander Werth, *France, 1940–1955* (1956) (Beacon); Herbert Lüthy, *France Against Herself* (1955); Philip M. Williams, *Politics in Post-war France* (1954); Nathan C. Leites, *On the Game of Politics in France* (1959); *Dorothy M. Pickles, *The Fifth Republic* (1960) (Praeger); and *Jean Lacouture, *De Gaulle* (1966) (Discus). On the latter, the brightest light is shed by his own memoirs.

Britain   General works: R. C. K. Ensor, *England, 1870–1914* (1949); Charles L. Mowat, *Britain Between the Wars, 1918–1940* (1955); Keith Hutchinson, *Decline and Fall of British Capitalism* (1950); A. J. P. Taylor, *English History, 1914–1945* (1965). Henry R. Winkler, *Great Britain in the 20th Century* is an excellent pamphlet. The Victorian age should be approached through *George M. Young, *Victorian England: Portrait of an Age* (1954) (Oxford); Asa Briggs, *Victorian People* (1955); F. M. L. Thompson, *English Landed Society in the Nineteenth Century* (1963); and Cecil B. Woodham-Smith's rich biography, *Florence Nightingale* (1950). Simon H. Nowell-Smith, ed., *Edwardian England, 1901–1914* (1964) is basic for the beginning of the twentieth century. Also recommended: Mary E. Edes and D. P. Frasier, eds., *The Age of Extravagance: An Edwardian Reader* (1955); *George Dangerfield, *The Strange Death of Liberal England, 1910–1914* (1935) (Capricorn); and *Anne Fremantle, *This Little Band of Prophets: The Story of the Gentle Fabians* (1960) (Mentor).

The interwar years are covered by *David Thomson, *England in the Twentieth Century, 1914–1963* (1964) (Penguin); *Arthur Marwick, *The Deluge: British Society and the First World War* (1965) (Norton); *Robert Graves and

Alan Hodge, *The Long Week-end: A Social History of Great Britain, 1918–1939* (1941) (Norton); and the biographies of James Ramsay MacDonald by Godfrey E. Elton (1939); of Stanley Baldwin by George M. Young (1953); of Neville Chamberlain by Keith G. Feiling (1946); of John Maynard Keynes by *Roy F. Harrod (1951) (St. Martin's); and of Ernest Bevin by Alan Bullock (1960). The postwar years are treated by David Thomson (above); Francis Williams, *Socialist Britain* (1949); and Ernest S. Watkins, *The Cautious Revolution* (1950).

For the history of the empire, its rise and fall, see Charles F. Mullett, *The British Empire-Commonwealth, Its Themes and Character* (1961) or the works of Nicholas Mansergh, *The Multi-racial Commonwealth* (1955) and *Commonwealth Perspectives* (1958).

Spain Raymond Carr, *Spain, 1808–1939* (1966) is the basic source of information. John B. Trend, *The Origins of Modern Spain* (1934) may still be usefully referred to. See also A. Ramos Oliveira, *Politics, Economics and Men of Modern Spain, 1808–1946* (1948). The important period of the Republic and the Civil War is treated in the following works: *Gabriel Jackson, *The Spanish Republic and the Civil War, 1931–1939* (1965) (Princeton); José M. Sanchez, *Reform and Reaction: The Politico-Religious Background of the Spanish Civil War* (1964); *Gerald Brenan, *Spanish Labyrinth: An Account of the Social and Political Background of the Civil War* (1960) (Cambridge); and *Hugh Thomas, *The Spanish Civil War* (1961) (Harper & Row). See also *George Orwell, *Homage to Catalonia* (1938) (Harcourt, Brace & World); *Stanley G. Payne, *Falange: A History of Spanish Fascism* (1961) (Stanford) and Payne's *The Spanish Revolution* (1970) (Norton); and, for later events, *Herbert L. Matthews, *The Yoke and the Arrows: A Report on Spain* (1957) (Braziller).

The Habsburg Empire *A. J. P. Taylor's *The Habsburg Monarchy, 1809–1918* (1948) (Harper Torchbook) provides an excellent short account, while *Arthur J. May gives a detailed one in *The Hapsburg Monarchy, 1867–1914* (1951) (Norton). For the major problem of the monarchy, see Robert A. Kann, *The Multinational Empire: Nationalism and National Reform in the Habsburg Monarchy, 1848–1918*, 2 vols. (1951). The fall of the empire is well described by *Oszkar Jaszi, *The Dissolution of the Habsburg Monarchy* (1929) (Phoenix) and, more recently, by *Edward Crankshaw, *The Fall of the House of Habsburg* (1963) (Popular Library).

Austria: The economic consequences of the Empire's disruption are reflected in Leo Pasvolsky, *Economic Nationalism of the Danubian States* (1928); the history of the Austrian Republic itself, in Mary MacDonald, *The Republic of Austria, 1918–1934* (1947); Charles A. Gulick, *Austria from Habsburg to Hitler,* 2 vols. (1948); Julius Braunthal, *The Tragedy of Austria* (1948); and Gordon Brook-Shepherd, *Anschluss: The Rape of Austria* (1963).

The Hungarian Lands C. A. Macartney, *A History of Hungary, 1929–1945,* 2 vols. (1957) is fundamental. See also the good book badly written by Rudolf L. Tokes, *Bela Kun and the Hungarian Soviet Republic* (1967); Owen Rutter, *Regent of Hungary: The Life of Admiral Nicholas Horthy* (1939); and, for very recent history, Leslie B. Bain, *The Reluctant Satellites: An Eyewitness Report on East Europe and the Hungarian Revolution* (1960); or François Fejtö, *Behind the Rape of Hungary* (1957).

Eastern Europe *Hugh Seton-Watson, *Eastern Europe Between the Wars, 1918–1941*, 2nd ed. (1946) (Harper Torchbook) is an excellent introduction, along with his *The East European Revolution* (1956) (Praeger). For more recent developments see *C. A. Macartney and A. W. Palmer, *Independent Eastern Europe* (1962) (St. Martin's) and *Stephen A. Fischer-Galati, ed., *Eastern Europe in the Sixties* (1963) (Praeger). Samuel H. Thomson, *Czechoslovakia in European History*, 2nd ed. enl. (1953) and Elizabeth Wiskemann, *Czechs and Germans* (1938) are useful for the troubled history of Czechoslovakia. Polish history should be approached through the good brief survey of Hans Otto Meissner, *A History of Modern Poland* (1966), and Titus Komarnicki, *Rebirth of the Polish Republic* (1957). For the dark years of the war see Tadeusz Cyprian and Jerzy Sawicki, *Nazi Rule in Poland, 1939–1945* (1961).

For more recent events: Paul Zinner, ed., *National Communism and Popular Revolt in Eastern Europe* (1956), whose documents help one to understand Flora Lewis, *A Case History of Hope: The Story of Poland's Peaceful Revolutions* (1958). *Leften S. Stavrianos, *The Balkans, 1815–1914* (1963) (Holt, Rinehart & Winston) is a handy synthesis of complex problems. So is *Robert Lee Wolff, *The Balkans in Our Time* (1967) (Norton). R. W. Seton-Watson, *A History of the Roumanians* (1934); Thad W. Riker, *The Making of Roumania* (1931); and Henry L. Roberts, *Rumania: Political Problems of an Agrarian State* (1951) are recommended for Rumania, whose Communist period is reflected in Ghita Ionescu, *Communism in Rumania, 1944–1962* (1964). For Yugoslavia, see Jacob B. Hoptner, *Yugoslavia in Crisis, 1934–1941* (1962); George W. Hoffman and Fred W. Neal, *Yugoslavia and the New Communism* (1962); and Fred W. Neal, *Titoism in Action* (1958). More general, but highly readable: *Rebecca West, *Black Lamb and Grey Falcon: A Journey Through Yugoslavia* (1941) (Compass).

Turkey George E. Kirk, *A Short History of the Middle East*, 4th ed. rev. (1957) should be useful, along with *Bernard E. Lewis, *The Emergence of Modern Turkey* (1961) (Oxford). The meeting of Turkey and the West, and subsequent developments, may be traced through William Miller, *The Ottoman Empire and Its Successors, 1801–1936* (1966); Roderic H. Davison, *Reform in the Ottoman Empire, 1856–1876* (1963); Joan Haslip, *The Sultan: Life of Abdul Hamid* (1958); Serif Mardin, *Genesis of Young Ottoman Thought* (1962); Arnold J. Toynbee, *The Western Question in Greece and Turkey* (1922); and Donald E. Webster, *The Turkey of Ataturk* (1939).

The United States James G. Randall, *Civil War and Reconstruction* (1937) is still dependable. Also interesting are Donaldson Jordan and Edwin J. Pratt, *Europe and the American Civil War* (1931) and Julius Pratt, *America's Colonial Experiment* (1950). On American expansionism, see *Albert K. Weinberg, *Manifest Destiny* (1935) (Quadrangle) and Walter Millis, *The Martial Spirit* (1931). For Latin America, see Daniel Dawson, *The Mexican Adventure* (1935), concerning the French fiasco of the 1860's; James F. Rippy, *Latin America and the Industrial Age* (1944); and *Herbert L. Matthews, ed., *The United States and Latin America,* 2nd ed. (1963) (Spectrum).

The Great Crash, 1929 (1955) (Sentry) by John Kenneth Galbraith, discusses the traumatic breakdown of 1920's prosperity. Two good works on the New Deal are *The Era of Franklin D. Roosevelt,* by D. W. Brogan (1950), and *William E. Leuchtenburg, *Franklin D. Roosevelt and the New Deal* (1963) (Harper Torchbook). See also *Allen Guttman, ed., *American Neutrality and the Spanish Civil War* (1963) (Heath) and *Richard Fenno, Jr., ed., *The Yalta Conference* (1955) (Heath).

The postwar posture of the United States is treated in *Eric F. Goldman, *The Crucial Decade and After: America 1945–1960* (1960) (Vintage) and John Kenneth Galbraith, *The Affluent Society* (1958) (Mentor). For a more general evaluation, see *George F. Kennan's brief and lucid *American Diplomacy, 1900–1950* (1951) (Mentor).

The Material Revolution

Technology and Production   William L. Thomas, ed., *Man's Role in Changing the Face of the Earth* (1956) is a massive volume, packed with information about every aspect of this problem. An optimistic view of the impact of technology upon social life is J. Fourastié, *Machinisme et bien-être* (1951). Other aspects and other views are to be found in Kingston Derry and Trevor I. Williams, *A Short History of Technology* (1961); *Sigfried Giedion, *Mechanization Takes Command* (1948) (Norton); Ludwig F. Haber, *The Chemical Industry in the Nineteenth Century* (1958); and *Lewis Mumford, *Technics and Civilization* (1934) (Harcourt, Brace & World). See also Frederick Pollock, *The Economic and Social Consequences of Automation* (1957); Thomas C. Cochran, *The American Business System: A Historical Perspective 1900–1955* (1957); *Frederick Lewis Allen, *The Big Change* (1952) (Harper & Row); and Michael Tracy, *Agriculture in Western Europe* (1964).

Medicine and Hygiene   Among works on modern medicine and its role in modern society, the following are the most useful: Richard H. Shryock, *The Development of Modern Medicine,* rev. and enl. (1947); Howard W. Haggard, *The Doctor in History* (1934); *Paul de Kruif, *The Microbe Hunters* (1939) (Harcourt, Brace & World); R. Sand, *Vers la médicine sociale* (1948); Nathaniel W. Faxon, ed., *The Hospital in Contemporary Life* (1949); and *Charles Wilcocks, *Medical Advance, Public Health and Social Evolution* (1966) (Pergamon).

Science and Thought   For a basic reference work, consult *John T. Merz's monumental *History of European Thought in the Nineteenth Century,* new ed., 4 vols. (1924) (Dover). See also Carl T. Chase, *The Evolution of Modern Physics* (1947); *Leopold Infeld, *Albert Einstein: His Work and Its Influence on Our World* (1950) (Scribner); *Bernard Barber, *Science and the Social Order,* rev. ed. (1962) (Collier); *Jacob Bronowski, *Science and Human Values,* rev. ed. (1965) (Harper Torchbook); *Arthur S. Eddington, *The Expanding Universe* (1958) (University of Michigan); W. P. D. Wightman, *The Growth of Scientific Ideas* (1951); William Esslinger, *Politics and Science* (1955); and J. A. Y. Butler, *Science and Human Life* (1957). For more specific problems see John C. Greene, *The Death of Adam: Evolution and Its Impact on Western Thought* (1959); Walter Hollitscher, *Sigmund Freud: An Introduction* (1947); *Benjamin N. Nelson, ed., *Freud and the 20th Century* (1958) (Meridian); *Ernest Jones, *The Life and Work of Sigmund Freud* (1961) (Anchor); *Philip Rieff, *Freud: The Mind of the Moralist* (1959) (Anchor); *Paul A. Robinson, *The Freudian Left* [Reich, Roheim, Marcuse] (1969) (Colophon).

Religion   Revealing and still important is *Andrew D. White, *A History of the Warfare of Science with Theology in Christendom,* 2 vols. (1896) (Dover Free Press). James H. Nichols, *History of Christianity 1650–1950* (1956) is a factual and reliable general work. See also John N. Figgis, *Churches in the Modern State* (1913); Waldemar Gurian and Matthew A. Fitzsimons, eds., *The Catholic Church in World Affairs* (1954); *Karl Jaspers, *Man in the Modern Age* (1957) (Anchor); *Walter Rauschenbush, *Christianity and the Social Crisis* (1963) (Harper Torchbook); Adrien Dansette, *Religious History of Modern France,* 2 vols. (1961); Michael P. Fogarty, *Christian Democracy in Western Europe, 1820–1953* (1957); Kenneth S. Inglis, *Churches and the Working Class in Victorian England* (1963); Reinhold Niebuhr, *Faith and History* (1949); and the essays in *Sidney A. Burrell, ed., *The Role of Religion in Modern European History* (1964) (Macmillan).

The Way They Lived

The Countryside   *Robert Redfield, *Peasant Society and Culture: An Anthropological Approach to Civilization* (1956) (Phoenix) is a theoretical study. More factual are Hubert H. Tiltman, *Peasant Europe* (1934) and H. Pourrat, *L'Homme à la bêche: l'histoire du paysan* (1949), as well as M. Augé-Laribé, *La Révolution agricole* (1955), already cited. For more specific studies, see R. Thabault's wonderful *Mon Village* (1944); *Gordon Wright, *Rural Revolution in France: The Peasantry in the Twentieth Century* (1964) (Stanford); *Lawrence W. Wylie, *Village in the Vancluse* (1957) (Harper & Row); and Edgar Morin, *Commune en France* (1967).

The Cities   Govind S. Ghurye, *Cities and Civilization* (1962) is an excellent introduction, along with *Constantinos A. Doxiadis and Truman B. Douglass, *The New World of Urban Man* (1965) (United Church); William E. Cole, *Urban Society* (1958); Paul K. Hatt and Albert J. Reiss, eds., *Cities and Society*, 2nd ed. (1957); and *H. Wentworth Eldredge, ed., *Taming Megalopolis*, 2 vols. (1967) (Anchor). Two classic works deserve attention: *Max Weber, *The City* (1958) (Free Press) and Lewis Mumford, *The Culture of Cities* (1940). H. Lavedan, *Histoire de l'urbanisme*, Vol. II, *Epoque contemporaine* (1952) is also useful. Colorful details in Lawrence Wright, *Clean and Decent: The Fascinating History of the Bathroom and the Water Closet* (1960) (University of Toronto), and Alison Adburgham, *A Punch History of Manners and Modes, 1841–1940* (1961) and *Shops and Shopping* (1964). See also Hans Selye, *The Stress of Life* (1956).

The Working Classes   Gilbert Stone's *A History of Labour* (1922, rather old) is still useful. More up to date is Walter Galenson's *Labour in Developing Economics* (1962). Very interesting and more theoretical are H. Dubreuil, *Le Travail et la civilisation; esquisse de l'histoire et de la philosophie du travail* (1953) and A. Touraine, *La Conscience ouvrière* (1966). Also suggested: Robert Theobald, *The Rich and the Poor* (1960); *Andrew Shonfield, *The Attack on World Poverty* (1960) (Vintage); and *Lee Rainwater and Karol K. Weinstein, *And the Poor Get Children* (1960) (Quadrangle).

For concrete social conditions, see G. Duveau, *La Vie ouvrière en France sous le second Empire* (1946); M. Collinet, *Essai sur la condition ouvrière, 1900–1950* (1951); Ferdynand Zweig, *Men in the Pits* (1948); *Val R. Lorwin, *Labor and Working Conditions in Modern Europe* (1967) (Macmillan); and John Hilton, *Rich Man, Poor Man* (1944).

Food   John Burnett, *Plenty and Want: A Social History of Diet in England from 1815 to the Present Day* (1966) and Richard O. Cummings, *The American and His Food; a History of Food Habits in the United States*, rev. ed. (1941) are factual and interesting. Norman W. Desrosier, *Attack on Starvation* (1961) and the older book by Frank Carpenter, *How the World Is Fed* (1928) have a more general scope. See also Noel Curtis-Bennett, *The Food of the People* (1949) and the pioneering study of R. N. Salaman, *The History and Social Influence of the Potato* (1949)—not limited to this period.

The Bourgeoisie   *Charles Morazé, *The Triumph of the Middle Classes* (1967) (Anchor) traces the rise and growth of the bourgeoisie. Lewis Corey, *The Crisis of the Middle Classes* (1935) marks the beginning of its decline. P. Bleton, *Les Hommes des temps qui viennent; essai sur les classes moyennes* (1956) and especially Nikolai Berdiaev, *The Bourgeois Mind* (1934) are strongly recommended. Also useful, Joseph A. Banks, *Prosperity and Parenthood: A Study of Family Planning Among the Victorian Middle Classes* (1954).

Women See Joseph A. and Olive Banks, *Feminism and Family Planning in Victorian England* (1964) and the works of Cecil W. Cunnington: *English Women's Clothing in the Present Century* (1952), *Feminine Attitudes in the Nineteenth Century* (1936), *The Perfect Lady* (1948). Specifically on the theme of emancipation, see *Eleanor Flexner, *Century of Struggle: The Woman's Rights Movement in the U.S.* (1968) (Atheneum); Aileen S. Kraditor, *Ideas of the Woman Suffrage Movement, 1890–1920* (1965); William L. O'Neill, *Woman Movement: Feminism in the United States and England* (1969) and *Everyone Was Brave: The Rise and Fall of Feminism in America* (1969); Page Smith, *Daughters of the Promised Land: Women in American History* (1970); Kate Millett, *Sexual Politics* (1970). Basic sourcebooks are *Mary Wollstonecraft, *A Vindication of the Rights of Woman,* edited by Charles W. Hagelman, Jr., first published in 1792 (1970) (Norton); *John Stuart Mill, *Subjection of Women,* first published in 1869, included in several collections; *Simone de Beauvoir, *The Second Sex* (1953) (Bantam); *Betty Friedan, *The Feminine Mystique* (1963) (Dell). Irene Clephane, *Towards Sex Freedom* (1935) is relevant but thin. The following may also be of use: *Mary Ellmann, *Thinking about Women* (1968) (Harcourt Brace Jovanovich); Virginia Woolf, *A Room of One's Own* (1929) and *Three Guineas* (1938); Arthur H. Hirsch, *The Love Elite: The Story of Woman's Emancipation and Her Drive for Sexual Fulfillment* (1963); *Helen Gurley Brown, *Sex and the Office* (1964) (Pocket Books); Adele B. Lewis, *From Kitchen to Career* (1965).

The Victorians See *G. Kitson Clark, *The Making of Victorian England* (1962) (Atheneum); *Steven Marcus, *The Other Victorians* (1966) (Bantam); Peter C. Quennell, *Victorian Panorama: A Survey of Life and Fashions from Contemporary Photographs* (1937); *Walter E. Houghton, *The Victorian Frame of Mind, 1830–1870* (1957) (Yale); *William L. Burn, *The Age of Equipoise: A Study of the Mid-Victorian Generation* (1964) (Norton); and Asa Briggs, *Victorian People* (1955) and *Victorian Cities* (1965) (Harper & Row).

The Modern Age

See Hajo Holborn, *The Political Collapse of Europe* (1951); *George Lichtheim, *The New Europe: Today—and Tomorrow* (1963) (Praeger); *Richard Mayne, *The Community of Europe* (1963) (Norton); and Michael Shanks and John Lambert, *The Common Market Today—and Tomorrow* (1962). For a more speculative approach, see Eric Fischer, *The Passing of the European Age: A Study in the Transfer of Western Civilization and its Renewal in Other Continents,* rev. ed. (1948). R. L. Delevoy, *Dimensions du XXe siècle, 1900–1945* (1965); Henry S. Hughes, *An Essay for Our Times* (1950); Kenneth W. Thompson, *Political Realism and the Crisis of World Politics* (1960).

Education and Popular Culture For the complex problems of modern education, see the works of Frank P. Graves, *History of Education in Modern Times* (1915); Adolph E. Meyer, *The Development of Education in the Twentieth Century* (1939); and G. A. N. Lowndes, *The Silent Social Revolution* (1937). Widely differing examples of excellent educational history are David Newsome, *Godliness and Good Learning* (1961), about the way in which the ideal of muscular Christianity evolved in British schools; and A. Prost, *L'Enseignement en France, 1800–1967* (1968). See also Howard C. Barnard, *Short History of English Education* (1947); Stanley J. Curtis, *Education in Britain since 1900* (1952); F. Ponteil, *Histoire de l'enseignement, 1789–1965* (1966). The phenomena of popular culture should be approached through the studies of *Raymond Williams, *Culture and Society, 1780–1950* (1958) (Harper Torchbook) and *The Long Revolution* (1961); *Bernard Rosenberg and D. M. White, eds., *Mass Culture*

(1957) (Free Press); and *Lee Loewenthal, *Literature, Popular Culture and Society* (1961) (Pacific Books). More specific, but very interesting, *Henry N. Smith, *Popular Culture and Industrialism, 1865–1890* (1967) (Anchor). *Sui generis* speculations on contemporary trends are in *Marshall McLuhan, *Understanding Media* (1964) (McGraw-Hill) and *The Medium is the Massage* (1967) (Bantam). Fascinating and also more comprehensible: *Richard D. Altick, *The English Common Reader: A Social History of the Mass Reading Public, 1800–1900* (1957) (Phoenix) and Richard Hoggart, *The Uses of Literacy* (1957), on changing tastes in reading and entertainment among the working classes. There are no good works on entertainments as social phenomena, but one can refer to Ronald H. Coase, *British Broadcasting: A Study in Monopoly* (1950); or consult the encyclopedic *Histoire des Spectacles* (1965), edited by Guy Dumur.

Concerning sports, the works of Peter C. McIntosh are the most useful: *Sport in Society* (1963); *Physical Education in England since 1800,* rev. ed. (1969), whose scope is broader than the title suggests; and *Landmarks in the History of Physical Education* (1957). There are two compendious works in French: B. Gillet, *Histoire du Sport* (1965), brief and handy; R. Caillois, ed., *Jeux et Sports* (1967). See also Eugen Weber, "Pierre de Coubertin and the Introduction of Sport in France," *Journal of Contemporary History,* Vol. 5, No. 2 (1970) and "Gymnastics and Sports in fin-de-siècle France," *American Historical Review,* February, 1971.

Literature and the Arts   The best introductions here are the works themselves. More generally, however, reference can be made to *Eugen Weber, ed., *Paths to the Present: Aspects of European Thought from Romanticism to Existentialism* (1960) (Dodd, Mead); *E. H. Gombrich, *The Story of Art* (1956) (Praeger); and *Sigfried Giedion, *Mechanization Takes Command* (1948) (Norton), cited previously. Beyond these see Stephen T. Madsen, *Sources of Art Nouveau* (1957); Nikolaus Pevsner, *Pioneers of the Modern Movement* (1937); *Alfred H. Barr, Jr., *What Is Modern Painting?,* 10th ed. (1968) (Mus. Mod. Art); Theodore M. Finney, *A History of Music,* rev. ed. (1947); Hugo Leichtentritt, *Music, History, and Ideas* (1950); Mary G. Colum, *From These Roots: the Ideas That Have Made Modern Literature* (1944); *J. M. Richards, *An Introduction to Modern Architecture* (1956) (Penguin); *Helmut and Alison Gernsheim, *A Concise History of Photography* (1965) (Grosset & Dunlap).

There are convenient volumes on various artistic movements in the World of Art Library: François Mathey, *The World of the Impressionists* (1961); Hans Richter, *Dada* (1965); *Patrick Waldberg, *Surrealism* (1965) (McGraw-Hill); and *Lucy R. Lippard, *Pop Art* (1967) (Praeger). John Rewald has written two beautiful and detailed studies: *The History of Impressionism* (1946) (Mus. Mod. Art) and *Post-Impressionism from Van Gogh to Gauguin* (1956). *Herbert E. Read's *Concise History of Modern Painting* (1959) (Praeger) provides a handy survey.

More details are furnished by good biographies of leading composers: Lawrence and Elisabet Mary Hanson, *Tchaikowsky* (1965); Siegfried Kracauer, *Orpheus in Paris* (1938), on Offenbach; *Winton Dean, *Bizet* (1948) (Collier); *Ernest Newman, *Wagner as Man and Artist* (1924) (Vintage); George Martin's excellent *Verdi* (1963); or *Igor Stravinsky's own *Autobiography* (1936) (Norton) and his other vivid writings—or see the biographies of leading literary figures.

Fiction   Until their slow death in the 1950's and 60's, novels of the past century have piled up in such numbers that we can give here only a highly selective list of those most revealing for the social historian.

For provincial life under the Second Empire, *Gustave Flaubert's *Madame Bovary* (1857) (many editions) provides a classic picture. Less read but perhaps more revealing is his *Sentimental Education* (1869) (Penguin), whose hero's moral disintegration under the impact of reality culminates in 1848 and soon after. Flaubert's nephew, *Guy de Maupassant, would carry on the family tradition of social criticism—especially in *Bel Ami* (1885) (Popular Library). Contemporary English life and values are reflected in the works of William Makepeace Thackeray and Charles Dickens; a somewhat later German period in a novel like *Theodor Fontane's *Effi Briest* (1894) (Penguin; Unger). The greatest literary achievements of the style would come from Russia, where *Leo Tolstoy portrayed the society and life of his own time in *Anna Karenina* (1875) (many editions).

Conditions of working-class life in the late nineteenth century are grimly described by Emile Zola in *The Dram-Shop* (1877); *Germinal* (1885) (Penguin; Scribner). The rather grosser life of the German bourgeoisie in the novels of Heinrich Mann are more useful to the social historian than those of his more famous brother. Both men wrote their best works before 1914. In the case of *Thomas Mann, *Buddenbrooks* (1901) (Vintage) is the tale of a bourgeois family's decline; *The Magic Mountain* (1924) (Vintage) that of the confusion of a whole civilization. One may compare this with *Jean Barois,* by R. M. du Gard (1913, 1969) (Bobbs-Merrill), the story of a Frenchman's life through the half-century preceding the First World War (and through the Dreyfus affair), facing all the problems of the *fin de siècle*.

The depression is better understood from novels than from economic analyses. See Hans Fallada, *Little Man, What Now?* (1932) for Germany and Walter Greenwood, *Love on the Dole* (1933) for England.

The intellectual quest for commitment can be traced through *André Malraux, *Man's Fate* (1933) (Vintage); *Ignazio Silone, *Bread and Wine* (1937) (Signet); *Ernest Hemingway, *For Whom the Bell Tolls* (1940) (Scribner); *Arthur Koestler, *Darkness at Noon* (1941) (Bantam); to the utter despair of *George Orwell's *1984* (1949) (Signet). The pattern of hope and disillusion behind that evolution is spelled out most clearly in *R. H. S. Crossman, ed., *The God That Failed* (1950) (Bantam; Harper & Row).

The Latest Age

For the aftermath of the war, see Wilfrid F. Knapp, *A History of War and Peace, 1939–1965* (1967); *Richard F. Fenno, Jr., ed., *The Yalta Conference* (1955) (Heath); *Herbert Feis, *Between War and Peace: The Potsdam Conference* (1960) (Princeton); *Arnold J. Toynbee, *The World and the West* (1953) (Meridian); *George Lichtheim, *The New Europe: Today—and Tomorrow* (1963) (Praeger); Jacques Freymond, *Western Europe since the War* (1964); Hugh Seton-Watson, *Neither War nor Peace: The Struggle for Power in the Postwar World* (1960); and Robert C. Mowat, *Ruin and Resurgence, 1939–1965* (1966), providing general surveys of the situation, of which Lichtheim's is the most suggestive. *David Rees, *The Age of Containment: The Cold War* (1967) (St. Martin's), and John A. Lukacs, *A New History of the Cold War,* 3rd ed. (1966) focus on that particular struggle. On the problem of European unity: L. Armand, *Le Pari européen* (1968) is excellent.

Some of the major issues facing us are tackled in *Herbert Marcuse's *One Dimensional Man* (1964) (Beacon) and *Reason and Revolution,* 2nd ed. (1963) (Beacon), strongly recommended for understanding the philosophy of a scholar whose influence upon the present generation has been great. Beyond Marcuse and more optimistic is *Michael Harrington, *The Accidental Century* (1965) (Penguin), a brilliant and incisive discussion of our times, their dangers and their promises. Some of the tendencies they criticize have been described in works like *David Riesman et al., *The Lonely Crowd,* rev. ed. (1950) (Yale); William H.

Whyte, *The Organization Man* (1957) (Anchor); and *Vance O. Packard, *The Status Seekers* (1959) (Pocket Books), studies of American society leading the way, where Europe and the rest of the world are likely to follow. Other aspects of our time are discussed in Eric Fischer, *The Passing of the European Age,* rev. ed. (1948); *Robert L. Heilbroner, *The Great Ascent: The Struggle for Economic Development in Our Time* (1953) (Harper Torchbook); *Raymond Aron, *The Century of Total War* (1954) (Beacon); Andrew Shonfield, *Modern Capitalism* (1966); *M. M. Postan, *An Economic History of Western Europe: 1945–1964* (1967) (Barnes & Noble). For the politics of developing nations, see the book of that title edited in 1968 by Gabriel A. Almond and James S. Coleman. Also R. Dumont and B. Rosier, *Nous allons à la famine* (1965), John Russell, *World Population and World Food Supplies* (1954), and the various writings of Jacques Berque.

On the revolt of youth, the best running comment may be found in the pages of periodicals of the 1960's—especially *Encounter* through 1968–70. For the New Left of the late 1960's, see *Paul Jacobs and Saul Landau, eds., *The New Radicals* (1966) (Vintage), and *New Revolutionaries. Left Opposition* (1969) (Apollo), edited by Tariq Ali. For a swift general report, see *Stephen Spender, *The Year of the Young Rebels* (1969) (Vintage). The American situation has been described in a plethora of books and articles—among them *Kenneth Keniston, *The Young Radicals* (1968) (Harcourt, Brace & World). For what happened in France see *H. Bourges, ed., *The Student Revolt* (1968) (Hill & Wang), which also reproduces a rather famous interview between D. Cohn-Bendit and Jean-Paul Sartre. For criticism of radical views: R. Aron, *La Révolution introuvable* (1968); for the comments of a friendly but critical witness: Epistémon, *Ces Idées qui ont ébranlé la France: Nanterre 1967–68* (1968).

The Third World   The literature on this score becomes out of date as fast as it is printed. But here are a few suggestions: on the evolution of East and Southeast Asia, see George M. Kahin, ed., *Governments and Politics in Southeast Asia* (1959); Frank M. Trager, ed., *Marxism in Southeast Asia* (1959); *Amry Vandenbosch and Richard A. Butwell, *The Changing Face of Southeast Asia* (1966) (University of Kentucky); Charles A. Fisher, *Southeast Asia: A Social, Economic and Political Geography* (1964); Harold C. Hinton, *Communist China in World Politics* (1966); and Hugh Borton et al., *Japan Between East and West* (1957).

On Africa, some of the most stimulating works are in French: for example, R. Dumont, *L'Afrique Noire est mal partie* (1966), and G. Balandier, *Sociologie actuelle de l'Afrique Noire* (1955). But see also *D. O. Mannoni, *Prospero and Caliban* (1964) (Praeger), an analytical view of relations between colonist and colonized; P. Gordon Walker, *The Commonwealth* (1962); and J. Dufey, *Portugal in Africa* (1962). Richard Bourne, *Political Leaders of Latin America* (1970) and the works of L. Mercier Vega, *Roads to Power in Latin America* (1968) and *Guerrillas in Latin American* (1969) are skeptical and thought-provoking. An original work whose suggestions go beyond the area it covers is *John J. Johnson, *Political Change in Latin America: The Emergence of Middle Sectors* (1958) (Stanford). Boris Goldenberg, *The Cuban Revolution and Latin America* (1965) is reasonably dispassionate on a passionate subject. Equally involved are those writing on the Middle East, a subject on which most people take sides or are pushed into doing so. See Don Peretz, *The Middle East Today* (1963); Bernard Lewis' expert *The Middle East and the West* (1964); John Marlowe, *Arab Nationalism and British Imperialism* (1961); and, dealing specifically with Israel, Christopher Sykes, *Crossroads to Israel* (1965) and Walter Z. Laqueur, *The Road to War 1967* (1968). One might also consult the interesting geopolitical essay of *John P. Cole, *Geography of World Affairs,* 2nd ed. (1963) (Penguin).

INDEX